Frank Paul Organ

Six Cultures

❧
❧
❧

Studies of Child Rearing

CONTRIBUTORS

John L. Fischer   Hatsumi Maretzki

Ann Fischer   William F. Nydegger

John T. Hitchcock   Corinne Nydegger

Robert A. LeVine   Kimball Romney

Barbara B. LeVine   Romaine Romney

Thomas W. Maretzki   Leigh Minturn

SENIOR INVESTIGATORS

Irvin L. Child, Yale University

William W. Lambert, Cornell University

John W. M. Whiting, Harvard University

John Wiley and Sons, Inc.

Six Cultures

Studies of Child Rearing

❉
❉
❉
❉
❉

Edited by Beatrice B. Whiting

Laboratory of Human Development

Harvard University

New York and London

SECOND PRINTING, APRIL, 1964

Library of Congress Catalog Card Number: 63-8908
Printed in the United States of America

Acknowledgments

✲
✲
✲

The research reported in this volume represents the collaboration of individuals from three universities, Cornell, Harvard, and Yale. It could never have been undertaken or completed without the unwavering commitment of the participants to a charter which represented a compromise between their interests and individual biases. The completion of this volume and the volumes to come is a tribute to their faithfulness, tolerance, and patience.

We are deeply indebted to many people and institutions for their advice and help. The opportunity to do the study was provided by the generous support of the Social Science Research Council, the Behavioral Science Division of the Ford Foundation, and by a United States Public Health Grant, M-1096.

Various faculty members at the three universities helped in designing and planning the research. A list of these and other contributors will be found in the introduction to this volume, but we wish to express special gratitude to Robert R. Sears, Pauline Sears, Eleanor E. Maccoby, and Alfred L. Baldwin, who have continued to give valuable advice to the project.

While in the field, the authors were assisted by graduates of local universities and schools who acted not only as interpreters but also as informants and friends. The aid that these students gave was invaluable. We wish to thank Nariyuki Agarie, Gurdeep Jaspal, Simeon Nyashae, John Okiamba, Felix Ombasa, Laurence Sagini, Sri Shyam Narain Singh, Taurino Singson, Muriel Eva Verbitsky, and Kiyoshi Yogi.

We are deeply grateful to all the staff and students of the Laboratory of Human Development of Harvard University who read and helped edit the monographs. Marilyn Johnson, Celia Kalberg, and Dorothy Tao were particularly devoted assistants. We wish to express our appreciation to numerous other people for reading and commenting on some or all of the monographs, especially Masanori Higa, Geraldine Kohlenberg, and Morris Opler.

We wish to thank Louis J. Chiaramonte for helping to select and reproduce the photographs and for taking the photographs of Orchard Town. We are indebted to Irene Pipes for her help with the index.

We are especially grateful to the families in Nyansongo, Khalapur, Taira, Juxtlahuaca, Tarong, and Orchard Town, who were not only cooperative informants but helpful friends. We hope that the children we studied will become proud members of the adult world into which they were born and that this volume will contribute to mutual understanding so that they may live in a friendlier world.

BEATRICE B. WHITING

Harvard University
January, 1963

Contents

✿
✿
✿

Introduction

This volume is the first of a series of publications reporting research undertaken in 1954 by a group of social scientists from Harvard, Yale, and Cornell universities. In its broadest conception, the research was aimed at exploring cross-culturally the relation between different patterns of child rearing and subsequent differences in personality. It was designed to study the degree to which the treatment a child receives in the first years of life determines his behavior and in adult life influences his perception of the world, his philosophy, religion, and code of ethics.

Theories of the relationship between specific types of treatment in early childhood and subsequent personality difference have been advanced by psychologists and anthropologists. This project was set up with the hope of being able to test some of these hypotheses on the basis of material collected in a standard manner in six parts of the world where families have divergent ways of life and theories and methods of training young children.

In tracing the history of this project one should begin with the work of Margaret Mead, Ruth Benedict, Edward Sapir, Ralph Linton, Abram Kardiner, John Dollard, and other pioneers in the field of culture and personality whose work formed the foundation of this study. Such an account, which would demand an essay on the entire new discipline that grew out of the integration of anthropological and psychological theory, is not practical in this introduction.

Specifically, the impetus for this study came from the cross-cultural work on socialization done by two of the senior investigators, John W. M. Whiting and Irvin L. Child, while they were colleagues at the Institute of Human Relations at Yale University. The results of this research were published in *Child Training and Personality* (1953). Using

1

theories of disease as measures of adult personality, the authors attempted to test certain psychological theories relating the treatment of the basic behavior systems in infancy and childhood to adult personality characteristics.

The data on the 75 societies used in these studies were taken from published ethnographies which varied greatly in the detail and areas of coverage. The dream of the investigators was to send field teams out to get comparable detailed material on 100 societies. As a first step in accomplishing this aim, the present study was planned.

In 1953 the Committee on Social Behavior of the Social Science Research Council sponsored a seminar * and a conference † to discuss cross-cultural work on socialization. As a result, a *Field Manual for the Cross-Cultural Study of Child Rearing* was prepared (Whiting et al., 1953), and Whiting and Child persuaded William W. Lambert of Cornell University to join them in seeking funds to carry out a comparative study of child rearing. A generous grant from the Behavioral Science Division of the Ford Foundation made it possible to carry out these plans. The fieldwork and part of the analysis and writing of five of the six reports in this volume were financed by this grant. Later analysis and editing were supported by a grant from the United States Public Health Service.

Intensive planning for the study was carried on at Cornell, Harvard, and Yale during the following year under the direction of the senior investigators, William W. Lambert, Irvin L. Child, and John W. M. Whiting. During June and July of 1954, a Social Research Council Summer Conference was held at the Laboratory of Human Development at Harvard. All the research personnel, with the aid of David Aberle of Michigan, Alfred Baldwin, and James J. Gibson of Cornell, and Robert Sears of Stanford, wrote the *Field Guide for a Study of Socialization in Five Societies*. This volume presents in detail the research plan, the hypotheses to be tested, and the research devices which were agreed on by the field teams and senior investigators.‡

The five original field teams started fieldwork in the fall of 1954 and

* The contributing members of this seminar were Barbara Chartier Ayres, Hildreth Geertz, George Goethals, Charles Holzinger, Edgar Lowell, Eleanor E. Maccoby, Kimball Romney, Richard Salisbury, William Stewart, and John Thibaut.

† Attending this conference were Robert R. Sears (Chairman), A. L. Baldwin, R. A. Bauer, Irvin L. Child, L. S. Cottrell, Jr., Leon Festinger, J. L. Gewirtz, A. Inkeles, Harry Levin, Gardner Lindzey, Eleanor E. Maccoby, Carson McGuire, G. P. Murdock, B. Paul, J. M. Roberts, T. R. Sarbin, Pauline S. Sears, M. Brewster Smith, R. L. Solomon, John W. Thibaut, and John W. M. Whiting.

‡ Published in mimeographed form by the Laboratory of Human Development, Harvard University, 1954.

spent from 6 to 14 months in the field. Although the original design of the study called for a sample of societies whose culture had been already studied by ethnologists, the temperament and motivation of young anthropologists are such that they tended to choose groups who are relatively unknown and who, often for some personal reason, appealed to their interests. The actual groups chosen represented a compromise between the advantages of previous coverage and these personal interests, in addition to providing the great range of differences desired by the project planners. Kimball and Romaine Romney of Harvard chose a group of families in the Mixtecan barrio of Santa Domingo in the town of Juxtlahuaca in Oaxaca province, Mexico. Leigh Minturn Triandis and John Hitchcock of Cornell selected a group of families of the Rājpūt caste in the town of Khalapur in Uttar Pradesh in northern India. William and Corinne Nydegger, also of Cornell, chose a group of Ilocano-speaking families living in hamlets in northern Luzon in the Philippines. Thomas and Hatsumi Maretzki of Yale chose the village of Taira in Okinawa. And John and Ann Fischer of Harvard moved into a neighborhood in Orchard Town in New England.

In 1955 a sixth team, Robert and Barbara LeVine, left for Kenya, Africa. They were financed by a Ford Foundation fellowship and a National Science Foundation predoctoral fellowship.

To help insure comparability of data, a central clearing house was set up at the Laboratory of Human Development under the supervision of Beatrice B. Whiting. Field notes were mailed in periodically, and field problems were discussed by correspondence. To prevent bias, the sample of children for each team to observe was picked by the staff at the laboratory from the census material.

The research design, agreed on by all the field teams, was set up to measure as accurately as possible the child-training practices and the hypothesized individual and cultural differences in personality, particularly in the areas of aggression, dependency, and the internalization of various mechanisms of behavior control—areas of particular theoretical interest to the senior investigators at Cornell, Yale, and Harvard universities, respectively. Previous research had been done in these areas at the Institute of Human Relations at Yale, at the Iowa Child Welfare Station under the direction of Robert Sears, and subsequently at the Laboratory of Human Development at Harvard University. The research conducted at the last two institutions had focused on a study of individual differences among groups of mothers and children in Iowa, Massachusetts, and among three different cultural groups in the Southwest. Cross-cultural research on aggression was conducted by

Lambert and Triandis at Cornell (1959), on self-reliance and responsibility at Yale by Barry, Child, and Bacon, (1959) and on socialization techniques in the Southwest at Harvard by Whiting, Chasdi, Antonovsky, and Ayres (in press).

In designing the research reported in this volume, an attempt has been made to assess individual as well as cultural differences. This is one of the unique aspects of the design. The hope was to test hypotheses concerning the relations of child-rearing practices and consequent personality, both intraculturally and cross-culturally. In the first instance, 24 mothers in each society were studied as individuals in their relationship to one of their children, and each of the 24 children (ages 3 to 10) was observed and interviewed in a standard manner in the hope of detecting behavioral and personality differences. The cross-cultural measures included material on child-training practices and also religious beliefs, theories of disease, recreational activities, and so on collected by standard ethnographic techniques.

A word should be said here concerning the nature of the unit which each field team chose to study. It was decided to choose a group large enough to yield an adequate sample of individual families. For our design this meant a group of at least 50 families would be needed to draw our sample of 24, since at least half the families would have grown-up children or children under 3. On the other hand, we wanted a group who knew each other and shared beliefs, values, and practices. Furthermore, the ethnographic techniques which we intended to employ—to be used with maximum efficiency—require a small group. Each team therefore chose a community of between 50 and 100 families, which was for them their unit of study.

Implicit in the research design is a general concept of the relation of personality to culture, which may be presented as follows: The ecology of the area determines the maintenance systems, which include basic economy and the most elementary variables of social structure. In other words, the type of crops grown, the presence or absence of herding, fishing, and so on, depend on the nature of the terrain, the amount of rainfall, the location of the area vis-à-vis centers of invention and diffusion. These basic economic conditions determine in part the arrangement of people in space, the type of houses, and household composition. These in turn set the parameters for child-rearing practices.

It is obvious that ecology does no more than set gross parameters for the social structure. Within these parameters, the nature of the composition of households, neighborhoods, and other social groups will lead to variance in child training. Whether or not a grandmother lives in the house, or whether other relatives are close at hand, will influence a mother's behavior toward her child.

It is assumed that different patterns of child rearing will lead to differences in the personality of children and thus to differences in adult personality. Since personality may only be inferred, the problem of measurement is difficult on both the individual and the cultural level. Individual children may be given tests of various kinds, interviewed or observed. On a cultural level, one may analyze the patterning of child or adult behavior, for example, the games and recreational activity, the rituals or ceremonial life, or one may assess the beliefs about the supernatural, theories of disease, or popular folk tales in terms of personality dimensions.

The chart presented below indicates this conceptual system in a simple manner.

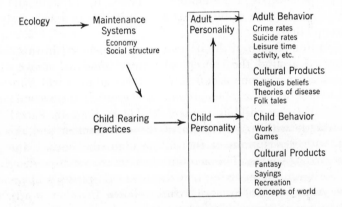

To summarize the conceptual background in another way, the researchers viewed ecology, economics, and social and political organizations as setting the parameters for the behavior of the agents of child rearing. They viewed child behavior as an index of child personality and adult behavior and beliefs and values as indices of adult personality. The causal relationships implied in this scheme are open to discussion, and such discussions, with present available knowledge, ultimately end with a problem similar to that of the priority of the chicken or the egg.

This volume presents the cultural material. Subsequent publications will present the analysis of the individual measures: the mother interviews, child interviews and Thematic Apperception Tests, and the child behavior protocols. It is worth noting, however, as stated in the *Field Guide,* that "One of the hallmarks of the research project is the emphasis on systematic observation of behavior and the development of flexible questionnaire methods which focus upon concrete actions, with projective techniques taking a clearly secondary, but related place." The choice of these methods for assessing personality was the result of the senior investigators' previous disappointment in their attempts to relate doll play and other projective tests to other measures of behavior.*

The cultural material presented in this volume will be used to make a preliminary test of our hypotheses. Further tests will be made on the basis of the individual differences in the behavior of children and the methods of child rearing reported by the individual mothers. Both these analyses will be presented in later publications. A preliminary report of the analysis of the mother interviews by Triandis and Lambert has already been published (1961) and their detailed analysis is near completion.

The outline of each of the six monographs included in this volume is organized around the conceptual system presented above. There are two main parts: one a description of the adult world into which the child is born—*the ethnographic background,* the second an account of how the child is trained—*child training.* In Part I, each account starts with a description of the environment and the local setting, with descriptions of the village plan, the houses, and their interior arrangements. The account then moves on to a description of the daily routine of living and the economic pursuits of men and women. A chapter on social structure follows. In other words, these chapters describe the maintenance systems, the parameters which set the stage for child rearing. The selection of material for the remainder of Part I is also theoretically determined and includes either descriptions of adult behavior or the cultural products which seem to be the best indices of adult personality.

In order to explain the selection of behavior and cultural products, it is necessary to return to the discussion of the dimensions of personality selected for focus by the senior investigators. As noted, the hypotheses to be tested were focused on aggression, dependency, and the internalization of various mechanisms of behavior control. William Lambert and the Cornell group, because of previous research, were most interested in aggression, Irvin Child in dependency, and John Whiting and the Laboratory of Human Development in the

* For a detailed discussion of behavior observation, see Lambert (1960).

problem of the development of internal controls which have been variously labeled as guilt, conscience, and super-ego.

It was the conviction of the researchers that the areas of study had to be limited and clearly defined if standardized material was to be collected. Chapter 1 of the *Field Guide* is a description of the "systems" of behavior which were chosen for study and the hypotheses which the investigators hoped to test. It is impossible to include a detailed description of the theory in this introduction, but in order to understand the material presented in this volume it is necessary to at least present a summary of the behavior systems and the nature of the hypotheses.*

The nine behavioral systems include succorance, nurturance, self-reliance, achievement, responsibility, obedience, dominance, sociability, and aggression. In the most general terms, succorance is defined as asking others for help; nurturance, as giving help or emotional support; self-reliance, as doing things for one's self; achievement, as striving to meet internal standards of excellence; responsibility, as performing one's expected role duties; obedience, as attempting to meet the demands of others; dominance, as attempting to change other's behavior; sociability, as making friendly approaches to other individuals; aggression, as hurting others. It was assumed that each of these systems of behavior would exist in some form and degree in every society in a recognizable form and could best be identified as responses to specific universal situations. For example, given a situation in which an individual encountered difficulty, whether he asked for help or solved the problem himself would indicate the relative strength of his succorance or, in contrast, his self-reliance. A measure of nurturance would be the frequency of the spontaneous giving of help or the reaction to requests for help or the perception that others need help.

Returning to the present volume, in describing the adult cultur e of each society we have included material which we consider relevant to these nine behavior systems.

The chapter on social control is included because it gives information on the frequency of brawls, fights, crimes, and other conflicts and describes the techniques which the society has devised either for preventing such conflicts from arising or for stopping existing conflict. Comparison of this material gives indices of the expressed aggression of the adults and the existence and type of internalized controls. It will be noted, for example, that the incidence of rape is high in Nyansongo, that litigation is frequent in Khalapur and Nyansongo,

---

* For a full discussion of behavior systems see Child (1954).

and that there are few cases of physical violence in either Taira or Santa Domingo barrio, Juxtlahuaca.

The chapter on medical practices and theories of disease is included because variations in such belief systems were found useful indices of personality by Whiting and Child (1953) in their cross-cultural study and in later studies by Whiting (1959). Similarly, the analysis of man's relation to the supernatural was fruitfully analyzed by Spiro and D'Andrade (1958), Whiting (1959), Lambert, Triandis, and Wolf (1959). Mourning behavior and death ceremonies have also been studied cross-culturally (Friendly, 1956).

It was hoped that the analysis of the use of leisure time might be made along dimensions relevant to the nine behavior systems. The man who prefers to be alone in his spare time would be rated less sociable than one who always seeks the company of others. The amount of teasing or playful wrestling in leisure settings, or even the amount of pleasure derived from cock fights, might be used to rate the degree of preoccupation with aggression. The amount of time spent practicing skills might indicate the need for achievement. Whether or not men seek the company of women, men and women, or only men, is of interest in assessing personality; similarly, whether a man chooses to smoke, eat, talk, drink, dance, or play games. The nature of popular games can be analyzed along lines suggested by John Roberts (1957).

Part II of the ethnographies is organized chronologically, beginning with pregnancy and childbirth and continuing through preadolescence. The time spent on the observation of this age span made it impractical to study systematically the lives of the adolescent children. The only exception to this is the monograph on the Nyansongo group in Kenya. The LeVines were particularly interested in the effect of initiation ceremonies on the Nyansongo boys and girls. For this reason they selected three age groups for study: the 3-to-7, the 7-to-10-year-olds, and the postinitiation boys and girls. The Nydeggers included a brief chapter on adolescence in their monograph. The other field teams did not feel that they had enough knowledge to include such a description.

The age span covered in the individual chapters of the six descriptions of socialization differs, each division being made on the basis of the age groups and the transitions recognized by the members of the society. Thus in Khalapur, India, where socialization is not broken by clearly defined stages, there are only three chapters. In Taira, Okinawa, on the other hand, there are named stages and sharp transitions, and the Maretzkis have followed this pattern in describing socialization. Weaning from the breast and back is an abrupt change in an Okinawan child's life. The transition from kindergarten to school age is also clear and dramatized. Before school age a child is "senseless," according to the mothers, and cannot be properly trained.

Within these chapters an attempt has been made to cover the parent's or parent surrogate's treatment of the nine behavior systems and the child's response to socialization. Obviously some of the behavior systems are not relevant in infancy. In general, the early chapters concentrate on the handling of succorance, the mother's early contact with the child, the number of other individuals who share in the early care of the child, and their responsiveness to the demands of the infant. Among the hypotheses advanced in the *Field Guide,* several concern the consequence of indulgence in infancy. As stated: "Indulgence in infancy, a large number of nurturing agents, and mild transition from infantile indulgence into childhood will produce: (1) a trustful attitude toward others, (2) general optimism, and (3) sociability." It is also stated that training with respect to succorance will tend to influence sociability.

It is hoped that, on the basis of the information presented in the chapters on infancy, the reader can compare indulgence in infancy and the number of nurturing agents. The comparison of weaning from the breast and from complete dependence on caretakers should make it possible to evaluate the severity of the transition. For the consequent measures one may turn either to the description of the behavior of older children or to the behavior and belief systems of adults. Is it true that, comparatively speaking, the Juxtlahuacan Mixtecan child is more friendly and sociable in later life than the Nyansongan? In infancy, the Mixtecan is constantly held or carried close to the mother's body, enveloped in a shawl. The Nyansongo child is tended for periods of time by a less consistently responsive 5-to-8-year-old child. In adult life, are the Juxtlahuacan Mixtecan adults more optimistic and trustful than the Nyansongans?

With the onset of weaning, other behavior systems become important. Training for self-reliance and the associated punishment for succorance are universal problems, but the degree to which this new behavior is expected of 3-year-olds varies from one society to another. The Orchard Town 3-year-old is feeding and dressing himself while the Khalapur Rājpūt child of the same age may still be dressed and fed by his mother. Similarly, as mentioned earlier, the abruptness of the shift in expected behavior varies. The handling of aggression against parents, siblings, and peers is also a universal problem which all parents and socializers must face at this time. Probably closely associated with this behavior system is training for obedience and respect.

The *Field Guide* contains many hypotheses about the antecedents of aggressive behavior in children and adults and stresses the techniques used by parents in the handling of aggression as well as their model behavior. Specifically, one hypothesis advanced is that permissiveness on the part of parents for teasing behavior should be reflected in the increase of observable unprovoked aggressive behavior on the part of children and adults. Is it indeed true that the Tarongan child who is "playfully" teased by his parents and other adults from early childhood instigates aggressive behavior more frequently than a Rājpūt child whose parents do not "playfully" tease their children?

A second hypothesis concerning the handling of aggression states that children will be less apt to retaliate to aggression if parents and socializing agents punish any expressiveness with regard to anger. Again, the Khalapur Rājpūt child whose mother dislikes all expression of emotion, even excessive joy, and the Juxtlahuacan Mixtecan child who is taught that he will sicken and die if he eats while angry should be less aggressive when provoked than the children of Orchard Town.* It will be noted that a distinction is made between unprovoked and provoked aggression. A further distinction is made with regard to instrumental aggression, where a person tends to select aggressive means for attaining his ends. Comparisons between the handling of aggression in childhood may also be used to explore hypotheses as to the conditions which lead to the displacing of aggression to others, the use of fantasy to express anger or the projection of one's own desires to hurt others. Here for consequent measures one can turn to theories of disease and the nature of the supernaturals. The theory would predict that those societies which punish aggression most severely would project their anger into the supernatural world and believe in dangerous and malevolent beings or attribute superhuman evil capacity to humans and believe in sorcery or witchcraft. To date, the best socialization variables for predicting the belief in witches and sorcerers is a combination of polygyny and the severe punishment for sex and aggression (Whiting, 1959). Of our societies, the Nyansongans are the most ridden with the belief in these superhuman individuals. Their treatment of aggression is therefore of particular interest. It is also of interest to speculate whether there is some relation between the Tarongan parents' treatment of aggression and teasing behavior and

* For further discussion of the hypotheses regarding aggression, see the *Field Guide for a Study of Socialization in Five Societies*, pp. 18–22.

their belief in whimsical spirits who must be avoided and not annoyed.

Each monograph on socialization also includes an extended section on techniques used by the socializing agent. Our theory stresses the importance of rewards and punishments for the specific types of acts included in the nine behavior systems. It includes, however, theories as to the differential effect of various types of rewards and punishments and the conditions under which they are administered. Rewards may be material, such as food or money, or immaterial, giving love and acceptance or praise and prestige. Privileges may also be used as rewards. All types may be given after good behavior or used to incite desired behavior.

Punishments depend on two types of sanctions: injury or abandonment which may have as referents several types of agents—parents or authority figures, peers, the self, or supernatural agents.

These rewards and punishments may be given for different reasons. The locus of evaluation may be a specific response of the child, some consequence of his action, or the child himself as a person. In other words, one may praise a child because he does a chore well, because he has helped his mother by doing the chore, or because he is a good boy.

The nature and strength of internal controls—mechanisms which keep an individual from breaking the rules of a society—are thought to be related to techniques and agents of socialization as well as to the strength of a child's identification with the same and opposite sex parents (Whiting and Child, 1953; Whiting, 1960; Burton and Whiting, 1961; Bacon, Child and Barry, in press). To determine the strength of these internal controls we hoped to observe the differences in children's behavior in the presence and absence of socializing agents. On a societal level, we predicted that when a boy's identification with the same sex parent is weak, there will be a higher incidence of crime.

We expected to find that authority figures would be important as sanction agents in the adult culture: when there was marked differentiation of authority within the nuclear family; when discipline was carried out by or in the name of the head of the house; and when responsibility and obedience training were emphasized. We expected peers to be important agents when there was little differentiation of authority within the family, when the right of discipline was not focused and self-reliance training was emphasized. If these hypotheses are correct, we would expect consequent differences in the social control systems.

For most of the societies, the period from 6 to 10 emphasizes responsibility training. A comparison of the chores assigned to boys and girls during this period, the rewards and punishments for good or bad performance or omission are an index of the training in this behavior system. The age at which different types of chores are assigned gives a clue to the age at which a society considers a child to have "sense," to be capable of reason, and it indicates the beliefs about the nature of the learning process. It will be observed, for example, that the Khalapur Rājpūts believe children learn primarily by observing, and hence they do little direct instructing. One type of responsibility is training children to care for younger siblings or cousins and neighbors. This training may start very young, as in Taira and Nyansongo, or may be late and unimportant, as in Orchard Town.

The size and composition of play groups and the attitudes of parents on friendliness are described for each age grade. It was hypothesized that sociability would be related both to training in nurturance and to the treatment of succorance, but initial comparisons would indicate that nurturance is probably more closely related to training for responsibility and dominance than to friendliness.

In planning the research the senior investigators were also interested in discovering age and sex differences in behavior which might be universal (Barry, Bacon and Child, 1957). Is it true that in spite of radically different treatment in infancy and early childhood in the six societies, boys and adult men are always more aggressive physically than girls and women and that girls and women are always more affectionate than men? Are there regularities in behavior which hold across cultures? Does succorance always decrease with age and dominance always increase? Although these are questions which cannot be answered from a comparison of the six societies alone, consistent age and sex differences should be followed up by further research.

The reader will be aware that in spite of the research design, the data are not always comparable, that in the different areas studied, some monographs have better coverage than others. These variations are due not only to the personalities, interests, and training of the fieldworkers but also to the nature of the culture of the societies they chose to study.

Although this volume concentrates on the material that the researchers felt was theoretically relevant, it is hoped that readers with different conceptual systems and different hypotheses concerning human behavior will find it possible to make some relevant comparisons between the six societies. Those who were concerned with the project have developed new insights and new hypotheses. Some of these can be studied, but for many, the relevant data are not detailed enough and must await further studies. It is our belief that this is inevitable in the field of social science and that progress comes from being willing to state hypotheses, test them, derive new theories and plan new research to test these.

BIBLIOGRAPHY

Bacon, Margaret K., Child, Irvin L., and Barry, Herbert III. A cross-cultural study of correlates of crime. *Journal of Abnormal and Social Psychology*, in press.

Barry, Herbert, III, Bacon, Margaret K., and Child, Irvin L. A cross-cultural survey of some sex differences in socialization. *Journal of Abnormal and Social Psychology*, 1957, 55, 327–332.

Barry, Herbert, III, Child, Irvin L., and Bacon, Margaret K. Relation of child training to subsistence economy. *American Anthropologist*, 1959, 61, 51–63.

Burton, Roger V. and Whiting, John W. M. The absent father and cross-sex identity. *Merrill-Palmer Quarterly*, 1961, 7, 85–95.

Child, Irvin L. Socialization. In G. Lindzey (Ed.), *Handbook of Social Psychology.* vol. II. Cambridge, Mass.: Addison-Wesley, 1954.

Friendly, Joan P. A cross-cultural study of ascetic mourning behavior. Unpublished honors thesis, Radcliffe College, 1956.

Lambert, William W. Interpersonal behavior. In P. H. Mussen (Ed.), *Handbook of Research Methods in Child Development.* New York: Wiley, 1960.

————, Triandis, Leigh M., and Wolf, Margery. Some correlates of beliefs in the malevolence and benevolence of supernatural beings: a cross-cultural study. *Journal of Abnormal and Social Psychology*, 1958, 58, 162–169.

Roberts, John M., Bush, R. R., and Arth, M. Dimensions of mastery in games. Stanford, California: Ford Center for Advanced Study in the Behavioral Sciences, 1957 (mimeographed).

Spiro, Melford E. and D'Andrade, Roy G. A cross-cultural study of some supernatural beliefs. *American Anthropologist*, 1958, 60, 456–466.

Triandis, Leigh M., and Lambert, William W. Pancultural factor analysis of reported socialization practices. *Journal of Abnormal and Social Psychology*, 1961, 62, 631–639.

Whiting, John W. M. Sorcery, sin and the superego: a cross-cultural study of some mechanisms of social control. In *Nebraska Symposium on Motivation.* Lincoln: University of Nebraska Press, 1959, 174–195.

————. Resource mediation and learning by identification. In I. Iscoe and H. Stevenson (Eds.), *Personality Development in Children.* Austin: University of Texas Press, 1960.

————. Socialization process and personality. In F. L. K. Hsu (Ed.), *Psychological Anthropology.* Holmwood, Ill.: Dorsey Press, 1961.

————, Chasdi, Eleanor M., Antonovsky, Helen F., and Ayres, Barbara C. The learning of values. In E. Z. Vogt and J. M. Roberts (Eds.), *The Peoples of Rimrock.* vol. I. Evanston, Ill.: Row, Peterson & Co., in press.

———— et al. Field manual for the cross-cultural study of child rearing. Social Science Research Council, New York, 1953.

———— et al. Field guide for a study of socialization in five societies. Cambridge, Mass.: Laboratory of Human Development, 1954 (mimeographed).

Nyansongo:

A Gusii Community

in Kenya

✿
✿
✿
✿
✿
✿

Robert A. LeVine

Barbara B. LeVine

Contents

About the Authors

Robert and Barbara LeVine chose a Gusii community in Nyaribari in the hills of the South Nyanza District of Kenya. During their stay they lived in the official residence of the chief, who prefers to live in his own home. This house was at Keumbu, about a quarter of a mile from a community of scattered homesteads which were selected for the study. Robert LeVine was an advanced graduate student in the Social Relations Department at Harvard who had been on the staff of the Laboratory of Human Development during the year when the other teams had been in the field. He had assisted in checking the comparability of the material as it was mailed in and had the advantage of profiting by the experiences of the field teams as reported in their journals and correspondence. Because he was interested in initiation ceremonies, he agreed to replicate the study, varying it to include a sample of older boys and girls whom he wished to observe and interview after initiation. Barbara LeVine was a graduate student of psychology at Boston University. She participated in the female initiation rites, observing, photographing, and dancing with the women in settings in which men were not allowed or had to remain in the background. With the aid of an interpreter, she did the mother interviews.

The LeVines used four interpreters during their stay: Simeon Nyachae, the chief's son; Lawrence Sagini, a teacher's college graduate who was headmaster of a nearby school and contributed valuable information and help. These two men offered their services gratis because they lived nearby and were interested. Felix Ombasa, a health officer, worked with the LeVines from April to August 1956, and John Okiamba from October 1956 to May 1957. Both men were graduates of the Nyabururu Roman Catholic Intermediate School and spoke English.

Robert LeVine is at present a member of the Committee on Human Development and teaching at the University of Chicago.

Part I

The Ethnographic Background

❀
❀
❀
❀
❀
❀

Chapter 1

Introduction

On the eastern side of Africa, astride the Equator, lies a cool, fertile highland region with green hills and snow-capped volcanic peaks ranging up to 17,000 feet above sea level. Surrounded and bisected by semiarid plains and vast hot savannahs, the relatively small strip of well-watered highland in Kenya has attracted dense African populations and the largest European settlement in East Africa. The southwestern tip of the region, wedged in between the White (i.e., European) Highlands on the east and the arid Lake Victoria shore lowlands on the west, is the African reserve known as Kisii Highlands, home of the Gusii people. The Kisii Highlands (hereafter referred to as Gusiiland) are located (see map 1) in South Nyanza District, 50 miles south of the equator, 40 miles north of Tanganyika, and 30 miles east of Lake Victoria's Kavirondo Gulf, which is visible from its higher hills.

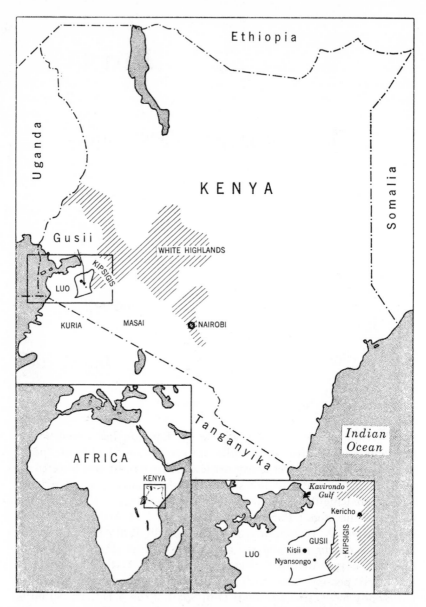

Map 1. Map of Kenya showing Gusiiland.

Gusiiland, situated at cool, 5000 to 7000 foot elevations above sea level, consists mainly of long, gently sloping hills and a smaller number of steep ridges and escarpments. Running between the green hills are swampy streams and rivers, fed by more than 80 inches of rainfall annually.

The appearance of Gusiiland has been likened to that of the Scottish Highlands and, indeed, few characteristically African features strike the eye. The hills are devoid of indigenous trees, removed in the course of expanding cultivation some years ago. Nowadays dark green groves of Australian black wattle trees and scattered eucalyptus and cypress occasionally interrupt the patchwork of crudely terraced fields and pastures. Dotted across the cultivated sides of the hills, in no pattern discernible to the casual observer, are the round, thatched-roof huts and granaries of the Gusii people. The inhabitants of one such dotted hillside forming a local community were the subjects of the field study reported here from December 1955 until May 1957.

The Gusii are a dark brown Negroid people of medium height who number more than a quarter of a million. Their language places them within the Bantu-speaking * majority of subequatorial Africa, but their entry into the highlands some two centuries ago isolated them from other Kenya Bantu peoples: the Kuria, whose language is mutually intelligible with Gusii, live 35 miles to the south, while the related Logoli and Luhyia are more than 80 miles to the north, and the more distantly related Kikuyu live 130 miles away in the east. The immediate neighbors of the Gusii are tribes of unrelated language families: the Nilotic-speaking Luo to the north, west, and southwest; the Nilo-Hamitic Kipsigis to the east, and the Nilo-Hamitic Masai on the southeast. The Gusii fought with their neighbors and lost a segment of highland to the Kipsigis while leaving an uninhabited buffer strip at the boundary of low-lying Masailand. Except for intermittent cattle raids, relations with the Luo inhabitants of the lake shore were more peaceful, and no serious conflict over territory seems to have occurred.

The entire Gusii people recognize a common ancestor, Mogusii, who is thought of as the founder of the society and the person after whom it was named. Despite the recognition of this common ancestry and a common cultural heritage, however, the seven tribes of Gusiiland did not traditionally constitute a unified group. They not only combined for military operations against the Kipsigis but also engaged in warfare against each other. Each tribe, in its turn, far from being

* Bantu is a language family containing many languages which are similar but mutually incomprehensible.

a unified political group, was an alliance of the patrilineal clans in a defined area which recognized a common ancestor and totem animal distinct from those of other tribes and which acknowledged the possibility of compensation for homicide within the alliance. There were, in every tribe, one or more clans which were considered the original inhabitants of the area, directly descended from the founder-ancestor, and others who were thought of as later settlers adopted into the tribal genealogy. The "descended" clans tended to be few in number but large in population, while there were many small "adopted" clans and clan fragments in a tribe. Some of the latter were refugees from interclan conflict in other tribes. Because of their numerical strength and hereditary position, the descended clans were in some respects politically dominant, and any tribe-wide military or judicial leadership a tribe might have would be contributed by one of the descended clans.

Each clan, however, was for the most part an autonomous political unit with its own territory and powers of decision making. Clans of the same tribe feuded with one another, that is, they engaged in prolonged relationships of mutual hostility involving spear fights and the abduction of women. Interclan hostilities within a tribe could be terminated by negotiation and the payment of compensation in livestock. The fact that clans were exogamous and had to take wives from one another in orderly marriage ceremonies must have exerted some pressure against the indefinite continuance of feuds, but it did not prevent them from occurring. Thus the clans of a Gusii tribe were traditionally drawn together by intermarriage and joint participation in intertribal warfare, but nevertheless they engaged in hostilities against one another.

In 1907, Gusiiland came under British administration and became a part of South Nyanza District along with adjacent Luo areas. Each of the seven Gusii tribes became an administrative "location"; one of these is Nyaribari Location in which the community of Nyansongo is located. The population of this location in 1948 was 42,670. Much of its 100 square miles was formerly no-man's land between Gusiiland and Masai and has only been settled since 1930. The population density of Nyaribari, though varying widely within the location, averages over 450 per square mile. This is not the greatest average density in Gusiiland and does not approach the thousand and more per square mile found in other parts of the western Kenya highland, but it is a heavy population load for even a fertile soil being tilled by primitive methods.

Nyansongo is less than a quarter of a mile from Keumbu, the administrative center of Nyaribari. Located at Keumbu are the chief's office, tribal police quarters, the location assembly hall, a prison cubicle, and the official chief's residence, in which we lived. There is a Roman Catholic primary and intermediate day school where 400 students are taught by Gusii teachers. On the other side of a dirt road from the chief's office and school, there is a market, a neat rectangle of Gusii shops and restaurants bordering a grassy field where cattle are traded and soccer is played. Ordinary Gusii homesteads and fields surround Keumbu, and the public grounds themselves are used as pastures by nearby people. The road running through the area is the main route from South Nyanza to the Kericho tea plantations and ultimately to the capital city of Nairobi. It is a narrow winding road, with a dirt surface that converts readily to intractable mud during the rainy seasons.

Nyaribari Location is characterized by continuous settlement with no pronounced geographical subdivisions. To its residents, the important affiliations are to kin and work groups and to influential men. In selecting a group to study, we chose the neighboring families who were members (population 208) of a large work group. We have called this group the community of Nyansongo.

Nyansongo consists of 18 homesteads, scattered over the slopes of a long hill on both sides of the main road to Kericho. Proximity to the chief's camp and market on one side, and to the chief's private homestead on the other, figures importantly in the life of the community. The immediacy of the road is also important, for on it one can take a bus 8 miles to Kisii township, district headquarters and commercial center, or 50 miles in the opposite direction to employment on the tea plantations. Despite such easy access to organs of government and centers of Western influence, Nyansongo is relatively traditional in its way of life, adhering to many of the beliefs and practices characteristic of Gusiiland before its conquest by the British 50 years ago.

Nyansongo is roughly divided into three neighborhoods, each of which consists of a number of nearby homesteads of the same kin group who comprise a small work group for frequent agricultural cooperation. [The residents of the smallest neighborhood belong to Bonyamosicho subclan (see map 2), while those of the other two belong to different branches of Omobea subclan (designated A and B on the map).]

Each of the 18 homesteads in Nyansongo is a residential cluster of one to eight houses (see map 3). The clustering is not pronounced because the houses of co-wives and brothers are usually separated by a cultivated field, and there is also a tendency of homestead members

to build their houses near a boundary disputed with another homestead. The result is what appears to be a random dispersion of houses,
but in fact the network of paths almost always makes it easier to get
from one house to another within a homestead than across homestead
lines, which are sometimes marked by fences and hedges. The residents
are usually a man, who is homestead head, his wives, their unmarried

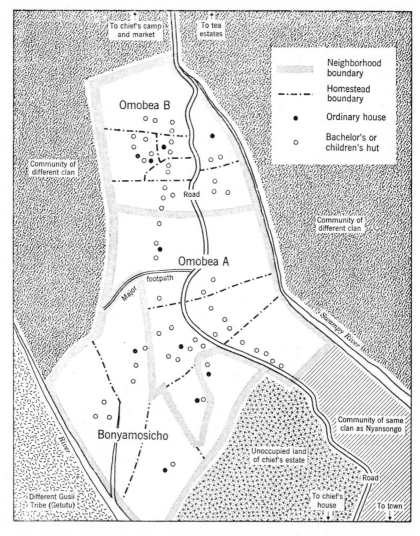

Map 2. Nyansongo community.

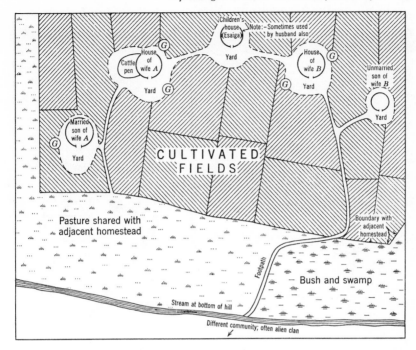

Map 3. Contemporary Gusii homestead in densely populated area.

children, their married sons with wives and progeny, and the head's mother if she is alive.

Houses are round structures with mud and wattle walls, floors of dried mud and cow dung, and water-tight conical roofs with neatly concentric thatching. They last five to ten years, the oldest one in Nyansongo being 12 years old and very shabby. There are two doors in an ordinary house but no windows, and the smoke from the fireplace drifts up to the top of the roof cone and seeps out through the interstices of the grass. The high roof of the house allows the construction of an overhead loft where grain for everyday use is stored in a large basket. There are two rooms (see Figure 1): (1) *enyomba* (which also means "house" in general), considered the wife's preserve, which contains the fireplace for cooking, the bed on which wife, husband, and small children sleep, and a partitioned entrance foyer in which the adult sons of the wife may eat without being able to see her posture while cooking or the interior part of the house containing the bed; (2) *eero*, a room reserved for the husband's entertainment of guests and where his stool, drinking tube, and other personal possessions are

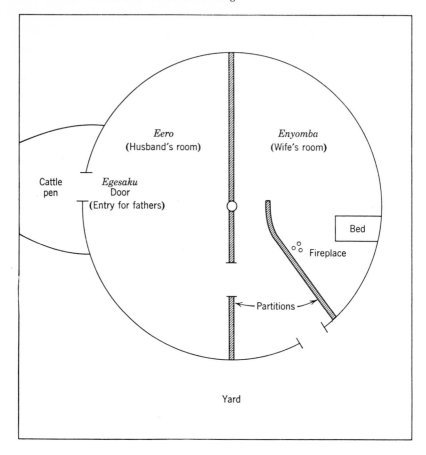

Figure 1. Traditional Gusii house.

kept. He also lies there when ill. This room has its own entrance through the cattle pen, and classificatory fathers of the husband may enter the house only through this door, never through the main entrance in the wife's room. The main entrance of each house faces downhill, toward the nearest stream or river. The yard in front of the main entrance is the scene of many daytime activities: the grinding and winnowing of grain, the play of children, the consumption of food (but not beer) with guests, and the casual visits of neighbor women who sit nursing their infants and gossiping. From the yard one can see down the hill, observe passersby on the road or to and from the stream, supervise the boys herding cattle in the pastures below, and even watch people of another clan on the opposite hill across the stream.

The house described above is the standard one in which a woman, whether or not she is a widow, lives with her unmarried children. A smaller house (*esaiga*), with one room and one door, may be used as a children's house for boys from the whole homestead who are aged 6 to 12, as a bachelor's house for one initiated but unmarried male aged 12 to 20, or to house an aged widow whose larger house fell into disrepair. In the early years of their marriage a couple may inhabit the husband's previous bachelor house, but eventually he builds a standard unit for his wife, and each secondary wife must have one too. Later on he builds a children's *esaiga* in which he may occasionally sleep when he is not rotating among the houses of his wives (see map 3). Each wife has a granary near her house for storing the grain from the fields allotted to her. There is always a field beside the wife's house in which she is cultivating vegetables or grain, but at any one time about half of the fields shown on the diagram are likely to be lying fallow.

This setting of dispersed homesteads, containing separated houses and surrounded by sloping fields and pastures, is the context in which Nyansongo individuals grow up, spend most of their adult lives, and die.

☙
☙
☙

Chapter 2

Basic Economy *

GENERAL BACKGROUND

Traditionally the Gusii combined agriculture and animal husbandry, and do so today although other means of earning a livelihood are now available. In the days before British administration, cattle herding was more important to the Gusii and tended to overshadow cultivation in social significance if not actually for subsistence. Economic aggrandizement was seen primarily in terms of the acquisition of large herds of cattle through breeding and raids on neighboring clans or on other

* For further material on the Gusii economy, see LeVine (1962a).

tribes. The importance of cattle, sheep, and goats in the Gusii prestige system and diet has diminished over the years in the face of a growing cash economy and because of the reduction of herds, initially occasioned by cattle epidemics and government restrictions on cattle villages, and presently by the increasing shortage of grazing lands. The young men, who once herded cattle and raided for more, now find employment on European plantations and in cities.

In the past, land was abundant; homesteads were widely dispersed across the hillsides; and cultivation was undertaken to supply the eleusine (finger millet) necessary for daily subsistence. The ready availability of land and vaguely defined property rights permitted lineage groups to move around considerably within the Gusii territory rather than remaining fixed to a particular piece of land. The pressure of a rapidly increasing population, the introduction of new crops, and the possibility of obtaining cash through agriculture have turned the primary economic attention of the Gusii away from cattle and to their extremely fertile soil. Corn, which requires less arduous cultivation, now rivals eleusine as the major food crop, while sweet potatoes, bananas, legumes, and tomatoes are commonly grown as well. Coffee is the primary cash crop, but surpluses of all crops are sold for shipment to other parts of Kenya. Thus the people of Nyansongo are now predominantly an agricultural people, but animal husbandry and outside employment serve important supplementary roles in their economy.

The Gusii standard of living is higher than that of many peoples living in "underdeveloped areas"; they are better fed, better clothed, and have more purchasing power than most peasant farmers in North Africa, the Middle East, and East Asia. Despite this relative prosperity, which is more than adequate for the satisfaction of their basic needs, the level of economic anxiety and preoccupation in Nyansongo is high. In part this is due to the economic changes of the past 50 years. The population has tripled in these years, and land, once abundant, now is fought over. The system of land tenure and land inheritance, understandably vague in the past, has in the modern era pitted brother against brother, neighbor against neighbor, and kin group against kin group in a struggle over land rights and ownership. The large amount of land litigation in Gusiiland is symptomatic of this struggle and the problems of population and economics that lie behind it. Middle-aged Gusii can remember a time when land and livestock were much more plentiful than they are now, and they witness the increasing population making them scarcer every year. Since employment and trade are regarded as supplements rather than substitutes for the life of the fields and pastures, it appears to many that the economic basis of their existence is gradually slipping away.

A further source of economic anxiety is the high value set on personal wealth. A Nyansongo man desires land, cattle, and money partly for the prestige that accrues to him. The size of his herds and number of his wives are visible signs of his affluence. The extent of a particular individual's wealth is a complex function of his father's wealth, the number of heirs with whom he had to share his father's wealth, the number of his daughters whose marriages bring in cattle, and his own personal efforts to acquire property through work and trade. In general, an individual is fiercely jealous of a neighbor who is slightly richer, deferential to one who is much richer, and fearful of the jealousy of those who are poorer. Wealthy men are respected and poor men despised: indeed, the term for "poor man" is an insult in the Gusii language.

Jealousy of a wealthy man is as great if his riches were acquired through honest work as if they were inherited, a situation which has become an obstacle to the Agriculture Department's program of encouraging extraordinarily competent Gusii farmers to develop their land to yield more than their neighbor's farm. The wealthy live in fear of poisoning, witchcraft, and sorcery at the hands of their jealous neighbors. Fear does not inspire the wealthy to share with others less fortunate, however. On the contrary, they use their wealth to dominate their inferiors through loans and threats of expensive litigation. The proverb, "The poor man's property belongs to the rich man," indicates that such domination is a familiar pattern. In spite of covert jealousy and resentment on the part of the poor, it must be emphasized that they automatically accord their wealthy neighbors a degree of respect and deference which insures domination by the rich. No poor man would dare to contradict or criticize a rich man of his own generation in a face-to-face situation unless there were a state of sustained hostility between their kin groups.

Thus in Nyansongo, as in most communities, there are one or two wealthy men who are the acknowledged leaders and whose opinions on local affairs are granted extraordinary weight. Although there is open recognition of economic inequality, there are no social classes among the Gusii. Often a rich man uses his influence (or wealth in the form of bribes) to establish legal claims to property belonging to a less influential person or to extort excessive fines from a neighbor for a minor offense. Unless such actions are overruled by a higher authority, they go unchecked, for Gusii consider themselves powerless to rebel against a person of superior wealth. Besides, those who are victimized are likely to be the influential man's debtors and dependent on his favor. This domination is prevented from persisting across generations by the likelihood of a rich man taking many wives and siring many sons. His wealth is thus fragmented in a generation. Furthermore, there is no feeling of solidarity among the wealthy, as expressed in the proverb, "Rich men fear each other." Traditionally a rich man preferred the company of his poorer relatives, whom he could dominate, to that of other rich men, who were viewed as rivals for local political power. This pattern persists, but today it is even difficult for a rich man to move his residence.

HOMESTEAD ECONOMY

The agricultural cycle in each Nyansongo homestead is based on the seasonal distribution of rain. All of Gusiiland has the two rainy seasons characteristic of Kenya highland areas. In Nyansongo the "long rains" come in April, May, and June, while the "short rains" occur in September and October. In July and August there may be occasional rain, but the December to March period is usually hot and dry. With respect to the major crops of corn and eleusine: January–February is the time for bush clearing and ground-breaking; March–April for sowing; May–June for weeding; and September–October for harvesting the grain. In July and August sweet potatoes are cultivated as "insurance" in case there is a poor grain yield. After the crops are harvested, social activities requiring food can begin, and November and December are filled with visiting and house building.

Bush-clearing and ground-breaking activity is concentrated on those fields which were allowed to lie fallow and probably used as grazing land. Once the undergrowth is cut down with machetes, the ground-breaking is accomplished either with a hoe, which is traditional and was once made by Gusii ironsmiths, or with a plow and a team of oxen. No one in Nyansongo owns a plow or oxen, but some people rent them from neighbors or borrow them from relatives outside the community. When they are borrowed from relatives, beer is served in return.

The exact time of planting is based on an individual's estimate of when the long rains will begin in earnest. Those who plant early worry about whether or not the rains will come soon enough to allow their seeds to germinate. Those who wait too long may find that the rains have come early, making the ground muddy and the planting more arduous. The sowing of corn can be performed with little additional preparation of the soil, but eleusine cultivation demands a finely pulverized soil, carefully weeded. This latter task is painstakingly performed by striking large clumps of earth with a hoe and shaking out the weeds and vines. When the whole field is soft and finely prepared, the eleusine seed is broadcast on it. In conformity with government instructions, all bushes, weeds, and vines are piled up along that edge of the field which lies lower on the hill, thus producing a crude contour terrace line.

Toward the end of the long rains, the crops must be weeded. Weeding corn, which is planted in rows, is a simple task for someone equipped with a hoe. Eleusine, which the Gusii insist on broadcasting despite the Agriculture Department's efforts to the contrary, requires a person to kneel down and pluck each weed by hand—a slow and tiresome job. By July and August, when all the weeding is finished, there is little to do but wait for the crops to ripen.

Just before the harvest, granaries begin to run low and food anxiety is common in Nyansongo. The midday meal is eliminated in most households, and all adults limit their diet drastically. Social visiting is at a minimum, since usual hospitality norms cannot be met. People know they cannot expect their neighbors to feed them or give them drink. Women visit their own kin, however, to beg for food and are usually only given bananas. These are often in full supply throughout this period, but bananas are only considered suitable for snacks, and informants took care to explain that they are not considered "food." Some women also plant small fields of sweet potatoes, beans, and peas to provide a supplementary food supply, for these can mature during the short rains. Solitary handicraft activities, such as basketmaking, may also be carried out at this time.

In October, when the harvest finally begins, initiation ceremonies provide a pleasant excuse for the resumption of neighborly social life and the consumption of large quantities of food and beer. The high point of these festivities is reached at Christmas, which is celebrated as a drinking feast even by the pagan Gusii. As the New Year begins, fences are built or mended to keep livestock away from the fields which will shortly be broken. Thus the cycle begins once more.

Today as 50 years ago before the British came to Gusiiland, work is organized according to age and sex. In the past, women and middle-aged men worked the fields, young men lived out in cattle villages to herd and raid, uninitiated children herded sheep and goats, and old men discussed cattle and settled local disputes. The abolition of the cattle-villages by the government in 1912, and the subsequent development of employment opportunities outside the district, effected some changes in this arrangement. With young men often away working for cash, children now herd cattle as well as sheep and goats, and women are burdened more than ever with agricultural activities in addition to their domestic chores. Women and children now do all the milking of cows, although women were once not even permitted to enter the cattle-villages.

Of the 28 adult males in Nyansongo, 24 have been employed at some time in their lives outside South Nyanza District. Although most have gone no farther than Nairobi (250 miles from Nyansongo), a few have been to places such as Egypt or the Congo. They have worked as artisans, policemen, and domestic servants as well as agricultural laborers. At the time of the field study, four men were Kenya policemen stationed outside the district, coming home only for vacation once every two years. Seven others worked away from home at some time during the 1955–1957 period, but these regard their employment as temporary and spend as much as a year at home before going out to seek work again. Some of the men who came home at this time never plan to seek jobs again. Five men in Nyansongo were living at home and were employed by the chief as agricultural laborers, guards, and servants on his estate. The others who had been employed outside the district had returned long since to devote themselves to their land, livestock, and lives as traditional Gusii men. Thus more than half of the adult males in the community derived income from employment during 1955–1957, and over two thirds of those employed in that period were living away from home.

Men who are at home devote themselves mainly to nonroutine tasks: the clearing of bush for a new field, plowing, building or mending fences, building houses and granaries. In addition, they take charge of the coffee garden if the homestead has one, supervise the children in their husbandry duties, and occasionally hoe corn and vegetable fields before planting.

It is women, however, who are responsible for most of the hoeing, sowing, weeding, and harvesting as well as grinding the grain, cooking, gathering firewood and wild vegetables. Children and adolescents are commandeered by their mothers to ease the female work load. However, the most difficult and time consuming of Nyansongo agricultural chores, weeding eleusine, is now performed exclusively by adult women, although it is said that in the past some men did it very skillfully.

The current division of labor by sex is the basis for the two different types of work groups in Nyansongo. Women of neighboring homesteads organize themselves into cooperative groups for the performance of routine agricultural activities. This type of group is called *egesangio,* which literally means "an equally shared thing," and a strict equality is its dominant theme. In hoeing corn, for example, the group spends a morning in the field of each of its members and then begins the round again. Each woman in the group keeps strict account of the amount of time spent in the fields of others and is jealous of any inequalities, insisting on her rightful share. When the *egesangio* weeds eleusine, the strip of field each woman is required to weed is measured with a rope, and arguments often develop over whether or not a woman has done her full share.

To perform nonroutine tasks which cannot be done alone or which have been delayed until they must be accomplished in very little time, men use a different arrangement. If a man wants to clear heavy underbrush from a fallow field or to build a house for a new wife, he will invite neighbors to come and work on the job intensively. In exchange, he will serve his visitors the beer his wife has brewed for the occasion. If the task is agricultural, the men may send their wives and daughters to do the work while they partake of the beer. The usual aim is to finish the work in one day. House building, of course, takes many days and the men do a large part of it themselves, for women are considered competent only to smear mud on the walls and are even forbidden to thatch roofs. (This restriction is apparently designed to preserve sexual modesty.) This exchange of work for beer the Gusii call *risaga,* and men recognize two groupings of homesteads on which they can call for *risaga.* There is a "small" *risaga,* restricted to the neighboring homesteads, whose women make up the *egesangio* or cooperative work group, and the "big" *risaga,* which includes more distant homesteads. The community, Nyansongo, is one "big" *risaga* which, taken as a whole, defines a territorial unit within which homesteads may exchange beer for work but outside of which the exchange does not take place.

Although much of a homestead's agricultural produce is used for subsistence, some is also bartered or traded for cash. Coffee is marketed through a tribally owned cooperative which pays individual growers for their raw coffee beans. Surplus corn and eleusine are sold at Keumbu Market to traders who pay a price fixed by the government's Maize Control Office, sold in town on the black market at a higher price, or traded illegally to the grain-hungry Luo tribesmen. Continuing a traditional practice, Luo traders bring bags of salt they mine in their country into Gusiiland on donkeys and receive grain for the salt the Gusii must have for their cattle. A number of enterprising Nyansongo women walk 10 miles to a market on the border on Tuesdays and exchange grain for Luo pots. Later in the week they take the pots to a Gusii market at Keroka, another 8 miles from their home, and sell them for cash. These women act as "middle-men" in both the physical and economic sense.

Besides dealing in surplus grain, Nyansongo women bring bananas, oranges, cabbages, and other vegetables into the Kisii township market and sell them for cash to African market traders who in turn sell them to the Europeans and East Indians of the town. Native beer is sometimes brewed and sold for cash in beer shops in Keumbu market or to men in the community. The sale of black wattle bark to the government for export as leather tanning extract was important until the end of 1956 when the permanent collapse of the world price on natural extract destroyed its market value. Thus Nyansongo families nowadays see their agricultural activities as directed toward the market and cash returns as well as toward their own maintenance.

The desire for Western consumption goods has kept apace with opportunities to acquire cash through agriculture and employment. Nyansongans want and feel they need cash for clothing, school fees, kerosene lamps, blankets, sugar, tea, medicine, bus fares, and bicycles to mention only the more common items. In the face of these desires, the developing land shortage and overpopulation are a source of considerable anxiety. The Agriculture Department estimated an average of 7 acres per homestead in Gusiiland in 1956. Nyansongo seems to be more densely populated, but many families are allowed by their chief to cultivate sizable plots on his adjacent estate, which, since they are not charged a rental fee, helps them greatly. Even if the homesteads of Nyansongo do average 7 acres when the chief's land is included, 7 acres tilled by basically primitive methods are not enough to supply the contemporary wants of a Gusii family. Thus, as mentioned earlier, many Nyansongo men seek employment on European plantations and in the cities.

Although livestock no longer occupies the central place it once held in the Gusii economy, it is still important today. Most families in Nyansongo keep a herd of three to six cows although the family herd may be increased temporarily to as many as 15 cows, when bridewealth is paid for a daughter. Such bridewealth cattle must be used quickly for another marriage, payment of debts, or sold for cash, because the grazing lands of Nyansongo are not adequate to support such herds. A few of the wealthier men in the community have larger herds, but they are kept for them by relatives living in areas of more abundant pasturage.

Cattle are useful in the homestead's daily diet, but the great value derived from their role in the marriage system makes them too expensive to be counted on for subsistence. Cow's milk is used daily; it is allowed to sour in calabashes and then eaten. Few people nowadays can afford to kill a bull simply to eat, but beef is sometimes bought in the market, though it is eaten in small quantities. Gusii conservatism has focused on the use of cattle in bridewealth, and unlike many other Kenya tribes, they refuse to accept cash as a substitute. Thus a young man whose family does not provide him with the necessary cattle must use over $400 of his job earnings to buy cattle for a legitimate marriage. Since cows are the most costly and valuable negotiable property owned by Nyansongo men, they are a great source of ambition, jealousy, gossip, quarreling, and litigation and are loaned, bartered, sold, inherited, and stolen.

The ownership and transfer of cattle are masculine prerogatives and the preservation and allocation of the herd a typically male preoccupation. Cattle are still regarded as the soundest form of investment for a man who has adequate pasturage: they multiply themselves and can readily be turned into cash in an emergency. No man is counted as truly wealthy who does not have a sizable herd to draw on for his own plural marriages and those of his sons as well as for the payment of fees to professional sorcerers, witch smellers, and medicine men. Cattle are thus marriage licenses, savings, health insurance, and prestige symbols.

Sheep and goats are less valuable than cows in terms of cash and marriage, but they have a prominent place in religious sacrifices and the entertainment of guests. Diviners usually specify the use of a sheep or goat of a particular sex and color for funeral and medicinal sacrifices, and such orders are always obeyed. A man of above-average means shows respect to his visiting in-laws or matrilineal kin by slaughtering a goat or sheep for them to eat, while a poorer neighbor kills a chicken for their consumption. A majority of Nyansongo families do not keep sheep and goats; instead they buy one or reclaim one that is owed them whenever a need arises, as when a medicine man asks for a goat as a fee for a curative potion. Every family has chickens, which are commonly given as gifts or sold in the town market, as are the eggs they produce.

In sum, the people of Nyansongo are fairly prosperous agriculturalists who supplement their subsistence and cash crop cultivation with employment and market trade and who have retained pastoralism largely for prestige and ceremonial purposes. They have a high level of economic anxiety, arising partly from overcrowding of the land and partly from economic values which emphasize invidious distinctions based on wealth.

❦

❦

❦

Chapter 3

Social Organization *

The social universe as Nyansongans see it is made up of units of increasing size and inclusiveness from the family to the nation, all of them referred to by the same term, *egesaku,* and all composed of a group of men who recognize a common patrilineal ancestor and occupy a common territory. *Egesaku* in its most general sense thus means "lineage," although it can refer to the group of father and sons in a single homestead, a lineage at one of four levels between family and clan, a clan, one of the seven Gusii "tribes," the Gusii people as a whole as contrasted with other ethnic groups (each one of which is also termed *egesaku*), or a nation such as Kenya, the United Kingdom, or the United States. Each unit within the Gusii ethnic group is spoken of as *egesaku* when considered as a separate entity, but when considered as one of several segments of a larger social unit, it is called *enyomba,* "house." Thus each social unit is thought of as subdivided into "houses," a pattern based explicitly on the polygynous extended family, as described below.

In the Nyansongo ideal, each *egesaku* has both genealogical and residential unity. Thus the Gusii people as a whole are descended from a man named Mogusii, and the territory they occupy is Bogusii. The males of Omobea subclan (the predominant one in Nyansongo) are descended from a man named Omobea, and their territory is called Bomobea. The social realities do not always correspond to this ideal.

* The structural material in this chapter owes much to Mayer (1949, 1950b). For additional material on the Gusii family, see LeVine, "The Gusii Family," manuscript.

For example, genealogical connections between clans and tribes are obviously fictionalized. Furthermore, the clans and many of their component lineages have suffered a certain amount of territorial dispersion, especially since the recent migrations to previously uninhabited areas of Gusiiland. There are also some local units which are based primarily on residential proximity and reciprocal work obligations and which do not correspond with lineage groups. These local groups are vaguely defined and loosely organized, however, and lineage ties still have an overwhelming influence on Nyansongo life.

Table 1 lists those social units (1–6) which are referred to by special terms (as well as *egesaku* and *enyomba*) in the Gusii language, and it also includes the two largest entities, the tribe and the Gusii people.

Table 1 Gusii Social Units
(Numbered in order of increasing scope)

SPECIALLY NAMED LINEAGE UNITS	TERRITORIAL UNITS	TRANSLATION OR MEANING
	1. Omochie	homestead
2. Abanyamatati		mourning lineage
	3. (Small) Risaga	neighborhood
	4. (Large) Risaga	local community
5. Riiga		"hearthstone" lineage
6. Eamate		clan (including numerous lineages)
	7. Tribe	alliance of clans
	8. The Gusii People	the seven tribes

Several units which are not designated by special terms have been omitted from the list. These are the mother-son unit within the homestead, which is simply called *enyomba,* and two types of lineages which can exist between the "hearthstone" lineage level (5) and that of clan (6), namely, "clan-house" and "subclan." (See Table 1.)

The composition and functions of these social units are described below, but it is noteworthy at this point to mention that adult Nyansongans are much more conscious of being members of homesteads, lineages, and clans than they are of their *risaga* membership, for both neighborhoods and the local community are unnamed ("Nyansongo" is an ethnographic pseudonym) and command no loyalty in and of themselves. The uniformity of clan membership in the local community and the rough correspondence of its neighborhoods to lineage fragments allow Nyansongans to regard these territorial units as localized lineages and provide a kinship framework for relations within the community.

The basic residential unit in Nyansongo is the household, consisting of a married woman and her unmarried daughters and uninitiated (prepubertal) sons. The woman's husband may also live there, but his residence is not necessarily constant, since he may be dividing his time among the houses of several wives, sleep in the children's house occasionally, or be away working for long periods. As mentioned earlier, the house is divided into two rooms, one called *eero,* in which the husband entertains his guests, and one called *enyomba,* which is the wife's room, where she cooks and performs other domestic chores. That the house as a whole and the household as a social unit are also called *enyomba* (plural *chinyomba*) indicates the primary association of the house with the wife and her activities. The children eat and sleep in the house with their mother and help her in producing and preparing food for the household. Land adjacent to the house is used for growing some of its food, particularly vegetables, but the woman is allocated larger plots of land by her husband on a yearly basis. Eventually the wife and her children become associated with those plots which are near their house and which they have cultivated, and this is the basis for later claims to legal rights over the land. When the sons marry, they build their houses near land used by their mother and use adjacent plots which have been allocated to them by their father. Granaries containing the produce of its land stand near each household and belong to it, subject to limited rights of disposal by the woman's husband. Each household also has a herd of cattle associated with it, consisting primarily of the cows given as marriage payments for the woman's daughters, and these cattle are to be used, if her husband approves, by the sons of the woman to obtain wives for themselves. As the sons grow up, marry, and establish houses near their mother's house, they continue to think of themselves as one "household," and the term *enyomba* is used to designate the sons of one mother even after their mother has died and they are all living in separate houses of their own.

The mother-child household, though basic, is not an autonomous unit; it is related to the larger family by links of marriage and paternity. Polygyny is viewed as the ideal form of marriage. In Nyansongo 15 men are monogamists, 11 men have two wives each, and 1 has three wives.* Of the married women, 21 are plural wives,† 19 are monogamous wives or widows, and 3 are the unattached widows of a polygynist continuing to live as co-wives. Despite the roughly equivalent number of polygynous and monogamous adults, more than two thirds of the community's children have polygynous parents. This is due to the fact that a sizable proportion of the monogamous men are young husbands whose wives have not yet given birth or have done so only once. By the time they have many children, these men will probably have taken additional wives and thereby become polygynous parents. Thus a large majority of Nyansongo children grow up in polygynous homes. In this respect Nyansongo is not exceptional, for in adjacent communities there are men with four and five wives and even a few wealthy elders with as many as eleven wives and scores of children.

Plurality of wives and offspring is a major ambition of Nyansongo men. Four is said to be the ideal number of wives because the households of the wives are linked in successive pairs within which bridewealth loans may be contracted and which are inheritance units. Thus the first is so linked with the second, third with fourth, and so on. An uneven number of wives is considered a troublesome and incomplete situation. The first four wives are titled—first is "the ash-sweeper," second, "the helper," third, "above the cattle pen," and fourth, "the gate." Later wives have no such traditional titles.

Each wife has her own house, separated from that of her co-wife by at least one field or pasture in a conscious effort to prevent (or contain) dissension. Every wife has to bring the husband a basket of porridge at least once a day, and although he cannot consume all that is brought, he eats at least a mouthful from the basket brought by each wife. The rest of the food is then taken back to be eaten by the children. The husband sleeps with the several wives in their houses according to his pleasure, staying the longest period of weeks with the youngest and fairest. He is supposed to honor each woman's desire to have children at regular intervals, regardless of his preference.

Ideally a Nyansongo wife should obey her husband at all times and be deferential to him. She should accept his allocation of land and cattle and consult him before she takes any important action. She should respond quickly to his demands for food and drink, and pro-

---

* Two men have plural wives who did not live in Nyansongo during the period of field work; the men are counted as polygynists, but their nonresident wives are not included in the enumeration of women.

† Included are leviratic wives living with brothers or cousins of their dead husbands.

vide hospitality for his guests. He will not be pleased if she spends too much time away from her domestic duties at home, and he will be furious if she allows anyone to eat from his basket of food before he has done so, no matter how late he is.

There are several potent sanctions a polygynist can use against a wife who disobeys him or violates a cultural rule. Refusing to sleep with a wife is not only a gross sign of his displeasure but also, if it lasts long enough, a withdrawal of her only means of achieving status and prestige—her capacity to bear children. As there are severe supernatural sanctions against adultery, it is difficult for her to escape this punishment of the husband. More often, however, the husband publicly refuses to eat the food of the offending wife. He may even break the basket and throw the food on the ground. In doing so, he is said to "refuse her" (using the verb *okogira*), which literally refers to the refusal of food but carries with it the implication of sexual and emotional rejection. A 10-year-old Nyansongo boy once gleefully informed a friend of an incident in which his father, displeased by the failure of his second wife (not the boy's mother) to weed his coffee garden, had angrily spilled onto the ground the food she brought him and smashed the container in which it came. Wife-beating is also a common and socially accepted practice, and although it may accompany refusal of food or sexual rejection, the latter two are more potent in a polygynous family. Each wife wants to be her husband's favorite and to have her children favored by him over the children of other wives. Consequently, she may be easily hurt by signs of the husband's emotional rejection.

When a rebuked wife acknowledges her guilt, she goes to her parents for a goat to effect reconciliation. Bringing the goat to her husband, she cooks for him twice. The second time he eats her food and they become reconciled. An older wife may act as mediator in disputes among the wives, but there is no institutionalized pattern of seniority or authority among them.

Most Nyansongo wives are so spontaneous in their performance of the chores which are expected of them and so automatic in their respect for important masculine prerogatives that their husbands do not need to issue commands. On minor issues and family matters, a wife may loudly proclaim her opinions, but she expects to be ignored by her husband, and this is what usually happens. The taciturnity of husbands and the garrulousness of wives sometimes give the impression that women have more authority in the family than they in fact do. Husbands refrain from exercising their authority, or in some cases from even paying attention to their wives, until they feel that the wife needs correction or an important decision must be made. They then expect obedience and may use punishment if it is not forthcoming. Two Nyansongo men are notorious for having wives "who rule them." Both are monogamists, for their domineering spouses succeeded in preventing secondary marriages. The wife of old Osano, a woman in her 60's, interferes with her husband's responses to questions and answers them herself. Their adult sons have committed a number of sex and property crimes, but Osano is unable to control them. Nyakoe, a man in his 40's, who has a minor judicial position, is not so subordinate to his wife in talking to visitors, but it is obvious that she has more control over the children than he does, and he appears to listen to her advice on many matters. She is widely reputed to be a witch and has been publicly accused. Both couples are considered deviant in Nyansongo because of their reversal of the acceptable authority relationship between husband and wife.

Despite their desire for polygyny, Nyansongo men recognize that it brings them trouble. Dissensions among co-wives is one of the most common themes in Gusii folklore. One proverb is: "Another child-bearer is like an ancestor spirit at the outside wall." This is interpreted as meaning that secondary wives bring hatred which can result in murder and invoke the wrath of the spirits. There is a special word, *engareka,* which means "hatred between co-wives," and a folktale about how *engareka* caused the first cooking of porridge.

Long ago, before the Gusii cooked food, there was a man who had one wife. He wanted to take a second wife but she opposed it bitterly. He took a second wife anyway, and when she had her first baby, she naturally stayed in the house for about a week. During that time the first wife brought her food. The first wife thought that if she made the porridge very hot over a fire, it would kill the second wife. When she served it to her, she noticed it made the second wife perspire and was certain it would work. But after the week was over, the second wife was fat and healthy and said she liked the hot porridge. After that, people cooked their porridge instead of leaving it uncooked.

This folktale expresses the real emotions that characterize Nyansongo wives. Many a first wife is extremely opposed to her husband's taking another wife, and this is a frequent cause of quarreling. Women realize that monogamy gives them much greater power in the family, and some of them are determined to retain that power. The wife of a monogamous husband can punish him by refusing herself to him sexually or by refusing to work in home and garden. She most often does this by going to live with her parents for a week or more. When the precipitating quarrel has concerned the husband's taking a second wife, he mav be sufficiently cowed by her desertion to give up the idea.

On the other hand, though, he may become convinced that a second wife is needed to free him from exclusive dependence on her. Once he has a second wife, the situation is reversed; *he* is the one who can punish by abandoning one for the other, and they become dependent on his favor.

For example, Manyara, a Nyansongo man in his 30's, had a rather dominant wife, Kerubo, and three children. When he began negotiating for another marriage, Kerubo ran away for some time and then came back. Manyara married the girl anyway and took her to a European plantation where he worked for a few months until she became pregnant. Being somewhat fearful of Kerubo's wrath, he wanted to present her with the *fait accompli* of the girl's pregnancy so that no pressure could dissolve the marriage. Kerubo refused to be more than barely civil to the girl, although, like a good wife, she sent food to the new house where the newlyweds were living. The new wife had a miscarriage and subsequently suffered from swollen breasts. Under such conditions she could hardly fail to assume that her misfortune was due to Kerubo's ill wishes (through witchcraft). Several months later, Kerubo complained privately that Manyara was spending all his money on fancy dresses for his bride, while she and her children went in rags and had no money to buy medicines for the youngest daughter's bronchitis. The animosity in this polygynous situation was so great from the start that only with difficulty will Manyara be able to keep it from resulting in open conflict. By his second marriage he forced Kerubo into submission but inadvertently turned her hostility against the new woman, who cannot but reciprocate eventually. Such ill feeling among co-wives is the price of polygyny.

Each wife tends to be the husband's darling when she is the latest and to maintain that position until he marries again. A Gusii proverb admonishes, "Never throw away an old grass ring (used for carrying pots on the head)," meaning that the older wives should not be neglected, but polygynists are said to "grow old toward the gate," that is, to prefer younger wives (such as the fourth, "the gate," last in the ideal pattern) as they get older. This tendency in itself causes jealousy among the wives. In addition, any inequality in the distribution of gifts or money, or in the number of children born and died, or in the amount of education received by the children, adds to the jealousy and hatred. A woman who becomes barren or whose children die almost always believes that her co-wife has achieved this through witchcraft or poisoning. She may then attempt retaliation.

Although bitter hatred may develop between co-wives, there are some Nyansongo families in which they get on well and cooperate closely. In one case, three co-widows maintain nearby households in conspicuous amity, which they attribute to their husband's deliberate attempts to foster good will before his death 17 years ago. At three homesteads where the co-wives are disparate in age—two of the older wives have children the same age as their co-wives—there are amicable relations among the women. In these cases the younger wife has accepted domination by the older, working with her in the fields, asking her advice and help in child care, gossiping casually with her in the afternoon, and so on. Where co-wives are closer in age, they may be superficially polite and cooperative but harbor grudges which result in their not talking for months at a time.

The husband who attempts to foster good will between co-wives is rare. Ordinarily he takes measures only to prevent already existing hatred from becoming expressed in violent acts. The usual provocation is the wife's refusal to do something for the husband on the grounds that the co-wife has not been doing her share. The husband, aware of the bitterness between them, takes the occasion to punish the one he regards as responsible. He may beat her or reprimand her semipublicly, so that neighbors can hear it. One morning Ogaro was reprimanding his second wife, Nyaboke, a young woman who has a girl of 12 and one of 8 and who has not been able to conceive again, while her older co-wife, Moraa, produces a child every two years. He was outside Nyaboke's house, shouting at her:

Moraa (first wife) is about to give birth and you won't work and go out drinking everywhere, coming back late at night. You may think because you don't have small children you can go wherever you want. But there are many women who have no children and they're obedient to their husbands and work hard. If you think it's me who is not giving you children, I'm not forcing you to stay here. Go somewhere else and see if you get children there.
Nyaboke: One time I was ill and Moraa didn't help me and didn't bring me anything.
Ogaro: If that is the case, then don't you go to her or help her now, but you obey me. (Turning to an old man): I'm about to leave for work at Kericho and I want you to tell her to obey me and keep feuds from occurring in my homestead. (Turning back to Nyaboke): I didn't want to quarrel, but you quarreled with her (Moraa's) daughter and you seem to want her not to have children. I didn't stop you from having children, it was God, and you can go accuse God if you want. When you were ill, I took time to take you for treatment, and most of the property, like the goat (for sacrifice), for that purpose came from Moraa's house. Well now I'm returning to work and if you follow me there I'll kick you and beat you, and you'll never see a cent from me again . . . You always claim that Moraa is given more. When I give you each five shillings, you say I've given her ten. And when I give you each a pound of sugar, you say I've given her five pounds. And it's the same with meat.

This case illustrates the troubles arising from the inequalities in child-bearing capacity among co-wives and the way in which the husband treats the jealousy when it is abruptly brought to his attention. So long as the wives have a superficially friendly relationship, however, he is unlikely to make threats or humiliate one or the other of them.

THE EXTENDED FAMILY HOMESTEAD

The extended family homestead is a clearly defined social and territorial entity which includes one or more mother-child households. It has such autonomy as a residential unit that educated Gusii refer to it in English as "village," although it is much smaller than a village in the ordinary sense. The residents of a homestead are: the man who is homestead head, his wives, his unmarried children, and his married sons and their wives and children. It is thus equivalent to the polygynous extended family as a local group. The homestead has its own land and cattle and is separated from other homesteads by boundary hedges, trees, and jointly used pastures.

Although there is a word in the Gusii language which means homestead (*omochie*), a particular homestead group may be referred to as the *egesaku* * or "patrilineal descent group" of its head. In this sense it means the head and his sons, his male descendants, who continue to live there throughout their lives and whose sons will live there too. The descent group is thought of as being divided into several *chinyomba* or "households," each one composed of the sons of a particular wife. Full brothers, who actually grew up in the same house (*enyomba*) —that of their mother—comprise as adults a symbolic household distinct from the sons of other mothers within the descent group of the homestead. This division is spatially represented (see map 3, p. 25) by the fact that married sons build their houses nearer to the houses of their mothers than to the houses of the father's other wives; it is represented in behavior by closer and friendlier relations between full brothers and their wives than between half-brothers and their wives. Many of the hostilities between the co-wives are thus passed on to their sons.

The homestead head is traditionally a patriarch with much control of family resources. He takes charge of all transactions from the nego-

* Literally, *egesaku* refers to the side entrance to a Gusii house from the cattle pen. The application of this label to the descent group apparently refers both to the identity of that group with its herds of cattle and to the fact that patrilineally related elders must enter the house through that door.

tiations for a daughter's bridewealth to the purchase of coffee seedlings. All the land and cattle of the homestead legally belong to him despite their "temporary" allocation among the several households. When he dies, the property is inherited by his sons (or closest heirs in the male line), supposedly according to his last instructions. Legitimate claims to property left by the father, however, are based by the son on which fields were cultivated by his mother and how many head of cattle, sheep, and goats were associated with her household. The cattle given as bridewealth for the daughters of a woman and any animals or grain acquired through her own efforts are thought of as belonging to her household and being reserved primarily for the marriages or inheritance of the woman's sons. The homestead head has the power to use such property for his own secondary marriages or for the marriages of sons of other households under certain circumstances (Mayer, 1950b: 27–29), but by doing so he establishes a debt between the household of the new wife and the one from which the cattle were taken. Such debts are never forgotten, and if not settled during the lifetime of the homestead head, they come up as inheritance disputes afterward. Thus the division of the homestead into mother-son units figures importantly in the allocation and inheritance of property.

In the relationship between a Nyansongo father and his adult son, formality, respect, and obedience are key qualities. The son is expected to act deferentially to his father, never contradict or embarrass him, and certainly never shout at him regardless of provocation. The father, however, may shout at the son and scold him abusively for misdeeds. Father and son may never bathe together, see each other naked, or discuss sexual topics in the presence of each other. Even their jointly hearing a sexual discussion or witnessing the copulation of animals is embarrassing. A son may want to ask his father to help him buy medicines to cure venereal disease, but he must confess his contraction of the disease through intermediaries rather than experience the shame of discussing it directly. This sex avoidance and embarrassment between persons of adjacent generations are called *ensoni* and will be discussed for other relationships later. In Nyansongo thought, the quintessence of *ensoni* in the father-son relationship is the rule that the father must never enter the house of a married son; both daughter-in-law avoidance and general privacy from the homestead head appear to be involved in this. A good son is not only deferential but also obedient, and the father's commands may involve his son's marriages, economic affairs, and the welfare of his children. The son is dependent on his father for cattle to marry with, land to cultivate, and the favor that will help him establish himself as an heir in good standing when the father dies. Although a son may go off and earn money outside the district, it is rarely enough to provide him with a full bridewealth at a young age. Furthermore, the father expects the son to bring him expensive gifts, such as blankets, lanterns, supplies of tea and sugar. Some sons are unwilling to share their earnings with their fathers, particularly because where money is concerned, they fear the father's turning it over to his other sons for immediate use in bridewealth or school fees. In general, however, sons do share their earnings, are glad to help their brothers in education, if not in marriage, and bestow gifts on their fathers. The obedience of contemporary sons may not be as great as it once was, but except in economic crises, Nyansongo filial piety would rank high on a world-wide scale.

In everyday interaction, Nyansongo adult sons and fathers do not overtly display the dominance-submission relationship which holds between them. A son will stay out of his father's way for the most part, and a father does not attempt to interfere with the daily movements and activities of his sons so long as they are not disruptive. But a father takes very seriously the rules of the relationship, refusing, for example, to enter a son's house for a chair for a visitor, even though there is no one else to get it and he wants to provide for his guest. In matters of marriage and property, the dominance of the father, and his severity if not respected, becomes manifest. The father of one Nyansongo son who sold a cow for school fees had him arrested by the Kenya police and burned down his house while he was in custody. A father may also put a curse on a disobedient son and beat the latter's mother. Most sons are keenly aware of their father's powers to punish them, and they obtain paternal permission before making any decision to allocate property.

Mother-son relations, by contrast with father-son, are more informal but also involve sex avoidance. Mother and son may argue freely without fear of offending each other so long as obscene expressions are not used. A son respects his mother but is not deferential to her, and their interaction has a relaxed, lighthearted quality that is never found between father and son. In terms of sex avoidance, the adult son may not go behind the partition (see Figure 1, p. 26) in his mother's house; he must be served food by her in the foyer of the house or outside. The explicit reason for this is sexual modesty, since the son should not see his mother squatting over the cooking fire with her dress pulled up on her thighs and should not be in the presence of her marital bed. Sexual activities and obscenity must not be an object of their joint attention, and here again deep embarrassment may be experienced if one breaks this rule or accidentally intrudes on the privacy of the other. When this happens, one party or the other leaves the scene, and the occurrence is not mentioned afterward.

The mutual loyalty of mothers and adult sons is a pronounced characteristic of Nyansongo families. A mother never admits to outsiders that her son has done wrong, no matter what the opinion of the community. One woman whose dead son had been a notorious thief would not concede this about him, even though the whole homestead was allegedly endangered by antitheft magic as a result of her refusal. A widow whose son had been deserted by two successive wives complained bitterly about the moral character of the wives even though circumstances indicated that her son was impotent, which is a legitimate ground for divorce. When rambunctious women destroyed a potato field of the same widow during female initiation ceremonies, her son ran out to chase the women and threatened them with punishment. This reciprocal protectiveness is a recognition of their common fate, for a son acquires his share of the patrimony through rights established by the mother and her daughters, while a mother gains helpers in her daughters-in-law and is dependent on her sons and their wives when she is old and feeble.

The *ensoni* feeling of sexual shame is considered by Nyansongans to be at the very core of their morality. In the homestead it is strongest between father and daughter or daughter-in-law, next strongest between father and sons, less between mother and son and weakest between mother and daughter or daughter-in-law. Among siblings of the same sex, it is only felt if there is a difference in age of a decade or more and even then may not be strong or permanent.

The homestead head uses his traditionally dominant position *vis-à-vis* wives and sons to keep conflict between the several households at a minimum. In such conflict a mother and her adult sons will act as a unit, with sons defending their mother against the father's favoritism, and the mother pleading with the father not to punish or disinherit a disobedient son even though she knows he has done wrong. Most polygynists find it necessary to maintain an attitude of impartiality with respect to their several households in order to avoid fanning the flames of family strife by undue favoritism. Those who are wealthy or have many wives have nearby houses of their own separate from those of their wives where they can spend time without arousing jealousy. A polygynist also has *emonga*, that is, land the produce from which is not allocated to the households but kept for his own use. Impartiality and a forceful, domineering manner constitute the Nyansongo formula for a successful homestead head. Even when friendly and cooperative relations among wives and half-brothers are maintained in the conduct of everyday affairs, however, an unequal occurrence of personal misfortune may mobilize latent aggression between households in the form of witchcraft or sorcery accusations. When the homestead head dies, the homestead most often dissolves as a social unit, each married son tending to form his own homestead on the land left by his father, with his mother and perhaps an unmarried brother continuing to reside there. In the acrimonious disputes over inherited property, one or more of the sons may decide to move elsewhere if land is available. Since the land is rapidly becoming filled up, more sons are now forced to remain at their father's homestead after his death, and land holdings are consequently becoming fragmented into smaller pieces.

THE LINEAGE SYSTEM

The patrilineal descent group of the Nyansongo homestead is the nucleus of an extensive system of patrilineages which plays an important part in the organization of Gusii social life. As with the descent group of the homestead, only men are full members of this system, and descent is traced through the male line to a common ancestor. Several related homesteads whose male members are descendants of one grandfather recognize themselves as a single mourning group * (*abanyamatati*) and observe a rule of ritual head-shaving at each other's funerals. They also eat the sacrificial meat together at the funeral and were at one time responsible for providing compensation for a homicide committed by one of their members. Two or more mourning groups together compose a *riiga* † ("hearthstone" lineage); its male members are usually descendants of one great-grandfather or great-great-grandfather. The *riiga* lineage is the largest kin group within which there is much hospitality and intimacy and was in some areas associated in the past with the joint herding of cattle by young men. Several related *riiga* lineages form a "clan-house"; two or more clan-houses compose a subclan; and several subclans make up a clan. The amount of subdivision within a clan varies from one area to another, particularly with size; a large clan often recognizes many more units between the *riiga* and clan levels than does a small clan. The clan ‡ is a large patrilineage which was often an independent political-

---

* For the exact relationships involved in the mourning group, see Mayer (1949: 18–19).

† *Riiga* literally means "hearthstone" of which a house has three, and metaphorically denotes subdivisions of a clan. See Table 1, p. 37.

‡ We follow Mayer (1949: 9–10) in using the word clan to refer to the maximal exogamous lineage, called *eamate* in the Gusii language.

military unit before British administration, and it is also the largest exogamous unit, requiring its members to marry outside the group, and the maximal group within which kinship terms are used. Thus the proximate Gusii lineage system is made up of kin groups increasing in inclusiveness and generational depth from homestead group to clan, all based on the principle of tracing descent through the male line to a common ancestor.

The lineage groups in Nyansongo are not intact lineages for the most part but fragments of kin groups whose other members either remained in older settlements or moved to different ones in Nyaribari during the migration to new areas that began in 1930. Every man in Nyansongo is a member of a hearthstone lineage (and hence of a subclan and clan) which has members in other communities; some persons even have fellow members of their mourning group living elsewhere. Despite their territorial dispersal and the cessation of their joint military activity, lineages of hearthstone level and below do have some corporate functions based on inheritance rights in each other's property. If a man dies without sons, his brothers inherit his land and cattle; if he has no brothers either, then property is inherited by those lineage members who stand closest in relationship to the deceased. If a whole mourning group were wiped out, its property would be inherited by a mourning group of the same hearthstone lineage, and so forth. In similar fashion are widows inherited, except that the heir must be of the same generation, and the widow has some freedom of choice. These inheritance rights, though residual, produce a sense of common interest in members of a lineage even when they are not living near one another. Many of the contemporary inhabitants of Nyansongo settled there at the invitation of fellow lineage members who took up residence there first. The military defense of joint property is no longer a consideration, but lineage members have been known to share the expenses of litigation in order to keep a disputed piece of land from being taken by someone of a different lineage. In general, a lineage of any order tends to act as a unit only when its interests are endangered by outsiders; such occasions are fewer nowadays than 50 years ago.

A striking feature of the Gusii lineage system is its use of the family idiom in the conceptualization of relations between descent groups. As mentioned above, just as the descent group of the homestead is called the *egesaku* of its head, and is made up of *chinyomba* or households, so a lineage of any order is the *egesaku* of its founding ancestor and is made up of subdivisions called *chinyomba*. This usage is perfectly consistent with the terminology referring to the homestead, since lineage members trace their ancestry back to a particular homestead head and, furthermore, often distinguish segments of the lineage by reference to his different wives and their households. The genealogy of a lineage is its history from its origin as a polygynous family to its present state. Lineages also suffer from the same internal dissensions as homesteads; the larger they are, the more segments or "households" they have, each one of which is jealous and suspicious of the other. Thus not only the same nomenclature but also some of the same motivations characterize both polygynous families and the lineages for which they are points of origin.

The family analogy also affects the rules of behavior among members of a clan. One's real father and mother are called *tata* and *baba*, respectively. All men of one's father's generation within the clan are called *tatamoke,* "little father," and clanswomen of the parental generation are called *makomoke,* which English-speaking Gusii translate as "little mother." In like manner, clansmen of the grandparental generation are called "grandmother" or "grandfather," and those of one's own generation are considered, if not called, "brother" and "sister." Nieces, nephews, and other clanspersons of that generation are called "my child," and those of the grand-nephew generation are called "grandchild." Thus for a given individual, the entire clan is made up of several generational layers, to each one of which he applies one or two terms derived from relationships in his immediate family.

There are definite rules concerning the individual's behavior toward persons in each of the generational layers. The parental generation is made up of his *abansoni,* that is, the persons in whose presence he experiences *ensoni* or sexual shame. Just as he must avoid physical immodesty and sexual discussion in the presence of his real parents, so must he practice such avoidance with respect to his "little fathers" and "little mothers" throughout the clan. The avoidance rules for classificatory parents are not quite as strict as those within the homestead group, for example, while a real father may not enter a son's house at all, a classificatory father may enter one room (*eero*) of the house and only through the cattle-pen doorway (*egesaku*). Furthermore, a man's father's brother (his "little father") may be his own age or younger, contrary to the implications of the paternity relationship. In such a case, serious avoidance does not begin until one of the parties has married, and it becomes stricter as they get older. The reserve of real father and son, however, is never reached, and a man may make passing reference to publicly known sex crimes in the presence of his father's brother while he could not do so within hearing of his real father. Hence, though behavior toward clansmen of the parental generation is patterned after customary behavior toward real parents, avoidance is not expected to be as intense in the case of classificatory parents.

Many incidents occurring in Nyansongo, where everyone belongs to the same clan, indicated that *ensoni* between adjacent generations is not merely a matter of formal etiquette but a feeling experienced by individuals. A beer party discussion of venereal disease and adultery was abruptly stopped by a group of men when a classificatory daughter of some of them arrived on the scene. When a middle-aged woman was describing supernatural punishment for adultery to the ethnographer, her real daughter and a classificatory daughter-in-law giggled for a while, then retired to another house in the homestead, and warned away other visitors of their generation. During the female initiation ceremonies, when women, especially those of middle age, are permitted to disregard verbal and physical modesty as they sing and dance in public places, the younger men—their classificatory sons—assiduously avoided these places whenever possible. When by ritual necessity or accident they were present at such occasions, the men displayed signs of acute embarrassment and fled at the first opportunity. Sexual embarrassment is more intense between persons who are not only of adjacent generational layers but also of opposite sex. An informant expressed the mortification experienced by the crowd at a magical ceremony when two chickens happened to copulate, by saying, "It was shameful; 'fathers' and 'daughters' were there."

Feelings of sexual shame can be avoided by conformity to the avoidance rules for persons of adjacent generations. With kin of the parental generation within the clan (and parents-in-law outside) one may not: shake hands (customary greeting between equals), sleep in the same house (except for adjacent generation females), bathe together or see each other naked, engage in joking insults (which are usually obscene), discuss sexual topics freely, or argue freely. The last mentioned rule is sometimes considered separately as "respect" (*ogosika*), since it is a prohibition on verbal aggression rather than sexual immodesty as such. In general, the attitude of respect is more important for conduct toward "little fathers" and sex avoidance more important with "little mothers." The maintenance of properly restrained behavior causing embarrassment to no one is facilitated by the use of an elaborate euphemistic vocabulary for sex and bodily functions in discussion between adjacent generation persons.

The rules governing relationships between clansmen not of adjacent generations require less restraint and involve less embarrassment; they lack the elements of sex avoidance and respect which characterize classificatory parent-child relations. This lack of restraint is particularly striking in relations between an individual and his real or classificatory grandparents. He may discuss sex and insult them jokingly. In fact, the characteristic pattern of interaction in this relationship involves obscene insults, humorous inquiries about sexual activity, and deprecation of the other's sexual competence. Despite the reciprocal nature of this warm, joking relationship, real grandparents may make economic demands which must be respected by the grandchild. If a classificatory grandparent is approximately the same age as the grandchild, their relations are as free and equal as if they were of the same generational status. Great-grandparents, however, are "like parents" and must be treated with the respect and sex avoidance required in adjacent-generation relations.

With clanspeople of one's own generation, classificatory brothers and sisters, one may shake hands, enter each other's houses, and argue. Sexual shame as such is not felt with these generational equals, but cross-sex avoidance is nevertheless practiced, at least in public situations. For example, a young man may bathe at the river with his male same-generation kin, sleep in the same house, and discuss sex topics with them, using obscene expressions. All of these are prohibited with *female* kin of the same generation and clan, who are barred as sex objects by the incest taboo. Despite the fact that this taboo is frequently violated by young adolescents, boys are afraid to treat such girls in a familiar way in public because of the possibility of discovery by someone of the parental generation. In general, however, it is within the same generation in a clan that relationships of the greatest intimacy and freedom are carried on.

To summarize, the Gusii lineage system is a set of organized social groups based on common descent through the paternal line and on varying degrees of common locality and mutual interest. Lineage structure and growth are explicitly conceived of in terms derived from the polygynous family homestead, which is the nuclear unit of the system. Each lineage up to and including the clan is stratified into generations whose relationships are explicitly patterned after, though not identical with, customary relationships in the family. Sex avoidance and unilateral respect characterize the relations of adjacent generations, while less restrained behavior is possible for persons of alternate generations and those of the same generation.

LOCALIZED KIN GROUPS

All of the inhabitants of Nyansongo community belong to a single clan, Abanyaribari, the largest clan in Nyaribari Location and the one to which the chief belongs. There are three neighborhoods in the community, each one consisting of a separate lineage fragment. The smallest neighborhood, on the side of Nyansongo nearest to the chief's estate, is composed of four homesteads of the chief's subclan, Bonyamosicho, which was formerly represented in the area in larger numbers. Each of the four homesteads is closely related to only one of the others. The other two neighborhoods contain seven homesteads apiece of the Omobea subclan. In one of them the oldest males of the seven homesteads trace their ancestry to two wives of a common great-grandfather; in the other, the homestead heads are descended from three wives of a common great-great-grandfather. Many of the other descendants of these ancestors are living in similar communities elsewhere in Nyaribari Location. The lineage fragments composing the three neighborhoods of Nyansongo are on friendly terms, despite the fact that they do not have a common subclan affiliation. In fact, two homesteads have most of their neighborly relationships with homesteads outside of their own lineage groups; both are on neighborhood borders and have been involved in quarrels with their own kinsmen. Thus Nyansongo is a one-clan community composed of three lineage fragments living in somewhat vaguely defined neighborhoods.

Clan membership gives residents of Nyansongo some sense of common identity, particularly because the community borders on the communities of two alien and formerly hostile clans with whom Nyansongans intermarry. Even those families who have out-clan neighbors living nearer to them than anyone else have a minimum of contact with these unrelated people. All of their visiting, beer drinking, and cooperative work arrangements are with their Nyansongo clansmen. Where Nyansongo bounds a community of the same clan, however, active social relationships are carried on across the border, to the point that it was difficult to determine the community to which such borderline homesteads primarily belong. The social interaction of Nyansongo homesteads is thus conditioned by clan affiliation as well as by mere spatial proximity.

COMMUNITY AND NEIGHBORHOOD

The local community is defined here as the largest unit of contiguous homesteads which recognize the reciprocal obligation to participate in the trading of work for beer, known as *risaga*. The unit is thus equivalent to what the Gusii call "large *risaga*." Ordinarily, natural features such as streams or groves of trees define some of the boundaries of this group. Community members are members of the same clan, though they may be of different lineages, and as part of the *risaga* relationship, they recognize a one-day ban on heavy work for each other's funerals and hold their initiation ceremonies jointly. Each community is made up of several neighborhoods. A neighborhood is a cluster of homesteads whose members belong to the same lineage (either mourning group or *riiga*) and who work and visit with one another more frequently than they do with other members of the same community. The neighborhood is roughly equivalent to the "small *risaga*," more frequently used for trading work for beer than its larger counterpart. The women of one neighborhood tend to form a single cooperative work group (*egesangio*). Although the neighborhood is a territorial unit within the community, its boundaries may not be marked by any natural features. Homesteads at the boundaries of two neighborhoods may be more closely related to one by descent but work with the other. Homesteads bordering other communities of the same clan may shift their orientation from one community to another, causing uncertainty as to the exact boundary. Neither the community nor the neighborhood has any formal organization or institutionalized leadership.

SOCIAL SOLIDARITY

Although the people of Nyansongo cooperate in work, recreation, and ritual, and although their relations are conditioned by kinship regulations, they value homestead privacy and autonomy over neighborhood solidarity. The local community as an unnamed segment of a continuously settled area, with no formal political organization of its own, does not inspire special loyalty in its members. The settlement of dispersed homesteads has no public place or building as a spatial focus for group sociability. Accidental meetings of persons from different homesteads occur on the road, along the paths, and at the stream, but prolonged gatherings occur only at private residences and tend to be small. Despite the subdivision of the community along neighborhood and lineage lines, there is no factionalism, partly because the community has too few joint activities around which factions might crystallize. Individual homestead groups frequently develop antagonisms with one another and sometimes break off relations, but such quarrels usually arise within neighborhoods and lineage fragments rather than between them. The result is that there are no strongly cohesive groupings of homesteads in Nyansongo.

✺
✺
✺

Chapter 4

Daily Routine

The activities of the Nyansongo family are not regulated by accurate calculation of time but by the sun and the press of seasonal circumstances. Each married woman (except the newly married, who eats at the house of her mother-in-law) has her own house, fields, and granary and is responsible for the cultivation of the fields as well for preparing food for her unmarried children (most of whom live in her house), her husband, and overnight visitors. With so many tasks to perform it is not surprising that the adult woman of the house is the first to rise in the morning, often at dawn, and after quickly dressing, builds a fire on which to cook eleusine gruel for the family's breakfast. On some mornings in the seasons of greatest agricultural activity, pressure from her cooperative work group to leave early forces the woman to provide her husband and children only with cold leftovers from the previous evening's meal.

Adult men arise later than their hard-working wives unless they have to attend a case at the African Tribunal Court, for which they may leave before dawn to make sure they arrive during the morning session. If a man does not have any specific task to do in the morning, he will eat and sit awhile, wrapped in the blanket under which he slept, before getting dressed. The children get up and eat when they want, though rarely much later than their mother, and they do not bother to dress until a few hours later. The boy or boys responsible for cattle herding must let the cows out of their pen next to the house and take them to the pasture before 8:30 A.M. Men and older children dash cold water on their faces in the morning, but washing is not considered a necessary part of the daily routine, except by adolescent girls. Each individual goes into a grove of trees or a bushy pasture for elimination, in order to insure complete privacy. Leaves serve as toilet paper.

Morning at the house is punctuated by the comings and goings of the individual residents. The woman of the house goes to work in the fields and leaves a child at home in charge. The boys are out in the pastures with the livestock, and girls carry pots of water home from the stream below. The man of the house may be occupied at home with mending fences, building a house, or tending to his coffee garden, or he may be helping a neighbor perform these chores in return for beer. If he goes to court or to see the chief or a government official for some favor, he will be away from home for the better part of the day. Despite the apparent dispersal of men, women, and children, it is often the case that no one is far from the house. The woman may be working a field adjacent to the homestead; the cattle pastures are nearby; and the stream is only a few hundred yards down the hill. Thus, except for those families who live nearer to the chief and cultivate land on his estate a mile or two from their homes, homesteads are not deserted during the daytime, for many family activities take place within shouting distance of home.

At 10:30 or 11:00 in the morning, the boys bring the cows home to be milked, and if the mother has been working nearby, she does the milking herself. She may cook a meal for the children at this time, particularly if breakfast has been inadequate and they are hungry. Such a meal may be simply boiled sweet potatoes or, if the father or guests are present, it may consist of baskets of dry maize or eleusine porridge (cooked by boiling meal in water) with beans, soured milk, or a spinach-like wild leaf called *chinsaga,* as a condiment. A large piece of dry porridge is taken by hand and cupped into shape so that it can be used to pick up some of the condiment. Meat can be used as a condiment, but the people of Nyansongo cannot afford meat; grain porridge predominates in their daily diet.

During midday, the women do not continue their cooperative cultivation but return to it either in the cool of the late afternoon or the next morning. At home, besides preparing the midday meal they attend to the grinding and threshing of eleusine, fetch water from the river, direct the work of the children in various tasks, visit one another, and pack kerosene tins full of corn kernels to be taken to the power mill two miles away for grinding into meal. If they expect to entertain guests or neighbors in the near future, the women bury grain flour and germinate eleusine in the earth for several days and fry it into small hard pieces which, when diluted with boiling water, make the beer the Gusii love so well. The boys take the cattle down to the stream to drink at noon, and girls continue the tasks their mothers have ordered them to perform. Local litigation takes place in the early afternoon and is an occasional focus of attention for adult men in the community. Otherwise there are no distinctive afternoon activities.

There is no rigid daytime schedule which the people of Nyansongo follow; each adult varies his schedule from day to day on the basis of family needs, neighborhood events, and personal inclination. As the day ends, however, individual activities converge into set routines which vary only with age and sex status. Women collect firewood in pastures and fallow fields. As they move about in the dusk, they are often frightened by the eerie shapes of bushes and trees which they imagine to be wild animals. Because of this tendency, the Gusii call the period of day in which the sun sets "women's eyes."

For married men this is the time of day for beer parties. Any Nyansongo man meeting a friend or neighbor in the late afternoon will ask where he is coming from and if there is beer there. Many men will find their way to the house of one who is serving beer to his neighbors. Each one brings his own 4-foot long bamboo drinking tube, puts it into the pot of boiling beer, and sits down inside the house to drink. Married women are allowed to drink a bit of the beer, but unmarried men are excluded from the house to avert the possibility of a quarrel with their elders when intoxicated. Despite such preventive measures, beer parties are often the scenes of bitter quarrels among neighbor-relatives, and most Gusii crimes of violence take place during or after a good deal of such drinking. Singing of traditional songs and individual dancing (mostly arm and neck movements) go on, but the pleasant atmosphere can easily be broken by a belligerent boast or deliberate insult aimed at one man by another, if both are drunk.

In the house where a beer party is not in progress, the wife prepares a meal of dry porridge and condiments for her husband and children. The children eat from one basket, and a separate basket of porridge is prepared for the husband. If he is at a party at which a large quantity of beer prolongs the gathering until late at night, the wife and children eat by themselves but leave the husband's food intact to be eaten by him on his return.

Fear of the dark drastically limits nocturnal activity in Nyansongo. Witches are most feared at night, but there is also a widespread (and incorrect) belief that hyenas are at large in the area and that they harm humans. Women are much more reluctant to go out at night than men, who by adolescence have overcome some of the nocturnal fears of childhood. Married women who walk miles away from home by themselves in the daytime are at night too frightened to go 20 yards to another house in the homestead unaccompanied. Unmarried men are the most frequent voyagers in the night, seeking sexual liaisons and arranging dancing parties with young girls whose fears must be constantly allayed. The men themselves carry kerosene lanterns to still their own apprehensions.

House-bound at night by fear, the family retires not long after the evening meal. All clothes are taken off for sleeping, and a woolen blanket covers the husband (if he is there), wife, and small children, who sleep at their mother's side in ascending age order. The traditional bed is simply a raised portion of the dung floor covered with cowhides near the hearth where cooking takes place. Most Nyansongo families, however, have purchased wooden bedsteads with hand-tied rope webbing. In the rainy season, when nights are cold and damp, the cooking fire is kept going for warmth; at other times the house is warm enough from the evening meal, since the thatched roof lets out only a limited amount of smoke and heat. Goats, sheep, and chickens sleep inside the house. Old widows sleep in their own houses but sometimes have as companions girls from the homestead who are considered too big to sleep with their mothers when the father is present in the house. The older boys sleep out in a small hut of their own.

✤
✤
✤

Chapter 5

Sex and Marriage

Three traditional rules provide the setting for Nyansongan sexual and marital behavior: (1) No one may marry into his own clan, for all of its members are classified as relatives. Intermarrying clans are traditional enemies and in the past carried on blood feuds, as expressed in the Gusii proverb, "Those whom we marry are those whom we fight;" (2) At marriage the wife must go to live at the homestead of her husband and his parents. There she is granted economic rights and a legitimate social position neither of which would be obtainable had she remained at the home of her own parents. Eventually a woman becomes incorporated into her husband's kin group, but as a newly-wed she is conscious of being a stranger in the enemy camp; (3) A respectable marriage requires the payment of cattle and goats to the bride's father, in number and quality satisfactory to him, before she takes up residence at her husband's home. The bridewealth cattle give the husband exclusive sexual rights over the wife and the custody of all children to whom she gives birth. If he dies, these rights are inherited by a real or classificatory brother of the husband. The rights may only be relinquished by the husband's clan on return of the entire bridewealth.* Thus the marriage system of Nyansongo is characterized by clan exogamy, patrilocal residence, bridewealth, and the levirate.

Girls are 15 years old on the average when they marry, while males average 18 to 20 years old at their first marriage. There is more variability in age on the male side, since the possession of the bridewealth cattle is required and proves a temporary barrier for many of the less fortunate young men. For example, a youth who lacks livestock, and has no uterine sisters whose bridewealth he may use, is likely to be 25 or 30 before he can afford marriage. On the other hand, a boy from a family which is exceptionally wealthy in cattle or which has a disproportionate number of married female children may be married when he is barely pubescent and recently initiated. There is no such inequality among girls, however, because their marriages bring wealth to the family and they may become secondary wives of older men if no eligible bachelors are available.

For most individuals, sexual activity begins long before marriage, although premarital liaisons are not approved by older people and must be carried on privately. Young people are particularly afraid of having their sexual activity come to the attention of their parents or other persons of the parental generation. A circumcised boy has his own hut within the homestead and is not subjected to intense supervision by parents so long as he is discreet enough not to bring his sexual behavior forcibly to their notice. From the age of 14 or 15 onward, boys are active in seeking heterosexual affairs, concentrating their efforts at first on girls in their own community. Since such girls are of their own clan and sex relations with them constitute incest in the eyes of elders, these affairs are extremely surreptitious and fraught with anxiety. The Gusii, unlike surrounding cultural groups, do not practice partial or interfemural intercourse before marriage; with complete penetration, the fear of pregnancy and subsequent parental and community reaction are considerable.

During the female initiation ceremonies, adolescent boys of a single

* The amount of bridewealth returned is diminished in proportion to the number of children the woman has borne; if there are three live children, nothing is returned, and the children remain with their father's kin group.

community, in a practice called "taking by stealth," sneak into houses where groups of adolescent girls of the same community are sleeping and attempt to have intercourse with them. The girls are usually successful in rebuffing them, but a few boys achieve a hurried and fearful act of coitus with girls who pretend to be sleeping. Despite the fact that this is a traditionally condoned practice, a boy who impregnates a classificatory "mother" or "daughter" under such conditions is regarded by the community as a serious offender against sexual morality.

In Nyansongo "taking by stealth" is becoming infrequent and in any case is limited to the brief period of annual female initiation. More commonly, boys of 14 to 18 seduce younger girls of the community, taking them to their own huts at night or meeting them in a wooded place near a stream. Other boys of this age turn to cows and other livestock for sexual gratification; when discovered, they are not severely chastised, as they are considered to be just "trying out their sexual organs." The cow must be disposed of by expelling it from Gusiiland, however, and a young man who repeatedly committed bestiality or did so at a later age would be thought to be insane and possessed by spirits. Homosexuality at this age or any other is regarded as inconceivable and occurs rarely if ever. Masturbation is also extremely rare, if it occurs at all.

When a youth reaches the maturity of 17 or 18 years, he turns to girls outside his own community and clan for sexual relationships. One reason for this is his fear that continued intercourse with girls of his own community will result in pregnancy and an incest scandal. This fear has a realistic basis in the fact that, as the boy gets older, he chooses as sexual partners girls who are losing their adolescent sterility and are more likely to conceive. Nyansongans believe, however, that it is the male whose reproductive powers are increasing. Another reason for the older unmarried male to seek sexual partners outside the community is that he has more confidence in himself than he did when he was inexperienced and is therefore ready to approach strange girls in the marketplace. The youth of 18 also has more opportunity than before to meet girls outside his own clan, for he is more frequently included in the marriage parties of his classificatory brothers. In fact, such a youth, if cattle have been made available to him through the marriage of his sister, or his father's wealth, may be looking for a wife himself and is old enough to be considered a prospective bridegroom when he enters the territory of an alien clan.

The marketplaces, at nearby Keumbu or Kegati (3 miles in the other direction), located at clan boundaries and free of parental surveillance, are favored places for young men and women of different clans to meet.

Marriage feasts provide other opportunities for such meetings and for explicitly sexual encounters. Further opportunities arise out of in-law relationships and the visiting involved in them. For example, it is assumed that a young man will try to seduce the maternal cross-cousin (mother's brother's daughter) of his half-brother or paternal cousin when she comes to visit. Premarital contact can also be initiated at community boundaries, along the road and paths leading to it, and at streams used by members of different clans. The liaisons arranged at these relatively public places are consummated in the privacy of a young man's hut or an isolated grove.

Nyansongo girls are not frank about their sexual feelings; they feign extreme reluctance even when they will yield quite easily to sexual advances. Young men woo them with gifts, flattery, and serenading. The girls try to prolong this initial stage of courtship, delaying the overt sexual advances of their suitors. Some girls appear to lead on eager young men in order to procure gifts and attentions at the market-place. Even when a girl goes willingly to a youth's hut or into the woods with him, she puts up some resistance to his sexual advances. He expects this and enjoys overcoming it, taking pleasure from her protestations and cries of pain. Aside from this patterned pose, most girls have sincere misgivings about premarital sexuality. They fear the disgrace of premarital pregnancy as well as public discovery of simply engaging in coitus on a particular occasion, with the resultant reputation of being a "slut" (*omokayayu*). They also fear parental punishment for such scandals, since the parents of a girl are eager to maintain her good reputation so that a substantial bridewealth will be offered for her. To this end, parents punish their marriageable daughters for staying out too late and straying too far from home. A youth's mistaking a girl's sincere reluctance for mere pretense can lead to rape, which is very frequent among the Gusii.*

Premarital liaisons are often quite brief; a couple may have inter-course on one or two occasions and thenceforward seek different part-ners. A young man who repeatedly seeks coitus with the same girl will have his actions interpreted as encouraging her to elope with him. She may also attempt to persuade him to marry her legitimately (i.e., with bridewealth). Many young men, however, do not consider it proper to have sexual relations with girls they intend to marry; consequently, they terminate affairs quickly and are constantly in search of new sexual partners. In general, individuals of both sexes have a few sexual encounters with each of a considerable number of persons before mar-riage.

* The frequency and etiology of rape are described in detail in LeVine (1959*b*).

The sexual motive for marriage is prevalent among young Nyansongo men. Since premarital patterns of sexuality do not permit easy access to females or protracted relationships with them, marriage is viewed as a means of obtaining a stable sexual partner. Older people often say of a rapist or violator of incest regulations, "Why doesn't he get married?"—implying that this would solve his problem. This is not to say that young men do not desire legitimate offspring, the enhanced social status of a married person, and the labor services which a wife owes her husband. Sex is only one motive for marriage, but it is more pronounced among the Gusii than among many other African groups where premarital sexual freedom is greater.

Any discussion of contemporary marriage in Nyansongo must take account of the legitimate marriage procedure based on tradition and the increasingly frequent unions which deviate from traditional practice and are considered illegitimate. In this discussion, legitimate forms will be described first and then deviant practice.

Before he can arrange a legitimate marriage for himself, a young man must be permitted by his father to use some of the family's cattle for bridewealth. Even if the marriage of his uterine sister has provided the family with bridewealth, the youth must obtain his father's consent to use that bridewealth for his own marriage. A son who does not bother to obtain paternal consent may find himself arrested for theft by tribal policemen on the basis of a complaint registered by his father. A father may withhold consent in order to use the bridewealth for his own secondary marriage or because he wants to punish a particular son; in the latter event the cattle might be granted to a different son for his marriage. A family which is cattle poor and has more sons than daughters is often rent by the rivalry of sons over available cattle. When a man has obtained paternal consent for his use of bridewealth in marriage, he can proceed to select a mate. In so doing he must conform to Gusii incest regulations, which forbid not only marriage within the clan but also marriage with cross-cousins and others of his mother's kin group. Furthermore, he may not choose as a mate any girl whom his father had openly considered taking as a secondary wife, even if negotiations for the marriage had broken off early. This means that a wife must be chosen from among relative strangers. A young man will have met girls from other clans at the places mentioned earlier, and others will have caught his eye although he has not had social contact with them.

The appearance of a girl is an important criterion of her desirability as a mate. Girls who are considered beautiful are much sought after for marriage, while ugly girls have a slightly more difficult time getting married. Characteristics considered attractive in a girl are: brown skin (as opposed to black), firm and erect breasts (as opposed to those which are too small or too pendulous), smooth, soft skin, shapely hips and buttocks (as opposed to those which are too straight or too fat), full calves and thighs (as opposed to thin ones). Some men like their women stout, emphasizing the development of hips and buttocks, but this is not general. Facial characteristics are also important although more difficult to formulate. Small eyes, a narrow mouth, and a space between the upper incisors are considered attractive in girls. Opinions of Nyansongo youths differ on preferred features, but they all take physical appearance into account in the process of mate selection.

Once a young man has decided on a girl whom he is not prohibited from marrying and whom he considers attractive, he finds an intermediary (*esigani*), usually a young man of her clan who is his friend or distant kinsman. Sometimes a marriageable youth selects an intermediary before he has a particular girl in mind, and the intermediary helps him choose from among available girls he knows. In either event, the intermediary is someone in a better position than the prospective groom to obtain information about the girl and her family. There are two questions the intermediary must answer: What is the girl's sexual reputation? and, Is there witchcraft in her family? In answering the first question, the intermediary reports the girl as having a bad reputation only if she has achieved some notoriety as a "slut." He may in fact know of some premarital affairs she has had; yet he will tell the prospective groom she is chaste unless her sex life has involved a scandal. This is because no Nyansongan wants to know the details of his future wife's sex life; so long as her general reputation is not bad, he is free to think of her as innocent and chaste, an image which she herself helps to foster. If the intermediary indicates that she has had premarital intercourse, which most girls have, the prospective groom is likely to reject her.

The witchcraft issue is an important one in mate selection. If there is known to be witchcraft in a girl's family, then it is deemed likely that she herself practices witchcraft and will cause trouble in any family she marries into. The intermediary is responsible for conveying information of this type to the young man and his family, and it is not uncommon for a girl to be rejected on the basis of witchcraft in her background. A Nyansongo girl whose marriage was arranged found the betrothal broken off after her mother was accused of witchcraft by neighbors. It was said that the girl remained unmarried beyond the usual age because of her mother's reputation as a witch. In many cases, however, the evidence is ambiguous, since a family believed by some to contain witches may be considered witch-free by other people in the same community. Hence the intermediary must often decide which set of rumors to pass on, and bias in favor of the girl's family is inevitable. Furthermore, the family of the marriageable young man hears rumors from sources other than the single intermediary. They must dismiss some rumors and accept others, at least tentatively. In consequence, when a bride comes to her husband's home, she may not be entirely free of the suspicion of being a witch.

A final task of the intermediary is to find out whether the girl has any disfiguring marks on her body which are not visible when she is dressed. To this end, he asks girls who are close to her and have bathed with her in a stream whether she had any childhood injuries which left scars on her body. The existence of such scars, particularly those resulting from burns, is sometimes mentioned as the cause for refusal of a prospective bride.

These, then, are the criteria which a young man with cattle uses in selecting a bride: her physical attractiveness, her sexual reputation, and the reputation of her family concerning witchcraft. The intermediary, besides giving the prospective groom information on these topics, informs the girl's father of the young man's interest. If the father has no particular objection to the youth or his family, he agrees to the match, subject to a satisfactory payment of bridewealth. Shortly afterward, the prospective groom comes with some clansmen for a dance at the home of the girl. During the dance, the girl and her female friends scrutinize the prospective groom. If the girl, seeing him for the first time, has strong objections, she may refuse to go through with the marriage, although fathers sometimes coerce their daughters into matches. One of the young men accompanying the groom sees the girl's father and invites him to come and see the bridewealth cattle on a certain date.

The inspection of the bridewealth cattle by the father of the bride-to-be is an important occasion, taking place four or five days after the above-mentioned dance. If he is an influential or wealthy man, the groom's family must slaughter a bull or he-goat for him to eat during his visit. Negotiations take place concerning the number and quality of the cattle as well as the number of goats and other articles, such as a macintosh for the father of the bride and a metal bowl for her mother. Sometimes the groom's father is cajoled into replacing inferior cows with better ones that he can borrow or increasing the total number. For example, although the maximum bridewealth set by the African District Council is 6 cows, a bull, and 6 goats (or 8 cows), several marital transactions in and around Nyansongo during 1956–57 involved 10 and 12 cows. Other times, however, negotiations break down—usually over the quality of the particular beasts offered—and the marriage is called off. If an agreement is reached, the father of the bride takes the cattle home with him. They remain at his home for a month. During that time the marriage may be called off by either side if any of the cattle die of natural causes or the intermediary brings some derogatory information to the groom's family. When this happens, the bridewealth is returned.

A month after the transfer of cattle, the bride must be taken from her father's homestead to the home of the groom. Among the adjacent Luo and other East African tribes, it is customary for kinsmen of the bride to fight with kinsmen of the groom and attempt to prevent her departure. With the Gusii, however, it is the bride herself who resists, or who hides herself underneath the roof of a nearby house, and her father, having received the bridewealth cattle by this time, may even help persuade her to go if her reluctance appears to be sincere. Five young clansmen of the groom come to take the bride and two immediately find the girl and post themselves at her side to prevent her escape, while the others receive the final permission of her parents. When it has been granted, the bride holds onto the house post and must be dragged outside by the young men. Finally she goes along with them, cying and with her hands on her head. This traditional resistance is usually token and not really intended to break off the marriage.

When the reluctant bride arrives at the groom's house, the matter of first importance is the wedding night sexual performance. This is a trial for both parties in that the impotence of the groom may cause the bride to break off the marriage and the discovery of scars or deformities on the bride's body (including vaginal obstruction) may induce the groom to send her home and request a return of the bridewealth. The bride is determined to put her new husband's sexual competence to the most severe test possible. She may take magical measures which are believed to result in his failure in intercourse. These include chewing a piece of charcoal or a phallic pod commonly found in pastures, putting either of these or a knotted piece of grass under the marriage bed, and twisting the phalluslike flower of the banana tree. The groom for his part is determined to be successful in the face of her expected resistance; he fortifies himself by being well fed, which is believed to favor potency, by eating bitter herbs, and nowadays by eating large quantities of coffee beans, valued as an aphrodisiac. His brothers and paternal male cousins give him encouragement and take a great interest in his prospects for success in the impending sexual contest. Numerous young clansmen of the groom gather at the homestead in a festive mood; chickens are killed for them to eat, and they entertain themselves by singing and dancing while waiting for the major events of the wedding night.

The bride usually refuses to get onto the bed; if she did not resist the groom's advances, she would be thought sexually promiscuous. At this point some of the young men may forcibly disrobe her and put her on the bed. The groom examines the bride's mouth for pods or other magical devices designed to render him impotent. As he proceeds toward sexual intercourse, she continues to resist, and he must force her into position. Ordinarily she performs the practice known as *ogotega,* allowing him between her thighs but keeping the vaginal muscles so tense that penetration is impossible. If the groom is young (by traditional standards, under 25), the young men intervene, reprimand the bride, and hold her in position so that penetration can be achieved on the first night. An older groom, however, is considered strong enough to take care of himself, and the young men wait outside the door of the house, looking in occasionally to check on his progress. It is said that in such cases a "fierce" girl in the old days could prevent the groom from achieving full penetration as long as a week. Brides are said to take pride in the length of time they can hold off their mates. In 1957, a girl succeeded in resisting the initial attempts of her bridegroom. His brothers threatened and manhandled her until she confessed to having knotted her pubic hair across the vaginal orifice. They cut the knot with a razor blade and stayed to watch the first performance of marital coitus by the light of a kerosene pressure lamp.

Once penetration has been achieved, the young men sing in jubilation and retire from the house to allow the groom to complete the nuptial sexual relations. They are keenly interested in how many times he will be able to perform coitus on the first night, as this is a matter of prestige and invidious comparison. He will be asked about it by all male relatives of his generation, and the bride will also be questioned on this score when she returns to visit her own family. It is said that the groom's clansmen also question the bride, in order to check on the groom's account of his attainment. Six is considered a minimally respectable number of times and twelve is the maximum of which informants had heard. They claimed that it was traditional to achieve orgasm twelve times, but that performances in recent years were lower.

An explicit object of such prodigious feats is to hurt the bride. When a bride is unable to walk on the day following the wedding night, the young men consider the groom "a real man," and he is able to boast of his exploits, particularly the fact that he made her cry.

After the wedding night, the bride remains at the home of the groom for a period ranging from two weeks to three months, following which she is allowed to return to her father's homestead (or "to her mother" as Nyansongans say) for as much as two months. When she comes home to her parents, the bride may plead for a termination of the marriage. One Nyansongo girl claimed that her mother-in-law was trying to teach her witchcraft—a common basis for divorce at this stage. The impotence of the husband is also a valid charge. The father of the bride may yield to her plea if her feelings seem so strong that she may desert her husband if forced to go back. Many fathers attempt to persuade or coerce their daughters into going back, however, particularly if the bridewealth cattle have already been used to bring another wife into the extended family. While she is at her parents' home, the bride, even if she intends to return to her husband, may accompany her unmarried friends to the marketplace, pretending to be unmarried in order to encourage would-be seducers to give her gifts. She does not have intercourse with them, however, for fear of supernatural sanctions against adultery.

Returning to her husband's home, the bride remains there and makes only occasional trips to visit her mother thereafter. If she does not become pregnant within a year, she may leave her husband for another man who offers to pay bridewealth for her. In such circumstances, the girl's father is obliged to repay the bridewealth of the first husband before or at the same time as he accepts that of the second. Many fathers do not refund the original bridewealth unless coerced, as attested to by the large number of indictments at the African Tribunal Courts for the "customary law" offense of accepting a second bridewealth without returning the first. Of the 51 legitimately married women residing in Nyansongo, 14, or 27.4%, had been married before with bridewealth paid. Most of these 14 left their first husbands because no children were born to them, but a few who were divorced already had children. Thus the first stage of marriage is a trial period during which the bride, who was so carefully selected by her husband and his family but had little say in the matter herself, can take steps to dissolve the union if she finds it unsatisfactory.

Up to this point the discussion has centered on the ideal case of the young man with an adequate bridewealth who is arranging his marriage in the traditional manner. In contemporary Nyansongo this ideal is no longer the most frequent practice. Scarcity of pasturage and the prohibition on raiding have put cattle into short supply. As the same time, cattle are absolutely required for a legitimate marriage, and the bridewealth rate has risen sharply. It takes the entire pay of a tea plantation worker for at least 40 months to purchase the cattle necessary for a minimal bridewealth. In consequence, many young men are priced out of the marriage market, at least until their sisters grow up and get married. Since fathers do not want their daughters to be married without bringing in bridewealth, they are tempted to arrange matches with rich old men who want second, third, fourth, or fifth wives and who are willing to pay considerably more than the going bridewealth rate for them. The young girls themselves want neither old husbands nor positions as secondary wives, if they can help it, so they tend to run off with young men who cannot afford the bridewealth and live as their concubines. This does not necessarily mean that they are renouncing sexual virtue, however, for the young men with whom they elope often promise to pay the bridewealth to legitimize the union as soon as they can raise the necessary cattle. In many cases this promise is fulfilled, and concubinage becomes legitimate marriage.

When a young girl has been persuaded by a youth to elope with him, she goes off to his house secretly and begins living there as his wife. She is accepted by the young man's family as if she were his wife. The elopement infuriates the father of the girl, who has been cheated of the bridewealth. He makes inquiries, finally comes looking for her at the homestead of her lover. Usually she has been forewarned and has hidden herself; the irate father cannot find her and eventually leaves. Sometimes he takes some valued articles from the homestead, feeling that he has been deprived of his source of bridewealth and might as well get some compensation. Some days later, the lover visits the girl's father, admits she is living with him, and offers a reduced bridewealth for her. The father may well accept in order not to lose everything. Even after such an agreement is made, however, one or the other party may renege. The father, on his side, may lure the girl home with the pretense that her mother is ill and then let her be taken by some young men who carry her off to a man who has paid the bridewealth. Or, he may get the chief's tribal police to retrieve her and arrest the lover on the "customary law" charge of removing a girl without the consent of her parents, which is punishable by the African Tribunal Courts. The young man, on his side, might never follow through on his promise to give bridewealth, in which case the girl may leave him after a few months or years to live with another man who promises her eventual legitimacy or to marry one selected by her father on the basis of his ability to make the bridewealth transfer immediately.

Romantic love appears to be a factor in elopement. Not only do girls dislike the idea of marrying older men but they are also positively attracted to particular young men because of their appearance, manners, and personalities.* There are cases of girls who have repeatedly run away from legitimate unions arranged by their fathers to live as concubines with particular youths by whom they are attracted. A girl may also leave her lover for a man with bridewealth only to return to the lover when he has raised the bridewealth needed to ransom her.

Of the 51 legitimately married women living in Nyansongo, 4 were known to have lived in concubinage elsewhere before their marriages. At least 5 women were living in the community as concubines at one time or another during 1956–57. Several Nyansongo girls eloped with men of other clans, and one of them was acquiring a reputation as a "slut" who runs from man to man, a reputation that would make it difficult for her to contract a legitimate marriage later on.

When a girl is first married, she sleeps with her husband in his bachelor's hut but cooks and eats in the house of her mother-in-law. During the first year of marriage, before she has harvested her own fields and has her own grain store, she and her husband will eat food grown in his mother's fields. Afterward, the bride is allotted fields to cultivate in her father-in-law's homestead, and she is then no longer dependent on her mother-in-law's food supply. If she gets along well with her mother-in-law, the new wife may cook and eat in the older woman's house until shortly after the birth of her first child. If their relationship is not a close and amicable one, the young woman may begin cooking in her own house sooner.

A legitimate bride is told by her parents, "We have been given their cattle. Stay there, obey them, do as you're told, and don't do anything to displease your in-laws." In consequence she acts shy and submissive to her parents-in-law at first. This shyness is said to disappear with her mother-in-law when she first becomes pregnant and with her father-in-law when she has given birth to her first child. No one gives orders to the newly arrived bride, for she is eager to do everything without being told. When there is no water or wood, she will fetch it, and she goes to work in the fields when she sees the others going. Her domestic work is scrutinized by her husband and parents-in-law, but they do not openly

* Girls prefer men who are young, have regular facial features and (preferably) a space between the top incisors, act in a suavely provocative manner, give them gifts, and make promises of material well-being and of attention to their desires.

criticize her. The young women in the homestead, wives of her husband's brothers, may jokingly criticize her lack of skill. They may call her by nicknames indicating that she grinds coarse flour or cooks bad food. Such an appellation embarrasses her greatly, but not so much as if her parents-in-law or husband had used it, in which case it would be so humiliating that she would report it to her parents and have the marriage called off unless an apology were made. As a married woman grows older and bears children, her confidence within the homestead increases. She develops an egalitarian and jokingly intimate relationship with her mother-in-law, although deferring to her on important occasions. With her father-in-law, avoidance and respect continue strong, but overt deference may not be as pronounced as when she first arrived.

A married woman never loses contact with her parents and blood relatives. They visit each other; they bring her gifts when her children are born; she borrows food from them when her granaries are running low; she attends their funerals. The brothers of a Nyansongo wife who had loudly complained that her husband was neglecting her in favor of a new concubine came to visit her husband and urged him to take good care of their sister. When a young widow was too pregnant to hoe her fields, her brothers brought a plow and oxen and did the job for her free. A woman has a special relationship with a wife purchased for her brother with the bridewealth provided by her own marriage. She may take food from this sister-in-law's granary without asking. Thus a married woman makes a new life and set of relationships for herself at her husband's home but does not give up her ties with her family of orientation.

In contrast with his wife, who comes to be on relatively intimate terms with her parents-in-law, a Nyansongo man always maintains a most formal and deferential set of relationships with his parents-in-law. They are always strangers and must be treated as honored guests when they visit. They may not enter the house of their son-in-law. They do, however, carry on a joking relationship with his parents. In like manner, a man has an egalitarian, joking relationship with his wife's brothers and sisters; with the latter, elaborate sexual joking is carried on.

In days gone by, and nowadays in areas of Gusiiland more conservative than the one in which Nyansongo is located, the final wedding ceremony could take place any time from days to decades after the start of cohabitation. It included an additional payment of cattle, aggressive interaction between the affinal groups in the form of wrestling matches, dancing contests, and reciprocal insulting of the bride and groom, as well as the placing of anklets of iron on the bride to indicate her married status. Many of the old and middle-aged women in Nyansongo wear such ankle rings. They are viewed as a symbol of marital fidelity, although the same degree of fidelity is required of a wife who does not wear them. The Nyansongo wife is not allowed to have intercourse with any man but her husband, although he is free to engage in extramarital sexuality. The possibility of sexual attraction between a woman and her husband's brother residing in the same homestead is recognized in some lewd songs but is actually considered a heinous offense.

The fidelity of the wife is ensured by a supernatural sanction described in Chapter 9. This punishment does not go into effect until the adulterous wife resumes intercourse with her husband. Thus it has the effect of inhibiting a wife's adulterous impulses unless she is willing to desert her husband and run off with a lover. When she does the latter, the husband can sue her father for return of the bridewealth and/or sue the lover for adultery, a "customary law" offense defined as living with a woman who is legally married to someone else. The bridewealth may be returned and a divorce granted, with the original husband retaining custody of the children. If the husband does not want a divorce and has other wives, he may do nothing, feeling that the woman will eventually return because her children will not be welcome at any homestead but that of their legal father, and she will want to be with her children (especially sons). When a repentant wife returns, a purification ceremony must be performed before the husband can resume sexual intercourse with her.

A Nyansongo woman may remarry after divorce, but if her husband dies, she cannot be married again. She may choose a genitor for her future children from among her husband's brothers and paternal cousins, but his responsibilities are purely sexual and procreative; they do not extend to her economic and social welfare. Children fathered by the levirate are known as sons and daughters of the deceased, who paid bridewealth for their mother, rather than of their physiological father. If a widow is very young, she may move her residence and live as a wife with a brother of her husband. If she is middle-aged and has a number of children, however, the man who is given sexual rights over her often does not live near her and she simply lives by herself with her children and co-widows, if any. Some widows are sexually promiscuous, but this is not widespread among them, for the same supernatural sanctions apply to their leviratic relationship as to an ordinary marriage.

Since the exclusive sexual rights of the husband over the wife are emphasized by Nyansongans, the manner in which these rights are exercised is of interest here. The conception of coitus as an act in which a man overcomes the resistance of a woman and causes her pain is not limited to the wedding night; it continues to be important in marital relations. Wives in monogamous homesteads never initiate sexual intercourse with their husbands, and they customarily make a token objection before yielding to the husbands' advances. The wife does not take an active role in the foreplay or coitus. Touching the husband's penis with her hand, for example, is punishable by ancestor spirits and must be expiated by a sacrifice. Most importantly, it is universally reported that wives cry during coitus, moaning quietly, "You're hurting me, you bad man" and other such admonitions. The men find this practice sexually arousing. The following statement by a 36-year-old husband suggests the attitude of the Gusii male toward his wife's sexuality.

> During coitus the husband asks her, "What do you feel? Don't you think it's good?" The wife says, "Don't ask me that." She will never say yes. When the woman cries and protests during intercourse you are very excited. . . . We are always mystified as to whether women enjoy it. But the wives in polygynous homesteads complain when their husbands neglect them, so they must like it.

There is good reason to believe that the reluctant sexual pose of wives is not feigned in all cases. Young husbands claim to desire coitus at least twice a night, once early and once toward dawn. In a number of monogamous marriages, however, this rate is not achieved, due in part to the stubborn resistance of wives. There are married women with reputations for refusing to have intercourse with their husbands for up to a week at a time. Such husbands are eventually moved to beat their wives and even send them back to their parents. In one case of this kind, the wife's distaste for coitus was the only major source of conflict between husband and wife. Among those monogamous wives who do not have antisexual reputations, however, refusal to have intercourse with their husbands usually occurs when they have quarreled over something else. Since family modesty prescribes the performance of intercourse in the dark after the children have fallen asleep, wives enforce their refusal by pinching a child awake if the husband is insistent. Such evidence suggests that for some wives at least the resistant and pained behavior in marital intercourse does not represent a conventional pose or an attempt to arouse their husbands but a sincere desire to avoid coitus.

❀
❀
❀

Chapter 6

Religion

The people of Nyansongo continue to believe in and practice the religion of their forefathers despite the efforts of Christian missionaries. Of the 70 adults living in the community, 28 have at one time or another been members of Christian churches. This group includes a few who were baptized during severe illnesses experienced while outside the district but who never practiced their new religion. By the broadest definition then, only 40% of Nyansongans can be considered Christians. Of the 28, nine (mostly women) attended church services during the period when fieldwork was carried out.

The Bonyamosicho neighborhood tends to be Seventh Day Adventist, since the chief and his elder brother had been Seventh Day Adventist evangelists 30 to 40 years before and had converted many in their subclan. The Omobea people tend to become Roman Catholics, and there is a growing trend in this direction among young girls who enjoy and look forward to the rituals and white dress of the Catholic wedding service. Two wives of Omobea men are from the Logoli tribe of North Nyanza District and belong to the Friends African Mission which is dominant there.

The Seventh Day Adventists and the Friends missionaries enjoin Africans to refrain from drinking native beer or liquor, making sacrifices, marrying more than one wife, and engaging in witchcraft and sorcery. With the exception of drinking, the Catholic mission sets the same standards for Christian behavior. The rules notwithstanding, everyone in Nyansongo drinks beer and participates in sacrifices; polygynous marriage is common even among younger men; witchcraft and hired sorcery are at an all-time high. Those who were once practicing Christians have for the most part given it up either because of involvement in polygynous marriage or of a pragmatic return to Gusii ritual to deal with illness or death. As a sophisticated Nyansongan re-

73

marked, "I don't believe they're good Christians when they're in trouble or sick. When a man is well off he can be a pure Christian."

Although Christianity is not widely practiced in the community, monotheism has begun to permeate the Nyansongo belief system. Some Nyansongans assert that it has precedent in their traditional beliefs, but regardless of the validity of this claim, the word *Nyasae,* used by African Christians of western Kenya to denote "God," is often heard. Nyasae occupies a position in Nyansongo thought equivalent to fortune or luck in our own, and events are attributed to Nyasae when an individual feels he has and can have no influence on their outcome.

The traditional religion of Nyansongo consists mainly of an ancestor cult which coexists in Gusii belief with a witchcraft-sorcery complex described in the chapter Death, Disease, and the Supernatural. The Gusii do not have an organized cosmology in the sense of a comprehensive set of conceptions of the universe and the beings and forces in it. They have a traditional history going back to Mogusii, founder of the national lineage, and continuing through the southward migration of the Gusii people, their segmentation into tribes and clans, their feuds, wars, and heroes. The personages of traditional history are the ancestors, and it is their spirits (*ebirecha,* sing. *ekerecha*) who are the major supernatural beings recognized by the Gusii. There is, however, little connection between the history and ritual observances concerning ancestor spirits, just as no connection is made between the ancestor spirits and the witchcraft and magic of living people. There is no priestly hierarchy nor are there any shrines in Gusiiland.

The people of Nyansongo view their religion as a set of demands made on them by the ancestor spirits—demands which must be detected and fulfilled in order to avert disaster. Characteristically, though, they do not resort to religious practices until the onset of misfortune or the appearance of a sign indicating that it is imminent. In consequence, religion is not an object of daily attention for Nyansongans, but rather a set of beliefs and practices which spring into action during an emergency when supernatural punishment is feared.

The ancestor spirits (*ebirecha*) are immortal beings lacking shape or substance, "like wind," living in a volcanic formation atop Manga, the most prominent escarpment in Gusiiland. In its most general sense, this category of beings includes all dead Gusii, but practically it refers to the male ancestors of the living members of one's lineage. In this sense, the ancestor spirits are simply the dead members of the lineage who in their postmortem form continue to take an interest in the affairs of its living members. They are not personified, however, and are identified only as "our grandfathers" rather than by any specific name or kinship designation. Like living "grandfathers," ancestor spirits make demands (especially concerning food) on their juniors, are easily displeased, and contribute little to the physical well-being of the homestead. The attitude of the living toward them is one of fear and deference, involving unquestioning obedience to their demands. The ancestor spirits are always considered right no matter how unreasonable their behavior might seem. They are to be appeased in order that they might not bother living members of the lineage.

A major source of displeasure to the ancestors is failure to perform funerary and other customary sacrifices to them or failure to sacrifice the right kind of animal. This is viewed as a deprivation of the food they desire. They are also displeased by intraclan homicide, adultery, and incest but may be propitiated by sacrifice after the commission of such crimes. When offended and not properly propitiated, the spirits can kill members of the offending homestead through disease or disaster (such as being struck by lightning or drowning), drive them insane, kill their cattle, ruin their crops, and afflict them with sterility. Before using such drastic punishments, the spirits send an omen to the offender as a sign of their displeasure; if he recognizes it as an omen, he has time to take remedial action and prevent major disaster. An aardvaark, python, or hyena seen in the daytime is considered a bad omen; the sight of a crane standing with its young, peculiar sounds emanating from a civet cat, jackal, or owl, the striking of one's granary by lightning, a hawk defecating on one's head—all these indicate that an ancestor has been offended. Some omens are linked to a specific type of punishment which follows if the omen is ignored. For example, if a man sees snakes mating and does not take the proper action, he will be made impotent.

When a man suspects that he has incurred the displeasure of the ancestor spirits or when he or his family are visited by misfortune, his only recourse is to visit a divine (*omoragori*). An intermediary between men and spirits, the diviner diagnoses the cause of the omen or misfortune and prescribes the type of propitiation needed. Diviners are middle-aged or elderly women who have learned their skill through a sort of apprenticeship to older diviners. When their apprenticeship is over, they are initiated into the profession by at least five senior diviners of the area in a ceremony called *enyangi*, a word referring to childhood initiation ceremonies and marriage ceremonies as well. In the ceremony, both senior diviners and novices rhythmically shake gourd rattles until they become possessed by the ancestor spirits and scream loudly. This part of the ceremony is private except for three mature men, but the next day a big feast is given, to which anyone can be admitted who leaves a small amount of money at the door step, and there is much eating, drinking, and dancing. The initiate can henceforth wear an iron clip on her necklace which signifies her status as an established diviner. Some women later go through another ceremony to become senior diviners who wear large cowrie-shell collars and can conduct the initiation of apprentices into the profession.

There are many female diviners throughout Gusiiland. In Nyansongo there was one well-established diviner, another who was initiated in May, 1957, and a third who began her apprenticeship at that time. They meet secretly with senior and established diviners from adjacent communities, but each woman practices by herself at her own house. The role of diviner is the most important role outside the family that a woman can occupy, but though it is a respected position, it does not endow her with extraordinary power or prestige. Since diviners' services are often required and usually paid for, the position carries with it monetary rewards.

Typically the diviner is confronted by a client whose wife has not given birth for an unusually long time. Her first task is to determine the cause of this affliction, and she does so by means of an oracle. One type of oracle involves the spinning of a small cup on the handle of a knife blade, which is stuck into the floor. Questions concerning possible offenses and omens are asked while the cup is spinning, and its coming to rest during a particular question indicates an affirmative answer by the spirits. In a variant of this, a gourd is balanced on a sharp implement in the floor; its falling off means "no" to whatever question is asked. Some diviners throw cowrie shells on the floor and read spirit messages from their configuration. Regardless of the method used, the diviner uses her knowledge of her client, first to demonstrate the efficacy of her technique and then to suggest a plausible explanation for his misfortune. She may be aware that he was out of the district when his grandfather died and thus unable to perform the customary role in the burial; she may have heard that the sacred fire went out during his initiation into manhood. Since both of these events are among the many ritual sources of irritation to ancestor spirits, the diviner can plausibly attribute his present misfortune to one of them. She also uses the oracles to search for omens with the prompting of the client himself, who may be eager to recall that he saw an aardvaark or found a lizard in his fireplace. Indeed some anxious people rush to the diviner as soon as they detect an omen. If the diviner, from her knowledge of the client's situation, believes that witchcraft is indicated, and if there are the proper omens to confirm it, she may suggest that her client is the victim of human witches rather than the offender of his ancestors.

Having struck on a credible explanation, the diviner prescribes a remedy. Unless witchcraft is considered the cause, in which case another type of practitioner must be consulted, the proffered solution is appeasement of the spirits through animal sacrifice. The animal to be sacrificed is specified in extreme detail: a black hen, a white ram, and so on. If the client desires propitiation of the spirits for a serious offense, such as incest, the animal is more likely to be expensive, that is, a sheep or goat rather than a chicken, and will also be rare, for example, an all-white he-goat.

A sacrifice to the ancestor spirits is conducted at home by the eldest male member of the homestead concerned, although younger men and men from other homesteads do some of the work involved in it. If a sheep or goat is to be sacrificed, it is suffocated with leaves outside the house and placed on its side inside the husband's room. The elder carefully cuts off the skin of the exposed side and inspects the visceral lining for an auspicious spot. If the spot is not found, another animal must be sacrificed, but this is rare. Many ritual details are attended to, which will not be recounted here. Stomach contents of the animal are smeared on the foreheads and chests of the individuals most directly involved in the occasion for the sacrifice, and the meat is divided among all relatives present. Much of the meat is eaten immediately without cooking, as Nyansongans also eat nonsacrificial meat. Although the meat is said to be drained of flavor by the spirits, who are "eating" it simultaneously, women and children greedily devour the intestines and forequarter, while the men who took part in the sacrifice haul away the choicest meat for later consumption.

The ancestor cult, whose role in social control is discussed below, does not encompass the entire traditional magico-religious system of the Gusii. Supernatural beliefs are involved in curing and preventing disease, ensuring agricultural success through the control of weather, and preventing crime within kinship units. Each of these functions has its supernatural specialists: professional sorcerers and witch smellers in the area of medicine, rain makers and hail stoppers for weather protection, magical detectives for theft control. Other part-time experts, who know rituals for removing different types of curses and protecting against specific misfortunes, abound in Gusiiland and are widely used by Nyansongans.

To summarize, the religion of Nyansongo in its essentials consists of belief in unpersonalized ancestor spirits who occasionally punish the living for ritual neglect or certain moral crimes, female diviners who interpret ancestor-sent omens and prescribe remedies for disease and sterility, and animal sacrifices to propitiate the spirits and thereby effect a cure. These essentials have not been markedly affected by Christianity, probably because they do not require constant observance but spring into action in times of stress when the desire to try anything that might help is very strong. Religious aspects of social control are described in the chapter dealing with that topic, and the most common magical beliefs and practices are considered in the chapter on Death, Disease, and the Supernatural.

Chapter 7

Recreation

There is little formalized or ritualized social life in Nyansongo. There are no drums, no group singing in the fields, and few organized group dances. Furthermore, even festive activities are not adorned by masks, wood carvings, or decorative art, all of which are virtually absent from Gusii culture. The people of Nyansongo generally take their pleasures in informal settings requiring little in the way of preparation, coordination, or ornamentation. Some of the situations which are arranged for pleasure are surreptitious; others are thought to be dangerous as well as enjoyable. Only the most superficial and fleeting forms of recreation are free from the danger of immoral or injurious consequences.

The sex and age divisions among Nyansongans are conspicuous in their recreational activities. Married men attend beer parties, occasional soccer games, and big public gatherings; married women visit each other, go to markets near and far, and conduct a few of the more expressive ceremonies. Young men and women meet each other in the marketplace, have parties of their own, and engage in sexual relations. Unmarried men are also involved in soccer as participants and interested spectators. Even when events like sacrifices and initiation rites bring whole groups of neighbors or kin together in what is partly a recreational context, the men and the women, the young and the old, have their distinct roles to play. Sex differences in expressive behavior are particularly striking, for the festive occasions in which women play a large part are characterized by much more gaiety, noise, and uninhibited words and movements than those presided over by men.

Every married man in Nyansongo has his own bamboo drinking tube, about 4 feet long and with a filter at the end, and some men carry them about, always ready to partake of some beer when it is offered. The beer is made of the fermented flour of maize and finger millet, roasted into hard, round balls, which are sometimes eaten between meals. The women, who make beer, put these granular balls into a large pot, which is placed in the middle of *eero,* the husband's room in the house, and pour boiling water into it. The top of the hot brew is poured off and drunk separately from a calabash or cup. Then the man of the house and his male guests, sitting on stools, put their tubes in and begin to drink. Although the filter in the tube keeps out the coarsest part, the hot beer is nevertheless very thick, sometimes approaching the consistency of oatmeal.

At most times of the year there are beer parties going on in Nyansongo every late afternoon, and a man may go to drink without being invited if he is on good terms with the host, particularly if they are close kinsmen or neighbors. Three to ten men usually sit around, sucking on their tubes and discussing events of the day. If the men are all of the same generation, they talk of sexual matters both real and fantasied, laughing moderately and enjoying the gossip. Such discussions are often terminated by the arrival of an old man or of a woman who is a classificatory daughter of someone present.

Although in the past women were excluded from drinking parties, nowadays they are permitted limited participation but are clearly there on sufferance. A woman enters the room, stands by a man whom she knows well, takes his tube when he is resting between drafts, and drinks some of the beer. She does not sit down, and she usually leaves in a few minutes to rejoin the women in the other room of the house, where they are boiling water and preparing food. If the liquid in the beer pot runs out, the men may shout at the women to bring more hot water. Occasionally an intoxicated man barks abusively at the women and tries to chase them out of the room in which the drinking is taking place. In spite of the fact that they must stay in the background during beer parties, Nyansongo women manage to drink enough on such occasions to get drunk regularly. A few of them are notorious for the frequency with which they get drunk and subsequently neglect

their duties as cooks and mothers, and one woman was severely reprimanded by her husband for this behavior.

Unmarried young men are barred from the room in which their
elders are drinking, although the youths are often given some of the
beer to drink outside or in a nearby house. The old men say this
prohibition is to prevent the outbreak of disrespectful behavior by the
younger men when they become intoxicated. It also serves to heighten
the exclusiveness and importance of the mature men as a drinking
group.

When beer is plentiful and guests are many, a drinking bout is
enlivened by singing and dancing. This is particularly likely to happen
if a man has brought his lyre, a traditional Gusii instrument, to accompany the singing, but unaccompanied singing is also frequent. One
man starts a song, then everyone joins in. The songs are traditional
Gusii melodies; some extol the virtues of famous leaders of the past,
while others have reference to contemporary figures, sometimes in a
satirical vein. The women join in the singing, and in the dancing that
begins soon after. During a song, one person gets up and moves his
arms rhythmically to the music, taking an occasional step forward as
he does so. The persons recognized as the most skillful dancers vibrate
the muscles of their necks, shoulders, and arms, while making very few
gross movements. A number of persons may dance simultaneously, but
each one does so individually; there is no coordination among them.
At a large, crowded party, there is little space for dancing, and someone
who wants to dance may have to wait until another leaves the floor. At
the height of such activities, however, everyone is participating by
either dancing or singing, and the atmosphere is one of restrained
hilarity.

Beer parties in Nyansongo have three dangers: violence, poisoning or witchcraft, and adultery. Alcohol is thought to make men aggressive, and quarrels among them are regarded as inevitable, beginning with pugnacious boasting and ending in physical combat. The
presence of respected outsiders and authority figures, such as in-laws,
ethnographers, and chiefs, has the effect of inducing a degree of restraint which is absent when only close neighbors and kinsmen are
there. Even then, men become more garrulous and bold, for example,
daring to ask the ethnographer questions about how Americans live,
which they had not previously brought up, and familiarly giving him
advice, which they did not do when sober. No aggression was observed.
In the absence of the ethnographer, however, incidents occurred in
which brothers attacked one another while drinking beer, as bruised

faces testified the following day. Drunken brawls are not taken lightly and often lead to litigation. Many men in Nyansongo openly express the opinion that beer parties should be kept small in order to prevent the occurrence of large-scale brawls.

A danger of beer parties less openly talked about is that one will be poisoned or bewitched. Some men believe that using their own drinking tubes avoids this, but the opinion is general that too much participation in beer parties exposes one to the secret poisons of one's enemies.

Women are thought to be made sexually uninhibited by alcohol, so that there is a danger that they may expose themselves indecently while dancing or be susceptible to seduction after the party. Typically an intoxicated woman who has left the party to urinate or to go home is accosted by a man who tries to take advantage of her condition by forcefully suggesting sexual relations. It is said that wives who are otherwise faithful to their husbands may be subjugated in such circumstances, but the only known case in Nyansongo during 1955–1957 involved a young mother of three children, widely regarded as sexually loose, who was seduced (raped, she claimed) by an unmarried man after she left a beer party. The young wives who get drunk most frequently are also those with generally bad sexual reputations. It is more acceptable for older women to become intoxicated, and they enjoy more toleration from the men at beer parties. By and large it is the sexual and aggressive potentialities of the men and women under 40 years of age that are considered most dangerous at beer parties.

Beer drinking in Nyansongo is not limited to the late afternoon and evening. If a man has a kinsman visiting him from afar or some neighbors helping him in the fields, he may serve beer in his house in the morning or early afternoon. In the months following the harvest, and particularly around Christmas, drinking may go on all day long. This daytime beer consumption is even more of a male activity than the parties described above, since the domestic activities of women prevent their taking part.

The unmarried people have their own parties at night in the bachelor huts of young men. Such parties are organized by a few youths who pick up girls in the marketplace and persuade them to attend. European beer is drunk rather than the traditional kind, and lively phonograph music provides the setting for dancing and eventual seduction. Some young men play guitars and accordians at such parties, adapting Gusii songs to vaguely Latin-American rhythms and melodies. In the 1930's unmarried men and women performed traditional dances publicly at markets, but an outbreak of rape in 1937 resulted in a permanent prohibition on such activities; nowadays they are much more private and somewhat clandestine.

Although Nyansongo women participate in the men's beer parties, this cannot be called their major form of recreation. The women more frequently mix pleasure with their work, which is very demanding and time consuming. While men meet over beer, women come together daily in their cooperative working teams, which give them the opportunity to chat, gossip, and joke with one another while cultivating the fields. In the afternoon, when they relax a bit or do some chores around the house like spreading grain on mats to dry, one or two women may drop in on another and spend some time talking. If she goes to the power mill, a woman engages in conversation while waiting in line to have her maize ground. However, going to the market in town or beyond one or two days a week is the greatest recreational event for a Nyansongo married woman. She gets dressed up in her best clothes and goes with a group of her female neighbors. There is always an economic justification for the trip—exchanging grain or vegetables for money, pots, or chickens—and a 15- to 20-mile walk is often involved, but seeing the town, looking over European goods in the shops, and the good-natured banter en route provide enjoyment over and above its ostensible purpose.

Apart from their weekly routine, married women conduct the most elaborate and raucous ceremonies in Nyansongo life. The initiation of girls, described later, is an annual revel for the females in the community, and they violate proprieties on that occasion as men never do. Initiation of female diviners, which occurs less regularly, provides another occasion for great rejoicing and, like initiation of girls, involves singing, dancing, and feasts. Unlike the latter, however, the festivities of diviners' initiation are held mainly indoors, and men must drop some money at the entrance in order to be welcome. The gayest and most elaborate indoor party attended by the ethnographers in Nyansongo was a diviners' initiation.

In ceremonies conducted by men, women often take a lighthearted attitude which is recreational for them and inconsistent with the seriousness of the males in charge. At the sacrifice of a goat to the spirit of a recently deceased Nyansongo homestead head, the women scrambled with each other for the pieces of meat allowed them. They devoured the raw intestines and forequarters voraciously, then complained about not getting more. The widow of the deceased took the lead in this good-humored fun, while the men solemnly performed the ritual and divided the meat according to traditional prescription. The female tendency to be boisterous in a formal ritual setting is also exhibited during the leading-in ceremony of the male initiation rites (see Chapter 16) and in the traditional marriage ceremony as described here and in Mayer (1950a). Women are expected to be highly expressive and even obstructive on such occasions.

Big public events outside the community attract men more than women and play a small but increasing part in the recreational life of Nyansongo men. Soccer is the most important of these; some of the younger men play it on the field at Keumbu market, where the two semiprofessional champion teams sponsored by the chief practice. Men young and old watch the game there and go to the stadium in Kisii Town to see the championship games, especially the intertribal matches. On one occasion when we drove a number of men to a soccer game in town they sang traditional Gusii war songs along the way. A year later, groups of Gusii and Luo spectators fought at an intertribal match. The indications are that soccer evokes great interest of the kind that men formerly had concerning military contests.

Political and judicial proceedings, regardless of their functional significance, attract male spectators on a large scale. The most regular of these is the Monday baraza (assembly) held by the chief, which is attended by men, especially older ones, from all over Nyaribari, who use the occasion to see their friends and kinsmen and to gossip as well as listen to the announcements and speeches which the chief makes in the formal session. Litigation at the African Tribunal Courts, a frequent activity of Nyansongo males, can be viewed as a diversion for many of the plaintiffs and witnesses, although it is obviously also much more than recreation. When the provincial commissioner visits Keumbu or the governor of Kenya Kisii Town, large crowds of men gather to watch and listen, and some of them bring huge calabash horns to sound as they dance in his presence or after he has left. On the occasion of the visit of Princess Margaret to Kisumu, the provincial headquarters 80 miles away, several young married men in Nyansongo donned their defunct policemen's uniforms and set off to see her. These events allow men in Nyansongo to relate themselves to the wider society in which they live, but it must be noted that a number of them participate only slightly in this form of recreation.

Chapter 8

Political Organization and Social Control

The Gusii are one of the many African peoples who did not have a centralized political organization before coming under European colonial administration. Political integration was at the clan, sometimes even local community, level, and there were no permanent governmental offices. Each clan and community had its own authority system in which elders and wealthy individuals had more power than anyone else. Warfare occurred among the seven Gusii tribes, and blood feuding was carried on between clans and sometimes between subclans and smaller lineage segments as well.

Beginning in 1907 the British pacified the area, established courts for the peaceful settlement of disputes, and appointed chiefs and other officials to rule the people. The Gusii political system of 1955–1957 was a combination of indigenous patterns of political behavior with the governmental structures introduced by the British. On the local level, particularly, the colonial system may be said to have been grafted onto pre-existing authority patterns rather than eradicating them. For this reason it is necessary to describe the traditional authority system of Gusiiland before proceeding to the contemporary political setting of Nyansongo.

TRADITIONAL LEADERSHIP PATTERNS

Leadership in traditional Gusii society was not institutionalized in a set of permanent positions with fixed powers.* An early district report states, "The chiefs have extremely little power and are far too

---

* A partial exception is Getutu tribe, which developed a limited form of hereditary chieftainship in the nineteenth century. Statements here refer primarily to Nyaribari tribe.

numerous." In fact, however, these were not tribal chiefs or clan chiefs in the usual sense but only nonhereditary local leaders who assumed power and performed some political functions. The indigenous authority system of Gusiiland is best understood by beginning with the extended family homestead, where the lines of authority were most clearly drawn, and then proceeding to larger units in the political system.

The traditional Gusii homestead was an internally self-governing unit. All disputes and rule violations arising within it were handled by the homestead head (backed up by the ancestor spirits) unless he called in an outside authority. The powers of the homestead head *vis-à-vis* his wives and sons were great and have been described previously. Unless he was a man of little forcefulness or discretion, his orders regarding the economy, defense, and marital affairs of the homestead were commands which had to be obeyed. Defiance of his will could bring punishment to wives and sons. He had supernatural and economic sanctions to use against recalcitrant sons, and he could beat his wives, humiliate them publicly, and reject them sexually. These sanctions the homestead head used to deter threats to his authority as supreme decision maker and to quell conflicts among his wives and sons. He did not need to use them frequently because his wives and children usually feared him and did not disobey him or come into open conflict with one another. Minor infractions on their part might provoke a threat by the homestead head; more serious or repeated infractions would lead him to apply sanctions. When the most serious crimes within the homestead occurred, however, the homestead head did not punish. Fratricide and incest within the homestead were considered punishable only by the ancestor spirits; propitiatory sacrifice and a peace-making ceremony would be performed. With respect to fratricide, the restraint of the homestead head is said to have stemmed from his desire to restore peace to the family rather than to perpetuate conflict by punishing one side or the other. A homestead head who was not a dominant personality or who wanted to impress his sons with his impartiality might call in his elder brother or some other closely related elder to help him adjudicate a case within the homestead. Extended families in which the father had died also called on similarly related elders for the settlement of internal disputes.

Cases of conflict or rule violation involving members of more than one homestead were brought to the attention of the "lineage elders" (*abagaaka begesaku*). This term did not refer to a council with a definite membership but to a group of homestead heads and other elders ("men with gray hair") whose membership would depend on the nature of the case being heard. If the case at issue was an inheritance dispute between two brothers, then several closely related patrilineal kinsmen of their father would sit as the lineage elders because they were representative of the small-scale lineage involved. If the case was an assault or witchcraft accusation involving two homesteads whose blood relationship was not very close, then all the older men in the community would be the lineage elders involved and would judge the case jointly. The composition of the group of lineage elders involved in adjudication could be expanded beyond community boundaries to the largest unit within which lineage ties and classificatory kinship were recognized, namely, the clan, but this of course did not mean that all the older men of the clan actually heard the case. This pattern of adjudication by elders is still operative in Nyansongo.

In the past, when the lineage elders sat as a court, they had no specialized agencies to enforce their decisions. Instead they relied on (1) self-help by the successful litigant, (2) general community respect for their age and the legitimacy of their role, (3) fear by the unsuccessful litigant of their power to curse, (4) oaths invoking the supernatural sanctions of the ancestor spirits, and (5) the military threat posed by certain wealthy and powerful men (known as *abatureti,* hut elders, because they provided a hut for meetings of elders) who played a large part in community decision making.

The lineage elders had the power to curse an unidentified thief or arsonist or someone who refused to comply with their order to pay a debt. Once they had decided to curse him, the plaintiff provided a pot of beer for them, and they would drink some but not all of it. Then they would hold their fingers over the holes in the tops of their drinking tubes, utter the words, "Let him become emaciated and die," and walk away without drinking any more from the pot. Holding the finger over the hole is said to be an imitation of suffocation. If an offender so cursed did not confess and attempt to put himself right with the elders, death or a great misfortune would befall him, since the ancestor spirits were believed to carry out the curse. If the offender decided to confess and reform, he brewed beer and killed a bull or he-goat for the elders. They would come and eat at his house, and after his public apology, they would spit beer on him to remove the curse. It appears that the actual uttering of a curse by the lineage elders was less frequent than their threatening to do so, which inspired sufficient fear in the offender to make him comply.

In many cases the elders did not have to render a decision themselves but were able to allow the litigants to take an oath which would be enforced by the ancestor spirits. The accused in a Gusii trial rarely admitted his guilt; consequently there was often a factual question to be settled. If someone accused of an offense or involved in a debt dispute were certain of being in the right, he could offer to swear an oath which would kill him if his testimony were false. When the litigation concerned whether a cattle debt had been contracted and was really owed, both parties might remove their clothes near a small, flowering tree called *omotembe* (*erythrina abissinica*). The plaintiff would seize the tree and challenge the defendant, swearing his own claim to be correct. When the turn of the accused came, he might demur, fearing death for a false oath. His refusal would be tantamount to confession, and he would be required by the elders to pay the debt. If he also seized the tree and swore he was telling the truth, then there was nothing more to be done except wait and see which one died or had death in his homestead. The first one to be visited by disaster might well settle the debt to prevent the total destruction of his family by the ancestor spirits. There were many different kinds of oaths, depending on the type of offense and the category of person involved. For example, an accused married woman could lay her unweaned child on the ground and step over it while denying the charge. If she were lying, the child would die. Ordeals, that is, supernatural tests by which the accused can reveal his innocence or guilt, were also used by the elders in certain cases and also freed them from the necessity to make judgments themselves.

A Gusii homestead was thought of to some extent as a military unit with the younger men being warriors under the command of the homestead head. On some occasions, for example, when homicide occurred, young men from the victim's homestead might attempt to retaliate against the family of the killer. This was not considered right, and the elders would try to prevent it, but everyone was aware of this possibility. The degree of deference accorded a homestead head by his neighbors thus depended on the military might he commanded as well as on his wealth and number of wives. A man who was wealthy in cattle could obtain many wives, who could bear many sons to augment the military capacity of his homestead. Thus a man with four to ten wives might have a formidable army of warriors bound in loyalty to him by the father-son relationship. If his community or lineage segment were attacked from outside, his sons might be largely responsible for the defense of the area. His poorer neighbors with their smaller families were aware of the fact that incurring his displeasure might jeopardize the protection from violence thus afforded them. Such wealthy men tended to dominate the judicial proceedings of the elders; hence defiance of the elders' decision was also defiance of them. Although they would rarely use their sons as officers of the court, the threat that they might do so was ubiquitous and aided the enforcement of the judgments reached by the lineage elders.

Regardless of his authority outside his local community, the most wealthy and forceful homestead head was dominant within it. He helped his poorer neighbors by making loans to them, judging their cases, and aiding materially in the defense of the area. At the same time, he used their dependence on him to dominate them and, to some extent, to exploit them. Two Gusii proverbs illustrate this: "The property of the poor monogamist is owned by the powerful man," and, "The property of the pauper is used by the rich." In all likelihihood he infringed on the property rights of others in the cause of his own aggrandizement, yet so long as his wealth and military power were unequaled, no one dared challenge his authority. Furthermore, it was often his son who was acknowledged leader of the cattle-village in which the young men jointly herded cattle.

Disputes and offenses involving individuals of different local areas within the clan were more likely to result in armed conflict than those occurring within local communities. An alternative, however, was the peaceful resolution of the conflict by conducting a trial with hut elders from the areas concerned (and from other areas, too, to lend impartiality to the proceedings) sitting in judgment. Poor elders with reputations for judicial wisdom might also be included in the impromptu tribunal, which was also thought of as the lineage elders. The success of such procedures in maintaining peace within the clan was apparently not very great, at least compared with those few areas of Gusiiland where something like hereditary chieftainship existed.

Traditional Gusii leadership was viewed as successful when it could contain and subdue the conflict resulting from lineage segmentation. As clans and their component local lineages grew in size over time, segments of equal size tended to break away from one another, to stress their autonomy and unity at the expense of the larger unit, and to view each other as enemies. This occurred in the minimal lineage of the extended family, where co-wives and their sons came into conflict with their coequals, as well as on the higher levels of lineage structure right up to the clan. The leader at every level was faced with the problem of maintaining order among conflicting segments, using his power to induce people to submit their disputes to him and the lineage elders rather than settling them by force. This order was more frequently achieved at the levels of the homestead and local community where the needs of economic cooperation and defense and the influence of supernatural sanctions reinforced the efforts of leaders to keep the peace.

Above the local groups, social control (in the sense of nonviolent settlement of disputes) was only achieved when a leader arose who was not only acknowledged as wealthier and more powerful than anyone else in the area but who also was willing to use severe physical punishments of offenders to maintain respect for his judicial authority.

CONTEMPORARY POLITICAL ORGANIZATION

In 1907, after the Gusii attempted to assassinate the district commissioner, who was establishing a government station in their territory, a British-led police force defeated them in battle and opened a new era in the political history of Gusiiland. Thenceforth the Gusii were administered by the district commissioner of South Nyanza from headquarters on the eastern edge of Nyaribari. He was the first man to command an effective monopoly of military power in the area, and he used this power to stop warfare and feuding among the Gusii, to abolish their cattle-villages, and to introduce a new form of government.

Gusiiland was rapidly transformed from its fragmented, stateless condition to a set of chiefdoms with specialized political roles operating within a system of colonial administration. Fifty years after the transformation began, however, many features of the indigenous authority system could still be observed in operation. The seven tribes of Gusiiland were converted into seven administrative "locations," each with its own chief. The chiefs are appointed by the Provincial Commissioner, but only from among the descended clans of the tribes they are to govern. Each chief has under him a number of "subheadmen" who used to function only in their own clan territories but were recently given multiclan territories in an action designed to reduce clan parochialism.

Three African Tribunal Courts have been established in Gusiiland, each with its president, vice-president, and two to four panels of elders, all drawn from the Gusii population. Although a specialized judiciary is an innovation, much of its procedure is indigenous. Traditional oaths are used in civil cases over land and custody of children. An *omotembe* tree is grown outside each courthouse for the most commonly used oath. Finally, "customary law" regulations are enforced Although the offenses covered in them are not traditional, these regulations seek to uphold with slight modification Gusii customs regarding marriage and property. On the other hand, however, the Tribunal Court is radical because it does not recognize the jurisdiction of the homestead head and because it is supposed to treat all individuals as equals before the law. Thus a son can sue his father and a wife her husband, actions which would have been unthinkable in earlier days.

The role of the wealthy judicial leader or hut elder (*omotureti*) has been formally recognized in the contemporary judicial system. Each one is supposed to be elected by the people of a given territory, and he hears cases in conjunction with the elected hut elders of adjacent areas. The lineage elders usually sit jointly with the hut elders and often influence their decision. Nowadays this local judicial arrangement is used as a court of first instance in land and property damage (usually cows eating crops) cases and can hear minor criminal cases as well. The hut elders have the power to award damages up to 200 shillings ($28.00) and can order prison sentences of up to three months, which must be confirmed by a Tribunal Court. They report their findings to the chief weekly at a public meeting, and he decides where the case should go from there. The hut elders in Nyansongo and elsewhere have a reputation for being eminently bribable and are little trusted by the people.

Over the chiefs and African Tribunal Courts is the district-wide apparatus of colonial government. This consists of the district commissioner and his administrative hierarchy, the resident magistrate and Kenya police, and the African District Council. The last is a legislative body, presided over by the district commissioner, on which all the tribes of South Nyanza (Luo, Kuria, and Suba, as well as Gusii) are represented by their chiefs and elected members.

Aside from the Council, other branches of district government are staffed at their top levels by British officials. Under the district commissioner there is a district officer in charge of Gusiiland, a district officer in charge of courts, and agricultural, medical, education, revenue, maize control, and public works officers. The district officer in charge of Gusiiland deals mainly with the chiefs, and the courts officer with the African Tribunal Courts, whose decisions he may reverse. The resident magistrate is the supreme judicial authority in the district, operating a court which hears all cases involving Europeans and Asians as well as the more serious African criminal cases. These latter include murder and manslaughter, arson, rape, theft, official corruption, the cultivation of marijuana, and the illegal distilling of "native spirituous liquors." The resident magistrate can give prison sentences up to 15 years and retains the power to order flogging, which he uses in cases of petty theft and other minor offenses. Cases of homicide and rape in which a sentence of greater than 15 years may be given are referred by him to the Supreme Court of Kenya. African cases are brought to the resident magistrate by the Kenya police, who have British officers, a number of outposts in the district, and considerable military equipment. This contrasts sharply with the African Tribunal Courts, which depend on complainants to bring their own cases to court.

In spite of the extensive British officialdom in South Nyanza, much of the responsibility for administration and law enforcement falls on the shoulders of the chiefs, who have considerable autonomy in the governing of their respective locations. There is no paramount chief or ruling council of Gusiiland; hence location chiefs are responsible only to the district officer and district commissioner but not to any higher chiefs. The district commissioner and district officer are infrequent visitors to any particular location, however, and this gives chiefs the opportunity to develop relationships with the people they rule which are independent of the dictates of colonial administration.

One of the outstanding characteristics of Gusii behavior within their contemporary political system is their litigiousness, for which they have been notorious in Kenya for decades. With a population of 260,-000, the Gusii supply their tribunal courts alone with almost a thousand cases a month and $50,000 to $60,000 a year in court fees. Many cases are appealed to the South Nyanza African Appeals Court and even higher; and the Court of Review, highest native appeal court in Kenya, visits South Nyanza more frequently than any other district. Almost every Gusii adult male has been involved in a court case; many have had ten or more. Land litigation and suits for the custody of children are most common, but assaults and sex offenses are also brought into court in great numbers. Lawsuits may be said to be a major preoccupation of the contemporary Gusii, and one of the reasons that the litigations are so protracted is the reluctance of persons to admit being in the wrong. The Gusii proverb, "No one cuts his own boil," applies to trial behavior, where the defendant will protest his innocence and fabricate stories in support of it to the end. A resident magistrate who had judged many Kipsigis cases in Kericho District was amazed and chagrined at the greater length of Gusii criminal trials due to the refusal of defendants to plead guilty regardless of completely incriminating evidence.

SOCIAL CONTROL IN NYANSONGO

In the 1930's, when the African Tribunal Courts were established, Gusii chiefs were deprived of their formal judicial powers. People continue to bring cases to the chiefs, however, according them a central role in the judicial process. This is especially true in Nyansongo, partly because it is under a powerful chief who has been in office for 30 years and partly because the community is located in the 2 miles between the chief's private residence and his official headquarters. The subheadman in charge of Nyansongo and the *etureti* (hut) elder of the community are both members of the chief's subclan, appointed to their posts by the chief without popular support, and are passive individuals commanding little respect from their neighbors. One is held in contempt by Nyansongans because he is dominated by his wife who is reputed to be a witch. Community residents by-pass the subheadman and hut elder living among them and take their cases directly to the chief.

When someone in Nyansongo has a problem with possible legal implications, his first impulse is to see the chief about it. Whether it is a land dispute, assault or stock theft, witchcraft accusation, or the elopement of a daughter, he will move as quickly as possible to see the chief. In the early morning there is a long line of litigants waiting at the chief's house, later in the day at his office, and they sometimes awaken him at night as well. For some, the chief is a legal expert who can advise on whether a case should be taken to the Tribunal, Kenya police, or hut elders. For others, who are themselves sophisticated in judicial procedure, a letter from the chief to the court or police is considered a necessity.

In many cases, however, the chief acts not as an intermediary but as a court, settling disputes, punishing, and issuing warnings. His actions in these cases go far beyond the legal powers granted him by the British authorities. Most frequently he is called on to adjudicate family squabbles and enforce the traditional obligations of nuclear family relationships. In Nyansongo a son quarreled with his mother over the fact that money he sent home was used for his brother's bridewealth. Tempers flared, and he struck her on the arm with a hoe. The homestead head, a weak old man, reported the incident to the chief, who had his tribunal policemen lock up the son for a few days in a brick hut at the chief's camp which is reserved for such purposes. During those days the son worked around the chief's camp under guard while the chief consulted the parents and tried to settle the case. In another case, two wives of a middle-aged man complained to the chief about their husband's neglecting them sexually in favor of a concubine from Ruanda-Urundi who, they were certain, was using love magic to hold his attraction. The chief ordered the concubine out of the district and gave her the bus fare for the trip. Such cases are everyday occurrences, often involving sons taking their father's cattle without permission, brothers fighting one another, cousins suspecting one another of sorcery. The chief deals with them firmly, often giving support to flagging paternal authority by dressing down sons, "discovering" their poll tax delinquency, or locking them up for a while. He also gives permission for persons to consult witch doctors of various types. Sometimes he reverses the decisions of the hut elders or insists on sending a case judged by them to the Tribunal Court. Despite the fact that his administrative location contains almost 50,000 people, no matter is too trivial for the chief to concern himself with, and he manages to dispose of the large number of matters which persons from Nyansongo and many other communities bring him daily.

The power of the chief is of benefit to himself as well as to others. He is by far the wealthiest man in the location, having 14 wives, a Chevrolet sedan, large herds of cattle, a sizable·coffee plantation, and five power mills for grinding corn. He is always well-dressed in expensive European clothing. The Gusii consider it appropriate for a chief to be wealthier than other persons, and if not outstandingly wealthy when appointed to office, he takes steps to acquire wealth as soon as possible afterward. The chief in charge of Nyansongo has been rich for many years, and some of his kinsmen have reaped economic benefits from his chieftainship as well. He does not share his political power with anyone, however, whether kin or not. His subheadmen tend to be obedient to the chief but not effective with the people, and it is said that he chooses men with such qualities in order to keep power concentrated in his own hands.

Except for some elders, the chief tolerates no contradiction or criticism at the weekly assembly meeting of the location. Most people are extremely deferential to him, but those who have defied him in some way find themselves ordered to court for tax delinquency or even told to leave the district if they wish to avoid dire punishment. The chief is surrounded by assistants—clerks, tribal police, bodyguards, chauffeurs, domestic servants, and field hands—who are available to do his bidding. Being a member of the chief's entourage is considered prestigeful and a means of eventually obtaining a political office, such as subheadman or elder of the Tribunal Court. One Nyansongo man gave up a job outside the district to become the chief's chauffeur; another did the same to become his cook. Ordinary residents of the location are sometimes pressed into service to perform an immediate task for the chief or one of his assistants. The tribal policemen, uniformed and armed but ill-trained guards which every chief is allowed to have, are most blatant about using their position to take advantage of fearful shopkeepers anxious not to offend them, and to extort bribes from suspected criminals.

The autocracy of the chief is resented by some but opposed by no one. Most people regard his power as vast, being backed up by the even greater power of the district commissioner. They respect his authority and appeal to it when they need to rather than protest against it. In spite of this, the chief is covertly suspicious of his subjects. He will not eat in the house of any person in his location, reportedly because of fear of poisoning, and he hires witch doctors to protect him from his enemies. This is consistent with the belief that the wealthy and fortunate are subject to the envious witchcraft of the less fortunate, but it is carried to quite an extreme in this instance. The private life of the chief is discussed by people in Nyansongo and elsewhere, but he is not expected to be a paragon of Gusii moral virtues. As with Gusii leaders of pre-British days, he is reputed to violate important kinship rules in the course of his own family life, but this does not seem to shake anyone's respect for his authority. Since his power is unsurpassed, there is no one who would dare attempt to correct his behavior.

The chief with his tribal police and the Kenya police with their patrol cars cooperate in law enforcement. In spite of their activities, however, criminals can evade arrest by escaping to the tea plantations 50 miles away where, as employees, they are protected from arrest by the European management or by bribing the policemen. To a large extent, then, the apprehension of offenders is dependent on the great responsiveness of the population in reporting offenses to the chief and the lack of willingness of criminals to resist arrest. Communities like Nyansongo do not have organized peer groups which aid in the detection and apprehension of criminals, and even the informal sanctions of their elders are nowadays authorized by the chief. Magical sanctions used by individuals and supernatural interpretations of death and disease remain important elements in the social control system, and their role in the control of specific types of offenses will be discussed below.

AGGRESSIVE OFFENSES

Despite their traditional pattern of feuding, Nyansongans believe that violence and aggression are evil and should be avoided. Women argue loudly with one another, though usually without strong emotion, but the men are particularly subdued and polite people. They rarely raise their voices to one another, and public brawls are extremely infrequent. There is no feeling that two men with a dispute should settle it with their fists or by any other direct expression, and when two men attempt it, there are always those who hold them back and try to calm them down. In transactions such as the selling of a cow, when bargaining has reached a deadlock and feelings are beginning to run high, the tension is relieved by smiling and laughing rather than by shouting. On many occasions we were amazed to see how polite and friendly a person could act toward someone with whom he was currently engaged in a serious dispute. It can be said that Nyansongo interaction, under conditions of sobriety, is generally characterized by an atmosphere of quiet and superficial good humor.

Such nonaggressive behavior often belies deep-seated ill feelings between Gusii individuals. This is recognized in the proverb, "People may be seen together but their hearts do not know each other." A case that arose in Nyansongo (described in Chapter 9) illustrates this concretely. When Mogaka died, his older widow made it known to numerous neighbors that she blamed two male neighbors, closely related to the deceased, with having killed him by sorcery. The two men knew of her charges, and they issued counter-accusations to other neighbors, imputing foul deeds to the widow's family. This was a serious and notorious situation in the community. But, a week after the death, when the sacrifice for the dead man was performed, not only were both men present and assisting in the ritual, but at the informal meal afterward, the widow was joking with them, good-naturedly encouraging one of them to take her younger co-wife as a leviratic wife, and so on. Their interaction betrayed none of the hostility they felt toward one another. Shortly afterward, the older widow was the sole complainant in the trial of one of the men for sorcery, and she uttered her charges publicly. This is a striking illustration of the Nyansongo ability to suppress aggression in direct interaction with the object of the aggression and their tendency to express it in back-biting and litigation.

Nyansongans are not highly sociable people, and they view their neighbors with considerable suspicion. "Homesteads are secret hiding places" is one oft-quoted proverb, and another warns, "A thicket has eyes," counseling caution about speech in the manner of our own wartime slogan, "The walls have ears." Sociability is equated with danger in two proverbs. "He who enters doors will be found with a swollen intestine," refers to a postmortem sign of death by witchcraft as the consequence of going into other people's houses. "Eat like the hide-dresser," is considered an admonition to stay out of trouble by eating at home like the dresser of hides, whose work prevents his visiting his fellows. Few Nyansongans follow the extreme advice of such proverbs, but they share anxieties expressed in them. Privacy is desired and available, and it gives individuals the opportunity to conspire and talk against each other. Everyone is aware of this, and thus when people come together for work and entertainment, which is rather frequently, each one comes with at least a slight feeling of distrust.

The unsociability which appears to give rise to aggression is itself a reaction to aggression, and the preferred method of handling it. "Bitter squash is of a different pot," means that people with a grudge will separate and not see each other. The hyperaggressive person is dealt with in the proverb, "A biting snake is pushed away with a stick," meaning, "Keep your distance." There is a definite tendency for Nyansongans to avoid volatile persons and alleged witches and to break off social intercourse with a family with whom they have a dispute. As soon as trouble between homesteads arises, paths leading from one to another are blocked, and visiting stops, at least for a while. When one of the men in the case mentioned above was judged guilty of the sorcery responsible for the death of the widow's husband, the elders ordered that there be no further social intercourse between the adjacent families, as a means of preventing any more aggressive action. If persons holding a grudge are forced into interaction by an accidental meeting along a path or at the homestead of a third party, they will ordinarily be polite and friendly. This is not considered wrong, as "insincerity" is in our own society, but a necessary expedient in order to avoid aggression. If one person is an alleged witch or notoriously quarrelsome person, the other would definitely be friendly in order not to provoke aggression, but he would also get away as quickly as is consonant with politeness. Mention has been made of the conscious spatial separation of the homes of co-wives in order to reduce their aggression. Young unmarried men are also spatially excluded from beer parties to prevent their becoming aggressive to their elders under the influence of alcohol. Nowadays they are given some beer, but must drink it outside the house or in another house. In the past, of course, young men lived in cattle-villages apart from their elders, which may have served the function of preventing intergenerational conflict on a daily basis. Currently, not only the presence of young men at home but also the overpopulation of the land makes separation more difficult than before and open aggression therefore harder to prevent.

A strong paternal authority is connected with the prevention of aggressive offenses within the homestead. Those homesteads in Nyansongo in which open conflict broke out most often between brothers were those in which the homestead head was senile or simply lacking in forcefulness when dealing with his adult sons. Where the father was a dominant person, he did not tolerate open quarreling, and the sons tended to remain peaceful under his authority. After the death of such a homestead head, the sons are quite likely to engage in aggressive encounters or to break off relations with one another, at least temporarily.

Although Nyansongans profess a negative attitude toward killing, in pre-British times homicide was often a necessity for defense and other military operations against out-groups. The extent of what might be considered an "in-group" varied from time to time and place to place in Gusiiland, depending on the balance between authoritarian leadership and divisive lineage tensions. Consequently the line between homicide as a military operation and homicide as an offense to group morality was difficult to draw. It can be said with certainty that homicide involving anyone outside the social unit here called the tribe was always part of legitimate warfare and homicide within the homestead was always a "criminal" offense involving expiation via sacrifice and other rituals. Intermediate cases within the tribe but outside the homestead might be settled by the payment of compensation equivalent to the bridewealth for one wife and sometimes by sacrifice as well, the probability of settlement being dependent on the relations between the lineage segments of murderer and victim.

Homicide under contemporary conditions in Gusiiland is treated as a police offense and is punishable by death (hanging) if the Supreme Court of Kenya decides it is murder and not manslaughter. That the retaliatory motive is still present is indicated by the fact that it is mainly in *intra*familial homicide cases that efforts are made to conceal, or bribe the police to conceal, the offense from the authorities. The family of the deceased wants to see the killer punished. Nyansongans, however, regard the process of Western justice with respect to murder as absurdly ineffective. Two middle-aged women once complained to us:

> When a man has committed murder, he should be hanged in front of a crowd of people rather than taken to Nairobi for hanging. When they are taken to Nairobi, people don't know whether they are really killed. If they were hanged in front of a crowd, people would know that bad things await those who murder others. Murderers should be taken to town, and everyone in the tribe should see them killed there. Now, when a man kills intentionally he's taken to prison for a year, and then people hear he has won his case and is free. Or he may bribe and get free, which is wrong.

Further investigation revealed that even among the semieducated Gusii there is strong doubt that convicted murderers who are taken to Nairobi are really killed there. Rumors are circulated to the effect that convicted murderers are kept in a large padded room in Nairobi and fed a great deal of food to make them fat while samples of their blood are taken. This is considered a far superior fate to being killed. Furthermore, cities like Nairobi are regarded by Gusii as corrupt places where one could bribe one's way out of execution, and they feel this theory is confirmed every time a killer is reprieved or acquitted for lack of evidence. Thus there is general disbelief that execution for murder is ever carried out.

The current Gusii homicide rate is fairly high. Table 2 is a comparison of the average annual rate of Gusii murder and manslaughter indictments during 1955 and 1956 with the rates for adjacent tribal groups, the Kipsigis and South Nyanza Luo, and with the rate of murder and *nonnegligent* manslaughter indictments in the urban United States during the same period.*

Table 2 Average Annual Homicide Rates per 100,000 Population Three Kenya Tribal Groups and the Urban United States, 1955 and 1956

Gusii	5.5
Kipsigis	4.8
South Nyanza Luo	4.5
United States, urban	4.85 *

* Statistical Abstract of the United States, U.S. Department of Commerce, 78th Annual Edition, 1957, p. 139.

Murders in Gusiiland ordinarily occur during or after beer parties at which relatives and neighbors are present. If in-laws or other respected visitors are present, there is little quarreling. But when the drinking group includes only intimates, sharp words are the very least that is inevitable. Alcohol seems to transform the quiet Gusii man into a loud, pugnacious braggart and to bring out his pent-up aggression. Intoxication in a familiar group is the most usual setting for murder in Gusiiland.

The motivations behind murder and other aggressive outbursts against neighbors and relatives usually involve economic factors. Land disputes and cattle debts can be at the root of bitterness that has been aggravated by years of litigation. A recent case from outside Nyansongo illustrates a fairly typical set of conditions that can lead to murder. An old man whose wife was dead lived for ten years with a widow at her

* Negligent manslaughter, mainly homicide due to auto accidents in United States, is extremely rare in rural Kenya. Population estimates used for the Kenya tribes are 1948 census figures plus 10%.

house. They quarreled bitterly and decided to divide their wealth in half. He took his share of movable articles to the homestead of his adult sons. One day he decided to return to live with the widow, and *her* adult son was home from work at the time. The son was annoyed, especially because he feared that the old man would stake a claim to half of the land which his mother worked, which according to custom belonged to the son. At a beer party, the son said, "They have divided the wealth and now he returns. I want to kill him—do you all agree?" The others present, who were drunk, laughingly agreed with him, thinking he was not serious. After drinking, the son found the old man going to sleep, hacked him to death with a machete, and carried the body to a river, where he deposited it in the water, first tying one leg to a tree. Eventually the body was discovered and the son arrested. This case contains the elements of economic anxiety, intoxication, and close relationship between murderer and victim that are typical of Gusii murder cases.

In traditional Gusii judicial practice, assault and mayhem were recognized offenses, and compensation could be obtained by the victim through litigation. If a person were badly injured and the services of a professional medicine man were needed, the assailant was required to pay the fee for his services as well as the compensation itself. The goat, sheep, bull, or grain that the elders awarded was intended to be food to help the victim recover from his wounds. If he died later on, full homicide compensation could be claimed. Thus there was traditional precedent for the concept of assault as a legitimate ground for civil action introduced by British administration.

The contemporary treatment of assault in the African Tribunal Courts combines Gusii concepts of compensation and the Western idea that it is a crime punishable by legal sanctions. The courts can order fines, damages, and prison sentences after one hearing. The fines and damages are commensurate to the injury and range up to $70; the maximum prison sentence is one year. Some assault and all mayhem cases are taken to the Resident Magistrate's Court, which has the power to order corporal punishment and longer prison sentences but does not award damages. The vast majority of assault cases, however, come to the African Tribunal Courts, where they constitute the most frequent category of criminal offense.

Assault is frequently committed by Gusii, and it is even more frequently a grounds for litigation. Some assault cases occur when men are drunk, and these are fairly likely to involve real injury. No matter how drunk or how slight the injury, it will be reported to the chief and an assault litigation will begin. The most frequent kind of assault case occurs in the following manner. Two neighbors with adjoining land disagree concerning their boundary; they may or may not be involved in a civil suit over the land itself. January arrives and it is time to break ground. Masoti begins plowing a pasture which he and Obwoge have been using for communal grazing and which contains the disputed boundary. Obwoge is aghast at this; he comes down with a machete and argues with Masoti about his right to cultivate the pasture. Masoti is adamant and pushes Obwoge away; the latter threatens him with the machete. Friends and relatives intervene and try to calm them down. The one who reaches the chief first claims he was assaulted and badly injured. At the hospital with a police form, he details an injury to his back or arm for which the doctor is unable to find evidence. At court the elders read the doctor's report, hear the complainant, eventually decide to dismiss the case for lack of evidence. Cases of this type pour into the courts in January and February, the plowing season. A variant of it is the case in which two neighbors have had a boundary dispute which has caused bad feelings. The cattle of one get into a field of the other. The owner of the trespassed property gets furious and shouts at the careless boy herder. He may slap the boy or threaten the neighbor if he himself is present.

The tendency of Gusii individuals to instigate assault litigation on trifling grounds is extremely strong, and Nyansongo seems typical in this respect. In a three-year period, 1954–1956, one of the three African Tribunal Courts in Gusiiland heard 1306 assault cases, of which only 478 or 36.6% resulted in convictions. At the Resident Magistrate's Court, where the more serious assault cases are taken, the Gusii surpass adjacent tribal groups in per cent of nonconvictions. This is shown in Table 3.

Table 3 Per Cent of Nonconvictions in Assault Cases by Tribal Group, Resident Magistrate's Courts of South Nyanza and Kericho Districts, 1955 and 1956 *

Gusii	39.5%
South Nyanza Luo	35.7%
Kipsigis	18.6%

* Court Records.

A certain number of Gusii (and Luo) nonconvictions for assault may be due to testimony so perjured that the court is unable to determine what took place. But the fact remains that the majority of Gusii assault charges are dismissed because there is no evidence that an assault occurred. The doctors who examine assault plaintiffs at the Kisii Hospital are rarely able to find marks of a determined attack.

Another category of aggressive offense, recognized by the Gusii though not by the British-imposed judicial system, is witchcraft and unjustifiable sorcery. There are many stories of young men who met witches at night and killed them with clubs. This is regarded as entirely justifiable, in fact commendable, homicide. In the daytime, however, a witch is not distinguished by dress from any other woman and is treated much like anyone else, even though people suspect she is a witch. To offend a suspected witch by accusing her or treating her impolitely would be to invite her wrath. In many ways she may be excluded socially, but this is done with extreme subtlety and discretion so that matters do not come to a head. Many divorces and separations occur because the wife is considered a witch by the husband, but this would not be stated overtly until she was gone. In general, the feeling is: If you are not prepared to kill a witch, do not offend her by revealing what she is. If a number of deaths in a community are attributed to witchcraft, then some action is felt to be necessary. In the past the most usual course of action after a public accusation was an ordeal called "going to the river," in which the accused had to pull an iron ring out of a pot of boiling water with both hands. If the hands were scalded, the verdict was guilty. Another kind of ordeal was used if a sick person were certain he was being bewitched but did not know who did it. Suspects drank a bitter liquid (*ekeroro*) and then ran around. Falling down and fainting was a sign of guilt. Persons incriminated by ordeals would be subject to lynching (*riyoyo*), that is, being clubbed to death by a mob of neighbors. The sons of the convicted witch might successfully defend her from the mob, but then they would have to pay compensation for anyone she killed. The mob execution of a witch was only done when she was notorious for killing people, but it was considered necessary at such a point because witches are thought to be incapable of reform.

Under the British administration, witch killing is murder, and since chiefs and elders no longer support it, alternative remedies for witchcraft have become popular. One is the hiring of a professional sorcerer (*omonyamosira*), a man, to bury medicine (*omosira*) which will combat the witchcraft poisons and act at a distance to kill witches. This is done not by the group, because elders disapprove of it, but by individual men who suspect their neighbors of witchcraft. Because of the high level of suspicion in the community, no one trusts his neighbor to use the sorcery only against witches but fears that it will be used to do away with anyone he hates or envies. In other words, each person fears that the other will use sorcery not for its ostensible purpose, to kill witches, but in the unjustifiable way that witches themselves use their magical powers. The use of sorcery, which has been largely imported from other tribes, has been increasing as has its concomitant suspicions. The professional sorcerers themselves are most feared as "witchcraft" murderers, and when death occurs in a community, the sorcerer may be blamed. One night in 1954, under such circumstances, a group of men smashed the skull of a wealthy sorcerer who had a reputation for unwarranted killing. His sons informed the police of the murder, but the culprits were never found because everyone refused to talk. Thus sorcery has become an increasingly popular witchcraft antidote, but it acts to bring new sources of aggressive conflict into Gusii communities.

Another contemporary way of dealing with witchcraft is to call in a professional "witch smeller" (*omoriori*). The witch smeller has the gift of being able to detect and root out the medicines hidden by the witch in the victim's house. He removes them in a dramatic way and warns the assembled throng, especially the women, to stop their witchcraft activities or he will have to identify the culprits. In general, however, he avoids fixing blame and focuses attention on removal of the injurious substances. This procedure has the general approval of Gusii constituted authority because it does nothing to increase suspicion or encourage witch killing.

Sometimes accusations of witchcraft or sorcery become public and have to be dealt with by authority in order to prevent witch killing. The Tribunal Courts refuse to hear witchcraft cases, but they will hear defamation cases brought by women who have been accused and want to clear their names. More frequently, however, the chief will order the elders to hear the case, as he did on several occasions in Nyansongo in 1957. If they decide the person is guilty, they issue warnings that such things must cease and sometimes order the alleged victims to stay away from the witch or sorcerer. No penalties are recognized for such offenses. The elders publicly oppose all witchcraft and sorcery and try to keep cases of it *sub rosa* as long as possible, for if they admit that it exists, they are encouraging retaliation. When a case becomes public, they try to reduce the conflict that led to the accusation rather than punish one side or the other.

SEXUAL OFFENSES

The sexual behavior of the Gusii is discussed in other sections of this work (Chapters 5 and 9) and elsewhere (LeVine, 1959*b*); hence this section will be limited to a review of those aspects which are relevant to social control and are not covered elsewhere.

Legitimate sexual intercourse among the Gusii is limited to the marital relationship; under any other circumstances it is theoretically punishable or a source of shame if discovered by someone of the parental generation. On the level of the family and neighborhood group, the social control of sex continues to be effected by traditional means: punishment by the ancestor spirits; *amasangia*, death because of adultery; intergenerational shaming. Father-daughter incest, for example, of which one contemporary case was reported to us, is treated as an affliction caused by the ancestor spirits who must be placated by a sacrifice. The offending father is not punished except for being forbidden to eat or drink milk from the cows in the daughter's bridewealth. Intraclan premarital incest outside the extended family is common but must be clandestine to avoid punishment.

The sanctions that can be used when classificatory father-daughter incest becomes public information are illustrated in a case where it resulted in pregnancy. A young man of 20 had a leviratic wife but was otherwise unmarried. One night during the time of female initiation he joined in *ogochabera*, "taking by stealth." He was drunk and had intercourse with a girl who was his classificatory daughter. She became pregnant while still unmarried, which is in itself a disgrace, and had a difficult delivery. During her labor, old women, in accordance with the belief that unconfessed sex offenses make childbirth difficult, had questioned her about her sex affairs. She confessed to having intercourse with 12 young men, whom she named, but the birth still did not take place. It is said that when she finally admitted intercourse with her classificatory father, delivery was immediate. This was taken as a sign of his guilt in the matter, and he was made to feel it. The girl's father and his own family reprimanded him harshly. He denied it at first and tried to run off, but he was ordered to stay home for three months so that the baby's resemblance to him could be noted. It is said that it was so strong that he had to confess. The girl's family contemplated accusing him in front of the elders but decided not to. In any event, he was stigmatized throughout the community and told when he came to beer parties, "You are useless; you may even steal our wives!" Because of this, he stayed at his own homestead and did not go out to beer parties until after the girl got married. Before the child of a supposedly incestuous union marries, the culprit will have to apologize at a feast in front of the child, its mother and legal father, and people from his own community. Such an apology (called *ogosonsorana*) is only necessary when the incest cuts across adjacent generation lines and has come to be known publicly; incest within the generation, even if publicly known, would not occasion such severe sanctions.

In the past, a Gusii man who discovered his wife *in flagrante delicto* had the right to spear and kill her lover. If he merely suspected a man of having sexual relations with his wife, he would question her about it. If she admitted it at all, she would claim to have been raped, and the husband would accuse her alleged rapist before the lineage elders. The elders could order an oath to be taken in which the woman stood naked astride a trench and the defendant, also naked, would pass through the trench between her legs, carrying a spear and shield. If his denial of guilt were false, he would be killed by the ancestor spirits. His refusal to take the oath indicated his culpability as a rapist, and the elders could slash and kill his cattle; no one of the husband's minor lineage could eat the meat of such cows.

Nowadays a husband may no longer kill his wife's lover under any circumstances. A Nyansongo man was told that his wife had sexual relations with an unmarried man in the community after a beer party. She claimed that she had fallen asleep in the house after leaving the beer party and that the young man had raped her while she was asleep. An indecent assault charge, to be heard by the local elders, was ordered by the chief. During their hearing they learned that the wife had the reputation of being promiscuous; the charge against the young man was immediately dropped. Had her reputation been cleared, the elders would have awarded damages to the husband. The latter would then have to perform a sacrifice with his wife before resuming marital relations.

While traditional means of controlling sexual behavior remain effective at the local level, where kinship sanctions are operative, increased contact between persons of different localities has resulted in a rise of premarital sexual activity, including rape. In the past, interclan rape or abduction would touch off a blood feud; today the typical rapist who is convicted of "indecent assault" serves six months in prison and pays a fine of $70. Many are able to escape the district before arrest, so that the charges are eventually dropped. The high frequency of rape has been a major problem in Gusiiland for over 20 years. Table 4 gives a comparison of the Gusii rate of rape (including indecent assault) indictments with the rate in the United States.

It can be seen that the Gusii have a phenomenal amount of rape. This fact is also revealed in Table 5, which compares the number of Gusii rape indictments in the Resident Magistrate's Court with those of adjacent tribal groups.

Homestead with fields and pasture.

Polygynous homestead with houses of two wives on right, children's house on left.

Men thatching a roof.

Men sitting in cattle pen watching girl's leading-in ceremony.

Woman carrying firewood and water pot.

Women weeding eleusine.

Boy and girl caretakers.

Mother nursing.

Children's group in pasture.

Children playing; boy with stick in charge of cattle.

Children tending cattle.

Brothers playing plow and oxen.

Clitoridectomy   *Circumcision*

Newly initiated girls shelling corn.

Divination.

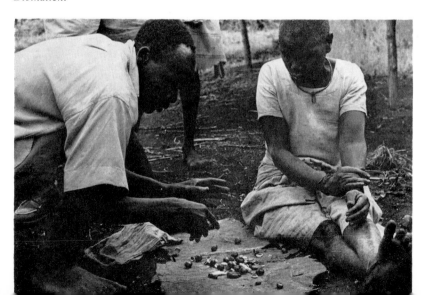

Table 4 *Average Annual Rate of Rape Indictments per 100,000 Population, Gusii and United States, 1955 and 1956*

Gusii *	47.2
United States, urban †	13.85
United States, rural †	13.1

* This is an extremely conservative estimate; the procedures by which it was arrived at are described in LeVine (1959b).

† Statistical Abstract of the United States, U.S. Department of Commerce, 78th Annual Edition, 1957, p. 139.

Table 5 *Number of Rape Indictments in Resident Magistrate's Courts, 1955 and 1956 and Populations, 1948, Gusii and Adjacent Tribal Groups*

	TOTAL NUMBER OF RAPE INDICTMENTS 1955–1956 *	1948 POPULATION
Gusii	13	237,542
South Nyanza Luo	6	270,379
Kipsigis	4	152,391

* A small proportion of the rape indictments are entered in the Resident Magistrate's Court, but this is the only court for which comparable figures are available.

This clearly indicates that the Gusii surpass adjacent tribal groups in rape rate.

THEFT

The Gusii traditionally had a clearly defined sense of private property with reference to domestic animals and grain. In each homestead the several "houses" had traditionally recognized claims to stock, but the homestead head was the formal owner of all herds and could allocate them as he saw fit during his lifetime. Theft within the homestead was dealt with only by him, while interhomestead theft brought judicial agencies and magical sanctions into play.

The Gusii are not shocked or revolted by the idea of stealing each other's cattle, as their Kipsigis neighbors are. Theft of cattle among the Gusii was only more serious than the theft of goats, sheep, or chickens in economic rather than emotional terms, and Gusii cattle were as fair game as those of another tribal group.

The rules of theft were relative to social distance. Raiding of alien tribal groups, Luo and Kipsigis, for cattle was highly approved of and frequent in the past. Cattle raids on other Gusii tribes were also permissible and frequent, although retaliations often resulted. Even the raiding of other clans within the tribe for cattle was proper under most circumstances, though not in areas where there was supraclan political authority. Within the clan, taking cattle, other animals, or grain belonging to another homestead was an offense and is more properly designated theft than appropriation outside the clan.

Controlling the theft of movable property in any society presents two distinct problems: identification of the thief, and treatment of the thief once he has been identified. In Gusii society there was no police force and no scientific method of detection; thus the identification of an unknown thief was difficult.

The solution was the application of magico-religious sanctions which were believed to affect only the thief himself and his family, although his identity was not known to the persons applying the sanctions. The thief would become so frightened that he would identify himself and could be dealt with as a convicted offender. Three procedures of this type were in general use before British administration. First, if a person found an animal or some grain missing and strongly suspected that it was taken by someone in the immediate vicinity of his homestead, he could summon his neighbors to a meeting. He would use the *obomera* oracle, rubbing leaves up and down on a greased stick and calling out the names of all neighbors present. The person whose name was called as the leaves stuck was the guilty one. In a variant form known as *amaera*, everyone present was asked to drink a potion (containing some earth that had touched the stolen article) which is supposed to kill the guilty one. The thief usually incriminates himself by refusing to drink. Second, in the case of a serious theft of several cattle that had not been committed by neighbors, the victim would invite the lineage and hut elders to his house to drink beer and curse the unknown thief. They would perform the drinking-tube curse, which would act to kill the thief. Ordinarily the thief would confess because of fear of the effect of the curse. Then he had to brew beer and kill a bull for the elders, and they would come and spit beer on him to remove the curse. The next day he would sacrifice a goat to the spirits and wear a goatskin bracelet. Third, if the theft victim preferred private sorcery to the elders' curse, he could hire a practitioner known as an *omokengi* to perform a kind of sorcery called *ogokenga*, which was used only against thieves. In one form of *ogokenga,* a hole was made in the watery stem of a plant called *omokubo,* and toads, ants, grasshoppers, snails, and crabs were inserted, along with rope from the stolen cow and earth from its footprint. The stem would be swollen with the articles introduced into it, and in like manner the thief's viscera would become swollen and he would die. Before a large crowd, the *omokengi* would hold up the stem and say to the anonymous thief, "You will die!" Elders in the crowd would shout, "Eeee! (Yes!)." An alternate procedure was to extract the bones and internal organs of a mole through a hole in its skin, fill it with the same articles just mentioned, and inflate the moleskin with air through a reed. It was taken to the top of a hill, where the *omokengi* shouted, "When the toad dies, you die!" Sometimes, instead of performing these laborious operations, he would shout a warning of the thief's death in the early morning for everyone in the area to hear. If this did not have the desired effect, he would undertake the rituals described. If the stolen animals were returned, the *omokengi* was given a hoe. This specialist in antitheft sorcery has been replaced in Gusiiland by the professional sorcerer (*omonyamosira*) and witch smeller (*omoriori*), both of whom are highly eclectic practitioners who perform any kind of magic (much borrowed from other tribes) for which people are willing to pay. One sorcerer is very fierce-looking and cultivates his reputation as a powerful, terrifying individual. Though he did not want to give away any secrets, he did make the following statement.

I am frequently called for in cases of theft. I mix a poisonous powder with the roots of certain trees, and then mix in earth from the place where the stolen article had been. I dig a hole there and put in the mixture and the freshly cut head of a black chicken. Then I put a curse on the thief and when he gets ill he confesses. But first I warn all the people around in a loud voice. Everyone is frightened; women ask their sons if they committed the theft. Most of the times after this the thieves return the stolen articles.

These, then, represent the range of magical procedures used to frighten thieves into confessing or returning the stolen property intact.

The second major problem in theft control is what to do about the thief once he is identified. In the past, if the owner caught someone in the process of stealing his animals, usually at night, he had the right to kill him without payment of compensation. Usually, however, this was not done for intraclan theft; litigation was more frequent. If the elders convicted a man of theft, he had to return what was stolen, or an equivalent, and provide a goat for the elders to eat. Both offender and victim ate it with the elders, and the thief was humble and quiet at the feast. If the convicted thief refused to repay the animals, the owner could either take them back himself with the moral support of the elders, persuade the elders to curse the thief, or, in some areas, appeal to the judicial chief (*omokumi*) for the use of his powerful wand to enforce repayment. An incorrigible thief would be warned by his family, who would eventually make it publicly known that he could be killed by anyone in the clan who discovered him stealing; alternately, he might be sorcerized by one of his victims. In general, however, the sanctions for occasional theft were rather mild, mainly involving repayment, provided the thief admitted both his guilt and the authority of the elders' order to repay what was stolen.

In many cases where the owner of a stolen animal claimed to know the identity of the thief, the accused maintained his innocence. Litigation before the elders was then necessary, and since in many cases perjured evidence made the facts difficult to ascertain, oaths and ordeals were often resorted to. If a stolen cow were found alive in a particular homestead, and the person in possession of it claimed it as his own, elders might order the following oath. The accused would hold the horns of the cow while the plaintiff cut off a piece of its right ear with a spear. As the animal shook the ear, throwing blood on them, the parties would state their claims in the form of a challenge. The animal could stay at the homestead where it was found, while the plaintiff retained the piece of ear. If at a later time trouble or deaths in the family caused one of the parties to concede that he was wrong, a cleansing feast would be held and the piece of ear produced at that time. When a person was accused of deliberately killing an animal belonging to someone else, he might be challenged to eat a piece of flesh cut from the wound on the body of the animal and stitched onto a sharpened stalk of napier grass. His refusal was a virtual confession of guilt; his eating it put him in danger of the usual spirit sanctions if he were guilty. In cases where the accused admitted taking the animal but claimed it to be rightfully his, the *omotembe* oath (described previously) would be used.

It is difficult to estimate the comparative incidence of Gusii theft. Statistics are not comparable to those available for American populations. In gross amount of theft complaints and theft convictions at resident magistrate's courts, the Gusii ran slightly behind both Luo and Kipsigis for 1955–56. The validity of the comparison is weakened by the fact that a breakdown for in-group and out-group theft is not available, and by the presence of European farms presenting unique temptations in Kipsigis reserve but not in the other two areas. The Gusii appear to have a reputation for an exceptional amount of theft among European farmers, and it may be that their theft rate is higher when they are living outside home territory. No type of theft is unknown in contemporary Gusiiland: organized rings of cattle thieves were discovered by the police during 1955–1957; robberies of shops and restaurants took place; sons frequently stole from their fathers. People in Nyansongo keep locks on their doors and do not leave valuables unguarded outside; children are sometimes left at home to protect the household against theft. Yet it would not be accurate to say that theft is an everyday occurrence nor that there is a pervasive fear of theft.

Nowadays the Kenya police are often called on for theft cases, and they provide a system of natural detection and enforcement which did not exist in the past. Belief in supernatural sanctions for theft have by no means died out, however. We administered a story-completion test to 27 Gusii high school pupils, who are among the most educated persons to be found in Gusiiland. One story they were requested to finish told of two teenage boys who steal a chicken undetected. Almost half of the pupils finished the story with the boys being identified through the use of the greased-stick oracle or poison ordeal and having to confess the theft. Thus magical means of identifying thieves play a part in the fantasies of even the more educated Gusii when confronted with the possibility of their own involvement in theft. The use of professional sorcerers for theft cases is common and is generally believed to be effective in causing the deaths of unconfessed thieves. The death of a Nyansongo man in 1956 was attributed to such a cause. Furthermore, traditional oaths are fully accepted and commonly used in the Tribunal Courts (at the request of the defendant) in civil cases of debts which often border on theft accusations. In general, then, there is a high level of belief in supernatural sanctions against unconfessed thieves.

CONCLUSIONS

The Nyansongans cannot be described as an extremely law-abiding group of people; many types of crimes occur in their community as well as in the wider society of which they are a segment. They are preoccupied with accusing each other of offenses, in court and outside, and no one is expected to admit his guilt. There is great reliance on the chief and courts, as well as on magical procedures, for the enforcement of cultural rules regarding sex, aggression, and property.

Chapter 9

Death, Disease, and the Supernatural

Nyansongans concern themselves with the interpretation of deaths and illness, and they see in the pattern of such events meaningful purposes and designs. No death occurs without firmly expressed opinions as to its "cause," and serious and chronic diseases often call forth interpretations as well. In the Nyansongo belief system, the same categories of supernatural explanation apply to all serious misfortunes and anomalies; thus a disastrous crop failure might be attributed to the same cause as human and bovine fatality, sterility, and congenital deformity.

This chapter covers Nyansongans' reactions to death and disease and their customary ways of coping with such events. The following topics are taken up: (1) medicinal practices which do not involve the supernatural; (2) emotional and ceremonial responses to death; (3) beliefs concerning witches (mentioned previously in Chapter 8), which are basic to an understanding of disease theories in Nyansongo; (4) theories of disease, involving not only witchcraft but ancestor spirits (discussed in Chapter 6) and sorcery (discussed in Chapter 8); (5) the ways in which contradictory diagnoses are resolved in concrete situations.

MEDICINE

A good deal of "naturalistic" medicine is practiced in Nyansongo. Medicine men (*abanyamoriogo*) have potions and pastes for sprains, diarrhea, pulmonary complaints, and heart ailments; indigenous surgeons (*ababari*) set fractures and cure backaches and concussions by the removal of sections of bone from the spinal column and skull. One Nyansongo woman whose head had been injured had two skull operations by a Gusii surgeon who removed sections of her cranium. Furthermore, even conservative Nyansongans are eager for Western medication, particularly injections and operations, and they pay exorbitant fees to poorly qualified Indian doctors in Kisii Town for remedies ranging from penicillin to diathermy. But these practitioners have little effect on the bulk of disease in Gusiiland. Although its elevation and coolness protect the inhabitants from sleeping sickness and other tropical ailments of the low-lying lake shore, Gusiiland is ravaged by pneumonia, typhoid fever (in the rainy seasons), bovine tuberculosis, intestinal parasites, and dysentery. Chronic malaria (with resultant enlargement of the spleen) is not uncommon, rabies is spread by numerous wild dogs, and fear of tetanus is the traditional explanation for the custom of removing the two lower incisors. Infant mortality is high, and so is the death of women during childbirth. Nyansongans are pragmatic about treatment and will try anything that promises help and that has the faith of someone they respect. When one remedy fails, they try another, running through injections, mepacrine tablets, sacrifice, and sorcery with no feeling of inconsistency. Diseases are so often in advanced stages before treatment is sought that even the best medical care would be of little use. Death from disease is thus a common occurrence,* and the outcome of any illness is fraught with uncertainty.

REACTIONS TO DEATH

Despite the high death rate in Nyansongo, death is not taken casually; on the contrary, it occasions elaborate ritual and the expression of intense emotions. The degree of ceremonial elaboration and emotional expressiveness varies with the social status of the deceased. The funeral of an infant, buried in the floor of the house, is humble, with little wailing and few people attending. When a wealthy, middle-aged man dies, however, kinsmen come from far and wide, and expressions of grief are profuse. Funerals of others fall in between these two extremes, with more elaborate funerals for married persons than unmarried, for men than women, and so forth. The corpse of an adult is buried just outside the house in which he lived, on the right side of the house for a man, on the left for a woman. Burial takes place in silence almost immediately after death, although the autopsy mentioned below may be performed first. The women of the family usually begin their wailing, which can be heard from far away, while the person is dying, but they must restrain themselves during the burial.

---

* This characterization is based on field observations; no death statistics were available.

After the corpse is buried, the women resume wailing, now even more loudly, sometimes sobbing and sometimes chanting in a stylized sing-song. They sing improvised eulogies of the deceased and attribute his death to the ill will of others. A Nyansongo mother wailed of her married son: "I'll never give birth again, and he's the one who caused me so much trouble in labor." Then she knelt on the grave and shouted, "You were my favorite son, you used to bring me sugar and salt and good blankets. Now you've gone below here. Why don't you listen to me and come back?" She ran into the son's house and emerged holding ashes in her hands, exclaiming, "These ashes—that's where I warmed myself last night hoping you'd come back, but you didn't." She ran back to the grave sobbing: "My Mogaka (his name), my Mogaka." The wife of the married but childless man chanted, "I'll never find a man who will love me as my husband did. I would have had a child by him, but maybe people were bewitching him." At another funeral, a married daughter of the dead man cried, "There was no one like my father, father, father! He was bewitched because he had so many cattle." When a woman is chanting a eulogy or wailing, she often goes into a slow, shuffling dance, moving her arms in rhythm with her legs. The wives of the deceased remove much of their clothing and either tie around their waists or actually don pieces of their husband's clothes, such as shirts, jackets, and hats. They continue to wail for 12 to 18 hours, sometimes longer, until they are too weak to go on, and yield to the urgings of the other women who want to give them food. Wives and daughters of the dead man have tears streaming down their faces while wailing and appear genuinely distraught, but women outside the immediate family wail loudly without other signs of deep grief. At night older brothers and sisters of the dead man stay with the widows to reassure them about the future and "keep them from killing themselves."

During the day of the burial, the males of the homestead and surrounding homesteads are silent and subdued. Their expression of grief is limited to facing the grave at one point and uttering a single note— "oooo"—which they hold for about a minute. The rest of the time they stand about silently, watching the women or chatting among themselves in low voices.

The day after the burial, the public funeral occurs. When the deceased is a married man, his wives and certain other close kin have their heads shaved at the grave. Some of the deceased's personal property is put on the grave. It may be his bed, if he had one, or the chair he most often sat on, with his clothes draped over it. His drinking tube and walking stick may also be included. By this time news of his death will have spread to his kinsmen near and far. Women from the community and from related families outside it will have gathered at the house of the deceased during or before the head shaving. Afterward, as other women join them during the day, this group wails with the widows of the dead man. The wailing on this day is more stylized and less grievous than the day before, although similar eulogies and accusations are sung. Men attend the funeral with spears, machetes, horns, whistles, and bells, as well as a few head of cattle apiece. They drive the cattle over the grave of the dead man while making a din by shouting, blowing the horns and whistles, and ringing the bells. Then they run about the grave thrusting the spears and machetes into the air.* Other men attend the funeral without cattle and pay their respects by facing the grave and singing one note, as mentioned above. Immediate relatives sacrifice two goats to propitiate the spirit of the deceased. Afterward the wives undergo a period of mourning of one to four weeks during which time they receive visitors and must not travel or bathe. A sacrificial feast at which the widows pick their leviratic mates ends the mourning period.

WITCHES

When a Nyansongan dies or is stricken by a serious illness, alternative explanations may be offered. One type involves the unprovoked aggression of witches or the wrongly directed magic of sorcerers; the other points to the patient's own acts as having caused either the ancestor spirits to punish him or a live person to retaliate through sorcery. Both explanations have an equal claim to validity in Nyansongo thought, but in specific cases one may be favored over the other. In this chapter we outline the alternative types of explanation and describe the process by which one interpretation rather than the other comes to be accepted in particular cases.

Before discussing Nyansongan theories of disease, it is necessary to describe their beliefs concerning witches. People in Nyansongo fear witches greatly and talk about witchcraft very frequently. In their belief, a witch (omorogi) is a person with an incorrigible tendency to murder his neighbors by secret means and with little provocation. In

---

* Although Gusii informants were not able to give reasons other than tradition for this behavior of the men, Wagner (1949: 453–458) describes similar phenomena for the related Logoli, attributing the cattle drive to a desire to pay respects to the dead man by wealth display, and the sham fight to recall the deceased's prowess in warfare.

theory a witch may be either male or female, but persons real and myth-ical to whom witchcraft is attributed are invariably women. Such women are believed to run naked at night, speechlessly carrying fire-brands and knocking on the doors of houses with their buttocks. Large groups of them are said to meet secretly at night to plan murders and to exhume and devour corpses. The eating of human flesh is supposed to enable them to run fast, although some are old women, and their muteness is attributed to their having eaten human hearts, which have stuck in their throats. Anyone who meets a witch may kill her if he can catch her, but a club must be used so as not to shed her blood. If you utter a sound while confronting a witch, you will die.

A person whose mother is a witch learns the evil art from her in childhood, but many women are believed to learn it later in life. A mother-in-law who is a witch may enlist her daughter-in-law, and women who have had great misfortune, such as the loss of many chil-dren, are regarded as specially susceptible to recruitment, since they want to retaliate against a world that has treated them badly. It is said that a woman who wants to become a full-fledged witch must first kill a close relative, usually her own child. After that she partakes of the conspiracies and cannibalism of the local witch group. Murder by witchcraft is effected by the planting of a "poisonous" substance in the roof, floor, or walls of the victim's house; it is thought to act at a dis-tance to cause disease and eventually the demise of the victim. The articles planted may be hair or feces of the victim, dead birds, bones of exhumed corpses, or actually poisonous powders, to mention but a few possibilities.

The question of whether there are women who conceive of them-selves as witches and run about naked at night is a real one. Highly educated Gusii youths claim to have seen them and relate detailed plausible accounts. Three living women in Nyansongo were mentioned as witches. One of them confessed to being a witch while drunk and later retracted the confession. Another indirectly admitted participa-tion in a witch group during an interview. Even if there are "real witches" in Nyansongo, suspicions and accusations run far ahead of substantiation. This is particularly obvious in cases where two families quarreling over land accuse each other of witchcraft, although none of their members may be considered witches by the community at large. Community opinion is fluctuating and inconsistent on the identity of witches, however, so it does not play a definitive role in settling such disputes.

An important aspect of Nyansongo witchcraft is that it is believed to be practiced by closely related neighbors against one another and by members of the same family against one another. The most frequently ascribed motive for it is jealousy of good fortune—greater wealth, better crops, more children—by a less fortunate person. A woman who becomes sterile is thought likely to practice witchcraft against those of her co-wives or wives of her husband's brothers who give birth regularly. Inheritance quarrels among brothers and half-brothers may also involve witchcraft accusations among their wives and mothers. Wealthy men fear the witchcraft of their poorer kinsmen.

THEORIES OF DISEASE AND DEATH

Witchcraft (*oborogi*) is always suspected when a Nyansongan has died. The proverb, "No one dies without carrying someone on his back" is interpreted to mean that all deaths are traceable to witchcraft. If the deceased were a homestead head or if the family has been suspecting witchcraft prior to the death, an autopsy may be performed. The examination is conducted to ascertain whether any of the internal organs are swollen. If so, the suspicion of witchcraft is confirmed. Regardless of what is found, however, the close female relatives of the deceased invariably make accusations of witchcraft in the course of their wailings at the funeral. At one funeral in 1956 the widow recalled that a neighbor woman quarreled with the deceased over trespassing cattle, and chanted her conjecture that the woman had bewitched him. At the funeral of a girl who had died in childbirth after we took her to the hospital, we were accused by her mother of having conspired with hospital attendants to kill her (no means were mentioned). Such behavior is an immediate expression of the grief and frustration of women at funerals, but it is often forgotten later on.

In some cases, however, accusations of this nature lead to violence at funerals. When a married woman dies without children, her kinsmen are extremely chagrined because they have to refund her entire bride-wealth, no matter how long she has been married. If she had been living in a polygynous homestead and had been infertile or unable to bear viable offspring, her kinfolk are doubly angered because they suspect witchcraft by her co-wives as the cause of death. When her sisters attend the funeral, they may destroy all her valuable possessions and grain stores to prevent the co-wives from benefitting by her death. In one such case the husband of the dead woman was attacked physically as well.

When an autopsy has been performed and signs of witchcraft are discovered, the men may decide to act on the confirmed suspicion, particularly if the deceased were a relatively rich and important person. A professional sorcerer * (*omonyamosira*) from outside the community is called for two reasons: (1) to retaliate against the witch, and (2) to protect members of the deceased's household from further effects of the witchcraft. The retaliation is accomplished by burying *omosira,* anti-witch medicine, in the grave itself or at some other place very near the house of the deceased. The *omosira* varies from one sorcerer to another; it may be a freshly killed black chicken wrapped in an article of the deceased's clothing or it may be a bottle containing a seed and some water. It is believed that when the seed germinates and splits, the witch will die. The sorcerer also performs a protective ritual known as *okoosia,* the making of incisions into which a powder is rubbed on the bodies of members of the immediate family. Just as an identical ritual protects a husband and adulterous wife from further supernatural sanctions, in this situation it wards off the future effects of the witchcraft that killed the deceased. Once the sorcerer has buried *omosira,* deaths and illnesses occurring in the next few months at nearby homesteads may well be attributed to its effect. The family which hired the sorcerer may be pleased at the success of the retaliation, but the family newly stricken by misfortune may not admit their responsibility for the previous death. The latter family may claim that the medicine is killing innocent people and report it to the chief. When the person is dying, they may ask the sorcerizing family to save his life by calling the sorcerer to take out the buried medicines and administer protective powders. If the sorcerizing family refuses, great bitterness against them will result, and they may come to be regarded as being like witches themselves. Thus a death may be attributed by family members to the illegitimate use of sorcery as well as to witchcraft by their neighbors; indeed, the distinction between witchcraft and sorcery may become quite vague in such cases.

Certain kinds of nonfatal illnesses may also be attributed to witchcraft. While dysentery, bronchitis, and malaria are believed to be susceptible of naturalistic treatment, if the family has previously suspected witchcraft or has had a series of misfortunes, a severe onset of such a disease may be thought of as witch-caused—particularly if the illness does not yield to naturalistic remedies. Sterility and mental disease, however, are always regarded as supernaturally caused, and the diviner rather than the medicine man is first to be called on in such cases.

---

* A professional sorcerer differs from a witch in being a male who can be hired to commit a magical murder; his profession is known and openly stated by him. Some sorcerers, however, have been suspected of using their powers to kill personal enemies and have been killed by their irate neighbors.

The diviner may diagnose either ancestor spirit affliction or witch-craft as the cause, but diviners always live nearby and know the situa-tions and fears of their clients well. The client is questioned about omens and mentions dead rats on the path, cut pieces of snakes and dogs found near the house, if witchcraft is his primary fear, whereas quite different omens point to ancestor spirits. If the first diviner does not give a satisfactory diagnosis, another will be consulted; thus the eventual interpretation of the disease is more dependent on the fears and anxieties of the patient and his family than on the arbitrary judg-ment of the diviner and her oracles. All three cases of mental disease which we had the opportunity to observe were attributed to witchcraft. In one, sorcery was used to combat it; a witch smeller removed the poisons in the second; and in the third case, that of a boy suffering from either mental retardation or psychosis, no remedy that we know of was resorted to. A witch smeller was also called in to cure a case of sterility. One young couple in Nyansongo had several infants who died and then a hydrocephalic child with a grotesquely enlarged skull. A diviner pronounced the deformity of their only living child the result of witchcraft by its grandmother, and the father of the child was re-ported to be learning professional sorcery to combat his mother's evil influence. Nonfatal but relatively incurable conditions, such as mental disease, sterility and deformity, then, are often attributed to witchcraft and less serious diseases may also be if patient and family are disposed to suspect witchcraft.

When a person suspects that he or his family are the objects of sor-cery, he views it as unprovoked and illicit malevolence, distinguishable from witchcraft only in that professional services were required for the evil magic. When a dead or dying person is known to have committed certain offenses, however, he is regarded as having brought sorcery on himself. This has already been mentioned for witches; a woman widely reputed to be a witch may die because of legitimate retaliation through sorcery. Sorcerers are also hired to kill unidentified thieves through magic, and the death of a man known to have committed theft may be attributed to sorcery by one of his victims. Finally, a man who refuses to pay a sorcerer for his services may become the latter's victim, and it is generally felt that his death was his own fault. Several deaths in Nyansongo were interpreted as the results of legitimate or justifiable sorcery: one of an old woman for witchcraft, one of a young man notorious for theft, and one of an elder who had failed to pay a sor-cerer. Interpretations of this kind resemble the ancestor spirit explana-tion of disease (discussed below) in that the affliction is regarded as punishment for an offense.

When a diviner diagnoses death or disease as punishment by ancestor spirits, she always names a misdeed of the patient as the ultimate cause. Sexual offenses, homicide (other than magical), and perjured oaths are the most serious of such offenses.* Another misdeed invariably punished by ancestor spirits is the neglect of proper mortuary rituals or the omission of a sacrifice for a dead ancestor. This is a residual category of offense, named by a diviner when she can think of no real misdeed committed by the person, because no one is entirely certain that he has done everything necessary for dead relatives. In addition, such ritual negligence is believed to be indicated by the occurrence of an intrafamilial offense, such as father-daughter incest or parricide, which is so serious that it is classified as a "madness" sent to punish the family by a displeased spirit. Numerous deaths and diseases in Nyansongo were attributed to supernatural punishment. A 10-year-old girl told us that her mother's co-wife had died in childbirth because a woman with whom her father was having an affair stepped over the birth blood. (This is *amasangia,* the spirit-caused punishment for adultery.) Even more frequent is the interpretation of impotence and sterility as spirit-caused conditions by diviners. Sacrifices to make up for ritual omissions are prescribed and performed over and over again until the condition improves or the patient gives up (or turns to witchcraft explanations). In general, when death occurs and the deceased is known to have committed a serious offense, the death and the offense will be linked in terms of ancestor spirits or justifiable sorcery; when an incurable but not fatal disease occurs, diviners are likely, if no serious misdeed is known, to fabricate a ritual offense to which they ascribe the condition.

Amasangia, the supernatural sanction against the infidelity of a wife, involves a somewhat special and elaborate set of beliefs. It can be incurred at any time after the transfer of bridewealth to the bride's parents. *Amasangia* literally means "sharing" and refers to the consequences of illicit sharing of a married woman's sexual attentions. *Amasangia* is caused by the adulterous behavior of a woman, but it directly affects her husband and children rather than herself. Nyansongans believe that if a woman has sexual intercourse with a man other than her husband and continues to cohabit with her husband, then when the latter becomes ill, her presence in the same room may cause his death. It is said that the sick husband begins to sweat pro-

---

* The homicide of a non-Gusii can lead to his spirit afflicting the family of the killer in exactly the same way as ancestor spirits do, but propitiation may require the performance of a special ritual in addition to sacrifice. It should also be noted that venereal disease is regarded as a punishment for sexual licentiousness without specific involvement of ancestor spirits.

fusely when approached by his adulterous wife; if he has cut himself, her attempt to bandage the wound will promote bleeding rather than arrest it. Some of the older polygynists will not allow their wives to visit them when they (the husbands) are ill, since they jealously suspect their wives of adultery. The "shared" wife may also unintentionally kill her child by her proximity to him when he is ill, and miscarriages are regularly attributed to adultery. Belief in *amasangia* appears universal among Nyansongo women, including Christians. They see it as punishment directed against themselves, for no woman wants to be a widow or to lose children. When a woman has committed clandestine adultery, she can avoid the evil consequences either by confessing to her husband and having a purifying sacrifice performed or by running away with her lover.

A second type of sanction enforcing marital fidelity is also part of the *amasangia* complex but is directed at men rather than women. When two men of the same clan have had intercourse with the same married woman, regardless of whether or not she is married to either of them, it is believed that a visit by one to the sickbed of the other will result in the death of the sick one. This is unimportant if the two men are distantly related and do not in any case visit one another, but it enters significantly into the relations of brothers, half-brothers, and first cousins. If one of them has an affair with a married woman, he must concern himself with whether any of the male clansmen whom he often visits has also had intercourse with her. Sometimes suspicion of adultery with a wife is aroused when a man becomes ill and finds that a particular half-brother or paternal cousin of his has not visited him. We knew of two young married men who were constantly seeking extramarital affairs and who would tell each other of the married women they had intercourse with so as to avoid sickbed visits if any of them were the same. Such collaboration to prevent supernatural punishment is rare; ordinarily *amasangia* acts as a check on male access to the wives of others.

DECIDING DIAGNOSES: PATIENT RESPONSIBILITY
VERSUS BLAME OF OTHERS

There are, then, alternative theories of disease causation extant in Nyansongo, and they are equally valid by Nyansongo standards. How is it decided which theory applies in a given case? No hard and fast rules of interpretation are laid down, and there are few simplistic formulations of the type which allowed medieval Europeans to conclude automatically that a leper had sinned. For example, when a woman has a miscarriage, she may attribute it to the witchcraft of her jealous co-wife, but her husband may see in it grounds for suspecting her of adultery, particularly if he has been away and has some anxiety on that score. Thus the theory selected to interpret a particular misfortune depends on the position and status of the person making the interpretation, and it often happens that a single event has entirely different meanings for different persons. Most frequently the patient himself (or, in the case of death, members of the immediate family) defensively blames the affliction on the witchcraft or unjustifiable sorcery of others, while neighbors, particularly men, are more likely to attribute it to misdeeds of the patient. When a thief dies, the women of the homestead immediately begin wailing and claiming that the deceased was bewitched. But neighbors, knowing that the dead man had committed theft and fearing that the sorcery medicine which they suspect killed him will kill anyone who goes to the funeral, refuse to take their usual part in the burial and other mortuary practices. Members of the deceased's homestead may not at first accept the fact of his guilt, but lineage elders will come and tell them that unless they make restitution and persuade the victim of theft to dig up the sorcery medicine, it will kill the whole homestead.

A case occurred in Nyansongo which illustrates this process. A young married man, Ongaki, son of Mogaka, was a notorious thief. He became seriously ill with a mysterious disease and seemed to be dying. Some elders came to him and urged him to confess so that his life could be saved by the appropriate measures of restitution, digging up the sorcery medicines and administering protective medicine. He maintained his innocence and blamed his illness on the unjustified sorcery of a neighbor whose family had a reputation for witchcraft. In January 1956 Ongaki died. His mother, the elder of two co-wives, wanted to bury sorcery medicines to kill the neighbor who killed him. Mogaka, father of Ongaki, opposed this on the grounds that the young man had probably been killed by the sorcery of a victim of his theft. Ongaki's mother insisted her son was not a thief and said she would take Mogaka's refusal as a sign that it was her co-wife, a much younger woman, who had killed him by witchcraft. Mogaka, realizing that his senior wife was threatening disruptive accusation within the homestead, agreed to hire a professional sorcerer so as to keep peace in the family. The sorcery medicines were secretly buried, but Mogaka, feeling that they would do no good, postponed payment of the cow that was the sorcerer's fee. In December of 1956 Mogaka had a severe attack of malaria and was suffering from pain due to a swollen malarial spleen. He refused to eat and became extremely emaciated. When a lineage elder asked him if he had any medicine buried, he denied it vigorously at first but intimated that he wanted to pay the sorcerer shortly before his demise in January of 1957. Almost simultaneously, Ongaki's widow bore a child (by her leviratic husband), which died a few days after birth. The funerals were poorly attended because of the widespread belief that the professional sorcerer had killed Mogaka in retaliation for the unpaid debt. Mogaka's widow steadfastly accused neighbors of killing him by unjustified sorcery and even ignored the fact that the two accused neighbors buried Mogaka to prove their innocence. (To bury someone whose death you have caused magically is believed to be fatal.) Eventually Mogaka's oldest half-brother returned from working outside the district and forced the widow to hire a witch smeller who removed poisonous substances from houses in the homesteads of the widow and the men she accused. The brother made a public speech about the evils of accusing others for troubles you yourself have caused. Later the widow confessed to several lineage elders that Mogaka did owe the sorcerer a cow, and it was duly paid. After confession and restitution, involving the widow's capitulation to the interpretation that Mogaka and she herself were responsible for the two recent deaths in their homestead, protective medicines were administered and accusations ceased.

Another case had similar elements. A young married man named Ogise came home to Nyansongo after having fought with British forces against the Mau Mau. He had had pains in his legs even before his military experiences and had reportedly been to doctors for them, but on his return he claimed a battle wound in his leg. He suffered for several months with an earache for which we gave him sulfa pills, but he refused to go to the hospital. When he seemed to be dying, he revealed that when he had killed Kikuyus for the government (not considered an evil act), the bodies had been left unburied, and perhaps their spirits were killing him. A diviner was consulted, and a hen sacrificed, but he died anyway. His older brother and another lineage elder inspected the corpse but did not find the battle wound he had reported. The elder brother said he simply died of disease, but a lineage elder said consensus was that he died of venereal disease contracted in his affairs with "low women" outside Gusiiland, had been ashamed to admit it to doctors, and had made up a story about a battle wound as a defense. Since no accusation of witchcraft was made (except the funerary ones of the bereaved mother) and since no magical sanctions were believed to be operating against the whole family, there was no need for the elders' interpretation of his death to be forced on the family if they wished to believe differently.

SUMMARY AND CONCLUSIONS

Nyansongans maintain contradictory explanations of disease, one of which views disease as a punishment for sexual, aggressive, property, and ritual offenses, while the other, more frequently used, blames it on the unwarranted malevolence of others. When a person becomes seriously ill, he tends defensively to adopt the interpretation which attributes the evil to others, much as a Nyansongo defendant in a trial always insists on his innocence. Lineage elders tend to adopt the punitive interpretation, especially if the patient is known to have committed offenses, and they try to persuade him to confess and perform the rites of absolution so as to save his life. When the patient dies without having confessed, close relatives, particularly women, often accuse others of murdering him magically. The elders then work to convince the survivors that their lives are in danger if they do not admit the dead man's guilt and do what is necessary to protect themselves from the sanctions that are continuing to operate. In doing this, the elders attempt to achieve two aims: (1) to save the homestead from annihilation by the supernatural punishment which the elders sincerely believe was incurred by the deceased and (2) to turn the blame of others into self-blame and thereby keep peace within the lineage. Thus, despite the fact that Nyansongo patients do not ordinarily blame themselves for their diseases, it is the role of authority figures to make them confess their guilt when it endangers the welfare of their family.

❊
❊
❊

Chapter 10

Formal Education

The Gusii did not take eagerly to the Western schooling which was first offered them in 1910. By World War II, the neighboring Luo were far ahead in education. In the 1940's the Gusii began to perceive the material advantages of schooling, and the desire for education grew rapidly until it now surpasses the government or mission ability to provide instruction. A contemporary myth tells of a great Gusii prophet who lived before the Europeans came, but who predicted that white men would come, take away Gusii children and give them white mushrooms. This prophecy, incomprehensible when it was uttered, is now understood to mean that schools would be established and that the children who attended them would be able to earn many shillings ("white mushrooms"). This story is typical of the Gusii view that education is a pathway to lucrative employment, and those parents who want their children educated emphasize the monetary rewards awaiting the educated man. Thus the payment of school fees is seen as an investment which will bring cash return.

In spite of this belief, however, and although Nyansongo is located a quarter of a mile from a school with eight grades and 400 pupils, only one child in the community was attending school in 1956. This 8-year-old boy was later joined by two adolescent boys who were first graders. Of the 28 married men in Nyansongo, 12 had attended school, a majority for two years or less, and this group included a few who attended for only one term and did not become fully literate. Four men claimed to have become literate without schooling. The married women are all unschooled and illiterate. The unmarried population includes only five males (other than the three boys who were pupils in 1957) and two females with a year or two of schooling. Thus Nyansongo is predominantly an illiterate community and does not show signs of change in this respect.

The most educated person in the community is a married man in his late twenties who went through seventh grade, speaks some English, and works sporadically as a brick mason on the Kericho tea plantations. He is not accorded unusual respect, in fact, his reputation is extremely low because of his numerous violations of sexual taboos among close neighbors and kinsmen. His education commands less attention than his deviant behavior, which is viewed as immoral and slightly mad.

When asked why they send so few children to school, Nyansongan parents plead lack of money for school fees, but this explanation is at odds with fact, for there are relatively well-to-do families whose children do not attend school, and poor families whose children do.* For the poor and powerless families education is seen as the path to wealth and prestige.

* The lack of education among Nyansongans is also related to their lesser involvement in Christian missions than many people in surrounding communities.

Many of the local economic opportunities in Nyaribari location are controlled by its chief, who in his thirty-year incumbency has acquired tremendous economic and political power. Much new land was opened for settlement by Nyaribarians, markets and power mills were built, and coffee cultivation was introduced during this period. Many persons of all the local clans shared in the benefits of this economic development, but the chief has favored members of his family and lineage, and to a lesser extent people of his subclan and clan, in the allocation of shops, jobs, and loans. His great prestige with the colonial government and his important positions in the African District Council and the Kisii Farmers Cooperative Union give him influence in the choice of persons for many well-paying jobs. He has used this influence on behalf of the selection of his own kinsmen and in barring persons of subordinate or "adopted" clans of Nyaribari from access to economic advantage.

The members of the lesser clans, some of whom have suffered from discrimination by the chief, have shown great determination to advance economically despite the obstacles he puts in their path. Some have explicitly encouraged their children to work harder than the other pupils at school, and to compensate for their membership in a less favored clan by advancing in education to the point where they have unique qualifications for important positions. These are usually obtained outside the district or in open civil service competition. This encouragement has had striking results. One young man from a poor family in a low-ranking clan, who grew up in a community adjacent to Nyansongo, received a B.A. from Makerere College, an M.A. from the University of Bombay in India, and became a labor relations executive with a large corporation in Nairobi. He is the most educated Gusii. Two men of a different low-ranking clan are regarded by the chief as special enemies. The son of one graduated from high school and was the only Nyaribari student in Makerere College during 1955–1957; a daughter of the other is one of the few Gusii women who has gone beyond primary school and speaks some English. Both of these educationally advanced individuals also grew up within a half mile of Nyansongo. By contrast, only one of the chief's numerous sons completed secondary school, and none of his daughters has had much education. Altogether, the educational advancement of his children has not been commensurate with the financial capability of their father to provide them with schooling. This is also true of the sons of the chief's brothers.

Thus the over-all picture of educational recruitment in Nyaribari is as follows. Young people from low-ranking clans, whose opportunities for economic advancement are blocked by political discrimination, have tended to go farther in school than the children of politically powerful families. Boys of the latter families obtain good jobs in local government despite their lack of high educational qualifications. In this context the educational backwardness of Nyansongo can be properly understood. Its people belong to the same clan as the chief, and one of its neighborhoods is made up of persons of his subclan. A number of Nyansongo men are employed by the chief as cook, chauffeur, guards, foreman of his field hands. Several families are allowed to use the chief's land without payment of rent. Certain men in the community who are not generally considered able have been appointed to minor political positions by the chief. In other words, residents of Nyansongo have access to the chief's favor and derive some economic benefits from their relationship with him. Given this relationship, which provides a sense of security unknown in the low-ranking clans, Nyansongans are not disposed to invest their scarce monetary resources in school fees or to push their children toward educational achievement.

The largest school near Nyansongo is a Roman Catholic mission school, but several smaller schools run by the Seventh Day Adventists, Friends African Mission, and African District Council are within a few miles. All of these, including the Catholic institution, are day schools staffed entirely by African teachers. The number of Nyaribari parents who want their children to go to school is so much greater than the number of places in the schools that many must be refused. Parents plead with the schoolmasters and attempt to bribe them in an effort to get a child into first grade or to win the readmission of one who was dropped for poor performance. This situation gives the teachers considerable power and even higher social status than they would otherwise have.

Most of the families in and around Nyansongo cannot afford to send more than one child to school. When asked which of their children they would choose to send, parents answer, "The most obedient child." No mention is made of specifically intellectual qualities, such as ability to learn. Parents seem to view schooling as a series of commands by the teacher which, if they are obeyed by the child, result in success. Failure is attributed to disobedience rather than to stupidity. The parental attitude is partly a recognition of the real dangers of truancy, for a disobedient child will go to the market or play with some friends rather than attend school, thus wasting the money invested in school fees. Truancy is a big problem, and though parents and teachers cooperate in controlling it, it is less costly to select a child whose obedience has been proven in the family setting than to risk sending to school one who seems likely to pursue his own pleasure and lie about having gone to school. Nevertheless, the adult view of education in terms of obeying commands is more general than a realization of the risk of truancy, and it sometimes results in the selection of a well-behaved child for schooling over his more clever and mischievous brother.

The first few grades are now taught in the Gusii language (Swahili used to be the norm) by teachers, most of whom have not gone farther than eighth grade themselves. English is introduced in fifth grade, and by eighth grade an average student can write a passable essay in English and carry on a limited conversation. The English of the eighth grade student in day school, however, is inferior to that of students in the mission boarding schools near Kisii Town. Academic subjects in the higher grades are taught by Gusii teachers who have completed high school and gone to teacher training college or liberal arts college. In addition to the standard British academic curriculum, the Catholic mission school near Nyansongo offers carpentry, agriculture, music, and physical education. Training in music is obtained by spending long periods in a drum and bugle corps which marches on the school playground. At morning recess and lunchtime, many of the boys play soccer, using small rubber balls when nothing better is available. They are great soccer enthusiasts and seem to play at every opportunity.

Pupils of both sexes must wear uniforms in good repair. For boys, who predominate at the school, this means a khaki shirt and khaki shorts; for girls it is a blue dress with white collar and cuffs. Children are sent home by teachers if they are not wearing the uniform on a particular day, but greater lenience is shown those whose uniforms are torn or frayed. Clothing is one of the school expenses of which parents complain, and many of them do not understand why uniforms are needed or that school authorities are firm in their demand for them. Children who do not go to school often have torn and tattered clothing and generally wear less than pupils. The school has pupils who walk as far as 10 miles every day from home to school; lunch is not provided by the school, and their mothers do not give them lunches to take along either. The wealthier boys are given a few pennies to buy bananas at the market during the noon recess; a fortunate few have relatives who are shop owners at the market and give them a meal. The majority, however, get nothing to eat from early in the morning until they get home in the middle of the afternoon or later, and this must have some effect on their performance in afternoon classes.

School discipline is strict. Teachers demand complete attention and order in the classroom. When the teacher walks into class, the pupils rise in unison and remain standing until told to be seated. Officially, only the headmaster is allowed to administer corporal punishment, and he must record each administration in a ledger which is examined by a visiting school supervisor from the mission. In fact, however, each of the teachers in the lower grades uses corporal punishment daily without even getting permission from the headmaster. Those children who have talked in class or otherwise caused a disturbance are made to line up in front of the class and one by one stand by the teacher to receive a few strokes with a wooden switch. Even outside the classroom the pupils are deferential to their teachers and responsive to their commands. Students in the seventh and eighth grades are put to work on the school's agricultural instruction plot as a punishment for misbehavior.

If the teacher derives some power by being the dispenser of a currently scarce and valued commodity and a classroom disciplinary agent, this power is augmented by the fact that the pupils do not return home for lunch and that many of them are 14 to 24 years old. In other words, he has daytime control over a number of physically mature individuals, and customary checks on personal power do not operate in his case because he is living at the school, away from his community and kin group. The seduction of girls in the 15 to 18 age range by their first or second grade teachers is a recognized abuse, and teachers are dismissed for such offenses when they are discovered. Many other extracurricular uses of the docile students are locally regarded as legitimate. For example, some of the teachers use the older boys to cultivate plots of land loaned to the teachers by persons in nearby communities. The boys are not paid for this, and the teacher reaps the harvest. Male students are also used as domestic servants in the houses of the resident teachers, even cooking for those who do not have their wives with them. In general, the older boys at the school are viewed by the teachers as a labor force which may be assigned to tasks personally required by the teacher. Neither the students nor their parents seem to take strenuous exception to this practice. In this sense, then, schooling is, as parents believe, an exercise in obedience rather than intellectual development.

Part II

Child Training

❧
❧
❧
❧
❧
❧

Chapter 11

·

Pregnancy and Childbirth

Nyansongo husbands and wives share a strong desire for offspring. Procreation is considered essential to marriage, and parents want as many children as possible, which is related to the dramatic population growth of the Gusii over the past half century. Both male and female children are considered valuable, males because they have a permanent stake in the welfare of the homestead, females because their marriages bring cattle to enrich the family. Insofar as mothers have a preference, it is for a boy, "to bury me when I die," "to take care of me when I'm old," "to bring a wife who will help me in work," "to build houses and mend fences." A girl is said to "go away (in marriage) as soon as she gets big enough to be helpful," and "she may even elope without giving us cattle." It is through her sons that a woman achieves an honored status in the family. Men traditionally want boys to perpetuate the lineage and defend its patrimony, but they realistically point out that having children of both sexes is far better than having too great a predominance of one sex. With all daughters, the minimal lineage dies out and its property is inherited collaterally; there is no one at home to help the parents when they are too old to grow their own food, and they become dependent on kin who are less interested in them than their sons would be. With a predominance of sons, the family has difficulty in raising bridewealth cattle for them to use in marriage, and they may remain unmarried until the age of 30 or longer. Short-range domestic considerations may also influence a mother's preference: if there are cattle and no boys to herd them, she will want a boy; if there is no one to help with fetching water and gathering firewood, she will want a girl. In general, however, Nyansongo parents desire to have both sons and daughters.

Women want to give birth once every two years until menopause, and their husbands actively concur. No formal post-partum sex taboo exists, but polygynists tend to stay with wives who are not currently nursing children. Many wives are eager for sex relations only when they want to conceive, and they do not want to become pregnant again until the child is about 2 years old and has developed some physical independence. Sometimes the space between children is less than two years, due partly to the Gusii belief that conception can take place only during menstruation. In monogamous families, children are more likely to be close in age, but women who have children too often are said to be oversexed.

Any unusual delay encountered by a woman who has been actively trying to conceive is viewed with alarm by husband and wife even if they already have several children. Childlessness is one of the standard supernatural punishments which can be inflicted by the curse of a father on his disobedient son, by the lineage elders on a serious offender against morality, and by the ancestor spirits on a man who has failed to make appropriate sacrifices, ignored omens, or sworn a false oath. Difficulties in conception, in addition to their frustration of the procreative impulse, arouse fears of such punishment and lead to efforts to propitiate the ancestor spirits. The husband goes to a diviner for diagnosis and often makes expensive sacrifices in order to cure the condition. If one sacrifice does not work, he will consult a different diviner. After several such attempts fail, the husband may begin to suspect witchcraft.

Childbearing is a matter of invidious distinction among co-wives in a polygynous family, and they are sensitive to any inequalities in the distribution of living children. Suspicions of witchcraft arise among them when a wife becomes sterile or has a miscarriage or stillbirth. A survey of Nyansongo women past menopause indicated that approximately half of the children born alive live to maturity. In this situation there are some women who have given birth repeatedly but have few or no children, and they often blame this on the witchcraft of their co-wives. When a woman first suffers a procreative disaster, she is likely to suspect the evil machinations of others. Should she become incurably sterile at a young age or lose so many children that her plight is abnormal, others may accuse her of witchcraft when they suffer similar disasters because it is assumed that jealousy has made her wish evil to them. Thus children are so desired by Nyansongo women that in polygynous families childbearing is competitive and gives rise to hostilities among co-wives.

The sterility or impotence of a husband is likely to result in the dissolution of the marriage. A young woman is not expected to remain with a husband who cannot father her children, since both her desire to have children and her marital fidelity are regarded as imperative. A young man in Nyansongo who was reputed to be impotent was deserted in turn by two legal wives, with consequent return of bridewealth. When a man becomes sterile or impotent later in life, the need for his wives to have more children may be honored by a clandestine breach of their obligation to remain faithful to their husband. Although it is regarded as shameful, the impotent man may allow his wives to have sexual relations with other men of their own choosing. Nowadays such a husband often takes employment outside the district so as not to be at home while his wives are being impregnated by other men. The adult children of such women may not accept this practice; they have been known to insult and even stone the men who are thus serving their father's wives. Children born of these unions are legally children of their mothers' legal husbands and have no relationship with their physiological fathers. All men suffering from impotence and sterility consult diviners (diagnosis usually involves snake omens) and perform sacrifices, usually without effect. Among the older bachelors are to be found those who proved sexually incompetent or sterile in an early attempt at marriage. Thus a procreative failure on the part of a man is disruptive to the marital relationship.

The need for procreation throughout their fertile years is felt so deeply by Nyansongo adults that irregularities in the ideal reproductive cycle arouse strong anxieties and cause disruptions in family relations. Despite the high mortality rate in infancy and childhood, the loss of a child at any stage of life is taken as a serious event. In order to establish a stable marriage, avert fears of supernatural punishment, and minimize dissension among co-wives, viable children must be pro-

duced regularly. The significance of childbirth for the Gusii of Nyansongo must be viewed in this context.

Infanticide is not approved of by the Gusii in any circumstances (unlike many other East African tribes) and does not occur. Such an act
figures in cultural fantasy as characteristic of witches who are said to
order a new witch to kill her own child in order to prove her power.
Abortion is also considered bad and occurs only in cases of unmarried
girls and brides who are about to escape the husbands chosen by their
parents. Women deny the existence of indigenous abortifacents and
claim that most abortions are attempted by deliberate jumping and
falling. Since the girls who attempt abortion want to conceal their
pregnancy and can confide in no one of the older generation, it may be
true that abortive techniques have not been highly developed. It also
appears to be true that most premarital pregnancies are not arrested
but result in childbirth. Infanticide and abortion, then, as methods of
disposing of what Nyansongans want most to preserve,—children—are
disapproved of and rarely occur.

Illegitimacy, that is, the birth of a child to an unmarried girl, is
regarded as an extremely disgraceful situation. The girl who discovers
that she is pregnant may frantically plead with her lover to marry her
or even come to live in his house without being invited. Sometimes
this results in marriage or concubinage, but more frequently young
men, cherishing an ideal of marriage to a girl with whom they have
not had sexual relations, run away to plantations or the city to avoid
such involvement. If the girl is young, her parents may press charges
of defilement in court and thereby scare the young man into marrying her. Often, however, the pregnant girl will not disclose the name
of her lover, and the best her parents can do is to try to marry her off
to a young man before her pregnancy becomes visible. If their attempts
fail, the girl has her child at home. She wears dresses which conceal
her condition as long as possible and afterwards remains at home, not
even visiting her girl friends, spending much of her time indoors to
avoid being seen. Her shameful condition is known and discussed
throughout the community. If she does not induce an abortion or miscarriage, she must undergo the ordeal of an illegitimate childbirth.

Nyansongans believe that a girl who conceives before marriage cannot deliver until she has revealed the name of her child's father. It
must be the name of the real father or delivery will not take place.
Thus when the girl who has previously refused to name her lover is in
labor, old women of her family and neighborhood demand her confession in severe terms: "Talk quickly or die!" They may even pinch
her and slap her in order to get a confession. If the man named is

someone of the same clan as the girl, the women will look for resemblance between the infant and the putative father during the first few months after birth. If a strong resemblance is found, then the man is disgraced (see Chapter 8, p. 103, for the handling of a case of this kind). If the accused is of a different clan and the girl is young, a defilement case may be brought against him at this late date, using the resemblance as evidence in an attempt to obtain damages or force a marriage.

Most frequently the unmarried mother is simply taken as a secondary wife by an elderly man wealthy enough to pay a high bride-wealth rate for proven fecundity but too old to be able to demand a girl of high moral virtue. The child becomes a legal part of the family of his mother's husband, but he has a lower status in the eyes of many in that family. Despite the social disgrace, then, the unwed mother may benefit her father by bringing an unusually large amount of bridewealth.

The Nyansongan desire for children is one of the strongest motivations in their culture, but it does have limits. The high value which they set on human fertility and reproduction is exemplified by their attitudes toward sterility, impotence, infanticide, infant mortality, and abortion. At the same time, their drive to have as many children as they can is modified by a concern for infant welfare, which prescribes a two-year interval between births, and by disapproval of nonmarital sexuality, as shown in the attitude toward unwed motherhood. Women who violate these limits on procreation are viewed as lacking in proper sexual inhibition.

Conception is believed to be a union of male semen and female blood; hence it can take place only while the female is menstruating.* There is no fear of menstrual blood. The male contribution to the child's heredity, that is, appearance and temperament, is considered greater than that of the female; in fact, resemblances to females are overlooked while those to the father are noted and mentioned. Menstruation is understood to be a monthly occurrence and is called *omotienyi,* which means "moon" and "month." When a woman who has resumed menstruation since the birth of her last child and has been cohabiting with her husband (or another male) finds that she has not menstruated for two or three months, she assumes she is pregnant. She is happy and tells her husband, who is also pleased.

A pregnant woman is not treated specially and is not subject to any restrictions. Women continue arduous physical labor until they no

* Even many of the more educated Gusii retain the belief that conception takes place only during menstruation.

longer feel capable of it. Although illness during pregnancy is a valid excuse to refrain from work, all women observed in Nyansongo performed normal domestic and agricultural tasks until about a week before giving birth. Some women claim they are "stronger" during pregnancy and can work harder. If a pregnant woman felt weak and wanted to sleep more and work less than usual, her husband and related women would help out. Cravings for particular foods, such as bananas or eleusine grain, are recognized and indulged. Some women are said to be more quarrelsome when pregnant, and others demand that their husbands stay at home throughout the gestation period. Morning sickness is known, and one particular form of it involves the wife vomiting whenever she sees her husband or even when she sees his clothes in the morning. There is no medicine used for such conditions.

A miscarriage is considered a pitiful event, though not as grave as the death of a living child. The foetus is buried in the floor of the house rather than outside because it was not yet ready to "leave the house," that is, the womb. If the woman who suffers the miscarriage has been suspected of adultery, she will be encouraged to confess her misdeed so as to prevent further harm from befalling the family. If she has had bad luck with previous births, the possibility of witchcraft or spirit affliction may be seriously entertained.

Human parturition (*okogonkia*) is distinguished in the Gusii language from that of animals (*okobiara*). When a woman feels the labor pains and contractions, she notifies her husband's mother. Birth is to take place in the mother-in-law's house (which is in the same homestead) because it is not proper for a mother to enter her son's house, and she is required to assist in the delivery. If a woman is visiting her own parents when she goes into labor, she may give birth there, but her mother-in-law will be called to assist. The first time a woman gives birth is a big event because her fear of the process is very great and also because there is no way of predicting what difficulties may develop. While only two or three women are present at a later birth, the first one may attract a large crowd of older women. At first the mother-in-law is in charge of the situation, with the wives of husband's brothers and of husband's paternal uncles also present. A skin is laid on the floor near the mother-in-law's bed (not on it), and the woman in labor lies on it, flat on her back with her knees bent. It is common for a woman who has not given birth before to be terrified, crying and holding her legs together. When this happens and labor has gone on for a while, women in the community are called and the woman's mother is sent for. On one occasion of this kind, at least 15 women were present, including the oldest woman of Nyansongo, who came from the most distant part of the community. A middle-aged neighbor was sitting behind the 18-year-old girl in labor and was supporting her in a sitting position identical to that used in the clitoridectomy operation. Under such circumstances the women tell her to be brave or she will kill the child. In particular, they say that holding her legs together will suffocate the baby. Sometimes they pinch her, beat her, or slap her to force her to aid the contractions. They often hold her legs apart forcibly. To add to the commotion, some woman may impatiently urge her to confess adultery in order to ease the delivery. An experienced woman may take charge of the situation; if her measures result fairly immediately in birth, she will be rewarded with flour.

Men are not called on in childbirth unless an emergency develops, and even then their role is a limited one. The husband is supposed to stay out of the house in which his wife is in labor, not because of a taboo but because the wife does not want him to see her at such a time and would be extremely angry if he approached. When delivery is long and difficult, however, the women attending will tell the husband to dig up the roots of a bush called *chinsaga*. It is believed that such difficulty is caused by the baby being stuck some distance from the opening, and that the juice of these roots, which are chewed and sucked, will dissolve adhesions in the womb and allow the child to come out. Another remedy for prolonged labor involves a man who is a classificatory brother-in-law; it must not be the husband or an adjacent-generation person. The man is to hold the woman's nose and force his breath into her mouth to make the baby emerge from the womb. This is frequently resorted to, as it was on the occasion mentioned above, although men do not relish doing it. Thus a variety of medical and moral measures, some of them involving men, are used to hasten delivery, particularly when it is the woman's first childbirth.

The old women attending are so anxious to remove the child from the womb that when it begins to emerge, they sometimes deliver it too rapidly, causing the placenta to be retained. Such cases are common and, before the advent of Western surgical aid, resulted in the death of the mother. If hemorrhaging occurs, the mother is fed porridge and water, as much as possible, "to make blood." If she becomes weak from loss of blood and loses her appetite, she may be fed the internal organs of a goat and the soup in which they were cooked; this is also believed to replenish her blood supply.

Under normal conditions, when the child is delivered one of the attending women cuts the umbilical cord with a knife and puts ashes and colostrum from the mother's breast on the navel. The women clean the substance from the child's mouth and wash the whole body with water. Juice cooked from the leaves of a pumpkin squash plant is fed to the child to wash out his first feces. On the evening of the day of birth, a bit of liquid porridge is put into his mouth to stimulate the food he will be taking before long. Actually, however, the child is nursed at the breast from its first day. Colostrum is considered healthy; "it makes the child fat." When the afterbirth emerges, the new mother herself wraps it in leaves and throws it into the bush while on her way to the stream where she will bathe. On returning to her mother-in-law's house, she will rest there with her newborn child for four to five days. During that time she will do no work except to gather some firewood and leaves to wipe away the child's excrement. If the mother-in-law is dead or feeble, the woman will stay at her own house during this period and will be helped by her co-wife or other nearby women. There is no seclusion or prohibition on visiting, and the husband may be sleeping in her house at the time.

Once the child's umbilical cord drops off, food is prepared for guests, and the women who attended at the birth come to name the child. Up until this time the neonate is called *Mosamba Mwaye,* "the burner of his own home," indicating that he has left his previous habitat (the womb) and cannot return to it. Now one or two names are chosen with the approval of the child's paternal grandmother and mother. There are many criteria for determining the name: the weather conditions or other events occurring at the time of birth, evil omens seen before the birth, previous condition of the mother with respect to childbirth. Most frequently, however, the name of a recently dead person of the same sex in the father's family is used for the first name and the name of a dead person on the mother's side for the second and less important name, which may later be dropped. The women eat, and then the child's paternal grandmother or a classificatory grandmother shaves its head and bounces it up and down in her arms, saying, "We shall call you _____." If the mother has had numerous infant fatalities before, a small top knot will be left on the child's head and maintained until his initiation. No men are present at the naming and shaving ceremony. After it, the new mother returns with her baby to her own house and begins to work as soon as she is able, doing even the hardest chores usually within a month.

Nyansongans conceive of the neonate as a fragile thing, especially susceptible to malevolent influences which can kill it through disease. Thus there is no idea of beginning to train it at this stage, for every effort should be expended to satisfy its needs and ensure its survival.

Chapter 12

Infancy

The infancy of Nyansongo children can be characterized as the period between birth and weaning, when the greatest amount of attention is paid to their needs and the least effort is directed toward their training.

In this stage the health and survival of the child are a source of anxiety to the parents, although this is not apparent until the child actually becomes ill. With the exception of an occasional amulet worn on the wrist to prevent stomach trouble and teething pain, few measures are taken which are specially designed to protect the child from disease; action is reserved until the onset of the disease. When an infant develops diarrhea that lasts for several days, the mother becomes extremely worried and usually hires a medicine man (*omonyamoriogo*) to administer potions orally and make small incisions on the child's body. The practitioner may be paid a goat or two, a substantial measure of the mother's concern. In general, such minor diseases inspire greater worry and more immediate action in infantile cases than in those of older persons.

Infants are particularly susceptible to the "evil eye" (*okobiriria*), not because they are young but because their skin is still light brown and therefore delicate. Adults whose skin is light brown are also thought to be affected by it, as are light-colored animals and trees with red flowers. When the child's skin develops a darker hue and rougher texture, however, the evil eye is no longer a danger. Although men have been known to have it, it is mostly women who have the evil eye. When such a woman looks at a child whose skin is still brown, any small things near the child—grain, feathers, flowers, wool of a blanket, ticks on a domestic animal—will cling to his skin. If not removed in time, the objects will work their way through the soft brown skin, lodge in the visceral organs, and kill the child. The practice of the evil eye is said to have been introduced by Kipsigis women who were sold into the tribe as wives when there was famine in Kipsigis territory. It is unconscious and not controllable by the person who has it, so that when such a woman gives birth she is forced to focus her eyes on eleusine grain held in front of her to absorb the evil effect and prevent it from reaching her infant. Therapy for the effects of the evil eye on infants resembles that used among the Kipsigis. When parents notice the adherent substances on the child's body, they rub his whole body with clarified butter, which is thought to remove the harmful materials. This process, called *okongura,* must be done without talking about the evil eye, for its evil is felt to be more effective when it is mentioned or even thought about. Some informants said a specialist is hired to do the rubbing, but other parents claimed to do it themselves. If an infant dies, it may be said that the therapy was not applied soon enough, before the stuff had penetrated the child's skin, for once it gets inside the body, no cure is possible. Internal organs, particularly the heart and liver, are thought to be so soft and sensitive that their being touched by any foreign object will cause death. Nyansongo parents are quick to notice adherent particles on their infants' skin, for they are most anxious to prevent the onset of the fatal disease.

The lack of strength and motor control manifested by all infants is attributed in part to their "hot blood," which makes them weak and fearful of a cold environment. The superior strength of adults and older children is thought to be caused by their experience with cold, which has made their blood firm and resistant. This belief does not lead to a determined exposure of children to the cold, but it may help to account for the relatively little concern which Nyansongo parents have about the warmth of naked infants and children on chilly days. The only medicines used to facilitate growth are herbs given to infants during the first three months of life to promote the growth of teeth.

CARETAKERS

The infant's most intensive relationship is with his mother, who nurses him. The Gusii word for breast feeding (*okogonkia*) is the same word as that which means "to give birth," and this identity conveys the importance of breast feeding to the infant in Gusii thought. A mother is expected to feel rather exclusively about her nursing infant, as expressed in the proverb, "Someone else's child is like cold mucus (i.e., disgusting)." Women do not nurse each other's children. The infant sleeps in his mother's arms at night, is carried on her back when she goes on long trips, and is not far from her when she is near the house. During much of the day, however, the mother is working in nearby fields and around the house, and the infant is carried and cared for by a child nurse (*omoreri*, from *okorera*, "to take care of").

The nurse, 6 to 10 years old, is usually an older sibling and plays an important part in the infant's life. In the cases of 24 Nyansongo children of different families whose mothers were interviewed, 19 had been cared for by child nurses, 4 were cared for exclusively by their mothers (who were unable to commandeer a child for the job), and 1 was taken care of by an old, ailing grandfather. Twelve of the child nurses were sisters of their infant charges, 2 were brothers, 2 were fathers' sisters, and there was one each of mother's sisters, father's brothers, and father's sister's daughters. The pattern of mothers using their younger sisters in the caretaking of their first and second children was observed to be more common than this sample indicates. Mothers who have no children of their own to act as nurses and who cannot find an unoccupied child of the right age in their husbands' or parents' homesteads consider themselves unfortunate, since they get little more aid from other adults than anyone else. They are forced to carry their infants around to a much greater extent. Twelve child caretakers remained with their infant charges until the latter were walking, 6 for two years or more, and 1 for only two months, since she was the preceding child and was too small to manage the growing infant. Typically, then, at least until he walks, a Nyansongo infant spends a good portion of the daytime being carried and cared for by a sister 5 to 9 years older than himself. In no case is he left alone; there is always someone nearby to attend to his needs.

FEEDING

Attending to the infant's needs is thought of primarily in terms of feeding it. There are no feeding schedules; the mother nurses whenever the infant cries and does not try to anticipate his hunger. At night the mother sleeps naked under a blanket with the child in her arms, even when her husband sleeps with her. The one-year-old infant may sleep beside the mother rather than in her arms, but no farther away than that. Ordinarily he may feed when he wants to without crying to wake her up. In the morning the mother gets up at dawn, picks up firewood outside the house, and cooks food until the infant cries, then nurses it. Shortly afterward, she turns him over to the child nurse and goes to work in the nearby fields. When the mother is hoeing, sowing, and weeding corn, the infant is often left at the house with the nurse in the following manner. He lies on a cloth beside the nurse or is carried on the latter's back in the house and yard; the nurse sometimes visits friends at adjacent homesteads with her charge on her back. During the eleusine weeding season, however, the infant is bound to the mother's back as she weeds from a kneeling position. On the mother's back, the infant's cries are heeded almost immediately, and she stands up, loosens the cloth, and nurses him. More frequently, however, the mother is doing agricultural work which requires movements too strenuous to be done with a baby on her back. If the field is as much as a mile away and the infant is not yet used to eating gruel, the nurse brings the infant along and holds him at the side of the field. If the field is nearby, the nurse stays at the house until the infant's crying cannot be silenced by other means (such as shaking and feeding gruel), then either calls the mother to come or brings him to the mother for nursing. If the mother does not have a child nurse for the infant, she may lay him on a cloth at the side of the field in which she is working.

When the infant cries, the mother may drop her hoe immediately to nurse him, or she may continue working for a while before heeding his cries. If the crying is insistent, however, no woman will let it go on as long as five minutes without attempting to nurse the infant. The observed variation within this limit was also found in the answers the 24 mothers gave when asked how quickly they generally attended to their crying infants: 7 said they take immediate steps to satisfy the infant's needs; 7 stated they would do so *unless* they were working; 7 specifically mentioned letting the infant cry for a few minutes if they were working; 2 indicated that they would not respond immediately to crying under any conditions; and 1 mentioned letting the infant cry if he refused the breast. Thus Nyansongo mothers vary in the extent to which they allow their agricultural (and household) chores to delay their response to the crying of their infants.

Since the dress of the modern Nyansongo woman is not parted in the front, the mother must pull her breast up to the neckline in order to nurse the child. With little more than the nipple protruding from the dress, she holds the child to it. The mother usually does this mechanically, without looking at the child or fondling him, and she often continues conversing with the other women and older children.

The women usually stop working in the fields before noon to avoid the midday sun and do not resume until the cool of the late afternoon. In the interim, the mother returns to her house, feeds the older children, and nurses the infant if he cries. During the time the mother is working around the house, putting out grain to dry, grinding, and so on, the nurse continues to carry the child on her back, handing him over for nursing only when he cries. The mother may have to leave the homestead to go to the power mill to have corn ground or to fetch water and collect firewood and edible leaves. Since all of these activities require her to carry heavy loads, the mother cannot take her infant, and he must remain at home with the nurse. At such times the infant may become hungry and have nothing to eat if he has not yet become used to supplementary foods. In general, however, the Nyansongo infant does not go long without being nursed by his mother once his hunger has been expressed in crying.

Traditionally Nyansongo infants were fed eleusine gruel from birth, or a few days afterward, as a supplement to mother's milk. The gruel (*erongoori*) was administered by force feeding: cupping her hand against the infant's lower lip, the mother poured gruel into it and held his nose so that he would have to suck in the gruel in order to inhale. Eventually he learned to drink it from a bowl-like calabash. Nowadays, partly because of mission teachings, early force feeding is coming into disfavor and gruel is being introduced at a later age. Middle-aged mothers in Nyansongo, used to the old system, still use force feeding and begin it within the first month of life; Christian wives of nearby schoolteachers abjure force feeding and wait until the infant is 6 months old before feeding gruel. Young but conservative Nyansongo women fall somewhere in between. If the mother dies in childbirth, the neonate is most likely to be given cow's milk, although it may be nursed for a short while by a grandmother (real or classificatory) who has milk in her breasts. After a week it is fed a mixture of gruel and cow's milk, which becomes its entire diet. This is also done in the case of a mother with completely dry breasts, although there is root medicine given to women whose breasts are not producing sufficient milk. Ordinarily cow's milk and other adult food are not given children until weaning. The early introduction of gruel is viewed as a convenience for the mother. She leaves some with the nurse, with orders that the infant is to be fed it when he cries. Under such conditions, the mother may go off for a considerable time during the day without making the infant go hungry and without being bothered every time he cries. When she is at the house, however, she is much more likely to nurse the infant than let him eat gruel. In our judgment mothers always leave more than enough gruel for their infants' needs during the day. The nurse is usually quick to feed it to the infant when he cries, and indeed she often pushes food into his mouth after he has shown that he does not want more.

There seems to be no particular problem about infants not wanting to eat their gruel or refusing the breast often. The only feeding problem mentioned by informants was that of an infant who wants the breast too often. The mother eventually becomes annoyed and refuses it, although she will relent if it keeps on crying. Some mothers are said to get angry at such a demanding child and to slap it lightly. In the main, then, the infant's needs for food are well taken care of.

OTHER RESPONSES TO CRYING

Feeding is not the only response which Nyansongo caretakers make to infantile crying, but it is by far the most nurturant of their responses. Mothers recognize a kind of crying during the first three months which cannot be satisfied by nursing, and they call it *enyancha,* which means "the lake." Some view it as a disturbing stimulation of the child's genitals caused by the wind from Lake Victoria; others think it is a kind of stomach trouble and have potions to feed the crying infant during the night. Most often at night, however, the mother puts on a light, binds the infant to her back and walks about in the house, shaking him up and down. With the side of his face pressed tightly against her back, the infant is frequently silenced by jostling in this position. In the daytime, child nurses also use shaking, either on the back or in the arms, as a means of calming a small infant who cries but refuses food. If the mother is at hand, the nurse may turn the infant over to her for breast feeding, but if he continues crying, the mother ordinarily turns him back to the nurse for shaking rather than do it herself. The shaking is not accompanied by kissing or hugging but sometimes by tapping on the child's body. Nurses train infants to get into position for going on the back when the baby-talk word *titi* is uttered. When the nurse wants to carry a one-year-old, either because of his crying or her own desire to move elsewhere, she kneels with her back to him and says, "Titi, baba" (mother) or "Titi, tata" (father), and he clutches her back and spreads his legs as she hoists him up.

A common way of quieting older infants is to frighten them. When a one-year-old on a nurse's back begins whimpering, she will say, "Aso, aso, esese," which is a way of calling a dog. There may or may not really be a dog nearby, but the calling of it (or, more rarely, a cat) is intended to make the child think that the animal will come and harm him if he does not stop crying. This often works to silence him. The infant is prepared to respond in this way by his mother, grandmother, and other caretakers, who often point out animals of any kind—cows, chickens, dogs, insects—and label them all *ekuku,* who "will bite you," a name (again in baby talk) which is supposed to inspire terror in the child. The mother and grandmother believe that this fear is good because it will safeguard the child from actual harm incurred by animals, such as being stepped on by a cow, and also explicitly because it can be used by a parent to control the child's behavior, particularly excessive crying. When we visited one homestead, one mother said to her 2-year-old, "You always trouble me by crying at night. Now Getuka (the investigator) is going to take you away. Will you agree to be taken in his car to his home?" The child screamed, "No, no!" and clutched his mother. When we were about to leave the homestead, another woman said to us for the child's benefit, "You'll come early tomorrow to pick up this child." After four months of such comments, whenever we approached the child and mother together, the little boy would run away screaming, although he had not done so originally. Nyansongo parents consider this amusing. When a toddler followed his mother and some other women who were on their way to the market, he was picked up by his mother, brought over to the ethnographers, and told, "They will eat you!" The child screamed and finally ran back home amidst the laughter of the women. These are not peculiar reactions to ethnographers or white people but represent a determined attempt on the part of Nyansongo mothers to frighten their children with animals and strangers in order to make them more subject to parental control. Such fear training begins before the child can actually speak and is one of the first kinds of verbal cues learned by the infant.

TEMPORARY CARETAKERS

Aside from the mother and child nurse, few other individuals participate in the care of an infant. It is rare, for example, to see a man holding an infant or paying much attention to it. Occasionally a young father was observed with his child in his arms when the mother was away, but this was exceptional. Of 21 children with living fathers, only 11 were reported to have been cared for by their fathers between the ages of one and six. Even many of the 11 do not represent true cases of the father as caretaker, as when a mother said, "Yes, her father also took care of her. Especially when she was sick, he would try to get medicine." Another mother who answered affirmatively stated that when she was not present, the father would tell the child nurse to cook food for the infant. Such caretaking does not involve actual contact with the child and is typical of the father's participation in child care. Women who reported that their husbands were not at all involved in child care made such statements as, "The father doesn't take care of small children." One woman said her husband claimed that as an old man he couldn't look after children; another said that if her husband heard of a beer party he would just go and leave his infant son alone. In addition to their aloofness when at home, many fathers spend a good deal of time working outside of the district.

Females in the homestead play a greater part in temporary caretaking than males. In polygynous families, co-wives sometimes take care of each other's toddlers and feed them when the mother is away for the afternoon or the whole day. If the child nurse is 8 or 9, however, she may be left in charge of the small children, especially if the co-wives are not on good terms. If the child's paternal grandmother is living, she may also act as baby sitter in the absence of the mother. When still active in agricultural work, however, the grandmother spends less time with her grandchildren than one who is blind or feeble and has nothing to do but sit with children. In Nyansongo a blind grandmother and a feeble great-grandmother helped rear the babies of their homesteads. Older siblings, aside from nurses, sometimes play a part in child care, and in families where there is more than one sister between the ages of 5 and 9 the responsibility is shared to some degree, although one of them is definitely charged with the duty by the mother and performs it more frequently. Initiated unmarried girls supervise child nurses, but rarely play the latter role themselves, since they are freed from that chore by their newfound status. The wives of brothers in an extended family may care for each other's children in much the same manner as co-wives. In most cases, however, caretakers, aside from mother and child nurse, are clearly secondary, playing that role sporadically and for short periods. Mothers recognize that the other women in the homestead are also busy, and they do not rely on them greatly in matters of child care.

AFFECTION

The Nyansongo mother does not act very affectionately toward her infant, although other caretakers may do so. It is rare to see a mother kissing, cuddling, hugging, or cooing at her child. Individual variability among mothers on this score is considerable, but in the main it is not done. As described above, the mother nurses the child mechanically and only occasionally takes it from the nurse when unprovoked by its crying. Most mothers observed saw to it that their infants did not get into trouble and were not neglected by the nurses but intervened only when they felt the nurses or the infants were doing wrong.

When things were going smoothly, the mothers tended to remain aloof. The caretakers who were most affectionate were nurses, grandmothers, and occasionally fathers' brothers' wives. When she is alone with the infant, the child nurse frequently hugs him, kisses him, tickles him, and indulges him in other kinds of affectionate play. Sometimes, however, she does this in a rough manner which tends to alarm the infant and other times she ignores her charge in favor of interacting with her peers. There is, then, little consistency in the nurse's affectionate behavior, and it may not always be communicated to the infant as nurturance. Grandmothers exhibit overt warmth and nurturance, repeatedly kissing an infant left with them, sometimes lightly biting its feet or hands. Fathers' brothers' wives have occasionally been seen behaving this way also. Perhaps the discrepancy between the amount of nurturance displayed by the real mother and that by other caretakers is due to the mother's fear that such an exhibition on her part might provoke the ill-wishing jealousy (*okoema*) of people watching her and her child. A grandmother or other person, however, would be motivated to show that she loves the child and wishes him no harm. We have no information on the truth of this nor on whether mothers are more affectionate with their children when completely alone with them. The mothers of older children all stated that they had left flowers and leaves or tins to beat on for the nurses to distract their children when they were infants, but we rarely saw such articles in use during the observation of infants. The only observed case of a toy frequently used for distraction was that of an infant whose hand had been badly burned; he was given a gourd rattle to shake with the other hand to draw his attention from the pain.

Despite the fact that mothers do not display a great deal of affection toward their infants, it is always to his mother that the frightened toddler will run, and he typically attempts to follow her even when she wants him to remain with the other children.

CLOTHING, CLEANLINESS AND WALKING

The Nyansongo infant is loosely wrapped in a thin, store-bought, cotton cloth which is also used for binding him to the nurse when he is a bit bigger. Sometimes the cloth is laid out as a groundcloth on which the naked infant lies, and we have seen this done in the cold of morning when it must have caused some discomfort to the child. The belief that the bodies of infants are excessively warm and must become hardened through exposure to cold may account for this behavior.

In some of the wealthier and more acculturated families, infants wear cotton shirts (if male) or dresses (if female) from as early as 6 months, but it is as frequent for them to be naked until weaning. Feces and urine are wiped away with soft fuzzy leaves collected by the mother for that purpose, but the mother does not try to anticipate the child's excretion. Most mothers are very casual about it and show no sign of disturbance when their infants soil the cloth and the mother's person as well. Sometimes their response is not immediate, but eventually they wipe up the excrement with the leaves, cleaning the infant, cloth, and themselves. No attempt is made to effect sphincter control during infancy. Mothers are said to suck mucus from the infant's nose, but we have only seen them pull it away with their fingers. Nurses and grandmothers also wipe away mucus, but all caretakers are rather erratic about this. The cloth or shirt the infant wears is typically filthy and not frequently washed. Infants themselves are bathed approximately twice a week with cold water; little effort is made to keep their skin free of ashes and dirt between baths, although, as mentioned earlier, adherent articles such as feathers and wool are viewed seriously as signs of the evil eye. Masturbation is considered bad, and on one of the few occasions when we observed an infant touching his genitals, his sister-nurse (8 years old) threatened him with a large stick and told him to stop.

Both mothers and nurses encourage infants to stand at about the age of one year. The most frequently used method is to hold the child in a standing position by his hands and say "person-pole, person-pole" over and over quickly as he remains on his feet. This is done in a good-humored way and may be the focus of family attention on a particular occasion. In general, however, nurses help the children in such motor advances during the time the mother is away. This is the case with walking, for example. Although some mothers do this themselves, the usual practice is to have the nurse guide the infant in walking in the cold dew of the early morning, which by cooling the "hot blood" of the child's feet makes them firm and is supposed to reduce his fear of walking. The nurse sets the child on his feet in the grass and says "Ta, ta," encouraging him to walk toward her. Although most children are taught to walk in this fashion and are able to walk well before they are 2 years old, there is no emphasis on early walking as an accomplishment.

If a mother becomes pregnant early (i.e. before her infant is 18 months old), she will put pressure on the nurse to teach the infant to walk as quickly as possible and will devote more of her own efforts to that end as well. This is because it is strongly felt that a child should be able to walk and not need the care of a nurse by the time its "follower" is born. Attainment of motor skills is not, however, a particular source of pride for the parents or of rewards for the child. It is viewed by parents as a prerequisite for the adequate care of the subsequent child but one which is fraught with danger. The cryptically worded Gusii proverb, "Lameness is up" means that when a child gets big enough to walk by himself, he will be confronted with physical dangers and may be so badly injured as to become lame. To some extent this is a realistic fear, for children who are learning to walk sometimes stumble into the fireplace and get burned. Three toddlers in Nyansongo were severely burned in this way during our stay.

SUMMARY

The foregoing picture of Nyansongo infancy needs to be modified for children of certain status. Girls and boys are treated alike in infancy, except that a string of beads is put around the girl's abdomen, and sex-typed dress is used by some of the more Westernized families. The oldest child of a particular mother is most likely to be cared for by the mother herself rather than by a child nurse, and the last child is least likely to be pushed toward walking or other independent behavior. A child born after many have died or a boy born after only girls have survived becomes the center of attention and is treated with more care and affection.

The general picture of the Nyansongo child as he emerges from infancy is that of a dependent, fearful individual, capable of making demands on his mother and other caretakers for food and protection, but unaggressive, quiet, and timid in his approach to the physical environment and to strange things.

※
※
※

Chapter 13

Weaning

Weaning is the first of a series of drastic changes which take place in the second and third years of the life of a Nyansongo child. The other changes are the birth of a sibling, replacement in the mother's attentions by the new sibling, the beginnings of responsibility and aggression training, and toilet training. In this chapter we shall describe weaning from the breast and then proceed to the later changes in the order in which they occur in the child's life.

In accordance with the Nyansongo value of postponing weaning until the child can walk fairly well and take care of himself to some extent, mothers try to prevent conception during lactation. This they do by refusing to have intercourse with their husbands while they are menstruating, as this is thought to be the only time during which conception can take place. As might be expected, such a practice is not invariably effective, and some births do take place before the older child has attained the desired maturational stage, occasioning early weaning. Women who have several children so closely spaced are criticized by other women for being oversexed and inconsiderate of the infant's welfare. Such success as people in Nyansongo do have in conforming to ideal rules of child spacing is due to the polygynous setup in which a husband can spend most of his time with nonlactating wives, to the absence from the home of many employed fathers, and perhaps to psycho-physiological factors as well. The fact that monogamous families produce children more frequently than wives in polygynous families indicates that plural marriage has an effect on child spacing even in the absence of a formal post-partum taboo on sexual intercourse.

Weaning begins within two months of the time the mother discovers herself to be pregnant. Numerous reasons are given for this timing: that milk from a pregnant woman causes diarrhea in the child, that the mother fears her suckling will use up milk intended for the unborn child, that mother's breasts dry up during pregnancy. Since some mothers do not complete weaning until the eighth month of pregnancy, none of these beliefs can be accepted as universal. The feeling which is probably most common to Nyansongo mothers is that the child, now thoroughly used to cereal foods and strong enough to walk by himself, should be prepared for his replacement as the primary focus of the mother's attention.* One mother told her preweaning child that bitter substances were on her breasts (although this was not true and she shortly afterward nursed him) in order to "prepare him for weaning." Although this in itself is not typical, it indicates the kind of reasoning which mothers apply in beginning weaning as soon as

---

* There was no indication that the resumption of parental sexual relations was experienced by the child as a deprivation or replacement by the father. Such a possibility cannot be ruled out, however.

they discover their pregnancy. The feeling is strong among Nyansongo women that there must be no competition between older child and infant for the mother's attention, and weaning during pregnancy is one step toward preventing such conflicts. Thus weaning should not begin until the child is thought capable of getting along without considerable maternal attention, and yet it should be completed before there is another child born whose demands for attention must be given priority.

Although Nyansongo people, particularly women, do not ordinarily keep track of dates and time periods taken up by events, some fairly reliable figures on age of weaning were collected. In a sample of 24 women, each of whom was questioned concerning only one of her children, the average age at which weaning was reported to have begun was 20.7 months, and the median was 19 months. The range was from 11 to 30 months. At the lower end of the range, the early weaners were wives of monogamists who became pregnant "too early," as some of them apologetically put it. The children who were weaned later than 24 months were last children whose mothers, having reached menopause, allowed them to nurse almost as long as they wanted. The last child (*omokogoti*) is considered very fortunate in that he never has to relinquish his mother's breasts nor her attention to a younger sibling.

METHODS OF WEANING

The word for weaning in the Gusii language is *ogotacha,* which literally means to stamp on or to step on. The painful aspect of the weaning process for the child is thus explicitly conceptualized, and there is the general belief that the more severe the mother is with the child she wants to wean, the quicker and more smoothly will the goal be achieved. The estimated time between onset of weaning and its completion ranged from one week to six months among the mothers questioned, but most reported that they accomplished it in one or two months. The methods in use among mothers include putting bitter substances (pepper, goat dung, juice from sour fruits) on the nipples, slapping the child, burning his arms with a caustic plant juice, ignoring his cries in the daytime and wearing a dress that prevents access to the breasts at night, sending him to live with a grandmother, giving him large amounts of solid food to make him forget the breast. Of the 24 women questioned, 16 used bitter substances regardless of what else they did, 4 others used slapping alone, 2 made few attempts to wean at all because the children in question were their last, 1 fed the child solid food to make him forget, and 1 mentioned only that she kept her dress on at all times. Eight of the 16 mothers who used bitter substances mentioned supplementary techniques: 3 slept with their dresses on, 2 slapped, 2 fed quantities of solid food, 1 turned the care of the child over to its paternal grandmother, 1 sent the child to sleep with its father at night. Although none of the mothers interviewed sent children to live with maternal grandmothers in order to effect weaning, this is a recognized practice, and there were two children from other communities living with their maternal grandmothers in Nyansongo during our stay. It is said that mothers who cannot bear to be severe enough to wean their children themselves send them away in this manner. The child who lives with his grandmother for a few months during weaning is usually fed a great deal and receives much nurturant attention from her. If he stays at home, as the majority do, nighttime during the weaning period presents the most serious problem. The child continues to sleep next to his mother and naturally tries to suck at her breast for nocturnal comfort and nourishment. Some mothers continue to sleep naked but keep their backs to the child, in contrast to the practice of moving the suckling every time the mother turns over so that he will always have access to the breast. Others, as noted above, sleep with their dresses on to prevent nursing, and attempts to ignore the child's demands seem to accompany this. Some mothers send the child to sleep in the house of a co-wife, which is considered a rather drastic measure for so young a child.

Sometimes daytime may also be painful for a child, as the following case demonstrates. A 30-year-old mother of four girls expected her husband, a policeman working outside of the district, to come home on vacation and impregnate her. She felt that her youngest child, 22 months old, was big enough to be weaned and that the process should be begun even before the husband returned. The child had been walking well for some time, and the mother wanted to have her weaned by the time she was 2 years old. On one occasion after the onset of weaning, we observed the child sitting on her mother's lap for 20 minutes, crying continuously and occasionally pulling at her mother's high-necked dress. Throughout the period of incessant crying the mother was looking at pictures we had brought and talking animatedly with a visiting neighbor. Only once did she pay any attention to the child's cries, shaking it briefly and then continuing her conversation as the child resumed crying. At one point, when the child's cries were loudest, the mother was laughing at a remark made by the other woman. Despite her almost unbelievable (to the observers) capacity for ignoring the bawling of the child being weaned, this woman was not less nurturant than other mothers in her treatment of her other children. Interestingly enough, she reported in an interview two months later that the child observed gave her no trouble during weaning. Her behavior, while perhaps not typical of Nyansongo mothers in general, at least illustrates the diminution of response to the child's demands for attention that can result when a mother is determined to wean. Many mothers did report trouble (crankiness, etc.) during the weaning period, and it is a commonplace among the older women that children being weaned are troublesome. Since virtually all of them are accustomed to solid foods long before weaning begins, it can only be concluded that the disturbance of the children during weaning is due to a certain degree of emotional abandonment by their mothers.

The only method reported of comforting a child during weaning is feeding it quantities of solid food. It is doubtful that this allays the frustration of the child's desire for the close physical, dependent relationship of nursing, especially during the night. Thus, although Nyansongo mothers vary with respect to nurturance, it is most usual for them to avoid and/or punish the child during the weaning rather than offering another kind of emotional comfort to replace the breast.

THE BIRTH OF A SIBLING

Since weaning usually begins during the mother's pregnancy, it is ordinarily followed a few months later by the birth of a sibling. The mother may inform the child that a little sister or brother is on the way, but whether she does or not, she hopes that the child will be nurturant to the new arrival. Such an attitude on the part of the newly weaned child is not always achieved without considerable training, however, as is illustrated by the following case. Nyanchoka, the younger of two wives of a middle-aged man, had her second child when her first daughter, Moraa, was 25 months old. Moraa witnessed the birth of her sister and ran off to the house of her mother's co-wife, crying, "My mother has killed a hen; I don't want to be there any more." She cried a great deal but returned toward evening to find her mother holding the neonate. Moraa said, "Take away the hen; I want to sleep next to you." When Nyanchoka refused to sleep without the infant in her arms, Moraa went back to the elderly co-wife, who had no small children, and slept with her. After six nights with the co-wife, Moraa returned to her mother voluntarily and was gently and repeatedly shown that the neonate was her sister and not a chicken. She soon wanted to hold the baby and be affectionate with it, and during the following three months, Nyanchoka taught her how to hold it and to be very cautious about sitting or stepping on it. During the same period, Moraa, who had previously been taught to chase chickens and dogs away from drying grain, showed a strong tendency to beat every dog and chicken she saw with a stick until she had to be punished for doing so. She also engaged in acrobatics and boasting to attract the mother's attention, although her efforts in this regard tended to annoy rather than amuse Nyanchoka. This sequence of behavior illustrates that the birth of a sibling and its important place in the mother's attention are disturbing to the child who has been replaced and that the Nyansongo mother trains and punishes to control the dependent and aggressive manifestations of this disturbance.

Often a child does not easily accept the diminution in maternal attention which follows the birth of his younger sibling, and severe punishment results. The feelings of both mother and replaced child are most likely to come to a head when the mother has to make a long trip or work in a field. She will take her infant or have the nurse take it but refuse the urgent demand of the older child to go along. Often the older child follows the mother, crying bitterly, and in 22 out of 24 cases, mothers reported caning their children for such behavior. The mother feels particularly strongly about the older child crying when she is holding or carrying the infant because the crying is interpreted as *okoema,* murderous jealousy. In other words, the succorant cries of the older child are held to mean that he wishes the death of his younger sibling.* Since such aggressive motivations are considered reprehensible, the child is punished for them. An observed incident will illustrate the intensity which emotions can reach in such cases. Nyaboke is the younger of two wives of a policeman; she and her co-wife are very friendly and cooperate closely in work and the caretaking of children. Nyaboke had sent her 2-year-old son, Manyara, to his maternal grandmother for weaning, and he had returned after a while. The infant developed dysentery, causing a great deal of anxiety to his mother. One morning when he was ill, she left Manyara, her 2-year-old, with the co-wife and a group of children who were helping the co-wife smear mud on the wall of her house. As Nyaboke left, infant in her arms, to visit a neighbor living higher on the hill, Manyara began to run after her, calling her name. Nyaboke chased him back to the homestead, a stick in her hands. Manyara was crying hard, but his mother threatened him with the stick and told him to sit down and wipe his nose with a leaf. He did so but continued bawling violently. Nyaboke

---

* No children were observed or heard of who tried to harm their newborn siblings.

struck him across the legs several times, then picked up the infant and began to walk away again. As Manyara again began to follow, the co-wife threatened to tie him up with some rope and, when this did not work, beat him on the feet with a stick. He continued screaming and trying to follow his mother. Suddenly the co-wife told him to go ahead and follow Nyaboke, who had turned around and come back again. She beckoned Manyara to come to her, and when he did, she caned him sharply on the legs. The co-wife pushed him into his mother's hut and locked the door as Nyaboke went off for good. Locked in the hut, Manyara continued screaming his mother's name, and eventually the co-wife sent her daughter to let him out. He began crying and calling for Nyaboke again, and when the girl shut him up in the hut once more, said, "I've stopped now," and did not resume crying after she let him out again. Nyaboke blamed her son's behavior on the fact that he had lived with his grandmother, who did not cane him enough. On the afternoon of the same day, Nyaboke was home and Manyara quietly approached. She said to him, "You're always crying. I'm going to tie you with a rope and then I'll buy a *kiboko* (rhinohide whip) and beat you with it." An 8-year-old female cousin on her way back from the river said to him, "I see you're quiet now, Manyara; you realize you did wrong." Although emotions ran high in this instance because the infant's illness made Manyara's "death wish" seem more dangerous, it is typical of mothers to punish a replaced child severely for crying when the mother is holding the infant.

Children who cry frequently or throw temper tantrums during the period following the birth of a sibling have to face severe punishment and threats even when the mother is not holding the new baby. Nothing annoys a Nyansongo mother more than a child who cries "for nothing," that is, a child who cries when he does not want food and has not been hurt. We observed a child of about 30 months crying loudly and long after his older brother hit or pushed him slightly. His mother, who was sitting beside him and thought his crying excessive for the amount of hurt he had suffered, hit him on the head with a piece of grass and continued doing so, saying "Quiet!" each time until he would tolerate being hit without making any sound. One mother reported that she warned her small child, "If you cry, I'll throw you out in the darkness and you'll be eaten by hyenas." Children who are threatened and beaten learn to be quiet, to refrain from crying, and to stay at home without trouble when their mothers go away with younger siblings; actual temper tantrums are infrequent. Usually the child stays at home with an older sibling whom he follows to a field or other homestead where other children are playing. When the group of children goes somewhere, the little 2-year-old is always desperately afraid of being left behind. We frequently saw children running and crying after older children who were moving a bit too fast. Despite the anxiety, however, a small child is rarely left behind, for the parents hold the older children responsible for its care.

TOILET TRAINING AND RESPONSIBILITY

Another event in the child's life which takes place shortly after the birth of a younger sibling is training in sphincter control. The primary aim of such training is to teach the child to defecate in bush or pasture some distance from the house; urination control is a secondary consideration. The approximate average age for the onset of toilet training is 26.7 months, and the median is 25 months. It is most commonly a three-stage process. First, the mother takes the child to an uncultivated field or pasture near the house several times to show him the correct procedure. (Some mothers, instead of teaching, simply tell the child to imitate what the older children do.) Secondly, when the mother feels he has had enough instruction, she will cane him for daytime defecation in the house and yard but not for nighttime infractions. At this stage the child ordinarily wakes up the mother when he wants to defecate at night, and she puts him in a corner of the house or outside, depending on her own fear of the dark. In the morning the mother sweeps out the feces. In the third stage, the child is punished for defecating in the house even at night, for he is supposed either to perform his elimination in the daytime or to wake up someone to accompany him outside at night. Infractions at this time are punished by caning and by making the child sweep out the feces himself, as the mother points out to him what he has done. The amount of time mothers reported for this training ranged from a week to a year, with the majority around a month. Some mothers who trained quickly attributed it to the fact that they were "serious" about it and punished severely for infractions. A significant minority of mothers took a year to train and seem to have been undisturbed by whatever the child did in this regard.

Proper habits concerning urination, though not stressed seriously as early as bowel control, are acquired by the child gradually as an adjunct of bowel and modesty training. Three-year-olds have learned to urinate away from the house, although boys occasionally do it within sight of adults, and not much more than that is required of them. Neither boys nor girls of this age wear any garments around the lower half of their bodies, so soiling of clothes is not a serious problem. The infrequency of observing 3-year-olds in excretory activities suggests that they learn modesty of this kind quite early.

A final change in the child's life that takes place after the birth of a sibling is his induction into the performance of tasks. If he is the oldest, he will be required to carry food to his mother from her co-wife or mother-in-law during the lying-in period. Many other little tasks are given all children during the first few months of their replacement, and the mother consciously does this to distract the child from his desire to continue as the exclusive object of her nurturance. The chasing of chickens from drying foods, carrying things from one adult to another, and even helping the older boys in herding cattle—these are the beginnings of a responsibility training that is intensified in later years.

In summary, the period between 18 months and 3 years is one of severe punishment for the child's infantile dependency behavior, and there are the beginnings of new behavior patterns in his learning simple tasks and his orientation toward other children with whom he is now forced to interact more than when he was primarily oriented toward mother. What effect on sibling attitude is produced by the neonate's place in this rough transition can only be speculated on, but our guess is that strong feelings of jealousy and hatred are engendered but prevented by parental punishment from being expressed in behavior.

Chapter 14

Childhood: The Years from Three to Eight

This chapter covers the period in the life of the child from the year following his replacement by a younger sibling to the time when the boy begins sleeping outside of his mother's house and the girl prepares for her initiation. For both sexes this is approximately a five-year period—the years from 3 to 8—uninterrupted by schooling, for hardly any Nyansongo children attend school.

STATUS OF THE CHILD

As Nyansongans themselves view it, the training of the child in the proper patterns of behavior takes place largely in the years between weaning and initiation. Although many behavior patterns improper for adults are tolerated up to the time of initiation, the child is expected to show signs of his readiness by some adult-like behavior beforehand, and this must be taught during childhood. The period from weaning to initiation is a longer one for boys, who are initiated between 10 and 12 years of age, than for girls, who undergo it at 8 or 9. Girls are said to "grow up more quickly" and are therefore ready to be initiated into adulthood at an earlier age. Until initiation, a girl is referred to as *egesagane* and a boy as *omoisia,* usually translated by English-speaking Gusii as "uncircumcised girl" and "uncircumcised boy." Both terms are strong insults when used among adults and are even considered insulting by the children to whom they can be properly applied. They carry the connotation of inferior status. In some sense, childhood is the most inferior status position in the Nyansongo life cycle. During infancy the child is the object of maternal attention, and few demands are made on him. After weaning, however, it is not too long before the child is at the beck and call of everyone around, with no one younger or more inferior for him to order about. During this stage the child is also most subjected to physical punishment by elders attempting to curb his impulsive activities. These are some of the reasons why the words for "boy" and "girl" connote inferior status and are used as epithets. Nyansongans believe the child who can walk and talk requires punishment in order to learn correct behavior, and he has few rights or privileges that must be respected by elders.

Despite the low position of childhood in the hierarchy of age-statuses, it is not viewed as unrelated to adulthood. Indeed, adults see in the behavior of individual children foreshadowing of their adult characters: a troublesome child will become "bad," while an obedient child, who is restrained, responsible, and respectful of his parents' wishes, will turn out to be a "good person." This does not mean they are completely fatalistic about the character development of children, but they come to regard some children as responsive to parental training, and others as incorrigible.

SLEEPING AND EATING

The Nyansongo family goes to sleep early in the evening except when a beer party is in progress. Children are allowed to stay up during a beer party held in the house, but smaller ones often fall asleep in the arms of mother or grandmother or lie down to sleep on the floor despite the noise. On ordinary nights, the mother sleeps with her infant and husband (when he is home and not staying at the house of another wife). One or two of the younger children are usually huddled close to the mother, especially when the traditional, slightly raised, hide-covered, dried mud bed is used. When the more common rope-spring bed on legs is used, they may sleep on the floor beside it or in a nearby children's house (*esaiga*) outside. Nights in Nyansongo are cold, and it is customary to sleep naked under blankets not far from the cooking fire which burns all night.

In the morning the mother is usually the first one up, building up the fire for cooking, nursing the infant, and preparing to work in the fields. If she plans to work in a small garden near the house, she may do some of this while the children are still asleep and return later to dress and feed them. The family then sits down to some gruel, the children drinking it either out of a dish of their own or out of a dish which has first been used by the father and mother. During the period of intense cultivation, the mother is often in such a hurry to join her cooperative work group that she leaves leftovers for the children to eat. The leftovers may be remnants of dry corn or eleusine porridge (*obokima*), sweet potatoes, bananas, or cooked squash. Sometimes they are inadequate, and the children are hungry during the morning. If a sister 8 years old or more is home, she may cook some gruel, but sometimes she is off hoeing herself, and the smaller children get food from a co-wife or grandmother. When the mother returns at midday, the children tell her they are hungry, and she hurries to cook for them before doing any other work. If she left hastily in the morning without cooking, she may come home as early as 10:30 A.M. to feed them, particularly if she is told they are hungry. At those times of the year when she is home during the day, or on a rainy day, she will cook for the children whenever they are hungry and ask for food. The midday meal may consist of boiled sweet potatoes or the more traditional dry porridge eaten with cooked beans, spinachlike leaves, curdled milk, or meat. There is usually a good deal of food available at this time, enough to satisfy the children until late afternoon or evening. During the afternoon, especially between October and January, children often break off corn stalks in harvested fields and chew and suck the sugary pulp inside. The evening meal is ordinarily eaten just after sunset at about 7:00 P.M. and consists of dry porridge by itself or with one of the condiments mentioned above.

The predominance of starch in the diet means Nyansongo children must eat stomach-bloating quantities of porridge to obtain necessary nutriments, and such quantities are generally, though not always, available to them. Mothers usually feed children on demand except when they have recently eaten and have conspicuously bloated stomachs. One reason given for refusal under such circumstances is that the child will become so heavy and sluggish with food that he will be unable to leave the house or yard to defecate. There are instances of children who continually ask for food, but feeding problems involving reluctance to eat are extremely rare, and some mothers regard such behavior as inconceivable except when a child is momentarily angry at his mother.

Nyansongo mothers consider providing food as their primary responsibility to their offspring, and there is evidence that food constitutes an important symbolic bond between mother and child. One third of the women interviewed concerning their reactions to an obedient child spontaneously mentioned giving or promising food, and some stated they would favor the more obedient child over his siblings in the apportionment of food. Forcing a child to miss one or more meals is used as a punishment for children of 6 and over, but some mothers find it difficult to refuse to feed even a misbehaving child, and this punishment is often reserved for serious offenses. One widow, a somewhat overprotective mother, expressed the generally felt association of maternal care with feeding when she said of her 14-year-old initiated son, "I take care of him—he's a young child. I'll let him go when he is married and has a wife to cook for him."

During July and August, when grain stocks are running low and the harvest has not yet begun, the family suffers a food shortage which is experienced by children as well. Adults voluntarily limit their eating during this time, and children may go without eating from early morning to evening. Small children are fed as usual because "they will cause trouble if they are not fed" and they "do not understand." From the age of 5, however, the child "can understand when the mother says there's not much food," and she begins limiting his consumption. If he cries for more at first, he will be fed a little bit of food from time to time but not as much as he wants and is used to. If he is persistent in his demands, the mother will cane him and say, "We have no food and you're still crying for more. You'll get food later." Informants report that children at this time cry and trouble the mother a great deal. The increased cultivation of bananas may be alleviating these preharvest shortages to some extent, but most Nyansongans consider bananas suitable for small snacks rather than for meals. Once the harvest is in, cereal food becomes plentiful, and eating, visiting, and ceremonial feasts become the order of the day.

The mealtime situation provides some important lessons in the rules of family behavior for the Nyansongo child. The father's dry porridge is served in a separate basket and must not be touched by the children even if the father is not present when it is served. Any man who came home late from a beer party and found that someone had taken some of the glazed top of his porridge would be enraged and would threaten his wife with sending her back to her parents for a gift of reconciliation; a second time he might really do it. When he eats the porridge, the father may finish less than half of it and give the rest to the children, but they are not to presume on the privilege. A polygynist receives a basket of food from each wife at every meal (though not more than twice a day), and he takes at least one mouthful from each, thus breaking the glazed top with his fingers. At his signal, the wife may bring the rest of it back to be eaten by herself and the children. Sometimes, however, the mother will serve all the uninitiated children their food in a single basket or dish separate from that of the father, and they sit around it together. Eating with the hands from a basket placed on the ground poses few problems of table manners. Some children are unusually greedy and tend to deprive the others of food; they are known as "black-stomach children." The mother warns such a child not to take so much but does not beat him, and eventually she may serve him his own dish of food rather than try to reform his behavior. She also tries to compensate the others by giving them more food when the black-stomach child has taken theirs. Thus the child learns to yield precedence to his father but not to his siblings in the sharing of food.

CLEANLINESS AND CLOTHING

Nyansongo individuals, in general, bathe infrequently, and children are no exception. Mothers take little interest in their cleanliness, although they encourage them to bathe at the stream with their siblings and friends of the same sex. Boys who are herding cattle sometimes take off their shirts and splash around in the water; girls, copying their nubile sisters, are probably somewhat more systematic about washing but do not appear to be very clean until initiated. (It should be noted that before the recent introduction of soap, smearing with clarified butter rather than washing was customary cleansing practice and was performed mainly for special occasions.) Hands are invariably rinsed in water before eating, the basin of water being passed from one person to another, and food is rinsed from the hands after eating, passing the same basin around again. Mothers regularly shave the heads of both boys and girls and inspect their toes for chiggers, which they patiently remove.

Although cleanliness is not stressed, the child learns a set of attitudes about the body at an early age. By the age of 3 the child knows the names of all parts of his body, and he has also learned that his parents give different names for some of these than his siblings of the same sex. The parents call the penis a "tail" when they have to refer to it, while other children use coarser expressions. When he is 3 and 4 years old, the child's naive use of obscenity, which he has learned from older siblings, provokes mirth and embarrassment in parents, and he is punished for it and warned against it. By the age of 5, most Nyansongo children have an extensive obscene vocabulary and a euphemistic one, and they have learned that only the latter may be used in the presence of adults. Masturbation is wholeheartedly disapproved of by parents, and children are beaten for it. It is extremely rare even in young children. Both boys and girls learn to conceal their defecation and urination by doing it in the privacy of the bush, and it is rare to see even a 3-year-old eliminating.

With respect to dress, modesty is more stressed for girls than for boys. In some families girls as old as 5 may be seen early in the morning playing outside the house naked, except for a string of beads around the abdomen, while in others one never sees girls unclad from the age of one. This variation bears no apparent relationship to the wealth or cultural conservatism of the family. Girls of 6 and older are never to be seen without a dress or some garment which, no matter how tattered, covers them from knee to navel and usually to neck as well. From their fourth year onward they are taught to sit with their legs together and skirts down. Even if a girl goes naked on some mornings and is seen that way by visitors, when she is wearing a dress and sitting so as to expose her genitals, her mother or father will sharply order her to "sit well." Boys, on the other hand, may wear clothes which do not cover their genitals until initiation, that is, until ten or twelve. They usually wear pullover shirts with long tails that reach to mid-thigh. When they sit down, however, their genitals are usually exposed and they are not instructed to sit modestly, since the uncircumcised penis is considered immature and asexual. Beads are not worn by boys.

For both boys and girls, dressing involves putting a garment over the head and slipping arms and head into the appropriate openings. Small children are dressed by their mothers, who eventually teach them to dress themselves at ages ranging from 2 to 5. More than half of the mothers interviewed said they began expecting their children to dress themselves without help at 3 or 4 years of age, but many of the others put it off until 5. Since small children often go naked in the cold of the morning and since their clothes are scanty and lightweight, it is possible that unhealthy exposure to the elements occurs, especially on chilly days during the rains.

RELATIONSHIP TO MOTHER

A Nyansongo mother is responsible for the care and training of all her uninitiated children. They live in her house, are fed by her, and look to her for support and protection. If they become seriously ill, she may be held accountable. If her child gets into mischief at another homestead, she must face the irate adults of that homestead. If one of her children continually misbehaves, she may be beaten by her husband for her failure in child training. The burden of this responsibility is even greater for widows and women whose husbands are working outside the district. With the formal responsibility goes a strong emotional attachment between mother and child, which is vigorously attested to by mothers and children, although it is often not a conspicious feature of their observable interaction. The worst insults used among uncircumcised boys are those which derogate another's mother, and the son's defense of his mother's reputation is paralleled by a mother's passionate and partisan attempts to protect her offspring from the ill will of others both inside and outside the homestead.

Despite the almost solitary responsibility of the mother for her children and the striking solidarity of the mother-child unit against outsiders, Nyansongo mothers are overburdened with an agricultural and domestic work load which limits the attention they can pay to their weaned children. In consequence, they delegate a good deal of caretaking and training to older children in the homestead, and they reduce their maternal role to what they consider its bare essentials. These include providing food for the child whenever he wants it, seeking cure for his illness and redress when he is harmed by others, and correcting his misbehavior when it is brought to her attention. Her responsibilities in regard to food production and infant care make it impossible for her to give continuous succor and support to the uninitiated boys and girls, and she becomes impatient with them if they repeatedly interfere with her work, make trivial or unnecessary demands of her, or are capricious and difficult to satisfy. Most Nyansongo mothers will use any device they deem effective to stop the crying of a child so that they can switch their attention to something else. On the other hand, since this lack of attention is more often dictated by necessity than by principle, the warmer mothers respond with great indulgence to the child's demands when they have time, are in a good mood, or when it is the last child and there is no infant to care for. This results in inconsistent nurturance of the child. Another important consequence of the mother's heavy work load is that she trains the children to share it with her as soon as they are able, emphasizing responsibility and obedience training. Thus the children learn to help their mothers as well as to avoid making too many demands of them. In the remainder of this section, the patterns of mother-child interaction are described in greater detail.

With the exception of the older uncircumcised boys and those who go to school, most children spend at least half of the day within shouting distance of the mother. Although she does agricultural work, some of the fields are near the homestead, and cultivation is seasonal, reaching low points during the July–August ripening time, and the November–December postharvest interval. During these times, and for parts of days in working seasons too, the mother is around the house, spreading grain to dry, grinding it, milking the cows, mending clothes, brewing beer, entertaining visitors. On the other hand, due weight must be given to her by no means infrequent absences from the homestead, absences occasioned by duties other than work in the fields: taking corn to the power mill, visiting her kin, taking crops to sell at the market, gathering firewood in the late afternoon, and fetching water from the stream at other times of the day.

When the mother is at the house, her interaction with the children is limited because of her involvement in domestic chores and the needs of the infant. Ordering the children to perform errands, reminding them of their regularly assigned tasks, and scolding or punishing them when they do something wrong or dangerous—these comprise a large proportion of the content of mother-child interaction. The child can bring himself to the mother's attention by doing something "bad" (or failing to do what he has been told) or by going to her for help. When he asks for food, the mother is more likely to comply than for any other kind of request. Of 24 mothers who were asked what they did when their child between 3 and 6 years old asked for help, 14—interpreting the "help" primarily as food—said they always give him what he wants. When they are busy doing something else, however, only 7 indicated they provide immediate help, 10 reported refusing immediate help, telling the child to wait till mother is finished, telling him to help himself, or beating him for being so demanding, and 7 said they stop work right away *only* if the request were for food. If the child is thirsty, he is told to get water himself from a pot in the house, but food must be cooked for him by his mother.

Perfunctory or punitive responses by mothers to childhood succorance are elicited by other kinds of requests. For example, some of the mothers questioned about what they do when their children fall down and hurt themselves said they blow on the wound, pat it, or hold the child and say, "Oh, I'm sorry you've hurt yourself. Don't cry; you'll be better." But half of the total sample reported saying, "Don't cry; it's your own fault. No one has hurt you," without offering any other comfort. The aim is always to stop the child's crying quickly, and when he has learned to bear small hurts stoically, the mother pays no attention to them. A child of 3 to 6 years of age who attempts to have his mother dress him when she knows he can do it himself is unlikely to be successful. Twelve of the 24 mothers said they punish for such a request, with caning the most frequent method used, while 8 reported letting the child go naked or telling him to do it himself. Of the rest, only 1 definitely stated she complies with such requests, and 3 said they vacillate between refusal and compliance according to their moods. A typical sequence begins with the mother of a child who has recently learned to dress himself yielding to his request but warning him that *he* must do it in the future. If he asks her to dress him again, she becomes angry and canes him. What angers a Nyansongo mother the most is a child who cries "for nothing" or who goes on crying after attempts have been made to comfort him. All mothers reported caning their children for such behavior. Usually the mother asks him what the matter is or if he wants food, and if he does not reply, or refuses food but continues crying, she beats him severely. Nyansongo mothers have little patience with children who make excessive demands for attention and support.

One kind of plea for help which does win the mother's attention is that of a child who has been hurt by another child. Nyansongo mothers investigate such situations and try to achieve redress for their own children if they feel it is deserved. As indicated above, the mother feels that if the child hurts himself, little can be done, but if someone attacked him, she can take action by scolding the attacker or telling his mother. The underlying notion appears to be that it is more justifiable for a child to cry when he has been injured by someone else than when the cause is accidental or his own fault. That children are affected by this value judgment is demonstrated by the fact that they were observed to cry much louder and longer when injured by another in the presence of the mother than when there were no adults present. They have apparently learned that they can achieve retaliation through the mother if they make a fuss when she is there to witness it. This connection between succorance and aggression is consistent with the maternal attitude toward early sibling rivalry. As described in the last chapter, the mother considers the cries of the replaced child as hostility to the neonate and punishes accordingly because hostility to the neonate is disapproved. In later childhood, she tends to equate his succorant cries with justifiable hostility against an unprovoked aggressor, and she is willing to help him by obtaining redress.

The Nyansongo mother discourages what she considers overdependence, but she does not put her children on their own or expect them to be intrepid and fearless. On the contrary, children spend their days under a maternal injunction against going more than a short distance from the homestead except on errands, and at night they are not allowed out of the house. In fact, mothers give instruction in the dangers of the night to instill what they consider a healthy fear of the dark. Half the mothers interviewed said they mentioned hyenas, although there are none in Nyansongo, in their warnings. One said, "I used to frighten Okemwa by saying, 'If you go out, a hyena will take you. I saw a hyena waiting for you by the fence.' I did that so he wouldn't go out at night." Another reported, concerning her daughter, "I'd warn her, 'Don't you go out at night; you'll be taken by hyenas.' I know hyenas don't take children but I said it to frighten her from going out at night." Most of the mothers who did not report warning of hyenas mentioned witches, "wild things," "something which will eat you up," "men and animals who will take you away," or unspecified dangers. Although they do not themselves believe most of the specific warnings, Nyansongo women are genuinely afraid of the dark and convinced that witches who might kill their children are outside at night.

The discouragement of daytime adventurousness serves Nyansongo mothers by keeping the children near the homestead for chores and errands; the fear of nocturnal dangers gives the mother a potent threat to use in curbing the child's misbehavior, particularly crying or crankiness at night. Thus, although she is not receptive to some of their demands for attention and support, the mother also limits her children's self-reliant behavior by restricting their freedom of movement and instilling in them fear of the external environment. Together with the importance of the mother in providing food and settling quarrels, this discouragement of self-reliance keeps the Nyansongo child dependent on his mother even when she pays relatively little attention to him.

Mothers do not play with their children, fondle them, or display affection for them openly. Even an indulgent mother, by Nyansongo standards, does not initiate nurturant interaction with her child but yields to many of his requests and demands. The child comes to his mother when he wants something, and she does not ordinarily proffer goods or emotional comfort unless she has been asked to do so. Praise is extremely rare, as mothers believe it can make even a good child "rude and disobedient." Over half the women who were asked what they do when a child is very obedient answered that they feel happy about it but neither say nor do anything to the child, though some indicated they praised him to others in his absence. Another one third of the mothers reported they give extra food or other material goods or that they promised the child such things. Only two out of 24 mothers said they praised their children for good behavior.

A child who is good can expect to have his requests for clothes and sweets complied with more than one who misbehaves, but the relationship is an indirect one in those families which have little cash to buy the articles regardless of how good the child is. In any event, even when the child is good and the family well off, he must ask or even beg for the desired thing. This is frequently successful.

The mother-child relationship is relatively informal, allowing the most relaxed interaction between persons of adjacent generations that can be found in the Nyansongo social system. This is especially so for the uninitiated children, who are allowed into the mother's cooking place, where she squats "immodestly" with her skirt pulled up onto her thighs, and who may make slightly obscene references within earshot of the mother and argue with her without being punished. She is distinctly more tolerant of childish deviations than the father. Even so, mothers expect considerable deference from their uninitiated children, and most of them do not tolerate overtly disrespectful or aggressive behavior. Nyansongo mothers overwhelmingly reported severe punishment, beating and depriving of food, as their response to being struck or insulted by a child, and some regarded it as inconceivable that their children would do such things. One woman said to her child while caning him for "abusing" her verbally, "I'm not your peer; you must respect me. If you don't respect me, you won't respect any elders." Others said they would refuse to cook for a child who had been disrespectful to them until he came back and apologized. In a few Nyansongo families, sons beat their mothers or cow them with threats of physical violence, but such boys are at least 10 years old and are recognized as behavior problems by the community at large.* More frequently, children respect the authority of their mothers and do not attempt to hurt them regardless of the provocation.

TECHNIQUES OF SOCIALIZATION

To train her children and control their behavior, the mother uses fear more frequently than reward. Although the child can no longer be frightened by domestic animals as in infancy, the mother inculcates other fears, mentioned above, of hyenas, witches, and vaguely defined creatures of the night. The small child who annoys his mother by crying at night is warned, "If you don't stop crying, I shall open the door and call a hyena to come and eat you!" or, "I'll throw you out in the dark and you'll be eaten by hyenas." Great effectiveness is claimed for this method of silencing a child. As he gets older, the child's general sensitivity to dire threats and warnings remains important as a behavior control, even though the content of the warnings becomes more realistic. The mother makes exaggerated threats about killing the child, tying him up in the house, and having his father deal unmercifully with him, resorting to actual punishment when these threats do not work.

The methods of punishment used by Nyansongo mothers are caning, i.e., beating on the legs and buttocks with a tall weed or thin branch, depriving of food, reprimanding, chasing from the house overnight without a blanket, withholding clothes, and assigning laborious chores. In terms of frequency, caning is the overwhelming choice for use with children aged 3 to 6. As one mother said, "If you want to teach a child anything, you must cane him." When a mother first sees her child doing something she disapproves of, she may curtly ask, "What are you doing?", tell him to stop, or threaten him with punishment. If this does not work or if the misdeed is one she feels strongly about, the mother canes the child and reprimands him simultaneously. In reprimanding, the mother often expresses the idea that the deviation is a foreshadowing of worse offenses and immoral character development, which only caning can prevent. One mother reported telling her 3-year-old son while beating him for masturbation, "If I don't cane you, you'll go on like this and might even do it in front of people." Disobedient

* These cases are discussed in chapter 16.

children are told, "If you don't obey me, since you are my child, you'll never obey anyone," and "You're falling into bad ways and won't be a good child." A mother beating her daughter for sex play said, "You're becoming a slut!" Another girl neglecting her chores was admonished with, "You'll probably elope * and leave your parents with nothing!" These pessimistic prognostications inform the child of the reason for the punishment; they also connect a trivial misdeed with an evil character trait or immoral type of person, tending to make the person rather than the act the primary locus of negative evaluation.

As the child becomes older, methods of punishment other than caning become more frequent. More than 85% of the mothers questioned mentioned caning as first in importance for children between 3 and 6 years old, but less than half of them said they used caning most often on children near the age of initiation. One reason for this is that the major alternative to caning—food deprivation—is considered too cruel for small children, who "lack the sense" to understand why they are being refused what their mothers always grant them. Another reason for less frequent caning of older children is that the behavior of the child himself may make it unnecessary or ineffective. If the child of 6 or older has learned to be "good," that is, obedient, then he can be corrected by the verbal warning or rebuke of his mother; she need no longer beat him to enforce compliance. If, on the other hand, his early training has not produced the desired results, the mother may give up trying to eliminate his deviations by caning. There is a widespread belief that effective training by physical punishment presupposes an appropriate response on the part of the child: "Caning is for a child who controls himself." As one mother said, "Some children are so bad that you can cane them until you are tired and they are still bad, and you leave them alone." Nyansongo parents disapprove of continuing the use of physical punishment on a child who does not respond to it: "After all, I don't want to kill him!" Furthermore, many a boy of 6 or older is able to run away from his mother when she attempts to cane him. Thus, if a mother concludes that caning does not reform her child or that she cannot catch him when he does something bad, she ordinarily resorts to excluding him from one or two meals. Should she become extremely angry, she might banish him from the house for the night. The father or adult brother will be called in to administer beatings for serious offenses. To summarize, in early childhood, caning by the mother is the most common type of punishment. As the child grows older, the mother resorts more frequently to food deprivation, banishment, and referral to father when punishment is

* That is, marry without payment of bridewealth.

required, or she uses verbal correction if the child is above-average in obedience. Except in unusual cases, however, caning is not completely eliminated from the mother-child relationship until initiation.

Several of the less common methods of punishment used in Nyansongo are quite severe. Children are sometimes chased out of the house at night, when it is chilly and frightening for them, and they must sleep without blankets in the children's house or in the house of a nearby relative. Similarly, a mother punishing her child in the early morning may withhold his clothes, forcing him to suffer the cold and shame of nakedness outside or remain in the house. A widow reported chastising her 6-year-old daughter as follows for sex play with little boys: "I snatched her dress and left her naked and chased her out of the house at night . . . letting her walk in the cold and cry behind the house. Then I let her in in the morning." A punitive measure often mentioned for an extremely delinquent child is to tie him to a post in the house for a few hours. Punishments of this sort, though not frequent in the life of any child, seem to have a strong impact, for they are vividly recalled in adulthood by the individuals who experienced them.

Nyansongo children over the age of 6 develop the capacity to turn banishment by the mother to their own advantage as a means of evading punishment, and their mothers do nothing to discourage it. For example, a girl who has failed to carry out an order may find that her mother orders her out of the house, implicitly refusing food and shelter. The girl goes to her grandmother, whose house is a few steps away in the same homestead, eats and sleeps with the old woman, and returns the next day to her mother, whose anger has abated and who forgives and forgets. When the mother has been seriously offended by the original misbehavior, that is, when it was actively disrespectful, she will require an apology, but she does not beat a child who has run away and returned, even though he has obviously not suffered. The older children sometimes anticipate this sequence by escaping to the house of a relative or friend in the neighborhood as soon as they see their mothers become angry enough to punish them, thereby managing to evade punishment altogether. The Gusii practice of extending hospitality without questions to any child of neighboring kinsman contrasts with the Kipsigis custom of refusing to feed neighbors' children at any time, on the grounds that they may be trying to escape parental food deprivation. The Gusii feeling is that the mother's desire to punish her child is a private matter between her and the child which need not be enforced by anyone else. The child learns that if he can succeed in avoiding his mother during the first flush of her anger over his deviation, he may comfortably escape punishment, particularly if he acts somewhat subdued and contrite on his return.

Children are aware that punishment is contingent on the mood of the mother. If she is irritable, she may punish for something she ignored on a different occasion. If she is in good spirits, her threats and warnings need not be taken seriously. She may tolerate a particular misdeed once or twice but not more, and her intent to punish, once aroused, can be softened by a show of remorse (some children reported pretending to cry in order to avert a beating) and dissipated over time if the child absents himself. Thus the child knows his mother's sympathies, moods, and inconsistencies and takes advantage of them to avoid punishment whenever possible. There is great variation in severity of discipline among Nyansongo mothers, but many expect their children to indulge in some defensive maneuvering—falsely denying, feigning remorse, running away—after wrongdoing, and they are willing to overlook it or be manipulated by it if the wrongdoing is not excessive.

RELATION TO SIBLINGS AND PEERS

The interaction of the Nyansongo child with other children takes place within conditions set for him by his mother. Mothers do not want their children to be social isolates; on the contrary, they see positive advantages for the learning of language and other desirable behavior in the small child's association with a group of the same or slightly older age. Nevertheless, they place numerous restrictions on the extent of this association, restrictions which are gradually relaxed as the child grows older. Two thirds of the mothers questioned did not permit their children to move outside the neighborhood of nearby homesteads before they were 6 years old. In many cases adjacent homesteads or the contiguous stream were the farthest points allowed. Others set limits which were almost as narrow. One women stated, "Once you let a child walk about freely, that means he is old enough to be circumcised." While this is an extreme statement, it does express a feeling common to Nyansongo mothers. They want the children to perform their chores and errands without distraction, and they also fear that in wandering beyond the neighbors with whom his parents are most friendly, the child may get into trouble for which the parents will be held responsible, or that he may be harmed by others. Two thirds of the women said they discouraged association with children who fight. For many it was most important to protect the child in this way from the aggression of other children, while some mothers were also concerned that their children would acquire bellicose habits. A few mentioned telling their children to avoid peers who use obscene language or steal. For various reasons, then, most mothers do restrict the movements and contacts of their small children, and this frequently results in such children associating almost exclusively with their siblings, half-siblings, and closely related patrilineal kin. Wider associations are looked upon as disruptive to the child's assigned work as well as possibly harmful to him.

Within the limits set by the mother, the place where the child spends most of his daytime depends a good deal on whether the family has cattle. When there is a herd of cattle in the family, the oldest uncircumcised boy is in charge of herding, and the younger children down to the age of 3 tag along with him in the pastures, which are contiguous to the residential area. When the family has no cattle, the children are expected to be at the mother's house unless authorized by the parents to leave it. At the house, the oldest uncircumcised girl is considered by the parents to be in charge of all the younger children and the safety of the house itself. If she is there, some of the others may wander off to adjacent homesteads and, if they are older than 6, even a mile or two to the market or stream, but the house must not be left unguarded for fear of theft, and the infant must not be left unattended by its caretaker.

The importance of cattle in determining where the children spend their time can be illustrated in the case of a family which had no herds at home before the eldest sister married. Prior to her marriage, the three youngest children were always at the mother's house under the supervision of the oldest uninitiated girl, and the son of 10 was either in the house or yard with them or off fishing with his friends. The arrival of 12 head of bridewealth cattle brought about a distinct shift in the locus of their daytime activities. The older boy, formerly footloose, was now constantly occupied with tending the herds in a nearby pasture where his younger siblings followed him, and he often had to exhort his sister to return to watch the unattended house.

The physical isolation of the homestead from others in the neighborhood is also a determinant of childhood social activity. In the above case, because the family had a large pasture of its own which bordered on unoccupied land, herding did not bring the children into contact with peers from other homesteads. Frequently, however, a pasture is shared by related families of two or three contiguous homesteads and becomes a meeting place for as many as seven children who herd their cattle together. Aside from such herding groups, in which no more than half of all the children participate, Nyansongo has no organized children's groups. Where the homestead is physically isolated from others in the community, the sibling group tends to be most important.

This narrow range of friendship and association, even for the boys who herd cattle, is reflected in their somewhat exclusive and suspicious attitude toward outsiders. Older children said they would not play with a strange child unless they knew who his father was, and some claimed they would not associate with any strange child but would tell him to go home even if he were friendly. The only uninitiated child who had friends outside the circle of nearby homesteads was also the only uncircumcised boy from Nyansongo attending school, and his friends were boys he had met in school.

At home and in the pastures, older children dominate younger ones. To some extent this is promulgated by parents, many of whom said they felt it important for one child to be in charge of the others and tell them what to do, and who select the oldest of a group of children for the position of leadership. As mentioned, the oldest uninitiated girl in the homestead is usually charged with responsibility for the children at home and the oldest uncircumcised boy for those herding cattle. Since the parents may hold the appointed leader accountable for misdemeanors by and harm befalling the younger children, he is highly motivated to keep them in line and boss them around, though he is not permitted to punish them. In herding groups consisting of children from several homesteads, the oldest dominates the others, ordering them about, occasionally beating them, taking whatever articles they own. This latter aspect is recognized in the proverb, "The small boy's stick belongs to the older (uncircumcised) boy." Whenever we gave something to a boy in a herding group, it was appropriated by the oldest one even if he did not want to use it for himself. Parents consider such behavior natural and even proper, but they do not accept the idea of the group or its leader dominating a boy so as to make him ignore or violate his parents' wishes. In fact, parents do not entirely recognize the existence of children's groups beyond those of siblings, and they try to maintain direct control over their children regardless of the amount of peer activity.

Adult supervision of children is impossible for much of the day, since adults are often too far away to keep an eye on the youngsters. Boundary hedges, corn fields, groves of trees, and various bushes act as barriers to communication between the women working in cultivated fields and the children at a homestead or between adults at the homestead and the boys herding in the pastures. These physical barriers, combined with the absence of adults from the neighborhood for at least part of the day, leave the children free of supervision for considerable amounts of time. On the other hand, this freedom may be unexpectedly terminated in several ways. Much of Nyansongo is a long hill sloping down to a stream, and standing on the hill one can inconspicuously watch activity at certain places above and below. Several fathers occasionally stand in front of their houses peering at the pastures below to observe the movements of their sons and livestock. Furthermore, winding paths to the stream traverse the pastures and connect the homesteads, and the very foliage which shields the children from the view of others can suddenly yield forth a visitor, a woman fetching water or an adult sibling returning to the homestead, who may scrutinize the child and report any mischief observed to his parents. Hence the children's freedom from adult supervision, though lengthy, is intermittent and precarious. In this respect the boys herding cattle have a distinct advantage over children restricted to the homestead, for the pasture offers more constant cover for activities of which parents disapprove.

ACTIVITIES OF CHILDREN'S GROUPS

What do Nyansongo children do when they are relatively unsupervised? This can be answered best by illustrations from two "groups" which were intensively observed for four months. The first is the largest herding group in Nyansongo, with a 10-year-old leader from one homestead, three brothers aged 3 to 7 from another, and another set of three brothers, the oldest aged 5, from a third homestead. The most permanent members of the group are the three oldest, who are responsible to their fathers for the care of the cattle, while the younger children spend much of their time at home rather than in the pasture. Herding together from about 8:30 A.M., the boys bring the cows back to their homesteads during the morning for milking and sometimes return again to have a meal at midday. Other times, mothers send food to them in the pastures, and the girl who brings it eats with them. At about 1:00 P.M. the boys take the cattle down to the stream for water, and they splash around beside the cattle, put rocks and mud together to block channels of the stream, and sometimes take off their shirts and swim. The 10-year-old leader, a boy noted for his disobedience and mischievousness, frequently directs the herding instead of participating in it himself. For example, when he is playing in the stream and sees the cattle going astray higher up on the hill, he will order one of the two other responsible boys to get them, and his order is usually obeyed. Herding is mainly a matter of moving the docile cows from place to place by beating their rumps with a stick. When they are grazing in a particular spot, there is little to do, and the boys turn their attention to other activities until someone notices that the cows are about to enter someone's garden, and then there is a rush to bring them back into place. The other activities away from the stream include climbing trees and trying to shoot birds with homemade sling-shots, which all Nyansongo boys had in 1956–57, watching buses and cars on the road and discussing whose they are and what they look like, and, most commonly, fighting with each other. A fight is some-times started when a younger boys insults an older one, saying *omoisia* (uncircumcised boy) or *ngoko* ("your mother," interpreted as mean-ing "your mother's vagina") when the older one pushes him or orders him to do something unnecessary. Other times the oldest boy jokingly insults a younger one in the same way or shoots a berry at him with his slingshot in order to provoke a tussle. Occasionally a younger boy cries when he is hurt in a fight but usually there is more bluffing, chasing, and grappling than exchanging of blows, and good humor prevails at the end. Fantasy play, almost nonexistent among Nyansongo children, was witnessed twice in this herding group—once when a 6-year-old boy fashioned a plow out of wood and hitched his younger brother to it and once when the 10-year-old leader built a "house" of reeds. These boys got into trouble over aggressive encounters with girls passing through the pasture. This was altogether the most lively group of children in Nyansongo and probably also the worst behaved by com-munity standards.

A group of children which gathers in a different part of Nyansongo is much more amorphous and variable in its composition. Its core con-sists of the children and grandchildren of three widowed co-wives who live in a homestead cluster along with their married sons and the married sons of two other deceased co-wives. The group of children from this one homestead alone can amount to 10 or 12, with the most permanent members being 9-year-old female twins who were in charge of two head of cattle and their 6-year-old brother who eventually took over the cattle when they were initiated. They herded the cattle in a small, level pasture very near the houses of the homestead, with no obstruction between residence and pasture, and were joined at different times of day by several 5- and 6-year-old girls from the same homestead, carrying their infant charges, and some boys ranging in age from 2 to 5. Since the pasture is level and adjacent to the road, it is a gathering place for children, primarily girls, from one of the three Nyansongo neighborhoods. Few of the children who join the twins there are herding cattle themselves; they are on the way to or from the stream with pots, taking care of infants, or taking time off from agricultural work to join their friends. At times there may be no children from adjacent homesteads joining the core group; other times 15 children congregate near the road. Their interaction is much less lively and aggressive than that of the herding group described above. The girls cuddle, play with, and carry about some of the others' infant charges; they whisper secrets about one another and giggle; they watch and comment on activity on the road, particularly the buses and who is going into town; they rarely fight. The proximity of the homestead with some adults usually about, and the lack of a common group activity, seem to account for the relatively subdued behavior of this group. When many of the same girls were fetching water and washing clothes at a rather secluded spot along the stream, they were much more animated, pushing and shoving one another, criticizing and jokingly insulting each other, splashing water good-humoredly, and so on.

Among the children who rarely gather in sizable groups such as the two described above, and who associate mainly with siblings and one or two cousins, interaction tends to be even less animated. All the boys of about 6 or more had slingshots, but aggressive encounters are infrequent, and when they occur, they are taken more seriously and emotionally within the sibling group than the casual fights in the pasture in a less closely related herding group. Long periods of inactivity are interspersed between tasks ordered by parents. The amount and kind of activity, however, vary considerably from one isolated homestead group to another.

THE CONTROL OF AGGRESSION

Parental control, its implementation and evasion, is a factor of primary importance in the aggressive and sexual behavior patterns of Nyansongo children. The basic fact is that parents disapprove and discourage any display of overt aggression and sexual interest, and Nyansongo children learn, for the most part before they are 5 or 6, that they must not fight or indulge in sex play in the presence of adults. Any adult stops children he sees from doing such things, and, if a parent, he is likely to punish them. The following discussion takes up aggression first, and then sex.

Mothers play an active part in the resolution of aggressive encounters within children's groups. Over two thirds of the mothers said they take some action on discovering their children involved in a fight.

The actions reported include investigating the cause of the fight ("conducting a trial," as some of them say), telling the children not to fight, reporting to the mother of the attacker and demanding that he be punished, and beating her own child for his part in the fight. Typically the investigation comes first, with the mother questioning participants and eyewitnesses as to who provoked whom and how. Her next step depends both on her assignment of blame and on whose children are involved. When the children are all hers, she may cane an attacker who struck without being provoked, tell the victim that he got what he deserved, or cane both of them for their mutual responsibility in the matter. When her child is struck without adequate provocation by another's, she complains to his parents; if investigation reveals her child to be the unprovoked aggressor, she canes him on the spot. Mothers indicated that they have a concept of just retaliation by their virtual unanimity in stating they chastise their children, mostly by caning, for beating too severely a child whose insult was slight. The general picture is one of a mother who is willing to interfere in her child's quarrels and mete out justice *when* a fight is brought to her attention.

Nyansongo mothers want (1) to discourage aggressive habits in their children and (2) to protect them from the aggression of others. In order to achieve the first objective, they urge their children not to fight, warn them of the dangerous consequences, and cane them when they provoke fights. In reacting to an offense committed by her belligerent child, a mother makes explicit which forms of aggression she considers worse than others. The most frequent response of mothers to physical aggression against other children is caning, but to verbal abuse and insult it is reprimand, indicating that the former deviation is regarded as more serious. Attacking one's own siblings is not considered as bad as doing the same to outsiders; in fact one mother reported telling her son, "Don't beat strangers; beat your own brothers and sisters." Injuries resulting from fights between children of different homesteads can lead to litigation and payment of compensation, and parents are acutely aware of this. Often when a neighbor reports that his child has been beaten, the mother of the attacker canes her child and says, "Do you want us to have a court case?" It is worse for a child to pick on someone younger and smaller than himself than for him to pick on someone of his own age and size. Parents are often extremely angered by a beating rendered to a smaller child, and even when it is a sibling and justified as punishment, it is regarded as usurpation of a parental prerogative. Finally, a fight started by a boy against a girl is considered more serious than a same-sex encounter, partly because girls are regarded as weaker and partly because of the assumption that the boy had a sexual motive. Fights among girls, which appear to be rare, are thought to be less likely to result in injury because of the feminine lack of strength. Hence, while mothers disapprove of childhood aggression generally, they explicitly prefer verbal hostility to physical violence, fights with siblings to those with strangers, attacks on age-mates to attacks on younger children, and encounters with peers of the same sex to heterosexual conflict.

To protect their children from the attacks of others, and to prevent their participation in serious brawls, some Nyansongo mothers (though not a majority) actively encourage them to report to mother when struck by another child. Actually, most mothers in discussing such matters assume that the child will report without encouragement. Less than half as many women (one eighth of the total) encourage their children to fight back when hit, and even these were at pains to say that they tell the children to retaliate *next* time he is struck but not to go back and fight with the child who just beat him. They fear that in the latter case they would be accused by the other child's mother of inciting violence which might result in injury. This is a serious accusation between parents. It is clearly what one mother had in mind when she reported, "I never encourage Nyangau to fight back; I tell him whenever he is beaten to come to me and I'll report that child to his parents and ask them if they sent that boy to fight my son." Mothers do carry through on their promises to achieve retribution for their reporting children by complaining to the attacker's parents. On one occasion a woman from an adjacent clan came to the homestead of the mischievous herding group leader mentioned earlier; numerous relatives were visiting the boy's dying father. The woman, accompanied by her 9-year-old daughter, shouted angrily to all present that the 10-year-old boy had encouraged his younger ortho-cousin to beat her girl on the arm when she was on an errand. Several men at the homestead looked at the girl's arm, which had a small swelling. The woman shouted, "If I meet the child who did this I'll beat him even if his mother is present!" An old woman from nearby said, "It is terrible what they did. Those boys are wild and bad." Mother and daughter stormed off. The boy's father then told his adult son from his deathbed, "Don't try to beat him now because he might hide. Wait till he returns with the cattle." In this case the mother of the victim was particularly aroused because the injury, though slight, was visible and had been inflicted by boys of one clan on a girl of a different clan. Another common reaction to a child's complaint of being beaten by children outside his homestead is to advise him not to associate with those children any more.

Mothers do not try to fight every battle for their children. A child who complains to his mother of being insulted and verbally abused by peers may well be told to retaliate in kind, particularly if the children are the same age. More than one third of the mothers encourage verbal counterattack, apparently feeling that a child should return an insult but not a blow, and some of the others said they ignored the complaint or simply told the children to stop. Even apart from the differential reaction to physical and verbal aggression, there is the feeling of some mothers that the child's reporting of being attacked is itself aggressive, since it can lead to the accused attacker being punished by his parents, and should not be encouraged any more than is necessary. Such women share the more widespread attitude that if a fight is serious enough to result in a visible injury, then the victim will report to mother, while if it is not that serious, has not been witnessed by an adult, and was carried on among closely related same-sex agemates, then it is probably not worth the difficulty of reconstructing from the contradictory fabrications of the participants. For this reason, most mothers close their eyes to the fighting that goes on in herding groups unless it is forcibly brought to their attention by accidental proximity, injury, or complaint by other parents. But they do not give their overt approval to aggressive activity.

THE CONTROL OF SEXUAL BEHAVIOR

The sex play of children elicits even greater disapproval than fighting from Nyansongo parents. More than three fourths of the mothers questioned said that they would cane their 3-year-old children on discovery of masturbation and older children on discovery of heterosexual play. The drastic punishment administered by one mother to her young daughter for sex play is described above; it is typical of the intense reactions reported by Nyansongo mothers to the manifest sexual behavior of their children. However, Nyansongo women are aware that there is secret heterosexual activity in the pastures; when they sing to the girls at their initiation, "You have been the wives of the uncircumcised boys," they are alluding to this activity. As one mother of a boy said concerning the possibility of his sexual relations with little girls, "If he does it secretly and no one knows, it doesn't matter, but if he is discovered doing it anyone may cane him and when he comes home, I scold him." Another mother stated concerning the same situation, "I would cane him very badly, thinking, 'After all, it is the natural thing to do but since I found them at it I must cane severely.'" Aside from accidental discovery, parents most frequently are informed of the heterosexual activities of their children when a girl has resisted the sexual advances of one or more herdboys who then proceeded to strike her or shoot at her with a slingshot. In such cases the girl reports to her mother and shows her marks of the scuffle, and the mother complains to the boy's parents, who scold and beat him. Nyansongans generally make the assumption that an aggressive act committed by a small boy against a girl is the result of a frustrated sexual attempt, and thus it is considered doubly bad when made public. When they are not made public—which means that no child has been hurt enough to complain to her parents—then such violations are part of the permissable private life of children which parents do not attempt to supervise.

RELATIONSHIP TO FATHER

Children do not have the intensive contact with their fathers that they do with their mothers. Of the 24 children whose mothers were interviewed, 11 have fathers who are alive and live at home all the time, 6 have widowed mothers (2 with recent leviratic husbands), and 7 have fathers who are alive but whose work takes them out of Nyansongo for extended periods of time. Thus about half of a sample of children could be characterized as having fathers absent or erratically present in the homestead. Even when the father is living at home he leaves the bulk of child care to his wife and older unmarried children. In the case of a widow, her oldest adult son tends to take on the disciplinary functions of the father with respect to younger children.

The Nyansongo father is viewed by his child as an awesome and frightening person, and with some justification. Fathers do not play with, fondle, or praise their children, and, unlike mothers, they do not feed them or comfort them when hurt. The patterns of deference to the father involved in eating and mealtime activity have been described earlier. In addition, and most importantly, fathers are more severe and inflexible disciplinarians than mothers. One of the most common of boyhood memories of Nyansongo men is being beaten by their fathers for neglecting the cattle. Fathers teach at least their oldest sons how to herd, and they later check up on their herding every now and then, telling them where to take the cattle and how. When a father hears his son has allowed the cows to eat crops in a neighbor's field, he is quick to cane and scold. For example, one father who had returned from employment to hear that his son was a neglectful herder was observed standing sternly with his son in the pasture, holding a stick with which to thrash the young boy for any signs of recalcitrance. Fathers employ physical punishment for other types of offenses as well and can also order the mother to deprive the child of food. Sometimes a mother who has been so ordered relents and lets the child have some food when he begs for it. She is often more lenient to the child secretly while the father demands punishment, and most Nyansongo children seemed to associate softheartedness and inconsistency with their mothers, punitiveness and supervision with their fathers. The mother, however, helps to build up the terrifying image of the father by warning and threatening the child that she will get his father to beat him for misbehavior. As boys get older and are less easily controlled by their mothers, paternal discipline becomes more important. Furthermore, children are warned not to injure or touch various objects around the house so as not to arouse paternal ire.

Unless he is a monagamist who remains constantly at home, the father does not always sleep with the mother of any particular child, and when he does sleep in the house, he and the wife wait until the children are asleep to have sexual relations. As children grow older, they are excluded from sleeping with the parents, and it is usually the father who takes the initiative on this score because of his sexual embarrassment. He excludes girls at an earlier age, mostly 5 to 6, then boys, who are told to sleep outside at 7 or 8. The girl goes to sleep with the mother's co-wife or, even more frequently, a grandmother. Boys are sometimes sent to the grandmother's also, but it is more customary for a children's house (*esaiga*) to be erected for them, where they can sleep with older brothers. Although the children's house is near that of the mother and there are older siblings present, many Nyansongo boys find sleeping there a very frightening experience at first. This is their initial experience sleeping apart from their mothers, and they are sometimes so overwhelmed by fear of animals and witches in the dark that they run crying back to the mother's house. It is notable that this initial period of sleeping out is required only when the father comes to sleep with the mother and is ordered by the father. One can guess that, especially for boys, who when they sleep out do not have mother surrogates, the shock and terror of the nighttime separation from the mother is associated with the father's coming there to sleep and may be viewed by them as a replacement of themselves by the father.

RELATIONSHIP TO OTHER ADULTS

The relation of the Nyansongo child to adults other than parents is for the most part explicitly patterned after the mother-child and father-child relationships, although less intense in form. Children are taught to respect all persons of the parental generation, and they may be chastised by such adults who catch them misbehaving. Adults are said to be more cautious nowadays about beating misbehaving children who are not their own because they fear litigation if the child is thought to be injured. The likelihood of a particular person administering a punishment any more severe than scolding is dependent on the friendliness of his relations with the child's parents. If two brothers are on extremely good terms, one will think nothing of punishing the other's children, but if they are distant and hostile, they are afraid that punishment of a child will be misconstrued and lead to legal action. So it is with co-wives, who discipline each other's children if they have a close relationship but keep hands off if they are not speaking, for fear of being accused of witchcraft should a beaten child fall ill. In any case, adults feel a minimal responsibility of reporting a child's observed misbehavior if serious to his parents. They nevertheless extend hospitality to children who are escaping parental discipline, as mentioned previously.

A major exception to the above picture of respect and parentlike relations with adults is the case of grandparents. They are much warmer and more jovial toward their grandchildren than other adults are, and children learn that they need not respect them in the ordinary sense. Grandparents initiate sexual joking with young children, and insults, including sexual abuse, flow back and forth between them in a manner which is almost as relaxed as that of agemates. A child must never strike his grandparent, however, and he tends to obey the older person's imperious commands despite the surface egalitarianism. The house of a resident grandmother within the homestead is a useful refuge for a child being disciplined and for girls whose fathers are sleeping in their mother's houses. Although grandparents rarely play a part in the punishment of children for important offenses, they were observed curtly ordering a grandchild to stop mischievous acts and even caning slightly once or twice.

RELATIONSHIP TO ANIMALS

Nyansongo children view animals more in terms of fear and aggression than as objects of nurturance and warmth. The fear of hyenas and wild animals inculcated by mothers has already been mentioned. In herding, boys sometimes beat the rump of a cow more than is necessary to make her move, and they also throw stones at cows to herd them from a distance. No particularly close relationship between children and cattle, sheep, goats, or even dogs and cats, was observed. Boys of about 4 and 5 occasionally beat dogs, particularly puppies, with sticks, much as they would an animal in herding, and the cries of the puppies elicit no negative reaction from adults, some of whom find it amusing.

TRAINING IN OBEDIENCE, RESPONSIBILITY AND SKILLS

The "good child" as viewed by Nyansongo parents is the obedient child who does what his parents tell him invariably and without question. Obedience rather than enterprise or initiative is considered to be the key to success in the contemporary setting, and parents state that the child selected to attend school (in those families which send any children to school) is the obedient one who will do what the teachers tell him and thereby make progress in school. Smartness or brightness by itself is not a highly valued characteristic, and the Nyansongo concept of intelligence includes respect for elders and filial piety as vital ingredients. An obedient child, according to Nyansongo thought, is also responsible, that is, he performs the tasks and chores regularly assigned to him by his parents with a minimum of supervision. Parents begin obedience and responsibility training very early, often as soon as a sibling is born. The child begins by carrying dishes of food from one house to another within the homestead. As time goes on, more and more errands of this kind are demanded of him. When the father wants to smoke a cigarette or the mother her pipe while sitting in the yard, any nearby child will be sent for a coal from the fireplace to ignite the tobacco. When visitors come, a small child is sent into the house for a stool. When a beer party is planned, children are sent to notify neighbors, and once it is underway they may be sent to other houses to borrow pots, kettles, and cups. An adult will never get something for himself if he can order a child to do it, even if the child is farther from the object than he himself is. Older siblings can

also command the labor of the smaller children for their own purposes, and we have seen boys who were herding remain sheltered by a
tree, building a fire to warm themselves, as they sent their little brothers
shivering into the rain to collect twigs for the fire. Disobedient or
dawdling children are very likely to be caned by their parents or older
siblings.

The training of boys in herding by their fathers and older siblings
has been described; it begins at an early age. Three-year-old girls are
taught to carry small pans of water from the river to the house on their
heads, and as they get older, they carry increasingly large pots on their
heads with grass-ring supports. The female equivalent of the boy's
punishment for neglecting cattle is the chastisement of the girl for
dropping and breaking a pot. The mother is angered by such an occurrence and will cane a girl of 6 or older very severely for the carelessness which has cost the family a fairly expensive object. Girls of 7 and
8 are usually so apprehensive of maternal punishment that they cry
after dropping a pot. One 9-year-old girl in Nyansongo broke a pot on
her way to the river and sat down gazing into space with tear-filled eyes
for 15 minutes before summoning the courage to inform her mother.
Mothers claim they do not cane for such an offense if the girl is weeping on her return. The emotional reaction of the Nyansongo girl to
her breaking a pot is much stronger than that of the boy who allows
the cattle to damage crops, even though the latter is a worse offense.
Girls are, in general, considered more responsible than boys, and informants offer as proof of this the observation that in families which
have no young boys, girls herd cattle in a very conscientious manner,
while boys are noted for recklessly running off to snare birds and fish.
As mentioned, girls 5 and older often serve as baby tenders. If a girl
were to leave the infant for any reason, she would face very harsh punishment by the mother; a beating for this offense was witnessed on one
occasion. Chores are not so sex-typed for uncircumcised children that
boys cannot be used to act as nurses for infants, and it is often done in
families lacking small girls. When boys are nurses, they are required to
be as responsible as girls in their care of the infant.

Both boys and girls as young as 3 years old have been observed helping their mothers hoe a field for a short period of time. Usually they
spontaneously ask to be allowed to do it and appear to enjoy it very
much. Girls show more initiative in this regard than boys, and two
6-year-old girls in Nyansongo cultivated their own plot of corn from
hoeing to harvest without any prompting from parents. By the time
they are 6 or 7 both boys and girls do a considerable amount of hoeing
in previously cultivated fields. Girls go on to learn the weeding of

eleusine, harvesting, and other of the painstaking agricultural chores which men rarely participate in. Girls are also taught to shuck corn, grind eleusine, and cook porridge by their mothers.

*
*
*

Chapter 15

The Initiation of Girls

The initiation ceremonies for both sexes are among the most important events occurring in Nyansongo. They are organized on the basis of *risaga*, that is, by local community rather than by lineage. Mayer (1953a: 9–10), in his detailed ethnographic account of the ceremonies, states:

. . . the initiation cycle is woven into the life of the neighborhood in such a way that nobody remains altogether unconcerned. Children too young to be initiated themselves are occupied in carrying food or running errands; they are awakened at night to hear the bull-roarers and to listen to the dramatic dialogue which is shouted loudly for their especial benefit. The older boys and girls, who have already been initiated but are not yet married, play a very important part; indeed, apart from the actual operation and the adults' beer-parties, they organize and carry out most of the rites and celebrations themselves. Some are formally engaged as sponsors or as circumcision-leaders, and many others volunteer to escort the novices to and from circumcision and to assist at the performance of the mysteries. All young people, as long as they are not married, are free to attend the parties which take place . . . at the home of one novice after another. All of them may, if they wish, take advantage of the special sexual license associated with the seclusion both of boys and girls. The young married people are less closely involved, but maturity brings the right to be entertained at the beer-drinks with which all parents celebrate their respective children's entry into and emergence from seclusion. Among the old people, some will be needed to take part in the ritual, for instance, in blessing the novices at the end of seclusion and burning their bedding.

Both male and female initiations involve genital operations and both occur annually, just after the harvest, lasting from October to December. They are performed earlier in western Gusiiland, where the harvest is earlier, and generally sweep through Gusii country in a west-to-east direction. Female initiation precedes male initiation by a few weeks in each community and is more elaborate ceremonially. The words for the genital operation (*ogoroka*) and the seclusion or novitiate (*obware*) are identical for boys and girls, and they are similar in format, although the content of the ceremonies and their consequences are quite distinct.

It is the girl herself who decides when she will undergo initiation. Unless she is at the maximum age for it, her parents will not press her to have it done in any particular year; they wait for her to show a desire for it spontaneously and without prompting. Most girls want to be initiated, not because the ceremonies themselves are attractive, but because they desire to leave the status of "little girl" (*egesagane*) and enter that of *enyaroka* (literally "a circumcised thing") or *omoiseke* (an unmarried girl). There are three components to the girl's conscious desire for initiation. The first is that she wants to put behind her the tasks and chores of childhood and assume those of an adult female. Acting as nurse for infants is almost always a responsibility of un-initiated girls, as few of the older ones want to be so house-bound, and their wishes in this regard are respected by their parents. In families lacking boys, girls often must herd cattle until their initiation, but are not allowed to do so afterward on the grounds that "it is for boys to do." The tasks they look forward to as initiated girls are proper women's work: hoeing, weeding, and harvesting of crops, grinding corn, cooking food, carrying water in large pots and pans on the head. None of these jobs is as confining as caring for infants and cattle, but, in addition, they are valued for their own sake as enjoyable and (relative to childhood chores) prestigeful feminine occupations. The second component involves the girl's wanting to avoid the aggressive encounters peculiar to childhood. Many girls state that they find being called "little girl" (*egesagane*) offensive, and they object to being fought and insulted by the younger children. Taking into account the Nyansongo equation of heterosexual aggression with sexuality, it is clear that implicit in such statements is a rejection of childhood sexuality. The girl wants to be the object of attention by circumcised boys, not by the lower-status rowdies of the pasture. As her aspirations for initiation increase, she rebuffs her former playmates' sexual advances, and they begin insulting her, shooting at her with slingshots, and so on. She assumes that initiation will terminate this annoyance, for she knows that parents have little tolerance for aggression directed against initiated girls by uncircumcised boys.

The third aspect of her desire for higher status is her fear of being left behind by her agemates. If she knows that the girls of her age in the neighborhood or community are planning to be initiated, she will ordinarily want to go with them, partly because their willingness allays her individual fears of the genital operation, partly because she wants to remain on an egalitarian basis with her friends. If they are all initiated in a particular year, and she is left behind, she will be excluded from social relations with them. Several girls said they did not want to be called "little girl" by their old friends, and they felt very strongly about it. One of them, an 8-year-old named Nyanchama whose mother refused to have her initiated because of the expense and disruption of the inadequately housed leviratic * homestead, experienced the abandonment which other girls fear. When her agemates from adjacent homesteads were being jubilantly led back to their houses from the clitoridectomy operation, she began crying. An unmarried girl involved in conducting the initiation took pity on her and said, "We'll take you tomorrow; we'll convince Mogaka (Nyanchama's leviratic father) that you ought to go." An older woman shouted, "Why aren't you circumcised when all your peers are?" The mother of one of the girls who had just had the operation performed, said, "If you come to abuse the other girls, you'll see what will happen!" Nyanchama sobbed bitterly at these unkind remarks, and during the next days starved herself in protest against the refusal by her parents.

In summary, three factors lie behind the Nyansongo girl's wish to be initiated: (1) her desire to graduate from childish and boyish chores to adult female ones, (2) her desire to avoid the sexual and aggressive molestations of uncircumcised boys, (3) her fear of being ostracized by her female agemates when they are initiated.

Regardless of whether or not they favor her initiation, the parents, particularly the mother, try to give the aspiring girl the impression that they consider her too young for it, that they cannot afford it, and that it would be too much trouble. In some families this attitude is sincere, but most frequently the parents want their discouragement to spur the girl on to proving herself ready for the important step. As the parents put it, they want to see evidence of *okongainia*, a verb which is variously translated "to be intelligent" and "to have sense." In the case of a girl, "having sense" means primarily being willing and able to do the work of an adult woman around the house and, to a lesser extent, in the fields. She should be able to grind a fine flour with the grinding stones and should perform these duties without having to be ordered

---

* A marital relationship between a widow and her deceased husband's brother or other kinsman. In this case the widow had moved to a small house at the brother's homestead, and there was no hut which could be used for seclusion.

and reminded by the mother. There is an assumption on the part of Nyansongo parents that any girl who has enough "sense" and serious- ness of purpose to do these things well will be able to undergo the painful operation of clitoridectomy without screaming or running away. A girl who runs away from the operation is terribly stigmatized as a coward (enkuri), and her social disgrace is compounded by the offense to the spirits which demands sacrificial propitiation. These consequences of her possible cowardice are what parents fear most, and their discouraging attitude is intended as a safeguard against her go- ing to initiation without the mature determination to carry her suc- cessfully through the painful experience. Observation and interviews of 8- and 9-year-old girls proved that the parents' ruse has considerable effect. A few weeks before initiation many of them said they wanted desperately to be initiated but were afraid their mothers would pre- vent them. In consequence, each girl began demonstrating her womanly competence. Some harvested whole fields by themselves; others spon- taneously ground flour, kept the house stocked with firewood, and carried water from the stream in the largest-size pans.

There was considerable variation in the motivation and performance of Nyansongo girls during the preinitiation period in 1956. Some of them had assumed adult domestic duties as much as a year before and made no special effort to prove themselves in the few weeks before initiation. A few were more afraid than desirous of initiation and did not accelerate their usually below-average attempts to perform woman's work. The majority wanted initiation badly, though they had some fears, and made heroic efforts to prove themselves capable. Right up to the day that initiation began, they had no idea whether or not they had convinced their parents that they had "sense," but they had become determined to join their agemates even in the face of parental op- position.

When communities to the west have begun female initiation, the mothers of the oldest of the uninitiated girls in the community let it be known on what day they are taking their girls to the home of the specialist who performs the clitoridectomy. It is not necessary for all girls who want to be initiated that year to have the operation per- formed on that day, but most will want to go along, with the oldest of their group leading the way. In Nyansongo, the girls of one of the three neighborhoods within the community did not undergo the oper- ation until more than a week after the others. Each girl whose close agemates are going will wake her mother at 5:00 A.M. and ask for the one or two shillings needed to pay the operator.* The mother typ-

* The operator charges according to the size of the girl; "bigger" girls are charged two shillings instead of one.

ically pinches the girl and tells her she is too small; this is to test her determination and courage. If the girl still insists on going, she leaves the house naked except for a cloth on her shoulders and accompanied by her mother. In the chilly dawn they meet the other girls with their mothers and proceed to the home of the operator, the women singing songs along the way. The operator is usually a middle-aged woman with a reputation for skill in clitoridectomy who lives within 2 or 3 miles of the community, though not necessarily in it.

In Nyansongo, the first and largest clitoridectomy ceremony took place not at the operator's home but at the homestead of twin girls who were being initiated. The initiation of twins was considered a rare and lucky event, and all the other girls wanted to have the operation at the home of the twins on the same day. The attraction of this event was so strong that even a girl not more than 7 years old managed to have it performed, and girls came from an adjacent clan. All in all, 13 girls had the operation that day at the home of the twins, with more than 50 women watching. Some of the girls ran ahead of their mothers and were gruffly greeted by middle-aged women who pulled the cloths off their shoulders and pushed them back, telling them they were too young: "Go herd cattle! Go home!" This was again testing to make sure the girls wanted to go through with it, and they did, demonstrating their determination by trying to push their way into the open place by the side of the homestead where the operation was being performed. A crowd of women surrounded a stone on which the girl to be operated on was seated. A woman squatting behind the girl supported her back on her knees and, with her arms thrust under the girl's arms, firmly held the girl's hands over her eyes. This grip served to prevent the girl from seeing what was going on and from moving her arms or the upper part of her body during the operation. The operator spread the girl's legs, put white flour on the genital area, and cut off the head of the clitoris with a sawing motion of her small knife. As soon as the piece of flesh had dropped to the ground, the crowd of women began trilling loudly, gaily screaming and shouting and, in some cases, dancing individually. The girl was then led over to the side of the house to squat, shivering under the eaves at the sides of the girls who had gone before her.

Most of the girls underwent the operation without mishap, but two of them gave more trouble than the rest. A girl from Nyansango refused to spread her legs and was subsequently slapped and cajoled into doing so by her mother and other women. She got up and ran away once before the operation was begun but was finally subdued and went through with it. The other girl, from a different clan and community, **tried to get away before the operation, eventually escaping after it had** been half performed. Although a sheep of redemption was not required of her, the stone was changed after her escape, indicating that her act had brought ritual impurity to the stone, which might have contaminated others. Both girls had histories of overdependence on their mothers and of crying easily when injured by playmates. In the case of the girl from Nyansongo, the rumor went around that her mother had been a coward at clitoridectomy and so naturally the daughter was too.

When all the girls have had the operation and the operator has been paid, they are led, walking stiffly with pain and covered only by cloth on their shoulders, back to the homes of their respective mothers. The women who lead them, including their mothers, begin the joyous obscenity and rowdiness which is expected of them on this day. In Nyansongo, the mother of the twin girls took off most of her clothing and danced and sang in front of her house. The 30 others from the community danced in a nearby pasture, arranging themselves in a circle and moving their hips to and fro. The words of all the songs were concerned with some aspect of coitus.

A week later, in a different Nyansongo neighborhood, the mood was even less restrained after the clitoridectomy ceremony. Bosibori, a middle-aged widow whose last daughter had just undergone the operation, led the expressive activity when the girls were being taken home. During the singing she and another woman of the same age put their arms around each other's waists and simulated sexual intercourse. In the atmosphere of hilarity, two young married women beat each other with sticks that are used to represent phalluses in the dancing. Jerking her abdomen against a road bank and shouting the obscene word for coitus each time, Bosibori noticed that the women were giving in to fatigue and cried, "I'll not give you food because I saw no one dancing with her skirt up like this." She hoisted her skirt up around her thighs and three other women followed her example. A young man from Nyansongo hurried by on the road as the women continued, and they intensified their hip movements for the benefit of a truckload of men going to the tea plantations. When her daughter collapsed momentarily by the road, Bosibori put her in the shade and resumed dancing. Some women told her to wipe the girl's blood from her hands but she jubilantly answered, "No, this is my own child," and smeared it on her own face. As the procession reached her house, Bosibori picked up a hide mat for her daughter to sit on in seclusion, but the mother first ran about with it in front of her as if it were a shield. Several women poised their sticks like spears and jabbed at the mat in mock combat. The songs included ones with the following words:

My brother-in-law (i.e., husband's brother), my brother-in-law,
Don't put me on the ground, don't put me on the ground.
You'd better have a mattress to put me on if you have sense.
Catch me at the waist and leave me before the cock crows.

A young man married a girl,
He put her on the bed,
Found she had no pubic hair,
He was very surprised, saying what kind of girl have I?
She may not bear children.

The use of obscene language, expressions of desire for prohibited sexual relationships, public mention of the sex act and its mechanics, immodest exposure and hip movements—all of these ordinarily shocking acts are expected and performed by women leading the novices back from the clitoridectomy operation. Although the performance is public, men try to avoid it so as not to suffer the inevitable embarrassment. Another notable aspect of the women's behavior is the playing of the male sex role: holding sticks which represent phalluses, singing songs of sex from the man's point of view, engaging in mock military combat, and even singing as one woman did:

I want to be a man, not a woman
I don't know what's happening at my (parents') home,
If I were a son I'd be at home and not here,
And I'd not have so much trouble.

Although the atmosphere is one of almost frantic hilarity, the women indulge in insulting, fighting, and destructive behavior which would ordinarily be taboo. For example, one middle-aged woman said to another, "You uncircumcised girl, what keeps you in the house when we take girls for circumcision? Is it your husband who keeps you?" The epithet and joking reference to marital coitus would be insulting in everyday social intercourse. Mention has been made of the young women beating each other with sticks; friendly tussling was also observed. Most striking is the wanton theft and destruction of crops. When the women accompanying her daughter arrived at Bosibori's house, they pulled up more than half of her potato garden, gorging themselves on raw potatoes and taking others with them. She became furious and tried to stop them, but they said, "This is a happy occasion; we can do anything, even annoy you." Three older women tied all the potato shoots into bundles and carried them away to plant in their own gardens. The group also trampled all the unripe maize in a small field near the house. At the houses of other women whose daughters had just been operated on, accompanying neighbors grabbed numerous ears of ripe corn from their fields. This license is expected, and even when carried to excess, as at Bosibori's, it is not recognized as ground for legal action or any other kind of retribution.

Each girl is left squatting behind a granary or some bushes near her mother's house, where she is hidden from sight until afternoon. The mother cooks food, and then, in midafternoon, the initiated women of the community gather to lead each girl into a month-long seclusion in her mother's house.

In bare outline,* the leading-in ceremony requires that several men, one of them the father or classificatory father of the novice, be present and sitting in the cattle pen, that the novice be led from her hiding place to the mother's house so surrounded by women that the men cannot see her, and that a ritual, in which a very old woman dances with a basket of flour while archaic songs are sung, be performed at the entrance as the girl is brought in. The theme song of female initiation, the *esimbore,* is sung, including the words:

> She is going to pass through the cattle-pen,
> She was a wife for uninitiated boys,
> Now she is a wife for initiated youths.

Informal behavior in the afternoon is at least as raucous and unrestrained as it was in the morning. If the girl's real father is present, the women jeer at him, emphasizing his exclusion from the house during his daughter's seclusion: "Where will you find a place for coitus now? Tonight you'll have to go behind the house, like chickens!" Sometimes they insult him with, "You're too old for coitus!" The men react with embarrassment and (sometimes mock) annoyance at this behavior, and occasionally they are goaded into returning an insult; in which case the women may saucily lift their skirts to embarrass them further. On one occasion a respected polygynist became so angered by the immodest conduct of a husky widow that he tried to whip her with a branch, but she tussled with him and threw him to the ground. Younger men were also observed wrestling good-humoredly with the insulting women. Many obscene songs are sung, some of them mentioning the name of the novice's father, as the women jerk their hips suggestively and move the phallic sticks, which most of them now hold, up and down or punch the fist into the palm of the other hand in a coital rhythm. At one leading-in the women staged a skit in which one of them played the father of the novice trying to enter the house and another took the part of his wife keeping him out during the seclusion

---

* Ceremonial details omitted in this account can be found in Mayer (1953: 27–29), although there is some subcultural variation between Nyansongo and the area he describes.

period. A moralistic song heard at one ceremony was, "A slut shouldn't sing and be happy about other women's children, lest the newly circumcised child follow the character of that slut."

When the girl has been led in and the dancing has subsided, her mother brings out food for the women to eat. They scold the hostess in abusive terms for the insufficiency of her food; at one house the women danced around holding the vegetables in their fingers and singing a demand for meat. They also pull grass out of the roof and steal corn from the fields. Among themselves, the women continue the insulting and aggressive behavior of the morning; two usually dignified matrons were observed in a rough-and-tumble wrestling bout which bordered on open hostility but ended in the humorous spirit in which it had begun. The leading-in ceremony and associated festivities are repeated at the house of each novice, in the order in which they had the clitoridectomy operation performed.

It is obvious from the above description that the girl herself recedes into the background while the women leading her use the joyous ceremonial occasion as an outlet for their usually concealed sexual interests and their antagonism toward men. The novice, preoccupied with her pain, dazed from several hours' hiding outside in the midday heat of the dry season, and overwhelmed by the noise and confusion of the female crowd, may be only dimly aware of what the women are singing and doing. In subsequent years, however, she will participate more consciously in the festivities which follow clitoridectomy and attain an awareness of its meaning for women which was not possible for her as a novice.

While the female novice is in seclusion in her mother's house, life goes on as usual in the house except that her father (or any circumcised male) may not enter and she herself may not leave (except for elimination). The exclusion of the father is mandatory even when it causes hardship, as was the case for one man both of whose wives had daughters initiated at the same time. Having just returned from employment and not realizing that both would be initiated, he did not begin to build a separate house in which he could sleep during the seclusion until it was rather late. Although the initiation of the daughters was postponed as long as it could be, when they went into seclusion, his new house had no roof on it. Nonetheless, he slept there throughout the month, being occasionally rained on during the night. The mother is not limited in her activities except that she must feed the novice a great deal of food, which is believed to aid in the healing of the clitoridectomy wound. The girl receives visitors, including her "instructor," and seems to have an enjoyable time. On several nights she is introduced by initiated girls to the "mysteries" (*chinyangi*) of female initiation. There is a ritual with obscure meaning (Mayer, 1953: 29–36), a great deal of singing (some of it involving archaic words not understood by contemporary Gusii), and provocatively sexual dancing in the nude at which it is said that boys sometimes peek. Any male caught watching might be severely beaten, however. A phallic object is constructed, which the novices are shown but which men cannot see without payment of a fee. On some nights when the older girls are sleeping with her, boys come and try to have intercourse with them (not with the novice) with varying degrees of success.* The theme of the nocturnal seclusion activities, ceremonial and otherwise, is primarily sexual and involves no direct instruction or hazing of the novice. At the end of the month a further ritual takes the girl out of seclusion, and she is smeared with butterfat and decorated with beads given by all the women of the neighborhood. She is said to be a "bride" (*omoriakari*), and she promenades around the marketplace and even in Kisii Town with other newly initiated girls similarly decorated. Both her parents and the newly initiated girl exult and rejoice in her new status.

After initiation, the life and behavior of the girl, although she is only about 9 years old, are conditioned by the prospect of her marriage. First of all, in contemporary circumstances, it is considered necessary for an initiated girl to be well dressed and neatly groomed. She may no longer wear the rags and tatters of childhood and is presented with one or more new store-bought dresses on her emergence from seclusion. At this time she begins to wear a head scarf and to spend long hours every day washing herself and her clothes. This emphasis on cleanliness is peculiar to girls between circumcision and marriage, for little girls and married women are not so attentive to their appearance. It is typical of girls of 9 and 10 years to go to the stream, ostensibly to fetch water, and to remain for several hours washing legs, arms, head, and garments with soap. Mothers fume at this behavior, especially when it delays cooking, but they appear to do little about it. In their concern about appearance, girls of the early postinitiation years, look for signs of physical maturity in themselves and each other; they can be overheard remarking on the first development of breasts in their friends. When they reach adolescence, they go to the market in groups, to be seen and eventually approached by boys and young men.

Another major consequence of initiation for a girl is the establishment of close relationships with the girls of the neighborhood or community who were initiated in the same year. After initiation, these girls tend to work together and to go to the market in a group. In the plant-

* This is "taking by stealth," described in Chapter 5.

ing season following their initiation, the girls of one of the neighborhoods in Nyansongo worked cooperatively in the fields every morning.
In fact, the name of the rotating women's cooperative work arrangement, *egesangio,* is closely related to the word which designates an age-
mate, *omogesangio.* The social ties based on the initiation experience
are relatively short-lived for girls, however, for the girls are too dispersed after marriage to continue them. Nevertheless, this initiation
work group, which lasts five or six years, is the basis for the sociability
of women when they are married and work in similar groups.

The problem of controlling the behavior of contemporary adolescent
girls is a difficult one for Nyansongo parents. The basis of the difficulty
is that the girl is oriented toward young men who give her gifts and
flatter her, expecting in return that she will yield sexually or even elope
with one of them. Parents, on the other hand, view an adolescent girl
as a family member who must of necessity leave home for marriage
and who can at least reimburse the parents who took the trouble to
raise her with a handsome bridewealth in cattle. What they fear most
is her running off with a reckless young man who has no cattle and,
secondly, her becoming pregnant or gaining a reputation as a "slut,"
both of which tend to make her undesirable as a wife. In the contemporary situation, the fear of a girl's eloping and leaving her parents
without the bridewealth cattle which are their traditional due is a real
one, for scarcity of cattle and high brideprice have made elopement
more frequent. But parents fear it so greatly that it colors all parent-
daughter relations. In an extreme case, a recently initiated 9-year-old
who failed to carry out an order of her mother was told by a neighbor
woman at the stream, "So you disobey your mother! You'll probably
run off and leave them without cattle!" Since the average marriage age
is approximately 15, the problem of elopement does not usually loom
very large until the girl is 12 or 13. At that time, the parents, especially
the father, experience ambivalent feelings toward the daughter. The
daughter is beginning to misbehave, showing a disregard of her
mother's orders, and staying away from home more than her parents
think she should. They want to punish her to arrest the kind of behavior which they believe will lead to wantonness and elopement, but
they fear the punishment itself will give her an added incentive to
leave home and injure her parents economically. This conflict is illustrated by the case of a Nyansongo father who proudly showed us a
phonograph and records he bought to entertain his 15-year-old daughter
at home so she would not have to go out to wild parties for such
amusements. When, several months later, she came home from market
after dark, the father became enraged, beat her severely (which fathers

are not supposed to do to initiated girls), and threatened to kill her. This is a common situation and often ends, as in the case cited, with the father hastily arranging her marriage to a man who is able and willing to pay cattle. The girl desires the romance and attention offered by young men but is afraid to commit herself sexually and emotionally because of the strong pressures and punishments of her father. In the most typical situation, the girl engages in sexual intercourse with different boys in great fear of discovery and pregnancy. All girls have sexual relations before marriage, although it is impossible to estimate the average frequency of such relations. If the father does not act fast enough in arranging a proper marriage to someone she will agree to live with, she may resolve the conflict by eloping with a man of her choice who pays no cattle to her father. Thus the Nyansongo girl, destined to leave home on marriage and never return to live there, becomes increasingly difficult for parents to control after initiation has brought her into the status of unmarried womanhood.

⚐
⚐
⚐

Chapter 16

The Initiation of Boys *

At the age of 8 or 9, when Nyansongo girls are being initiated into womanhood, the boys are still mere children who have not yet begun to aspire to adult status. Many of them are still timidly experimenting with the frightening prospect of sleeping outside the mother's house, and neither they nor their fathers and brothers will consider them even slightly ready to graduate from being "little boys" (abaisia, sing. omoisia) to "circumcised men" or "warriors" (abamura, sing. omomura).

The uncircumcised boy of 8 to 12 is usually the chief herder of cattle in the family and sometimes one of the major behavior problems as well. Unlike the girl, in the preinitiation period, he is not

* Many ceremonial details omitted in this account can be found in Mayer (1953a: 10–25).

being progressively introduced to the kind of life and tasks which he will have as an adult; rather, he has a distinct way of life that does not prepare him for the future. Three problems can develop during this period, involving (1) dependency on the mother, (2) irresponsibility, and (3) aggressive and sexual offenses.

Although he has begun sleeping outside his mother's house, the uncircumcised boy does not ordinarily do so every night but only when his father sleeps with his mother. For the sons of monogamists this may be every night, while for sons of polygymists, widows, and men who are working outside of the district, it may be less frequent. Even so, if there are circumcised brothers sleeping in their separate hut, the boy may be persuaded to sleep out with them rather than with his mother at every opportunity. Of the children studied, sons of widows were found sleeping outside the mother's house at the latest age, 9 to 10, and one of them was reported to be so terrified by noises when he first tried it that he ran back crying to his mother during the night. Even when the boy is accustomed to sleeping away from the mother regularly, he is comforted by the knowledge that he can return to sleep occasionally if he wants to, and he may sit near the mother in her cooking place in the daytime and beg food, money, and permission to go places. Ordinarily the mother does little to discourage this; indeed, the boy of this age is clever at so manipulating his mother's behavior as to be rewarded for his dependence. It should be noted that this close relationship with the mother, particularly in the case of boys who do not have cattle to herd, may involve the boy's learning and practicing the most typically feminine chores, namely, grinding and cooking. All of this may be disturbing to the father, older brother, or whatever adult male is closest to the family. Even the possible sexual connotations of the boy's closeness to his mother are explicitly thought of. Nyansongo men claimed that in days of old when all of a boy's circumcised brothers were living away in cattle-villages, boys remained sexually innocent until a later age. The abolition of the cattle-villages and the presence of older boys at home are the cause, they claim, of the lowering of the age of circumcision because boys gain sexual sophistication at a younger age and have to be moved away from their mothers earlier. Whether or not this historical explanation is true, there can be no doubt that a father feels it is improper for a boy of 10, whom he knows to have some sexual knowledge, to be in such a close relationship with his mother, especially sleeping near her and sitting with her while she squats to cook in the house. In the context of the customary avoidance between mother and adult son, such dependency is viewed as fraught with sexual overtones. This is one reason why the father feels it would be good for the boy to be circumcised and initiated into adult status.

Another aspect of the boy's behavior which presents a problem to his parents is his irresponsibility. Although he is in charge of herding cattle, sheep, and goats, the boy's adventurous spirit takes him off hunting birds, fishing, and climbing trees with the other boys of the same age. Sometimes he leaves the cattle in the care of a younger brother who may not be capable of handling them; sometimes he goes off without making any provision for their care. Eventually, the cows do some damage; there is a law suit, and the boy is punished by his father, but usually he continues to find ways of evading his duty to the herds. Mothers find that boys of 10 to 12 disobey them, refuse to do assigned tasks, disappear when called for, go long distances from home and return erratically. In some of the most extreme cases, the boys take to stealing and become serious threats to neighborhood property. Some mothers say they will not beat boys of this age for fear of retaliation; food deprivation is typically used by mothers under such circumstances. But the father, if he is present, may be increasingly called on to discipline the boy, and this may be another reason for his wanting his son to be circumcised.

A third problem presented by an uncircumcised boy to his parents is his aggressive and sexual behavior. As the oldest sibling in his herding group, he is liable to bully and terrorize the younger ones to a point which parents consider reprehensible. An even more certain source of trouble is in his relations with younger girls who are already initiated. An initiated girl expects to be treated like a woman, and especially by uninitiated boys. But a 10-year-old boy is not prepared to accept a 9-year-old girl as worthy of respect. If the younger initiated girl is his sister, he may continue to order her about and to insult her as he did before. She will report this to the parents, who scold him for insulting his initiated sister. If the girl is not a sister, the boy may wish to engage in sex play with her as he did sporadically in the bush before her initiation. Now, however, she spurns him as a little boy, and he is so infuriated that he beats her or shoots at her with a slingshot. Girls invariably report such attacks, and their mothers come raging to the parents of the boy about it. The boy is often beaten and scolded by the father for such behavior, but it is considered more effective to get him circumcised so that he will not continue in an inferior status to younger girls. The boys who postponed their circumcision for several years were the greatest behavior problems for their parents; they were noticeably more disobedient, disrespectful, and overdependent on their mothers than other boys of the same age, and one of them was frequently accused by adults of sexual and aggressive offenses as well as theft of small articles.

The majority of boys are eager to be initiated and to become big men who can go away to work on the tea plantations or begin school. Like girls, they do not want to be left behind by their agemates when the latter are circumcised. Boys are more impressed by the awesome kinship duties of adulthood than girls; they seem to realize initiation means giving up dependence on mother and the relatively reckless, mischievous life of the pastures, and they are somewhat frightened. Furthermore, they know that male initiates are subjected to painful hazing as well as the circumcision operation, and this adds to their apprehensiveness. In spite of these fears, the average boy comes to want to be initiated spontaneously. He proves that he "has sense" not only by continuous sleeping in the children's house but also by wearing shorts to show he is developing a proper sense of modesty, and sometimes by doing agricultural work to indicate seriousness of purpose. The extent to which the father pretends to be skeptical about the boy's fitness in order to spur him on, or coaxes him toward initiation, depends on whether the boy is eager for it; in which case the father would be skeptical, or reluctant, requiring coaxing.

Before the day when the other boys in the community are going to the circumciser, a boy who wants to be initiated must choose his sponsor from among the initiated but unmarried boys who are of the same generation but who are not actual brothers. The sponsor is in charge of one or several novices during their seclusion and is assisted by a second boy whom he appoints. The novices shave their heads the day before and sleep at the hut of an initiated boy, not necessarily the sponsor or his assistant, who will escort them to the circumciser. Several escorts of the same age sleep there.

They rise in the middle of the night, for it is customary to reach the circumciser before dawn. The older boys may treat the novice roughly and, as a final test, try to frighten him with stories of the pain and how bad it is to be a coward. If the boy persists without crying, he bathes in the cold water of a stream and proceeds naked toward the house of the circumciser, about 2 miles from Nyansongo. The older boys buffet and shout at the novices along the way. Parents and classificatory fathers may not attend a boy's initiation, but brothers, classificatory brothers, and unrelated women who happen to be nearby may witness it. The boy is led to a special tree, and he stands back to the tree and arms above his head against the tree in readiness for the operation. In contrast to the girls, who are held tightly for their clitoridectomy, boys have to face circumcision on their feet and unsupported by another person. The circumciser kneels before the boy to perform the operation, and the older boys and men, standing behind the circumciser, aim spears and clubs at the boy's head, shouting continuously throughout the operation that he will be killed if he moves or shows signs of pain. A number of boys interviewed before circumcision expressed the conviction that they would be killed if they cried or tried to escape. The boys who were observed did not move during the operation; they looked up into space or at the men threatening them with spears with expressionless faces. After the quick operation, the boy is led away with his newly circumcised agemates, holding the penis (to prevent bleeding) with one hand and carrying a branch of a bush (*ekerundu*) used in many rituals as a fertility symbol.

In the afternoon the novices are led into seclusion by classificatory brothers who sing the *esimbore* for male initiation, with the words:

> Uncircumcised little boys have had pain!
> The circumciser has taken our penis;
> He has made you a spear and a hard shield.
> Fight the Kipsigis, fight the Kipsigis!
> Fight the Abatende,* fight the Abatende!
> Uncircumcised little boys have had pain!
> Mother's clitoris, mother's clitoris;
> Mother's pubic hair, mother's pubic hair.
> Uncircumcised little boys copulate with mother!
> Uncircumcised little boys have had pain.

The next to last line is interpreted as referring to the fact that before circumcision a boy's mother could touch his penis and sleep in the same house. The men singing this song are much more sedate than their counterparts in female initiation; they simply march slowly. Furthermore, unlike their female counterparts, the men affected by Christianity are embarrassed by the obscene lyrics and even sing bowdlerized versions on some occasions.

Mothers and other related women are unable to see the novices, for the latter are shielded by blankets and the crowd of singing men. The women express their jubilation by trilling and running about lifting their skirts immodestly. The whole affair is much less elaborate and lively than the girls' leading-in ceremony. Unlike girls, who are secluded in their mothers' houses, male novices are led into a newly built house which two or three of them will share during seclusion. There is considerable ritual paraphernalia associated with seclusion and the postcircumcision rites of initiation; bull-roarers, a fire that must not be allowed to go out, a particular kind of grass (*esuguta*)

---

* The Gusii word for the Kuria, the linguistically related people to the south of them.

stuck into the floor of the hut, which must not be allowed to wither. The mothers of the novices prepare food and send it to them, but no one else may eat the leftovers. Much food is needed for the novices "to heal their wounds." Boys of different seclusion huts meet each other outside, primarily for hunting. Until about 10 years ago, they would steal chickens from homesteads in the neighborhood without reproach, but now the fathers of novices who do so are faced with lawsuits and the practice has virtually died out. Married persons are barred from entering the seclusion hut, although others may come and go freely. In or out of the hut, however, the novice must not be seen by classificatory parents. He carries ashes with him outside to throw up as a warning when persons of the parents' generation inadvertently approach. There must be no fighting among the novices in the seclusion; a sacrifice would have to be performed if an outbreak occurred. The boy's life in seclusion is generally an enjoyable one, although he must carefully follow ritual prohibitions on dressing, bathing, and licking his lips as well as rules limiting social intercourse.

Hazing by other boys is an essential feature of the seclusion period, although it is not so severe as that found in many other East and South African societies. On the third night after circumcision, an indoor event known as *esubo* is conducted by the older boys. The novices are forced to eat a number of caustic and nauseating substances which the older boys tell them are delicious foods. Refusal to eat brings a beating. They are threatened with being eaten by an animal called *enyabububu* and are then shown that the noises attributed to the animal are made by a bull-roarer. Another bull-roarer is used outside the hut, with an announcement for the benefit of women and children that a great beast is swallowing the novices. Soon after, the older boys announce that the beast has vomited them up again. Toward the end of the night, the novices are beaten with nettles, made to pull up pegs near a fire with their teeth, and have their fingers twisted in long bows. Although formalized hazing occurs on this one night only, older boys can come and torment the novices throughout the initiation period. They may tell a novice to call for his mother, then beat him when he does so, telling him he's a man now and shouldn't need to call her. Sometimes they explicitly warn him against further familiarity with mother and stress the keeping of initiation rituals secret from women. Direct instruction rarely goes further than this, but there can be no doubt that the novice understands the moral lessons presented to him in this manner. All boys are aware of the respect and avoidance rules of adult status long before their initiation, and hazing helps to make them realize that the rules now apply to them.

Traditional ceremonies of emergence from seclusion involve several cycles of cleansing, blessing, anointing, and feasting. Most significant is the anointing of the boy's forehead with white earth by the father, who promises to "respect" the boy (i.e., to refrain from beating him) and commands the initiate to respect him in turn. Underlying this ritual is the assumption that, morally, the boy is now a finished product. Having learned the correct rules of behavior through the instruction and chastisement of his parents, he is thought to have no further need of the physical punishment used as a teaching method for children. In our opinion, the majority of Nyansongo boys accept the moral trust of their fathers with great solemnity. Fathers whose sons were particularly delinquent in their preinitiation behavior entertain the hope that initiation will have made them "sensible" enough to behave properly when put on their own, although there is some cynicism about this under contemporary circumstances.

The difference between boys' and girls' initiation sheds some light on the meaning and function of the male rite. The girl is accompanied to the genital operation by her mother and secluded in her mother's house; the boy is kept apart from his parents from the time of his leaving the house to be circumcised to his emergence several weeks later. The girl is held down during the genital operation, while the boy must stand to face the knife alone. The girl is confined to her mother's house during seclusion; the boy's seclusion in a special house involves going out to meet others for adventures in hunting and theft. In short, initiation encourages boys to be self-reliant, to do without parental support, to endure hardship unflinchingly, to cooperate with related agemates, and to venture forth with weapons. There is no such encouragement for girls, and this is congruent with the fact that the girl leaves her mother's house, not at initiation but at marriage, five or six years later, when she will be transformed from *enyaroka,* "a circumcised thing," to *omosubaati,* a young married woman. Initiation, however, is the only formal change of residence and status for the young male, who moves permanently from his mother's house to his own hut nearby and becomes *omomura,* "young man," which he continues to be after marriage, until his son is circumcised and he becomes *omogaka,* "elder." The emphasis in female initiation is on sexual stimulation, while in male initiation, sexual avoidance and respect for parents are stressed. In augmenting and manipulating her sexual attractiveness in postinitiation years, the girl becomes increasingly inconsiderate of her parents' wishes and commands. The initiated boy, however, is more respectful and obedient than he was as the footloose roughneck of the pastures. While they are not pleased with the girl's misbehavior during adolescence, parents do not consider it unnatural nor try to correct it more than is necessary to assure a legitimate marriage. "If she is bad, let her husband beat her," Nyansongo adults say of the unmarried girl, adding that once she is initiated it is not the place of the parents to punish her. The boy's behavior continues to be the concern of his parents, for he never moves away from their homestead, and physical punishment by the father is replaced by economic and supernatural sanctions after his initiation. The parental concept of initiation as a moral finishing school for boys and the lack of such a concept for girls thus appears to be related to the patrilocality of Nyansongo marriage.

After initiation, the boy assumes adult responsibilities. In the past he joined other warriors in the cattle-villages for defense of the herds and raiding other groups. Nowadays, after a few years he usually goes off to work on the tea plantations or in the city. When he is home he helps his father build houses and mend fences, and occasionally he supervises the herding of his uncircumcised brothers. Living in a separate hut within the homestead, he eats food cooked by his mother and brought to him by younger children. His relations with his mother become more distant although still affectionate. In the past it was mandatory for a boy to give his mother a goat before entering her house after initiation, but this custom is rarely practiced nowadays. In any event, he may not enter the cooking and sleeping area of her house and must avoid obscene language or any mention of sex in her presence. His sex life is now private as far as his parents are concerned. They make no mention of the girls he brings to his house, and no longer punish him for participation in sexual relations. His father expects great deference and obedience from him when he is home and financial contributions when he is working away from home.

While young initiated boys usually have stiff, formal relations with their parents, they tend to spend a good deal of their time with boys of the same age, usually from the same neighborhood or community. If they were circumcised in the same year, regardless of whether or not they shared a seclusion hut, such boys are *abakiare* (sing. *omokiare*), "pals," and this means they can hurl obscene insults at each other and deride each other without offense being taken. In a sense, the pal relationship is the mirror image of the father-son relationship; all conditions are reversed. Whereas the son is bound to his father by kinship and economic obligations, nothing ties him to his pal except shared ephemeral interests. While he must respect his father, he can jokingly but sharply insult his pal. Sex is a forbidden topic for discussion with the father but is foremost with the pal. Pals cooperate in seducing girls together in their youth, but the permanence of their relationship depends on their actual kin and residential relationships to each other. Regardless of whether the specific relationship in continued, the pattern of contrast between intergenerational relations and peer relations becomes solidified in the postinitiation period and perpetuated throughout the life of the Nyansongo male.

BIBLIOGRAPHY

LeVine, Robert A. Omoriori: smeller of witches. *Natural History*, 1958, **67**, 142–147.

———. An attempt to change the Gusii initiation cycle. *Man*, 1959*a*, **59**, 117–120.

———. Gusii sex offenses: a study in social control. *American Anthropologist*, 1959*b*, **61**, 965–990.

———. The internalization of political values in stateless societies. *Human Organization*, 1960*a*, **19**, 51–58.

———. The role of the family in authority systems: a cross-cultural application of stimulus-generalization theory. *Behavioral Science*, 1960*b*, **5**, 291–296.

———. Wealth and power in Gusiiland. In P. J. Bohannon (Ed.), *Markets in Africa*. Evanston, Ill.: Northwestern University Press, 1962*a*.

———. Witchcraft and co-wife proximity in southwestern Kenya. *Ethnology*, 1962*b*, **1**, 39–45.

———. Witchcraft and sorcery in a Gusii community. In J. Middleton and E. Winter (Eds.), *Witchcraft and Sorcery in East Africa*. London: Routledge, Kegan, Paul, in press.

———, and LeVine, Barbara B. Studying child rearing and personality development in an East African community. In *Anthropology in Africa Today*, Annals of the New York Academy of Sciences, 1962.

———, and Sangree, Walter H. The diffusion of age-group organization in East Africa: a controlled comparison. *Africa*, 1962, **32**, 97–110.

Mayer, Philip. The lineage principle in Gusii society. *International African Institute Memorandum 24*. London: Oxford University Press, 1949.

———. Privileged obstruction of marriage rites among the Gusii. *Africa*, 1950*a*, **20**, 113–125.

———. Gusii bridewealth, law and custom. *The Rhodes-Livingstone Papers Number 18*, London: Oxford University Press, 1950*b*.

———. The joking of pals in Gusii age-sets. *African Studies*, 1951*a*, **10**, 27–41.

———. Two studies in applied anthropology in Kenya. *Colonial Research Studies*, *No. 3*. London: His Majesty's Stationery Office, 1951*b*.

———. Gusii initiation ceremonies. *Journal of the Royal Anthropological Institute*, 1953*a*, **83**, 9–36.

———. Ekeigoroigoro: a Gusii rite of passage. *Man*, 1953*b*, **53**, 3–6.

———. Witches. Inaugural Lecture, Rhodes University, Grahamstown, South Africa, 1954.

Wagner, G. *The Bantu of North Kavirondo*. London: Oxford University Press, 1949.

The Rājpūts

of Khalapur, India

❆
❆
❆
❆
❆
❆

Leigh Minturn

John T. Hitchcock

Contents

About the Authors

Leigh Minturn obtained her Ph.D. in social psychology from the Social Relations Department of Radcliffe College and Harvard University. At the time of her participation in the project she was a research associate of the Psychology Department of Cornell University. She was unmarried at the time and arranged to work at one of the field stations of the Cornell India Project, a project under the direction of Morris Opler of the Anthropology and Sociology Department of Cornell. This arrangement enabled her to take advantage of the housing and facilities of the field station and to utilize material gathered by the other investigators.

Leigh Minturn was assisted in her field work by Gurdeep Jaspal, who acted as her interpreter and recorded the behavior observations of the children. Gurdeep Jaspal received her B.S. from Women's Christian College in Dehra Dun and her M.A. in sociology from Luchnow University. As co-worker and interpreter, she assisted not only in the interpretation of language but also in an understanding of Rājpūt culture.

John Hitchcock, a Ph.D. in anthropology from Cornell University, was field director of the project during the time that the research was in progress. He was working on a study of the political life in Khalapur.

John Hitchcock was assisted by Sri Shyam Narain Singh, who served as a co-worker and interpreter. The latter's unstinting assistance, sense of humor, and affection for the Rājpūts of Khalapur were of uncalculable value. Patricia J. Hitchcock also helped her husband in collecting data and greatly lightened the burdens of administration.

John Gumperz gave valuable linguistic assistance to the project. S. C. Dube and Mrs. Leela Dube helped by making available field notes on aspects of Khalapur life not studied by either of the authors.

Both authors wish to express their deepest appreciation and affection to the people of Khalapur, and particularly to the Rājpūts of Khalapur, who are the subject of this article. We wish to thank them for their kindness, patience, and hospitality. This is their story; we sincerely hope that we have told it well.

Leigh Minturn is a member of the Department of Psychology at the University of Illinois. John Hitchcock is a member of the Department of Anthropology and Sociology at the University of California at Los Angeles.

Part I

BY JOHN T. HITCHCOCK AND LEIGH MINTURN

The Ethnographic Background

❧
❧
❧
❧
❧
❧

Chapter 1

The Setting

South of the Himalayas, the great mountain chain which forms a natural boundary between India and countries to the north, lies a vast alluvial plain. It is watered by the broad, slow-moving Ganges and its tributaries. The region is very fertile and its western half—most of it now a part of the state of Uttar Pradesh—was the cradle of Indian classical civilization. Khalapur, one of the many thousands of villages in Uttar Pradesh, lies between the Ganges and its large tributary river Jumna. The village is about 90 miles north of Delhi and is so close to the Himalayas that the foothills and snow-covered peaks are visible on clear days (see map 1).

The climate is monsoonal, and a hot, wet summer is followed by a comfortably warm winter and a very hot, dry spring. In April or early May, after the winter crops have been harvested, a scorching wind

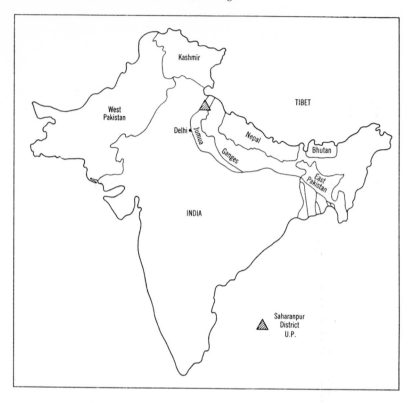

Map 1.

from the western desert begins to blow. It is ladened with dust picked up from the barren fields. The atmosphere becomes yellow and opaque and dust is everywhere. Small twisters sometimes whirl across the plain, and occasional dust storms blacken the sky and lower the visibility to a few hundred yards. In the heat of the day, temperatures rise to 110° F or higher.

Violent thunder and hail storms often precede the summer monsoon by a month or more. These harbingers of the longer and steadier rains are called the "little monsoon" and sometimes cause severe damage to any grain which is still standing in the fields. The heavy rain-bearing clouds of the true monsoon arrive toward the end of June, and from then until the end of September almost all of the 40-inch average yearly rainfall occurs. The usual pattern is rain for a day or two, followed by a few days of sunshine, with each succeeding day becoming increasingly humid and hot, so that the renewal of rain is a welcome relief. Throughout the monsoon insects are abundant, and toward the last of the period the incidence of malaria shows a marked rise.

With the retreat of the monsoon in September, temperatures gradually fall. By November and December nights are cool, and occasionally there may be a light frost. There is some rainfall during the winter, and during these wet periods the weather can be uncomfortably damp and chilly. On the whole, however, the winter months are moderate, clear, and very pleasant.

Culturally the region where Khalapur is located shows a strong Muslim tinge. It was part of Hindu kingdoms and empires until the thirteenth century, but after this, like much of North India, it fell under the sway of Islamic invaders from western Asia. Muslim rule reached a climax during the sixteenth and seventeenth centuries when most of North and Central India was united under the Islamic dynasty which produced Akbar, the great contemporary of Queen Elizabeth of England. Although Muslim power in North India suffered a gradual decline in the eighteenth century, descendants of Akbar continued to occupy their Delhi throne until 1858, about 50 years after the British had become the real power in this section of India. Like most villages in the area, Khalapur shows many evidences of this prolonged Muslim and west Asian contact. The custom of purdah, or seclusion of women, which the high status village families observed probably was taken over from the Muslims. A Hindu temple was recently built in Khalapur, but prior to this the most prominent religious structure was a large domed memorial to a Muslim saint. Hindustani, the language of the villagers, is a blend derived from Sanskrit, Arabic, and Persian. Prior to the adoption of a different script after independence, the schoolchildren learned a Persian form of writing, and most official records also were maintained in this script. Nearly 400, or approximately 8% of Khalapur's population, are followers of Islam, and their number includes some of the landowning families.

The center of Muslim and west Asian influence in the neighborhood of Khalapur is Bhudana, a town of some 25,000. Once an important seat of Muslim provincial rule, it lies about 4 miles northeast of the village and today houses a world-famous center of Islamic learning.

The headquarters city of Khalapur's administrative district is Saharanpur, a large manufacturing and railway center. Villagers sometimes are required to travel there in their dealings with the government, but most often they go to Bhudana, which besides being an important religious center is also the headquarters town for the district subdivision (*tahsil*) in which Khalapur is situated. Here the villagers find such government facilities as law courts, a land-revenue collection office, a dispensary, and a police station. A hard-surfaced road and a major railway pass north and south through Bhudana. Going north by bus or rail one can travel to Saharanpur (some 36 miles distant) and to other major cities of northern Uttar Pradesh and the Punjab. Traveling south 12 miles one comes to Muzaffarnagar, the headquarters city of the adjoining district, and four or five hours later to Delhi. Many people from Khalapur travel frequently within a radius of 100 miles. Although there are many women who have not seen large cities, most of the men have visited a number of them.

Two decades ago a sugar mill was constructed in Bhudana, and at the same time another was built on the railway about 8 miles to the south. Both mills process and purchase cane grown in the village and together have brought a considerable increase in prosperity to the landowners of the area. Another factor of great economic importance is the Ganges Canal. A branch flows near Bhudana, and two distributaries carry water to Khalapur and make it possible to irrigate almost two thirds of the village land.

Approaching Khalapur along the Bhudana road, one passes lines of creaking bullock carts carrying loads of sugar cane stalks to the Bhudana mill. The drivers sit on the yoke and urge on the straining bullocks by making loud popping noises with their tongues. The carts are accompanied by clouds of dust. Occasionally a returning cart bumps past, with a jingling from bells on the necks of its trotting bullocks. It may carry small purchases made in the Bhudana bazaars or sometimes a veiled wife who has been met at the station after a visit to her parents. The few cyclists, most of them with a cloth market bag dangling from their handle bars, hug the narrow, unrutted strip along the edge of the road.

The road enters the fields of Khalapur long before one can see the village. The fields are separated by earth ridges or irrigation ditches, and in many of them one can see farmers at work. Some are guiding a light wooden plow behind their team of bullocks, shouting at them, goading them with a stick, or twisting their tails. In a cane field a man is cutting down the tall, reddish stalks of the standing crop while another strips off the leaves and tops. A number of men move through the fields with huge loads of fodder on their heads. They have bundled cane leaves, grass, or grain into large cloths which they balance with a bamboo staff carried across their shoulders. The burdened farmers are following the network of paths leading through the fields to the village. They move smoothly, with the characteristic hip-swinging jog of persons who carry heavy loads on their heads.

About half a mile from the village, the road passes beside a large mango grove. Monkeys chatter from the dark green leaves. A group of women with heads and faces covered by their white saris walk in the shadows. They carry brass trays and have come to make offerings at a small, conical shrine erected to honor a male ancestor of their family.

After leaving the grove, the road passes between a group of white-plastered buildings. They house, respectively, the cooperative seed store, the Cornell Project, and the new high school. The high school is large and impressive. It was begun about four years ago, soon after India became independent, and some buildings are still in the process of construction. There are classrooms, a boys' dormitory, an office, a kitchen, a diesel-driven irrigation well, and a fenced plant nursery.

A few hundred yards straight ahead, the village itself can be seen. It is a very large village, with a population of slightly over 5000. Its houses are partly hidden in the many trees which have been planted to provide shade. The closest buildings are strung out for a quarter of a mile along the edge of a stream. They are of all sizes and shapes and closely packed together. Greyish, sun-baked adobe alternates with white-washed brick. The tall, curving spire of the Hindu temple rises above the trees. Behind it in the center of the village one can glimpse some of the taller buildings. They rest on an extensive mound, built up from the brick, broken pottery, and tumbled-down adobe that have accumulated during the many centuries people have been living on the site.

Where the Bhudana road enters the village, the brook widens to form a fair-sized pond. Some years ago those who entered the village here had to wade, but now there is a brick and masonry bridge built by the sugar mill. It is wide enough for bullock carts to cross. Yet even with the new bridge, when the rains have been heavy, one sometimes has to wade, for the brook floods its banks and covers the approaches. The pond is used for watering cattle and on hot days farmers or their sons bring the family buffaloes there to be splashed and cooled. In a field just beside the bridge, there is a clump of trees where herd boys often play hookey while their cattle rest in the shade.

The village neighborhood nearest the bridge is the one in which this study was made. The men's houses of some families face the brook and are separated from it only by a small field and a road. Houses and cattle compounds of other families form the easternmost end of the village and in this direction straggle out from the densely packed site into a sandy, barren field. The neighborhood is marked off from adjoining portions of the village site by tortuous lanes and footpaths.

Although Khalapur's jumble of cattle compounds, angled-mud and brick walls, new houses, tumbled-down houses, and narrow, muddy lanes appear patternless, in the minds of the villagers the site where their houses are situated has many clear divisions. There are seven subdivisions, called *paṭṭī* (see map 2). These divisions hark back to a system of revenue collection no longer in use. There is also division into smaller neighborhoods, some reflecting recent revenue divisions, others the boundaries made by lanes and paths. In some of these neighborhoods. washermen, goldsmiths, leatherworkers, sweepers, or Brāhmaṇ priests predominate. In the neighborhood in which this research was done (see map 3) the people all are members of the Rājpūt landowning class. Only after long acquaintance would an order growing out of caste and kinship begin to emerge.

People who are not well acquainted with Indian society think of the caste system as a fivefold division consisting of Brāhmaṇs, or priests; Kṣatriya, or warrior-rulers; Vaiśya, or merchants; Śūdra, or artisans, servants, and laborers; and Untouchables, or persons who are regarded, somewhat paradoxically, as being entirely outside the system. If such divisions ever really existed and served as a means of organizing so-

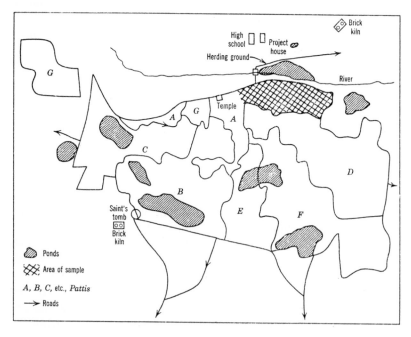

Map 2. Living site of village of Khalapur showing paṭṭī *divisions.*

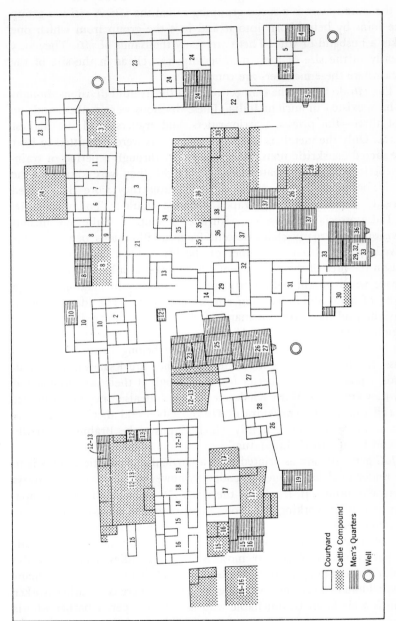

Map 3. Neighborhood of study.

Courtyard
Cattle Compound
Men's Quarters
Well

213

ciety, it was many centuries ago in ancient India. Today the basic unit of the caste system is a social grouping called the *jāti*. A *jāti* is a group one joins by being born into it and it is the group from which one takes a husband or wife. There are many thousands of *jāti*. They vary greatly in the size of their membership, as well as in the size of the area where these members are concentrated.

The *jāti* do have some connection with the fivefold divisions thought to have existed in ancient India. These divisions were ranked, and the first three—the priests, warrior-rulers, and traders—had the highest status. Only the members of these three orders were permitted to hear the sacred Sanskritic texts. Since they went through a period of training believed to give greater spiritual insight, they were known as the "twice-born," and as a mark of their status they wore the "sacred thread," a circlet of string draped over one shoulder. Today most *jāti* in India associate themselves with one or another of the five ancient divisions, and many claim descent from an illustrious personage believed to have been a member of the "twice-born" orders. For this reason the idea of the five ancient classes serves as a kind of organizing device which might help a stranger to a locality in making a rough order of many unfamiliar *jāti* encountered there. The idea is not always helpful, however, for many of the lines are blurred. In a given region or village there are those who claim they belong to one class while their neighbors claim they actually belong to another, lower class. In Khalapur the goldsmiths claim they are Kṣatriya. The landlords, whose claims are better founded, laugh at their pretensions and say they are Śūdra. Many Khalapur villagers are also uncertain whether to call the washerman Śūdra or Untouchable, and there is also some doubt about whether a family which claims to be Brāhmaṇ actually should be accorded this status.

Jāti generally are associated with a particular occupation. This is to be understood as a general tendency, however, for there are always many exceptions. In Khalapur there is a *jāti* whose traditional occupation is leather working, but none of its members will skin dead cows or make leather articles. Everywhere in India agriculture is an occupation in which members of any *jāti* are apt to be engaged either full or part time. In Khalapur most Brāhmaṇ families depend for the major portion of their living on farming, and there are some Brahmans who seldom or never perform priestly duties. There is a leather worker who is a clerk, an Untouchable who is a shopkeeper, a barber who is a minor government official, and another who has become a tailor. The list could be extended, but these examples are sufficient to show that the relation between *jāti* and occupation, while viable in a very general way, is one that in any particular case is very likely to break down. This is especially true in the many villages like Khalapur where new occupations are being introduced as old ones become unprofitable.

Members of a *jāti* usually are found in a number of neighboring villages. Some *jāti* have little political solidarity; others are fairly cohesive and may be represented by strong legislative and judicial councils. *Jāti* are characterized by shared customs regarding such matters as religious belief, dress, and food, and often these customs serve to differentiate them clearly from other *jāti* in the locality.

Relations between the members of different *jāti* are subject to a number of rules which operate in contexts having to do with sex, touch, eating, drinking, and smoking. Most of these rules give expression to the idea that some *jāti* are capable of polluting others. The Brahman, who has the highest ritual status, can be polluted by various forms of contact with others but is not himself polluting. That is why Brahmans are in demand as cooks or as water dispensers. In general, *jāti* having the same or nearly equal ritual status can eat and drink together without fear of pollution. More and more restrictions apply as the ritual distance between *jāti* increases. The rules are complex and variable. A few from Khalapur will serve as illustration.

When Rājpūt landowners of the village are sitting together, they all smoke, using the same hookah stem, although they suck the smoke through their fists so that their lips never touch it. If a Brahman were to join them, he either would be offered a separate pipe, or every time it was his turn to smoke, a different stem would be inserted in the hookah base. He would also be offered the place of honor, at the head of the cot, and Rājpūts would move away to make room for him. If the Brahman were orthodox and his Rājpūt host wished to give him some cooked food, he would offer him only food that had been cooked in clarified butter or *ghī*. Food boiled in water would be unsuitable. If a goldsmith came to join the group, he would be offered a place on one of the cots; but a water carrier or potter would be expected to squat on the ground some distance away from all the others. This is the situation in only one social context, however. If a Brāhmaṇ and an Untouchable were working together in the fields, as they often must, the rules of distance and even of touch would not be observed, at least by the younger men. The Brāhmaṇ and the Untouchable would tug together on the rope used to lash the load of sugar cane to the bullock cart. The Untouchable also would help hoist a load of fodder to the Brāhmaṇ's head and in doing so would touch the portion of the Brāhmaṇ's clothing in which it was wrapped. In neither case would the Brāhmaṇ feel he had been polluted.

The relations between *jāti* have never been static and are always in the process of redefinition. Upward mobility, although a slow process, always has been possible. In each region the path of mobility is defined by the customs of those who are highest in the ritual hierarchy. If the local Brāhmaṇs refrain from eating meat and drinking wine, then a *jāti* that adopts these customs lays claim to a higher status. If it is a small group within a *jāti*, its members strengthen their claim if they refuse to intermarry with those who refuse to make the change. In time the new group will become a separate *jāti* and will feel somewhat superior to the group of which they were formerly a part. Another path to higher status, and one which also has brought about a proliferation of *jāti*, is the idea that some occupations are polluting. Making wine or working in leather are occupations which preclude rise in ritual status. Groups that give up these traditional occupations in time separate themselves from those that do not. The nonleather working *jāti* in Khalapur is a case in point.

The twin concepts of *dharma* and *karma* are of basic importance in the ideology of the caste system. The concept of *dharma* has a wealth of connotation but a core meaning is "a way of life appropriate to one's status." Quite simply it means that a potter should be a good potter and should follow the rules governing relations between himself and other members of his *jāti*, and of other *jāti*. By doing this he wins for himself, by the workings of *karma*, a better station in his next reincarnation. He is a potter in this life because of deeds he performed or failed to perform in his last. Besides accounting for one's status, the concept of *karma* accounts for the good or ill fortune one may suffer during the course of one's life. Although the full meaning of these terms is untranslateable *dharma* connotes duty and *karma* connotes fate. Both ideas have religious sanction.

Landowners, who were the subject of this study, belong to a *jāti* claiming descent from the ancient warrior-rulers, or Kṣatriya. Throughout Indian history there have been groups of kinsmen who at various times and places have achieved political power. Generally these kinsmen were organized as patrilineal clans, that is, they were groups of men, all of whom believed that they could trace their descent, if they went back far enough in the male line, to a single man who was the progenitor of them all. The children of these men, both boys and girls, were also members of the clan. The wives, however, were not, for it was the rule that they had to come from a different clan. A powerful clan generally validated its claim to the status of Kṣatriya by securing a genealogy. In the genealogy the descent of all members of the clan was traced back to one or another of the semidivine Kṣatriya heroes whose lives and deeds were recorded in the ancient Sanskritic epic literature. And when members sought wives, they picked them from among clans that had established similar claim.

As a matter of historical fact, it is probable that many of the clans which achieved this status are descended from invading tribes that entered India from Central Asia prior to the arrival of the Muslims. Later, during the period of Muslim invasions, many of these clans, now calling themselves Rājpūts, or "sons of princes," fled to Rājputāna, a dry and forbidding mountainous area to the southwest of Khalapur. The kingdoms they established there were in existence throughout the Muslim period and continued as seats of Rājpūt courtly splendor until India became independent. These kingdoms were a center for resistance to Muslim rule, and the heroism and derring-do of Rājpūt groups and individuals today are an important part of folk tradition throughout India.

Some Rājpūt clans, or portions of them, after offering fierce resistance to various Muslim armies—tales of these exploits are also part of widespread folk tradition—drifted north or south into the mountainous regions of Central India or the Himalayas, and some may have gone as far as Nepal. Many of them remained in North India. Most were landholders, and many were persons of considerable local influence. Muslim rule varied in extent and efficiency, and sometimes a group of Rājpūt clansmen were able to set up petty kingdoms in opposition to the reigning power. There were also Rājpūts who took important posts in the Muslim central administration or who ruled provinces as subordinate chiefs.

It is impossible to say with any certainty from which area the Rājpūt clan to which the landowners of Khalapur belong came. According to their own traditions, they moved into North India from Central India sometime during the early centuries of Muslim rule. Their numbers swelled, and as opportunity arose they took up land in northwest India, in the region where the Ganges and Jumna debouch onto the plains. Calculations based on their genealogy suggest that Khalapur, as part of a general southward movement, was taken by a clansman and his sons sometime during the fifteenth century. The descendants of this man, with their wives and children, now number over 2000. No other caste group in Khalapur is as large by half, and the few other caste groups claiming equal length of residence in the village say they came as retainers of the founding family. Today the Rājpūts hold over 90% of the land and regard the village as theirs by right of conquest and 400 years of possession.

Following the usual pattern, the Khalapur Rājpūts and the other members of the clan to which they belong—many of whom have a similar position in a large number of surrounding villages—validate their claim to Kṣatriya status by means of a written genealogy. This is kept by a professional genealogist whose family has served in such a capacity for generations. His home is in Rājputāna, so that he forms a link with the heartland of Rājpūt tradition. He journeys once a year to visit various clan villages and keeps a careful record of births and deaths in the male line. His charts trace the male line back through a succession of historical and mythical figures to Rāma, the divine hero of the epic poem Rāmāyaṇa.

Things the Rājpūts say about themselves show how they tend to create their self-image in terms of their putative and, to a degree, their actual past. For instance, during a conversation in the village it was remarked that a highly placed official was a good administrator. "And why not?" replied a Rājpūt man. "He is a Rājpūt. He belongs to a ruling race, and they have been doing this work since time immemorial."

Because the Rājpūts do consider themselves potential rulers and warriors, their self-image causes many of them to have markedly ambivalent feelings about their present occupation of farming. It is proper that they should own the land but not proper that they should have to farm it themselves. It is regarded as demeaning to become so heavily involved in farm work that one does not have ample leisure.

The fact that many Rājpūts now are more heavily engaged in the actual day to day routine of field work than they believe they should be is the result of the interplay of many factors over the course of centuries. To meet Rājpūt status requirements, the ideal farm is one where there is enough land so that it can support the family owning it as well as the tenants and field workers who will work it. The founder of Khalapur must have had such a farm. As time went on, however, a number of developments made it more difficult for all of his descendants to maintain a similar economic base. It is a rule among the Rājpūts in this section of India that all the sons have a right to an equal portion of the parental estate. It can easily be seen that seven or eight grandsons who partition the estate are going to be less well off than their grandfather as far as the size of holding is concerned. One way the constantly increasing pressure on the land was taken care of was by putting more and more untilled land under the plow. Another was to move off and capture or found another village. But there was a limit to both processes, and in time many Rājpūts were much more like small farmers than they were like landlords.

The pressures bringing this state of affairs about were eased somewhat by the fact that up until the latter part of the nineteenth century the predominant economic pattern was subsistence farming, with a heavy emphasis on herding. There were common lands on which cows and buffaloes could graze and many Khalapur farms apparently were large enough to support tenants and laborers, as well as the landlord family, if all the latter wanted was grain enough to eat, and sufficient reserve to carry it through a bad season.

By the end of the nineteenth century the pattern of farming had changed. The British established more peaceful conditions, and the railways connected the farms of Khalapur and other villages with local and world markets. It became easier and more profitable to sell grain and, later, sugar cane for money. And there were desirable things to use the money for—chaff cutters, which greatly eased the burden of farming, kerosene lanterns, water pumps, mill-made cloth, and many other items of the new economy. Farming not only became more profitable but also such developments as the Ganges irrigation system made it more secure. This, and many other factors which made life a little easier, increased the population. Hence, at the same time that land was becoming more valuable and difficult to obtain, there was also a much greater population pressure being exerted on it.

Among the things that happened in Khalapur as a result of these developments was that the common grazing lands, with the support of newly instituted British legal machinery, were parceled out among individual Rājpūt families. Some families began to work their lands hard in order to obtain a surplus of grain, which they sold for money or to other farmers who had had bad luck or who were not as industrious. When those who had borrowed grain defaulted, legal machinery and its supporting police power were brought into play, and the debtors forfeited a number of rights in their land. They thus became tenants to Rājpūts who were better able than they to take advantage of the changing times. As a result, just prior to independence, a few Rājpūt families in Khalapur—and this pattern was repeated in many other North Indian villages—held a high proportion of the land. They were true landlords. Many other Rājpūts, on the other hand, were either small farmers or were small farmers and also tenants of other Rājpūts. After independence a law was passed in Uttar Pradesh (U.P. Zamindari Abolition and Land Reforms Act, 1952) which reduced the holdings of the larger landlords. Furthermore, tenancy was made illegal. Since there were few farmers left who were wealthy enough to hire all the labor needed to work their farms—a fact which was partly the result of increasing labor costs—many had to begin doing much more actual field work. In the sample studied, there was one Rājpūt farmer who had to learn to plow when he was over 40.

It may be said, in summary, that with regard to field work many Rājpūts in Khalapur and elsewhere in the region, during much of their history at least, seem to have been able to maintain a kind of genteel poverty. In the late nineteenth and early twentieth centuries this became easier for a few and more difficult for many; and today it is difficult for almost all.

In view of their self-image it is understandable that Rājpūts who now are having to do farm work, especially plowing—which is felt to be particularly inappropriate—have a desire to justify and explain the situation. Such justification sometimes takes the form of a mythico-historical tale, as when a Rājpūt told how the Muslim conquerors gave small parcels of their land back to the Rājpūts so "that the regular contact with cows and bullocks would make them patient and calm and they would become like the earth they plowed, all broken and scattered." "Rājpūts," he added, "should be given their own work and that work is not beating the hind end of a bullock."

In line with their image of themselves as warriors, the Rājpūts think they are larger, stronger, and more virile than other caste groups in the village. When one Rājpūt father heard that a primary school teacher was taking the students outside the village to participate in an athletic event, he said, "I am not going to let my son participate. Rājpūt boys do not have to participate in athletics. They are already stronger than other castes."

When discussing the new universal adult franchise, another man complained, "These are critical times because now we have to fight (the members of other castes) with the vote. Formerly it meant something that we were bigger and stronger men."

It is a traditional Rājpūt value to be touchy on points of honor and unafraid to pursue a quarrel to the point of violence when prestige is at stake. This behavior still characterizes the Khalapur Rājpūt. During the course of the study there was a killing as a result of a Rājpūt quarrel, and a number of fights with staffs occurred. The Rājpūt is not, however, quick to take his revenge. He may plot for years to avenge an insult to himself or his family. Outward hostility should not be shown while retribution is being planned lest the enemy be forewarned. As one Rājpūt put it, "We like to wait until our enemy reaches the edge of the pond and then we push him in."

Throughout the nineteenth century the Rājpūts of Khalapur and their kinsmen in nearby villages were a problem to the British because of their cattle thieving, their marauding for grain (especially when crops were poor), and their unremitting resistance to revenue collectors. The police and some government officials still speak of Khalapur as a criminal village, and some of the village Rājpūts still do augment their incomes through cattle theft.

The past century, however, marked a considerable lessening of both thieving from outside the village and feuding within it. With regard to the former, this is partly because the times no longer called for such activity. The increased irrigation and communication facilities greatly decreased the incidence of crop failure and famine. And with regard to the latter, more adequate police protection, the establishment of courts, and the founding of schools tended to mitigate the reliance of sheer force as a method of settling disputes. Also significant is the fact that the village has been strongly affected during the past few decades by two reforming leaders.

In the twenties and thirties a young Rājpūt named Pṛthvi Singh inaugurated a period of cooperative endeavor during which many projects and reforms were carried out. Under the leadership of this man, a temple and a school for teaching Sanskrit and religion were built. It was a time, the villagers say, "when the cart was running nicely." The major stimulus accounting for the success of this leader was the Ārya Samāj movement, which both molded Pṛthvi Singh and prepared the people to accept his programs. This movement, which was a revivalistic and reform movement within Hinduism, was strongly ascetic in emphasis.

Many of its teachings, although present in Hinduism, ran counter to Rājpūt values, and one of the effects of Pṛthvi Singh's teachings was to strengthen values which previously had not been emphasized so strongly within his group. The Ārya Samāj opposed meat eating, drinking, opium eating, and smoking, and many Rājpūt men gave up these practices. Despite Pṛthvi Singh's influence, most Rājpūts now smoke, many drink and eat meat, and some eat opium. But it is partly a reflection of his strengthening of the ascetic; Brāhmanical strand in Hinduism that many feel they must justify indulgence in terms of their warrior heritage.

Although Pṛthvi Singh sometimes was authoritarian and used force when crossed, his conciliatory methods, concern for the village as a whole, and a desire to minimize external and internal conflict are the traits for which he is most remembered. He gave the villagers—and the Rājpūts in particular—a new conception of their own potentialities and in many ways laid the foundations on which the reform leader who is now the village's key figure was able to build.

This second leader, though a Rājpūt, comes from outside the village. He was able to channel the enthusiasm for India's independence into support for building the new high school, of which he is now the principal. He also is the medium through which the influence of the Congress Party, the party of Nehru and Gandhi, reaches the village.

At present, then, the Rājpūts are a people whose values are undergoing change. One still finds allegiance to old Rājpūt values, and there are many powerful men in the village who exemplify them. These values, however, have been countered to some extent by more peaceful conditions and by outside movements from which two very influential leaders derived much of their authority.

If answering quickly and without thinking, a Rājpūt will say that Rājpūts everywhere are members of the same *jāti*. Difficulties arise, however, as soon as there is a problem of marriage. To limit the discussion just to the region around Khalapur, there are some groups of kinsmen calling themselves Rājpūt whom the Rājpūts of Khalapur regard as upstarts. Occasionally a Rājpūt from the village has taken a wife from one of these groups, but it has always led to much criticism and, in the past, often to a refusal to share the hookah with the remiss caste brother. These groups as yet have not been able to validate their claims to true Kṣatriya status. There are other groups who are accorded the status of Kṣatriya, but who are not wholly acceptable as marriage partners because the Kṣatriya hero from whom they claim descent is regarded as slightly inferior. But in actual fact this objection seems to be of much less importance than the former objection, and, practically speaking, the *jāti* of the Rājpūts of Khalapur includes their own clan and the members of any recognized Kṣatriya clan close enough for intermarriage. These considerations localize the *jāti* of the Khalapur Rājpūts in an area with a radius of about 100 miles, an area which includes some ten or more acceptable clans.

Almost all North Indian villages are composed of persons belonging to a number of *jāti*. In Khalapur some 30 are represented. They vary among themselves in the extent and definition of their social organization. The Rājpūts in Khalapur, for example, are clearly and explicitly a portion of one of the clans in their *jāti*. They always have lived in the village, and only a few outsiders have ever been able to obtain any of the land. The members of other *jāti* in the village, with the exception of the Brāhmaṇs and perhaps a few others, have moved to the village recently, taking the place of others who have left. Few own land and hence do not have one of the basic prerequisites of high status. They know their *jāti*, but their relation to other kinsmen within it, or to illustrious mythical ancestors, is not recorded or defined with any precision, partly perhaps because they have never owned much land. We will speak of all *jāti* segments in Khalapur as "caste groups" regardless of their varying types of social organization.

The Rājpūts and the other caste groups of Khalapur form a complex web of economic interdependence. Each Rājpūt family is dependent for services on families belonging to nine other caste groups, and these families in turn are dependent on the Rājpūt families they serve for most of their food. Water carriers and sweepers come to a Rājpūt house every day, the former to bring the daily water supply—a task of special importance, for wives cannot leave the courtyard—and the latter to clean the latrines or carry off refuse, a job which only an Untouchable can do. Every family, in addition, is served by a carpenter, blacksmith, barber, potter, washerman, and leatherworker. Carpenters and blacksmiths make and repair agricultural implements; barbers shave, cut hair and fingernails, and play a key role on ceremonial occasions; potters make a large variety of clay pots and other utensils, including the jugs in which water is carried and stored; the washerman washes clothing and bedding; sweepers make cow dung cakes and carry away refuse, and the women also act as midwives. The leatherworker removes dead cattle and supplies his clientele with a few simple leather articles, such as a whiplash and parts of the bullocks' harnesses.

Each family also has a Brāhmaṇ priest who assists on ceremonial occasions. Some priests, as noted earlier, have given up their traditional role and obtain a living from their land. Only a few priests in the village devote all of their time to ritual matters. These are the Brāhmaṇs who know how to read and write and how to conduct the marriage ceremonies. The remainder of the priests divide their time between their farms and the ritual needs of their clientele, the majority of whom are Rājpūts. Today priests are called less often than they were in the past. A major reason for this was the Ārya Samāj movement. It had an antipriest bias and taught that each family head was himself capable of carrying out any religious rites which were necessary. The coming of the schools also weakened the position of the Brāhmaṇs, who in the past were prime repositories of whatever learning was found in Khalapur. These developments have made an increasing number of Rājpūt families reluctant to give the full traditional payment to their Brāhmaṇ priest. The priests, in response to these changes, have shown an increasing tendency to give up their traditional calling. And were it not for the fact that the women are much more conservative religiously than the men, it would seem that the decline in the functional importance of the Brāhmaṇ would be even more marked. An index of women's greater conservatism in ritual matters is the fact that, unlike most men, they will bathe and wash their hair if they inadvertently come into contact with an Untouchable.

Part of the payment for services performed by members of these nine caste groups consists of a number of customary benefits provided by each of the families served. These include such things as food on many ceremonial occasions throughout the year and the right to cut fodder and fuel from the fields. The major payment consists of grain. These payments are made twice a year, after each of the two food-grain harvests.

This system of economic interdependence, known in its widest ramifications as the *jajmānī* system, is based on mutual need and lack of economic alternatives. It reflects a subsistence rather than a money economy, and many of the strains to which it now is subject arise both from the growing number of different jobs which are open to villagers and to the increasing use of money. Aside from mutual need, the controls in such an economic system are diffuse and cultural, although on occasion sanctions involving either deprivation or force are involved. Culturally the relations between a Rājpūt family and its servants are colored by a semifeudal ideal. The Rājpūt is supposed to be paternal and benevolent, the servant loyal and deferential. The relation between servant families and Rājpūt families should persist generation after generation, like the relations between nobility and their retainers.

Actual relations, of course, have always been a compromise between allegiance to these ideals and many other competing interests. One finds that Rājpūts who are dissatisfied with a servant will shift to another. This usually is not a severe economic blow, for servants work for many Rājpūt families and for members of other castes as well. There have been instances, too, when a servant left a Rājpūt with whom he was dissatisfied. The system always apparently has shown fluidity of this kind. Animosities sometimes are aroused, however, and then it is the Rājpūt who tends to have the upper hand. A powerful Rājpūt family has been known to drive a disliked servant family from the village. The servant families are not always totally without recourse, especially when less powerful Rājpūt families are involved. A servant may be able to obtain the support of neighboring Rājpūts with whom he is on good terms, or he may be able to secure the intercession of a powerful village leader with a just bias. Some caste groups also have considerable solidarity and, in addition, are purveying a service which the Rājpūts would find it hard to do without. This is true of the sweepers, who on a number of occasions have been able to bring quite a lot of pressure to bear by threatening to "strike." However, a caste group like the water carriers has a much weaker bargaining position. They are a comparatively small group, and now that pumps are being set up in many of the women's houses, a "strike" by them is becoming a less effective weapon. There have been occasions when the interests of all the serving castes were seriously involved, and as a group they were able to present a strong front. By this method on one recent occasion they were able to secure an adjustment of the biannual grain payment.

Some of the caste groups formerly a part of this system either have dropped out entirely or are in the process of dropping out. This is true of the weavers and tailors, and there are other groups, such as the potters, blacksmiths, and carpenters, who are tending to shift to an item by item cash payment basis, and at the same time are tending to work for anyone who will pay them.

The labor of almost all of the caste groups in the village is drawn on at the time of the two yearly harvests. For many of them, the portion of the harvest earned in this way is a vital supplement to what often is a meager yearly income. One of the most important of all caste groups to the Rājpūts is the group of Untouchables who no longer work in leather. They represent about 13% of the total population, and many of them are hired as manual laborers. They plow, make adobe houses and walls, do the difficult spading required when the sugar cane is young, gather fodder and chop it up in the chaff cutter, and perform a number of other services requiring hard manual labor. Occasionally they also obtain a field or two from the Rājpūts on a sharecrop basis.

Members of the many other caste groups in the village work at a variety of occupations. Some do much the same work as the Untouchable laborers. Some, including an Untouchable, run the 30 small shops which supply such items as spices, sweets, cigarettes, needles and thread, vegetables and grain. Some work as herders, a few make grain or popcorn, press oil-bearing seeds, or act as bearers and messengers. There are goldsmiths and shoemakers and some who take wadded cotton and fluff it so that it can be used for restuffing pillows, quilts, and mattresses. There are two doctors, one following traditional Hindu, the other traditional Muslim methods. There are also a postman and a number of school teachers. There is such a variety of occupations, in short, that there is someone in the village to meet almost every need.

Although not part of the village caste system, one of the most interesting aspects of village life are the individuals and groups continually moving in and out, many of them following their traditional *jāti* occupations. There are bangle and cloth sellers, a group of colorful, wandering metalsmiths, and a similar group which makes wooden combs. There are Muslim cattle dealers and a man who cuts and trims the bullocks' tails, keeping the hair for making brushes. There are wandering minstrels and occasionally a troupe to put on one of the traditional folk dramas. There is a man who cleans out ear wax, another who doctors sore eyes. There is an exhibitor of a five-legged cow, and a man who makes a living by pretending to be something he isn't —usually a mailman with a fake telegram or letter.

✹

✹

✹

Chapter 2

Social Organization

In the Rājpūt neighborhood selected for study, the largest and most conspicuous houses are some of the men's quarters. Each of these buildings consists of a platform 4 to 6 feet in height surrounded by a retaining wall of brick. One ascends the platform by a series of steps. The height of these platforms lifts the occupants above the dust of the lane, keeps the cows, buffaloes, pigs, and dogs from intruding, and gives the occupants a good vantage point from which to see what is going on, at the same time lending them a certain eminence. Many of these platforms are shaded by trees. When not working, the men of the family and their friends sit together on these platforms, smoking the hookah.

At the far end of the platform, farthest from the lane, there is an open arcade, or porch, which is roofed. Behind the porch is a larger room with two or more doors, entering onto the porch. On each side of this large central room are smaller rooms used for storage. A chaff cutter often is kept in one of them.

The men of the family sleep in these quarters, and when not in the fields they spend most of their time here. During the rains or in the winter when it is cold, they sleep in the large central room, completely swathed in a cotton sheet and resembling white cocoons. Otherwise they sleep in the same fashion outside on the platform. Prosperous families build their men's quarters of brick. Poorer families have quarters of mud, often consisting of nothing more than a small hut without a platform or any extra rooms. The size and type of construction of these houses are an indication of the wealth and status of the family. Bullocks often are tethered in front, and their number, breed and condition also are a reflection of family status (see figure 1).

The other important part of the Rājpūt dwelling unit is the women's house. Since the Rājpūts have adopted the custom of purdah, the women must be carefully shielded from the gaze of the casual passerby. The women's life, therefore, goes on within enclosed courtyards, which may be located behind the men's quarters, across the street from them, or some distance away. The women's rooms open into the courtyard, never to the outside. These windowless rooms serve as storerooms and as bedrooms when it is cold or rainy (see figures 2 and 3). Most of the time household activities go on in the sunny open courtyard. The principal articles of furniture is the all-purpose string cot, which is used for sleeping, sitting, baby-parking, grain drying, and dish draining. The floor of the courtyard is surfaced with a mixture of water and cow dung renewed every seventh day. When dry, this forms a hard, dustless, water-absorbent surface which is very functional. There is

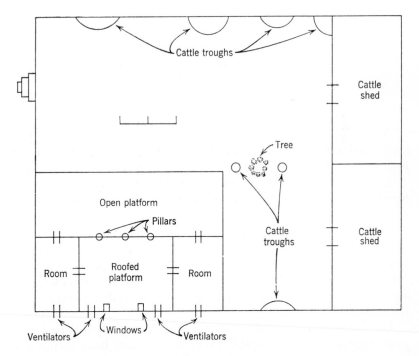

Figure 1. Men's platform and cattle compound.

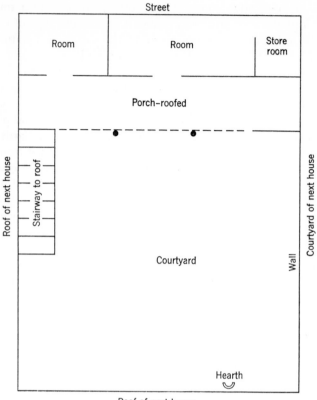

Figure 2. Typical women's house.

usually a drain in one corner of the courtyard through which wash and bath water can funnel out into the street. The drain is sometimes used as a woman's and children's toilet, although some of the women's houses have a small walled-off portion which is used as a latrine and is cleaned daily by the sweeper.

Like the men's quarters, the houses of the women vary in size and materials used in their construction. Most families have women's quarters which, in part at least, are constructed of mud-plastered adobe.

Part of the courtyard may be set aside as a cattle compound for cows and buffaloes. As added protection against theft, bullocks also may be tethered here at night.

The family cooking is done on the hearth, a mud, U-shaped fireplace about a foot square and 6 inches high, usually built against one of the courtyard walls. The cooking pot rests on the mud support, and cow dung or wood is burned beneath it. The hearth is given a new coating of cow-dung paste every morning in order to make it ritually pure for the day's cooking.

All but a few of the village lanes are narrow and wind in and out among the houses in a seemingly endless maze. They are often bordered on each side by the high, windowless walls of the women's houses. A second village thoroughfare is formed by the flat rooftops of the women's houses. Several courtyards may be connected in this way, and staircases, ladders, or footholds in the courtyard walls make these roof-top "lanes" readily accessible. They are often used by the women for interhouse visiting when they do not want to be seen by the men.

The everyday clothing of the villagers is simple. The men wear a *dhotī*, a garment which consists of a length of cotton cloth wound about the waist, pulled between the legs, and tucked in. The upper garment is a cotton shirt. Many of the younger men now wear the "Gandhi cap" made popular by the Congress party, although the more traditional turban is still very common among the older men. When working in the fields, the men often drape their heads in a folded

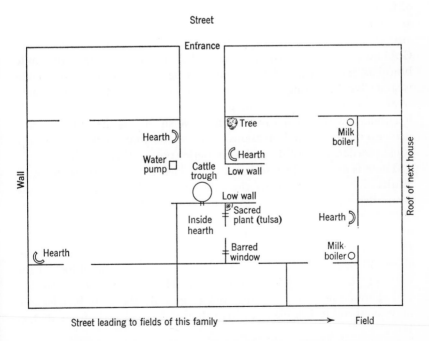

Figure 3. Large double courtyard of two extended families.

square of heavy cotton cloth. This is the cloth used to tie up the bundle of fodder they carry back to the village when they return. Schoolboys often wear cotton pajamas with long tailed shirts, which are not tucked in. Some schoolboys also wear leather oxfords or sneakers, although most men wear leather slippers made in the village. All members of the family go barefoot around the house, and many put shoes on only when they go to town or attend ceremonies. Many men carry a long bamboo staff, which serves for driving cattle, carrying loads, and as a weapon. These staffs are sometimes bound with heavy wire and studded with nailheads. Some even have a metal-spear point. When altered in these ways, they are lethal weapons.

Styles in women's clothing are more varied. They wear saris, loose baggy pants, and sometimes long, full skirts. All three of these are worn with cotton shirts, fashioned like the men's shirts and worn with the shirt tail out. When wearing saris, the women drape the end over their heads; when wearing skirts or pants, they also wear a head cloth, for adult women must keep their heads covered as part of the custom of seclusion. Most of the elder women wear tight, black, cotton pants, a style of clothing which has not gone out of fashion. The women are fond of jewelry and all except widows wear it. The most common type of bracelets are glass bangle bracelets, which fit tightly over the wrist and must be broken to be replaced. Silver and imitation gold bracelets are less common but are also worn, particularly for festive occasions. Gold nose plugs are worn in one nostril. Gold earrings and silver ankle bracelets, hair clips, and belts may also be worn. All married women wear a silver "wedding ring" on the second toe of each foot. The women wear their hair in one braid down the back. The braid is usually lengthened with a string braid. Black eye shadow is the only common makeup on ceremonial occasions. Some of the younger women use lipstick, powder, nailpolish, and a cosmetic spot on their foreheads.

There is no special winter outfit. Sleeveless sweaters may be worn by adults of both sexes during the cold weather. The villagers may also wrap themselves in shawls or in padded cotton bed quilts to keep warm.

Children of both sexes wear simple cotton shirts until they are 4 or 5 years old. Usually this shirt is their only clothing. In cold weather they may wear cotton pants, padded jackets and bonnets, and rubber shoes. Their hair is cut close to the head except for a small lock at the back of the head which distinguishes Hindu men from Muslims throughout their lives. At this young age only the glass bangles and occasional ankle bracelets distinguish the dress of girls from that of boys.

The center of life for Rājpūt women and children is the courtyard, as the men's house platform is for the men and adolescent boys. In the courtyard the women sleep, take care of the children, and cook for the men and boys who come into the house for meals. The women who share a courtyard usually are the wives of brothers, their young children, their unmarried daughters, married sons' wives, and their sons' children, two or three generations related in the male line. Of 36 families studied, 28 were extended families; 9 with two generations, 16 with three generations, and 3 with four generations. Eight of the families consisted of a husband and wife and their children, but in all but one of these cases the nuclear family had split off from a larger household within the last few years or had recently lost a senior parent.

The average number of women and children per courtyard in the extended families is about seven—three of whom are adult women. (Twelve households had two adult women, 5 had three, 5 had one, and 6 had over four.) On the average they feed five or six men and adolescent boys. There are two large double courtyards, one of which has a total of 25 mouths to feed—with six adult women to do the cooking.

There are fewer men's dwellings, for related men from neighboring courtyards may share the same platform. Four brothers, for example, with wives living in three different courtyards shared the same sleeping quarters and spent many leisure hours together there.

After the courtyard and men's house groups, a third important social unit is the joint farm family—the group of males who own and work land in common, plus their wives and children. Although the ideal pattern is for brothers to continue to own and operate the father's farm after death, in practice brothers usually divide the land. The joint farm family, therefore, tends to be a smaller social unit than either of the two groups who share a sleeping area.

Lack of congruence among the membership of these three social units is often the result of quarrels between the wives confined in the same courtyard, a situation leading them to exaggerate small annoyances. The easiest and least disruptive solution of such tension is for the conjugal family to build a separate hearth within the courtyard. Sometimes, however, the courtyard is divided into separate compartments by building a wall down the center, or a completely new women's dwelling unit may be constructed. The men may continue to share the same men's dwelling and may continue to own land in common.

At the beginning of a cycle, a courtyard may consist of a mother and father, a married son and his wife and children. They eat together at a common hearth and share a single women's house. The men and adolescent boys share a single men's dwelling, own land in common, and work together in the fields. Ideally the young sons will marry and continue to live with their parents and raise their children in the common courtyard. The ideal, however, is seldom realized for long.

The first break in the pattern usually comes when a man and his wife decide to have a separate hearth. This step may be taken with overt good nature and willingness on both sides and may be rationalized on the basis of convenience. More frequently, however, as mentioned above, it results from tension and quarrels among the women. It is a weakness of the ideal extended family that fractionating is inevitable but not accepted emotionally.

Although not always regarded as desirable, separate hearths are no real threat to the extended family, for basic patterns of authority and of property allocation and economic cooperation are not broken. The older women still have charge of giving out the daily ration of food. The father runs the farm. Further division, however, is a threat to basic patterns. The division of the courtyard into two sections by building a wall, or the setting up of a new household, entails the division of property: the milk cattle, furniture, and food. Now the mother-in-law no longer has to be approached for the daily ration, and the young wife has a source of pocket money, for she can sell small amounts of grain at the store and spend the money for bangles without permission of her mother-in-law.* At this stage, however, land remains intact.

Further divisions may be more drastic. The land may be divided up among brothers, or brothers and cousins, at the death of the older generation, thus setting up separate joint farm families. The men may still share a dwelling and their wives a courtyard, but the economy of each family is now distinct.

Fathers remain active authority figures until they are very old men. As the sons get older, they take over more and more of the hard work in the fields. The father devotes most of his time to managerial jobs, such as driving the cane to the mill, collecting payments, attending marriages, keeping abreast of village affairs, and making purchases in town, although many continue to help in the fields at peak work seasons like harvest and planting. As they grow older, the sons also take more and more responsibility for their individual families, with the father having a say in how the farm as a whole is managed and guiding

---

* During the fieldworkers' stay, two major family quarrels occurred which resulted in the division of the courtyard of the women's houses. In one case the personality of one of the wives was the direct cause. In another courtyard, a low wall had been built, and although the children and cousins conversed over it, the adult women were not on speaking terms. This division was the reflection of a fight between an uncle and his nephew.

the group in its political and marriage relations. The father never really retires as long as he is sane and able and the family stays together. Rather, his activities and authority are gradually curtailed.

If brothers stay together at the death of their father, the eldest son usually takes over the father's role. However, if a father thinks that one of his younger sons is more capable than the eldest, he may delegate authority to him, or an older brother may voluntarily relinquish his authority to a younger brother who is more capable or more suited to the role. Some Rājpūt families cannot afford to educate the first son because his services are needed in the fields, but they will usually try to educate a younger son.

The rank of the wives within the courtyard depends on the relative authority of their husbands. The head woman may be very authoritarian in her treatment of her daughters-in-law and sisters-in-law. Probably the greatest conflict arises when an authoritarian sister-in-law takes over at the death of her husband's mother.

Since it is the extended family which is valued most highly, the primary emphasis is placed on the solidarity of this unit, and the nuclear-conjugal family relationship is ideally kept subservient. When quarrels arise, a man is supposed to side with his father and brothers rather than with his wife.

Most of the women who share a courtyard come from clans living in villages to the south and southeast of Khalapur and as brides are strangers to the village, although occasionally they may be related to their sister-in-law or come from the same village. In two cases in our sample, brothers married women who were sisters. Such marriages are considered desirable on the grounds that sisters should be able to live peacefully together. In both of these cases, however, the sisters fought bitterly. In the two other cases sisters married men of the same village subdivision, or *paṭṭī*, but of different lineages.

The life of a woman is surrounded by restrictions imposed by purdah. Women may visit neighbors, particularly if their houses connect with each other and they can go over the roofs unseen by men; but for visits to more distant neighbors they must wait for ceremonial occasions. Although ceremonies are quite frequent, the vast majority of the time must be spent in the courtyard. As a woman grows older, the restrictions of purdah are relaxed. The end of childbearing and the marriage of sons and daughters mark the increase of freedom, especially in the less strict, lower status families. The strictness with which purdah is observed varies not only with social status but also with education. Many young educated people are beginning to question the custom.

In a girl's childhood village, she and the men of her caste group generally belong to the same clan. Any sex relations would be incestuous, for men and women of the same clan regard each other as "brothers" and "sisters."

Even as widows who may not remarry, women usually remain permanent members of their husband's house. A young widow lives in the courtyard under the direction of her mother-in-law much as she did prior to her husband's death, and her husband's kinsmen have the responsibility of looking after her and her children and for arranging the children's marriages.

Some widows complain that they and their children are being cheated by their affinal kinsmen, and occasionally an older widow with maturing children who feels this way will wish to take over the management of her share of the estate. Unless all the husband's close kinsmen are dead, and even then on occasion, this arrangement can lead to tension. There is little difficulty if her sons are responsible and are able to do the field work. But if they are still too young, she must get others to farm the land for her, usually on a sharecrop basis. This means that she herself often must leave the seclusion of purdah and go about the village alone. Even if she is a fairly old woman, this always stimulates gossip, and her affinal relatives are annoyed because it damages the family reputation. More serious than this, however, is their fear that she may allow herself to be duped and lose some of the land. This fear is greatly strengthened if the widow has no sons. Statutory law now permits a daughter to inherit village land, which means in effect that her husband, a member of a different clan, must join the village community or, at the very least, see to the management of some of its land. Regardless of its legality, such a situation is a very serious breach of village customary law, which has always held that no wife, daughter, or daughter's husband could inherit land. This rule was a very important one and still is adhered to with deep emotion. It was a means of excluding persons who were not members of the village landowning caste group, and in large part it accounts for the fact that this group has been able to maintain almost complete control of the Khalapur land through all the vicissitudes of the past 400 years. Thus it is not surprising that a widow with an only daughter who insisted on managing her own estate and let it out on shares was severely beaten by her husband's kinsmen.

There is much variation in the treatment of widows, and this is a consideration much in the minds of most fathers when they are selecting a husband for their daughters. A number of village families have well-founded reputations for dealing justly with their widows and for taking good care of them and their children. In one family of the sample there was an elderly widow who was treated with great deference and who in the large women's house had become something of a matriarch.

Few widows return to the homes of their parents permanently, although they may often go there on visits. The reason stressed by informants is that the widow's leaving would indicate her husband's family was negligent in their responsibility or too poor to take care of her. If she has sons, the husband's family will wish to have them grow up as part of their kingroup, and they will want the mother to be there to take care of them. There is a strong feeling, too, that a wife's first loyalty is to her husband's house and that it should be lifelong.

When a woman returns to her own village to visit her parents, she does not observe purdah and can go about freely. As a general rule, high-status families in North India do not marry within the same village. The custom partly reflects and is supported by a situation such as is found in Khalapur, where most of the landowners belong to the same clan. Since daughters of the Rājpūt families are regarded by the men of their home villages as "sisters," with whom a union would be incestuous, purdah restrictions are felt to be unnecessary. A young bride usually returns home for a protracted visit after the first months or weeks of marriage and spends about half of the first eight years of her married life in her mother's home, sometimes visiting for a year or more at a time. She is treated as a special guest with no household duties. She spends her time visiting friends, chatting, singing, and playing games. A servant in her mother-in-law's courtyard, in her village of birth she is a vacationing guest. The emotional ties of women to their parental homes are so strong that they persist throughout life, no matter how happy the adjustment to the husband's village may be. Even grandmothers return to their villages and sometimes take their grandchildren home on visits.

Land is the most valuable property which passes from father to son, jewelry the most valuable which passes from mother to daughter. A man cannot sell his wife's jewelry without incurring strong social disapproval, so that this property usually remains in the female line. Much of the extensive dowry which a wife brings to her husband's house is turned over to the mother-in-law who distributes it among the members of the household or includes it in the dowries of her own daughters.

Virtually all the cash assets of the Rājpūt family are obtained through the sale of sugar cane and wheat. Most of this is sold by the men and they keep the accounts. Grain that is not sold at the threshing floor is stored in the women's quarters for family consumption. The surplus of this grain provides the women with a small independent source of income. They use it to barter for items at the village store and sell small quantities for cash, using the money to buy cloth or bangles from the traveling merchants. Women do not usually consult their husbands before making such purchases. The women may also have some control over the cash obtained from the larger sales. Cash is usually stored in the courtyard, for safety's sake, and some men go to their wives when they want money. One woman, whose husband had recently died, said:

> My husband would never buy anything—even if it cost only two pice—without asking me. I had all the money and everything in my hand.

Ordinarily a woman would not refuse money to her husband. We did see one mother refuse to give her son money to buy a new shirt on the grounds that she had recently made him one and that he did not need another. The fact that he was a grown man, married, and the father of two children did not abate her firmness.

The children are not given a regular allowance. It seems to be permissible for them to take grain from the house and use it to buy things at the village shops. Usually they ask their mothers for this, although they may take it without asking. This is not really regarded by the women as stealing. One woman stated that her little girl often took grain without asking her, and she knew about it but said nothing. We observed only one instance of acknowledged theft of this sort. A boy had taken several rupees from his mother without her knowledge, and she was very upset about it. We never heard of children taking anything from their aunts or from other people within the house. It seems to be a characteristic of the Indian household that each member (except for the youngest daughters-in-law, who must ask their mothers-in-law for everything) is fairly autonomous in petty cash matters.

There is relatively little property belonging specifically to the children. They have exclusive use of their own clothes, although these clothes may be the hand-me-downs of an older sibling. Toys are few. Children may possess a cloth ball or toy, a doll, a hoop, a toy cart, but they do not have the great accumulation of toys which causes so many property disputes in American homes. Property ownership is not an important matter for children.

On either side of the courtyard walls live families who are apt to be closely related—members of the same lineage who trace descent from a common male relative. In the area studied there were six lineages represented, 20 of all the families from one lineage, 5 from another (other 4 families of lineage not in sample), 4 from another (other 4 members not in sample), the remaining 4 from three other lineages.

Khalapur as a whole consists of 34 different Rājpūt lineages. With one exception, all are descended through the male line from the Rājpūt founder of the village.

The members of a lineage tend to live in a contiguous area forming a neighborhood closely connected by kinship ties. Ideally the lineage should be close knit, cooperative, and loyal. It is the group to which members should be able to turn for financial assistance and help on ceremonial occasions, as well as for political backing and physical help in quarrels. Some lineages approach this kind of unity. Others are torn by dissention. Over the past two decades, quarreling among the members of one lineage, part of which is in the sample, had led to two deaths, and the opposing factions seldom speak to one another and do not participate in each other's ceremonies.

Each of the seven *paṭṭī* or subdivisions of Khalapur is inhabited by a different number of different castes, but in each the Rājpūts are the most numerous. In four of the *paṭṭī*, the Rājpūt lineages all trace descent from a single man. The descent patterns in the other three are more complex, but generally it is true that Rājpūts in each of the seven are more closely related to one another than they are to the Rājpūts in the others. The fields of the *paṭṭī* members lie for the most part on the side of the village nearest to their *paṭṭī*. The families in this study belonged to the *paṭṭī* with the largest population, including 602 Rājpūts representing ten lineages. The sample consists of 24 of these families forming a neighborhood unit within it.

Marriage invitations are concentrated within the *paṭṭī*, and occasional informal councils are held at the *paṭṭī* level. The voluntary consolidation of land holdings was begun on a *paṭṭī* basis, and *paṭṭī* are the units for a number of Community Development Programs.* Rivalry is often expressed in *paṭṭī* terms, and claims are made that one *paṭṭī* has more prestige or power than another. But although *paṭṭī* are perceived as units, and although their members sometimes cooperate, there are numerous occasions when *paṭṭī* lines are crossed by ties of friendship, neighborliness, political alliance, and other forms of cooperation.

Beyond the *paṭṭī*, for the men especially, the permanent social unit of the most importance is the Rājpūt village caste group. Although this

---

* The Community Development Projects were conceived of and partly implemented by the government of India under the First Year Plan. They were designed to further rural community development in such fields as agriculture, education, public health, and public works. Khalapur is a member of a Community Development Project Block which was inaugurated in the fall of 1953. Its effects had not yet been strongly felt in the village when this study was being made.

group often is divided into opposing units, all the Rājpūts of Khalapur nevertheless have a sense of community. It resides in their knowledge of a shared ancestry and in common loyalty to many traditional forms of behavior. It is symbolized by such tangible evidences of common endeavor as the village itself, the religious school specializing in the teaching of Sanskrit and the traditional Hindu way of life, the Hindu temple, and, most recently, the new high school. It also is seen in their desire for political unity even in the face of frequent failure to achieve it, and in this sphere it is symbolized by the caste group councils which meet to decide on matters of importance to the group as a whole. The village is the stage on which most Rājpūts act out their lives, and the caste group is the audience whose approval or disapproval touches one of the most sensitive of all sources of self-esteem.

Outside Khalapur the Rājpūts share a sense of close kinship with landowning members of their clan in a number of neighboring villages. These ties to surrounding and dominant groups are an important source of psychological security. There is much friendly visiting and ceremonial participation among the Rājpūts of these villages, and occasionally elders from each village meet together to decide on matters of common concern.

Almost every Rājpūt has one or more very close friends outside of his own immediate kin group. Often these friendships have grown up in boyhood and frequently begin in school. A few are said to be rooted in youthful homosexual experience. No ritual marks the entrance into such a relationship, though the institution of ritual sisterhood is found among Rājpūt women. These friendships result, however, in the mutual expectations of loyalty and support characteristic of ritual brotherhood elsewhere in the world. Once established, there is an opportunity to give ritual expression to a relationship of this kind during a portion of the marriage ceremony. One of its hallmarks is the approval with which each party to such a friendship regularly speaks of the other, a trait which is very noticeable in the general prevalence of critical gossip. It also is seen clearly during a serious illness, when the friendship is expressed in deep concern and tender ministrations, such as cradling the sick man's head, or traveling and staying with him if a trip to the hospital is necessary.

These friendships are among agemates, and they cut across neighborhood, *paṭṭī*, and even village lines. One of the best known examples was between two elderly men, one from Khalapur and the other from a Rājpūt village some miles away. The two were so supportive that they were jokingly said to be "the grandfather of each other." Occasionally such friendships even cut across caste group lines, though they never existed, so far as we know, where ritual distance between two men was very great.

Friendship groupings of lesser intensity exist among many of the men who live near one another. These cliques draw their membership from different lineages, *paṭṭī*, and caste groups. Men who belong to them often cooperate in field work, assist in arranging and putting on marriages, and borrow and lend implements to one another. The most conspicuous are groups of elderly men who meet together almost daily in various sections of the village to smoke the hookah and talk. These groupings also tend to be age graded.

Aside from clan members generally and an occasional very close friend, the ties outside the village which are most important for the men are those with relatives by marriage. As is usually the case in societies where great stress is placed on the male line of descent, there are warm and friendly feelings for the men of the mother's family, especially her brother. When a Rājpūt is in such serious trouble that he wishes to leave his family and village, he is very apt to go to his mother's brother. This happened when a young Rājpūt was being subjected to much social pressure because of a romantic attachment between him and a lower caste girl. Easy, friendly relations are also common between a man and his wife's father and brothers. The husband usually accompanies his wife when she goes to visit her parents and returns to pick her up. On both occasions he often stays for a day or more, and most men look forward to these visits. Although the husband is treated with some deference by his wife's people, for they are culturally defined as somewhat lower than he in status—a fact which may account for some of his pleasure—the general tone of the relationship is comradely and without strain.

In village life, formal associations are almost nil. There was a statutory village court prior to independence, and now there is both a court and a legislative and executive council. Neither, however, includes more than a few of the Rājpūt caste group. Some Rājpūts have been active from time to time in local or national political parties. They have attended meetings and campaigned for their candidate in Khalapur and other villages. A few are members of government-sponsored organizations, such as the village cooperative and the sugar cane growers' union. But even when all organizations are taken together, only a small fraction of the Rājpūt population is involved. Social life comprising lineage kinsmen, friends, neighbors, and affinal relatives is by far the more significant aspect of most Rājpūts' lives.

A woman's deepest emotional ties for many years tend to be outside her husband's village with her own parental village. Inside the village a woman's ties are primarily with other women of her husband's family, who are invited to the family ceremonies and who are likely to live nearby. Women also visit neighbors from other lineages, and individual women may make efforts to visit friends from their own village who also have married into the village. Some women form friendships which are ritualized by the ceremonial exchange of a head cloth and the sharing of a meal from a common bowl.

The adult Rājpūt men and women in Khalapur have a dramatically different life and clearly differentiated status and roles. Men control the economic welfare of the family. Although women can own property legally, it is very difficult for them to support themselves and manage their own legal affairs. A woman could only attempt to do this through her sons or brothers. Although women may vote, they cannot attend political meetings or speeches to inform themselves. Men have the power to veto any suggestions made by the women. Women are discouraged from getting more than a rudimentary education (see Chapter 11). Most men wish to keep their wives in purdah, although it is a luxury, since to do this the men must do without their help in the fields and hire servants to help them run the house. The men control even the physical movements of their wives. A man, if angry or inconsiderate, may beat his wife, refuse to try and provide medical care, and may even prevent or cut short her visits to her own home, or refuse to call her back from a visit to her own family.

The subordinate status of women is further emphasized by the custom that women must crouch on the floor and pull their saris over their faces when in the presence of their husband or any man older than their husband. This custom is so pervasive that young women usually cover their faces even in front of older low-caste serving men. This is a sign of respect for the man's status. Covering the face in the presence of one's husband is also a sign of respect for his mother, another of the customs designed to protect the mother-son relationship from being threatened by the son's attachment to his wife. When a man has entered the house for his meal, he will quickly retire into a room or behind the wall of his hearth. The women are then free to move about their business quietly. His meal will usually be served to him by his mother, if she is living, or by an adult sister. Only if some woman of his own family is not present or does not wish to assert her prerogative will his wife be allowed to serve his meal.

Because of this custom, the men always announce their presence with a warning cough before entering the household and when possible send a boy or the youngest male present on errands to the courtyard, since the younger the man, the fewer are the women who must keep purdah from him. When the eldest male enters, the entire court-yard is immobilizd until he has been safely attended. In nuclear families the wife usually does not cover her face before her husband but only because the man usually requests her not to continue this custom.

The symbols of woman's status inferiority are easy to perceive. The ameliorating factor in the status inequality of such a social organiza-tion, however, is the strength of the bonds which exist between mothers and sons and between sisters and brothers. Adult males are taught that they should be respectful and considerate to their mothers and be-cause of their early, prolonged intimate contact with her are influenced by her wishes. The mother feeds her son even after he is married and even has strong influence on his marital life. She runs the family as long as she wishes to assume the responsibility.

Ideally a man and his wife are not allowed to talk to each other in front of the older members of the family. Since the mother-in-law is virtually always present in the courtyard and the young wife cannot leave the courtyard, this means in effect that the young couple may converse only surreptitiously at night.

A husband is not supposed to show any open concern for his wife's welfare; this is the responsibility of his parents. If the wife is sick, the mother-in-law and father-in-law see that she goes to a doctor; if they do not, neither she nor her husband should complain. The villagers report one or two cases where a woman has remained childless for years and, despite the great importance of having children, has not seen a doctor because the husband was too shy to ask his negligent par-ents to take her.

The restrictions, imposed on husband and wife in the presence of others, particularly the mother-in-law, are to avoid jealousy and con-flict and to ensure that the extended family takes precedence in im-portance to the nuclear. The presence of five nuclear courtyards in the sample which have recently separated from the extended family may be an indication of a new trend in the adjustment to this problem or may simply represent an age-old pattern.

After the death of the mother-in-law, a woman can talk to her hus-band in the presence of her sisters-in-law. When her sons marry, she assumes a new and prestigeful role. She is now in charge of the young women and is released by virtue of her relative age from many of the restrictions of purdah. Age in the courtyard brings respect, and every bride can look forward to the day when she assumes this role. There are some women who in spite of purdah and the status inferiority of women become very powerful. In many ways it would seem as if in her young years a woman's relation to her husband is primarily sexual and procreative, and that with age and the death of his mother it may become more one of a companion or even an advisor.

The relationship between a brother and his sister or female cousins also seems warmer and less restrained than the marital one and is considered sacred. A sister, even after marriage, may sit with her face uncovered and converse freely with her male relatives. There are ceremonial days when the strength of this bond is publicly recognized. On Brother's Day sisters fast for the health of their brothers and receive a present of a few rupees from their brothers in return for these good wishes. This festival occurs shortly after the festival honoring a locally worshipped goddess. When the clay figure of the goddess, which has been plastered on the courtyard wall, is removed, a smaller figure of her brother is put up in her place.

✻
✻
✻

Chapter 3

Daily Routine

Life in Khalapur, as in any agricultural village, is paced to the slow and ever-recurring round of the seasons. By day life tends to move according to the sun and at night to the constellations. A man will raise his arm toward the sky and say he will meet you when the sun has risen that far. Or two men in the fields will argue over whether the star Sirius has risen high enough for it to be time to switch the flow of canal water from the field of one to the field of the other. Life also moves in the well-defined patterns of caste and ritual. A man must be asked three times before he will come to a wedding feast, and the last invitation must be delivered by the barber or some member of the family just prior to the beginning of the meal. But for all its measured toil and ritual patterning, one is impressed by the spirit, and sometimes the rough and raw vitality, with which Rājpūt living is suffused. Their greetings and laughter are loud and hearty, their friendship demonstrative. Brāhmaṇs by contrast seem much more distant and restrained. In physical type the Rājpūt men range from the spindly and small, or even washed out and apathetic, to those who show a tendency to be portly. Yet the dominant impression is of men who are robust, muscular, and fairly tall. Some, by any standards, are strikingly handsome. If they seem bigger than other caste groups in the village, no doubt it is partly because of their better diet, though it also has something to do with their confident presence and bearing. One cannot know them for long without sensing, unlikely as most of the props may be, that somehow they have acquired a tinge of the princely and medieval.

The village day begins before dawn when the temple priest blows his horn. This signal calls the sleeping villagers from their cots to start the day's work. How soon the call is answered depends on the morning's division of labor. In the courtyard, the daughter-in-law who is to make breakfast emerges before her sisters-in-law. Grandmother may decide that grain needs to be ground. Perhaps there is a calf to feed or milk to churn. These early morning tasks bring some women from their beds while the daughters and children of the house are still sleeping soundly.

In summer the men must get to the fields early and do the morning's work before the blazing sun drives them to a noonday siesta in the shade. On cold winter mornings they enjoy lingering in the warm quilts, going to work after the chill has lifted and the dust of the roads has become warm for bare feet.

But winter or summer, one by one the villagers arise, and, taking a small brass pot filled with water (the Indian version of toilet paper), they take care of elimination. The younger daughters-in-law use the courtyard's drain or latrine, if there is one; the children may use the streets. For everyone else, the fields are the "facilities." The men may go alone, the older women always in groups; but every gray dawn finds the fields filled with silent, white-cloaked figures performing the first task of the day.

The toilet completed, the women return to the courtyard, wash, and begin the day's work in earnest. Grandmother may go to her churning or grinding, or she may decide to rest and smoke hookah while she waits for breakfast. The hearth must be given its first purifying coat of mud each morning before it can be used. If the family eats breakfast, then the fire must be laid and unleavened bread cooked for all members of the hungry household, and the daughters-in-law whose turn it is to make breakfast have a few busy hours.

Gradually the children emerge from their beds, stumble sleepily into the street or to the drain, and return to wash their faces and huddle, shivering, around the hearth fire waiting for breakfast. If it is winter, they may gather brush and build a bonfire in the courtyard for added warmth. Some people drink only milk to break their fast; others eat a good breakfast. The men finish feeding and milking the cattle before they come into eat. Finally, when the men and children are out of the way, the women have their meal. Eating is a strictly private matter in the village. Each man eats either at his own hearth or men's quarters. Each woman takes her food into her room or into a corner of the courtyard where she can turn her back toward the other women. Children are fed when they demand food and may eat together or separately, depending on whether or not they get hungry at the same time. Since the family does not gather for a meal, the dining hour is not fixed but is a matter of individual convenience.

If an individual wishes to bathe, he uses water from a pot or pail. The women bathe in the courtyards behind screens of cots, placed on edge. The men bathe by the village wells. Both sexes remain clothed while bathing and, when finished, wrap clean dry clothes around themselves, dropping their wet clothes from underneath the fresh ones without ever exposing their bodies.

After breakfast the men leave for the fields or return to their quarters to smoke the hookah and talk. During the morning the women sweep the floor, gin cotton, spin or mend clothes. If there is a daughter to be married, they make things for the dowry. If a festival day is near, they may be busy plastering and whitewashing the house. There is always woman's work to do. The children go to the streets to play. The schoolboys collect their books, slates, and pencils, put them in bookbags or tie them in a rag, and start off in the general direction of school, where they will arrive sooner or later. The older boys who are not in school drive the village cattle across the bridge to the grove of trees by the side of the pond. Every morning several hundred cattle leave the village by this bridge, and every evening they return the same way.

By about 10 o'clock in the morning, when the school officially opens, most of the students have arrived. They settle themselves on the open sunny platform, and from then until noon they sit chanting their leslons, teasing the boys next to them, or just staring into space, to be jolted back to reality by a sharp reprimand from the master. The boys with the cattle have collected and quieted their herds and are playing hockey or *kabaḍḍī* under the shade of the trees. The younger children are playing less organized games in the streets or on a vacant men's quarters. The women start cooking lunch about this time, and in every courtyard a pot bubbles on the hearth. The men are off working in the fields unless it is the slack winter season, when they may be away arranging for a marriage, fighting a court case, or visiting in the village, discussing local politics.

Around noon, the task of feeding the men of the household demands attention. When work in the fields is light, the men come home to lunch; but if it is harvest or planting time, they prefer to have lunch carried out to them by an older daughter or son. The women pack rice, pulses, and unleavened bread into pots or tiffen carriers, tie them with a cloth, and balance them carefully on the head of a child and send him or her off on the long walk to the fields. The older men may come to the courtyard for their lunch, or it may be brought to them at the men's quarters by a daughter or son. The boys come home from school, and the herders, leaving a few of their number in charge of the cattle, also return for their noon meal. When the women have fed everyone and forced their reluctant sons back to school, or at least out of the house, they again snatch enough time from the day's routine to eat their own lunches.

Now the day is at its hottest. The sun beats down relentlessly. The heat shimmers over the fields and is reflected from the mud walls of the courtyards. Shadows are scanty and everywhere the villagers seek shade. The women huddle with their spinning or mending along the narrow shadow of a wall, shifting as the sun shifts. The men pull their cots under a tree on the men's quarters or under the roof of the rear sleeping quarters. The schoolboys crowd for seats under the trees; the herders abandon their games for conversation; and when they must start their cattle on the long walk to the fields, their pace is slow. In the fields the men leave their plows and squat in groups under a lone tree or rest in a mango grove and eat their lunches. The small children return to their homes or seek the shade of a friendly tree for their play, and their voices are muted. Even the dogs look for a cot to sleep under. In the summer work ceases entirely during the middle of the day. The men work in the fields before the dawn and after dark, and everyone takes a siesta during the middle of the day.

Around 4 o'clock in the afternoon the pace of work quickens again. The children start returning from school; some have chores to do, others return home only to throw down their books and run out to play. The women start preparing the evening meal. In the fields the men get ready to go home. At dusk, around 5 o'clock, the road to the village is once again a crowded thoroughfare. Men and boys carrying loads of fodder on their heads, men driving plows or bullock carts, an occasional youth on a bicycle, and from all directions the lowing, slow-moving cattle—all must filter once again back across the narrow bridge and into the village. This is the time of day so often described by Indian poets, when the dust from the hooves of the returning cattle catches the light of the setting sun and the ground dissolves into a yellow-red haze.

As night falls, the men and boys feed and water the cattle, the women prepare to feed their men again, and the children return from play to try teasing some dinners from busy mothers. The bats emerge from the rafters and become darting black shadows in the dying light. The cattle stamp restlessly and then become gradually quiet as they are fed.

Around 8, the men come into the courtyard for their evening meal. Once again the efforts of the women are concentrated on serving food to their men. Only when the men have left do the women eat their own dinners.

By now the oil or kerosene lanterns are lighted, making small yellow patches in the darkness of the courtyard. The women sit and gossip. If there is a good storyteller in the house, she may tell stories to the children or to the other women. The young daughters-in-law may play games or retire to corners to whisper about their husbands, their joys or disappointments in the home of their in-laws, or to reminisce about their own villages. In the men's quarters the men visit each other, smoke the hookah, and talk of farming or politics. Gradually the children drift off to bed, to be joined later by mother or an older sibling or cousin. One by one, in courtyard and men's quarters, the villagers climb into their cots, cover themselves from head to foot with quilts or sheets, and at last the village sleeps—but never completely. All night a few are stirring. A man slips into the courtyard to call his wife quietly from their children to a separate cot and then returns as silently to the men's quarters, careful not to disturb the occupants of the still cocoons. Another man gets up in the night to check the cattle. A mother stirs in response to the crying of her baby. And if the crops are nearing harvest time, the fields are full of silent sentinels guarding them against the thieves who prowl in darkness. After harvest, farmers plow their fields and the tinkle of bullock bells may be heard far into the night, for the moonlight is bright and cooler than the rays of the sun. In winter the night's stillness may be pierced by the barking of jackals, with an occasional answer from a vigilant watchdog. But these are only periodic interruptions of the silence—intermittent movements in the stillness —for it is night and the village may sleep until the horn of the priest calls it once again from slumber to meet the toil of a new day.

Chapter 4

Basic Economy

The village Rājpūts are landowners and farmers. All families in our sample own their own land and live on the produce of this land. If the family can afford it, they hire low-caste men and women to work in the fields. In such cases the Rājpūt men merely direct their servants, and their own work is slight. But in all except the wealthiest houses, the Rājpūt men do their own farming with the help of their sons and perhaps some servants. When a man's sons are grown, he retires and leaves the work of farming to them. Therefore wealthy men and older men are likely to have plenty of leisure.

The principal crops are wheat and sugar cane, both of which are cash crops, that is, they can be sold for money instead of being consumed or bartered. Cane is sold at the nearby sugar mills and provides the largest income, with wheat coming second. Maize, corn, rice, millet, cotton, hemp, barley, oats, peas, mustard, several kinds of fodder, and various pulses are also grown. Potatoes and other vegetables are both bought and grown.

The plowing is done by hitching the bullocks of the humpbacked Indian cattle to a simple wood and metal plow. During the principal harvests, the crops are transported from the field in bullock carts. The daily loads of fodder and grain are carried back by the men and boys on their heads. Both cows and water buffaloes are kept for milk.

The villagers harvest two major crops a year: the *khārif* crop, gathered in the fall, and the *rabī* crop, gathered in the spring. The fall crop includes maize, rice, several kinds of pulse, cotton, hemp, and some other minor produce. The spring harvest, which is called *rabī*, includes wheat, barley, oats, peas, and mustard. Sugar cane, considered to be a separate crop, is harvested in the late fall and early spring.

The lives of the farmers have a seasonal rhythm patterned around the needs and yields of their land. October and November are two of the busiest months of the year. Most of the *khārif* crop is harvested and the *rabī* crop planted. The men leave for the fields early in the morning and may work long into the night. Some of them actually live in the fields and have their food brought to them there. These months also mark the first of the cane harvest, and carts must be readied for trips to the sugar mills. Toward the middle of November, when the first of the winter rains are hoped for, work begins to slack off.

December, January, and February are comparatively easy months, the only work being occasional irrigation of the *rabī* crops, collection of fodder for the cattle, tillage of the fields in preparation for cane planting, and trips to the sugar mills. During their leisure hours the farmers are to be found sitting on the platforms of their men's quarters, smoking hookahs and visiting. Many marriages take place during the winter months, and the village is noisy with blaring bands. The sale of cane provides the villagers with money for minor luxuries and trips to visit relatives. February is one of the most beautiful times of the year. The mustard and peas are in flower and the wheat has tassled. In the fields and in the village, groups of men are seen sitting around a fire roasting peapods and wheat tassles for a between-meal snack.

By mid-March the tempo of work begins to increase. Some cane fields are still being harvested, others are being plowed, others planted; in still others the thin, dark green shoots of the new cane are being weeded. Some fields are being sown with the millet and cotton of the *khārif* crop, and preparations are being made for the fast approaching *rabī* harvest. On the men's platforms the older men roll strands of hemp between their palms to make the ropes which will soon be needed to tie the harvested crops. Implements are repaired, and arrangements are made for obtaining the necessary extra labor.

Harvesting is a period of intense activity. Rain and hail may fall, and it is important that the ripe crops be gathered promptly. Load after load of grain is hauled to the threshing floor, where it is stacked in high, rectangular piles. For threshing, grain is spread on the ground and bullocks are driven round and round in a circle over it, their plodding feet separating the grain from the stalks. The grain is then winnowed from the chaff, a process hastened by the hot wind which is already beginning to blow. Some of the threshing is done by the women who beat the stalks on the courtyard floor or pound them with sticks.

The period following the *rabī* harvest marks another brief respite from field work and is another season when marriages are held.

The monsoon rains, which begin the middle of July, begin a period when long days must again be spent in the fields. Much of the *khārif* crop is sown at this time, and the paddy fields must be manured. During July the paddy is transplanted, and the wheat fields are plowed again and again between the rains. Toward the end of August, the maize has reached the stage where it must be guarded from thieves and from marauding monkeys and deer. Thatched watchmen's huts are erected in the more distant fields.

In September, as the rains gradually cease, some of the rice and cotton and maize is harvested and the stalks of new cane are now so high that they must be tied together so that they will not blow over. The wheat fields are plowed more frequently, and by October, when the last of the *khārif* crop is being harvested, they are ready for sowing, and the yearly cycle is repeated.

During this yearly cycle there is never a time when there is no work to be done. If for no other reason, daily trips to the fields must be made to bring fodder to the cattle. During the winter months, however, there is comparatively little work. The three periods of peak activity occur during April and early May, when the *rabī* is harvested; during late June and July, when the *khārif* is planted; and from September to November, when the *khārif* is harvested and the *rabī* is planted.

Rājpūt women do not work in the fields, although the young girls and older women may pick cotton and the leaves of pulses, which are used as a vegetable. But once the grain is in the house, it is the job of the women to process it. After the threshing, the grain is dried by spreading it on cots in the courtyard. Each house has a small, metal-lined husking pit in the floor of the courtyard. The dried grain is put in this pit and pounded with a heavy, metal-capped stick. Finally, it is winnowed in hand-winnowing baskets. Ready for use, it is now stored in mud jars or mud-covered baskets (plastered over if it is to be kept for some time), which are kept inside the rooms of the house.

In general, the handling of food occupies a good proportion of the women's time. The principal diet is rice with a potato or vegetable curry, eaten with *rotī* and *ghī*. *Rotī* is the generic term for several kinds of round, unleavened bread (not unlike tortillas). *Ghī* is clarified butter made from curd and is used both for frying and for pouring over food. Both the rice and the curry are cooked over the hearth in large brass pots. The "breads" are first cooked in small, slightly concave pans, then put directly into the side of the hearth to puff, and finally stacked in a dish by the side of the fireplace. Whole spices are ground by placing them on a flat stone or board and crushing and pulverizing them with another stone. Unrefined brown sugar, called *gūr*, is also eaten and used in making various kinds of sweets. In the summertime, the women make vermicelli (thin spaghetti) from wheat flour by rolling it with their hands.

Milk, both from cows and buffaloes, is an important part of the diet. Men usually do the milking unless the cattle compound is within the women's quarters. The milk is boiled in large pots on a special hearth. Most of it goes into the making of *ghi* and curd, although boiled and sweetened milk is sometimes drunk.

Popcorn and sugar cane are popular between-meal snacks for both children and adults. Most of the children are very fond of popcorn, which they take themselves to one of the village shops to be popped. This is eaten without butter or salt. The children also eat quantities of sugar cane, particularly at the beginning of the cane season. We have seen children consume 6 feet of sugar cane during the course of a morning.

An interesting aspect of the division of labor between the sexes is caused by the fact that the women are vegetarians. Those Rājpūt men who like meat must get it and cook it themselves in the men's quarters because their women will neither touch it nor have it in the house. Some of the men keep chickens for eggs and meat.

The principal fuel for cooking is cow-dung cakes. The making of these cakes is one of the tasks usually performed by the low-caste sweeper women who daily clean latrines and sweep out the cattle compound but the Rājpūt women frequently make at least part of their own supply.

After food problems, the other major occupation of the women is the preparation of clothing. The cotton, harvested in September, is ginned by the women on small hand gins—a process which keeps them busy throughout October and into November. After ginning, it is taken to the mill to be fluffed, and then it must be hand rolled into long, loose swatches for spinning. The spinning goes on all through the winter and spring. Rājpūt women do not do their own weaving, however. After the thread comes off the spindle, it is wrapped into skeins on a wooden frame and taken to the weaver. The fabric produced is then used for bedclothes and some of the coarser clothing for men. All finer materials are purchased, and most of them are fashioned into wearing apparel by the women, although some are sewn by the village tailors.

When a girl in the family is going to be married, the women will help to make the various things required for her dowry. These include baskets, papier-mâché bowls, hooked and woven sitting-mats, children's toys, and household decorations made of cloth. This activity begins several months before the marriage.

There is a marked tendency toward sociability in the women's work habits. All the women in one household are likely to do the same kind of work at the same time. For spinning, there may even be a gathering from several households. Chatting is a favorite occupation. Some women smoke the hookah as they talk.

Chapter 5

Politics and Social Control

In the traditional system of social control, each of the caste groups of Khalapur has much autonomy. In the larger groups, the major responsibility for social control rests in the hands of a few elderly and respected men. When problems arise, they meet together in councils called *panchāyats*. Their functions are both legislative and judicial. They adjudicate disputes and in cases involving violations of caste group rules, especially those relating to sex and marriage, they focus public opinion and bring pressures to bear on the culprits. When a change is to be made in caste group rules, such as whether or not the group will continue to perform a particular service, they are the focus for the decision-making process. One or more of these men also act as representatives of the group when it deals with other caste groups in the village or with government officials. Among some caste groups, the lines of political solidarity extend beyond Khalapur and include *jāti* members in other neighboring villages. Occasionally the leading men of the caste groups in each of these villages will come together to discuss an especially difficult dispute or to make a decision of importance to the segment of the *jāti* which they represent.

If the village as a whole presents a picture of semiseparate layering, it is also true that there is considerable segmentation along family lines within each of the caste groups. Each family head is a focus of authority, and there are strong feelings that disputes within the family should be settled by him. These feelings are especially strong among the higher castes. These castes also show a further form of segmentation, reflecting the social and residential cleavage between men and women. A Rājpūt woman who is head of the women's house has considerable authority of a legislative and judicial nature, although it is exercised in a very limited sphere.

The focus of social control within the Rājpūt caste group is a number of men who are called "prominent (literally 'big') men." It is a relatively easy matter to identify them. As one informant said, "You can get the answer from any child you see playing about." In the subdivision of the village where we did the most intensive research, there is general agreement among the adults on the names of ten men.

All ten of these men are married and middle-aged. Thoroughly acquainted with the customs and procedures of a generally conservative group, they also are said to be "strong." The major sources of their strength are ownership of land enough to give them relatively moderate to great wealth (all have farms larger than the farms of about half the other Rājpūts of the *paṭṭī*) and the support of a number of friends and closely related kinsmen, especially sons. Because of their manpower and wealth they have leisure necessary for performing the duties of a prominent man. Their wealth also enables them to command valued symbols of status. As a group they arrange good marriages for their children, with large dowries, big feasts, and affinal relatives who themselves are people of status. Most have large, brick men's houses, and although seven are illiterate, all but two have educated sons.

The prominent men function as opinion formers, advice givers and wielders of verbal sanctions. Some of them move about the village from men's sitting place to men's sitting place, finding out what is going on and discussing the latest developments. Others very rarely move about in the village. They are usually to be found sitting at their own place, and those who wish to see them gather there.

On important ceremonial occasions, such as marriages, two or three of the prominent men of the village are invited to attend. They lend the sanction of the caste brotherhood to the proceedings, and they form an authoritative panel which can decide on moot points of ceremonial procedure which sometimes arise. When a large sum of money changes hands during the ceremony, it is handed to them, and they count it aloud, thus making the transaction public and figuratively stamping it with the seal of their authority. On these occasions one of the prominent men is asked to make the customary gifts to the family servants. As an elder who is versed in the customs governing intercaste relations, he certifies to the correctness of the payments, protects the reputation of the man who gives them, and forestalls bickering.

Perhaps the most important role of the prominent men is sitting on the decision-making and adjudicatory councils, or *panchāyats*. The size of a *panchāyat* varies from two or three prominent men, plus other interested persons, to a group of 50 or more, which may include prominent men from other villages. Only one intervillage *panchāyat* was held during the course of the research. A man who had promised to marry his daughter and (in a very unusual transaction) had taken a sum of money in return for permitting the marriage had refused to honor his promise. The *panchāyat* was able to bring sufficient pressure on him to make him change his mind.

Decisions which affect the Khalapur Rājpūt caste group as a whole are made by *panchāyats* consisting of most of the prominent men. If all are not present, those who are must be able to "speak for" the others if the decision is to be binding. *Panchāyats* at this level are held to consider such matters as a candidate for village office or changes in the marriage ceremonial. Some *panchāyats* are called on a *paṭṭī* basis, and in these meetings all elderly heads of Rājpūt families in the area usually are present even though some may not be prominent men.

The most common form of *panchāyat* is the small council of three or more elders. Such *panchāyats* do not represent any particular geographical unit. They are called when there is a dispute between two men. The aggrieved person selects the prominent men he wishes to hear the case, and the meeting is held at his men's house. His only obligation is to supply plenty of tobacco for the hookahs. The defendant also is asked to appear, and the council listens to both sides. The familial tone of these small *panchāyats* encourages truthful statements as well as discussion of other and perhaps more basic sources of hostility Truth is also encouraged because the prominent men usually are aware of the facts, and sometimes a man is asked to take an oath in which he asks the deity to bring him bad fortune if he is lying. During the course of the research, small *panchāyats* were held to consider the following matters: disputes over rights to land, water and trees; petty theft, both of articles of clothing and of crops; a decision on whether a man should accept land offered him in the village of an affinal relative (where he, as an outsider to the landowning kin group, would have been unwelcome); and a Rājpūt's use of physical violence against a stranger. Decisions often are made in the form of a compromise. In some cases, such as those having to do with crop stealing, the primary motive of the accuser may be to shame the wrongdoer, and an apology will be accepted.

Although the informal systems of social control tend to operate autonomously, there sometimes are occasions when caste group lines are crossed. This frequently occurs in neighborhoods that consist of both Rājpūt and lower caste families. Rājpūt prominent men are asked to mediate in disputes between Rājpūts and their lower caste neighbors. They also are called on when disputes among members of lower caste groups can't be settled by their own elders.

The operation of the informal system of social control is illuminated by considering some of the different types of disputes or kinds of conflicting interests it must handle. One area of conflict involves the Rājpūts and other caste groups in the village. When such conflicts do occur, the scales are tipped heavily in favor of the Rājpūts because they are so much more powerful than any other group. The primary basis for their power is economic, but there are other important contributing factors. Traditionally the land on which non-Rājpūt families built their houses was regarded as the property of the Rājpūts. Recently the legal basis for Rājpūt claims to ownership of this land has been destroyed by the government. The feeling that they are the rightful owners tends to persist, however, and the threat of eviction still is an effective weapon in their hands. The Rājpūts also are in a position to threaten to prevent lower castes from using the fields for latrine purposes or for gathering fodder. Their ascendancy is further enhanced by sheer numbers and by beliefs associated with the caste system.

The superior power of the Rājpūts was shown when an Untouchable group, in an attempt to raise their status, refused to perform their traditional task of removing dead cattle. The Rājpūts were concerned because they were inconvenienced, and, more important, they saw the move as a threat to the social order. By threatening the various kinds of deprivation mentioned above, they quickly were able to bring the group back into line.

In matters which do not involve serious conflicts of interest, the Rājpūts are more ready to meet demands or to make compromises. When the volume of a traditional measure was officially decreased, the hereditary service castes, who are paid in kind and according to units of this measure, were adversely affected. They were able to obtain an adjustment in a large *panchāyat* which included their caste group leaders and Rājpūt prominent men. Under some circumstances an individual Rājpūt can be made to bend a little before lower caste pressures. When a member of the Untouchable sweeper caste group was beaten because he allowed his pigs to damage a Rājpūt's potatoes, his caste group—which has unusual solidarity and provides services the Rājpūts are very reluctant to do without—was able to obtain at least the semblance of an apology from the Rājpūt concerned. In effecting the outcome, however, an important role was played by a number of

Rājpūt prominent men who lived nearby and would have been adversely affected by a sweeper "strike."

Within the Rājpūt caste group, conflicts of interest may be roughly grouped according to the relative strength of those who are involved. There are many conflicts involving members of Rājpūt families who have neither large farms nor large followings. The occasions for conflict between members of these families are the same as those between stronger families, but the aim and outcome often are different. In conflicts between weaker families, the ostensible cause generally is the real cause. The poor young man steals crops because he is short of fodder for his animals or because his family is short of grain. Or he steals from a men's house platform because the purchase of clothing or tobacco represents a fairly serious drain on his resources.

Disputes between poorer and weaker men usually do not involve violence, though occasionally, as a result of repeated provocation, a man may lose his temper and attack another, especially if he catches him red-handed and the two start arguing. A more frequent recourse is to call a *panchāyat* of prominent men. These *panchāyats* often obtain satisfaction for the man who has been wronged. Since the person who has committed the misdemeanor is weaker than the prominent man handling the case, he fears the sanctions they may apply. If they threaten to go to court against him, for example, he knows they have a good chance of winning. He also knows that they or their supporters can harass him in various ways by "speaking against" him or by creating other difficulties, such as taking some of his crop or depriving him of water. He knows that these forms of chastisement lie behind the appeals which are made to a concern for his own reputation or the reputation of his neighborhood, *paṭṭī*, caste group, or village.

When a conflict results from a wrong done by a strong family to a much weaker one, the system of informal control generally is ineffective. Once when a young Rājpūt, Dharam, stole another's wheat and when the latter, who had only a few close kinsmen and a small farm, approached a prominent man for help in organizing a *panchāyat*, the elder gave him this advice:

> You don't have a shoe in your hand * and aren't in a position to do anyone any harm. If I organize a panchayat, Dharam might do something else to you. If you take the matter to court, you won't be able to get witnesses. Dharam comes from the largest lineage in the village. You'd better keep quiet and not get him down on you.

---

* Beating someone on the head with a shoe is a stylized form of insult, since the head is sacred and leather is impure.

As a rule, however, strong families do not engage in petty theft of this kind. If they do, as happened in this case, it generally is the act of some younger member of the family, not of an older and more responsible person or the family head. The fact that the family head does not take action against his own son, grandson, or nephew is an example of how emphasis on family solidarity often interferes with processes of social control which are supposed to uphold values associated with the larger social unit—the whole Rājpūt caste brotherhood or the village.

In conflicts involving two or more strong Rājpūt families, the meaning of the difficulty generally is different from what it is when two weaker families are involved. There are some conflicts between strong families in which the ostensible issues actually are the basic issues. This was the case, for example, when a strong Rājpūt family used chicanery in an attempt to attain title to a valuable piece of vacant village land. In many other conflicts, however, the ostensible is not what is of primary importance. In such quarrels the end sought is not so much material benefit—a few square feet of property, for instance —as the immaterial gains deriving from a demonstration of power which is relatively greater than one's rival.

In every generation situations arise in which a few previously weak families acquire leaders who are not only able but also proper Rājpūts in the sense that they respond to values calling on them to establish a strong family and to become prominent men. In addition, some of them also have been given an allocation of men and land on which they can build a domain. One way in which such a family can make its influence felt is by acquiring the recognized symbols of status, such as housing and good marriages. The head of the family will also seek to demonstrate in little ways that he and the kin group he leads are persons to be reckoned with. This does not mean that the process is consistently rational and planned. From what has been said above, it is clear that village life is full of many small points of potential conflict. The family of strength can and does demonstrate on a number of occasions that it can defend its own interests. It may have been deprived of some of its land in a prior generation. In this generation it wins the land back in a court case. A few demonstrations of capable leadership and the ability to attain its ends in competition with other families—plus the appropriate symbols of status—move the family toward a position of prominence and attract other weaker families into its political orbit. Its head becomes a prominent man, and the family, together with its alliances, is recognized as a significant power cluster in village affairs.

A prominent man cannot afford to alienate his own kinsmen and friends. If he does, at least to any very serious extent, he is no longer a prominent man. He no longer is "strong." This is why it is usually impossible to obtain his support in cases involving these individuals. Even when a number of prominent men agree that steps should be taken against a person who is supported by only one or two other prominent men, they will be reluctant to proceed because they know that even this much opposition has power enough to cause them trouble. They are not like judges backed by an obedient police force and proceeding against a single deviant individual. For this reason it is difficult to take effective action against strong families. There are stories of strong families that drove others from the village. The ousted families were not able to return until death had changed the composition of the family that opposed them. Apparently murder cases in the early nineteenth century (when not occurring within the family itself, in which case usually nothing was done) brought forceful retaliation by kinsmen and friends. Today such cases are generally handled by the police and the state courts. In the past, according to our possibly partial evidence, the only form of deviance which a strong family could not get away with was an act which threatened the purity of the bloodline. A generation ago a man who impregnated a village "sister" and then attempted to kidnap and sell her to a man in a distant province was outcasted and driven from the village. It seems very probable that today similar strong action for a like offense would be taken. However, there has been a weakening of some of the rules in this sensitive area. A generation ago a man who married a widow or who married a girl from a clan whose claims to true Kṣatriya status were suspect would have been denied hookah privileges with the rest of the caste group. Today it is not possible to obtain the consensus necessary to deny the hookah to men who are deviant in this way. There are at least two younger Rājpūts who have married into clans generally agreed to be of low status. There are murmurs of criticism but nothing more. There was some attempt to deprive a man of hookah privileges who some years ago married a girl who was technically a widow, but only a few of the Rājpūts would agree to carry out the sanction.

The informal system of social control among the Rājpūts is further strained by another process characteristic of village political life. This process seems to be triggered in part by Rājpūt values, which stress pride, sensitivity to slight, and arrogance toward anyone conceived of as a potential rival. A man who becomes strong enough to throw his weight around, so long as he knows he cannot be met by superior opposing force, often will do so. There is also a belief that a Rājpūt family should take revenge for a wrong, and it is felt that an appeal to the informal system of social control is a sign of weakness in a strong family. Apparently, too, a family which acquires a relatively good holding, and especially a number of sons—and is, in addition, a family which has not been prominent—experiences what may be best described as a kind of power intoxication. It is difficult to describe in other terms the act of a family which took possession of some land under circumstances so provocative that they could not help but realize that the step would be met by forceful retaliation, with a good chance of a stick fight that would lead to a killing. As a result of the interplay of factors such as these, there are strong families which become involved in feudlike assertions and counterassertions which may go on for many years. Occasionally there is something of genuine material consequence at issue, but more often the occasions of their quarreling would, under different circumstances, be of little moment. What is really at issue is the relative power of the two families and their supporters. This type of conflict can lead to violence, especially if the competing groups come into contact with one another when they have been drinking. This happened during the course of the research, and during the ensuing fracas a man was killed, a man who ironically and unfortunately had never been a prime figure in either of the two contesting groups.

Paralleling the informal political structure in Khalapur there is a formal political structure. It is the creation of the state government. Before independence, there was a formal, government-sponsored village court presided over by one of the prominent men. Shortly after independence, as a result of changes in the state law, this court was given enhanced powers, and a number of procedural changes were made. It was hoped that these changes would make it more effective in settling minor cases cheaply, expeditiously, and justly.

The village court has handled much petty litigation and in many ways is serving a useful function. It often serves as a backstop for failures of the informal system, which generally is tried first, and a number of cases which otherwise might have gone to the town courts, with resulting expense and prolonged hostile competition, have been successfully adjudicated.

The court has often failed, however, and much of the difficulty can be understood in terms of the picture presented above. Since the court operates in Khalapur, most of the judges are Rājpūt prominent men, and they are subject to the usual sort of pressures. Technically they are government officials. But the concept of "office" and duty to an "office" is not highly developed. To the Rājpūts, the judges are primarily kinsmen and members of their own caste group. Thus when caste group interests are involved, it is difficult for the judges to make just decisions. The police are distant and their ministrations often undependable. There is nothing similar to a bar association or any other kind of group which can provide support at all comparable to the support provided by judge's kinsmen and village alliance. The difficulties are enhanced by the fact that there often is a conflict between statutory law, as set forth in the laws of the land, and village customary law. A just decision according to one concept is unjust according to the other. As a result of these factors, the village court tends to operate successfully or unsuccessfully in much the same way, and for much the same reasons, as the informal system of social control. The prevailing attitude, which both gives it its due and recognizes its failings, was well summarized by a Rājpūt when he said of the court: "It is better to have a broken down bullock in the cattle compound than no bullock at all."

At the same time as the new village court, a new legislative and executive council was created. This body was revolutionary in that members were to be elected on the basis of village-wide adult franchise. There were provisions also to ensure representation for the Untouchables, and the body was given the power to tax, to spend money on village improvements, and to allot certain village lands.

The new council also has run into difficulties, and the villagers for the most part regard it with the same misgivings as they do the court. A basic difficulty stems from the fact that the council rests on a new conception of what village government should be. The idea that all village caste groups should have an equal voice in village government and the idea of making decisions by ballot and by majority vote run strongly counter to long-established custom. In addition, the elective system has enabled the lower caste groups to pose a threat to the long-standing Rājpūt hegemony, since in combination they can outvote them.

Very broadly speaking, it can be said that the new council, during the time of the research, mainly represented the interests of a Rājpūt power cluster. Partly for this reason and partly because the villagers did not really understand the nature of the new governmental instrument, it was doing more to create dissension than to rally the support of the various caste groups of the village or to guide them, with a degree of harmony, toward a more democratic and effective village administration.

Outside the village the agencies of social control of most importance to the Rājpūts are the police and the courts of justice. The police officials with whom the Rājpūts have most contact are stationed in Bhudana. Higher police officials have their offices in Saharanpur. For

Khalapur, the lowest echelon of the state judiciary is the courts of Bhudana. Cases which are appealed from these courts go to Saharanpur and may eventually go to still higher courts located in cities outside the district.

The police are regarded with suspicion and dislike. This attitude is partly due to Khalapur's history. Its residents frequently violated statutory law, and the police were the representatives of authority with whom they were most often at odds. Aversion to the police was also heightened when a detachment was stationed in the village during the latter part of the nineteenth century in order to prevent the Rājpūt practice of female infanticide. In the pursuance of their duties the police necessarily had to violate purdah restrictions, and this caused much resentment. The villagers generally maintain that police contacts more often involve bribery, extortion, and brutality than retribution for wrong-doing.

The negative attitude toward other government officials is much less strong than in the case of the police, and many higher officials of the district and state are regarded with respect. Since independence, the villagers feel that officials at the higher levels are much more accessible. One Rājpūt said that if he wished, he could go right to Nehru.

It cannot be gainsaid that the processes of village government and social control are subject to much strain, nor that this is especially true among the Rājpūts. A more precise estimate of the degree of strain is apparent in answers to a query about the court cases that men in the sample of families used for this study recall being involved in, either directly or as witnesses. Thirty-eight men, ranging in age from about 25 to 65, were asked to mention any court cases they had participated in during the course of their lives. Eliminating duplication, 59 separate cases were mentioned. The main figures involved, with few exceptions, were Rājpūts in the *paṭṭī* where the neighborhood studied is located. Assuming the oldest man was involved in his first case when he was 25, the period covered is 40 years. Over half the cases involved disputes concerning the possession of land or the allocation of income derived from it. About a quarter involved theft, and the remainder concerned such matters as loans of money, water rights, and assault. Seventeen of the cases had taken a violent turn, and in three of them men had been killed. These data, of course, underestimate the number of disputes. Some court cases in which the men are known to have played a part are not mentioned, and a large number of disputes never reached the courts.

A noticeable feature of the lives of Khalapur Rājpūts is suspicion. With the exception of their close kinsmen and friends, men tend to be uneasy about the motives of other Rājpūts in the village. In part this seems to be a concomitant of the fact that family retaliatory power is an important factor in social control. If the other family can get away with something, it is felt they may do so. This is one reason why a high-status family tries to free one of its men from the burdens of farm work so that he can keep his finger on the village political pulse. It also stems in part from the fact that taking revenge is looked on as normal, even obligatory, and that preparations for taking it are concealed. After so many generations of living together, with the amount of jockeying for status and power that goes on, there are few families that cannot think of a number of others whose members may be waiting for a chance to make a move against them.

The women are more openly quarrelsome than the men. Tempers have no chance to "cool off" in the close quarters of the courtyard, and minor irritations build up into open hostility. A woman with whom this matter was discussed agreed that the women fought so much because they could not leave the courtyard. She said that if they could take a walk for an hour, most of the quarrels would not occur. Quarrels often begin over some minor matter. Two women may disagree over the cooking or the children, and the bickering begins. In an extended family, the other women usually take sides, and eventually all the women are lined up against each other. Neighboring women, hearing the rumpus, come to add their voices' worth to the quarrel so that finally the courtyard is filled with angry women. Such an extensive performance, however, does not occur frequently. The women vary considerably in how often they quarrel. We were told that in some houses the women fight daily, in some once a week, and in some not for months at a time.

In any case the quarrels between sisters-in-law are usually not of long duration. Seclusion has the effect of terminating as well as precipitating disagreements. Tempers may flare, but if the women of a courtyard cannot get along with each other, they have no one else to turn to for company. After a quarrel, women may not speak to each other for several days or even one or two weeks, but a wise mother-in-law or loneliness coupled with the restrictions of purdah may help resolve the hostility. An extremely angry woman may show her vexation by going to bed and refusing to eat. When this happens, some woman from the house or a neighboring house may act as peacemaker. In some cases quarrels between sisters-in-law result in permanent unfriendliness. As discussed earlier, the women may insist that their husbands divide the courtyard by building a wall.

The women, like the men, sometimes engage in aggressive gossip and joking when they are not on good terms with each other. When the women are really angry, they are more likely to voice their charge directly, calling witnesses if necessary.

If women are habitually on bad terms with the women of other houses, they stop visiting each other. Often the women's visiting habits follow the patterns of the men's quarrels, that is, they do not visit the families with whom the men are on bad terms. However, women's quarrels are seldom championed by the men. The village women in general believe that the men fight less frequently but more seriously than they themselves do—a belief in which we concur. As one woman said:

The men do not fight, but if they do, it is dangerous. They will start abusing one another and then start fighting with staffs. Like on Holi—the men had a fight and that man was killed. The fights that go on from generation to generation are the fights of men and not of women.

⚹
⚹
⚹

Chapter 6

Marriage

Because the life of women is so curtailed by the custom of purdah, it is not surprising that they look forward with pleasure to any ceremony which allows them to leave the courtyard and associate with other men and women. Among the most exciting of these occasions is the marriage ceremony.

The weeks or months during which marriages are celebrated are the most festive of the ceremonial year. During these seasons almost every day marks the arrival or departure of a wedding party. Some arrive in crowded, honking buses, but most make the journey as far as Bhudana by train and then travel to and from the village in long lines of bullock carts. The platforms of many of the men's quarters are filled with guests, and groups of village women dressed in brilliant saris hurry through the lanes on the way to houses where ceremonies are in progress. Throughout the marriage season the village rings with the trumpets and trombones of wedding bands and the blare of popular Indian movie songs which are played over amplifying units hired in one of the nearby towns.

There are certain times of year when no marriages are ever held, for these periods are inauspicious. Auspicious times during the balance of the year depend on astrological calculations, and, as a rule, marriages take place in November and part of December and in May and June after the harvest. Most families prefer the latter period because food stocks have been replenished and the warm weather makes it easier to provide for large numbers of guests, since they can sleep in the open and without heavy bedding.

A family must arrange marriages for all of its daughters. A failure to do so is unheard of in the village and would be met with severe censure. There is not the same social pressure to see that all of the sons are married, but a family will make every effort to get wives for them, especially the eldest. Girls are generally married at 16 or 17. The marriage of a boy may be delayed until he is 18 or 20, especially if he is a student.

When a girl is old enough to be married, her family must begin the search for a suitable groom. Marriage negotiations are sometimes conducted by the girl's father, particularly if he is the head of the house. But it is more usual for the father to obtain the help of elderly relatives. Information about eligible boys is often obtained when a member of the family, or a relative, goes to another village to attend a marriage.

The range of choice is limited by a number of factors. Since some Rājpūt clans are more highly regarded than others, the negotiators will try to make an alliance with a family belonging to a clan of high standing. Another limiting factor is the location of the groom's village in relation to Khalapur. Traditionally wives have come from the south, and daughters have been given in marriage to the north and northwest. Distance is also a consideration, and few marriages are made in villages which lie beyond a radius of about 100 miles. Most Rājpūt villages very close to Khalapur are eliminated because the Rājpūts in them are clan brothers.

Within these limitations, the selection of a suitable groom requires a delicate balancing of many factors. The reputation of the groom, his age, health, looks, and schooling are important. The relative social and economic standing of the two families must be weighed. It is desirable, if possible, for the girl's family to make an alliance with a family having a somewhat higher status than hers, since this enhances their prestige in their own village and ensures that the bride will not be discontent with her husband's social standing. But aspirations of this kind must be trimmed according to the amount of dowry which her family can afford and, finally and most important, by a decision as to whether the girl would be well taken care of, both as a wife and a widow.

When a decision has been reached and a boy's family has agreed to the match, a ceremony is held at the men's quarters of the boy's family. The negotiators who represent the family of the girl present a sum of money to the groom-to-be, plus small token payments to the members of his family and some of his family servants. Since the status of a wife's family is always subordinate to the status of the groom's, this aspect of the new relationship is shown by the very respectful and deferential way in which the elderly representative of the bride-to-be's family presents the gift of money to the groom-to-be. It is also clearly sym- bolized by the eating pattern. Since members of a girl's family are not supposed to take food in the village of her husband, when food is served at the end of the ceremony by the family of the groom-to-be, the representatives of the bride-to-be's family refrain from eating. This is an indication that the preliminary marriage agreement has been sealed.

An auspicious date for the marriage is determined by astrological calculations made by a Brāhmaṇ in the village of the bride, and the groom's family is informed of the date by letter carried by the bride's barber.

As the date approaches, both the family of the groom and the family of the bride have much to do. The head of the groom's family must see that arrangements are made for the ceremony and feasting which will take place before the groom sets out for the bride's village. Those who are to attend the groom as members of his marriage party must be in- formed and arrangements made for their transportation.

By far the greatest burden of a marriage is borne by the family of the bride. The money for the dowry represents the savings of many years, and often a family must go into debt in order to provide a sufficient amount. (About a century ago the necessity of marrying all of the daughters in the family, plus the heavy financial burden which their dowry represented, led to the practice of female infanticide among the Rājpūts, although it was also caused, according to some informants, by the reluctance of the male members of the bride's family to assume a subordinate status in relation to the members of the groom's family.) The dowry also includes expensive jewelry, kitchen utensils, and large amounts of clothing and bedding. Some of these articles will have been collected well in advance, since mothers often start putting things aside for their daughters' dowries soon after they are born, and when they are older, the daughters themselves make many of the articles which will be included in their dowries. But much of the bedding and clothing and some of the kitchen utensils and jewelry often remain to be purchased. Arrangements must also be made for housing and feeding the groom's marriage party and for feeding guests from the village and family servants.

A number of preliminary ceremonies center about the bride and the groom separately, but the most important ceremonies take place when the groom and his party have come to the village of the bride, where they remain for three days of ritual and feasting. On the third day the groom and his party leave the village, taking the bride with them. The new bride seldom stays at her husband's village for more than a month or two. The date of her return to her parents' home is decided during the marriage ceremonies, and at the appointed time her brother or some other male member of her family comes to get her. She may remain in her parents' village for as long as three years, but she usually stays no longer than a year. When she again returns to her husband's home, she takes a large number of gifts for the members of her in-laws' family. She does not return to her own village until the birth of her first child.

Although children do not participate directly in the marriage preparations and ceremonies, they have ample chance to view the proceedings from first to last. For months before the marriage, the conversation of the women centers around the event. In the bride's family the women are busy making baskets, bowls, and mats. The children see the preparations and mounting excitement. At the various ceremonies leading up to the wedding and at the wedding itself, the children, in restless, giggling groups, hover in the background, watching with eager interest.

The marriage proceedings are particularly significant for children in that they provide a clear and dramatic picture of the drastic changes in a girl's life following her marriage. During the ceremony which marks the sending of a letter to the groom's house to set the date of the wedding, the girl, hidden in some dark corner of the house, weeps, by herself. This weeping is not a ritual mourning but a genuine expression of grief.

When a new bride enters her husband's house, she is put "on display" every afternoon for several days. All the women of the family's lineage are invited to see her and her dowry. The bride, her sari pulled over her head and face, sits huddled on the courtyard floor. One by one the visiting women lift her veil and peer at her face, while the bride, with lowered eyelids, struggles to turn away. Having seen the bride and perhaps commented on her looks, the visitor turns to an inspection of the dowry. The mother-in-law displays the various items and tells her visitors how many utensils and pieces of clothing the bride has brought to the house. Each woman is comparing the dowry to those of other families, and the older women may verbalize these comparisons and make slighting remarks about the quantity and quality of the goods, or they may praise the dowry to the detriment of some other family who has recently acquired a bride. By the middle of the afternoon, the courtyard is full of women busily talking to each other and catching up on the latest news. No one speaks to the bride, and it would be shameless for her to join the conversation. She must not even be caught looking at any of the visitors. Although she may peek through her sari while it is over her face, she does not lift it, and she must keep her eyes lowered when anyone lifts her veil to look at her. The children, both those of the family and those who have come with their mothers, watch the proceedings, and occasionally a little girl, with a troubled expression on her young face, stands thoughtfully viewing the silent figure huddled in the midst of the chattering women.

A daughter-in-law must cover her face in front of her mother-in-law, older daughters-in-law, and husband's sisters until the birth of her first child. Actually this custom is seldom strictly observed in practice, since it interferes with work, but when visitors are present, a young daughter-in-law will usually pull her sari over her forehead and sit at a lower level than her in-laws.

The bride's return to her home after two or more months for a prolonged visit suggests that in a sense the first marriage ceremony functions as an initiation ceremony—preparing the young girl for adult female life.

❧
❧
❧

Chapter 7

Religion

Sometime in India's prehistoric past, probably around 1500 B.C., horse riding people from the area of the Iranian plateau began pushing across the Hindu Kush, through the mountain passes, and into the land of the Indus valley and its tributaries. Here they found a highly civilized people who lived in fortified cities, had a written language, used copper and silver, and traded with the peoples of the Middle East. Possibly the first wave of invaders, and surely subsequent waves, spoke Indo-European. The religion of these invaders is contained in a collection of hymns, ritual texts, and philosophical treatises called the Veda. Agreement on the sacredness of these texts plus the system of caste—which is supposed to rest on Vedic authority—are the two most general characteristics of Hinduism. During the course of its long development, however, Hinduism has become a great religious storehouse, encompassing a myriad of gods, sects, beliefs, and customs; and each caste, each region, each village, and even each individual may choose a slightly different set of beliefs and customs from this vast diversity. In Khalapur, as elsewhere, the Rājpūt men and other high-caste men have a quite different religious life from that practiced by their women; the old differ from the young, and each caste emphasizes a slightly different set of ceremonies and customs.

The two most important gods of Hinduism are Śiva and Viṣṇu. These gods are sometimes represented as two members of a trinity of gods, Śiva being the god of destruction, Viṣṇu the god of preservation, and Brahmā the god of creation. Brahmā has never been the focus of as much religious devotion as the other two members of the trinity and is now reputed to have only two temples in all of India.

Śiva is represented throughout much of India in the form of a *lingam,* or phallic-shaped stone, the base of which rests in a stone structure called the *yonī.* The *yonī* is shaped like an oil lamp and represents the female principle. Closely associated with this representation of Śiva is his bull Nandi; a figure of Nandi is often placed beside the *lingam* and *yonī.* These three figures are the central figures in the Śiva temple at Khalapur.

Viṣṇu, in his role of preserver, has appeared on earth in the persons of Kṛṣṇa and Rāma. The exploits of these two god-heroes are recorded in two great epics, the Mahābhārata and the Rāmāyaṇa. In the Mahābhārata Kṛṣṇa helps five brothers recover the kingdom which they have lost to their scheming cousins in a dice game. Rāma, hero of the Rāmāyaṇa, save the world by killing the demon Rāvaṇa, who has stolen Rāma's wife, the beautiful Sītā. This epic has special importance for the Khalapur Rājpūts, since they consider themselves to be descendants of Rāma.

Today Śiva and Viṣṇu, although far from impotent, are regarded as passive, whereas their consorts Pārvatī and Lakṣmī are the active members. This contrast between the quiescent male principle and the active female principle is reflected in attitudes toward men and women. Women are regarded as flighty and less dignified than men, and it is believed that women's sex drive is stronger than that of men. This belief justifies early marriages and supports the stereotype of the immoral widow.

In addition to the major gods, some worship of various animals and natural objects may be traced to the Vedic tradition. In the Veda fire, the sun, and several rivers are addressed as gods, and these entities are still regarded as sacred throughout India. Water has purifying, as well as cleansing, properties, and the daily bathing of high-caste Hindus is practiced as much for spiritual as for sanitary reasons. Bathing in sacred rivers or temple ponds is a regular part of worship at religious festivals, and often water is used in ceremonies for purposes of purification. After cremation, the ashes of the dead are finally consigned to some sacred river or canal. Fire may also be used for purification. Dishes which have become contaminated may be purified by passing them through fire. Fire also figures largely in the wedding ceremony.

The worship of trees is prevalent in Khalapur and, like many other elements in Hinduism, may stem from a non-Vedic, non-Aryan religious strata. There are a number of trees around the village which are associated with spirits. One mango tree is supposed to have been a man at one time and is worshipped each year at the time of a festival known as *Ekādaśi*. A Brāhmaṇ goes to another tree to receive the offering of milk made by those whose cows and buffaloes have recently calved. *Pīpal* trees are considered sacred and are also associated with ghosts, which they sometimes house. The *nīm* tree is considered to have both medicinal and magical properties. Its twigs are used for brushing teeth; its leaves are sometimes used in medicine; and its branches are hung over doorways to protect the family from ghosts. Many courtyards have a small *tuḷsī* or basil bush growing in them. This bush is thought by some to be a Brāhmaṇ girl who was miraculously changed into a tree to escape the advances of a Muslim man who had kidnapped her. There is a song about the *tuḷsī* bush which says:

> Where *tuḷsī* is standing, there Kṛṣṇa took birth.
> Ghosts surround the courtyard where god is absent
>   and *tuḷsī* is not standing.

Although they did not consider cattle too sacred to slaughter and eat, the Vedic writers held cows in high regard, used them as their standard of exchange, and identified them with earth, nourishment, and motherhood. This symbolism has persisted, and cows are today the most sacred of animals in India; it is the gravest of sins for a Hindu to kill a cow or eat beef. In many cattle compounds one sees old bullocks whose days are long past. They will nevertheless be cared for and fed until they die. All of the five products of a cow—milk, curd, butter, urine, and dung—are considered sacred. For this reason cow dung is used in the construction of religious idols, as a plaster to purify the cooking hearth, and as a poultice for the wounds of cattle. Its sacredness explains why many Rājpūt women make their own dung cakes for fuel.

Some animals are sacred because they have come to be associated with particular Vedic gods or have appeared in post-Vedic legends. Thus monkeys are sacred because of the important part that the monkey god, Hanumān, playing in helping Rāma to recover his wife from the demon Rāvaṇa. The villagers sometimes threw food to the monkeys living in the village mango groves. Snakes, sacred to Śiva, are also worshipped on a special day. This worship, however, is chiefly designed to persuade the snakes to stay away from the houses. When found, snakes are usually killed, particularly when found within the village. A number of other animals are considered to be sacred in various parts of India. In Khalapur, cows, monkeys, and snakes are the only animals regularly worshipped, although some villagers accord sacred status to some other animals, such as peacocks and antelope.

It should be noted that since all forms of life are sacred to some extent, reluctance to kill an animal does not necessarily mean that it has some specially sacred status.

As is well-known, there are Hindus who carry pantheistic doctrine to an extreme, taking elaborate precautions to avoid killing any living thing, even inadvertently. In the village no one takes such an extreme position, but the doctrine forms a part of the belief system of those who are strict vegetarians, and there are many villagers who are re-luctant to kill wasps, flies, and even bedbugs.

Although an observer might well conclude, from the large number of spirits, deities, animals, trees, and natural entities that figure in vil-lage worship, that Hindus are polytheistic, this is not true, strictly speaking. The religion of the Ṛg Veda is largely polytheistic, but in the last book of the Ṛg Veda there emerges from this pantheon the idea of a single world soul or deity who encompasses all of the various gods, goddesses, and forces of nature. This concept is found fully developed in the Upaniṣads, theological texts written in the sixth century B.C. The philosophers of the Upaniṣads conceived of the material world as an illusion. The only true reality exists in the world soul, Brahman. Man's soul, the Ātman, as well as the souls of animals, plants, and even inanimate objects are merely separate manifestations of this world soul. These writings give the basis for the impersonal monotheism of sophisticated Hindus and provide a theological basis for the Vedic tradition of pantheism.

The Rājpūt men in Khalapur adhere, in greater or lesser degree, to these beliefs, and even the women, although much of their worship is directed to lesser figures, clearly express a belief in a supreme deity.

The strength of Muslim influence in the past may be seen in the small contemporary Muslim Rājpūt community. The Hindu Rājpūts esteem this group and consider its members to be blood relatives, although they do not intermarry with them or share the same hookah. There are strong ties of friendship among a number of individual Muslim and Hindu Rājpūts.

Muslim influence may also be seen in the ritual centering around the Muslim saint's shrine. The spirit of the place is generally invoked by the women in any ceremony designed to protect people or animals from harm. It is believed to have special power to protect children and to cure disease and barrenness.

Rājpūt bridegrooms make an offering at the shrine before leaving the village to obtain their brides, and the women of Rājpūt families make annual offerings at the shrine. The saint's special service to the village is the protection of village crops from locusts and hail storms. When the crops are damaged by hail, as they were in the spring of 1955, many believe the disaster is caused by an offense to his spirit.

The strongest, most recent influence on the religious life of many Rājpūt men is the Ārya Samāj movement. This sect, founded in 1875 by a Brāhman named Dayanand Sarasvati, represents a reform movement within Hinduism. Sarasvati objected to the proliferation of caste groups and worship of the numerous local deities. He advocated a return to the religion of the Veda. Sarasvati claimed that the Veda represented a purely monotheistic religion and, further, that all modern scientific discoveries and theories are stated in these texts in germinal form, claims which may well be disputed by more objective scholars. The community which he set up grew rapidly, and Ārya Samāj teachers began to preach their teacher's ideas in many parts of India. These teachers were very critical of beliefs in minor and local gods and goddesses. They preached against idolatry, maintained that all castes, not just the twice-born castes, had the right to study the sacred texts, and that worship could be performed without entering a temple or utilizing the services of a Brāhman.

It was, however, a less extreme version of this doctrine which was introduced into Khalapur by the Rājpūt leader Pṛthvi Singh. Pṛthvi Singh enlisted support from conservative as well as "liberal" Hindus. He persuaded the Rājpūt men that it was not proper for them to worship at a Muslim saint's tomb, then the only major religious structure in the village, and pressed for the construction of a Hindu temple to Śiva. Thus, although Ārya Samājists destroyed temples in some villages in their efforts to suppress idolatry, they were instrumental in constructing one in Khalapur. With the construction of the new temple, the worship of the saint declined. Men are now taken to the temple rather than to the tomb to take an oath when a *panchāyat* wishes to test the truth of their statements. The people most strongly affected by this new movement were the men of a number of high-status families in the subdivision of the village from which the sample for this study was drawn. The strict Ārya Samājist accepts only a core of the widely shared beliefs which form the background of village Hinduism. Most important for him is the belief in an absolute, impersonal, and all-embracing spirit. He feels that only a few ceremonial forms have true religious significance, and he speaks slightingly of much of the ritual activity which goes on, calling it "women's work." He believes that the all-embracing spirit cannot be moved by offerings and that the only way of approaching Him is through personal prayer.

For the women and many men, the spiritual realm is more complex. The name of Rāma is often mentioned by the women in their prayers, whereas the major gods and goddesses are worshipped chiefly during various calendrical festivals in their honor. At other times the women's worship is primarily directed to various disease goddesses, local spirits, and the family ancestors. The worship of disease goddesses is fairly widespread in India. In Khalapur the goddesses are conceived of as 101 sisters. The few who are actually named are thought to be responsible for such epidemic diseases as smallpox and cholera. In their benevolent mother aspect, they may be worshipped on other occasions, when the women are appealing for general protection and good health.

The two most important local godlings are the Muslim saint and the village's guardian spirit, whose shrine was built when the village was founded. In this area of India every village has a shrine built to consecrate and guard the village site. Both this spirit and the Muslim saint are regarded as protectors of the village. Other shrines in or around the village are associated with spirits whose worship is believed to be efficacious in the prevention or cure of a variety of ills. One of these spirits, for example, is believed to have the power to prevent one from getting thorns in one's feet; another prevents boils. In addition, there are several *satī* shrines in honor of women who destroyed themselves on the death of their husbands.

Besides the worship of these many gods and spirits, the worship of family ancestors plays an important part in the religion of the women.

Indeed, some of the women define their religion as ancestor worship. The ancestors are invoked in virtually all prayers and festivals regardless of what other spirit or deity may be involved. Many women utter the name of Rāma and the male ancestors every morning on arising. Usually the ancestors are worshipped for three generations, that is, for as long, generally, as the person is remembered.

Almost every family in the village has one or more small shrines in the fields built in honor of ancestral spirits. It is believed that the spirits of men who have died unmarried or childless or who have met a violent and untimely death and thus have been taken from life before they were willing to leave it are most likely to remain on earth and cause illness to members of their family or to bother them in the form of snakes or dangerous insects. These spirits often appear in dreams or speak through some person they have possessed. At such times they usually request the construction of a shrine where they may live and where offerings may be made in their memory. When the family members build the shrine, they request the spirit to live there and cease bothering them. Worship at these shrines is generally irregular and is carried out by the women. There is one family in the village, however, whose women make offerings at the ancestral shrine every month.

Because the villagers believe that there is an auspicious and an inauspicious time for beginning certain acts, they stress astrology and the reading of omens. The Brāhmaṇs are the astrologers of the village, and some of those who are literate have books in which there are astrological tables. One of these Brāhmaṇs is always consulted when the date of a marriage is to be set, or when a new house is to be lived in, or a new business enterprise undertaken. The reading of omens does not necessarily require a specialist, for their interpretaton is common knowledge. When a dog shakes his head so that his ears flap, those who see him take off their shoes and shake the dust from their feet. This act symbolizes a fresh start after seeing an inauspicious sight. The calling of a crow indicates that a guest will soon arrive. Most people are reluctant to start out on a visit to anyone immediately after they have sneezed or to make plans when the jackals are howling. There are innumerable omens, so many, in fact, that no one takes all of them seriously.

The idea of a sacred place, such as a temple or a shrine, is combined with the idea of an auspicious time with the result that there are certain days, or hours within the day, when it is most appropriate and efficacious to go to sacred places and perform ritual activities. The crossing of time and place is most conspicuous on the occasion of a *melā,* or religious fair. The most significant *melā* for Khalapur occurs once a year in connection with the worship of the goddess Balsundrī, whose temple is located in Bhudana. The town of Hardwar, where the Ganges leaves the Himalayas and enters the plains, is a major Hindu sacred place not far from Khalapur. A *melā* is held at Hardwar every year, and every 12 years a portion of the river at Hardwar becomes one of the holiest places in all India, and pilgrims come from all over the country in order to bathe there.

The seasons are marked by many festivals, observed primarily by the women. Many honor one of the major gods or goddesses: Daśarā is sacred to Durgā, the Mother Goddess, and commemorates the day that Rāma vanquished the demon Rāvaṇa; Dawālī, the beautiful festival of lights, celebrates both the wedding day of Viṣṇu and Lakṣmī, the goddess of wealth, and the return of Rāma to his capitol after Rāvaṇa's defeat; Śiva's wedding day is celebrated in the festival of Śiv Rātrī, the night of Śiva, the only day of the year when the women worship at the Śiva temple. Gias celebrates the awakening of the gods, who sleep during a portion of the year, whereas Janmāṣṭamī honors Kṛṣṇa's birthday. During the important festival of Khānāgat the Brāhmaṇs serving the family are given food for 16 consecutive days, to honor the male ancestors. There are also two fast days kept by the women, one for the health of their husbands and one for the health of their sons.

Certain patterns of worship are common to most of these festivals. Offerings usually consist of water (which is often used to bathe the image representing the divinity), sweets, bread fried in *ghī*, and tiny earthenware lamps, whose cotton wicks have been soaked in mustard oil and lighted in offering. Many of the calendrical rites involve fasting. Such fasts are usually kept by women, but men may also fast on important occasions. Sometimes the fast requires not eating throughout the day, but often it consists only of abstention from such foods as cereal grains, so that fasts are, in general, mild.

Almost all ceremonies are celebrated by the cooking of special kinds of food, the most common being various sweets, milk preparations, and fried breads. The village women frequently begin their descriptions of ceremonies by saying: "We cook sweets and fried breads on this day."

Another feature of these rites is the giving of presents, usually in the form of food, to the family servants. Providing food enough for servants, as well as for family, and offerings keeps the Rājpūt women busy on these festival days.

In ceremonies, the family is the most important unit, and among the members of the family it is the women who take the most interest and participate most actively. Many ceremonies are carried out without the help of any religious specialist, but there are some which require the presence of a Brāhmaṇ. In many ceremonies where the Brāhmaṇ is present, one of his significant functions is ritual eating. This fact has led some of the women to complain that Brāhmaṇs have invented festivals so that they could be fed.

The Rājpūt men usually do not keep fast days or participate actively in the calendrical festivals. Some of the men most influenced by Ārya Samāj say that they are aware of these festivals only because they receive particularly good food on these days. In some of the festivals, however, the men play a part. They participate in the Janmāṣṭamī celebrations, and a few of the younger men engage in the general horse-play and throwing of colored water that takes place during Holī, the spring Saturnalia. Although Rājpūt men elsewhere in India do homage to their weapons on the festival day of Dasarā, in Khalapur the custom has almost completely died out. Stimulated by the Community Development Project, which provided musical instruments, a small but enthusiastic group of men, including a few of the younger Rājpūts, meets weekly in the newly constructed village council house to sing religious songs. Occasionally some of the older Rājpūt men gather on a men's house platform to hear one of their number read aloud from a book such as the Rāmāyaṇa.

The Hindu expresses his religious beliefs not only in ceremonies and prayers but also in the customs which guide his everyday activities and his relations with other people. The religiously supported concept of *dharma* defines one's duties as a member of a caste, one's duties as a man or woman and a man's duties at different ages during his lifetime. In traditional Hindu thought, the ideal life of a man was divided into four stages. In the first stage he was to be a celibate student. In the second it was his duty to become a father and to raise a family. In this stage it was not sinful to enjoy sexual pleasures, nor was it wrong to be concerned with the accumulation of wealth and the enhancement of the prestige of one's family. The pursuit of these goals became sinful only if such activity became so all-absorbing that it couldn't be given up when the third stage of life was reached. This stage began when a man had arranged for the marriages of his sons and daughters and his children had begun to raise their families. Ideally it was appropriate at this period for a man and his wife to retire to a forest and live there as celibate hermits, devoting themselves to a life of religious contemplation. No men and women of the village carry out this doctrine literally, but it is common for a man to begin to give up the management of his farm after his sons have married, and it is considered unseemly for a woman to conceive after a daughter-in-law has come to live in the house. In the fourth and final stage of life, a man and woman were supposed to give up all worldly possessions other than simple prayer beads, an antelope skin used as a sitting mat, a few items of clothing, and a begging bowl. They were supposed to become wandering hermits, concerned only with the salvation of their souls. No Rājpūts of the village have taken this final step, but the power of the ideal is seen in the genuine respect which is accorded many of the *sādhūs* who pass through the village and occasionally spend some time in one of the village orchards. There are some *sādhūs* who are regarded as insincere and meretricious, and they are accorded no respect. Even so, they are always able to obtain alms in the village.

The four stages of life are differently valued. In accordance with the strong other-worldly emphasis of Hinduism, those who have entered the third stage are accorded more respect, a sentiment which is reinforced by the increment in status which men and women acquire as they grow older. But this does not mean that any of the stages should be omitted. Ideally a man should fulfill the obligations of all four.

The beliefs that the ultimate meaning of existence lies in an attempt to renounce it and transcend it and that the ordinary concerns and claims of daily living are in a sense unreal and a barrier between the soul and its true destiny, are reflected in the high value placed on ascetic practices and in a respect for those who have renounced worldly concerns. A man who gives much of his time to devotional practices is called a *bhagat*. A certain respected elderly Rājpūt is known by this title. He lives a life of simple austerity, performing daily ceremonies, and he says he is attempting to atone for sins committed in his youth.

The concept of *dharma,* and the desire to store up spiritual merit, helps to explain the readiness with which villagers give alms, both to holy men and to beggars, for giving alms is defined as a meritorious act. It is especially commendable to feed a Brāhmaṇ, and it is regarded as wrong for other castes to take food from Brāhmaṇs. A Rājpūt may eat with a Brāhmaṇ friend, but he will usually leave a token payment.

When the philosophers of the Upaniṣads developed the idea of the absolute world soul, or all-encompassing deity, they also developed the idea that the true end of each soul, and thus the ultimate meaning of existence, is reabsorption into the One. Until this reunion is achieved, the soul must progress through a repetitive cycle of birth, death, and rebirth, or reincarnations. All forms of life, from insects and animals to human beings, represent stages of life at varying distances from reunion with God. One obtains release from this cycle only through many meritorious deeds performed in successive lives. Increasing asceticism marks a man's progress toward this goal, and the popular veneration for the wandering holy men stems from their presumed nearness to this final goal. The ordinary person acknowledges that the attachment to earthly desires places him a long way from his final release.

The stage into which each soul is born is the result of *karma*. A Rājpūt man explained this concept by saying that God keeps something which resembles a court file. During the course of a man's life his meritorious deeds and thoughts are entered on this file, together with his sins. The file is first consulted when the man dies. At this time the balance between his good deeds and his bad deeds determines the length of his soul's stay in a "small heaven." This heaven is described as a place where the soul has a "good house, good food, and good clothing, such as it did not have upon earth." The file is consulted a second time when the soul is to be reborn. This time the balance between good deeds and bad determines the status into which the soul is to be reborn.

Variant interpretations of the doctrine of reincarnation were given by the women. For some of them, reincarnation simply meant an endless succession of rebirths without ultimate release. For some, the reward for virtue was rebirth into a higher caste; for others, it was greater comfort in the next life. One girl felt that the highest reward would be rebirth into one's own household. Some thought it was possible to be reborn into the body of an animal; others did not. Some women held that faults and virtues were preserved in successive incarnations; that is, if one was a thief, one would continue to be a thief in the next life. This kind of belief is illustrated in the following story, told to us by a Rājpūt woman:

> Once there was a man and his wife who kept fighting with each other. When they were born again, the husband was a donkey and his wife was a crow. The crow kept sitting on the donkey and pecking at it.

Most observers of Indian village life have commented on the prevalence of fatalism. It is commonly said in the village that what will happen to a person is written on his forehead at birth. The doctrine of *karma* sometimes merges with that of fatalism. One man said he was sure Nehru must have committed some sins in a previous life, for in this life he had no sons. But usually the doctrine of fatalism and the doctrine of *karma,* with its implications of freedom of choice and opportunity to improve one's lot, are kept separate, and the villager is not bothered by any logical inconsistency. When he is faced with a situation which surpasses his control in spite of any efforts he may make, the appropriate concept is that of fate. The women frequently refer to fate as an explanation for various misfortunes, perhaps because they have so little autonomy over their actions.

Not only are individuals born and reborn in successive lives, but the entire universe is periodically destroyed and recreated. In each cycle there are four stages, each progressively shorter than its predecessor, and representing also a decline in health, happiness, stature, longevity, and morality. The age of the universe in which we are now living is the *Kali-yuga*, the last and worst of the four. It is believed that this age will be brought to a close when God sends a divine warrior to kill all evildoers and begins the cycle all over again. Since the fourth age is characterized by an extreme disregard of *dharma*, there are many villagers who see the new rights and aspirations of the lower castes as expectable aspects of the deteriorated times. There is a strong tendency to compare the present unfavorably with the past, and there are few who express sanguine hopes for the future. Most Rājpūts, whose superior status has been severely threatened by the reform movements of the new government, feel that they were much better off under British rule, and even those who see a change for the better will hold that any real and lasting improvement in human affairs must await the next recreation of the universe.

The children are not concerned with these more general religious beliefs and attitudes. They hear the religious stories and songs told and sung by the adults and learn the ceremonial largely from observation. There is no formal religious instruction.

The villagers take their religious ceremonies rather casually, and except when a Brāhmaṇ is present in the house, the ceremonies are not solemn occasions. The children are almost always present during household ceremonies. Little girls may participate actively to the extent of joining their mothers and aunts in keeping a fast, but this is likely to be in the spirit of fun, and children are never required to fast. There is a sex difference here too: little boys fast less frequently than little girls because men do not fast as often as women, and the children's participation is largely imitative.

They may, however, help with some of the preparations, such as the making of the figure of a goddess, which is plastered on the courtyard wall during one festival. During one festival the children run through the village with flaming rags and at another they set off firecrackers.

There are few instances of special religious status for children. Little girls (i.e., virgins) are compared to goddesses because they are pure. They are often called "goddess," and in some ceremonies young girls are given offerings of candy or money. In ritual feeding, a girl may sometimes substitute for a cow or a Brāhmaṇ. Sons should perform funeral rites for their father, but they are usually adults before this duty falls to them.

❉

❉

❉

Chapter 8

Disease and Medical Practices *

Until the 1920's the death rate in all of Uttar Pradesh was extremely high (Bacon, 1956: 37–43), and the fear of disease must have been great. Although epidemics of plague, cholera, smallpox, and so on, since this time have been largely curtailed and famine is more easily prevented because of improved transportation, disease is still a major problem.

Many types of diseases are recognized by the Rājpūts. Diagnosis is based primarily on symptoms, and treatment varies with the type of disease. If one cure fails, a series of other diagnoses and treatments follows. Disease may be caused by the improper functioning of the human body, the needs of which are described in Hindu and Muslim medical texts, by the ghosts of ancestors, or by goddesses and godlings whose nature or function is to give disease. The ancestors may become displeased because they have not been accorded proper ceremonial respect. The goddesses and godlings may punish men for sins of omission committed in this life or in some previous existence. Since one cannot know one's sins in a former life, the actions of the gods are for all practical purposes unpredictable. The supernatural may also be manipulated by individuals through sorcery or the unwitting possession of an evil eye.

Although certain symptoms may be associated with one type of ex-

---

* A large part of the material in this chapter was taken from the Cornell files. Special help in understanding and interpreting the material was contributed by Jack Planalp's doctoral thesis.

planation rather than another,* there is no consistency of diagnoses, and a series of cures may be tried one after another, each implying a different theory of causation. Although the men and the younger and more educated people tend to lean toward traditional or Western medical theories, the women and less educated men tend to favor supernatural explanations. While a man may be seeking the aid of a doctor in a nearby city, the women at home are anxiously offering prayers and food to the family ancestors or to the goddess held responsible for the sickness. An individual may try various types of cures successively or simultaneously.

There is a tendency, however, to diagnose the illnesses of children as supernatural in origin, evil eye being the greatest threat to infants and the epidemic diseases attributed to the goddesses and godlings as the next most frequent.

The diseases most commonly attributed to the more naturalistic causes include pneumonia, stomach-ache, thread worms, eye trouble, coughs, colds, and diarrhea in adults. These are thought to result from the improper care of the body. Leela Dube, in a paper on Khalapur medicine, points out that the villagers have adopted a simplified version of the traditional theory and that their beliefs about proper diet and the regulation of the body are a simplified version of ancient medical texts which contain elaborate instruction about the ideal daily routine, including exercise and cleanliness of the body as well as instruction about food and drink.

Cures which involve fasting or special diet are based primarily on the theory of the nature of certain foods. As Leela Dube (1956: 5–6) writes:

The villagers distinguish between foods that are "hot," that is, which have heat producing effect and foods that are "cold," that is, which have a cold producing or cooling effect. There are also foods that are intermediate between these two and thus are neither "hot" nor "cold." Some foods are constipative, some are laxative. Another distinction is that of catarrhal, billious and flatulent foods. Some foods are supposed to have all three of these properties, some are considered to have two of them and some others may be believed to have only one. There are many commonly used foods to which villagers attribute none of these properties.

In addition there are certain foods like ghi and nuts which are supposed to be particularly strength-giving. Some foods are regarded as better than others in respect to increasing the blood supply in the body. One distinction is that of dry and wet foods. Dryness accentuates the hot quality of a food while wetness accentuates its cool quality.

* Dr. Woodruff's (1959) study of theories of diseases in southern India suggests that a more intensive study might reveal more consistency of symptom determining diagnoses.

The way in which foods are classified in Indian villages varies from place to place, and in Khalapur there is variation from person to person. But many villagers would include as heat producing such items as onion, potato, cane liquor, tea, mangoes, oils, *ghī*, and buffalo milk. Many also would agree that spinach, lemon, and curd are cold, and cow's milk neutral.

In line with these beliefs about diet, it is interesting to note that a number of the older Rājpūts insist that the health of the younger men has been adversely affected by the new varieties of seed the government is distributing. Although better in yield and appearance, it is felt that the crops lack nutritional value and make the young men weak and unable to compete with their elders in agricultural work. Widespread physical deterioration also is attributed to the use of vegetable oil substitutes for *ghī*.

Besides proper food, the villagers emphasize the importance to health of daily bathing, regular elimination, and sexual moderation or abstinence. Village men frequently refer to excessive sex activity as a cause of minor illness, and the longevity of several men is attributed to complete abstinence in their later years. A young man is expected to keep his wife satisfied and beget sons but should not overindulge. When overindulgence is most likely, sanctions sometimes are applied to prevent him. A groom's older sister may regulate the sexual activity of the newlyweds, and his father or uncle may reprimand him or even recommend that his bride be allowed to visit her own house for a time if he sleeps with her too often. (It should be noted that although sanctions of this kind are phrased in terms of the groom's overindulgence, they also in part reflect concern for the new bride.) Sexual intercourse is thought to make men in particular weak and susceptible to disease because the loss of one drop of semen is considered the equivalent of the loss of 40 drops of blood.

Smallpox, chicken pox, measles, and cholera are generally associated with particular disease goddesses referred to as *mātā* or *mai* ("mother"). These goddesses are thought to be sisters, and although informants disagreed, they are most frequently reported as numbering 101. No woman, however, could give the names of more than five or six. Smallpox is named "mother" (*mātā*) after the goddess, and chicken pox is referred to as "little mother." There are shrines to various of these goddesses in the village and its surrounding fields, which the women visit to make offerings. Since smallpox epidemics usually occur in the summer, it is believed that the goddess enters the village at this season. The presence of the goddess is synonomous with the disease, and it is believed that she resides in or near the sick person. Prevention involves keeping the goddess from entering the house, and treatment involves persuading her to leave. Both for prevention and cure, pots of water are placed on the roof of the house to keep the goddess cool or to persuade her not to enter the house or to reduce her power if she is already present. When the patient is recovering, the family performs a ceremony to remove the goddess politely from the house. Like the disease, the goddess is thought to be unpredictable, coming and going like the wind. It is hoped that offerings at the shrines will please her and persuade her not to manifest herself, although there is a contradiction in the ritual themes, for sometimes it is thought she visits a family because they please her.

Certain symptoms are attributed to possession by ghosts of the dead. Possession may be active or passive, the former causing bad dreams and trances, the latter lingering illness. In the trance, the voice of the ghost may speak and make known its wishes.

All persons become ghosts after death but remain so only until after the death ceremonies. If the death ceremonies are not conducted properly, however, a person will remain a ghost. People who have met unnatural deaths or have died in the prime of life while still having worldly desires are very apt to remain ghosts. There are two categories of such persons: suicides, people who have been murdered or killed by ghosts, or who have been killed in accidents fall in the first; unmarried men, men who have not had sons, and women who die in childbirth are examples of the second.

In general, women are more susceptible to possession by ghosts than men, and certain women are more susceptible than others. Girls on the eve of their marriage are sometimes possessed, but even more frequently young daughters-in-law residing for the first time in a strange household become possessed by some hostile spirit. Such possession makes these young brides temporarily the center of concern and attention despite their low status. The ghost is feared, and his demands, spoken through the patient, must be obeyed. The case is reported of a girl possessed by a ghost who became very aggressive, demanding only candy and abusing both her in-laws and the practitioner, who only succeeded in persuading the ghost to depart after it had made a shrewd bargain.

Menstrual difficulties are often associated by women with ghosting. Men are more apt to attribute menstrual disturbance to heat which rises from the lower part of the woman's body to her brain and makes her think she is troubled by a ghost.*

If a ghost simply "sticks" to a person, he becomes ill. A baby whose

* See Jack Planalp's field notes.

mother had died in childbirth is in great danger, since the ghost of the mother is apt to return and "stick" to the child, causing illness or death.

In general, any malingering, undiagnosed illness is likely to be attributed to ghosts. Such patients are taken to magical practitioners called *sianas* rather than to a doctor for cure. There are several such *sianas* in Khalapur and in neighboring villages who are expert in exorcising ghosts and may also perform sorcery. Their cure is usually to persuade the ghost to possess the patient (to "play on" the person in village parlance) and state its wishes. The practitioner then either persuades the ghost to depart to its proper abode in the ancestor's shrine or transfers the ghost to himself and takes the responsibility for taming it. If the ghost will not leave the patient, the practitioner may become possessed himself or he may use an assistant to reveal the identity of the ghost. Another method of expelling a ghost is to put it in a pot and bury it in some field so that it will stick to some person who passes the burial. Obviously anyone may unwittingly fall prey to a ghost in this fashion; however, daughters-in-law returning from their village to their husbands' home seem to be the most frequent victims.

Illness also may be caused by deliberate or inadvertent sorcery. A barren woman may steal and bury the hair of a child and so kill the child and become pregnant. Certain individuals who are believed to have accidentally eaten feces as babies have power to cast the evil eye. A person may not know that he possesses this power, but the act is willful in the sense that the evil eye is an envious eye. Although children are particularly susceptible to the effects of the evil eye, especially if they are unusually handsome or healthy, any person, animal, or even crop which incites envy may fall victim. A man who has an exceptionally good crop puts a blackened pot in the field to ward off the evil eye, and the owner of a good buffalo or cow which is about to freshen ties colored strings to the horns or legs. Black palm prints are sometimes painted on each side of a doorway to ward off the evil eye, and a black spot is painted on the baby's temple or foot.

Although specific cures are associated with different diagnoses, characteristically many techniques are tried simultaneously and in succession. These include diet, herb medicine, Western medicines and massage, prayers and offerings as well as treatment by people skilled in magic, such as wandering holy men, or *sādhūs,* and *siānas.* No matter what the theory of causation, treatment for almost all illnesses involves food restrictions, which are designed to restore the balance of bodily functions. During some acute illnesses the patient may abstain from all food for several days. The villagers also treat patients with a large variety of local medicines, some of which are purchased at the bazaar and some of which the villagers make themselves. Various herbs and plants are common ingredients in these medicines, which may also include such diverse substances as powdered pearls, soot, and honey. Massage is an important part of the treatment of many diseases. When a man is sick, his friends will gather at his bedside to keep him company and massage his limbs. Often this massage is for comfort only, but for sprains and muscular pains its purpose is curative as well. Oil is used for some massages and as a poultice for skin diseases, although cow dung seems to be the most popular poultice. Bleeding, both by cupping and leeches, is not so important for most therapy, but it is mentioned as a treatment for ringworms and bruises.

Some *sādhūs* treat sickness as well as cases of ghost sickness and sorcery. Accidents at birth or in later life bestow certain powers. Babies who enter the world feet first develop power to relieve swelling in the groin by stroking the affected parts with their feet, and men who have killed a rare species of brown bird are called on to cure a cattle disease with their touch. One Rājpūt has a method for protecting humans and animals from the effects of mad dog bites, and people travel long distances to seek his services.

There are three doctors in the village, who combine knowledge of traditional Indian medicine with a knowledge of Western theories and practices. They combine traditional treatments with such things as antibiotic injections. In general, villagers do not consult these doctors until they have tried a number of other remedies. They may visit a doctor and a *sādhū* or *siāna* simultaneously.

The differences in medical treatment of men and women is a function not only of the fact that women believe more in supernatural explanations for illness but also of the restrictions imposed by purdah. Men, particularly wealthy men, will go to the government hospital at Bhudana or even to Delhi if they consider themselves seriously ill. Such expert aid is almost never sought for women. Seeing a doctor involves a breach of seclusion which is undertaken with reluctance, and the women seldom get beyond the village doctors who can visit them in the home. It is not uncommon for a man to go to a doctor in behalf of his wife. One man, leaving his sick wife at home, traveled all the way to Delhi to seek aid for her. Even when the doctor does see his women patients, he must make the diagnosis and conduct his treatment without a physical examination, since this would constitute an unpardonable breach of modesty.

Purdah is not, however, the only explanation for the better medical care received by the men, since the same relative lack of concern may be seen for the health of little girls. Of some 90 children in the neighborhood of this study, almost two thirds were boys. Struck by this unbalanced sex ratio, we questioned 36 women about the sex of their children who had died after birth, that is, not including miscarriages and stillborns. The over-all infant mortality rate for both boys and girls was 33%; for boys it was 25%, and for girls 41%. (Sixty-one children were reported to have died.) These women were, therefore, losing almost twice as many girls as boys in childhood. A test for the differences between percentages shows that this difference would occur by chance only once in a hundred times.*

This differential death rate reflects the prevailing preference for sons. The phenomena is not peculiar to Khalapur. There is an excess of male population throughout India. This excess is most pronounced among such high-caste groups of Northwest India as those represented by the Rājpūts of Khalapur. Until the turn of the century, the village Rājpūts practiced female infanticide. This custom died out under governmental pressure. However, with an over-all childhood death rate of one third, lack of prompt or prolonged medical treatment for girls may be responsible for tipping the balance. This is not to say that all girls are neglected—they are not. But the villagers always expect quick results from medical treatment and will change doctors if the cure is not effective. With a girl—particularly if the family is poor—they will become discouraged sooner, and if she fails to recover, may stop treating her. The four sick babies in the neighborhood who were receiving little or no medical aid were all girls.

The interviews with the afore-mentioned 36 mothers indicate that the child mortality rate is highest from birth to 3 years and declines sharply after that age. Seventy-eight per cent of the 46 dead children had died before the age of 3 years. Usually the mother did not know the cause of death, often attributing it vaguely to "a fever." Malaria or diarrhea may account for some of these deaths. Nine children were reported to have died of smallpox. Dysentery, boils in the mouth, stomach infections, and lack of milk on the part of the mother were also reported to have caused some deaths. One child reputedly died of sorcery, one from the evil eye, and one from the effects of having seen a corpse.

We interviewed the mothers of 23 sample children concerning the diseases suffered by the sample children. Their reports are summarized in Table 1.

* For further information on surplus of males, see Subcontractor's Monograph, Cornell-8, HRAF-44, *India: A Sociological Background*, vol. 1.

Table 1 Incidence of Disease

DISEASE	NO. OF CASES	PER CENT OF CHILDREN
Typhoid	5	22
Pneumonia	7	31
Mātā (smallpox or chicken pox)	12	52
Malaria	16	70
Measles	6	26
Sore eyes	19	83
Boils	12	52
Colds	6	26
Infection	4	18

Most children contracted malaria and sore eyes repeatedly, both diseases being more frequent during the summer months. The seriousness of these two ailments varied. Reaction to malaria may be severe or mild. Similarly, for some children, eye infections yielded readily to the local red medicine, which so often appeared on the faces of children, while others had more trouble throwing off the infection and might even develop fever from it.

Although the children contracted a number of diseases, serious accidents were rare. Mothers commonly reported that the children bumped and cut themselves, but none of the children had broken any bones, and only two had received serious injuries—one, a boy, when he fell from a cart into a ditch and injured his knee, and a little girl when her irate father shook her so severely that he either sprained or dislocated her shoulder.

The high rate of disease affects the attitudes of parents toward children. Almost every baby wears a necklace containing charms to ward off illness. Delicate children are objects of concern, and adults sometimes openly express their doubts for their survival. When discussing the future life of a child, a mother would sometimes add ". . . if he lives." One mother who had lost two daughters reported that she was reluctant to become too fond of her 8-year-old daughter or to buy good clothes for her for fear that this child also would be taken from her. Sickness and death are very much a part of the villager's experience, and the fear of them is never far from their minds.

Chapter 9

Death Ceremonies *

Since earth, fire, and water are all sacred elements, a body may be properly disposed of through any one of these mediums or a combination of them. In practice, all three elements usually enter into the disposal of the dead. Thus, in the procedure used with most adults, the dying person is first laid on the earth, the body is cremated, and the ashes are consigned to water. Burial or disposal of the body in a river is practiced when the deceased is a child or a person who has died of an epidemic disease. Some sects of *sādhūs* bury their dead.

This differential disposal of the dead can be partially understood in terms of the Hindu's beliefs about spirits. When a person dies, the divine and impersonal aspect, the soul, immediately goes to heaven, but the more personal aspect—the aspect which differentiates one from the others—lingers in the vicinity of the home. The elaborate ceremonies which follow the cremation of a body are primarily designed to ensure the safe passage of this personlike shade into the world of the ancestors. If the ceremonies fail in their purpose, the shade will become a malevolent ghost and haunt the family, causing trouble and sickness. When the body is buried or consigned to a river, there is no elaborate ceremonial. These latter forms of disposal are, in effect, "short cut" methods and as such are reserved for those whose shades are considered to be willing to abandon the pleasures of this world without elaborate persuasion. Children fall into this category because they have not yet known and enjoyed worldly pleasures; *sādhūs,* because they have already voluntarily renounced them.

The reasons for not cremating persons who have died of epidemic

* In writing this section the author has used material from the thesis by Jack Planalp (1956) as well as the field notes on Khalapur. Dr. Planalp worked in a village several hundred miles distant from Khalapur but with a similar group. The main outlines of funeral customs are the same for large numbers of the Indian population.

diseases probably stem from the belief that these diseases are sacred, representing, as they do, the visitation of a disease goddess. Therefore persons who die in this fashion are already touched by a goddess and do not require further purification by fire. The practice has the obvious practical advantage of allowing for rapid disposal of bodies at a time when many people are dying. The death ceremonies, in a somewhat attenuated form, may be held for such persons after the epidemic has abated. When they are held, a figure of the deceased is fashioned and used to represent the corpse.

When a person is about to die, the area beside the cot on which he is lying is made ritually pure by plastering it with cow dung. The person is then lifted from the cot and laid on the ground. The cot is impure, and it is felt that a person should breathe his last on a spot of sanctified earth.

After death, the body is washed and prepared for cremation. When a married man dies, his wife comes to touch his feet; at the same time her jewelry is removed and her bangles are broken over the feet of the corpse by the wife of the barber. When the body has been sewn in the funeral cloth (which must always be newly purchased), the first of several offerings to the spirit of the dead is made. This consists of a rolled piece of dough made of barley flour and water, which is placed on the dead person's chest. Offerings of the same substance are made on the way to the cremation grounds and during the period of mourning, assuring the re-embodiment of the spirit and hastening its progress to heaven. The bedding and the clothes of the deceased are given to the family sweeper.

When married women of the deceased's lineage receive news of the death, they come to help prepare the body and express their regrets. Together with the women of the household they beat their foreheads, breasts, and thighs and raise their voices in the high-pitched tones of ritual wailing. A family will be criticized by neighbors if the women's wails are not long and loud, and one woman said that when women mourned properly, their bodies should show the bruises of their self-inflicted beatings. The wailing reaches a peak when the men of the family arrive to remove the body to the cremation grounds, usually not more than two or three hours after death. In marked contrast to ritual wailing, grief, when wailing is not required, is expressed in complete silence. As the body of a mother-in-law was carried away, a daughter-in-law beat her head against the courtyard wall and had to be restrained by the other women, but the dead woman's teen-aged, unmarried daughter stood on the sidelines, holding the baby of her wailing aunt, with silent tears coursing down her face.

The body is carried by four male members of the family (preferably sons and grandsons of the deceased) to the cremation grounds, a place just outside the village designated for this purpose. Only men, close relatives and friends, join the funeral procession, which is led by the chief mourner, preferably the eldest son of the deceased. The body is tied to a stretcher which is made of the boughs of the sacred *nīm* tree, usually prepared by the family carpenter. Members of the family carry logs of wood or bundles of straw, and one carries a pot of clarified butter and another a piece of burning cow dung. Other mourners pick up twigs on the way, for no one should go to the cremation grounds empty handed. At a particular spot about half way to the grounds, the body is lowered to the ground, and the men who have been carrying the body take up different positions beside the bier. In the past the chief mourner had his head and moustache shaved at this time, but now the barber merely cuts off a token lock of hair.

After the body has been placed on the pyre, which is made of cow dung and wood, and after the mourners have placed their bits of wood, straw, and twigs on the pyre, the family Brāhmaṇ throws *ghī* and sacred and aromatic substances over the corpse. All but one pole of the stretcher on which the body was carried are also placed on the pyre. The chief mourner lights a bundle of straw from the burning cow dung which was carried by one of the mourners and moves quickly around the pyre setting it ablaze. All the mourners squat on the ground, and while the Brāhmaṇ recites sacred verses, the chief mourner throws the last of the *ghī* and other sacred substances into the fire. He picks up the remaining pole of the stretcher and makes seven ritual passes from the ground to the head of the corpse, signifying that he has broken its skull. The importance of having sons is due in part to this portion of the cremation ceremony, since, to ensure the safe passage of a man's shade into the world of the ancestors, it should be a son who "breaks" his skull. After making the final ritual pass, the chief mourner flings the pole all the way over the pyre. All the mourners then stand up and walk slowly back to the brook which runs in front of the village.

After ritually cleansing themselves in this stream, the mourners walk to the vicinity of the men's quarters of the deceased. On the way they strip some of the leaves from a *nīm* tree. They squat on the ground near the men's quarters, chew up some of the leaves and spit them onto the ground. The *nīm* leaves provide further ritual cleansing, and the spitting is said to symbolize a complete severance of any connection between the mourners and the dead person.

The family of the deceased observes a number of restrictions for the next 13 days, especially in regard to eating. The chief mourner, who is ritually impure, is subject to more severe restrictions. He must sleep on the ground and is not permitted to sit with other men or smoke the hookah with them. If possible, he should remain quietly in one place, usually a corner of the men's quarters.

On the third day of mourning, the chief mourner, the family Brahman, and sometimes the family barber go to the cremation site and gather the ashes and bones. The ashes are put in the brook or into one of the irrigation canals, both of which are said to connect with the Ganges, but, if possible, the bones are saved to be taken to Hardwar for consignment to the sacred Ganges itself.

During the next nine days the family may make various offerings to the deceased's shade and engage in ritual bathing. Women of the deceased's lineage come to the family's women's quarters every afternoon and sit with the bereaved women in silence, a silence which may occasionally be broken by remarks about the virtues of the deceased and the family women who cared for him. On the 11th and 12th days of mourning, more balls of barley dough are offered.

On the 12th or 13th day after the cremation, male relatives and friends plus affinal relatives come to attend a feast and a ceremony. All the affinal relatives bring cloth, sweets, and money. The gifts from families into which daughters have been married cannot be accepted and are returned to the donors with some additional money, but one of the pieces of cloth given by one of the other affinal relatives is taken, and in a ceremony at which a Brāhmaṇ officiates, it is tied around the head of the chief mourner and worn as a turban. The villagers say that this ritual act symbolizes the transfer of authority from the deceased to the chief mourner. The ceremony also serves to remove the last vestiges of impurity from this man, and after it he can sit with others and share the hookah. Meanwhile the lineage women visit the courtyard for the last time and wail again. The Brāhmaṇ also purifies the house on the 12th or 13th day. After this ceremony, the shade's journey to heaven is considered complete.

Funeral feasts occasionally are elaborate, and many guests are invited, particularly when a respected elder of a prosperous household has died. But most are small and include only a few close friends and relatives. Whenever such feasts are held, the family servants are also fed.

If the deceased is a married man, his wife may go to bathe in the Ganges sometime after the funeral feast. There she gives her old clothes to sweepers and dresses in a new white and borderless sari, which is given to her by her family. She also puts on the silver bangles of a widow, which have been provided by her own family. After bathing, she provides a meal for the attendant Brāhmaṇ. If the deceased is a man of importance, a feast similar in nature to the 13th-day feast may be held a year later on the anniversary of his death.

Children who die before the age of about 12 are usually not cremated. If they have not yet had their hair cut in the ceremony usually held when the child is about 5 years old, they are never cremated. A child between the age of 5 and 12 might be cremated with the attendant ceremonies if his family were wealthy and he was a favored or only son. Such an event, however, would be rare.

Since there are no large rivers near the village, children are usually buried beside one of the village ponds. Rarely is a child's body taken to a river for disposal.

The body is taken from the house by the man of the family. After burial, the wooden handle of the spade is left behind, but the metal part, being too expensive to abandon, is retained. The men who perform the burial wash in a stream or well. To signify cremation, a piece of burning cow dung may be placed in the child's right hand until it scorches the flesh. This practice is also present with river disposal. After a burial, in the evening a piece of burning cow dung in a piece of a broken water jug is placed near the grave. Two small earthenware pots of milk and a small earthenware lamp are also placed there. It is said that these things are placed near the grave to prevent animals from digging up the body.

The family may fast for a time, but this is not required.

✤

✤

✤

Chapter 10

Recreation

Leisure time in the village is usually spent in the company of one's own sex. Men gather in their open courtyards and talk and smoke. The daily family gatherings are probably the most spontaneous and friendly. Men also frequently visit other men's quarters and discuss state and local politics, economics, and gossip. Some of this visiting is in the line of practicality and could not be said to be motivated by carefree sociability. Rājpūt men of an extended family are well advised to be on good terms with as many other Rājpūts in the village as possible. A man who is not your friend is a potential enemy, who may be drawn into the hostile camp in time of a dispute. As one prominent Rājpūt man stated: "It is easy to get court cases going, even false cases, if a family is not social and does not go to meet people in the village. I don't accept a family as a good family unless there is at least one person who can go around the village and meet people. This is one of the most important things."

In line with maintaining friendly relations, the Rājpūts have a definite code of etiquette for hospitality. Although strangers may be viewed with some suspicion, they are treated cordially unless there are serious grounds for doubting them. Men must be offered the hookah and should be offered food. There is an attempt to emulate the gracious manners of the traditional feudal court. One of the defining requirements of a good daughter-in-law is that she be able to cook large meals for guests.

Visiting is one of the most important forms of recreation for the men. There are a few Rājpūts who seldom leave the village, and two have retired almost completely from the village and their families, living a lonely life of seclusion in small shelters in the fields. But these men are exceptional. Most Rājpūt men, young and old, leave the village fairly often to attend the marriages of friends or relatives. Brothers often visit their sisters' families, and when their sisters' children are married, they are expected to be present and to bring gifts. Some of the older men make occasional trips to quite distant pilgrimage spots, and whole families sometimes go by bullock cart to those which are closer. Men often have to go to the city—to deliver cane, to pick up their payment, to buy liquor, meat or tobacco, to make small purchases needed by the women for the household, to purchase jewelry for marriages, to attend court cases, and to visit various government offices. Many of the men have friends in Bhudana, and a few have friends in the more distant larger cities. They look forward to visiting them whenever their business takes them to these centers. Many of the younger men and some of the older will also attend a cinema if time permits. A few of the younger men occasionally visit prostitutes. A few of the men are interested in state and national politics, and they sometimes leave the village to hear the speeches of candidates or to meet them personally.

Traveling singers, players, and astrologers are an appreciated source of amusement and relaxation. A few of the young men have harmoniums. They have learned to accompany themselves as they sing local folk ballads and current cinema favorites. They and their friends will gather for singing, sometimes on a men's house platform and sometimes in small huts in the fields or orchards. The temple attendant has a good voice, and a number of the younger Rājpūts gather to hear him sing and to smoke Indian hemp (*Cannabis indica*) together in a hand-pipe which they pass from person to person. Occasionally an Arya Samaj preacher comes to the village. His preaching consists of homilies, interlarded with jokes and songs in the folk manner. He is accompanied by a harmonium, a drum, and small cymbals. These presentations are popular and always attract a large crowd. The village constantly is being visited by *sādhūs,* and the older ones especially are welcome on the men's house platforms. There is one holy man who comes to the village regularly every spring from a nearby pilgrimage center. He makes his home in a field under a large tree, and many of the Rājpūts stop by for a talk with him as they pass to and from their work. He is much respected, and his remarks on the virtue of asceticism and on the glories of the ancient Hindu way of life are frequently quoted. On one occasion a well-known, retired Rājpūt robber visited friends in the village and attracted a large and appreciative audience.

There is much camaraderie of a more informal nature in the fields, especially among the younger men. One of the characteristic village sounds is their calling to one another across the fields. Those in adjacent plots meet together to rest and warm themselves before a fire and to eat their noonday repast. Lower caste field laborers usually are welcome members of these groups.

There is variety in village recreational life. But all else is peripheral to conversation, a never-palling source of pleasure. Once past school age this form of recreation has an unchallenged place among the men. They talk with animation, gesturing forcefully. A joke, a salty phrase, or a well-aimed riposte are much enjoyed, and even on solemn occasions talk is punctuated with laughter.

Similarly, the women in a courtyard spend most of their daily life talking and gossiping with one another as they work. As Patricia Hitchcock describes it:

The young daughters-in-law of the family visit in one room and then another of the same courtyard. While they talk, they work with their hands—knit, embroider, etc. They tell about what happens in their own homes in their parents's villages. The young daughters-in-law play games before dark with the young children. They play hide and seek, dog and cat, and jacks with stones. The older women sometimes tell stories in the evenings, often about the ancient kings and about ghosts. A literate woman sometimes reads to the group. This may last until 10 or 11 in the evening. Great pleasure is afforded by painting simple designs on the walls for religious ceremonies and marriages. The designs may be original but are all in the same style. Music is popular and the women play drums and dance. One courtyard has a victrola which is very popular.*

The women's conversation covers many subjects. They talk about borrowing and lending grain, about marriages and new brides. They discuss the whereabouts of their husbands, whether they have come home from the fields, the health of the cattle, and other practical problems. They may criticize others, perhaps for stinginess or other deviant behavior at the time of a marriage. Any unusual event is discussed with animation, and, during our stay, the Americans at the Project House were a constant source of conversation. There is also a good deal of joking and gossiping of a sexual nature.

Intercourtyard visiting is frequent among the older women, who may pass through the streets and who have delegated much of their work to their daughters-in-law. Among the younger women, whose households demand the observance of strict purdah, visiting is sometimes possible over the rooftops. Visits to the home village are frequent and looked forward to with happy anticipation.

Religious ceremonies and births and marriages are most welcome interruptions to the daily routine. The religious calendar provides many such days, which involve festive preparations. Although the religious aspects are important, there is joy in both the preparations and the get-togethers. Perhaps the most eagerly anticipated event of the year is a fair or *melā* (a religious fair), held in the spring, when in most families all but the youngest daughters-in-law enjoy a day's release from the confines of the courtyard. At this time some of the hair-cutting ceremonies take place, and the women make offerings of food or money to the goddess of the local temple to ensure good health for their families. The women come early in the morning and spend the day enjoying the sights and participating in the fun. They shop for sweets, jewelry, cosmetics, and other luxuries as well as more practical items, such as metal trunks. The children, accompanying the women, also have a gala day. They may ride on the crude carrousel or ferris wheel, stare curiously at the *sādhūs* who always frequent the *melās*, or, if lucky, persuade mother to buy them one of the many toys displayed for sale.

One man always accompanies the women to the *melā*, to drive the bullock cart, but, as in other social settings, most of the men part company from their women. Since the *melā* comes in the middle of the busy harvest season, the men usually attend at night, visiting a movie

* See Patricia Hitchcock, field notes.

and the circus or watching the dancing of the female impersonators and the antics of the clowns who provide a side show along one border of the fair grounds.

Although the *melā* is a particularly festive occasion for the women, providing for many their one yearly trip beyond the confines of the village, all religious festivals are times for sociability. Often preceded by fasts in honor of some goddess, they include feasting, with the elaborate preparation of special dishes. The house is decorated with wall painting and other ornamentation. The family servants come to receive food, and there is visiting between courtyards, conversation, singing, and often dancing. The women dress in their best sarīs and sometimes get new clothes for the occasion. They wear their most valuable jewelry and cosmetics. Some women may take offerings to the ancestor shrines or other village shrines. Although some women who are in purdah make these excursions, the younger daughters-in-law give their offerings to an older woman or to an unmarried girl to take for them.

The most unlicensed ceremony takes place on the day after the spring festival of Holī. Many of the usual patterns of respect and avoidance are abandoned. Teen-age boys may throw colors at the new brides, and both boys and girls may enter courtyards and break water pots. Any woman who is outside her courtyard is apt to have dyes thrown at her. The sweepers have a band and dance and sing through the streets. Many of the village men drink heavily.

Weddings with all their preparations and ceremonies are events which are enjoyed by both men and women and involve the largest groups. At such times the entire neighborhood has a chance to visit each other and share in the fun and excitement.

When visiting players come to the village with musical dramas, the men usually attend by themselves. The female impersonators who sing and dance in the dramas are not considered proper entertainment for women.

⚜
⚜
⚜

Chapter 11

Education

Although the Rājpūts belong to a culture with a rich heritage of art, music, and literature, and although they also are one of the elite twice-born castes, a high percentage of the village Rājpūts are illiterate. The traditional role of warrior did not require that a man be literate. More recently, however, education, for men at least, has assumed new importance. With the coming of the sugar mills, the average farmer was brought into everyday contact with business methods in which paper work played a very significant part. If he could not read, someone had to tell him how much cane to plant, how much to cut and when, how much it weighed and was worth, and when to come and get his payment. For some decades, knowledge of the law and court procedure has been an important means of protecting family interests. In the present, literacy is becoming increasingly valued as an avenue to job opportunities in the lower echelons of the government bureaucracy. Although some of the poorest families need the help of at least some of the sons in the fields, almost all families now try to have at least one or two boys educated. The educated boy is usually a younger son, the first son having been recruited as a full-time field hand. Most Rājpūt families can educate all sons if they wish. The inferior status of women has meant that education for them was virtually nonexistent.

The increasing emphasis on education among the Rājpūts can be seen in the statistics of enrollment in the boys' primary school. Of the 200 students enrolled in the school, 167 are Rājpūts. The breakdown on the remaining 33 students is 6 Moslems, 6 Brāhmaṇs, and 21 from the other castes. The large proportion of the Rājpūt boys reflects, of course, both the predominance of Rājpūts in the village population and the greater wealth of the Rājpūt families. Nevertheless, they are clearly more education-minded than other castes in the village, including the Brāhmaṇs, to whom the role of educated teacher traditionally belongs.

A breakdown by age shows that education is a very recent development among the Khalapur Rājpūts. Only 24% of the men in our sample families who are over 40 have had any education. Of the men between 20 and 40 years of age, only 38% are literate, but 70% of the boys and young men between the ages of 6 and 20 have been to school or are currently enrolled in school. Clearly the great increase in education for men has occurred during the last 20 years. Extent of education has also increased since the high school has been built. Before that time anyone wishing to continue beyond the primary grades could only choose between attending the religious school * or seeking further education outside the village. Only four men in our sample had any high school education. One of these is a teacher in Bhudana, a second is a government clerk in Bhudana, the third administers a farm, and the fourth is a member of the legislative and executive branch of the village council.

The rather dramatic increase in the literacy rate of males does not hold for the feminine population. Most men still believe that teaching a girl to read and write will only encourage her to write to her family begging to come home whenever her in-laws displease her. Furthermore, because the educated city women usually have servants and are not in seclusion, the men also believe that an educated girl will not cook and keep house and will become restless in the confinement of the courtyard.

On the other hand, there is gradually developing a body of opinion to the effect that a girl should be able to write home and complain if she is unhappy in her husband's house and that an educated girl, being presumably wiser to the ways of the world, does not need the protection of purdah to ensure her virtue. In any case, the statistics for the women in our sample families show an increase in literacy during the last 20 years, although a very gradual one. Seven per cent of the women over 40, 5% of those between 20 and 40, and 14% of

---

* The religious school (*pāthṭhālā*) is situated a short walk outside the village to the south. The school was conceived of by Sucheet Singh and supported by other members of the Ārya Samāj reform movement. At the time of research there were 25 students, all of them members of the three highest castes. There is a principal and two teachers. The boys lead an austere life. Sanskrit is emphasized, but the curriculum includes Hindu, civics, geography, natural science, and mathematics. A high proportion of the students attend this school until they pass the primary stage and then shift to the high school. The school is supported by the income from 20 acres of land; 5% of high-caste doweries in neighboring villages goes to the school; and one stalk of cane is taken from every load of cane brought to the mill from these villages. The Rājpūts of Khalapur contribute 10 pounds of grain per plow.

Men's platforms and cattle compound; closed porch and rooms in building at left.

Boys taking cattle to graze. They are walking on the walls of irrigation ditches.

Men chopping fodder with bladed wheel.

View of the rear of a men's quarters showing porch and bedrooms.

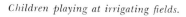

Old man smoking Hooka on men's platform.

Children playing at irrigating fields.

Boys playing game similar to jacks.

Double courtyard shared by group of brothers.

Typical single courtyard.

Women spinning.

Women weaving.

Women nursing during haircutting ceremony.

Ten-year-old girl carrying year-old boy cousin.

Six-year-old girls picking water chestnuts.

Eight- and 9-year-old boys bringing fodder from fields.

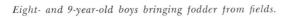

the girls between 6 and 20 are literate or attending school. The older educated women come from exceptionally wealthy and "cosmopolitan" families.

These statistics probably indicate a slight improvement in the educational level of women. It is impossible to be sure, however, since the women over 20 are primarily wives who have married into the village, whereas the women under 20 are primarily daughters of Khalapur. It is possible, therefore, that the figures reflect merely a higher educational level among the Khalapur women as compared with those of other villages. The educational opportunities for girls are still limited to the five grades of primary school, for the high school is open to boys only. Many parents withdraw their girls from school after the fourth grade. Since they have usually mastered enough knowledge to be able to read and write by the end of the fourth year, the fifth year is often regarded as superfluous. Only 40 girls, mostly Rājpūts, attend the girls' school, as against the 200 students in the boys' primary school.

The boys' school is located on the temple platform and the men's quarters of the village council, which is adjacent to the temple platform. There are a number of rooms behind the platform. Classes are held on the open platform, in the rooms, and on the roof of the building. Most of the younger children sit under a large tree on the temple platform. In the winter, during the coldest months, they bring mats; otherwise they sit on the ground. Situated in another part of the village, the girls' school consists of one large room in an open terrace and garden. The school grounds are enclosed by a high wall. Weather permitting, classes are held outside, and when it is unusually cold, hot, or rainy, they are held inside.

The primary school term runs from the first week of July until the end of May. There are several vacations of a week or more and a number of one- or two-day holidays during the school term. Until September, the school day begins at 7 A.M. The morning session runs until 11 A.M. and the afternoon session from 3:00 until 5:00. From October until March, when the weather is cooler, the morning session runs from 10 in the morning until noon and the afternoon one from 12:30 to 4:00. During the winter months many of the boys come to school at 7 or 8 o'clock so that they may have a longer lunch hour. Supposedly, the hours in the morning before the school opens are to be used for study, but there is only one teacher present as monitor, and frequently the boys' bookbags remain unopened. The boys' school has five masters.

There are two teachers in the girls' school. The headmistress is an intelligent and sensible woman, but the assistant teacher is far less competent. During the months of October and November, when the headmistress was on leave, many of the mothers stopped sending their girls to school because of the incompetence of this younger teacher. The discipline in the girls' school is far better than in the boys' school, and the girls spend most of their time studying.

The curriculum for both primary schools is almost identical. For the first two years the children are taught reading and writing, numbers, multiplication tables and simple arithmetic, and general knowledge. In the second year, art is added to the schedule. The third year sees the addition of history and civics, and in the fourth and fifth grades geography is included in the curriculum. The boys are taught farming in the third, fourth, and fifth grades, and the girls are given some instruction in sewing.

Learning is primarily by rote; the children write either on a regular blackboard-type slate or, more commonly, on a wooden slate which is coated with a whitewashlike substance and then written on in ink. The teacher traces the letters on the slate with a pencil, and the children go over them in ink. They learn their multiplication tables by chanting them in unison.

The fees for the boys' school start at one anna, or about 6¢ a month for the first grade, working up to about 46¢ a month for the fifth grade —not a significant drain on the finances of any but the poorest families. The girls' school, on the other hand, charges no fees at all because, according to the headmistress, the villagers would not pay anything to send their daughters to school.

The villagers' interest in education is practical rather than scholarly; hence their attitude toward academic achievement is very casual. They do not press their children to attend school, get good grades, or encourage them to study. As mentioned earlier, a high percentage of the parents themselves are illiterate, and they cannot successfully help the children with their studies. Moreover, their fatalism and the fact that in extended families such educational decisions may be made by the head man prevent the parents from making extended plans for their children's education. We asked a number of mothers how long they wanted their children to attend school. By far, the most common answer to this question was, "It is in his fate, no matter what I want." Even the most educated father, the only man in our sample who holds a white-collar job rather than farming for a living, says about his son's education, "You can never know about the future, or what is going to happen. A man may have high ambition, but only that is fulfilled which is in nature's wish. It depends on his luck. I may wish that my son will become a collector (the highest official in a district), but it is only that which is in his fate."

Because of this attitude, attendance at school is far from regular. Illness, no matter how mild, is always an accepted excuse for non-attendance. We often found children playing actively in the streets who insisted they were too ill to attend school. Since the mothers are in purdah and the fathers in the fields, there is no one to check on whether or not the child actually goes to school once he leaves the house. The headmaster of the boys' school says that usually about 20% of the students are absent in the morning and about 40% in the afternoon. The younger boys do not attend classes in the afternoon, which accounts for the larger number of absentees at that time. The girls play hookey less from their school, probably because those who are in school are better motivated.

Even when parents do send their children to school, attendance is not regular. Parents may take their children out of school when their services are needed at home, for example, during the harvest season. Furthermore, if children do not want to attend school, they seldom are forced to go. Both boys and girls occasionally complain that the teachers beat them, and some children refuse to attend school for this reason. We saw an older boy who was acting as monitor hit two younger boys and make them cry. And, we also saw one master teaching a class and holding behind his back a rather ominous-looking Indian club, but we never observed the teacher actually hitting a child. Probably such events did occur from time to time and were used by children as excuses for not attending school.

As the boys progress in their education, the lackadaisical attitude changes. There is a marked difference in the behavior of the younger and older boys in the primary school, the older ones being far more studious. The boys who elect to continue through high school must work hard. Their examinations are supervised by the government and held in another town. The students are therefore in a competitive atmosphere, which is not true of the primary schools.

Part II

BY LEIGH MINTURN

Child Training

✳
✳
✳
✳
✳
✳

Chapter 12

Pregnancy and Childbirth

The bearing and raising of children are considered appropriate and natural functions of the middle years of life. Parents have a social and religious obligation to marry their daughters; and girls, unless seriously deformed or mentally aberrant, are always married. Persons who die childless are believed to become ghosts. Since they have not in life fulfilled their role of parent, they are still bound to the world of the living by their desire to finish their incomplete life cycle in that world.

The fact that one important belief in sorcery revolves around the desire for children is further evidence of their importance. It is believed that if a woman is childless, she may steal the birth hair of a baby—for sorcery purposes. She gives this hair to a *siāna* who puts it in a pot with five different kinds of clothing. He then buries the pot, accompanying the burial with appropriate incantations. When this is

301

done, the child whose hair has been cut dies, and the childless woman becomes pregnant. Reports varied as to the effectiveness of this procedure. One woman said that the child usually did not die but always got sick; another, however, warned us never to go near a childless woman. We found only one woman, Mrs. Rāmchand, who thought that such sorcery had actually been performed on her son. This woman, having only one child, born after 12 years of marriage, was very concerned about his health. Nonetheless, all the women knew of this practice of sorcery and were probably on guard against it.

There are other less violent ways for a childless woman to become fertile. A shrine near the village is believed to be an auspicious place to pray for children, and barren women sometimes make offerings at this shrine. A woman with children may pray for a barren friend on Hōī, the day when she gives offerings for the health of her own sons. Mrs. Rāmchand's sister-in-law had prayed for her during her 12 years of barrenness. On Hōī day, the grateful Mrs. Rāmchand was dyeing a headcloth to give to her sister-in-law. She had promised to give her a yellow headcloth on Hōī for five years, in thanks for her successful intervention.

In the matter of sex, sons are greatly preferred to daughters. Evidence of this preference is demonstrated dramatically at birth, with the elaborate birth ceremonies which are usually held for sons only.* There are several reasons for this preference for boys. The family prestige depends largely on wealth and manpower; boys are potential farm hands and fighters for the family name, and, since the society is patrilineal, they are the bearers of the family continuity. Also, a son is necessary for the performance of certain funeral rites at the pyre of his father. Without a son, a man's salvation is jeopardized. A girl, on the other hand, is always a financial liability. She requires an extensive dowry at the time of marriage, and she is committed to making gifts to her husband's household when she returns to visit him for at least the first few years of their marriage. Furthermore, since a girl must marry into a family of higher status than her own, her male relatives are always subservient to the men of her husband's family. Many of the men do not take kindly to this inferior position.

Until the turn of the century, the prejudice against girls was expressed in the custom of female infanticide.† Today, as we mentioned

* These ceremonies are sometimes held in an attenuated form for girls.

† The British outlawed infanticide in 1848. A government officer was sent to the village about 1900 to enforce this law. Because of his necessary violation of purdah restrictions, he was murdered by some outraged men. However, government pressure and Ārya Samāj influence brought an end to infanticide as a widespread custom. although isolated instances of it probably still occur.

in Chapter 8, differential medical treatment still causes twice as many girls as boys to die before reaching maturity.

There does seem to be some compensatory status for girls. When asked whether they would wish for a girl or a boy when pregnant, the women either expressed no preference, saying that it was in the hands of Rāma or that they wished for a boy. But when asked whether they *liked* boys better than girls, the women were as likely as not to express a preference for their own sex. They said they were fonder of girls because girls go away to their husband's homes, while boys stay with their parents. This attitude seems to reflect a sentimentality about girls which is not accorded to boys.

At present most couples prefer to have at least one daughter, since the giving of a daughter in marriage is a virtuous act, which, according to Hindu tradition, every man should perform during his lifetime. But a family with a dearth of sons and an excess of daughters is considered unfortunate indeed.

Although the Indian government sponsors a birth-control program, knowledge of birth control had not yet reached the village women. No contraceptive methods are used in the village, although some of the women asked about American practices. They realized that "medicine" was available for this purpose but were vague about its nature. Education, expense, and the high child-mortality rate are probably the three most important factors standing in the way of an adequately planned parentage program.

Certain methods for abortion are known to the villagers. One elderly lady was reputed to perform abortions, and some informants mentioned the use of a medicine which is inserted in the vagina to dilate the cervix. Abortion was certainly not frequently practiced, however. Probably it was usually practiced only for cases of illegitimacy.

Since sexual immorality, particularly among women, is a great disgrace to the family, and therefore a carefully guarded secret, it is difficult to estimate the frequency of illegitimate births. At best one can state some of the conditions under which they might occur and the probable reaction to such events.

Strict sexual mores and early marriage mitigate against premarital affairs for girls. Since any scandal about an unmarried girl will not only reflect on the family but also greatly decrease her chances for a good marriage, Rājpūt parents react with immediate and violent indignation to any remark against their daughters' virtue. Nevertheless, stories persist that the girls sometimes have affairs with boys from the village when they are working in the fields. An illegitimate baby, born to an unmarried girl during our stay, was delivered by the girl's father, who then killed and buried it. The village women were highly critical of the parents for having raised their daughter so badly but made no comment about the killing of the baby. Furthermore, the village officials took steps to see that the police would not investigate the incident. Murder of such children is evidently accepted as a necessary step for the preservation of the family honor.

The illicit affairs of married Rājpūt women would usually occur either in their own villages or with a relative of the husband who has access to the courtyard at night. A woman who conceived in her own village and was unable to hide this fact would probably be abandoned by her husband and his family. If the pregnancy occurred in the husband's house, he might accept the child as his own rather than face a scandal, particularly if the father were his superior.

Since neither abortion nor contraception are normally used, the only check on pregnancy rate is the post-partum sex taboo. This taboo on intercourse should last for two years after the birth of the baby. The reason given for the custom is that intercourse will make the mother's milk bad and cause the baby to become weak and sickly.

The census material shows that the taboo is not always observed, at least not for the full two-year period. There are a number of families who have children at two-year intervals; an interim of more than two years between children usually indicates that a child, now dead, was born during that period. If one examines only the children of parents who are now over 35 years old, one finds that the modal age between these children is three years, as one would expect if the couple were observing a two-year intercourse taboo between each child. Younger parents, however, are more likely to have children at two-year intervals (see Table 2).

Table 2 Birth Rate as a Function of Age of Parents

	MOTHER OVER 35	MOTHER UNDER 35
Children born 2 years apart or less	6	14
		$P = .03$
Children born 3 years apart or more	13	7

The birth rate is not influenced by whether or not the couple is living in a house with a mother-in-law. Evidently the period of the taboo is being shortened by the younger couples, and mothers-in-law are often no longer able to enforce the restrictions. Certainly, at present, the custom presents no significant check to the birth rate. The average number of living children per family is between four and five, but six and seven living children are not uncommon. Since about one third of the children born die before reaching maturity, we estimate that the average woman, whose husband survives throughout her childbearing years, bears from seven to nine children.

Pregnant women do all of their regular work but are careful not to strain themselves. They have a number of dietary restrictions. Among these are milk, cold rice, a pulse dish, food which is either excessively hot or excessively cold, and spicy foods such as pickles. The reports concerning the length of time that milk should not be drunk varied from after the first four months of pregnancy to the last month of pregnancy. The explanations for this taboo also varied. One woman said that milk made the Fallopian tubes septic; another said that the baby would get too big; and a third explained that milk and the baby were considered to be the same.* Some women report a craving for mud during pregnancy, and some eat mud or clay at this time.† Women are prohibited from having intercourse during pregnancy. No ceremonies are held, since men of the household are not supposed to know that a woman is pregnant, and a ceremony would publicize the fact.

When the labor starts, the mother retires to her room, and the family sends for a midwife. They are often not very prompt about calling the midwife. Since blood is considered to be unclean, the Rājpūt women will not deliver children, clean up after a birth, or change bandages on the mother, and midwifery is traditionally the profession of Untouchable women. In Khalapur the wives were usually of the Bhangī or sweeper caste. Although there is a government-trained midwife resident in the village, most of the sample families would not use her, for she refused to return after the birth to change bandages, a service which the Rājpūts consider as important as aid in the delivery of a baby. Furthermore, the government midwife brings an Untouchable woman to cut the cord and clean up, necessitating the payment of two persons.

While the mother is in labor, a sickle, knife, and plowshare are placed near her bed, and a shoe is turned upside down near the foot of the bed or under it. Many women procure a paper with prayers on it from a village Brāhmaṇ, which they look at to aid the delivery.

Only one birth was witnessed during our stay in the village. The

* This information is taken from the field notes of Dr. Leela Dube.
† This craving may be due to calcium deficiency.

baby had arrived and the midwife was cleaning up. The following is an account of this incident:

The midwife was there. The baby was lying beside Mrs. A. It was a boy. Mrs. A.'s mother-in-law and an older woman were helping. Mrs. A. was sitting on her feet in the characteristic Indian squatting position. She had each foot on a brick so that she was somewhat elevated from the floor.* She was sitting just beside her bed, facing it. She was wearing a petticoat, blouse, and head shawl. Behind her was a pile of ashes. A small pile of flour was on the floor a few feet away from her. There were blood and water on the floor around her. Part of the afterbirth was on the floor underneath her. The midwife tore off a piece of cloth from an old piece of clothing and removed the afterbirth with it. She pushed this into the pile of ashes, which she was evidently going to use to sweep up with. Then Mrs. A's mother-in-law held out a pot of water to Mrs. A. and she washed her hands. Then the mother-in-law helped her onto the bed. Mrs. A. removed her petticoat, which was wet and bloody. When she was seated on the bed, the mother-in-law took a piece of cord from out of the cloth braid in her hair and gave it to the midwife. The midwife pulled at it and it broke. She rejected it. The mother-in-law then took off another piece from the end of Mrs. A.'s braid. The midwife tied the baby's cord with this. The other woman handed the midwife the vegetable cutter. (This is a curved knife mounted on a board. The women put one foot on the board to hold it while slicing vegetables.) The midwife cut the umbilical cord with this knife. Then she rubbed the baby with flour. She pinched its breasts and then cleaned the eyes and nose with her finger. The mother lay on the bed and pulled the quilt over her. She was moaning slightly. However, she did not seem to be in much pain, and the baby's head showed only slight deformation. We were informed that it had been an easy birth.

In the room, watching the midwife at work, were seven children, one of them holding a small baby. They were all watching quietly, and none showed the least signs of fear or upset. When Mrs. A lay down on the couch and covered her head, moaning, her son (age 2) got a little frightened and whimpered briefly but did not shed any tears. His grandmother spoke to him and he stopped. A few minutes later he was running around happily in the courtyard.

After finishing with the birth, the midwife buries the afterbirth by a rubbish heap. She bathes the baby and sometimes the mother. She comes daily to the household and cleans the cot, washes the soiled clothes of the mother and baby, throws away the mother's bandages, and cleans the room with cow dung. She also removes the excrement of the mother and the baby. The mother is not allowed to go outside the room to eliminate until the ceremony of Jāsūtan. Until then the midwife must come into the house to remove her excrement. The length of time that a woman is in confinement varies with her age, how she feels, and how many other women there are in the household

---

* Birth sometimes takes place while the mother is in bed. The squatting position is an alternative.

to take over her tasks. She should remain in bed for 10 to 14 days and do no work for 12 days after that. She cannot start cooking until she stops bleeding because until then she is unclean. The mother, except for the Bahari ceremony, does not change her clothes for from 14 to 22 days. At the end of this time she puts on new clothes, and her old clothes are given to the sweepers. During her confinement no one may touch her eating plate and glass, which are also unclean. When the mother's confinement is over, the family cleans the room and purifies the mother's eating utensils by burning coals in them and washing them in Ganges water. After this the midwife cannot enter the house.

On the day that the baby is born, the mother eats sweets, a special corn dish, and a dish of pulse. The mother is fed as much *ghī* as she can consume, and many of the women eat a great deal after their babies are born. She may also be fed a dish which is a mixture of sugar, water, *ghī*, almonds, coconut, and dry ginger powder. This diet is considered to be healthy for the new mother and is continued for 20 days. The mother is not supposed to drink milk for some time after the baby is born. Again the length of time reported for this taboo varied from 15 days to one and one quarter months. The baby is fed sugar and water when it is first born and is given mother's milk from one to three days after its birth. The baby may also be fed a dish consisting of about one cup boiling water, caroway seed, two puffed sugar candies and a pinch of ashes. Before nursing begins, a sister of the husband washes the mother's breasts with Ganges water or milk. For this she receives a present of jewelry. Sometimes the sister-in-law clamors for a particular piece of expensive jewelry. If the child is a boy, particularly a first-born son, her request is usually granted. If no husband's sister is present, another woman acts as a substitute. She receives only a nominal gift.

There are four ceremonies connected with the birth and early childhood of a village baby. The first is the Bahari ceremony, which occurs on the first Sunday of a boy's life. The second is the Chotilī ceremony, when the baby is 5 or 6 days old. The third is the Jāsūtan ceremony, on the baby's tenth day. The fourth is the Mundan hair-cutting ceremony, usually held when the baby is about a year old.

The differential status of boys and girls is apparent from birth. The midwife is paid twice as much for delivering a boy as for delivering a girl. The birth of a girl occasions no public ceremony. One informant, in fact, declared that when a girl is born, the mother hides, although this is an overstatement. When a boy is born, on the other hand, a sweeper is called to beat on a drum before the door of the happy household, announcing to the village the advent of a son. The Brāhmaṇ women are summoned to sing special songs, and the branch of a *nīm* tree is put over the door of the mother's room for good luck and to keep ghosts away. This singing and drumming are repeated every day for ten days. A yellow cord is placed around the waist of male babies.

The first ceremony in a boy's life, the Bahari, may find him any-where from 1 to 6 days old. The Bahari is usually held only for boys. It takes place in the late afternoon of his first Sunday, and to it are invited all the women from the family lineage and any other close female friends of the family.

Preparations for this ceremony are elaborate. The Brāhmaṇ women who serve the family make abstract designs of cow dung decorated with green and yellow dots. These are "painted" on the courtyard wall on each side of the mother's room and represent all of the gods and goddesses. The Brāhmaṇ women say that these designs are in honor of the ancestors. On the floor in front of the door to the mother's room is placed a square design made out of rice-water paint. This pattern is a sign of respect for the baby and mother.

Since the birth, the mother and child have remained in bed in the mother's room. She is still considered unclean. Now, however, she is bathed, her hair is washed, and she dresses in new clothes. Outside in the street, the sweeper man is drumming; in the courtyard the Brāhmaṇ women sing. Both Brāhmaṇ and low-caste women bring contributions of *dūb* grass, for which they are given money. The grass symbolizes that they wish the family to prosper, as the grass prospers. A low wooden stool is placed beside the design at the mother's door and before it two or three bowls of food and a bowl of water.

When everything is ready, the mother comes out of the room and sits on the low stool, holding her baby. She greets the guests and they bless her. A woman, usually an elderly one, sits beside the mother and gives her water from a bowl. The mother sprinkles this water onto the food, and then the food is given to the Brāhmaṇ women. Each member of the family and each guest offer money and a handful of grain to the "ancestor" designs, and these gifts also are given subsequently to the Brāhmaṇs. Sometimes the wife of the family barber is present and touches the fingernails and toenails of the new baby to indicate that she will cut the child's nails when he gets older. After this brief cere-mony, the mother again greets her guests and returns to her room. There she is permitted to break the fast which she has kept all day by eating a paste of sugar and *ghī*. She resumes her soiled clothes and re-mains in them until she completes her period of seclusion and returns to her normal working life.

The details of this, as well as other ceremonies, vary from time to time. Instead of having the Brāhmaṇ women sing the ritual songs, sometimes the guests themselves sing them. The type of grain blessed by the mother differs with the season. The amount given in payment to the servant families may vary somewhat. But the general ceremonial pattern remains the same.

The second ceremony, called the Chotilī, is held on the fifth day of a baby girl's life and on the sixth day of a boy's. For this rite, a red sacred thread is tied around one leg of the mother's cot, and a small figure is made out of cow dung to represent the goddess Bahamatā, maker of children. This goddess is one of the 101 sisters concerned with disease; she receives homage only at the Chotilī ceremony. The family women offer whey, grain, and a tiny oil lamp; they invoke the names of the ancestors, of Mātā the smallpox goddess, and the goddesses Balsundrī and Bahamatā. The family may invoke the names of 5, 7, or 9 such deities, including local gods, goddesses such as the Bhumia and Darga, the Moslem saint, and ancestors. The baby receives its first costume, which may be either a cloth to go around his stomach, a shirt and cap, or both. These clothes are called Chotilī. These are colored for girls and white for boys. Women from other houses in the lineage present gifts of grain to the mother, and the ceremony is over. Afterward, they hide the figure of Bahamatā in a room of the house for good luck.

Jāsūtan, the third festival, occurring ten days after the birth of a boy, terminates the family's rejoicing over a new son. On this day the boy's yellow cord is exchanged for a black one. It is the last day that the sweeper drums and the Brāhmaṇ women sing. It is the end of the holiday from spinning, observed by the women of the lineage out of affection for the new son of the house. Apparently in some cases the Chotilī ceremony is performed on Jāsūtan, although it is more common to clothe the child on its fifth or sixth day.

According to some accounts, a wealthy family gives a feast on Jāsūtan for one unmarried girl from each Rājpūt family in the *paṭṭī*. In the sample studied here, there were no families which observed this custom, but the family Brāhmaṇs are fed and sweets distributed to the other houses in the lineage. It was stated that at least one Brāhmaṇ must be fed on this day in order to ensure the cleanliness of the kitchen.

A boy is not named on the day of Jāsūtan but may be named any time after this date. Until babies are named, and often during the first year or so of their lives, they are called *lālā* (masculine) or *lālī* (feminine), an affectionate term literally translated as jewel.

Choosing a name is always difficult, particularly for a son. He cannot be given the name of any man in the family or any of the in-law's families, since there will then be some women who will not be able to say this name out of respect to the older man who bears it. The names of older women must also be avoided for girls, although here the rule is not as rigid. Many women liked to give their children a name which included Rām so that one would take the name of Rām whenever one said the name of the child. Names with Dēvī (goddess), Dēv (god), and Rāj (king) in them were also common. Generally a woman has several possible names in mind, and the baby might be called all of them until one is settled on. In some cases the baby is 6 months old before the final name is chosen. Naming a child was, therefore, a casual and informal procedure.

After Jāsūtan, the cow-dung designs placed on each side of the mother's room are taken down and sometimes replaced with hand prints made in rice water, which are good luck symbols.

The first hair-cutting ceremony usually takes place during the child's first year of life. This, like the Chotilī ceremony, is performed for both boys and girls, and there are three occasions on which it may be done. The first and most usual occasion is the spring religious festival for Balsundrī, held in Bhudana. A second possibility is the Shakumbri religious festival, held in the fall in a town about 80 miles distant from the village. Because it is so far away, the villagers do not often get to the mela or "fair"; but some manage it and may perform the hair-cutting ceremony at that time. A third and fairly common practice is simply to go to the family shrine and offer the hair to the ancestors. According to report, the ceremony follows the same general pattern wherever it is performed. The birth hair, cut any time from 12 days to a year after the child is born, is offered to the goddess as a gesture of consecration. This hair is material which can be used for sorcery purposes. Offering it to the ancestors or to a goddess, therefore, presumably consecrates the child and protects him from harm.

When the hair-cutting ceremony is performed at the family ancestor's shrine, a Brahman and a barber are called. They go to the shrine with the family. The family barber cuts the child's hair, and it is placed between pieces of unleavened fried bread and left there. We asked what happened to the hair and were told that the dogs eat the bread and the hair blows away. But since the hair has been offered to the ancestors, it cannot be used for sorcery.

Although there was no opportunity to observe a hair-cutting ceremony at the ancestor's shrine, we did see one at the Balsundrī mela. This was performed on a little boy from our village. We traveled with them by bullock cart, leaving the village at 4 in the morning and reaching the mela grounds about 6:30 A.M. The usual order of proceedings at this *melā* is described in the section on religion. On this particular visit, the hair-cutting ceremony was performed right after the baby's mother and older sister had washed at the bathing pool inside the temple wall and changed into clean saris. The mother carried the baby boy to a barber, who was sitting just beside the temple platform busily clipping the hair of the numerous babies brought to him. He held the baby and ran his clippers hastily over its head, leaving tufts of hair here and there. Then there was a brief bargaining over the price, which ended with the mother giving the barber 2 annas, half of what he had asked. Collecting hair and baby, the mother then went to the door of the temple and threw inside the birth hair and the newly purchased sweets as gifts to Balsundrī. This was the end of the actual ceremony, and the women went on to perform other customary rites or worship at the temple before leaving to spend the day shopping at the fair grounds.

⚜
⚜
⚜

Chapter 13

Infancy

Rājpūts consider their children to be "pure." This means that they are holy, God resides in them, they have committed no sin and cannot distinguish between good and evil. Some women say that babies remain in this state of purity until they begin to eat solid food. Some commented that children are born with their hands shut because they are sent from God fully equipped and do not want anything from the world.

The villagers believe that "The fate of a child is written on its forehead at birth." There are days on which it is considered unlucky to be born, and children born on these days will come to no good end. But, in general, the villagers consider that the child's fate, while divinely predetermined, cannot be known.

Because of the high death rate among young children, their health is a matter of concern and anxiety. Babies are believed to be particularly susceptible to certain kinds of supernatural dangers. Sorcery by means of birth hair has already been discussed. Necklaces of various kinds and protective charms are worn by babies up to the age of a year and a half. An elaborate version of such a necklace worn by a boy whose mother had lost several children contained the following charms:

1. A charm, which had been given to the mother by a *siana*.
2. A paper with charms written on it.
3. A package of tiger's meat to make the boy brave.
4. Four silver ornaments—a moon, a flower, a bow and arrow, and one unidentified ornament—to ward off smallpox.
5. A shell, some red beads, and several cloth packages for which the informant could give no function.

Not all children wear such charms, and only a few wear necklaces as elaborate as the one described. But many small children, particularly boys, wear a simple thread with one or two charms or coins on it.

The evil eye is another danger which threatens children. The evil eye is put on a child by someone who is jealous of him. Handsome people of any age, since they are the objects of jealousy, are susceptible to the evil eye, and all small babies must be protected against it by a black dot on the temple or foot, which is worn continuously during the first few weeks of life and may be worn on occasions for several years. Mothers of handsome children are warned that they should not dress the children well and make them look pretty lest they incite envy. One must never praise a child by saying that it is pretty or exceptionally big and healthy. Such praise may bring bad luck to the child and leave the praiser open to the suspicion of throwing the evil eye. Beliefs about the children's susceptibility to the evil eye varied. Some women were firmly convinced of the reality of this danger, whereas others believed that all illness was determined by the will of God. Some worried only about handsome children, and still others feared for all children.

Another danger to children is ghost sickness. Ghosts may stick to children when they are sleeping and make them ill or may possess them, causing them to laugh, dance, and sing. The family must then take the child to a *siana* who may determine why the child has been bothered by the ghost. He can drive out the ghost but is not able to predict the behavior which the ghost causes. One mother said that she did not let her child go out after dark in the village because of the danger of ghosts.

Finally, all boys wear a black cord around their waists, which sometimes has a charm or two on it. Although some women said that it was worn simply "for fashion," its chief function is to make the vein in the penis grow straight. If the vein does not grow straight, it is believed that the boy will be impotent. Boys wear this cord from infancy on, and some men evidently wear it throughout their lifetime.

Once the birth ceremonies are over, the women return to their usual household routines, and the new baby causes little or no further disturbance to the usual pattern of living. All babies sleep with their mothers for several years. Girls may sleep with their mothers until they are 8 or 9 years old. During the day, when the infant is not in need of food or some other attention, it is placed on a cot with a quilt or sheet entirely covering it, to protect it from insects and envious glances. Babies are often so well hidden by piles of quilts that one cannot detect their presence. Generally, unless the baby cries, no one pays any attention to it, and it lies well covered in the midst of the busy courtyard until it expresses its demands in loud and persistent crying. Children, particularly boys who have been born after several years of barrenness or after the death of several children, may be accorded more attention.

When the baby cries, adult response is usually fairly prompt, but if the mother is busy with a task, like cooking, she cannot leave, and the baby may have to wait. Most mothers said that they would leave their work or try to finish it to pick up a wailing infant, but a few women reported that they might let the baby cry for an hour or so.* We observed three sickly, probably unwanted girls who cried often and were left to cry for extended periods, but these children were definitely exceptions.

Whether or not the mother receives assistance from the other women of the household depends largely on how well they get along with each other. Although the women are generally not unfriendly to any children, each woman cares for her own children exclusively if the women are on bad terms with each other, but if the courtyard is a friendly one, the women help each other out. In such a courtyard the crying child may be picked up by any woman or older child. If the baby continues to cry, it may be passed from one woman to another while each tries her own devices of distraction and consolation. Grandmothers sometimes offer their milkless breasts as pacifiers. If nothing is effec-

* The promptness of response to a crying infant was a point on which the mothers were questioned. Out of 24 mothers, 21 said that it was their practice to pick up a crying baby and try to pacify it in some way. Nine said they would do this at once, 9 said they would pick the child up as soon as possible or in a few minutes, and only 2 said they would delay for any length of time. Eight mothers said they left their work to pick up the baby, 6 said they would carry the baby while they went on working, and 5 said they would finish their work and then pick up the child.

tive, it is assumed that the baby is hungry, and the mother-in-law or aunt will take over the work of the mother so that she can stop to nurse. During the months when the baby is too old to lie quietly on a cot and too young to walk itself, it is, if possible, turned over to an older girl to carry when the mother is busy working. As a rule, this caretaker will be an older sister, but a cousin may take the child if the sisters-in-law are on good terms.

The role of the men in the care of infants is negligible, except for a few elderly men who are too feeble for farm work and have retired from active participation in the village political scene. To such old men are relegated the tasks of rope making, baby tending, and guarding the cattle. Such men may spend the day in the cattle compound or on the men's platform. John Gumperz reports that some spend most of their time making rope and playing with a baby. If there is such an elderly grandfather or great uncle in the family who is willing to take on this role, the baby may be given to him instead of to an older child. However, since it is unusual for villagers to reach such an advanced age, most babies do not have such a doting male as a companion. It is more common for an uncle to take the baby to the men's platform for an hour or so, but when the child begins to cry or fuss, it is quickly returned to the women.

If the mother is very busy and has no one to help carry the baby, she may resort to the use of opium to put the baby to sleep. The women agreed that this was not good for babies and should be used only as a last resort. One busy mother administered two grains of opium a day to a baby that was a few months old. When under the influence of the drug, it was impossible to awaken the baby even by vigorous shaking.

Whether or not the baby is tended and amused by other women, an older child or an elderly male, the mother retains the responsibility for feeding, dressing, and washing her own child. She is the one with whom it sleeps and until it is weaned, no substitute caretaker will carry the infant far from its food supply.

From the time that the mother's breasts are ceremonially washed and she begins to nurse the baby, it is nursed on demand. One informant said that young babies were nursed every 30 to 35 minutes and, when older, three or four times a day. Since the baby sleeps with its mother, night feeding is no problem.

Mother's milk is considered to be the best milk for the child. Some women believe that it is sufficient food for the infant, and no supplementary feeding is required. If the mother has no milk or insufficient milk, supplementary milk is given. Goat's milk, which can be purchased, is supposed to be best for this purpose, cow's milk next best, and buffalo's milk least good. One mother, who did not lactate, fed her child on powdered milk, but this is the only instance we know of where powdered milk was used. Supplementary milk is given either by spoon or from a small brass nursing bottle which is shaped like a round pot and has a small spout in the side for the nipple. These pots are about 2 to 2½ inches in diameter and hold only an ounce or two of milk. Wet nursing is uncommon. We were told that some sisters-in-law would do this, but most women did not like to nurse another woman's child.

Reports as to the age at which supplementary feeding is started varied from six months to two years. Our observations indicated that generally children were regularly given some solid food, a piece of bread or a little candy or rice, at about one year, but that very little solid food is given before this age. Some mothers believe that solid foods fed to a nursing child cause dysentery. If the milk supply is not sufficient at this time, the mothers feed the child some cow's milk. Mothers who think that their milk provides sufficient nourishment may delay longer before giving solid food.

Babies are not diapered; they wear only a short shirt and sometimes a cap or scarf on their heads. When put on a cot, they are laid on a sheet which then serves the purpose of a diaper. When the baby is being held by someone, it is simply held away when it urinates. Sometimes the mother sits the baby on her own feet while it urinates. Since the urine is quickly absorbed into the mud floor of the courtyard and the hot sun dries the moisture in a few minutes, accidents of bladder control on the floor present no problem. At night the mother holds the baby away from the bed if the urination awakens her. Some mothers did complain that their babies wet them frequently because they slept too soundly.

Bowel movements are regarded somewhat less casually. The mother tries to anticipate the baby's bowel movements and holds him over the courtyard drain or a pile of trash in the cattle compound at what she considers to be the appropriate times. When the baby does eliminate on the floor or on someone's clothing, he is quickly removed from the feces and washed. The feces are also cleaned up at once. The women are particularly careful not to let the baby get smeared with his feces or play with them because it is believed that a person who has accidentally eaten feces as a child will have the power of the evil eye. Although the women sometimes show mild disgust at a baby's bowel movement, their reaction is surprisingly mild considering the extreme disgust attached to adult feces, which can be removed only by a sweeper, the lowliest of the Untouchable castes in the village.

Because of the relaxed attitudes of the women, neither feeding nor elimination present a problem for the Rājpūt baby—the same cannot be said, however, for bathing. This is a most distressing experience, which the baby must face daily. Babies, like adults, are given "sponge baths" with water from a bucket or pot. No villager immerses himself in water except when bathing in a river. The mothers ordinarily do not use soap when washing the babies, but they rub the eyes rather vigorously with the heel of the hand and often are not very gentle in their handling of the baby during the bathing process. Babies usually cry and struggle violently while being bathed, and they particularly dislike having their face and eyes washed.*

Although the infants and small children wore nothing but shirts, we saw no evidence of masturbation. Whether or not the babies masturbate while hidden under their covering of quilts we were not, of course, able to observe. Since infants are usually carried when they are not sleeping, they do not have much opportunity to masturbate. The only instances of handling of genitals that we noted occurred with a boy about 1½ years old. One day, while sitting on his mother's lap, he took his penis in his hand and said "penis" several times. His mother laughed and said, "He is showing you his penis." Some time later we saw this child's aunt playfully pull the child's penis while joking with him.

The life of the Rājpūt baby is, aside from the daily bath, bland and free from stress, but it is also free from deliberate creative stimulation. A person in the village is viewed as a member of a group rather than as an individual. According to the religious beliefs, he represents one incarnation of a soul that may have appeared on earth a million times and may appear on earth a million times again in the future and that is but a fragment of the universal world soul. The individual does not, as in Christianity, represent a unique event in the world's history. The sex and health of the child are the important characteristics which will determine its individual future. Assuming that the child will live to maturity, its future life can be predicted with great accuracy. A boy will become a farmer; a girl will be a farmer's wife. A boy born into a wealthy and powerful family may now have more diversity in his choice of occupation. He may become a government worker, perhaps even a governmental official. Such diversity will, of course, increase in the future, but at present such exceptions are still rare. It is to a large extent true that the fate of the child is written on its forehead at birth. Throughout his or her lifetime, the person will function in a group; seldom, if ever, will he be called on to act independently of the group,

---

* The custom of massaging babies with oil, popular in other parts of India, is not common among Khalapur Rājpūts.

let alone oppose it. Whereas a mother who conceives of her child as a unique individual emphasizes how he differs from other children, the Rājpūt mother, for whom all people are but transient elements in a permanent group structure, insists that "all children are alike."

This attitude is, no doubt, accentuated by the fact that the village mother has had far more experience with children than a mother raised in an isolated nuclear family. She has grown up in a household where the advent of a new baby was a fairly common occurrence. She has seen babies born, seen them nurse, seen them live and grow up, and seen them die. She has probably cared for a younger sibling or cousin herself. Furthermore, she has her own children in the company of older women to whom childbirth is a familiar experience. Therefore babies are neither the objects of interest nor the objects of anxiety that they are in this country. A mother does not fear that her child is sick every time it cries; she knows better. But, by the same token, she is not as delighted with its smile because she also knows that all babies smile. She therefore continues with her usual routine, attends to her infant's needs but does not hover over it or "drop everything" to rush to its side. If there is sufficient help, someone will comfort the child; if there is not sufficient help, she may resort to opium to quiet the child while she gets her work done or she may use some other device to amuse the child.

The elderly men who sometimes care for babies may "play" with them, but usually neither the women nor the girls who go about their own activities with a baby on their hips spend much time interacting with the child. The baby receives attention only when it cries or fusses. When it thus exhibits distress, the mother, another woman, its child nurse, or even a young child of 4 or 5 will attempt to sooth the baby back to quiescence. When it becomes quiet, its distractor leaves it. Adult interaction with babies is generally aimed at producing a cessation of response rather than a stimulation of it.

The concept of educational toys is foreign to the Rājpūt, and there are few toys of any kind. Some infants had plastic rattles or painted wooden animals which their mothers gave them. More commonly the toys were hand-made cloth balls brought by a new bride or returning daughter-in-law. One mother sat her toddler beside a stool with a woven seat. She then scattered grain on the stool, which the baby picked off and ate, grain by grain. When he had finished, he waddled expectantly over to his mother, and the process was repeated.

Because of the belief in the evil eye, a visitor who followed the American custom of admiring the baby, praising its unusual healthiness, good looks, or well-kept appearance would cause panic rather than pride, and a village mother would no more show off her baby to the admiration of a visitor than an American mother would deliberately expose an infant to a contagious disease. Even during the birth ceremonies the baby remains well hidden, wrapped in his mother's arms, and no visitor makes an attempt to see the child.

Thus the baby spends his first two years as a passive observer of the busy courtyard life. He is never alone, never the center of attention. He spends his first months sleeping on a cot, covered with quilts. Later, when he is more wakeful, he moves from cot to hip. His child nurse may carry him out to the streets or to a neighbor's house, but since he is still being nursed, he is not taken far. If his mother leaves the courtyard to attend a ceremony in a relative's house, she will take him with her, but such excursions are rare. It is quite common, however, for the mother to return home to her own village for a visit during this period. Here she is relieved of her household duties and spends her days visiting with her relatives and friends with her baby on her hip. Sometime during these years the child will be taken to a *mēlā* for his hair-cutting ceremony. This will probably be the child's most extensive excursion during this period.

A baby spends little time crawling. Sometimes, unattended, he may set off across the courtyard on his own, but someone usually grabs him before he gets far. Since the women do most of their work on the floor, the food dishes, grain dishes, and so on are usually lying somewhere. This makes a crawling baby something of a nuisance, although there is little that can hurt him except the hearth fire and an occasional spinning-wheel spindle or knife. If the infant is crawling toward some area where it is not supposed to be, or playing with some object which it is not supposed to have, an adult simply removes either the baby or the object rather than attempting to coax the baby to give up the object or to crawl away. Occasionally the process is not so simple, as the following observation illustrates:

J. (boy aged 6 months) fell into the spindle when Mrs. S. (his mother) was spinning. She picked him up and scolded him; then she gave him to her sister-in-law, Mrs. D. Mrs. D. kept facing him toward the other courtyard and telling him to go there. A lady from the other courtyard called him, but he kept crawling back. Mrs. D. would shake her fist and say, "Should I break your mouth?" Finally she hit him on the back. The baby just smiled. Eventually he cried a little. His mother called him to her, picked him up, and put him in the other courtyard. One of the women in the other courtyard was cleaning a parrot cage. The baby watched her do that, and the women of the other courtyard gave him something to eat.

When the child is ready, he learns to walk; he is not encouraged or rushed in this process by adults. Only once did we see a grandmother and older sister, each holding the hand of a baby who was laboring to take his first steps. One family had a wooden walker, consisting of a cross T-bar on three wheels, with an upright handle built on the cross bar of the T. We were told that the family had bought this for a boy who was slow in learning to walk. This was the only walker we saw in the village, although they were sold at the spring *mēlā*. When the child does learn to walk, he may still be carried when taken outside the house, but he now wanders about the courtyard on his own. He may venture just outside the door to look at the street. A fond father or uncle may take him for a visit on the men's platform, or he may follow an older child to the men's quarters. But he still is not allowed far from the house, and he is still an observer rather than a participant in the busy life around him.

☆
☆
☆

Chapter 14

The Preschool Child

Until the child acquires the use of speech, he is not considered to be teachable, and no demands are made on him to modify his own behavior. A mother may place an infant's palms together in the gesture of "Namaste," the Hindu greeting, or shout at a crawling baby who ventures too near the hearth, but no systematic demands are made on the child until he can walk and say a few words. From this time on he is considered able to respond to directions and may be punished for failing to do so. He is still considered too small, however, to learn from verbal instruction. He can be told to do something that he already knows how to do, but it is believed that young children learn new activities best through observation and imitation rather than instruction. The years from infancy to school are a transition period during which the child moves from observer to participant in the life of the village. This transition is a gradual one with no clear signposts to mark its beginning or its end. The time required for the transition varies from one child to another, depending on how urgently his services are needed by his family, but all make the journey in their own way and in their own time.

As far as sleeping arrangements are concerned, the preschool child is still a baby. He continues to sleep with his mother and may do so for some years. When a new baby arrives, the older child is usually moved to a cot, with another sibling, at least temporarily. However, the child may later return to the mother's bed. It is not uncommon for a mother to sleep with two or even three children.* Children are not encouraged to take naps and seemingly do not sleep during the day except during the hot season, when everyone takes an afternoon rest. Their sleeping hours are much the same as adults', only longer. On cold mornings the mothers encourage children to stay in bed until the fire is well started and breakfast is ready, but too much sleep is considered by some mothers to lead to laziness, even in youngsters, so ordinarily the children are up shortly after the women.

The first systematic demands made on the child are that he stop nursing and that he eliminate in some appropriate place. Both weaning and toilet training usually occur during the second or third year.

The mothers reported three reasons for weaning a child—illness, failure of the milk supply, and pregnancy. Of these, pregnancy is the most usual. A few mothers reported that their children stopped nursing of their own accord. Mothers usually nurse through the first months of pregnancy, but they try to wean a few months before the birth of the new child. Several mothers reported that their milk stopped during pregnancy. Since children are usually born two to three years apart, most children are weaned between the ages of 1 and 4, the mean age being 3. Children whose parents observe the post-partum sex taboo on sexual intercourse for the full two years, are, of course, likely to be weaned later than children whose parents ignore or attenuate the period of the taboo. If the mother does not become pregnant again, she usually nurses the child as long as her milk supply lasts. In such cases the child may be nursed for five or six years.†

* In our sample there were two households in which adult men slept in the women's courtyard. In one of the largest of the courtyards, two cousins about 19 years of age slept with their respective wives, aged 15 and 17. Neither couple had produced offspring yet. The most aberrant case is that reported for a household consisting of two married brothers but not any parents. It was reported that the father, aged 25, slept in the house and shared a cot with his 3-year-old daughter and that the 7-year-old son shared a cot with his mother.

† When interviewed, four mothers said they weaned between the ages of 1 and 2, six said between the ages of 2 and 3; eight said between the ages of 3 and 4, and three mothers said they nursed for five or six years.

Most mothers said they had no trouble weaning their children. A few reported that the children had troubled them for three or four days. One mother said that her child cried off and on for 20 days; this was the most extreme case of emotional upset due to weaning reported to us.

Chillies or *nīm* leaves, which are bitter, may be put on the breast to aid in a difficult weaning, but since the mothers are reluctant to use such punitive measures, they rarely resort to this practice. Two mothers told us that they were using *nīm* leaves to wean their children, but in both cases we saw the children nursing without protest. One mother held the leaves in her hand while nursing but did not use them. A milkless woman, usually a grandmother, may give a child her breast to keep it quiet if the mother is busy, but pacifiers, other than the breast, are not used during weaning. The fact that the children are usually getting supplementary milk and some solid food before weaning is instituted seems to make it a relatively easy adjustment. The children we saw did not show signs of emotional upset, and, according to the mothers' reports, the children rarely tried to resume nursing after the birth of a second child.

As mentioned earlier, most children are given some solid food between six months and a year. The first solid food is bread; later grains of cereal and bits of candy are added to the diet. After weaning, the children eat the same food as adults. If there is a shortage of milk, it is saved for the children. Other foods may be substituted for particular dishes that the children dislike, but the limited diet does not allow for extensive substitutions, and the children quickly learn to accept the adult diet—spices, peppers, and all.

Most mothers reported that their children had learned to eat by themselves before the age of 2. Several reported that they had learned this before one year, but this undoubtedly referred only to bread and bits of cereal. It should not be assumed, however, that because 2 year olds have mastered the skill, they are allowed to feed themselves regular meals. Some mothers continue to feed children their regular meals until they are 3 or 4 years old. One reason for this practice may be that the mothers feel it is quicker and easier to feed the child than to let him eat by himself. Religious beliefs concerning food pollution probably contribute to this prolonged feeding of children. Food which is left on the plate unattended becomes polluted and should not be eaten. For this reason adults cannot be interrupted in the middle of eating. Learning to finish eating all that has been served without interruption is therefore part of the process of acquiring adult eating habits, and one of the "naughty" behaviors which mothers frequently mention is making a mess while eating. Some mothers may prefer to feed their children until they can count on proper eating behavior.

Children are not encouraged to eat if they are not hungry, and we saw no children who were "feeding problems." The only problem of the village children seemed to be to get enough food. One of the things that mothers complained of was that young children nagged them for food before it had been cooked. Since cooking is a slow process, most women try to keep a supply of bread and left-over rice to take the edge off the children's appetites until dinner is prepared. We frequently heard children ask for food and complain that they had not been served enough. Food was also mentioned by the mothers as a reward for good behavior.

When the child can walk, he is led to the courtyard drain, to the cattle compound, or to the street just outside the house to urinate or defecate. Adults may make a "squizzle" sound to encourage urination. Later, when his mother sees him squatting, she encourages him to go by himself to the latrine or the cattle compound—if there is one—inside the courtyard. Most children learn to eliminate in the proper spot during their second year, although some do not go by themselves until the third year. Since adults urinate in public, the children can learn the procedure through imitation, and since children ordinarily wear only shirts, they have no clothes to remove for elimination; thus the learning process is not difficult. During the winter the children sometimes wear pajama trousers. However, if the child is not yet toilet trained, he wears trousers with the crotch cut out—the very opposite of diapering.

We saw one little boy during successive stages of this learning process. On one occasion he went to his mother, saying, "Water, water." His mother promptly carried him to the courtyard drain, where he urinated. A month or so later he was toddling to the drain himself.

For some time after the children have learned to go to the drain in the daytime, they may still wet the bed at night. If the night is cold and rainy, the mother may encourage the child to urinate in the room. A few mothers reported that their children refused to do this and always used the courtyard. The last stage of this learning process is learning to use water to wash after a bowel movement. Mothers do this for babies and young children. By the age of 4 or 5, the children have learned to do this themselves and may sometimes be seen eliminating by a stream and washing themselves. The adult attitudes about human feces and their association with the Untouchable castes are undoubtedly communicated to the child, but no direct punishment of accidents was observed. The training seems to present no real problem for adults or children.

Children are usually bathed by adults until they are 5 or 6 years old, but although personal cleanliness is highly regarded by adults, who bathe daily, it does not seem to be regarded as so important for children of this age range. Babies are kept clean and their nasal discharges are removed. However, once the children are old enough to play around the dusty village streets, they and their clothes are often quite dirty, and I doubt that all mothers bathe their children daily, although they are, however, required to wash their hands before eating. Runny noses and eyes are particularly common at this age, and the children frequently have eye infections which are quickly spread through the lamp-black eye makeup, which is taken from one container and used on all the babies and young children of the family. Luckily the fear that elaborately groomed children will contract the more serious variety of evil eye prevents the regular use of this makeup. It is usually reserved for festival occasions.

At this age, warm-weather clothing is similar for both sexes. All children wear a shirt. In the winter the boys may be bundled into padded jackets and cotton pants or sleveless sweaters. Babies and young children may also wear padded bonnets in cold weather. Mothers seem less particular about warm clothing for girls, who do not wear padded jackets. Little girls may wear adult clothing, a sari or pajama trousers and overblouse or a sleeveless sweater if the day is chilly, or they may simply add a headcloth to their shirt. Some of the wealthier families have black rubbers for children to wear on cold days, but most children go barefoot the year round. On winter mornings and evenings when it is really cold, both children and adults wrap themselves in quilts.

The hair of young children is cut close to the head except for a small lock in the back called the _chōtī_, which distinguishes Hindu men from Moslems throughout their lives. The hair of girls is cut during this period because the villagers believe that it will grow thicker if kept cropped for some years; also the short hair makes lice easier to eliminate. Girls also have a _chōtī_, and often a cloth braid, a miniature version of the ones worn by the women, is attached to this tuft of hair. This braid, glass bracelets, and sometimes ankle bracelets are usually the only items of clothing which distinguish the preschool girls from the boys.

The mother has the primary responsibility for feeding, dressing, and washing her own child. If the mother is very busy, an indulgent mother-in-law may feed or bathe a young child, but for the most part, the older women consider that they have reached an age deserving of some leisure, and they expect their daughters-in-law to care for their own young as well as attend to the household tasks. Actually there was a living grandmother in less than half of the families studied.

In theory, disciplining should be carried out by the oldest person present. Within the courtyard this would usually be the grandmother, a grand-aunt, or the wife of the eldest son. In practice, among the women at least, this rule is not strictly observed. It is true that the younger wives are reluctant to discipline the children of their older sisters-in-law, and daughters-in-law would rarely scold the children of the mother-in-law. They do not, in other words, scold the children of women who outrank them unless perhaps the child is bothering them personally. This does not mean, however, that the oldest person present punishes the child because, in general, no woman, not even the mother-in-law, will punish a child if his own mother is near and has also seen it misbehave. If the mother is in another part of the courtyard and the women are on good terms, an older woman may reprimand a child, but serious scoldings are usually administered by the mother, and a woman hardly ever strikes a child that is not her own.

The role of the grandmother in discipline depends on the grandmother's personality. In general, she is more lenient with the children than the mother and is more likely to scold the mother for being too harsh than she is to scold the children. In extreme cases of incompatibility, a grandmother may send the mother home, keeping her child and refusing to recall her until pressure is exerted on her by the girl's family. When this happens, the grandmother replaces the mother as major caretaker. If the mother dies, it is the grandmother or great-aunt who is likely to care for the child rather than an aunt. The grandmother may continue to care for the child even after the father marries again.

The custom of having the oldest person present discipline children is evidently more strictly followed by the men. Several men said that they are shy of scolding their children when their father or uncles are present. A man may feel free to discipline his children in the courtyard but not on the men's platform. The father often remains a fairly stern and remote figure to his children, although this is much less true now than it used to be. Traditionally, as one of the mechanisms to promote the solidarity of the extended family, the father was expected to trust the welfare of his children to his father and brothers. He was the disciplinarian, and they were the defenders. A man, out of respect for the extended family and perhaps because of sexual connotations, was supposed to interact with his nephews rather than his sons. At present this custom, while still considered ideal, is seldom observed.

One elderly man told us that his father had scolded him but never played with him, and he had never held his son, only his nephews. Now, he says, times have changed—the brothers have more tendency to separate, and each man interacts with his own children. At the pre-school age, the children of both sexes are usually with women, but as a shadow of things to come, the men begin to exert more control over the boys, while the disciplining of girls falls to the mother. Men are not supposed to reprimand their older daughters; such matters should be carried out by the women, and a few men are reluctant to reprimand their daughters even at this young age. In general, fathers are probably more severe in their punishments of the boys; but a few mothers said that their husbands were the lenient ones.*

Aside from the parents, older brothers and sisters feel free to shout at or even slap an erring child. Within the courtyard an older sibling is more likely to be unofficial second disciplinarian than an aunt. If a child misbehaves outside his home, neighbors usually feel free to shout at him. Such a person is usually a man, since the women stay in the courtyards.†

Regardless of who disciplines the children, the villagers agree, in general, on the methods of discipline. Despite individual differences in the handling of children, and some variance between the discipline of the men and that of the women, there is a clear consensus of opinion which forms the norm of the villager's socialization techniques.

The core of this consensus is the belief that praising children "to their faces" will spoil them and make them disobedient. As one man put it, "If we praise, the child will think we love him too much and then he will not be under our control." Some men were of the opinion that children obeyed men better than they obeyed women because the women "loved them too much." This phrase "loving too much" also occurs in the women's discussions of children, for when asked, "What do you do when your child has done something good?" the women said that they loved him "very much." Despite the belief that praising is wrong, mothers reported that they do praise children, using such phrases as "You have done good work," "You are a queen (king)," or "You look very nice like that." In examining our observations, how-

* When asked, "Who scolds your child when all the adults are present?", 8 mothers said that either they or their husbands did; 3 said everyone in the house; and only 1 said the grandmother. When asked, "Who in the house usually sees that the child behaves well and who forbids him?" 7 mothers named themselves; 4 named themselves and their husbands; 8 said everybody; 2 said the father; no one named either grandparent.

† Thirteen out of 17 mothers said that older siblings punished the children, and 14 out of 24 said that neighbors sometimes punished them.

ever, we find only one recorded instance of a mother praising her child. When her 4-year-old daughter presented her with some dishes she had just washed, this mother said simply, "Oh, you have washed the dishes, good." It may be that some mothers were somewhat reluctant to praise children in front of us, but I doubt that our presence reduced the normal frequency of praise to any great extent. In general, the village women seldom praised their children.*

Although it is bad to praise children "to their faces," it is permissible to praise them when they are not present or to hold them up as examples to other children. In the best of form, one should use only nieces and nephews as role models and leave it to the other members of the family or neighbors to use one's own children as good examples. This technique, perhaps because of the increasing residential segmentation of extended families, is seldom practiced. Very few women are so firm in their friendship that they will hold up each other's children as examples to their own. On the other hand, most women in extended families are probably reluctant to lavish praise on other children for fear of being accused of spoiling them. A careful impartiality in children's disputes, although not always achieved, is by far the safest course. The mother-in-law, similarly, must be careful in her use of praise or she will be accused by the women in other houses of "playing favorites" and causing dissension among her daughters-in-law. The men of the family are subject to similar pressures. Among the men, it is the grandfather who is most likely to love the children "very much." These patriarchs usually confine their attention to the younger children, and the descriptions of their behavior in this connection sound more like doting grandparent behavior than systematic attempts to reinforce certain responses. Certainly, considering the infrequent use of praise by the women and its reputedly less frequent use by the men, one can only conclude that the village child is seldom complimented for specific good behavior.

The use of tangible rewards for good behavior is equally rare. Only 6 out of 24 mothers said that they sometimes gave small presents, usually food, to children when they were good. About one half of the women mentioned that they promised trips to a nearby town or a visit to a relative in return for good behavior. Such trips are made relatively infrequently, however, and do not serve as immediate rewards. Pocket money or a little grain to buy candy is given to children, even young children, but not necessarily as a reward for good behavior. In our

---

* The reluctance to praise young children may also be related to the belief in the evil eye.

work with the mothers we never saw them give children rewards or special privileges for being good.

In general, then, reinforcement is used sparingly in socialization. The mothers do not often capitalize on the child's love for them by rewarding their actions with praise, nor do they use material objects to encourage good behavior. Instead they rely almost solely on punishment to control children. By far the most common punishment reported in interviewing, and by our observations, is a simple scolding, often consisting of a curse or a derogation. We recorded some 24 scoldings in our observation protocols. Sometimes this scolding is nothing more than a curse, ranging from the mild "Go away," to such terms as "immoral widow," or "sister seducer," or simply "Go to Hell." The stronger curses are more likely to be used by older children than by the women. More commonly the scolder calls the child by a derogatory but not obscene name. "Chamar," or "Bhangī," both Untouchable castes, were commonly hurled insults. "Monkey" is also used. "Let the dog bark" is a phrase indicating that the speaker disdains to notice the culprit's behavior. Such insults point to the absence of the expected caste behavior and threaten loss of status. Ridicule is also used frequently. When interviewed, one half of the mothers said they laughed at their children and make fun of them when they were naughty.

Sometimes other mothers are used as the sanctioning agents in such statements as "They will say the sweeper is crying." "They will say you are a dirty boy." Such derogatory statements come closest to love-oriented techniques, since they threaten the child with loss of support. The source of the support, however, is the social in-group rather than the mother herself. Similarly, some men reported that when they are displeased with their sons, they announce this publicly to the other men of the men's platform. It is probably at such times that a man is likely to praise a nephew and cite him as a good example. The technique might best be called status oriented rather than love oriented, since it capitalizes on fear of lost status and consequent abandonment by the social group rather than fear of loss of love from a particular person.

Other types of scoldings involve the threat of physical punishment. A mother may reprimand her child with a sharp "Stop that! Do you want a beating from me?", or she may go so far as to threaten to cut off the ears of a naughty child.* This threat is so obviously a hoax that few children take it seriously, as can be seen in the following exchange between a mother and her 4-year-old daughter:

* To pull a person's ears is a great insult.

Mother: I will cut off your ears.
Daughter: Oh, I will see how you cut off my ears.
Mother: Really, I am telling you, I will cut off your ears and send them to
           the mill, and they will make flour and we will have bread from that.
Daughter: Don't be silly.

Again, some of the mothers in threatening the child with physical punishment or removal from the group invoked supernatural agents, animals, and, more recently, Americans as the punisher. About one third of the mothers said that they frightened the children most commonly with ghosts, who will take them away and presumably kill them. The terms *hāvā* and *lūlū* are also used to frighten children. These words denote something frightening and may refer to ghosts, animals, such as dogs, wolves, and jackals, or Americans. Some mothers frightened children by telling them that the Americans would give them injections, take them away, beat them, or even eat them. Jackals and wolves were used chiefly to quiet children who fussed at night. During the winter months jackals can be heard barking in the fields at night, a sound that must lend considerable weight to the threats.

Another method used to frighten children is to lock them in a room of the house. The intent is to frighten the child, since the rooms are windowless and completely dark when the door is closed. Thus, locking a child in such a room would be more like locking him in a closet in America, except that the room is bigger than a closet. The mothers considered this a rather severe punishment and used it rather rarely.

A number of women claimed that frightening the children with ghosts and locking them in a room were not effective because they were not frightened. It seems impossible that in a culture where the women, at least, are genuinely afraid of ghosts, the children would not be frightened by them. It is more likely that the strong value placed on bravery by the Rājpūts leads the women to insist that nothing frightens their children. The fact that the men strongly disapprove of the women's practice of frightening the children on the grounds that it makes them timid, and do not use this practice themselves, indicates that it was not ineffective. This disagreement about frightening children seems to be the only sharp divergence between men and women on matters of discipline. It is understandable that the women use supernatural agents to control the children, whereas the men do not. The men are less likely to believe in ghosts, place more emphasis on bravery, and have more authority than the women. It is enough for a man to frighten a child with his own wrath; he does not need the aid of a ghost.

Men sometimes use a mild form of isolation as a punishment. A number of men said that they sometimes sent children to the corner of the men's platform or inside one of the men's cubicles when they were naughty. This would not be nearly so frightening as being shut inside a room of the courtyard. It is more common for the men simply to send the children to the courtyard when they are naughty. The women may send them out to the men's quarters for the same reason. One woman humorously said that children sometimes go back and forth from courtyard to men's quarters all day long. This practice is clearly more a "buck-passing" technique to get rid of obstreperous children than a device for punishment by isolation.

Children are not threatened with the wrath of gods or ancestors for being naughty. Using fear of the gods or fear of the ancestors for such a purpose is evidently considered improper. All of the women interviewed denied doing this, one protesting indignantly that it would be a sin because ancestors are to be respected, and one should not make fun of them.

Although physical punishment is often threatened, it is less often administered, particularly to young children. Almost all mothers reported that they slap their children sometimes, if their scolding is not heeded. Some mothers beat their older children, but many said that a threatening gesture is sufficient. We did not observe many cases of physical punishment, but our presence may well have decreased the frequency of such punishment. The village mother is reluctant to create a scene when company is present. Older children are less inhibited and do occasionally land a blow on a young child. One blow with the hand is usually the extent of the punishment—children were not held and beaten; however, the threat of such a blow as the ultimate sanction is ever present.

None of the mothers punish children by withholding rewards. "What we have, we give; the thing we do not have we cannot give," was the most common answer to this query. The answer reflects, in part, the relative scarcity of tangible rewards at the mothers' disposal. Since money is not regularly given, it cannot be effectively withheld. Mothers who are themselves confined to the house have little to offer by way of special entertainment to children whose social mobility is considerably broader than their own.

A number of mothers interpreted the question about withholding rewards in terms of food, which they said was the only thing the children asked of them. Although fear of upsetting a balanced diet would probably not dissuade the village mother from sending her child to bed without his supper, withholding food was never used as a disciplinary technique because refusal to accept food is a common, culturally pat-

terned way of showing extreme displeasure. Since a person may not
accept food from anyone of a caste lower than his own, refusal to accept food from a person may be a serious insult. The ultimate caste
sanction, outcasting, consists, in part, of refusing to eat or smoke with
the outcasted person. Adults commonly show their displeasure by
wrapping themselves in a quilt, retiring to their beds in stony silence,
and fasting until someone persuades them to forget their anger. Even
older children sometimes walk away in a huff, refusing to speak to
someone who has insulted them.

Refusing to speak to a person, like refusing to accept food from him,
is a serious breach of etiquette, usually reserved for major disputes
among adults. When mothers were really displeased with their children, however, they would sometimes show their anger by refusing to
speak to them. About one third of the mothers said that they sometimes
stopped speaking to their children. Several of the mothers who did
not use this technique explained that the children were too young to
understand it. Needless to say, the mother's silence lasted only for a
matter of hours, whereas the silence between feuding adults may last
for years. The child may have interpreted this silence as withdrawal of
love by the mother; yet, because of its cultural significance, it has the
implication of a group as well as an individual sanction.

Aside from the periodic shouts of "Don't," the village women do
very little to guide their children's behavior. Since children are thought
to learn from observation, they feel little need to reason with children,
to explain the demands made upon them, or to spend time instructing them. The content of the mother's scoldings does not contain a
description of desired behavior. The scoldings are little more than the
briefest condemnations. They are never developed into long, explana-
tory lectures. The few chores required of children are simple enough to
be learned through observation, perhaps with the guidance of a few
simple instructions.

As we have said, the villagers occasionally use other children or, less
frequently, adults as role models to guide children's behavior. This
technique is not, however, used frequently and certainly is not employed as a deliberate teaching device. The heroes and heroines of
epics and myths probably function, to some extent, as role models for
children. Stories are not told to children, but the women sometimes
amuse themselves in the evening by telling stories to each other, and
some of the men read the religious epics in groups or relate tales of
great Rājpūt warriors and rulers. On festival days someone may relate
the festival's origin myth. The children, as well as adults, listen to

these narratives and hear of the bravery of Arjuna and Pṛthvī Rāj, the wisdom of Rāma and the obedient devotion of his wife, Sītā. However, identification with these epic figures is not evident in the children's play nor in their fantasy responses on interviews or story completion. We conducted a short interview with the children as well as a story completion test. The children always completed the stories briefly and realistically; fantasy figures never entered the story. When asked "Who would you like to be if you could be anyone in the world?" almost all of the children named a family member despite the fact that we gave them a long list of characters, including such figures as bandit, king, queen, god and goddess, from which to choose. The children's only imaginative play is adult role play, in which the boys play at farming and the girls at cooking. Once, just after the *melā*, which had a circus, we found a group of children playing circus, but we never saw them pretend to be kings or warriors. Certainly the adults, particularly the men, identify with their epic heroes. Judging from behavior, however, this identification may not take place in early childhood, probably not until adolescence.

All of the socialization techniques employed by the adults are probably less effective in the modification of the children's behavior than the observation and imitation through which the children gradually absorb the skills, customs, and values of their group. As the villagers say, the children learn from observation. The preschool period might be called the period of observation and imitation for the Rājpūt child. He is considered too young to learn from instruction; very little is expected of him; and he spends most of his day observing the busy scene around him. As a babe in arms he was carried from the house by his child nurse; he saw the children playing; he might be taken into a neighboring courtyard or, more rarely, to a ceremony. Once weaned, housebroken, and walking, his sphere of observation widens. He may spend more time with the men. Sometimes a fond uncle will take a young boy to the fields with him. Two small boys spent most of their time in the fields with the men, but since young children tire easily and are likely to become a nuisance in the fields, most preschool children remain in the village. If the child is a boy, and the mother is alone in the house or very busy, the grandfather may assume a position of major caretaker. Two 3-year-old boys spent much of their time with their grandfathers. Both of these men were too old for active field work, and neither was powerful enough to assume the role of "Big Man" that many of the wealthier and more prestigeful men assume in their declining years. Once the child can walk, the grandmother is more likely to take him with her when she visits a neighbor, and from this time on, the children attend all of the birth ceremonies and weddings of their village even if the mother must remain at home. Children may accompany their mother, aunt, or grandmother on a visit to her parent's village. When not with an adult, the young children tag along after the 5-, 6-, and 7-year-olds, who are themselves too young to be working. Since the courtyards are crowded, they play in the streets, on the empty men's platform, or by the pond in the road and fields just outside the village. Usually the children do not venture more than a quarter of a mile from their homes, and they are seldom far from an adult. The 3- and 4-year-old children are frequently seen standing on the outskirts of a game of tag, "rooting" for an elder brother who is playing shells, smiling vaguely at a group of boys who are "plowing" a field, or following an older brother or sister to the pond with the water buffalo.

As the children grow older, they begin to participate in the games and activities. Children of about 4 to 8 have relatively extensive social contacts. Their daily social interactions are not hemmed in by restrictions that segregation of sexes imposes on the adult social life. Most mothers would probably have prevented their children from playing constantly with lower caste children, but since they do not live in the neighborhood, there was little chance for such friendships to develop, and we did not observe children playing with Untouchables. Children of different lineages play together if their houses happen to be close together, and children move freely from one house to another even though their parents may not have been on speaking terms with the adults of the house for years. Only one woman said that she did not like her children to play with children of women with whom she was not friendly, and her statement was probably made to insult her sister-in-law, with whom she was quarreling and who was present during the interview.

We were impressed by the fact that the women did not take their own quarrels out on the children. Men's quarrels, on the other hand, result in blood feuds which may go on for generations. Probably for this reason men are more concerned with impressing upon their sons that they should know their enemies. Fathers stated that they told their children not to be friendly with people with whom their fathers did not talk but to speak politely to their father's friends.

Strangers from other villages are unpredictable and tentatively suspect, and some fathers warned their children about them.

We tell them that you should not believe people from a different village. You never know what they will do at what time.

For the most part, however, visitors from outside the village, particularly those with whom the children would have contact, are visiting in-laws and guests, toward whom the children are taught courtesy.

If any man from another village comes and the child knows that the friend of his father is here, then if the father is not there, he will give him the hookah, and talk nicely to him. Even if a man comes whom nobody knows, the children will ask him to sit down, and if it is time for meals, then they will give him food.

The difference in training of boys and girls is reflected in the child interviews. When asked how they would react if a strange child tried to be friendly with them, 8 of the 10 girls said they would be friendly, whereas 5 of the 9 boys said they would not be friendly.

The mothers prefer that the children play in groups rather than alone.* When asked if they preferred some playmates to others, the mothers were reluctant to name specific children they did not like but stressed the fact that they did not want their children to play with children who fought. More than half of the mothers stated that they liked their children's friends and, when asked to specify those they would choose as playmates, usually named the playmates we most frequently observed with their children. Mothers summarized their feelings by stating they preferred children who were nice and did not fight or have bad habits.

The adults pay little attention to the activities of children unless there is quarreling or trouble, so that the children's recreation is informal and without adult supervision. A great deal of the play of younger children consists of almost random activity. They chase each other, tease each other, climb on a vacant cart, or play seesaw on a wagon wheel that is lying beside their house.

The children have relatively few toys. Families do possess toys, but they are likely to be *objets d'art* rather than playthings. One family showed us a collection of painted plaster dolls which they had made. The only time we ever saw them was on this one occasion when they were displayed for our benefit. Only once or twice did we see children playing with such plaster figures. A few of the girls have rag dolls, but they very rarely play with them. Some girls have sets of toy cooking utensils with which they play. Two of the children in one of the wealthiest households had toy grain grinders which their grandmother had given to them, and some had toy scales. The boys sometimes have small, wooden bullock carts, some made by the village carpenter, some,

---

* When asked in the parent interview whether they liked their children to play alone, 18 of the 23 mothers stated that their children should play with others, not alone.

crude affairs which they make themselves. These may be a block of wood with two wheels attached or one solid wheel with a bent piece of sugar cane for an axle. The boys also make bows and arrows for themselves and play with small iron hoops which they roll with a stick.

The adult segregation of the sexes influences their role play. The village boys and girls do not join forces to play house or other fantasy play modeled on adult life. Both sexes, however, have their own type of fantasy play which is modeled on adult work. As mentioned earlier, the little girls play at cooking and the boys at farming. One child in the sample studied was particularly fond of playing at cooking. She had a set of toy dishes, and she would build herself a hearth out of three stones and go through the exact motions of making bread. She used either mud or potsherds for her bread, rubbed "oil" in the frying pan, patted the breads, fried them on the "fire," turned them, put them in the "fire" underneath the pot to let them puff, took them out, flattened them, and stacked them on a dish beside her. It was an exact copy of the motions that an adult woman goes through in making bread. When she finished playing, she washed the dishes and stacked them, and washed the floor in the place where she had cooked. Another bit of imitative play observed with this child was her cooking spinach with water in a small pot. She put it onto the hearth and carefully stirred it. She even blew on the "fire," as do the adult women.

Although the role playing of this girl was unusually detailed and accurate, the making of mud breads is a fairly common play activity of the little girls. Their favorite place for doing this was at the edge of the village pond, where there was plenty of mud at hand for the dough.

When the little boys play at farming, they sometimes make rather elaborate imitations of fields and then irrigate them. More often the play is somewhat simpler, as in the following observation:

A group of boys were playing at sowing. They had long sticks and were pretending to plow. They said, "Let's grow wheat." Some of the boys started scattering dust like seed. They were following boys who were "plowing" the ground with sticks. They said, "Brrr, brrr, brrr," which is what the men say to the cattle. Then they leveled the ground with a stick by rolling it along the ground.

The preschool child is free to play most of the time, since little work is expected of him. He gets little training in responsibility. The first chore that may be assigned to the child is shopping, a necessary task which the women, confined to the courtyard, cannot do. Children are sent, with handfuls of grain clutched in their shirt tails, to the nearest store to buy spices. Sometimes they take grain to be popped. Usually an older child is chosen for this task, but if none is available, a 4- or 5-year-old may be sent. One mother, alone in her courtyard with a 3-year-old son, sent him to shop for spices. This boy also served food to his grandfather, for it is not customary for a woman to serve her father-in-law. The shop is several hundred yards from the neighborhood, and the way lies through the maze of twisted village streets. Such excursions are the longest trips that the young child is likely to make alone. Aside from shopping, little girls may occasionally wash a dish or two, and either girls or boys may bring water if the daily allotment brought by the water carriers runs short. One 5-year-old boy took the cattle to water by himself, but this task is usually left to older children. Children also serve as messengers to the men's platform. All of these chores are irregular and brief. There is little feeling that children should be given work for the purpose of developing a sense of responsibility. Children are asked to work only when their services are needed. Mothers are particularly lenient with girls in this matter, since a girl is considered to be a guest in her own home. The mothers often emphasized that since a girl must work so hard in the house of her husband, she should not have to work in her parents' house.

In some families the eldest son may be singled out for more training in responsibility. There is no clear pattern, however. Some parents said that they gave him special training, since the management of the farm and the authority of the extended household would ultimately fall on his shoulders. They stated that he had some special status even as a child. Younger children are encouraged to obey him, and he in turn is taught that he has the responsibility for other people in the household, that he must be fair to them, take care of them, and be industrious in running the farm. As one informant said:

We advise the eldest son to help his parents when they get old, and give good advice to his younger siblings. We tell the younger brothers to obey the eldest boy. As soon as the oldest son is old enough to be running the fields and finances, the father gives him all the responsibility and retires. The father trains his son until he knows how to do it. We stress obedience to the elders equally for the elder and the younger son.

Other parents stated that the status of the eldest son was not different. There are several possible explanations for the divergence in pattern. The parent may elect to turn over the position of headman to whichever son he considers the most capable. As mentioned above, the eldest son may be the least educated, for his help may be needed in the fields during the school years. A third reason may be the breakdown of the extended family pattern and the frequent division of land after the death of the father.

Self-reliance training is almost as scanty as training in responsibility. Mothers still dress, bathe, and serve food to children of this age; sometimes they still feed them. When the children want something, they ask their mother rather than try to solve the problem by themselves. The extent to which the mothers reinforce this dependency is seen in their often repeated phrase, "What we have, we give." The children may be scolded for nagging for food before it is ready, but this is a condemnation of the unreasonableness of the demand, not of the request itself.

During the preschool period the children learn to determine the appropriate sources of various kinds of aid. Although they are free to play in a neighbor's house, they do not stay for dinner. Food is not casually shared, and a child learns to go to his mother when hungry. Cooked food is served to the children by an adult. However, the children eat grain, sugar cane, and candy between meals. If the family has a common food bin, the children may help themselves from it. If the food stores are divided, they must take cooked food from their parents' hearth and grain from their parents' bin, which is usually inside the wife's room. Within these limits the children are usually free to help themselves to small quantities of grain without asking permission. Similar caution must be observed toward all the aunts' possessions, money, clothes, jewelry, and so on. However, each woman keeps her belongings securely locked in a trunk so that there is little lying around to tempt a child into trouble.

The extent to which the children were capable of insistent demanding was brought home to us almost daily. Although the children do not ordinarily ask anything of the adults of other houses, my interpreter and I were exceptions to this rule. Whereas other adults would quickly discourage any approach of this kind, our role in studying the children required us to be nonpunitive. The children discovered very quickly that they could pester us without being punished. Throughout our stay we were rarely out of earshot of the whining cry, "Give me my photo." Since we took photographs of the children daily, and sent the films to Delhi to be developed, it was impossible to give the children all the pictures that had been taken of them, although we passed out as many as we could. No amount of explanation could silence their demands, nor did the mothers reprimand their children for this persistent begging. Many mothers were, in fact, only slightly less demanding in this regard than their offspring.

In general, the apparent lack of self-reliance in both adults and children is one of the first characteristics that strikes an American observer. The children's interview included two questions about succorance. We asked what the child would do if he or she were having trouble in some task (schoolwork, herding cattle, or fixing a toy). Eleven children said that they would ask for help, and 6 said they would do nothing or abandon the task. Only one 10-year-old boy said he would solve the problem himself.

Children usually seek help from adults rather than peers. As the children grow older and spend more time outside the home, playing in peer groups, succorance becomes a somewhat less notable part of their behavior. In the first place, peers can provide fewer rewards than can adults. Also, children generally are less responsive to succorant behavior. We asked a number of children whether or not they would assist a friend who needed their aid in schoolwork, catching a stray cow, or fixing a toy cart. Ten children said they would help, and 8 said that they would not. When asked what they would do if a friend fell and hurt himself, 10 said they would help or get help, and 8 said they would do nothing.

Although the parents' behavior encourages the children to make frequent requests, parents do not place much emphasis either on training them to comply with the requests of others or on training them to be spontaneously nurturant. Four out of 6 of the mothers of preschool children said that they thought their children should help younger children when they were in trouble. The remaining 2 mothers said that their children were as yet too young to do this. Only a few mothers, however, could remember an incident in which their child had, in fact, helped a younger child, perhaps because the children are more likely to seek aid from an adult than from a child. The fathers were similarly vague on the subject, one father commenting that only good-natured children would help younger children. In practice, the children follow the adult pattern of giving aid only when it is asked and often only if the supplicant is insistent in his demands. Children were not punished for failure to give help unless they refused to give alms to a beggar or food to a servant who had come for her daily pay, nor were they praised for generosity. Therefore the children's nurturant behavior depends largely on their temper of the moment and the quality of their relationship with the person who is in need of assistance. Sometimes they completely ignore the need of their playmates and siblings as in the following instance taken from an observation protocol:

Sr. (boy aged 4) came out of the room with a ball. He knocked down Sa. (brother aged 1½) in the doorway. Sa. was crying slightly and could not get up. Sr. paid no attention.

Girls are more likely to exhibit nurturant behavior toward babies and younger children. For instance:

Sh. (girl aged 5) was eating bread. R. (brother aged 1) was sitting beside her, and she gave him some of her bread, saying, "Take, eat. Do you like it? It is sweet." . . . The baby was crying. She went up to him where he was lying on another cot. She said, "Don't cry, who hit you?" . . . She brought the baby to the grandmother, gave him to her, and sat beside them saying "Brrrrrrrrr" to the baby.

As judged by their verbal reports, the mothers place primary emphasis on obedience and the training of passivity, begun in infancy. When asked, "Whom do you call a good boy or a good girl?", they were able to answer the question adequately, although their answers were usually brief. The most frequent answer to this question was that a good child is one who obeys. Several women also said that a good child should study, should not fight, and should respect its elders. However, inasmuch as respecting one's elders includes such behavior as using the proper greeting and kinship terms, and speaking politely, and since obedience is also a sign of respect for elders, the concept of an obedient child is undoubtedly closely linked with that of a respectful child. Since these kinship terms denote respect, the continued insistence that children use them keeps the lines of authority clear and "sets the stage," as it were, for ensuring that children will obey their elders.* According to the interviews, obedience, politeness, and peaceableness were the most emphasized virtues. There were no consistent differences between mothers' descriptions of what was expected of a good boy and what was expected of a good girl. In practice, obedience is stressed somewhat more for girls and bravery for boys; but both sexes are expected to be both obedient and brave, although in the contexts of different tasks.

The mothers were also asked, "Whom do you call a bad child?" or "What sorts of things do you punish your children for?" Stubborn demanding of attention was the most frequently cited negative characteristic. This concept was phrased by the women in a number of different ways, for example, "When he is stubborn," "When he troubles me," "When he cries for nothing," "When he will not listen," "When he will not stop crying," or "When he insists on having food which I cannot give him." Another frequently mentioned fault was fighting or abusing: "Those children who fight and abuse among themselves," "Those children who hurt others." These two were by far the most frequently mentioned causes of punishment. Other faults included less frequently were stealing, getting dirty, spilling food (spilling milk from a pail or

---

* In several instances, mothers deplored to us the fact that the proper use of kinship terms was becoming less frequent. We even heard children praised—a rare event—for the correct use of kinship terms and we heard mothers commended for requiring this amenity of their children.

spilling food when eating), and not working. These answers clearly indicate that the mothers desire a child who will simply do what he is told, stay out of trouble, and not demand too much.

The Rājpūt children do not strike an observer as being particularly well trained. One reason is because of the pattern that a strong or repeated request is required before a villager, adult or child, will comply, unless the request falls within the limits of some customary obligation, and such formal obligations do not affect the children. Thus it is often necessary for a mother to ask a child several times to do something before the child complies.* Since mothers are usually lenient with small children, they sometimes do not comply at all. The custom of seclusion of the women fosters disobedience to some extent, for the unruly child is safe from pursuit if he simply leaves the courtyard. When we interviewed the children, 14 out of 16 said that they did run away when their mothers scolded them, so it is a common method of avoiding punishment for wrongs committed outside the house, since it is difficult for the women to check on the child's story. Mothers commonly lose their tempers and shout at disobedient children and then "cool off" and forget the matter without having exacted obedience. Consequently it seems that the children learn more about how to weather the mother's emotional storms than they do about obeying her will. On the rare occasions when the grandmother scolds the child, she is little more effective. Since the grandmother is usually more lenient and permissive than the mother, the children know that grandmother is a "softie."

The men, by virtue of their higher status, evidently expect and receive more obedience with less effort than do the women, at least when the children are in their presence. However, even their discipline is by no means perfect. Dr. Gumperz cites an incident where a Rājpūt man sent a boy on an errand. When the boy did not return, he sent another boy to find him. When the search proved unsuccessful, he simply dispatched the second boy to run the errand. He was apparently not upset by the first boy's disobedience.

Another reason why obedience is often more in evidence in preaching than in practice is that the authoritarian hierarchy of village social

* When asked whether they expected their children to obey at once or whether they gave them a little time, 12 mothers said they should obey at once, 3 said it depended on the urgency of the work to be done, and 6 said they give the children some time. When asked, however, if they always followed up any shirking on the part of their children, 15 out of 19 mothers said they sometimes let it go when their children did not carry out orders. The attitudes of the fathers are similar to those of the mothers except that the men make more of a distinction between work which is urgent and work which can wait.

structure requires that people shall be obedient to persons who are above them in status but domineering with persons below them in status. Therefore, within the framework of the social structure, dominance is considered to be a desirable trait. Each mother in the sample was asked whether she thought her child should direct the play of his peers or whether this made the child bossy. Even the mothers of preschool children usually said that being the leader is good and a mark of intelligence. The fathers expressed similar opinions.* Thus, although obedience is emphasized, dominance is tacitly encouraged. Since the mothers almost never clarify their expectations to the children, some of the reluctant obedience to adults may well be due to the fact that the child is not clear about what behavior is required in what circumstances.

The following is an example of the preschool childrens' responses to their mothers' demands.

Mrs. H. is preparing dinner. Her daughter Bw., aged 4, is sitting beside her trying to open a tin can containing chillies for seasoning. Her son Bb., aged 6, and her nephew M., aged 4, are also present.
Mrs. H. says to her son: Go and give the cattle water.
Bb.: I will go after some time.
Mrs. H.: No, go now.
Bb. leaves, shouting crossly: I won't go all the way to the pond. I will come back from the well.
Mrs. H. to daughter: I will put chillies in the chutney.
Bw.: No. I don't like chillies.
M., male cousin aged 4, takes shell from Bw. She screams and he returns it. Later he takes it again.
Mrs. H. shouts to him, "Don't do that" and he gives it back.
M. to Bw.: You open the tin.
Bw.: No, I won't open it.
Mrs. H. to Bw.: Give me the tin. I will put in the chillies.
Bw.: No, no, no.
Mrs. H.: No, I am keeping your chutney separate.
Bw. continued to play with the tin.
Mrs. H.: Don't do that, you will drop all the chillies.
Bw. let go of the tin and leaned against her mother sulking.
Mrs. H.: Will you eat now?
Bw.: Yes, bring it for me.
Mrs. H.: Will you eat it with chutney?
Bw.: Yes.
Mrs. H. got some water and started feeding her daughter.

The interviews show that training in the inhibition of emotion is also begun during the preschool period. The mothers reported that

* Fifteen mothers thought it was good for their children to dominate, 5 thought this was not good, and 2 mothers said it depended on the situation.

they stop the children when they get too excited, laugh too much, cry, or become angry. Occasionally mothers would even scold or punish children when they cried, even if they hurt themselves, as exemplified in the following:

> We were visiting R.'s house in the evening when M., a 4-year-old girl, fell off the cot and landed on her shoulder. She cried loudly. Her teen-aged sister came over to her and said sharply, "Get up. You did not get hurt. Get up." I put on the flashlight briefly in order to see M. in the darkness, and the sister, in an effort to distract the crying child, pointed to the light and said, "Look, look at that." M. went on crying. Her mother, who was several yards away at the hearth, shouted very crossly, "I will beat you if you don't stop crying. I will throw the big spoon at you." M. continued to cry, although not quite so hard. No one paid any further attention to her. Eventually she stopped.

A number of children corroborated this observation, stating that their mothers punished them for falling and hurting themselves.* Probably the Rājpūt emphasis on bravery is partially responsible for this unsympathetic attitude.

Although parents say that they discourage outbreaks of anger and aggressive behavior, they in fact sometimes ignore or even reward such behavior. The severity with which such behavior is punished depends on the status of the person to whom the aggression is directed. Theoretically aggression directed at adults is a graver offense than aggression directed at peers, which often goes unpunished. On the other hand, small children sometimes become angry with their mothers, aunts, and grandmothers, "scolding" them and, less frequently, hitting them. When this happens, the mothers sometimes scold or hit the child, but sometimes they ignore the outburst. In the extended family, issues are seldom so important as keeping the peace. This is true of quarrels among adults, and the same attitude evidently holds for the misdemeanors of children. When we asked the mothers of all the children, "What do you do when your child gets angry when you or your husband do not let him have something or are angry with him?" 12 of the women said that they would give in to the child at this point and console him or give him what he wanted, 4 said they would discipline him, and 3 said they would ignore him. Five women either repudiated the question or failed to answer it. Half of the mothers, then, report that they give in to their children when the children become angry with them. Insofar as this practice is followed, it probably re-

* When asked what they would do if they fell and were hurt, 7 children said they would ask for help, 3 said they would fix the hurt themselves, and 9 said they would ignore it. A number of children mentioned that if they hurt themselves, they would be punished by their mother.

wards the expression of anger and undermines the mother's authority by increasing the frequency of the child's challenges of that authority.

Quarrels among children of approximately the same age are usually ignored by the women until actual blows are struck or until a child cries or complains. When the mother does not know who started the fight, she usually makes no attempt to find out. Women are sometimes reluctant to scold their sister-in-law's children or children from other houses for fear that it will be said that they scold other people's children but never their own. When she finds her child fighting with neighbor children, she will usually scold her own child, perhaps slap him, and give the other children only a mild reprimand or send them home. If her child is fighting with the child of a sister-in-law, the mother's action depends a great deal on her current relations with the sister-in-law, and whether the sister-in-law is above or below her in the family hierarchy.

In general, however, almost all mothers, not only of preschool children but of older children as well, discourage fighting in their own children. When asked what they did if their children got into a fight while playing, 20 of the mothers said they punished their children, and 4 said they determined who was at fault and punished the offender. Three out of 24 mothers said that they sometimes told their children to fight back, but the other 21 said that they never did this, and several were quite shocked at the idea of giving the children such bad advice.

The children engage in a good deal of minor bickering, name calling, snatching of objects, and semiaggressive teasing or "horseplay." More serious quarrels are infrequent, for parents intervene before they reach this point. If a fight occurs outside the house, only a young child who feels he has been unfairly treated by an older playmate will go crying into the house to report to the mother. Older children, knowing they will receive no sympathy, keep their fighting to themselves. Only once did I hear a child try to justify his attack to his mother with the explanation, "She hit me first."

The type of aggression that is most likely to invoke swift retribution from the parents is that which is directed against a young sibling or cousin. This situation applies chiefly to the older children who may become angry at a preschool child, but it can also apply to a 4-year-old hitting a 1- or 2-year-old child. The deciding factor here seems to be one of inequality in physical strength. In such contests the bigger child receives most, if not all, of the blame. If, however, a boy is fighting with a sister who is older than he but not appreciably stronger, both will be scolded. Bullying, then, is strongly discouraged.

Sibling rivalry is conspicuous by its absence. This is not to say that the children do not fight with their brothers and sisters, but they do not show hostility or resentment to a new baby. Only one child displayed open resentment to a newborn sibling. This child was a 2½-year-old boy named Kheer, the first son of a young woman who was visiting her parents' home. The only other child in the house, except for the baby, was a 10-year-old boy. The mother had an unusually large supply of milk and so continued to nurse both children. Once we saw Kheer try to push his baby sister away from the breast and nurse himself. Another time we made the following observation:

S.D. came walking along the road. She was carrying her baby girl. Her son Kheer was following her, crying. She said that he wanted her to carry him also. As he came up behind her, she sat down on the road, and he knocked her off balance. He then hit the baby several times, walked around his mother, and hit her on the back several times. The mother laughed and said, "Are you trying to kill baby?"

Three factors seem to contribute to this striking lack of sibling rivalry.

1. Adults are not overly affectionate with children of any age. Infants are usually not given special attention beyond their physical needs. They are not cuddled or played with. Consequently the older child, never accustomed to being the center of his mother's attention, does not feel displaced in her affections by the new arrival.

2. In an extended family household women are present who can replace the mother in taking care of the older child when her time is demanded by the new baby.

3. In an extended household it is unusual for any child to have the experience of being the first-born child within the household. If he is the son of one of the younger brothers there are some older cousins present. If he is the son of the oldest brother, there are usually uncles and aunts in the household who are still children; since the women marry so young, it is not uncommon for grandmothers to be of childbearing age or to have preadolescent children.

Because of these circumstances the child is always a secure member of a group, but he is never an important individual. His needs are cared for, his reasonable demands met, but he never monopolizes his mother's time.

It seemed to us significant, in this connection, that Kheer came from a household containing no other young children and that his mother was in her own home and therefore had no household duties. As a result, he got an unusual amount of attention before the birth of his sister. Obviously further research is necessary to test these hypotheses. We present them here merely as a tentative explanation for the striking lack of sibling rivalry.

Temper tantrums seldom occur. Only twice did we see a child lying on the floor and screaming in a real hysterical tantrum. On the first occasion the child, a girl, was ignored; on the second, a 6-year-old boy was taunted by his mother and aunt and an older cousin who shouted at him, "Are you the only child here that you are fussing so?" When very angry, the children, like their mothers, may retire to their beds and refuse to eat. This performance, however, is also rare.

Young children are often not punished for being rude to the low-caste servants. The caste hierarchy can be clearly seen when such incidents occur. Children are also generally not reprimanded for being rough with animals. Almost every household has a dog, and a number of children have puppies. Although not deliberately cruel to them, they are often rough in their treatment. They may pick up the puppy by one leg or throw it. Such behavior is ignored by the adults; indeed, the children are only imitating the adult pattern with regard to most animals. Adults will hit a dog that happens to be in their way, and, as mentioned previously, the men sometimes twist the tails in driving their bullocks until they are broken in several places. Since cows are sacred, they are accorded more respectful treatment.

The following observation is an extreme example of a child's aggression but illustrates the mother's lack of concern.

M. (girl aged 6) picked up a puppy. She twisted it so that one of its paws scratched her face. The puppy had nothing to do with it. She hit the puppy and threw it on the ground. I said to stop before I remembered myself. The puppy hid under the cot. She chased it to the other side of the cot. She grabbed both its paws and dragged it across the courtyard. She hit it again, and the dog finally retreated under a cot in the far corner. A few minutes later she was holding it again. She twisted its leg and it howled. K. (interviewer from project house) hit her and said to stop. She threw the dog on the floor, and it ran out of the house. About ten minutes later she hit it again. This time the mother intervened, but she hit it once more after the mother had told her to stop. The dog again retreated, and she lay on the floor and hit her mother's and K.'s feet. The mother had been present throughout but had not intervened until the last.

No specific ceremonies mark the transition from one age to another. The age of 5 or 6, however, may be marked by the performance of a second hair-cutting ceremony involving a pilgrimage to some shrine to thank a goddess for preserving the child's life. If a woman is particularly concerned about her child's health, especially if she has lost several children, she may vow to a goddess that she will offer her the child's hair and other gifts if the child lives to a certain age. Since sons are more highly valued than daughters, these ceremonies are usually performed for boys. One mother had performed two hair-cutting ceremonies for each of her four boys. She had offered the birth hair of her sons to the Bhudana goddess, and, when each had reached the age of 5, she took them to the Sakumbrī fair to offer their chōtīs, along with bread and sweets to the goddess Sakumbrī. Another mother said that she intended to leave her son's hair uncut until he reached the age of 5 and offer all of it to Sakumbrī. Another mother, concerned over the possible use of her son's hair for sorcery, offered his chōtī to the Bhudana goddess.

The aforementioned ceremonies and the Hōī fast for sons are the only ceremonies specifically concerned with children. The initiation rites of vesting boys with the sacred thread of the twice-born castes have become part of the marriage ceremony for the Khalapur Rājpūts.

⚘
⚘
⚘

Chapter 15

The School Age Child

The changes to be described in this section come about gradually, as does the transition from infancy to the "preschool status." Chronological age is of no interest to the Indian mother, and there are no named age grades. There are no linguistic terms which differentiate children as they mature—one is a child until he becomes an adult.

At about age 5, the child is gradually taught to identify with the members of his or her own sex. Boys and girls, who until this age have been treated very much alike, now begin to face somewhat different experiences. The casual observer will first notice this change in the children's clothing. As mentioned previously, small boys and girls are usually dressed alike, but from the ages of 4 to 6, they begin to wear adult clothing, first on special occasions and then more regularly, so that by the middle of their sixth year most children have completed this external transition.

Girls may wear either saris or the loose trousers, shirt, and head-cloth, and most of the girls have outfits of both kinds. Since the shirt and pants are easier for an active youngster to manage, they are the more usual outfit for the 6- and 7-year-olds. After this age the girls are more likely to be seen in saris. Girls begin to cover their heads as soon as they wear adult-styled clothing, although even preschool age girls sometimes wear a headcloth with their shirts. Adults, however, insist that girls cover their heads in public until they are adolescent.

Along with the change of clothing, the girl's hair is allowed to grow; as soon as it is long enough it is braided, and a cloth braid is added to increase its length. When it is sufficiently long and thick, it is dressed in the elaborate fashion of the adult women: a number of small braids are made from one side of the head to the other; these are then woven into each other at the back of the head and finally meet in the one long braid. This coiffure, once completed, is left untouched for several days. Sometimes, usually between the ages of 5 and 8, the girl's ears and one nasal septum are pierced. Since the gold nose plugs and earrings worn by the women are nǒt usually purchased for a girl until she is about ready to be married, most preadolescent girls wear small twigs in these holes. The ears are usually pierced a year or two before the nose because the women say that the nasal aperture will become enlarged if pierced when the girl is too young.

Boys simply add short or long pajama pants to their shirts. The dhōti, an older style of clothing, is usually not worn by boys, except for special occasions. When children begin wearing adult clothing, they more or less follow adult standards of modesty. Parents vary as to the strictness with which they enforce these rules. One mother shocked her neighbors by allowing her 7- and 9-year-old sons to attend school without trousers; another sometimes allowed a 7-year-old girl to leave the house wearing only a pair of shorts. Both of these incidents, however, drew criticism from neighboring women. At this age children are expected to remain covered, at least outside the house.

A second, more subtle change in the children's lives occurs as the responsibility for their care falls more and more to the parent of the same sex. This shift of caretakers takes place gradually, usually over a period of several years. Its timing and extent depend largely on the size of the family. Children of small or nuclear families, whose services may be needed by both parents, move more freely from men's platform to courtyard then do the children of the larger extended families. Boys may be sent out to the men's quarters to sleep occasionally but may not move out permanently until they are 12.

For girls, who have always spent most of their time with their mothers, the change is not great. They continue to spend their evenings listening to the women tell the stories that transmit the background for the complex ceremonial tradition and emphasize the virtues of a good Indian wife. The chief change for girls comes in their gradual expulsion from the men's platform, where they played so freely when they were younger. They may still play on the platform when the men are away, or loiter for a while when sent on an errand, but it is considered somewhat immodest and disrespectful for them to stay among the men for extended visits. Furthermore, since fathers are not supposed to punish their daughters, and since this prohibition is more carefully observed as the girls grow older, the disciplining of girls falls entirely to the women.

There is no similar prohibition against mothers punishing their sons, and mothers continue to discipline boys but often ineffectively. Many of the older boys were not only disobedient but also rude to their mothers. The boys' increased awareness of the low status of women in village society probably contributes to the ineffectiveness of their mothers' discipline. A rather extreme example of such difficulty is illustrated by the following observation.

Mrs. Singh is attempting to persuade her sons, Bīr, aged 9, and Patrām, aged 7, to leave for school. Bīr is sulkily trying to push his foot into his oxford without untying the lace, which is knotted. Patrām is in the bedroom taking things out of his mother's cupboard.

Having failed to persuade him to untie the lace, Mrs. Singh tries to help Bīr put on his shoe, but he pulls her hair. In retaliation, she hits him and they start wrestling. After considerable struggle, she pins her son to the ground and beats him with a shoe. Bīr hits her back, crying loudly. He grabs a stick to continue the assault, and his mother with some effort tears it from him.

After temporarily vanquishing her eldest son, she turns her attention to Patrām. Discovering him in the bedroom, she beats him, exclaiming, "I will see how you will go to school. You sit there and do not come out of the room at all. If you just step out I will beat you. You are just like daughters-in-law, not to go out at all."

Meanwhile Bīr is sitting on the courtyard floor, crying loudly and defiantly tying one knot after another in his shoelace.

Having effectively reduced Patrām to tears, Mrs. Singh returns to the court, sits down with her 2-year-old daughter Lālī and begins to fondle her, but with the warning, "If you do like this, you will also get a beating." Bīr, balefully eying the favored sister, threatens, "I will bury her." His mother laughs and mocks him, whereupon he returns to his room, wraps himself in a quilt, and lies down on his cot. After a minute he emphasizes his displeasure by getting up and closing the door.

"Go on, close it," says his mother. "Bolt it well and don't come out." At this command, Bīr promptly opens the door and returns to the courtyard. He procures some scissors and begins cutting a piece of cloth on which some grain is drying. "Go ahead, do that, but don't go out," proclaims his mother. Bīr abandons the cloth and begins to cut his hair.

Meanwhile Patrām has left the room where he is supposed to be cloistered and stands sniffling in the courtyard. At this point a 3-year-old girl from the neighboring house wanders in and begins playing with the toy push wheel belonging to Lālī. Lālī looks quite distressed at this encroachment on her property. Bīr, with an evil glint in his eye, takes the wheel from the neighbor girl. She appeals to Mrs. Singh but is crossly told that the wheel does not belong to her. Bīr rolls the toy out of the house and then returns it to the child, looking at Lālī to see what she will do. His maneuver is successful, and she tries to retrieve her wheel, which he promptly reclaims and wheels away. As Lālī returns weeping to her mother, Bīr vents his anger on the neighbor child, hits her, and sends her home crying.

As Mrs. Singh comforts Lālī, telling her not to talk to her brothers, the two boys finally gather up their bookbags, and despite their mother's prohibition on leaving the house, go off. When we asked whether or not they had gone to school, Mrs. Singh said that they had probably gone to play, since they would not go to school after being beaten.

The most striking example of loss of maternal control over a son concerned a 12-year-old boy, Sham, whose father had died when he was 11 months old. His mother had virtually no control over him. His 19-year-old brother, of whom he was somewhat afraid, was the only member of the family who could discipline him. The following interview excerpt will illustrate the difficulty faced by this mother.

Q.: When Sham is naughty, do you ever send him inside the room alone?
A.: Yes. I lock him in the room. Yesterday he ran away and I chased him. He ran in one room and then I chased him there and he ran in the other. Finally he ran out of the house and I could not catch him.
Q.: Do you ever take the name of ghosts, etc., to frighten him?
A.: When he was young I would frighten him with ghosts. I would say, "Don't fight or I will call the ghosts," or "I will call the police." But he is very bold and is not frightened. He would say, "I will beat the police."
Q.: Do you ever frighten Sham by telling him you will send him to another village or town?
A.: I am scared to tell him this. This is how he frightens me. He says, "If you scold me, I will go away." He says that he can get food anywhere. I took his earrings away because I was afraid that he would run away and sell them." (This boy had frightened his mother badly at one time by running away to a neighboring town and staying there for two or three days. She had given him grain to sell, and instead of bringing the money back, he had spent it.)
Q.: Do you ever take God's name to frighten him?
A.: No one is frightened of God. He is not afraid of anyone. He will go anywhere at night. Reeshmī (her daughter) is afraid to go out at night, but not Sham. . . . Neither police nor ghosts can frighten him. If I lock him up, he tries to break a door. He is not afraid, so now I say that I will jump into

the well or go out of the village if he is not good.Then he is scared and sorry.

Q.: Do you do this most often? Or do you beat him most often?

A.: I have left off beating him because it hurts my hand. I beat him very hard and he just says, "Oh, that's nothing." So I say, "I will go away, and your brother and sister-in-law will be cruel to you."

Q.: Do you ever beat him with a stick?

A.: Yes, sometimes, but I cannot do that because I feel very bad.

Evidently this mother has reached the point where threats of suicide are her only effective means of controlling her unruly son. Luckily most boys have a father or uncle to take over discipline when the mother's control becomes inadequate.

Although this custom of differential caretaking is sanctioned by the belief that men are the best teachers for boys and women for girls, it sometimes leads to disagreement between parents who, in individual instances, do not approve of the action of their spouse. One man reported that if men do not think their wives are sufficiently strict with the girls, they will beat their wives, since retaliation against their daughters is denied them. Evidently such action can also be taken for the opposite reason because more than one woman could recall instances when husbands had scolded or beaten their wives for being too harsh with daughters. One informant, for instance, recalled the following incident from her own childhood.

Once when my mother was milking three cows, I untied the calves. She had told me not to do it. She was so angry that she threw a pot at me, and it cut my leg, which bled. She pushed me out of the house and I was crying there when my father found me. He went in, asked why she had done this, and beat my mother with a sugar cane. Then as soon as he left, mother started beating me again for having told him.

The mother is usually on the receiving end of such disagreements, since only a very bold woman would reprimand her husband for his treatment of their sons.

Although the men may reprimand their wives for severe treatment of the children, particularly the girls, they are usually more severe with boys than are the women. Probably the men do not utilize physical punishment more frequently than their wives, but when they do, it is likely to hurt more, not only because of the greater strength of the men but also because they are more apt to beat older boys with a stick or shoe, whereas women must frequently use only their hand. This seemed to be particularly true of the younger men. We noted that several 8- to 10-year-old boys were most afraid of an older brother or cousin. On inquiring, we found that such 18- to 20-year-old men, themselves low men on the family pecking order, not only assumed the disciplinary role of the elders but also administered this role with particular severity.

Since some of the men are severe in their use of physical punishment, tender-hearted mothers may cover up for their sons to protect them from father's wrath. Once we entered a household just after a mother had discovered that her 11-year-old son had stolen some money from her. She was very upset and loudly bemoaning her son's bad character. When he returned, she hit him several times, demanding to know what he had done with the money and threatening that when she told his father, who was out of town for the day, "He will beat you until you are dead." Despite this violent scene, we discovered the next day that she had not reported the incident to her husband and had failed, herself, to make the boy tell her what he had done with the loot.

The move to the world of men means that the boys are exposed not only to stricter discipline but also to masculine values, which differ, at least in emphasis, from those of the women. The daughters will soon marry out of the village and play no active role in village life, but the sons must be taught the patterns of loyalty and hatred which define the social groupings with which they must live throughout their lifetime. Therefore, whereas the wives usually do not extend their quarrels to their children and may welcome in their courtyard the offspring of families with whom their husbands are feuding, the men pass on their animosities to the next generation. It is they who point out the men's platform of an enemy lineage and warn their boys not to sit there or play with the children from that family. It is they who define the trustworthy, the untrustworthy, the relatives, the enemies, the false friends, and the neutrals who make up the participants in the intricate web of village factionalism.

Since the men live in a world in which they are surrounded, in fact and fantasy, by potential enemies, they cannot, as do the women, adopt a categorically negative attitude toward aggression. Although it is deemed best to remain on seemingly cordial terms with one's enemies, and although disputes are usually fought out in the arena of the courtroom when they do break into the open, nevertheless one can never be sure when a hotheaded, drunk, or tradition-minded Rājpūt will decide to settle a grievance with a "conversation of sticks." A youth, therefore, must stand ready to defend himself and his family in physical combat.

This does not mean that the men encourage aggression indiscriminately. Like the women, they say that they stop the children when they see them fighting and scold them. When questioned by Gurdeep Jaspal and me, a few of the men reluctantly admitted that they sometimes told their sons that they should fight back if attacked. Others, however, insisted that they never told their sons to fight. In view of the military tradition of these men and the fact that the adult men must defend their crops from thieves, and sometimes themselves or their relatives from attack, their answers seemed understated. We felt sure that the sons must be receiving more aggression encouragement from their fathers than the fathers were reporting. Hoping that they might be more honest in their answers if interviewed by a man, we requested one of the Indian men in the project to repeat parts of the father interview. Mr. Narayan Singh was kind enough to do this, and our conjecture proved to be correct. He interviewed nine men, asking them, among other things, "Do the men say that a boy must defend himself if someone hits him?" and "Do they say that a boy must defend another child from the family if someone attacks him?" Eight of the nine men said that they told the boys they must fight under these circumstances, and the ninth said that the mothers taught them this. Two other men said that women as well as men told their sons to defend themselves.

Evidently the men stop fights if they see them occur, but they do train their sons to defend themselves and their relatives. One should be peaceful, but one must defend oneself if attacked. The men's reluctance to discuss the topic shows their own conflict in this area.

The men reported, both to us and to Mr. Singh, that they did not instruct their sons in the art of staff fighting. This, they insisted, "They learn themselves." Some men said that they told their sons to hit the cattle with the staff (in order to herd them), and in this way they learned to use it. The following is probably an accurate description of how the boys learn to manipulate the staff.

In this way they learn. That when they are in the fields grazing their cattle, they hit the cattle with the staff. Then the children start fighting themselves and they beat each other with small sticks. Then like this slowly, they learn how to fight. While playing also they learn. They beat the other one and the other one beats them. Nobody teaches them this thing. They learn by themselves.

In general, the fathers' attitude might be summed up in the maxim: "Do not start a fight, but if someone starts a fight with you, finish it." The children do in fact readily retaliate when attacked, and they soon learn to appeal to a relative or friend for aid in their defense. This aggression training is given traditional sanction through the occasional reading of the Rāmāyaṇa and the Mahābhārata and the relating of stories about the bravery of Rājpūt warriors. There are many such stories which may be read or told by men in the course of an evening's entertainment.

Although girls are probably punished more severely for aggression, and although the cultural ideal for women condemns aggressiveness, a girl growing up in a courtyard is apt to witness bickering and verbal fighting among the women, and her mother's techniques of scolding and punishing are often expressive of anger. When questioned on the interviews as to what they would do if another child teased or hit them, there was little difference in the responses of boys and girls. Twelve out of 18 children said they would not hit a child who teased them, but 14 out of 16 said they would hit a child who hit them. The children, then, did retaliate to direct aggression.

The following observations give some idea of the kind of quarreling which is likely to occur among the children.

Biirwattī (girl aged 14), Raaj (boy aged 5), and Preem (girl aged 6) were playing on the road. Angurī (girl aged 8) came along the road. Angurī was carrying a dish of mud on her head. Biirwattī was with Angurī. She said to Angurī, "You take this home." (The mud.) Angurī: "I'll take it after some time." Raaj was lying on the road. He threw sand on Biirwattī. Biirwattī said, "Do you want to get a beating from me?" Preem threw sand on Angurī. Angurī threw back. Preem said, "Now don't you go and tell your sister. You have also thrown."

Dhuum (boy aged 10) went into the kitchen where his older sister was cooking. He said, "Give me some hot water." Sister: "You take it yourself. I won't give it to you." She got up and shook her fist at him. Their mother shouted at her, "Don't be silly." The sister hit him several times with a stick from the fire. He hit back at her. She hit him harder than he hit her but neither hit very hard. The sister sat by the chūla and picked up the tongs and shook them at him. Dhuum picked up a wooden sandal and shook it at her. The mother shouted, "Are you not ashamed of yourselves?" To the daughter she said, "Go and sit down and do not fight." Dhuum put on the sandals and went out.

Mukmal (girl aged 6) and Preem (girl aged 6) had a tussle. Mukmal said to Preem, "I'm going to beat you, bad character's widow. I'll set you right. Leave me, leave me." Preem was holding her and hitting her. Preem was stronger than Mukmal and she could not hit back so she was shouting. A big boy who is a relation of Mukmal's came along the road and Mukmal said, "Tell Preem to let me go." He grabbed Preem, who kept tight hold of Mukmal. Then Preem let go of Mukmal and held on to one end of her headcloth while Mukmal had the other end. The boy swung the two of them around him in circles, like cracking the whip. He was holding Mukmal while doing this. He let go and Preem grabbed Mukmal again. They were still tussling at the end of five minutes.

Although several competitive games are popular at this age, particularly with the boys, no one seems to take winning too seriously. An informal version of field hockey is played almost daily by the herd boys in the morning when their cattle are gathered under a grove of trees just outside the village. The game is played with a ball and the staffs which the boys use to control the cattle. As there are no goal posts, no goals, and no referee, the game consists mainly of the two opposing teams chasing the ball back and forth. Also popular is a hockeylike game played with a wooden stick ¾ of an inch long and pointed at both ends, which substitutes as a puck or ball. The players hit this puck with sticks, spinning it in the air, and attempting to hit it again in midair. It may be played alone or as a group game. Both of these games afford practice at handling a staff.

Older boys play a team game similar to the American game of Red Rover, played on a field which is divided into four equal rectangles placed lengthwise like the markings on a football field. The field is usually about 30 feet long and 15 feet wide. Members of two opposing teams line up at each end of the field. One member of a team attempts to run across into the section held by the opposing team, touch a member of the other team, and get back across the center without being tagged. While running, he keeps repeating, "kabaḍḍī, kabaḍḍī, kabaḍḍī" without drawing a new breath. If the boy is tagged, the opposing team wins a point; if he gets back to the middle line, his side wins a point; if he goes over and comes back without touching any boy, or is not touched, there is no score. The other team can only tag the boy when he is in the end section. A variation on the rules of this game is that if the boy is tagged, he is out. This game is potentially an aggressive game, but boys usually content themselves with tagging each other, although occasionally they will bring a boy down by tackling him.

Boys occasionally play a tree tag. The boy who is "it" attempts to tag the boys who have climbed a tree with a stick.

As popular as the first three games is a less strenuous one played by both boys and girls, which involves skill in pitching shells or small stones. The object is to toss the shell into the hole or to hit one of the opponent's shells. If a boy succeeds in doing this, his opponent forfeits his shell.

A variety of jacks is also played by boys and girls with seven or eight shells or pebbles. There are several variations of this game, involving manual dexterity; sometimes the children start by tossing the shells into the air one at a time, catching them, and increasing the number after each successful try; sometimes they try to catch the shells on the back of their hands; sometimes they throw one stone on two fingers and try to catch it again.

A third game of skill (tangī-tangī) is popular with both sexes and is similar to American hopscotch. Five squares are drawn in a row. The player throws the stone into each square consecutively and, hopping on one foot, tries to kick it out.

Little girls play a game similar to tag—frequently on the men's sleeping platform. All the girls stand in a group while one stands at a distance. She sings the following lines:

> Hul-hul a fly comes.
> The rest of the girls shout:
> If it comes, let it come
> The lone girl says:
> It will eat, it will drink.
> The girls say:
> Let it come.

All the girls then run round and round, and the lone girl tries to catch them.

When the play groups are mixed, the older children direct the play of the younger ones. They keep the small observers out of mischief. When girls and boys play together, the boys usually dominate the girls, although personality differences may upset the pattern. In short, the dominance pattern of the children follows the adult lines of authority, but, even as with adults, the tacit approval given to the dominant person may allow children with forceful personalities to assume ascendency over others who are structurally classed as their superiors. This does not mean that the older, stronger, or more dominant children bully or coerce the others. The mothers generally agreed that they would scold or beat children who persistently demand their own way with the other children. Individual dominance must not be allowed to upset group solidarity. If the child can successfully dominate his peers, well and good, but if his demands provoke a quarrel, he is punished. Again, this implicit "rule" is derived from adult standards.

Although the recreational activity becomes more organized and varied as the children grow older, they have less time to devote to play, since a portion of their day is allotted to school and work. Most children now perform at least a few chores fairly regularly. The girls may wash dishes, sweep, tend a baby, serve food to the men on the men's platform or bring food to them in the fields, pick water chestnuts, leafy vegetables, and sometimes cotton in season, bring extra water from the well, and wash clothes. The boys run errands, particularly for the men, water and pasture the cattle, bring fodder from the fields, and help the men with field work.

The extent to which the children must work depends largely (for girls) on the size of the family and (for boys) on the size and wealth of the family, since the custom of not requiring work of children if an adult can perform the task holds for older as well as for younger children. A family with few women, even if wealthy, requires the services of its girls, but a wealthy family can hire field hands, and even if short on manpower, may dispense with the services of the sons. Many families consider that school is a sufficient chore for a boy. Although some schoolboys may be expected to help with the farm only on weekends or during the harvest, others must skip more frequently or give it up altogether. Since school is not considered important for girls, they are more frequently withdrawn from classes during harvest seasons.

Children who are not in school usually have more work than those who attend classes. This is particularly true for boys, for a girl may be withheld from school because of the conservatism of her family, whereas a boy is not withheld unless the family needs his full-time services.

There are two boys in our sample, Shēr and Narayan, who did not attend school and who worked regularly. Shēr is 10 years old and Narayan is 7. Shēr's work is to pasture the family cattle. Every morning he drives the cattle across the bridge to the grove of trees standing just across the pond. Here he and the other herd boys play hockey while their cattle mill around under the trees. At noon Shēr returns for lunch, leaving his animals in the care of some other boys. In the afternoon he and his friends drive the herd to pasture on cut down fields. Small groups of boys and cattle leave the procession as they reach their families' fields. Shēr's fields are several miles from the village, and when he reaches them, only three or four friends of the group that started from the village remain to spend the afternoon with him. When he and his friends have herded their cattle safely into the center of a field, they sit down to rest, talk, or perhaps wrestle to pass the time. The afternoon is pleasant and leisurely, but the boys must always keep one eye on the cattle lest they stray into a neighboring field and invoke the ire of the property owner. Such an event will bring at least a flood of abuse for their carelessness, and in a community where so many grudges lie barely dormant, the results may be far more serious. It is dangerous to let cattle stray even into the fields of a relative if the family members are not on good terms with one another. One of Shēr's friends, Rājsingh, let his cattle stray into the field of an unfriendly uncle. The uncle and his wife were so enraged they invaded Rājsingh's home and beat his mother so severely that they knocked out one of her eyes. Shēr, whose uncle is also unfriendly, is careful to keep his cattle in bounds.

Narayan's family needs his services as fodder carrier as well as cattle tender. Narayan and his older brother leave their house between 7 and 8 A.M. and drive their few head of cattle to their fields, which are situated about 3 miles from the village. At noontime Narayan turns back to the village, often bringing a heavy load of fodder on his small head. After eating his own lunch, he returns to the fields, carrying food for his brother and father. At twilight he returns again with his father and brother, carrying another load of fodder or vegetables.

Of the girls—Dēvī, 10 years old, Rēshmī, aged 7, and Ohmwattī, aged 8—only Dēvī, the oldest, had extensive duties. Ohmwattī sometimes cleans dishes and sweeps for her mother. Although she has a 1-year-old sister, she does not carry her, perhaps because the baby is quite sickly. Rēshmī is a rather rebellious child who evidently does not care for her female status; she always uses masculine verb endings as though she were a boy. Her mother has trouble persuading her to be helpful, although, as we shall see, she is credited with less work than she actually performs.

Dēvī belongs to a family burdened both by poverty and lack of manpower. Her father is dead, and Dēvī and her mother live with her uncle Shanner and his wife, Dēvī's grandmother, her brother Rīrkā, and her male cousins Mugala and Baby Natū. Rīrkā and Mugala help Shanner in the fields after school and on weekends. Almost daily they may be seen trotting along the road with bundles of fodder so long that one must bend down to recognize them. When work is heavy, they must leave school. Dēvī's grandmother, old enough to ignore purdah restrictions, also goes to the fields to pick fodder and vegetables and carries large bundles of them home on her aged head. Dēvī is the steady baby carrier for her infant cousin, and when she goes on visits in the village, he is almost always on her hip. She also takes food to her hard-working uncle in the fields. She sometimes sweeps the floor, cleans the hearth, and, if the family exhausts their daily supply of water, delivered by their water-carrying girls, she brings an extra pot or two from the nearby well.

Adult recognition for this increase in the childrens' responsibilities is meager. Although one of the most frequent forms of praise reported by the mothers, when interviewed was, "You have done good work," we seldom heard a mother actually say this. Rather, there seemed to be a general tendency to belittle the tasks of children. Granting that the chores required of most children are neither long nor arduous, even those children who did work regularly were not accorded recognition. For instance, Narayan's mother, when asked about her son's chores, reported that he did not do very much work. It would seem that walking an average of 12 miles a day, and carrying a load for 6 to 9 of those miles might be considered a rather arduous undertaking for a slightly built 7-year-old boy, but his mother was not impressed.

Rēshmī's mother provided us with our most amusing example of this tendency to underrate the amount of work done by children. We interviewed her on this topic, and she responded as follows:

Q.: Can you tell us which work Rēshmī has recently learned?
A.: She has not learned anything special, but she can clean one or two utensils. . . .
Q.: What is Rēshmī's regular work?
A.: Besides the utensils, what does she do? What she will do, the immoral widow?
Q.: How often does she wash the utensils?
A.: (Sarcastically) Oh, she does them daily. No. Only sometimes.
Q.: How often? Every eight or nine days?
A.: She usually never washes them, but sometimes one or two she takes and washes.
Q.: How do you get her to do it?
A.: She does not do any work. Now I am telling her to take the baby girl and she won't do it.
Q.: Do you often ask her to take the baby?
A.: Every day she takes the baby, but I have to scold her and then she takes her.
Q.: What do you want of Rēshmī? That work which you tell her to do, should she do it at once, or do you give her a little time?
A.: What work? She does not do any work. Supposing you ask her. Sometimes she will bring one or two buckets of water from the well. That is all.

In one breath the mother denies that Rēshmī does any work, and in the next she mentions another task which the child performs fairly regularly.

Schoolwork is similarly ignored by most parents. Although education, as has been said, is by no means universal, even among the high-caste groups, at present most boys and a number of girls attend school. Since the school system is segregated by sex, those who do attend are effectively isolated from opposite-sexed children and adults, six to eight hours a day for five days a week, barring special holidays.

Although the Rājpūts send more of their children to school than do any other caste in the village, devoted scholarship is a rarity. The headmistress of the girls' school manages to keep her little band of students quiet and in their places, and the fourth and fifth grade boys spend most of their school time at least looking at their books or reciting, but the younger boys spend most of their time in minor horse-play. Their work is continually interrupted by frequent borrowing of books, pens, ink pots, and so on, usually accompanied by a good deal of bickering about who owns what.

Jagdish (boy aged 10) was in school, writing with some chalk on the floor. He turned to a boy and picked up a pen. He asked, "Whose is this?" The boy said, "It is mine." Jagdish picked up another pen and asked again. This time the boy did not reply. Jagdish took the pen and gave it to a boy in the corner. Then he sat down and wrote on his slate. A boy started using Jagdish's ink pot and Jagdish objected, saying, "Use your ink pot, not mine." He threw the boy's ink pot away from them. The boy said angrily, "I bought it for two pice."

The older boys sometimes take it upon themselves to stop the horseplay of their younger schoolmates. Indeed, some of the older boys act as official monitors and, like the older brothers and cousins, sometimes discharge their duties with a sharp blow. The following is a fairly typical example of the "study habits" of the beginning students and the attempts of a self-styled monitor to control them. All of the boys are Rājpūts.

Pralard, Puran, Jaipāl, and Bharat (all 6 or 7 years old) are sitting side by side; opposite them is Rūp, an older and stronger boy. They all have their slates and bags in front of them. The boy next to Bharat is attempting to write on his slate but is prevented by Bharat, who is twisting his hand. The boy keeps calling for the master (teacher) in a plaintive voice.

Jaipāl gets up, moves to the opposite row and then moves back. Puran follows him on both moves. Pralard is singing to himself.

Bharat twists the boy's hand again. He calls for the master.

Jaipāl again gets up. He pushes a boy sitting opposite him. He then backs away, returns to his seat and makes faces at him.

Rūp looks up at Jaipāl severely and says, "Why aren't you writing?"

Meanwhile Puran and Bharat are having a tussle. Seeing them, Rūp comes over and shakes his fist at Pralard.

Finally the master comes over and Rūp, seeing him, returns to his seat.

Although Rūp holds no official sanction with regard to the four boys, he does exercise a certain amount of control over them by virtue of possession of two of the three major sources of power of Rājpūt men, age and strength. The third source of power, wealth, does not enter into leadership patterns of the children. This informal control among the children is exercised among members of the same caste. Indeed, the Rājpūt children are in contact with only a few children of other castes in school, and they seldom associate with them. Their interactions while in school are primarily with their friends, relatives, and neighbors, all of whom are also Rājpūts.

Most parents do not press a child to attend school against his wishes. The teachers report that the school usually has about 80% attendance in the morning and about 60% in the afternoon. None of the younger boys attend school in the afternoon. Evidently their mothers feel the all-day session is too much for them. Any minor illness is sufficient excuse for remaining home. Furthermore, since the mothers are confined to quarters and the fathers are busy in the fields, there is no one to check on whether or not the children, after leaving the house, actually arrive at school. Since many parents are themselves illiterate, they cannot help the children with their homework, but older brothers and cousins, who have been to school, are seldom enlisted to supervise the work of the younger children. In fact, the children do very little homework in the afternoon. The possibility that they worked in the evening seems very remote in view of the poor lighting available to the villagers. In general, the parents show little concern for scholarship, and children do not expect them to. Out of 400 behavior observations, there was only one instance of a child seeking approval for good scholarship.

M. read his schoolbook to his brother. Every so often he would say, "Is it all right?" to the brother. He looked at us and smiled.

One can discern a number of reasons why children are not rewarded for working. We have already said that the attitude that a daughter is a guest in her own home leads mothers to be reluctant in demanding that their daughters work. The men, who consider farming a degrading occupation for Rājpūts and who hire, if possible, low-caste field hands, are unlikely to communicate to their sons any enthusiasm for work. Furthermore, the adults are impatient with the inept performance of children who are just learning a task and are more likely to scold the child for his awkwardness than praise him for his enterprise. A girl, just learning to spin, is ordered away from the wheel because she breaks the thread; a boy trying to feed grass into the fodder cutter is pushed aside by the man at the wheel; a boy who has brought a bread container from the bedroom in an attempt to feed himself is scolded and beaten by his mother when he drops it; a girl is making a fair attempt at embroidering on the petticoat that her friend has started but is told by her aunt to stop because she is ruining the work. In this way children are often discouraged from learning new tasks or undertaking work that is not well within their ability. The work they do is judged, not in terms of a reasonable expectation for children of a given age but in comparison with adult performance. Narayan works considerably harder than other neighborhood boys of his age. When his mother reports that he works very little, she can only mean that his contribution to the family manpower pool is meager in comparison with the amount of work done by his father and older brother, a comparison that naturally puts Narayan at a disadvantage.

In this atmosphere it is not surprising that the children are not notably self-reliant or conscientious. At school the boys seem unable to keep track of their own pencils and ink pots, and their books are often torn and dirty. When the work is difficult, they consult another student. Outside of school the children seldom undertake a task beyond their ability, nor do they persist in the face of difficulty. As reported earlier, when asked what they would do when having difficulty in some task, only one child in the sample said that he would attempt to solve the problem alone; all others reported that they would abandon the effort or seek help.

According to their reports, however, the children enjoy working. When asked to choose their favorite activity, 3 boys and 2 girls chose schoolwork, and 2 boys and 4 girls chose some household or farming task. The remaining 3 boys and 2 girls whom we interviewed chose some sort of recreational activity: playing a game, attending the *mēlā*, eating sugar cane, and so on, as their preferred pastime. Observed popularity of adult-role play confirms these reports. It may be that the children were giving socially acceptable answers. It seems probable, however, that, like most children, these children envy adult status, are anxious to grow up, and would be willing, if not eager, to shoulder increased responsibility if their parents were not so sparing of encouragement and impatient with their mistakes.

BIBLIOGRAPHY

Boquet, A. C. *Hinduism*. London: Hutchinson's University Library.
Blunt, Sir Edward (Ed.) *Social Service in India*. London: His Majesty's Stationery Office, 1939.
Carstairs, G. Morris. *The Twice-Born*. London: Hogarth Press, 1957.
Crooke, B. A. *The Popular Religion and Folklore of Northern India*. Westminster: Archibald Constable and Co., 1896, Vol. 1, 2.
Dube, Leela. Diet, health and disease in a North Indian village. Department of Anthropology, Cornell University, 1956 (Manuscript).
Dube, S. C. *Indian Village*. Ithaca: Cornell University Press, 1955.
——. *India's Changing Villages: Human Factors in Community Development*. Ithaca: Cornell University Press, 1958.
——. Some problems of communication in rural community development. Cambridge, Massachusetts: Massachusetts Institute of Technology, 1956.
Hawkridge, Emma. *Indian Gods and Kings: A Story of a Living Past*. Boston: Houghton-Mifflin, 1935.
Hitchcock, John T. A dilemma of dominant caste politics in a North Indian village. (Manuscript.)
——. Leadership in a North Indian village: two case studies. In R. L. Park and I. Tinker (Eds.), *Leadership and Political Institutions in India*. Princeton: Princeton University Press, 1959.
——. Surat Singh, head judge. In J. B. Casagrande (Ed.), *In the Company of Man*. New York: Harper, 1960.

————. The Idea of the Martial Rājpūt. *American Journal of Folklore.* 1958, 71, 216–223.

Lewis, Oscar. *Village Life in Northern India.* Urbana: University of Illinois Press, 1958.

Macdonell, A. A. *India's Past: A Survey of Her Literature, Religions, Languages, and Antiquities.* Oxford: Clarendon Press, 1927.

Planalp, Jack. Religious life and values in a contemporary North Indian village. Unpublished Ph.D. thesis, Cornell University, 1956.

Subcontractor's Monograph, Cornell-9 HRAF-56, *Uttar Pradesh,* Human Relations Area Files, Inc. New Haven, Conn.

Subcontractor's Monograph, Cornell-8, HRAF-44, *India: A Sociological Background.* Vol. 1, 2, Human Relations Area Files, Inc. New Haven, Conn.

Subcontractor's Monograph, California-3, HRAF-33, *India: Government and Politics,* Human Relations Area Files, New Haven, Conn.

Subcontractor's Monograph, California-1, HRAF-32, *The Economy of India,* Vol. 1, 2, Human Relations Area Files, Inc. New Haven, Conn.

Steed, Gitel P. Notes on an approach to a study of personality formation in a Hindu village in Gujarat, *American Anthropologist,* 57, No. 3, Part 2, Memoir #83, June 1955.

Woodruff, Gertrude Marvin, An Adidravida settlement in Bangalore, India: a case study in urbanization. Unpublished Ph.D. thesis, Harvard University, 1959.

Taira:

An Okinawan Village

Thomas W. Maretzki

Hatsumi Maretzki

Contents

About the Authors

Thomas and Hatsumi Maretzki chose the village of Taira on the northeast coast of Okinawa. Thomas Maretzki was an advanced graduate student in Anthropology at Yale; his wife, a graduate of the University of Hawaii who had worked for one year on the staff of the Gesell Institute's nursery school in New Haven, Connecticut. The Maretzkis rented half a house in the village. They were assisted in their work by Nariyuki Agarie, a graduate of the State University of Iowa and subsequently a graduate student in psychology at Yale University, and by Kiyoshi Yogi of Naha. Although the Maretzkis did not have children to speed their participation in community life, Mrs. Maretzki's knowledge of Japanese and her exceptional gift with young children were invaluable aids. She seldom moved about the village without an entourage of small, devoted children.

The Maretzkis returned to Okinawa in 1960. Unfortunately time did not permit the incorporation in this monograph of any data collected on this later expedition. Thomas Maretzki is now teaching at the University of Hawaii.

Part I

The Ethnographic Background

✤
✤
✤
✤
✤
✤

Chapter 1

The Setting

THE ISLAND

Okinawa lies a day's voyage by steamer to the southwest of the Japanese island of Kyushu. Leaving Kyushu, the ship passes along the Ryukyuan chain until it reaches Okinawa, the largest of the islands. Land is never completely out of sight until the ship enters the port of Naha, capital of the southern Ryukyus.

The Ryukyus are part of a long string of islands which, beginning in the north with the Kurile Islands and Sakhalin, run all the way south, including Japan, the Ryukyus, Formosa, the Philippines, and the Indonesian archipelago. In their offshore position on the Western rim of the Pacific Ocean, the Ryukyus are within access by small craft from Japan, Korea, and China. This geographic position of the Ryukyus puts them within the sphere of influence of several countries, a fact which has been a determinant in their historical development and an important factor in speculations about prehistoric events.

Until further archaeological evidence permits greater certainty, the original settlement of the Ryukyus is believed to have taken place predominantly from the Asiatic mainland, with occasional influx from the southern islands, Formosa, the Philippines, and Indonesia (Kerr, 1958). Surviving culture elements of great antiquity support these theories. Most frequently cited are a basic form of Shinto, characteristic of the religion, and the shamanistic role of the priestesses. Specifically, the "curved jewels," formerly worn by all priestesses, are mentioned as apparent links with the neolithic cultures of Japan.

On the other hand, sporadic contact with the islands to the south is evidenced by culture traits, such as raised houses of tropical design (common to all of Japan) and perhaps the practice of "mother roasting," a period of recuperation after the birth of a child during which the mother is kept near a fire. This custom is widespread in Malaysia (Cole, 1945:155).

Linguistic evidence points to a separation of Okinawan from a common proto Japanese language about 1500 years ago (Hattori, 1954). This may indicate a southern movement of peoples from Japan under the pressure of the Yayoi people who introduced the wet rice complex into southwestern and central Japan at this period. That this was not the earliest settlement of the Ryukyus, however, is evidenced by remains in the Ryukyus of the earlier Jomon period.

From the first mention of the Ryukyus in Chinese annals of 605 A.D. until the end of the nineteenth century when Japan formally annexed the islands, they stood in a curious relationship of dependency toward China and Japan. Both nations claimed suzerainty over the kingdom of Okinawa with its royal court in Shuri and extracted tribute. Eventually the Lord of Satsuma in southern Japan extended his sovereignty over the Ryukyus. But with ties to China remaining, Okinawa participated in both Chinese and Japanese culture, which disseminated through the urban trading center of Naha into the outlying areas. It is this intermediate cultural position which still gives Okinawa a peculiar character, although it long ago became part of Japan and abandoned direct contacts with China.

In 1872 Japan formally declared its claims on the Ryukyuan kingdom, and after deposing the last king in 1879, made the Ryukyuan islands a province of Japan, with the capital at Naha. Between this time and the present, intensive contact with Japan has led to an overwhelming absorption of Japanese culture, a willingness on the part of Okinawans to adopt Japanese ways and to identify with Japan as their home country. Nevertheless, many aspects of Okinawan life still suggest an earlier phase in which independent developments gave the islands their own particular culture.

The Okinawan people, approximately 655,000 as counted in 1954, live in an area of about 454 square miles. Their major economic activities have traditionally been agriculture and fishing. In 1945 a long, peaceful existence was brought to an abrupt end during the final battles of World War II in the Pacific. As a result of world conditions Okinawans have been placed under American administration for an indefinite period of time. Today large numbers of men—and some women—find employment as unskilled and semiskilled laborers with the American forces. Gradual training for highly skilled jobs widens these opportunities for employment. Indirectly Okinawan life is influenced by Americans through stimulation of trade, building, and improved health conditions. Land requirements of the American forces in some areas also have influenced the settlement pattern. While these changes have affected the entire island to some degree, the greatest changes are noticeable in the central part around Naha where American administrative and military personnel are located. The village of Taira in the northern province of Kunigami, where the present study was located, had been subject to relatively few of these postwar changes in 1954. Isolated since earliest times because of mountainous terrain, this part of the island participates, as it probably always did, marginally in cultural influences which affect the center of the island. A great deal of cultural stability has therefore been preserved until the present day.

Nevertheless, it is useful to remember that the population of northern Okinawa is linked with the rest of the island by an efficient communications system. Roads connect almost all settlements in the north with the central island, and a bus transportation system extends its service into the remote areas. But long before all villages were connected by road with the center of Okinawa, people of Kunigami province traveled by foot over the many trails which traverse the mountains, and, since the turn of the century, many have left their home villages. Some went to Japan as laborers; others settled in the Japanese-controlled Islands of the Pacific, and some families joined the numerous Okinawan settlements in South American countries.

LANGUAGE

Taira people are bilingual. Okinawan, which linguists consider a separate language, has many regional dialects, some of which are not mutually intelligible. The speech differences are so great that even two neighboring villages have noticeable dialectical variations. Japanese is the second language.

Okinawan is spoken in almost all households. The first words learned by the child from his mother or others around him are Okinawan. The child is praised or scolded in Okinawan; he learns Okinawan terms for numbers, names for plants, tools, and other implements used around the house. A curious exception in this pattern is the use of kinship terms. Taira children start using Japanese kinship terms in infancy with one exception—in some families the grandmother is addressed by the Okinawan term.

Knowledge of the Okinawan language is said to have been helpful to Americans during the war in distinguishing the local people from Japanese. Japanese has been the official language in Okinawa for over 60 years. It is taught and used in schools exclusively until the upper grades, when foreign languages are introduced. Everybody who has gone to school learns Japanese, and only the oldest persons in Taira speak Okinawan exclusively.

Young children, even though they learn to speak Okinawan first, soon pick up Japanese words and phrases. While their Okinawan vocabulary is limited to everyday experiences, the child's horizon is widened gradually by the use of Japanese terms. First formal efforts to teach Japanese are made in kindergarten, and teachers quickly succeed in eliminating the use of Okinawan in class. Even in play groups of school-age children, Japanese is usual. Children frequently censure each other for occasional slips or shifts to Okinawan.

Taira adults vary in the use of language. Simple, routine matters in daily living are mostly discussed in Okinawan. This language is also predominant in small, informal social gatherings and in emotionally tense situations, such as domestic quarrels. Furthermore, the priestess and her assistants conduct all religious ceremonies in Okinawan. People resorted to Okinawan in our presence when they did not want to be understood. On the other hand, village meetings and gatherings of village leaders or visits of teachers and other officials are conducted in Japanese.

THE PEOPLE

The majority of the Taira people are of short, stocky build, with heavy bones. Their hair growth is strong, their skin dark. A light skin is one of the rare, desired body attributes. It was the opinion of some that the descendants of the noble families who came from Shuri, however, are taller and slender, with a prominent, curved nasal ridge.

Until they feel confident in the presence of strangers, Taira people appear quiet and restrained. It is considered a virtue not to show one's emotions, and Tairans consider the expressiveness of Americans childish. Actually they are gay, talkative, and given to laughter, especially the women. Men are quiet unless stimulated by alcohol, but both men and women may lose their composure in emergencies. A notable exception is their placid reactions to the threat of disaster from the ever recurrent violent storms.

THE COMMUNITY, ITS HISTORY
AND NATURAL ENVIRONMENT

Taira is one of the northern villages on the northeast coast of Okinawa in Higashi township (see map 1). Today it is home to over 700 people who make their living—as did their ancestors since early times—from the surrounding fields, forests, and from the sea. The Okinawan name for the village, Taira, means "sloping fields." The character used for writing the prevalent Japanese version, Taira, means "flat, plain, good."

Since the family records were lost during World War II, it is necessary to depend on oral traditions for reconstruction of the history of Taira. Unfortunately, the desire of many Okinawans to establish a relationship between their local families and the former royal courts casts some doubt on the accuracy of these traditions.

According to these traditions, the first village to be settled in the vicinity of Taira was the neighboring community Kawata. After the Hokuzan kingdom in Nakijin (on the northwestern Motobu Peninsula) was conquered by the southern Okinawan kingdom of Chuzan in the fifthteenth century (Kerr, 1958:85), the second son of the Lord of Hokuzan is said to have escaped northward into Kunigami province. Unitokogami, the fleeing nobleman, arrived near the present site of Kawata and established himself in a cave around the year 1477. He is still revered today as founder of the village in a yearly spring ceremony when prayers are said in front of the cave. The oldest Taira families trace their descent in the male line from Nizenya, the "main house," he founded. Taira was settled around 1550 by two families tracing descent from this "main house." The descendents of these settlers are the two main "houses," or family lines in Taira, and for several centuries Taira must have been a small, closely knit community of interrelated people.

Between 1875 and 1895, when the court life at the old capitol of

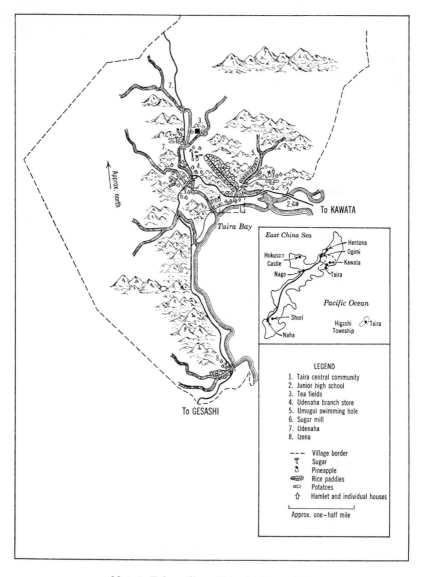

Map 1. Taira village (Higashi Township).

Shuri was broken up under Japanese influence, many families of noble origin moved into the country to become farmers, and the village grew in size. These people settled mainly outside the central village in areas where land was available. One family moved into Taira proper, forming the third "main house." Although it still maintains feeble ceremonial connections with Shuri, it gave up its noble title shortly after coming north and moved its ancestral tomb to the community. The noble families who settled in the valleys and hills preserved their distinctive traditions until the end of World War II. Their noble descent was noted in the population register, and intermarriage with commoners was discouraged.

Except for these Shuri migrants, few outsiders seem to have settled in Taira prior to World War II. The residents on the southern part of the island, especially the residents of Naha and Shuri, consider northerners rustics. Although this part of the island was often used as a hiding place by political and criminal refugees from the south, who are said to have founded nearby villages, none of them made their home in Taira.

The original settlers of Taira were reluctant to accept later arrivals in their midst. Because of the fear of spirits, foreign to the village, they prohibited the burial of the newcomer's dead near the tombs shared by the members of the "main houses." To this day the funeral urns of a family who came to Taira about 60 years ago and later intermarried with settled villages are kept in a cave, away from all other tombs.

Higashi township was established in 1922. The area had previously belonged to Kushi township to the south, but the great distances between villages and the mountainous character of the country made efficient administration very difficult. Furthermore, some Higashi inhabitants felt that because of temperamental differences and divergent interests they should separate from the southern township. Since 1922 contacts have been predominantly with Ogimi township to the northwest and the town of Nago, 16 miles away. Once the road connecting the two coastlines was completed in 1936, Taira's isolation decreased considerably, and it became the administrative seat of Higashi township in 1946.

Taira also became the home of the high priestess. In the period prior to direct Japanese administration, her office was under the jurisdiction of the Shuri court (Lebra, 1958), and her predecessors must have been appointed by the Okinawan kings. Taira may have been chosen as the seat of the high priestess in lieu of Kawata because Kawata lacks the good rice land which traditionally went to the high priestess by royal decree. Some of this rice land is still in the hands of the living priestess.

Although a number of important shrines and worship places are located in the Kawata area, the main shrine is in Taira.

To this tranquil area the activities of World War II brought a great upheaval. Although the main stream of refugees from the south, following threats of United States troups' invasion, did not reach this northern area, Japanese guerilla forces settled in the hills of Higashi township. This, and the constant warnings from the Japanese of the "terrors" of American occupation, caused the population of all villages to take refuge in the mountains, carrying along what few possessions they could, including livestock. Families were separated and individuals lived in constant fear of soldiers from both sides. Nightly excursions to the fields to harvest whatever could be found helped to maintain a meager diet. It is characteristic of the stresses of this period that among the children of central Taira only one was born in 1945.

The war ended for Taira people when American troops had cleared the northern areas of Japanese troops. In this action several villages were destroyed, among them Taira. The present economic struggle of Higashi township, an area which was always handicapped by lack of farmland and poor soil, is partly due to the war. On the other hand, the demand for lumber for an island-wide reconstruction program lent a temporary boom to the economy. In the process, however, forests which had been heavily cut before the war fell prey to rapid and poorly planned cutting. At present the whole township is in the throes of economic readjustment.

In the past 50 years, Taira, like the rest of Okinawa, has sent some of its overflow of population to various areas in the world, including Japan, and especially to the industrial areas of Kobe and Osaka, Saipan, and Brazil. At least five of the families in central Taira lived either in Japan or the Pacific Islands and returned shortly after World War II. Emigrants to Brazil have stayed with the exception of one prominent person who returned to Taira several years before the war. Some of the families lived as many as 18 or 20 years abroad, and several children in the study were born in Japan and returned to the village as infants. Among the villagers are many who have served in the Japanese Army in Asia or in the South Seas.

The repatriation of these families does not seem to have caused any serious disturbances to the village, since many people were killed during the war and several families moved to the city. An exodus to the outlying areas of the village also provided room for returnees, so, although rice land is scarce, there is still some uncultivated farmland, admittedly mostly of poor quality.

The community is dispersed. In the outlying parts, as far as 2 miles from the center (see map 1), the houses are scattered between the paddies or farm lands in sections which form subvillages or wards. As mentioned above, settlers from the south took up residence in these areas. Recently families from the main village have also moved to the more remote parts of the community, such as Udenaha, because they can reach their fields more conveniently. Although the name Taira refers to the political unit of main village and outlying parts, including Udenaha and Izena, most references in this study pertain only to the central community. Its 60 households, with about 330 individuals, form the primary social unit from which the sample of 24 children was chosen.

Central Taira nestles along the inner shore of Taira Bay, which opens into the Pacific Ocean. At this point the median range mountains recede from the coastline. Behind the village, rice paddies spread in a crazed pattern at the bottom and on the terraced sides of several valleys which are separated from each other by sparsely wooded hills. Here and there the red earth of an eroded section shows like a scab through the green slopes.

In traveling by road from the south, most people choose the highway along the East China Sea coast, which is connected with the road which crosses the island. Higashi township is entered through a low saddle in the mountains which separate the two coastlines. To the right and left begins Taira's forest. Central Taira is reached through a winding lane bordered by pine trees. To the left the view opens into one of the neatly cultivated rice fields, backed by the hills on whose flat tops and terraced sides village people cultivate their farm lands.

The central village itself lies on a sand bluff, separating the valley from the ocean, so that there is a slight drop toward both sides (see map 2). The main road runs the length of the village. Except for the thoroughfare, which is dirt and gravel, the side roads are not surfaced, and after heavy rains puddles form and remain for more than a day, to the delight of children who play in them.

When Taira was destroyed during World War II, along with its houses went much of the foliage which once served as a windbreak. A few fukugi trees * line the main street, and hibiscus hedges here and there hide some of the houses from a first inspection. There are bushes around the edges of the village.

The war-time destruction is hardly apparent on a first walk through the village. Along the main street, lined by houses, one finds the rice mill, a substantial new building of concrete and wood, the police sta-

* A small- to medium-sized evergreen tree with a narrow, upright, very dark green crown of leaves.

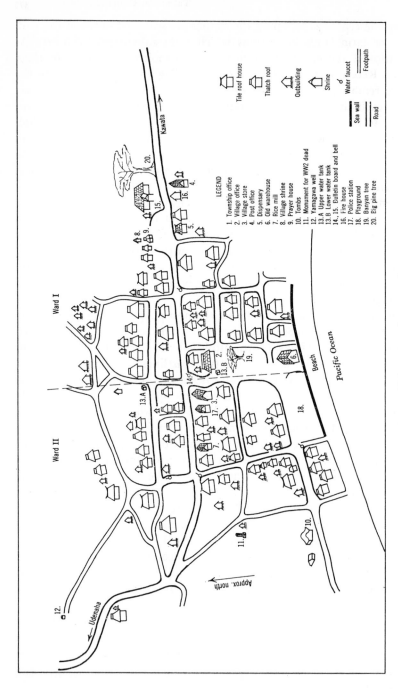

Map 2. Taira, central community.

LEGEND

1. Township office
2. Village office
3. Village store
4. Post office
5. Dispensary
6. Old warehouse
7. Rice mill
8. Village shrine
9. Prayer house
10. Tombs
11. Monument for WW2 dead
12. Yamagawa well
13.A Upper water tank
13.B Lower water tank
14, 15. Bulletin board and bell
16. Fire house
17. Police station
18. Playground
19. Banyan tree
20. Big pine tree

Tile roof house
Thatch roof
Outbuilding
Shrine
Water faucet
Sea wall
Footpath
Road

Ward I
Ward II
Kawata
Udenaha
Pacific Ocean
Beach
Approx. north

tion, a frame wood building, and the main store. On the eastern end of the village the road opens into a little square in front of the simple, open prayer house with a small concrete shrine in back, housing three sacred stones. Beyond these is the township office crowned by a mighty pine tree of tremendous and symmetrical proportions, acclaimed by Taira people to be the oldest existing pine in Okinawa. Across from the office are the post office and the dispensary.

Closer inspection of the village shows former house sites which were not rebuilt. Some still have empty concrete shells or single concrete walls and abandoned pigsties or storage sheds. Some of the vacant lots are used as potato fields, others as play areas, the favorite being a large house lot surrounded by a concrete wall, near the main store.

Houses are set back a short distance from the roads and paths, and most face south. In spite of the hedges and trees, the house is easily accessible from the street—its orientation is therefore toward the community as a whole and, as will be seen later, open to visitors who can enter freely without going through winding garden paths and knocking on doors or entering through long corridors and passages. Each house lot is small, ranging from 1300 to 6050 square feet. Houses are set so close to each other that neighborly conversations from one to the other can be conducted without leaving one's premises. Although some privacy is attained by the hibiscus hedges and fences, few secrets can be kept from neighbors.

There are several focal areas where people frequently meet and interact. The main store is a geographical center. Its two bulletin boards make it a natural congregating point. The banyan tree, overshadowing the village office and the lower water tank, is another such place, and on any day of the year scores of children can be found on or under it. In prewar times it was flanked by important structures, but now the empty lots, which are adjacent, form a green which is used on good days for village meetings.

South of this green, and close to the water, stands the old warehouse, a concrete structure with tile roof which once served as a storage center for agricultural products shipped south by boat; now it serves as a village meeting playground, especially on rainy days. The open space around it, bordering on the sea wall, is also used as a play area and as a gathering place for young adults. Here people prepare firewood for sale and stack it to be picked up by the village truck. Houses once stood near the 10-foot sea wall but were not rebuilt after the war.

To the north of the store lies the upper water tank. Until several standing faucets were installed in 1955, this used to be another place where people met frequently. Water is diverted from a stream a mile above the village and piped into the upper and lower tanks where people fill their buckets which they carry home on a shoulder yoke. Both tanks always attract children. Before faucets were installed, the two spigots on each tank were closed with a wooden stopper which the children often pulled to get a drink or water to play in. An open lot surrounding the upper water tank is another popular play area.

On the eastern side of the village below the main road lies a flat sandy plain, separating the actual beach from the houses above. Children are frequently found playing there or walking along the beach to the mouth of the Noro Mata and Fukuji rivers, which reach the sea about 400 yards away. To the west of the central village lie the tombs and the monument for the war dead of the village.

Many hills around the village drop off vertically toward the south; these drops are partly effects of the geological conditions, such as karst depressions, partly caused by erosion of drainage during the heavy rains. Narrow paths, leading up the steep claylike hillsides, are slippery and very treacherous during rains. On the way to school in Kawata, the neighboring village, children have to pass a section of the road where river and rains have washed away the bank so badly that a misstep on the edge of the road could lead to a fall of more than 50 feet.

The little river which runs through parts of the valley behind Taira is another gathering place of children. A path alongside it leads into the hills and mountain forest lands. Seven minutes walking along this path takes one to Umugui, a natural swimming hole which also serves as one of the favorite laundry places. During the summer the river offers several other popular swimming spots downstream from Umugui. There is also a little concrete bridge in the rice fields beyond the houses, where adults and children go to wash laundry and sometimes pots and pans. Yamagawa well is a water hole, lined with concrete, near the northwestern part of Taira. Before water faucets were installed, girls frequently went there to wash their hair and do laundry.

Children go to the fields to look for flowers and berries or, in the case of older boys, to cut grass for animals. Distances covered by any child depend, of course, on the age. Younger siblings under 5 accompany the older ones to places beyond the area, but no expeditions extend to areas that are not also regularly traversed by adults in the course of their daily duties. Perhaps because of the multiple rivers and water sources, the beach offers less enticement than one might expect. On some days a group may decide to play on the beach, but since sand is also available throughout the village, everybody will soon shift back to some other area inland.

Tropical plants, bushes, and trees grow at sea level. At higher elevations one finds temperate zone forests. Typical for the area are numerous grasses growing along the mountainside and on top of hills. Among them, the most permanent in appearance and use are miscanthus grass and a dwarf bamboo. Panadanns bushes line the beaches and areas close to them. Pine trees are common. Fukugi trees grow in the village but also in the hinterland. Here and there cycad palms lend the scenery a special tropical touch. Wild flowers grow almost all year.

The heavy underbrush is the habitat of several species of poisonous snakes for which the Ryukyu Islands are notorious. The most common, the *habu*, a pit viper, feeds on rats and other small animals and often enters the actual village area. Since rats outnumber humans in Okinawa by an approximate ratio of three to one, these snakes find ample food. Their search sometimes takes them into the rafters of thatch-roofed houses. This danger is present from March until October. People are bitten if they happen to step on the hidden reptiles or sometimes while they sleep. Children are taught by their elders to be careful, and during our study no children were bitten.

Insects are another source of irritation. Mosquitoes attack quite viciously during the summer; fleas, which live in the sand and in straw or reed mats, inflict bites at any time but are seldom carried in clothes. Flies do not seem to annoy the villagers although they are thick wherever food is left in the open and near the pig pens and outhouses.

The number of motor vehicles passing through Taira is small. A few heavy lumber trucks and an occasional U.S. Army vehicle drive through the main street. Four buses daily, two in the morning and two in the afternoon, connect Taira with other villages in Higashi township and the rest of the island. Because traffic is sparse, and it is difficult to catch a ride, persons intending to leave the community in the middle of the day often take the 50-minute walk to the other side of the island where buses pass every 30 minutes on the coastal highway. Villages frequently take trips to the nearby provincial market town of Nago or even to Naha, the capitol.

THE CLIMATE

In spite of Okinawa's subtropical geographic position, it has distinct seasonal differences demanding appropriate adjustments in living routine and clothing. Temperatures in the Taira region may reach a minimum of 38 degrees in January and February and a maximum of 96 degrees in July or August. The average daily mean temperature, however, shows much less variation. From the low 50's in early winter it rises to the low 80's in midsummer. The relative humidities, having daily means of 70% in January and February and 82% in July and August, may often reach an uncomfortable 96% preceding or following one of the many rain squalls in the hot season.

From January through March, winds blowing from the northwest to north carry cold, damp air from the Asian continent across the East China Sea. Although many houses in Taira are somewhat protected by bushes separating them from the open valley behind, nevertheless, house doors are often kept shut during this coldest part of the year.

March and April offer a pleasant, balanced climate. Winds are east to southeast, rainfall is low, and temperatures reach the high 60's. The rainy season begins in late May and lasts until late June. During these four weeks it sometimes rains steadily for one or two days, and adults are forced to give up working.

Children take shelter during the worst downpours, but they reappear outside even before the rains are over to play in puddles or little streams running down the streets. During this time floods and landslides occur.

Midsummer is often so hot and humid that villagers frequently comment on their discomfort. This is one of the busiest agricultural seasons, but exhaustion causes many people to take naps during noon hours. Work efficiency decreases, and fewer daily trips are made to the mountains. Children also stay at home in the afternoon. It is believed that the heat causes severe headaches. The hot season gradually gives way to a few weeks in late October, November, and early December which correspond in climate to an early fall in northeastern United States.

Typhoons are known to have hit Okinawa at almost any time of the year. The most dangerous season for these violent storms, however, with wind velocities of over 50 miles per hour, is from late June until October. An extensive warning system exists, and Taira, though remote and without radio, is notified immediately by telephone of storm warnings, sometimes days in advance. Taira people hardly need such warnings. They can sense the oncoming storm and often predict one correctly before the official forecasts confirm that a storm is approaching the island. Since 1955 was one of the rare years in which no major storm hit the island, no firsthand description can be given. The damage is always considerable, not only to crops and trees but also to houses and other property.

CLOTHING

Today the clothing of Taira people is predominantly Western. Until World War II some fine silk materials for dress were woven in the village, but work clothes were bought in the stores in Nago and Naha. Men and women wear simple, drab, patched, or torn clothes which are laundered frequently. Almost everybody still has a few pieces of U.S. Army fatigues which were handed out immediately after World War II; some have Japanese uniforms.

Women wear cotton skirts and blouses, men cotton trousers, rolled up to the knees for work in the fields, and shirts. During the cold months old jackets are added. Men almost always wrap towels around their heads to hold back their long hair or, as they say, to absorb perspiration. Women also cover their heads with towels during work. Most men and women wear some underclothes; both wear pants, and most women wear slips.

Young girls are more fastidious about their daily dress than older women and all men. An adolescent girl is always well covered, unlike an older married woman who may leave her blouse open to give the baby easy access to the breast. During the heat of the summer, when men take off their shirts, old women follow their example. Most married women just work in their slip and skirt during the hottest part of the summer.

On special holidays or for trips to the city, people have better clothes. Many of these are bought by both men and women from the itinerant, secondhand clothes peddler who visits Taira several times a year before the major holidays. Some old women and a few old men still wear the dark, silk kimonos of prewar days for dress, but usually women wear one-piece dresses or two-piece suits with blouses and men Western suits with white shirts and sometimes ties. Not everybody has shoes to go with special outfits. Wooden clogs are worn by both men and women, even with Western clothes, more commonly than sneakers and shoes.

Although a Western-style hairdo as pictured in magazines or seen on American women in the central part of Okinawa serves as a model to the younger Taira women, few can afford to have their hair done in the city. Sometimes a teacher or the wife of an official returns from a trip to town with a permanent wave. Most older women wear their long hair tied in a bun at the back of the head. Younger girls who have finished school wear their hair short and straight. The priestess' daughter cuts hair in a barber chair outside her house. Men go to her for a shave; but since this happens only about once a week or less, they have a stubbly beard much of the time. Men have their hair cut infrequently. From adolescence on they prefer long and unwieldy hair, combed to one side.

Almost no women use lipstick, but a few put on rouge for special occasions. More and more of the younger women use some make-up when they travel to the city, in spite of rather rude teasing from other villagers that they look like prostitutes.

During the hot summer most people have straw sun hats which can be bought at the local store after the rainy season. They cost little and last until the end of the heat. Umbrellas are the only rain protection during wet days, since the raincoats and hats formerly made of palm thatch have almost completely disappeared.

DWELLINGS

All but two houses in Taira are postwar structures. The first postwar structures were small and hastily built of local, mostly inferior materials. In the last few years families have built more elaborate houses with several rooms, substantial walls and roofs, and made of quality Japanese hard woods, which will resist rapid deterioration. Only a few of the present houses, however, compare in size and workmanship with the large prewar farmhouses.

On the whole, housing in central Taira is inferior to outlying parts of the community and other surrounding villages. Two house types are found: the simple, temporary house or hut with two or three rooms and a kitchen, covered by a thatch roof; and the larger, more substantial house with either thatch or tile roof, four to six rooms and a kitchen.

All houses have common characteristics. They are elevated from the ground so that a 20 to 24 inch space is left underneath the floor, which is sometimes used for the storage of potatoes and firewood. The floor plan is uniform for all houses of either type (Figure 1). Living rooms, also used for sleeping, are always located in the front part of the house. A smaller room located at the right rear of the house is used as a bedroom or for sick people and parturient mothers. The kitchen is on level ground so that a step has to be taken to enter the eating corner from the kitchen. Even the simplest huts have a thin wall which separates the rear bedroom and kitchen from the front part. All outside doors are sliding panels which move in a wooden track so that the whole front of the house may be opened. A visitor can tell immediately if somebody is home and, if an informal caller, will sit on the elevated

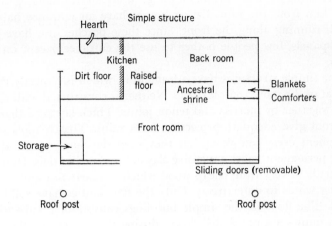

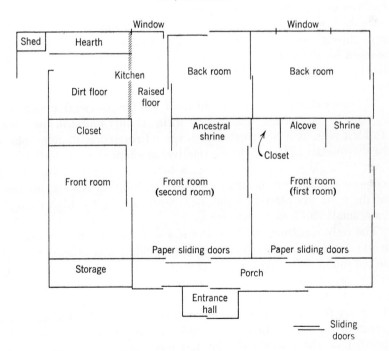

Figure 1. House plan showing simple and complex structures.

floor, resting his feet outside on the ground. An overhanging roof protects him from the rain. Larger houses have an entrance hall and a porch running along the front. Since these porches also have sliding-door panels, few people bother to use the entrance except on formal visits.

The simple structures have a framework which is basically the same as that of the more complex ones. Neither is constructed with nails but held together by mortise and tenon joints. Thick layers of thatch or a tile roof give adequate protection from rains. Thatch roofs need replacement every few years, but they keep the house cooler than the more permanent, more expensive clay or cement tile roofs. House walls are made of very thin, cheap wood which weathers fast and cracks, allowing winds to enter freely. Only the new houses have solid double walls. The floor in the simple buildings consists of planks which in many houses are not nailed down; during the winter months the cold penetrates through the wide slots between the boards. Better houses have ceilings and doors to separate the "first" and "second" room in the front of the house, as well as solid floors.

Smoke from the open fireplace in the kitchen rises into the roof and seeps through the thatch. Poor eyesight, common among children, is believed by the villagers to result from smoke-filled houses and poor lighting. In the evening, dim light is provided by one or two kerosene lamps.

The ancestral shrine, a built-in shelf for the ancestral tablets, has its place in the "second" room. This shrine is only found in the homes of oldest sons. It is not treated with special reverence. Photographs of the deceased as well as of living relatives are kept there as well as personal belongings—a letter, money, a bottle of sake, or gifts. During religious holidays of ancestral worship, red hibiscus flowers, the color for the dead, are placed on the shelf. Since the shelf is high from the floor, small children cannot get at it.

The only furniture in all houses is a low table on which food and drinks are served. Everybody sits on the floor, legs crossed and feet tucked under their thighs in the case of men or put behind to one side in the case of women. Very few houses in Taira have the thick, padded straw mats found in the homes of more well-to-do people in Okinawa. But every family has several thin mats of woven reed standing in one corner of the room; these are spread out for guests to sit on or for a member of the household who lies down during the day. Storage shelves are used in simple houses, but in the better houses mattresses, comforters, and hard pillows are kept in a built-in closet space during the day. On sunny days women air the bedding by spreading it over walls, fences, or in the grass.

There are no uniform sleeping arrangements. The larger the family, the more corners of the front rooms and rear room are occupied. Since the number of comforters is limited in most families, two or three members of the family share one. Father and mother do not always sleep together, and, even if they do, an infant may sleep between them. When there are several children, another child may sleep next to the father, so that in one row there may be mother, a baby, father, and an older child. One or two children usually sleep with the grandmother in another corner. In several families an older sister may sleep with younger brothers; in others, two elder brothers, or an older sister and an older brother, may sleep next to each other. Children do not usually sleep at other people's houses, but when they reach junior high school age, a girl may stay with a girl friend or a group of boys may sleep together at one house.

A simple desk and chair are kept in each house where children go to school. These are put in one corner of the front room, except in large houses with a third room in front, which is reserved for schoolchildren of the house, who also sleep there. Around the study corner, books are kept on a crate or shelf. Only the biggest houses have a niche in their "first" room. Paintings and scrolls, used to decorate alcoves before the war, have been lost, and few people have acquired replacements. Many families decorate rooms by pasting pictures from magazines and newspapers on the walls. Some have reproductions of the Japanese Crown Prince Akihito, others scenic pictures from Japan.

Only a few recent buildings have inner sliding doors with paper screens. The paper is often left off during the hot season and put on before New Year. If children or cats are around, the splendor does not last long, and even an adult's hand frequently punctures the screen in trying to open the door. Holes are left unrepaired for the remainder of the year.

The eating corner between kitchen and rear room is the place where most families gather in the evening, especially during the winter. An informal caller may join them there. If it is cold, a brazier is put in the center, filled with pieces of charcoal on top of old ashes to provide heat for those sitting around it. These braziers vary in type: the poorest families use the bottom of an oil drum filled with ashes; others use pottery jars or small wooden boxes lined with metal.

Crockery used in most houses is of a simple type. If breakage occurs, as it often does, a cup or bowl can be replaced for a few yen at the grocery store. Well-to-do families may have an extra set of teacups, which are used for guests. Several families also own lacquer ware, but it is not in daily use. Like cups and bowls, chopsticks are simple and inexpensive. They last a long time and are seldom lost. Children do not use household equipment in their games. Instead they find broken dishes, old cans, and other discarded items in the trash heap.

The kitchen has no equipment other than the open fireplace with three hearth stones and a shelf above it on which a salt column, symbolizing kitchen deities, is kept. During the last few years, the Ryukyan government Home Extension Service has been trying to introduce brick stoves into farmhouses. Several families now have this kind of stove although it is expensive to build.

As far as can be superficially discerned, the home is kept clean. A visitor usually finds the floor of the house free of dirt. Footgear is taken off before entering, and children are reminded to wash their bare feet before going into the house. Less care is given to the area around the kitchen.

Outside the kitchen stand one or two jars to store water. A dipper is kept nearby, and children playing in the vicinity or adults often walk to one of these jars for water, which they drink out of a dipper. There may also be an array of pots, pans, crates, baskets, and other equipment piled up around the kitchen. Knives and hatchets are openly left around among the equipment behind the kitchen.

The courtyard is an important place for domestic activities. Here women and girls wash dishes, mix pig food in large kettles, make bean paste in a hand stone grinder, and prepare grain for storage. There are vegetable patches in one corner of the yard, chicken coops, pigsties, goat pens, and an outhouse in another. Most garbage is fed to the pigs; the rest is thrown over the sea wall to roll down onto the beach.

✲

✲

✲

Chapter 2

Daily Routine

There are few clocks in central Taira. Except for the township office, post office, and village store, only two or three families own a timepiece. Twice a day, at noon and 10 o'clock in the evening, a clerk strikes an empty oxygen bottle with a wooden mallet to mark the time. The noon bell tells people in the fields and mountains that it is time for the midday meal and helps those who have a clock to compare the time. The evening bell indicates that it is time to end the day. School-children do not need a clock, since they get up early in the morning and go to school soon after, knowing that they are probably early. For most adults, daylight and sun position are enough to tell the approximate hour of the day. Some take arrival and departure of the bus, four times a day, as a point of orientation.

Old women are the first to rise in the morning. Long before dawn during the winter, or with the first light of the summer day, they get up and start a fire to boil sweet potatoes and heat the soybean soup. Blue smoke rising through the thatched roof into the early morning sky indicates that life in the village has begun. Children soon awake. The door is pushed open and a sleepy child appears to urinate off the edge of the house. Men are the last to rise. Considering the effect of the sake which they may have consumed on the preceding evening, it is remarkable that they are able to wake up so soon. By 6:30 the sleepiest person has risen.

The addition of outer clothes to the underclothing in which most people sleep is simple. Cold water splashed over the face and a quick turn at the toothbrush is all the toilet needed to begin a new day.

The task of folding comforters and taking down the mosquito net falls to one of the older children or to the mother. Older children and young girls help to carry water from the tank, the first task that has to be done after getting up. After breakfast, women feed the pigs. By about 7 o'clock everybody is ready for work. On a good day people leave for the mountains or start toward their fields—schoolchildren are on their way, too.

By 8 o'clock, except during very poor weather, the village is left to the old people and young children. Little boys and girls hang around, waiting for kindergarten to start at 9 o'clock. Play begins for them after they leave the house in the morning and does not end until evening.

For men and women, the routine of work in fields and forests is prescribed by seasonal activities which demand their special attention, but there are daily chores, such as digging potatoes, picking vegetables, and collecting feed for the animals and firewood for cooking. Only a few men who go to the mountains, taking their midday meal along, are away all day. The rest come and go during the day from the rice paddies, potato fields, or forests, so that there is repeated contact between children and their parents. A young child, even if left in the care of an older sibling or the kindergarten teacher, therefore has a chance to see the mother. Men and women who have gone to the mountains return with their first load of wood around 10 o'clock. The mother will return again around noon and prepare the midday meal: noodle soup, fried cabbage with dried shrimps, perhaps rice, and always sweet potatoes. After lunch there is a short rest period. During the hot summer months this rest extends to an hour or more, and on the hottest days people lie in their houses sleeping during the noon hours. Midday is also a time for social interaction. There is some visiting back and forth. Old people always seek each other's company, and younger ones back from the fields or forest may join them for a while.

Toward evening blue smoke indicates again that food is being prepared. Pigs are fed by the women in late afternoon. Then women, young girls, or boys fill water buckets and carry them home. After 5 there is a heavy run on the tank or faucets, and this is often the time when families start preparing a bath. It takes until dark to warm up an oil drum filled with water and heated underneath by scraps of wood and twigs. People take their bath after dark. Since the bath house was destroyed during the war, ablutions take place outside near the tank under a faucet or in an old oil drum in one's backyard.

Young men who return from the mountains wash their horses in the sea. The women who sell fish call on each house at this hour to peddle their wares. The village store, which has only seen a few customers in the morning and during noon, now has its busiest hour. Mothers send their children to buy noodles, kerosene, rice, or seaweed or else they come themselves, a baby on their back or the toddlers following them.

This is also the hour when the young men and women gather to do joint work in the fields of their association or to play volleyball on the playground. Meanwhile, all forest workers have returned and busily cut the last pieces of firewood, bundling them before the store clerk comes along to buy the load. Some adults sit near the playground and watch the children.

Work goes on until dark. Only then do families gather for the evening meal. During the summer this may be as late as 8 o'clock. For many families this is the only time during the day when everybody gathers in the family circle. At this time family affairs may be discussed and plans made for the next day's work or other pending matters.

The evening meal consists of rice, a bean paste or noodle soup, and some fish. Meat is served occasionally if a goat is killed or on holidays when someone has slaughtered a pig. Most families cannot afford to buy more than small portions of meat, which are fried or made into soup. Nothing is wasted and leftovers are kept for the next meal. The majority of people are fast eaters, and chopsticks move from bowl to mouth quickly and deftly. Some families eat silently, others enjoy talking during the meal.

Before and after full moon, people like to go out after supper and gather in small groups by the store to talk and smoke or to visit each other. Less running back and forth is observed during dark nights. There is also a seasonal variation in that respect. On cold winter nights, or when it rains, doors are closed early, and visitors slip into the house by the side kitchen door. On warm nights all houses are open, and one can see people sitting in their living room by the light of a kerosene lamp; passers-by just call over and then go in for a chat. Guests are served tea, bits of brown sugar, and other sweets. Men get together at this time and start talking over a cup of sake. A relative or neighbor, bottle in hand, walks in and joins the party. Here and there somebody pulls a samisen out of the corner and starts singing.

Evenings are also the time for village meetings, finance group meetings, family gatherings, and other formal get-togethers. Several times during the week a light shines from the village office or the store office, where some of the village leaders meet to discuss community affairs. In the winter, household-head meetings or other general meetings are called for 8 o'clock; in the summer they do not start until 9 o'clock. In the absence of clocks, few meetings ever start on time.

The young men and women have their get-togethers at the clubhouse in Udenaha. Both sexes attend, sometimes for lectures by a village official on village affairs, sometimes for lessons in bookkeeping and the use of the abacus in business, for which one village leader dedicates his time, or for other educational purposes. Once a week they have a social evening with discussion and sometimes folk dances. On nights when no meetings are scheduled, young men gather at someone's house to smoke, drink, or sing together. If enough sake is available, parties can become noisy. Occasionally a fight or quarrel starts later in the evening after everybody has drunk steadily. Such interruptions on quiet evenings are rare and seldom occur more than once or twice a month. Loud singing at midnight or later, a group of gay men knocking on somebody's door, these are the only disturbances an early sleeper may experience if a party is held somewhere.

By 11 o'clock mosquito nets are hung in the rooms and comforters spread on the floor. Except in the house where men gather to drink, quiet descends over the village around that time. Individuals, however, may be seen until long after midnight. Taira goes to sleep late, and although people claim that everyone gets eight hours of sleep, it is more likely that the majority of adults have to be satisfied with six and a half hours.

✻
✻
✻

Chapter 3

Basic Economy

INTRODUCTION

Taira depends on its fields and forests for a living. Rice and the sweet potato are the principle staple crops; wheat, beans, and vegetables are additional subsistence crops. Firewood and building materials, sugar, pineapple, and silk are main sources of cash. Tea is raised for home consumption.

Since the few rivers around Taira are short and the valleys narrow, the area available for wet rice cultivation is limited. Farm land for sweet potatoes is also not too abundant in this mountainous region and is located either on the gently sloped hills or on a few plateaus between valleys. Here and there it rises on skillfully terraced steps along the steep sides of mountains.

The size of land holdings and the quality of soil partly determine whether a family is able to grow additional cash crops or merely subsist. The average holding for each family is about 5 acres of rice land and 6 acres of other farming land. Yet it is important to note that the range and quality of this land vary widely. Some families own only 1½ acres of rice land and an acre of other farm land, while others own as much as 14 acres of rice land and 12 acres of other farm land; good rice paddies produce three times the quantity of poor ones and are wet enough to allow for two crops per year. Of the 141 families questioned, only 15 grew enough rice to be self-sufficient; 123 had to buy extra rice, and only two families raised a surplus for sale. All families grew enough vegetables for home use, and only 18 bought sweet potatoes. Sixty families grew a surplus of vegetables and 16 a surplus of sweet potatoes.

But actually no family is entirely self-sufficient, for each needs to purchase foodstuff as well as ready-made clothes, manufactured mostly in Japan, more substantial building materials, such as better grades of wood, tiles, and cement, tobacco, alcoholic beverages, sweets, toilet articles, some medical supplies, and other luxuries. Farmers buy their tools; students their books and writing materials. Finally, cash is needed to pay taxes.

In addition to the utilization of sugar, pineapple, firewood, and building materials for cash, Tairans also raise pigs for sale to slaughter houses, and some families derive an income from raising silkworms and producing tea. Fishermen sell fish inside and outside the village, and a small group of people are salaried workers or have an income from specialized services.

Village leaders fear dependence on rapidly dwindling forest resources, still the main source of ready cash. They realize that the present modest living conditions of all families could be much improved if Tairans concentrated on increasing the cultivation of subsistence crops and farmed more intensively to raise cash crops. Most people lack this insight, however, and live on a day-to-day basis without much thought of the future. This is an island-wide problem which has the attention of central government agencies, and a great deal of educational propaganda comes to the village through government channels.

AGRICULTURE

The productivity of the land varies not only with its quality but also with the industriousness of the owners. Farmers who show foresight, those who seem to be under less pressure for immediate cash, take off more time from forest work to cultivate fields during planting season. The village headman and council members remind everybody during village meetings and informal discussions that work in the fields should not be neglected. With the approval of the whole community, the first and 15th of each lunar month have been set aside for farming. On these two days it is forbidden to go to the forests to cut wood. Such agreements are usually observed (as a rule), and they help to achieve their purpose but are not completely effective.

Rice is planted and harvested twice a year. The first rice is prepared in January when seeds are put into special beds where they are left to grow into young shoots until March. Until about 30 years ago it was said that all people seeded rice on the same day while prayers were offered at the village shrine by the priestess. Today key agricultural events are still marked by small ceremonies in which the priestess beseeches or thanks the gods, but the actual day for planting is determined by weather and the condition of seed.

When the rice is transplanted in March, the whole family spends long hours in the paddy. Then the paddies swarm with people; some prepare the soil by spreading fertilizer, others stand in the ooze to set the seedlings. Transplanting is done by mutual assistance groups, which will be discussed later in this chapter. They guarantee everyone a sufficient number of helping hands during the painstaking, rapid work, which has to be finished within a limited time. In a few days the whole paddy area suddenly turns from brown into the tender green of the young shoots. Once planted, intermittent weeding is all the care that is needed.

In July the rice turns brown and is ready for harvest. This is an event of joy for the whole village, for young rice is most delicious and loved by everyone. By then vacations have started, so that schoolchildren can help to cut rice and carry bundles to the spot where it is threshed in treadle-type machines, located either near the field or behind one's house. As soon as the rice is threshed, the grain is carried to a place in the village where the wind blows freely. There a woman holds a flat winnowing basket filled with grain at an angle to let the breeze separate the chaff from the grain. The first rice is cut by men and offered at the family shrine before the whole family eats a specially prepared gruel. Rice is usually stored in one or two oil drums in the kitchen-side corner of the front room. Better houses have a metal-lined storeroom. Once a week a supply is taken to the miller to be hulled and polished.

Those whose fields are sufficiently wet plant a second crop, and the cycle is repeated once more in midsummer, with the second harvest falling in late December.

Sweet potatoes can be planted throughout the greater part of the year if the soil is not too dry. They take from five to seven months to grow to full size. Although less popular than rice, no part of the plant is wasted. The large tubers are consumed, the small ones are usually fed to the pigs; the young leaves are used as vegetables, the older ones cooked into pig food. Slips are cut and used for planting a new crop.

The preferred variety of potato (*tadushi imu*) is grown in the dry paddies during the second rice season. To plant this potato, the soil must be piled up to form a long, narrow, flat-topped mound. One of the hardest jobs for farmers, this is done by men in the humid heat of a midsummer day. Women set the slips after the earth has been moved. These potatoes are the only variety which are thought to improve with storing and are kept under the house or on a special shelf on the rafters.

Onions, giant radishes, beans, and cabbages are also raised on farm lands. Night soil is rarely used for such vegetables nowadays but is still used on potatoes. Several of these vegetables as well as others are raised by women in small "home-garden" plots.

The hardest working period during the year is in July and August. Within a few weeks after the rice harvest, the soil must be made ready for the second rice crop or the soil must be prepared for dry paddy potatoes. This is also the time for planting the chief sugar crop. All this takes place during the hottest time of the year, when efficiency is greatly reduced by heat and humidity.

Sugar harvest and processing fall in the period between January and March. One field after another is harvested by the owners after arrangements have been made for a date when the cane can be processed. Such arrangements are made with the director of the Taira cooperative, who supervises operations of the sugar mill which is owned by the cooperative. The whole family helps on the day of processing. Women carry bundles of branches and light firewood to heat the kettles. The operation requires the help of someone to feed cane into the small, diesel engine driven press, some to carry the pulp away, and others to watch the kettles in which extracted juice is boiled down to molasses. Finally, a few persons stir the brown residue in wide, open pots until it becomes stalted. Then it is put into tubs that hold about 132 pounds.

The agricultural market for cash crops was totally disrupted at the end of World War II. There was no immediate outlet for sugar products; crops had been destroyed or neglected, and the sugar mill was demolished in the fighting. But by this time most people were too satisfied with the great returns from forest work to invest much time and energy in a crop which takes a year and a half to show any material results. Nevertheless, sugar was the first crop to find a market again.

Pineapple, introduced recently in Taira, has a promising future. Tea is still grown in small quantities, but few families grow more than they need for their own use, although it is a good potential cash crop for this area.

ANIMAL HUSBANDRY

Raising pigs is an important source of cash income for all households in the village. Even the poorest families own at least one, but few families have more than two; in the central village the average is about 1.2 per household. Pigs are given special care and attention.

Before a piglet is bought, its feeding habits are carefully observed by the buyer to determine future growing potential. It is then kept in a sty; pigsties are either in the yard near the house or in a cluster of stables on the north edge of the town. Twice a day women cook the food in large kettles and ladle the liquid food into a trough. Nowadays pork is rarely consumed in the village except for special holidays, when several families may slaughter pigs and sell part of the meat to everybody through the local store or preserve some of it by salting. Most farmers, however, wait for the meat buyer from the southern part of the island from whom they receive a good financial return.

Goats are raised for home consumption. They are never left to graze but are quartered in a goat pen near the pigsty and fed on grass cut from uncultivated land. Seven families in the central village have horses. Their main use is to carry firewood from the mountains. The small breed looks like a cross between a horse and pony and seems especially adapted to climb the steep trails. They are also used for plowing and for pulling two-wheeled carts. The owner of a horse may more than double his income from forest work. Horses are frequently rented out for half the day's income from wood carried by them.

Silkworm raising, an important source of income in Taira before the war, is only now being resumed by some Tairan families. The larvae are supplied through island-wide silkworm raising associations, which repurchase the cocoons after they are spun. To raise silkworms, a substantial house is needed so that rats cannot enter and eat the worms. The temporary postwar structures with holes and cracks in the walls and roof are inadequate. Only a few recently built houses can be used. One family keeps growing worms on shelves in the front room. Most of the mulberry trees were lost during and after the war. Plans have been made to plant new trees. Young girls feed the mulberry leaves to the gluttonous worms who require constant attention. When the worms are ready to create their cocoons, they are taken off their diet, and the cocoons are cleaned and sorted out. Silkworms can be raised four times a year if there is an adequate supply of mulberry leaves. Their sale brings a good income, which can become a substitute for cash earned in forest work.

FISHING

Fishing is a much less important source of livelihood than one would expect in a coastal village and is a low-prestige occupation. Only two of the permanent Tairan families fish; the majority of the fishermen are migrants from the surrounding islands who come for a season, leaving their families behind. A few families have moved in permanently. The fishermen supply Taira, but most of the catch is peddled in the Nago market by the fishermen's wives. Some of the more enterprising and mercantile-minded women in the village buy up fish and peddle it for a profit.

Two or three times a year, during February or March, large fishing boats from Henza Island land in Taira with whale meat. All the able women look forward to making extra cash at this time, for whale meat is considered a delicacy in homes where meat is rare. Blubber is eaten and used as frying fat. The distribution of whale meat is arranged by one village woman whose fishermen relatives from Henza supply it in response to her request. She acts as agent, distributing the meat to the women on consignment.

LUMBERING

The main source of immediate cash for most families is firewood. Forest land in the mountains is owned by the township and the village, except for some woods near the fields, which are personal property. The township permits the village to exploit a certain region surrounding the community in return for payment of a forest tax. This tax is levied on firewood bundles or on lumber sold by villagers. Everyone in the village is free to cut wood in the designated area in any amount he desires. This, however, does not imply that unlimited cutting is possible, for resources have been utilized so heavily that most forests near the village are almost cleaned out, and it has become increasingly difficult to find wood. Reforestation has only recently been introduced on a serious scale. Often villagers are found trespassing on land owned by the central Ryukyan government in order to cut from the less depleted forests there. Government officials are sympathetic to the villagers' plight, and they tend to dispose of such transgressions with a stern warning.

Men and women, and during vactions, some children over 12 years, go to the forest. Most people prefer to walk and work in small groups. To reach a place high up in the hills, they may have to hike almost a mile from the center of Taira. The steep, narrow paths made by woodcutters traverse the mountains. Following the approach trails during the day, one can hear voices and the sawing of wood from many directions. All lumber people carry a short handsaw and a heavy bush knife which they use interchangeably. After sufficient trees have been cut and cleared of branches, a large bundle of firewood is carried to the village. Most forest workers make four or five trips a day into the hills— two or three during the hot summer season. As the afternoon ends, they sit down along the road in the village or nearby to prepare firewood bundles. Pieces of wood are inserted through a bamboo loop of standard size, prescribed by the cooperative store, until a tight, uniform bundle is obtained. The last piece has to be driven into the bundle by force. All over the village one can hear the knocking of wood pieces which marks the end of a forest worker's daily labor. Each household works independently and sells firewood to the cooperative. A store clerk travels around the village in late afternoon, checks all bundles, and issues credit slips to each household; these can be changed into money at the store. The following morning the truck, owned by the cooperative, carries the firewood to Naha or Itoman where it is sold to a dealer who redistributes it to individual consumers or public bathhouses. The northern part of the island has always supplied firewood to the population of southern Okinawa to be used for kitchen hearths and bath stoves. In recent years kerosene kitchen stoves have become so popular that the depletion of wood resources tends to coincide with decreasing demand.

TRADES AND PROFESSIONS

Other ways of making a living exist. A few artisans in Taira derive part of their income from wage labor. A number of Taira men earn their living by carpentering, although they do most of their work in the south. They return occasionally when their services are needed for local house building. When working on local construction, they are paid in money, free lodging, and meals. There are also a few part-time resident carpenters who, whenever they are not employed in house building or repairs, spend their time farming and cutting wood. New buildings are usually put up between the beginning of the second rice crop and the New Year.

Several persons are salaried township or village officials. They are paid monthly and work a 44-hour week, not counting many extra meetings and duties connected with their work. All office workers however have fields, either their own or those of their parents, where they spend Sundays helping in agricultural pursuits. During rice planting season, they are given special time off to attend to their fields.

Also among the salaried workers are store employees, a full-time director with assistants and clerks. The clerks are always young people just out of school who receive nominal wages in return for a seven-day work week. The township office employs as janitor a girl who keeps the office in order, serves tea at any time during the day, washes dishes, and helps to cook meals for entertaining. Her family owns one of the largest houses in the central village and more land than most others. No social stigma is attached to her job; in fact, most Taira girls would consider it a privilege to exchange their mountain work for her kind of employment even though they would earn no more. Another girl, employed by the local "doctor" as nurse and maid, lives with the family, eats with them, and sleeps with their children. Only one farmer employs a hired hand, a man from another township.

Among others living on a salary is the postmaster. His father held the same office, and his son is now trained to succeed him as the third in line. The rice miller, a man from outside the village and married to a Taira woman, and the "doctor" also depend for most of their incomes on specialized services. The latter owns his dispensary and small hospital. He receives some financial support from the township government. His services to people are compensated for either in cash or kind. Patients who are unable to pay at once will bring rice to his house after the harvest. These remunerations, pig raising, and other side activities make him, along with the rice miller and the postmaster, the wealthiest person in Taira. Local male school teachers also own fields, to which they give time in the afternoons and Sundays to help their wives.

The priestess and her assistants, although they are religious specialists, are not paid in money for their services. They participate in daily work like the rest of the village. Only when performing services outside the community is the priestess paid a small fee. Within the village she receives the food and sake which are offered in the ceremony, whether she is called by a family or prays at the village shrine on a general holiday.

DIVISION OF LABOR BY SEX AND AGE

Men and women are equal partners in everyday economic activities, both in agricultural and forest work. Only a few occupations are clearly differentiated by sex: fishing, the handling of horses, and the carrying of night soil are done exclusively by males; housework and the care and feeding of pigs predominantly by women. Some agricultural work is considered too heavy for women, for example, the turning of the heavy sods in the rice paddy; nevertheless, women and younger girls often do this work along with the men and boys if time runs short. There are some women who prepare their farm land without the help of their husbands.

In mountain work, women produce almost as much as men except that they do not handle the large logs. Even pregnant women make three or four daily mountain trips, sometimes up until the day of childbirth. Only the mode of carrying wood, like any load, differs for the sexes; a man uses a carrying stick supported on his shoulder, with two bundles attached to each end; a woman carries bundles on her back, tied and held in place by a tump line tied over her forehead. Women can carry loads of 100 to 120 pounds in this manner.

Men seldom carry water from the tank or faucet to the house; this is considered women's work, although younger boys are expected to help at times. Work in the potato fields is mainly women's responsibility. Their hands are also preferred in rice transplanting, where dexterity is needed in pulling out the tender shoots from the seed bed and replanting them in straight rows at measured intervals. Occasionally a young man helps, and boys sometimes try to work along with their sisters when they learn transplanting. Both men and women sow the seed beds. In special activities, such as house building, a more distinct division of labor can be observed. In any building activity, men do the structural work and women carry materials and cook for the men. The same division of labor is found on community projects, road building, fencing against wild pigs, or repairing the water pipes. In general, however, no special comment is made if either a man or woman performs work usually done by the opposite sex.

Men and women work in the fields and forests from ages 15 to 60. When they approach 60, men like to "retire." If possible, they turn over their responsibilities as household heads to their eldest sons. From then on, they tend to stay home more and more. They can still help with less demanding work, making bamboo rings for firewood bundles, sawing wood, or doing odd jobs around the house. Approaching old age, most men become economically useless and in other ways contribute little to society. For old women, quite the contrary is true. Even grandmothers who are well over 60 seem strong and active. Most of them go to the fields to plant or harvest potatoes or other vegetables. One woman, well into her sixties and bent over from arthritis, took long walks to distant potato fields, with a heavy load of slips or potatoes in a basket on her back, a hoe on top of it, supporting herself on a stick. Other grandmothers look after the youngest children, thus freeing the mother for work. Old women also cook, help bundle firewood, and look after the sick. Even if they are too old for any work, like two oldsters over 80 years, they can still hold the youngest grandchild. Two exceptional old men, brothers of almost the same age, pass their time by making rope bags and mats from the fiber of the fan palm. Both are active as financial experts, investing money here and there and lending it for high interests in various shrewd transactions.

INFORMAL AND FORMAL COOPERATION

Cooperation plays a prominent part in Taira economy. Assistance is always given for major tasks, such as preparing grass land for farm use or house building, or for work which must be done quickly, such as transplanting rice or harvesting and milling sugar. In fact, since wet rice cultivation depends on assistance in any culture that works its paddies by hand, it is noteworthy that the term *iimarū,* used in Taira for labor exchange in planting and harvesting, is also extended to other mutual assistance. The term, literally translated, means "gathering by rotation." A family who plans a project that needs the help of others makes an informal arrangement with relatives or neighbors to help for one or more days. This is simply done by notifying individuals that such help is needed. No one, unless he has urgent reasons, would refuse to comply with a call for assistance. If it is a small task, a few close relatives are asked. In most larger undertakings, it is the neighborhood group that lends a hand. These mutual-assistance groups usually form within the central village and within each of the geographical clusters of the outlying village, although close relatives from other parts of the community may be called. However, the most recent arrivals in Taira, all present members of one family line who have the same surname, act jointly in reclamation of neglected fields to strengthen their economic position.

Return services are expected, but nobody would admit that there is any thought of equal compensation and would not even joke about the matter. There is a strong feeling that calculated thinking is unseemly not only among relatives but also among unrelated neighbors. One man, when asked what would happen if a person refused to comply to a request for help, answered, "There is no such dirty person, and if there were one, he would be an outcast." During the rice planting season, persons helping in another's fields will shortly be helped themselves. In housebuilding, a long time may pass until those who aided will need aid in return.

Except for people over 56, pregnant women, and mothers of children under 3 years, every adult past school age, male or female, is required to work on community projects if called by the village head. Officials may pay the village for exemption from this duty. There are two kinds of community corvées, those in which every adult and qualified member of a household has to participate, and those in which only one household representative is required to attend. As many as 12 days a year may be spent by each villager on road construction, clearing of village land, improvement of village-owned tea fields, or in similar projects. In some cases, where the central government has granted support, this work may be compensated by a small payment. More often, however, it is a free contribution to the village effort.

The strength of deeply rooted cooperative behavior seems to have been an essential factor in introducing formal cooperatives successfully in this area. The northern village of Oku is credited with being the first community in Kunigami province to organize a cooperative store in 1906. Initiative for this organization was provided through the Japanese administration. Taira was the first village in present-day Higashi township to establish a cooperative. In 1918 the village was poverty stricken, and village leaders, the president of the Young People's Association, one of the teachers, and others, made a study of the Oku organization. They then convinced the Taira headman of the great possibilities. Over the years the Taira cooperative supported by the majority of Tairan households, through buying of mountain products, marketing, running the store, and sugar production, tried to improve the village economy. One immediate result was that the indebtedness to money lenders from outside the village, especially to the owners of sailing junks which transported mountain products south, could be avoided. Up until the war the cooperative flourished and improved economy.

The end of the war found the village cooperative totally defunct, and it took several years to restore the organization. At present it owns the store, the sugar mill, and the truck. It also controls the use of the village-owned tea fields in which everybody has the right to grow at least one row of tea bushes.

Shares in the cooperative are held by households, and almost everyone in Taira is a member. The two directors and several officers are elected by shareholders. Actually the directorship does not change often, and the most influential leaders usually hold the office. They may initiate measures which will aid the village economy, but they have no absolute power: a check and balance system protects the people. As one person put it, "It is always necessary to have a few persons outside the business so that they can check what is going on. If people of the highest status are all engaged in it, there is no one who can check it and nobody who would dare to." The accounts are checked and audited, and reports are made to the members.

It is characteristic of the cooperative that it works closely with the political organization of the community and that it is an integral part of the village. In certain ways it has taken over some financial functions of the village, supplying it with funds which would otherwise have to be raised through village taxes.

The cooperative buys all firewood that has been produced by the households at a uniform price, thus giving families a great deal more security than they had in days when selling was done on a competitive basis. Since the firewood market fluctuates, the cooperative often takes a loss which would be hard for individuals to bear alone.

The truck which takes the forest products to the city returns with goods for the store. All shareholders' purchases are recorded. Dividends are issued once a year. They are actually small. Part of the profits are used to finance new shares for each household. Every shareholder now owns an equal number of shares. A limited saving system has also been resumed by the postwar cooperative. The small amounts which have accumulated (few families are able to lay aside money for long periods of time) are withdrawn around New Year or on other occasions when special purchases are made.

Although the cooperative would like to finance individual projects, such as building, buying livestock, and agricultural expansion, sufficient funds are not available. Mutual finance groups are formed to extend this type of credit. A person who needs money to finance a project asks others in the village to form a partnership in which everybody who agrees to participate pays the same amount monthly, on a prearranged date, into the common fund. A different person takes a loan each month. It usually goes to the lowest bidder, except that the first loan is given to the person who asked to form the group. The difference between the bid and the actual amount collected is paid out as interest. Each person has a guarantor who is made responsible in case the actual participant is unable to make his monthly payment toward the fund.

Mutual finance groups are formed between any persons, based on their willingness to participate at a certain time, either because they themselves need a loan or, as happens in a few cases, because they hope to make some money from the interest. The obligation to pay is taken very seriously, although it can create tremendous hardships on individuals who have to make quick temporary arrangements to borrow money elsewhere in order to meet their monthly payments. Since several finance groups are formed simultaneously in the village, and an individual may belong to more than one, this system can create more problems for the community than it helps to redress. Village leaders therefore think that the cooperative could take over the loan functions at low interest rates more effectively.

Concern about improving village economy is genuine and foremost. Since the whole island has common economic problems, many suggestions for developing sound village economy originate from the central government. There are many associations and movements which all aim at the same result. Their number is staggering and bewildering to the outsider. In Taira, concern for improvement of conditions is a program of the Women's Association and the Home Improvement Group, associations who try to introduce such changes as better stoves, making of bean paste by villagers, and saving during feasts. There is also an Agricultural Promotion Association which is concerned with improvement of agricultural practices, promotion of cash crops, and reduction of forest work. All these organizations, along with the cooperative and the village government, work together. An individual may be a member of several. Persons with enough knowledge and experience to assume responsible positions are limited in number, and the same persons appear as leaders in various groups. This puts a heavy burden on them, since few days pass during which their attendance after work is not required at one meeting or another.

Taira assumed a leading position in the township in improving agricultural and general economy, especially by promoting sugar development, pineapple growing, and tea raising in recent years. Meanwhile, low income and general poverty are a constant concern to everybody but do not seem to result in constant anxiety. Security, as will be pointed out in other contexts, is provided by being a member of the kinship group and, in the wider sense, of the village as a whole. This helps to share burdens and thus reduce their weight.

✽
✽
✽

Chapter 4

Property

Rice paddies, farm land and some grass land, trees on private land, a house site and house, as well as livestock and tools, are owned by the heads of households. Land is registered in the household head's name, and he has sole right to dispose of it. Ordinarily younger sons have no right to their father's property, but a man may will property to them. If there is no will, however, everything reverts to the eldest son. Despite this, several families of younger sons were found to have land holdings equal to those of eldest sons.

A widow with young sons may hold land in trust for her sons or, if there are no male heirs, may inherit the land outright. Divorcees and spinsters may also acquire land by purchase, and there are several women in Taira who are household heads and owners of real estate.

Because of the war and a general shift in population, much land and many house sites have changed owners, and former wealthy families are no longer the largest landowners. When they returned, several families with small prewar land holdings were able to raise the necessary cash to buy land.

There is little sentimental attachment to a particular plot of land, and households have never been associated with particular plots. Rather, land is considered a necessary commodity, and thus it frequently changes hands. This sentiment may derive from the communal land-holding system with its periodic redistribution of plots to individuals, which was found throughout Okinawa until abolished under Japanese administration at the turn of the century.

Forest land from which villagers derive an income is owned by the village. Being a member of the community confers the right to use village forests, subject to regulations made by the village. Of particular interest is the village-owned tea field, which the village cooperative controls. The field has been subdivided, and each household in the community is entitled to the use of one of the equal-sized lots. A small yearly payment is made to the cooperative, which passes these proceeds on to the village to pay salaries for officials and other expenses.

Tenancy was never a problem in the Taira area. Under the old system everyone was entitled to land. The final distribution in the change to individual ownership gave everyone sufficient land. Although many new landowners sold and mortgaged their property in other parts of Okinawa, one source states that "in the villages of Kawata, Taira and Miyagushiku . . . none of 348 families was found landless . . ." (Tamura 1927:292 translation). Today several families hold mortgages on their land, usually for loans to put up new buildings or some other capital investment. Nevertheless, a shortage of rice paddies is obvious, since a part of the land around Taira is owned by people from the neighboring village, and an extension of paddy land in this mountainous district would be feasible only with the aid of irrigation projects.

The renting of property from persons who have moved to the city is not uncommon and is a means of bolstering one's own rice or farm land. People who move out of the community, either temporarily or for longer periods, may rent their land or let relatives and even nonrelatives use it. In most cases no compensation is paid for the use of farm land, although in rare cases where the owner continues to live in the village, some agreement is made to share the harvested crop. Rice paddies, however, are rented for half the crop. The owner returns from the city during harvesting time to help in cutting and threshing the rice. If unable to return, he may hire a person to help or to make adjustments in the division of the yield. Taira people do not rent their paddies or farm lands for money. An exception may be made in the case of outside fishermen who move into the village and who may rent a small area of land from a villager. In a few cases land has been left in the care of a family member by a relative who went overseas. One of the most substantial farmers in Taira holds several such properties, part of which he owns and part of which he holds in custodianship for a relative overseas. In such a case he is entitled to exploit the land without any compensation for the departed family member.

Almost all local families own their houses and house lots. The thought of renting a room or house for money is somewhat foreign to the village, and in the case of the authors, "rent" for two rooms, as originally suggested by the owner of the house, was nominal. Fishermen, however, have to rent a room or a whole house. Their rent is an informal arrangement of payment in kind, fish, or other sea products. In addition, bachelor teachers from outside the community who require room and board are sometimes put up without compensation, and they agree, perhaps, to give some help with studies of the landlord's children. Only the village "doctor" takes transient guests, mostly visiting officials from the city, who pay for lodgings.

Although the household head is a legal owner of the family property, there is a feeling that it belongs to the family and everyone in the household identifies himself with his land and house. This is expressed in the language. A person who is asked, "Whose rice paddy is this?" would answer that it is the household's or "ours."

In addition to the communal land holdings and the property of the cooperative described earlier, the following items are shared. The government supplies a breeding boar to each village; it is then left in the care of one farmer. This animal is available to pig owners for studding on request, and a small charge is made for the upkeep of the boar. A few tools are jointly owned by several households. Threshing machines were bought jointly after the war by two or more families to defray the high cost of such equipment. These families could be neighbors or relatives. Today many are complaining that joint ownership works hardships during the busy harvest season when there is heavy demand for the machines. As a result, everybody wishes to own his own machine as soon as he can afford to. For tea harvesting, special clippers are owned by the village cooperative and loaned to people as they need them. Since tea harvesting, though seasonal, is not done by all families during the same day, sharing of these tools presents no difficulties.

Property of others is very much respected. Stealing among villagers is almost unheard of, except for some pilfering of green vegetables and fruits by children. Only one case was reported during the field-work period—a person tried to take some goods without payment from the community store. When a village meeting was called, and it was announced that the person's identity was known to the store manager, the merchandise was later replaced. Willful damage to fields is similarly strictly forbidden. No child would really think of doing such damage. But there are no formal rules about trespassing. Movement across other people's property is completely free and unchallenged.

Chapter 5

Political Organization and Social Control

THE TOWNSHIP

Administratively Taira village is part of Higashi township, an area of approximately 30 square miles with six independent villages spread over a distance of about 15 miles along the coast. Taira is centrally located and since 1946 has been the seat of the township administration. Higashi is one of several townships in northern Okinawa. It is responsible to the central Ryukyuan government at Naha which has branch offices at Nago, the nearest town to Taira. Control over communities such as Taira by a central government is of ancient date. The Okinawan king levied taxes throughout the island and held political control over the villages until establishment of Japanese administration.

The township office is headed by a mayor who is elected for four years by popular vote. He nominates an assistant mayor who must be confirmed by the township assembly, a council of 16 representatives who are elected from all the villages. The Assembly meets two or three times a year to enact local ordinances, to confirm the mayor's appointments, and to approve the annual budget.

The administrative organization of the township consists of five departments, which are responsible for carrying out central government policies. The Finance and Education Department is concerned with tax collection and general school affairs. The Industrial Department acts as controlling and advising agent in all matters of subsistence and cash production. Financial help for farmers is channeled through this department. Attached to it is an Agricultural Extension Division agent who is concerned with individual farmers' problems. A General Affairs Department is in charge of office administration; it is also responsible for keeping the population registry, with vital statistics and relevant information on all township residents.* The Welfare Department investigates relief cases and receives applications for support from the poorest families. The Health and Sanitation Administration is primarily concerned with preventive work. Representatives from these five departments are supposed to visit all the villages in the township frequently to inspect and to discuss regulations. The officials and personnel of the five departments are drawn equally from all the villages and commute daily by foot, bicycle, or bus.

The township administration links the central government and individual villages. Numerous requests for central government aid, originating in each community, are sent through the township office. The government in turn deals with each community through the township administration. Contact between township and the villages is maintained by weekly meetings of all village headmen with the mayor and his staff. The village headman is responsible for carrying out township and central government ordinances.

THE VILLAGE

The village headman is elected once a year, in June, from a slate agreed on beforehand during informal discussions by villagers. There is no campaigning; in fact, the elections are treated more as a necessity than a politically important event, and neither before nor after do they incite much public discussion. This democratic process of elections is of post-World War II date. Before the war, the council of village leaders accepted a new headman only if the choice pleased them, so that the headman at that time was virtually appointed. Villagers remarked that "listening to public opinion is a recent change."

The village is still experimenting with the mechanics of a free election. Votes are still restricted to household heads, but the Taira Women's Association and Young People's Association tried to change this in 1955. Although they did not succeed, a concession was made by permitting "representatives" to vote for their household in the absence of a household head, provided the voter was 20 years of age. The elec-

---

* The old registry was totally destroyed during the war. A new one is being prepared with the help of the people. It no longer differentiates between persons of noble and common descent. Information on crimes committed by people, sentences passed by courts, and other information, such as diseases in the family, like mental illness, is also omitted now.

tion itself is arranged and supervised by an *ad hoc* committee. In 1955 written ballots were cast and counted immediately so that the result was known within a few minutes after the last ballot was in.

In contrast to a position in the township administration, which carries high status, equivalent to that of a teacher, the village headman's job is considered a community service and carries little prestige. This does not mean that the headman should not be an individual of high qualities. He must be at least 25 years old; he has to have sufficient education, especially knowledge of Japanese writing characters, to read government documents and to do the required clerical work; he has to be a good accountant and must be proficient in working with the abacus, since all tax collections are supervised by him; he must be community minded and able to enforce regulations in a friendly but efficient way. The rewards are small, the salary less than that of most township officials. The office is held most frequently by young men who have not been out of high school too long. Most recent headmen are between 25 and 30 years of age. Serving in this office may mark the beginning of an administrative career, either in the township office, in the village store, or in business outside Taira. The clerk, appointed by the headmen to assist in village administration, is also a young man. He too is likely to be headed toward an administrative career.

Each village is subdivided into wards, set up originally by Japanese administration to effect greater control over families through the warden. He is a subagent of the headman, and at present he functions mainly as a channel for communications, a useful function in a village like Taira, which covers a large geographical area. Regulations, village meetings, and special events are announced through the warden, and he is often called on to collect delinquent taxes. However, he has little authority and functions more as a neighbor who takes care of necessary contacts between residents and the village administration. Ward members elect him to his honorary office for a one-year term.

Village affairs are discussed and legislative action concerning the village initiated by the village council. This group is now partly elected, partly composed of holders of essential offices, such as heads of associations, members of the township assembly, and township officials who live in Taira. The 26 members of the Council are responsible for measures affecting the community, and the headman relies heavily on their advice. Most councilmen are middle aged; few are over 50 years old. Since the head of the Women's Association and the nurse are members, there are at least two female representatives. The youngest councilman is usually the head of the Young People's Association.

It is apparent that leadership in the community is always exercised by a limited group. The council represents almost all potential leaders. Education and experience in the outside world are the most important qualifications. This is a change from the old days when wealth was also an important factor. An example of a member of township assembly and village council is the man who lived for many years in Brazil (see Chapter 1, p. 374). His leadership is widely recognized and partly due to his successful use of modern farming techniques. Another village leader is a graduate of an agricultural high school, a man of superior intelligence and qualifications who ranked high in an island-wide civil service examination. Another former headman, and now a council member, was born and raised in Japan of Okinawan parents. Although unfamiliar with local dialect and practices, he is well versed in things Japanese and is a financial expert.

The full village council seldom meets. Instead, local matters are discussed among a core of its most active leaders. Noncouncil members, such as the postmaster, policeman, or teachers, may be invited to some meetings. A discussion may start because several villagers want to set aside a special day during which nobody is permitted to go to the mountains to cut firewood, so that more work can be done in the fields. Such a proposal, if approved by the committee of council members, need not be brought before the entire council. Since no formal vote is taken by the council as a rule, friendly discussions decide the issue. Such a decision is then taken directly to a meeting of registered household heads which is held monthly or whenever there are a number of matters to be discussed and voted on. They are presented point by point, first by the headman, next by one or more council members; then discussion is opened to the whole meeting and eventually a vote is taken. This is done in a very relaxed manner and without actually counting the votes, since discussions have continued until there is a general consensus in the group.

Minor matters of immediate importance, such as tax collections, plans for celebrating a holiday, or maintenance work on roads and ditches in parts of the village, are taken up between the headman and wardens in weekly meetings.

The household head meeting is attended by many women who are either registered household heads or have been sent by their husbands or fathers as representatives. Some men may actually be unable to attend; others are disinterested. Failure to send any family representative over 18 years old to a village meeting results in a fine of 20 yen. At one meeting when it seemed as if more women than men were present, the headman joked, "Let's call it a Women's Association Meeting." The women answered, "We are just nice to our husbands, so we attend." As on all occasions women usually sit together on one side or in the rear. Few of them participate during discussions. The most active spokesmen for the women are the head of the Women's Association and one or two of her close assistants. If a discussion concerns such matters as liquor and food for celebrating certain holidays, a woman may speak up. Mothers bring their infants along and hold them in their arms or nurse them when they get restless. Sometimes a child feels uncomfortable and starts crying, and the mother is forced to leave the room.

In general, Taira people do not enjoy being leaders or playing a dominating role. There are no bosses who attempt to force issues or dictate policies. Even people who have definite ideas on how to effect changes would not attempt to assume full responsibility by disregarding the advice of others. "Power" is not associated with responsible positions and village leadership. The headman and clerk perform a duty, often loathed by them and never too highly rewarded by others. A man commands respect for his education, age, sound advice, and exemplary behavior, not for the office he holds. Moreover, all villagers are friendly neighbors, and the man who is presently headman still remains a relative or neighbor to everybody. There is more prestige associated with township offices. The mayor, who holds the highest position, is a man of age and experience; he commands a great deal of respect and has been elected to that office because of the high esteem in which he is held. Occasionally one hears of power hungry persons who are unscrupulous and authoritarian, but they are rare.

FORMAL CONTROL

Formal control of law and order is in the hands of the police. A detachment of the Hentona district police is located in the village, and one policeman is constantly stationed there. He lives with his family in a building which also has a small office. Recently a telephone with direct connections to Hentona was installed. The policeman and his wife are from another township.

The policeman's main duty, according to villagers, is to protect them from the occasional outside burglars or from fugitives from the south who come north to hide in the woods. The announcement that such a person is on the loose creates much excitement and anxiety. A second important duty is the control of the shore line. Smugglers and illegal entrants from the Japanese island of Yoron, just to the north of Okinawa, land along the coast. Although one man with only a bicycle can hardly control effectively several miles of coastline, since the only road to the outer world leads through Taira, the policeman can at least check all transients. Another important duty is to prevent the use of explosives by fishermen, a difficult if not impossible assignment, for he must catch the fisherman *flagrante delicto* when he lands with fish killed in this way. There is no indication that villagers assist the policeman in detecting offenders.

Policing the village itself is not a difficult job. The absence of crime and the low incidence of quarrels, disputes, and brawls would seem to make policing unnecessary. Nevertheless, the policeman interferes at times in disputes. He considers it his duty when actual blows are exchanged and somebody is hurt. In such a case he "investigates," takes notes, and makes a report to the police department. During the entire field work, reportable incidents occurred at about the rate of one a month; in the two or three cases where violence occurred, the matter was settled peacefully later, although the policeman kept a record of it. The rare quarrels which do occur are usually the result of drinking or domestic disagreements, generated by financial problems.

The policeman plays the role of judge and jury. In one case a young man hit a woman and was temporarily detained by the policeman until he made apologies to the victim. In disputes over business transactions, the policeman often arbitrates. In a dispute in which a Taira woman was accused of cheating a trader from another village, the policeman heard the case and ordered the Taira woman to make refunds over a period of time. The villagers seem to accept such arbitration. Serious disagreements seem to be unthinkable, and everyone fears public censure and ostracism. Court action is extremely rare and is referred to the provincial courts in the town of Nago.

The policeman is given high status by the villagers and commands respect. He remains, probably by his own choice, a neutral person in village affairs. He attends village functions, where he is given a place among village leaders. Being friendly with many families, he visits and is visited by other men. It was noted that fishermen sometimes send a special catch to the policeman. But since this is a courtesy which is also common among farmers with regard to nonfarming people, such as teachers, one should not think of such actions as bribery. Mothers use the policeman as a threat in disciplining children. "If you do such a bad thing again, I'll take you to the police station." This, however, does not seem to instill any fear of his person, but rather a respect towards the general area in which the policeman lives. Village children play freely with the policeman's children, but his courtyard is entered less frequently by children than that of other villagers.

The head of the General Affairs Department at the township office is charged with supervision of public order. It is not clear how much this is a self-assigned task. During several occasions, when an alarm went out for fugitives from the south, he would accompany the policeman or investigate himself. In cases of death, both he and the policeman have to make a report.

The Young People's Association may serve as a vigilante in emergencies such as fires, floods, tornadoes, and other disasters. When a military jeep was reported to have been stolen near Naha and driven on the dead-end road running north, the young people in all villages on the way erected road blocks and were ready to help catch the thief. The group would act together in a similar fashion at any threat from outsiders.

The headman can only enforce local ordinances insofar as he is able to persuade people to comply. He is not concerned directly with crime or disturbance of the peace. Exceptions are such matters as stealing sugar cane or letting chickens run loose so that they enter every yard. For such acts, money fines can be imposed. One warden still has a tag which used to be given to the man whose chickens ran around freely. The offender had to pay the fine and keep the tag until he detected someone else's chicken running loose. Then he could pass the tag on to that person. Such measures are no longer used. But the underlying principle of public censure and fear of ridicule continues to operate in village social control.

Public censure is used along with fines to ensure attendance at village meetings. Roll call is taken before each meeting so that the absence of individuals is made known to the whole group. Similarly, when tax collections became more and more delinquent, it was decided to have ward meetings in which everybody would be reminded in public to pay his share. Those who were unable to do so would have to state their reasons. As soon as this new plan was announced, several people got up during the meeting to pay outstanding amounts to the headman. The school uses similar devices to achieve better attendance and scholarship. During home visit week, about once a year, a meeting is held for all parents and the statistics for attendance for each village are read as well as scholastic performances for each community.

INFORMAL CONTROL

What other people might think is uppermost on everybody's mind. Children are reminded by their mothers not to play alone lest people would think they are unpopular. They are told not to fight lest others think badly of them or make them responsible for the consequences. Censure by gossip is common, but criticism is seldom made directly to a person's face, and the target of extensive gossip is often unaware of it.

An exception to this was the case of a junior high school girl who left her mother and stepfather and went to live in the city. The incident was known to all villagers within a short time, and gossip was rife, but referring to the case directly in the presence of the mother was avoided. When the mother finally heard the gossip, she contended that the story had been circulated by a certain family, singled out the woman of that house (who happens to be one of the few Christians in Taira) and told her in no uncertain words that she, as a Christian who wants to do good and others to be good, should know better than to spread evil gossip.

Concern with the affairs of other villagers is, of course, a result of the general intimacy between people. Not only one's immediate family but also anyone in Taira is aware of what happens to others in the community, and the right to such knowledge of private and family matters does not seem to be denied by anybody. People ask and receive answers, and news travels rapidly from one house to another. In considering the fear of censure and its effectiveness in social control, however, one should not forget that, conversely, the concern of others for one's life leads to a feeling of belonging and the expectation of help and affection.

Children are part of the gossip channel in that they are talkative and report news. They do not seem to invent malicious stories but do join in fun making at other people's expense.

Being too malicious is censured. Older people still remember that they heard in their youth about old wicked women who could bring a curse on others. The term for curse still connotes a person who is disliked or who snoops excessively in other people's affairs.

If possible, nobody is deliberately made subject to public exposure in case of wrongdoing. A township official, who by virtue of his office was also a member of the village council, showed little interest and responsibility toward the community. When the village meeting deliberated whether township officials should continue to be made members of the village council, his name was not mentioned, although the case was discussed at length in public. The final decision was to give him another chance. This, too, is characteristic of community behavior. Ostracism and complete rejection of serious offenders against the community would be a most serious punishment. This in itself would give the community a bad standing. A common front toward the outside is preferred, so that all drastic actions are left only for extreme cases. Rather, one tries to get along, even with a deviant person. Individuals between whom disagreement exists act friendly toward each other in public.

A deep sense of mutual obligation and duty not only toward immediate relatives but also toward members of the entire community, and even certain strangers, appears in many contexts. Any villager feels a sense of obligation to participate in mutual assistance, and someone who fails to live up to this obligation is severely criticized. A person who commits a crime is said to have no feeling of obligation, and it seems clear that the infrequency of transgression, either the violation of mutual help codes or more serious infractions, is held in check by fear of censure.

The Japanese moral code, which stresses obligations and feelings of indebtedness and gratitude toward those from whom favors have been received, is obviously related to such social control forces or is in fact identical with them. Japanese ethical training was part of school training before World War II, and it is still deeply valued and followed. That any close-knit community tends to foster such forces of control is common knowledge. Yet the positive attitude toward obligations and their elaboration in interpersonal relationships is noteworthy and characterizes an important aspect of Taira life. It is learned early, as we found out when one mother said about her 4-year-old daughter: "She understands the idea (of obligations and indebtedness), although she does not know the concepts." When the family receives a gift, the little girl asks, "Shall we take some fish (a counter present) to them?" In spite of the positive value mentioned, there seem to be few compulsions connected with obligations. Actions appear spontaneous rather than forced. Of course, these obligations are of importance in determining contributions of individual households at weddings, funerals, and other occasions where interpersonal ties are cemented.

✴
✴
✴

Chapter 6

Social Organization

In every society an individual belongs to a number of groups, overlapping in membership and differentiated by function. A resident of Taira is no exception. Some groups are open, that is to say, new members may be recruited and present members expelled. In others, which are closed, membership is automatic and inevitable, depending in no way on the behavior of the individuals involved. We are here concerned with these latter groups whose membership is determined by sex, age, kinship, and rules of residence. Whether an American male lives in Connecticut or California, in the city or the suburbs, is to a large degree a matter of his personal preference. This is not the case for everybody in Taira, although there are people who at any time may leave the village to seek their fortune.

There are two types of households in Taira: those of oldest sons, who live in the house of their parents, and those of younger sons, who establish a nuclear household of their own, which may be near the house of their father. Many young sons, however, leave the central village and settle in its outlying districts or move to the southern part of the island. Whereas formerly many younger sons moved to Japan or to one of its prewar South Pacific mandates, or to Hawaii and South America, since the end of World War II employment opportunities around U.S. Army installations absorb many such migrants. The oldest son is required to live in his parents' house and eventually take over the duties of a household head. Unmarried younger sons remain in the household until they marry or leave the parental home for work elsewhere.

For a woman it is customary to move to her husband's home if he is an older son or into a house in his village if he is a younger son. In the old days this usually involved simply a move in the village, since the preference was to marry a woman from the same community. Nowadays there is no clear-cut preference; a woman from central Taira may become the bride of a man from that part of the village, from one of the outlying parts of Taira, or from another village, usually to the north. Of a sample of 55 marriages, 26 of the wives were from Taira, 29 from other villages, five of which were immediately adjacent.

The composition of the household, therefore, changes for the individual during his lifetime, and it is not the same for all persons in the village. Several children not only have their parents and at least one paternal grandparent but also paternal aunts or uncles who live under the same roof. If the father is a younger son, only one's parents and siblings are household members. Since houses are small and space is very limited, all these members of the household live in close face-to-face relationship. Women tend to outlive men, so that there are many more old women living with their married sons than old men. This is why children have a grandmother more often in the home than a grandfather (see Table 1).

Table 1 shows the composition of 60 households in central Taira. It is probable that the effects of war dislocation have increased the number of nuclear households and account for at least one of the matrilocal extended households. Some of the fragmentary households, classed as nuclear, consist of just a widow or widower and an unmarried son or daughter.

Table 1 Household Composition in Central Taira

Total population	328
Number of households	60
Nuclear households	36
Patrilineal extended households * (3 generations)	18
Matrilocal extended households	4
Not classified	2

* In households classified as extended, grandparents of the youngest generation present are distributed as follows: grandmothers 14, grandfathers 4, both grandparents 4.

Relationships and status within the household are ordered according to generation, age, and sex. As will be discussed later, the status of women in general is high. High status of males, especially the first-born male in the family, must be considered as representing an ideal which is not reflected too distinctly in day-by-day interpersonal relationships, although birth order and sex are significant in ancestor worship and in representation of households. Ideally the younger generation members defer to the older people. Normal behavior, however, more frequently reflects a warm, personal relationship that, although not devoid of respect, tends to minimize differences and stress familiarity rather than distance.

Besides his membership in a household, the individual is part of a larger descent group, a "main house" in which all the members are related through the male line. Most of the "main houses" in the village trace descent to the founder of Taira. They represent three old lineages. The remaining belong to two more recent and unrelated lineages.

The houses of older and younger sons are distinguished, the term "stem" referring to the house of the founder and the descending line of his oldest sons and the term "branch" to those of younger sons who have set up separate households in the village or elsewhere. Through the decades, as the branches grow into unilineal descent lines of their own, new "main" houses are formed.

Originally descriptive names were given to each household. These names indicated a "stem" family or one of its branches. The "Big East House," a reference to the lineage as well as to the homestead itself, probably split into several branches. These, the homes of younger sons, were known as "Little East House," or by a further derivative, "Behind Little East House." Sometimes the rank order of a younger son was used to name his house, such as "Second East House." This house order system is no longer in existence in Taira, but a few of the names are still in use to indicate houses, and individuals are frequently referred to as "the person of such and such a house," for instance, "the grandmother of the East House." *

Although every individual is aware of his membership in a "main house," these descent groups have little importance except in religious life and death ceremonies. Members of the same "main house" revere common male ancestors and share in the upkeep of a common tomb in which their remains are placed at death. Funerals and the veneration of deceased members of the "main house" bring the kin group together several times a year. Women, although entombed with their husbands, visit the "main house" of their father to pray before his ancestors' tablets and make offerings. If they were born in Taira, they may first take offerings of rice and sake to the shrine of their husband's paternal ancestors; then later in the day they prepare for a ceremony in their own "main house."

The descent group also functions in other religious contexts. The oldest woman of the main house acts as priestess for the lineage, and she or another older female may visit the sick and assist their relatives with prayers and practical help. Descent group affiliation does not affect such daily concerns as lending help to others in economic tasks, though some of the descendants of early Taira settlers seem to feel more obligation in this respect than members of the more recently arrived lineages. Lineage affiliation does not determine the choice of a marriage partner. However, although members of the same "main house" or lineage may marry each other provided they are not first cousins, such unions are rare. Marriage with maternal first cousins is also forbidden.

An individual also holds membership in other kin groups which have only a loose structure and few functions. These are the relatives

* Individual surnames among commoners are of recent date, introduced after the Japanese assumed administrative control and required their adoption to establish a population registry. Family names had been in use among the Shuri gentry.

on one's mother's side and, after marriage, the wife's family. In seeking mutual assistance for rice planting, house building and other undertakings, such relatives may be approached. In other words, kin, neighbors, and members of the same geographical section of the village participate almost equally in mutual assistance groups. Maternal relatives join in family celebrations and in the discussion of family matters. Since many decisions are made jointly with the help of relatives, there are frequent occasions for the kindred to gather in the evening at one house or another.

Each Okinawan also belongs to an age group. As will be described in the section on socialization, beginning at kindergarten an Okinawan becomes associated with a group of boys and girls who will remain his companions through school. As a member of junior high school he will join the formal Student's Association, which is responsible for certain community projects. High school students and all unmarried young adults belong to the Young People's Association, which is both a social group and a cooperative work group.

After marriage there are several associations which one may join. Adult married women who are under 57 belong to the Women's Association, which is affiliated with an island organization dedicated to "modernizing" women's lives. The organization is lead by a few women who are in contact with the district and island organization. They attempt at semisocial gatherings to introduce changes aimed at easing the burdens of daily life and the pressure of poverty. For example, they are trying to influence the women to return to making their own bean paste rather than spending precious cash. The leaders show the women how to make bean paste and encourage them to set aside one work-free day a month to catch up with neglected housework. Many of the efforts of the organization, however, are not too successful. Most women go back to their homes and find that the accustomed ways are easier to follow. One has learned to live with economic pressures and tradition and established custom is a strong force. So the few forward-looking women have a difficult task in rallying others.

Both adult married males and females may also join an organization similar in objective—the Home Improvement group. Although the men who are village leaders belong to this association, the majority of the members are the same women who are leaders in the Women's Association.

Before World War II there was an association of older men.* Although this group seldom, if ever, meets, it still sends a representative to the village council and to a few village functions.

* Apparently of relatively recent origin.

Both adult men and women also belong to mutual assistance groups, mutual loan associations, and to the work groups described in Chapter 3. All individuals between 16 and 57 are expected to cooperate in community work projects. All households are members of the village cooperative. Since most villagers look to the cooperative for help in improving their economic conditions, this draws them together in a familial way.

It will be noted that age and marital status are prerequisites for membership in most of these associations and that only one is exclusively for women and one exclusively for men.

Taira culture is essentially egalitarian. Personal status is not ascribed by membership in social classes or achieved by the accumulation of wealth. Furthermore, although power and respect are the attributes of certain village offices, such as headman and school teacher, these only give rank *ex officio*. An ex-headman has no higher status than one who has never held such an office.

There are factors, however, which do differentiate Tairans as to personal status. Men have somewhat more power and command more respect than women; adults must be addressed respectfully by children; older siblings have more authority and privileges than younger; and in recent years the educated are somewhat more respected and are more likely to be chosen to hold office than those with the minimum required amount of schooling. And since education often leads to better jobs, greater wealth is sometimes associated with status, though not a necessary prerequisite.

The status of women in Okinawa, although, ideally, inferior to that of men, is in reality relatively high. Many cultural forms are based on the principal of male superiority, which Japanese values tend to reinforce, but there are numerous indications in daily life that women command a comparatively high degree of respect and power. It is difficult to assess to what degree status differences have been influenced by contact with Japanese; the importance of women in religious affairs suggest their higher status prior to the introduction of the Japanese school system in Taira.

As will be discussed in the chapter on religion, although the veneration of one's father's ancestors is the core of one part of Okinawan religion, the ceremonies are run by the women. The oldest male of each main house and the household head in each household are nominally responsible for keeping the tablets of the ancestors on his house shrine, but the actual upkeep of this ancestral shelf and the bimonthly offerings are performed by the women. If no direct male descendant is available to keep the ancestral tablets, a widowed woman retains them in her house until a male can assume the responsibility for them. The propitiation of the natural deities is lead by the village priestess—and she is assisted by a group of women.

Taira women are essential to the financial well-being of the family. Their role in both agriculture and lumbering is equal to that of the men. Since there are few kinds of work which women cannot do and do not engage in, a widow or single woman, although handicapped, can support herself and her family. Several women, whose husbands died during World War II or who have been divorced, support themselves and their children. One Taira woman supported her four children while her husband left for Japan to help a sick brother. She worked the household fields and sold fish. Her husband, who was expected to return after three weeks, remained away for six months. Once or twice he wrote his family to ask for money; his wife and sister obliged. Even old women remain active members of the family. They contribute to the household economy by working in the potato fields, cutting firewood, and doing other useful work around the house.

Such economic independence gives women a place in the family which cannot easily be challenged by a male who theoretically can claim preferential treatment. Perhaps a man is more dependent on his wife than she is on him. Men never cook. They expect the womenfolk to look after house affairs. A wife, although she does not usually own the land on which she works, has the same rights as her husband to the village forest lands. There she cuts firewood like the men, cooperating with the husband in preparing it for sale. Most of all, pig raising is her concern, and this gives her an important hold on the purse strings.

There is no uniform rule as to who keeps the money in the family. In some households the husband takes care of all financial matters and hands over small sums of money to the wife for daily use. In these families it is either found that the wife does not contribute heavily to subsistence or that she is from another village and is somewhat intimidated by her husband and unable to find security in having relatives close by. Such women are meek or at least restrained and solicitous of their husbands.

There are numerous cases, however, in which women handle all money affairs. In one such home the husband is a township official. His wife, although from a distant village, is a forceful character and follows economic pursuits independent of her husband. He is glad to let his wife handle finances, although he retains ultimate control over them. The more common situation, however, is almost equal responsibility in economic matters between the sexes. Where this is the case, the wife takes charge of household funds while her husband controls larger spendings.

Many quarrels between couples originate from financial matters. Disagreements happen frequently when a husband returns home intoxicated late at night. His wife may blame him for using money which she has put aside for a special purchase; from this incident the argument turns to family finances in general. As words become more heated, the woman holds her own, telling her husband in no uncertain terms that he is a squanderer. Some husbands settle such an argument by hitting their wives.

Decisions are seldom made by one person in the family. The more important the issue involved, the more people within the family are consulted. A husband and wife may discuss whether to buy or sell a pig and make a joint decision. They also decide mutually on the buying of seed rice and other agricultural matters. Men concern themselves with the building of new structures or the addition to old ones. On the other hand, women make decisions affecting the daily life of children. They determine if a child needs new clothes, if he should be taken to the doctor, or accompany the mother on a shopping trip to the city. Some fathers take an interest in their children's study habits and accomplishments at school, but few are consistent in supervising their children in this respect. Here, too, mothers seem to have a much greater influence. Girls are likely to receive even less attention from their fathers than boys. In cases of decisions that can vitally affect the future of the whole household, members of the husband's and wife's family, if they live in the village, gather to discuss plans.

Although women are less active politically than men, they participate in village meetings as representatives for their families. With the exception of the Women's Association leaders, their participation is more passive than that of the men. But although they seldom speak in public and sit together at the back of the meeting, women nevertheless exert a great deal of influence on community affairs. Their influence is felt even more in meetings of mutual finance associations.

It is unlikely at this point that a woman in the village would run for political office. Several recent developments, however, indicate a steady increase in their political participation. The headman who was elected to office in 1955 is responsible for an innovation which reflects this trend. He selected his clerk by means of a competitive examination which was open to both young men and young women. Two girls who had graduated from high school were among the candidates. They were defeated by a young man to whom the job was given because of his high score. Under American influence, universal suffrage and equal representation have been introduced and formally adopted in some village affairs, although the household head vote—traditionally mostly male—is still maintained in many cases.

The Women's Association is the main force behind the attempts to give women greater equality. The spokesmen for this group do not proclaim equality for women as such as the important goal but express hopes that women's life can be made easier by reducing their work load and providing more conveniences for them, such as better stoves. Attempts are made to give a woman more time to spend at home instead of in forests or fields and to reduce the expenses involved in preparing for holidays and special celebrations. The opinions of the Women's Association carry weight in village affairs. This, as one old woman pointed out, is a considerable change from earlier times. There had been a Women's Association before the war, but women were still barred from participation in village meetings at that time, and the only place where they could make themselves heard in village matters was at the meeting of the individuals required to do periodic labor for the village.

The situation at the time of fieldwork with regard to the attempts of women to gain more recognition and the role which men play in this respect is illustrated by a celebration of Mother's Day—an event which came to Taira quite recently from the outside. The women decided to observe it by taking off from their daily duties during the afternoon. The Women's Association made all arrangements, so that it was not a day dedicated by children or adult men to the mothers, but a day that the mothers celebrated themselves. Nevertheless, for the meeting at the old warehouse, where mats had been spread and food prepared, there were also tables arranged for the male village officials, such as the headman, village council members, and the policeman. They started the affair by treating the women to a few speeches in which the importance of motherhood was eulogized by such observations as: "A man can be great only if he has a mother who is making him great," and (from the policeman): "Mothers are an important factor in preventing juvenile delinquency." After this initial hourlong introduction, the leader of the Women's Association declared that festivities could now begin and that she "did not care how much sake the women drank as long as they were happy on this day." The children, who had been told by their teachers to help their mothers on this day by cleaning house and freeing them from some of their chores, gathered near the building, received some feast food and played as usual, and men—with the exception of the invited officials—worked as usual. It was an affair organized by the women leaders, which, though a little slow in starting, turned into a gay carousing for the older women, who were less inhibited than the younger ones and needed little encouragement to drink and dance.

The daily life of a woman is more monotonous than her husband's and she has less leisure and recreation. After a day of hard work, men sit down alone or in groups to spend the evening in relaxation with a bottle of sake. After a short time they show signs of pleasant intoxication and all burdens of life seem to disappear. Such recourse to carefree diversion is generally denied women. Instead, they are loaded down with household chores and care of infants and guests after a day of work in fields and forests. They spend their little free time exchanging news with other women or talking with other family members or visitors who assemble around the charcoal fire in the back room during winter evenings. Only women of advanced age feel free to join the men in drinking at home.

Men have greater sexual freedom. They are at liberty to have affairs with other women outside the village and on trips to the city may visit tea houses and afterwards enjoy the favors of a prostitute if their pocket books allow.

Status differences based on age are reflected in the social structure and clearly denoted in the kinship terms. There is a special term of reference and address for "first son" and "first daughter" and for "older brother" and "older sister." As mentioned, ideally the oldest son assumes responsibility for the household, for his parents, and for the ancestral tablets. Even if he leaves his parental home temporarily or permanently for the city, where economic prospects are better, he remains the nominal household head and sends money back to his family. Theoretically the oldest male may retain authority until death, although in practice most men retire from this position at the age of 61. Their retirement is made official by an entry in the population registry. They continue to live with their oldest son and act as advisors and critics. A man's loss of authority with age occurs around his late fifties and early sixties and is evidenced not only by his retirement but also by his loss of the right to vote in village meetings. Veneration for age itself therefore, does not exist. Actual behavior toward the grandparental generation, all the members of which are addressed as "grandmother" or "grandfather" regardless of actual kinship, is warm, mildly playful, and indulgent. Disrespect, however, is absent.

It is characteristic of the relationship between children and grandmothers that in addressing nonrelated old women, the suffix -san, which denotes respect, is most often dropped for the "grandmother" term. As the child gets older, the familiar suffixless form of address is used less and less frequently, though girls seem to retain it longer than boys.

The strength of one's ties to the community as a whole regardless of actual kinship is seen not only in the use of the term "grandmother" and "grandfather" in addressing all members of this generation but also in the similar use of the terms "uncle" and "aunt" for all members of the parental generation. Those who are not known well or who have high status are addressed by the appropriate kinship term with the suffix -san added.*

Achieved status is recognized by special terms of address. The teacher, school principal, the doctor, the village headman or mayor are addressed by their titles. Taira people combine familiarity with formality by calling a young teacher from the same or neighboring community by the first name, then adding the title "teacher." †

In summary, although affiliation with a patrilineal descent group and kinship ties with kindred influence certain aspects of life, over and above these ties is the identification with the community, which is drawn together by bonds of economic and social interdependence. Individual leaders serve their term of responsibility and then return to the egalitarian community life, which is comparatively free of competitive strife.

✤
✤
✤

Chapter 7

Courtship, Marriage, and Sex

Most marriages in Taira take place when both men and women are in their early or middle twenties (see Table 2). It is perhaps most note-

* This refers to the use of Japanese kinship terms which are prevalent in Taira— see Chapter 1, p. 370.

† The use of first names may also help to identify individuals since many persons have the same surname—this explanation, however, is not in contradiction with the statement concerning familiarity.

worthy that so few women marry before they are twenty and that many marry in their middle and later twenties. For those whose formal education ends at the age of 15 there may, therefore, be an interval of five to ten years until matrimony.*

One might ask whether sibling position affects marriage age, either because first-born must marry first or because of the inheritance pattern, young sons seldom inheriting either a house or land. The record of 59 marriages in central Taira shows no clear pattern in this respect; oldest sons and daughters do not seem to marry earlier more frequently than those in lower ordinal positions. A more plausible explanation for late marriage is that young men tend to spend some time after school outside the community and, prior to the war, even outside the country. The rationale for a period abroad is in part economic, but "wanderlust" or curiosity undoubtedly contribute. Furthermore, there is no doubt that the period between the end of school and marriage is an extremely enjoyable one, for now work and duties are mixed with comradeship and amusements in contrast to the new duties and responsibilities one assumes with marriage and children. This is especially true for women.

The most striking fact concerning Taira marriages is that among the total of 59 unions, 18 wives were older than their husbands. Marriage records from the other parts of Taira reveal the same age discrepancy. In comparison with Western countries, and what we know of most other societies, this discrepancy is unusual. Similar findings were suggested from studies in Japan. Here, however, the explanation seems to be that such marriages tend to occur between a first son and a woman who is older than he because a mature woman is desired to take over responsibilities as an oldest son's wife. In Taira only nine (one half) of the age reversals involve marriages of oldest sons. Since there are 29 first-born males included in the sample of 59, the proportion of age reversal marriages of oldest sons is no greater

---

* There were no dependable data to indicate whether the present trend toward a relatively late marriage represents a change from a previous pattern. Informants' statements suggest that marriages took place at an earlier age in past times, perhaps prior to the turn of the century. Other references to marriage in Okinawa would support this information. The *Civil Affairs Handbook, Ryukyu Islands,* Office of the Chief of Naval Operations, 1944, states that: "The usual age of marriage as reported in 1925 was 18 or 19 for men, 17 or 18 for women. An analysis of the marriage statistics for 1934, however, indicates that the average age at marriage was about four years older. In 1937, the average was reported as 27 years for men and 24 for women" (page 64). The rapid increase in age between 1925 and 1937 suggested by this source can only be accepted with reservations.

than one would expect, and we may conclude that the oldest son explanation does not hold for Taira.*

Table 2 Marriage Statistics for Central Taira

1. Age of men and women at first marriage
   Total cases: 59
   For the period: 1904–1953

AGE OF MARRIAGE	MEN	WOMEN
16	—	2
17	—	2
18	2	4
19	4	4
20	5	11
21	4	3
22	10	5
23	3	8
24	7	3
25	2	4
26	2	1
27	3	2
28	4	2
29	1	3
30	2	—
31	1	—
32	—	—
33	—	1
34	—	1
35	1	—
36	—	—
37	1	—
38	1	—
39	—	—
40	1	—
Not listed	5	3

In the old days, apparently, there were many gay and unrestrained courtships of men and women on the beach after dark. During our fieldwork we did not observe open courtship. The expression of affec-

* Unfortunately, we did not recognize the large number of these cases while in the field; hence we failed to ask informants for their explanations and rationalizations. The age reversal tends to underscore the relatively high status of women vis-à-vis men and may be instrumental in perpetuating it.

tion between couples is not seen in public. Men and women are teased by the community if they are seen standing and talking together. One or several boys teasing a girl would be the boldest advance seen in public. Although, even at night, we never observed couples pairing off in or near the village, we were told that a boy and a girl would arrange private meetings. It is our impression that there is more self-consciousness about love-making than there used to be.

Although there is little occasion for intimacy between a couple during times when other villagers are around, young men and women associate frequently in larger groups during the week in community-wide activities of the Young People's Association. During the many hours which are spent in club meetings, work projects, and other social activities, there is a comraderie between young men and women which effectively neutralizes the formal social distance that is maintained in the traditionally separate seating arrangements. There is, nevertheless, a certain embarrassment and almost clumsy behavior of young men toward the better poised and adroit girls, at least in the presence of strangers like ourselves.

Young men may seek intimacies with girls of other villages, but in doing so they risk the ire of the young men there. It is also possible that a Taira girl agrees to an intimate relationship with someone in another village where she may feel safer from detection. Young men are more likely to seek a girl with whom an arrangement for a meeting away from her home can be made. The girl, of course, suffers public disapproval if the couple is detected, while a man is not subject to the same criticism. In contrast to girls, men have many more opportunities for sexual relationships without public censure.

Sexual attraction does not seem decisive in selecting a mate for marriage, although beauty is appreciated in a woman with long, black hair, a dark arched eyebrow, fair skin, a prominent nose, small mouth, and large eyes. Younger people are beginning to adopt some of the American standards of beauty, which are introduced through movies and magazines via Japan. Although the concept of romantic love is gaining in popularity, arranged marriages still outnumber love marriages in Taira. Even if a young man and woman reach an agreement about marriage, there follows a formal arrangement by their parents with the help of go-betweens, a trusted neighbor or a friendly couple, or a person who commands status and respect. If a man or his family are interested in arranging a marriage with a girl, the go-between notifies her family. Eventually word will reach the girl. If the suitor has not previously indicated his interest to the girl, she may voice her feelings and wishes to her mother, father, or to some other relative. If she objects violently, the matter may be dropped. If the go-betweens succeed in making arrangements, they become the special friends and patrons of the young couple, officiating at the marriage ceremony and attending the rituals during the first week after the birth of all the couple's children.

The first engagement event is a small family affair at the bride's house, attended by a few close relatives of the couple, who ceremonially eat rice from the same bowl. The food is contributed by the groom's family. From this time on the groom may spend evenings and nights at the bride's house, where he is permitted to have sexual intercourse with the girl. For a man whose girl lives in the same village, the day is now divided between work for his own household and helping the girl's family in the field. The groom receives supper from the girl's family, who encourage him to stay for the night. The couple is never seen together in public, although the girl also helps occasionally at her groom's house.

The second engagement party is held some later time, also at the girl's house. All the relatives of the bride whom she wishes to introduce to the groom and his family are invited. The groom also invites his relatives and friends. Food and drink are supplied by the groom. Since this may be quite a burden, the bride urges him not to hurry in planning for this party. At this engagement ceremony, relatives and friends congratulate the male members of the bride's family and some of the close female relatives, the mother and sometimes an aunt, or the grandmother. Short speeches are exchanged. The girl's father, in response to well-wishing, may point out that the girl is inexperienced and that she needs guidance and education from the groom's family. The groom also toasts his father-in-law, tells him that he will do his best, and thanks him and his wife for their permission to marry.

The actual marriage ceremony may be postponed until much later. One reason for the long engagement period is to see whether the girl becomes pregnant, or as one person said, "To see if the seeds match." There are also economic considerations. The ceremony takes place at the groom's house. The go-between, his wife, and a few friends go to the bride's home to accompany her and her relatives and friends to the groom's house. The elaborateness of the celebration depends on the wealth of the groom's family, but since the war, all families have economized in this as well as in other ceremonies. The cost of the wedding is carried by the groom, but it is to some extent offset by small money gifts which guests contribute. The groom gives the bride's family a certain amount of money—in one case about 2000 yen (approximately $17.00) or two thirds of a well-to-do Taira family's monthly cash income, earned by several adult members in joint work, or equal to about one half of a teacher's monthly salary. The girl brings a dowry consisting of furniture, household utensils, and other things, so, as one person said, the groom is repaid in one form or another. In former times the men had to pay a fine to the parents of the bride if she married out of the village (Suttles, personal communication; Tamura, 1927 translation:44).

Even under present conditions the wedding ceremony is colorful compared to most other private ceremonies. All guests attend in their best clothes and the bride wears a special kimono and a special wig hair dress. She is seated next to the groom, who wears Western-style clothes instead of the traditional silk kimono. The whole ceremony is presided over by the go-betweens. While preliminaries take place, the bride sits almost motionless. Her face expresses what Glacken describes as "undescribable gloom" (1955:218). This continues even through the climax of the event, the ceremonial exchange of wine which symbolizes the union of the participants. During this part of the ceremony the guests, who have been enjoying food and sake and talking amicably, give this moment a solemn meaning by their silence. Speeches by the go-between and other notables follow. The virtue of the bride and her family and of the groom are told and acknowledged by a thank-you address by the groom. Parents of the couple sit close to them but have no other function than to accept congratulations. The bride then goes around introducing herself to the guests.

Children are not present at this event. They line up outside the house and peek through openings to see the bride and watch the guests, who start dances as soon as good food and wine take effect. After the formal part of the wedding, the feast ends like any such event in the village—with great gaiety. The bride acts as hostess; she changes from her kimono and heavy hair dress into more suitable clothes and sees that the guests are well taken care of. The length of this feast depends, of course, on how much food and drink the family is able to provide. Finally, when all guests have left, the bride and groom retire to the bedroom which has been reserved for them, sometimes furnished with one or two pieces, a chest of drawers or a Western-style closet supplied by the bride's family. The bride also provides the comforter for the marriage bed. Friends of the groom may play a prank and replace the normal-sized comforter with a small one, "so that the marriage is consumated quicker," as they say.

Sexual relations between husband and wife are not discussed in public except in jocular references. In spite of the intimacy of household members in the confinement of a small house, one attempts to keep others from noticing sex activities. Keeping sex a private matter does not mean that there is a feeling of shame or guilt. It is considered a natural function, and although they do not discuss marital relations, men feel free to mention sex and its pleasurable aspects. Such conversations seem to cause some embarrassment among the younger women but are thought entertaining by older ones.

To men, sex, like food and drink, is to be enjoyed and indulged in. Women, too, enjoy sex but are more reticent and give much less overt expression to their desires. There are stories about women who are sexually aggressive, but they are either characters in the folklore or women of a neighboring village who are said to be this way "because they don't work hard enough." Men enjoy sex activity until an advanced age. One man over 60 whose wife had long been dead twice took a young woman as second wife; in both cases the women left him after a short period, but dissatisfaction with his sexual capacity was supposedly not the cause. Several children in Taira were fathered by men who had passed their sixtieth birthday. People believe that potency depends on physical well-being and age, but that it can be produced by a special drink consisting of sake in which a poisonous snake, the *habu,* is steeped. As soon as one finishes drinking this brew, its effects should be felt. Sake, meat, and eggs are also thought to increase potency.

Women's breasts are considered sexually stimulating. Men like to caress the breasts and the skin in general. Kissing occurs during foreplay only among some younger couples; older people do not care for it. In a room or house, shared with others, few couples undress fully for intercourse. Moving the baby to one side of the mat or mattress, a husband joins his wife.

There are no pre- or postparturition taboos; relations continue throughout pregnancy and are resumed about a week after childbirth, when the wife has taken her first bath. Men tend to disregard the public health nurse's urging that women be given a little longer rest.

That extra marital affairs do occur is evidenced by the presence of illegitimate children. But the mothers are likely to be widows or girls who for one reason or another did not get married at the usual age. Deformity may be a reason for not finding a husband. Two children in Taira were claimed to be the issue of an incestuous relationship between a man and his widowed daughter. Although the children were conceived and born outside the village, people became suspicious after the family returned to Taira. Because the putative father failed to deny paternity strongly, villagers felt certain that their suspicions were justified. Both children were slightly retarded, and people believed that this fact added even more proof.

An illegitimate child is loved by everybody and treated like any legitimate child. The bastard's name is listed in the registry under his mother's and his illegitimacy noted. Since World War II the distinguishing red ink mark is no longer used in recording these children. Unless the mother marries the child's real father, the offspring has no legal rights of inheritance. If she marries another man, the child may receive affectionate treatment from the stepfather, but he remains legally her son. Socially such a child does not suffer any form of ostracism, but adults make references to his status within his earshot. One such girl proudly said that people had told her that she was half-Japanese.

Legally a man cannot have more than one wife, but there are cases of multiple marriage even in Taira. It takes a substantial income for such an arrangement, since a second wife is given a separate place to live. A younger "wife" is usually taken if there is no male heir born by the legal wife or if the marriage remains childless altogether. A man, formerly a resident of the village, took a young concubine late in life after his sons were killed during the war. She bore him a son, apparently with the consent of the first wife, since there was amicable interaction between the two although they lived separately. The husband registers such children as his legal offspring.

Two modes of divorce are possible. A couple may agree to separate and call a family council of parents and relatives on both sides. The township office is then notified and separation acknowledged. Once children have been born, such divorces are not too frequent, at least there were few cases of divorced women with children in Taira. A husband may initiate a divorce by telling his wife of his desire to separate. Extra-marital relationships of the wife would be sufficient cause, as would be sterility, which is interpreted as her fault. In Taira a settlement within the family is the more frequent mode of divorce although relatively rare. One official estimated that the rate of divorce for the whole township is two per year. Among the 59 marriages we found listings for five subsequent divorces. During fieldwork, many debates about modernizing divorce laws were held among members of the Women's Association, which advocated the abolition of the unilateral emphasis that gave husbands all the rights and wives almost none. Only a crime committed by a man would be sufficient cause under existing law to permit the wife to initiate a divorce.

＊
＊
＊

Chapter 8

Religion

The religious beliefs of people in Taira and their ritual practices recognize the existence of two different sources of supernatural forces. The old Okinawan religion, which is still practiced by many persons in the village, centers on beliefs in a host of nonhuman spirits that inhabit certain localities. A historically more recent Confucian-Bhuddist influence from China and Japan has added to these beliefs the veneration of ancestors who, in their divine state after death, control many activities of the living. Under the influence of these two forces, the animistic and the ancestral, life must be conducted in such a way that both remain appeased at all times by proper worship and performance of ritual as well as by avoidance of actions which might offend these supernatural forces.

Even though many younger people laugh away the adherence to beliefs, especially in animistic deities, there is much evidence that the life of almost all people is controlled by fears, anxieties, and desires for appeasement stemming from these religious beliefs. Although historically the animistic and ancestral religious beliefs were separate, they are synchronized at present so that it is not always possible to make a clear distinction between each system (Lebra: 1958).

The supernatural beings of nature live all around the village. There are mountain deities, deities of the sea, of the well, of trees, and other places. Any localities connected with productive activities, such as the store, the sugar mill, the sugar press, and the village truck, have their own deities. There is also the Deity of Fire, associated with the hearth and the house. He is represented in three hearth stones found in most simple kitchens. Three upright small stones, resembling the hearth stones, are the divine symbols in the village shrine where all these supernatural beings are worshipped.

The supernatural beings living in and around the village appear

432

like "owners" of the concrete objects which they inhabit. These objects can be made subservient to human needs if care is taken not to offend the deities. As long as proper ritual observances are performed, humans need not fear their hostility. They are addressed in prayers and chants, and people make offerings to them at several ceremonies during the year. No one in Taira, including the priestess, has any exact knowledge about their characteristics, and there is no theological dogma, but people know that when building a house, for example, one must announce his intention to the deities and pacify these spirits who have been carried with the lumber from the mountains or with gravel from the beach and the sea. They must be thanked for letting the builder use such materials and sent back to their natural abode. Before the house is finished, the surrounding plot of land must be cleared of all evil spirits. Neglect of such ceremonies can turn supernatural beings into adversaries. One family who neglected proper rituals on their house lot when they built their home tried to appease angry deities by holding a ceremony a year after the house was finished because bad luck had befallen members of the household. Although most supernatural beings can be pacified by proper observance of rituals, there are some who are inherently malevolent. These ogres may be seen in the form of fire balls or in some other shape or physical appearance.

The worship of these nature deities and the observance of ceremonies in their behalf are in the hands of the high priestess and her female assistants. In former times each main house, later each village, had its own priestess. The present high priestess in Taira derives her office from a much later institution, a nation-wide hierarchy of religious officials established by the Okinawan king in an effort to combine religion with political influence and supervision in the villages. Today the high priestess has no association with the central government; the Japanese abolished the system. The hierarchy of female religious officials (see Lebra: 1958), those representing main houses, and the chief village priestess is no longer clearly delineated in Taira, since representatives of several offices have left the island or died, and the vacancies have not been filled. The high priestess has taken over most of the religious functions. Her chief assistants are older women from the two main houses. While these three women officiate, several other women are in attendance as helpers. In spite of the diminishing role of animistic religion in the daily life of younger people, the high priestess still enjoys prestige in the community. She is exempted from communal labor in recognition of her status.

The present high priestess is a woman in her fifties who works and lives like other villagers, spending most of her time in the fields and around her home. She has children and grandchildren, but the father of her children no longer lives in Taira. She regards the continuation of the old ceremonies as her holy duty even though she has to do without most of the accustomed material support from the village and in spite of disbelief and lack of participation. She has sought in vain to have the village make necessary repairs on the simple village shrine near the township office and on the little hut where the ancestral tablets of her predecessors are kept.

While many of the former ceremonies have been discontinued, the priestess is still called on to officiate at house-building ceremonies, to purify the lot, to offer prayers when the beams are raised, and to conduct the dedication when the house is finished. If the owner is moving out of an old house, the priestess notifies the fire deity so that he will follow to the new abode. On other occasions the priestess conducts prayers at the village shrine or at one of the other sacred places near the village. Many of the prayers are succorant—requesting the aid and blessing of the gods in accomplishing a certain goal. In general, as Lebra has pointed out (1958), ceremonies of asking for help are more numerous and elaborate than thanksgiving ones.

On New Year's morning the priestess prays at the water well. Since so many ceremonies have been abbreviated and are no longer carried out in traditional detail, the priestess apologizes for short cuts in her prayers. If she fails to offer prayers in all prescribed spots, she pacifies the deities by facing in the direction of the sacred place where the ceremony should have been conducted. Although the priestess is clearly best qualified to enter into communication with the deities, many older women seem to possess such power also, and if the priestess' assistants are not present, another older woman can function as her helper.

For these ceremonies food for offerings is contributed by the village. The priestess, in a white gown, kneels, flanked by her assistants, also in white, in front of a tray of sake, rice, or other food for the deities. Charcoal incense sticks are burned while brief prayers asking the deities for a successful crop, thanking them for a harvest, or whatever is appropriate to the occasion are mumbled. On certain occasions the women sing chants. After these ceremonies, the priestess, her assistants and the few others present, usually old women, share the food offerings.

One of the most dramatic ceremonies is held on Boat Race Day in lunar June. Priestesses from several villages gather near Taira. During the ceremony the Taira priestess stands in the middle of a circle formed by the other priestesses and helpers. beating a drum as the women chant. The tempo becomes more and more frenzied, and at a certain moment a bell rings. Nobody knows who rings it, and no amount of questioning elicited any information other than that this was done by divine action.

Ancestral worship is equally important in the life of Taira people. Each house of an oldest son has a shelf with a shrine in the main living room. On this shelf the family keeps the ancestral tablets, each representing a deceased ancestor of a recent period. The tablets for whole family lines are kept on the shelves of the main houses. Through this system a family maintains continuity between the living and the dead. Although a deceased person is believed to become a buddha or a god who ascends to heaven, his presence is still felt by the living relatives. If they fail to make the required offerings on the first and fifteenth day of each lunar month, or otherwise neglect religious duties toward the ancestor, misfortune may come to the family. At the same time, the worship of common ancestors holds branches of the larger kin groups together.

No village adult died during our stay, but the funeral practices for adults described by Glacken (1955) and Pitts et al. (1955) for other villages in Okinawa are similar. Seven years is the age limit for a child burial, which is simple and does not require attendance of people other than immediate relatives and perhaps one or two neighbors.* During the study an 8-year-old boy died from an illness and was given a full funeral, which is similar to that of adults.

The funeral must take place at the first outgoing tide after the body has been prepared and dressed. Accompanied by family, residents of the ward, and mourners from other parts of the village whose number depends on the prominence of the dead, the body is carried on a simple, open litter to the tomb area just west of the central village (see map 2). Women feel free to show their emotions, while men remain outwardly calm. Until decomposition takes place, the body remains in a tomb used by the whole village for temporary entombment. Like other village ceremonies, funerals are less elaborate now than they once were, perhaps to the relief of all concerned, since death is highly anxiety provoking, and nobody feels comfortable during the prayers and the ritual farewell to the corpse at the tomb. The participants receive a cup of sake before leaving the tomb area to cleanse them of the pollution of death. Some people still prefer to return to the village by a different route so that the spirit of the dead person will be fooled and unable to follow.

* The reason for this is possibly that the younger child has not yet fulfilled his filial obligations.

After death, memorial services are held in the home of the deceased every seventh day until the 49th day when a more elaborate ceremony concludes this period, and a permanent tablet is installed on the house shrine. On this day, too, offerings to the deceased change from white rice to red-colored rice, indicating the end of the mourning period. From now on, observances in memory of the dead are held on the first, third, seventh, thirteenth, twenty-fifth, and thirty-third anniversary of death. These are small family affairs at which special food is prepared and offered at the shrine before it is consumed.

The body is left in the tomb for at least three years until a propitious day when the whole village decides to wash the bones of all those who have died within the preceding three to seven years. On Bone Washing Day little groups of family members gather around the coffin. They take out the bones, clean them, wrap them in a white cloth and place them in an urn. Women do all the cleaning of bones because it is believed that they have more power to expel the evil. They weep freely, and even some men find it hard to restrain their emotions. Young children are kept away from the tomb area at this time. The urns are then placed inside the family tomb, which has been opened for this purpose. Remains other than bones are burned with the coffin.

Every lunar March ancestral services take place at the tombs, attended by many members of the kin groups to whom each tomb belongs. Some come from the city or other villages for this occasion, including women who have married into another kin group. This celebration of the dead is more serious than other religious events. Offerings of sake and special delicacies are made and then eaten by the family group. One family, sitting in picnic style around the tomb after their prayers, even began to sing and dance—probably to the delight of the ancestors who in their life must have enjoyed many a good feast and dance. Tombs of other relatives may also be visited for short prayers and other offerings.

Spirits of the dead are harmful only if the deceased is not from the village. For this reason new residents formerly could not bury their dead near the village. Even now, recent settlers in the central village have no tombs and keep their dead in urns in a cave, and the residents of outlying houses or field houses have a separate tomb area altogether. If a stranger happens to die in the village, measures are taken to prevent his spirit from doing harm. The body of a fisherman from southern Okinawa was brought to shore after a storm. There it was left for several hours on the beach under a tent in the hot sun until relatives arrived in a hired car to take the body home. Even then people did not carry it through the streets but along the shore to a spot nearby where the car could pull up.

Communication with ancestral or family spirits lies in the hands of individual households or the larger kin group. In general, as with the nature deities, women maintain the relationship. The oldest woman in the house prays and makes offerings in front of the divine shelf or by the tombs. Sometimes the high priestess, whose only regular role in the cult of ancestors centers around the mythical founder of the village to whom vague references are made, is asked to conduct a special prayer for a family at its ancestral shrine. Such invitations are usually the result of consultation with another religious practitioner to whom one turns in case of misfortune.*

Those who are considering a special undertaking, such as building a new house or moving to another one, or transporting ancestral tablets from one home shrine to another, seek the advice of a diviner, the *sanjinsō* or *yekisha*. This expert, always a man, consults books on the workings of the universe, special astrological calendars from which he can predict events by using a horoscope calculated on the birth date of the person seeking advice.

Although it would seem from the attendance at ceremonies that older people, mostly women, are the supporters of religion, even the most modern of the Tairans seem to share beliefs in the power of the supernatural forces and are loath to make an open break with traditions. One may verbalize that the old religion is just "superstition," but when it comes to dealing with adverse events, when somebody suggests that perhaps the *yuta* should be consulted, or a special offering is in order, or when the old special wine of the gods is prepared from rice for Boat Race Day, then many of the apparent apostates cooperate. To some extent this is done to appease the older people, but fear of neglecting duties, especially toward ancestors, is probably much stronger in general than people's behavior would suggest. Religious influence, then, which controlled so many facets of village life in former days, still acts as a strong force in uniting the members of families and descent groups as well as in binding together the community as a unit separate from other communities.

* See Chapter 9 for description of the *yuta* or shaman.

Chapter 9

Disease and Medical Practice

From a world-wide point of view, Okinawa is not one of the most diseased and famine-ridden areas. Still, the statement referring to pre-World War II times that "the inhabitants of the Ryukyus do not enjoy particularly good health" (*Civil Affairs Handbook, Ryukyu Islands,* 1944, p. 145) applies as well to the present. Although Okinawans have been subject to the special concern and control of both Ryukyuan and American authorities since World War II, general health conditions, particularly in the area of some major diseases, have not materially improved in the past five years. In 1954, 13,318 new cases * of communicable diseases were reported for all of the Ryukyus (Civil Affairs Activities in the Ryukyu Islands, vol. II, no. 2, 1954, pp. 176–177), or approximately one person in every 60 was affected. Among these, tuberculosis rated second highest (after venereal diseases), accounting for 2307 new cases or one in approximately every 333 persons. To these figures must be added patients from previous years whose cases are still active, in order to comprehend the severity with which this and other diseases affect the island. A further constant threat is dysentery and Japanese encephalitis, which occasionally affect villages like Taira with sudden epidemics. Another slightly less severe disease of constant concern is trachoma (1583 new cases reported in 1954). Less serious but quite prevalent are skin diseases and intestinal parasites. There are still several new cases of leprosy reported annually for the Ryukyus.

Taira, during our study, was spared any of the dangerous epidemics just mentioned, and even tuberculosis seemed to have a relatively low incidence in the village. There were several cases of pleurisy among some older students, some of whom had to stay home from school for an extended period of time. On the whole, serious communicable

* For a total population of 782,564.

diseases seemed to be below the expected rate for Okinawa, in general, and we had the impression that Taira people are healthy on the whole. Only one case of leprosy, which had been removed to a special hospital on the island of Yagaji, was reported from Taira.

Among the children there were frequent complaints of intestinal diseases. Most children seem to lodge a variety of parasites, mostly hookworms and tapeworms, and many were subject to skin ailments. One girl had a severe case of what was thought by the nurse to be congenital syphilis. The skin of her whole body was covered with sores which were a constant source of irritation. This 4-year-old never appeared in the company of children other than her younger sister. She would stand in front of her house, her face swollen, her head stooped from discomfort and embarrassment. Almost all children have impetigo and various kinds of rashes. During the summer these cover their faces and parts of the body. Almost all have marks of boils which have plagued them in the course of years.

Because sickness is always a threat, it creates fear, and any explanation which may restore some hope is important knowledge. Although some Western or modern theories about disease have been introduced recently through the school and the village nurse, they filter into every house only slowly and do not materially affect what has been handed down as popular knowledge from older members of each household. Most Taira people are probably quite eclectic in their beliefs as well as in their choice of treatments, so that it would be difficult to ascribe to them any single body of theory of disease.

Home remedies, often applied by old women, are widespread. The most popular ones are blood letting and the use of *moxa* cautery. Whenever people agree that there is "bad" blood in an adult's or child's system, it must be removed. There are many phenomena which are accounted for by the presence of "bad" blood. Visible signs such as eczema of the skin or swellings are such indications, but malfunctioning of certain organs, the stomach, liver, kidneys, can also call for the removal of "bad" blood. Mothers expose infants as young as five days to the treatment, which may be preventive as well as curative. Pointing to a bluish green area on the infant's back (not the mongoloid spot), whether real or imagined, the mother swabs the area with sake before she or the grandmother make numerous $\frac{1}{4}$-inch incisions with a razor. After the blood starts to ooze out of the tiny wounds, more sake is rubbed into the skin. The mixture of blood and sake is caught and rubbed on again and again until all the undesirable blood has been drained.

So many Taira babies have eczema that this treatment takes place frequently and may be repeated as many as four times during the first year of a child's life. An older child occasionally undergoes this treatment for a case of violent impetigo. Even a horse may be bled in this way for loss of appetite or other symptoms of disease.

A woman whose face had been struck in an unusual display of temper underwent a blood letting soon after a swelling appeared. Her neighbor from across the street, a farmer like everyone else, sterilized her cheek with iodine and then cut it with a razor until the blood flowed freely. After a night's rest, the woman appeared outside her house without any signs of swelling and seemingly recovered.

As was pointed out previously, many diseases are believed to be caused by supernatural forces: the ancestor spirits, spirits of those who have just died, and natural deities and evil spirits who wander around at night. The ancestors expect proper respect and attention and in general are benevolent unless neglected. Spirits of those who have recently died are most dangerous if the deceased is from another village. For deceased villagers one is careful to purify oneself after the funeral. The doors of each house are shut at night to protect against the evil spirits of the night air. Disease is less frequently caused by natural deities who have been neglected or mistreated.

In case of sickness or other unfortunate events in the family, somebody may go to consult the *yuta*, a shaman who communicates with the supernatural. She discovers the cause of misfortune with the help of rice oracles and through powers of divination received through visions and hallucinations. There is no *yuta* living in Taira now, so that people have to travel to the other side of the island, an hour or more on foot, if they want to learn about the source of some evil. Taira people make many such trips to consult this shamanistic specialist. The most common cause of misfortune discovered by the *yuta* is neglect of ceremonies to the ancestral gods or, less frequently, the neglect of ceremonies to the natural deities. Although the *yuta* stands in no direct connection with the high priestess, she may suggest that her client ask the priestess for special prayers to rectify the negligence. In such cases, then, the competence of individuals in the family may not be adequate to deal with the ancestral world, and the priestess enters into family religion.

Some Taira parents still find an adoptive parent for a sickly child in the belief that his own ancestors have caused bad health, and that this can only be remedied by making a formal arrangement which transfers ancestral responsibility for the child to another family. The child remains with his own parents and only visits his foster parents during the New Year and the midsummer Buddhist *Bon* Festival, which honors ancestors, and perhaps at one or two other occasions during the year. On these occasions his parents take gifts of tea, noodles, and whatever else they can spare to the foster parents. During their visit the foster parents present the gift as an offering on the ancestral shrine and pray to their own ancestors, the guardians of the foster child. It is believed that this may help to offset the adverse effects of the child's own ancestors.

In spite of some treatments, such as blood letting and moxa cautery, which seem harsh to the unaccustomed observer, Taira people are extremely concerned about their sick. Illness, and most of all the need to remove the patient to the local dispensary or to a hospital in town, involves the whole family. No one likes to leave a sick person alone. His family and friends attend to him in such numbers that the small rooms are never large enough to hold all. The security given in everyday life by the presence of relatives and neighbors in the village continues during the critical period of illness. In the case of a fisherman from the south who was washed ashore in his boat after a storm, township officials kept the man continuous company in his dispensary room even though he was close to death. Female relatives cook meals and look after the comfort of a hospitalized person. This means that a young girl or an older woman will leave her usual work for days or weeks to attend the patient.

Because of intimacy in the home and visits to the sick, children are quite familiar with illness. A mother who has to go to the hospital takes her youngest child with her. After burning moxa weeds on her skin for two weeks had failed to cure a nephritic condition, one woman went to the hospital in town, taking her 8-months-old daughter although she did not have enough milk to nurse. The infant had to be given bottled milk prepared from cans. Meanwhile the older children remained under the care of their father.

There is, however, little concern with children who have minor ailments. A school child may be excused from attending classes. In one case a boy stayed home from school with stomach pains. He was happily playing with younger children in the street. One of the adult villagers walked past, stopped after seeing him, and inquired: "Why aren't you in school today?" When told by the boy that he had an upset stomach, the man ordered him to go home right away and stay inside or go to school. The boy's mother, although aware of her son's discomfort, did not pay any special attention to it.

Preventive medicine is officially the responsibility of the public health nurse. She advises people on proper preventive care, inoculates children against whooping cough, diphtheria, and other diseases. She also acts as an advisor to mothers on child care and occasionally helps with a birth if the doctor is unavailable. If a case is diagnosed as tuberculosis, the public health nurse teaches the family how to treat the patient in the home by giving him rest and drugs provided through her. Isolation, though recommended, is not carried out effectively, as might be expected from the general treatment of sick in the village.

Like most public offices in Okinawa, the nurse's carries with it a large load of administrative duties. Between these and attending meetings and lectures at Nago hospital, there is relatively little time to cover the long distances between villages. Taira is fortunate to be the residence of the nurse, and when occasionally a nurse from another township comes to help her with inocculations, the children crowd around her and say: "We want 'our' nurse to do it."

The dispensary, or small hospital, in Taira is owned and run by a former medical corps man in the Japanese Army, referred to as "doctor." After the war the government gave permission to a number of former army medical personnel to practice on a limited scale in the villages. The Taira practitioner takes the place of a midwife, gives first aid, and diagnoses simple illnesses. If there are no complications, a patient requesting medical care may be kept at the dispensary, where a family member and the doctor's "nurse," a young female servant, attend to all his needs. If the doctor is confronted with a complicated birth or a case requiring surgical skill, he refers the patient to a private clinic in Nago or to the public hospital there. The township gives financial aid to the doctor to maintain his establishment.

Penicillin has become the doctor's stock in trade, and other antibiotics and drugs are liberally administered via the hypodermic needle. But the doctor does not restrict himself entirely to the use of recognized Western medicines and practices. He may recommend special diets to which people have resorted for a long time, such as goat soup, which is believed to cure colds. Although the doctor has a high status in the community, most persons do not rely on his advice alone but resort to other practitioners and their remedies.

Until a few years ago a popular medical practitioner, the bush doctor, resided in Taira. After his death nobody took over his work, and now many people have to travel far to receive treatment from a bush doctor in another village. His methods primarily include the use of moxa cautery, burning mogusa weed on the patient's skin, and accupuncture by the use of a fine golden needle. He may also prescribe a certain diet and the use of special herbal remedies, which the patient prepares for himself. Those who have great confidence in the bush doctor's competence, particularly older persons, do not consult the Taira doctor at all.

In all their dealings with sickness and its prevention, Taira people are severely handicapped by their economic conditions. Even families who have accepted them cannot afford to buy the recommended drugs. Furthermore, the choice between the bush doctor and the trained medical men in town is sometimes determined by lack of money to pay for the more expensive services.

Cleanliness of the village and general sanitation are theoretically under township control. Except for superficial biannual inspections, nothing much is done about them. Perhaps the Women's Association, once they carry out plans to take over this function, will be more effective.

There are several cases of physically deformed, mentally deficient, and mentally ill persons. A young man of about 20 years, born as an idiot or imbecile, lives in the back of his parents' house, protected from the gaze of outsiders. His family provides well for him, and when no stranger is around to embarrass the family, the grandfather may take him out to attend a village event. Another young man, who was normal, one day began to frighten his family and eventually the whole village by outbursts of violence. He attacked other persons and property. Nobody really knew how to cope with the situation, since the single mental hospital in Okinawa could not keep him longer than six months, and everybody realized that he was sick, not evil minded, when he broke bottles and other glassware in the village store. The family tried religious treatment and locked the man up but never for long, for he had intermittent periods of calm and seemingly rational behavior. Another man, during a busy day, complained of sudden headaches. Soon afterward he became severely depressed and attempted to commit suicide, quite an infrequent phenomenon in the Okinawan village.

❋
❋
❋

Chapter 10

Formal Education

The Japanese school system, which was introduced to Okinawa in the 1880's, reached Taira by 1891. At that time a small school was established in the village. Some of its early graduates are still alive and recall that in their quest for education, adolescents and even adults attended the elementary grades. The introduction of a formal school system in the village marked the beginning of changes in the culture; the Japanese language was introduced, and teachers transmitted Japanese culture as part of the curriculum (Kerr, 1958). It is found today that people too old to have attended school—which in the early years was not compulsory—are the only ones who do not speak Japanese and who are illiterate. Their number is small, probably less than 3% of Taira's population.

The school was moved about 40 years ago to nearby Kawata village, where a substantial schoolhouse was built. Today the elementary school is located there, about a one-mile walk from central Taira, but 3 miles from the outlying subvillage of Izena. The junior high school lies halfway between Taira and Kawata. During the war all school buildings were destroyed, but two new permanent structures for the elementary school were finished in 1954; one of these is a wooden building with a tile roof, the other an all-concrete, flat-roof structure of simple, modern design. Four classrooms and a teacher's room are located in these buildings. The remaining temporary, thatched-roof huts with three more classrooms will disappear as soon as the school rebuilding program is completed.

Built against a hill, the school has spacious grounds in front for sports and play. Classrooms for 30 to 35 students are fairly adequate in size and, in the new buildings, are well lighted by glass windows on sunny days but dark when skies are overcast because of the overhanging roof, which protects the hallway outside the classrooms from frequent showers, and the lack of artificial lighting. A building immediately behind the classrooms houses latrines, separated for boys and girls, although both pass through the same passageway where boys use the urinals. Equipment is extremely poor and a great problem for principal and teachers. Simple, rickety desks and chairs of unfinished wood are bought or made by parents for their children. They are standard in design but differ in height according to the size of the child. Many first graders' furniture is made with future growth in mind, while some older students have outgrown their desks and chairs. An older sibling may pass on his table to a younger one if it is still serviceable after several years of nonchalant treatment.

Teaching aids are few. A small organ is available for music lessons and is carried by several boys on the shoulders to the classroom where it is needed. Sometimes a teacher accompanies a singing class on a mouth organ. Visual aid material, maps, pictures, and charts are displayed in school rooms along with students' physical measurement tables and sometimes a chart indicating their birthdays. There are also exhibits of students' drawings, which enliven the simple rooms. Each classroom has at least one blackboard built into the wall. By withdrawing removable walls in the new building, individual rooms can be converted into one large auditorium with a small stage for special occasions.

The personal equipment carried by students, other than books, consists of notebooks, pencils, a ruler, abacus, and, for those who can afford it, crayons and drawing paper. Sports equipment is also scanty, and replacement budgets are too low to remedy the situation. Students bring their own tools for garden and agricultural work as well as for work on the school grounds.

The teachers' room has desks for each teacher and the principal and a large table in the center for meetings. A small corner is reserved for a kerosene stove to prepare tea. There are also two cots for the teacher who remains on duty as night watchmen or for a child who feels ill during school hours. No privacy is provided for teachers, since students enter the room on any pretext or crowd around the windows if something attracts their curiosity.

Upkeep of the school is the responsibility of teachers and students; the only paid help is a girl who acts as janitor, nurse, and servant. The students, supervised by their teachers, tidy up classrooms after school, scrub walls and floors at regular intervals, take care of the hallway, cut grass, and weeds, and clear ditches on the school grounds. When school repairs are needed, teachers and parents help if no specialist's work is needed, as in repairing the thatch roof of temporary buildings.

The present school system, although under American supervision, follows the Japanese pattern. A six-year elementary school education and three years of junior high school are compulsory. After graduation at about the age of 15, students can enter high school if they choose and can qualify by passing the extremely rigid entrance examinations, which eliminate a considerable number of applicants. High school students have to move to Ogimi in a nearby township where they room and board while attending school.

The curriculum in the Okinawan schools is on the whole similar to that in Japan. Japanese language continues to be the medium, and textbooks, as well as other school materials, are purchased from Japan. Children therefore continue to be familiarized with the culture of Japan as were their parents in the days before American administration. A number of changes have taken place since that time, however. Since the Ryukyus are at present under an independent administration, all symbols and paraphernalia pertaining to the Japanese Imperial House and to the Japanese nation have been removed from the schools.

Nevertheless, the school remains, in the eyes of the villagers, as a rallying point for ties with Japan.

No attempts have been made until the present to introduce Okinawan culture other than by a few occasional references to Okinawan history or folklore. Teachers, during discussion of reading material, refer to home life, farm work and mountain work to illustrate points made in the books.* School is the first opportunity for Taira children to become acquainted with the world outside their own village and to relate their own experiences to the rest of the island, Japan, and other parts of the world. Since Japan is the dominant subject of reading material, however, it is clear that no awareness of being "Okinawan" is developed.

Teachers, many of whom are young, are devoted to their work and to the children, even though their pay is hardly commensurate with their high status in the community and does not represent adequate compensation for the long hours of teaching and administrative work that demand most of their time. In addition, the community in which the teacher lives makes demands on him as one of the educated, able leaders. Both men and women teach. Some of the younger ones who follow the urgent call for teaching positions do not have much training beyond a high school diploma. During the summer, special teacher training courses are now conducted by university professors from Japan and the University of the Ryukyus. Graduates from the University of the Ryukyus Education Department are still too few in number to reach a remote country school, such as the one in Kawata. Most teachers come from one of the surrounding communities; others, mostly bachelors, are from other parts of the island. Children are therefore well acquainted with many of the school teachers, some of whom are neighbors, relatives, or friends of the family.

The extremely modest appearance of teachers does not detract from their status and authority. The relationship between students and teachers is a mixture of respect, as dictated by custom, and intimacy, as a result of mutual affection. A conscientious teacher comes to know his students well during the school year and takes an active interest in them. Children can tell if a teacher is enthusiastic about his work and often establish a warm relationship with him. During our stay, the first two grades were divided into two sections, taught by women, while male teachers taught the upper four grades.

The school day starts at 8:30 with a study period before the formal meeting of the teacher and students on the open grounds in front of

* Some practical work in gardening begins in the upper elementary school classes. Only Junior High School students work in the fields as part of their curriculum.

the school. Classes are held from 9 o'clock until noon with one recess. After an hour for lunch, lessons resume for all grades above first. Classes, sports, and cleanup end between 2 and 3:30 in the afternoon, the highest grades staying the longest.

All grades receive instruction in Japanese writing and reading, arithmetic, science, music, and drawing. Social science is introduced in the second grade. Since each class has one teacher for all subjects, shifts from one to the next subject may come in the middle of an hour. The greatest amount of time is spent in teaching Japanese reading and writing. At first grade level the simplified syllabary is taught, followed in the second grade by another syllabary and the first Chinese characters.

Parents maintain contact with the school through a Parent-Teachers Association, called by the American abbreviation, PTA. Every household is a member. Those with children of school age are regular members who pay 15 yen (12 cents) a month; others are supposed to pay 5 yen but have become so delinquent that their fees have been dropped. The actual PTA work is done by a committee from each village, including the headman and the heads of the Women's and Young People's Associations. The main purpose of the PTA is to support the school in some of its maintenance problems. Attendance of all parents at a general meeting occurs only once a year when elections of officers take place and the PTA budget is discussed and approved.

The principals of both schools are represented in township affairs and in the associations of their own community. Contact between village leaders and school representatives is therefore frequent. Since education taxes are the single largest tax item which villagers pay (80% of the total tax), this representation of the principals is a necessary but burdensome duty for them.

Township education taxes are supplemented by government subsidies. School taxes are paid by all households according to their income and average about 515 yen ($4.30) yearly. Since 1952, government orders require education taxes to be levied separately from other taxes so that people are aware of the amount destined for education; tax collection is one of the main problems in village administration, and school principals are sometimes called on to explain the need for such taxation and the obligations of individuals to carry their share of the burden.

The administration of funds and general school matters are the responsibility of an official in the township finance department. During 1954–1955, 310,344 yen ($2586) were collected by the township in education taxes. The government subsidy amounted to 3,716,397 yen

($30,970) for the four schools in the township. The largest expenses are salaries, construction, and maintenance. Money is also provided for conferences, supplies, and other items on the school budget. The PTA budget serves to supplement the regular school appropriations, which are always insufficient to cover all expenses.

The concern with educational matters is carried into the community in another way. Taira has established a so-called scholarship incentive fund for which money is contributed by the village store and some prominent Taira businessmen from the city, such as the former mayor. This fund is used to give awards, usually notebooks or pencils, to all students, double amounts to those with outstanding attendance records. Honor students are not singled out. The largest part of the fund is used as financial help to families with one or more high school students and to widows with schoolchildren who have no other breadwinner in their family. This is another example of direct support of education by the community.

As with all matters concerning village life, participation of parents in school affairs and an interest in the school's goals and problems depend greatly on the educational and economic background of individual families. For this reason, scholastic standing of children is frequently a reflection of the interest and encouragement they receive at home. Incentive is therefore to some extent passed on from successful parents to their children, and if one can speak of a succession in leadership, it is partly determined by this instruction.

✤
✤
✤

Chapter 11

Recreation

No one can remain in the village of Taira for long without recognizing that its people have a happy faculty for enjoying themselves during those periods which they can spare from their work. The daily routine is broken by a good number of rests and holidays, and the full and unburdened indulgence in social activities at such times, without any apparent aftereffects of remorse or physical incapacitation, is a characteristic of this village. Excessive or orgiastic feasting which might interfere with work duties of the following day or days is absent. Leisure events spent in groups are joyful and desirable to all, untinged by hidden motives of social compulsion or conformity, which marks so many recreational activities in a culture like ours.

The village calendar does not include a weekly rest day, although government offices are closed on Sunday. Rest and holidays for the majority of villagers are regulated by religious and agricultural events which, in former times, were observed at least once during each lunar month. Although some of these have been simplified or given up in recent times by people whose participation in the old religion has diminished or by those who seek a sounder economy by urging greater production of crops and accumulation of savings, when it comes to observing and enjoying holidays, even the most rational village leader forgets his concern for the time being. The elaborateness of celebrations may be less today, as a result of economic pressure, than in former times—the spirit hardly could be. To know and appreciate the sense of humor and the wit of the people, one has only to attend their parties. During other times these qualities are less expressed—though they are never completely absent. If the naive comment that Okinawans are "childlike"—an observation which Westerners in describing them have permitted themselves—can be taken to have any foundation in fact, it could only be that like many children they are capable of complete absorption and indulgence in fun when the occasion is proper. For the Taira person such indulgence cannot be achieved without food, drink, music, and dance. These are the main components of entertainment which help to elicit gaiety and good humor, whether during holidays observed by families in individual homes, or those of the descent group main houses, or in village-wide celebrations, which are extremely common. These ingredients also appear during more informal hours of relaxation, each day after work, when there are small gatherings here and there, though on a more modest scale.

Since calendrical holidays, whether of a family nature or community-wide, have many aspects in common, we may mention some of these in general. Most gatherings begin in the late afternoon and last until late at night although never until daybreak. These are the rare times when people can dress in their best clothes and by doing so shed, perhaps, symbolically all associations with everyday routine.

The sequence of events at any kind of celebration is somewhat like a veil dance during which one layer of formality after another disappears. A formal period precedes not only all village-wide celebrations

—held at the old warehouse, the village office, or, during warm days, outside—but also introduces all family or small group events. This is the time when guests arrive, polite greetings are exchanged with everyone in the order of his relative status, and a seat is found in accordance with it. Everyone sits quietly and politely, men with legs crossed tightly in front, women resting their buttocks between their heels. The conversation is somewhat stilted and reluctant. Meanwhile the hostess and her female helpers set cups before each guest, and they, or the male host himself, may pour tea.

Village celebrations of an official nature, such as "Mother's Day" (see Chapter 6) or the reception of the newly elected mayor, or New Year, are times for oratory of a sober nature. The village dignitaries and honored visitors, frequently seated at tables overlooking the community on the floor, each give a speech consisting of lengthy inventories of events and accomplishments. Sometimes food and drink are not served until the last one has spoken, but more often the situation is mellowed by the simultaneous serving of food and drink, which add to the inspiration of the speaker and the enthusiasm of his listeners.

Special dishes are associated with different holidays, and food, when served, begins to dispel some of the formality. Even if there are no speeches, it gives everybody something to do and talk about, and as we shall see shortly, more effective stimulants follow soon. The ice is broken. The food set before guests may be red-colored rice, which is served at joyful events such as New Year, or white rice, which is prepared when the dead are commemorated. For agricultural holidays the special food is made from the harvested crop, rice or potatoes. A feast plate may also include some pork, cooked in soya sauce, or presented in a mixed dish of vegetables; sometimes, it may be deep fat fried dumplings, either plain or with brown sugar stirred into the batter, or red and white fish cakes, or even several of these together. Less expensive foods, such as noodles and fried fish, are also served during feasts. Tairans have a sweet tooth and eat with relish the pound cakes and cookies which accompany or follow a meal. There is a sufficient quantity of food for the many guests, and whatever they cannot consume during the party, they may wrap up in a newspaper and take home.

Once food is set before the guests, the emptied tea cups are refilled, but this time with sake. This helps immediately to loosen the formal atmosphere which still prevails, at least after one or two cups have been emptied. Before this happens there may be, especially during weddings, family affairs, or the Mayor's reception, a polite exchange of cups between two men, who fill each other's and present it with a little ap-

preciative statement or an introduction. It is polite to make the rounds
in this fashion, to sit before another guest, fill his cup and utter some
polite phrases, then wait for a return compliment.

By the time men—and a little later women—have been served food
and drink in some quantity, there is no more stiffness in the room, for
with every cup of sake animation and voice volume increase. Speeches
that have not yet come to a conclusion show definite signs of inspiration; each speaker who sits down is trumped in eloquence by his successor. Long after serious oratory has been dispensed with, a happy
celebrant may get up and sonorously hold forth. During fieldwork
the authors were frequently the aim of such addresses. In one of them
a farmer, quiet and serious during everyday routine but known for his
merriment and wit when in his cups, held forth on a future visit to
Taira by these Americans. "There will be skyscrapers," he said in a
booming voice, "subways, wide lanes and bright lights," and on he went
to the delight of everybody.

On such occasions Tairans display their skill in playing with words
and their ability to act and mimic. The assistant to the headman,
similarly quiet on ordinary days, several months after our arrival came
into a room where the authors were present during one of the many
post-New Year celebrations. At an advanced stage of merriment himself,
he turned to his host and by way of introduction said that he had just
come from Hong Kong. "Oh, from Hong Kong," the host said, "that
is why you cough so, kong, kong, kong," adding that he himself came
from New York (pronounced in Japanese similar to *nyūyoku,* meaning
"a bath"), whereupon the arriving guest went into the motions of
someone taking a bath, saying "ah from *nyūyoku,*" and so the fun
went on, mostly as a take-off on the American guests who were present.
This reminded the clerk of another story at the expense of the authors,
which he told with gusto. "That first day he came to Taira, Maretzki
came up to me when I was carrying pebbles from the beach and asked
if he could help since he was going to haul pebbles too. Then he
started to introduce himself, and I only understood 'Umaretsuki'
(similar to Japanese for 'temperament') . . . I waited and waited for
a story, but nothing followed. I did not know what to say." He had
never repeated this story during many sober encounters.

At another event, when several teachers were present, one of the
men, after much gaiety, turned to a female teacher whose husband had
left for the city to find a job and called over: "Hey, your mosquito
netting must be wide now, huh?" The woman blushed, covered her
mouth with a handkerchief and laughed.

The evening is never old before one man, or several who are known for their special skills on the samisen (a three-stringed banjolike instrument covered with snake hide), open the singing and dancing with the first, traditional song, *Kagiyadefu,* a solemn and slow piece which is rendered in the forced, nasal voice peculiar to Okinawan song. Immediately after this, the tempo changes, the music takes a fast, stirring beat, and the first dancer, a man, gets up. Dances at social events can be performed by a single man or a woman, or by several dancers of either sex, but traditional group dances are done by women only. Taira people like to dance some of the many Okinawan dances in which a story, sung by the vocalists, is acted out. For example, a popular dance deals with a fisherman and his catch. A hat, hastily put on, and a basket under the arm suggest the role of the dancer, his body and hand movements the actions. No one is much concerned with accurate or highly artistic rendition of these familiar dances; many performances become simply improvisations in which one male dancer is joined by other men or women who, dancing freely, add their own versions to established movements. There is much applause and laughter from the audience around the dance floor, which sings and animatedly claps hands in rhythm to the music. As all, men and older women, imbibe more sake, they become gayer, and more talents are unleashed. Amusing presentations of a husband and wife, in which sometimes aggression and sexual interaction are acted out playfully, are received with great hilarity by the audience. If such a suggestive performance is given by an old woman and a young man, it seems to appear even funnier. As they get tired, dancers leave the floor, making room for others.

Not everybody participates with equal lack of restraint. Younger women do not drink sake and show much more inhibition; they dance established versions of Okinawan dances in group performances if called on, usually before the merrymakers take over. Often a mother, young child in arm, cannot resist. Passing the infant to a relative or a girl sitting nearby, she joins other dancers and becomes carried away by the spirit of the event. On one occasion a young woman, seeing her aged mother display her talents on the dance floor in comical movements to the delight of everybody, angrily demanded that she come home right away, only to be rejoined with a taunting remark by the old lady, who defiantly swallowed some more sake and continued her entertainment.

Not a single event that we attended was marred by any serious unpleasantness. No guest was ever seen to become sick, although some men drank themselves into a stupor. Here and there a paper screen may be broken as a result of a tumbling body, or a hard bang against a thin panel may set the house shaking. But the end of such a feast would be nothing more uproarious than a group of singing celebrants seeking further entertainment from house to house. The occasional quarrels after drinking, which are mentioned elsewhere, seemed much more frequent where only a small group of men indulged after work, especially younger ones. No major holidays ended in dissonance.

The main events for family celebrations are lunar New Year, *seimei,* a period in spring during which descent group ancestors are revered and *Bon,* a commemoration of the dead in the fall. At these times families are reunited with relatives from other villages or the city. These events are observed in the home or in front of the ancestral tombs. During *Bon* young men and women go from house to house, performing traditional dances for this holiday in front of the assembled families.

Celebration of special birthday cycles and agricultural events, such as the day when ditches in the paddies were cleaned in former times, are observed by villagers as a group. An important religious event for the community is Boat Race Day in lunar June. On lunar August 15, the celebration of the full August moon, some villagers present stage performances and dances at a public celebration.

In general, it may be said that families gather as a unit on those days on which ancestors and deceased family members are commemorated. The village jointly celebrates events which are either based on local religion or on agricultural events. The only national holiday which is now in existence was established by the post-war Ryukyuan government. It is observed by school and government offices but not by the people.

Sport events form another category of holidays. The most important one falls in October when both in Japan and all over the Ryukyus athletes compete against each other. Athletic meets take place for several weeks; for the village the biggest event is the competition of all athletes in the township on *undokai* day. Everyone leaves work and takes picnic food to the track at the junior high school where each village competes against the others. This lasts all day.

Wrestling matches are part of entertainment during outdoor celebrations in the early summer. They are mainly an affair for young men. Occasionally an older man who feels strong enough challenges a younger one. The villagers sit around a large circle near the beach, watching the fights while they eat holiday food and drink sake. On Boat Race Day Taira and the neighboring village of Kawata race fishing canoes against each other. Spectators at this event are enthusiastic supporters of their favorites. After the races this holiday ends like any other, in celebrations with dance and drinking.

Part II

Child Training

✲
✲
✲
✲
✲
✲

Chapter 12

Pregnancy and Childbirth

The custom of "trial marriage" stresses the importance Taira villagers put on a woman's ability to bear children, for it is imperative that there be heirs to carry on the family line. The first child is usually born within one or two years after marriage. Taira people would be extremely surprised if a child is not born soon, for children, especially male offspring, are desired. A barren wife faces the possibility of annulment of her marriage by her husband or even her husband's parents. Should this action be disagreeable to her husband, she may still be forced to take the lesser role of co-wife. A fertile woman who fails to bear a male child may suffer a situation not unlike that of a barren woman. Pregnancies, however, arouse a great amount of ambivalence in attitude.

Most women welcome pregnancy happily, knowing that they are fulfilling their role as a woman. Nevertheless, some women complain of the economic hardship incurred as a result of large families. A few of the more outspoken mothers complain bitterly against the old people who expect them to continue bearing children until three male heirs are born. Men desire male heirs, and one son is not enough: the favored number is three. Informal interviews reveal that in spite of the cultural preference for sons, mothers welcome daughters, who grow up to be useful helpers. Even if women protest when they feel tired of bearing children, they submit to their husband's demands. Since Japanese given names are used today, the practice of naming a girl Sueko (end child), to indicate that one considers her to be the last, is often resorted to. If this proves insufficient and another follows, she might be called Tomeko (stop child). In one family the wife gave her baby girl the name Sueko to indicate that she did not desire any more children. Her husband, however, disagreed, for he wanted another son, and registered the child without his wife's knowledge under another name.

Although the older generation, which has supported large families, looks on birth control measures with distaste, the young mothers circulate information published in Japanese magazines and by the Okinawan public health department on this matter, and a few families actually use contraceptives. However, in general, public health nurses have found it extremely difficult to discuss matters like birth control, abortion, and infanticide with villagers. "We suspect that these measures are practiced everywhere. Of course, with the system of registration and public health nursing, infanticide is hardly possible; however . . . we could not say. . . ." * It is interesting to note that in Taira there are mental defectives but no physical defectives. Abortion is legal with a doctor's consent, but informants claimed it was not practiced. There are illegitimate children born in the village.

"The seeds, they must match. If they do not match, then it cannot be," explain the villagers. They continue, "It is like planting a field, however; if the soil is hostile to growth, nothing can happen." Thus the villagers express their theories of conception.

Cessation of menstrual periods signals the start of pregnancy, and the sudden craving for a particular kind of food forces the woman to acknowledge the fact. Informal interviewing and casual observation reveal that morning sickness is not usual. Women rarely miss a working day in the fields and mountains even in the early stages of pregnancy. One male who failed to appear for work with the rest of the male population of the village was the butt of many a joke. "How now, you are taking over the task of your wife?" teased the men and women.

Malfunction of the kidneys is not uncommon among pregnant

* Personal communication from public health nurses.

View of central village, Taira.

House and yard.

Preparing rice paddy.

Cultivating rice.

Women washing at water tank.

Women transplanting rice.

Woman transplanting.   *Carrying wood.*

Children catching small fish.

Girls washing their laundry.

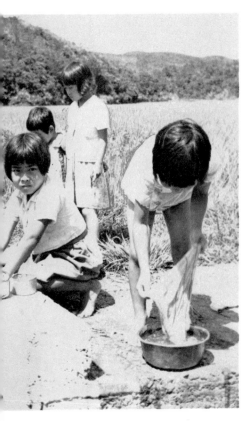

Carrying water while their mother is recovering from giving birth.

Boy harvesting.

Young girl carrying baby sister.

Boys wrestling.

Playing house.

*Mother about to nurse her
daughter says, "Now say please."*

women in Taira. Three young mothers, who continued to work despite the discomfort and pain of swollen extremities, consulted with the doctor in the nearby town, and a fourth described this condition, which had prohibited her from any but the most simple and undemanding work. The old people look upon unusual pregnancies in askance. "Work, good, hard physical labor is what we did and we never had any difficulties. Young people pamper themselves."

Special foods and advice are proffered the expectant mother for the benefit of the baby. "Eat this so that you will have lots of milk for the baby. Remember that spicy things are bad for the baby. Do you recall the one who was born with a great patch of hair on its arms? Its mother was frightened by a great big cat while she was carrying that child," comment villagers to the mother. Some husbands indulge their wives' cravings for special delicacies like expensive imported fruits.

To keep the baby in position, a sash is wound several times about the pregnant woman's abdomen by a midwife or some old woman.

In the "old days" it was not unusual for a woman to return from the mountains or fields carrying her newborn. Grandmothers recall with relish the days when "Women paid little heed to their condition, did hard work, and had their babies without a whimper." "The women to-day pamper themselves," snap the wizened grandmothers watching an expectant mother resting between trips to the mountains.

As the day of parturition approaches, the expectant mother schedules her work to remain as close to the house as possible. When labor starts, she retires to the back room of the house, which is situated next to the kitchen. The medical practitioner, or in his absence a midwife,* is called to assist in the delivery. The husband's mother, if she lives in the house, or other older related women attend. A man may be present during his wife's first delivery but at subsequent births will wait with some of the women in the front room. In the old days a woman was supported by her husband or someone else in a half-sitting position. Nowadays, however, women give birth lying down. Only rarely does a woman in labor cry out in pain. Soft crying is permissible, but any loud demonstration would elicit contemptuous comments from the older women. "If you had worked hard, the baby would not be so big, then labor would not be difficult," is an often heard retort.

Informal interviewing revealed that birth takes place in a large number of cases during late evening or early morning hours. Usually children of the house sleep on undisturbed. Should they awake, they are kept out of the delivery room, although the youngest may be allowed to enter to visit with his mother shortly after delivery.

The newborn is bathed in tepid water then bundled in blankets,

* At present there is no midwife in Taira.

kimonos, and diapers. He is placed under the blanket next to the mother and given a gauze nipple dipped in tea and sugar to suck, which is often his only food for as long as two days if lactation is slow. Meanwhile the afterbirth is wrapped in straw and left under the floorboards in the kitchen to await the outgoing tide.

Tea is now served in the front room, and the birth is discussed by the women who assisted. On one such occasion, the father and grandmother showed a little boy whose sister had just been born a great deal of affection. The father held the boy in his lap, and both adults told him that he was now a big brother.

At the first hour of the outgoing tide, old women—the grandmother of the baby, relatives, and neighbors—wrap the afterbirth in rice straw and bury it in a specified place outdoors behind the hearth. The purpose of the ceremony is to ensure that the child will be happy and sociable. To the accompaniment of laughing, loud clanging of pots and covers, and calling to each other, the women circle the house. When the burial is completed, they chant loudly, "May this baby always laugh and be pleasant." A stone is then placed over the burial mound so that the infant will not be frightened in his sleep, an emotion which is inferred from the jerking of a young infant while asleep.

Until about 10 years ago a ceremony was performed by descendants of noble families from Shuri over the newborn to ensure success in his future role. For boys, a winnowing basket was propped up against a hoe on which a clump of soil and grass rested. While the father's mother held the child in one arm, she shot an arrow with a bow into the basket. This act was to make certain that the child would become a good hunter (provider) as well as a successful farmer. The grass on the hoe symbolized strength. A girl, on the other hand, received a miniature loom constructed especially for such occasions, which was to assure her success as a weaver of cloth. A spool of banana fiber was presented along with the loom.

There is a story that long, long ago an infant was born on the beach. Immediately after he was born, as he still lay on the sand, a crab crawled over his chest. This infant grew up to be a strong, famous man. Shuri descendants still have a custom of grandmothers holding a newborn boy in their laps and releasing a small crab, which scurries over the infant's chest. These practices, however, are absent in central Taira now and are rarely found in the outlying settlements of predominantly Shuri descendants.

Formerly mother and child were confined to the darkened delivery room next to the kitchen and at the rear of the house for seven days, while an open fire was kept blazing in the brazier near the mother.

Today the *yukajiru* ceremony held on the fourth day ends the seclusion. A group of close relatives gather to ask for the good health of the child and to make food offerings to the ancestors.

On the fourth or fifth day a name is selected for the newborn. In the old days rice oracles presided over by an old woman were consulted to ensure that the name consist of the proper combination of Japanese writing characters, an essential for the well-being of the child's personality. Today family elders and the local teacher are consulted. In the pre-Japanese periods, temporary names were used until a permanent name was given. This practice was intended to fool the spirits during the early years when the child was thought to be particularly susceptible to spirits.*

On the sixth day after birth the mother is allowed to take her first postdelivery bath; the room which she has occupied with her baby is cleaned and aired, and preparations begin for the *mansang* celebrations. For this event the mother's parents try to be present, especially if it is a first child. Friends and relatives in the village attend. A female elder of the patrilineal kin group or the priestess prays behind a tray of rice, rice wine, and incense so that the child will sleep peacefully and not cry at night. Thanksgiving prayers are offered to the ancestors and the nature deities for the health of both mother and child.

When the prayers are completed, a man sings the *mansang* song to the accompaniment of a samisen. The father of the baby then rises to dance briefly, sits down, and writes with brush and ink on a white sheet of paper the name and birth date of his child. The paper is then hung on the wall near the alcove. Meanwhile the special song is being concluded:

> Coming from the darkness to light,
> This baby was received as a treasure
> And the mother is being celebrated.

Food is then served, and the guests discuss the name and admire the newborn. Like all parties, the celebration ends with song, dance, and wine drinking.

The *mansang* celebrations mark the end of the most critical period for the infant. From now on he may be taken outdoors. At the month's end, his parents may take him to see his maternal grandparents in their village, to offer food at the ancestral shrine of the mother. This is called the first walk. Sons who have left the paternal village for the city return with their infant to observe this day.

* Hanging an irregularly left-woven rope in the delivery room to keep out evil spirits which might harm the newborn, is no longer done in Taira.

There are no food taboos during pregnancy, and after birth mothers can continue to eat what they wish except for certain "hard" foods, such as octopus, whale meat, and certain kinds of fish which are believed to stop the flow of milk. To stimulate lactation, the mother is given papaya boiled with flour and noodles or a medicine made from herbs.

Chapter 13

Infancy

The infant is considered a helpless, pitiable treasure who is incapable of knowing, understanding, or learning until he is around 6 years old. If this senseless child is treated affectionately and indulgently, he will grow to be a healthy, happy adult.

With the spread of Japanese influence throughout Okinawa, according to informants, there evolved another belief, which in Taira is complementary to the idea of the senseless child. This new belief is vaguely conceptualized by most young parents but was verbalized concretely by at least two sets of parents. "Children are the gift of gods.* They are godly until they are 7 years old." Exoneration of misbehavior on the part of the child under 7 (6 years according to Western count) conjures up in the mind of the observer a picture of willful capricious gods who are totally unpredictable. A shrug of the shoulder and a phrase which completely defines both attitude and resignation in Japanese is, "helpless, against one's will." Because children are godlike in nature, they do not know any better; because they do not know any better they are godlike in nature. Just why and how a child outgrows this temperament could not be explained by the parents. These beliefs foster the extreme indulgence, protection, and nurturance of young babies. Their physical and emotional needs are attended to constantly, with a great deal of affection.

* This notion may well have been influenced by Christian as much as by Japanese ideas.

In addition to meeting with physical and emotional needs, the child must be protected from the nurtured by the numerous supernatural forces in the form of malevolent and benevolent spirits which operate to influence the course of an individual's life. There are lucky and unlucky days, years, and tides, which are believed to determine the fate of a person. Females born in the year of the monkey are considered unlucky, for they are thought to outlive their male contemporaries. Men dislike marrying them. Supplications are made and precautionary measures taken by adults to secure the newborn's life, happiness, and health.

Ancestral spirits influence the development and fate of the child. Occasionally a child who is the victim of ill health during his early years is adopted by a couple whose ancestral spirits are thought to be more favorable than his own on the dictate of the fortune teller. By mysterious calculations involving birth dates of the principals, the fortune teller uncovers some incompatibility and advises adoption. The child remains with his parents but worships the ancestral spirits of his adoptive parents. In this way parents seek to ensure the well-being of the child.

Mother interview data indicate the awareness of Taira people of the variations in personality among children of one family. Adults do in a large measure adapt their actions in accord with these differences. They recognize hereditary influences, but although a mother may comment on the similarity of temperament with regard to her child and other members in the family or kin group, there are no ideas or beliefs that the souls of deceased are inherited. Usually the mother, in describing the characteristics of the child, rarely goes beyond likenesses which can be attributed to herself or her husband. She is at a loss to explain the "very different child." "My eldest son has my nasty temper whereas my second daughter is not like either of us, very strange. All the others have a little of myself and my husband in them. We often wonder how it is that she is so unlike either of us."

A child born with two cowlicks predicates a "problem" to his parents. Parents often explain, "Oh, this child is very naughty, for as you can see, he has two cowlicks." Children often search each other's heads, and on discovering two instead of the single whorl, they shout in glee, "Naughty, naughty." One 4-year-old cuddled and hugged his newborn sister after searching her head. "You have two cowlicks just like me! You and I are 'naughty,'" he whispered to her. Turning to the adults in the room, he snapped his small bright eyes and grinned impishly as he reported his discovery joyfully.

Twin births are disliked only because they place a burden on the mother and family. "Nursing two babies at once on a diet as meager as ours is too difficult," explain the mothers, and they also point out that multiple births cause great economic hardships.

Infancy in Taira, in congruence with the concept of the nature of an infant, is a period of indulgent and affectionate nurturance. Except for a brief period during the initial month of life, the baby is rarely left to lie on the floor to sleep, and during this period the mother or grandmother is always close by to pick him up at the slightest whimper. From the time he is a month old until shortly before the arrival of the next baby, he is constantly carried during the daytime on the back of another, an adult or an older child. At night he sleeps next to his mother. His carriers include parents, paternal grandparents, unmarried aunts and uncles, older siblings in an extended household, and parents and older siblings in a nuclear household.

Those mothers who have read or heard that it is good for babies to cry occasionally never have an opportunity to test it. "The old people feel sorry for the baby and insist upon prompt attention," complain young mothers with "modern" ideas. The immediate response of adult and child caretakers to an infant's cry is to take him to his mother, who promptly nurses him. The breast is thrust into his mouth whether he is hungry or not. "Pitiful!" exclaim old grandmothers and rush to pick up the infant. More often than not it is the newborn's father or older sibling who orders the mother to do so with the same expression.

There is the belief that the first four months are a trying period in which the "bad" habit of crying is formed; therefore every attempt is made to keep the infant comfortable and quiet. One mother described how she and her husband took turns eating their evening meal because one of the children had formed such a bad habit. "We would take turns carrying him and walking around the yard and eating. There was nothing else we could do. Both of us did not like to have babies cry." Another mother told of how her whole family converged on her every time the infant whimpered. "Hurry and nurse it . . . must be hungry . . . may be sick . . . so pitiful!" they would say to her.

It is imperative that a mother have enough milk. She is given special foods and told not to get overtired. She is advised to avoid foods that could pass on properties which might be harmful to the child. Sometimes she has more milk than her infant can consume. One such fortunate mother nursed the baby of a mother whose milk supply had failed. Women who have a plentiful supply of milk are also sought out when mothers find it necessary to work at some distance from the village. In these cases reciprocal arrangements are made so the baby need not go hungry for very long.

There is no specific or preferred posture for nursing. While the mothers are in confinement for the brief period following delivery, they often lie next to the baby and feed him. Sitting while nursing is the most common posture, but mothers frequently nurse while standing or squatting. The baby is held loosely and the mother is relaxed. If others are about, she will carry on a lively conversation and occasionally pat the baby gently on or around the region of the buttocks. When alone, she holds the baby with one arm, talks softly, smiles, and with her other hand tugs gently at the baby's limbs. Each feeding is leisurely; the breast is never withdrawn from the infant's mouth. More often than not he suckles his fill and falls asleep.

It is as natural to suckle one's infant at a village meeting as it is to do so in the privacy of one's home. A common sight is that of a mother sitting and listening intently to speeches while cradling her suckling infant loosely in her arms. On buses, in market places, or at large public intervillage gatherings, one is sure to encounter such a scene.

The breast is used to soothe a baby when he is ill, irritable, or in distress from pain. This was quite evident when all the babies in the village were being given a series of innoculations for diphtheria and typhoid. As the injections were given in one large open room, the cries of the infant being innoculated prompted others to cry. Invariably the mother offered the breast to the baby.

After the birth of a child, the mother sits at home during a short rest period, watching happily as neighbors, friends, and relatives continually drop in to admire the newborn. Sipping tea, the visitors offer bits of advice, exchange the latest gossip, ask to hold the infant, and take their leave with the standard phrase: "Take care of yourself." It is a pleasant interlude, but as the family resources begin to dwindle, there is a slight but perceptible change in the attitude of the mother toward her newborn. The constant stream of visitors, for whom tea and some small tidbits must be offered, and her nonparticipation in the regular economic activities prove to be a drain on the family budget, in spite of the fact that the mother and her husband have worked with extra diligence in the months prior to parturition. The mother begins to talk about the approaching feast day and the need to get new clothing for the older children. She asks anxiously about the condition of the firewood market and starts to plan her inevitable resumption of work in the mountains and fields. In spite of her feelings of protectiveness and pity for the young baby, she begins, bit by bit, to reinstate her normal routine. Although she continues to cuddle, kiss, and affectionately nurse the infant, she thinks of the good weather and of how she might have been able to make one more trip to the mountains before noon but for the fact that she had to return to attend to the infant.

If a grandmother is available, the mother straps the 3-to-4 months old baby onto the grandmother's back in the morning and goes off to the mountains with her husband to haul firewood or to the fields to cultivate sweet potatoes. For the first six months she returns to the house frequently during the day to nurse the infant. It is likely that while the infant demands feeding at short intervals, a mother will work in or around the village. At one of the locations for firewood bundling she can make the bamboo rings, fit the cut wood into them, and stack the bundles.

Throughout the morning hours grandmother, with the infant on her back, wanders about the village. Occasionally she offers her dry breast to the bawling infant who cannot seem to wait until its mother returns from the fields or mountains. If the mother is nearby, she hurries so that the infant does not cry for long. When the hour for lunch approaches, the grandmother hurries home to begin preparations for the noonday meal. As she walks, the infant's head bobs up and down, forward and back precariously, but it continues to sleep undisturbed.

After lunch has been eaten and the infant nursed, the adults in the household sip their tea and rest for an hour or so. Within that hour the mother may play with the infant or nap with it nestled in her arms. Rousing themselves from the noon nap, the adults return to the mountains and fields. The infant is again strapped to the grandmother's back, but this time as she slowly wends her way to the main thoroughfare, she calls out to someone in a house which boasts one of the few clocks in the village. "Hey, what is the time there?" The answer will quicken her pace, for it is near the time for an older sibling to return from school. As she reaches the main street, she joins other grandmothers as well as mothers who are anxiously scanning the direction from which the schoolchildren return. Each admires the infants on the other's back and exchanges timely topics of the day, but as the minutes pass and no children appear, they begin to grumble about the "irresponsible siblings who *must* be playing on their way home." At last the older child returns, and the grandmother hurries home with her charges, promptly transfering the infant onto the back of the older sibling. The old woman rushes to get her hoe and basket, mumbling to herself about the quantity of potatoes she should harvest for the next day's use.

An older child who ignores the crying of his infant charge will be criticized severely by his peers. If the mother happens to be in the fields and away from the village, the young caretaker jiggles up and down to soothe the baby on his back. As his cries become frantic, the caretaker's peers will pat him on his buttocks and try to placate him by guiding his fingers to his mouth.

For the nuclear family with no other caretaker except the mother, the newborn proves to be a problem. One such mother complained that she could not do anything efficiently with a baby on her back. She was able to go to the fields to harvest potatoes but had to leave the laden basket until the afternoon to carry it home, for at that time the neighbor's child returned from school to look after the baby. In payment for baby-sitting services she had planned on buying the neighbor's child a dress for the next New Year.

In the nuclear family with school age children, the mother works around the house and in the nearby fields in the morning and rushes off to the mountains when her relief returns in the middle of the afternoon. Thus the infant which brought so much joy to the family and gave its mother respite from the rigorous routine for a short time becomes somewhat of a burden to all. Nevertheless, the baby continues to be indulged, pitied for his helplessness, and the object of affection.

It is important to note, briefly, the father's attitude and behavior during this initial period. Although only females were born during this study, interviews suggest that a male birth elicits a somewhat more solicitous behavior on the part of the father toward both mother and infant than a female one. The father will discourage the mother's early resumption of work and may even feel encouraged to carry the male infant despite the fact that children are deemed "women's work." Ostensibly, however, he seems embarrassed and disinterested in the whole matter be it a male or female. Congratulating visitors find that after a few polite exchanges the father will retire to a corner in the house as attention focuses on mother and child. After sitting out what seems a proper length of time, he will mumble some excuse or other and leave the house to do some chore. The observer visiting the household on the occasion of the birth of a fourth daughter found gloom and disgust in the father's expression. A male visitor who sat trying to convince the father that daughters are quite useful, too, received only contemptuous stares. His wife sat dejectedly holding the infant loosely in her arms. In contrast, a visit of the same purpose to another household on the birth of a fourth daughter revealed similar but notably less intense reactions on the part of the father. Perhaps because of the existence of one male heir he felt less threatened.

There is a tenacious belief in Taira that the female determines the sex of the child. If the woman fails to produce a male heir, the man can take on a second wife. The woman who is delivered of her third son is the envy of others who have none or only one son to their credit, for she has achieved what is considered to be the ideal in a wife. Thus the first mother with four daughters was treated with outright disgust and contempt by her husband, whereas in the second instance the mother was receiving the normal treatment of disinterest with minor solicitation.

The constant stream of visitors during the first month gives the other children in the household a sense of importance. Whenever an older child has a chance, he stresses the fact that there is a newborn in the house and reports the identity of the latest visitor to scores of admiring peers. He is the envy of the lot when at last he is allowed to carry the infant and play. But the envy is short lived, and the older sibling's pride withers rapidly when he finds that this is just another baby to be carried and cared for constantly. As the baby gains weight and no longer sleeps quietly for extended periods of time on the back, the older sibling begins to run and hide when he sees his mother approaching with the baby.

A few days after the birth of an infant, the fieldworker visited a household and found the older siblings all crowded in the back room with the mother and child. One of the girls, a 5-year-old who was unusually sturdy and large in build, was teased by her mother. "Hey Hanako, let's give the teacher this baby, all right?" said the mother, winking on the side to the fieldworker. The little girl looked anxiously at the fieldworker and slowly edged over protectively toward the infant. She shook her head slowly and deliberately for some minutes, indicating that she would not assent to giving her baby sister away. At this point the grandmother entered the teasing and told the little girl that the baby would only prove to be a burden when she had to carry her later on, but she continued to shake her head. As the mother handed the baby over to the fieldworker, the girl burst into tears and cried out, "No! No!" All laughed and assured her that the baby would remain in the household.

Several weeks later, Hanako proudly paraded her newest baby sister for all her playmates to see. Many begged to carry the infant "for just a little while" to no avail. When her older sister returned from school, she reluctantly gave up her charge in deference to age and experience. This went on for about two months until one day the fieldworker came on the mother calling frantically around the village for Hanako and the older girl. The older girl successfully evaded her mother, but Hanako was discovered and the baby was strapped to her back. Hanako frowned and tugged at the straps that were straining at her neck muscles.

At a still later date, Hanako, with her baby sister strapped to her back, played on the beach. At one point, when all the children were scattered over the beach and no one else was nearby, Hanako edged up to the fieldworker and asked, "Would you like this baby, teacher? Here, take her," she said wearily. Asked why she had changed her mind, the little girl smiled shyly, squirmed uncomfortably for a moment, then whispered, "She's too heavy." Her 3-year-old sister, off in the distance at that point, began to scream and cry at being left so far behind. Hanako turned to look back once, then walked on as the 3-year-old squatted on the sand and screamed to be carried. At that moment her mother appeared to nurse the infant, and Hanako ran to her. She bounded swiftly away to the 3-year-old as the mother started to nurse the baby. Returning a few minutes later with the 3-year-old on her back, Hanako deposited her disgustedly, panting heavily from the weight. "Shall we give baby to teacher, Hanako?" asked the mother, and without any hesitation Hanako this time nodded "Yes." The mother laughed and said, "Hah, she has had enough of her already. When the baby was tiny and cute, she was so eager to carry her and wouldn't give her to you, but they all get tired of babies in time." And with that the mother began to rock the baby back and forth in her arms. Smiling affectionately, she kissed and hugged the cooing infant and murmured, "Nobody wants you, eh?" Because she was an unusually outspoken mother she confided, "I think I have had enough too, here, I give her to you!" She laughed as she continued, "How can I make money, feed and clothe the children when I have to rush back from the mountains to nurse this baby."

When the child is about 6 months old, he is subjected to a painful operation which prepares him for the introduction to solid foods. The area around the navel is moxa-cauterized. Nine little brown dots in three rows of three attest to the practice of burning a special kind of grass on the skin in this area to protect the infant from various digestive complications. The child thus treated, the mother will begin to supplement breast feedings with rice water, milky white in appearance, that is spooned out of the boiling pot of rice. Sometime later, before the child is about one, bits of sweet potato and special kinds of fish mashed between the fingers are thrust into the mouth of the infant as he sits on his mother's lap at mealtime. Gradually he is given more and more solid foods until, finally, at the age of 2 he is eating rice, unmashed fish, potatoes and vegetables, but nursing is continued until the mother becomes pregnant. Usually, however, weaning is not started in earnest until the mother is three months pregnant.

If the infant has a fever or "bad color," he may be subjected to another painful experience, blood letting. Incisions are made on those parts of the body which are thought to be affected, and blood is drawn and caught in a cup. The area is washed with sake. The mother often suckles the baby and holds him while the grandmother or some other older person performs the operation.

Babies are diapered and swaddled until they are about a year old. For the first two months their wet and soiled diapers are changed frequently; however, as time goes on, less attention is paid to wet diapers, although those soiled from excreta are promptly changed. Infants are checked often during the raw winter days, but because they are bundled so heavily, there is hardly any danger of their contracting colds as their mothers fear. Severe urine burns and annoying diaper rash are more common than colds among young babies.

Although care is taken to keep the infant as clean as possible during the first year of his life, this attitude changes as the child grows older. This is in large part due to the mother's inability to devote much time to her offspring once she has resumed full participation in economics activities. Depending on the season of the year, babies are bathed from every third or fourth day to once a week. They are bathed almost daily during the first two months of their lives as a result of the insistence of the village nurse. Water is heated on the kitchen hearth and poured into a small washpan. Mothers test the warmth of the water by immersing their arms up to the elbows and adding cold or hot water as they see fit. Soap is gently applied either with a soft washcloth or with the hands and rinsed off by splashing. On chilly winter days the bath takes place indoors, but on the hot sunny days it takes place right outside the kitchen door. In drying the baby, the mother places him in a large towel and pats the dampness from his body. She is careful to dry the skin at the joints where rash is likely to erupt. Except for the very poor, all families keep a bottle of talcum powder, which is applied right after the bath. Throughout the bath, the mother talks softly to the baby, smiling and tickling him. The atmosphere of the bath at this time contrasts sharply with that of a later time when the child is 2 and 3 years old.

Although there is hardly any possibility that the infant at this time would be able to smear himself with excreta, the opportunity for doing so is present later when he no longer wears diapers but is still untrained. It rarely happens, as the child is almost constantly watched by a caretaker. One mother reported disgustedly that her infant smeared herself from head to toe when she had left her diaperless on the floor for a few minutes. She had assumed that the child had completed elimination and had gone out to rinse the soiled diaper.

When the infant is anywhere from 22 days to 10 months old, the mothers start trying to anticipate urination before the baby wets his diapers. Each mother trains herself to her child's particular cues, squirming, peculiar facial expressions, and so on, or keeps a kind of mental time check. Holding the infant in a semisitting position out over the edge of the porch, and supporting him under his knees with her hands and at his back with her chest, she coaxes gently, repeating "shi-shi" until he urinates onto the ground outside. If the mother is successful in her efforts, she hugs, kisses, and praises the infant. On the other hand, if she does not reach him in time and he is already wet, she will hold the child over the wet diaper and say "shi-shi." This is to ensure that he has fully eliminated, or if the interval between diaper checks has been long, to make certain that he does not need to urinate again before putting on a fresh change. In these instances she does not praise unless the infant does urinate or eliminate at her coaxing, but she does not punish him for urinating in his diapers.

Although mothers may desire bladder control to develop, their statements do not indicate that they conceive of holding the child out as training. In discussing the practice, mothers seemed more concerned about the number of diapers they had to wash or buy. With a great deal of pride one mother reported that she never had to wash a diaper except when it was soiled with feces. Another bragged that she had only had to buy diapers once, and this was for her first child. Treatment of bladder control at a later period raises further doubt that this practice is meant for training purposes. Pertinent here, too, is the belief that children are incapable of learning at this early date.

While a few mothers who have the time to look after their babies continue to avoid wet diapers, most of them eventually abandon the routine and leave it to the child to train himself. When they resume normal activities following childbirth, an older sibling takes over the care of the infant, and the mother does not instruct the older child to continue the practice. Fear for the safety of the baby keeps her from doing so. Once she straps the baby onto the young caretaker's back, she expects him to remain there until she or another adult unstraps him. Teen-age caretakers seldom bother to change wet diapers until it becomes unbearable. If the grandmother is the chief caretaker, however, she will continue the practice. For the greater part of the first year, the infant urinates in his diaper, frequently wetting his caretaker. Just before the child turns one, most mothers will reduce the amount of swaddling and diapers. Almost immediately after he has passed his first birthday, she will stop diapering him and substitute a short shirt or a dress during the summer and kimonos during the cold weather. This is the period which proves most trying to the young caretaker. Unless the baby is filthy and evokes much comment from others, however, they ignore the condition. The following examples illustrate common occurrences during this period:

H. (an 8-year-old girl) carrying her baby sister on the back is playing on the beach. She straightens up suddenly with a wry expression on her face. "She urinated, wet," she exclaims, standing up and spreading her dress at the back which is completely soaked. The baby is bare-bottomed and crowing happily at the older children playing around her. The older sister waves her dress briefly in the wind, then squats to continue her play. When asked if she was not going home to change, she exclaims that she would dry soon enough, and, as for the baby, she was dry. The day is warm and windy and the dress dries off rapidly.

K. (a 7-year-old girl), baby sister on her back, is squatting with other girls, drawing in the sand. As they draw figures in the sand, the baby breaks wind and defecates. It is a rather noisy operation, and the other girls watch fascinated and somewhat amused while K. keeps on sitting unconcerned. (The baby's bottom is bare so that the feces drops on the sand.) One of the girls laughs and comments on the feces dropping. K. says, "I will let my mother clean the ground." The other children walk away, spitting,* showing some disgust. All through this K. squats calmly, letting the baby eliminate undisturbed. She tells the baby "Finish defecating quickly," but she is not impatient, rather absent-minded.

Probably the earliest cleanliness training is the gentle withdrawal of unclean objects from the child, with statements of "Dirty, dirty." As he begins to respond to facial expression, the mother will show her disgust, shake her head and say, "Dirty!"

Infants may be patted or manipulated around the genital area by an adult. Old women like to tweak a little boy's penis and jokingly say, "What is that, what is that?" Female infants are quickly covered with exaggerated expressions of shame whenever they are exposed for diaper changes. Petting of genitals by an adult is used mostly to soothe the child. It would be severely rebuked, however, if attempted by a child caretaker.

When the child is a year old, a simple ceremony is held. After a short birthday prayer, the child is offered a tray with food, an abacus counter, pencil, book, and money. The audience waits expectantly to see what the infant will choose. The pencil portends a writer, the money a

---

* Expectoration at the sight of unpleasant things, such as dead animals or a pile of feces, is common among children and adults. Children pass a pile of dirt, spit at it, and cover it with dirt by a careless kick before continuing on.

financier, the abacus a mathematician, the book a scholar, and food a glutton. The villagers did not seem to place much credence in the choice. Mothers laughed when asked what choices their children made and commented, "It's something to talk about, but many times we can't even remember which child chose what!"

The child continues to be carried on the back until the next sibling is born, the interval being between about two or three years. By the time an infant is a year old, he has been taken through every nook and cranny of the village. He has also seen all the adults and children of the village and has witnessed the economic and social-ceremonial activities. Whereas he slept most of the time when he was young, he now begins to participate in what goes on about him. He claps his hands in glee in response to his older sibling's delight over some aspect of play or raises his arm in defiance of another child who attempts to strike at his older sibling. In spite of the fact that he is capable of crawling or learning to walk within the second half year of his life, he is kept on the back. He does not protest or clamor to be put down; he seems to prefer being carried to being left to crawl.

Caretakers are too busy with work or play to let the child crawl about freely, so there is no crawling stage in Taira. Older siblings are too involved in play to sit and patiently watch a crawler. The older child would also be severely punished should the infant pick up some object and swallow it or injure himself in his crawling. One 8-year-old found that the 10-month-old sister she toted on her back took to standing on the ground and jouncing up and down every time she squatted to play. After several unsuccessful attempts to stop this annoying behavior, she unstrapped her and allowed her to crawl about freely. The older girl became so engrossed in the game that her mouth dropped open and eyes turned round with fear when one of her playmates shouted, "Hey! the baby put some dirt into her mouth!" Immediately she rushed to "flush" the baby's mouth out with her fingers and promptly strapped her onto the back again and continued playing despite the uncomfortable jouncings. The baby did not protest at being restrapped; she just jounced and played with her hands.

A mother who sits and plucks sweet potato leaves off the vines for hog feed works more efficiently with the baby on her back. Crawling around on the loose floorboards near the fire pit or over the edge of the raised floor, the child would require constant attention. On one occasion the observer was sitting and talking with a mother who was weaving a bamboo basket in her front room. The floor was littered with bamboo shavings and slats. As the mother worked, she was relaxed. She turned and twisted the sharp ends of the bamboo slats, leaving pointed ends swinging in the air, and dropping the huge knife in a careless fashion on the floor near her. Suddenly there was the sound of a crying baby and her eldest girl appeared with the 8-month-old on her back. Unstrapping the baby, the girl plopped her onto her mother's lap. Instinctively the mother pushed the basket, bamboo slats, and knife away as she unbuttoned her blouse to nurse the baby. When the baby had had its fill, the mother called to the little caretaker to come and carry her. The older child called out that she was going to get a drink of water and disappeared around the house. She entered through the back and called to the baby to come. The baby crawled over but was attracted on the way by the big knife. Instantly the mother snatched it away, and the baby started to move toward the sharp pieces of bamboo. In desperation the mother picked up the baby and called crossly to the girl to come immediately. The older child obeyed, and the baby was strapped onto her back. "Now go and play somewhere," instructed the annoyed mother.

Another instance of similar nature took place in the frontyard of a place which that day was the scene of "house playing." A grandmother watching the activity decided to let the year-old baby on her back down to join in the play. "Eh, go and play with your older sisters," she smiled and said to the child as she put her gently down on the ground. The child started to crawl over to the group but stopped and sat very quietly staring ahead for a minute. The grandmother, who had disappeared into the house, reappeared. "A-yah!" she exclaimed as she looked down to see the baby scratching the damp earth about her. The baby had urinated and was puddling about so that in that brief instant she had thoroughly soiled herself as well as her clothing. Grumbling and scolding, "Dirty, dirty!" she picked up and carried at arm's length the baby, who was smiling and gurgling. The old woman cleaned the baby at the water barrel and, dressing her in clean clothes, promptly put her on her back again.

The only children who were allowed to crawl about were the sons of two fishermen. Fishermen's wives, compared to the farmer-woodsmen's wives, have a great deal more leisure time. They buy their potatoes and rice with money from the sale of fish. The men send their catch to the market via the bus, so their wives, except when they accompany a catch to the city, have only to care for the house and a pig and are free to watch their children as they crawl about.

In summary, the infancy period is characterized by consistent nurturance. Mothers, grandmothers, and child baby-tenders are helpful and demonstrative in their affection. That they value such behavior is further evidenced by their conscious teaching of young children to copy their behavior. When several mothers and their children are gathered, a mother of a year-old child will coo, "Cute baby" as she strokes a friend's infant's head. She smiles at her child, takes his hand, and repeats the action. A spontaneous response such as this on the part of a year-old child would evoke admiration and voluble praise from the audience. A year and a half old boy became the pride of his mother when he approached all little children with a highly nurturant attitude. He had learned his lesson so well that he considered children of his own age babies because they were smaller than himself. Walking up to them, he would bend down, pat their heads patronizingly, and take their hands to guide them along.

Equally important to the Okinawan parent is a friendly child who is well liked by everyone in the village. A happy, smiling personality is ideal, and it is this wish for the child which leads grandmothers and mothers to perpetuate the custom of burying the afterbirth of a newborn to the accompaniment of laughter and appeals to the spirits to ensure this characteristic. Adults constantly try to get infants to smile by talking and making funny sounds and faces. Even young children approach infants clapping their hands together in an attempt to elicit smiles.

Treatment of children during this initial period discourages expression of self-reliant behavior. As described above, except for rare and very brief intervals during the day, a child is strapped onto someone's back from the time he wakes up in the morning to the time he is put to bed at night. The child is carried about in this fashion from the age of one month until he is almost 2 years old.

❋

❋

❋

Chapter 14

Weaning

When a mother discovers that she is pregnant again, usually about two years after her last delivery, she begins to think of weaning her child. Most mothers nurse the last child until they are about three months into their term, but one mother reported that she nursed her first son until the day before the second was born. Curiously, the determination with which mothers wean contrasts sharply with their very indulgent nurturant handling of the young child, who now encounters a period of withdrawal.

There is a month-long period of what seems, to the observer, indecision and vacillation on the part of the mother. The child is refused the breast, but, if he persists and becomes vociferous in his protests, the mother nurses him. She and others present, however, are no longer solicitous and protective. Derisive comments are directed against him, and, finally, at the end of the month drastic steps are taken. When mothers stated in their interviews that it took four or five days to wean, it usually meant after the final drastic measures were taken.

The child who has slept beside his mother from birth is simply put to sleep with an aunt, grandmother, grandfather, father, or older sibling. In some instances an overnight trip to the city proves extremely convenient for the mother, who leaves the child behind instead of taking him with her as usual. If merely denying the breast does not work, big patches of black paper used for toothaches, backaches, and bruises are pasted on the chest, and the baby is told that the mother is suffering from pain there. "The black paper frightens them and we pretend to wince with pain if the child tries to nurse," report mothers. The black paper proves to be very effective. When this device is not used, another similarly drastic in nature is resorted to. Red pepper or bitter medicine is rubbed into the breast so that the child attempting to suckle is promptly punished with a very unpleasant burning sensation. Frequently a combination of these techniques is applied to wean what a mother terms a very difficult child.

Shaming is a technique that is directed not only to the child but also to the mother. "Ah, shame! Hide the breast," says the mother to the child, or, "Hide, hide, drinking mother's milk!" says she, pulling one end of her blouse flap over the suckling child's head.

On one occasion an old man approached a mother who was nursing her 1-year-old. Immediately the mother pushed the child's head down to acknowledge the elder's presence. The old man, on the other hand, pulled the breast, taking the nipple from the child's mouth. "A big baby! You should not be drinking your mother's milk!" he scolded in a growling voice. As the little girl started to scream and cry, he laughed and, squeezing the breast, squirted milk into her face. The mother laughed with him, then mocked an attack on the old man to pacify the crying child.

Another technique which uses threat to the mother was applied very effectively in the case of a boy who did not respond to red pepper or black paper. The mother described how she tried to fend off the boy one day by simply refusing. As he fussed and cried there was a loud clanging of the pots in the kitchen. The boy stopped crying and looked at the mother who pretended to be very frightened. "Look now! There! It's a big rat coming for your mother's breast, let's hide it, quick, quick!" And with that she buttoned her blouse hurriedly and took the boy in her arms. She laughed as she described how she reminded him thereafter about the rat and how he ran to her and held onto her breasts protectively.

For the child, this whole interim period is a stormy one filled with tantrums, whining, and obstinancy. At no time, however, does the child resort to thumbsucking or other breast substitutes. For older siblings who are his caretakers, this period is a very unpleasant one. Many things displease the child. If his caretaker squats, he screams to have him stand; if he stands, he whines to have him walk. Frequently the sibling caring for him reflects the changing attitude toward the child, and, jiggles him up and down impatiently with a frown and curt comment, "What is it!"

As far as actual nourishment is concerned, weaning should not be so traumatic. Long before weaning commences, when the child is about one, he is given a spoon with which he can learn to feed himself. If families can afford it, they purchase new spoons and special small-sized rice bowls as well as chopsticks for these novices. When the budget is so limited that purchases of new implements are impossible, adult-sized ones are used, and often as not the tablespoon used for cooking and serving proves useful.

At mealtime the entire household sits in the back room, which is next to the kitchen. The head of the family sits nearest to the raised hearth, and the rest of the members form a circle to the left and right of him at a low round or rectangular table. The baby sits on his mother's or grandmother's lap. Usually the mess resulting from this early training period in self-feeding is ignored. The adult holding the novice in his lap occasionally picks up the dropped rice and thrusts small pieces of fish or vegetable into his mouth. Only when he bangs the table excessively with his spoon do his elders mildly chide him. At first the adult holding him will absently reach for the offending arm and slip some food into his mouth. Later they will begin reprimanding him by scowling and glaring at him saying, "Me-me!" (child talk for "eye," meaning "I look at you disapprovingly.") But all this is done in a very gentle way, and often when the novice bursts into tears from fright of the disapproving response, he will be hugged, laughed at, and told, "No, no, no." In this manner the child is taught his early table manners.

As the child approaches the age of 2, the mother begins to praise him for eating without messing but still does not scold him if he fails to do so. He is the center of interest at the table, and his grandparents as well as older siblings encourage him with smiles and expressions of approval. At this time he loses interest in the spoon and is attracted to the chopsticks, which everyone else at the table uses. As he struggles to handle the sticks, the adult holding him sets them in his hand. Holding his hand, with the chopsticks held in the proper position, they guide him a few times; then, as he protests and indicates annoyance at being restrained, they leave him to experiment for himself. This ritual is repeated at each meal, but the child is fed from the adult's chopsticks until he has mastered the technique for himself. The child is not hurried along in his experimentations or learning attempts. The adult praises each fortunate action and quickly slips food into the smiling, open mouth, and the child continues without protest.

Before each meal, people in the village raise their bowls and chopsticks slightly and bow their heads momentarily, murmuring, "Itadakimasu" (a polite signal that the meal is about to be partaken). Similarly, at the conclusion of the meal, the bowl is raised with a brief nod of the head, but this time the expression offered is "Gochiso-sama" (to indicate it was a treat . . . feast). Two very outspoken and good-humored mothers would nurse their young babies, then take the little hands, fold them over each other, palm sides up, gently push the bodies forward, and say, "Gochiso-sama!" Serious training in this aspect of eating etiquette, however, is left until the child is learning to feed himself.

Weaning, then, does not involve a dramatic change in all aspects of the diet of a child, and in many ways may be most traumatic as a withdrawal of the indulgent nurturance of the mother. With the arrival of the new baby, a further step in the emotional weaning takes place. The child is denied his mother's back, for she now has a new baby to tend and eventually to carry.

Treatment of succorance during weaning contrasts sharply with that of the infancy and early childhood period. Unless there is a grandmother or older siblings in the family, this is the time of real deprivation for the child. He is ridiculed, shamed, and punished for demanding to be carried. It is a time marked with temper tantrums, extended periods of crying, and sullenness. Without doubt, this is the most trying stage in the life of a Taira child. Until the words, "You are a big brother or big sister" take effect, he is the most miserable creature alive in the village.

Weaning from the back often occurs at the same time as weaning from the breast; if not it occurs within six months. While this study was being done, eight children between 18 months and 2 years were weaned from the back as well as from the breast. Temper tantrums in which the child would sit down and scream his head off, hurl dirt and stones at his mother, older siblings, or adults who stopped to have a kind word with him or to ridicule him, and incessant whining were symptomatic of the repercussions of abrupt withdrawal. Sulkiness, stubbornness, and tyrannical behavior, however, are short lived. The child finds that although this kind of behavior brought immediate and rewarding responses in the past, he now faces further withdrawal or punishment as a result. The mother impatiently screams back at him to stop crying, and siblings simply leave him behind to keep up with his own pace or drag him along forcibly and uncomfortably, with threats of punishment if he refuses to cooperate. As if to heap more abuse on deprivation, he finds the newly arrived baby the center of the household and taking his place at his mother's breast. He is encouraged and discouraged by turns. "You are an older brother or an older sister. You do not drink your mother's milk now. And see how big you are and such a good child," now encourage visitors. "Come here, hurry!" scream older siblings or mother when he fails to keep in step with them on walks. For about three months the child's bleary eyes, tear-streaked face, and woebegone expression are unquestionable evidences of the most unhappy interval of his childhood.

In an attempt to continue "ruling" the family, he goes into frequent rages. He demands anything and everything in sight, concentrating on the breast and on being carried. Desperately he screams and cries. Finally he sits on the ground and refuses to move. If his caretaker does not pick him up at that point, he will simply lie prone and cry hysterically. Usually adults scream back at him and start walking away, whereupon the child quickly picks himself off the ground and runs after the retreating caretaker. In this way the child's control is broken. Furthermore, he is ridiculed, shamed and scolded for his "babyish" behavior. Only the grandmother, with whom he sleeps at night, responds to his dominating behavior. During the day, he whines, wheedles, and makes numerous demands on her.

Obviously family structure determines in part the severity of the deprivation. The child who lives in a household with a grandmother and perhaps older siblings will have someone to indulge him. The first child of a nuclear family, on the other hand, will not have these supports and thus finds this time severely depriving. The child in a nuclear family with a number of older siblings to support and meet his dependency needs will find the transition difficult but will suffer less deprivation. If there is a grandmother or older siblings in the house, he can still claim some infantile support until he is about 4 or 5 years old. They continue to comfort him when he cries, help him in dressing, bathing, and eating. "Go ask your grandmother or older sibling," instructs the mother when the child requests aid. Or, if she happens not to be busy, she will help him herself.

Mothers in extended households complained that grandparents often intervened on behalf of the child and made disciplining very difficult. The kindergarten teacher remarked on the differences between children who have grandparents and those who do not. "Those who do not have grandparents are much easier to handle, they don't cry so easily and do many things for themselves. My child always runs to grandfather whenever I scold her (there is no grandmother in the house) . . . and we mothers end up by being scolded by the old folks," she remarked.

It is not an uncommon sight to see a child crying and running to his grandmother on being reprimanded by his mother. With carrying, hugging, and venting anger against the mother, the old woman comforts the child. Children soon learn that if no one else complies with their demands, grandmother or grandfather will grant them satisfaction.

Grandmothers often will protect and indulge children of the village other than their own grandchildren. One day as the fieldworker sat talking with two mothers and watching their children play, the question of Okinawans' dislike of children's crying, and of overindulgence of grandmothers arose. The year and a half old boy of one of the women at that instant got one foot over the lower rail of a fence. As the child watched others climbing the fence, he tried to lift the other foot. He howled as he discovered the feat too difficult. The mother made no move to go to the boy's aid but instead sat laughing at the "foolish predicament he got himself into." Suddenly from the house across the way rushed a grandmother. She picked the screaming boy up and examined him for bruises. When she spotted the mother sitting within eye- and earshot, she rushed over with the boy and started to scold her. "What are you doing sitting there! Just looking at your crying child! Why didn't you go over and help him . . . see what the matter was anyway?" And with this she put the child in the mother's lap and gave her a slap on the back. The old woman then went home and hysterically reported the incident to her family. The mother, meanwhile, laughed and told her boy, "Just like your grandmother, can't stand to hear you cry even when you are not hurt!" She then went on to say that both she and her husband ignore the boy's crying in situations where he could help himself, but the boy's grandmother immediately runs to soothe and aid him. Generally it may be said that in extended households, grandmothers tend to prolong the dependence period and discourage independence and responsibility.

The relationship between grandfather and grandchild is more restrained. Although grandfathers may be seen carrying children or doing things for them, there is always a discreet distance between them, the result of early training in respect and deference to male elders. Children do not tease their grandfathers as they do their grandmothers. Older boys, in their late teens, may carry on a superficial joking relationship with their grandfathers, but they must be careful not to show disrespect. The male elders in turn show greater affection for the male child than for the female. When both grandparents are living in the house, the child, whether male or female, is more likely to direct his succorant appeals to grandmother rather than grandfather.*

Mothers, themselves, are often not too consistent in their training for independence. They will feel sorry for the child when he is first weaned and allow him to stay close to them until the birth of the next sibling. On the other hand, they will encourage the little 2-year-olds to imitate older girls and boys, particularly in their baby-tending role. A mother will strap a "doll" on her daughter or son's back. The "dolls" are usually rolled blankets or jackets, for real dolls are expensive and rarely bought in the village. Older children and adults do not fail to comment to a child carrying such a burden. They praise him for being such a good caretaker; they pretend to see the "baby" sleeping and report this to him. If the strapping becomes loose, they call to him and reassemble the "baby" and the pinning. The doll is never played with or manipulated. Thus the 2-year-old gets praised for emulation of the responsible and nurturant behavior expected of older siblings.

Perhaps it is this role training that explains in part the absence of aggression toward the newborn sibling, which might well be expected with such a short interval between weaning from the breast and back and the birth of the next child. The fieldworker did not observe one instance of such hostility. If there is any hostility expressed, it is against the mother in outbursts of temper and against those who ridicule or try to comfort the displaced child. The grandmother's aggressive actions against the mother may encourage the child in this behavior

* Only 4 out of 24 sample children lived in the same house with a grandfather.

as well as comfort him. The support and the nurturance of his older brothers and sisters help in softening the blow and may also function as role model behavior. Even children who had shortly been weaned were observed responding very nurturantly and affectionately toward their newborn siblings. It is difficult to rely wholly on the premise that the greater emphasis placed on the child by his grandmother and the constant attention paid to his status as an older sibling would nullify any aggressive intents. The wistful statement made by a 10-year-old in the form of a wish to be his baby sister because she is loved and indulged by everyone certainly indicates envy as well as the child's clear view of the protection and nurturance given to young infants.

In summary, this period is an unhappy interlude for the Taira child. He is forced to give up the indulgencies of infancy. He is punished for demanding behavior and must now confine dominating behavior to his grandmother. He must shift his dependence from his mother to his grandparents and siblings and finally to his peers. He does this only after a period of stormy protests.

Chapter 15

Kindergarten

It is necessary to define the term "kindergarten child" as it is used in Taira. The group includes all children from weaning until the age of 6. The younger ones are carried to the morning sessions, whereas the older ones go on their own. Kindergarten may thus be likened to a mass baby-sitting session. An adult, scolding an 8-year-old who smears mud all over concrete walls, by calling him a kindergarten child is belittling his intellectual maturity. Finding a newly planted field trampled, an adult will quickly volunteer: "Oh, it must have been the kindergarten children; they don't know any better."

Taira adults feel that children under 6 years "do not have sense." Because of this belief, they are considered uneducable. Serious training and instruction pertinent to the standards and values of Taira society are therefore generally postponed until the child is believed to be endowed with this mysterious capacity to "understand and know." Kindergarten children pilfer from gardens, have temper tantrums, and attack each other physically, but very little enforcement takes place. "They are only children, we can't expect them to know any better," say adults.

In spite of this distinction, there is not a complete laissez-faire handling of the still "senseless" child. On the contrary, the child is subject to a number of restrictions. Adults assiduously attempt to train him to say "Please" and "Thank you," "Good morning," "Good day," and "Good-bye." One mother and her eldest daughter were observed trying to teach the youngest child, an 8-month-old girl, to say "Thank you." A piece of brown sugar was extended, withdrawn, given and taken from the baby until she had twice performed the act indicating "Thank you." Mother and daughter took the baby's hands, folded one over the other, palm side up and raised it, saying at the same time, "Ah-ah," baby talk for "Thank you." The situation was not without fussing and screaming on the part of the young child.

Adults often push the young child's head down to say "Hello," and, if he lets out screams of protest, all laugh hilariously. The child inevitably joins in the laughter and the adults taunt, "Know-nothing." Three and 4-year-olds playing in the dirt along the lanes are picked up and taken to the faucets for a wash down and a scolding, "Dirty! Cat!" Although such enforcement occurs, it is negated when the child starts crying. "Here, here, don't cry; mother was bad" (for scolding you) placates the adult, hugging and cradling the child.

One mother complained that her tomato patch was constantly being raided. When asked whether she knew who was doing it, she said, "Yes, they are kindergarten children." Questioned further as to why she did not scold them or talk to their parents, she said, "It's no use, they are too young to talk to, and besides, I would not like to talk to their mothers because, who knows, my own girls who are under 6 years old may be doing something like that too."

Playing with water is the favorite pastime of young children. During all times of the day a group of them gather at the water tank or at faucets to puddle and "wash." When the water supply was limited, adults would pause in passing by to scream, "Eeyah!" once, then go on, shaking their heads while the children paused only momentarily to look up and then continued with their play.

In the morning, after adults have departed for the fields and mountains and older children have left the village for school, the kindergarten child leaves home with two or three sweet potatoes in his hand to gather with others his age under the great banyan tree at the lower water tank. On rainy days he proceeds to the empty warehouse. There is no compulsion to go; he can join another renegade at the upper tank or on the beach, if he feels inclined to. As the group grows, games of tag, marbles, and rope jumping are started. By the time the kindergarten teacher arrives on the scene, the children have organized themselves into numbers of little groups and games. She carries the big drum from the village office to the banyan tree, and, even before she drums to signal the start of the session, little girls are lining up in front of her. The boys, as if to assert their maleness, play on, disregarding her until she calls sternly to them. Soon a line of boys forms next to the line of girls. As the teacher instructs all to straighten the formations by putting hands onto the shoulders of those in front, boys begin tickling each other and slapping in time to the song of the kindergarteners. The teacher frowns at the boys and tries hard to suppress an amused smile, for the sounds of the childish voices are so incongruent with the brazen attitude. With her drumsticks she reaches over to lightly tap a head, a buttock, and an offending arm. Soon there is order, and she bows slightly, saying, "Good morning, students." The children respond with, "Good morning, teacher," the boys exaggerating the politeness with deep bows and shouting voices. The teacher smiles, then instructs all to stand up straight to sing the kindergarten song. Roughly translated it goes, "We are kindergarteners. . . . We play together well. . . ." There are motions to go with the song, and the girls, with their serious concentration to be perfect in their performance, contrast sharply with the improvisations of the boys. The teacher ignores this and interrupts her singing occasionally to laugh and reach over with the drumstick to restrain a particularly disturbing boy.

When the song is completed, she comments on the excellent singing performance and then goes on to ask how many children remembered to wash their faces and hands before coming to kindergarten. There is an embarrassed twitter among the girls and a few downcast eyes, but the majority proudly raise their hands. As she examines the children, she comments that those who are negligent should be ashamed. From among their ranks a voice calls out, "Teacher, teacher! I didn't wash my face and hands, and I am not ashamed!" A little girl comments, "Fool thing!" The teacher finally hears his insistent cries and has him repeat his information. She tries hard to look disapproving, but laughs spontaneously instead as she lightly whacks his buttocks with the drumstick, saying, "What do you mean, you have not washed your hands and face and you are not ashamed!" She turns to inspect the children one by one, still smiling and commenting on a dirty ear and unkempt fingernails. One or two girls stand fearfully, almost in tears, while others subject themselves to inspection with aplomb. The boys by now are mocking the teacher by inspecting each other and commenting on the failure to meet the test. A few little girls disgustedly say, "These boys, wish we did not have to have them!"

After a brief lecture on cleanliness and orderliness, the teacher asks all to count the number of children present. Immediately there is bedlam as all start to count aloud. She quickly takes a count herself and waits for the first child to answer. As she listens to the shouts, she points out the child who has the right answer and says, "That is right, now let us count together. You, Sachiko, at the head of the line, one, next, Nariko, two. . . ."

Following this counting, the teacher may present a simple lesson in manners. She tells each child down the line to answer with a crisp "hai," then to state his name in full. The oldest girls respond obediently and help their 3- and 4-year-old siblings. As she approaches the line of boys, she frowns and nods. Each boy shouts his answer and name in spite of her protests to the effect that she is not hard of hearing. From somewhere near the end of the line comes a loud voice, "Hai, Taira, Saburo-san!" She quickly moves over to the possessor of the voice and taps the boy on his cleanly shaven head. The noise of the tap is sharp and clear. It induces a hearty round of laughs from all the children. The censured boy stands rubbing his head and smiling at the teacher as she tells him that he knows well one does not use the honorific suffix with one's own name.

The teacher does not attempt to present further lessons. Instead, she asks what kind of games the children would like to play. Shouts of "Race, race!" drown out her instruction to organize into teams. From the back of one 6-year-old girl she unstraps a screaming infant. With one arm cradling the infant, she drums to spur on the runners. From the direction of the village store, a grandmother comes slowly shuffling to join the group. She points out the 2-year-old on the back of his 5-year-old sibling who is starting off on his share of the run. The mother of the screaming infant comes running down the path to relieve the teacher of her burden. She sits nearby on a fence stone to nurse the baby and spur the runners on. Other adult passersby stop briefly to watch the runners, encourage them with shouts to run a little faster, clap their hands to congratulate a winner, and console a loser with advice to try harder the next time.

After the races the children sit and sing songs with the teacher. In their sitting positions they "act out" the songs with motions of their arms. The teacher releases her hold on the drumsticks as a 4-year-old attempts to hold his hand over hers and he continues to beat out the rhythm of the songs. While finishing the last song, she traces lines for the snail game on the sandy ground. A 5-year-old girl, singing the final words of the song, impatiently tugs at her hand. Taking the stick from her hand, the girl erases the teacher's lines and painstakingly tries to make a perfectly round spiral. She stands back to look at the finished "snail," hands the stick back to the teacher, and returns to her place.

The snail game involves teams of two groups of children. One member of a group takes his position in the inner end of the spiral, while the other stands at the outer end. At a signal from the teacher, both run toward each other as fast as possible to cover as much of the length of the line as possible. When they meet, they play a game similar to the American "rock, paper, and scissors." The loser gives up his turn to another member of his group who has to start at the beginning of the opposite end while the winner runs from the point at which the "toss" took place. At the point of meeting, another toss takes place, and the first contestant to reach the opposite end of the spiral wins a point for his team.

Another favorite game of the kindergarten children is "choosing sides." Two mixed groups stand opposite each other and at the signal one group, hand in hand, moves forward, gaily kicking their feet toward the other members of their group. "We will take, Yoshiko," they sing as they swoop in a semicircle to encircle the chosen one, who attempts to run away while her group tries to run interference. Then the next group has a turn. There is no real "winning" in this game, but the children enjoy the united chasing and united defense.

After playing organized games from about 9:30 until 11:15, the children are temporarily disbanded while the teacher goes to prepare the powdered milk, which the children look forward to eagerly. Often the promise of milk serves as a powerful incentive to attend kindergarten for even the most incorrigible renegade. The children all scatter to run home for their small tea cups in which the coveted drink is served. As the teacher approaches the banyan tree from her home, bucket of milk and dipper in hand, she smiles to see the two lines already formed. "Today, we will serve the girls first because the boys were first yesterday," she announces, and immediately there is a shout of disapproval from the boys and a few menacing scowls and upraised arms with clenched fists directed toward the girls. The little girls smile smugly back at the boys, and a few return the hostile threats. The most aggressive boys and girls soon become involved in a tussle, and the teacher serves notice that milk will be withdrawn for the day if order is not restored. The observer feels that in her reprimand to the guilty parties there is slightly more emphasis in the censure of the female child, whether she is really more responsible for the disturbance or not. There is a tone in her voice which implies that "females do not fight; boys, well, boys can't be helped." The children are quick to sense this, particularly the guilty boys, who strut about brashly when the teacher turns her back to start serving the milk.

When all the milk has been served and drunk, the teacher starts the farewell song for the day. Again the song is fairly shouted out, but for a brief moment serenity reigns when the teacher bows her head slightly to say, "Students, good-bye, until tomorrow," to which the students respond, "Teacher, good-bye until tomorrow."

In spite of the competitive content of the games and lessons which the teacher presents to the kindergarten, the observer finds few expressions of achievement motivation and competitive spirit. There is little to indicate that children at this age are interested in winning or excelling. Perhaps the remarks of a 4-year-old boy who reported to his mother on the activities of kindergarten are adequate to summarize the attitude of most kindergarten children. "Mother," he said, "Saburo is first in the races, Tetsuo is second and I am third, always third." To which the mother replied, "If you would try a little harder tomorrow, you may be first." The child looked at the mother questioningly, and the next day he reported that while he thought he tried harder he was again third. The mother again encouraged him, but with a broad smile the child said, "But mother (and the mother explains the expression on the child's face as one of 'You don't understand') I am third! Saburo is first, Tetsuo is second . . . and I am third!" The mother went on to explain to the fieldworker that the whole idea was hilariously funny to the child and the fact that the mother would take the subject so seriously was even funnier.

Furthermore, once the winners are determined, the game is concluded *in toto* as far as the teacher and the children are concerned. There are no congratulatory remarks beyond the clapping of the appreciative audience. No references are made to yesterday's winners or today's possible winners. During performances the teacher may encourage a child here with a positive comment, censure an unruly child there with the stick, but the whole atmosphere of child-teacher interactions is affectionate, indulgent, and relaxed. When a child is being reprimanded, the teacher takes no great pains to conceal her appreciation of the humor involved in the situation, and her affection for the "senselessness" of children at this age is expressed while she is making a token effort.

There are no toys to play with in kindergarten, no way in which to express one's creativeness except in perfecting and improvising song-dance performances. Lacking paper and crayons or paint, children crouch to the ground with the teacher to trace "pictures" in the sandy ground with their fingers or small sticks. The beach provides a rich playground on days when the teacher suffers laryngitis as a result of a cold and is unable to lead songs and direct the play verbally. Collecting shells, learning their names, examining washed up bits of seaweed and fish, exploring exposed stretches of rivers at low tide are real lessons in nature for the kindergarten child as he discovers these things himself and experiments without the direction of formal lessons. If he desires more information about things, he is free to ask the teacher; if he does not, no pressure is put on him to learn and know.

The kindergarten phase is a happy one for the child. Under the direction of the teacher, who may be the mother or sister of one of his peers, he passes the two hours, from 9:30 to 11:30, of the morning, then goes on to play in and around the village for the rest of the day. He runs home only when he is hungry or when it is mealtime. And he hurries back to rejoin his peers for free play for the rest of the day.

Adults put little restriction on children's movement. They are free to occupy any part of the home and run around at will. Before entering the house, everyone takes off his shoes; a rag lies on the ground to wipe dirty feet. Few children spend any length of time indoors, however, during daylight hours. If weather forces them to stay inside, they are found either in one of the front rooms or in the cooking area to the back.

Despite the occasional motor vehicle traffic through the village, adults show little concern, for the kindergarten child has been well exposed to rules of safety in this respect. At the sound of warning horns, children run to the side of the main road and into the yards. The few brazen little boys who dare to chase vehicles and attempt to hang on to the rear bumper are severely reprimanded by those nearby.

A 4-year-old boy who had run out of the way of a lumbering truck stood watching as it rounded the curve and entered the village. Adults waiting for the vehicle to pass chatted idly and scanned the passengers to see if there were any familiar faces. Suddenly the 4-year-old leaned forward and threw a small branch he had in his hand under the tires of the passing truck. At once the driver, passengers, and by-standers screamed. "Fool one!" The passengers waved a warning finger at him, and he was berated by the village adults standing with him. "That was a dangerous thing to do. If you do that another time, you will be taken to the police station!" they threatened. The boy looked down at the ground and nodded to acknowledge his wrongdoing.

On the whole it can be said that children seem to decide for themselves how far they can move around. Underlying the action of most is a dislike of venturing into unfamiliar grounds, and this largely restricts the territory commonly covered. Most children travel in groups of more than two, an aspect of Taira children's behavior to which reference will often be made.

The area of tombs is generally avoided by children, except by those who pass there to walk to the mouth of the Udenaha River or over the narrow, fragile bridge across it. While children do not fear the bodies of the dead, they express a fear of spirits. But during ceremonies for the dead, children accompany adults and participate in the social gatherings in front of tombs following the prayer. When the body of a fisherman was brought up on the shores of Taira after a typhoon, scores of children of kindergarten age roamed to the beach to take a peek beneath the canvas which covered the corpse. The policeman who officiated on the occasion impatiently waved away the kindergarteners, and when the schoolchildren returned in the afternoon, they also had to be warned to stay away.

In the central village itself, few places are closed to children. The village office building, of which only a section is reserved for office space, quite often attracts children. It is a convenient temporary shelter during rain squalls and a cool spot during hot weather. The village headman or his clerk may complain about too much noise and chase a group out, but this does not discourage them from returning soon afterward. The open prayer house, too, is a place for play, and no objections are voiced by adults, including the priestess and her assistants. These buildings are village gathering places, and children, as essential members of the community, have free access to them. The situation is different with regard to the township office and the post office, which children never enter except on special errands.

Children are familiar with dangerous spots, such as steep hills, and show amazing skill in maintaining balance, even when the ground is wet and the dirt is loose. On a picnic hike of a little under 4 miles, kindergarteners ranging from 3 to 6 years scampered across a frail, wide-slatted bridge, up and down over slippery clay paths and over rocky terrain with only a 30 minute stop to eat their lunches. In a group of about 15 children only two 3-year-olds slipped and cried to be carried down unusually steep inclines and over the rickety bridge. None seemed exhausted although many roamed off the paths to forage in the bushes for berries and laurellike flowers from which they sucked nectar.

Journeys outside the village are rare for most children. It is usually the infant still at the breast who is taken on shopping trips to Nago, the nearest town, or to neighboring townships to visit maternal relatives. When whale meat was marketed from the village on weekends, a school age child was taken along to carry the infant because the mother was burdened with her basket of meat, but this was infrequent. Few children have explored their township beyond Miyagi, a village 5 miles to the east of Taira or Gesashi, 4 miles to the southwest.

Children also rummage through the garbage heaps, where they find useful things like tin cans, bottles, and discarded bits of vegetable with which to play house or store.

During the harvest and planting seasons, children accompany adults to the rice paddies and potato fields near the village. Mats are spread out on the dikes and kindergarten children gaily dangle their feet in the oozy mud while "keeping watch over the sleeping infants." Those who whimper to help are given small sheaves of rice to carry to their fathers and older brothers, who thresh them in the dry fields or on the flat grounds bordering the paddies.

Many 4-year-olds are adept at handling knives. As implements like knives, hatchets, pronged hoes, sickles, rakes, and saws were often left within reach of children, it was not unusual for them to use them. Although many cut themselves, adults do not seem to take special care to put them out of reach. Children of kindergarten age are frequently scolded for playing with sharp instruments, but with persistent crying or begging they usually gain reluctant consent.

During all holiday events, children participate without much control from adults. Young children are carried by their mothers as they make the visiting rounds or sit on the floor in the building where the whole village congregates. Toddlers explore the surroundings and, finding themselves in the middle of the dance floor, are gently pushed aside and handed back to their mother. Older children hang around while food is served; then they disappear to play games of their own. During sport events, track meets, wrestling, and at dance performances, children are as interested spectators as their parents. Nobody would think of leaving a child at home on a holiday, and nobody would demand that the child sit quietly through lengthy speeches or ceremonies.

Children learn dances from kindergarten days on, either by watching or by coaching from an older person, a friend, one's older sister, or mother. Sometimes they are called on to perform for adults, or a special children's performance is given under the direction of the kindergarten teacher. Adults enjoy these dances as much as if they were done by grownups. They are amused and delighted if a little girl

wiggles her hips and otherwise makes movements that are not permitted in the classical Okinawan dance.

Kindergarten children are usually asleep by 8:30 in the winter and
9:00 in the summer. They sleep an average 8 hours. Ten o'clock is
considered to be proper bedtime for all people. The village bell is
rung to remind everyone that the day has ended. The entire family
sleeps on the mattresses spread on the floor with wooden pillows. In
winter the heavy quilts are taken down. Children vary in their bedtime. Those who feel tired fall asleep soon after the evening meal.
Often the grandparents lie down with the small children. If children
accompany parents on a visit, they lie down in their father's or
mother's lap, or on the floor to sleep. Since not all adults go to sleep at
10:00, older children may stay up longer, particularly during moonlight nights. Few children take naps except during the summer, when
the heat makes everyone drowsy and slows down work during midday.
Once in a while a young child goes home to lie down for a nap.

The kindergarten child's day has been an active and carefree one.
He is seldom alone. "Do not play alone, go and play with others. If you
play alone, people might think that others dislike you," instruct parents in Taira. Anyone passing a child playing alone would remark,
"How lonely he seems." Furthermore, mothers worry about a child
being alone "because he is more apt to do naughty things or get into
dangerous play."

A 4- or 5-year-old may sometimes find himself being a caretaker, but
generally he is not considered very reliable, and being a "senseless"
individual, he is not held responsible by the village for anything that
might happen to his charges. It is the mother who is held culpable and
is censured in this case.

One mother was severely criticized by her neighbors when she punished her 4-year-old boy for abandoning his 2-year-old sibling. The
children had been sent out to play. When the older boy came home
for supper, he faced an angry mother who berated him for thinking
only of his own pleasure and leaving his little brother on the main
road and to the dangers of passing trucks. She spanked the boy, tied
his hands and legs briefly, and left the crying child behind when she
went to the village store with his younger sibling.

In another case, a grandmother grumbled about the "laxity" and
irresponsibility of the mother. A 5-year-old was carrying her month-
old sibling who was sleeping on the back in a twisted position due to
loose strappings. "Come here! Your mother, where is she . . . how
could she leave this child with you! Almost falling . . . ," the old
woman mumbled as she unstrapped the peacefully sleeping baby and

cuddled it in her arms. The 5-year-old in this case was disappointed at being relieved of his charge, but no doubt would have been happy to be absolved of any blame in the event that the baby had fallen and hurt itself.

Most 4- and 5-year-olds, therefore, find their nurturant efforts frustrated, for they are considered too young to carry their younger siblings. They are told that their necks will hurt, they are not strong enough, and that they will be dwarfs if they started to carry such a heavy burden from such an early age. A sturdy 5-year-old, nevertheless, finds that if he is persistent enough, his mother will allow him to carry his infant sibling for short periods of time with close supervision. It is on these short jaunts that the child basks in the shower of praise and is richly rewarded for his nurturant behavior. Several mothers reported how their 4- and 5-year-olds take pride periodically in mopping up floors, setting tables, and clearing up after a meal. "They don't really do these chores, they help at it, but we let them do it because they like to. And if they don't feel like doing it, we don't say anything," report these mothers.

Frequently kindergarten children accompany their mothers to the potato fields in the afternoons. There they play in and around the plants or "help" their mothers. One 4-year-old girl pointed out with pride that she goes with her mother to their fields to "clean dirt off the potatoes" which her mother has dug before placing them in the basket. Boys of 3 and 5 were observed "assisting" by following adults' instructions to drop the seed potato into the hole at planting time. Generally adults dislike taking children to distant fields, for they beg to be carried near the half-way point. Occasionally a young child who has been on such a trip is toted back in the grandmother's empty carrying basket or in one of the suspended shoulder-yoke baskets of his grandfather.

During the kindergarten period, constant pressure is put on the child to learn sphincter control. The child goes pantless until he attains this goal, which is usually achieved by the age of 4. There is little formal bowel training. Children simply crouch and defecate. Grandmothers or mothers clean up the feces as soon as they see them. Younger children eliminate all over the village, but by 3 they usually restrict themselves to their own yards. When there are grandmothers in the family, bowel training seems to be taken over by them. Not infrequently the old woman can be seen standing over a child in the yard or cleaning up both the child and the yard. She is generally the one who gently coaxes the child to use the outhouse when he is old enough and physically able to straddle the opening over the pit. The practice of allowing the child to eliminate wherever he chooses is necessitated by the structure of the outhouse, a concrete tank covered with a slotted wooden board or loose planks.

Girls may go pantless until they are completely toilet trained but must wear dresses. Since clothing distinguishes those who have been toilet trained, girls proudly compare bright printed panties while boys sport nondescript short pants. Untrained boys wear short shirts or cotton kimonos in summer or flannel ones in the winter.

Accidental wetting of pants and bedwetting do not present much of a problem to parents. Children, however, appear to be embarrassed in such situations. Mothers claim they do not scold or shame the children. It seems to be more of a threat to the child, who realizes his newly gained status and recognizes the accident as infantile behavior. A few children, ranging from 4 to 11, suffer from eneuresis. An 11-year-old, according to the mother, wakes himself and rinses out his wet clothing without waking anyone else. She felt that he was suffering enough and so refrained from saying anything about it.

As seen in the description of the kindergarten session, constant pressure is placed on the child to keep himself clean. A mother seeing a dirty child will laughingly tell him to go sleep with the rats. There is a nasal affliction which is common among children up until the age of 8. Whereas the mother or grandmother tends the infant, sucking the mucus out of his nose, they do not aid the weaned child. During the preschool years, the child, with a well-practiced movement of the arm, smears the discharge over half his face, onto his kimono or shirt sleeves, or wipes it impatiently with his grimy hands. The resulting appearance prompts others to tease, "Dirty faced cat," or to question sneeringly, "Did the rat walk over your face?" It seems, however, that boys are less interested in cleanliness and tolerate dirty and unkemptness for a longer period of time than girls. By the time they are 3 years old, girls are conscious of their appearance, but this may be because they frequently accompany older girls to the wells and rivers when laundering is being done. As it was the usual procedure to end the task with washing heads and delousing, the girls were less soiled than the boys at this age. Five- and 6-year-old girls are praised for going to the well or river to wash their own clothing and heads if they go with older children. If they go alone, they are severely scolded and punished. When the faucets were installed in the village, 4-year-old girls assiduously tended to their grooming, spurred on by the praise and admiration of adults. Girls may be punished, on the other hand, for using too much soap or washing too often. One mother complained that her 8-year-old girl used to be such a stickler for cleanliness and good grooming but was at present always a mess. One of us was present at the home one day when a group of younger girls came by to call the 8-year-old to accompany them to the river to wash their heads. The girl dashed around the house and yard searching for a nonexistent bar of soap and finally was crossly told by her mother that there was none and that she really did not need washing. Nevertheless, the girl gathered some hibiscus leaves, which she tore and mashed to extract a slimy, soapylike substance, and left with the other girls to wash her hair. Regular bathing between the age of 1 and 5 is sporadic. During the summer it is more frequent, for the older children take their younger siblings to the rivers for bathing and swimming.

At irregular intervals during the winter young children are bathed behind the house, near the kitchen doorway, by their mothers or older sisters. A little hot water added to the cold eases their discomfort. During the holiday season mothers and older girls were observed dragging and carrying screaming 2- to 4-year-olds to the bath.

As children get older, exposure of genitals is much less serious in the case of a boy than in the case of a girl. Little girls are told to sit like their mothers with their legs together and are never permitted to expose their genitals. This is true even for those young girls who are still without pants. Occasionally boys tease a little girl by shouting, "Your vagina is showing." Sexual manipulation between children, either homosexually or heterosexually, was never observed. The following observation illustrates the response of an older sibling to her 4-year-old sister, who attempts to imitate a urinating boy.

A group of girls were playing with a ball and K. (4-year-old boy) came along. The girls objected to his presence and began to chase him away. K. then reached in his fly and brought out his penis. He began to urinate, pointing his penis up at the girls. The girls screamed and scattered to get out of reach of the urine. K. chased them briefly, urinating all the while, then stopped to finish. Just as he finished, M. (4-year-old girl), lifting the front of her dress, started to urinate in a standing position. Halfway done, she started to squat, but before she started to squat, her sister saw what was happening and yelled out in an angry voice, "M!" . . . then she went over to give the little girl a slap on the head.

Exhibitionism between boys occurs, and a urinating demonstration among boys with an erection is occasionally seen. Such behavior is not condoned by adults. Girls, however, almost always urinate alone at a short distance from the group. Children are shamed if one refers to their genitals as they approach school age. The separation between boys and girls, which increases with greater age, also discourages mutual play or sex experimentation.

There are few other demands made of the kindergarten child. He can still try to get his way by crying, and his mother willingly continues to give him food when he asks. One parent remarked that it was much easier to meet the child's demands. Observations confirmed this statement. Many adults simply say "Yes" and promise things to children which they promptly forget. Obedience is not expected except for conformity with safety rules. Until shortly before he starts off to school, the child's disobedience tends to be excused. "No, no!" says a mother to her year-old child who may be waving a piece of sugar cane around her head from his perch on her back. The child continues, and the mother pushes the stalk aside each time she is hit. "Know nothing," she says as she rearranges the stalk, to avoid being hit. "Don't mess the yard," screams a grandmother. "Stop puddling in that mud," shouts a father. "Go and bring me the hoe," commands a mother. To all these requests the child may turn a deaf ear, and chances are that he will escape being punished for not complying. Mothers admitted that they allow their children a great deal of leeway concerning obedience.

By instilling fear into the child about the dangers of the well, river and beach, the main road and paddies, adults attempt to enforce the rules of safety. Their attempts are negated, however, when they allow children of this age to play in these areas in the company of older siblings. No one coming across schoolchildren trailed by kindergarteners censures or points out the danger of these places; however, should an adult or older child come upon a group of kindergarten children playing alone at the river or beach, a word of caution or reprimand is sure to be offered.

In a village such as Taira with its closely situated houses, dry thatched roofs, and light wood walls, the danger of fire is very real; therefore the rule with respect to playing with fire and matches is stringently enforced regardless of the age of the child. One mother of a 4-year-old boy found smoke rising from the backyard one day. She went to the source of the smoke and found her 4-year-old busily striking matches and trying to whip up a fire. His 4-year-old companion was scurrying about for pieces of brush and paper with which to feed the fire. "I scolded him roundly, spanked him and tied his hands. I threatened to put him in a basket, then suspend the basket from the rafter posts the next time he played with matches. He was so frightened that I doubt whether he will ever play with matches again."

Aggression in children up to school age is generally tolerated although adults do not approve of such behavior. Because they feel that preschool children change their minds and moods so rapidly, adults do not interfere with their altercations. Parents laughingly explain,

"Play and fight are children's work." As one mother reported, "It is no use. They fight and then before you know it, they are friends again. In Japan, parents often interfere with children's fights, but we here in Okinawa don't believe in doing so. It is much better to let them alone unless they injure one another. The way it is, it would make an adult look like a fool to interfere." Some parents attempt to channel aggression by calling a wrestling match between boys who start arguing. In this way, rock throwing and fighting with sticks are avoided, and the boys can work off their anger, but hitting, biting, and pushing, as well as rock throwing, were observed among children of this age. As the children approach school age and gain facility in language, they resort more and more to verbal aggression; however, as will be discussed later, some physical aggression is carried over in the behavior of boys toward girls. At no time is aggression toward younger children tolerated.

Only after exhaustive questioning can one get parents to admit that they train their children to retaliate. "Never fight; if someone hits you, just walk away, for you (in thus showing your strength to resist) will win the fight; fighting is bad," instruct mothers, according to the mother interview. Informal talks nevertheless revealed that parents disliked it if their children are underdogs all the time.

Boys are expected to be more aggressive than girls, who are, ideally, docile, gentle mannered, kind, reserved, and considerate. In some ways adults seem to train little boys to be aggressive. Beginning in infancy they tease and bully them, holding their arms and restricting them bodily, withdrawing desired objects and pretending to scold and hit. They glean great amusement at the expense of the child if he screams and strikes out in anger. The adult expresses surprise and mock anger. Finally, when he cries, everyone will laugh while the mother retaliates by playfully slapping the aggressor. While most of this kind of teasing is restricted to male infants and young boys, female children are not exempt.

Irritable, pushy children do not exist in Taira. Those who try to get things by "walking over others" do not get far, for children ostracize and avoid them. One 4-year-old, observed over a period of months, altered his methods of acquiring goals from pushing and bullying to socially sanctioned techniques, such as asking, waiting his turn, and sharing. The change was startling. Adults passing on a group of children that included this former bully no longer had to scream warnings at him, and his mother felt she did not have to "look after him" any more. During the time of this study, only the children of a recently arrived fisherman and his wife were ostracized by parents as being far too aggressive and ill behaved. The children played with them but never sought them out and often deserted them en masse when disagreements arose. Taira villagers blamed the parents in this case for being too lax and quarrelsome with each other.

Peer groups are another of the major agents of socialization for the young child. Child interview data intimate that censure by peers arouses much more anxiety than censure by parents. Refusal to comply with the demands of his peers in the face of punishment from his parents for complying raises in the mind of the child, the question, "Will he hate me for not doing what he asks?" Consequently the child chooses the support that is available to him the greater part of his day and calculates the risk of adult censure quite logically.

In despair, one mother described how her 5-year-old boy rushes into the kitchen daily and demands to be given his lunch standing on the dirt floor. Despite his parents' instructions to wash his feet and sit properly on the raised portion of the room to eat, the boy scrambled on all fours and hung his unwashed feet over the edge and shoveled his rice down his throat because "his friends were waiting for him."

As mentioned above, the village as a whole acts as another socialization agent. However, although various members shout warnings in attempts to stop children from disapproved behavior, they do not punish them. Their function seems to be one of casual reminding.

When a child turns 5, he is faced with a dramatic change. Parents now begin to treat him like a school child. New independence and responsibility are expected, and an attempt is made to prepare him for first grade.

✤

✤

✤

Chapter 16

First Grade

Entry into first grade constitutes a change of status for the child in Taira. It means more than just less play time and adjustment to strict routines, for now he is considered capable of knowing what he is doing. He is made to feel and understand that all the things he did as a kindergarten child are reprehensible. His long walks to and from school give him a sense of independence in spite of the fact that classmates and siblings accompany him. The adulation of kindergarteners, who hang on to everything he reports about his new experience, creates in him a sense of superiority which he never fails to emphasize. "You don't know how to write your name . . . see, this is how you write . . ." he fairly sneers at the wondering, admiring 3- to 5-year-olds and scratches the syllabary in the sand with his fingers.

MORNING ROUTINE

The first grader rises early the morning of his first day of school, rushes out to the pot of water standing in the yard just outside the kitchen door, splashes the cold water over his face, brushes his teeth, and re-enters the house. He shivers a bit in the cold, damp morning air as he struggles to wiggle out of the clothing he wore the day before and into an outfit specially designated for school. He remembers that he has a new pair of canvas shoes and runs out to wash his feet. Clothed and shod he peers into the darkness of the house, waiting impatiently for signs of stirring. From around the corner of the house his grandmother mutters as she goes about her task of starting the fire under the soup pot.

While his mother and grandmother prepare breakfast, he sits looking through his new books; a reader, penmanship notebook, an art book, a music book, and a nature science book. His father is the last to rise, and as he goes stumbling out to wash, his mother calls for someone to amuse the baby who has meanwhile awakened. His older siblings, who are still preparing themselves for school, feign surprise as the new first grader moves to the baby. "Yah! Look, the first grader is all ready!" they laugh.

As the morning meal of rice and soup is hurriedly eaten, the adults instruct the first grader not to disgrace himself and to listen to the teacher. Already the cries of other first graders are urging him to be off to school. The older siblings leisurely gather books and lunches together, but the first grader runs out to join his classmates. All question each other excitedly for "forgotten things." Their mothers stand admiringly, but a few are disgruntled. "It is still too early to start. You are not to be in school until a half hour before the beginning bell," they warn. A sympathetic old woman volunteers, "Go, it is a long way and you will take longer to walk," she advises as the little group starts off. One or two anxious mothers accompany the group "to see that they will be all right on their first day of school."

Walking down the road to school, the child smiles proudly as adults comment, "Hah! See how he struts, that big first grader!" He moves to the side of the road as a big lumber truck comes rumbling along and remembers the warnings about the steep bank near the river. The older schoolchildren, walking more leisurely, lag behind and keep a close watch on their younger schoolmates.

SCHOOL ROUTINE

When they reach the schoolyard, the older children run to their rooms to drop their books so that they can play unencumbered, but the first graders cling to their books and lunches. Gathering into little groups according to their villages, they inspect each other at a discreet distance. As the elementary school is situated in the neighboring village of Kawata, which is visited frequently by Taira villagers, the children exchange notes on the extent of their acquaintance with this bigger, older place.

At last the bell is sounded by one of the teachers. Immediately there is a cry to gather. Each class forms two lines in front of their respective teachers. There is bedlam in the first-grade lines as the only boy from one village is directed into the boy's line and separated from the three girls with whom he had walked to school. The principal calls out impatiently for all to straighten the lines. He calls out signals, "Extend arms forward, palms down, fingers barely touching shoulders ahead." Teachers survey the lines and call out to those who mar them. Arms are dropped. Girls are instructed to stand with their arms to their sides and boys with their hands folded behind them, their feet slightly separated.

From his perch on a 3-foot-high concrete block, the principal calls out the signals again, and the whole procedure of lining up is repeated; this time, however, he holds them at attention in a formal position. In crisp tones he calls out, "Pupils, good morning!" Instantly the children respond, "Teacher, good morning," bowing gravely. There is some confusion in the first-grade lines, but the teachers quickly attend to it.

Standing once more in a relaxed position, the students listen thoughtfully to the principal's message. He welcomes the first graders and commends them for their orderliness but warns them to behave like first graders and not kindergarteners. There is an amused ripple from the ranks of the older children. Instantly the principal turns a disapproving eye on them. He continues with a long list of rules concerning classroom behavior as well as safety. Finally the students are dismissed to march to their classrooms. In their eagerness the first graders break ranks and are sternly commanded to stay in line.

The first-grade rooms are located in a temporary, wooden, thatched structure. The sides are open, and the dirt floor is hard and swept clean. As the group enters the room, a wild confusion develops as each child searches for his desk. The children with new desks have little difficulty, as they had played with them for days at home until they were brought to school earlier, but those who have inherited outgrown older siblings' desks and chairs are in sad disarray. Amid the screams and shouts of two roomsful of first graders, two high pitched female adult voices call for attention. Gradually the voices diminish on both sides of the thin wall until only the two teachers' voices are audible.

Roll call is taken after instructions are given as to how one is to answer, ask to be excused, and to sit. After a brief consultation just outside the door, the two teachers organize their groups into two lines, males in one and females in the other. The observer standing just outside the windows of both rooms hears identical speeches on the merits of using the toilets before school starts. Continuing, the teachers locate facilities for the boys and those for the girls. The boys are allowed to go first, then the girls.

Back from the toilets, the little girls obediently march to their places and sit quietly at attention with their hands folded on their desk tops. The boys are noisily making their way to their places. Giggling and pushing each other, they knock into chairs and tables, annoying the girls.

During the first week of school, the teacher's chief task is to make the first graders stop talking and playing in class. On one occasion when numerous appeals, threats, and commands had failed, one exasperated teacher remarked to the fieldworker, "Just like kindergarteners." Then she turned back to the children and called out loudly, "First graders!" "Yes!" shouted the children. "You are first graders, remember that. You are not kindergarten children who don't know anything or don't understand what teacher is saying. For those who cannot understand and do not listen, I will arrange for demotion to kindergarten, understand?" "Yes," replied the children sheepishly.

"Because so much time is taken in orienting the child the first day of school, we can only have a short lesson," explains the teacher apologetically to the observers. The parents nod appreciatively. A printed syllabary hanging to one side of the blackboard becomes the focus of attention as the teacher raps loudly at it with her pointer. She taps at the first figure and reproduces it on the black board, verbalizing it at the same time. She asks the children to imitate her, using their index fingers to follow the order of strokes. With their arms raised, the children reproduce the figure in the air. Five figures of the syllabary are reproduced in this way, and after reading it off several times, time is called. Just before the children are excused, they are told to learn the five figures. This is their first homework assignment.

It is 10:35, and from the direction of the principal's office, the recess bell can be heard. The teacher explains that after 20 minutes of play, the class will again convene for 1 hour and 20 minutes. The boys are allowed outdoors first and the girls follow. There is a flurry of excitement as older siblings appear to question the first graders on the activities of the morning. The children are reminded that this is also the time to go to the toilets.

The older boys and girls are already organized, and games of sham battle, volley ball, hopscotch, and marbles are in progress. The first graders wander in and out of other classrooms, then around the playground, where the various games are being played, until the bell signals them to return to their rooms. They return with a newly gained sense of confidence. The boys, who had been surreptitiously turning their heels in the well-worn marble holes on the dirt floor all morning, move the last row of desks and chairs just a few inches to clear the field for the game. The last few returning girls are given a rude shove to hurry along to their seats, for the boys are eager to start the game. With a great deal of shouting, magnified from the first-grade class next door, the boys begin their game of marbles.

While the teacher checks her records and consults numerous slips of paper on her table, the girls call to each other to check on books, contents of their lunch boxes, and plans for the afternoon. Finally the teacher raps for attention. The boys continue their game of marbles unconcernedly, and the girls scurry back to their seats. There is a wave of giggles as the raps reflect exasperation. "Where are the boys?" questions the annoyed teacher. There is no answer, but the few remaining boys and girls who have heeded their parents' and older siblings' advice to behave all turn their heads toward the back of the room. The teacher carefully picks her way through the closely lined and crowded room. The marble players are so engrossed in their games that they do not see her until she taps one head, then two, saying, "I have called you. Don't you know that recess is over?" Sheepishly a few walk off to their seats. A few smile broadly and run off to evade the pointers. Suddenly a high voice calls out, "The principal! The principal!"

The principal smiles as he approaches the classroom but soon begins to frown. He sees that the boys have been misbehaving. Returning the slight bow of the first-grade teacher, he stands just inside the door, looking over the boys with a disapproving eye. Immediately order and quiet reign.

After a short review of the morning's lesson, the teacher picks up each of the books which has been issued to the children. As she explains the contents of each, she names them and lectures on the care and use of books. She interrupts her talk when she notices two children without books. Because' they had no older siblings and their parents had failed to appear two days before to pay for and receive their textbooks, these children had none. She quickly jots down their names and the name of the village from which they came and assures them that they will receive their books the next day.

At 12:15 the children are sent out to wash their hands and told to eat their lunches. It seems that the most wanted, long awaited event of the school day has finally arrived, for even the best behaved children break into a run before they reach the door. The teacher's plea to walk out of the room goes unheeded.

Those children with elaborate lunches and containers proudly spread their meals out on the desk. Rice balls, a fried egg seasoned with soy sauce and bits of scallion, a touch of soybean paste, and a sliver of fish, packed by the proud mother of a family of some means, are exhibited freely. With some reluctance another lunch, consisting of rice balls, pickled vegetable, and a bit of bean paste, is shown. Those with three or four sweet potatoes and a small handful of vegetable mixed with soybean paste or with sweet potatoes alone slip out bits of food from their closed containers in quick, shy movements. When the girls have satisfied their curiosity as to the contents of each other's lunch boxes, they begin to exchange bits of egg for pickled vegetables, soybean paste with scallion for a sweet potato or some fish. The boys do not exchange portions of their meal but instead eat silently and swiftly.

Standing beside their desks on which lie books and empty lunch boxes, the children face the teacher. "Students, good-bye!" "Teacher, good-bye!" answer the children in unison. Older siblings and the few mothers who accompanied the first graders to school gather. The questioning is rapid and amusing. "What did you do, did you behave, did you eat all of your lunch, did you learn anything?" Without waiting for answers, the older siblings, who have to remain in school until 2:35, begin to recite the rules on walking home and to reiterate the dangers of vehicular traffic, steep banks, snakes, the beach, and the river.

RETURNING HOME

The first graders leave the schoolyard reluctantly, but once they reach the road their footsteps quicken. The boys shuffle along to see how much dust they can raise, for they are not so concerned about their new canvas shoes with rubber soles. The girls stop to dust off theirs at regular intervals with such comments as: "When they get very dirty, we can take them to Yamagawa well and wash them," or, "My mother says I cannot have another pair for a long time because they are so expensive," or, "On rainy days I will walk barefoot to save my shoes."

"Ai! Fool one!" suddenly exclaims one of the girls. The others turn to look at her, then follow her gaze. The boys, who have left the road, thus disregarding one of the cardinal rules of safety, are scurrying about in the bush in search of wild berries. They stand above the road eating their finds on the spot and exaggeratedly mimic the girls' censure on their behavior. There is a rumbling noise, and the girls stop on the side of the road to let the lumber truck pass before continuing their walk. An adult sitting on top of the wood in the back of the truck shouts, "Eh, get out of the bush before the snake strikes!" The girls giggle and watch the shamefaced boys scramble down the embankment to the road. They carry on a lively exchange of stories of snake victims, turning occasionally toward the boys with meaningful glances.

The midday sun is hot. The dry sandy dirt of the road reflects the heat of the sun, and little beads of perspiration run down the flushed faces of the first graders as they plod wearily homeward. Suddenly one of the girls lifts her wide-brimmed straw hat, "Oh, how cool it feels when the wind blows through the hair!" she exclaims. With a sudden burst of enthusiasm, the other girls lift their hats. Surreptitiously the boys imitate the girls.

The junior high school comes into view and with it the bridge over the Fukuji River, and beyond it the land bridge leading directly into the village of Taira. Spirits immediately lift, and the children's pace quickens. As they enter the village, they assume an assured appearance. Their posture is upright and proud. They parade past the main street where mothers, grandmothers, and siblings wait. Each one is greeted by bystanders. Hurrying home, they put their books away carefully, change their clothing to that designated for play. The girls, eager to assume their new status and the responsibilities that go with it, hurriedly sweep and mop the floors of the house. The boys, who are less interested, rush out to play. Those with younger siblings are promptly entrusted with caretaking duties, and mothers and grandmothers go off to the fields.

At 8 o'clock each evening, even before the village bell is sounded for schoolchildren to start studying, the first graders are on their way home from their after-supper play time. On a quiet, still night their voices are loud and clear and their recitations spirited in comparison with those of the older children.

OBEDIENCE TRAINING

Not only in school is new behavior expected of the first grader. He must now be more obedient toward his elders. Adults, however, differentiate between commands for the performance of tasks and rules of safety. The standard, or more specifically the ideal, would be to command unquestioned obedience in both cases. The practice falls far from this mark, for adults lack persistence and consistency in the treatment of task performance. Obedience to rules of safety, however, is enforced with greater consistency.

There is, of course, the disposition of the adult at the time when obedience is expected, which the child learns to discriminate very early. Children are more apt to obey their elders when the latter are tired and irritable after a hard day's work than when they are relaxed. It was interesting to observe children teasing parents and escaping obedience when the adults were relatively relaxed. "Bring me those things there," a parent would command a child. The child would laughingly shout "No," and run away without punishment. For this disobedient act a child would be spanked if the parent were tired and harassed. "If you do not listen well to adults, you will grow up to be a good for nothing, a criminal," warns a mother. But adults in their inconsistent handling fail to impress on children the virtue of obedience.

It is interesting that, in their relationship with adults other than their parents, children are often more obedient. People of special status and authority enjoy greater obedience from children. Teachers and village officials usually find their orders fulfilled. Shortly after the new water faucets were installed throughout the village, children be gan playing with them excessively. Parents scolded, shooed, and threatened the children to no avail. Finally the village headman took steps to enforce the rule forbidding children to play with the faucets. Passing a faucet one day, he came upon a 9-year-old turning the water on and off. "You come to the office later. You know you are not supposed to play there," he said sternly to the boy. Later the boy reported to the office. The clerk, in the absence of the headman, instructed the boy to bring 10 yen and his father to the office. The boy ran home and returned to the office with 10 yen and told the headman, who had returned meanwhile, that his father was not back from the fields, so he was unable to accompany him. The headman's wife, in relating the story to the fieldworker, described how surprised and amused her husband was to find the boy so obedient. Because he had just assumed office a week earlier, he had not expected compliance with his orders.

An obedient child is rewarded with verbal praise and admiration by adults. He is told that he is a good child and that he has "a good head." If he is capable of anticipating commands and quick to comply with hints, parents of other children urge their children to play with him.

TECHNIQUES OF SOCIALIZATION

Although the child has learned many types of preferred behavior by the time he is 6 and has been rewarded and punished for many acts, his entry into first grade is a time of increased discipline and a suitable time to discuss the techniques used by Tairans in socializing their children.

Examination of the different techniques reveals that the most important and reliable of these is the denial or withdrawal of love. There is a good share of physical punishment, threatened food deprivation, and shaming. Praise and rewards are inconsistent and haphazard. Reference to a "God" is common, but there exists no complex system of instructive myths, stories, or prayers. Training in skills is highly informal.

The technique of withdrawal of love or support is a curious double-edged one. If we take the position of the child, we would conclude that he shows a deep sense of confidence in the bond between himself and his mother when he "runs away from the house" after a severe scolding or spanking. He runs away in the belief that he will arouse the anxiety of his mother and recover a love or support, which he has temporarily lost as a result of some transgression. This belief is reinforced when his mother does search for him and takes him home. Furthermore, she serves him the dinner which he was to have been deprived of as punishment. This theme apprears not only in reality but also in the children's projections in the verbal TAT's.

There are, however, threats of withdrawal of love by the mother which evoke great fear of actual loss of love among children. These fears are based on the fact that, in contrast with the foregoing examples, no happy ending can be expected from this threatened punishment. The child is no longer confident that his mother's feelings will soften in the long run when she says to a disobedient son: "We will sell you to the Itoman fisherman." The boy has undoubtedly heard stories of little boys being sold to southern Okinawan fishermen. Such words make him quake with fear, and he promises to obey. Girls, on the other hand, are told they will be "changed for money" and made to live a life of virtual slavery in the house of strangers. These threats have a realistic basis; children know that until recent times boys were sold to fishermen and that girls paid off their parents' debts by working in a house of prostitution or for a farmer who accepted the extra hand instead of money for his debt. At least two persons still live in the village who had such experiences when they were young. One woman can testify to the mistreatment which she received from her masters during indentured labor, and such stories of many cases which are widely known are passed on to children.

At present a new twist has been added to the old theme. Mothers silence a crying child with, "If you don't stop crying, we will give you to the Negroes." Now and then a grandmother will point to a jeep full of soldiers passing by and warn, "Eh! Come home now or we give you to the Americans." The response is usually immediate. The frightened child runs home, clutching onto his grandmother's kimono while the old woman cackles with amusement.

Some mothers threaten their children with running away themselves and leaving them with their fathers. This technique proves just as effective as the former, for a child's concept of support or love with respect to his father is never clearly defined.

One mother, after a particularly exasperating day, thought she would make good her threat to run away from the house. She packed some clothes in a bundle and started off in the direction of the main road. Quickly ducking around houses, she ended up a couple of houses away from her own and sat sipping tea with her neighbor in the back room. Meanwhile, the child, who had been hiding from her mother all day to avoid chores, discovered that her mother was missing. She started to search the village and was told by cooperating adults that they had seen her mother leaving the village with a bundle of her clothes. The child became frantic and ran around the houses. When she finally found her mother, she was crying hysterically. After this, the mother reported that all she had to do was to threaten to run away and her children would obey.

Young children between the ages of 3 and 6 who have frequent temper tantrums are subjected to an experience which is apt to have lasting effects. Since Taira adults like teasing play, when a mother needs the aid of a neighbor to teach the naughty child a lesson, she has no difficulty. A mother who was having trouble keeping her youngest son, aged 4, from whining and crying all the time talked it over with her next-door neighbor. The neighbor, an old grandmother, suggested a plan to put a stop to this nonsense. That night, as the child whimpered and whined to attract his mother's attention, the mother warned, "If you don't stop that, the ghost will come." The boy wailed louder. From between the hedges down the lane, there suddenly came the sound of slow, shuffling footsteps. "There, there! Listen! Here it comes to get you!" called the mother to the boy, who had stopped his whimpering to listen. The boy sat round-eyed watching the clearing in the hedge until suddenly there appeared the apparition. He screamed and ran to his mother, who stifled his cries with, "Eh, now, if you cry, it will take you away, shush!" The fear-paralyzed boy could only nod his head. The next day the old grandmother screamed with laughter as she reported the incident to others in the village. She had worn an old straw hat, a large black coat, and wooden clogs. In the dark she could be distinguished only as a dark, formless "blob" scuffling along. Warnings thereafter to the boy took the form of, "If you cry, we will give you to the ghost."

A heavily bearded, jolly and well-liked octopus fisherman who carries a large bag and talks with a booming voice was requested to walk past another mother's house when her boy became too demanding. "There, see now, here comes the man with the big bag to carry you away because you are so naughty." As the boy huddled up to his mother, she chose that moment to extract from him a promise to be a good child.

All mothers reported that they talk or scold first, and if the child does not respond, they spank. Only two out of the 24 mothers interviewed disclaimed spanking at all. Usually mothers spanked the child with their hand but seven mothers said they use a piece of firewood or bamboo. One mother laughingly reported that she uses "anything she can lay her hands on at that moment" to punish her 10-year-old boy, because if she did not, he would disappear.

Physical punishment is much more frequent than the mothers' interview answers would lead one to believe. In parent-child or sibling interactions observed by us, the scolding or talking was usually simultaneous with a sharp crack on the head with the knuckles or a slap on the buttocks. It is true that a great deal of leeway is generally given the child, but mothers home from a strenuous day in the fields are more apt to scream and spank at the same time.

Tying of hands or feet for several minutes, or as much as an hour, is considered appropriate punishment for those who trespass into forbidden areas or play with taboo things like matches. Sometimes the child's wrists are tied with a piece of rice-straw rope to the front house posts. One 4-year-old boy wandered down to the beach to play with his 3-year-old cousin despite repeated warnings from his mother to the effect that this area was dangerous. Because he disobeyed this rule, he was tied hand and foot. In addition, he was spanked because at the same time he had abandoned his younger brother in the village to go to the beach with his cousin.

Another type of physical punishment, which is often threatened but rarely used, is cauterizing a piece of skin on the neck, back, or hands with moxa. Children in play situations frequently act out giving moxa to a naughty child with a lot of teasing and mock anger. "Come here, you naughty one, we will give you moxa," they scream to each other. A 4-year-old girl was cauterized by her father when she threw her chopsticks on the floor in a fit of anger. Because he believed that food was not only the product of hard labor but also a sort of blessing from the gods, he felt that this very painful enforcement was just.

Grandmothers, in particular, use pinching to enforce some rules of etiquette. If a child forgets and extends his foot toward another person, she will take the flesh of the leg between her thumb and index finger, lift it and with a quick twist administer a punishment which is very painful. After the initial experience, all she has to do is to put her hand in position for pinching to her lips and breathe out audibly as if to say, "I'm warming up!" and the child will correct himself.

Older brothers and sisters are apt to be "quicker with the hand," according to mothers. Generally they agreed that this may be the reason for their effectiveness in handling their younger charges. Frequently all an older sibling needs to do is to raise a warning hand, look disapprovingly, or call with a stern voice when his charge is about to misbehave.

Although mothers do most of the spanking, scolding, and talking, children fear their fathers a great deal more than they do their mothers. Mothers claim that this is true in most cases and offer an explanation: "Maybe this is because the children know well our strength. They don't know their father's strength but believe somehow that it could be much more painful." One could, of course, relate this to the cultural concept of maleness as opposed to femaleness as discussed previously.

Praising and rewarding are techniques that are administered in a very haphazard fashion in Taira. While the child is still very young, up until he is about 2, praise and rewards are lavished on him for almost anything. If he responds to his mother's entreaties to hand over a stick with which he might hurt himself or to bow when meeting someone, he is hugged, kissed, and told over and over, "Good child, good child."

As the child grows older, these extravagant displays of praise and reward lessen. Instead the child may receive promises of something good to eat or a coveted article of clothing in return for some good deed or commendable behavior. Generally the child has to remind his mother many times before he is actually rewarded. By the time the child is of school age he takes these promises with a grain of salt and usually forgets them himself. Only when the children were questioned by us on rewards did it become obvious that parents promised a great deal more than they could ever hope to produce. For, from the plain view of economics, no family could purchase all the goodies pledged for good behavior. Nevertheless, for younger children these promises mean something, and they always look forward to the day when their mothers will color their evening rice red or make them some fried dumplings. Rewarding a child with food proves to be as effective a technique of socialization as threatening to deprive him of food.

Occasionally, in a rare burst of enthusiasm, parents may reward a child to make up for all the empty promises. During one of the rice harvests, a 10-year-old boy worked alongside his parents with as much concentrated effort as any adult. All day he stayed in the fields without running away to join his playmates, as some other boys his age did. At the end of the day his mother prepared some festive food. She colored the rice, and the dinner was a merry one. The man from next door who had helped out that day sat drinking sake with the boy's father. "Here, why don't you have some sake, you did as much work as any of us," offered the father. Neighbor and mother urged the boy on and laughed merrily as the boy sipped a bit of the sake.

Even before he is able to understand the significance of the words, a child in Taira is praised and censured with "good child," and "naughty child." Especially during infancy, mothers will tease babies by gently slapping them and saying over and over with mock anger, "naughty child." When the child is about 5 months and capable of responding to smiles and a disapproving eye, his mother will murmur affectionately, "good child," to encourage and praise. She will open her eyes wide, assume a disapproving look, and scold, "naughty child, naughty child," to discourage and censure him.

A 7-year-old girl was carrying a large winnowing basket filled with potato peelings from her uncle's house to her own. Behind her trailed her 3-year-old brother who was well known for his crying. Suddenly, for no apparent reason, the little boy started to scream and cry for his sister to carry him. The 7-year-old tried to no avail to get the boy to follow her. She shifted the basket to her head, stooped down, and the boy scrambled onto her back. With some effort she stood up, one hand on the basket and the other around the boy's buttocks. The boy clung to his sister's neck and grinned. "Naughty child," murmured the field-worker's companion, a 23-year-old girl. To the 7-year-old girl she then turned and said admiringly, "Good child that you are!"

"Be a good child and do this . . ." instructs an adult to a child. "Naughty child that you are, making your sister cry," one child is chided by another. Praising and punishing by referring to the person of the child as the locus of evaluation are most frequent. The child's action itself, or his response to a particular situation, is usually not evaluated. Very few adults set a standard which is intended as a guide to the child's performance of a task. Therefore children who have completed a task do not ask themselves: "Did I do it well?" or "Did I do it poorly?" If scolded for inadequate performance, the child may echo reprimands by saying to himself: "I was bad to do it that way," or "I was bad to do that" and not: "That was a bad thing to do."

Words which evaluate the person rather than the action are generally applied only to children under 12, although occasionally one hears a young adult say to another teasingly, "Ah, good child," in praise or "naughty child" in response to being tricked.

Of the 24 mothers interviewed, only three reported they did not refer to a deity to control their children's behavior. This deity is always present, always watching and can be depended on to punish the erring child. To the child, this god is a being to be feared, although he is told that not only his misbehavior is observed but also his good behavior. "The divine being is everywhere. When you are alone and do something bad, you might think that no one knows about it, but the god knows and he will punish you," warn mothers. This technique of control is very useful in Taira, where the children spend a great deal of time without adult supervision.

In the houses of first sons there are family altars upon which memorial tablets of family ancestors are placed. Children from these homes are told that their deceased grandfathers are now divine beings and are watching them. In one such family a 4-year-old boy was told by his mother that, since he was naughty, the divine ancestor would punish him. She pointed to the picture of his deceased grandfather and the memorial tablets on the altar. The little boy looked up to the shelf and then to his mother. "That's only a memorial tablet," he said sneeringly.

Not many children are as skeptical as this 4-year-old. A hunchbacked storyteller sometimes comes to Taira. This man is a preacher for a Japanese sect which combines Japanese nationalistic teachings and concepts of proper conduct and healthful living with a belief in a supreme being. He appeals to children and reinforces the belief in the sanctioning power of God. Occasionally a Christian missionary visits the village, and the children look forward to his bible readings, which also reinforce the belief. In addition, the children of the two Christian families help to caution others, warning of divine omnipresence and knowledge.

Shaming and ridicule as techniques of socialization are used to a fair extent. An older child's shortcomings may frequently be compared with a younger's achievements. However, some form of verbal lashing is usually accompanied by direct physical punishment, whether it be merely a slap on the buttocks, a crack on the head, or a whipping.

Several mothers summed up their flexibility in handling their children by saying, "I have so many children and it seems that each one is different in some way. For some children one thing works and for others you have to think of other ways. You cannot scold this one because she is so sensitive. The boy you cannot scold because he would get so angry he would not be able to understand the wrong he did."

Nevertheless, it is important to point out that mothers in Taira, for the most part, do not spend as much time with their children as do their counterparts in a more wealthy village. Their work day is long and strenuous. They return home exhausted and impatient. During the long rainy spells, when work in the fields and mountains is impossible, mothers have to stay home more often than usual. At such times they manifest an irritability with respect to the numerous demands children make upon them that can be attributed partly to the fact that their long absence from home during a normal work day makes them forget children's cravings for attention; the loss of income during bad weather just increases their impatience.

TRAINING IN SKILLS

There are no complex systems of training in skills. Adults rely heavily on observation and imitation on the part of children; they seldom "teach" them to do things systematically. Parents were surprised and amused when questions such as "How do you teach children to transplant rice, harvest rice, or otherwise help in the fields?" were put to them. "We don't teach them; why they just learn by themselves," was the usual answer.

Children learn by observing and experimenting. Whatever adults are doing, children are present to watch their activities and overhear their conversations. Although parents do not seem to make any special efforts to have a child attend a function so that he might learn adult ways, they take their children to the fields, parties, public meetings, and rituals long before they consider them ready to absorb any learning.

In the fields, children play among rows of vegetables. When a parent, grandparent, or older sibling stops for a rest to have a cup of tea, the little ones pick up a hoe and attempt to imitate their elders. While rice is being transplanted, throngs of children sit on the dikes in the paddies, dangling their legs in the mud. They intently watch adults transplanting and weeding the paddies. Gradually they edge down into the mud to stamp with their bare feet in the ooze as they have seen adults do, until a warning shout arrests their educational water play. During the harvest season, groups of children carry mats out to the paddies and watch infants who need to be near their mothers for their feedings. While the infants sleep, the older children walk along the dikes, watching the work that is going on and clamoring to be of some help. Even a little child of kindergarten age stands by gloomily until an adult laughingly hands him a small bundle of rice sheaves to carry over to the threshing machine. By the time the child is 8, he has learned enough by watching to attempt cutting and tying small bundles of rice sheaves.

After the harvest, rice straw can be found in great quantities around the village. Some of the best straw is preserved to be made into rope. If there are rainy days, men will sit and twist the rice straw into rope, while 8- and 9-year-olds sit and watch. In a few days rope games and swings are in evidence everywhere. Little 4- and 5-year-olds stand by watching the older children, and soon they pick up stray bits of straw and twist them to no avail. A younger sibling whines as her movements fail to form rope. Her brother quietly takes the straw and without a word demonstrates the deft movement. She watches and tries again when her brother hands it back to her. She is unsuccessful. As she starts to whine again, her brother picks up a length of finished rope and gives it to her. She runs happily toward the playground, waving her rope in the air.

Although young children are not taken to the mountains, they can sit in the village afternoons and watch adults sawing, splitting, and working the bamboo rings used in tying faggots. Boys do not go into the mountains to cut firewood until they are about 10 years old, girls until they are 12, although they may have begged their parents for several years to let them help with cutting and hauling of firewood. But as long as they are still too young for mountain work, they try to use the cutting tools. Tools are left within reach of children so that opportunities for experimentation are almost unlimited. Only their size and weight deter the youngest children. A 2-year-old girl was seen imitating her mother by attempting to whittle off pieces of bamboo with a large 12-inch blade bushknife. A teen-age girl working nearby passed the little girl several times without saying anything. The little girl's father also worked nearby but, like everyone else, was too absorbed in his work to notice his daughter. Finally her mother looked up from where she worked, noticed the huge knife in the girl's hand, and saying in a loud, angry voice, "Why do you carry this, fool?" took the knife away.

Other small children pick up hoes and forks to try them in the yard or in the pigsty. Sickles and knives are used expertly by many 6-year-olds. Bandaged fingers and numerous little scars are evidences of learning and experimentation. Occasionally an adult will say to a 9- or 10-year-old. "Hold the sickle this way so you won't get hurt," but more often than not the child has already learned by himself. One 4½-year-old boy shinnied up the side of a feed box to get a sickle. There was no adult around to peel the long stalk of sugar cane he had been given, so, with expert strokes and handling of the razor-sharp tool, he shaved off the thick, hard skin. By the time his mother arrived on the scene, the child was busily chewing and sucking on a considerable length of the peeled cane. The mother was asked who had taught him to use the sickle, and she was at a loss for a reply. "I don't know! He must have watched us and learned by himself by trying it out!" she said.

Little girls watch their mothers cooking and doing other household work. By watching and asking questions they learn how to light a fire and when to extinguish it to cook a perfect pot of rice. They crouch with their mothers, who are busy with the laundry. It is not long before they pick up a small article of clothing and start soaping, rubbing, and rinsing just as their mothers do.

IMITATIVE PLAY

What children observe in adult life is frequently acted out in play situations. Before a girl is old enough to do all the household work alone, she can always find satisfaction for her desire to learn an adult role by imitating it in play. Playing "house" is an activity which all girls from the age of 4 to 9 or 10 indulge in constantly at all times of the year. The beach, yard, empty lots of uninhabited houses serve as locales for this play. Girls "act out" the role of the mother in the household in crude but painstakingly constructed "houses." Boys rarely join in this kind of play, which is not surprising, since males have very little to do with the day-to-day happenings in the house. Invariably there is a play store at which all the "mothers" converge to buy their daily supply of bean paste, noodles, or dried seaweed, but the most concentrated locale of activity is in the "kitchen of the houses." Here elaborate meals are prepared with sand for rice, grass roots for noodles, chopped up pandanus leaves for greens, and hibiscus for red coloring. Frequently during the vegatable season discarded carrots, cabbage, and turnips are used in make-believe dishes. Shells of all kinds serve as plates and bowls and sticks, into which cockle shells are wedged, as spoons. Bamboo pieces serve as chopsticks. An 8-year-old may spirit the real kitchen knife to chop up the "vege-tables" if the house-playing takes place near the home. Deftly she slices the carrots and turnips and mixes them into water. If she is fortunate, she and her playmates can use a temporarily uninhabited house in which the hearth stones and wire hung pot still remain, in which case she need not construct one out of small rocks. As she orders her "children" to go to the store for rice or salt, she jogs up and down to quiet the infant that fusses on her back. Finally the meal is ready to serve. The "family" without "father" all sit in the kitchen on their knees as she busily serves the various concoctions. There is a disturbance "outside," and she turns to look as one of her children shouts, "Oh, look what the boys have done!" "Fools! Go away!" she shouts as she runs after the laughing boys who have taken a few of the bamboo sticks that delineate the house walls. "We are robbers, robbers come to rob you!" shout the boys as they run away. After the "meal" is finished and while she is washing dishes, she hears someone calling, "Good day." She hurries forward and finds a 5-year-old boy standing at her door. "Want anything today?" asks the boy, unloading a bunch of grass. The "mother" smiles, amused, then she sorts through the grass and hands over some "money" and thanks the "peddler" as he goes on his way to the next house. The peddler turns out to be the same boy who was the robber. When his peddling bores him, he returns to robbing and finally leaves the scene entirely. As the "mother" returns to her kitchen to work toward her next meal, one of the "children" returns "home" with a bunch of flowers. As it is the fifteenth day of the lunar calendar, she hurries to put them into a small empty bottle. She places the flowers on the family shrine shelf along with "incense sticks." This done, she goes out to the "store."

After "marketing," preparations for the next meal begin; but as she works intently, there is a call. "Good day, excuse me . . ." calls a voice in high-pitched tones which are the essence of politeness and femininity. As visitor greets hostess, the etiquette of adult life is enacted with much finesse. "Tea" is brought in by an "older daughter," and polite talk is exchanged over it. Sitting quite properly on her knees, the hostess "bows her guest" out of the house as she has seen her own mother do countless times. And so it goes, day after day, little girls who never seem to tire of imitating their mothers until they approach the age of 10, when unmistakable signs of self-consciousness affect their behavior.

In other respects, too, the play situation is often turned into a valuable learning experience. These are play activities which are in reality beginnings of assuming responsibility toward economic contributions for the home. A kindergarten child follows his older sibling or mother down to the beach. The trip is made to collect seaweed for the pigs, but the young child just goes along for recreation. The young child, unable to discriminate between the different kinds of seaweed, drops into the basket whatever she picks up. She "plays at collecting seaweed." The older sibling silently picks out the undesirable variety and discards it. Many times the portion the younger child has collected is rejected, but before long, through observation and imitation, he learns to pick the particular kind of seaweed which is desired. The older sibling in many cases does not attempt to instruct by saying, "Pick the green, smooth kind that grows thick on the rocks." Instead, he may just nod or shake his head if the younger brings forward some for approval or disapproval.

On one gathering trip in the fields, a 10-year-old boy devised a game which actually was instructive in nature. He was accompanied by his two male cousins, 3 and 4 years old. They were hunting for a type of milkweed which was to be fed to the chickens. The older boy would walk on a way, carefully searching the ground, stop when he spotted some milkweed, and call to the younger ones, "There are some near the spot on which I am standing!" The two little boys would rush over and start examining the area carefully. With a shout one of them would drop to the ground, uproot the plant, and bear it triumphantly to his older cousin. Then the game would continue with the older boy saying, "Good child."

The relatively few restrictions placed on the young child are an important basis for learning. By being able to participate freely, children learn what is going on in their village from day to day. Since adults feel that children do not really understand what they are talking about, conversations are free and not couched in mysterious terms. The 10-year-old who is fully aware of the subject under discussion may giggle uncontrollably, but none of the adults pays attention to this. An adult giving a blow-by-blow description of the latest quarrel may even turn to a 10- or 12-year-old child for aid when he forgets a detail.

SOCIALIZING AGENTS

In general, mothers continue to be the chief socializers, with the grandmother and older siblings second in importance. From the child's point of view, the mother retains the closest bond with him throughout childhood, regardless of the grandmother's prominent role in his early life, and even though, in terms of time which the child spends with others, the mother gradually assumes less importance. It is to the mother that children turn for ultimate support, and to her is delegated the responsibility of child rearing in Taira. Although much of the responsibility for caring for children is given to siblings, the villagers hold the mother alone culpable, should a child deviate in his behavior.

The mother's ultimate responsibility for the child is not reduced by the fact that she may spend a great part of the day away from her offspring. Mothers frequently ask other children for the whereabouts of a son or a daughter. Just as the fieldworkers soon learned in what places they would be most likely to find a particular child, so mothers on the whole are aware of their children's favorite play areas. A mother occasionally inquires about her children's whereabouts without showing anxiety. The fieldworkers were once asked by a mother if they knew where her daughter, who carried an infant sister, was playing. They had not come home for the noon meal, which was unusual. The mother, however, did not search extensively, for the fieldworkers, a little later, noticed the two girls peacefully playing "house" in someone's backyard. They stayed for a good part of the afternoon, and the mother probably continued her usual activities.

The relationship between child and mother remains warm and intimate throughout childhood. A mother may be scolding, impatient, angry, or punishing, but to the child she is the center of the family.

In households lucky enough to have a grandmother, she becomes recognized as the person who is at home if something is wanted or if help and comfort are needed. It is interesting to note, however, that the relationship between children and their grandmothers changes decidedly as the child starts off to school. As if to assert his independence, the 6-year-old begins teasing his grandmother unmercifully. In response to her suggestions, the child laughingly refuses and pretends to run away or often pretends not to hear her. As she screams all kinds of invectives at the child, he giggles hilariously while running ahead. But he does not run as fast as he could. He allows grandmother to catch him, and there is much laughter from both of them. Actually the child rarely fails to comply with her wishes. Two girls, aged 8 and 10, and a young female adult aged 23 often saved a part of their share of goodies, given them by the fieldworker, for their grandmothers. The 10-year-old lavished further indulgence by taking her grandmother's clothing along with her own to launder on washdays.

Boys seem to differ somewhat in this respect. Although there is a very affectionate bond between them and their grandmothers, there is less of this kind of indulgent pattern. They will, however, at the time they start off to school, meet with the old women's demands to run errands, carry tools, and share with her the care of their younger siblings.

Because the society feels that child rearing is "women's work," males have little or nothing to do with the handling of children until the time when decisions as to their future have to be made. There need be only one qualification made with reference to the above statement and it is that fathers may serve as "last resort" disciplinary figures in the case of male children. For many mothers the most effective threat is to "report to father."

The father is not so forbidding a figure for the child of preschool age. Many observations show that fathers tolerate the kindergarten child who begs to be taken to parties or on laps while visiting with neighbors; however, an older sibling or mother was called as soon as the child began to fuss or show signs of fatigue. The kindergarten child often directs his succorant appeals to his father, particularly in a nuclear family, but the father in turn directs the child to his mother. Should there be any discrepancy in thought as to the way a child should be handled in specific problematic situations, the mother will defer out of custom to the father. Such cases, however, are rare, for men, in informal interviews, generally felt that "women knew better" where children's affairs were concerned. Only one out of 24 fathers believed that he should "train and discipline" the male child and his wife should confine herself to the female children.

The school age child seems to have more fear of his father. "If father is at home," reports one mother, "the children returning from school go about quietly putting their books away, clean the yard, study, then take the younger siblings out with them to play." She added, "If father is not at home, they drop their books on the porch and run out to play, leaving the house and yard in a mess and me with the babies!"

It should be noted that fathers spend less time at home than any other member of the household. Men who work in the mountains go out after the morning meal and often do not return until dark. A man returning at noon seldom sees the children, who are out playing or at school. Since there are no weekly rest days, children see their fathers mainly in the evening after dark or on holidays. But even then fathers spend their time visiting around or entertaining neighbors and relatives in their own homes. Contact with father is, therefore, only sporadic and is not affected by a special desire on the part of fathers to spend time with children. It should be noted, however, that the mere presence of the father in the house has an effect on the child's behavior.

Next to mother and grandmother, older children in the household are very important child-rearing agents. These are mostly the older siblings, but occasionally a young unmarried aunt or uncle who lives with the family looks after a child. Children between the ages of 5 and 12 take care of younger children; adolescent siblings or aunts do so to a much lesser extent. The obvious reason for this is that in the distribution of duties in the home, the care of a younger child falls to those who are not otherwise burdened with such responsibilities as exacting studies during junior high school or economic activities in fields and mountains, which begin after graduation from school. While adults, except for the old folks, are in fields and mountains, a young child spends much of his time on the back of the older kindergarten or school age sibling or as a toddler in tow of an older one.

Both boys and girls are charged with taking care of a younger child, but when possible, boys try to escape this duty by "making a deal" with their sisters. Girls are therefore more frequently seen caring for younger siblings, but when there are no older girls in the family, a boy must assume this responsibility. Often the novelty of having a tiny infant in the home, for instance, the first girl among several boys, causes older boys to volunteer carrying the infant. On the whole, boys are as reliable caretakers as girls.

The child on the back finds his child caretaker far less sympathetic and indulgent than mother and grandmother and more literal in applying rules of behavior. Young caretakers, under threat of severe punishment, tend to enforce stringently the rules of safety and permit a much narrower latitude with respect to obedience. Boys are inclined to give expression to their impatience with a younger one more easily than girls; nevertheless, a child taking care of a younger one knows that nurturant behavior toward his charge is a virtue, and failure to show indulgence and sympathy toward the little one is subject to severe reprimands by adults. Although a small child may be left with an older sibling for several hours, the older one knows where to find his mother or grandmother in case of a crisis. When the child on the back cannot be put to sleep by the rocking of his carrier, and indicates persistent discomfort by continued crying, the child caretaker knows that the limits of his competence have been reached.

There is some evidence that the young child-rearing agent follows the example of adults in deferring and giving preferential treatment to males. A young caretaker often seems to show more tolerance toward a little boy charge than toward a girl.

☘
☘
☘

Chapter 17

Latency

By the time a child finishes first grade, he has achieved full membership in the elementary schoolchildren group (age 8 to 12). His associations with kindergarten children are no longer as prevailing or intimate as they used to be. He has little in common with them, but since he still takes care of a younger sibling or plays games to which younger children are attracted, there remain frequent contacts between the age groups. The transition between first grade and second grade is in no way as pronounced as the drastic status change from kindergarten to first grade. Children feel it mostly as a gradually increasing pressure toward assuming more responsibility. The transition which takes place at a ritual level * during the early latency period, however, is not reflected in their daily life.

CHORES AND RESPONSIBILITY TRAINING

Although adults say that the elementary school student is still very much of a child who only toward the latter part of this stage can seriously be expected to contribute much to the tasks and duties in home and village; the children, in fact, do some work daily. Already in first grade, responsibility is approached with seriousness, girls exceeding boys in this respect. Children beg tasks, and obeying the school's directive to "help one's parents" seems to become the prime objective of first graders who have just proudly attained their new status. They plead to accompany their older siblings who, with much less zeal than the younger ones, gather giant African snails after a heavy rainfall, hunt frogs, dragon flies, and grasshoppers, or wash potatoes for the pigs. Adults consider some of these chores play. Although frogs and grasshoppers are fed to the chickens, and minnows and seaweed are added to the pig swill, nevertheless, adults would not seriously label expeditions to collect these responsible. On the other hand, if there is no available feed, as occasionally happens, the child will be scolded and berated for "thinking only of play and not of the hungry chickens." Four- to 6-year-olds are discouraged from these foraging trips, for the danger of snake bites and accidents in the paddies and on the beach is very real. Accompanied by older siblings, however, they, too, may participate.

Some tasks, such as fetching water and feeding the pigs, cutting grass for the horse and goats, washing down the horse, and gathering faggots for the hearth, are still too difficult for the first grade child. But some of them are attempted, at least by assisting older children.

Once the child starts off to school, he is made aware that he is

* In case of death, the child who has reached the age of 8 must be given a full-fledged burial, since in afterlife he becomes a buddha from now on. We had no indication that children were aware of this.

no longer one of the "senseless" by praise for responsible behavior. After a relatively brief period of fairly consistent verbal reward, however, parents assume the attitude that chores are not voluntary but compulsory, and they begin to pay more attention to omissions—reminding, threatening, and checking up on the children. Although punishment is rather inconsistent, a child of 9 or 10 finds his chances of escape very slim if he fails to be responsible. But if he carries out some task spontaneously, he may find himself amply rewarded. Children generally seem to react more responsibly to school duties than home duties. This may be because teachers utilize peer group control to elicit responsible behavior by rewarding and punishing in the presence of the whole class.

Girls assume caretaking of younger siblings earlier and more seriously than boys. A 6-year-old girl may be entrusted with a younger sibling during a whole afternoon. A boy, looking after a younger child, is more likely to abandon or neglect his charge than a girl. In families where there are several children of caretaking age, each is assigned a specific share of time. Inevitably the girls find themselves with the greater or entire portion of this duty, for the boys either simply refuse or evade assuming their share. This shirking of duty is partly supported by the mother, who, by her failure to enforce assignments, displays passive acceptance or approval of the boys' actions. A girl, however, invites censure not only from her mother but also from other girls for similar actions.

The most important factor in differential treatment of boys and girls is a cultural one. Most of the tasks or chores assigned to both are, on the adult level, performed by women. Cutting and gathering grass for horses and goats is men's work, but mopping floors, tidying and sweeping yards, fetching water, cleaning lamps, caring for chickens and pigs, and looking after children are all tasks that are "women's work" in Taira village. It is therefore evident that girls derive some intrinsic reward from them, whereas they may be intrinsically punishing for boys.

The difference in parental expectation with regard to children's increasing responsibility with age is reflected in these selected answers from interviews with mothers to the question: "What chores do you expect your child to do?" The mother of a 5-year-old boy said: "His work is to play down at the beach. But his older brother (11 years) is such a big help. . . . If I am busy, I may ask him to feed the pig, watch H. (baby sister) or clean the house, fetch water or wood, and Y. will do it without saying anything." The mother of another 11-year-old boy put it this way: "His job is to see to it that the chickens are fed every day. This is a job for him, and if he does not do it he gets a scolding. . . . My husband does not believe in letting him play too much, and so K. has to take his job seriously—otherwise he will get scolded by his father."

The mother of a 5-year-old girl, after mentioning that she washes her own hair and shoes, said, "The day before yesterday she helped me clean up the place after eating, and so I told her that if she would do this two times a day for me, she would get one yen. She said she would do it, but I don't expect much because she is still too young." The girl's father is a township employee, but giving one yen as reward is also done by other mothers when they feel that a child has done more than can be expected at that age. Of her 8-year-old daughter, a mother says that "she can mop the floor, fetch water, watch the baby, and serve rice into the bowls at dinner time. But she does not really have to do these chores regularly. Whenever I am busy I ask her to do these things for me," and she adds that her girl very seldom refuses, but "if she should not do what I ask her to, I scold her." And the mother of another girl, 7 years old, tells that her daughter's job is "to mop the floor every day. She knows that it is her responsibility and she has to do it. When she does not do it, she gets a scolding until she does it. She usually does it, though, without too much difficulty." Only a few mothers point to care of younger siblings as one of the duties. It simply seems to be taken for granted so much that it is not even mentioned.

An enthusiastic 6-year-old girl surprised her mother one day, not long after starting school, by taking the family laundry to the well and washing it. When she returned, she hung out the wash carefully to dry, then went out to join her playmates. The mother came home, examined the wash, and found that it still needed a good scrubbing. Quickly gathering the once-washed clothing, she hurried down to the well. She chose a path around the back of the house to avoid being seen by her daughter. That night she thanked the girl for doing the wash and helping her so much. "I did not want to hurt her feelings by telling her that the washing was still dirty. It was fortunate that she did not see me going down to wash it the second time, for if she did, she would have been discouraged and might never have done it again," reported the mother.

The community as a whole also makes some demands on these children of school age. Several times a year they sweep the streets and adjoining public areas in the morning, before they leave for school.

Children seem to have an ambivalent attitude toward greater pressures in responsibility training. When tasks are mere routine, interfering with playing and other favorite activities, they are not always discharged with enthusiasm. We have already referred to this in the discussion of child care. On the other hand, there are many expressions, starting actually at kindergarten level, which reveal identification with adolescents and adults.

To the question, "What would you like to do best?" there were such answers from boys as: "I would like to go to the mountains and earn money" (7 years), and "I would like to plant rice" (8 years); and from girls: "I would like to cook, and I would like to transplant rice" (7 years), "I would like to cook rice and soup" (7 years with a wide grin), and "I would like to teach other children calculation if they need help, and take the place of the teacher" (10 years), adding, "Then I can punish boys who bully girls, too."

We learned something more about the identification with older children and young adults, and perhaps a feeling of envy of their status, from answers to questions such as, "Who would you like to be most if you could be changed into anybody by magic?" and "What age would you be if you could be any age?" And, in answering, children also revealed something of their needs, motivations, and goals. A 7-year-old boy stated that, "I would like to be 15 years old, then I can go deep places to swim . . . and then I can go to the mountains and earn money and buy rice, noodles, and help father and mother." He then expressed achievement motivation in his answer: "I would like to become a scholar on plant roots. Then I will know why trees wither and die. I want to save them because otherwise people cannot make money. Then I will be happy and feel good." Although this boy's father is not one of the prominent village leaders, he seems here to express the feeling which, we believe, explains much of the responsible behavior in village leaders. We also see a desire for independence in the answer of a 10-year-old boy, "I would like to be 20 years, then I can go and do work on my own," and nurturance with an almost sanctimonious overtone, perhaps linked to hidden anxiety about aggression, in this response to the magic man query, "I would have him change me into a big, big person. Then I can go and hit anyone who bullies little persons . . . I can look all over the whole village and catch all bad persons and talk to them . . . I can make them all good." This answer, which expresses, again, achievement desires was given by an 8-year-old boy, "I would like to be 16 years old because then studies will be easier and I can wrestle like the *seinen* (young adults)," followed by "Make me into a township official because they have 'good heads' (are intelligent) and they help the people. Then I can buy food with the money I earn and save some for a new house." Other boys, too, revealed a combination of achievement-oriented and nurturant needs and over-all qualities of responsibilities which characterize leading adults in the community. But there are also dependence needs in boys, such as expressed by this 10-year-old, "I would like to be the youngest baby . . . because everyone loves that one" (in response to the question "If you could be anybody in the family, would you like to be a father, mother, or a baby?") But the answer of a 7-year-old boy: "I want to become father, then I can raise potatoes, rice, and other things" is more typical of the Taira boys in this age group than the previous one.

Girls were quite explicit in their nurturance motivation, but they, too, used answers to reveal other desires. "I'd like to be mother so that I can cook and go to the mountains" (6 years); "I'd like to be 14, then I can fetch water and go on real errands and get money," and by the same girl (7 years), "I would like to be like K. (a girl of about 20 years) because she is an employee of the *yakuba*" (the servant and general helper at the township office). Several girls wanted to be the age of their older sisters, because, as one (6 years) said, "She buys things for me and she can buy all kinds of things for me." A real strong dependence need and a reflection of economic privations in her family, one of the poorest in Taira, was revealed by a 6-year-old girl: "I would like to become someone else's big sister . . . like the Kawata (village) rice miller's . . . because then I can eat a lot of rice," followed by, "I'd like to be Y. (baby sister) because she is small . . . because she is not even in kindergarten and father and mother will take me around with them."

Taira female adults' roles are apparently well recognized and correctly interpreted by these girls, and identifications are appropriate. Only one girl referred to a professional career, open to women, but her answer reveals very practical reasons for achievement striving: "I'd like to be a teacher, then I can do well in studies and do all kinds of studying . . . can earn money. With that money I can buy clothes and hats. And when anyone speaks *hōgen* (dialect), I can hit them with a stick and give them all failing grades. . . . Then I'll feel good!"

SCHOOL ROUTINE

The school, like the parents, expects more of the 8- to 12-year-olds. The session is longer, lasting until 4:00 in the afternoon and reducing the time for play, tasks, and homework. A child now spends eight hours in the school setting. Children are more matter of fact about school. They are slower to start in the morning, often playing a quick game before leaving the village.

The school schedule is more routine but still flexible. Some of the students do homework and prepare for classes while others play until the morning school assembly. From their arrival at school until they leave in the afternoon, children are under moderate supervision but by no means subject to severe discipline from teachers. The atmosphere at school is friendly, almost intimate at times. There is nothing to frighten children, and none shows signs of unhappiness or anxiety as a result of being away from home and in another village. Most of the boys behave with little restraint, while girls are much quieter and more responsive to occasional reprimands from teachers seeking order. The classroom atmosphere remains informal through all grades. Children call out answers spontaneously or make loud comments. Some move freely in the room during lessons or leave for the toilet.

The informality in the classroom is also illustrated by the occasional presence of a teacher's young child, who is taken along by his parent if no one else can take care of him at home. Off and on, a student's younger sibling also sneaks in and sits quietly through a lesson. Physical privations are not considered conducive to learning. A child who was not able to sleep adequately during the previous night will not be disturbed if he falls asleep in the middle of a lesson. If on a hot, sultry summer day children are sluggish and fail to respond, teachers ease up on their demands accordingly.

The classroom situation may best be described by an excerpt from field notes, taken in the fifth grade.

The male teacher is going through some new expressions from their reading material with the class. Children have their notebooks open and, as the teacher explains, take notes. Boys interrupt by shouting something, a suggestion, an answer, a question. The teacher hardly disciplines at all. He does not object to interruptions. K. (10-year-old boy), who apparently tries to show off as observers enter, shouts as "crowded streetcars" are discussed by teacher, "What would happen if somebody beats you in a streetcar?" Teacher seems to disregard this question. A little later K. interrupts two more times. Boys and girls sit apart; about one third of the students are girls. The girls hardly speak up during the session. In discussing the word "insensitive" one boy shouts as example, "I am insensitve to teacher's scolding." This is accepted as an example. There are three boys who have taken their shirts off on this warm morning. Two put them on as observers enter. After a while the teacher says, "Let's close this now." Somebody shouts, "Arithmetic," and the teacher concurs. He then gives addition problems by rapidly calling for summations, 6 plus 13 plus 8, etc., about six to eight numbers. The difficulty lies in the speed. Boys raise their arms quickly, shout "Hai (yes)," and when called on give the answer. If it is wrong, as the first ones usually are, the teacher just points to somebody else and says, "Hai," until someone gives the right answer, sometimes not until six students have tried or until he has finally supplied the answer himself. Girls participate less than boys. K. raises his hand twice and twice has the wrong answer. The class then works at problems from the arithmetic book. One problem is read out loud by a girl. Students get up only when called on by the teacher to read from the book or from the blackboard. While listening to the problem which the girl reads in the customary high sing-song reading voice, the class is quiet although not everyone concentrates. The girls seem much more attentive. The teacher puts high numbers, ten million, etc., on the blackboard, which students have to read off. There is no embarrassment about giving the wrong answer. There is no kidding or teasing by others. If one can't do it, another student volunteers information, but there seems to be a lot of pressure provided by the constant raising of hands, which prompts even those who don't know to raise theirs and to make a blind guess.

Teachers, after the second grade, are always men. Their relationship with the students is informal, warm, and friendly. Living in the village, they are also a part of the social world in which the student lives. On the whole, they seem to have little difficulty in maintaining control over the class. Girls hardly ever present disciplinary problems. The disciplinary techniques used by the teachers are milder than parental ones. They rarely use physical punishments, limiting them to nose pulling or a light slap; they employ more commonly mild forms of ridicule and ostracism, such as standing a child in the corner. A child who continues to misbehave is scolded roundly in the presence of the class.

In interviews, teachers stressed the fact that they preferred reasoning and explaining to ridicule and shaming. They stated the belief that it was better to ask a child why he had done wrong or discuss his misbehavior with him. They also voiced a preference for positive measures, such as praise. Rewards, not unlike the silver and gold stars given in some American schools, are sometimes used.

Rote learning is one of the most important techniques of instruction, but teachers are striving to introduce new methods. A new lesson is first read by the teacher from beginning to end. Afterward the teacher discusses the topic and questions with students. Then various minor aspects of the reading are dealt with, and finally the teacher asks if there is anything that is not understood. After all points have been clarified, the new words used in that day's lesson are written on the blackboard. While writing, the teacher reads the characters aloud. The set sequence of strokes for each character is left for later practice. When all the new words are presented in this fashion, the teacher takes the textbook and reads the passage once more to the class. This is a signal for all to pay close attention to their books. After this, everyone reads to himself. For about five minutes bedlam reigns as discordant voices fill the room. Then a child is called by the teacher to read aloud to the class. The teacher may call on several other students before instructing all to read to themselves once more, for the last time. Should a child make a mistake in reading, the teacher rereads the passage. The lesson is concluded with instructions to study it that night. In the evening, back in the village, one is apt to hear loud, sing-song recitations of the lesson being read and reread. Elementary school students delight in verbal presentations of whole lessons on the spur of the moment during playtime. Talent programs are popular among 8-year-old girls, and at village or school celebrations in which students partic-ipate it would be unusual not to have at least two readings offered. The school also promotes oratorical contests in which long, memorized stories are recited. Rote memory, discussion with association of facts, familiar with the unfamiliar, and imitation, therefore, are utilized in these learning situations.

Although reading allows for a certain amount of creativity in timing and flexibility of inflection patterns, penmanship is a rigidly controlled practice. As the teacher writes the character on the board, strictest attention is required. There is precise order in the sequence of strokes, as well as unquestionable direction as to how to form them. The teacher counts 1, 2, 3, 4, 5, while writing the strokes on the board. All children have to raise their right hand and with the index finger write the character in the air, following the teacher's example. The character is written in this fashion four or five times before the whole class is sent to the blackboard in small groups to demonstrate that they have understood the principles of writing the character. This process uses imitation, repetition, and memorization in learning.

In the area of physical science and social studies, teachers are work-ing toward practical applications of concepts which were presented in the lessons. Resources are very limited and so is the potential of actual experiences which a northern Okinawan village child is likely to have during childhood. Applying concepts mostly remains in the realm of discussion in class and not as much has been done to widen the circle as educators wish. Excursions to the beach and mountains help somewhat to integrate and bring into association those facts, mentioned in textbooks, which have reference to the local environment. But how should a Taira child grasp, for instance, the meaning of a large hotel in the city, where travelers can stop, engage one or several rooms, have meals served either individually in the room or at the restaurant? The little Taira guesthouse, run by the doctor and to all extent and purposes a private home, is hardly an adequate model.

Learning by doing is, on the whole, an innovation in the school program. To find out what fifth- and sixth-grade students might have learned in the home by actually doing things, the school circulated a questionnaire which covered such items as: "Have you ever tried to make a simple telescope? Did you ever watch a plant grow from the time of seeding and make a scientific description of its progress? Did you ever build a small toolshed or other small structure by yourself? Did you ever make regular observations of weather phenomena and keep a record?" From our previous description of typical activities of Taira children, it is not surprising to learn that very few of these or similar experiences appeared on the answers in the affirmative.

At school, participation and learning by doing are found at least in a few instances. The basic skills of cleaning rooms by using rag and mop, as well as maintaining school grounds by cutting grass with a sickle and weeding with a hoe, may not have high educational value, but they carry over to the home and village situation. In the upper grades, students begin to do some gardening at school. Later in junior high school they work in their own small garden plots on the school grounds and in school rice paddies under teachers' supervision. Unlike the home situation, where learning also takes place by observation and doing, the teacher lays a foundation for solid knowledge by instruction and demonstration of proper techniques and by criticism of errors. The large number of students who work under guidance of a single teacher limits the practical value of such learning situations. It is evident, however, that there is an important qualitative difference between learning in the home situation and at school. Where the child does a chore in the village without trying to meet standards set by parents, the school child finds that the teacher scrutinizes his work carefully, judges, compares, picks and chooses the best performers from the poorer ones, and imposes standards for all to meet or excel. If a standard is set at all in the village, adults tend to either overlook it or simply fail to enforce it.

ATTITUDES TOWARD ACHIEVEMENT

Observations revealed there is a contrast between home and school setting in attitudes and treatment of achievement-oriented and competitive behavior. The classroom situation tends to breed competition. Eager attempts to answer questions and to get the teacher's attention by raising a hand and calling out suggest competitive spirit. There was little we observed in the village which seemed to bolster competitive behavior, except for some games and occasional wrestling and athletic practice. Parents discourage boasting in children and in our presence gave little evidence of fostering achievement. However, if we now let the children speak, and then mothers (unfortunately fathers were not interviewed), one might get a different impression of the parental role in achievement training.

In answer to the questions "How do you feel about doing something better than anybody else your age? When you're not the best, do you ever practice so you can do better?" the six boys in our sample agreed that they would like to be first. One 8-year-old answered: "Yes, I would like to be better than my classmates." "But," he adds, "no, I don't practice or study when I am not first . . . only sometimes. If I am last I would practice and study because I would get scolded by the teacher and my parents. . . . I would be ashamed because others would laugh at me. But if I am average, I won't do anything, I don't care." Two other boys implied that they would do little to improve their position if they were in the middle, or as one put it, "I do want to be first, but I don't do anything about it . . . not much anyway."

The fear of being scolded by parents is also expressed in the answer of four others in this group. Shame was mentioned only by one other boy, but among those who fear scolding at home were two whose parents are exceptional in stressing good performance at home and driving their children toward higher standards. They responded, as one might expect, with expressions such as: "Yes, I would rather be better than all others. . . . In the middle? No, I would rather be first." Only one of these two mentioned fear of scolding as an incentive.

Girls' answers differed slightly in the somewhat greater emphasis on performing well and making determined efforts in this direction. One reply, "Yes, I will study hard to become first. Even if I am in the middle, I will try hard so I can be first. I don't feel good being last," was essentially echoed by the five other school girls in the sample of six. Three, however, thought they would not mind too much being in the middle, though they would prefer to be first, and all seemed to agree with the statement of one that "it is no fun to be the last," and as one said (and the five others put it in similar words): "If I am last, then I would work very hard. . . ." Wanting to be first and doing something about it are, of course, two different things. But the intentions of girls to work hard are stated more strongly than those of boys. And, significantly, none of the girls mentioned fear of scolding or shame.

Does this mean, then, that girls have a higher achievement motivation than boys or are they just more responsible and obedient? At home girls have been trained to assume responsibilities at a slightly earlier age than boys and have, therefore, been exposed to more rewards for doing their tasks than boys—and also more scolding for doing them only in part or not at all, although the fear of being scolded is not verbalized. It may be that the desire to do well becomes an end in itself for these girls because of previous satisfactions and, possibly, fears. And to some extent, observations of classroom behavior and participation in studies by girls would bear out that they make more determined efforts to perform well in class.

Mothers' replies to the questions "How satisfied do you feel about how well your child does things?" and more specifically, "What do you do if he does poorly?" were uniformly positive expressions. All mothers said that they were not only happy with good performances but also actually encouraged good work at school by giving praise and often special food. Only three mothers of the boys who expected scolding said that they would do so if their child did poorly; two others suggested that they would talk to the child to make him perform better. The mother of one boy who stated that he would feel ashamed to be placed at the bottom said that if her boy "should do something poorly I would tell him that he has become 'useless, hopeless.'" None of the girls' mothers, on the other hand, indicated that she would scold their daughter for poor performance.

Mothers, then, though purporting to be interested in their children's performance in school, are actually using, at best, mild pressures toward satisfactory accomplishments. Although they genuinely feel a pleasure over good performance, we wonder if they express and enforce their sentiments toward children consistently enough, emphatically enough, and frequently enough to make an impact. We rather think that mothers who work in fields and mountains all day have little time and patience to concern themselves seriously with their children's schoolwork; and since their daily work is hardly an inspiration to the child to improve his scholastic activities, there is some question in how much parental influence is relevant here. Moreover, mothers are always under pressure from the teachers to urge their children to work hard and would respond to such an obviously weighted question in this fashion to a person to whom they accorded the same polite title in address, which they use toward their children's teacher, *sensei* (i.e., the interviewer). It is also a fact that teachers have had difficulty getting parents to cooperate in training their children to establish regular home-study habits. Fathers, on the whole, seem even less consistent than mothers in supervising schoolwork. The fact that most boys would like to be first but make concentrated efforts to improve their work only if they perform poorly suggests that parental discipline usually does not function effectively until the child has become severely delinquent in his studies.

If the desire to cheat in school is a measure of competitive pressures, it is interesting to note that there are few such attempts made during the examinations which are held several times a year. Nothing is done to separate the students whose tables are close together. Although the teacher remains in the classroom, he hardly proctors. However, the teacher commented that if a student is suspected of unfair practices, others will report his activities to the teacher.

An impetus for the development of competitive spirit has been the introduction by the Japanese of athletic sports into the schools. The communities participate annually in athletic competitions sponsored by the schools and other agencies outside the community. One is impressed, however, that these events have taken on the Okinawan pattern of a pleasant gathering where the older people can enjoy being sociable while the young men and women engage in various sports.

A few students have regularly assigned tasks and offices. Each class selects a monitor. The method of selection varies, depending on the teacher. In one class, candidates were taken at large, and the student who received the largest number of votes took the office. The monitor is responsible for the class during the morning assembly and during athletics. He sees to it that students line up and remain orderly. In the classroom he has the same responsibility, but we observed nobody discharging his duties in an authoritarian way, although some older boys liked to show their strength in a playful manner of bullying.

Girls could theoretically become monitors, and several votes were cast for them, but it is doubtful whether a girl could be effective among boys, who might be unwilling to follow her lead.

The student Red Cross chapter has a chairman in each class who makes collections under the teacher's supervision. Somebody may volunteer for such jobs as pouring milk during lunch hour. Other assignments have to do with the upkeep of a few school-owned goats, which must be fed during vacations too.

RELATIONSHIP BETWEEN BOYS AND GIRLS

Differential status of boys and girls, emphasized in child rearing from the time of birth, is clearly defined in many details of school routine. Boys are sent out first when it is time to leave the classroom; they head the lines; and they are given first turn at the equipment. The promotion of sex equality under American supervision of the educational program has met with only mild acceptance in the classes we observed. Although separate seating is avoided under post-World War II rules, a separation continues in fact.

Girls remain on the receiving end of much teasing and horseplay, more, it seems than one observes during associations of boys and girls in the village, which we will describe later. Teachers, like parents, expect the boys to bully girls. In one classroom, for instance, we heard girls complaining that the (male) teacher favors boys by calling on them all the time. This may encourage the dominant, aggressive behavior of boys toward girls. Hardly a day passes in school without several girls crying as a result of assertive boy tyrants. Occasionally a boy is punished, but usually he escapes with distinct pride showing on his face. Recently teachers have resorted to ridiculing those who intimidate girls, but the tradition is so strong that even if bullying on the school ground is curbed, there is a great deal on the road to and from school. Only the most vociferous girls do not seem to be cowed by such boisterous demonstrations and may adequately match in verbal repartee those boys who try to put them into place as well as provoking more teasing and aggression. To illustrate attempts at bullying in the classroom, we quote from an observation record (second grade).

. . . Whenever one of the girls gives a wrong answer, S. (Taira boy) shouts loudly; he is one of the most vociferous in class . . . Class then starts reading aloud, each pupil for himself . . . A boy in front of K. (Taira girl) turns around, hits her for putting her feet against his chair. K. continues kicking his chair, doesn't seem to mind boy's slapping. He is not really angry, smiles. Looking at observer, he stops slapping, pinches K. under desk.

In none of the observations on schoolchildren's behavior were there examples of Taira boys protecting Taira girls from the teasing of other village boys. Instead, during school hours boys tend to team up with boys, girls with girls, although among each sex there is a tendency to associate more with those from one's own community.

PLAY GROUPS

By midafternoon all schoolchildren have returned to the village, and play groups can be found in various locations. The more stringent requirements of school seem to have been forgotten. Hardly any students of the elementary grades study immediately after returning from school. For two hours or more they spend their time with peers and younger siblings.

A play group comes into existence when two or three children meet in the street, in the corner of a garden, or in one of the many open lots and village places. All Taira children are intimate with each other because since early childhood they have been together during the greater part of the day. There is always a slight preference for one another among some children, either because they are close neighbors of the same age and sex, or cousins, or otherwise congenial. Although these special friends associate more often with each other, they do not exclude other children who want to join their play. Once children attend school, association on the basis of sex and age becomes more distinct. The total composition of a play group, however, shifts from day to day and from locality to locality. If one group starts a game, other children in the vicinity soon join to form a new group to play a similar game nearby. Such a play group numbers from two to ten or more children. Most frequently, however, groups are composed of children of the same sex and similar age.

There are several factors, however, which lead to variations in this general pattern. If a school age girl is the oldest in the family and has several younger siblings to care for in the afternoons, she will frequently be found in the company of younger girls and hence younger boys, the play groups being more mixed at the younger ages.

M., a 7-year-old girl with three younger sisters (ages 4, 3, and 1) was usually found in a large play group composed primarily of younger children. In contrast, S, a girl of 10, was found in smaller groups. Although she has no younger siblings to tend, she frequently cares for a neighbor's child. Her charge, however is an infant who is still carried and does not yet seek the companionship of other young children. S. interacts less frequently with other children not only because of the age of her charge but also because she is older and hence has more duties at home and in the fields. Furthermore, she was born in 1945, a year when few other children were born in Taira.

K., a boy of 10, is similar to S. in that he has no siblings who need care, the youngest being a 4-year-old girl who can travel with her 7-year-old sisters. In contrast to S., however, he interacts more frequently with children of the same sex and same age or older.

AGGRESSION BETWEEN BOYS AND GIRLS

We have touched on the relationship between latency boys and girls in school, implying that the bullying which occurs frequently there is less frequent in the community. Boys sometimes tease girls but less persistently and less often than in school. Since boys associate mostly with boys, and girls with girls, and since contact between sexes of the same age takes place mostly in group names, it is seldom unfriendly. Teasing among boys, and teasing among girls, is common, so that it would be hard to maintain that between the sexes it is more frequent. Once in a while, boys will keep girls out of their game, or girls will be annoyed when boys join them. Some of the kindergarten boys, as we have mentioned, like to be the disruptive agents in peaceful house-keeping games by assuming the role of a robber or wild animal. Two 5-year-old boys who generally enjoy teasing others select girls as their target now and then. Sometimes girls are just the objects of general-ized aggression, as in the case presented below. M., a 5-year-old boy, first interacts aggressively with another 5-year-old boy, F., and then turns on a girl.

F. has picked up a piece of pink paper and comes carrying it up to M. He holds it against his chest, stands in front of M. and smiles. "Give it to me," says M., and F. just stands smiling, mumbling, "Hmmm, maybe," but does not hand it over. M. rushes him and attacks him with his fist and takes it away from F. who stands laughing. M. rolls the paper around the end of his stick and walks down the lane toward a group of kindergarten-age girls.

Y. (4-year-old girl) comes walking up from behind M. M. turns around and raises his stick menacingly at her. Y. looks anxious, maneuvers quickly around him to join the girls, and laughs nervously. M. smiles smugly, walks back to boys.

When provoked, the girls will often fight back, and they score equally well, especially in verbal aggression. At other times they accept the teasing good humoredly, as seen in the incident of a 10-year-old girl, S., who is teased by a 7-year-old boy, A., described in the following protocol.

S. is guarding the can in a can-kicking game. A. (who has been playing a rubber band game with another boy nearby) looks up, smiles, goes running over to the can and kicks it with his foot, yelling, "Safe!" S., whose back is turned to him, jumps, turns around and sees him. "You're not playing this game," she laughs and A. laughs and goes back to his own game.

RELATIONSHIP BETWEEN SIBLINGS

As mentioned above, the caretaking responsibility and the tendency of younger siblings who are beyond the carrying stage to follow an older brother or sister keep siblings together a great deal during play. When an older brother has to mind a younger sister, he is usually not overly protective. He seldom defends his sister from teasing and sometimes is more aggressive to her than he would be to others if she interferes with his activities. There is, of course, a great deal of variation due to personality. A 5-year-old boy (one of the teasers described above) sometimes pushes his younger sister, and she runs home crying. An 11-year-old boy, on the other hand, when he takes care of his four younger sisters, or some of them, is usually quite protective and nurturant.

A record of the behavior of T. (7 years), his younger sister H. (4 years), and other boys illustrates a brother-sister interaction. T. and other boys have made a swing and T. is sitting on it while A. (5-year-old boy) and H. try to get turns:

A. tries to get him off the swing. H., who expected that her turn would come next, whines "nisan (older brother)" and while A. tries to get T. off, she keeps on whining, "This should be enough." T. replies, "This is A.'s turn"; while A. is trying to get on the swing, H. starts crying and goes into the house. Apparently an adult is in the house. T. follows, voices are heard, but not understood. T. returns after a moment and helps F. (another boy) push A. on the swing. H. seems to have stopped crying. We heard no adult scolding T. or talking to H. H. returns, no longer crying. She stands behind T. whose body swings back and forth while pushing A. H. pushes T.'s swinging body to help him. A., F., and H. sing in rhythm, "one, two, three," etc. After song is finished, H. says, "Brother, it is my turn next." T. ignores her, but A. gets off the swing and H. sits on it. H. swings by herself. T. orders A. to help him push the door next to the swing open. A. complies. T.'s mother passes, does not say anything. After the door has been opened (and more room gained), T. and A. push H.

The presence in the background of T.'s mother may have something to do with his change in behavior toward H., or it may be that he wants her to wait her turn and do it his way. T. is very much in control of this situation, even among the boys. The swing is constructed on the edge of his parents' house. But T., on another occasion, when his aunt asked him to wash her daughter's (T.'s 4-year-old cousin) feet after she had waded in the muddy paddies, complied agreeably and was quite nurturant and indulgent with the younger girl. With H., too, he is more cordial at other times. Perhaps what bothers him, and other boys of his age, is the interference of younger sisters with boys' play.

To sum up, between boys and girls of school age there is not a very close relationship, each sex being quite strongly oriented toward members of its own group. Brothers and sisters, on the whole, fall into this pattern, except that the succorance-nurturance relationship between younger and older continues, though moderately. Although separation of sexes is found in the kindergarten pattern, it is more pronounced in latency, since the activities of peers are more and more differentiated by sex.

RELATIONSHIP TO PEERS

We asked the children a question in an attempt to measure how they would resolve the conflict between having to do a chore and the call of friends to join in play. All boys (in the group of six) agreed that they would do their work first, four mentioning fear of being scolded. One boy worried about what his friends might think if he does not join them soon: "Will they not think badly of me?" adding, "Sometimes I have gone out without finishing my work and then I would worry about getting scolded. It's 'bad,' but if my friend persists, I would go and join him without doing my work." And another admitted, "If mother and father are not at home, I would go and play without finishing my work, but then I would worry about getting scolded."

Strangely enough, five of the girls answered that they would do their work first, but if their father and mother are not home, they would go out and play; at least four say so, while the fifth boldly says, "If friends come and call me when I am doing my chores, I will go and play without finishing," but this girl, coming from a poor family, is less secure than others and more anxious to be a part of the group. Several girls mentioned the fear of being scolded. Only one, the sixth, replied,

"I would do my work first and then go out to play, whether my parents are home or not."

The mother of a younger boy reported that he is so anxious to rejoin his playmates that he barely gives himself time enough at home to eat his meal. It is our feeling that it is not just the desire to play which pulls children away from assigned tasks, but the urge to be with peers. The attitude of mothers encourages play groups. They tell their children: "Do not play alone; go and play with others. If you play alone, people might think that others dislike you." As one mother put it: "It looks so lonely when (my child) is playing alone." Only one mother, whose child-rearing methods in general deviate from those of others because she and her husband set high achievement goals and standards for their child, said that she would like to have her son play alone occasionally. In this way she hoped he would devote some time to educational activities. It is interesting, however, that several mothers mentioned the names of other children whom they considered unsuitable playmates for their child, either because they were too bossy, or too aggressive, or had otherwise undesirable qualities in their judgment. If, however, there is selectivity among children on the basis of their parents' desires, we were not aware of it.

Peers assume increasing importance as socializing agents as they grow older. Schoolchildren of the same age watch and control each other so that there is hardly need for interference by adults. Older children remind younger ones who neglect a crying young sibling to attend to his needs. Failure to respond to the succorant pleas of a younger sibling meets with disapproval. Peers rarely interfere directly with the activities of others, but do so by remarks to each other, and by other indirect means through which they achieve compliance or conformity. There are some obvious situations when outright commands by an older child are needed. For example, when a 3-year-old girl pulled the plug from the concrete water tank and was immediately frightened by the stream of water pouring out, a 6-year-old girl nearby called, "Close it," and watched as the little one hurriedly put the plug into place. Hardly ever does one hear children taking the role of an adult in trying to demand conformity from peers with rules set by adults. Only the boy mentioned earlier, whose parents make determined efforts to train him toward responsibility and achievement, occasionally attempts to correct the behavior of peers by talking like an adult. He always does it in a quasi-nurturant, responsible manner, perhaps because he strongly identifies with his father, one of the village leaders.

Parents do not like their children to become "leaders." Almost all of them disapprove of dominance in their children: "It would be terrible if my child would tell this child and that child to do one thing or another and they would get into trouble." The fear expressed here, and in similar statements, is obviously that leadership entails responsibility in case anything goes wrong, and parents do not like to be put in a position where they or their children could be blamed.

The Western observer, perhaps, is most impressed with the ability of children to manage their own affairs. Fights occur, and disagreements crop up frequently, but almost without exception these matters are settled within the group and without dramatic scenes in which adults become involved. There are no violent fights or quarrels which break up groups and cause prolonged hostile feelings among children. Least of all did we find bullying and harassing of younger children by the older ones, although younger ones are often assigned inferior roles in play by the older children.

ACTIVITIES AND GAMES

In part, at least, the tone among these play groups is set by the surprising variety of activities that children engage in during the year, innumerable games which come and go in cycles, but which have a village-wide appeal while they last. All of them are played with a minimum of equipment and a maximum of inventiveness and enthusiasm. There are few toys which parents can buy their children, and fewer still which they make for them. This situation is met with great ingenuity. Children use any objects available to them—discarded household equipment, empty cans, boxes, or whatever they pick and gather from trees, bushes, and the ground. Round stones, peas, and seeds serve as marbles; an empty carton becomes a truck or boat. Wooden sticks, bamboo, an old bicycle wheel without a tire find some use. Suddenly one day children run about with helmets made of cabbage leaves, swinging little pistols made of a piece of bamboo, or a stick as a dagger. Girls gather shells and gravel on the beach and carry pieces in their dress pockets. In the absence of dolls, girls have a younger sibling to act the part of "child" in realistic play. Babies, however, are never used in such games.

Boys and girls like to play games of skill. Girls often pull out five stones from their pockets and play a kind of jacks. There are also many versions of ball games in which one girl performs several stunts with a ball while she sings a song. If she makes a mistake, another one gets a turn. Teams of two girls at a time play hopscotch, which they call "parent and child game."

An old Okinawan game of skill on which early Western visitors have frequently commented is still a favorite of Taira boys, 5 years and older. This is a kind of stick-ball game. A wedge-shaped piece of wood 3 to 4 inches long and pointed at both ends and a striking club are used. Children whittle both with a knife. This game is played by two or more players, and the purpose of the game is to get the wedge into a hole. The game requires a series of skillful manipulations of the wedge with the club. It is an exciting and competitive game. Each player is awarded a number of points for certain accomplished acts. Although boys are quite absorbed in this play, there are rarely any arguments and the winner hardly ever shows any pride. Winners seldom boast after a game, and the observers felt that the satisfaction is really gained from the performance, not from having outdone others. Girls sometimes join the boys in this game.

Boys and girls, separately or together, play other games of skill, such as marbles. A challenge by another starts a game, sometimes of two, sometimes of four or six players. There is usually a kibitzer around who becomes involved. Two games in the same play area are not uncommon while spectators wait for their turns later.

Equally common, but frowned on by the school because of its gambling character, is a rubber band game. The store uses rubber bands to tie packages. Children carry a number on their arms. Each player chips in a number of bands, two or more, depending on agreement. The person who starts the game is decided on by tossing. The rubber bands are put on a cement or wooden surface, a step or block with a ledge from which the rubber can drop down. They are placed at some distance from the ledge. Then they are moved toward it, either by hitting the ground with the palm of the hand, slightly cupped so that air escapes, or by blowing. The rubber bands drop over the ledge, and the person whose rubber band first overlaps with another wins the stake. This game continues until one player has won all the rubber bands. Parents object to the game only if the children buy rubber bands instead of collecting them.

Boys like to practice skill in sports. Wrestling, a national sport in Japan and the Ryukyus during spring and early summer, is taken up by boys who copy young men and older students, and for several weeks wrestling matches get spontaneously under way. Prior to the annual island-wide athletic meets in September, boys practice high jump, broad jump, and relay running. There is much practice for the mere fun of it, but few signs of involvement with attaining outstanding performance. Losers are not teased or ridiculed, although a good performer is occassionally given an encouraging remark by others who practice.

Group games are usually played after the schoolchildren have returned to the village. One of the popular games is a version of prisoner's base similar to that played in the United States. This game is played with much yelling, laughing, and noisy challenging. Equally popular is a version of "kick the can." This game is exciting and fast moving. It is a game which can lead to arguments, since one must trust the honesty of the person who is "it" and claims to have seen another player. Brief arguments arise and are quickly settled. Part of the fun seems to be teasing and challenging the tagger.

These are games that children may play on any day in the year. During holidays they are sometimes asked to entertain adults with dances. Little girls learn the traditional Okinawan dances from kindergarten days on, either by watching or by coaching of an older person, a friend, one's older sister, or mother. Neither kindergarten nor school programs include the teaching of such rich Okinawan heritage as classical dances. Boys do not begin to imitate the burlesque dances of their male elders until adolescence. But they are sometimes invited, together with girls, to present group dances or little plays for the adults. Adults seem to enjoy most the performances of Okinawan dances by little girls who may have learned the rhythm and movements but not the restraint of serious adult presentations. They are delighted if a 6-year-old, dressed in bright-colored costume, innocently wiggles her hips in a rather suggestive way.

Children who perform for adults show no stage fright. At school, where little sketches are presented on the stage, there is a complete ease in improvising. Nobody is embarrassed if he forgets a line, a song, or a cue, and the recitation contests which we have already mentioned are carried out with much zest.

Schoolchildren are supposed to remain at home after 8 o'clock in the evening to do their studies. This rule is encouraged by the school but rarely enforced by parents. Many children, boys and girls, appear outside after dark, and on moonlight nights they often resume their playing. Off and on, a couple of elementary schoolboys are attracted to the store where the village truck arrives with goods from the city after nightfall. There they stand in the dim yellow light of the kerosene lamp, watching, helping, or just listening to some of the men who come to have their sake bottles filled. If a bath has been prepared for their families, their turn will come sometime after the older males in the household have had theirs. By 10 o'clock children have finally disappeared from the street and paths.

BIBLIOGRAPHY

Civil Affairs Activities in the Ryukyu Islands. United States Civil Administration of the Ryukyu Islands, 1954, vol. II, no. 2.

Civil Affairs Handbook. Ryukyu (Loochoo) Islands. Office of the Chief of Naval Operations, Navy Department, OPNAV 13–31, 1944.

Cole, Fay-Cooper. *The Peoples of Malaysia.* New York: van Nostrand, 1945.

Glacken, Clarence J. *The Great Loochoo.* Berkeley and Los Angeles: University of California Press, 1955.

Hattori, Shirō. On the method of glottochronology and the time depth of Proto Japanese. *Gengo Kenkyu (Journal of the Linguistic Society of Japan),* 1954, 26, 27; 29–77.

Higashi Son, Industrial Department Survey. Compiled by Noboru Miyagi and Seian Iju, 1954 (mimeographed).

Kerr, George. *Okinawa: The History of an Island People.* Rutland, Vt. and Toyko: 1958.

Lebra, William P. Okinawan religion. Unpublished Ph.D. thesis, Harvard University, 1958.

Pitts, Forrest R., Lebra, W. P., and Suttles, W. P. *Post-war Okinawa.* Pacific Science Board, National Research Council, SIRI Report No. 5, Washington, 1955.

Tamura, Hiroshi. *Ryukyu Kyosan Buraku No Kenkyu (A Study of the Ryukyuan Communistic Villages).* Tokyo: 1927. Translation in manuscript, 1956.

The Mixtecans

of Juxtlahuaca,

Mexico

❋
❋
❋
❋
❋
❋

Kimball Romney

Romaine Romney

Contents

About the Authors

Kimball Romney received his doctorate in anthropology in the Social Relations Department of Harvard University (1955). His wife Romaine attended the University of Colorado. The Romneys selected a Mixtecan barrio in the town of Juxtlahuaca in the province of Oaxaca in central Mexico. They had two children, Becky, aged 7, and Bobby, aged 3. A third child was born in Oaxaca during their stay and spent the first months of her life being cared for by the women of the barrio. The baby has a Mixtecan name and Mixtecan godparents and is considered a member of the barrio. Two teenagers lived with the Romneys and helped both with the daily routine of living and with fieldwork. Romaine Romney had little opportunity after the first few months to do formal fieldwork but spent her time with the other women marketing, cooking, attending church and fiestas, and caring for the young children. Bobby, a vigorous and active boy, was a source of fascination and pleasure to his less active and less boisterous Mixtecan friends. Becky did creditable fieldwork on her own. Muriel Eva Verbitsky, a graduate student at the University of Mexico, acted as an assistant to the Romneys and did most of the mother interviews and many of the standard observations of the children. Duane and Barbara Metzer, as well as Robert Ravicz, also contributed to the work. The Romneys spent nine months in the field and returned the following summer. They lived in an adobe house which was specially built for them but was similar to the surrounding Mixtecan houses.

Kimball Romney is now a member of the Department of Anthropology at Stanford University.

Part I

Ethnographic Background

✷
✷
✷
✷
✷
✷

Chapter 1

Setting and Overview

Santo Domingo barrio is part of the town of Juxtlahuaca in the state of Oaxaca, Mexico. The cultural heritage of the 600 barrio members we studied derives basically from the Mixtec Indians whose culture was flourishing in the area before the time of Christ.

The barrio itself is located on the site of a pre-Columbian Mixtec town and represents a continuation of many aspects of Mixtec culture up to the present. We know from documentary evidence that the first Spanish priest came into Juxtlahuaca in the 1620's and that six Spanish families took up permanent residence in 1636, at which time construction of the original Catholic church began.

Today the Mixtec-speaking peoples number approximately 250,000 and occupy an area of about 10,000 square miles in the north and west parts of the state of Oaxaca. We know from archaeological data that they have occupied this general area for at least 2000 years. In a number of respects, the impact of conquest was different in degree from other parts of Mexico. It occurred with little armed force, and there was relatively little compulsory emigration or labor in mines, for the rough terrain made exploitation uneconomical.

Although priests penetrated the area early in introducing religious changes, the basic subsistence patterns have been little affected. The addition of some fruits and vegetables was supplementary: maize, beans, and chile have remained the basic diet. Even the introduction of oxen and the plow have failed to affect greatly the pattern of land exploitation. Thus the intrusion of Spanish culture elements in the Mixtec area has involved little change in such features as land usage, subsistence patterns, residence, and certain aspects of village organization.

THE REGION

Mexico is a mountainous country with only some 7% of its land being described as level or rolling. The state of Oaxaca, lying at the juncture of the Eastern Sierra Madre and the Sierra of Oaxaca, is also mainly mountainous. The rugged terrain is cut by narrow river valleys whose slopes rise steeply to high peaks and ridges. The long summer rains make raging torrents out of the otherwise sluggish streams. Communities are consequently somewhat isolated from one another.

The state of Oaxaca is divided into 28 districts. Juxtlahuaca is a village or town located in the extreme west central part of the state (see map 1) and is the *cabecera* or head town, roughly equivalent to a county seat, of a district of the same name. The district is approximately 54 miles from north to south and 48 miles from east to west. This 3000 square miles is further divided into *municipios*. These *municipios* may be thought of as towns together with a large surrounding area inhabited by scattered hamlets and isolated families. Thus there is no land between *municipios,* for all the land and the people living on it belong to some *municipio.*

If viewed from above in three-dimensional perspective, the topography of the district is seen as a steep-sided valley shaped much like a tilted trough running from south to north with the lower end to the north. The sides are formed by mountain chains of over 10,000 feet, and the floor is comprised of the narrow valley of the Mixteco (or at this point, it is sometimes called the Juxtlahuaca) River, a valley that nowhere reaches 2 miles in width and that in most places is no wider than the river. The sides of the valley are cut by numerous steep-sided gullies

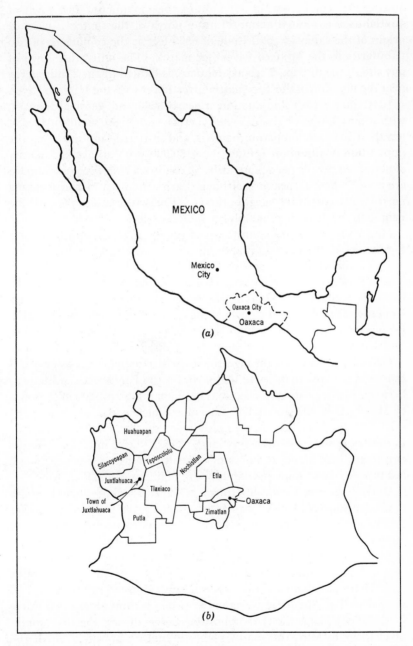

Map 1. (a) Map of Mexico showing state of Oaxaca. (b) State of Oaxaca showing Juxtlahuaca and surrounding districts.

547

and ravines cut by streams that drain the mountains. The town of Juxtlahuaca is located about 20 miles north of the southern head or origin of the valley at an altitude of 6500 feet at the confluence of two tributaries to the Mixteco River (see map 2). The only other town of any size in the district, Tecomastlahuaca, is located about 2 miles away near the junction of the Tecomastlahuaca River with the Mixteco River.

Juxtlahuaca, with a population of nearly 3600, and Tecomastlahuaca, with a population of about 2500, together with eight small villages of less than 500 each, numerous hamlets, and scattered families, bring the population of the *municipio* to about 30,000, with an average density of about ten people per square mile. Juxtlahuaca and Tecomastlahuaca are mostly Spanish speaking, although each contains a Mixtec-speaking *barrio* or community neighborhood. Otherwise, practically all the people in the district speak only an Indian dialect.

Map 2 shows the two main towns of the district. It is approximately 5 miles across the map, so that about 25 out of a total of 3000 square miles for the whole distirct is shown in the map. It takes about half an hour to walk from Juxtlahuaca to Tecomastlahuaca, or from Juxtlahuaca to Santa Rosa, while it takes about four to five hours to walk from the valley floor to the crests of the mountains, which are, of course, far out from the area shown by the map. It is also important to point out that much of the level ground in the district is shown in the map.

One enters the valley through the town of Huajuapan, a commercial center of the area that lies to the north on the Pan American highway between Mexico City and Oaxaca. Huajuapan is about 200 miles south of Mexico City and about 120 miles north of Oaxaca. There is a dirt road between Huajuapan and Juxtlahuaca that may be traversed only in the dry season in jeeps or very large trucks. The 65 miles between the two towns take about 14 hours of difficult driving. A similar, though less traveled, road joins Juxtlahuaca to the highway via Tlaxiaco.

During the rainy months, roughly May through September, both roads are impassable, the former lying in a river bed and the latter following a mountain ridge on which slides are frequent. An alternative method of entering the community is in small aircraft. A cleared field at the north end of town serves as a dry-season landing strip, but planes cannot land if the strip is muddy, and they do not fly on cloudy or rainy days. Hence, for some of July (when it may rain ten days or more) and virtually all of August and September (when it rains almost two thirds of the days) plane travel is impossible. Even during the dry months of October to May, the use of planes is limited by winds which rise every afternoon and continue with some force until well into the night.

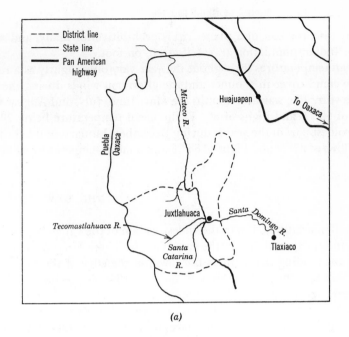

(a)

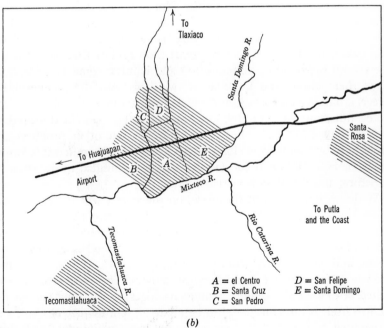

A = el Centro   D = San Felipe
B = Santa Cruz   E = Santa Domingo
C = San Pedro

(b)

Map 2. (a) District of Juxtlahuaca showing town of Juxtlahuaca. (b) Town of Juxtlahuaca showing barrios and adjacent towns.

In any case, the cost of a plane trip is prohibitive for many, and most of the Indian population travel, if at all, on foot.

Mean temperatures throughout the year vary only slightly as a result of the cloud cover in summer and the afternoon winds during the rest of the year. The warmest months are May, June, July, and August with lows of 50° F and highs of 86° F; the mean temperature being 70° F. The coldest part of the year is during December, January, and February, with lows of 32° F and highs of 86° F and a mean temperature of 60° F.

THE TOWN

Juxtlahuaca, then, lies in the widest section of the valley between the river and the mountains on the east. The road from Huajuapan, which skirts the landing strip, enters the town on the edge of the plaza. The large, whitewashed adobe church, built in 1633, is the first landmark one sees. Beyond the church to the south is the treeshaded town square or park containing two water fountains, several benches, and a circular speaking platform or *kiosco* that faces toward the *juzgado* or municipal buildings. These buildings house the administrative offices for the district as well as the jail and barracks for the local detachment of soldiers. The market, an open roofed structure, is located on the south side of the square, and Friday is market day. It is on Fridays that people from the several surrounding communities and hamlets come into town to trade their wares, and the market overflows into the cobblestoned streets around the square. A few traders from warmer areas carry fruits, coffee, nuts, and other products up from near the coast for this market day. Pottery, corn, fruits, beans, and innumerable other products are brought in by people from closer villages. Very little handicraft is found in the market. On any other day the market is confined to the covered structure, and the plaza is virtually empty.

Within a few blocks of the plaza, on the streets which converge on it, are the telegraph office, the post office, and the two schools (one federal and one private Catholic). A number of small general stores open onto these streets and sell canned and packaged foods, clothing, yard goods, and hardware. A vacant building is rented occasionally during the winter for showing of old Mexican movies. This section of town is called *el Centro*, the center. Around its edges lie the four *barrios* (el Centro itself is not considered to be a barrio). On map 2, el Centro is designated A, and the four barrios, Santa Cruz, Guadalupe, San Pedro, and Santo Domingo, are designated B, C, D, and E respectively. The people of el Centro are purely Spanish speaking and consider themselves superior to other residents of the town. Santa Cruz is also Spanish speaking and is composed of farmers and handicraft people only slightly lower in general prestige than people of el Centro, whom we shall call townspeople. Guadalupe is composed of very poor, Spanish-speaking people who have moved to Juxtlahuaca from surrounding Indian hamlets only within the last generation. They have very little land and live by making charcoal and working for low wages for townspeople. San Pedro, again, is Spanish speaking on the whole, although many also speak Mixteco. Many of its people are only one or two generations removed, culturally speaking, from being Indians. They are generally progressive and would rank above people in Guadalupe in prestige. Everyone in Santo Domingo, on the other hand, speaks Mixteco, although most also speak Spanish. Santo Domingo barrio contains approximately 600 people as compared to about 3000 for the rest of the town combined.

THE BARRIO

Santo Domingo barrio is composed entirely of Indians. They are distinguishable from Spanish-speaking townspeople, although not primarily by physical type, for both groups are relatively short and brown skinned with black hair which is naturally straight. (The town population does include a few blonds and redhaired people, but the Indian population does not.) The basis for the distinction is cultural rather than physical and is most clearly seen in language and dress.

Mixteco is the first language a barrio child learns and the only language some of the oldest barrio people speak. Most people between these extremes speak Spanish as well, but Mixteco is used at home and in most of the daily routine. Spanish is used when it is required—in dealings with the priest and nuns and with merchants in el Centro, none of whom know any Mixteco. Barrio meetings and all the events of the barrio fiestas are conducted in Mixteco, but if a non-Mixteco guest is present, the conversation will be carried on in Spanish as a courtesy. Schoolchildren are under pressure to use Spanish at school and frequently also use it at play. Children of preschool age, especially those who have no older siblings, hear Spanish much less and do not learn it until shortly before they are ready to enter school. However, young children who spend a great deal of time with an older sister who has learned Spanish begin to learn it from her, for she will often use it, except for expressions of endearment or warnings given under stress.

The typical, conservative costume of barrio men is homemade of coarse, white cotton material. It consists of a pair of trousers which reach to midcalf, where they are tied, and which are secured at the waist by wrapping and tying in back. They have neither buttons nor pockets, but a pocket for carrying money is improvised by tucking a small cotton bag into the waist band. The long-sleeved, collarless shirt has a concealed pocket on the inside left front in which are carried cigarettes or tobacco and sometimes folding money. Huaraches, a locally made leather sandal with heavy rubber sole, are worn on the feet. Every man has a sombrero. A plaid wool blanket or serape, sometimes with an opening cut for the head, is used for warmth outdoors in the early morning or at night. It also serves as a covering for sleeping.

Many barrio men have an alternative set of clothing, a shirt and pants made of a heavy cotton material and purchased ready-made. This costume, in fact, predominates except in wet weather, when frequent changes of clothing are necessary, but old men and very poor men wear only the typical costume. The trend toward this ready-made outfit is illustrated by the fact that only a small percentage of Indian boys wear the white cotton costume. In other respects, boys dress much like their fathers except that they do not always have huaraches. They wear no underclothing, although during the coldest part of the year they may wear two shirts. The boy's serape is made by cutting a wool or cotton blanket in half. A hat is not a necessary piece of clothing for boys, although most boys do have them. These sombreros are purchased new for the fiesta in July, and a child wears his hat as long as it lasts, but no new one is purchased until the following year. This may mean that a boy has no sombrero for the rainy season, in June and early July, for the fiesta is on July 24, and the new hat is purchased only a week or two before.

Indian women wear a hand-embroidered, white cotton blouse and a printed cotton skirt which reaches almost to the ground—both homemade. They cover their heads and shoulders as well as carry their infants with a rebozo, a long, dark blue cotton shawl. This rebozo and the characteristic way in which it is draped are the mark of a Mixteco woman throughout this part of the state. Women are traditionally barefoot. They carry money in a cotton bag tucked inside the blouse. Small loads are carried in handbaskets woven locally, and heavy loads are carried in a *tenate,* or carrying-basket, on a tumpline across the forehead. The hair is worn in braids which either hang down the back or are wrapped around the head. Earlobes are pierced for earrings, but not all women wear them. No make-up of any kind is worn.

Unlike the men's costume, the women's costume is worn by all adult barrio women without exception or alternative. However, a trend toward a ready-made costume for women is perhaps observable among children and adolescent girls. Little girls wear one-piece, knee-length dresses of printed cotton, often a slip, and sometimes panties, although the latter are not necessary for girls under 7. Like their mothers, they are barefoot and wear the rebozo whenever they are outdoors, regardless of the weather. Adolescent girls wear a knee-length printed cotton skirt with blouse (not embroidered) or a one-piece dress. However, the traditional costume is still the basis of the trousseau and is worn by all recently married girls.

The dress of barrio people provides them with relatively little protection against the elements. Children rarely have a change of clothing; when the clothing is drenched in a sudden rainstorm, the wet rebozo or serape is simply turned over or turned around rather than changed. Unless there is cooking in progress, there is no fire over which to dry wet clothing, and the child must often sleep in clothing still wet from a daytime shower. For many children the rebozo or serape is their only covering at night, even though it may often be quite cold. During the day the wind is chilling, especially if one is wet, and even during the dry season it may blow dust or dirt so hard that it is difficult to see across the street. Similarly, the rebozo may protect the head from direct exposure to the sun but is hot to wear in full sun. During the hottest part of the day the streets are almost deserted except for occasional playing children, and resting in the shade at this hour is not uncommon.

Santo Domingo is set off from the rest of the town by a clear geographical boundary. A deep *barranca* through which a stream runs lies at the southern end of town and separates it from el Centro. Santo Domingo is referred to locally as *the* barrio, and we shall adopt this practice. The barrio occupies about the same area as the remainder of the town, with the result that one sixth of the total population lives on onehalf the total land (see map 3).

The moment one crosses the natural boundary, the barranca, the distinctive features of the barrio become apparent. None of the barrio's streets is paved in any way except for an occasional pathway of stones. Two or three of them, those which lead across the barrio toward el Centro, are as wide as a road and flat. The others slope more or less sharply and are narrow, rocky, and cut by gullies. During the rainy season most of these become intermittent, muddy streams, and at planting time, water diverted from the river for irrigation runs down several streets from the hillside.

The houses along the streets are separated from each other by occasional cornfields or fields of alfalfa. Although some present a blank, windowless adobe wall, the back of a room that opens on the inner

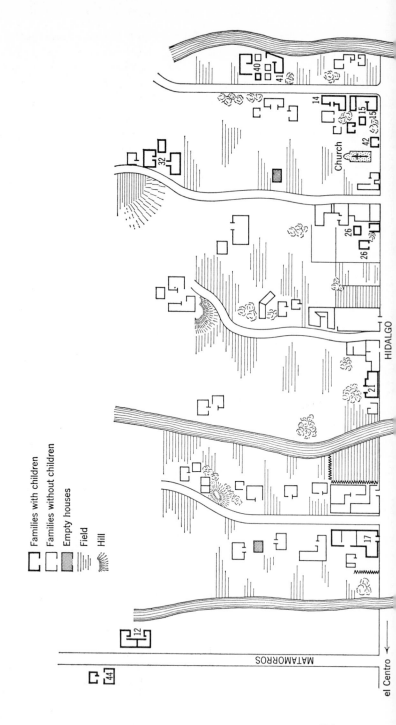

Families with children

Families without children

Empty houses

Field

Hill

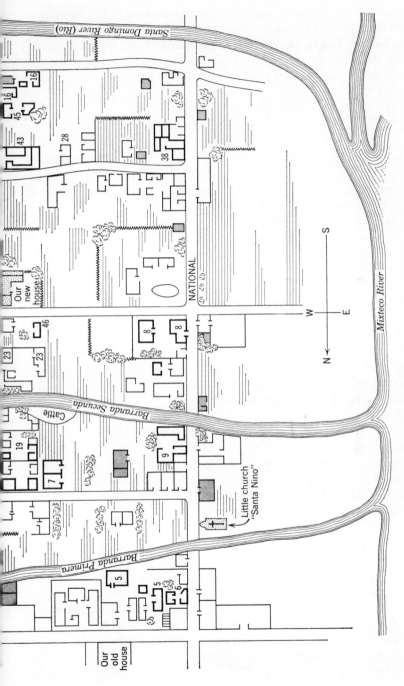

Map 3. Barrio of Santo Domingo, Juxtlahuaca, Oaxaca.

courtyard, most houses in the barrio are set back from the street in a grassy courtyard. The yards have fruit trees, low shrubs, and sometimes flowers. During the dry season the village looks sunbaked, while during the rainy season the corn is in various stages of growth, and the vista is green and luxuriant.

THE HOUSE AND COURTYARD

Ideally, a group of siblings, together with their wives and families, will occupy separate dwelling units surrounding a common courtyard. We designate this cluster of structures and accompanying courtyard by the term *compound*. Each nuclear family typically maintains separate sleeping and cooking facilities and eats apart from the others while it shares the courtyard and engages in a number of common activities with the other families. There are two distinct kinds of structures within a compound, even in those cases where it is occupied by only one family. These two structures are the cook shack and the main room used for sleeping, storage, and visiting. We shall refer to the main room as the house and understand that all cooking takes place in the cook shack located adjacent to or near the house.

The arrangement of the compound varies a great deal but almost always includes a house and cook shack for each family. The women, children, and older people spend most of their time within the compound, while the adult men are usually away at their fields during the day. Children play with and are cared for by their siblings and cousins within the compound, and the majority of their play activity, especially in the early years, is confined to the area.

The usual house in the barrio is rectangular, one room, windowless, and with only one door. It is made of adobe and usually has a tile roof. The adobe is made by members of the barrio and is available during all times of the year except during the rainy season. The houses have a gabled roof with heavy beams that are hand cut. These beams form the frame for the tiles that are placed from bottom to top to make the roof. These beams are brought from the mountain sides by burros and are later cut by hand. There are few hung doors, but doorways have a high wooden doorstep that one must step over and usually down into the house. Many have only boards for a doorway or a small fencelike partition that may be put up at night or when the family is out. The floor is dirt and is usually rough in some spots, particularly where there has been frequent walking and sweeping.

Horizontal beams along the top of the room form a space used for storage. There are no two-storied houses in the barrio. Houses, on the outside, are all adobe, unplastered, and unpainted. A few of the houses are plastered inside and painted white, with a strip of color around the bottom as a border.

For a very few families the cook shack is the only structure, but this is the rare exception rather than the rule. The cook shack is always made of sticks or of palm, not adobe, and generally has a thatched rather than tile roof. The hearth is sometimes in the center of the room but usually is back against a well-blackened corner. There are no ovens or other special construction for cooking, the only equipment consists of large rocks or broken pots turned upside down around a small fire to form support for the cooking pot or the flat *comal* for tortillas. Wood is usually used as fuel but little is kept inside the cook shack, most of it being stacked in the yard. There is a great deal of smoke in the cook shack when a fire is going, and if a child wants warmth or if the mother needs help, he must remain in this stuffy, smoky room, often with tears running down his face from smarting eyes.

Every house has an altar inside the main room, never in the cook shack. It is always up off the floor on boards, or planks on boxes, or perhaps on a table. Tables and chairs are made in the barrio by two carpenters and can be purchased fairly cheaply; so several families own them. Also, small woven chairs can be purchased very inexpensively from travelers from the mountains. Prints or colored pictures of the saints, some framed or some unframed, and perhaps even an image, will be found on the altar, but very seldom will a crucifix be seen. There will always be flowers of some sort in tin cans, sometimes fresh, more often faded or withered. Dried-up flowers seem to be as acceptable as fresh ones. There may even be some dusty paper ones. Candles are usually found on the table, but only the very small ones purchased at the store are upright. All the others lie flat on the table until the time comes to use them. They are very important in all ritual functions. There is always a container for the special Indian incense, *copal*, which also finds its way into all ritual activities.

Many other little items that might be pretty or interesting are found on the altar table, such as gourds, pretty stones that the wife might like, or some colored paper streamers. It often appears that the altar is merely a convenient place to dump all the odds and ends that sometimes come in handy and that the people do not want on the floor. The altar may become a very untidy spot in a room that is otherwise quite neat. It is customary for visitors to cross themselves in front of the altar on entering and leaving the house. This practice, however, is not rigidly adhered to except on such special occasions as fiestas.

The main room usually contains a chest or a trunk in which extra or fiesta clothes are kept. This chest is usually the bridal chest, presented to the girl at her wedding, although all sorts of family clothing are later kept in it. It may be very simple or ornately varnished, painted, or carved. However, it is usually kept up off the floor on planks or a trestle.

Corn on the ear is often stored in the main room and carried to the cook shack for shelling as needed. Granaries as such are very rare.

Most people sleep on the floor on palm mats that are made in the village and are very cheap. These are also used to sit on, and a woman grinding usually kneels on an old one or a piece of one. Every household, even the poorest, has several palm mats.

There may be a few chairs, generally small ones, close to the ground, much like a child's chair. The chairs are usually offered to guests as a form of respect, and almost every house has at least one or a substitute like a smooth log or small box to offer. When the man is in the house, he commonly sits on the chair or on the wall bench while the woman will sit on the mat on the floor. At all the fiestas this same pattern is carried out, the men sitting on the benches or the chairs around the walls of the room and the women sitting on the floor on mats. Perhaps if one sits on one's heels, as the men do, it is easier to sit on a chair or bench than if one sits on one's legs or with crossed legs as the women do. Perhaps an early habit of sitting controls the way in which furniture is later used. There is little other furniture in the house.

Most families do have a good collection of pottery or dishes, none of which is made in town but which is brought into market from the mountains by villagers who make them on the hillsides. Each house has several kinds, and some have many of the same type. There are usually the following: cups and bowls of various sizes, the clay *comal* for cooking tortillas, the lime pot, the pot for boiling corn, the bean pot, a large bowl for washing, and a water jar.

Water is brought to the home from the *barrancas,* the small tributaries of the river, or from wells. All of the people with wells tend to share the water with whomever asks, and some courtyards may have as many as six outside families entering once or twice a day for water. There is no monetary payment for this water, but flowers, a candle, or a choice bit of food may be carried to the wife on occasion.

No courtyard in the barrio has a bathroom or even a privy. People go to the fields or the river banks or to a particular corner of the courtyard, leaving the rest of the courtyard clean. The roads are also kept clean. Every householder is required to clean the street outside his house each day or whenever it is dirty, and in general the people of the barrio are careful, so that the streets are usually clean. The only dirty sections are those by vacant lots where there are no houses along the road. Almost all the yards and houses are kept very orderly with everything in its place.

In the courtyard outside the cook shack many pots can be seen drying on the ground in the sunshine. Inside the shack, implements and tools are hung on the walls or kept very neatly in one corner. The Indians seem to be careful not to have a great many things around for which there is not a definite use. They do not put things away and save them for the future. If they should come upon or be given an item for which they have no use, they either find a use for it or give it to someone else. There are not many things in the houses that do not receive frequent use.

COMMUNITY BUILDINGS

On one of the wider streets of the barrio is a corner store of the type found in el Centro, the only one that exists in the barrio. The non-Indian storekeeper (who is the barrio's only resident "outsider") sells primarily refreshments—soft drinks, candy, cigarettes, and locally made beer—and deals largely with people passing through the barrio on the way to el Centro. Barrio people buy candles, matches, aspirin, and mentholatum there, and children go there to spend a few centavos on sweets.

Farther down this same street, at the geographical center of the barrio, is the church, the religious center of the barrio. The fiestas, which are the major social and ceremonial events, are held in the church and its yard. It is in the barrio church that the images of Santo Domingo and Santiago, the patron saints of the barrio and of the town, respectively, are housed. It stands on a piece of open ground, one of the few plots in the barrio that is owned by the Indian population. Like the main church in el Centro, it is whitewashed adobe and very old. It is much smaller than the main church and is furnished inside with only a few movable benches instead of pews. (Most of the worshippers sit on the adobe floor or stand.) It has a high bell tower that is climbed by barrio men to ring the bell to announce a mass or a fiesta or a death in the barrio. The priest from el Centro comes to the church to hear confession on Saturday evenings, and early on Sunday morning (before mass in the main church) he says mass in the barrio. Weekly mass is attended mainly by women and children under 12. A nun and one or more young assistants come to the church from el Centro every

Thursday afternoon to give a class in catechism for children, and from 15 to 35 children under 12 attend more or less regularly. They gather before church to play in the churchyard, and they also meet there on the fringes of adult fiesta activities. Of particular interest to children are the preparations for fiestas—the construction of decorative arches and of fireworks displays—which take place in the church courtyard for several days before each fiesta.

The common civic center for the barrio is the *comunidad*. Because of the encroachment of townspeople on the land of the barrio, the comunidad is today separated from the barrio by town houses and fields at the northern edge. It consists of three large rooms surrounding a very large, bare courtyard. The more social, rather than religious, aspects of major barrio fiestas are set in the comunidad, as are the meetings of old men of the barrio to discuss matters of common interest. Children visit the comunidad during fiestas when their parents attend. They sometimes cross the yard on the way to school, but they are rarely to be seen there alone at any other time. (This fact may be related to the present location of the comunidad in el Centro, for barrio children tend to stay within the boundaries of the barrio for reasons we shall discuss below.)

BARRIO BOUNDARIES

At the southern edge of the barrio is the river. It is swift and narrow as it comes down from the hillside, but as the slope becomes less steep, the river widens and slows its pace. High on the hillside, some of the water is diverted into a canal that carries it through the streets of the barrio to irrigate fields in the valley. Lower down, the river is used for bathing and washing of clothes. Washing at the river is done about once a week, but bathing there is less frequent during the cold months. The river is enjoyed as a beautiful place, as well as a practical one, and adolescents use it as a setting for courtship. Young children may go with their older sisters while the latter wash clothes and flirt with boys. The river is forbidden to small children alone.

Beyond the river on the south and west are the fields owned and worked by barrio men. The farthest of them are as much as an hour and a half's walk away, and many others are half an hour away from the village. Men go to the fields when there is work there throughout the growing season, and when a boy is 12 years old, he goes and works beside his father. Younger boys do not go to work but many carry their fathers' midday meals to the field and stay to return with them at dusk.

Women and girls, as well, go to the fields at planting and at harvest; then the whole family lives in a temporary shelter for four or five days, eating and sleeping there until the work is finished. If there is a new baby in the family, the mother usually does not go on these expeditions, and small children are sometimes left behind with a grandmother or other relative.

Children must learn to walk long distances early. If the whole family goes to the field, all but the baby must walk the complete distance. A child does not ask to be carried but the father or an older sister may volunteer to carry a 2- or 3-year-old the last part of the way if he is lagging behind and detaining the family. The small children will also walk up the hillside 1 or 2 miles to the river each Sunday for bathing or washing of clothes.

The hills rise steeply on all sides of the barrio and its fields. Firewood is there for the taking, and families, including older children, make semiannual trips during the slack season to gather it. Herds of cattle, belonging to townspeople, and sheep, which some barrio members also own, graze on the hillsides. Few children play on the hillside unless they are watching a grazing herd. Early in the spring, children go with great enjoyment to collect flowers, which are used to decorate altars in the church and in homes. On these excursions an older sister or an adult is always present to supervise the younger children. The walk is exhausting for the youngest of them, and it is not surprising that they do not venture this far often.

There are few dangers in the barrio for children. There are almost no harmful snakes or animals in the natural environment and few poisonous insects. Only the oxen, which plod down the street during the work day, and the sheep and goats on their way to and from pasture must be avoided. All adults or older children warn younger ones to get out of the way when these animals approach and, if necessary, move them to safety.

For the typical barrio adult male the universe is spatially limited, and his horizon does not extend much beyond the valley he knows so well. This is not because he has never seen or visited other localities; most males have visited Oaxaca or Puebla at one time or another, and during the war some even got to the United States as unskilled laborers, although none stayed long enough to learn any English. These outside cities, so briefly visited, are part of the Indian's universe only in a most casual sense. Their local focus and main identifications center around the barrio itself. This localization of identification is even more striking for the women and children. None identify much with the larger town of Juxtlahuaca, let alone with the state. If outside the community and asked where they are from, they answer, "barrio Santo Domingo, Juxtlahuaca," or sometimes just, "the barrio," if the questioner is acquainted with the region.

The Indians regularly attend only three fiestas outside their own community—in Copala, Tecomastluahuaca, and Santa Rosa. Only adults and nursing infants in their mothers' arms go to Copala. Copala lies about eight hours south of Juxtlahuaca and has an annual fair and fiesta that draws people from a very wide area, including several adjacent districts. Indians from several different cultures and languages attend, and it is a great adventure for the barrio members. Copala is occupied by Trique Indians who speak a language very different from the Mixteco used in the barrio. In a real sense, Copala represents the southern boundary of the real social universe of the barrio, and though people know the names of villages, only a few men have ventured much farther south than Copala. (This statement does not apply to the townspeople, who have a much wider outlook and frequently trade great distances.) Santa Rosa is shown on the map, about 2 miles down the valley, and is only about 30 minutes' walk away. These people are very close to the barrio and are said to have moved from the barrio a few generations ago. Although the barrio, on the whole, tends to be endogamous, when people do go outside for marriage partners, they generally look to Santa Rosa. It is the only village, according to the barrio Indians, where Mixteco is spoken without an accent. The main fiesta in Santa Rosa, a religious event, is in August and is heavily attended by barrio residents. The annual fair in Tecomastlahuaca, on the other hand, is mainly a commercial affair, but many barrio members attend for the excitement of the large crowds it attracts. Children may go to affairs in both Santa Rosa and Tecomastlahuaca with their parents. Other than visiting in Santa Rosa with relatives, however, children very rarely go beyond Juxtlahuaca and the fields and hills immediately surrounding it. Under no circumstances would a boy or girl under 14 go as far as Santa Rosa without an escort.

Children rarely go even to el Centro without their parents or, if alone, without a legitimate errand, for el Centro is separated from the barrio not only geographically but by sociocultural barriers as well. Townspeople, in contrast to Indians, speak only Spanish and place a low value on Mixteco. They dress in Western-style, though rural, clothing, both men and women wearing shoes (although frequently without socks). The rebozo is worn by townswomen as well as by Indians, but in town it is brightly colored and is never draped in the Indian fashion. Coats also substitute for the rebozo in town. Women of el Centro often wear their hair loose, or curled by permanent wave, and many use make-up. Men of the town wear ready-made clothing of better quality than the average Indian's. Thus, even before he speaks, the barrio member is immediately recognizable as an Indian.

Indians are different from townspeople, and townspeople attach a negative value to this difference. They look down on the people of the barrio, and barrio people avoid interacting with them whenever possible. Townspeople and barrio members do meet at the market and in the stores of the town. (The food habits of the two groups are sufficiently different that such encounters are not as frequent as one might suppose. Indians consume no canned goods and buy very little meat, while town diet is varied.) At the market, interaction is limited to the specific act of buying and selling, and the Indian waits until all townspeople have been served. He is sometimes refused service altogether and is from time to time addressed or referred to in a derogatory way. The prices he pays and the prices he receives for his products are set by the townspeople.

Formally, the whole town is under the political leadership of an elected president. In fact, the barrio takes no part in the election of the president (or any other officials of the state or nation) and participates little, if at all, in the political affairs of the town. A representative of the barrio, the *regidor,* appointed by the president, has a certain amount of autonomy in barrio affairs. He is empowered to call for labor when the barrio streets or irrigation system or church need repairs, and all adult males in the barrio are required to serve their turn. He and his two assistants are also responsible for the selection and installation of the *mayordomos,* whose role as organizers of barrio fiestas we shall discuss later.

The barrio maintains its own church and celebrates its own annual series of fiestas. However, on a number of occasions throughout the year barrio people attend the main church. When they take part in processions originating in the town church, Indians walk at the end of the line. During the *Posadas* of the Christmas season, in which a procession ends in a private home, townspeople enter the house and Indians remain outside. When food is served, the townspeople are served first, the Indian men at the same table later, and the Indian women, on the floor in the kitchen, last of all.

Among adults, derogation of Indians by townspeople and deference to townspeople by Indians seem to be the accepted pattern of behavior. Among children, however, open aggression is not at all uncommon. Barrio children on their way to market or to school are in danger of attack, either verbal or physical (stone throwing), by town children. Since they are trained not to fight back, they are in real danger of being hurt. It is thought best by barrio parents for the child to remain in the barrio, which is his home, and not to go into the town, where he may come into conflict. Some give this reason for not sending their children to school.

The most important product of this social situation is an *esprit de corps*, a sense of solidarity among barrio Indians that is unknown in the town. Membership in the barrio community is highly valued by those inside it.

SOME BARRIO ATTITUDES ABOUT THE WORLD

Before going into detail about the cultural context of the child training practices, we would like to present a few reflections of the adult view of life and the universe. This should give the reader a quick preview of the general nature of the temperament of the people we will be talking about.

The basic assumption of the Indian man about the world in which he lives seems to be that it operates according to certain rules or laws ultimately controlled by that part of the universe which we would call the supernatural. He also believes that the general plan of things is ongoing and immutable and therefore that man must learn certain patterns of action and attitudes to bring himself into conformity with this scheme of things; that if he does so, he will receive the minimum amount of punishment and the maximum reward. There is the feeling that some suffering or misfortune is inevitable, but there are certain ways of avoiding it or mitigating it once it has fallen. In the Indian scheme of things in the barrio, the individual seems to be somewhat submerged in the group, that is, the individual exists as a member of a group that is adjusted to nature, and by following its pattern, he survives and prospers.

The barrio man recognizes change but does not project these changes into the future. He lives more or less in the timeless present, in which the known pattern is continued indefinitely. The barrio man identifies with the land, and there is a reciprocal relationship between the *milpa* (cornfield or cultivated place) and the man. The man's fulfillment, in one sense, comes from his opportunity to work out this adjustment between himself and his land, and it is interesting that he always works it with others. He seems to get the same pleasure from working with his friends in their fields as he does in his own fields. The Indian, as contrasted with the Spanish element in the town, sees the weariness that comes from physical toil as one of the facts of life, and he receives the approval of his fellows for working.

One might say that in his relation with other men in the barrio the Indian pattern is adjustive and permissive, while within the town the Spanish pattern is one of ordering and dominating. The statuses of leadership in the barrio, such as the *mayordomos* and *regidor,* are thought of as obligations rather than something to be striven for competitively. Every man from the barrio who follows the pathway of the culture and gains the respect of his fellows may expect to assume positions of prominence during his lifetime. However, these statuses are not thought of as a restrictive group of prizes for which many must compete and few attain. Envy and competitiveness are regarded as a minor crime. An Indian in a position of prominence never gives orders to his fellows. He may point out the pattern to be followed in a ritual or suggest practical modes of action, but this is in the manner of dispensing knowledge, not of dominating others either by force of personality or by authority of position. Age gives knowledge and wisdom and is respected as such.

Group decisions are made by consensus rather than by majority rule or dictatorial fiat. Perhaps it can be said that almost all the patterns of social activity in the barrio lead toward merging with the society rather than individual distinctiveness. The approved way of doing things is to live and let live and to adjust to other human beings to avoid conflict. This does not mean highly organized cooperation, although men do work together in groups that move from one field to another. However, each family has its own property, and each individual family goes about its business, not interfering with others although cooperating within a wide range of activities, such as planting and harvesting.

In the barrio, when a man takes a post of public responsibility, for example, as *mayordomo,* his wife shares the honor and responsibility. The man and woman in the barrio, as husband and wife, form a cooperative unit in the pattern of adjustment, and to this working team are added the children when they reach 8 or 10 years of age. Exploitation of one sex by the other is atypical, and children are not dominated primarily by physical or other heavy punishment. Bickering and fighting by teammates are not characteristic. Again, it seems that adjustment without friction is the goal, and, if this proves to be impossible, withdrawal rather than domination is the answer.

Overt interest in sex is fairly rare in the barrio; this is not to say that there is no interest in sex but rather that sex is regarded as necessary and natural. From the barrio point of view, the use of sex for exploitative purposes is inconsistent with their attitudes, just as are all other forms of exploitation of human beings. Sexual power does not add to the luster of the individual within the barrio.

Just as there seems to be no compartmentalization or stratification of the society among the Indians, similarly, there is no compartmentalization of the universe and supernatural matters. What we might call the supernatural is not clearly distinguished in the barrio; rather, the universe is seen as a more or less integrated whole. Among these nominally Catholic people there still persists a basic notion that the planting ceremonies, the rain-making ceremonies, and so on, operate without any distinction between empirical and spiritual world.

In the barrio, the personality of the typical individual—provided of course that his routine is not interfered with too much by the townspeople—is relatively more secure and better integrated than that of the townsperson. The Indian seems to follow the approved patterns of culture without any strong motivations toward special rewards, distinctions, prominence, or the like. This is evident, for example, in the work patterns of the Indians, in which they follow with the utmost diligence the standard routine, such as milpa work, corn grinding, and so forth. This same careful following of pattern is similarly followed in such ceremonial activities as the fiestas and the cofradia ceremonies. For a great many reasons, it seems that the Indian maintains a personal security so long as he stays within the framework of his culture and is able to follow the pathways without a great deal of deviation. However, we should say that the barrio person does not show an extreme of flat emotional reaction. The *abrazo* or semiritual embrace is given, for example, although not with a great show of enthusiasm. Joking is characteristic, but somewhat constrained. On the other hand, within the patterns of their life—and this is particularly noticeable in the fiesta pattern—a great deal of flexibility is allowed as long as the major outlines of the pattern are followed, so that though they appear somewhat compulsive, this is not carried to the extreme. They are not given to overexpression of emotions, though they can on occasion give vent to their emotions in an explicit way.

In the following chapters we shall outline the cultural context of child training practices, as well as the practices themselves, in an attempt to show how children are equipped to take their places in barrio life.

Chapter 2

Daily Routine

The day begins in the barrio household between 5:30 and 6:00 A.M. The woman gets up from the mat on which she has slept, smooths her clothes, perhaps shakes her rebozo and throws it around her shoulders. She does not stop at this hour to wash her face or arrange her hair, for she must start the fire, heat the coffee (if there is any) for breakfast, and begin the preparations for the rest of the day's meals. Firewood is kept stacked in the courtyard, and she goes outside to select some pieces for the day. She lights the fire with a match, tends it until it is going well, and then puts a little pot of water into the coals to boil for coffee. If she plans to have her corn ground at the mill, she must go at once. When she returns, she takes the *masa* (coarsely ground corn) to the metate for its second grinding. If she is doing all of the grinding herself, she will have ground it through once instead of taking it to the mill. While she is grinding, her husband awakens and gets up. She may stop her grinding to serve him some coffee and a cold tortilla or two which have been stored since the preceding day. When he has eaten, he goes to his field if it is nearby and does not return until breakfast time at about 9 o'clock. Meanwhile the children awaken. A mother does not stop grinding corn to attend to the children as they get up. There is little dressing to be done, for children as well as adults sleep in all their clothing and need only shake out their rebozos or serapes and put them on again. The children often sit outside in the sunshine to get warm and wake up. Then they too eat a cold tortilla before beginning to play or to help their mother.

The woman is occupied with the making of tortillas until breakfast time. The children play in the courtyard or in the cook shack while she works, and she seldom notices them unless some difficulty reaches her ears. The oldest of the little girls is in charge of the younger children and watches them play. An older boy may take this opportunity to lead the burro or other animal to pasture, or he may split firewood in the yard. The family gathers at about 9 o'clock to eat the morning meal. The time for this meal, as for all others, is not set and may vary widely from day to day, but the content—cold beans, fresh tortillas, and chile—is always the same. The man and boys are served first, all sitting on the floor, the woman waiting on them and sometimes making tortillas as they eat them. After eating, the man goes outside and sits in the sun while the children are fed, and then he returns to the fields. When the younger children have returned to their play, the woman and older girl (if she has been helping with the meal) sit down to eat. After the meal, the woman washes the bowls in clear water and sets them aside. She washes the empty bean pot also and leaves it ready for the beans she will soon set on the fire for the midday meal.

During the morning the woman of the household may go to the market (if it is Friday) either to sell some garden produce or to buy food. On other days she might make purchases in a store. However, many small items of food are obtained by barter within the barrio, among friends, and this sort of exchange is carried on later in the day. When a woman goes to market, she may take her children with her. It may be necessary for them to sit with her quietly for several hours at a time. There is never any noise or interference from these children. They are simply there. Nursing infants, who might create a problem, are usually left behind, often with a woman friend or relative who can nurse the baby if the mother is delayed. A mother of a young infant might send her daughters or her younger sons to the market or the store rather than go herself. Adults and children alike tend to go about their errands with dispatch. Women, especially, do not stand in the street to gossip with friends. They greet neighbors in a friendly way but do not stop to converse. Even if a woman should meet her husband in the street, she does not talk with him at any length until they have reached home. In contrast, in the market place itself there is a great deal of conversation between women who sit next to each other hour after hour.

At home there are many tasks to be accomplished before noon. Preparations for dinner begin soon after breakfast is over. Beans are winnowed by pouring them from one hand to the other, then rinsed and placed in a pot of water on the fire. Corn is removed from the ear and boiled in lime water, then drained and ground. Children—girls of all ages and younger boys—may help with the preparation of beans and may carry corn from the storeroom and help to shell it. Only older girls grind corn. Water must be brought in for use in cooking and for drinking during the day. The source of water is usually a well at some distance from the house, for not all households have wells; those with water share it with their neighbors. The woman will often leave her children in the care of their older sister and go to get water herself, for this is considered heavy work. However, children of all ages, both boys and girls, can and do carry water. Poultry and pigs must be fed by the woman or the younger children. The house must be straightened up and the house and courtyard swept. The woman rarely does this herself unless she has no children, for girls and younger boys do the work under her supervision.

An older daughter may go once a week to the river to wash, a task which requires spending the whole day. For this reason, a mother with a nursing infant is not usually called on to do the laundry, nor is a woman who has full responsibility for the preparation of meals. If there is a relatively unoccupied woman or girl in the compound, she goes to do the washing. Otherwise mother and children go to the river together, and the children play while the mother washes and spreads the wet clothes on the grass and on bushes to dry in the sun.

For much of the average morning the woman is either away from home on an errand or, more frequently, bent over the fire and the metate in the cook shack. Children who sit in the kitchen near their mother may be asked to hand her a utensil from time to time, to bring a piece of firewood from the yard, to chase the chickens away from the corn, or to drive the dog from the doorway. They may munch a cold tortilla, a piece of fruit, or a handful of pumpkin seeds as they watch her work.

Children of school age may spend the morning and the afternoon at school, coming home for dinner between 1:30 and 3 o'clock. However, only about half of the barrio's school-age children go to school at all, and even those who do attend do so irregularly. Thus, when their morning chores are finished, many barrio children are free to play. Some children play alone, particularly those who live in nuclear households and have only infant siblings or siblings much older than they. More often, children play in courtyard groups that include their siblings and their cousins. While children in the courtyard are young, play groups may include both sexes under the direction of an older girl in the family who is entrusted with the care of the younger boys and girls. As soon as they are old enough to do without a caretaker, boys tend to play with other boys and girls who have no caretaking responsibilities tend to play with other girls. When boys and girls beyond the toddler stage play together, they usually play on the boys' terms.

The man of the household may or may not come home for dinner. If his field is within easy walking distance from the house, he may be at home for both breakfast and dinner. If it is farther away, he may wait until breakfast is over before he leaves, and in this case breakfast is served well before the usual 9 o'clock. He also stays in the field until late in the day, and his dinner is brought to him there by his wife or often by an older boy who is not yet old enough to work in the fields for a full day. The boy stays with his father after dinner and returns home with him at the end of the day.

If dinner is not yet ready when the man arrives, he may take a few minutes to play with his children or sit among the children while he chats with the friends or kinsmen who have come home from work with him. When dinner is ready, the man and boys are again served first; when they have finished, they may smoke a cigarette outside. The man generally does not return to the field after dinner, but neither does he spend the late afternoon at home alone. He gets together with other men in his compound or in another to visit or to do business. The talk centers around the crops, prices, and coming fiestas. He may spend the time making something—leather goods, adobes, tile —which he will later sell. He may gather materials to build a new house at some future time. He may work with other men on the decorations for a fiesta. Older boys may spin tops or shoot marbles with friends in the street. Later they may cut hay for the animals and bring the animals home to be fed.

Meanwhile the woman and girls clear the kitchen after dinner, putting aside the leftovers—beans, tortillas, and chile—once again for the evening meal. (Second helpings, at least for children, are discouraged, and food left over after a meal is saved rather than distributed.) Then the woman may visit a neighbor, usually going with some sort of excuse, for example, an exchange of food or a question about plans for a coming fiesta. When this small business has been taken care of, the women sit and visit at length. The guest may be offered coffee, fruit, or squash cooked in brown sugar, for "little gifts make for good friends." The women may comb and delouse each other's hair and that of the children who have come along on the visit. Corn may be shelled by all of the women present. Some of them may sew or embroider. The children play in the courtyard largely unnoticed.

Instead of visiting in the afternoon, a woman may engage in some money-making project at home, such as butchering a pig and rendering the lard for sale, toasting pumpkin seeds, gathering greens and herbs, or picking fruit. Such activties are often shared by other women in the compound.

At dusk water is carried from the well for evening use. The fire is built up and the tortillas reheated or, less frequently, made fresh. Supper—leftover beans and tortillas with chile—is the end of the day for the family, and after the dishes are put away and the corn set to soaking for the morning, the adults sit and talk around the smouldering fire. Candles and ocote are used sparingly, so the room is usually dark, except for firelight, long before bedtime. The children lie down and sleep when they are ready, and even the adults are usually asleep by 9 o'clock.

Special events require a number of alternative routines. On Thursday afternoons some children of school age go to catechism class at the barrio church. On Sundays some women arise earlier than usual in order to attend mass, but not all women go, and attendance is rather irregular at best. Children may or may not go with their mothers to mass. Also, on Sunday, many people go to the river to bathe. The whole family may go at once, but more often the women of a compound and all the children go together. The bath takes place soon after noon, during the warmest part of the day, and the hair is washed and clothing changed. There is much visiting and chattering in such a group. On Sunday afternoons some barrio men play softball on a field at the edge of the barrio using equipment that they own cooperatively. A few younger, generally single, barrio men spend Sundays drinking with their friends, and there may be a drunk or two in the streets of the barrio on Sunday evening. These are the exception rather than the rule, except on fiesta occasions.

During the week the man of the household may, instead of going to the field, engage in some special semiskilled work. He may make or lay adobe or tile or do carpentry on contract, and while he is working, he may receive a midday meal from his employer. This is particularly true if he is working for another barrio person. On other days he may take part in a cooperative work group in the field of a friend, and on these days, he eats a festive meal with the group. During the dry season he may be called on to help on the same basis in the construction of a friend's house. The woman of the household that has requested cooperative help prepares the meal for the workers with the aid of her daughters and other women in her compound.

A man's labor may also be required by the regidor. The *tequio*, or communal work, includes planting and tending corn in the communal fields, street cleaning, repairs or improvements on the church, and so on. The church bell rings to announce the time, but the 30 men needed on any given day are notified in person beforehand. Records are kept by the regidor of each man's participation. The *tequio* is seldom accompanied by a communal meal.

Fiestas of all kinds alter the daily routine, even when the household is not directly involved in them, for the gift of food from someone else's fiesta makes it unnecessary for the woman to prepare a meal for the family. Besides providing good fare fiestas offer an opportunity for visiting and drinking. Barrio saints' fiestas also entail entertainment—dances, dramas, fireworks displays, and the movement of crowds. They include special masses which are attended by the majority of barrio residents. When the man of the household is a member of the society that is responsible for the fiesta, the routine is even more strikingly changed. For several weeks preceding the fiesta, especially if it is an important one, much of the man's time and energy goes into preparations for the event. He takes part in the purchase of food, liquor, cigarettes, and ritual necessities, such as candles. He participates in the gathering and arrangement of materials used in decoration of the church and adornment of the saint. He may help to build a structure on which fireworks are to be displayed. He spends much time in meetings with the other members of the society, planning and collecting money. On the days of the fiesta itself (which may last from two or three days to as long as two weeks), he rises early, attends mass, and then gathers with the other men of the society for a breakfast served by all of their wives. After breakfast they drink and smoke and make speeches until dinner. Between dinner and evening they drink again and watch the ceremonies that mark the particular fiesta. After dinner there are fireworks, a drama, or, often, a dance in which everyone participates until very late. Children sit and watch the dancing until they can stay awake no longer. Then they often go to sleep on the floor or in the arms of their mothers or sisters.

The woman whose husband is deeply involved in a fiesta is responsible for helping to prepare the food. Under the direction of the *mayordoma*, the wife of the head of the society, she works with other women (at grinding and tortilla making and the cooking of meat) from early morning until late, sometimes even sleeping in the fiesta cook house. The work is hard, but the interaction with other women is pleasant, and fiestas are anticipated with much excitement. Children may go with their mothers to the fiesta site, and here, as in the market, they sit and watch without interrupting. The youngest may be tied onto the mother's back while she works. Sometimes younger children are left at home with an older sibling; in this case, the woman leaves the fiesta at about 10 in the morning and again at 4 in the afternoon to take some of the fiesta food home to her children. Sometimes a woman arranges to do part of her work at home, for example, grinding and making a batch of tortillas. Then she sends her daughter with the finished tortillas to the fiesta place, and her share of the food is sent home to her. On fiesta days, meals are irregular, but children wait without complaint until their mother returns, and they enjoy the special meal when it is ready.

In general, barrio men spend very little time with their families. They are at home only briefly during the day, and even then their attention is often absorbed by business and the society of other men. Men are sometimes affectionate and playful with their children (especially the youngest) and often show pride in them before visitors. They are occasionally asked by their wives to discipline unruly sons. However, the only children who interact at all intensively with their fathers are boys of 12 years and over. Boys of this age work in the fields every day and begin to participate with the other men of the compound.

Similarly, barrio women are occupied almost full time with their primary responsibility—the provision and preparation of food for the family. When they are not busy in the kitchen, they are relaxing—always with hands at work—with other women in their own courtyard or a neighboring one, or they are chatting with others while selling fruits in the market. The youngest child and the oldest daughter receive more attention from their mother than any of her other children. A nursing infant must be attended to by his own mother whenever she is present, and, in addition to routine care, he receives many expressions of love, both verbal and physical. The oldest daughter, on the other hand, needs little care but much instruction. The mother teaches her to fulfill the feminine role by example, often calling her from play to watch some operation in order that she may learn to perform it. As the oldest daughter learns more and more of the appropriate role behaviors, she comes to interact with her mother and the other women of the compound as a woman among women.

Neither men nor women are often found playing with children. Thus children between infancy and young adulthood spend their days apart from adults for the most part. However, their play is often imitative of adult role behavior. They are content to watch adults at work and to be near them without doing anything else. They are happy, especially when very young, to perform little tasks for the adults around them. The daily routine in the barrio belongs to adults, and children observe it and practice it, first playfully and later in earnest, until they too are grown.

Chapter 3

Economy and Diet

All the men in the barrio, save one, earn their primary living through the cultivation of maize. Since most of the land in the valley belongs to townspeople, barrio men farm land on the hillsides for the most part. A few families own irrigated valley land near their houses and plant corn there. Many are tenant farmers; they plant the plots adjacent to their houses and split the crop with the landowner who lives in town. In addition, all men in the barrio may work land that is communally owned by the barrio, and the produce of this land belongs to them as usufruct owners. The communal land is in the hills, and a fee of 50 centavos per *maquila* (approximately 4 pounds of seed) planted is paid into the communal treasury for the use of the land. All barrio men also contribute labor toward a collective harvest of corn on part of the communal land, the sale of which benefits the barrio treasury.

Corn may be planted four times each year, depending on the type of land and the availability of irrigation. The first planting, which depends solely on irrigation, is about the first week in February and is called "early seed." It is harvested in late June and early July. The second planting, called "half irrigation," takes place between the first and the tenth of March. It is irrigated twice, and the rest of the moisture comes from the rain. Corn planted at this time is harvested from the twentieth of July through early August. The third planting depends entirely on rain, taking place between March 20th and April 1st (by which time some rain may be expected). It is called "cloud seed." Harvesting of this crop takes place in late September and the first days of October. The fourth planting, called "rain seed," takes advantage of the *temporal*, the heaviest part of the rainy season. Seed is sown from April 25th (the day of San Marcos) through the first few days of May, and the harvest is reaped in mid-October. Planting high in the mountains takes place in late February and March and harvesting in late November and on into January, depending on the time of planting.

The first step in preparing the land is the *barbecho* or breaking of the land. This is done with a crude wooden plow tipped with metal, pulled by a yoke of oxen that the owner of the field may own, borrow, or rent. After the plowing, the field is left for a month; then a second plowing, again using oxen, takes place. This plowing is called the *revuelta* or "turning over," and its purpose is to break the earth into smaller pieces and keep it from drying out. The field is left for another three months after the *revuelta*. Then, again with the plow and oxen, furrows are made in the soil. Within a month, the first rain comes and the field is planted. A hole is made with a *coa* or digging stick, a little water is poured into it by hand, and four to six seeds are dropped in. If beans or squash are being planted also, the seed of these are placed in the same hole. The hole is covered, and the sower moves on to the next spot about a meter away.

When the corn in the field, or *milpa,* is about a foot high (in about a month) the first weeding (*limpia*) takes place. The ground is turned over with a plow. A second limpia is performed in three weeks to a month, depending on the amount of rain. A third limpia is done by hand or with a hoe and consists of pulling out the weeds that have grown up close to the corn stalk and of heaping up the earth in hills around the base of each corn plant. The weeds pulled are used to feed livestock and may be brought in little by little instead of being harvested and stored all at once. When the corn has dried on the ear, the *pisca,* or harvest, takes place, the corn being removed from the stalks and carried unshucked to storage areas in the owner's house. The land is immediately prepared for another planting if it is flat and not stony. Hillside land and land full of stones are allowed to lie fallow for one or two years between plantings. High in the mountains, the fallow period is as long as four years.

If the field is irrigated, irrigation takes place for the first time ten days before the barbecho; next, a month after planting, twice more a month between the second and third limpias, and perhaps a fifth time if the soil is sandy. The irrigated field is left fallow until the following January when it is irrigated again, and the cycle repeats. The use of water for irrigation is regulated by the town government through the regidor and is subject to a fee.

Both planting and harvest are attended by the entire family, and usually four to six men in addition to the owner of the field help with the work and receive food and reciprocal help in their own fields in return. This system of cooperation holds true only within the barrio, for when a barrio man works for a townsperson, he is paid by the day and receives no meals. On the day of planting, the owner or some other member of the family (even one of the women) walks slowly around the field sprinkling aguardiente (a distilled sugar-cane liquor used in all ceremonial contexts) on the ground. Incense is burned and a candle lighted, and over these, prayers are said to the "owner of the earth" asking him for a crop this year as in other years. The aguardiente is interpreted as the first drink the earth receives—a kind of nourishment given to the "owner of the earth" in the hope of nourishment, in the form of a good crop, in return. Rarely now, but formerly often, the head of a turkey, chicken, or sheep was planted in the center of the field and stood for the earth's first food. After the earth has been offered drink, the people drink also and the planting begins.

Similarly, at harvest time, aguardiente is sprinkled on the ground before the assembled men begin to remove the ears from the stalks. When the corn is finally heaped up in the owner's storehouse, a candle is lighted and incense burned, and the family gathers around the mound to pray, giving thanks for a good harvest and asking that the corn last for a long time. When a stalk with three ears on it is found, it is brought back to the house intact and placed upright in the center of the mound of ears in order that the rest of the corn remain plentiful throughout the year.

Prayer is thought advisable, for farming is always hazardous, and many barrio families operate on a very narrow margin. Although irrigated land is twice as productive as *temporal* (yielding 120 *maquilas* per maquila sown, in contrast to about 60), it is scarce because of the physical limitations of the valley and the fact that it is owned primarily by the townspeople. As a result, it is expensive, and few barrio men can afford to plant enough of it to ensure a surplus. Many families cannot plant enough corn to meet their needs throughout the year. A few, who have become wealthy by barrio standards in ways we shall discuss below, have enough surplus to sell to merchants in el Centro and to outsiders who come to market. The average family grows enough corn to feed the household and the livestock and to pay for the bare necessities in the way of clothing. Food items that are not home-grown, of which some are staples, and extraordinary needs such as medical care, life-cycle ceremonies, and contributions to barrio fiestas must usually be financed in other ways.

OTHER SOURCES OF INCOME

Livestock is one supplement to family income, although it requires initial capital and is therefore differentially distributed among the households, depending on their wealth. Every household has some poultry—turkeys or chickens—for it is relatively inexpensive to feed and is an essential part of most household and community ceremonies. No one can afford to be without a chicken or turkey in case of an emergency. Chickens provide eggs that can be sold in the market or traded in the stores. Eggs are not eaten, as a rule, because they bring such a good price. Many families have pigs which may be sold or slaughtered, primarily for lard. Pork is part of one important ceremonial dish prepared for the patron saint's fiesta in July.

Most families have a burro or two, rarely more. These animals are useful for transporting corn from field to storehouse or market and for carrying wood from the hills. A few families have sheep or goats in small numbers. Very few have cattle, and horses are even more uncommon. Some of the barrio's cows are milked and the milk sold, largely in el Centro. Several men have teams of oxen which other men sometimes pay to use. Responsibility for the care of livestock is fairly clearly defined, women and young children attending to the pigs and poultry and boys (and, less often, men) to the burros and other large animals.

Alfalfa is grown by about ten barrio men and used to feed their own animals and to sell to others. Alfalfa must be irrigated once after planting, and during the year of its growth cycle, it can be cut five times. Since it requires even more hand labor than corn, the help of other men is always requested, and the first cutting is divided among them. The owner of the field receives all of the rest of the harvest.

Wage work within the barrio is unknown, but barrio men sometimes do farm work for townspeople, even though wages are extremely low. Better pay can be earned in Tlaxiaco, in the mines, or in the sugar refinery at Atencingo, Puebla. Several men, or occasionally a whole family, will go there to live and work for a period of weeks or months.

Half a dozen men have been as far as the United States as *braceros* for six months or more, and the wages accumulated during these periods have made one or two of these men rich by barrio standards. The land on which the barrio's wealthiest man plants some 35 *maquilas* of corn a year was bought with his American earnings.

Several men have part-time specialties which provide them with additional income. One man carves the wooden masks worn during the religious drama performed at the fiesta of the patron saint. Another bakes the bread served during this fiesta, a task which takes three to five days, and is reimbursed in food (enough for his family as well as himself). Several men serve as butchers at the fiesta and are paid in food. One man with grown sons still at home leaves them in charge of the milpa and makes regular trips to Copala to sell corn which he has bought for this purpose. The young men of another family work as carpenters in el Centro. Several others make or lay adobe or tile which they sell in the barrio and in town.

Many other small money-making projects are engaged in by women. Indeed, while only a few men have part-time specialties, nearly all women earn money in one or more ways. A great number of women make tortillas for sale. A woman who is fully involved in this activity will grind and prepare tortillas three times a day and will either take them to market or send a little girl to sit and sell them there or to deliver them by prearrangement to houses. Many other women sell products of their gardens—fruit, tomatoes, chiles—in season, or send their daughters to do so. A few women are well-known as expert embroiderers and sell blouse decorations to others. One or two have sewing machines and make clothing to order for other barrio people. (The one man who is not a farmer also has a sewing machine and does tailoring for men.) Women with no other means of support, widows primarily, gather firewood in the mountains, sell it to buy corn, and then make tortillas for sale to meet their daily needs. One barrio woman bakes bread, and several others prepare chocolate on order.

Among women, only young girls work for wages outside the barrio. Some of them work for families in el Centro, but wages there are less than half the daily rate for men, work is hard and demeaning for the most part, and fringe benefits are few. Many of the girls who are servants work as far away as Oaxaca and Mexico City for months at a time.

FOOD

Corn and beans are the basis of the barrio diet, and everyone in the barrio eats them daily from the time he is a few months old. Beans occur in wide variety. Of the five colors, the black, brown, and red are all grown in the barrio; spotted ones seem to grow wild and are brought in by mountain people on market day, and white beans grow at some distance away and are brought in by merchants. Beans are prepared by simmering them in a clay pot for many hours and are served with salt as the only seasoning.

Corn of four colors is grown in the barrio. The white is considered the best and may be used in all of the dishes made with corn. The yellow is in second place and is used mostly for tortillas. The red and the blue-black are harvested early and do not keep very well. These latter are eaten boiled, on the cob, having been picked before they have dried. The white and the yellow varieties are rarely served in this way.

Of all the ways of preparing corn, the tortilla is by far the most common. These thin, unleavened cakes are served with every meal and take the place of tableware, for people use them to carry food from the plate to the mouth. In the preparation of tortillas, the maize is first soaked overnight in lime water to soften the hulls and then ground on a *metate*. Many women nowadays take the boiled corn to one of two motor-driven mills located in el Centro on the edge of the barrio, although not all feel they can afford this luxury. Each morning quite early a line forms outside the mill, and women chat while they wait their turn. Since grinding corn is a woman's job exclusively, one of the mills is even run by a woman. Little boys do not go to the mill alone; and if they go with their mothers, they stay outside while the grinding is done.

Tortillas may be cooked twice, and this operation transforms them into *totopo*, a crisp, flat cake that can be carried on journeys for two or three days without spoiling. Maize is also prepared as *atole*, a gruel made of very finely ground corn with milk and water. For this purpose, milk, rarely used in any other form, may be bought by the cup from a passing vendor. Atole is the first solid food given to the nursing infant and is also served to invalids and the aged. Corn is also prepared as tamales, which are balls of corn dough enclosing meat or beans, wrapped in corn husk or palm leaves, and boiled. Still another way of preparing corn is *posole*, a festive dish, much like hominy grits, made with meat.

A great variety of chiles is used in cooking; and chiles, either whole or ground with tomato, are served with each meal of beans and tortillas. A sauce used with meat on festive occasions is made almost entirely of chiles of different kinds, ground to a fine paste on the metate, and cooked. Townspeople consider the Indians' use of chile excessive and have great difficulty in eating barrio ceremonial food for this reason. Only a small amount of chile is grown in the barrio, despite its importance in the diet, since climate limits its cultivation. Most of the chile consumed in the barrio is bought in the market from merchants from the coast. Salt, the only other seasoning in daily use, is also brought in from the coast or from the north and purchased at the market. Garlic, onions, pepper, cinnamon, and cloves, used in festive cooking, are purchased as needed. Other herbs which are used in preparing meat are gathered in and around the barrio, where they grow wild.

Meat in the form of chicken, turkey, beef, or pork is a luxury food and is consumed only at fiestas. However, various sorts of fiestas arise very frequently, on the average of once a week throughout the year, and therefore meat is not as minor an item in the diet as might be supposed. All kinds of meat are boiled, and various herbs are used as seasoning. Meat may be served in broth or in a chile sauce. It is held in a tortilla and eaten with the fingers.

Several kinds of fruit grow in the barrio. Pomegranates, bananas, avocados, and papaya are used at home and bartered or sold to other households. In addition, pineapples are occasionally bought in the market. Fruit is eaten casually, between meals, and is enjoyed by adults and children alike.

Squash may be cooked as a vegetable, with chile and herbs, or as a sweet, with brown sugar. In the latter form it is often eaten between meals, especially by children. The seeds of the squash are dried and toasted and served as another type of between-meal snack. Tomatoes are used primarily as a sauce with chiles added. Greens of various kinds, mostly gathered in the hills, are sometimes served boiled with a meal, but they are not an important part of the diet.

Coffee is drunk on arising by those families who can afford it. Coffee beans are bought from merchants from Copala and other coffee towns to the south. The bean is toasted on the comal, shelled by hand, and then ground on the metate. Coffee is made by boiling the coffee powder with a lump of dark, unrefined cane sugar.

Chocolate and bread are almost exclusively festive foods. The cacao bean is toasted, shelled, and ground like coffee. Next, however, the paste is ground again with white sugar and stick cinnamon and patted into small, round tablets. These tablets are dissolved in hot water to make the chocolate. Some women seem to be particularly able chocolate grinders, and they are sometimes hired to grind large quantities of chocolate for a fiesta. Chocolate is often served with bread as an early morning festive meal. The bread may be bought in the barrio, where one woman makes it regularly, or in el Centro stores. It is made into rolls, some white and some sugar-frosted. Once a year a special kind of bread, ordinary in shape but different in the proportion of shortening and in the use of eggs, is baked by a barrio man and assistants to be served at morning meals during the patron saint's fiesta.

Candy is eaten occasionally, for this is usually what a child buys with any money he may be given as a reward for obedience. It is available in the barrio's one store and in the stores of el Centro. Cigarettes are smoked by men on ceremonial occasions, rarely at other times. They may be bought at the store or rolled by hand from local tobacco. Wild tobacco is also chewed "to give one strength for one's daily work."

Aguardiente, a strong liquor made from distilled sugar-cane products, is drunk on all ceremonial occasions, often in great quantity. Men
drink much more than women and are sometimes taken home at the
end of an affair by their sober wives or by their children. On certain
occasions, depending apparently on the supply of liquor or the inclination of the hosts rather than on the type of ceremony, women are
vigorously encouraged to drink. However, only one woman in the
barrio has been seen drunk, and she is the subject of much amused
comment in the community. Beer is also drunk by some barrio men,
although its use is infrequent partly because of its greater cost. It tends
to be confined to ceremonies in which townspeople take part, for the
people of el Centro deplore the barrio's enjoyment of aguardiente
and often refuse to drink it.

The food and drink used daily are purchased in very small quantities, for there is never much money on hand in the average barrio
household. Raising the cash for a major expenditure—a fiesta, for
example—usually demands a major money-making effort. Corn or
alfalfa or an animal must be sold or some family member must work
for wages for a time. In an emergency, money may be borrowed, often
from a kinsman or *compadre*. Wealthy townspeople are sometimes
approached for a loan, but this is infrequent because the interest rate
is about 10%.

CEREMONIAL REQUIREMENTS

The fiestas celebrated by the individual household on the occasion
of the marriage, birth, or death of one of its members are partially
supported by contributions of a few pesos from each family that attends. Nevertheless, much of the cost of the food—which may be served
or distributed to the whole barrio—cigarettes and liquor, the incense
and candles, the fireworks and the services of the priest must be
borne by the family. The families of a bride and groom exchange sets
of clothing for the couple. The family of the deceased provides the
coffin. The *padrino* of the principal in any ceremony may help pay
for liquor, cigarettes, decorations, and so on, and a baptismal *padrino*
is especially likely to contribute clothing for the child, but all such
contributions are voluntary. The less formal meals which are served
to those who help with planting and harvest are always somewhat
festive. Meat and aguardiente are essential. Contributions of money
or liquor by the participants on such occasions are less frequent.

In addition to the above fiestas, which involve even poor families in the expenditure of money for ritual purposes, there are many fiestas of great community significance which are financed largely by those who can best afford it. Each of the major barrio saints has a *mayordomia,* a group of men who share the cost of the fiesta for the particular saint in a given year. The *mayordomo* bears the greatest financial burden, but his *diputados* share it, and contributions from invited guests may be expected. The expense involved in these ceremonies varies greatly, the mayordomo for the patron saint's fiesta being expected to put on the biggest show. Men are selected for these offices largely on the basis of their economic capability.

In comparison to any of these ritual requirements, the cost of curing illness is usually relatively minor. A great number of common ailments can be treated by the family itself with herbs or rituals which cost nothing. For more serious conditions a *curandero* or *brujo* may be summoned from the barrio or from a neighboring community. Midwives are employed to assist at a birth. Only rarely do barrio people consult the doctor in el Centro. However, such medicines as aspirin and mentholatum are rather widely used. They are bought in town stores at little cost.

OTHER NECESSITIES OF LIFE

Clothing is bought to wear for the first time at the fiesta of the patron saint in July. (However, not every member of the family has new clothes every year.) Some clothing is bought ready-made—the shirts and pants of men, huaraches, sombreros, rebozos, and serapes are sold in local stores. Hats are manufactured outside Juxtlahuaca and are imported in great numbers. Just before the big fiesta, they are sold at higher prices than during the rest of the year. All other clothing is made at home from yard goods bought in el Centro. The sewing may be done by hand, especially on blouses and on men's traditional clothing, but is often taken to a barrio seamstress who does it on her machine for a fee. The tailor mentioned previously makes Western-style shirts and pants for men.

Most adults have two sets of clothing, one to wear and one to wash. The very poor sometimes have less than this amount of clothing, but the rich seldom have much more. Extra cash tends to be invested in the family business in the form of land or animals or to be spent in community ceremonies. Little is used for personal adornment and relatively little for enrichment of the diet. Children, even of middle-income families, may have only one set of clothing and must either wrap themselves in a rebozo or blanket while it is laundered and dried or wear it dirty. Two children who attend the Catholic school wear school uniforms provided by their respective el Centro godparents. The barrio children who are in public school have no special school clothes. Worn clothing, especially men's work clothing, is mended and remended.

All household utensils, furnishings, and tools are purchased, and none of these are made anywhere in the barrio. Included are such items as pottery, baskets, metate, mano, rope, and mats. Chairs and wooden chests are made by el Centro carpenters. Metal tools—knives, machetes, hoes, coa and plow points—come from Oaxaca and are bought in el Centro stores. Even the less durable of these utensils— the pottery, baskets, and mats—need to be bought only infrequently, while the wooden and metal objects and the mano and metate may be bought only once or twice in a lifetime.

Resin-soaked pine, which is burned for light, may be cut in the mountains or purchased from the Indians of neighboring hamlets. A few families use kerosene lamps.

The nonfood items required for ritual are also largely purchased. The candles in common use are made in el Centro, although the mayordomia of the patron saint makes pure beeswax candles once a year for use in the church. The incense, copal, is a pine resin which can be gathered in the mountains but is often bought in the market from people who live in the mountains. The pictures of saints used on household altars are bought in el Centro stores. Although the decorations used in the church during fiestas are partly of store-bought crepe paper and cotton cloth, flowers and greens which grow in the area are an important material in adornment.

It is clear that the barrio household, only partially self-sufficient with regard to food and medicine, is even more dependent on the people of el Centro as manufacturers or middlemen for most of the other necessities of life. Housing can theoretically be obtained without spending much money, for most of the materials of a thatched adobe hut are free for the taking, and cooperative labor is used for the construction. Adobe is made of local clay and straw by the owner himself or by another barrio member (whom he pays). Roof beams and supports may be cut in the mountains. Doorsills and the infrequent doors are made locally, and thatching materials for cook shacks are gathered in the surrounding hills.

Tile for the roof of the main house must be bought in el Centro and laid by an artisan who charges for his services. A new house is therefore a major undertaking, and only the wealthy can build one simply for the sake of greater comfort. A house may last for generations, and many a barrio member is born and dies in the same one and passes it on to his children. A young married couple may live with the husband's parents, in which case another fireplace in the cook shack and perhaps another room on the main house are added. The couple will, sooner or later, build their own separate house.

PROPERTY OWNERSHIP AND INHERITANCE

Everyone owns his clothing, and whatever he has worn (except his blanket) is buried with him when he dies. All other possessions— the utensils of the woman, the tools of the man, the land, the animals, and the family house—are divided among the immediate family after the individual's death. If a man has not made arrangements for his inheritance in advance, his widow is in charge of the distribution of property among their children. (A man's own siblings will not inherit from him unless he has no children.) Both men and women may inherit, although a daughter will expect to receive less than her brothers. Land and animals may be divided equally among the children, or the eldest son may be given more than the others and be placed in authority over his younger brothers and sisters, especially if they are much younger. The house is usually kept by the widow until she remarries. Then it may be sold by the children and the money divided among them or it may be bought by one of them from the rest, who are then expected to leave it. In any of these situations, disputes may arise among siblings. A widow may attempt to forestall an argument by having the town judge preside over the distribution.

OVERVIEW

The subsistence of each barrio household is based, essentially, on one crop. Cooperative arrangements and participation of the whole household easily handle the labor problem. However, land availability limits the production of corn to the extent that it is often difficult to feed the family, much less to buy the many food items which supplement corn in the diet and the even more numerous items of clothing and household equipment. Very few of the necessities of life are made at home or obtained free. Opportunities within the community to supplement the family income are limited and relatively little exploited—industry is nonexistent and animal husbandry is of little economic importance. It is difficult to make ends meet in the barrio, and it is virtually impossible to become rich.

One can either remain poor, then, or leave the community in search of wealth. Many barrio people have chosen the latter alternative. However, leaving the community need not be permanent. Once having become relatively wealthy, it is possible to stay wealthy on one's return home. By investing his savings in land in the barrio, a returned laborer can produce a surplus of corn which allows him to reinvest in land, animals, and so forth, and thus to increase his income steadily through the years. Short of this, it is possible to improve one's financial condition in a more limited way by working long enough to pay for a new house or to pay off a debt. In either case, there is a commitment to permanent residence in the barrio on the part of most of those who leave it. Young girls come back before they are too old to marry, and men come back in time to accept a mayordomia. Most people seem to prefer to live in the barrio, more or less accepting its standard of living, rather than to seek a higher standard of living by leaving it permanently for the outside world. While the fact that money goes farther in the barrio than outside is certainly relevant, there is clearly more than economics behind their choice. The experience of barrio people with non-Indians has given them no reason to expect a warm welcome in the outside world.

Since human warmth matters to them, being a member of the barrio community is important in itself, and people are willing to spend money to increase their acceptability as members. A man may go away to work primarily in order to pay the expenses of a mayordomia, and the rest of the community notices and is gratified (or not) by the amount that he spends on food, liquor, and entertainment. Ceremonial spending, even at the household level, is subject to community comment. When the death of a rich man is announced, it is sometimes said that "a bull has died," meaning that a bull rather than a cow will be killed for the funeral feast. Tradition and opinion demand that those who have wealth share it, to some degree, with the rest. Respect and honor are the rewards for this kind of service to the community. On the other hand, display of wealth in personal adornment or consumption of alien foods is likely to be widely criticized. The economics of this situation can perhaps best be summarized in the words of Eric Wolf (1957) who describes the closed corporate peasant community (of which Juxtlahuaca's barrio is an example) in the following terms.

> Closed, corporate peasant communities . . . maintain a body of rights to possessions, such as land . . . (they) put pressures on members to redistribute surpluses at their command, preferably in the operation of a religious system,

and induce them to content themselves with the rewards of "shared poverty" . . . They strive to prevent outsiders from becoming members of the community, and (place) limits on the ability of members to communicate with the larger society. . . . (Their) internal function . . . is to equalize the life chances and life risks of (their) members.

Closed corporate peasant communities . . . will strive to force co-members to redistribute or destroy any pool of accumulated wealth which could potentially be used to alter the land tenure balance in favor of a few individual families or individuals. Purchase of goods produced outside the peasant sector of society and their ostentatious display also rank as major social threats, since they are prima facie evidence of an unwillingness to continue to redistribute and destroy such accumulated surplus. They are indications of an unwillingness to share the life risks of fellow villagers according to traditional cultural patterns. Among most peasant groups, as indeed among most social groups anywhere, social relations represent a sort of long-term life insurance. The extension of goods and services at any given moment is expected to yield results in the future, in the form of help in the case of threat.

People of the barrio, then, generally feel the need of the life insurance their community can provide and are willing to pay for it in terms of continued residence in the community and distribution of surpluses according to traditional rules.

❧
❧
❧

Chapter 4

Family Organization and Kinship

THE EXTENDED FAMILY

The typical family in Santo Domingo is an extended one. While a nuclear family, which characterizes our own society, consists of a husband and wife, together with their children, an extended family may include married brothers, together with their wives and children. As we shall see below, the families in Juxtlahuaca most frequently contain two or three nuclear families within the same household.

These extended families are housed together within a jointly owned compound which consists of a large area that generally has several rooms and cook shacks around a common patio area. A compound has its limits defined by an adobe wall or, less usually, by a wire or wooden fence. Within the compound, each of the individual rooms is thought of as belonging to one or another of the family members. The patio area, however, is the common property, so far as use is concerned, of the whole family. The compound area will also include two or three cook shacks in which the adult women prepare food, as well as sheds for the burros and chickens and pigs.

Residence is ideally patrilocal, that is, at marriage the wife would move to reside with her husband, and the new couple would reside with or near the husband's father. When interviewed, people of the barrio say that such patrilocal residence is to be preferred. In actual practice there is a great deal of variation in residence patterns. A number of circumstances make it desirable for the husband to join his wife and live with or adjacent to her family. The major determinant as to whether or not a newly married couple will reside near the husband's family is the availability of space in the prospective compound, together with the relative economic position of the family. When the husband comes from a lower economic group, and his compound is already crowded, the couple may elect to live with the wife's family if there is room in that compound. In the event that there is no room in either of the compounds, the couple will tend to reside as closely as possible to one or the other set of parents; so, although they are not living in the same compound, they are very close, and the day to day interaction amounts to virtual membership in the extended family. Thus, for example, related children living in adjacent households frequently play together and interact very closely with each other regardless of the fact that they do not all share a single patio area and common compound.

The question arises as to whether to count adjacent families who are related and interact frequently as nuclear or extended. We have checked on the total barrio, counting them first one way and then the other. If we count them as nuclear families, we find that one third of the families in the barrio would be classed as nuclear families. On the other hand, if we count on the basis of interaction, relationship, and adjacency, then over four fifths of the families in the barrio live in extended families. For purposes of socialization, we feel that the second criteria is a better one to follow. On this basis, only 3 of the 22 intensively studied families would be counted as nuclear families.

The same distinction also affects the extent to which the ideal patterns of patrilocality are carried out. The ideally stated pattern of preference for patrilocal residence is not borne out by an actual statis-

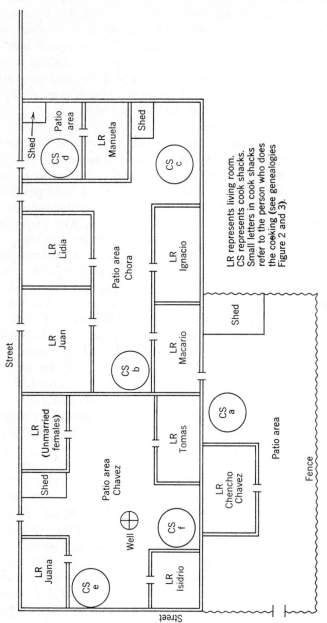

LR represents living room.
CS represents cook shacks.
Small letters in cook shacks
refer to the person who does
the cooking (see genealogies
Figure 2 and 3).

Figure 1. Typical barrio residential arrangement.

588

tical count. The relationship between adjacent families in the barrio as a whole is as frequently linked through females as through males. This judgment assumes that the criterion of interaction and adjacency is more important than sharing a single common patio area. If the more stringent criterion of sharing a common compound patio is invoked, then the ideally stated pattern of patrilocal residence has an edge of about two to one (i.e., about twice as many extended families are related only through males as there are extended families including both male and female adults).

A detailed examination of one or two residential arrangements will illustrate the organization of the extended family. Figures 1, 2, and 3 present a typical floor plan and the genealogies of some interrelated households.

An examination of Figure 1 illustrates several characteristic features of the compounds of the barrio as a whole. Note that there is no rigid pattern for the arrangement of the rooms and cook shacks within the compound area. This is true of the barrio as a whole, and an examination of the arrangement of all of the compounds in the barrio fails to reveal any two that are identical.

Despite the variety of arrangements, there are other characteristics that are true of almost all compound areas. There is always a common entrance from the street into the patio area. That is, members of the family can enter into the patio area, which is a common family

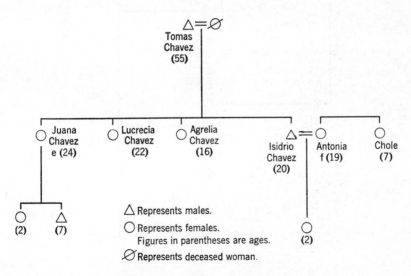

Figure 2. Genealogy of Chavez family.

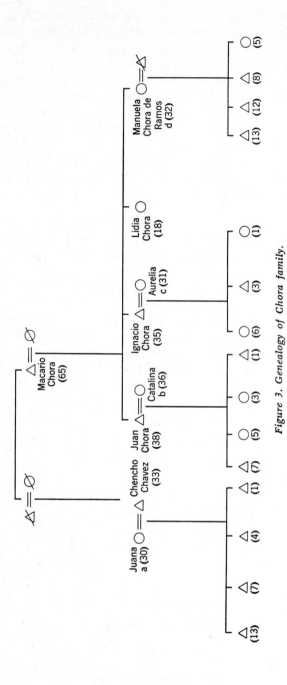

Figure 3. Genealogy of Chora family.

area, from the street without going through their individual rooms. In about 10% of the compounds in the barrio, there are additional private entrances. One private entrance illustrated in Figure 1 is the door from the street that goes directly into the living room of Juan Chora.

It is to be noted that each compound also contains cook shacks. The cook shacks in Figure 1 are all indicated as being round. This is generally the case, although some of them may be rectangular in shape. Also note that there is provision for a shed for animals in each of the compounds. In only one of the compounds illustrated in Figure 1 is there a well. In the barrio as a whole, approximately one out of ten compounds has a well.

The entrance from the patio area of Chencho Chavez into the room of Macario Chora and from there into the patio area of the main Chora compound indicates a rather close relationship between Chencho Chavez and the Chora family, and, in general, the compounds of closely related people may have common entry ways. This makes the problem of rigidly defining the boundary of a compound virtually impossible, and it illustrates the necessity for thinking of extended families in a flexible framework. As these families develop through time, it is possible for them to merge compounds or to partition a single compound into a series of smaller compounds. For example, on the large genealogy of the Chora family, it will be noted that Manuela Ramos is a sister of Juan and Ignacio Chora. As can be seen from the map, Manuela maintains a separate small patio area and cook shack. At one time Manuela's house was connected by an entry way to the common patio area of the Chora compound. Today we would have to consider her as occupying a distinct compound because there is no common entry way from her area into that occupied by her brothers. There is no set rule about when divisions of compounds might take place, and there are other compounds in the village in which married brothers and married sisters do live together in the same compound. Judged on the amount of interaction that takes place between Manuela's children and the children of Juan and Ignacio, Manuela's family could be considered part of the same extended family as her brothers.

The difficulty in distinguishing between closely related adjacent families is illustrated again in the position of Chencho Chavez, who is related to Juan and Ignacio as a cousin and who spends a good deal of time with his family in the compound area of Juan and Ignacio. (Chencho Chavez is more distantly related to Tomas Chavez and is living where he is because of his relationship to Macario Chora and not because of his relationship to the Chavez household.)

All adult women who have children who are not yet adults have cook shacks, as can be seen if we match up the genealogies to the cook shacks in the map. These are indicated in the figures with small letters. Elderly people—for example, Tomas and Macario—eat, in general, with the family of their eldest child if they live in the same compound. Thus Tomas Chavez eats with his daughter-in-law Antonia while Macario eats with the family of Juan Chora.

The ideal pattern of patrilocal residence probably influences the organization of the extended family in such cases as the families of Chencho and Manuela, both of whom are heads of households that are related through females, but neither of whom share the main Chora compound. However, there are several examples in the barrio of situations where an adult brother and sister do live in a common compound with their spouses and children. Thus the practice of separating the houses of brothers and sisters is not always carried out in the same way that it is in this particular family. Although much of the primary child care is allocated to a true sibling when one of an appropriate age and sex is available, one of the cousins frequently takes this responsibility when one is not available. Thus, for example, the children of the four families represented on the Chora genealogy in Figure 3 play together and have child caretaking responsibilities with very little differentiation between those who live in Manuela's family and those who live in the patio area of the main Chora family. This is not to say that there is no distinction, but only that the amount of interaction is very great and that the differences and distinctions made between the children who live within the compound and those who live in closely related compounds are very small from a child's point of view.

It is also important to remember that each of the individual nuclear families eats separately and that this is invariably the case throughout the barrio.

The internal organization of the extended family needs closer examination. We have seen that the extended family consists of a small number of nuclear families, together with various older people and a few other dependent relatives, as illustrated by the sister of Antonia in the Chavez family. Within the wider extended family, each nuclear family, consisting ideally of husband and wife and their children, occupies a distinct room and has use of a distinct cook shack. Thus, while there is a great deal of cooperation within the extended family, the individual nuclear families do maintain identity as separate and important social units. In the next chapter we will examine the functioning of these units as well as the complete family in its relations to the barrio as a whole. Let us return our attention now to further aspects of the internal organization of the families.

Economic arrangements within the family are best mirrored by the assignment of people to a particular cook shack. This defines the group that is economically responsible for food and its preparation. Though the children of a compound, or adjacent compounds, may play together in an undifferentiated way all day, and though the men may leave to go to the field, the nuclear family reassembles for major meals. In addition to the nuclear family, elderly people or younger dependent people will join a particular nuclear unit for purposes of eating. The food used by a particular woman in cooking is kept separate from that of all other women in the compound. For example, in the main Chora compound, Juan's wife is assigned one cook shack and Juan's father, Macario, eats with them, but their personal belongings and economic resources are kept separate from those of Juan's brother Ignacio. Lidia, an unmarried younger sister of Juan and Ignacio, eats with Ignacio. Thus we have a situation in which there are two adult couples who live in the same compound and share the use of the patio area and the shed for animals but who keep the produce of their fields separate from one another. In some compounds the woman who is economically responsible and occupies a cook shack may have no husband or male for support. An example of this situation is Juana Chavez in the Chavez household. Here, Juana is economically responsible for herself and her two younger sisters. They get some help from their brother Isidrio, but to a very great extent, they take care of themselves. In case of real economic need, families within the same extended household come to each other's aid, even though it is ideally stated that they are responsible for their own subsistence. The farmland belonging to an extended household is owned individually and not corporately. The houses within a compound are also individually owned. However, if a house is standing empty, its owner would certainly give permission for any close relative to occupy it and become a member of the extended family.

Thus, if an individual was in need, he would first turn to other members of his extended household for economic aid. If there were not enough resources within the extended family as a whole, he would appeal to close relatives in other extended households. There is a great deal of sharing of food and other resources within the extended family, but informal track is kept of the exchange of food and other items, and it is expected that the exchange will be reasonably equal.

One of the more important functions of the extended household is to increase the probability that an older child will be available for the caretaking of younger children. If we count all of the families in the barrio, we find that there are more cousins acting as caretakers of younger cousins than there are older siblings caring for younger siblings. Women with infants will also call on other women in the same extended household to care for their infants while they are away at market or otherwise occupied outside the compound area. So we find that the wife of Juan Chora will occasionally leave her youngest boy with the wife of Ignacio Chora. Sisters-in-law residing in a common household will even, on occasion, nurse each other's children or infants if necessary.

Older people within the extended family are respected but are not dictatorial heads of households. Thus, for example, Macario Chora and Tomas Chavez, in the households under discussion, are respected, but they do not give orders to their children and in many respects are dependent elderly males. They may not even be very active in work outside the household, but they would contribute the produce from any land they might have to the household in which they live and particularly to the group with which they eat.

There is no head, in any recognized or institutionalized sense, of the extended family as a whole. Rather, the adult men who are still in the prime of life all maintain more or less equal status, and each has complete freedom to carry on his affairs as he sees fit. The elder brother may have prerogatives in the community not yet obtained by the younger brother, but the elder brother does not have authority over the younger.

KINSHIP TERMINOLOGY

One of the indicators of family organization is the way in which people classify their relatives terminologically. The family organization in Santo Domingo is mirrored very nicely in the local kinship terminology. Figure 4 shows in diagrammatic form the way in which the barrio people classify their relatives. Each box in the diagram represents a category of relatives that are called by a single term. In each box we have included a crude English paraphrase for the kind of relative and have followed this with the Mixteco term in parentheses. The horizontal lines in the figure represent differences between generations, and the vertical lines represent distinctions made in terms of closeness of relationship. The closest relatives are direct relatives who stand in direct lines of ascent or descent or are full siblings. A second category is labeled collateral relatives, which includes the spouses

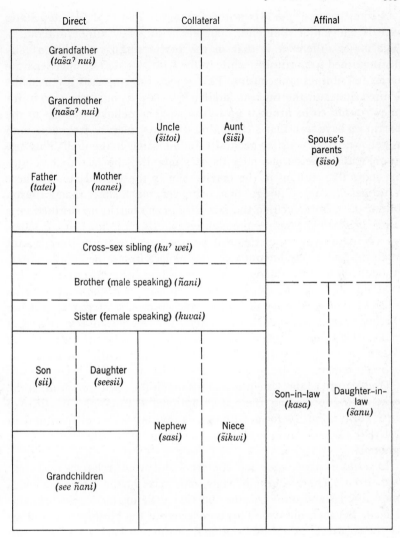

Figure 4. Kinship terminology of the barrio.

of collateral relatives and one's spouse's collateral relatives. The third major category includes one's wife's direct relatives and one's direct relative's spouses. Thus it can be seen that there is a single term for one's wife's mother and father and their parents, and, in turn, there are terms for one's children and their spouses. These last terms are further distinguished by sex.

A comparison of the Mixtec terminology to that in the United States reveals one major difference, together with a few minor differences. The major difference is that in the barrio siblings are not usually distinguished from cousins, while in the United States, we have separate terms for siblings and cousins. This reflects the emphasis given in the United States to the nuclear family. It is rare in our own society for one's cousins to be brought up in the same household, whereas in the barrio we have seen that a child almost always interacts frequently and closely with his cousins, generally in the same household. This terminological difference represents or symbolizes the fact that cousins are more like siblings in the barrio than in the United States, where a brother or sister is thought of as being very much closer than a cousin. Minor differences include the fact that in the barrio no distinction is made between the sex of grandchildren. Also, in the United States, we are more likely to distinguish great-aunt or great-uncle from aunt or uncle, and a grand-nephew or grand-niece from a nephew or niece. Another interesting difference is in the sibling and cousin terminology. Where English distinguishes only the absolute sex of the relative being referred to in the terms of brother and sister, the Mixtec system has three terms: one is used between relatives of opposite sex, that is, a male to his sister or female cousin and a female to her brother or male cousin, another is used between males, and still a third is used only between females.

One feature of the system is that although the term for cousin is the same as that for sibling, there is an optional addition of a modifier to distinguish them. In former times this option was never used and in everyday usage today it is still most common for this distinction to be ignored.

In terms of experience and contact with various relatives it is clear that, from a child's point of view, one plays in the compound with one's siblings and one's cousins and that little distinction in behavior is made between the two. This is reflected in the kinship terminology by the relatively minor and optional distinction between cousins and siblings. On the other hand, one looks to one's own parents for food and for the primary responsibility in caretaking and discipline. This is demonstrated in the eating patterns, in the sleeping patterns, and in the separate rooms for the nuclear families. Thus father and mother and son and daughter are closer than one's uncles and aunts and nephews and nieces. Since one's uncles and aunts from both sides of the family are likely to live close by with their spouses, one would not expect a distinction to be made between different kinds of aunts and uncles and whether they were related through blood or by marriage.

In this respect, the system is very similar to English. On the other hand, one's spouse's parents and one's children's spouses do not necessarily grow up in the same household; thus one assumes a new relationship with them upon their marriages, and they are clearly distinguished from other relatives.

There are no strongly patterned behaviorial preferences or customs among the barrio people. One is supposed to be helpful and responsible for one's relatives, but there are no taboos or strong patterns among relatives such as mother-in-law avoidance or joking relationship.

RITUAL KINSHIP AND FAMILY FIESTAS

As in many other parts of Mexico, ritual kinship is highly elaborated in the barrio. By far the most frequent term of address overheard on barrio streets is the term "compadre" or "comadre," indicating some kind of ritual kinship. There are nine occasions which result in ritual kinships. Ranked in order of most to least importance, they are as follows:

1. Baptism
2. First mass
3. First communion
4. Confirmation
5. Wedding
6. Raising of the cross after death
7. New house
8. Private saint
9. Animals (mainly for children)

Let us illustrate the concepts involved in this relationship by discussing baptism. When a child is born, the parents choose some couple they would like eventually to be the godparents of the new child. If the couple chosen agrees to the invitation, they become related by the term "padrinos." Padrinos are future godparents of the child and future compadres to the parents of the child. Unlike some systems in which the emphasis is placed on the godparent-godchild relationship, Santo Domingans put the emphasis on the compadre relationship, or the connection between the parents and godparents. The new padrinos then become responsible for certain duties such as arranging and paying for the baptism of their future godchild and providing a new set of clothes for the occasion. It is also their duty to supply a meal for the guests during the compadre ceremony.

Let us outline an actual example. One couple has an infant for whom it invites another couple to become godparents. The future godparents (padrinos) then arrange for the baptism. On the evening when the infant is to be baptized, there will be a procession to the church where the ceremony will take place. The padrinos go to the home of the parents, dress the infant in a new outfit, and carry the child to the church at the head of the procession. After the priest baptizes the child, the padrinos and guests return to the home of the parents of the infant, where food is served to everyone present, and then a ceremony is performed.

This ceremony consists of a series of speeches by a speaker representing the parents and another speaker for the padrinos in which the values of the ritual kinship tie are extolled. Ritual gifts are distributed between the two families. Afterward, the families and relatives of the parents line up opposite the families and relatives of the padrinos, and everyone in each line embraces everyone in the other line as they pass each other. It is on the occasion of the ceremonial embrace that the compadre relationship is solidified. After this ceremony, everyone who has taken part in the embraces calls each other "compadre." The padrinos have become compadres of the parents and godparents of the infant. The relationship between the infant and his godparents is permanent, and one is supposed to have respect for his godparents and be able to call on them in times of trouble, but the more significant relationship is the reciprocal one between compadres.

As can be seen, the proliferation of ritual kinship ties is very great in that the relatives of both parents and godparents also become ritually related.

There are regularities in the ceremonies in which ritual kinship ties are formed and in the duties performed by the actors in the ceremonies. Since all of these elements appear in the ceremonies connected with baptism, we may use it as an example in the following discussion. The ceremonial round that results in the formation of compadre relationships is always initiated by some person or persons in behalf of some occasion, object, or person(s). The initiating party is most frequently a married couple, in which case the initiative would be taken by the husband. Less frequently the initiative is taken by an individual.

The occasions that provide an appropriate setting for the initiating party to act are implied in the names of the kinds of compadre relationships listed previously. In the example of baptism, the parents of the new infant are the initiators in behalf of the infant. First mass, first communion, and confirmation are also appropriate occasions. In funeral ceremonies it is the cross which must be raised at the end of nine days that provides the appropriate object for the initiation of a compadre ceremony. The completion of a new house also sets the occasion for a couple to initiate a compadre ceremony.

Regardless of what sets the occasion for a compadre ceremony, the initiator's first action is to invite some person or persons to be padrinos of the object or event that sets the occasion for the ceremony. In the baptism ceremony they are said to be padrinos of the infant being baptized. In the case of a funeral they are padrinos of the cross. Similarly, there are padrinos of a new house and padrinos of private saints, and so forth. For baptism, first mass, first communion, and confirmation, a married couple is invariably chosen as padrinos. For a wedding two married couples are chosen, while for the funeral cross there are five, and for a new house, four. In the case of private saints and animals, only one couple is chosen.

For every ceremony the padrino has certain invariable responsibilities. For example, he always has the responsibility for "dressing" or caring for the object of which he is a padrino, for example, infant, cross, house, and so on. Thus, in the case of baptism, he supplies the clothes that the infant wears during the procession and baptism. For first mass or first communion or confirmation, the padrino would supply a new outfit of clothes. Similarly, for the wedding, the padrinos provide new clothes for the couple to be married. For the cross, house, saint, animals, and so on, the padrinos would be responsible for decorating or dressing the object.

A second invariable responsibility of the padrinos consists of arranging for a priest to bless the object or to carry out and consummate the ritual that constitutes the occasion for the ceremony. His services are needed on all the occasions and the padrinos arrange for his coming and pay for his services.

Another invariable aspect of the ceremony is that the padrinos and initiators of the ceremony must engage in the ritual meal. In almost all cases the meal follows the services of the priest. In a few cases where this is inconvenient or impossible, the meal may precede the services of the priest. In all cases in which the ritual meal follows the services, the ritual embrace takes place at that time. Otherwise it will take place after the services.

All of the above features are invariable, even though they may occur in rather attenuated form. For example, the ritual meal may not consist of anything more than hot chocolate and sweet bread. Features in the ceremony that are subject to variation include the size and elaborateness of the ceremony, whether or not speakers for the two sides are formally chosen and participate in the ceremony, as well as the number of padrinos involved in the ceremony. Two examples in addition to the one given on baptism may aid in giving an idea of the amount of variation and importance invested in the *compadre* relationship. We will discuss those connected with animals and with the completion of a new house.

During February of each year a special day is set aside for the blessing of animals by the local priest. On these occasions, if a youth or older child desires to form a compadre relationship with a friend, he may do so by inviting the friend to be a padrino of an animal. If the friend accepts, it becomes his responsibility as padrino of the animal to dress and decorate the animal with crepe paper and ribbons and to carry it down to the central part of town where it is blessed by the priest. Then the padrino of the animal returns the animal to the house of its owner, and the children or youths have a meal together and go through the ritual embrace and become compadres. The resulting relationship is not necessarily permanent and tends to be recognized only so long as the participants find it convenient. It is discussed here to illustrate the total range of compadre relationships that is possible. The animal involved may be a pet or farm animal; it does not matter. The mood surrounding this little ritual is as playful as it is serious. It is taken very lightly by adults. However, it is exceedingly popular, and the central church courtyard is always full of a weird collection of animals, ranging from birds to bulls, on the day designated for the blessing of the animals by the local priest.

The compadre relationship is also formed when a new house is completed. In this situation the owner of the house invites four people to be padrinos of the house, that is, future compadres. These padrinos decorate (dress) the house and arrange for the priest to come and bless it, following which there are a ritual meal and the ceremony involving the ritual embrace between the family who owns the house and the families of the padrinos. All who embrace thereby become compadres.

Some general remarks on ritual kinship may be useful. It is significant to note that it is the collateral tie between compadres that is stressed and not the lineal tie between godparents and godchild. This is a very dominant theme in the barrio and is consistent with the annual circulation of membership in the cofradias. The custom of having someone speak for the principals during the ritual corresponds to the practice in the cofradias of a speaker for the mayordomo. The term padrino is also used reciprocally between future compadres.

It should be pointed out that the importance placed on a com-

View of house from inside courtyard.

Women weaving.

Woman carrying basket.

Man plowing.

Girl imitating mother.

Woman making tortilla.

Young girl caretakers.

Fiesta, showing musicians, masked dancers, and spectators.

Women visiting in a courtyard.

Casual caretaking.

Playing house.

padre relationship varies with the importance of the original occasion which gave rise to the association, baptism being the most important and the blessing of animals, the least important. For the more important type of compadre relationships, the children of compadres would extend terms for brothers and sisters to each other. Consequently, if you heard two men call each other brother, it may mean that their parents are close compadres or it may mean that they are in fact brothers or cousins. The compadre relationship is the one that is frequently called on when one needs more labor than can be supplied by one's true relatives. If a man needs help in putting up a house, he may call on his compadres to help him; or if a man needs many helpers during harvest, he will call on his compadres. In these situations he will pay for food and refreshment after the task is done. There is no exchange of money for these kinds of services.

In addition to the fiestas involving compadre relationships, there are a small number of occasions for which it is appropriate to give private fiestas. The main kinds of private fiestas are those for harvesting a field, for celebrating one's birthday, and for celebrating the anniversary of the death of an important relative. On any of these occasions it is appropriate to give a large meal for everyone involved and to serve aguardiente. The harvesting of fields is almost invariably accompanied by a private fiesta at the end of the day's work. Birthdays are frequently celebrated in a similar way, as is the anniversary of the death of a parent or, more rarely, of a spouse.

✻
✻
✻

Chapter 5

Barrio Social Organization

The most important set of customs relating to social organization in the barrio is the "cofradia" organization. A cofradia is a society organized for the purpose of sponsoring celebrations in honor of various saints. In Santo Domingo a cofradia refers to a group of people who are organized into a society whose function it is to honor a particular saint. Most of the cofradias hold a celebration on that saint's day; in addition, they hold a midyear celebration. Other cofradias may honor the saint for a whole month.

An example of the first type of cofradia is that organized to honor Santiago, the patron saint of Juxtlahuaca. The largest ceremony of the year is held during the days preceding and following July 25th, the day of Santiago. The midyear celebration on January 25th is a smaller ceremony, also sponsored by the cofradia, to honor Santiago. An example of a cofradia that involves no large celebration but honors a particular saint for a longer period of time is one called Heart of Jesus. This is celebrated during the whole month of June, with a special mass on June 29th.

The cofradias are composed of groups of varying numbers of people, from as few as 3 or 4 to as many as 40 or 50. Each cofradia has a leader or mayordomo. The mayordomo, as well as the rest of the members, or diputados, of the cofradia, serves for a period of one year. It is the duty of the mayordomo and his helpers to sponsor a celebration to honor the saint for whom that cofradia has responsibility. The celebrations may vary from year to year, depending on how much economic surplus the community may have. In years of drought the celebration in honor of the patron saint Santiago may be fairly small, while in good years the celebration would be very large.

There is a total of nine cofradias in the barrio; thus, including midyear celebrations, there would be approximately 18 fiestas in honor of saints during the year. Not all of these celebrations would be participated in by all the members of the barrio, but approximately five or six during the year are important enough to involve everyone, and some would include invited guests from several of the surrounding Mixtec villages. The nine cofradias in the barrio are listed below in approximate order of importance.

1. Santiago
2. Santo Domingo
3. San Sebastian
4. San Marcos
5. Padre Jesus
6. Santa Cruz
7. Virgin of the Rosario
8. Heart of Jesus
9. Heart of Mary

The first six mentioned above are all composed of men, while the last three are made up entirely of women. The activties of the women's groups differ slightly from those of the men's groups. For example, the duties of the female cofradias extend through a whole month, during which time the women place flowers in the church daily and arrange for special masses. Those cofradias composed of men give celebrations centering on a particular saint's day, as well as the mid-year celebrations.

The functioning of the major cofradias can best be understood by referring to a specific example. We will describe the celebration sponsored by the cofradia responsible for honoring the day of the patron saint of Juxtlahuaca, Santiago. The fiesta we observed had been preceded by a year of good crops and was considered a relatively large one. The mayordomo was assisted by 45 helpers. While the main day of the celebration was July 25th, the program participated in by all barrio members and people from several other towns included the five days from July 24th to July 28th. Some weeks before the main festivities began, the cofradia sent out invitations to surrounding villages to invite their musical and dancing groups to participate in the celebration. In addition, they invited the members of 12 of the surrounding Mixtec villages to come as guests.

The celebration is always financed by contributions, in decreasing amounts, from the mayordomo, his helpers, and guests. For this one, the mayordomo contributed 1500 pesos, each of his helpers contributed the equivalent of 250 pesos, either in the form of money or goods, while guests contributed 3 pesos. All of these contributions are classed as voluntary donations. It may be noted parenthetically that any time an individual in the barrio accumulates any money, great pressures are put on him to participate in an important cofradia either as a helper or as a mayordomo. When one considers that the average income of a barrio male is about 3 pesos a day, one can understand the extent of the economic sacrifice made by a mayordomo and his diputados.

When a mayordomo or helper is chosen to serve in a cofradia, his participation is considered voluntary and includes not only the services and contributions of the male but also the contributions of his family. Each member of the cofradia is responsible for furnishing several days' work on the part of his wife. In the vast majority of cases, it is only married men who participate as helpers or mayordomo in the cofradia. If a man does not have a wife, one of his relatives will serve in place of the wife.

This fiesta in celebration of Santiago is considered an Indian celebration, and the townspeople do not attend except for a token appearance at the dances and music during the major days. Beginning on the 17th of July and continuing to the 25th, special masses are given in the church each day. Each of these masses is arranged, sponsored, and paid for by a particular member of the barrio as a contribution to the over-all celebration in honor of the patron saint.

As we observed on July 24th, the musical groups and guests began to arrive and to congregate at the community house of the barrio. A musical group or band consisting of several wind instruments, together with a drum and fife and violin, came from each of four villages. Thus, by 10 o'clock in the morning there were five musical groups playing music in the community center. The music continued for five days with no time out during the evening. The groups took turns, but one or another played day and night for the five days. In addition, four dancing groups—Chareos, Chilolos, Rubios, and Moros—assembled and provided entertainment for the guests during most of the daylight hours. These groups consist of from 5 to 30 members, all in costume, and each group performs a kind of dramatic story. The dance of the Moros, for example, consists of two lines of dancers facing each other, dancing forward and back, swinging their machetes as swords, re-enacting the fight between the Christians and the Moros. All of these dances date from the colonial period in Mexico, when they were introduced by the Spaniards, and have since evolved from these early dramatic dance forms.

The middle of the day of the 24th, the music had begun playing and the dancers had each given a performance. Then a procession was organized with the mayordomo and his helpers at the head, followed by the band and dance groups, with the guests bringing up the rear. This procession, preceded by fireworks and other festive activities, went to the barrio church. At the church the image of the patron saint, which is a figure approximately 5 feet high of Santiago seated on a horse, was removed from the church, and a benediction in his honor was delivered by the priest in the churchyard. A smaller image, approximately 2 inches high and made of silver, was also blessed. Then the larger image was returned to its position in the church while the smaller image was carried by the procession to the courtyard and house of the mayordomo, where it would stay for the remainder of the celebration. In the courtyard of the mayordomo, the musicians continued to play and the dance groups to perform while the helpers went to their respective homes to gather together their contributions for the festivities. During the course of the afternoon, turkeys, chickens, and cattle to be used for food later in the ceremony were gathered together in the mayordomo's courtyard. Around 4 o'clock in the afternoon, these animals and other foods had been assembled and decorated.

The mayordomo, his family, and friends carrying his contributions, followed by the helpers with their families and contributions, made up another procession, which returned to the community center. The year that we observed this procession there were 3 beef cattle, 80 turkeys, and 50 chickens, together with numerous gallons of aguardiente and many bags of cocoa beans and other foodstuffs.

On returning to the community center, the men of the cofradia, together with their wives, immediately began the slaughter of all of the animals and the preparation of the food. In the evening at the community center a meal was served to all the assembled people, and the dances and fireworks and music continued on into the evening.

During all the time the celebration was going on at the community center, the males composing the cofradia sat inside the large community room around a single, very long table. It is their duty to sit there, to make speeches, and to eat and drink during all five days of the ceremony. They leave the room only to participate in the processions and the masses, and they catch what sleep they can while sitting at the table.

The second day, July 25th, which is the major day, is primarily focused around a religious procession in which the large image of Santiago is paraded completely around the village of Juxtlahuaca. Stops are made at each of the four corners of the village, and the saint is placed inside a previously prepared temporary shelter in which an altar has been arranged. The priest blesses the saint at each of these stops. This is one of the processions in which townspeople participate to a much greater extent than they do in the others. In the early afternoon after this religious procession, the main banquet takes place. The beef slaughtered the night before is served with mole and specially baked bread and other festive foods. The evening is devoted to a special church service, after which the major fireworks and dancing resume in the community center.

The third day of the fiesta continues the dancing and music and eating of the preceding days, with one additional special event. This event is a ritual meeting between the officials of the Spanish-speaking part of town and the barrio officials. During this special ceremony the presidente or mayor of the town, together with other town officials, meets with the Indian officials of the barrio and the cofradia inside the community house. Official greetings are brought by the mayor and his group to the barrio officials. An exchange of gifts is made between the two groups, and several speeches are made in which the recurring theme is the maintenance of good relations between the two parts of the community. The cofradia is represented by a specially designated speaker, not by the mayordromo himself. The mayor of the town reaffirms his delegation of certain authority and independence to the barrio officials. In turn, the barrio officials reaffirm their willingness to obey the laws and customs of the town. Town and barrio groups of men are then served a special meal by the wives of the helpers, after which the town officials depart and the general festivities continue.

The following two days of the fiesta continue with music and dancing during the day and some fireworks at night. Inside the community house, the men devote themselves to the business of choosing a new set of helpers for the cofradia for the following year. They also have to make an accounting of the finances and belongings of the cofradia, and they go through a ceremony to transfer these belongings and responsibilities to the new mayordomo and his helpers. On the last day there is a procession from the home of the old mayordomo to the home of the new, and the new mayordomo and his helpers then officially take over the duties for honoring the saint for the coming year.

The preceding description of a ceremony given by a cofradia should give the reader some idea of the nature of the ceremony. Let us call attention to a few of the more salient and general features of the ceremony as a whole. That it is a ceremony in which the Indian barrio takes great pride is apparent. That the barrio holds these kinds of ceremonies while the townspeople do not sets it off as distinctively Indian. That a ceremony as large as this one is a significant economic drain on the part of the community that can least afford it is also noteworthy. Clearly, such a fiesta pattern makes it impossible for the Indians to accumulate any amount of capital. The men in the barrio view membership in a cofradia as both a duty and an honor. However, the way in which the men cooperate to produce such a celebration makes it impossible, also, for any single person to maintain any special prestige or privileges. The fact that a new group of men takes over each year means that each adult male in the barrio will have served in several cofradias during the course of his life. If a cofradia gives a particularly successful celebration, people will talk about it for a few years, but no other rewards are entailed.

Thus the honoring of a patron saint is seen as reflecting on the barrio as a whole and not as raising any individual above any others. The behavior of the cofradia meetings is democratic and equalitarian. The same thing is true of the women's behavior in the preparation of food in that no one woman directs the activities of the others; instead, they all do their part without prompting or direction.

Many of the ceremonies are rather small and may include only

200 or 300 people in the barrio; but a general feature of all cofradia ceremonies is the inclusion of music, dancing, drinking, and serving of a meal. These items are a minimum requirement in the celebration of any saint's day by a cofradia.

Chapter 6

Social Control

Social control mechanisms may be defined as the various devices used by a society to ensure conformity to the rules of the society and to control the aggressive impulses of its members. Uncontrolled aggression would pose a serious threat to the social organization of the barrio. The discussion of social control will emphasize the control of aggression among adults.

Before describing reaction to physical aggression and occasions that may lead to aggression, it is important to point out that the more serious crimes, such as homicide, would be handled within the framework of the regular court systems in Mexico. The following discussion focuses on the mechanisms used within the barrio to minimize aggressive outbursts. No attempt will be made to describe the wider court system of Mexico as it is practiced in the central part of town.

It is rare for a conflict between members of the barrio to reach the Mexican court system. Conflicts do arise between members of the barrio and townspeople, and these frequently reach the formal court system. This is partly because the townspeople are not under the influence of the factors operating within the barrio to reduce aggression and conflict.

No barrio member was involved in a court case during our year's residence in the field. No cases of theft nor accusations of theft came to our attention, and despite the fact of numerous opportunities, the investigators never lost any material goods during the year. Adultery between members of the barrio does not reach the formal court system but is handled within the barrio, as will be reported below. On the other hand, if a person from the center of town were to attack a barrio girl, it is reported that her family may well take the case to court; otherwise there would be no possible way of punishing the offender or receiving justice.

During a year's study in Juxtlahuaca, we observed only one case of overt physical aggression among members of the barrio. This particular episode will be described in some detail, for it illustrates many salient points. It took place during a group house-building fiesta in which the roof of a house was being completed by a group of approximately 20 men, while the women were gathered around the cook shack preparing food to be served when the task was completed. Several men were on the roof of the house passing up tiles; several others were on the ground carrying materials and handing them up to those on the roof.

The task was just about completed, and the men had begun to drink; the bottle of aguardiente was being passed with some frequency. A young man named Pedro was drinking somewhat more heavily than the others while engaged in placing tiles at the very edge of the roof. A certain amount of by-play in the form of verbal joking was going on in a good-natured way with Pedro as a particularly prominent participant. As the drinking and bantering gained in momentum and the task neared completion, two or three men began pointing out to Pedro that his work was getting a little sloppy. They invited him to get off the roof and stop working and indicated that they would join him presently.

At one point a couple of men corrected Pedro's work by replacing some tiles. Pedro objected to this and said that he was perfectly capable of placing the tiles. While the men tried to humor him, he slipped and fell from the roof. His falling from the roof was not caused by any kind of physical scuffling; it was an accident caused by Pedro's partial drunkenness and by his tripping. When he fell to the ground, a fall of about 10 feet, people first looked to see whether or not he was hurt, and then everyone laughed uproariously. Nothing was hurt but Pedro's pride, and he wanted to climb back up on the roof and work.

At this point two or three men attempted physically to stop him and to humor him into staying on the ground. Pedro struck out at the men who were trying to prevent him from going back on the roof. The response of the men whom he struck was to move back and to try to cajole him into complying with their wishes. It was also clear that there was consensus among the men that Pedro had had enough to drink, that his effectiveness as a workman was impaired, and that it would be better if he sat quietly for a period of time. The men backed away to the street adjacent to where they were working; Pedro followed them and tried to pick a fight by hitting one or two of the men with his fists. None of the other men returned the blows, and several of them, including his closest friends, crowded around and put their hands on Pedro's shoulders, attempting to calm him down. He continued in his aggressive manner for three or four minutes, and all of the men became very anxious to quiet him. Finally, two of his friends persuaded him to sit down and take it easy and to forget further work.

There are several things to note in the above episode. One is the typical pattern of beginning to drink just before a task is finished, in anticipation of the food and drink which invariably follow work groups of this sort. The second thing is that none of the men returned Pedro's blows. Yet another point to notice is the fact that the men saw humor in the clumsiness of Pedro's falling from the roof. This is a very typical reaction on the part of male adults in particular and, to a lesser extent, of female adults in the barrio. We will note in the discussion of socialization that the reaction of an adult to a child's falling or accidentally hurting himself changes from nurturance to ridicule at the particular stage that marks the boundary between early childhood and late childhood. Another thing to stress is the amount of concern shown by all of the men for Pedro's aggression. They were clearly disturbed and wanted to do everything possible to calm him down and to avoid any aggressive behavior.

When interviewed afterward about the cause of Pedro's aggression, the men reported that this was extremely unusual behavior. They remarked that Pedro had gone to the city to work in the past and there had picked up the habit of smoking marijuana. During the morning of this occasion, he had been smoking marijuana; and, in their opinion, it was only a combination of the marijuana and drinking that could give rise to and account for such aggressive behavior. They reported that there were two other individuals in the barrio who had picked up the habit of smoking marijuana and that this was a particularly bad habit. Although they seemed to feel that it was a person's own business, they did consider that it was sad and unfortunate when such a thing happened.

When informants were asked about other causes of aggression, they reported that in the past, women, political factions, and land disputes were the most usual causes of aggression.

They reported that men sometimes fought over women but that this was very rare. There were no cases of men resorting to physical aggression over women during the year that we were there, and most reported episodes had taken place at some time in the past. If a man discovers that his wife has been sleeping or flirting with another man, his aggression may be taken out, according to informants, on either the other man or the wife. Although they did not remember any recent examples, they reported occasions when men beat their wives for sleeping with other men. They also reported episodes, again none recent, of men fighting over women. There was one case that was re- membered from an earlier generation of a man being killed in a fight over women. During the field period we had occasion to learn of cases in which a barrio wife was known to be sleeping with another man, but there was no physical aggression as a result. On one occasion we actually observed an informant discover another man in bed with his wife, and his response was to shrug his shoulders and to walk around the block. We do not know what happened subsequently, al- though we never observed or heard of any repercussions. On another occasion we observed an episode involving a married man and an un- married woman who were discovered in bed together. This fact be- came common knowledge in the barrio, and the result was a good deal of gossip directed toward both the man and the woman. Two days later, the woman went to stay with some relatives in Mexico City for a period of a month until the gossip had died down. The man re- mained in the barrio, and, other than gossip, there were no observable repercussions in his relation to his wife and family and to the other members of the barrio.

During election years the people in the center of town are extremely active and acrimonious in the political campaigns. Although the In- dians in the barrio have relatively little political power, several of the men are able to exert their right to vote. During this time emotions ride high and are fanned by the more aggressive people of the town, where physical aggression in the form of fights between men is not unusual. Any and all means of political persuasion are used during campaigns, including economic pressure and threats in the form of ambush and shooting by the townspeople. The political leaders in town attempt to attract the more progressive male adults from the barrio to their side and urge them to proselyte in their behalf. On these occasions it is reported that barrio men will sometimes find themselves in opposite factions and that, in the past, this has led to fighting among barrio members. Our field session took place during an election year, and it was apparently a quiet one, for there was no physical aggression in the form of fights generated in either the barrio or the town, but the informants reported that it is more normal for the townspeople to get into fights than not. The general attitude among the more level-headed elders in the barrio is to advocate noninvolvement in the political affairs of the main part of town, and there is a great deal of gossip to the effect that it is bad to get overinvolved in politics.

The problem of land disputes is a recurring one and most frequently pits the barrio men against the townspeople, although on occasion there can be disputes between members of the barrio concerning privately owned irrigated land in the valley.

One of the possible causes of aggression, which was specifically denied by informants on direct questioning, is drinking. This corresponds to our observations at the fiesta, where the men generally drank a great deal during the ceremonies but were never observed to become loud or aggressive.

We observed that the barrio people conform rather closely to their customs and are relatively free of aggressive outbursts and serious crimes. Two interrelated questions arise from such observations. First, how is such conformity to the group's standards maintained, and, second, how are the aggressive impulses so effectively controlled? Several very powerful social control mechanisms are at work in the barrio. The remainder of this chapter will be devoted to describing these mechanisms and attempting to interpret their success.

One approach to an understanding of why barrio members are so conforming and nonaggressive is to analyze the various types of possible punishments or threats of punishments for nonconformity, including aggressive outbursts. Many societies have a mechanism for imposing fines, jail sentences, or physical punishment for crimes against the society or its members. There are no such mechanisms within the barrio, and the barrio members seldom resort to the formal courts which do use such punishments. Thus the threat of such things as fines or jail sentences is not a primary mechanism of social control within the barrio. Still other societies use mechanisms such as gossip, backbiting, or threats of sorcery as mechanisms for social control. It is true that there is a certain amount of gossip within the barrio, and beliefs about sorcery do exist. However, the gossip is not of a very malicious nature, nor it is a preoccupation among the people. Similarly, almost no people in the barrio believe that they have been victims of sorcery. No one in the barrio is thought to be a sorcerer. Even though most of them believe that sorcerers exist in other villages, they are not preoccupied with the menace of sorcery. Thus such mechanisms as fear of sorcery, fear of malicious gossip or backbiting, or fear of physical punishment will not account for the degree of conformity observed in the barrio. We must look for other mechanisms of social control.

We believe that ostracism from the social life of the barrio is one of the realistic threats for compelling conformity and one of the important mechanisms of social control. Participation in the social life of the barrio and social acceptance are particularly important to the barrio individual. Emphasis on collateral ties is greatly elaborated in the family and social organization of the barrio, and the threat of ostracism would constitute an important deterrent on an individual's behavior.

One of the values in barrio social life is participation in the fiestas sponsored by the cofradias. During these fiestas the men sit in the main room of the community house and engage in social drinking. The drinking patterns during this time (and some observed deviations) provide insight into the importance of ostracism as a mechanism of social control. The pattern of drinking is highly stylized and has high symbolic meaning to the people of the barrio. We will describe it in some detail because of its importance in its contribution to understanding the role of ostracism.

As soon as the men congregate in the community room on any official confradia fiesta, a speaker for the mayordomo will stand and make a welcoming speech. The speech always contains references to the cohesiveness of the barrio group and to the necessity for maintaining ritual and ceremonial continuity with the past. At the end of his speech he invites the mayordomo to drink with him. A tray with two shot glasses on it is handed to the speaker, and he fills both of them with aguardiente. The speaker and mayordomo then salute each other and down the drinks in one gulp. It is obligatory for them to finish the entire shot. The tray is then passed on to the next individual at the table, and he salutes his neighbor at the table in the same way. The tray with the glasses and the bottle is passed around the entire table in this manner. There is a large bottle containing several gallons of aguardiente in the corner of the room, and each time the small bottle is emptied, it is replenished. It is obligatory for each man to drink with his neighbor at the table. In case one does not finish the entire amount of aguardiente, his penalty is that the glass must be refilled and he must drink again. There are no customs that allow an individual under these circumstances to refuse a drink. This differs from customs in other parts of Mexico where one may take the drink and pour it into his own bottle to save it until later or take only a sip, symbolizing his acceptance of the drink. By the time the tray reaches the head of the table and everyone has had one drink, another speech will have been made, and the tray will then make another round. This continues all during the time of the fiesta, which means that, for a small cofradia celebration, it will continue for a period of 12 hours or so; but, for a large fiesta, the men may be drinking, practically day and night, for a period of three days or longer. The result is that every man drinks either very close to his capacity or, more commonly, beyond it. It is perfectly acceptable for an individual to pass out at the table, and it is rather common during the longer fiestas. During the time that a man is unconscious, he is passed in the round of drinking; however, when he comes to and sits back up to the table, he is obligated to take his turn when the bottle is passed around.

The manifest function of this drinking pattern as stated by the men is that it represents solidarity and acceptance within the group. They recognize that the pattern is very different from that in the central part of town and say that it sets the Indian off from the Mexican. They also say that it symbolizes acceptance of the Indians and of the whole cofradia organization and the round of fiestas that it entails.

As an outsider we might interpret this pattern as having an aggressive as well as a sociable function. If we ask the question as to who is being aggressive to whom, the only answer is that a group of peers are being mutually aggressive among themselves. In this sense it is a high price to pay in order to stay in the round of ceremonies at the bario-wide level represented by the cofradias. To the extent that it does function as a mechanism for peers to dominate peers in a self-reciprocal type of way, it is a covert and unrecognized mechanism. The men would certainly deny that it had any aggressive or mutually dominating function.

Two other aspects warrant examination. One of these is the function of drink in other contexts and the second, more important, is the question as to what happens if a person is unwilling or unable to participate in such a round of drinking. The question concerning the use of alcohol in other contexts will be answered first. In other ceremonial contexts, for example, compadre ceremonies or private parties such as birthdays or harvest parties, alcohol is used in much the same way it is in the cofradia ceremonies. There is less drinking, with a few exceptions which would include weddings, where a great deal of alcohol is consumed. However, the patterns of reciprocal drinking are pretty much the same in other fiesta contexts, although not quite so formalized; the bottle is not passed around in a definite order, but most individuals drink about the same amount, and if invited to drink on these occasions, they must accept.

Outside of the fiesta context, the barrio men almost never drink aguardiente or other alcoholic beverages. There is one marginal person in the barrio who does drink in nonfiesta contexts, but he is not a full member of the barrio. He is the one individual who is not engaged in farming as a primary occupation and who is a marginal person in many other respects. Aside from this man, only a few of the younger barrio men drink in nonfiesta contexts and then only rarely. Thus the prevailing pattern for the consumption of alcohol is to drink very heavily in the fiesta context and not at all between times. Questioned about whether or not they desired alcohol between fiestas, the men in the barrio always responded as though this were a peculiar question because obviously one drank only during fiesta occasions. Most of the men accepted this drinking pattern as the only natural and imaginable one possible. A few of the very elderly men reported that they thought there was too much drinking at the fiestas.

Alcohol, or aguardiente, is used in one or two ritual contexts. For example, before a field is planted it is used to feed the earth god and is poured in each corner of the field. In summary, aguardiente is used almost exclusively in a social context, either between men or between man and spirit. It thus has acquired a high social, symbolic value and represents social solidarity at the conscious level for barrio people.

The second question concerns what happens when an individual is unwilling or unable to drink during the ceremonies. There are three or four men in the barrio who claim, for physiological reasons, that they are unable to drink aguardiente. These men are all excluded from attending any cofradia function. Two of them had been highly respected men with important roles in cofradia organization in the past. They were now ostracized from such participation. None of these men had the full respect of other barrio members, nor were they considered to be full-fledged members of the barrio. When referred to by other barrio people, they were frequently classed as being closer to the townspeople. In addition, they clearly paid a price in terms of being deprived of the emotional and economic security afforded by barrio members. It will be remembered that the cofradia fiestas are the major occasions on which every member of the barrio eats meat and other special fiesta foods, so that the economic function of food distribution is withheld from the families of the men who do not drink.

The threat of ostracism is one important way of ensuring participation in the barrio-wide cofradia organizations. It would be invoked primarily as a punishment for not conforming to the ritual aspects of the cofradia ceremonies, particularly participation in the ceremonial drinking pattern. The threat of ostracism does not seem adequate, however, to account for the degree of control of overt aggression observed within the barrio. It does not account, for example, for the lack of any great aggressiveness in the ceremonies themselves. Another mechanism relating to aggression remains to be discussed.

The low level of overt aggression observed among the barrio members may be accounted for, at least in part, by two factors. The first factor consists of the training in the control of aggression during childhood. This will be discussed at length in Part II. The second factor has to do with a set of beliefs concerning aggression. These beliefs will be the concern of the remainder of the chapter.

Members of the barrio share an elaborated set of beliefs concerning the relationship between aggression and illness. Anger, aggression, jeolousy, and related kinds of emotions are believed capable of causing illness which may result ultimately in death. These beliefs are very strongly held and are related to the stress on self-control of aggressive impulses.

The way in which these beliefs account for various kinds of phenomena may be best illustrated by the examination of a case history from field notes. It concerned a woman, whom we shall call Catalina, who supplemented her income by selling tortillas in the market place. All people who occupy any space in the market are expected to pay a very small tax for the space they occupy there. One market day when Catalina was selling her tortillas, the tax collector came around to her place in the market to collect the tax. By mistake, he attempted to collect the tax a second time from her. She tried to explain that she had already paid her tax, and an argument of a very mild nature ensued. Shortly afterward, she confided to her friends in the market that she had felt very angry about this double imposition and that she did not feel well and was worried about having become so angry. She thereupon left the market in the afternoon and went home. She became increasingly ill during the evening and died about midnight. The cause of her death was attributed to the illness that was caused by her aggressive feelings. All of the people in the barrio accepted this as the explanation. The event was reported to the children and talked about in front of them and used as an object lesson for the importance of controlling one's feelings.

The well-internalized belief that anger or aggression can lead to illness and possibly death is a strong deterrent to placing oneself in a situation that may lead to anger or aggression. When the validity of such a belief is reinforced or demonstrated by actual deaths, as in the case of Catalina, it becomes a very potent deterrent to aggressive behavior and thoughts.

Chapter 7

Disease and Curing

Illness is common in the barrio. Although some of it is chronic (for example, rheumatism, certain types of dysentery, and malaria among those men who have worked in hot country), much illness is seasonal. The winter months bring colds and flu with their complications (earache, eye inflammation), especially among children. Measles strike yearly in the heat of the spring before the rains begin, and here again children are the principal victims. In the rainy summer months intestinal diseases are common. Barrio people recognize the seasonal distribution of kinds of illness to some extent by their tendency to lay the blame for an epidemic on the weather. For example, one woman explained the occurrence of much illness one summer by saying that in the previous year the rains had come earlier, and so by June the water was no longer muddy and there was little sickness. The association of muddy water and sickness in her thinking seems likely. April and May are said to be good months for taking a purgative, perhaps to prepare for the dangers of summer. Again, measles is said to occur at about the same time each year, when the sun is so hot that it heats the blood and produces a rash as the heat seeks a way out of the body.

Although the weather helps to explain the widespread occurrence of illness in the barrio, the illness of an individual is usually thought to have much more specific causes. Some few conditions—for example, wounds, burns, poison ivy, and malaria—are believed to be caused by the physical agents with which they are associated in Western medicine. Poison ivy is contracted by touching or being near the plant, and malaria comes from the bite of a mosquito in hot country. Most diseases, however, are assigned causes of other kinds. In order of importance, these include: (1) disturbed emotional states such as fear and anger, (2) ritual contamination, (3) magical seizure by sorcery, and (4) improper diet or regimen. Supplementing these categories in the ex-

planation of individual illness is the belief in differential susceptibility to illness. Susceptibility is increased by abnormal bodily conditions brought about by exertion, excessive sweating, body exposure,
wounds or blows, as well as by the conditions of pregnancy, parturition,
menstruation, and menopause. Weakness may also be due to extreme
youth or to old age. The illness of a particular individual is interpreted in the light of his condition (weakness or strength) and his
recent experience, as well as his symptoms.

Fright is "like a heat in the stomach," taking away the appetite and
producing fever, sleeplessness, and general apathy. It may follow a fall,
especially a fall into water, or the unexpected sight of a snake, or any
other event which produces fear or shock. (Among these other events
is the sight of aggression, "seeing some person kill another person,
or seeing someone else pushing somebody from behind into the water.")
Anger as well as sometimes causing illness and sometimes death is also
believed to cause pain in childbirth and miscarriage in those who
are weak for one reason or another. One type of weakness which is
relevant here is an overabundance of bile or, rather, a tendency for the
bile to be discharged readily into the stomach or the liver. The danger
of illness following anger is greatest before breakfast because the bile
sack is fullest then. It is considerably less after eating, for then food
supports the sack, and the bile is less likely to be released. Another
type of weakness is due to pregnancy, which entails the danger of pain
or miscarriage. Still another is due to menstruation, which makes the
pores hollow due to loss of blood.

Ritual contamination may cause excessive crying in an infant, illness (fever and vomiting), or bodily deformity. It comes from a number of sources. One of the most common is the evil eye. People who
have unusually bright, staring, or hypnotic eyes are thought to cause
illness or harm merely by looking at another person. It is possible for
this person to contaminate the individual unconsciously as he (or, more
frequently, she) admires him, but some cases of evil eye are said to
have been deliberately caused by a witch. Infants are particularly
vulnerable to the evil eye, especially when they are sleeping and hence
defenseless. Another kind of contamination is *mal aire,* a term which
includes two rather different concepts. One is simply evil air, which
may enter the body and cause illness. Gas in the intestines is interpreted as "air inside" and is a cause of worry and loss of appetite in
many barrio people. Night air is evil, and people go outdoors at night
rarely and then with nose and mouth covered by the rebozo or serape.

The second concept translated as *mal aire* is a dark shape which
may be encountered at night. This shape frightens the victim, and

fright is formally the cause of the resulting symptoms. However, the symptoms—fainting, dizziness, "absence of breathing," half-consciousness—are quite different from the usual result of fright. The same symptoms are reported for the result of an encounter with the *tabayuku,* or owner of the earth. The *tabayuku* appears only to men, and always in the shape of a woman—the particular woman whom the man is thinking about at the moment, whether wife or lover or someone else. The *tabayuku* takes the victim to her cave and kisses him. She offers the victim many wonderful things—all the things he has wanted—and asks that the victim pay her for them with a kiss. Afterward the victim returns home half-crazed, and unless he is cured, he may die.

Evil air also emanates from the body of a dead person. It can cause a swelling on the back of the head of a newborn infant if either he or his mother is exposed to it.

Sorcery can cause insanity as well as other forms of illness. It is sometimes used by one person who is angry with another. The person who bears the grudge does not do the witchcraft himself. Instead, he hires a witch in el Centro or, more often, in one of the neighboring towns. (There are said to be no witches in the barrio.) The witch may steal the soul of the victim by sending out his *nagual,* or animal counterpart, and illness results. Alternatively, the witch may make a small figure of wax or clay in the shape of the victim and stick cactus spines into it. The figure may have an opening where the stomach would be, into which is placed the stub of a candle previously used at a wake. The witch buries this figure near the victim's house at night in order to cause his illness.

Improper diet or regimen can cause a great variety of illnesses, and diet is considered so important to well-being that those barrio people who consult the town doctor usually ask him to prescribe a special diet for the patient in addition to the medication he suggests. Proper diet is defined in terms of a complex of ideas that attributes hotness or coldness to foods. These attributes do not seem to be consistently related to the actual temperature of the material. For example, meat, fat, chocolate, and mangos are hot foods, while water is cold, and *papauza,* dry toasted tortilla, and aguardiente are apparently neutral or "refreshing." Neither the hot nor the cold condition is good or bad in itself. Rather, good health depends on equilibrium between the internal condition of the individual and the condition of things which affect him. Illness may result from adding hot to hot or cold to cold; taking a warm bath in hot weather or a cold bath in cold weather may produce headache and fever. Similarly, it may follow an excess of hot foods; it is said that people in Copala, who eat "nothing but mangos," suffer greatly from diarrhea. Illness may also come as a result of mixing hot and cold in a particular way; one can develop pains in the arms after grinding chocolate if one washes in water. Anger is especially likely to cause illness if one eats hot foods (pork, fat) while in the hot condition or if one bathes, turning one's hot condition suddenly to cold. As might be expected, the wrong type of food can also aggravate illness which already exists. It is bad for a sick person to drink either cold water or hot liquids; so he is given lukewarm water exclusively.

The hot-cold complex is important, then, not only in diagnosis but also in the treatment of illness. Avoidance of the type of food which caused the illness is one aspect of curing. Another is the administration of cooling or refreshing foods or herb baths, when the illness is regarded as a hot one. Diarrhea is treated by avoiding all hot foods and by eating refreshing or neutral fruits and dry tortillas. A person with a cold may be given a sponge bath in aguardiente mixed with mentholatum and camphor, or mentholatum and candle wax may be applied to his throat, temples, and the sides of his nose. Mejoral, a patent pain-killer, is considered refreshing and may be given in small quantities to children with colds. Fainting and nausea may be treated by application of a cooling herb, *ruda,* to the back of the neck and by drinking a mixture of lemon and bicarbonate of soda. Dizziness after an encounter with *mal aire* or the *tabayuku* is treated by blowing aguardiente from the mouth all over the patient's body and by applying a great number of herbs—*ruda* and myrrh and others. Anger-caused illness and illness due to fright are treated in much the same way. In the case of measles, several steps in the treatment participate in the hot-cold complex in different ways. First, a mixture of aguardiente and mexcal is blown over the patient's body to cool the skin and bring the rash to the surface. He is protected from wind, which might shock the body and drive the rash inward. (When the heat represented by the rash stays inside, the patient usually dies.) Then, some days after the rash has appeared, he is given a sweat bath. Barrio people explain that the heat of the sweat bath is a refreshing heat.

The sweat bath, which is used in combination with various herbs for fevers of other kinds and for rheumatism as well as for measles, is administered in a more or less permanent structure in the courtyard or house of the patient. Some barrio households have a *baño de refresco,* a sweat bath built of adobe, but most build a *baño de toro,* a temporary structure, when it is needed. The *baño de toro* is made by arching bamboo poles to form a framework some 6 feet long and 3 feet high. The framework is placed over a fireplace built with four adobes set in a square. A fire is built in the fireplace, and rocks the size of a softball are piled on top of it. The rocks are allowed to heat for several hours; in the meantime, small leafy branches (brought from the river) are tied together in bunches to form dusters. Finally, the framework is covered with several layers of mats, and the patient and his helper (a woman relative or a profession curer) go inside. Behind a blanket which covers the doorway to the bath, they undress. Water is thrown onto the rocks so that steam rises from them. Then the helper brushes the patient well with the bunch of branches for 20 minutes or more. On emerging from the bath, the patient wraps in a blanket and lies down. He should be given only warm water to drink, but he can have anything to eat that he wants. The sweat bath may be repeated several times at two-day intervals before the cure is considered complete.

In addition to herbs, patent medicines, and baths, a number of rituals are employed in curing illness. Illness caused by the evil eye is sometimes diagnosed by examining the inside of an egg for telling signs, and it can be cured only by the touch of the person who caused the contamination. In other types of illness in children, the patient may be taken to church for an *evangelio,* a short and simple service in which the priest reads scripture over the head of the child, and a candle is lighted. (Evangelio may also be read for children who are not ill as a prophylaxis.) There is some indication that the professional curers of the barrio use rituals or prayers in curing. It would be surprising if the belief in illness caused by fright (*espanto*) were not accompanied by some kind of ritual to retrieve the soul of the patient from the spot at which it was lost, for this combination of beliefs is common in Middle America and, indeed, occurs elsewhere in the Mixteca. Some curers are said to know how to suck foreign objects (inserted by witches) out of the patient's body. Divining the outcome of illness by means of an egg is also reported. The egg is rubbed on the afflicted part of the body and then stood on end. A small piece of incense is placed on top and lighted. If the heat of the burning incense breaks the egg, it is expected that the patient will die.

Ritual means are also taken to prevent illness. Babies often wear a pointed shell on a cord around their necks to prevent coughs. They can be protected from contamination caused by the presence of death and from spells cast by witches by a bag of selected herbs which the mother wears tied around her waist.

Curing may be attempted by members of the patient's immediate family, in the first instance. Herb remedies for simple illnesses are widely known, and aspirin is often bought in local stores. Often, also, the patient is given no medication at all but is allowed to rest and is given little food until the disease goes away of its own accord. Illness which is vague (e.g., headache, slight fever, listlessness) and not alarming in its symptoms may be tolerated by the patient and the family for days or even weeks. At some point, which differs in each household, the illness is defined as serious and treatment is begun. Home remedies and store-bought medicines are usually tried first, and it is when they have no effect that a professional curer is sought.

The barrio has several professional curers, all of them women who also serve as midwives. Their methods include the rituals described above, and it is they who apply the more elaborate herb baths required in cases of fright and anger. If the illness is judged to be caused by witchcraft, a witch from a neighboring community may be called in to cure it.

Local _curanderas_ charge less and are generally more trusted than the town doctor, but barrio people occasionally consult the doctor. A resident doctor in Juxtlahuaca is a rarity, the only ones in recent years having been recent graduates doing their six months of required social service. To a considerable extent, they share the feeling of el Centro people toward the Indians and behave toward them in much the same way. Barrio people who visit the doctor are likely to be examined briefly or not at all and to be sold medication at greater than usual cost. Nevertheless, some families take their sick members there when the illness defies local treatment and they have the money. Frequently they ask for injections, one of the services that only the doctor can perform. While injections have the confidence of some barrio people, others fear them. It is rumored that the recent death of a barrio child was caused by one of the doctor's injections.

Praying to the saints may be an adjunct to any cure for an illness. An ill person may go to the church where the statues of the saints are kept and make a special prayer on an individual basis to the particular saint. The typical procedure would be for the individual to light a candle for the saint and to make an informal prayer to him. In a few cases, an individual would go to the priest and ask for a special mass or service. The practice of promising a saint a special mass if he will cure an illness is also known, although very rarely used. On the whole, the part played by the saints in curing is a nominal one and is primarily an adjunct to other methods.

Although illness is an everpresent concern in the barrio, it does not seem to be a dominant one. People make an effort to avoid illness by eating properly and behaving prudently (avoiding anger, aggression, and ritual contamination). When they become ill, they tend to wait patiently until they are well again. If the illness is severe or of long duration, they attempt to cure it—first by the means which are nearest at hand and least expensive, next by means which are thought more certain but also cost more, and, finally, by any means at all up to a given economic limit. Death, when it comes in spite of everything that has been done, is seen as a loss but also as an end to suffering, and it is accepted "if God wishes it."

⚘
⚘
⚘

Chapter 8

Funeral Ceremonies

A bell in the church is rung to signify that a death has taken place. This sounds different from the one signifying time for church; this one is rung a long time, very slowly. It is rung by male members of the deceased's family—sons, brothers, cousins, and so forth. When the men finish ringing the bell, they go out into the street and tell the people who has died. No special person is necessarily called to pronounce the death, in contrast to societies in which the padre or the eldest member of the family is expected to make this announcement. All the close family is gathered together immediately, including aunts, uncles, cousins, sons, daughters, father, mother, husband or wife, as well as particular compadres. They all sit with the body throughout the night, with candles burning. No special person is required to stay with the body, for instance, the mother or the husband, but all the members of the family who are able to come do so.

Women prepare the body of a woman for burial, while men prepare the body of a man. There is no bathing or washing of the body or combing of the hair. It is left just as it was when the person died except that new thick stockings and special death shoes made of palms, like huarches, are placed on the feet. If the deceased is a woman, her rebozo is placed around the head, covering her face and almost all of the body down to the feet. The arms and hands are folded over the chest. Dry cotton is placed in the nose and ears, but no other special preparations are used. A small white bag of heavy material is prepared, and inside it are placed two tablets of chocolate, ten cents worth of finely ground sugar in a separate bag, a tiny beater for mixing chocolate, two special, tiny, coarsely ground tortillas, two pieces of the meat that the family had for their last meal together, a bottle of water, and a spool of thread if it is a woman. If the person knew how to write, a pencil, small envelope, and paper are also placed inside the bag. This bag is supposedly laid over the shoulders, crossing under the chin and over the mouth. In addition, all the old clothes of the deceased are laid inside the coffin. If there is anything new that has not actually touched the body, it can be kept by the family, but all other clothing should be placed with the body. Serapes or blankets are not put in the coffin.

The corpse is laid in front of the family altar, where all the saints' pictures are placed together. There are many flowers gathered by the family and many that are later brought by the mourners. There are many candles—the small altar candles, the white candles used for light, and also the very tall, special fiesta candles, which are brown. These brown candles have all been blessed at the annual fiesta. The Indian incense, *copal,* is in its special dish in front of the body and is lighted as soon as death occurs. The body itself is placed on boxes to get it up off the floor until a casket can be prepared. A crucifix is not necessary on the family altar, but a special cross of vines is arranged on the dirt floor in front of the corpse. Palm mats are placed on the floor in front of the body for mourners to sit on. All the guests go first to the chief mourner, that is, the mother of a child or the husband or wife as the case may be, and to this person they give their gift of money. Most also bring candles or flowers or both. If a close friend or compadre is sick, he is not supposed to go to the wake, since there is bad air present, which makes it a dangerous place for a sick or weak person.

On entering the room of death, the mourner immediately goes to the altar, kneels in front of the chief picture or statue, and crosses himself. Then he lights the candle he has brought and places it somewhere on the floor near the corpse. Flowers are similarly placed nearby. Next the mourner retreats and sits on the floor on a mat. Praying is not obvious. The people merely sit and watch. They may talk quietly with one another. Drinks are served to the men, who may be off in one corner, and sometimes there is a great deal of joking and laughing. It is not necessarily a very solemn, quiet occasion.

The body must be interred before 24 hours have passed. If death occurs early in the day, the burial may take place the following morning; otherwise it always takes place late in the afternoon. It does not necessarily entail a visit to church nor is it necessary for a priest to officiate. He may come to the house if he is asked, but this involves a payment. Even if the priest does come to the house, he does not go with the body to the cemetery. However, even for the poorest, a song or prayer is said, and often musicians are invited to the house to play the music. A body must be buried during the daytime, never after sundown.

Food is served to all persons attending the wake. The type of food varies according to the amount of money in the family, on how much time there is in which to prepare it, and how much help is available. It can be anything from a simple repast of chocolate and bread to a complete meal with chile and turkey or beef. Food is served until time for the funeral procession to start, at which time the church bell is rung again to signify that it is time for the people to gather. All who care to may walk with the body up to the cemetery. They follow it in two lines, the women on one side of the street, the men on the other. Everyone walking in a funeral procession, not including children, should carry a tall candle. If one does not bring his own, it is up to the house of the deceased to supply one.

Children attending a funeral may not enter the room in which the body is laid out, but all the household or patio is open to them; they are fed the same food as the parents, and they are allowed to run and play freely. However, few parents bring their children because there might be bad air. Many children seem to enjoy walking in funeral processions, and their parents often bring them to this part of the ceremony. A small boy usually walks first, carrying the incense; then come the four men carrying the coffin. It is interesting to note that in every funeral we saw, the family of the deceased, no matter how poor, had provided a coffin. There was a great deal of variation in its ornamentation. For the people walking in the procession it is not necessarily a solemn or very sad occasion. True, there is no singing or dancing, but neither is there any wailing or weeping or any noise except the talking of the people walking in the lines. No one supposedly weeps at a funeral except the mother and perhaps the husband or the wife. The other people merely come to show their respect, not to weep. In fact, it is often difficult, when entering a house, to tell from the outward signs of cooking and preparations whether it is a wedding or a funeral.

The body is taken to the cemetery, which has one section for the Indians and one for the townspeople. The Indians are all buried with a cement slab over the top of the grave. It does not stand upright as a tombstone but lies flat on the ground. Since the Indian section is a small part of the cemetery, the graves are very close together. In fact, skeleton parts are often found during the digging and are simply thrown out with the dirt; no one seems to think anything about it. There is no special blessing at the grave. The hole has been prepared earlier by men who went up in the morning to do their duty, armed with two bottles of aguardiente. Often they are the men who will also carry the corpse back to the cemetery, which is high up on a hill and quite a climb. These are male members of the deceased's family, and they are not paid in money but are merely given drinks and a meal.

The casket is lowered into the grave; all the flowers that have surrounded the body in the home are placed on top of the casket; and then the clods of dirt are thrown over the flowers. Many persons throw handfuls of dirt to start the covering. Thanks are given at the graveside to those who have helped in any way, including special thanks to the particular society that lends the sacred brown candles. These thanks are expressed by some male members of the deceased's family. After the thanks, most of the women leave the cemetery, not waiting to see the grave filled and the ground level again. (It is interesting to note that the mothers or particular mourners do not go to the cemetery. When we asked why the mother of one woman who had died did not come, we were told that she had cried so much she could not stand to walk in the hot air up to the cemetery with all that bad air.) During the burial people have been standing or sitting on the cement stones that are gravemarkers. They seem also to step from grave to grave, as they are going out from the cemetery, without any particular thought that they might be walking on corpses. As the sun goes down, the majority of the men come down from the cemetery, finishing up their refilled bottles of aguardiente, talking and laughing with their shovels over their shoulders.

There are then eight days of visiting with the family. On the evening of the eighth day, there are candles around the altar, and on the ninth day "the raising of the cross" occurs. A bell, the particular low-ringing death bell, is rung in the church late in the afternoon to signify that it is time to gather for this particular ceremony. All persons attending bring the usual candles and the pesos for the house of mourning. The house altar is fixed as usual with the pictures of saints, the tall brown candles, the many vases and cans of flowers on the table and on the floor surrounding it. On the floor in front of the saints' pictures there is a cross, about a foot high, made out of plant leaves which are very white on the ends and so waxey in appearance they seem to be made of porcelain. A close relative of the deceased keeps the cross after the ceremony. In front of the cross on the floor there is a wooden box with a cross drawn on it with powdered lime. The numbers one to five are marked in ink around it.

These numbers are used to designate the five padrinos of the cross. Each padrino, especially chosen for this occasion, brings a tray of flowers and a large, special glass with an altar candle in it. As each padrino enters, he kneels, crosses himself, and places his candle on one of the inked numbers. When all five padrinos have entered, the ceremony can begin. Until this time, a dish of corn is served to all who enter, although many only come as far as the gate, hand in a peso, and leave. But careful note is made of each arrival, the gifts of food are sent to all whether they came in or not. Special palm spoons are made with which to eat the special cold dish, *pesole*. It is the job of one of the older men of the family to sit in the sun and carve these hundred or so spoons.

The ceremony always occurs at night, and so one fire is built in the path before the doorway to the house and another in the inner courtyard before the room of mourning. These two fires are supposedly only for light to guide people's feet and not for any signficant reason. A large dish of pesole and also a small one of mole are set on boxes on each side of the cross.

When all the padrinos are in attendance, the singing can begin. It is led by a man, usually, who sings a verse, after which a woman attendant or young girl who knows the responses very well leads the audience loudly. Three times a long group of prayers are said with the man alone leading and the woman and the rest of the audience responding. As the prayers start, all the people kneel. Each group of prayers takes from 20 to 35 minutes; thus by the time the third series comes along, many of the people are very tired. Nevertheless, all of the women, with their rebozos wrapped around them and their eyes looking downward, kneel on the dirt floor or on palm mats. Many of the men, however, are only partially kneeling and many are almost asleep by 11:30. Very few children attend this ceremony, and those who are present sleep beside their mothers. At the end of each series of prayers there is a breathing spell for relaxation and resting the knees. Everyone sits back and talk starts immediately—gossip of the village and other notes of interest. Many of the men step outside to have a drink and a walk in the night air, but the women usually remain inside the room.

It is interesting to note that few of the mourners' family are present —the women, that is. They are all outside by the cook shack preparing a meal to be enjoyed when the prayers are finished. At the end of the third group of prayers, the leader goes up in front of the cross, which is flat on the ground and completely surrounded by flowers, usually in tin cans, takes a flower, and dips it in a small cup or dish of holy or blessed water. He kneels and sprinkles the cross with holy water from the flower. Then he puts his lips to the cross, gets to his feet, and walks to the side of the room. This same performance is then repeated, first, by all the men in the room. It is a very orderly procession. Each one steps up, kneels down, sprinkles the cross, kisses it, gets to his feet, and moves off. There is no obvious social prestige involved except that the men of the deceased's family go first. After that there is no seniority or status preference, just whoever happens to be sitting along the wall as each one takes his turn. When the men have finished, the majority of them leave the room, and then the women do the same thing, going up to kneel and kiss the cross. When everyone in the room who cares to has performed this little ceremony, two men of the deceased's family return, carefully pick up the cross and carry it out into the open air, and stand with it there for a few moments. Then they return and place the cross upright on the family altar. This concludes the raising of the cross, and the people start talking and laughing and joking.

The musicians come in, and pesole is served to everyone. By this time it is usually between 11 and 12 o'clock at night, but the people, even those who have been sleepy the hour before, become wide awake and laugh and joke as they eat. Then gifts of food are sent around early in the morning to all who did not attend but who sent their little gifts of money, as well as to comadres or compadres of the family to whom the family of the deceased owes gifts. Then, as people are leaving, gifts of candles to light the way may be given to those going home in the darkness, since few people have flashlights and none have Coleman lanterns. So it is, at midnight, little bands of people can be seen walking down the street together. They pause to talk, then separate, and then two candles or two lights go on down the street.

The death of a child is treated quite differently. Children who are young, 12 or under, who have not been through confession, are called angelitos, and these "little angels" go directly to heaven. There is no need for the nine days of prayer and the raising of the cross for these little children, for they become angels the moment they stop breathing. They are dressed in long white robes trimmed with the color of the particular saint of that month. For example, if a little girl dies during June, she is dressed in the colors of the Virgin Mary, for this is her month. If a little boy dies in May, he is dressed in red and white, the colors of Jesus, for May is his month. Also, if a very small child dies, he may be dressed in the particular color of his saint's day, always combined with the white and gold. The long white robe has a gold belt with little gold tinseled slippers. A crown is placed on the child's head and a flower in each hand. The flowers may be waxed or artificial, or they may be real flowers. Also, a canopy of gauze is usually raised over the head to make almost an altar of this little angel. The baby's eyes are not closed; they are staring straight ahead in order to see God immediately. Four candles are placed on the table beside the child at each corner—north, east, south, and west.

Part II

Child Training

✦
✦
✦
✦
✦
✦

Chapter 9

Introduction

People in the barrio divide life into more or less distinct stages. Individuals in each stage are thought to possess certain qualities and characteristics that set them apart from individuals in other stages of life. Practices and beliefs concerning the various behavior systems vary according to the stage of development of the child. There are ideas about the kinds of behavior that are appropriate for individuals in each stage as well as special privileges and responsibilities associated with increasing maturity. In this section, the socialization of the behavior systems will be described and discussed in the framework of the stages of life as seen by the people of Santo Domingo barrio.

The first stage is that of *infancy*. The Mixteco word used for infants means "in darkness" and implies that the infant has no "awareness." When speaking Spanish, Santo Domingans use the term "creature" in referring to infants. About the time the infant is weaned, at the age of 1 or 2 years, he gains "awareness" and enters the second stage, which is *early childhood*. The Mixteco word for this period means "this child now knows." Early childhood continues until the second set of teeth is replacing the milk teeth. This marks the beginning of *late childhood* and takes place in the sixth and seventh year. At this time the child begins to have the capacity to reason. The fourth stage, *youth*, begins when the child becomes actively aware of sex. In theory this begins at age 12. Until the age of 12, a child who dies is thought to become an angel; beyond that age he becomes responsible for his status in the next world.

Despite these ideas, the differences between late childhood and youth are much less marked than between the earlier stages of life. Full maturity or *adulthood* is reached with economic independence, which is generally associated with marriage. In talking with Santo Domingans, one always hears them say that adulthood begins with marriage. It happens that there are about a dozen men in their twenties or thirties in the barrio who have never been married. When asked whether he is adult or not, the Santo Domingan will say, "Yes," and then point out that he is economically independent, and this is what really distinguishes him from a youth. Sixteen is the age given to mark the beginning of adulthood.

The people agree that the stages outlined above are the ideal. They recognize, however, that in practice numerous factors can speed up or slow down development in any specific case and thus there is variation about the stated transition points. For example, the youngest child spends more time in early childhood than his older siblings. Or again, if a woman has two children close together, the older one is weaned earlier and thus enters early childhood sooner than otherwise.

With two rather dramatic exceptions, the transition between stages of life is gradual and continuous for the barrio child; one stage blends into another with no sudden shift in expectations, and what has gone before is consistent and preparatory for what follows. The two exceptions are: (1) the transition from infancy to early childhood, marked by abrupt weaning and a shift from sleeping with parents to sleeping alone or with siblings, and (2) the transition from early childhood to late childhood, marked by a change in the amount of succorance allowed and nurturance given the child, together with increased expectations in responsibility, self-reliance, and obedience, all backed up by a shift in techniques of discipline.

The infant up to the age of 2 differs from an adult in two respects besides those that are apparent in size and knowledge. Infants are thought of being, along with other animals, without awareness and the ability to reason. It is thought that no learning takes place until the infant develops awareness. Awareness grows and increases slowly and naturally without human help or interference, beginning at the end of the first year of life and continuing until it is fully developed at the age of 2. The ability to reason does not develop until the age of 7. Like awareness, reason matures without human intervention. Near the end of the sixth year, a child will begin to show evidences of reason, and by the age of 8 it will be a fully developed characteristic. Since the ability to understand and learn behavior appropriate to adulthood depends on the ability to reason, children younger than 6 are not expected to begin to behave like adults, and their behavior cannot be judged as morally good or bad.

Every individual gains awareness and reason much as he cuts teeth or matures physically. It is recognized that some may develop these qualities at an earlier or later age than others, but every individual, in the natural course of events, will mature in these respects just as surely as in physiological traits. Since every adult has these abilities, they cannot account for observed differences between individuals.

"Every person has his own character. Some people are happy, some are mean," say the Santo Domingans. Such differences are believed to arise through two kinds of factors: inheritance and learning. A child inherits its personal characteristics through the blood. Even though rearing and learning do and can affect these characteristics, a person never loses his blood, and eventually it will come out. For example, if one has a bad temper, it can be explained in terms of the father or mother or some relative having had bad temper. Characteristics inherited in the blood may lie dormant for many years before showing up in behavior. It is common for some inherited characteristics to first show up at marriage, for example, jealousy in women.

One inherits blood from both the mother and the father, and most characteristics would come from them, although on occasion one might get the blood of a more distant relative, such as an uncle or aunt or grandparent. One inherits more from the father or mother, depending upon which one is the most dominant and energetic. One of the values held very highly by the barrio people is that a husband and wife should be about equal in dominance and energy, and it is believed that inheritance of blood is usually equal from each parent. Where differences were said to occur, however, it was more commonly found that women were thought to be more energetic and dominant than their husbands rather than the reverse. Corresponding to this belief is the idea that the mother's blood is stronger in more children than the father's blood.

Differences in siblings are thought to arise because not all children of the same parents get the same blood. Even if they get blood in the same proportion from each parent, the children will come out differently because, "Some of them get the blood of a parent and some of them get the dominant blood from an aunt, an uncle, or other relative," says a Santo Domingan.

The way in which inheritance and learning are related in the development of an individual is very neatly summed up by Juan Chorra, one of our informants. "One's character comes from the blood, but what one learns is very important. One learns until these things that one learns become a habit. Habits are very hard to get rid of."

Parents are responsible for the training of their children. They are believed capable of shaping the development of the child and are expected by the community to do the best they can. If, despite everything a parent can do, the child does not turn out well because of bad blood somewhere else in the family, the parent is not held responsible. On the other hand, if the parent does not give the child adequate training and the child turns out to be bad, then the parent is felt to be responsible. The beliefs are sufficiently flexible to allow the Santo Domingans to shift blame according to their attitudes toward the parents. When asked why specific people turned out as they did, the choice of explanations seemed to depend on the following variables: how well the parent is liked, the standing of the family in the community, the number of bad relatives, the degree of resemblance between parents and child in other respects, and so on.

Personality is most maleable between the ages of 6 or 7 and 12. Before the age of 6, the child is not thought to possess sufficient reasoning power to really learn effectively. After 12, it becomes increasingly difficult to change the basic character of a person until he reaches adulthood at about 18, when it becomes impossible to alter his character. At this age, the results of earlier learning and training are fixed; the final effects of blood show themselves, and one's character is fixed for life. The good parent is the one who feels responsible for his children until they marry. If the community consensus is that a parent has done his duty for his children, he is not judged responsible for his children after marriage.

The above sketch presents an idealized version of the barrio theory of development. There is great variation in the way in which this ideal is translated into practice. The following chapters will trace the process of socialization in some detail and introduce observational and interview data.

✻
✻
✻

Chapter 10

Pregnancy and Childbirth

To bear many children is viewed by barrio women as a desirable and natural part of life. The ideal is to have many children of both sexes while still young, since children are viewed as a natural part of life and as economic assets, especially as providers for old age. If there are several children, the burden will not be too great for any one of them.

The beliefs about children as a natural part of life are summed up in the phrase, "Children come as the rain." The rain comes in season; there may be periods of drought, but it always comes. Without rain to support the crops, the barrio could not exist. So it is with children. They come one after another, with shorter or longer periods between. But without children, the barrio could not go on.

Economically children contribute much to the family. At cooperative works in the barrio, each family is expected to contribute its share of labor, both male and female. Families who do not have sufficient children to fulfill these obligations would be expected to hire outside help or call on other relatives. Either of these would involve extra burden, for calling on other relatives would obligate one to repay in kind later. Also, within the family itself, children begin early to help their parents; girls help their mothers with younger children and in household tasks, while boys help their fathers in the fields and with the animals and other male tasks. Thus, while on the whole there is little over-all preference for a child of one sex over the other, a father prefers sons who will help him, a mother prefers daughters who will help her.

Families who have only children of one sex receive the sympathy of the other barrio members. Chencho Chorra and his wife had three boys and a girl, for example. When the little girl died, Chencho and his wife showed more grief than was usual at the death of a child, and the barrio was very sympathetic and said, "The poor woman, now she has no one to help her." Salazar, on the other hand, has four girls and no boys. Everyone feels that it is a shame that he has no one to help him with his work. On occasions when he has to call on relatives to help him with his share of a cooperative work party, the men say, "It's too bad you don't have any boys to help out."

The birth of a healthy, well-formed child is always an occasion for rejoicing. Of all the fiestas, the one given soon after a child is born, when he is baptized, is most joyous.

Traditionally, and still to a considerable degree, a couple without children is not considered married. It is only with the appearance of the first child that the woman is said to have demonstrated her womanhood, and the couple becomes a family. There is one couple in the barrio who have lived together for several years but have no children. Everyone feels very sorry for them, and they express great desire for children. Some people explain it by saying they were too old when they were married, while others say that they are being punished for something they have done in the past. Their situation is viewed by themselves and others as unnatural, and they do not enter into full participation of the barrio social life as a consequence.

Several kinds of preparations are used to induce pregnancy. A common one is made from fresh pine resin which is boiled with three roots from a corn plant and taken hot. Another preparation is a brew made from a sage plant.

Women who want to control the number of children they have are viewed with considerable disapproval. They have techniques which they believe will control conception as well as cause abortion. They believe that drinking water in which a metal worker has washed his metal tools when they were hot will prevent conception, but this is thought to be both bad and dangerous since it not only prevents pregnancy but also causes sickness. When the weather gets cold, the woman's feet will swell, and when the moon comes out, her belly will be painful. Abortion can be produced by taking the squeezings of a dozen cold lemons. These practices are highly disapproved of in the barrio and are attributed mainly to townspeople.

Infanticide, or the killing of newborn infants, is only practiced when a child is born "with the face of an animal." Children who are deformed in other ways are reared much like normal children.

Conception is known to result from sexual intercourse. Children learn this at an early age by asking questions about cattle that are brought together for breeding purposes. There is little secrecy about the matter although there may be some jesting by the men.

A woman knows she is pregnant when "her moon disappears," that is, when menstruation stops. The first person she notifies is her mother or her mother-in-law if she lives in the latter's courtyard. They are in charge of advising the husband and the fathers of both the husband and wife. The woman is embarrassed if others are told, especially if it is her first pregnancy. The rest of the family become aware only when her belly begins to swell. There is modesty, though no secrecy, about later stages of pregnancy.

If a pregnant woman feels like eating something on a whim, it should be satisfied lest she suffer a miscarriage or a premature birth. It is part of a husband's duty to provide his wife with the foods she desires, and there are no restrictions as to what she may eat. However, it is believed that eating too much causes painful childbirth.

There are no special taboos on a pregnant woman's activities during pregnancy. She continues to grind for tortillas, wash clothes, and engage in other normal work. The only precaution mentioned is that she should not carry heavy objects. A couple may continue to have sexual intercourse up to the time of birth. No special positions are used for the protection of the fetus.

Nausea during pregnancy is not unusual during the first three months. It is thought to be a natural condition of pregnancy for certain women, not a reflection of character and not related to other qualities she might have.

When a woman feels that the baby is going to arrive before it is due, she takes steps to prevent the miscarriage or premature birth by drinking a concoction brewed from the leaves of *Santa Maria*, a species of *artemisa*, and other herbs. This is supposed to "fix" the fetus so that it sticks better inside and does not "fall out early." The two major causes of miscarriage are thought to be the frustration of some food craving of the mother and lifting heavy objects. Premature babies, when they survive, are given no special or differential treatment, nor are there any special beliefs about them.

About a month before the baby is expected, special treatments are supposed not only to keep the fetus in the proper position for birth but also to loosen the fetus gradually so that birth will be less painful. A midwife massages the hips and stomach gently with warm oil of almonds.* The massages are sometimes done by hand, and sometimes,

* In other areas of Mexico, the massages are sometimes very vigorous, and in Tzintzuntzan, Foster attributes many miscarriages to the heavy massaging.

after being rubbed with oil, a rebozo is used. The rebozo is pulled back and forth around the woman's stomach. The midwife also puts catalan in her mouth and blows it on the buttocks and hips of the pregnant woman. This also is thought to help loosen the child and make childbirth less painful. These treatments are given about once a week during the last month of pregnancy.

There are many beliefs current among barrio people about the effects of the experiences and behavior of pregnant women on their children. If a pregnant woman sees the eclipse of the moon, the baby will "lose moisture" and will be born with defects caused by the lack of moisture. Harelips and defective extremities are most commonly given as examples of such defects. A pregnant woman should be especially careful about how she speaks of others. Bad gossip about others or direct aggressive statements can affect her unborn child. For example, if she said to another person, "You have the face of a fox (or other animal)," her child might be born with such a face. Although some recognize a hereditary factor, it is a common belief that twins are caused by a woman eating double or twinned fruit, especially a double banana. Not all women admit to this belief, and some skeptics tend to joke about it. On one occasion we happened to run across a double banana and offered it along with some single bananas to several women. Although they laughed and joked, none of them would take it. The twinned fruit does not need to be eaten during pregnancy to produce twins, and even young girls avoid it. Twins are not feared, but neither are they desired since they are thought to be more trouble than other children.

Not all defects of infants are thought to arise from the experiences or actions of the mother during pregnancy. Some arise by chance or providence. Mothers also expressed the belief that the unborn child might be deformed "just because he wants to." The beliefs of the people in the effects of the experiences and actions of the pregnant woman are strong enough, however, so that in no case did we observe practices contrary to the beliefs.

The course of the first pregnancy is very similar to that of subsequent ones although women seem more fearful after their first delivery. There is some difference in the husband's and wife's attitudes toward pregnancy. Women's attitudes vary from a somewhat fatalistic acceptance to pleasant anticipation. The men exhibit more anticipation and generally prefer larger families than their wives. The women would be content with an average of four children, while the men would prefer about six. Due to the high rate of infant mortality, most couples never have more than four to six surviving children.

These differences in the attitudes of the husband and wife are related to several factors. Girls tend to marry younger than men because, according to Mexican law, marriage cannot take place before compulsory military service. Although this law is sometimes circumvented, men are generally over 20 at marriage, while a girl would be considered undesirable if not married by that age. Becoming a mother raises the status of a woman somewhat, but the improvement in status is much greater for a man. When he becomes a father, he moves from youth to manhood and acquires a new independence.

Ideally a man will be more affectionate and thoughtful of his wife's needs during her pregnancy. This ideal is generally reflected in practice for the first child or two, but after this time there is no observable difference in a husband's behavior during the pregnancy of his wife.

When a woman is ready to give birth to a child, a warm vapor, like steam or smoke, appears where the infant's head is to appear. With the appearance of this vapor and the commencement of pains, the midwife, the mother, the mother-in-law, a compadre or two, the husband, and any others who might come to help, are sent for. The birth takes place in the house of the couple having the child, and the people who are to aid, along with the girl's father, assemble there. No children or other men should be present.

The woman kneels with her knees well separated on a woven straw mat which has been laid on the dirt floor for the purpose. To help her make sufficient exertion, she is given two raw eggs to eat. These are broken directly into her mouth by the midwife or one of the other women present. When the pain begins, she is given a bitter tea made from *artemisa,* which is supposed to help expel the child. If the woman tires from holding her posture too long, she may get up and walk around. The women present also rub her belly with almond oil.

When the child begins to emerge, the midwife places herself in front of the mother to receive the child, while the husband, or sometimes another woman, holds the mother down strongly by the waist. At this point, a wide sash is adjusted around the woman's waist. The husband assists until the infant is born and until the sash is adjusted. If the sash is not put on tightly and adjusted properly, the woman could get sick and die, since it is thought to prevent the blood and the placenta from rising and is said to help expel the placenta more rapidly.

The mother must continue to exert herself to expel the placenta. She does this by blowing in a bottle and by chewing a few leaves of *yerba buena,* mint with salt, to help in her exertion. Sometimes her throat is tickled with a feather or finger to cause nausea in order to aid the expulsion of the placenta. After the placenta has been discharged, it is placed in a rag and rolled up in the straw mat and placed in a tree so that the child, when he grows up, will be able to climb trees. The placenta should be very clean because if any dirt gets on it, it may affect the eyes of the child. Once the afterbirth is expelled, the mother changes her clothes but does not bathe or touch water. If pain continues after birth, the mother takes a special tea brewed without sugar.

In case of delayed births, the mother lies down on the mat and a rebozo is put around her waist. The two ends of the rebozo are held by the midwife and moved first toward one side and then to the other, sliding over the body with steady pressure in a rotary movement. No one knows why births are delayed. Some attribute it to God's will.

If the child is in an improper position for birth, the midwife corrects it by external pressure and massage. In no case does the midwife put her hand inside the mother. If the child begins to be born hand first, a needle is used to prick the little hand so that it will pull back inside and the mother is placed almost on her head with her legs upward. The midwife then blows on her so that the baby will straighten out.

When the baby is born, if he doesn't want to cry, the midwife blows a little warm alcohol near his heart. The baby is immediately placed on a new straw mat with a clean cloth. His umbilicus is tied with a thread and is cut above the tie with scissors which have been heated with a candle made of grease. After the cord is cut, the exposed end is burned with a candle. The cord is then passed through several squares of cloth previously prepared for the purpose with center holes. Grease is rubbed on the cord and the squares of cloth. The body of the child is then greased with almond oil, and it is dressed in a tiny shirt. The baby is given a spoonful of oil. This is said to clean out his stomach. The infant is then given to his mother, and they lie down together.

During the first two days, the infant is fed by some woman other than the mother. Any woman who is currently nursing her child may offer her services. The mother squeezes the colostrum from her breasts during this period unless there are no other women available in which case, the infant is given a little tea and the mother gives him the breast the second day. To encourage the flow of milk, a green herb spice is toasted and ground into a paste for the mother. The paste is rubbed on the back between the mother's shoulders and on her hips and around her breasts.

Grease is rubbed on the umbilical cord until it falls off. When it falls off, it is kept wrapped in a little rag and used in the preparation of an eye wash used in the treatment of children's eye diseases. The cord of a male child is used to treat a female child and vice versa. Once the umbilicus has fallen off, the child is bathed in lukewarm water and rubbed with almond oil.

After birth, the mother is supposed to rest in bed 40 days. She sleeps alone with the infant in her arms and does not resume her sexual life for two months. In practice, she may get up a little before this but almost always confines herself to the inside of the house and never does any hard work. She must not touch a needle, hold a broom, or do any lifting. When she does begin to get up, she does it very gradually. Women may visit her, bringing bread, chocolate, a peso for clothes for the child, or some other small gift. They do not look at the infant, for if something happened to him, they might be accused of "evil eye." During the first few days the mother can only drink chocolate and broth and eat meat of chicken or a crisp, toasted tortilla of a special type. She cannot eat chile, greases, pork, black or green beans, or any "cold" foods. She can drink atole, white broth, warm tea, and should neither touch nor drink cold water.

Two or three days after birth, an herbal brew is prepared for the mother. She washes herself with this mixture and then goes back to bed. Six days after birth, the mother is given her first sweat bath. Before entering the bath she loosens her hair and rubs her head with "a good piece of Juxtlahuacan leather." She can only wash her hair during the 40 days. If she were to cut it on any account, it could "go inside" and death could result. In the sweat bath she is assisted by two female relatives. Her head is washed twice and then her body is bathed. She must take between 12 and 15 of these sweat baths before she is considered recovered.

We have almost no reports of women dying in childbirth, and childbirth is not considered dangerous for the mother. The case is very different for the infant. During the year of the study several infants died immediately or soon after birth, and an analysis of the genealogical material confirms the high rate of infant mortality. The average woman in the barrio has borne twice as many children as are surviving. Not all of these children have died right after birth. The period around weaning, as reported later, is also very hazardous. The figures cannot be taken as too accurate, but 20% mortality due to advanced miscarriage, premature births resulting in death, and infant deaths, is a conservative estimate. When an infant is born prematurely and dies, he is buried in the cemetery as is a fetus that is born dead or dies at birth.

Chapter 11

Infancy

After birth, the infant is wrapped in soft, usually old, clothes and held in the arms of the mother. For the first eight days he is close to his mother continuously, either in her arms while sleeping or being rocked during the day. After this time the infant may be put in a small, shallow, wooden cradle which hangs from the ceiling by ropes. There he sleeps for short periods during the day.

The first few weeks of life are considered very dangerous for the new baby, who is thought to have little resistance. There is much reality to this belief, for he is susceptible to diarrhea, parasites, and other ever-present ailments. Infants, particularly under the age of 2 or 3 months, are especially prone to the effects of "evil eye" and witches. This is one of the reasons given for confining the mother and child to the house for the first 40 days. As mentioned in an earlier chapter, an infant is not exposed to the dead at funerals.

The first 8 to 15 days, while the mother stays in bed, and the remaining time of the 40 when she sits around the house without doing very much work, no one but the family is supposed to see the baby lest he become sick and die. A sleeping baby is particularly vulnerable, since he is unconscious and cannot protect himself. This is one of the reasons a rebozo, or cloth, is always kept over the face of younger infants. Older infants are covered while sleeping, partly to ward off flies and partly to protect them from "evil eye."

"Evil eye" may be caused unwittingly by a relative, friend, or stranger who covets the child and stares at him directly. It may be caused willfully by a witch. The most common symptoms are vomiting and fever. It may be cured by the guilty person touching the victim if the act is unintentional. Two examples from our case histories of "evil eye" will help to illustrate the concept further.

The first example concerns unintentional effects of staring. Reina, a young girl of 13, attended a fiesta with her parents. An older woman looked at Reina several times during the evening because "she liked Reina." The next day Reina became ill with a fever and vomiting. Several remedies were tried without effect. Finally, the older woman was called; she came and touched Reina, and then the illness went away.

The second example concerns intentional effects of "evil eye." A couple in the barrio had no children and were very sad because they could have none. A young unmarried girl had an infant daughter, and her mother suggested that she give it to the childless couple. She did so, and the couple was very happy. When the baby was 3 months old, an old lady reputed to be a witch from Santa Rosa (a small village about 2 miles south of the barrio) came by one day and looked at the infant. The next day the baby came down with a high fever. She had this fever for 20 days, and nothing seemed to help her. A *curandera* (a woman who cures illness) was called in and tried everything she knew of to cure the baby. One day the infant rallied slightly and opened her eyes. That night, at midnight, the mother heard a knock at the door. When she opened it, she saw no one. On re-entering the room she saw a large, black cat walking around the mat on which the child was sleeping. She tried to hit the cat with a stick, but the stick "went through the cat" and she could not get it away. Then suddenly the cat disappeared. At three the next afternoon, the child died.

In talking with several people about this case, the following beliefs were brought out. Everyone agreed that the infant died from "evil eye." The witch was said to have a "strong" eye. Some of the people thought that the cat had been sent by the witch, while others said that it was just unfortunate that such an evil animal came when the child was already so ill that she had no defense against it.

Infants must be protected from the effects of witches. Informants said there were no witches in the barrio but named one woman in the central part of town and one woman in Santa Rosa. More distant towns were said to have many witches. The witch in town is said to attack only children under 3 to 4 months of age. When asked how they knew the woman was a witch, people say, "She goes out every night, and no one sees her going or coming." The following episode is attributed to the work of the witch in towns.

A mother awoke one night to find her infant daughter gone from her side. The mother jumped up from her bed and hurried to the door, calling the infant's name. She found her child on the step crying hard. The baby had blood beneath both ears and under her chin. No one was visible in the street in any direction. The mother comforted the infant; and the next day, she called in a curandera. The curandera cured the child and there was no lasting ill effect.

There are various ritual precautions that may be taken to ward off "evil eye," witches, and other evil influences. The mother frequently puts scissors, or even crossed sticks, at the head or the foot of the crib to cut any evil powers. Small nuts, not carved in any special way, are prepared by boring a hole through them so that they may be tied to a string which is put around a new baby's wrist to ward off evil.

To protect infants from "evil air," small caps are put on their heads. Since there is, in fact, a great deal of wind and many drafts which enter through the thatched or roughly tiled roofs, this precaution serves practical, as well as ritual, purposes.

Not all illness in infants is attributed to witches and "evil eye." We have records of five infants who died from measles during the period of the study. The disease was not thought to be caused by any outside agent, and deaths resulting from it were treated as due to natural causes. Death is said to result when "the measles don't come out, but turn inward and cause death."

Young infants are rarely taken out of the house and, in theory, should not leave the house for 40 days after birth except to be baptized. The mother is constantly close to the child. In practice, the 40 days' rest for the new mother is not strictly followed. Because of the press of work and other factors, the women will occasionally enter the courtyard; near the end of the 40 days they may even walk to the market or to the house of a relative. On these occasions the infant is carried in the mother's rebozo, but no part of the infant is ever exposed to air or to sight. For the first year the infant is carried in a prone position. It would be considered very bad manners for anyone to show any curiosity about seeing the infant. After a year the child may sit in the rebozo swing.

Mothers do not burp their new infants over the shoulder until they are about 4 months old, since it is thought dangerous to hold the child up over the shoulder before he can hold up his own head. They say that a new infant is "like a tender flower—you would break the stem." The backbone of the new infant is also considered to be very weak, and one has to handle the infant very carefully to avoid injuring it.

The responsibility for the care of an infant falls primarily to the mother, especially during the first four or five months. In the interviews, we asked the mothers who had spent the most time with their children when they were infants. Three fourths of the mothers responded that they had. Older sisters and grandmothers account equally for the remaining quarter of the cases. We also asked mothers who would take care of the child in case the mother was busy. One third of the mothers responded that they themselves would work with the children on their backs, while the other two thirds indicated that someone else would take care of their infants. The people mentioned, in order of frequency, were as follows: sisters, grandmother, and then aunt. All but 20% of the mothers indicated that someone other than themselves took care of the infant at least part of the time.

In general, our observations indicated that the mother is almost the exclusive caretaker during the first 40 days. After that time, the extent to which other older females participate is highly related to their availability. If there are older sisters in the household, they invariably take over a large share of the caretaking after the first two months. If there are no older sisters, then the grandmother or aunt will take over this function, if such a person happens to live in the compound or is close by. The empirical rule seems to be that the mother has the primary responsibility, but if the household is such that an older female is available to share in this task, she is pressed into service by the mother when she is busy or when she leaves the household for marketing or to wash clothes. In one family where there were only older brothers in the household, they sometimes took over the caretaking duties. This was commented on in the barrio and was thought to be an undesirable state of affairs.

Slightly less than half the mothers indicated that persons other than themselves had nursed their infant child. Most frequently mentioned was the aunt of the child; one grandmother was mentioned. In every case but one, however, the substitute was a close relative.

The other half indicated that no other woman had nursed their children but explained that this was because there were no other women in the extended family capable of nursing the child.

When a substitute nurse is used, it is most frequently during a short period when the mother is absent from the household and does not take the infant, as, for example, a trip to the market or to the stream for bathing or washing clothes. Actually, in these cases the mother most frequently takes a nursing child along with her, and it is only during the transition stage to early childhood that she might leave the child at home. Generally, when the mother is present, there is no substitution. Rather, one of the other women in the household might temporarily take over some of the grinding duties and other work of the mother. It is not at all uncommon for a mother to carry on simple tasks like shelling corn while she is nursing, nor is it uncommon to see mothers nursing their children in the market while carrying on trading activities there. The following exerpt from an interview gives an example of one mother's attitude toward substitute nurses.

Q. When he was still nursing, at times you allowed someone else to give him the breast? Did you not? That is, someone else like a sister or female friend?

A. Yes. Josefa gave him her breast because sometimes I would leave him sleeping and I went out, and if he woke, she would nurse him.

Q. In what situation did you allow Josefa to breast feed Abel?

A. Only when I was not there. If I was there, even if I was busy, I gave him the breast. Because if some other woman nurses them, it can do harm. I ate nothing fresh, no pineapple, coconut nor avocado nor banana or another kind of banana. Other women do eat these things but I do not. I took care of my milk so that it would not be harmful to the child. Some children get diarrhea and die if they take milk from other women than their mother.

Q. Was Abel allowed to breast feed whenever he asked?

A. Yes. She (referring to Josefa) gave it to him because she was there, and I had to go to the market almost every day. Abel's reddish hair he got from his mother, Josefa, because she nursed him a bit, so that she who gave him her breast is also his mother and he calls her mother. I tell him to call her mother so that he will love her more. (Note: Josefa is an aunt by marriage of Abel. Abel's mother's belief here that the child can inherit characteristics of the woman who nurses him, through her milk, is a distinct one, and no other mother mentioned this belief.)

Although fathers are generally affectionate toward their infant children, it is not thought to be their duty or responsibility to care for them. The father actually spends only a small part of the daylight hours in the household, for he is generally out in the fields. In the evening, or early in the morning, the father may pick up his infant child and jounce him on his knee for a short period, but if the child is wet or cries, the mother, sister, or grandmother will immediately take the responsibility of attending to the infant's needs. In the interviews, no mother reported that her husband aided in the care of the infant. Most reported that at night or during siestas or early in the morning, the husband might hold the baby for a moment or two, but nothing more.

Babies spend a great deal of time in their mothers' arms, and they are generally offered the breast at every little cry. They are rocked and go to sleep with the breast in their mouths, which thus serves as a pacifier. After the initial 40-day period, they sleep with both the mother and father.

Babies are never laid on the floor or placed on mats until they are a year old. During the day they sleep in a wooden box or cradle with a palm mat on the bottom and a rebozo over their head. The cradle hangs by a rope from the ceiling in the main room of the house. It is swung back and forth periodically by the mother or other close female relative. An infant is held and rocked in arms to put him to sleep before he is placed in the cradle. An infant who wakes up and cries will immediately be taken from the cradle and held by some older female caretaker. Once he is old enough to be placed on the floor, his movements are unrestricted as long as he stays on the mat.

Small babies are kept rather clean and changed fairly often. They are bathed and rubbed with oil the first few days of life and later are wiped with water and a clean rag; generally no soap is used. The bath water is placed in the wooden tub, which is put out in the yard to be warmed by the sun. Water brought directly from the well or the river is not used, for it is considered to be too cold. Babies are not actually put into the bath bowl; rather, they are sponged off. Small children beyond infancy may be placed in the wooden bath bowl.

Infants are dressed in a cotton shirt with diapers made of rags or cloth. These are tied on with a separate length of material, not pinned as is our custom generally. The baby is wrapped in a square piece of wide cloth. In poorer families this may be an old rebozo; in others, soft cotton material is used. The blanket is wrapped lightly, not tightly, from the arm pits down. This restricts movement somewhat but not completely. Infants at this age are generally very quiet and do not exhibit much physical movement. For about 10 months they are swaddled in this way most of the day and always at night.

Older children, from about 6 to 12 months, are generally changed less frequently than small babies. After a baby learns to walk, he will frequently be seen in the courtyard without any clothes other than a ragged shirt, but no attempts are made to toilet train the infant.

Girls' ears are generally pierced the first week or so. No special ceremony is performed. A small hole is pierced with a needle or pin by the mother or aunt, and a thread is drawn through the hole and tied in a little loop. The thread is merely to keep the hole open until the child may begin to use earrings—usually in late childhood and then only on special occasions.

An idea of the general behavior of the mother with respect to an infant is probably most easily communicated by excerpts from an actual observation. The following observation was taken of a mother with her 1-year-old boy. The setting is inside a cook shack where the mother and several other women are engaged in cleaning up after a meal at a fiesta.

The mother has one arm around the child, and he is standing and moving around her, holding on tightly to her all the time. The mother talks and smiles at him and wipes his face with her hand. He begins to cry, and the breast is immediately offered; he nurses for about a minute and a half and then stands up, holding onto the mother's arm and drops her breast. He makes many goo-ing sounds, and the mother answers in "cuddly tones." He cries again, and the mother holds his face and looks into his eyes, then the child reaches inside her dress for the breast and pulls it out. The mother unsnaps the blouse, and the child stands on her knee to nurse, the mother continuing to dry the dishes. He nurses for two minutes and then drops the breast again. The mother refastens her dress and continues work, talking to the women around her. The child stands on her legs as she is kneeling and he pulls at her earrings and her hair. The mother does not appear to notice this. The child cries again, and the breast is offered again, for the third time in ten minutes. He nurses two sucks and pushes it away. The mother refastens her dress and shows no annoyance. The child cries a little, and the mother looks around and gets a tortilla and breaks off a small piece and gives it to him. The child takes it and starts sucking on it and is quiet.

☙
☙
☙

Chapter 12

Early Childhood

The transition from infancy to early childhood is marked by several changes in the treatment of the child, the most important of which are weaning and a change in sleeping arrangements. During infancy the child sleeps in the same bed with his parents or, more rarely, in a cradle next to his parents' bed. At the transition into early childhood the child begins sleeping with his siblings rather than his parents. Thus children in both early and late childhood sleep together. The third important change is that the care of the infant, which has been primarily in the hands of the mother, is transferred to older siblings or cousins.

The parents' conception of the nature of the child at this stage differs in some important respects from the concept of the child as an infant. One of the more important of these ideas is the belief that the child develops or gains "awareness" on entering early childhood. The child is conceived of as being aware of himself as a distinct entity as well as developing awareness of other human beings as individuals. A child of this age, however, is not thought of as having developed the capacity for reason. In Mixtec belief, the child in this early stage is capable of learning by sheer repetition but is not thought of as having the capacity to learn by reason; nor can a child of this age recognize right from wrong, and he is not expected to be responsible for his behavior.

One of the more interesting ways in which this belief is related to the attitudes and behavior of the adults and older children toward a child is in the amount of nurturance given to children in this stage. For example, when a young child falls or hurts himself by any means, he is immediately nurtured and given comfort by an older sibling or cousin and is never ridiculed for the behavior because it is taken for granted that he does not know any better. As we shall see in the next chapter on late childhood, this attitude undergoes great change, for then the child is conceived of as having the ability to reason and to distinguish right from wrong. In that stage he would be ridiculed rather than comforted in such a situation.

Relatively little distinction is made between the treatment given to boys and that given to girls at this stage of life. Both boys and girls are carried around a great deal by the older children, and there is no distinction made on the basis of sex in the amount of nurturance and attention received from the older caretakers. The relatively simple tasks required of children are undifferentiated with respect to the sex of the child. The young child is not seen as making any contributions to the labor supply of the family; rather, this period is one in which the child is learning some simple skills by imitation and demonstration.

Weaning generally takes place at the age of 1 or 2 years. Ninety per cent of the mothers reported that they had weaned their children by the age of 2. Those who nursed longer than two years mentioned that there were no younger children and that this accounted for their nursing the child to the age of $2\frac{1}{2}$. Nursing may continue well into pregnancy. Almost all mothers, however, stop nursing during the fifth or sixth month of a new pregnancy. Some reported that the milk was not "good" beyond this time, that it would turn sour and might make the nursing child sick. Another frequently mentioned reason for weaning at this time was the amount of energy and strength available to the mother, the feeling being that it was just too difficult physically to carry a baby of some size and still continue to nurse.

The most striking uniformity of weaning is the abruptness with which it takes place. Weaning was abrupt in all but one case of the 22 mothers intensively studied. Half of the mothers used a bitter herb or dirt on the breast to discourage nursing. The herbs mentioned included saliva and *yerba maestra*. Just over a third of the mothers reported that they used the technique of leaving the child with a relative for a couple of days. Thus we see that although there is variation in the time of weaning and in the techniques used, there is almost complete uniformity in the abruptness with which weaning takes place. After weaning, when the baby cries, he is frequently given a liquid, such as coffee or milk, as a substitute for the mother's breast. This is one of the very few uses of milk in the barrio, for it is considered an expensive luxury under normal circumstances. Also, during the day the child may be given bits of food, such as a tortilla to chew on. After the initial break, the mother does not offer her breast to the child again. The child will continue to sleep with the parents for a short time, but after weaning, he will sleep by the father rather than by the mother in order that he not be drawn to the mother's breast at night when he is in a sleepy state.

Excerpts from one of our interviews on weaning might provide some additional appreciation and insight into the attitudes of the mothers concerning weaning.

Q. How old was Abel when he was able to eat alone, that is, without aid?
A. He began to eat alone when he was nine months. I gave him his broth in a plate and he ate it. He picked up the plate and he also took his cup of water all by himself.
Q. How old was Abel when you ceased giving him the breast? Or, when he ceased nursing?
A. He was one and a half years old. As I have no children after him, he was the last.
Q. But before that you gave him a little bit to eat of other things?
A. Yes, I told you, he began to eat at four months of age.
Q. Did you take the breast from Abel little by little or in one fell swoop?
A. At one time.
Q. Did Abel not complain as you took the breast from him? Did he cry or yell?
A. Jesus, he didn't pay any attention. I put him to sleep with his eldest brother. He didn't even cry. Yes, he cried when he nursed because then he wanted something better to eat.
Q. Did you or did you not give him the breast again?
A. No more. I took it away all at one time and he didn't complain about it.
Q. Did you put anything or apply anything on the breast in order that Abel would not ask for it?
A. No. I tied up my breast so that he would not pay any attention. I tied it with a little handkerchief so that he wouldn't find my breast. Some people put saliva, that bitter herb on the breast, or they paint it with something,

that is, with some charcoal, but my son wasn't foolish and I didn't have to do that. He drank his atoli and ate his tortilla. I am too poor to give him cow's milk. Just hot tortilla and toli.

Q. Did you not give him something distasteful to eat when he asked for the breast in order that he would not ask for it again?

A. No, I didn't give it to him. I gave him sugar cane because that is good when one is taking the breast away from the child because it is sweet and has water. The child can chew it and they forget to want to nurse. When they cry one could clean off a piece of sugar cane and that should suffice. Then they forget they want to nurse.

Not all children take weaning so easily as Abel. Many mothers reported that the period following weaning was a difficult one. They reported that children cry more frequently during the two to six months following weaning, and the child experiences, for the first time, the discomfort of being allowed to cry on occasion without receiving as much nurturance as he would formerly have received. Before weaning, the infant would almost invariably be offered the breast or some other comfort when he was fussy or crying. During the transition period immediately after weaning, fussing or crying does not inevitably lead to being nurtured. An observation taken during a fiesta in which about 20 women were in the community house preparing food will illustrate this point. A small boy aged 3 was sitting by his mother, who had a 3-month-old infant strapped to her back in a rebozo. The boy had been weaned about six months earlier. The observation follows:

Juan is sitting by his mother's knee while she is sorting and cleaning beans. The mother gets up to go outside the room to change the infant's diaper (they do not change diapers in the room where there is food cooking). Juan begins to cry as the mother disappears out the door. He continues to cry and the mother does not return and he is crying loud enough for her to hear him outside. None of the other adults in the room offer him any assistance. He continues crying for four minutes and finally one of the other women tells him to keep quiet, that the mother will be back. Gradually he slows down and stops crying but continues to gulp sobs, and tears continue to run down his face. The mother becomes engaged in other activities outside the door and returns only after fifteen minutes. By this time Juan has stopped crying but still sobs intermittently. The mother goes over to him and he cuddles up against her. There are no words exchanged between them. The mother offers him a tortilla and sits quietly beside him and he leans against her and goes to sleep five minutes later. (When the mother returned, the infant was asleep in the rebozo on her back.)

This observation is not presented as representing the most typical behavior, since an examination of all of our observations taken on children in early childhood indicate that it is relatively rare for nurturance to be withheld for as long a period as indicated in the above account. The observation does illustrate, however, the insecurity of the child following weaning and also demonstrates the fact that several adults would withhold nurturance on occasion during that period. In a more typical situation in the household, the mother would withhold the nurturance formerly given, but she would encourage and insist on the older siblings providing the nurturance for the young child. They would see it as the duty of the older sisters and cousins to provide the care and nurturance of the young children. It is the mother's duty to care for the infant, but a mother cannot accomplish all her work if she has young children under foot also. In a real sense the mother is weaning the child away from herself as the major source of nurturance during the several months following actual weaning. For example, the mother no longer carries the child in the rebozo. Thus weaning involves physical separation as well as withdrawal of the breast. The transference of the primary caretaking responsibilities from the mother to the sibling group, however, is not an abrupt one like weaning from the breast. It takes place gradually, beginning at about the time the child is weaned. However, the child still continues to spend a good share of the time with his mother, and generally it is not until about a year after weaning that he spends almost all of his daytime hours with the older sibling caretakers.

In general, however, after weaning, the response to succorant appeals on the part of the child are less immediate, particularly if there is no apparent need. One very frequently reported undesirable behavior during early childhood is "crying without any reason." Several mothers reported that a young child who cries for some reason is immediately nurtured and comforted, and various attempts are made to alleviate his discomfort. But they also reported that when children cry without any reason, that is undesirable behavior. With the exception of two mothers of young girls, all the mothers of young children reported that they would either scold or physically punish such behavior. This report on the part of the mothers of the younger children corresponds with the observational material. The mothers believe that the frequency of crying without reason increases following weaning. The observational evidence indicates that this is a realistic appraisal by the mothers, although it does suggest that withholding of previously given nurturance, rather than punishment, is the most frequent response. Oddly enough, the mothers of older boys report that they would comfort the child, while the mothers of older girls report scolding or hitting as the main response. We do not have any adequate explanation for the responses of the mothers of the older boys.

Weaning is also related to the problem of health. The mothers report that this is a dangerous time from the point view of the health of the child. Given the rather poor diets of the barrio people, it is our impression that this period is indeed a dangerous time. The child's resistance to various kinds of ailments seems to be low in the months following weaning, and although we do not have definite figures to document this, it is our distinct impression that the frequency of illness during the year following weaning is relatively high compared to the year preceding and the years succeeding this period.

As nearly as we can tell from an examination of the observation protocols, no special stress is placed on obedience during early childhood. It is not until around the time when the child enters late childhood that special stress is placed on obedience. Although, in the interviews, the mothers reported that obedience is desirable for children of this age, from observation we would judge that this is more of an ideal value on the part of the mothers than it is a principle put into practice in the training of the child. A quote from an observation on a 3-year-old girl will serve to document this point. Six children between the ages of 3 and 8 are playing around a large rock at the side of a house in one of the larger compounds. Three separate piles of cornstalks are scattered around the rock. At the time the observation begins, some of the children are sweeping with the cornstalks while others are walking on the cornstalks or sitting on them.

Cortina (the 3-year-old subject of the observation) has been walking around the rock and now begins to collect some plain sticks from among the stalks. She stands alone at one side of the pile, cleaning a stick from its dried outer husk. She is very intent on her work. She has about five sticks cleaned in her hand. She then wanders away from the piles of cornstalks, still holding the sticks in her hands, and enters one doorway of the closest room. She comes out immediately with a small chair in one hand and the sticks in the other hand. At the corner of the house, Odilia (a female cousin, age 6) reaches for the chair and tries to pull it away from Cortina. Cortina turns her back and pulls the chair. Odilia lets go of the chair, and Cortina carries the chair around to the side of the house and puts it on the ground. Juana (another female cousin, age 7) is sweeping the ground close by where Cortina places the chair. As Juana begins to sweep closer to Cortina, Cortina picks up the chair in her hands and holds it waiting for Juana to finish sweeping. Cortina then puts the chair back on the ground. She leaves her chair with the sticks on the seat and goes in the house and brings out another chair. Cortina's father and a male compainion enter the compound and pass Cortina as she comes out with the chair. The father asks her to bring the chair over to the other room for his compadre to sit on. Cortina continues walking around to the side of the house with the chair. (It was not evident whether she didn't mind her father or was just going to get another chair.) She walks up to the chairs and sits on one as her father comes around and takes the other chair. He does not say anything, and neither does she. (There is no noise or crying or any special recognition as he takes the chair.)

The father's request for a chair, which was ignored in this case, seems like an ideal opportunity for obedience training if there were any stress on it at this age. This observation is quite typical, and we have several examples of parents making a request of a young child and not following up when the request was ignored. Almost never, during the earlier stages of early childhood, does either parent stress obedience in situations of this kind.

In the interviews, in contrast to the observations, mothers of girls reported that their children were obedient. In response to the question, "When you ask or tell your child to do something, does he do it right away, or does he delay?" five out of six of the mothers of young girls reported that their child obeyed right away. Mothers seemed to be more realistic about their sons' behavior, for four out of six of the mothers of the young boys indicated that their children would delay or not obey at all. The same contrast was noted in the answers of mothers of older children. In a mother's view, then, girls respond to requests or orders immediately, while boys delay or do not ever respond.

We also asked the mothers, "What do you do to your child if he delays?" Half the mothers of the younger boys responded that they would scold, and half responded that they would hit the child. This contrasts in an interesting way to the responses of the mothers with older boys, who unanimously reported scolding as the only technique of punishment. Mothers of girls reported equally as much scolding and hitting for both younger and older girls. The moderately frequent response of the mothers reporting the use of physical punishment did not correspond to the data gathered by observation. Not once during our entire stay did we see a parent strike a child. Since, in another context, every mother interviewed reported the use of physical punishment, there seems little doubt that on occasion parents do strike their children, but this is a relatively rare occurrence and probabaly takes place mostly in private.

In response to a general question on the technique of punishment preferred by the mothers of the younger children, we found that all but two said that scolding was a more frequent and preferred kind of punishment than physical punishment. Isolation of a young child was mentioned by four mothers as a form of punishment. It is conceived of as being relatively harsh and may be used on occasion if a child fights back. The report that physical punishment is more frequently used on younger boys than on older boys reflects the increasing differentiation in the treatment of boys and girls in late childhood. During early childhood it is apparent that boys and girls are treated very much the same, while, in the later stage, use of physical punishment is reported to continue for the girls but not for the boys. Our interpretation of the interview material, in conjunction with the observational data, is that obedience is ideally desirable from children in early childhood but that, in practice, it is seldom required or enforced. The mothers also stated that they used an embrace, praise, or material rewards for obedient behavior. The reported use of these various rewards for obedience was also greater than that which we noted in the observational protocols.

Returning to the observation reported above, the dominance-submission relationship between Odilia and Cortina should be noted. It will be remembered that Odilia, aged 6, reached for the chair Cortina, aged 3, carried and tried to pull it away. Cortina resisted and Odilia gave up. Obviously Odilia would have been physically able to take the chair away from Cortina. Situations of this sort almost never lead to any overt aggression or scuffle among children in this age group. Observations of many situations similar to this one indicate one of two outcomes. The first is the one observed in the above episode where Odilia reaches out for the chair and, when it is not proferred immediately, gives up the attempt to take it. The other outcome that we have frequently observed would be for Cortina to give Odilia the chair with no further comment. One could argue that the gesture of Odilia's putting her hand on the chair is a nonverbal request for the chair, in which case the nonverbal answer would be either "No" as in this case, or "Yes" if the request had been complied with. The important point is that these situations almost never lead to any further aggression. It should further be noted that the sex of the interactors does not seem to make any difference in the responses. In other words, had Odilia been a boy, Cortina's response would probably not have been any different; or contrariwise, had the younger child been a boy, one would not predict a different outcome.

A final aspect of the same observation that deserves attention is the nature of the activity of a group of young children. The activities are not organized or integrated in any way. The children are playing close to one another, but they do not have common goals, and the amount of social interaction is relatively small and diffuse. Organized games do not begin until late childhood. Further insight into obedience and types of playing may be gained from an observation taken of two children at the very end of the period of early childhood. The two girls are Elidia (age 6) and Juana (age 7). They are cousins living in the same household and are playing in the yard at what might be called making dinner or preparing food. They are playing under a tree close by a great-aunt (age 80) who is sitting under the tree, sewing. As the observation begins, Juana is trying to knock some dry leaves off the tree to crumble for the play food.

As Juana hits the branches of the tree with a stick, the dried leaves fall on the aunt and her work. The aunt tells Juana to stop hitting down the leaves, but Juana continues to knock down the leaves. Then the aunt asks Elidia to pick up the leaves that have fallen on the sewing materials of the aunt. Elidia comes around and picks them up off from the aunt's materials. Elidia then shows Juana what a big handful of leaves she has. Juana pays no apparent attention, continuing to hit the leaves down. Elidia takes some leaves in her skirt and goes over to the side wall of the house and makes a pile of them. Then she returns to the tree and points up to a big one telling Juana to get that one. Juana does not pay any attention. Elidia gets more leaves in her skirt and takes them back to her pile. Juana calls that there are some more to pick up on the other side of a big pile of logs. Elidia comes immediately and climbs over the pile of logs (with some difficulty) and picks up some more leaves. She walks back around the pile of logs carrying what she can. Juana calls that there are more, so Elidia returns close to Juana. At this point Juana walks away toward the house. Elidia tries to pick up all the leaves, but there are too many, and the wind keeps blowing them out of her hands. (She shows no visible reaction to the wind blowing the leaves.) She then gets an armload of leaves (rather than carrying them in her skirt as previously) and walks back with them around the logs to her original pile of leaves. She returns to pick up all the leaves that the wind hasn't blown away. She then forms a large neat pile of leaves and drops them through her hands. Juana returns with some pieces of old pottery to play with. Elidia offers Juana some leaves. (She points to the pile and says "Have some.") Juana takes about half the pile of leaves.

It is to be noted that the aunt places no special stress on insisting on obedience from Juana. Nor does she give any visible rewards to Elidia for compliance to her request to remove the leaves from her sewing materials. This lack of special attention to obedience during early childhood is quite representative of our other observation protocols. Again and again we have observed opportunities where obedience might appropriately be stressed in early childhood, but the occasions are not used to instill obedience in any way.

The amount of interaction between the children playing is also quite typical in this observation. Relatively little conversation goes on between children of this age, and although they are playing in a common area and with similar materials, the amount of interaction in any organized way is small. The slightly older girl, Juana, does initiate more suggestions than does Elidia. In terms of caretaking duties, Juana is just entering the stage of late childhood. Since there are other older girls in the same household, however, Juana is not really being pressed into a caretaking role in any important way at the time of the observation.

Children in early childhood spend most of their time playing in the courtyard with siblings and cousins. In light of this fact, the responses reported below of mothers to the interview question as to whether they preferred their children to play alone or with others were surprising. Fifty percent of the mothers reported that they would prefer their children to play alone. Both sex and age of child made a difference in the response received from the mother. The older the child, the more frequent would be the response of preferring the child to play alone, and this response was also more frequent from mothers of girls than it was from mothers of boys. One third of the mothers of young boys and one half of the mothers of young girls preferred them to play alone. This difference between boys and girls is even more striking in the older age group of late childhood. There, one third of the mothers of boys reported they would prefer them to play alone, while all but one of the mothers of girls so reported. The reasons given by the mothers for this preference indicated that it was mainly desirable because it cut down on the probability of ordering other children around or of getting into a fight. Since all of the mothers are very concerned and preoccupied about any aggressive behavior, we interpret their responses as indicating a high value on avoiding any situation involving the possibility of such behavior. Thus the ideal statement shows a preference for playing alone despite the fact that in reality the children are almost always playing with close relatives. This anxiety concerning aggression undoubtedly does affect the amount of play allowed by the mothers with other than very close relatives. Our observational material clearly demonstrates that play groups for both early and late childhood are composed almost exclusively of children who are closely related and very seldom include distant relatives or any other outsiders.

The mothers' concern about aggression is further revealed by an analysis of the responses to the following question, "What do you wish your child to do if another child looks for an argument with him and when the other child wishes to fight with him?" All of the mothers of young children indicated that they would want their child to come home immediately if anyone attempted to pick a fight with him. Almost all of the mothers of early-childhood children indicated that they would use hitting as punishment to prevent their child from fighting back when attacked. There was only one mother in the entire sample who would encourage her child to fight back, and she was the mother of one of the older boys. She was also the only mother in our sample who had not been born in the barrio. Her responses to several questions concerning aggression and achievement were different from those of any of the other mothers. To prevent fighting back was the only reason for which almost all of the mothers reported that they would use physical punishment. This again points up the special concern with aggressive behavior. We also asked the mothers what sort of punishment they would use if a child attempted to order around other children of his own age. Such behavior was thought to be undesirable by all of the mothers, and all but one reported that they would use scolding as the technique of punishment. The sex of the child would make no difference in the treatment for either fighting back or ordering others around. This is further evidence for the relative lack of differentiation between the training of the two sexes during early childhood. As we shall see in the next chapter, the differentiation between sexes begins to assume importance only at the beginning of late childhood.

The major part of "early childhood," then, is spent in the courtyard. Occasionally the child may accompany an older caretaker to the outskirts of the barrio, where the older siblings and cousins may be engaged in washing clothes or taking baths. The confinement to the courtyard cannot be explained by realistic fears on the part of parents, for the environment in the barrio is on the whole a benign one. There are no poisonous snakes or insects in the area, nor are there any dangerous wild animals. The oxen which are frequently herded through the streets of the barrio are very difficult to turn. Children are taught to keep out of their way and must get into a doorway or step inside a gate. All adults and older children will, if necessary, move to help them out of the way.

Only during parts of the rainy season is the child very frequently in physical discomfort. Then he may be drenched in sudden rainstorms if he is not in the courtyard. When he gets wet, he seldom has other clothes to change into and may become chilled and cold.

About a year after weaning, there are a series of new skills to be learned by the young child. These include such things as learning to dress and to urinate and defecate by themselves. The big majority of the mothers of young children reported that their children learned to urinate and defecate by themselves around age 3. (The mothers of the older children reported that their children learned this at age 2. We would interpret this reported difference as a drift in the mothers' memories rather than an indication of a real change in the age of training.) Since there is a complete lack of sanitation facilities in the village, toilet training is a relatively casual affair and is not given any special attention. Toilet training consists of learning to go to a particular part of the patio and to perform one's duties there rather than elsewhere in the patio. When not at home, it requires only that one step into a relatively unobtrusive place in order to perform one's duties. One is not supposed to defecate in the street but, rather, to step into the fields or at least off the path. Indians who come into town from the surrounding mountain areas are thought to be rather uncouth because they do defecate in the streets.

Toilet training begins after the child learns to walk and the mother takes him outside the house. "They learn to walk, then one teaches them, and they go out alone." All but three of the children in the sample were trained by 3 years of age. Urination just outside the doorway comes first, and then gradually the child learns to go out to the fields or to a corner of the patio alone for either function. Young children are usually without pants at this age, and training is rather simple. Most mothers said that they would talk to the child or scold him for errors, but others said that they did nothing, for the child would gradually learn anyhow.

The ability to dress oneself is acquired shortly after the toilet training takes place, generally between the third and fourth year of life. There are no reported differences in the age at which boys and girls acquire this skill. Since they sleep fully clothed, there is not any early morning rush to clothe oneself. On arising, a little girl shakes out her rebozo and wraps it around her shoulders and head. A small boy shakes out his hat, places it on his head, and is ready to start the day. If a change of clothing is necessary and available during the day, children are generally able to change without help by the age of 4.

In the interviews, the mothers of the younger children reported that these youngsters, both boys and girls, have few assigned duties and are treated with relatively great leniency. "They should play when they want to and help when they want to." The early tasks for young girls include going to get water with the mother or older sibling, piling up dishes after meals, learning about fire care by bringing wood and blowing on the fire, and running small errands. Before girls are strong enough to carry heavy water buckets or do grinding, they learn the correct posture and methods through imitative play. There is no caretaking in this group except perhaps to be nurturant to even younger siblings, but these girls do not have any responsibility for babies as yet. Boys in early childhood are starting to learn animal care and feeding and may walk with the father to nearby fields. They also run errands for the mother.

Most of their simple tasks are more in the nature of imitative behavior of the older siblings and cousins. Helping by young children often takes the form of apparently spontaneous help without being asked or without any kind of formal or overt instruction. An example of this is given in an excerpt from one of the observations on Antonia, age 5. Antonia's older half-sister, age 13, is sweeping the room when the observation begins, and Antonia is standing just outside the door.

As Aulalia finishes sweeping out the room, she begins piling dirt onto a mat and then folding the sides of the mat up together. Antonia runs, without anyone's saying anything to her, and lifts up the mat. She rolls it up and puts it on her head with the waste inside and walks over to the corner of the patio and dumps the dirt out of the mat and shakes the mat. She returns with the mat on her head and then throws it onto the floor in the middle of the room. She bends over, and with her hand brings together a small bit of trash that remains in the corner. Her younger sister, aged 1½, comes and attempts to help her. Antonia pushes her sister's hand away, gathers the trash into her own hand, and walking toward the door, she throws it outside. The wind carries the trash away.

The differential assignment of tasks according to sex of child is not drawn during early childhood. Boys of this age frequently do little tasks that are later assigned to girls as serious work. For example, carrying water is considered mainly a girl's task, as is sweeping. But little boys will participate in imitative activities of these sorts at an early age, when later he will not engage in such female tasks. In summary, the observational material quite definitely indicates that early childhood is pretty much free from any responsibilities for regular and serious tasks. It is sufficient that a young child not be a burden to his mother in terms of requiring time and attention and that he learn to play and to accept the caretaking of older female relatives. Our individual ratings show no difference in the responsible behavior of girls and boys at this age. There is some indication, however, that girls are already being trained for their future caretaking roles.

On the basis of our ratings, nurturance is the only behavior system in which we can detect a difference between boys and girls in early childhood. On the average, girls show many more nurturant responses than do boys of this age. There is also a relationship between the amount of nurturance shown and the age of the child. In general, there is a gradual increase in the amount of nurturance through the period of early childhood. Girls tend to show the nurturant responses earlier than do the boys. By the time late childhood begins, both boys and girls show a high frequency of nurturant responses. Thus during early childhood the difference between the boys' behavior and the girls' behavior is accounted for by the fact that the girls begin to show more nurturant behavior at an earlier age than do the boys. When it is considered that the girls will take on caretaking responsibilities at an early age, it is reasonable that their training with respect to the behavior system of nurturance would begin earlier than that for the boys.

Socialization of various kinds of sex behavior, including such things as modesty and imitative sex play and masturbation, is handled in a rather casual way during early childhood. There are no specific or severe rules concerning any of these activities at the beginning of early childhood. A young child may go around nude without causing any special comment or evoking any punishment or discipline from the caretaker. In contrast, during the latter part of early childhood, children will be lightly ridiculed for going around nude. Thus there is a gradual learning process regarding modesty during early childhood.

Masturbation and imitative sex play between small children are treated with equal casualness. Parents and caretakers tend to be very permissive concerning these activities at the beginning of early childhood and gradually extinguish such activities, mainly through ridicule, toward the end of that stage. The observations of these activities indicate that masturbation and imitative sex play are not particularly common although by no means unusual. The following observation provides insight into the attitudes concerning imitative sex play. This is an observation of 6-year-old Marina, who is playing in the patio with her 4-year-old brother, Alfonso, and her younger sister Chlorea, who is about 2. The three children are playing in sight of their mother and an aunt, who are sitting just inside the doorway sewing.

Marina draws close to Chlorea and says, "Now I will carry you." She stands Chlorea up, bends over, and takes Chlorea by the arms and carries her on her back and runs over to Alfonso. When Marina arrives in the middle of the patio, she throws herself to the ground and the two little girls fall into a sitting position. Marina laughs, saying, "Aye, yi, yi," as if she were very tired. (*Note:* She does this in jest, as in a game.) She gets up and takes Chlorea by the hand and steps toward the door. She then again picks up Chlorea and walks around the patio with her. She again throws both of them on the ground laughing. The two of them lay on their backs and both laugh, breathing hard from the play. Alfonso comes toward her and takes off his cotton trousers that he had on. He stands there nude and then throws the trousers over Marina. Marina gets up on her hands and feet, covered with the trousers and she cries, "Oh," from underneath them. Then she uncovers herself, sits down, and then stands up laughing. Alfonso throws himself upon her and cries, "Now I've got you," and the two children roll around on the ground kicking and laughing. Chlorea has gone a few steps away. Chlorea picks up a rock from the patio and puts it into her mouth. Marina watches, stands up and walks over to Chlorea, taking the stone away from her and hitting her on the hand, saying to her very seriously, "You shouldn't eat that." Chlorea begins to cry. Marina runs and again throws herself on Alfonso, and they whirl around on the ground. A teenage girl standing at the edge of the patio says, "Hurry up, Chlorea, run and hit Marina." At that moment Arelia Grusmon (mother of Marina) comes into the patio. She is carrying a basket. Marina stands up laughing, jumps on one foot, and cries, "Ah, my mother's come." Arelia goes into the cook shack. Marina returns and throws herself on Alfonso, who is lying on the ground still naked. The two children roll around laughing. Marina puts her finger in Alfonso's anus and laughing hits him with the other hand. The boy pulls her hair. She squeezes the boy's testicles with her hand and cries, "I'm going to hit you on the rear end." She laughs. Alfonso sits up and, also laughing, hits Chlorea lightly on the head. (Chlorea had stopped crying and had approached the other two children.) The little girl starts to cry again. Marina puts her arms about her and caresses her head; then Marina looks at Alfonso as if she were angry and says, "Go on, you donkey, get up." Alfonso again throws himself on her, and the two roll around on the ground laughing.

Two or three items of interest occur in this observation. In the first place, the amount of activity and physical exertion engaged in by the children is greater than is typical on the basis of other observations. This activity and excitement also affect the children's behavior toward their 2-year-old younger sister. Typically they would not allow the younger sister to cry, nor would they aggress against her even in jest. Marina's instruction to her younger sister about eating a rock is typical behavior and could be documented in many other observations. However, one would have expected her to nurture the baby after instructing her concerning the stone. The activity of the two children is undoubtedly related to the kind of sex play in which they were engaged and led to a somewhat higher amount of activity and excitement than is typical. This was generally true of the few cases we observed of imitative sex behavior. It should also be noted that there were older people, including adults, around who had seen Alfonso naked and who saw Marina and Alfonso playing together on the ground. None of these people took any steps to interfere or to interrupt the activity. Judging from other observations, it would be our guess that in about two years they will begin to ridicule behavior of this kind.

In summary, early childhood involves weaning, toilet training, learning to dress and feed oneself, learning to play with other children, and not to make too many demands on parents and adults. There is little perceived difference in the treatment of boys and girls, and the only area where sex difference in behavior was obvious was in the higher frequency of nurturant responses in girls.

In rating the children on the behavior systems, there were one or two findings with respect to the ratings that merit interest. The first of these was the discovery that frequently children from related households tended to cluster together on the ratings to a rather marked degree. This strongly suggests that if we had fine enough measuring instruments, we would be able to detect family differences in child-training practices. It is true that there may be some contamination effect of our ratings of closely related people; however, it is our strong belief that there are definite clusterings of child-training practices by various large extended families in the barrio. We were able to trace the genealogical connections among all of the 22 intensively studied families. We were then able to rate the degree of relationship between various clusters of families. An analysis of the ratings indicates that family differences account for a great deal of the variability of our ratings. In those behavior systems where there was no significant difference by sex or age of the child, the family differences accounted for most of the observed variability.

At one point in our analysis we attempted to distinguish between those children who were reared in nuclear families and those who were reared in extended families. It was our impression at the time that some of the children were reared in nuclear families. A closer analysis of the residence patterns and the interaction patterns between related families revealed, however, that none of the children in our sample were reared in a nuclear family situation. Even in cases where only one family lived in a compound, it turned out, on closer scrutiny, that closely related families lived very close by and that in fact the children of early childhood age were part of a group formed by the siblings and cousins and other close relatives. The social context for the children was equivalent to an extended family in all cases when judged on the criterion of interaction during the day and with caretakers.

We also attempted an analysis of the possible effects of position in birth order on the various ratings of the behavior systems. Because of the fluid residence patterns and the amount of interaction with other families who were closely related, we were unable to make any very clear-cut conclusions about the effect of birth order. The one exception to this pertains to the terminal child in a family. The last child in a family tends to enter the various stages at a somewhat older age than is true for other children. An example of this is the age of weaning, as reported earlier. The last child tends to be weaned later. The last child also tends to be trained later with respect to self-reliance, succorance, obedience, nurturance, and responsibility. No effects were detectable for dominance.

⁂

Chapter 13

Late Childhood

Although the transition from early to late childhood is difficult to pinpoint precisely in time, its implications for the child are dramatic in several respects. At the age of 5 or 6, the child encounters changes in the daily round of activities and increasing demands for participation in the simpler household tasks and the care of younger siblings. There are new patterns of interaction to be learned in school and with the Mexican children in the central part of town. Even more important are the adjustments to changing parental expectations that are supported by the withdrawal of earlier nurturance, changes in techniques of discipline, and increasing demands for responsibility and obedience. Clear cut differences in the socialization of males and females also appear with explicit clarity at this period of life.

It must be emphasized that the transition is not abrupt. Unlike the almost overnight transition from infancy to early childhood, the change from early to late childhood is gradual and generally takes two to three years to complete. It typically begins during the fifth year, although it varies from one child to another. In general, parents begin training girls earlier than boys. Similarly, they tend to postpone these demands and expectations for youngest children. Later in the chapter it will be seen that these variations are related to the need for labor to perform various household tasks, and that the age of transition depends, in part, on the family's labor requirements.

The parents' conception of the nature of the child at this stage differs in some important respects from the concept of the child in early childhood. Probably the most important is the idea that the child now has *reason*. Whereas earlier he could learn only by imitation, now he can be taught by reason and counsel as well and can understand the place his tasks have in the family and in life generally. A second idea is that the child at this stage is most malleable and teachable. Later he will become set and independent in his ways. Although youths are still somewhat teachable, it is felt that now is the ideal time to instill proper work habits.

The child's conception of himself reflects his new status. While the transition from early childhood is rather difficult with respect to the behavior systems of nurturance and succorance, the transition into appropriate and responsible role behavior seems to be rather smooth. When tasks are assigned to children of this age, they are generally discharged without any particular fuss or bother, although not always with any great speed. There are many behavioral indications that the child wants to join older people in their tasks and identifies with the roles of people older than themselves.

Probably the most pervasive and overt change is the nature of the participation in the daily round of activities; the part played and the tasks required in late childhood differ from those of early childhood in several important respects. Unlike the rather passive accepting position of the earlier period, these children, particularly the girls, become active participants with a variety of assigned tasks. Since these tasks occur throughout the day and are not limited to any particular time or activity, we shall describe them and the techniques used by parents to assure their performance.

In contrast to early childhood when the list of tasks was small, relatively undifferentiated with respect to sex, and seen by parents as practice for later responsibility, the tasks of late childhood are many, differentiated with respect to sex, and seen by parents as real contributions to the family labor supply. The girls' tasks mentioned most, in the mother interviews, in order of frequency and importance in terms of time, included the following: caring for younger siblings, carrying water, running errands that involve food, or going to market, keeping the fire, caring for small domestic animals such as turkeys and chickens, sweeping and other household tasks, serving food and washing small dishes, bathing self and younger siblings, and washing small items. Cooking, care of large cooking pots, heavy washing, and grinding of corn are not required until later. Boys' tasks include, in rough order of importance, gathering produce or fodder in the fields and bringing it to the house, care of large animals such as goats and burros, some light work in the fields, gathering firewood in close by hills and keeping wood neat in the courtyard, and running errands of various sorts. In general, the girls' tasks at this stage are greater in number and more time consuming. In families where there are no girls, the boys are usually expected to do some tasks normally reserved for girls, especially caretaking of younger siblings, caring for small domestic animals, and sweeping. The reverse is not usually true; if there are no boys in the family, the boys' tasks are done by the male head of the household or a male relative.

The kinds of tasks performed by older children and the differences between early and late childhood can best be illustrated from the observations. The following sequence was observed in the kitchen of the Ramos house, where Helena, age 8, is behind her mother, who is grinding corn for tortillas. Helena is sitting, leaning against the wall with her feet stretched out in front of her, eating a tortilla.

Helena's mother asks her to take a cup of water to her father. The child gets up, takes a cup from a box, comes up to the earthen pot, and crouching down, fills the cup from the water in the pot.

With the tortilla in one hand and the cup of water in the other, she goes out into the couryard. Since the door is closed, in order to open it she kicks it with her foot. The door bolts open. The child, back facing the kitchen, pulls the door again with her foot, and kicks it back to close it.

Helena walks toward the entrace of the room where her father, with another man, is making a drain ditch so that the rain water will not run into the room. The other man is her uncle.

In silence, she hands her father the cup with the water. Her father takes it, looking at the child without saying anything to her, and he drinks. The child stands there with her hands hanging down watching him drink as if she were waiting for something. Her father stops drinking and puts the cup on the ground while he talks with her uncle about the drain. Helena crouches down, picks up the cup from the ground, throws the remaining water on the ground, and runs back to the kitchen with the cup in hand.

She enters the kitchen, opening the door and leaving it open. She returns to the place she was before. She leaves the cup on the ground next to her and sits down behind her mother. She eats her tortilla in silence. Into the kitchen comes Helena's younger brother, who asks for a chair. Helena's mother looks at her and repeats the request. Helena gets up slowly. She takes a few steps and takes a small chair in one hand (in the other, she still has the tortilla) and carries it on her back as far as the child. She sets the chair down and remains standing looking at it. Her younger brother sits in the little chair, smiling.

Helena, with the same serious expression on her face, returns to where she was before, sits down, and continues to eat the tortilla.

The following observation illustrates the girl's part in helping with food preparation. It takes place in the cook shack of the Gutierrez family. Just outside the door, Mr. Gutierrez is talking to a neighbor woman who has come to buy corn. Juanita, age 7, is sitting in a corner behind the fire, cleaning beans by passing them from hand to hand and blowing across them. Across the room from her and close to the fire sit the mother, Manuela Gutierrez, and two younger sisters of Juanita, ages 2 and 4, who are sitting passively.

Juanita passes the beans from hand to hand three times. When she has finished this, she stretches and shakes her skirt, which has some dirt on it. She then takes a peach from the ground next to her, cleans it with her hand, and bites into it. She puts the peach down on top of the clean beans in the pot. She squats down on the ground and, with one hand, retrieves the beans which have fallen on the mat on which she has been sitting. She throws these beans with the rest into the pot and takes the peach, sighs, bites it, and stands up. With her left hand (in her right hand she has the peach), she cleans her skirt by shaking it.

She crosses the room, going toward a large basket, and fills her skirt with beans. She returns to the place where she was before, sits down, puts the peach on top of the pot of clean beans, smooths her hair down with her hands, makes her feet comfortable, picks up the peach and takes another bite.

For the first time Juanita looks at the group which is formed by her mother and her little sisters. The youngest sister had just asked for the mother's breast and the mother did not wish to give it to her, and the group had been laughing about this. Juanita shakes her hair with one hand, grabs a fist full of beans and begins cleaning them again. The mother stands up and, crossing in front of her, looks at her. In order to pass, the mother picks up the pot of beans and puts it on top of the metate and then is standing between the metate and Juanita with her back to the little girl. Juanita says in a gentle voice, "The pot." The mother, without turning around, asks, "What, my little daughter?" and Juanita repeats her request for the pot. The mother, without looking at her, hands her the pot of beans with one hand behind her, still with her back to the little girl. Juanita takes the pot, puts it to one side, opposite to where it had been before. She continues cleaning the beans.

The mother crosses to the other side of the room and sits down. Juanita remains crouched and reaches her arm over to hand the pot of clean beans to her mother without speaking. After Juanita hands the pot of beans to her mother, she stands up, scratches her arm, and goes to a corner, picking up a jar of water and handing it to her mother. The mother receives it and begins to clean the beans with water. Juanita remains looking at her. The mother says to her, "Hand me the dirty plates." Juanita takes two steps toward the metate and picks up a pile of dirty plates, which she hands to her mother. The mother takes the plates and says, "Bring me water." Juanita walks toward the pail. The mother says, "Not that pail over there. Over here." Juanita goes to the other pail, fills a gourd full of water (the gourd was floating in the pail of water), and takes it over to her mother, putting it on the ground next to the dirty plates.

There are several typical features to note about these two observations. First, there are constant demands made on the girls by their parents, especially by the mother. These requests are constant in contrast to the period of early childhood when few demands were made. Second, the parents make few nurturant responses toward the children in late childhood in contrast to their constant nurturant responses in the earlier periods. In the first observation above, it is interesting that Helena was required to comply with, or nurture, the requests of her younger brother by giving him a chair. Here the young child is gratified by the expenditure of the older child's effort. A third feature to note in both observations is that little reward is offered for the proper execution of tasks. Helena's father ignored her, and any expectation she may have had of appreciation for her behavior was disappointed. Similarly, Juanita received no overt special thanks for her work.

Before turning to the question of how such compliant behavior is learned, an illustration of typical tasks performed by boys of this age will be useful. The following episode involves three older boys, ages 7 to 9, engaged in the task of carrying corn husks from town to the barrio for feed for cattle.

Franco is sitting on the edge of the sidewalk with his cousin, Angel Chavez, waiting for his other cousin, Margerito Chavez, who is in a small store buying something. Next to the children is a great bundle of corn husks which they are watching while Margarito returns with the donkey.

Margarito arrives with the donkey and stands at the corner in front of the door where the corn husks are piled. He looks at the children and says, "Let's go." Then he looks at Angel and says, "Toss it to me," and points to the husks. Angel stands up and lifts the pile of husks, carrying it with difficulty. Franco, with a stick in his mouth, watches the proceedings.

When the children have placed the husks on top of the donkey, Franco stands up and comes close, rubbing the head of the animal and embracing his snout while pulling on the lead rope. The donkey moves, and the husks appear to be about ready to fall off. Margarito grabs them quickly and says, "Hey, grab the rope, Franco." Franco fastens the rope, rolling it up in his hand while the other children finish tying the husks on top of the donkey.

Franco leans over the head of the animal and asks, "All ready?" "All ready," answers Margarito, "Let's go." Margarito turns the donkey around, pulling it into the middle of the street, gives a little jump, and climbs on to the rear end of the animal. Franco runs behind and fastens a strap that passes over the tail of the animal, tightening the saddle.

Margarito gets the animal moving while Franco is running behind and finishing the tightening of the ropes. Then the donkey stops. Franco comes close and puts one hand on the saddle while the other is hanging onto Margarito's pants. He sticks one foot in the stirrup and gives a jerk with his body that pulls him up and climbs onto the donkey, sitting behind Margarito. With one hand he strikes the animal, who starts running through the streets toward the barrio, while Angel, on foot, runs behind.

These new duties are associated with various new techniques of discipline. In general, there is a great increase in the ratio of punishments to rewards. Whereas in early childhood, rewards and nurturance for compliance were the major techniques for training, in late childhood, punishment for lack of compliance becomes more prevalent. The child is now considered capable of understanding and is therefore punished for failure to carry out requests or commands, as well as being subjected to withdrawal of nurturant responses by the parent. Consider the following observation, for example.

Helena, age 8, is sitting on a small chair while her Aunt Rosa, age 9, stands behind her picking lice out of her hair. Helena squirms around in the chair. Rosa jerks on her hair to make her sit still. As Rosa pulls her hair, Helena turns her head and looks at Rosa sideways. Rosa says to her, "Sit still."

Helena's mother comes out of the cook shack and shouts to Helena that the turkeys are out in the street. Helena looks at her but remains sitting in the chair and waits to be deloused. A minute or two passes, and then Helena's father comes out of the kitchen and approaches Helena, telling her in a rather serious tone that the turkeys have escaped. Helena gets up and runs out to the street. A half a block away are the turkeys. Helena runs up the street until she comes to them.

When she gets up to the turkeys, she waves her arms and shouts at them in order to scare them in the direction of the house. She runs back and forth from one side of the street to the other, herding the turkeys in front of her. One of the turkeys attempts to escape into some plants at the side of the road. Helena crouches down, picks up a stick, and with it in her hand, strikes the bird, forcing it to go with the others. With the stick in one hand and waving her arms, she has the turkeys jumping around in the mud in the street and coming back toward the house. She herds them into the courtyard and goes up to the door of the living room and says, "Shall I leave them?" "No," says her mother. Helena continues waving her arms and herds the birds into another corner of the courtyard. She then turns them around and herds them into the house. The turkeys enter the room, making a great deal of noise. Helena throws the stick away and leans into the cook shack, looks inside, and then crosses the courtyard and goes to stand in front of her father without speaking to him. She looks at him. Her father goes into the room without saying anything. Helena looks at the turkeys and then counts them to see if they are all there. She again approaches her father and looks at him. He does not speak or recognize her presence by any overt move.

This observation illustrates the use of a threat of punishment for noncompliance and the lack of a reward, nurturant or otherwise, by the adults for the completion of the task. In the interviews, there are many examples of the mothers' indicating that caresses, embraces, and other nurturant responses are not given as rewards to late-childhood children as frequently as they were given in early childhood. For example, one mother, when asked what she does when her child complies with a request, answered:

Now that she's older, we don't kiss her any more. We don't embrace her. Her father does occasionally when he feels like it. I don't do it any more as I have two other children. When her papa asks her for something and she brings it to him, he might say to her, "Daughter, I like that."

Answers such as this, on the part of several of the mothers in the interviews, indicate that there is an explicit awareness that cuddling, embracing, and other forms of physical nurturance are no longer appropriate for children in late childhood. It should be noted, however, that obedience and the mastery of these new skills are not expected until later. Obedience to the father is learned earlier than obedience to the mother; the child always complies with the father's commands more rapidly than with the mother's commands. This is associated with the fact that he is more consistent in backing up every request with punishment for noncompliance. The mothers, on the other hand, are less consistent in following up their commands and not infrequently allow noncompliance to go without any disciplinary action, or they delay punishment much longer than the father does. Fathers demand obedience equally from sons and daughters. Mothers, on the other hand, tend to let sons "get away" with more than daughters.

The two following observations both involve mother-child interactions. The first illustrates a request to a daughter and the second, a request to a son. Neither observation involves punishment but illustrates, rather, the degree of leeway allowed before any disciplinary actions are taken, and, equally important, the difference between the obedience expected from boys and girls—boys responding more slowly and with less apparent interest.

Juanita comes in from the street and stands in the doorway of the cook shack, looking silently at her mother. She stays this way for a little while. Then Juanita looks at her mother and says, "Mama, this Socorro (little sister) doesn't want to take a bath." Juanita's mother ceases grinding and looks at Juanita, saying, "Tell her to hurry up; tell her to bathe." Juanita answers, "But she says she is going to wash her head." Juanita's mother replies, "Tell her, not now, tell her to hurry up and come."

Juanita remains standing, looking at her mother without moving. Her mother begins to grind, and then she raises her head and says again, "Go on, go on and tell her to hurry up, that I'm about to leave." Juanita enters the cook shack, walking toward her mother; she stops half way between the door and where her mother is sitting and asks her mother, "Where are you going?" Her mother answers, "Go on, tell her to hurry up now, that I have to take the food out." Juanita smiles and says, "Where?" Her mother answers rapidly, "I'm going up to the woods." (That is, the mother is going up on the hillside.)

Juanita walks toward the door and stops and leans against the door frame with her arms at her back. Suddenly she says, "I'm going now." She begins to run toward the street. She stops in the middle of the patio and looks at the back of the cook shack, then goes on, walking slowly. She crosses the street in front of her house and goes along a little path; then she walks along through the corn field. She walks along looking at the ground. After about a hundred yards, she comes to a water ditch where her aunt, her mother's sister, is washing. And Socorro, Juanita's sister, is completely dressed in the water ditch, washing her head. Before reaching her, Juanita moves her arms and cries out, "Socorro, run; Mama says she is going to take the meal out to the hill." Socorro straightens up while the soapy water drips down and asks, "Who went out to plant?" Juanita says, "No one; I didn't say anything to Mother, but she said that you should hurry." Juanita's aunt looks at the girls and then goes back to her washing.

In the above observation, we see the mother repeating several times a request to a daughter to take a message to a younger sibling. It is typical that the mothers frequently speak to their daughters more than once before the daughters carry out a command. However, most such episodes result in the daughter carrying out the request of the mother. Contrast this observation with the one below describing an interaction between a mother and son. In it, the mother repeats a request several times, and the son avoids carrying out the request of the mother. In this episode, Jubenal, aged 8, and his mother, with the baby, are sitting on a log in the open courtyard. His mother is picking over ripe tomatoes from a basket. She has just returned from the field where she has picked them.

Jubenal is squatted beside his mother, eating a tomato. He is holding it in his hands and eating it very carefully, taking small bites, letting the juice drip between his legs on the ground. His mother does not say anything and continues to place the tomatoes into two piles, one of ripe tomatoes and the other of green. She gets several ripe ones ready for cooking in one spot. Jubenal reaches his hand over to take another tomato, and his mother says, "Go get me that pot." Jubenal says, "Where is it?" and continues eating. He is now eating the second tomato that he took. His mother says, "It's inside the cook shack." He turns around without getting up, and it does not seem to be in sight. (They are outside, not inside the cook shack.) He seems to search for it with his eyes, but can't find it. His mother gives him a prod with her elbow and says, "Go look."

He gets up, wiping his hands on the back of his pants, and walks very slowly over to the door of the cook shack. He pokes his head inside, leaning on the door jamb, and peers around in what must be a dark room after the bright sunlight. He comes back and squats down beside his mother, reaching his hand for another tomato, and says, "I can't find it." His mother continues separating the tomatoes and says, "Oh, pshaw, now go and look. I told you right where it was in the corner of the cook shack." Jubenal remains for a moment to finish the tomato and then wipes the juice with the back of his hands and stands up quickly and runs to the cook shack and enters and fumbles around inside. He sticks his head out the door and says, "Where is it?" His mother says, "Just look." He turns back into the room and seems to continue searching. He was turning over mats and looking under them and could not seem to find any pot. (Pots are never kept under mats, which lie flat on the ground.)

His mother remains outside, separating the tomatoes for the next five minutes. During this time Jubenal remains inside the cook shack but does not look for the pot any further. His mother, when she has finished sorting the tomatoes, goes back and walks in, lifts up a little basket and picks up the exact pot that she wants. She gives him a look in the eye that is almost a grin and then turns and walks back outside. Jubenal grins at her, but no words are spoken.

The above two observations illustrate two general differences between boys and girls in late childhood with respect to obedience in parent-child interaction. In many of the observations, we encountered the sequence where a mother requests something of a daughter and repeats the request, but each time the request is repeated, it tends to get stronger and stronger until the daughter complies. The pattern with a son is very different in that, in general, the son either complies after being asked a few times or else worms his way out entirely. Mothers, with their sons, are not so likely to increase the strength of the request, although this does occur on occasion. Another feature that recurs is the flaunting, by a son, of the mother's authority in a mild, but definitely interpretable manner, as shown in the above observation where the son pretends to look for the pot, but it is rather clear that the mother, as well as the son, realizes that he is not making a serious attempt to comply with the mother's request and, in fact, succeeds in not complying at all.

Two factors would seem to be related to this difference in the behavior between boys and girls. The first would be the reality factor that a girl's tasks are more closely related to the needs of the household, which the mother is running, that is, the kinds of tasks that a daughter does for her mother may in some ways be more necessary to running the household than are the expected and accepted tasks for boys. The second factor that accounts for the difference in behavior between boys and girls of this age is the expected deference shown to adults. Girls are expected to be more deferent to adults than are boys of this age. This is certainly, at least in part, preparation for the adult roles, but it also reflects the somewhat earlier and stricter obedience training for girls. The two observations below illustrate this difference very clearly, for the settings are similar and involve deference to adults shown by a girl (in the first example) and then by a boy (second example).

Antonia is standing by a partially opened door, listening to loud music coming from a phonograph. (*Note:* this is an old, hand-wind type with an amplifier, like the RCA dog ad, but it is something very new to this area.) Antonia sways back and forth to the music, not tapping her feet, but keeping time with over-all body movements. Antonia leans back against the doorway and gradually slides to a squatting position. She cocks her head on one side, seeming to listen to the music. An adult male friend of the family visiting the household goes to the half open door and starts to go out and then looks down at Antonia at his feet and says, "Move, child," but not harshly. Antonia quickly scoots over to one side, and he pushes the door completely open and steps outside. Antonia moves back into the better position to see the proceedings as he leaves, still squatting. Some people step up to the doorway (but don't come in, just look), and Antonia quickly moves back to the other side of the door. As they leave, she scoots back against the wall in the semi-darkness of the room away from the open doorway. She sits down flat with her legs stretched out in front of her.

Compare the above example of deferent behavior on the part of a girl to a similar situation for Pedro. The following observation is taken during the day of the first harvest, which is a ceremonial and gay occasion. It takes place at the doorway of the cook shack in Pedro's household. There are many women around the house getting the food prepared to carry out to the field where the men have been working since early morning.

Pedro is sitting in the doorway where anyone entering or leaving the house must step over him. Many adult women, including his mother and aunt, are present. Pedro is leaning against the door jamb. This step is high, and his feet hang down inside the room. Pedro has one hand inside his pants. His head is on one side against the door. His eyes are half-closed, and he is making a choo-choo sound, something like a train.

Three women step over him, one at a time. Their long skirts brush against his legs. He doesn't move or appear to notice all the movement around him as his mother hands out baskets of food for the women to carry out into the field. He takes his hand out of his pants and wipes his nose with the back of it and then he turns over onto his stomach and hangs over the door sill, half inside and half outside, his feet hanging inside.

One woman stands at his head outside the room looking in, and her skirt almost covers his head. Three women go out the door, each lifting her skirt and stepping up over Pedro. One leans down and pats his head. He does not move or even look at her. He stays on the doorstep, and a dog from outside comes up and sniffs at him. He still doesn't move.

Pedro's sister comes up to the doorway and says to the mother, "I'm going to the field now," and turns back to the patio. Pedro gets up slowly, looks after her as she crosses the yard, and then runs after her saying, "Me, me." The sister walks to the side of the wall and gets a basket which she intends to fill with food. Pedro turns back to the cook shack and leans against the doorway. Most of the women have gone now. His mother comes to the doorway and says rather sharply, "Move." He backs slowly out of the way, but stays against the wall watching as she and the sister fill the basket that the sister had brought.

We would predict that, had Pedro been sitting in the doorway in which men were coming in and out, the adult men would have required Pedro to move out of the way and that after one reminder, he would have voluntarily moved away from the door on the approach of any adult male. We would also predict, however, that had a girl of Pedro's age been in the doorway, the women would not have stepped over her but, rather, would have required her to move away if she did not do so without being asked.

From the interview material and the observations, it is fairly clear that mothers, in fact, take more responsibility in the training of daughters than of sons and that fathers take more responsibility for boys. The women that we interviewed frequently made this differentiation explicit. For example, a mother, when asked what she does if her 8-year-old child delays in carrying out a request, replied, "I scold him, but when he does comply, I tell him, 'That's the way to do it; now you're acting like a big boy.'" Then the mother went on to say that the father was stricter than she was. She expressed herself as follows. "That's the way to do it with older children. It hurts me that their father makes them work, that he takes them away from the house when they're so young (speaking of 8- to 10-year-old boys), but I tell myself it's better that way even though it hurts me, because if I leave them alone and don't make them work, if I don't make them do it now, later on, they will turn out to be lazy." She then goes on to express pride in these boys who have just helped their father with the harvesting of the corn crop. In observations, this same mother was seen to allow these boys to get away without following up on requests that she would make to them.

Besides obedience and the learning of new tasks, there are three important new settings in late childhood which require new habits: school, caretaking away from home (e.g., bathing younger siblings in the stream), and work away from home (e.g., gathering wood in the hills or working in the fields with the father). The first new setting affects both sexes, the second is most relevant for girls, and the last primarily involves boys. The important common factor in all of these situations is that they involve being away from the immediate vicinity of the courtyard. Earlier, the child has been accompanied by a parent or an older sibling. Now, for the first time, he may be "on his own" in these new situations. School will be examined first.

Of the three new situations, the school involves the greatest adjustment, since this puts the child into a completely new environment that includes the teacher and students of the central part of town who look down on him and feel that the barrio child is an ignorant, dirty, poor, backward Indian. It is also important to note that it is an environment with which the parents of the present-day barrio children have had no experience, for none of them attended school. We know of only three barrio adults who attended school earlier than 1945. Even now, only about 50% of the barrio children of school age spend a significant amount of time in school. It is true that adult barrio members have learned to interact with the Mexican population of the central town. Most of these interactions, however, are highly patterned, with the barrio Indian definitely taking a subordinate role. Furthermore, most of the interaction between adults of the barrio and the townspeople are at a relatively superficial level and include such things as economic transactions in the market or in the stores of the townspeople. Also, on occasion, townspeople hire barrio persons to do various sorts of menial labor or farm work. The important thing is that the interaction at the adult level lacks the closeness, the constantness, and the intimacy that is inevitable in the school for those barrio children who attend at all regularly.

There are three problems which attending school poses. The barrio child must learn to interact with children who have been reared in very different ways and who react differently from the barrio children; the parents of their new agemates, although preaching equality, treat the barrio people as inferiors; and the language in school is Spanish rather than Mixtecan. And although barrio parents begin to teach their children Spanish around 4 or 5 in anticipation of their going to school, they are still not proficient in the new language. In short, the school involves a radically new and somewhat harsh environment for the barrio child. In discussing the school, we will first describe the general classroom situation and then the relationship between the barrio and central children.

The school is located in the central part of town, about a half a block off from the main square. It is between a mile and a 2-mile walk for the barrio children. By and large, the barrio children do not attend very regularly, with some exceptions to be noted below. The girls' attendance, on the whole, is more regular than that of the boys. Children frequently spend more than one year in the same grade. Of the twenty-four children in our sample, all who were in school were in either the first or the second grade. The school itself is an old, colonial-style house in that the rooms are all in a line and open on an arched corridor about 3 yards wide which faces a large yard. The school itself covers two sides of the yard. This large yard is used for playing.

The first grade teacher is a young woman of about 23 who was born in a neighboring village. She comes from an originally Mixteco family. Although she herself is very definitely of Mexican culture, she has relatives who still identify themselves as Indians. She seems to like her teaching, and she expresses herself in interviews about her own lack of understanding of the Indian children. She says that it irritates her very much that the Indian children speak Mixteco in class all of the time. She believes that the barrio children have a very much lower level of concentration than do the town children. She thinks that the parents of the barrio children are responsible for the lack of attention shown by the Indian children in keeping their copy books clean, attending classes regularly, and so on. In spite of her expressed attitudes, the observations in the classroom seem to indicate that she behaves toward the barrio children without preju- dice. As nearly as we could tell from the observations, she gives the barrio children equal opportunity. She does give more attention to boys than to girls, whether Indian or non-Indian.

The teaching method she uses consists of what is called in Mexico the global method. This means that she teaches reading and writing by introducing short, complete words which are formed by a small number of different letters that can be combined in different ways to form a great number of words. She writes the word on the black- board, reads it aloud, and then has the children copy it in their copybooks. She uses very few visual aids. She accounts for this by saying that the school is very poor. The aids that she does use are small cards with pictures with the word naming the object under- neath. There are only a few of these cards, and the children seldom handle them. The only other visual aids that she uses are drawings on the blackboard and colored sheets of paper which she hangs on the wall. On these sheets of paper are simple drawings, words, or mathematical operations. For example, $2 + 2 = 4$, and so forth. Four of the barrio children in our sample were in this classroom.

The other children in the sample are in the second grade, which is taught by a man about 40 years old who has some intellectual prestige in the central part of town. He writes long poems for all national holidays and reads them at the school festivals. While ob- serving in his classroom, it seemed that his behavior was oriented primarily toward impressing the observer. He tended to behave in an authoritarian fashion toward the children and, during the time of our presence, used literary forms of speech which he probably did not use on ordinary occasions. While in his room, we frequently saw definite cases of biased behavior toward the barrio children in his class. Examples of such prejudiced behavior will be given below.

The actual flavor of the classroom can be most vividly obtained by excerpts from an observation made in the classroom itself. The following observation was taken in the second grade. It illustrates several points about the school in general and about the second grade teacher in particular. Note the following points in it:

1. The classroom behavior as a whole is very informal and at times almost chaotic. This feature of constant movement and noise and individual conversations and interactions among the students is typical of almost every single observation we took in the schools.

2. It is to be noted that in the following observation, the teacher is giving out parts of a poem for the children to recite. The recitation of poetry is important to the children in this case, since they will recite at the fiesta on September 16th, which is Mexico's Independence Day and equivalent to our Fourth of July celebration. Thus all the children desire to participate in the fiesta. It is characteristic of the second grade male teacher, when giving out rewards of this sort, to give more opportunity to the children from the central part of town than to the Indian children of the barrio. In the observation below, he gives only one poem to any barrio child, and the way in which he ignores Alberto is typical of his behavior toward all barrio children in this kind of situation.

3. Note how Alberto reacts to the behavior of the teacher by displacing his hurt and aggression onto other students, after being rebuffed by the teacher. As the observation begins, the teacher has been reading poetry out loud and allowing the children to choose which poems they want to recite on Independence Day. The students listen until he finishes, at which time all shout at the same time, "Me, me, teacher, give it to me." The children stand up; the teacher makes them all sit down, and they laugh. As the observation begins, Alberto is sitting on a table with his feet on the chair.

Alberto stretches forward, his arms extended on the table and his body leaning toward his bench, doubled slightly at the waist. The teacher begins to read another poem. Alberto looks at the child who is sitting on his left and says to him, smiling, "This one is pretty." The other smiles also and repeats, "This is pretty." Before the teacher finishes, Alberto stands up on his bench, waves his hand, and shouts, "Me, teacher, me." The child who is next to him stands up and cries, "Me, teacher, me." Alberto, the other boy, and several others get up and run toward the teacher, surrounding him and raising their hands so that he might give them a part of the poem. The teacher hands the poetry to one of the central children. Alberto immediately turns around, and the boy who was his bench companion imitates him. As they are walking back to their seats, Alberto shrugs his shoulders, looks at the other, and says, "There are more."

The other boy sits down, Alberto returns to the teacher and stands facing him and says, "Teacher, shall I take this?" (He was referring to a sheet on which the poetry is written.) The teacher does not answer and begins to read another poem. Alberto returns to his place and sits on the table with his feet hanging toward the aisle, hands folded in his lap. He gets down, sits in his chair, stretches, lowers himself to the floor, and remains there listening. When the poem is finished, he runs down the aisle toward the teacher, but before he gets there, a group of children have already surrounded the teacher. In the middle of all this noise, Alberto raises his hand and says, "Me, teacher, you haven't given me a single one; you're not giving me any." The teacher gives the poem to Alberto's bench companion, who returns to sit down with a broad smile on his face and the paper in his hand.

When Alberto sees the other child with the poem, he again runs to the teacher, who is still surrounded by a group of children. Alberto tries to push apart two of them, sticking his head between the shoulders of the two, and looks over the teacher's arm. The teacher hands the last poem to another central child and says, "Now, there are no more."

Alberto, not getting any, goes back to his seat. Seriously, he looks at the other boy and says, "It's all finished." The child laughingly shows him the poem that he has in his hand. Alberto again returns to the teacher and asks him, "Are they all finished? Isn't there anything for me?" The teacher, who is speaking to another boy, does not answer him. Alberto returns to his bench and sits with his head between his hands. He stand up and shouts, "Teacher." When he doesn't get an answer, he sits down again. He looks at his bench companion and says to him, "Don't bother me." His bench companion laughs and stands up and then sits down again. Alberto hits him, givng him a punch in the stomach. The boy stands up. Alberto raises his foot under the table and gives him a kick at the same time. The other boy leaves, running. He stops a few feet away and looks back at Alberto with a smile. Alberto looks at him seriously. The other child moves away, and when he is a few steps farther away, he looks back and says, "You'll see," and then he goes and sits in another place. Alberto remains looking at the front of the room.

None of the observations taken in the first grade female teacher's room show as clear-cut bias toward barrio children. In the second grade, the barrio children have no effective way of relating to the teacher; rather, they have to adopt a subservient attitude toward him, and there are several examples in the observations of the kind of displaced aggression toward their agemates shown by Alberto in the above account. The first grade teacher does not adopt the superior attitude of the second grade teacher, nor does she ignore the barrio children, as he so typically does. The barrio children are much more frequently rewarded for their efforts at learning in the first grade class than they are in the second.

In the context of the school, the barrio child learns to cope with children from the center of town in various ways that differ from any techniques or behavior used earlier in their interaction with other barrio children. These techniques include the following: an increase in overt aggressive acts, such as hitting and kicking, telling falsehoods and lies about what one owns or what one's customs are in order to save face with central children, and accepting subordinate positions in games with children from the central part of town.

Although they receive some unorganized support and informal instruction from older friends and relatives from the barrio, these new types of behavior are learned primarily in games with age peers. For example, in the game, *carry the word,* barrio children receive practice in hitting in a socially sanctioned (sanctioned by the central part of town standards) context. The following observation on Hidelberto, age 8, in the school courtyard during recess, illustrates the game. The observation begins just as the children are leaving their room for the courtyard; the recess bell has just rung.

Hidelberto leaves the room running and stops just outside the door, where another child takes him by the shirt and asks him, "Don't you have any verse to say?" Hidelberto makes a gesture with his hand as if to say, "What can you do?" and then says with a very special accent, "Didn't you see? Man— they didn't give me any!" The other boy looks very serious, as if someone had died (but observer interprets this as a joke) and says, "I'm sorry, brother, I'm sorry." The two children then laugh together.

Hidelberto runs to the courtyard and gets in a line. The teacher goes back into the room, and the children begin to play a game called *carry the word.* (This game may be described as follows: the first boy in the line hits the one behind him and says to him, "Carry the word." This boy then passes the punch, or the blow, onto the following boy in the line. He is supposed to hit the boy in the line following him in the same place that he received the blow. At the same time, he strikes the next boy and repeats the words, "Carry the word." This is continued all down the line. The joke is that each boy that gets punched is supposed to be unaware of the game; and when he receives it, he passes it quickly to the following boy, so as not to break the chain. The boys make a great point in attempting to give the blow to the person next to him in a way that the other boys in the line do not know that it is coming.)

When the boy next to Hidelberto punches him in the arm and says, "Carry the word," Hidelberto, without turning around, punches the boy behind him and says to him softly, "Carry the word." The boy next to him then passes his punch onto the next.

When the line is finished, Hidelberto and several other boys begin the cycle again, saying, "Carry the word," and hitting the following boy in the line. The game soon becomes disorganized in that it breaks out in several parts of the line. In a few minutes, there is terrible confusion, and all are interchanging punches, laughing and shouting, among them Hidelberto, who hits his line companion three times when he should have hit him but once.

The teacher arrives (the second grade male teacher) and stands in front of the line. The children stop playing. Hidelberto leans one foot on the other and laughs while scratching his head. The boy whom he had hit before takes him by the collar and tries to throw him on the ground. Hidelberto shakes himself until the other boy lets him go. He turns around a few times and asks, "What time do you have?" (*Note:* Technically speaking, these boys do not know how to tell time.) No one answers him.

Other games played in the school context include hitting and other kinds of aggressive acts that would generally not be allowed in the barrio. In our earlier discussion of the socialization of aggression, we pointed out the severity of the barrio practices with respect to aggression and the suppression of any overt aggressive acts. In the school setting, the barrio child is thrown into situations which almost demand the use of some overt aggressive acts. Games, such as *carry the word,* are one of the ways in which barrio children learn to behave aggressively in their interaction with others. A barrio child who has been in school for a few months begins to hit and push beyond the context of play when he interacts with children from the central part of town. Since the school presents many frustrating experiences for the barrio child, we would expect that such frustration would be followed by aggressive acts on his part. And indeed, such is the case. However, most of the aggression on the part of barrio children observed in the school context, or in the central part of town, takes place under "safe" conditions or is displaced or masked in some manner. That is, the barrio child is seldom observed "sticking up for his own rights" in a manner equally aggressive to that of the children from the central part of town. Another response to instigation to aggression by the barrio children is to use some subterfuge to head off the necessity of the use of direct aggression. Techniques used here would include telling falsehoods, ignoring or redirecting the aggression, escaping the situation in some way, or accepting a subordinate position.

The barrio child is usually not able to fight or wrestle with comfort. So long as it is a game, or in fun, he participates with apparent ease, but the moment the situation gets serious, he attempts to retreat or tries to deny or ignore the aggressive component of the interaction with children from the central part of town. In the following observation we see an 8-year-old boy, Jubenal, showing some anxiety when a fight threatens to become serious. His response is to attempt to make a joke out of the whole affair. Significantly, he does not become openly angry, as a central child would probably do. As the observation begins, Jubenal is in the corridor adjacent to the playground, playfully punching with two other children. A group of children are looking at the two boys and laughing. Jubenal and the child with whom he is playing at the moment are roaring with laughter while they pull each other over the corridor, sort of wrestling against each other.

Jubenal and the other boy are scuffling with their arms around one another. Each one has his arms crossing the chest to the shoulder of the other. In spite of the fact that they are both showing strength, they are not apparently trying to harm each other. (It is clearly a game at this point.) The two are roaring with laughter. In one of their movements, they fall to the ground intertwined and scuffle around with first one on top and then the other. They go rolling around on the ground until Jubenal remains above the other boy. At this point, Jubenal stops his efforts. (*Note of observer:* It appears that Jubenal is hoping that the other will stop his efforts also.) While Jubenal looks down at the other boy, laughing and breathing heavily, he pulls up his pants which have slipped down, adjusting his belt with both hands. He is fairly red in the face and is breathing rapidly; his clothes are in disorder and his hair messed up. Both boys stand up and then the other boy begins to run. Jubenal lets out a yell, and runs after him. He catches him, and again they scuffle, with Jubenal's arms around the waist of the other boy. The two run, gripped in this fashion, while all the children who have been watching run behind them, following by a few yards.

Another boy who was following catches up to them and joins in the fray. The three run together through the little passage way in the corridor. Jubenal lets go of the boy and leaves the other two scuffling and fighting, still playfully, and watches them. Another boy comes running from the courtyard and grabs Jubenal from behind, as if he wanted to join in the fight also. Jubenal shakes himself loose, and with a push almost throws the other boy to the ground. Then Jubenal laughs. The two again put their arms on each other's shoulders, fighting and pushing. They both then try, with their arms on the other's shoulders, to entwine the legs of the other so they will fall to the ground. The two boys double at the waist backward and forward, breathing heavily, uttering small groans and ughs. Jubenal grabs the other boy by the shirt and pulls at it as if he wanted to take it off. While he does this, the other boy grabs him by the calf of the leg and throws him to the ground. Jubenal gets up (the other boy stands laughing in an expectant attitude). Again they scuffle, and this time Jubenal throws the other boy to the ground by the same system of grabbing at the legs. The other boy hits the ground quite hard. He gets up, no longer laughing, and grabs Jubenal by the arm, twisting it. Jubenal is laughing; but when he tries to free himself, he becomes rather serious (he just realizes that the other is no longer "playing"—that the other boy has become angry). The other boy then throws Jubenal to the ground. From the ground, where Jubenal is sitting, he says to the boy, "What are you doing?" The other boy raises him from the ground by pulling him by the arm and begins to shake him. Jubenal laughs again. The other child lets him go and runs through the courtyard. Jubenal adjusts his trousers and begins to run after him, following him with shouts. The children run round and round, taking turns chasing each other; they climb some stairs, they come back down, they run between other children pushing them and return, running through the corridor where they were. There they begin to fight again by interlocking their arms and placing their hands on the other's shoulders. The other child throws Jubenal to the ground between laughs. Jubenal falls on his back, and as the other let him go suddenly, his head hits the ground rather hard. With tears in his eyes, Jubenal cries and laughs at the same time, with the other children who are watching also laughing.

(Finally, Jubenal conquers the cry part and again laughs with the other children and begins playing again in a much more subdued manner.)

A child from the central part of town would have reacted to the last hard blow with anger and would not have shown as much self-control, nor would he have tried to fit into the group by making a joke and ignoring, insofar as possible, his apparently painful blow on the head. The observations in the barrio showed only scattered examples of boys scuffling with each other, and in none of our observations did they end in fights. In contrast, our informal observations in the school play yard indicated that scuffles ending in fights among children from the central part of town were not at all unusual. Barrio boys, in this school situation, avoided bringing such an episode to a close with overt aggression. By the time they reach the second grade, some of the barrio children begin to approach the direct expression of aggression, and on occasion, they use verbal aggression but generally avoid physical aggression. The following observation illustrates three aspects of aggressive behavior, or responses to aggressive behavior, on the part of a barrio boy. One is the use of verbal aggression against a central boy in defense of a friend from the barrio; the second is response to an aggressive act by the teacher; and the third is the response of ignoring aggression by a boy from the central part of town. This observation involves Jubenal again, who is sitting next to another boy from the barrio, Hidelberto. As the observation begins, Jubenal and Hidelberto are sitting together on the same bench at a table.

Jubenal is sitting, looking straight ahead, slapping the palms of his hands on the top of the table. (He appears relaxed and contented.) A boy from the central part of town walks down the aisle and makes a hitting gesture at Hidelberto, who is sitting next to Jubenal. Immediately Jubenal stands up on the bench and says, "This son of a gun," and pretends he is going to climb down and chase after the other child, who has by this time gotten out of the way. The teacher sees him and cries out, "What are you doing—one moment," and takes a few steps toward Jubenal with a little rod in his hand. (This rod is frequently carried by this male second grade teacher. During our observations, he frequently threatened with it, although he never actually struck a child in the presence of the observer. The children reported that he hits them with this rod on occasion.) Jubenal reacts immediately, sitting himself down on the bench, in a restful position but very straight, hands together quietly on the table, feet crossed one over the other. The teacher returns to his former position and turns his back.

When the teacher is not looking, Jubenal, from across the room, makes signs at the child who had made the hitting gesture at Hidelberto, as if indicating with his fist that he's going to get even later. (The gesture that he uses is a conventional one, and in Mexico is a defiant gesture that implies, "I'll take care of you later.")

Jubenal turns forward in his seat and speaks a few words to the boy in front of him in Mixteco. The teacher slaps the rod on the blackboard, asking the class to be quiet again. Jubenal sits up straighter than ever, seriously looking at a little girl who is standing in front of the class and who now begins to recite. He listens with much interest, hands joined, eyes fixed on the little girl, without moving himself for a few moments. (He was sitting almost rigid.) When the little girl finishes reciting, a central boy comes and punches him quite strongly in the back. Jubenal turns around and looking over his shoulder, he smiles at the boy who struck him. At this moment, another girl begins to recite, and Jubenal returns to his previous attitude, listening with much interest.

In this observation, the verbal and gestural aggression in the early part toward a central boy was a "safe" type of behavior for Jubenal in that there was the protection of the school class situation, and it was of a minor enough sort that it would not be followed up. The use of a threatening gesture with the rod by the teacher was immediately responded to, and in our observations was always responded to, by the students, although it is to be noted that immediately upon the teacher's turning his back, the students went right back to their horseplay. Jubenal's response of smiling at the boy who hit him rather hard in the back was quite clearly a refusal to return in kind the aggression of the boy from the center of town.

An example of telling a falsehood in response to what was probably a derogatory question from a child from the central part of town is contained in the following excerpt from an observation. This observation was taken in the first grade in the presence of the female teacher. Angel, the subject of this episode, was sitting in one of the front benches surrounded by a group of children, some standing, some sitting, some writing, and some chatting. The teacher is standing next to the group, talking with some of the children. Every once in a while she walks up and down the aisles looking at the rest of the children.

As the teacher moves away, Angel turns and follows her with his eyes. The teacher says, "Write 'as.' " Angel looks at his notebook, laughs, and writes, copying the notebook of the child seated to his left. He raises the notebook and shows it to the teacher, saying, "Is there an 'a' missing?" The teacher looks at it and says, "Yes, the 'a.' " Angel writes in the notebook and then puts down his pencil. Then he picks his notebook up in both hands, putting it on top of his head. The child who is seated in the seat ahead of him and who is from the central part of town turns around and asks him, "In your house, do you have a well?" "Yes," answers Angel. (This is not true.) Angel looks at him and says, "Look, look here," and passes his book rapidly before the other's eyes. "Fine," answers the other boy.

Angel gets up, stands on the chair, leans his hands on the table, and looks at what the child on the bench in front is writing. He wrinkles his forehead. He sits down again, stretches out, turns his notbook over, stands up and puts his elbow on the table, sucking the pencil in his mouth. The teacher looks at his notebook and says, "Let's see." Angel shows it to her. The teacher says, "Yes, now you've got it." She smiles at him. Angel looks at his benchmate, but this child is looking the other way. The teacher says, "Now, you're going to write the word 'chair.' " Angel writes rapidly in his notebook and raises it immediately, showing it, and saying, "Like this?" The teacher glances at him rapidly, saying, "No, not like that. There is a letter missing." Angel puts the notebook down and writes again. He raises it and repeats, "Like this?" "Yes, very good," says the teacher approvingly. Angel throws the notebook in the air and cries out, "Ay, ay, ay!" laughing contentedly and showing his notebook to the child next to him.

Another child from the center of town gets up and comes toward the teacher, standing between the teacher and Angel. He says to Angel, "Let's see the pencil." Angel withdraws the hand in which he has the pencil and does not give it to the boy. "Let's see," says the other, and he grabs the pencil from Angel's hand with a jerk. Angel smiles, and he gently removes the pencil again from the boy's hand. Then Angel holds the pencil tightly in his fist, pounding it on the table, and at the same time, tapping the ground with his foot. He closes the notebook and continues pounding on the table as he looks out at the street through the open door of the room.

There are three typical and characteristic actions to note in this observation. First is the use of a falsehood to head off a possible derogatory sequence, such as when the child from the center of town asks about a well. Angel responded to this question with a quick lie and then distracted the boy's attention with an irrelevant comment and gesture with his notebook. The second item of special note is the difference between the female teacher of some Mixteco background toward barrio children and the male second grade teacher who discriminates against the barrio children and never gives them a warm response. Angel's increased efforts and interest followed dramatically from her warm and reinforcing remarks and smiles. A third item of note in the observation was Angel's response to the boy who jerked his pencil from his hand. Angel's response of a smile to this somewhat aggressive act and his subsequent gentle removal of the pencil from the boy's hand typifies the subordinate position which the barrio children frequently assumed, and it shows how a smile may be used in an attempt to head off further aggressive acts on the part of town children. We have seen that attendance at school by barrio children requires many adjustments on their part. It is clear that previous behavior patterns are not sufficient to cope with the school situation and that behaviors and techniques rarely used in the barrio occur with great frequency in the school setting. In addition to the setting of the school itself, we should also mention an additional factor, that in order to get to school, the children are required to go through several blocks in the central area of town.

This brings them into contact with the central children who are playing in the streets and who frequently have some kind of interaction with the barrio children as they pass by. As younger children, any experiences a barrio child may have in the center of town are always buffered by the presence of an older caretaker. Even these experiences would generally be confined to small economic exchanges of a sort that do not entail extended and informal interpersonal relations with town children. Barrio children are discriminated against by the town children. In fact, many of the barrio parents report that the reason their children do not attend school is because the central children are aggressive toward them or hit them on their way to school. The parents will keep the barrio children at home rather than subject them to the aggressions of the town children. The following observation characterizes the relationship in the street between the children in the central part of town and the barrio children. In this observation, Jubenal is walking through the street returning from school. He is walking with another barrio child who is carrying a wooden hoe. Jubenal is carrying his own school books under his arm.

The two boys walk alongside one another in silence. In the middle of the street ahead of them, there are some central children playing a form of baseball. As they approach the group, Jubenal and the other child stop to look. Jubenal smiles at the children and makes motions as if he were going after the ball. (Quite obviously he wants them to invite him to play. The central children would probably not make such motions without being invited.) The boy with whom Jubenal was walking continues to walk while Jubenal stops. Jubenal watches him moving away, but he himself does not move. Jubenal begins to shout, "Now play. . . ." (It appeared as if his presence was being noted, but he breaks off his encouragement or statement in the middle.) The other child who was walking with Jubenal is now beyond the group and quite a distance from Jubenal. Jubenal looks at him and goes on walking very slowly and walking backward, still watching the game. The other boy stops, and when Jubenal catches up with him, he says to him, "Shall we play?" The other boy stands leaning on his hoe. Jubenal continues looking at the players and smiling. The other children from the center of town continue playing, but they do not recognize his presence nor do they invite him to join them. Jubenal remains serious, looking at the children with one hand in his mouth. When one of the children passes close to him, he smiles at him, but the central child does not pay any attention to him.

Jubenal, looking serious, scrapes his teeth with a finger. When another central child comes close to him, Jubenal cries out to him encouragingly, "How you play, eh?" The central child ignores him as if he didn't see him. Jubenal seems more serious. He puts his hands in his pockets and continues looking. The other barrio child puts his hoe on his shoulder and touches Jubenal's shoulder without talking, gesturing that they leave. Jubenal turns around, and the two go down the street, walking slowly. They pass by a small girl from the center of town. When they get next to her, Jubenal gives her a little kick which just misses her, and she shies away. When they get a few yards ahead of the girl, she takes a stone and throws it at Jubenal. It doesn't hit him, but the boys hear the noise and turn around and look at her. When they are about 25 yards from the baseball players, Jubenal turns around once more and looks at them; then he continues walking alongside his companion.

In addition to providing a vivid description of the general tenor of everyday interaction between the central and barrio children, the above observation again contains an example of displaced aggression, this time toward the little girl from town.

In our discussion of late childhood up to this point, our evidence has been based primarily on observational material and on the mother interviews. In reviewing the state of the various behavior systems in late childhood, we also have the evidence from the TAT questions administered to the children in this period. In the following discussion, we will review the evidence obtained from the TAT and child interview questions and attempt to interpret the answers in terms of the various behavior systems; then we will relate this interpretation to the evidence already presented. It is clear that the children's responses to the TAT questions represent a different level of data from that of the observation protocols and the remarks of the mothers in the interview situation. However, by combining evidence from each of these three sources, we should reach a better understanding of the behavior systems of late childhood.

The child's attitude concerning aggression is well illustrated in the responses to the TAT questions and the story situations for children. In general, the child will not admit to open aggression, even in his verbal responses to the story situations. For example, in response to the question, "A child is sitting under a tree. Another child passes, trips on a branch and falls, then he stops and says to the seated child, 'Why did you trip me?' But the seated child didn't do anything. What happens?" In only one response was there any resulting aggression shown in the story given in response to this situation. In the vast majority of cases, the child attributed blame to the other, but then went home and told his mother. In response to the direct question, "If another child hits you, what do you do?" the typical answer for both sexes would be represented by the following response. "I cry. No, I do not hit him, I tell his mother so that she will scold him." The aggression here is rather veiled in that one may tattle on another but would not engage in any overt aggression even though it was initiated by another person. This verbal response on the part of the children in answer to a hypothetical situation of direct instigation to aggression corresponds quite closely to the observations in the school, where the child, in fact, meets many occasions where other children instigate aggression. The denial of direct physical counter-attack in the TAT and interview responses corresponds to the infrequent use of direct counterattack to aggressive acts in the school situation. The counterpart to the veiled aggression implied in tattling in the TAT responses comes out in the observation protocols in the form of displaced aggression against a relatively harmless person or object and in "safe" types of verbal or gestural aggression.

Although there was only one example of direct aggression in the first person, the barrio children were able to tell aggressive stories if they did not involve the idea of any overt aggression on the part of the child himself. For example, stories told about the following situation frequently contained aggressive answers. "A child is standing in the middle of the street. An angry bull comes running down the street. What happens?" This situation is rather common in the barrio environment, and about 50% of the children indicated that the child went into a doorway, or that someone helped him into a doorway, or some functional equivalent of this response. On the other hand, approximately 50% of the responses indicated that the child was injured by the bull, and in 2 cases out of 12, that the child was killed by the bull. In the cases in which the child was injured by the bull, there was an immediate attempt on the part of some actor in the story, generally a mother or elder sister, to fix or mend or comfort the injured child. Thus 50% of the children were able to report and verbalize an aggressive act on the part of an animal, in this case, in a situation which does not involve them personally in direct physical aggression. In the observational protocols, we have several examples presented above where barrio children were able to engage in games, such as *carry the word,* that involved hitting and direct physical aggressive techniques in the guise of a play situation. This may be somewhat equivalent to shifting blame or, at the least, shifting responsibility for aggressive acts from oneself, that is, when aggressive techniques are used under the guise of play, the child does not see himself responsible for the use of direct aggression.

Two of the behavior systems, namely achievement and self-reliance, are very difficult to distinguish from each other as they operate in barrio children. With respect, for example, to a question such as, "If you're doing something and it's very difficult, what do you do?" more than half of the children of both sexes indicated that they would simply leave the situation; only one child's response indicated any value or emphasis placed on attempting to try harder or to persevere and keep at the task. Now, whether the fact that a difficult task would be abandoned indicates a lack of achievement orientation or a lack of self-reliance is a fine point. On the whole, we would tend to interpret it as involving both behavior systems. Neither are developed to any great extent in the typical barrio child.

In only 1 of the 24 mother interviews was there any emphasis placed on achievement. In the other 23 cases, there were no indications that the mother desired her child to strive to do things better than other children. The whole conception seems to be a desire that each child will learn to perform up to some minimum standard, but that there is no value in nor desire to go beyond this. It is generally taken for granted that all individuals will easily learn to perform up to these standards. For example, with respect to the task of learning to make tortillas, every mother would expect her daughter to make acceptable tortillas, but there would be no emphasis on making better tortillas than other women. In fact, the question simply would never arise. The situation is the same with respect to all of the normal skills and tasks generally engaged in by people in the barrio.

One variant case is of great interest in that it stands out in great contrast from the other families in the sample. This concerns a family in which the mother came from outside the barrio and from a Mexican family, so that marriage into the barrio was a definite lowering of status from her point of view. She is married to the only adult male in the barrio who does not support himself primarily by raising corn and beans. He works in the central part of town as a secretary in the mayor's office. He is one of the three adult males in the barrio who are considered literate. The mother dresses more like the people in the central part of town than like the women in the barrio. In addition, the husband's drinking patterns were more nearly like those in the center part of town. Also, he did not participate in the ceremonies of the barrio but rather was attempting to identify himself with the townspeople. He was the only person in the barrio that we observed who became aggressive when he drank. Thus, on several points, they were a variant family. By examining this mother's responses on the mother interview, we can illustrate the patterns of the other 23 mothers in comparison. This mother, in response to the question, "What work or task is expected of your child daily or weekly?" had the following to say:

He takes care of his burros, goes on errands for me, keeps the weeds down. He has himself four donkeys. He wasn't crazy. His uncle had an old female donkey which he was going to kill because she was ill and was no good any more for carrying things. The uncle said to my boy, "Do you want that burro?" He didn't think that the boy would say anything, but the boy said, "Yes, I do." After a short while, the donkey had a little son and then a little daughter and now, there are four of them altogether, and my boy takes care of them. He says, "You see, Mother, now I have 400 pesos all for myself. Some day I'll be able to sell my burros, and then after that, I'll get some more." Well, I think the boy is not so dumb to do that, and I tell him, "Very good, my son. You're doing very well. Guard your money. Don't turn out to be poor like your father." My husband certainly doesn't mistreat me, nor did he turn into a drunk, but he's pretty fouled up (i.e., poor). It's hard, you know, for me because my father had a lot of property and money. We even used to have cheese balls to sell, but when I left my house to get married, I became so poor and that's why it's better for my boy to be bright and take good care of his donkeys. He doesn't load wood; he only takes care of his donkeys now and does a few little things for me. When he's bigger, at about 16 or 17, he'll learn to work the ox team in the field. That's the only work there is here for men; but before that, he'll have to go to school. I don't want him to turn out to be as stupid as those of the barrio because—yes, we are very stupid, as I, for example, don't know what you are writing down on the paper, and it hurts me. Yes, he'll go to school.

This is the only example out of 23 responses to the question that contains any hint of an emphasis on achievement. The other mothers simply listed a few tasks and ended up by saying something like, "That's all." None of the other mothers volunteered any comments that would indicate that there was any awareness of a desire for the children to achieve above others. There were two mothers who mentioned casually, as a fact, that their children were going to school, but they did not indicate that this was in order to better themselves.

With respect to self-reliance, it seems that most mothers take self-reliant behavior on the part of their children for granted; there was no indication that they consciously encouraged self-reliance, although there are examples in the behavioral observation that can be interpreted as a parent allowing a child to attempt tasks that he could just barely handle when it would have been easier for the parent to step in and help. These cases probably represent some direct training for self-reliance.

The mother in the variant family, whose remarks were quoted above to illustrate her unique emphasis on achievement, differs in a systematic way from the other mothers in behavior systems other than achievement and self-reliance. For example, she is somewhat more defensive than the barrio women in general. It is our hypothesis that the severity and effectiveness of training with respect to suppressing overt aggression in the barrio children is inherently incompatible with the development of strong achievement drives and emphasis on the development of self-reliance. We would assume that a strong achievement orientation would necessarily involve competition, and that if the fear of expressing aggression is strong enough, effective competition would not be allowed to develop. If this is true, it follows that individuals who place high emphasis on achievement must, or would probably, handle aggression training differently than those who do not place emphasis on achievement.

It is interesting to look at the variant mother who expressed strong desires for achievement on the part of her son and to see how she handles the training of aggression for him. If our hypothesis is correct, we would expect her to be variant on the handling of aggression as a consequence, or at least, as related to her emphasis on achievement. As mentioned earlier, we asked all the mothers, "What do you wish (name of child) to do if another child looks for an argument with him, or when another child wishes to fight with him?" Every single mother in the sample, except this variant mother, indicated that she would not want her child to fight. In addition, every single mother, except the case in point, indicated that she would apply disciplinary action for fighting in the situation. The mother who encourages achievement and self-reliance gave the following answer, which is in distinct contrast to the other 23 mothers.

> I tell him not to look for an argument, but if someone else does, I tell him to stand up and fight. I tell him to only fight with his hands. He should not pick up a stone or anything, because that way you can hurt people. I tell him it's shameful. I tell him don't be rude, but don't give in either, because it's bad to have people get used to that.

This one case suggests, although the data do not allow validation, that low achievement and self-reliance are related to the extreme fear of aggressive behavior shown in the sample as a whole. Strong achievement strivings would seem to require the willingness to express some aggressive impulses. We do not wish to suggest any direct causal relationship but only to indicate that the three variables are interrelated in the training of barrio children.

The TAT questions revealed some interesting attitudes on the part of the children with respect to the behavior systems of nurturance and sociability. It is at the beginning of late childhood that the child is no longer nurtured for small accidents or difficulties into which he gets himself. This is one of the more trying things for a child, the fact that he is no longer comforted on occasions that would have elicited nurturant and comforting responses on the part of his mother when he was younger. In answer to the question on the TAT item, "What happens when many children are playing in the street and one is alone, standing nearby just watching?" a certain ambivalence with respect to showing nurturant sociability behavior revealed itself. There was also a sex differentiation apparent here. For the girls, two thirds of them gave an answer that indicated in the first part of the answer that the child would be ignored and left standing, and then later in the answer, the child would be invited to join the group. The following answer is typical of this two-thirds. "He just watches them. He is sad because he can't play too. No, they don't call him, but I tell him, 'Come, little child, come play with us,' or 'Come, let us play.'" There were four almost identical answers to this question, and it indicates a certain ambivalence in that the child is first left standing and then given nurturance and invited to join the group. The other third of the girls who responded to this question revealed no ambivalence, and their first and only response was one of inviting the other child to play, which indicated a straightforward nurturant and sociable response. For the boys, two thirds responded that they would just leave him there, and he would feel sad. Typical response of the boys would be, "Nothing. They don't say anything to him. He's just standing there." The other third of the boys would invite the child to play with them. A typical response of this sort is, "I start playing with him because the others don't call him, because they are playing a lot, and he has come all alone."

In balance, the girls responded with more nurturant and sociable responses than the boys in that all girls indicated that they would eventually make a nurturant or sociable response, even though two thirds of them would first let the child stand there without making an immediate response. On the other hand, only a third of the boys made any nurturant or sociable response. Another interesting thing in these replies from the children is that in every case where nurturance is given, it is phrased in the first person, with an implication that the other people do not invite him to play and that they are leaving him out. This, in a sense, would seem to be another example that indicates a shifting of blame or responsibility to others. This shifting of blame is associated with another idea mentioned earlier, namely, that tattling to one's mother is a common and typical response. For example, in answer to the question, "If another child hits you, what do you do?", the majority of both sexes indicated that they would tell their mothers.

The difference between the responses of boys and girls on the TAT items relating to nurturance and sociability as reported above relates to the differences in roles in late childhood. This difference in roles between boys and girls is further emphasized in a definite bifurcation of two new settings for the child of this age. These settings are caretaking away from home, for example, taking a younger sibling up to the river for a bath, and work in the fields for boys. Caretaking of younger siblings in settings in which the mother is not present inherently requires many nurturant responses on the part of a child toward a younger sibling under her care. That a caretaker sometimes delays a nurturant response toward a younger sibling, or sometimes gives a nurturant response only begrudgingly, is reflected in the TAT protocols reported above by the ambivalence of the answer given by the majority of the girls. There is ample documentation in the observational protocols that caretakers of this age frequently postpone or give nurturant responses in a begrudging manner. The fact that the boys begin going to the fields at this age and are not normally pressed into service as caretakers would allow them to offer or refuse to make a nurturant response with no particular ambivalence, and this is reflected in their responses; as we saw, two thirds of them chose not to make a nurturant response in the TAT situation. This also foreshadows the adult differentiation of nurturance, where the mother, in general, gives many more nurturant responses to her children than does the father.

Just as nurturance would seem to be an important behavior system with respect to the caretaking role, so we might expect that the boys' work in the fields would be connected with the behavior system of self-reliance. The observational protocols, however, do not seem to differentiate the sexes in any clear manner with respect to self-reliance. Actions on the part of the children that can be interpreted as self-reliant occur in the observations of both boys and girls. This may well relate to the fact that the caretaking role requires as many actions that we would interpret as self-reliant as does working in the fields. In any event, even though acts occur in the observation that we would interpret as self-reliant, we can find little, if any, explicit emphasis on it in the mother interviews and in the responses to the story situation.

BIBLIOGRAPHY

Beals, Ralph. Ethnology of the Western Mixe. *University of California Publications in American Archaeology and Ethnology*, 1945, 42, 1.
Dahlgren de Jordan, Barbro. *La Mixteca: Su Cultura e Historia Prehispanica.* Mexico: Imprinta Universitaria, 1954.
Fuente, Julio de la. *Yalalag, Una Villa Zapoteca Serrana.* Mexico: Museo Nacional de Antropologia, 1949.
Gay, Jose A. *Historia de Oaxaca.* Departamento de Educación del Gobierno del Estado, Oaxaca, Mexico, 1933.
Lewis, Oscar. *Life in a Mexican Village: Tepoztlán Restudied.* Urbana, Ill.: University of Illinois Press, 1951.

Parsons, Elsie Clews. *Mitla, Town of Souls.* Chicago: University of Chicago Press, 1936.

Pena, M. T. de la. Problemas sociales e económicos de las Mixtecas. *Memorias del Instituto Nacional Indigenista,* 1950, **2,** 1.

Redfield, Robert. *Tepoztlán: A Mexican Village.* Chicago: University of Chicago Press, 1930.

Whetten, Nathan L. *Rural Mexico.* Chicago: University of Chicago Press, 1948.

Tarong: An Ilocos Barrio

in the Philippines

❧
❧
❧
❧
❧
❧

William F. Nydegger

Corinne Nydegger

Contents

About the Authors

Mr. Nydegger was an advanced graduate student in the Anthropology Department at Cornell University; his wife, a former graduate student of anthropology at Wisconsin. When leaving for the field, they had a small girl, Elizabeth, aged 1½. A second child, Charles, was born at sea ten days out of Manila. They moved into one of the hamlets and set up housekeeping in a bamboo, thatch-roofed house. Two teen-aged neighborhood girls helped with the housework and daily care of the children. Taurino Singson, who holds a degree in sociology from the University of the Philippines and speaks fluent English, acted as interpreter and assistant during the fieldwork. The Nydeggers lived for over a year in the community, participating in the daily life. It should be noted that Elizabeth played with the children in the community, and the women constantly watched Charles' progress and advised Mrs. Nydegger on child care.

William Nydegger is currently a member of the faculty of the Department of Anthropology and Sociology at the University of California at Los Angeles.

Part I

Ethnographic Background

✷
✷
✷
✷
✷
✷

Chapter 1

The Philippine Setting

THE PEOPLE

The prehistory of the Philippines is unclear, but geological and archaeological evidence indicates that during the Pleistocene various land bridges via the Malay Peninsula, Sumatra, Java, and Borneo formed easy, if circuitous, migration routes for both animals and humans. Approximately a quarter of a million years ago a primitive human, similar to Java Man (*Pithecanthropus*), accompanied by now-extinct animals of the period, found his way to the archipelago (Beyer and de Veyra, 1952). This early man apparently disappeared about the end of the last glacial period—perhaps not long before or at approximately the same time that the first true humans made the last dry land migration. These were the Negrito (or pygmy) peoples, now confined to remote forested mountain areas of Luzon, Mindanao, Palawan, and a few other islands.

Of the present population, the largest part is made up of proto-Malayan (or Indonesian) and Malayan types. Although the routes of migration and the number of distinct groups arriving in the Philippines are subjects of considerable discussion (Beyer, 1948; Beyer and de Veyra, 1952; Kroeber, 1943; Cole, 1945), there is general agreement that at least three major migrations may be distinguished on the basis of both physical and cultural evidence in the present population:

1. Negrito (migrating probably 25,000 to 30,000 years ago)
2. Proto-Malayan (or Indonesian) (5000 to 6000 years ago)
3. Malayan (300 to 200 B.C.)

Accurate numerical evaluation of the percentage of these types in the present population is impossible. Authorities agree that the Negritos represent less than 1%, foreigners (Indians, Arabs, Chinese, Europeans, and Americans) something over 10%. The remainder is divided between proto-Malayan and Malayan, but there is disagreement as to their precise proportions.

The Ilocano ethno-linguistic group of Luzon belongs unquestionably to the third or Malayan type and is concentrated on the coastal flats, low hills, and valleys of the northwest coast. Physically they are typically Malayan in stature, feature, and color. Rather short (typical male, 5′ 3″; female, 5′ 0″), light-boned, well-built, and stocky, they resemble in this last respect their proto-Malayan mountain neighbors more closely than the Tagalog (also Malayan) population to the south. In body appearance little sexual difference is noticed, women being slightly shorter and broader hipped, but both men and women develop broad shoulders, strong, well-muscled arms and legs, heavy brows and wide jaws in maturity. Only one resident of the *barrio*, a woman, could be properly described as fat—a statement less true of urban areas.

Ilocanos are also characterized by moderately high, round heads and have a tendency toward broad noses and medium-to-thick lips, although a wide range is present. Cheek bones are prominent; broad, square faces and pronounced jaws typical. The occasional occurrence of epicanthic eyefold may be noted. Hair is black, coarse, and straight, accompanied by little body hair, eyes are dark brown, and skin color ranges from light olive to dark reddish brown. A suggestion of the mainland Chinese is discernible in the cast of facial features and light color of occasional individuals in the *barrio*.

THEIR PAST

Written history of the Philippines essentially begins with the first landing of a Westerner in the islands, recorded in the remarkable account by Pigafetta (1525), a member of Magellan's party on the first circumnavigation of the world. Although examination of Chinese, Javanese, Indian, Persian, and Arabian sources yields small items of information that give some insight into pre-Spanish contacts with the Philippines, the destruction by the Spanish of virtually all native documents seriously limits research. Just as controversy exists about original migration routes, so also do interpretations differ as to how direct and early were the contacts between the Islanders and Hindus, Arabs, Persians, Chinese, and Japanese. It does seem fairly certain that no permanent foreign settlements were established north of Pangasinan prior to the Spanish period and that the Ilocano had only sporadic coastal contact with itinerant Arab and Persian traders prior to 1000 A.D. and similar limited contact with Chinese and Japanese traders after that period.

In summary, except for limited trading there was probably little contact with the people of Ilocos before the sixteenth century. Although there is no direct evidence, it seems reasonable to believe that at least since the early part of the first Christian millennium people substantially similar to the modern Ilocano had populated the coastal regions.

The first recorded Spanish contact with the Ilocos area occurred in 1572 (Blair and Robertson, 1903, vol. 1, p. 33) when Captain Juan Salcedo and his men visited there. In 1576 Salcedo was recorded as being in Vigan with 100 men (Sande, 1903, vol. 4, p. 26), and the municipality in which the field work was carried out is included in a "list of villages reduced to the service of his Majesty" (Blair and Robertson, 1904, vol. 9, pp. 81–85) in a document assumed to carry a 1594 date. A church was established in the poblacion by 1670 according to both local tradition and church records.

In an unsigned and undated (1586?) "Relation of the Philipinas Islands" (Blair and Robertson, 1906, vol. 34, pp. 382–383), the following description is given of the people of "Ylocos": "They are husbandmen and possess very large fields. Consequently, it is a land abounding in rice and cotton. . . . That province . . . is . . . poorly populated by Spaniards. It contains many churches and Christians, and all the people are not wholly Christian because of the lack of ministers." Later observations and records indicate that the Spanish population continued to be relatively low while, if the present belief systems may be accepted as an index, a scarcity of ministers continued. Incidentally, this same "Relation" makes an observation that is frequently made by present-day visitors to the area: "They are a most cleanly race, especially the women in their houses, which they keep very neat and clean. They have a practice of going three or four times a day to bathe in the river."

During the seventeenth, eighteenth, and nineteenth centuries, Chinese traders began to drift into the area, but in most cases they were single males, establishing themselves one or two to a *poblacion* and frequently marrying Filipinas. The large Chinese communities, as found in the provincial capitols, tend to remain endogamous and hold themselves aloof from the local population. Even today the Chinese in the Ilocos provinces number less than 1500 out of a total population of 527,733 enumerated in the 1948 Census.

After the coming of the Americans in 1898 there was greater concern with "improving" the area. Although few Americans lived in the north, projects such as road improvement, water control, innoculation and health programs, and a school system reaching remoter areas began to have effect, especially during the first quarter of the twentieth century. The influence of Protestant missionaries, however, remained slight and was confined in the Ilocos to urban centers. During the field period there were approximately ten Americans—missionaries and expatriates—in each of the two capitol cities, while in the area between, the total American population was six—the fieldworkers' family and two veterans, one of the Spanish American War and one of World War II.

In addition to the educational campaigns connected with the above-mentioned projects, a new system of land titles was introduced. The effects of the former are difficult to estimate, but certainly pervasive and rapid change in traditional belief and value systems did not occur. Even the land title system appears not so much to have altered socioeconomic structure as to have consolidated the position of the landlord group. Classes stabilized, and a large quantity of developed land was claimed through title manipulation by wealthy and educated *poblacion* residents, some of whom had been Spanish administrative officials. Although great estates were not acquired, most of the tracts now supporting the upper-class *poblacion* group were obtained at this time. The independent farmer who was so deprived of his land had two alternatives: he could try to secure his own land title, an occasionally successful venture, or he could at that period register and open new, adjacent valley fields—small but fertile ones. Present land ownership patterns in Tarong indicate the use of both alternatives.

THEIR LANGUAGE

Although much work remains to be done on the classification of Philippine languages, all of them are accepted as belonging to the Malayo-Polynesian language family. Tangco (1951) lists 55 groups and 137 subdialects, but since many Filipinos are bilingual, most of the population speaks one or more of eight languages. Ilocano represents the third largest with 14.0%, 2,687,861 individuals. Because of bilingualism this is not an accurate figure, but does indicate the relative position of the Ilocano as an ethnic group.

At the present time reading material printed in Ilocano is limited to one periodical, a weekly story magazine, government bureau bulletins, Roman Catholic church literature, and a few miscellaneous publications such as almanacs. Although printed in standard English type, there is no standardized use of the alphabetical symbols, nor is Ilocano taught in school; consequently "reading" is usually halting pronunciation followed by word recognition. Dialectical differences in pronunciation, intonation, and meaning are numerous and extremely localized but mutually intelligible. Tarongans are adept both in identifying such dialects and in distinguishing rural from *poblacion* residents on the basis of their speech patterns.

THE PRESENT

On July 4, 1946, Philippine Independence Day, a smooth transition was made from a dependent status to an independent republic formally modeled after the United States (Tolentino, 1950). Political divisions inaugurated in Spanish times and continued under United States administration were retained. Those citizens of *regular* provinces such as the Ilocos (as opposed to those of *special* provinces, created to handle the problems of underdeveloped areas) found that the new status had little effect on the relations of the average *provinciano* with his government.

The strong national government, now defined by constitution and centered in Manila, continued as the source of major legislation and administration. Three major divisions, executive, judicial, and legislative, have similar duties but greater authority than their counterparts in the United States. Working through a bureaucratic structure, the system leaves little autonomy for the administrative subdivisions, the provincial, city, and municipal governments.

Provinces are the largest political unit within the national government but are directly analogous neither to states nor to counties in the United States, in some respects resembling both. Provinces elect only three officials, a governor and the two members of his council. Their duties are purely administrative and narrowly defined, for most provincial business—education, public health, constabulary, agriculture, law, etc.—is handled by bureau officers directly responsible to Manila, and no legislative power or taxation authority is granted the province.

Municipalities are the units comprising the province and are made up of *barrios*, smaller geographical units, one of which, generally the largest, is designated the *poblacion* and is the seat of government for the Municipality. More autonomous than the province, they elect a mayor and a municipal council with limited legislative power. The mayor has considerable authority over the local police and budgeting, while the council, elected at large but representing individual districts, may pass ordinances and levy taxes.

All actions of the provincial and municipal authorities are subject to review by the next higher echelon, but although both receive financial support from the national government, only the municipality has the right to increase its income through taxation.

The *barrio* is the smallest political unit and is usually composed of several settlements or housing groups known as *sitios*. According to the 1948 Census, a *barrio* consists of from 10 to 1000 houses. In the Ilocos region a rural *barrio* would rarely exceed 50 to 100 houses although a *problacion barrio* will be considerably larger. *Barrio* boundaries are not always stable; they are subject to fluctuation depending on the kin and social alliances of families living near their edges, but in general they follow natural geographic features. The *barrio* is in the charge of an elected lieutenant confirmed by the municipal government, but his authority is dependent on the force of his personality, for his legal power is minimal.

For purposes of this study, two adjacent *barrios* have been consolidated under the name *Tarong*. In the early part of the field period, an examination of genealogical data and sociometric choices clearly indicated that one peripheral *sitio* of six houses, which had its own name, was not integrated into the population to the same degree as the other *sitios*. At the same time, a small adjacent *barrio,* was intimately related and socially integrated with the larger *barrio*. Therefore it seemed appropriate to exclude the first and include this second unit in our sample, but more convenient to refer to the whole by a single name. Individual names and place names within the municipality studied are fictitious.

⚶
⚶
⚶

Chapter 2

Environment

THE POBLACION

When one drives north from Manila along the national highway, the gradual disappearance of advertisements featuring American trade names becomes apparent above San Fernando, La Union, the terminus of the railroad (see map 1). Congestion decreases, private automobiles become scarce, buses and trucks less frequent, traditional clothing more common, and nonchalant strollers and meandering livestock make driving increasingly hazardous. A change in locally made headgear is noted—pointed outside Manila, globular in Pangasinan, finally superceded by the woman's broad flat hat and man's gourd hat of the Ilocano. Beyond Rosario, the junction with the famous Kennon Road to Baguio, sharp green mountains rise to the right and overlook the South China Sea.

After Vigan the road bifurcates a series of charming, quiet *poblaciones,* each characterized by a large church and municipal hall on the plaza, a covered market nearby, and neat bamboo houses interspersed with more pretentious wood and occasional modern cement ones. Here and there a shaded *sari-sari* store displays a dusty Coca-Cola or San Miguel beer sign near which women stop to rest or gossip and men to discuss tobacco prices and the merits of their fighting cocks.

Outside and within the *poblaciones,* cow and bull carts outnumber motor vehicles, and the roadway is frequented by women carrying loaded baskets on their heads, men taking carabao to water, and children loudly enjoying the sunny day. Another square, gray church tower rises in the foreground, and the road passes the high school and

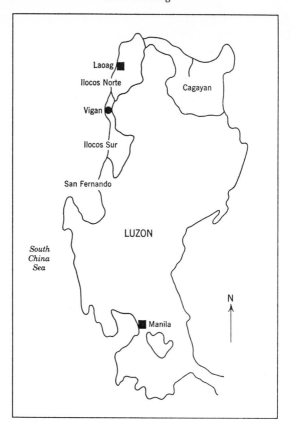

Map 1. The Ilocos region.

enters Poblacion,* midway between the port *barrio* and the mountains some 3 miles to the east (roughly 300 miles north of Manila).

Municipality is typical of the Ilocos. Of medium size, with a 1948 population under 15,000 and a Poblacion population well under 5000, it extends for some 10 miles along the national highway, varying in width from 4 to 6 miles. As one drives through Poblacion at a safe 10 to 15 miles per hour, a lumber yard may be seen, as well as two Chinese general stores and the usual complement of *sari-sari* stores. Predictably, Municipality's only church faces the plaza as does the usual statue of Jose Rizal and the municipal hall, which houses the postoffice and other government bureaus. Nearby is the upper-class resi-

* In the interests of clarity and anonymity, the *poblacion* in which the field work took place will be referred to as Poblacion and, similarly, the municipality, as Municipality.

dential area—the boundaries of which are formed by the traditional Holy Day processional route. Near the entrance to the weekly market, where people gather, a casual conversation quickly elicits terse and amused stereotypes of the local "*barrio* person." Described as poor but hard working, and in general honest and law abiding, it is immediately apparent that, with all of his virtues, he is somehow uninteresting and obviously not an appropriate subject for conversation with a visiting American. Summed up: "The people are simple and, you see, life in the *barrio* is very difficult." However, when convinced of the field team's determination to live in a "remote" area of Municipality, friendly aid was offered everywhere, accompanied though it was by incomprehension.

THE BARRIO

About 5 miles north of Poblacion, a narrow, graveled lane leads from the national highway across a broad, flat stretch of paddies toward a treelined gully a mile to the east. Here the lane drops sharply to a plank bridge crossing a shallow stream, which is the accepted western boundary of Tarong. From this point the lane not only loses its gravel surface but also dips, turns, and climbs alarmingly. After about a mile of this, during which time only three houses are visible, the lane passes the Tarong school, acting here as the boundary between Tarong and the adjacent *barrio* of Bantai to the south. The school grounds, well tended and flower ornamented are separated from the lane by a fence and surround a two-room stone and cement schoolhouse and three small, bamboo auxiliary buildings. The largest concentration of Tarong's population lives to the northeast and east of this point, with a small group of houses clustered near the school (see map 2). The lane continues to climb steeply to the east and into the next *barrio,* but this section can be managed only by jeep.

Since the lane is impassable after a rain and full of ruts and steep grades, traffic is limited to lumber or tobacco trucks and occasional jeeps. All traffic is exciting; the adults living along the lane run to the windows and their children to the edges of the yards, where they hang on the fences, watching excitedly and waving. Older boys may even be given short rides, which provide much the same thrill as a roller coaster ride in America.

Tarong encompasses approximately 2 square miles of what, at close range, seem to be sharp, twisting ridges and narrow, curving valleys—bewildering and haphazard. But from the far end of the

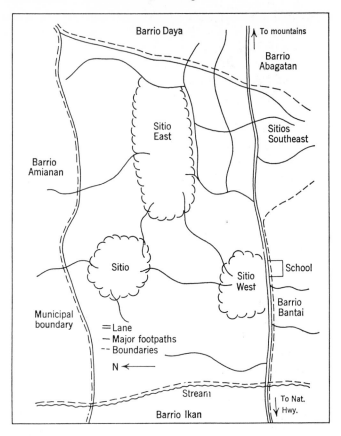

Map 2. Tarong and adjacent barrios.

barrio in the higher ridges, actually mountain foothills, the pattern is clearer—rugged mountains slope down bamboo-topped ridges and terraced valleys into the sea. It is a dramatic landscape; the mountains shift color and apparent relief constantly, limiting but not dominating the eastern view. The western sea, sparkling against the white coral shore, is seen from any rise and often appears suddenly through the bamboos along a path; at sunset every bamboo wall glows during the brief dusk.

The greater part of the day is hot and sunny in any season, making woven shade hats or umbrellas standard equipment. But as the monsoon winds shift in June, bringing a downpour from the mountains each day, gourd hats replace straw, the fields fill with water and the paths with mud. The rainy season continues through July and August, the paddies rapidly becoming the brilliant green of seedling rice. Then the rains taper off through August and September as the winds again shift, blowing coolness from the sea, and the fields turn tawny yellow, with dark green banana trees framing them. During the ensuing dry season, from December through mid-May, no more than one or two light showers a month are normally recorded; the fields and stubble turn brown and by April the paddy cracks are a foot deep, and a dust haze shimmers under the clear, hot sun. But with the first rain of the next monsoon, the air washes clean, the greens magically reappear, and paddy frogs croak all night.

The neighborhood living-groups, *sitios,* are connected by footpaths, which are myriad and form an efficient network for communication (see map 2). Between any two points are usually four or five possible pathways, the choice depending on their relative shortness, muddiness, roughness, the breadth of some to accommodate carabao sleds. It is literally impossible to be out of sight of some kind of path which will lead eventually to a house.

Walking toward Sitio East, where the field team lived, the broad bamboo-lined path runs east from the school area along a high ridge, then suddenly turns and drops into a valley. Ridges such as this provide the only land available for any use other than paddies, and houses are invariably found on them. When not needed for living space, they may be used for pasturage, for semicultivation of the cogon grass used for thatch, and for small vegetable patches. The ridges left to natural growth are covered with a brushy tangle of shrubs, low trees, and light bamboo. The heavy variety of bamboo is not found here, growing farther up in the mountains, but the abundant light bamboo affords the indispensable supply of easily worked woodlike material needed for house construction, kitchen equipment, containers, thongs, and innumerable objects in daily use.

Many wild fruits, vegetables, and roots are available in those brushy spots as well as leafy plants used for animal and sometimes human consumption. Among the Tagalogs to the south, the Ilocano are called the "Saloyots," in honor of one of the plentiful wild vines, *saloyot,* considered a weed in the south but eaten here when other fresh vegetables are scarce.

In contrast to the abundant plant growth on these ridges, there is little animal life except for birds and the omnipresent but harmless lizards. Snakes are rare; in fact, there are almost no dangerous wild animals. Birds are not plentiful probably because Tarongans of all ages, walking through these brushy areas, keep a sharp eye open for birds' nests. Tarongans watch the nests carefully and catch and roast the fledglings.

The valleys between the ridges are narrow, their steep sides partially, and their floors completely, terraced with earth dikes 2 to 5 feet high, most with stonelined cuts for drainage control. These dikes commonly support a path and a growth of banana trees.

Along one or another of these paths, someone can usually be seen crossing the valley; generally it is two or three women with loaded baskets on their heads, a few children running to or dawdling from school, a man moving between his scattered fields. At intervals throughout the day carabao slowly drag sleds of rice, cane, field implements, or perhaps hay over the path, and an old woman may bring a load of faggots home. Less commonly, visitors from a neighboring *barrio* cross, or a pair of peddlers follows the paths from *sitio* to *sitio*.

Such a path across a valley floor winds along the curving dikes and spans the drainage cuts by one or two bamboos, which are very slippery when wet. At the base of each drainage cut is a waterhole hollowed out by the force of the water pouring over the cut during the rainy season. Some of these waterholes are deep, occasionally 5 feet, especially at cuts below terraced hillsides. Since there are only three shallow streams in Tarong, two of which are dry much of the year, these waterholes provide the wallows essential for the carabao.

Scattered along the valley floor 15 to 20 feet below the house sites, are the open wells, their rims only a foot or less above the ground. Drawing water involves a laborious uphill climb with a heavy water jar on the head many times a day, but, in spite of this, water is generously used. Each isolated house has its own well, and in the larger *sitios* there is at least one well for every three houses. At almost any time of the day there is activity at some of the wells: in the early morning the men bathe; later the women come with young children to bathe, refill the household water jars, and wash clothes. The stone on which the clothes are pounded with flat wooden paddles is next to the well, and mornings are filled with their hollow "pok" echoing loudly along the valleys. During the day water is drawn when needed by women and girls, large cooking utensils are sometimes cleaned here, and men may splash the carabao between chores. At dusk water jars are filled for the night; men water the animals and bathe again.

THE SITIO

Approaching Sitio East, the dike paths climb sharply up the ridge sides and into the housing group, passing carabao tethered under shade trees, small bamboo huts enclosing open-pit toilets (each usually shared by two to three households), and a few small garden plots. Flies are present and annoying during the wet season, particularly in the vicinity of animals, but there are surprisingly few other insects. The brilliantly colored and gigantic butterflies are infrequently seen, and most of the insects, though alarming in appearance, are nonpoisonous and make excellent toys.

Only three insects are consistently killed—a fuzzy caterpillar believed to produce itches, and the small centipedes and scorpions, both of which not only cause skin rashes but may inflict painful stings. The malaria mosquito does not occur in this area, and mosquitoes are scarce except during the early rainy season both because of the lack of stagnant water and of the government's program of spraying houses and yards with DDT every year or two.

The *sitios* cover the tops of low ridges or cling to the sides of higher ones in order to be as close as practicable to the wells, and they follow the same pattern. The houses themselves are grouped into family clusters, partially surrounding and facing common yards which are contiguous and transversed by the main paths through the *sitio*. The yards vary greatly in size, the smallest we noted being about 15 by 25 feet, the largest 35 by 100 feet. The diagram (map 3) of Sitio East, the largest in Tarong, indicates this central path-yard space surrounded by houses, which resembles in function and appearance an elongated, narrow public square.

The location of a house in the *sitio* cluster is determined by a number of factors involving kin ties and land ownership, but obviously not by consideration of exposure or directional orientation. Facing a house away from the paths toward a view or a cooling breeze would not only be considered antisocial but would deprive the occupants of a large part of daily social interaction, for the greatest part of the time spent in the house resting or doing odd jobs is spent sitting on the porch or at a window, chatting with whomever may be in sight and watching activities in the yard and along the path.

The houses and paths are on intimate terms, the passerby being obliged to greet the houseowner by requesting the right to pass. The householder invariably grants this request and usually asks the passerby

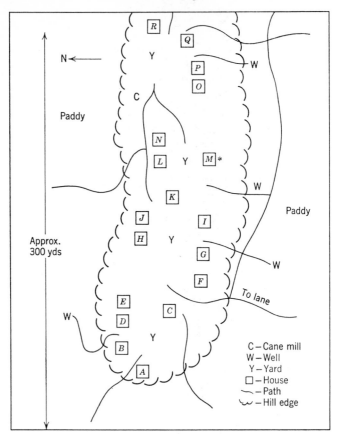

* Inhabitants of house *M* moved in with members of
house *N* to provide quarters for the anthropologists

Map 3. Sitio East. Inhabitants of house M moved in with members of house N to provide quarters for the anthropologists.

where he is going, a question to which a friendly directional answer is sufficient. These formalized exchanges are more than likely to start a short conversation, and such chats result in rapid circulation of bits of news.

The main path, broad and clean swept, wanders down roughly the center of the *sitio,* past houses, sturdy, elevated bamboo and cogon thatch granaries, and the rice-pounding areas. These areas, 6 to 8 feet square, are generally covered by an extension of the house roof and shaded on the sunny side by a bamboo screen. The floor is of carefully smoothed clay and dung cement with a large flat stone embedded in it upon which the rice is threshed. There are one or two stone mortars for polishing the rice and a rack of wooden pestles, 5 feet or more in length, used both for threshing and polishing. These areas are busy, convivial spots in the early afternoon, when two or more women and perhaps men gather to pound their rice, the rhythmic pestle beats being repeated across the valleys from each *sitio* to the next.

The yard itself is a pleasant area of clean, natural clay shaded by trees or roof extensions, ornamented with flowering plants at the house entrance, sometimes boasting a bamboo bench and always with a minimum of litter. It is given a thorough sweeping at least once a day, and stray tools, firewood, animal-feeding dishes, and carabao yokes are neatly stacked away under the houses when not in use. The yard is the focal point for much of the daily work of the women, most of the men's nonfield work, and the family's recreation. Here the infant first sees the outside world, children play, animals are fed, and the old people, past the age of field work, make their contribution by baby-tending and taking over light tasks. Formal gatherings are conducted here or overflow from the houses on such occasions as baptisms, birthdays, dances, weddings, and funeral feasts.

The yard is rarely empty or quiet. During the morning children race across it shouting; cats and dogs settle their differences; carabao tethered at the edge voice their general disapproval by blowing through their noses and stamping; chickens cluck to their wandering broods, and pigs grunt, searching for scraps of food. From nearby pastures cows and goats are heard as well as the clatter of a water pot from an adjacent porch, a baby crying. In the afternoon the strong rhythm of rice pounding is added and, near meal times, the crackle of kitchen fires. These intermingling domestic noises provide a comfortable background for the never-absent human voices, sometimes raised in anger but more often companionably chatting or crooning to a fretful child. At dusk the men return with the animals, and pig feed is cooked over an open fire, children play noisily, and adults visit each other's porches for a coconut shell of sugar cane wine.

THE HOUSE

The houses themselves are elevated some 5 to 6 feet, which, together with their bamboo walls and cogon grass roofs, gives an initial impression of fragility. However, both in material and design they are sturdy and admirably adapted to withstand wind and rain, yet they remain reasonably cool during the hottest days. Each house is two

rectangular units—a larger structure, the *sala-bedroom*, enclosed to the
ground, its hip roof steeply pitched as is the saddle roof of the second
and smaller kitchen. unit. The kitchen is open beneath and so are
the connecting porches, which have low pitched roofs. There is some
variation in size, but the over-all height of the houses is an average
20 to 25 feet.

Floor plans are similar as to number and relationship of rooms and
the placement of bamboo-shuttered corner windows but differ in size
(see Figure 1). Large, high, heavy wood posts and carefully selected
materials indicate wealth, but house size is dictated almost solely by
the number of occupants.

Wood posts 4 to 8 inches in diameter support the *sala* section, but
lighter wood or bamboo posts are used elsewhere. Wood joists and
beams are preferred, but, whether wood or heavy bamboo is used,
the joints and corners are either mortised and pegged or carefully
notched and tied with split bamboo thongs. Nails are used only
for supports for the hardwood floor planks or, occasionally, split
bamboo flooring. Nails elsewhere are considered evidence of slip-shod
workmanship as their use destroys the resiliency to seasonal drying and
swelling and the typhoon winds.

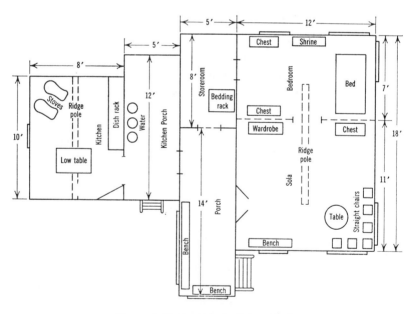

Figure 1. House plan (well furnished).

House walls are of split bamboo. Those enclosing the storage space beneath the *sala* are set singly, but those in other walls are set double and overlapping, affording excellent protection against wind and rain. A few old houses have upper *sala* walls of vertically set wide planks and shutters of wood, often with shell lights.

The walled space beneath the *sala* is used for tools, carabao sleds, large containers of food or wine, and the storage of rice—if there is no granary. It also functions as an addition to the men's work area, which is popularly the open space beneath and around the front porch. The house posts and beams make convenient suspension points for work and tools, and there is shade. This underporch space is also the favorite spot for children's play during a rain, storage of firewood, and the quartering of small animals.

The front porch juts into the yard and serves not only as the anteroom to the house but also as the locus of its daily activity and movement. It varies in size from 5 to 6 feet in width and approximately 10 or more feet in length and is constructed in the same manner as the house, being reached by a bamboo ladder securely set against the porch and loosely attached by a length of rope. This ladder is pushed away from the porch, the rope holding it perpendicular, when no one is home and at night. The porch's three exposures, only partially walled, and the slatted floor of bamboo splints create an airy space well suited to its social and work uses and a cool sleeping place for the hot nights of summer.

Furnishings on the front porch are rarely more than one or two narrow, wood or bamboo benches placed along the outer walls. Knives, combs, women's partially consumed cigars and talismans are wedged into the walls for storage. The porch is in constant use; neighbors stop in for a chat; friends passing through the yard from nearby *sitios* often rest a moment in the shade, bringing the latest gossip. At any time one or more of the adults is likely to be resting or working on a bench or the floor while the younger children clamber about or nap in a corner.

A low step down and a wide opening lead from the front to the kitchen porch, which is open at both ends and only partially roofed. The rear ladder enters the porch and is flanked by pottery basins of water for cleaning mud off feet and legs during the wet season. Water pots are generally kept on the porch, sometimes on a rack; occasionally there is a work table. Large wood and enamel basins lean against the walls. This is the usual place for doing messy kitchen chores, and toward the rear, the split bamboo flooring is set far apart to facilitate drainage into a constantly muddy puddle beneath the porch, odorless, for accumulation of decaying matter is prevented by foraging pigs and the generous daily use of water which drains down the nearest bank.

Kitchens, level with the kitchen porches, range in size from 6 by 8 feet to 9 by 12 feet and, being lighted only by the entrance and one small window, are dark and smoky. The two open clay stoves are 18 by 36 inches and a foot high, and walls near them are usually well smoked. The exposed thatch of the roof, although 12 or more feet high, is also soot-blackened, for there are no arrangements for the escape of smoke aside from vents at the top of each gable end. Fire would seem to be a likely source of danger here, because the stoves are rarely bedded in sand, more commonly standing on three short clay legs placed directly on the split bamboo floor. Open-flame, kerosene lamps stuck haphazardly into the bamboo of the walls contribute to the danger here as elsewhere in the house. Nevertheless, during a one-year period, only one minor kitchen fire was noted, probably because of the constant surveillance of stoves.

Use of the kitchen is limited to mealtime activities, although an aged person may occasionally curl up on the floor next to the stove on a cold night to take advantage of its remaining warmth. If the family is large, part of the kitchen porch may be walled off to provide a dining room containing a table and some benches, but usually the family squats around serving dishes placed on the floor or a low table in the kitchen.

All cooking equipment and a small wood pile are kept in the kitchen, all within easy reach of the squatting cook. Openwork baskets containing food hang from the rafters and a new basket may hang over the stove being smoked to strengthen the fibers and discourage beetles. Carrying baskets, rain hats, and tools hang from the walls or lean in corners, and sometimes a large chest of tobacco is placed near the stove to take advantage of the heat and dryness. From season to season, corn, tobacco leaves, or a stem of bananas are suspended from the rafters, disappearing as they are stored, cured, or consumed. The kitchen, like the rest of the house, is easily cleaned, and most debris falls through the floor. Frequent sweeping and occasional scrubbing with a coconut husk prevent the accumulation of dirt.

Opposite the entrance to the kitchen porch, a step or two up from the front porch, are the double doors, preferably wood, which open into the *sala-bedroom*. This room, normally 10 by 15 feet to 15 by 22 feet, is divided by easily removable partitions to form a smaller bedroom section at one end, the remainder functioning as a living room.

It is important to a Tarongan that his *sala* be both attractive and comfortable, since it is the place where guests are entertained. He lines the roof with basket-woven strips of bamboo exposing only the roof beams and the ridgepole. He takes pride in a well-laid, wide-planked hard wood floor and his wife equal pride in its care. She sweeps frequently and scrubs it daily by foot, first with a coconut husk, then with banana leaves to oil and polish it.

Comfort in Tarong is conceived largely in terms of coolness, and the house is built with this in mind. There are ventilators at each end of the *sala* ridgepole and above the cornice, the ridgepole itself is some 15 feet above the floor; the thatch eaves are deep, and each window has a shutter which may be slid to one side or raised as an awning.

The insect population is controlled by large predatory spiders and small house lizards. Bedbugs are controlled if not eliminated by frequent washing of sleeping mats and blankets. Cats keep the rats under control. The larger gecko lizards, however, are relentlessly pursued, for they bring bad luck into a building.

The simplicity of house design extends to its furnishings: minimal furnishings of the *sala* are commercially produced, simply designed, and precisely arranged so as to encourage sociability as well as to take advantage of the window placement. If surplus cash is available, a caned arm chair, an extra chest, or a mirrored wardrobe may be added. Wealth may be indicated by the quality of furnishings, but rarely by quantity.

Decorations in the *sala* are limited. The walls are invariably hung with a mirror and a number of large frames in which randomly placed photographs of funerals, weddings, and individuals are displayed. Also framed school certificates, occasional lithographed baptismal certificates, calendars, and political posters may be added. Gaudy pin-ups of movie stars, politicians, and so on, clipped from magazines, bedeck a number of *salas*.

The bedroom section is separated by portable 5- to 6-foot partitions or screens of bamboo or *sawali*, a draped doorway open to the *sala*. The bedroom includes approximately one third of the entire room space and the partitions are always removed for large gatherings of people. The bedroom also functions as an extra storage place. In addition to the bedding rack it contains a bulky loom in at least a third of the houses. Most families in Tarong weave at least some if not a large part of their own cloth, and a loom is shared by the women of neighboring homes. A bamboo bed is stored here or under the *sala* to be used for birth, illness, funerals, and such. Most Tarongans sleep on the floor although cane-bottomed beds—prestige items—are owned by some families.

There is a shrine, usually in the bedroom but always at one end of the house and at right angles to the ridgepole. It may simply consist of a candle and a colored lithograph of a favorite saint or the Crucifixion, or it may be quite elaborate—one or more wood or plaster Virgins and saints arranged on a table with two or three lithographs hanging above them. The shrine pictures and statues serve as talismans but take on added significance during funerals, weddings, and other special occasions when plates of food are placed here for the ancestor-spirits who reside about the ridgepole. Windows are hung with brightly embroidered or crocheted valances for celebrations.

Informal day-to-day use of the *sala* is similar to that of the front porch, but in cold weather many tasks are brought in out of the wind. Then the family huddles together in the closed room until an early bedtime. Clothing, as well as housing, is inadequate for the cool nights and rare cold, damp days of winter. Shoes are never worn for warmth, but towels, cloths, and scarves are wrapped around the head. Most people add an outer jacket of cotton. On cold nights more extra clothes may be added at bedtime, and each individual wraps himself in a cotton blanket and huddles into the family sleeping group. An old person may occasionally get up and start a small bonfire in the yard, where "others who are also cold may see it and come and talk to you." Everyone is quite miserable during the twenty or more really cold nights which occur during the winter.

If there are no visitors, evenings during all but the hot time of year are usually spent in the *sala*. On dark nights especially, evil spirits draw closer about the house, and a Tarongan feels safer behind closed shutters with his family, discussing the day's events or reading aloud from *Bannawag*. During the evening children are, one after another, wrapped in individual blankets and put to sleep on mats. As each member of the family grows tired, he unrolls his mat on the floor in his preferred spot—old people often near the door, parents with young children, adolescent and grown children in corners of the *sala* or bedroom. By 10 o'clock the dog is tied under the porch, the ladder is pushed away, and only roosters, challenging each other between *sitios*, or a young baby crying for food disturb the sleepers.

❉
❉
❉

Chapter 3

Economics

Land Usage

Tarongans as a group produce almost all their own food. The staple on which both the economy and the diet are based is rice, and a rice paddy is measured not in acres but in yield. The unit is a *uyon*, which is a plot of land large and fertile enough to produce approximately 5 bushels of polished rice per year. Since an average Tarongan family requires 35 bushels a year to subsist, they should own seven *uyones* of rice land. Only one fifth of the families own this much rice land. Therefore Tarongans tenant land, another one-fifth of the population in this way bringing their rice income up to the necessary level (see Figure 2). Most such landlords are from Poblacion but a few are Tarongans.

Tenantry arrangements are uniform, at least regarding rice. If the tenant is new, the landlord provides the seed rice and the tenant labor and necessary equipment. At harvest, the harvest help is first paid from the rice; then the remainder is set out to dry. The landlord comes to divide the crop formally: first seed rice is set aside, then the storage bundles are lined up, and the landlord selects his share—50% of the remainder. According to the provisions of the Rice Share Tenancy Law of 1946, the crop should be divided 75% for the tenant, 25% for the landlord. However, this 50-50 division customary in Tarong is considered fair by both tenant and landlord and does not, because of the high price of land, represent a high rate of return on land investment.

Landlord-tenant relationships in Tarong range from the informality customary between relatives to formal, involving a Poblacion landlord or occasionally, his agent. In either case the tenant is scrupulously honest and the landlord carefully generous. For if a tenant has had trouble with a number of landlords, he is assumed to be lazy or untrustworthy, and landlords will not accept him as a tenant. On the other hand, if a landlord is known to always press his tenants for more than he should, by custom, take, he will be unable to find tenants for his land. These considerations encourage each party to try to accommodate the other, and the visit of a Poblacion landlord will normally involve a goat feast provided by the tenant and compliments and minimal requests from the landlord. The rarity of agent-usage, placing landlord and tenant frequently face to face, undoubtedly encourages mutual respect and understanding of each other's problems.

Paddies throughout this area are small, the largest single paddy in Tarong producing 10 bushels of rice per year, the smallest one half a bushel. The commonest size paddy, producing about 5 bushels, may vary in square footage considerably, for the quality of soil and drainage varies. An average paddy of good land with good water control will be no less than a quarter acre and is usually somewhat more. The December 1955 price of such a paddy was about 800 pesos * and had been higher previously. These high land prices, the highest in the Philippines, are apparently due to the relative scarcity of flat land here and the competition between small landholders and farmers to buy the small plots one or two at a time. On the rare occasions when a Poblacion landlord sells a large number of paddies to another landlord, the price drops, frequently to two thirds the current rate.

Rice Production

The agricultural cycle in Tarong, as can be seen below, is a two-crop cycle, one wet (rice) and one dry (tobacco).

Early in June the rains begin, soaking the dry, cracked ground within a week. As soon as the soil is tillable and the paddies show promise of filling with water, men prepare the seed beds on well-drained hillsides, and women plant the seed rice. Squatting, they dig small holes with their fingers, drop in two or three grains, cover the hole, and dig another a few inches from the last. A seed bed holding enough seedlings to fill an average paddy takes roughly half a day for two women to plant. A half *uyon* of the sticky rice used in sweetmeats is considered sufficient.

Since the paddies must fill with water to a certain depth (10 to 12 inches) or the seedlings cannot be transplanted, and since transplanting must be done when the seedlings are about six weeks old, planting

* In 1955 the official rate of exchange was 2 pesos to 1 United States dollar.

Agricultural Calendar

Rainy season	June (first half)	Rice seed beds planted (6 weeks in bed)
	June—July	Paddies prepared and vegetables planted
	July (second half)	Rice seedlings transplanted
Rains taper off	August	
	September	Vegetables harvested
	October (first half)	Tobacco seed beds planted
	October (second half)	Rice harvest begun
	November	Tobacco planted in paddies and vegetables planted
Dry season	December	Rice harvest completed and tobacco transplanted
	January	Vegetables and sugar cane harvested
	February	Tobacco harvest begun
	March	Sugar cane harvested and planted
	April	Tobacco harvested
	May	Tobacco harvest completed

requires careful judgment of weather conditions. Tarongans take the measure of a farmer largely by his success in proper timing.

During the six weeks needed for seedling growth, the paddies are prepared for transplanting. Preliminary releveling if necessary and plowing is done when the ground has softened and minor dike repairs are made. When the paddy is well filled, final plowing and harrowing are done. By this time the water is no longer rushing across the paddies with the force it had earlier in the season, and drainage can be manipulated by filling or opening the cuts in the dikes.

No fertilizer is consistently used in Tarong—there are no compost heaps, nor is carabao manure utilized except for fortuitous droppings. Scattering of small twigs and leaves of a certain weed in the fields just before transplanting is practiced by only a few Tarongans.

When the paddies are prepared, women pull the seedlings. If the household is small or if most of its members are unable to plant, kin or neighbors may help, and are paid in rice at harvest time. Typically, one or two people do all the planting since help is scare at this season.

The seedlings are pushed well into the mud and spaced about 6 inches apart in precise rows. It is chilling, wet, backstraining work. The small sweetmeat making party given by most families when their fields are all planted is fully as much to celebrate the relief of planting being over as it is to encourage their ancestors' protection of the crops by the sweetmeat offerings in the fields at this time.

During the remainder of the rice-growing season, the fields require no further care except for water regulation and occasional minor dike repairs. There is now time to plant wet season vegetables and, toward the end of the season when the rains are light and the paddies drying, to prepare and plant seed beds for dry season crops.

When the rice is ready to harvest, work groups are arranged among kin and neighbors, ranging from 4 to as high as 18 people, a *uyon* field being harvested typically by 6 to 8 workers in a half day. The rice is cut with a special knife, a stalk at a time, then tied into bundles. A good worker is expected to harvest one half to one third of a *uyon* in one full day.

Payment for harvesters varies between communities, but in Tarong it is approximately one tenth of the rice harvested by the worker. In this way the average harvester can earn rice worth about 1.50 pesos in a day. It would take 80 days of such work to accumulate a year's supply of rice, and no one comes close to working this many days at harvesting.

After harvesting, the storage bundles of rice are set out to dry in the yards for a number of weeks. Then they are stored in the granaries, or in the storage space under the *sala*. No attempt is made to store rice for longer than one year, any surplus being sold or bartered within the *barrio*, for fresh rice is considered much superior to old and is definitely better flavored.

When rice is needed for consumption, one or two bundles are removed from the storage place in the morning, dried in the sun until afternoon, then threshed and polished. Normally a woman pounds one bundle every one or two days, depending on the size of her family, a chore that takes about 1½ hours. Two or three women from neighboring houses usually gather to work jointly. If there is to be a party and a large quantity of rice is being pounded, a large group, including men and older boys, will gather to help.

The rice is threshed on a flat stone by pounding with a wooden pestle, the grain pushed back into a pile after each few strokes by foot, the straws then collected for kindling. The rice grains are put into a stone mortar about 2 feet high and 1½ feet across, where they are pounded with the pestle till the largest part of the coating is removed. It is then sifted, and winnowed by tossing in a woven tray and the bran collected for pig feed. The rice is now ready for cooking. For certain sweetmeats, rice is pounded to flour in the mortar, a longer and more laborious process.

Most families do their own rice pounding, but some of the wealthier landholders have it done for them, sometimes by the portable motor-driven rice mill which comes from Poblacion a few times a year. More commonly their rice is pounded by their neighbors: the pounders receive one tenth of the rice they pound, a not inconsiderable source of rice (see Figure 2).

One additional source of rice income is harvesting in Cagayan, Luzon's north coast province, where a large number of Ilocanos have settled over the past generation as a result of government resettlement projects. Here, because of a labor shortage, the harvesters are paid a quarter of what they cut. In one of the municipalities in Cagayan, about 200 miles from Tarong, a large number of people from Municipality have settled, and Tarongans count many relatives among these settlers. The long bus trip to Cagayan does not seem so hazardous if you know there are relatives waiting to welcome you and take you into their home; thus a fair number of women, and occasionally men, go each year. These harvesters bring back not less than 5 bushels apiece, which makes up the rice deficiency in a number of households,

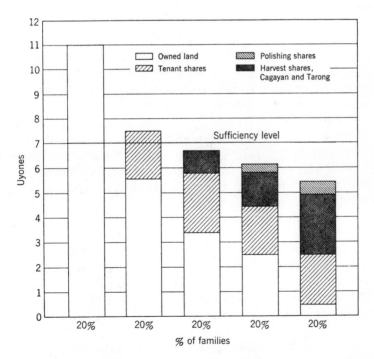

Figure 2. Sources of rice income.

only leaving about one fifth of the Tarongan households still badly short of rice (see Figure 2).

Fruits and Vegetables

Tarong has long been known as a fine eggplant-producing area, and this vegetable is consumed in larger quantities than any other. It is planted in seed beds, then transplanted to harvested paddies. They bear until the rains begin, at which time they become watery and flavorless and are uprooted for rice planting. When eggplant or other vegetables are grown on tenanted land, the landlord has a legal claim to 20% of the crop. In Tarong he may claim 33% to 40% but usually does so only in the case of cash crops.

Only eggplant can be profitably sold in the market and only for a short time. Excess produce is generously distributed among neighbors whose patches may be as yet unripe, while the family owning the over-productive field eats as much of the fruit as it can. Eggplant is not only the longest-bearing vegetable grown, but it is one of the few prevalent throughout the dry season. It is so omnipresent, especially during the last three months of the season, that parents frequently laugh about their children coming to the eating table and groaning, "Again eggplant!"

Mongo beans and corn are popular, because they may be dried, ground, and boiled with rice to extend the rice supply. At least 16 vegetables are grown. They are planted after rice harvesting and must be watered a number of times a week until the roots are established, generally within two or three weeks. This means carrying 5-gallon kerosene cans full of water from the wells to the fields and watering each plant with a coconut shell—a laborious and time-consuming task.

With the first rains these dry-season crops all disappear, and in June and July there are almost no fresh vegetables. Now the wild vine *saloyot,* mentioned elsewhere as a weed, is sometimes eaten from necessity. As the heavy rains taper off in September, a number of vegetables again appear. The most important is *tugi,* much like a white potato. *Tugi,* which grows wild and is common and cheap even in market throughout the harvest season, is the mainstay of poorer households, where it is used as a rice substitute. By the end of harvesting, the dry-season vegetables are beginning to bear, rice is available, and the *tugi* is largely forsaken although available for longer.

At any time of the year there are at least a few varieties of wild vegetables which can be gathered by families short of food or others desiring variety in their diet. In fact, to the American taste, two of the wild vines are among the best vegetables to be found in the area. Any of the vines, roots, and vegetable fruits growing wild on hillsides can be gathered by anyone, if care is taken not to disturb plantings.

Each house has at least one papaya tree that produces throughout the year, but with greater yield at the end of the rainy season. These trees provide a steady food supply, for few of the many fruits are allowed to ripen, almost all being picked when small and green and used as a vegetable. Also available most of the year are a number of varieties of seaweed, which are bought from the adjacent seaside *barrio* and are an excellent food, many being crisp and flavorful.

A large number of fruits grow in Tarong. Some of the many species and varieties ripen in the dry season; others in the wet season. Thus fresh fruit is available throughout the year. Coconuts grow only in the seaside *barrios*. Because coconut is required in sweetmeats and spirit offerings, they must be bought in market at some expense. This is also true of betel nut, which is chewed by many middle-aged and older men and women.

Of greater importance than all other fruit is the banana. The trees grow on the dikes and along the edges of the valleys, most farmers having about 100 trees in various stages of development. The bananas ripen throughout the year although they fill out more rapidly and are at their best during the rainy season. No part of the tree is wasted: the blossom and fruit are eaten; the stalk is fed to the pigs; the leaves are used as pot-liners and food wrappers. Because they are less seasonal than other fruits, their price is relatively stable, and they are the only fruit Tarongans regularly sell..

Domestic Animals

The only animal essential to the Tarongan farmer is his carabao, a major investment averaging 250 to 300 pesos for a trained, adult carabao in 1955. The health and strength of his carabao may seriously affect a farmer's productivity. Accordingly, signs and marks found on a carabao at birth are hoped to indicate its future strength and the length of its working life. Both males and females are worked, males being slightly preferred because of their somewhat larger size. Working carabao are generally castrated.

Carabao are traded and sold frequently at various special market places. A farmer with a little extra cash who is dissatisfied with his carabao trades it for a younger, larger, or better marked animal every few years. By the time a carabao is about 13 years, it is weak and is sold for butchering.

Each farming household has at least one carabao, preferably one for each adult male. Because of the cost of a working carabao, sometimes a calf is bought for a son; in this way it will be at a good working age for the boy when he is old enough to farm. More often the family carabao is bartered for a breeding female which can be worked until calving and almost immediately after, the calf trailing along to the fields. Female carabao are also available to be worked in return for their care, the first calf belonging to the caretaker, the second to the owner, subsequent ones alternating in the same way. This division of offspring is customary for all animals raised by tenants.

The considerable amount of care required by a carabao is the responsibility of the males of the household. The carabao are bathed at dawn and dusk each day even when not worked and four or more times when working. They must also be moved to graze, to shade at noon, and so on at least four times a day. Much of the carabao food is cut and brought to the animals, for they do not like the grazing on the hillsides and the farmer cannot let them graze close to planted fields. At times when food which the carabao like is scarce, the carabao may be force-fed cane leaves or other greens they normally reject. They are bedded on frequently replaced rice straw, tethered near the house, and any unusual activity on their part is immediately investigated. Tarongans even shave the straggly hair of their carabao, some saying this makes them easier to bathe, but most simply stating that they look better with their black hides smooth and glossy.

Although mainly used for the cultivation of rice paddies, carabao are also used as draft animals, for *barrio* lanes and paths, especially in the rainy season, are impassable to wheeled carts. Every farmer owns a homemade bamboo sled with wooden runners which his carabao pulls along the paths, and to this sled he may tie a large woven bamboo basket. Carabao cannot be used on the highway, for their hooves spread and are relatively soft, but these sleds can be taken along the shoulders of the road.

In addition to a carabao, a Tarongan family may raise a few cows for a landlord and almost invariably owns a pig, which is generally raised for sale. Butchering a hog in the *barrio* usually occurs for a large feast. Caring for the family pig is the wife's duty. Young pigs are bought at market, since pig breeding is seen as a low class occupation.

Pigs, like the carabao, are troublesome to care for. They are spayed to fatten them. They are tied under the house much of the time but allowed to forage part of the day. They are fed in the morning and evening, always laboriously prepared cooked food. The bulk of their diet is shaved and pounded banana stalk combined with ground corn or rice bran, the whole boiled to a mash.

Raising chickens can provide a small weekly cash income, but most households own small flocks because the *peste* (Newcastle disease) will often wipe out a whole flock. Women or older children feed the chickens ground corn, sometimes rice, but otherwise they are left to take care of themselves. The chickens generally roost in trees around the houses and are not penned; they are shooed out of houses constantly. The fighting cocks, however, are penned and carefully cared for by their owners. Despite the interest in cock fighting, only one third or so of the Tarongan men own such cocks.

Most families have at least one or two goats, which are slaughtered by the owner for goat feasts or sold locally for this purpose. The care of the family goats is entrusted to older children although the women of the family are ultimately responsible. Little effort is required; mostly the goats are moved from one grazing place to another, and brought to shelter. Since goats are plentiful, relatively inexpensive, and not large, they provide the favorite food for small feasts.

Although dogs are occasionally raised for meat, few Tarongan families do so—they are considered expensive to feed.

Another source of protein is fish. Since salt water fish are costly, most of the fish eaten in Tarong come from the paddies, for the mudfish bury themselves in the mud during the dry season and come up as soon as there is water in the paddies, at which time they are caught in bamboo traps. In addition, while the paddies are wet, some snails and many frogs are also caught. A few men weave nets and fish in the stream at the western boundary of Tarong, but this is sporadic, since it is time consuming and the catch is usually small. Salt water shrimp, octopus, and crabs are sometimes bought by those able to afford them in the seaside *barrio* Ikan.

The fields, and especially the wooded ridges, provide other supplementary foods including some birds and, at periods when they are prevalent, at least seven varieties of insects—mostly beetles, locusts, crickets, and certain ants. These insects are roasted or fried and are flavorful and well liked, but because of their short seasons and the difficulty of catching them in any number, they are only occasional tidbits, not a major part of the diet.

Sugar Cane Products

Cane has long been a major cash crop in Tarong although in the late 1950's it began to yield to tobacco. Its two products, brown sugar and wine, are valuable but are sold by only a few Tarongan households. The major drawback to cane as a cash crop is the amount of land required and its long growing season. Enough cane for home consumption can be planted in rotation in high paddies of dubious value for rice or in flat hillside stretches. But rice paddies must be given over to the cane for commercial production, and few Tarongans have enough rice land to do this on a profitably large scale.

After cutting, the stalks are taken to one of the six *barrio*-made sugar mills, which have a pair of vertical hand-hewn wood rollers powered by a carabao. These mills and the cooking equipment are usually owned by a number of kin-tied households and used by anyone in the *sitio*. Repairs are the joint responsibility of the users; the non-owners pay for use of the mill in this way, and also by gifts of some of the products. The cane stalks are twice fed into the mill while the carabao walks in a circle around it, slowly turning the rollers. Crushing alone takes the better part of a half day.

To make brown sugar this juice is boiled until it is reduced to a thick syrup, which is mixed with a little lime, poured into containers, and allowed to harden.

Wine is made by cooking raw juice for three hours, then adding crushed dried leaves of the *samac* tree. Some of the wine is also allowed to turn to vinegar for household cooking; some is sold; the rest is aged in large mud-sealed pottery jars that are usually stored under the *sala*. The wine is considered good after a year, when it is strong and clear, but is often drunk much earlier, when still cloudy.

Sugar boiling invariably is the occasion for a small party, since two or more households frequently process sugar cane at the same time. All the members of these households, as well as neighbors of the mill-owner, gather to watch and chat. While the syrup thickens, young children and old people squat about the pan with bamboo splints, dipping out and eating the sticky foam which rises to the top. When the boiling is almost finished, rice prepared in a variety of ways, or slices of banana or tubers, are tossed in and cooked until coated with a thick layer of sugar.

Tobacco

Most households grow native tobacco, half the families growing small extra quantities for sale. Tobacco production is laborious, involving initial planting in carefully tended seed beds, later transplanting to paddies, watering for two to three weeks, and handpicking worms and lice from the leaves at least once a week the entire growing season.

Men smoke thin homemade cheroots but Ilocano women prefer large thick cigars rolled from one or two leaves and at least a foot long. The cigars scarcely draw at all and are constantly relit, one cigar frequently lasting a whole day. To yield these large leaves, the plants are allowed to produce only 8 to 10 leaves; the rest are pinched. These large leaves, although requiring considerable paddy-space, bring the highest prices. However, great care must be taken to pick worms and lice from the plants, for discolorations or holes lower the value of the leaf.

Although aging tobacco for one year doubles its sale value, few Tarongans do so except for their own use because it is so troublesome. The leaves are stored in large chests in a dry place with sufficient banana leaves to retain moisture, and at least once a month all the leaves must be shaken, aired, and repacked with fresh banana leaves.

Since the time of the Spanish occupation Tarongans have grown various cash crops in addition to native tobacco—first indigo, then cotton, followed by eggplant and sugar cane products. Recently the growth of Virginia tobacco for Philippine American-style cigarettes has been encouraged by various government agencies, and the Ilocos area is considered one of the provinces with the best potential, having long been famous for the quality of its *native* tobacco. In 1953, spurred by some Poblacion businessmen who also acted as purchasing agents, small quantities of *Virginia* were planted throughout the Municipality. Virginia tobacco has proved more profitable than any of the previous cash crops, and in spite of the fact that it is even more work than raising rice, the financial reward makes it worthwhile.

In 1953–54 Virginia tobacco sold to buyers was then taken elsewhere in Municipality to be cured in the few available flue-curing barns. In 1954 a Poblacion businessman built a flue-curing barn in Tarong. Six Tarongans were regularly employed at this barn, and many women and older children worked part time stringing tobacco. In this way Tarongans learned the technique of flue-curing as well as its economic possibilities. In 1955 eleven households in Tarong built their own flue-curing barns. The owners felt that by being able to store the tobacco (something they were unable to do with green leaves), they could demand better prices, more stable payments, and increase their profits.

FOOD PRESERVATION AND CONSUMPTION PATTERNS

Only meats and a few vegetables are preserved by Tarongans, and, with one exception, the only method used is drying. Pork, beef, and carabao are generally bought a pound or two at a time, and since this quantity is too expensive to be consumed in a day or two, it is cured so that it will keep a week or longer. The meat is sliced thin, washed in vinegar, dried for a day in the sun, then diced and fried. Frogs and small fish also are cleaned and dried whole in the sun. The only vegetables dried are seaweeds, corn, and *mongo* beans.

The one food treated to another preservative technique is a tiny fish which is pickled in vinegar and salt, sealed in large containers, and aged. The fish gradually disintegrate, leaving a thick, grayish liquid, which tastes much like pickled anchovies and is widely used as a flavoring.

Two patterns of eating are followed in Tarong: if children of the household attend school, there are three full meals a day; after the children graduate, however, most families return to the older, and in many ways more suitable, schedule of two full meals and a snack or two.

Rice is preferred freshly cooked for each meal, but the morning meal may be left-over cold rice. At the noon and evening meals, the rice is served with a vegetable sauce and is flavored as well as salted by pickled fish, fresh ginger, or hot peppers. Most families manage to add bits of meat or fish to the vegetable sauce three to five evenings a week. If a number of small birds, fish, frogs, and so on have been collected or a chicken killed, these are roasted on spits over the stove fire for a special evening meal.

At the times when vegetables are plentiful or if one of the household women takes pride in her cooking, an extra dish of fried or boiled vegetables may be served. Frequently these extra vegetable dishes are sliced tomatoes or "raw" salad (for example, squash blossoms flavored with pickled fish), but if such foods cannot be peeled, they are boiled for a few minutes and never served really raw. Fresh fruits, especially bananas, are a frequent addition to the basic meal and may be served as a dessert. The time for extra dishes is at the evening meal, for then all the household is sure to be home—the eating times of its various members being haphazard when work is heavy or there are special school activities.

Family meals are eaten in the kitchen, the adults and older children squatting about either a low table or dishes on the floor; young children are held and fed by one of the adults. A bowl apiece for rice, either an individual ladle or a dish for the sauce, and bowls of water to clean the fingers are all the utensils required. The finger bowl is essential, for almost without exception Tarongans eat with the fingers in a prescribed fashion: the fingertips are used to gather some rice into a ball, which is then dipped into the sauce and popped into the mouth—a neater procedure than this description may suggest. For juicy foods not eaten with rice, the index and middle fingers are used as a scoop with remarkable dexterity. The fingers are cleaned frequently, but no water is drunk throughout the meal; as each finishes, he goes to drink from the kitchen-porch water pot.

Midafternoon snacks are likely to be gatherings of a number of households on a porch or under yard trees to chat and nibble in-season fruits, sweetmeats, or boiled peanuts. Children frequently eat cold rice or other left-overs at this time and adults may join them.

The poorer families follow essentially the same diet but can seldom afford meat, rely more on wild foods, and usually omit snacks. The difference in consumption between average and wealthy households is largely in quantity: extra money or rice for barter is used for more meat, canned or fresh fish, eggs, fruits, additional wine, market vegetables for variety, more brown sugar and commercial margarine. But all Tarongan women are cautious in their outlays for extra foodstuffs, and these expenditures remain small. Sometimes luxuries available in Poblacion, such as white sugar, are bought but only for special events. Nevertheless, a woman going to market frequently spares a few centavos for a tangerine, cookies from the bakery, or a bottle of carbonated drink for her children or grandchildren.

Feasts are required after baptisms, weddings, and funerals and may be given for other occasions. A feast is always held at noon and the guests eat in the *sala* from tables or the floor. The most common food is roast goat. Aside from this, the typical foods for large or small feasts are elaborated daily dishes: invariably there is twice as much rice as needed and, depending on the number of people to be fed, two or three meat sauces. A variety of meats is desirable, and for this reason, at large feasts, a few chickens, a goat, and a pig will be butchered rather than two pigs, although pig is never omitted, for the lard is needed. Some of this meat is roasted or braised and often served with a paprika gravy. A favorite and delicious dish at feasts where a pig has been butchered is vinegar-coagulated blood fried slightly with minced liver and seasoned with pickled fish and ginger.

A water pitcher set with six tall glasses is an expensive but indispensable article in a properly equipped household, and for large feasts these sets are borrowed, along with china and enamel dishes and spoons, from houses throughout the *sitio*. Occasionally neatly trimmed banana-stalk slices are used as plates, but the commercial china is much preferred; coconut shell cups never appear, the wine which precedes the meal always being served in glasses.

If the affair is too big for the *sala*, when this room and the porch are filled with borrowed tables and chairs for the guests of honor and important visitors, the rest are fed in the yard under a bamboo and palm-leaf canopy. Sometimes there are benches here—otherwise the guests stand to eat. If possible, a spoon and fork are laid out at each rice bowl at the *sala* and porch tables so that honored guests may eat Western style.

Although there is some chatting during the meal, the foremost concern is eating, and there is little general talk until dessert and water are served. Then long handtowels of finely woven native cloth are given out, one to a table. Next, the tables are cleared, and guests smoke, drink more wine, joke, and chat while the girls and women who have served the food eat in the kitchen, and the dishes are washed by a chattering group of as many neighboring women and relatives as can crowd onto the narrow kitchen porch. The children, who have been coaxed into eating some of all the food present, sit blinking on the floor, trying vainly to stay awake to listen to the joking.

Small, informal parties are generally held in the afternoon—to honor a visitor, celebrate a birthday, or simply because of a sugar boiling. Guests are always provided with sweetmeats. There is a standard menu for the various types of parties: soft-boiled eggs on rice are favorite foods for the breakfast parties occasioned by work groups or large numbers of overnight guests after important dances or wakes for the dead; chicken-rice stew is usual at death anniversaries, and so on.

The impressive aspect of Tarongan party cooking is the apparently endless varieties of sweetmeats that can be made from three basic ingredients: rice, coconuts, and brown sugar. There are at least ten distinctive kinds, differing in the proportions of ingredients, the way they are prepared, and the method of cooking employed.

TRADES AND SPECIALIZATIONS

In over half of Tarong's households one or more of the members are engaged in the practice of specialized, nonagricultural trades or skills. During the field period, approximately one half of the number of such specialists were women, representing six trades, men engaging in nine. This division of specialities reflects the customary sex division of such skills except for those marked with an asterisk—midwives, *ilots* and *sirkanos* may be women as well as men, though the post-partum *ilot* can only be a woman. The tobacco marketer is thought to be doing a woman's job.

Men	Women
10 Carpenters (2 old, semiretired, 1 "apprentice")	18 Traders (1 fish peddler)
3 Pig sprayers	5 Weavers
3 Midwives *	3 Seamstresses
2 Basket makers	2 Laundresses
1 *Ilot* (for sprains, dislocations) *	2 *Ilots* (post-partum masseuse)
1 *Sirkano* (medicine-man) *	1 Embroiderer
1 Rope maker	
1 Tobacco marketer *	
4 Musicians	

* Professions open to both men and women.

These specialties are a means of obtaining cash or rice and thus making up deficiencies in the total income, but very few people can maintain themselves in this way. Most Tarongans possess some of these skills themselves and to hire someone to do such work would seem wasteful. Wages and prices are low and only some carpenters and a few traders can be said to make a living from their specialties.

As can be seen from the foregoing table, most Tarongan women who earn money other than by farming do so by acting as traders. This activity ranges from "looked-down on" fish peddling to acting as middlewomen in expensive jewelry purchases. Of all the women engaged in trading, only two were not either widows or spinsters. Trading is thus the way that most single women in Tarong maintain themselves if they own little land.

One of the most successful of these women is Elena, a middle-aged spinster, who earns enough not only to support herself but also to provide many luxuries for her large family group. Lately she has been taking a teen-age niece on her trading trips as a companion and apprentice. Her dealings, although they show a shrewder business sense and more industry than most, are typical of the kind of activities in which such traders are engaged.

Elena goes to Cagayan twice a year, once at rice harvesting time and again during corn harvesting. While there, she not only works at harvesting but takes advantage of different values of goods in various localities to make a considerable profit. Salt is seven times higher in Cagayan than in Ikan, but the tiny fish for pickling are cheaper in Cagayan than Ikan. Therefore Elena bought salt and took it to Cagayan; there she traded some of the salt for fish which she pickled with the remaining salt. When the pickled fish was sold back in Tarong, Elena had made a 300% profit.

Tarongans are largely but not completely self-sufficient. Salt, some fish, coconuts and betel are the only foodstuffs regularly imported. The most costly necessary imports consist of iron tools and machines such as knives, chisels, scissors, pressure lamps, sewing machines and so on. Thread and ready-made cloth, pottery, soap, and jewelry are not manufactured in Tarong and require cash outlay.

ECONOMIC VALUES

Actual cash savings of most Tarongans are necessarily small; this fact cannot be taken as an index of the importance of saving. All members of a household contribute their earnings to the family cache, out of which the necessary expenditures of each are paid. No luxuries are bought without joint discussion. Money is not spent foolishly; one man who is an habitual drinker is the sole aberrant example. Even devoted cockfighters bet only if they can afford to lose and bets are small. The hesitancy to spend money on nonessentials is the primary reason for the constant borrowing of objects, sometimes a lifetime passing before they are returned to their owner or his children.

Savings are almost invariably kept in various hiding places in the house. Such secretiveness prohibits even peripheral members of the household knowing its precise financial status and allows a family to claim shortage of cash as an excuse for not loaning money to relatives —from whom one does not expect interest. Some savings, however, may be put into mortgages, a popular and highly profitable source of income, the mortgage holder receiving the entire crop.

Some of the savings are spent for necessary feasts or sickness expenditures and as part of children's marriage settlements, but by far the largest share is used for either land or education. Landed families continue to buy land as a profitable investment, and landless families are anxious to obtain some land of their own. In addition to the economic advantages of land ownership, there is also considerable social advantage. The social gulf in Tarong is not between the wealthy and poor as such, but between landowners and the landless. These landless families have essentially no voice in community affairs, and their greatest desire is to get even the little land which will give them the position of "respectable poor." For most this is an unrealizable hope, for at current land prices a poor family needs 25 years or more of steady savings to buy a *uyon* paddy.

PROPERTY: OWNERSHIP AND INHERITANCE

Custom and the *Civil Code* (1954) give both men and women of legal age autonomous control of their own personal property, but conjugal property is ordinarily administered by the husband. Conjugal property consists of the property settlement, usually supplied by the groom's family, earnings during the period of marriage, and additional property received by inheritance or gift which is designated as conjugal property by the donor.

Although the husband administrates the conjugal property, he can neither alienate nor encumber it without the wife's consent, and in the case of incompetence either spouse may take over complete control. At death certain obligations must be met, after which it is divided, one half to the surviving spouse, the other disposed of as designated by will. This law is observed in Tarong, although in the occasional disputed case legal action is not resorted to because of the cost of court proceedings and the small amounts involved. As with many other decisions, kin-neighbor pressures and the homogeneity of the community obviate major quarrels.

Traditional inheritance patterns are confirmed by the *Civil Code* for personal as well as conjugal estates. The testator in this case must reserve one half of the estate for the legitimate children; the surviving spouse usually has claim to a quarter; the other quarter may be freely disposed of subject to the rights of recognized illegitimate children.

In Tarong the ideal patterns of inheritance parallel the legal ones —with the "free quarter" of the personal estate preferably being given to the oldest child to maintain his role as group leader or to younger children to further their education. In practice, limited property holdings nullify the wish. At death an average couple owns little beyond a small field or two, hardly sufficient to have fed them, a small house that has already been given or promised to a child, and a bit of jewelry and cash, which are usually used for funeral expenses.

In giving property settlements to their sons at marriage, Tarongans plan on an equal amount for each child in lieu of an inheritance. Unfortunately this is rarely possible because of present-day land pressures, and the first married sons generally acquire most of the family lands, frequently the house, and much of the cash. Only the daughter of a very wealthy man may expect a small field of her own, although daughters of sonless families inherit equally.

Wills are said to exist in Tarong, but the field team never saw one although other documents were freely exhibited and explained. A "will" seems to be an expressed desire that certain properties shall accrue to designated heirs—a last wish that is not always followed after death. Presumably the child or grandchild, regardless of sex, who cares for a parent in his last years has prior claim to whatever property is left. A son usually collects this claim, but daughters and grandchildren find it more difficult. Possession at the time of death of a house or cash belonging to the deceased is usually accepted as ownership; jewelry has most often been distributed but, if not, is generally given to the designated heir. Lands tend to go to the holder of the most recent tax receipt, and it is this device that determines whether a strong-minded spinster or the son who has been cultivating the field will gain final control.

⁂

Chapter 4

Kinship and Marriage

Traditional history, confirmed by genealogical evidence, indicates that in approximately 1860 the area now called Tarong was settled by seven nuclear families. Four of these householders were relatives (two brothers, their cousin, and a more distant relative carrying the same surname), and all had expanded into the area from Poblacion and neighboring *barrios*. Of the 61 households that now comprise Tarong, all but six are descended from those original seven householders. The six exceptions descend from two families immigrating from neighboring *barrios*, the first a number of generations ago, the other more recently.

As of November 30, 1954 the population of Tarong consisted of 298 individuals. Their distribution by sex, age, and marital status is shown in Table 1. Ages were determined when possible by the use of birth or baptism certificates and ages under 40 are presumably accurate; those 40 and over became increasingly difficult to determine and some may be ten years from the real age.

Table 1 Sex, Age, and Marital Status of Residents of Tarong as of November 30, 1954

Age (years)	MALES (139)			FEMALES (159)			Total
	Single	Married	Widowed	Single	Married	Widowed	
0–1	4			1			5
1–3	5			6			11
3–6	13			16			29
6–10	13			11			24
10–20	29			27	1		57
20–30	15	4		13	7*		39
30–40	4	13	1	9	14	3	44
40–50	1	8	1	6	9	2	27
50–60		7		3	6	3	19
60–70	1	6	3	1	6	4	21
70–80		7	2		4	4	17
80–90		1	1		2	1	5
Total	85	46	8	93	48	18	298

* One of these women is separated from her husband.

The nuclear family is the basic socio-economic unit, and it is expected that a separate house will be provided for a couple at marriage. Sometimes this may be delayed until after the birth of the first child. Even if others, such as an unmarried sister, widowed daughter, newly married couple or aged parent, share a house, each unit tries to maintain its economic separateness when possible, particularly in the important rice supply. Although the rice may be harvested together and stored in the same granary, it is customary for each unit to contribute daily from its own store the probable amount of its consumption.

The nuclear family houses are clustered into predominantly patrilocal groups, one or more of these clusters making up a *sitio*. Of the 61 Tarongan households, 11 are scattered although never out of hailing distance of another, 12 are paired, 20 are in small *sitios* of three to seven households, and 18 are clumped into one exceptionally large *sitio*—called Sitio East. The house clusters and kin relationships within this large *sitio* are worth noting in detail, for they typify the ideal living-group.

As can be seen from Table 2 and map 3, all of the households are related through the patrilineal line to three men who lived approximately a century ago. Two of these men carried the same name and were known to be paternal cousins. The youngest generation of 11 of these households are all second cousins; this generation of another 5 are more distant cousins; thus only two households are not related to the entire *sitio* by bonds of cousinship. These two households, F and G, were left without close.kin ties in the neighborhood and are attached to Sitio East.

Of the women who have married into these households, one third have been from Tarong, two-thirds from its adjacent *barrios*. The only exception was a cousin from Cagayan. There is a tendency for sons to marry girls fom the same *barrio*. This generally is the *barrio* of their mother's origin and the girls are often related to the mother. There are at least four households in Tarong so ideally located that both maternal and paternal parents of the couple live in the same *sitio*. For example, in Sitio East, two sons of household K married two sisters of household N who were both their second cousins and neighbors. Each couple then built a house (L and M) in between the parental dwellings. The percentages of endogamous marriages have increased in Sitio East, as have *barrio* endogamous marriages, with each generation and are proof of the effect of parentally preferred cousin marriage.

About 80% of Tarong's households were patrilocal, which is more practical since sons are given some of the family land at marriage. Nevertheless, matrilocality occurs in about 15% of the households and occasions no comment. One small *sitio* was matrilocal, the family being wealthy and having no sons. Of the nine Tarongan households on or near the houseplots of the wives' parents, five were those of immigrating men married to Tarongan women who settled in Tarong instead of returning to their own localities. The four Tarongan men living matrilocally had all married women who had more land or land expectations than their husbands and it was expedient to reside near the woman's parents.

Only four, or 5%, of the households were neolocal. (This figure is

Table 2 Genealogies of Adults Currently Living in Sitio East

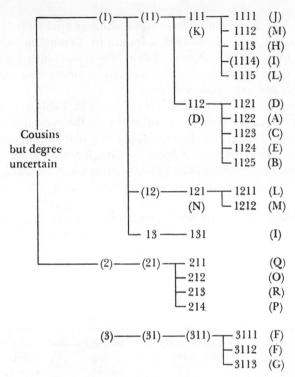

All numbers in parentheses represent deceased adults. Letters in parentheses refer to map 3.

underestimated since emigrants are not included.) Some of these families had moved for convenience to family lands, some as the result of kin group quarrels. Within a few generations, however, such a single household can swell to a *sitio* of some proportions. In addition to natural increase, related and unrelated families who are dissatisfied with their current location may join the new kin group, as well as the occasional family whose *sitio*-mates have all died. Houses are easily moved, and if close kin ties are broken by death and quarreling, a family may shift to another *sitio*. Few *sitios* grow to the size of Sitio East, in which *sitio* endogamy could be encouraged for a large number of young people.

Aging parents maintain separate households for as long as possible, sometimes taking in a grandchild to help care for them if their children have all married. Widows may return to their parents' households but are more likely to remain in their husbands' *sitios* if their children are nearing adulthood and if they can maintain themselves economically.

At the time of the study there was a disproportionately large number of widows and middle-aged spinsters in Tarong, apparently the result of the California-Hawaii labor migrations during the 1930's. Many of these migrants, married as well as unmarried, never were heard from and are considered dead.

Kin terms used by Tarongans are indicated in Table 3. It should be noted that they are identical to our own with the exception that older and younger siblings are distinguished, and that the sex of younger siblings and niece/nephew is ignored. The phrases *a lalaki* (male) or *a baba'i* (female) may be added to kin terms when required for clarification (e.g., *ading a lalaki*, younger brother; *ading a baba'i*, younger sister).

In common usage, only ten of the consanguine terms, some slightly altered, are sufficient both for reference and direct address (terms with

Table 3 Tarongan Kin Terms

Consanguine

grandfather	*lilong* *	older brother	*manung* *
grandmother	*lilang* *	older sister	*manang* *
great uncle	*onkl* (*ulitegko*, rare)	younger sibling	*ading* *
great aunt	*anti* (*ikitko*, rare)	sibling	*kabsat*
		cousin	*kasinsin*
father	*tatang* *		
mother	*nanang* *	son	*barok* *
parent	*naganak*	daughter	*balasangko* *
uncle	*onkl* (*ulitegko*, rare)	child	*anakko*
aunt	*anti* (*ikitko*, rare)	niece/nephew	*ka?anak*
		grandchild	*apok* *

Affinal

parent(s)-in-law of one's child	*abalayan*
parent(s)-in-law	*katugang*
spouse	*asawa*
sibling(s)-in-law	*abirat*
brother(s)-in-law	*kayung* (rare)
sister(s)-in-law	*ipag* (rare)
child(ren)-in-law	*manugang*

* Common classificatory terms. When so used, the *-ng* possessive suffix is omitted from *lilong, liland, tatang, nanang* and the *-k, -ko* possessive suffix is omitted from *barok, balasangko,* and *apok.*

asterisks in Table 3). The choice of term is based on the age class of the speakers. In English, for example, "son" can be used to any male young enough to be one's son. In Ilocano, any person is called by the kin term most appropriate to the relative ages of the speakers.

There is, however, definite up-aging as a form of politeness. When meeting a peer for the first time, the older brother (*manung*) or older sister term (*manang*) is always used. One of the first questions asked will be about relative ages of the speakers, but the correct younger sibling term (*ading*) will not be used until intimacy is fairly well established.

This up-aging as a form of politeness does not extend to the oldest age-class terms (*lila, lilo*), however. Any adult who could conceivably be thought of as appropriate in age to be your parent is *tata* or *nana;* only very old men and women are habitually called *lilo* or *lila* and this generally within the *barrio*. The exceptions to the general classificatory terms are relatives in the speaker's direct line of descent; a Tarongan calls his own grandfather *lilong* even if he politely calls another older man *tata*. To indicate respect, the formal *Apo,* much like "sir" in English, is used.

What the kin group means to one of its members can be best illustrated by example. Pasqual Navarro (Household L, map 3) is a married man 33 years of age, the youngest child of Ariston (Household K, map 3). Because he is the youngest child it is somewhat expected that he be aggressive and hot-tempered and he is without question both, but Pasqual still on occasion requests advice from his old parents, and his relations with them are good. Ariston's and Pasqual's families are in and out of each other's houses constantly, helping, gossiping, sometimes quarreling loudly.

Pasqual and his three brothers (Households H, J, and M, map 3) all take pains to gain the favor of their parents, for the old couple, instead of being almost impoverished as is common, are receiving a large monthly cash income from the insurance of a son killed during the war. This income permits the sons to borrow or beg now and promises land and cash to be distributed after the parents' death.

Pasqual, as the youngest son, received a smaller marriage settlement from Ariston than did his older brothers. Despite this, through the help of his wealthy and sonless father-in-law and by undertaking a prodigious amount of farm work, his annual income is only slightly less than that of his oldest brother Rufino, who is the wealthiest man in Sitio East. It is from this eldest brother, who has now succeeded his father as family leader, that Pasqual and his children can get often needed sponsorship. A man expects to turn to any older brother or sister, especially the eldest, as to a parent when necessary. If he is brotherless, he will probably attach himself to a closely related kin-group leader and establish a similar relationship.

Pasqual, however, is not typical and, being clever and having the ambition and drive usually attributed to an American businessman, he will probably succeed to Rufino's position as head of the family. Despite his birth position, it is unlikely that any of Pasqual's brothers will dispute his ascent. Pasqual's ties with his brothers are strong, and they not only do a considerable amount of work together but also are intimate friends, pitting their cocks together or gathering on one or another's porch in the evening to chat.

This kin group is not permanently united, however, for by the time Pasqual's children have married and grouped around him and the children of his brothers have done so also, each new patrilocal kin head will be the leader of his immediate kin group and the semi-authority Pasqual has over his brothers will have weakened. He and his brothers and their children will work together and consult each other, but major decisions will be made by the leaders of the smaller close-kin groups.

Prudencio, his daughter Elena (Household D, map 3) and his four sons (Households A, B, C, and E, map 3) form a kin group which differs from that of Ariston's. Prudencio owns a negligible quantity of land, and all his sons are poor and forced to tenant farm. Elena, however, as has been mentioned previously, is one of the most successful businesswomen in Tarong. Due partly to this, and partly to her position as the eldest child, Elena is in fact the kin-group leader and has great authority via her control of group finances. However, her authority is exercised in Prudencio's name, and when he dies it could be challenged by his eldest son. It is more likely that they will share the group leadership, but decisions will be in the son's name, since no man would refer to a woman as kin-group head: others would say, "Her molars are harder."

The attitude of most children toward their aging parents is ambivalent. On the one hand is the cultural prescription: "When parents begin to be infirm, you should treat them like babies. It is expected of well-behaved children that they will repay the same kind attention they were given as children." As one old man graphically put it: "When you are older, even should you feed your mother from the palm of your hand, you could never repay her for the trouble you caused her."

On the other hand is the frequent reality of impoverished parents consuming the scanty rice supply but incapable of productive work.

Old people can maintain respect only as long as they can maintain themselves or are at least of some use about the house; after this they are a grudgingly supported nuisance. When commenting on Prudencio's elderly wife pounding rice, Elena only half-jokingly replied, "She's still eating, isn't she?" If this seems harsh, it should be remembered that the food eaten by an old man or woman may quite literally be taken from the mouths of their grandchildren. Elena actually treats her parents very well, even buying rather expensive cloth for her mother's old-style clothes. Nevertheless, her comment reflects the basic attitude of a Tarongan toward old people.

There are even cases of parents being ill-treated by children who could well support them. An extreme example occurred about eight years ago when an old couple, homeless and landless, was forced to wander the *sitio* and sleep in the fields for three days while their eldest son and a daughter, both of whom were married and well off, wrangled over who was to take them in. At last the daughter assumed the responsibility, but the affair was still spoken of as shameful.

A common method of ensuring one's old age is by taking in a grandchild (preferably the second grandson) when he is about school age and providing him with food and clothing, often in greater quantity than he could expect at home. This child gradually takes over the farming and can expect whatever property might be left at his grandparents' death to come to him. This expectation, coupled with a strong feeling of obligation for his childhood support, ensures good treatment of the grandparents at the hands of this "second son."

Since marriages between relatives or at least nighbors are preferred, a boy or girl is encouraged as a child to look on his agemates in the immediate *sitio,* and especially his cousins, as future marriage partners. When he is old enough to marry (18 or so), a boy's preferences may be established through contacts at dances, death anniversaries, parties and feasts, where he will have met available Tarongan and neighboring-*barrio* girls. If he does not find a girl in this way, his parents will suggest someone, usually a cousin.

The essential quality the girl must have is chasteness. If she is known to be unchaste or has an illegitimate child, her marriage chances considerably diminish unless her family can force the guilty man to marry her. Generally this is impossible, for almost all the men so involved are already married. But such lapses among young marriageable girls are exceedingly rare. Beyond the age when she is marriageable except to an older bachelor or widower, that is about 30, there is only mild gossip at any sexual liaison she might have, and her social status or that of the children she might have is not greatly affected. The lovers of these older single women were generally from outside the *barrio*. The double standard is evident. Whereas a married man may go visiting, adultery by a married woman would be considered a serious offense. Although monogamy is the ideal and only sanctioned form of marriage, sororal polygyny does occur rarely. There was one case of this in Tarong and one in each of two of the adjacent *barrios*.

Further marital qualities desired in a girl are industry, maturity, and a cheerful, steady disposition, which will smooth her relations with her in-laws. A girl's beauty is admired but not sufficiently to ignore her other qualities. However, if her family is wealthy and socially important, her desirability is enhanced, and such a girl may be forgiven flightiness or lack of thrift. Although her precise age is irrelevant, generally the boy and girl are approximately the same age, but a few years' difference in their ages in either direction causes no comment. Great age differences are not considered wise but do occur, the man usually being the elder.

The characteristics essential for a Tarongan boy to be considered a good marriage partner are few: marriage settlement and industriousness. Attractiveness is noticed, but, as with the girls, is no substitute for ambitious hard work. Education beyond the Tarong school, rather than increasing the desirability of its possessor, either reflects the financial standing of his or her family, thus adding no new factor, or may put the boy or girl in a social status beyond the *barrio*-marriage market, as is usually the case with those who hold a teacher's certificate.

If the boy successfully courts a girl, a secret agreement may be reached between the young people. Such agreements are becoming increasingly popular and shorten the marriage discussions. Traditional negotiations may be completed within a minimal three meetings of the prospective in-laws: the father of the boy, a man known as a talented speaker and a variety of other relatives, but not the boy himself, go to see the parents of the girl. The request for the girl's hand is made in a stylized fashion and her parents respond vaguely. Hints of the marriage settlement to be offered may be made by the speakers for the boy, and if the suit is favored by the girl's parents, they will set a date for a second meeting within a week or two, when the girl's answer will be given.

The girl may appear at any time during the meetings and indicate her rejection of the suitor, usually accompanied by "I am too young" or a like excuse. If she does not show herself, it is proof that the boy's suit is at least under consideration. If the boy is a cousin, neighbor, or in some other way a desirable match, her parents will encourage her assent. But no girl is forced to accept a suitor against her will, and a good parent does not press too long a suit unwelcome to his daughter. A primary concern for both the girl and her parents is closeness of the marriage residence. "A girl should marry no more than a day's journey from her home"—a walk of two to three *barrios*. In any event, "If it was farther, the parents would not have met."

At the second meeting the girl's answer is given, and, if favorable, either another meeting date is set or discussions are immediately begun concerning the marriage settlement, given by the groom's father and, ideally, sufficient to make the new family self-sustaining. One by one the categories of the marriage settlement are discussed: money, work animals, house and plot, and land. The offerings of the groom's father are forced as high as possible by the parents of the bride. One or more further meetings may be required before negotiations are completed, the formal marriage settlement contract written, and a date for the wedding determined. A final brief morning meeting is held to discuss details of the large and elaborate feast, which is provided by the groom's family, and selection of wedding sponsors. The formal negotiations are concluded when the prospective fathers-in-law clasp their hands over which wine is poured. The average length of time from the beginning of arrangements to the marriage itself is four to six weeks.

By far the greatest number of marriages are performed in the Poblacion church. This is a simple early morning ceremony, which is looked on as a formality. Far more important is the subsequent day of feasting to which everyone related to or friendly with either the bride's or groom's family is invited. Most of the guests are assembled in the decorated *sala* by the time the couple, accompanied by a small party of friends, returns from the church. Upon entering, both bride and groom slowly circle the room, greeting each guest. The bride also embraces and tearfully says good-bye to her family and the "companions of her youth." Both then sit on either side of the family shrine where offerings to the ancestor spirits (plates of coconut-milk rice and bowls of wine) and two candles have been placed. On the floor in front of the shrine is laid a mat on which are placed two new white baskets heaped with well-polished white rice for the new household.

There is feasting and dancing in the yard, led by the bridal couple until midafternoon. At that time the guests are reassembled in the *sala,* and the couple again take chairs next to the shrine. One of the groom's sponsors now reads aloud the settlement contract, and at the mention of each item the audience shouts, "Is this correct?" The bride's father answers, "Yes, it is correct" and property transfer papers are signed if necessary. The sponsors then group relatives and friends of the groom on one side of a mat, those of the bride at the other, and a spirited contest begins in which each group tosses money onto the mat. The sponsors urge each side to equal the other's donations with cries of, "Who will buy the rice pot?", "Who will buy a basket?" When as much money as possible has been donated, it is then totaled, the amount announced (generally about 100 pesos) and presented to the couple.

The party now officially over, the couple accompanies the wife's parents to their house where they stay for two to four days after which a group of relatives of the groom come and "take them back" to his parents' house. Here they stay for the same number of days before moving into their own house.

Inexpensive civil marriages, also acceptable, are resorted to occasionally by couples eloping because of parental censure. But such elopements are uncommon, since the couple involved can, by sulking and threatening elopement, usually force the parents' consent if not their approval. Generally parental approval is granted after the marriage has been accomplished, a settlement is made, and the marriage formally recognized by the traditional feast. If the boy's parents remain adamant, however, no settlement or feast may ever be given and the couple remains poor and of little status within the kin group.

The civil marriage is sometimes a substitute for the more costly church wedding for poor families. In such cases a small party is usually held to celebrate the wedding, but the large feast is dispensed with, particularly if there is no settlement at all, for a family does not advertise its poverty.

There is a saying, "Getting married is not a joke—it is not like eating rice, when if it's hot you can always spit it out." And Tarongan marriages are remarkably stable. The concern of the parents of both boys and girls that their children be satisfied with their marriage partners and living arrangements, and the emphasis on marriages between relatives to make this transition easier partly explain this stability. Wives on occasion "go home to mother" in tears, but quarrels are usually smoothed over by both sets of parents and the wife returns. It is very rare for a woman to remain at her parents' house and break the marriage completely, and only one such case is now represented within the *barrio*. If such a break seems to be imminent, the parents of the girl especially press for a reconciliation. Since divorce is not recognized, the daughter cannot "marry" another man legally, and she and her children would be an economic drain on her father's household. Nevertheless, as with marriage, this is not forced.

Although a son is economically independent of his father at marriage, he in fact will not practice complete independence of action until he is much older, if then. Important decisions are rarely made without consultation with his wife, his parents, often brothers, uncles, neighbors. Too great independence indicates an asocial attitude suspect in a neighbor or relative, and this personality trait, being "all for himself," is the most objectionable a Tarongan may have.

The new bride retains her own surname and her close ties with her own family, gradually beginning to weave them with her husband's family. In spite of some strain with her mother-in-law and older sisters-in-law, to whom she, as a young bride, must defer for a number of years, by the time she has borne two or three children and is less able to visit for a length of time at any distance, she is completely at home in the company of her in-laws and accepted by them. The bonds with her own family lose some of their strength through lessening contact and scattering of family members and childhood friends, but are never severed.

The emotional transition at marriage is eased by the autonomy of the new household. No in-law would presume to take over the management of the new bride's house unless specifically requested during illness or childbirth. This is particularly true of the kitchen, which is a woman's private domain. Advice is constantly given, but there is no authority to lend it weight unless the husband chooses to argue in favor of his family's attitude. In general, however, a husband should and does stay aloof from such "women's" disagreements, and they rarely reach a serious state. After her first child is born, the new wife relies with greater frequency on the advice, help, and friendship of her husband's relatives, and soon she is a part of this intimate group —"we who share the same yard" replace the companions to whom she said good-bye on her wedding day.

Due in large part to pre-existing ties, the respective parents-in-law of the couple usually maintain excellent relations. However, the obligations to mutual aid, both work and money, which used to be part of this relationship have fallen into disuse, only remembered by the oldest generation of Tarongans.

Possible in-law suspicions as well as daughter and mother-in-law strain are formally recognized only at the birth of a child, especially the first—a period of potential danger to the mother. It is the specific duty and obligation of the mother-in-law to take proper care of her daughter-in-law, to see that she receives good medical care and follows her instructions as to taboos and required observances. For at least a month her every act comes to the attention of the in-laws and neighbors, and deviations from what is usual are much discussed. Should the daughter-in-law die, the mother-in-law must be able to show by her neighbors' evidence that she did all that could be done or else be suspected by her in-laws of fatal negligence. One rare case had occurred wherein the Tarongan parents angrily blamed the mother-in-law, who lives in the adjacent *barrio* to the east, for their daughter's death after childbirth and brought back the girl's sister who had married into the family so that her child could be born at their home—an insult which thoroughly disrupted her marriage. Fortunately such suspicions are not common due both to widespread general agreement regarding birth practices and to the frequent close kin-neighbor ties between the in-laws.

The first 25 or 30 years of marriage, starting after 20 for most women, are quite literally "the best years." She is productive, active, and reasonably independent. In return for doing her work properly, bearing children and remaining faithful to her husband, she is accorded the highest social status she will ever have. Furthermore, as her children grow older, they relieve her of many time-consuming household chores, freeing her for economic and social activities. If she is the eldest daughter-in-law, she will look forward only to the time when her mother-in-law, now well past menopause, is forced to relinquish her hold over the families about her. The role of unofficial leader of the daughters-in-law will then normally fall to the first married among them, who is usually the wife of the eldest son and family head, until her interest is in turn weakened in favor of keeping an eye on her own new daughters-in-law.

☘
☘
☘

Chapter 5

Social Organization

The community of Tarong is functionally dependent on an extensive although not formally structured system of mutual obligations, very few of which a member of the community can avoid. "How can a man live if he does not have neighbors to help him?" not only was a common response to questions by the field team but a frequently heard warning to wrangling children. The answer is, of course, "He cannot. Therefore he must get along with and help his neighbors or they will not 'see' him when he is in need."

And members of the community, putting this Tarongan golden rule into operation, are by American standards overpoweringly nurturant. But for the Tarongan the system provides an always ready reservoir of reliable support drawn even from beyond the confines of his *barrio*—an environment of greater security than Americans experience. In turn, each member of the community is obligated to offer such help and support to all others when they have need of it. To Tarongans the associated social interaction compensates for any inconvenience.

Within this over-all informal obligation system there are a few more or less formally structured organizations whose members have specific reciprocal responsibilities—the cooperative men's work groups. The most frequent type is the *tagnawa*, a loosely organized group of men varying in number and composition who, for one day, work together to help one member accomplish a task too complex for him to finish alone, such as house building and leveling additional land. The host furnishes materials when required, an elaborate noon meal, and a breakfast as well if the work day begins early.

Neighbors and kin within the *sitio* and brothers from without are obligated to attend each other's *tagnawas*, and for smaller jobs this number is usually sufficient. When a more ambitious project is undertaken or if the number of obligated close relatives is small, the man giving the *tagnawa* calls on a wider circle of helpers. By explaining to heads of kin groups and other leaders how many men the job requires about a week before the *tagnawa* date, the host is assured that approximately this number will arrive.

In accepting this help the host has also accepted the obligation to attend at least some of the *tagnawas* such leaders may give or suggest he attend. By helping at such affairs with some regularity a Tarongan builds up a kind of reserve in the system, and when he holds a *tagnawa* the men he has helped will dependably appear. *Tagnawas* are thus much like the barn-raisings of the American past, solving the same problem of major construction without payment.

At present, with the increasing amounts of cash available to Tarongans, some of the usual *tagnawa* functions are being replaced by contract labor. Semipermanent contract groups are for hire or the same men who would appear at a *tagnawa* are hired, although reduced in number. Many Tarongans prefer to hire contract laboi since the difference in expense is negligible and the *tagnawa* demands time and effort from the whole household. Nevertheless, Tarongans continue to hold *tagnawas* for the largest percentage of their major work projects, believing the use of contract labor offends their neighbors and does not so well satisfy their social needs.

More rigidly structured than the *tagnawa* is the *kompang*, a work group that generally consists of six to eight men; it is used for heavy field work, such as major dike repairs after a flood. The composition of a *kompang* varies, but the core is a small group of men who work adjacent land and who are maybe kin, neighbors, or good friends. (Occasionally men from other *barrios* join because of land proximity.) Such a group will become active when there are a sufficient number of its members with roughly equivalent work needs. The *kompang* group moves from one man's land to the next, the order dependent on the urgency of the work to be done; they spend a day at each project, and if the work has not been completed, more rounds are then arranged.

The obligations of *kompang* membership are serious, and a fine, equivalent to a day's labor, is levied on any member who fails to attend. This sum enables the other members to pay someone else to take the defaulter's place, but in practice absences are very rare and usually unavoidable. The reasons for joining a *kompang* are generally pressing and the advantages of membership in good standing obvious.

The many work groups adapted to different needs provide a dependable source of labor and skills upon which any Tarongan can draw. Good carpenters are often *tagnawa* or contract organizers. Even if a man has moved his house because of disputes within his kin group, although his small kin-neighbor work group is disrupted, he can still expect his brothers to appear at his *tagnawas* and he may very well remain within their *kompang*.

The nucleus of the Tarongan's obligation and interaction system is his *sitio*. Here live his closest kin and neighbors, with all of whom he has such constantly reinforced reciprocal obligations that they blend into a simple "one helps one's neighbors." Within this group, helping ranges from giving a hand with an unsteady sled basket, through preparing roast goat at a feast and helping tie new bamboo walls, to loaning substantial amounts of money. This is true even when close neighbors are unrelated. Except for the specific obligations between members of a direct descent line, this generalized neighbor obligation system overrides kinship degree and forms a strong bond of communality between *sitio* households.

This is particularly true for the women of the *sitio,* some of whom are unrelated to anyone living in it. These women are completely dependent on their sisters-in-law and other neighbors for their daily social interaction and for help with baby-watching, feast food preparation, and such tasks. Although the women do some field work, the largest part of their day is spent in and about the houses and yards, and friendships between neighboring women are frequently stronger than their kin ties. For, in addition to being daily gossip partners, these are the women who help during childbirth, who suckle the newborn until the mother has milk, who keep watch over children playing in the yard. They share with a neighbor the produce of their vegetable patch, help pound her rice, and take part in her parties and funerals. When rifts between neighboring women occur, their lives are so entwined that the quarrel can be maintained only if one of the families moves.

The Tarongan is a social man, and although he may plow alone, his amusements are never solitary. Practice cockfighting, sweetmeats or wine gatherings in the late afternoon, evening chatting, impromptu picnics and card parties, planned dances and the gossip of prayer meetings for the dead all require other people. Most everyday amusements involve the intimate neighborhood group, but throngs of people attend planned affairs, such as feasts and dances, which strongly resemble Jane Austen balls; here marriageable boys and girls dance self-consciously under the gimlet eyes of their elders. For these affairs, related or friendly people arrive from *sitios* nearby, from *barrios* some distance away, and, occasionally, even from Poblacion. The dry season is the time of the greatest partying, and a full moon is considered requisite for evening affairs.

In any small community where members so constantly interact, there are tensions, annoyances, fancied or real reasons to take offense. And a Tarongan has no hesitation about making his feelings loudly apparent to anyone within shouting distance. Stereotypically, women quarrel often but men are more silent, fighting with their bolos when angered. Nevertheless, bolos are used most often for threatening, not chopping, and men roaring imprecations and curses are heard not infrequently throughout a *sitio.*

Since it is shameful to fight with neighbors and relatives, such arguments occasion no family support and are quickly smoothed over. Although heated, they leave little bitterness; instead they seem to clear the air and are openly enjoyed and kibitzed by noninvolved *sitio* members. Recalling that recently two men had killed each other in a not far distant barrio as the result of a long-standing series of disagreements, a Tarongan woman said of her husband's violent quarrel with his cousin, "Now there are no secret grudges to grow more serious. It is all out in the open."

Differences between members of the close kin-neighborhood group occur; one woman was censured for her treatment of her sister-in-law, and one young man was openly laughed at as a fool. In another *sitio* there had been many quarrels involving a troublesome adolescent, and another family was thought to "mistake" neighbors' chickens for their own.

Momentary quarrels over money, proper division of a tobacco crop, not sharing a butchered pig or productive vegetable patch can all ripen into major quarrels but rarely do. The most common source of serious argument is insult. Men in particular are touchy about their honor, which is broadly interpreted, and an insult from a non-neighbor results in a bolo-brandishing response. The protagonists are usually forced back, protesting and led away by their companions, still hurling dire threats, which are rarely effected before a reconciliation.

The loudest and most violent quarrel observed involved a hot-headed man and his argumentative sister-in-law. Within a short time everyone in the *sitio* was gathered around watching with avid interest, many grinning. Sympathy was definitely with the man until he hurled an insult involving an incident from years past. His raking up the past after all these years was an inexcusable breach of social convention, and most of the onlookers shifted their sympathy to his sister-in-law, but, although there was discussion among them, no one interfered with the continued screaming of threats until a bottle was thrown. The group then quickly separated the two and the sister-in-law made plans to move out of the *sitio*.

Tempers simmered for a few days, but gradually the quarrel was forgotten by those not intimately concerned, and three weeks later, when the two concerned met on the lane, one said good morning. The other replied and when questioned said with a shrug, "She said good morning to me. Who am I not to answer her?"

In this way most quarrels end and are forgotten. Past disagreements should not and generally do not set the tone of present interaction, and forgetting quarrels is encouraged by all one's neighbors. And Tarongans do forget. After their immediate anger has subsided, their adversary is still their neighbor, one whose support they need. The other neighbors have little interest in the argument but only in its speedy conciliation, and "life is pleasant when you are all friends and drink wine together." Right, justice—such words have little meaning and atonement for any act is possible.

This willingness to forgive insult or injury is less apparent in quarrels involving members of two *sitios*. On occasions of great provocation most of the kin-group members of the participants support them actively, and something not unlike a mild feud may result.

Such a feud has been in effect for a long time between two *sitios*, flaring up three times during the field period, once in a fistfight. Derogatory comments about the members of the other *sitio* are common.

A common description of members in one *sitio* by those living in the other was, "Oh, those ones! They are always only for themselves!" On one occasion a man said angrily, "Let's go there and knock them all!" When reminded that his brother lives on the periphery of that *sitio* and two households of second cousins live within it, he answered, "Oh, no, we will start with second cousins and on down."

Despite quarrels and long-standing animosities, the members of the two *sitios* appear when required at each other's *tagnawas*, funerals, and parties. Quarrels are loud and therefore noticeable, but the everyday contacts between most *sitios* are neighborly.

At large parties, for example, everyone who has any claim on the host within a kin-oriented spatial area congruent with the size of the party is invited. And special care is taken to invite close relatives and often certain social leaders from nearby *barrios*—generally people of some wealth who are capable leaders in community and social affairs. Invitations to such major parties are rarely refused, but some people come diffidently, eager to help if needed, knowing they cannot afford to return the hospitality fully. Socially prominent families may come condescendingly from a feeling of personal obligation rather than from a desire to attend, which causes some strain, but the status-conferring benefit of their presence fully compensates the host.

Giving elaborate parties at which a large number of out-of-*barrio* guests may be lodged and fed for a day or two is one showy and accepted method of achieving social distinction and proclaiming one's economic standing in an essentially classless society. For example, the most elaborate party given during the field period was the annual feast and dance given by the most socially ambitious woman to commemorate the death anniversary of her husband.

It began with a breakfast served to approximately 25 helpers and early assembled guests, followed by the main feast at noon at which between 150 and 175 people were fed. An evening meal was eaten by about 50 who had come from some distance, and later the dance was held, during which time more food was served to at least 75 people. About 15 of the guests stayed overnight, and they were given an elaborate breakfast the next morning. In all, about 5 bushels of rice, 3 pigs, 10 kilos of carabao meat, 2 goats, 8 chickens, and innumerable head baskets full of a variety of vegetables and bananas were prepared. This is enough rice to feed one person amply for half a year and is at least a year's supply of meat for him. But none of the excess food was wasted. Perishables were distributed through the *sitio,* and for a week afterward the roof of the hostess' house was covered with trays of rice being dried for reuse.

In addition to the lavish supply of food, further social distinction accrued to the hostess by the presence of a number of important out-of-*barrio* people, most of whom she had carefully maneuvered into a position of obligation and so forced them to attend. Despite the fact that many of these Poblacion guests sneered audibly at the goat, the other guests, and the makeshift arrangements, their hostess was obviously delighted with them and sure of the success of her party.

Besides work groups and parties, the most important inter*sitio* relationships are effected by the school (see Chapter 9). A Tarongan's contacts with other *barrios* are, except for the school organizations, dependent on the location and kinship orientation of his *sitio* and on the location of his land, which largely determines *kompang* membership. If a *sitio* is close both spatially and in kinship affiliation to a *sitio* of an adjacent *barrio,* more interaction may occur with this *sitio* than with other Tarong *sitios.* But more often, distance interferes, and the interaction, while important to both *sitios,* is not as frequent as that occurring within their respective *barrios.*

That municipal boundaries do not inhibit interaction is evidenced by the many friendly contacts between Tarong and its adjacent northern *barrio,* Amianan, which is the southernmost *barrio* of the next municipality. Many of the children from Amianan attend the Tarong school, and there are some kin ties between the *barrios* because of intermarriage. Although Amianan is thought of as less intimately related to Tarongans than the other adjacent *barrios,* all of which are within Municipality, the neighborliness which exists has encouraged friendly attitudes in Tarong toward the whole of Amianan's municipality. Its *poblacion* is only slightly farther from Tarong than Poblacion, and a number of Tarongans attend its market regularly.

In general, Tarongans maintain friendly relations with *barrios* with whose members they have frequent contacts but are suspicious of strangers from even a short distance. Since contacts are most frequent with the adjacent *barrios,* these, with one notable exception, are regarded as friendliest, most trustworthy, and most dependable. This classification includes four of the five *barrios* which encircle Tarong: Abagatan and Bantai to the south, Ikan to the west, and Amianan to the north. In contrast most Tarongans avoid Daya, the adjacent *barrio* to the east, whenever possible and fear its residents unless they are very close relatives.

Dayan children attend the elementary grades of the Tarong school but rarely become part of Tarongan play groups; Tarongans going to the mountain *barrios* to buy their excellent native tobacco never forget their talismans, and few are so foolhardy as to accept a drink of water in Daya. Even at parties and dances attended out of obligation, many do not touch the proferred food, for Daya is believed to be the home of witches who poison by means of strange powers and mysterious substances.

Even nonresidents are subject to such attack. One member of the field team was bewitched while attending the Daya primary school graduation ceremonies so that a bamboo splinter in the heel of his hand festered and required surgical treatment. On his return from the Poblacion doctor's office, a small group of neighbors met him to express their shame that they had not forewarned him of the dangers to be met in Daya.

In brief, the relationships which form a Tarongan's social world are classified in the same three-part manner as his relationships with the physical world—that which is "here," that which is "near," that which is "far." Primary are the intimate kin-neighbor (or *sitio*) ties, these extended farther in directions established by other kin relationships. The resulting circle may be completed by work- and school-group acquaintances, but beyond the circle all are strangers and potentially suspect.

One facet of Tarongan thinking serves to reduce strains in all aspects of daily living, and seems especially pertinent to social relationships. This is what can be translated as fate or luck. The final determination of events in this world rests not in the "real" antecedent immediate causes themselves, but in one's luck. In contrast to the usual interpretation of "fate," this luck is neither personified, pre-determined, controllable nor consistent through time. It is only chance, as in throwing a die, which decides whether a given event will be lucky or unlucky and any event, as with the die, has equal probabilities for the occurrence of good or bad.

Talismans and signs of good or bad luck are seldom given great weight despite the reputed strength of their magical properties, for luck can overide them. One's personal responsibility for events is, of course, even less potent. And while God is granted the ability by some to "change one's luck," he is also beyond control and his intervention also a matter of luck. The attitude is not "What is meant to be, will be"; it is rather "What is, is." Luck then, is the tangible symbol of an unpredictability inherent in the real world. Noteworthy is the fact that one's social relations are not considered as indeterminate and luck-controlled as events in the physical world.

The implications of this acceptance of indeterminacy permeate Tarongan life but are especially clear in the universal attitude toward inequality of economic position and the most typical values regarding aspirations and attainments. The concept of luck enables the Tarongan to resolve without conflict the classic antithesis of the West: inequality is accepted, yet people remain equal.

A man's position is, in the last analysis, dependent on the vagaries of his uncontrollable, unpredictable, unearned luck. Though the value of hard work is acclaimed, concrete results of shrewdness or unusual ability are more often attributed to luck than individual skill. So then, one may envy a neighbor's fine clothes but can one sensibly decry his luck? In fact, what is envied is not the neighbor but his luck, leaving the friendship for the neighbor relatively unaffected.

There is consequently an acceptance of the inevitable inequalities of life without hopeless resignation. One does not rail against one's luck beyond momentary curses, for luck is not a purposive thing: the biographer is regaled with few tales of past misfortunes, no protests against the "injustice of life" since neither justice nor injustice are seen as absolute or immutable; rather he is simply told "It was my luck to be poor."

Only one woman out of all the residents of the *barrio* expressed bitterness over her family's poverty. In the presence of her sister-in-law she complained at length to a member of the field team, recounting past misfortunes and bewailing her current economic status till the sister-in-law, stung by the implied insult to her brother, retaliated: "You knew when you married that we were very poor (landless)." The intent of the remark was to insultingly remind the woman that there had been no fraudulent marriage settlement claims, thus implying that the woman's family had been equally impoverished. But also obvious in the tone of her retort was the general unreasonableness of such complaints.

In any event, who is to say that one's luck may not improve? The equalizing aspect of luck is here underscored: luck is unpredictable, reversible—hence status (especially economic status) positions are held only tentatively. Every man in lowly position knows his turn may come and, fully as important, so does the man in a higher position. Indeed, unless he blatantly mismanages his affairs, he will not be held personally responsible for economic losses.

Equality is maintained in the face of differential status. So too is a degree of hope—life is good even at the bottom of the ladder and, even here, one can hope to climb a rung or two (and be satisfied with this accomplishment). The possibility of climbing is admittedly slight for the landless minority but the belief is sufficiently potent here and realistic at the higher levels to maintain itself without skepticism, reinforced by the "class" cross-cutting interactions of daily *barrio* living.

This egalitarian outlook, along with the real possibility for and values attached to relative mobility, combine to provide motivation sufficient to ensure continuity of effort. However, the recognition of good luck as the most crucial attribute of a successful man makes success as uncertain as luck itself. This sets limits on aspirations that generally reflect a realistic appraisal of what can be accomplished. No more than this is expected of the Tarongan—thus he is not consumed and driven by wanting, but is reasonably content with what he has, placing greater value on the security of his affective relationships.

⚐
⚐
⚐

Chapter 6

Political Organization and Social Control

POLITICAL ORGANIZATION

At the *barrio* level, political and social leadership are synonymous, informal, and vested in the kin group or *sitio* heads. A large *sitio* consisting of a number of kin groups may have more than one such leader but, being neighbors, they generally work together rather than compete with one another. Occasionally women are kin-group heads and therefore *barrio* leaders but their roles are less overt, and they work officially only through the school organizations. Nevertheless, these women are listened to, and their influential support is sought by other *barrio* leaders.

Francisco is an excellent example of a successful *barrio* leader. Although not wealthy, he is well off and has sent his two children to Poblacion Institute. He is greatly respected and his influence extends beyond his kin-group. Because of his organizational ability and general good sense, a number of kin-group leaders outside Sitio East generally follow him in *barrio* affairs.

Francisco's activities are typical of *barrio* leaders. He guides and helps members of his kin group and his neighbors in reaching decisions; he organizes work groups or arranges the loans often necessary to put them into effect; he contributes time to marriage arrangements and money to godchildren, and provides at least one major feast a year by which he maintains his social position. Francisco is president of the PTA and its most forceful member, devoting most of his free time to organizing work groups, soliciting donations, and disseminating ideas introduced by the schoolteachers. He is a liaison not only between his *sitio* members and the school but also between his *sitio* members and the Municipal government, frequently effecting its regulations and most certainly affecting its elections.

As with the old-time ward heeler, for Francisco no question is too inconsequential to ignore, no service is left undone. And the result is demonstrable, grateful support of his requests and his leadership. When the present Councilor, Rufino, retires, it is quite possible that Francisco will lead the whole of the Sitio East area.

Rufino, Francisco, and Tarong's three other *sitio* leaders join together on many occasions, especially for school-sponsored projects, but no one of them exercises authority over any other. Even the head schoolteacher works with these men rather than directs them, and such authority as he may enjoy is dependent on their support.

The *sitio* is, in fact, the effective functioning unit politically as well as socially. The *barrio* is a far less dependable political unit. Nor is the *barrio* of any real importance as a unit of formal governmental organization. It is integrated into the Municipality, whose mayor, vice-mayor, and 11-man council are elected at large. The councilors are then assigned districts for which they act as representatives. Since each district consists of several *barrios* and since the representatives usually live in Poblacion, there is a wide gap between governors and governed at this lowest governmental level.

To narrow this distance, the system of *barrio* lieutenancy, inaugurated by the Spanish, has been carried over into the current governmental structure. This *barrio* lieutenant is a resident of the *barrio* appointed by the Municipality to represent directly the Municipal Council, and he is empowered to enforce Municipal laws and to report violations to the mayor or police. He may also, when requested, serve as a mediator to hear disputes, but he cannot, without a court order, impose judgments or fines. He receives no compensation, and his term lasts until he retires or until others petition for a replacement. Theoretically the lieutenant, being the titular head of the *barrio,* overshadows other leaders and is the medium through which official contacts with the *barrio* are made, but evidence suggests that leadership has generally been more widely distributed. Real leaders in the *barrios* have kept cautiously clear of the lieutenant's job with its many responsibilities, little authority, and no remuneration, and have conspired among themselves to see that a man is elected who is respected but not politically potent.

Elections other than for the lieutenants (which is by show of hand vote by one representative of each economically autonomous household) are similar to elections in the United States and are held to fill municipal, provincial, and national offices. The Tarongan is related to this formal political structure through Poblacion leaders to whom loyalty and support are given by whole families and kin groups under the guidance of their leaders. The Poblacion leaders are obligated in return to support these *barrio* leaders and their followers —the relationship is the same kind of personal one found between *barrio* leaders and their supporters and is maintained by the same network of mutual obligations. These Poblacion leaders are usually landlords, and the bonds of the landlord-tenant relationship serve to emphasize further the mutual obligations.

Throughout the formal governmental structure, at all levels, the political parties are of great importance, but their role is somewhat different than that of political parties in the West. The Poblacion leaders are associated with the two major national parties, with whose next-level leadership they maintain the same kind of obligation system as the *barrio* leaders have with them. To vote for every man on the party ticket indicates great loyalty to a personally known leader, not necessarily to the principles for which the party stands. If a family's loyalties are divided between leaders belonging to opposing parties, a conference is held at which obligations to the opposing men are evaluated and the distribution of family votes determined. There are occasional leaders—the late President Ramon Magsaysay is a good example—with enough *charisma* to attract votes from men obligated to other parties, but their occurrence is not frequent, and their effect is often limited to their own candidacy and not to their party. The political parties are rarely in themselves primary causes of voting behavior, but they are, by long support of their associated leaders, dear to the hearts of Tarongans, who vehemently argue their merits.

The registration records for the 1955 elections are very impressive: out of Tarong's 161 adults, 104 are eligible and all of this number are registered. The 57 ineligibles are almost entirely illiterate and cannot handle the ballots which require that all choices be written in full. This voting record indicates the Tarongan's interest in politics as well as his feeling of obligation to vote for his leaders. And in view of this personal concern it is not surprising that, as a campaign becomes heated, tempers also rise. When fights and brawls occur near election time, people nod and say, "Politics" with regret but also with understanding.

Throughout the 1955 campaign the candidates for Municipal offices toured the *barrios,* sometimes informally to chat with leaders, sometimes with wine and loudspeakers to hold a rally. Once about 40 women leaders of one party invaded Tarong, lustily singing party songs, and each party held at least one major rally with many speakers, more loudspeakers, music, and the inevitable wine. Rumors about candidates spread, election promises were discussed, and speakers at any event turned the occasion into a political platform.

Interest in politics is not limited to campaign periods themselves. At the Tarong school graduation a verbal battle broke out during the speeches, which were made by elected municipal officials of both parties. A particularly vicious attack on a popular official goaded Francisco, the PTA president, into a rage, and in his final speech he roundly denounced the attacker for his ready promises of help for the school, none of which had ever materialized.

As the performing schoolchildren looked on with interest, the Poblacion supporters of the denounced official gathered around him, muttering, many with hands on their pistols. Francisco's kin group vanished, to return again very quickly and greatly enlarged, with bolos prominently displayed.

At the conclusion of the program, everyone not concerned left hurriedly; children were whisked to safety while their elders stood watching the two groups of men glaring at each other. Despite the hysterics of a few women, the protagonists kept their followers calm, and soon each group had gone its way—but six months later, at a rally in the next municipality, a similar argument resulted in three deaths.

SOCIAL CONTROL

Except for capital crimes, which occur very rarely, deviant behavior is handled by informal action within the appropriate social unit. The head of the nuclear household is presumed capable of handling misbehavior within his household—especially that of minors. If a man cannot control a son who still lives with him, he receives scant sympathy from others: "It is his own fault. He was not severe enough when the boy was young." A rebellious child must have been consistently, and rather publicly, punished in order for his parents to be exonerated of blame for his later misbehavior.

The next larger unit of informal social control is the kin-neighbor group. Disagreements of consequence between members of this group should be mediated and resolved within the group: "For others to know of our quarrels is a shame to us all." The Philippine Civil Code itself encourages such settlements. Finally, disputes between kin-neighborhood groups within a *sitio* should also be handled informally if possible.

The strong dependence of Tarongans on one another at the local level makes such social control not only possible but very effective. The threat of ostracism and the loss of local support are far more powerful than the fear of a jail sentence. Such threats can be very effective even in such extreme cases as "blood feuds." A man from Daya vowed that he would kill a policeman, who had been responsible for the shooting of the Dayan's brother a few years previously. At a party in Sitio East, an abortive attempt was made on the policeman's life. The Dayan's uncle, a rich, childless man, who had been helping him financially, said clearly and before many witnesses, "If you do not hear what I say now, do not from here on expect me to help you in any hardship. I will not count myself as obligated to help you or protect you in the difficulties which will result from this act." The Dayan gave up his attempt and later cited this threat of severing family bonds as the major deterrent to carrying out his pledge.

Difficulties that cannot be settled at the *sitio* level by the kin group, or those involving two *sitios*, may be taken to the *barrio* lieutenant for a hearing if the parties so desire. Since the lieutenant has no official judiciary status, he can serve only as a mediator and press for reconciliation or recompense if the kin groups involved can be brought to some agreement. Despite the impotency of the *barrio* lieutenants in Tarong, pressures are strong to seek their mediation and to confine disagreements within the *barrio* just as they are confined, when possible, within the *sitio*.

If mediation proves ineffective, the next step is to bring the matter before the Poblacion justice of the peace, a step not taken lightly, for it involves litigation and most often expenses greater than the disagreement merits. Only two Tarongan cases in three years reached the justice of the peace.

A Tarongan has few dealings with the courts, since most disputes are handled at the *barrio* level and involve trespass and minor assault charges. Major crimes against persons and property, which must be handled in Poblacion or the provincial capital, are infrequent. Within Tarong there has been one suicide (an adult woman) and one murder within memory of the oldest residents. Throughout Municipality murders are infrequent and are usually the result of personal, long-standing grudges; however, Tarong's murder was the fatal stabbing of a girl by her jilted fiance. Occurring almost 25 years ago, it was still spoken of.

Banditry has been a problem in the Municipality at various times. Shortly after World War II, a small bandit group located near Tarong was driven out by the police, with no injury to the inhabitants. Since then Municipality had been free of such activity until toward the end of the field period when its southernmost *barrios* were terrorized by such a group, which killed three men within a few weeks before the police killed some of the bandits and drove the rest into hiding.

A wife found adulterous, although she should not be killed, could be thoroughly beaten by her husband with general approval. Adultery, however, is rare, and only a few tales of wives running away to live with other men could be recounted of still-living Tarongan women. Two cases of rape were spoken of, but neither were physical assault, rather, what Americans would term accosting. Both cases, one during the field period, the other more than 20 years ago, brought prompt and violent reactions, for both involved young, marriage-age girls. One resulted in a jail sentence and the other stopped just short of the formal courts because of parental pleas and promises of better behavior. Theft is very rare, members of a household being far more likely than neighbors to pilfer its cash hoard.

Although crime is punished effectively, lapses from the customary business ethic are not. Redress for unfair tenancy practices is difficult. A case in point involved a poor widow and her sister who are largely dependent on Rufino for work, for, owning no carabao they cannot tenant. The two women grew a large amount of tobacco for Rufino on his land, doing all the work except the initial plowing. The customary tenantry shares would have given them two thirds of the crop, and they hoped for half. However, at harvest Rufino's wife and aged father-in-law also picked (for a brief time) and the entire crop was divided into five equal parts, only two going to the widow and her sister. The difference in cash represented the food supply for a number of months, and the women openly cried over the unfairness.

They received considerable sympathy and promises of food, even from members of Rufino's kin group, but little else could be done. No one was in a position to force Rufino to greater fairness, rather, almost all the *sitio* was greatly obligated to his leadership and the women were related to no one of importance. But such dealings, if frequent, would weaken his leadership among others than his family group, and recognition of this serves as a partial check.

Everyday behavior is governed by the Tarongan's strong sense of identity with his *sitio* group, the intensive training in neighborliness that a Tarongan child receives, and the constant *barrio*-wide publicity of each Tarongan's acts, for someone always sees anything he may do. At evening porch gatherings, parties, prayer meetings—anywhere groups gather—the most common and most interesting activities are gossip about people not present and teasing of those who are among the group. This teasing although friendly is accurate in regard to facts and mercilessly embarrassing. Although one does not tease someone of much higher status, others of that status may, and so no one is exempt. It is an important child-training technique and a major method of enforcing proper social behavior.

Furthermore, the *sitio* and *barrio* can close themselves to one who, though lawful, behaves in too aberrant a fashion. Two Tarongans, a man and a woman, were ostracized in this way during the field period. The young woman, Maria, was ostracized because she was believed to be a witch. Her parents, living in Daya, were well-known witches and their daughter is believed to have inherited this power, having presumably used it a number of times to make Tarongans ill. Maria lived at the eastern edge of Tarong near Daya, and all her social contacts and her husband's economic activities were associated with Dayans. Maria was not spoken to by most Tarongans and was greatly feared.

The Tarongan man, Adriano, had inherited lands producing seven *uyones*, considerable wealth. Now all but a one-*uyon* paddy is mortgaged, and even Adriano has no hope of redeeming his property. The mortgage money has been completely dissipated in rum, and family finances are in such bad shape that Adriano's wife, who is from Ikan, now peddles fish in Tarong and nearby *barrios* for her relatives.

Adriano's drunkenness is as continuous as he can afford and very noisy. He rampages throughout the *barrio,* shouting threats and boasts and sleeping anywhere when exhausted. (He has delusions of being selected by the spirits to be an important medicine man, but no one else shares his opinion.) Adriano has beaten his wife so severely that she has often gone home, and once her brothers forced Adriano to appear in court because of the bolo slashes she had received.

Her brothers defend her but cannot support her and so encourage her return to Adriano in spite of his behavior. Partly as a result of this treatment, his wife has retreated into day dreams which occasionally frighten her so that she screams, "The devil is chasing me!" and runs crazily into her house.

To other Tarongans Adriano's behavior is contemptuous, and he is a favorite example to point out to a wasteful child, "So you are deaf to what I say? Do you want to become like Adriano and sleep in the fields?" Adriano's closest relatives in Tarong are only first cousins, so he has not been accepted into any neighbor group and is invited to no parties; if he does attend a gathering, he is not sent away but neither is he made welcome. He is hired now and again as a carpenter, occasionally accepted in a work group, and, when working, people are friendly but he is never visited socially.

Adriano's children, four boys and one girl all under 13 years, suffer perhaps more than their parents—there is no kin group to give them the additional support, training, and affection usually relied on; their clothes are not taken care of properly; their meals are sporadic, and the older ones must work hard helping their father farm, for he has no kin to do so, and then often watch him dissipate all the money they helped earn. Nearby children are told not to play with Adriano's children and most do not; at school they are shunned or laughed at, the boys sometimes fought with. It will be difficult for the children to marry respectably when they are older, for "See what his (or her) parents are—he may be the same!" However, if any of these children by obvious effort works hard and becomes a proper Tarongan, others will encourage him, and, if he succeeds without question, his past will be forgotten because, after all, "The son is not the father."

In striking contrast to the ostracism accorded Maria and Adriano is the tolerance of homosexuals and transvestites. Two males (both transvestites) and three females (one a transvestite) had lived in the area. Such persons are commented upon, joked about, but treated with propriety if they are otherwise respectable. The attitude was expressed by "It is their luck to be so. One would not berate a cripple for his bad luck so why the girl or boy who prefers the same sex?"

The important point is that the homosexuals seem to have conducted themselves in all ways save this one as decent, socially responsible neighbors. For a group with generally accepting attitudes toward personal idiosyncracies and toward sexuality, a preference for unusual sexual relations in no way outweighs the proper performance of social obligations. But when an Adriano or Maria consciously commits acts against the group, punishment is justified.

✻
✻
✻

Chapter 7

The Supernatural Environment

CHRISTIANITY

Artifacts of Roman Catholicism are widespread, but their functions have assimilated to and most often fused with those of the indigenous belief system. Evaluation of assimilation of Catholic beliefs to this system is more difficult, some reinterpretations of rituals and their significance apparently having been introduced by the church itself to simplify understanding of doctrine. However, if performance (with its explanations and attitudes) can be considered sufficient evidence, the Tarongan belief system has been enlarged rather than modified through its contact with the Catholic church.

"Jesus, Maria, Apo Dios (God)" have become the Tarongan trinity (the Holy Ghost is at best a confused concept), recognized as omnipotent and supreme, but in practical effect powerless and remote, for there is no contact with them—except perhaps in the dim and awful Poblacion church. Since supplication of spirits is useless, praying to

God for help or guidance is unknown. Only at the novenas after a death does praying occur, the text chanted aloud by a leader, the refrains by the predominantly female group.

Creation is generally attributed to God, but this is a matter of no concern to the Tarongans; other Biblical matter (including Crucifixion implications) is either unknown or hazily misunderstood by a few. The Christian afterlife has been modified: after death the spirit goes to Purgatory, known primarily because the term occurs with frequency in the novena texts, where it resides a brief time to accustom itself to its new condition. Then it moves on to Heaven where it may reside permanently, leaving at will to observe, from the ridgepole, the household it left at death. The latter abode, being of far greater interest to the spirit as well as more sociable, is generally frequented in preference to Heaven. There is no Hell although some spirits, especially those of evil-doers, wander an earthbound limbo as ghosts, malevolently seeking revenge.

Excepting for the occasional civil marriage, church baptism, marriage, and funeral rites, are never omitted. Baptisms are likely to be put off until a convenient date, often until after rice harvest,* for the ceremony at the church is brief, but the following noon feast is as large and elaborate as the family can provide. A child usually has two godparents, who attend the baptism and thereafter are expected to take an interest in the child's welfare, expressed largely in terms of occasional small gifts of money, the first at the baptism feast, and sponsorship of his wedding. Since the favor of those in power can be of considerable advantage, people of importance are sought as godparents and *sitio* and *barrio* leaders often are obligated in this way to a large number of families. But unlike the *compadrasco* system in Latin America, these obligations are not as strong as those toward one's own kin group.

That portion of a funeral involving the church or its priest is small: last rites are administered when requested but poor families, unable to donate money to repay the service and awed by the priest, rarely request them. Funeral services in the church vary as to elaboration, depending on the financial status of the household, but a Tarongan funeral prayer rarely lasts longer than 10 minutes and there is no further service at the cemetery. Funeral masses are not said, being too expensive and too presumptuous for a *"barrio* person."

---

* In Spanish times an infant had to be baptized within 3 days of its birth or the person bringing the child was flogged. This practice (attested to by Church records) undoubtedly contributed to the universal acceptance of the custom of baptism.

Among other church observances in common practice is the singing of an Ilocano translation of the Passion during Lent. Three or four women, at the house of a *sitio* leader, sing a semimelodic chant in a strange falsetto; the rest of the *sitio* members gather about the *sala* and porch to listen for as long as two hours. In addition, on certain religious holidays, such as All Saint's Day and Good Friday, no work is done, for it would bring bad luck or accidents. On Sunday no one leaves for market or works during the early morning hours; instead people wait until a time when "Mass must be over."

Although almost all Tarongans are Roman Catholic, three families profess faith in the Philippine Independent church—better known as the Aglipayan church, a Philippine-oriented group which followed a native bishop who broke away from the Roman Catholic church. But Tarongans show little concern over religious affiliation, and in general are unaware of any but superficial distinctions between faiths. The basic spirit-belief system, of far greater importance for daily living, is the same to all.

During the field period, religious instruction was introduced in the school, one half hour three days a week before the other classes. Permission slips for attendance had to be signed by the parents, but there were no refusals, even from the Aglipayans. The instructors were two unemployed teachers from Bantai who received a peso a day from the Poblacion priest for their work. The instruction was in Ilocano and English and was simple—a few prayers, songs, and religious stories. The children attended these classes quite regularly and enjoyed them, in no small part because of the chorus-teaching methods employed.

Except for baptisms, weddings, and funerals, contacts with the church are rare. Most Tarongans never attend mass. This was apparently less true 20 or so years ago when Poblacion had an active priest who established women's church societies. Five elderly Tarongan women had belonged to these and are the prayer leaders and the ones who baptize in emergencies. This priest had also held one mass a year in the *barrio* for three consecutive years before his reassignment.

His successor, the current priest, has allowed *barrio* religious activities to languish and finally disappear. No mass has been held in Tarong during his tenure. Twice a year, during the annual fiesta days in honor of Municipality's patron saint and during Holy Week, most Tarongans go to Poblacion to see the processions of the statues and, in particular, to attend the fiesta fair and the *Comedia,* a stylized musical play continuing throughout the three-day fiesta. Although there are a number of special church observances throughout the year, only these two are attended in any number by Tarongans.

The behavior of an average Tarongan woman who feels she should at least enter the church on these days (men feel less compelled to do so) is the best description of her attitude toward the church. Over her head she carefully arranges a black scarf and she may hold a handkerchief but not a rosary, for she either does not have one or does not know its use if her household owns one. Nervously she waits near the door until a few friends join her, all adjusting their scarves. Huddled together the women slide into the church past the holy-water font, which they do not use although they cross themselves. They stand for a little while, gaping at the candles and numerous statues lining the church; one may remember to bob in a haphazard genuflection. Then, retreating to one side, they watch the Poblacion people entering pews with assurance or moving along the side aisles, praying before the statues. In a few moments the women nudge each other, whisper a few words, and slide out through the doorway. Once outside, they take a deep breath, push back their scarves, and smile at each other shakily and with evident relief.

THE SPIRIT WORLD

In dark brushy places, at shadowed water holes, under large and isolated trees, about the houseyards, even within one's own house, the supernatural world is manifested—always unpleasantly for the Tarongan. Except for this general unpleasantness, the nature and circumstance of contact with the supernatural are unpredictable—a man can only shrug his shoulders, trusting to his talismans and to good luck. Still, this very unpredictability relieves the Tarongan of a large part of his concern over supernatural behavior, for no amount of worry or precaution beyond the usual can be of value. Although his shrug eliminates hope of controlling a future event, it also relieves him of anxiety and responsibility for the event.

Luckily one's house area is relatively safe from the intrusion of malevolent supernatural beings, only the spirits of Tarongan ancestors being commonly encountered here. These spirits, especially those recently dead, spend much of their time unseen and unheard about the houses, yards, and fields they knew best when they were alive and over which they still feel a proprietary interest. Their presence is noted by the rocking of a favorite chair, footsteps along a porch, creaking of a once-used loom. In general, the attitude of these ancestral spirits is friendly—often too friendly, wherein lies the danger. For if they touch a human, he is chilled and develops fever, headache, and often vomiting for which he must be cured by various simple remedies.

The danger from ancestral spirits is greatest immediately after a death, for the spirit is not used to his new condition and may try to greet his friends who have come to pray for him. There are a few common methods of avoiding this contact: pulling the lobe of one ear and repeating certain words when entering the *sala,* patting the forehead a few times, and so forth—all being discreet gestures to give no offense to the family. However, since the likelihood of a spirit being interested in the living decreases with time, these avoidance practices are used only for the first few visits after death. But children remain susceptible, sometimes developing this spirit-illness by lying about on porches or in doorways where spirits are likely to pass.

Ancestral spirits are remembered on all important occasions, and food is set out for them at the household shrine at all special events, such as feasts or candy making. Some Tarongans say to neglect this custom will result in stomachaches, but most feel it is merely a friendly gesture to include them within the family's activities. The food set out for the spirits is later eaten and brings good luck.

When the Tarongan moves farther from his *sitio* area, he does so with greater likelihood of meeting spirits who are maliciously rather than unintentionally harmful. The least dangerous of these are the *kiba'an* who are not greatly feared, for they do not kill or cause serious damage. The *kiba'an* are small, mischievous, humanlike creatures akin to leprechauns, who live in thickly wooded places. They resemble Filipinos except for their feet, which are reversed and leave a distinctive footprint, and their hair, which is very long and trails along the ground behind them. They take pride in the length of their hair and will steal human hair to tie onto their own; thus care must be taken when going through known dwelling places of the *kiba'an.* One woman in Ikan had lost all her hair to the *kiba'an* and was forced to keep her head covered with a scarf.

The *kiba'an* live much like humans and at times can be heard washing clothes, pounding rice, or cleaning pots at the wells. They too eat rice, often stealing it from humans and removing a quantity of the rice in such a way as to leave a perfectly cylindrical hole in that which is left. But, since the *kiba'an* are afraid of fishnets, these may be placed over such containers, and their contents will be safe. A few intrepid Tarongans have attempted to capture a *kiba'an* by the use of fishnets, for his captor can obtain a mantle of invisibility and a pot that will cook enough rice for a family even if only two grains are placed in it. To date, none of these attempts has been successful.

The *kiba'an* also cause children's skin diseases. The cure for these is to have a relative of the child go to the *kiba'an* dwelling place at night and leave a lit candle there. The person then calls: "I am giving you light now, but please go also and cure the skin disease of the child." This is generally effective because *kiba'an* like light but rarely can get it.

Far more dangerous, although seldom met, are the *black ones*, malevolent beings who change size and shape at will but always remain very black. They live in large, isolated trees far from human habitation and fall upon the unlucky man walking beneath their tree, crushing him to death. No Tarongans have been killed by the *black ones* to the knowledge of current residents, but many know and avoid specific trees inhabited by them. The only safeguard is to break sticks noisily in a show of strength when their presence is suspected.

Sa'ero, the most powerful and malicious supernatural beings, also prefer to live in large trees or in brushy dark places—anywhere people pass infrequently. These awesome beings may appear in any form to one by whom they wish to be seen, yet remain invisible to others about him. Most often their presence is indicated by a loud crack, as of a whip—the noise made by their very rapid flight through the air. When a Tarongan hears this sound or suspects their presence for any other reason, he turns quickly away from its source, for if he looks on them, they may "take his vital organs" and he will quickly die.

Sa'ero are invariably evil intentioned, even luring or stealing people from their houses to do them harm. And there is no sure protection against the *sa'ero,* for "only God they cannot overpower." However, a crucifix, the symbol of God, may turn them away or lessen their power, and the household shrine can generally be relied on to keep them outside. However, during the field period an old man was "taken" down the house ladder one morning, where, neighbors apparently interfering, he was left bleeding from the mouth and delirious. Continued attempts to take him were made by the *sa'ero* throughout the morning, at one point his relatives being compelled to restrain him from leaping out of a window in their company.

Fortunately Tarongans are not troubled by them frequently, for they are not numerous and so spread their malevolency over large areas. They remain somewhat remote and among more Church-conscious Tarongans are equated with the Christian devil: "The *sa'ero* were in early times in open combat with God. God is all good, the *sa'ero* all evil."

More often the *sa'ero,* for practical curing or precautionary measures, are grouped with the largest class of beings with whom Tarongans have the most frequent contacts—the *not-humans*. This rather elastic term also includes those beings attracted by the smell given off by fresh blood * and entrails. At birth, for example, if the spirits gathering about can "take the blood smell, they take with it the life of the child." In the same way the blood smell emanating from a bleeding cut or wound can cause death, and in such circumstances counteractive devices must be employed—ash applications for cuts, smoke for childbirth.

By far the greatest number of illnesses, accidents, and deaths are attributed to the *not-humans*. A girl falls out of a tree while picking fruit because she was pushed by *not-humans*. The traveler takes the wrong turning because the *not-humans* have changed the appearance of the pathways to confuse and mislead him. A woman miscarries because a *not-human*, jealous of her pregnancy, struck her. A man dies of a heart attack because he accidentally bumped against a *not-human* while cutting food for his carabao. The state of severe and sudden illness, such as a "stroke," is invariably ascribed to the angry retaliation of a *not-human* who has been hit in some way. During such epidemics as smallpox, it is the *not-humans* who carry the disease, standing outside houses at night calling "Apo" or throwing pebbles at the shutters. Whoever opens the door or shutter lets them and the disease into the house. One old man who, during the epidemic of 1919, lost his three children within a week to smallpox laid its introduction to the *not-humans*, "who were angry because I hit them when I was cutting firewood on the hill."

Although treatments for illnesses contracted through the anger of the *not-humans* are known, their value is uncertain. Daily precautions are of some value: talismans shield their owner from many harmful events; avoidance of dark and brushy spots minimizes contacts and, since complete avoidance of these spots is impossible, it is wise to warn the *not-humans* of one's approach by calling "You, you" or, if a bundle must be dropped or growth cut, "It's coming."

At night, such measures are less effective, for the *not-humans* follow the dark as it closes in about the houses. Tarongans fasten their shutters and stay indoors if possible; when they must go out, they carry a light and stay close to the house unless they are part of a safely large group. Only on full-moon nights, when additional light is almost superfluous, is it safe for Tarongans to gather in the yards to boil peanuts, chat, or practice dueling with long, hardwood swords.

Contacts with *not-humans* are, for most Tarongans, limited to the

---

* Menstrual blood, sexual discharges, and other exuviae, being normal, are not included in this category.

fortuitous and accidental, often unknown except through subsequent diagnosis. But a few men—less often women—have been in communication with supernaturals, and, after a period of erratic behavior and often illness induced by them, have become their intimates. These persons "who speak to those we cannot see" become medicine men (*sirkanos*), deriving special medicinal knowledge and diagnostic skills from the *not-humans* and able in conversation with them to effect remedies for supernaturally caused illness. However, such powers are dangerous, and relations with these men are colored by awe and fear.

Selection of individuals who will become *sirkanos* is sudden and inexplicable and rests entirely with the *not-humans*. A man has no presentiment of being changed, but the usual sign is a period of behavioral insanity, often including frenzied attacks on others, thought to be caused by the appearance of supernaturals. Most *sirkanos* recover and function normally. The following account of the selection of a *sirkano* now practicing in an adjacent barrio is typical.

The man, Pacifico, went one day to catch frogs in the paddies and found a very large one. He reached for it but it hopped away just as his hand closed about it. He went toward it again and it seemed to be larger than it had been! Again it almost allowed itself to be caught, escaping at the last moment and again it seemed larger than before. Pacifico continued to follow the teasing frog which got bigger at each jump until he realized: "This is no frog—it is one of the *not-humans*."

Turning, Pacifico ran home but, because of his great fear, continued to run as if crazy, hitting anyone in his way. His neighbors caught him and took him to his house where they tied him, while he struck out and shouted. He continued like this for some time, fighting with *those we cannot see:* he was afraid and did not want to accept the relationship. Finally he surrendered to them and became normal again—for if you do not give in they may cause your death—and he became a well-known *sirkano*.

Despite the danger, a man will occasionally withstand the *not-humans* successfully, refusing to accede to their demands. Prudencio Navarro of Sitio East, a skilled midwife, is one of these few. He was selected, with no forewarning, at the age of 25, shortly after the birth of his second child and while he was still acquiring his midwifery skills under the tutelage of a renowned old woman, Melchora. Here is his account of the experience.

I was near Ikan, harvesting maguey with a friend one bright moonlit night after plowing. The maguey was high there then and we gathered till very late. I had not fed my carabao so I went a little way off to cut corn stalks while my friend went home. Suddenly I felt very tired and lay down on the ground where it had been cleared. But I was restless and could not sleep, so I tied my carabao to a stake and started along the path home.

Near the lane I saw a small spotted dog coming toward me. It was hazy and only as big around as my wrist—like a new-born puppy. I bent and picked up a few pebbles to scare it away and when I looked up again it was as high as my knee! I was afraid and stopped, but the dog came closer and when it reached me it was as big as a horse! I had to look up at it. I started to throw a stone but before I could throw, it vanished—there was nothing there at all.

I knew then it had been one of those who are *not-human* and I was afraid and worried, for I still had a long way to go. I walked toward the brook and thought "They will be waiting for me there," so I took out my bolo, which was a long one and very sharp and shining. I tucked it under my arm, holding that arm tight against my side, for then it looks as if you had sliced your body. They are afraid if you do this. They think: "He is very brave—he even slashes himself with his own bolo and does not cry out!" In this way I reached home safely and was not further troubled.

I ate a large meal of cold rice, for I had not eaten since midday, and lay down to sleep on the porch where it was cool, with my head on the *sala* step. I slept for a little but was awakened suddenly—the house was crumbling, falling to pieces around me! I thought of the child, still unable to walk, and shouted and wrestled with the walls to save him. When I came to my senses there were many people around—it had been difficult for them to restrain me, so hard had I fought them. Melchora, then old, knew these seizures and helped hold me, muttering things no one else could understand.

I was not well for some time after this, and each night *those we cannot see* came to take me. I struggled and argued. My wife was frightened and awakened me because I shouted in my sleep and struck out. Many times she saved me. One night several appeared to me in a dream—some were white like Spaniards, some brown like us—and they told me if I did as they wished, they would help me get a midwife's license. But I answered: "I do not need a paper!" and they were angry.

One day after this, in the early dawn when I was grazing my carabao, I felt suddenly very tired and with no thought about it I lay down to rest. One of the *not-humans* appeared—like a Spaniard with a long beard—he wound a rope about my arm and jumped at me! I woke and jumped to my feet and pulled out my bolo, but he laughed and vanished. I went right home and became very sick—blood flowed from me with my feces.

That night they appeared again and told me what it was they wanted: they would give me the power to raise nine, even from death—but I would be the tenth to die! There were many more alluring promises, and I would have accepted if I had not had to die. But because of this, I refused their power and fought them. They made me very sick for more than a month— I could not rise from the mat, yet felt like a bit of cotton floating in the air —they almost destroyed me! Many *sirkanos* were called to save me, but they could do nothing. I was lucky, and finally those who were tormenting me became discouraged and left me. But if I had not been the tenth to die, it would have been an extraordinary power!

MAGIC AND WITCHCRAFT

The principles basic to all Tarongan magic are first that similar events are believed to produce similar effects; and second, that certain objects and certain rituals are believed to ward off undesired events or to bring about desired ones. The power in the former lies in the similarity; the power in the latter resides in the object or ritual itself.

The basis by which events are recognized as similar often seems far fetched to persons unfamiliar with Tarongan culture. Thus to dream of catching fish foretells good luck in money matters, and many a Tarongan, after such a dream, will feel justified in borrowing money to bet on a cockfight; or, a dream of having one's teeth pulled is believed to foretell the death of a member of the family. This latter omen can be counteracted by, immediately upon arising, breaking a pot in the doorway, or by biting the trunk of a tree to transfer the omen. As Tarongans, fond of a pun, explain: "You pull the teeth of the dream."

The Tarongan list of omens is long and a few examples will suffice to indicate their flavor. If a kingfisher calls from a perch near a house, something serious—perhaps death—will affect someone in that house. A mound of white ants under the house brings money to the household; "Its luck will grow as the mound grows." If a gekko lizard croaks outside the house, it foretells the arrival of a guest.

As has been suggested above, many of these omens can be negated by certain rituals or talismans. The talismans have much wider significance, however. They are of two kinds, the *anib* which protects against misfortune and the *talibagot* which brings good luck.

As one informant put it, "*Anibs* are our shield." They protect their owners against *not-humans,* against illness, against witchcraft, lightning, robbers, and so on. There is a cluster of long established *anibs* basic to ritual and used by all Tarongans to ward off ill. These are salt, garlic or ginger, hot pepper, wine or vinegar, *anglem* (various kinds and mixtures of smoke), and the Christian cross. This by no means completes the list of *anibs.* There are many of less wide acceptance than the basic list either because they represent personal beliefs or because they are out of fashion.

The use of *anibs* is exemplified by the following practices. It is believed that if one eats outside this will make the envious *not-humans* cause inflammations of the neck and mouth or a toothache. This danger may be avoided by sprinkling salt about before eating. Similarly, a pregnant woman is likely to arouse the envy of *not-humans* if she goes outside at night. She will be reasonably safe, however, if she loosens her hair, letting it fall over her face, and carries *anibs* of salt and garlic or ginger. Pepper *anibs* are believed to be especially effective against disease-carrying spirits and are hung outside the house during epidemics. For added protection a plate of salt is set at the top of the ladder. Another method of dealing with such spirits, was described as follows: "When you hear their footsteps and hear them bumping against the walls, open the shutter just enough and sprinkle vinegar or wine and a little salt out quickly. This will drive them away."

The other two *anibs* in general use, smoke and the cross, are also effective against thunder and lightning. The smoke (*anglem*) is produced by burning a mixture of substances slowly on embers in a small container, to produce as much smoke as possible. Generally bits of the "kitchen rag" are burned and certain leaves—often garlic or ginger; church incense when it can be procured is considered especially effective.

These generally accepted *anibs,* with the exception of the cross, apparently owe their counteractive properties to their strong taste or smell, which repels *not-humans.* Since they are always available, they are in constant use. To hang pepper on the wall when sickness is about is as casual a gesture to a Tarongan as our taking aspirin when we feel a cold coming on and has no more or less awesome overtones—both are simply sensible precautions. The effectiveness of the cross as an *anib* derives its power from the Catholic church rather than from its natural properties. A cross of any sort, even the sign of the cross, is a good *anib,* but one fashioned out of palm leaves which have been blessed in church on Palm Sunday is particularly strong. It is believed to be effective against sickness and thunder and lightning if it is hung in the window of the house. The household shrine statues or pictures are also *anibs* against bad luck in general.

Far greater in number and variety are those *anibs* used by many but not all Tarongans, and their functions are also more varied although none are required for ritual practices. The largest group of these are unusual roots, seeds, and nuts most often bought from *sirkanos* or Igorot and Tinguian peddlers from the mountains. But almost any distinctively formed object may have *anib* qualities and is likely to be tried by its finder. For example, from Cagayan have come a number of roots which startlingly resemble a human hand. Such a root, kept in a bottle of coconut oil, is very powerful and, when hung from the middle of the ridgepole, discourages all manner of bad luck, even robbers. The oil itself, in which the root is kept, becomes a strong counteractive agent to be used during the massage-cure of certain illnesses.

A potted spiky cactus, rare in Tarong, is a deterrent to witches as are, one man avows, the string of honey-combs hung from his porch. Those *anibs* specifically against witches are called *somang* and frequently not only shield their owner but also force the evil back against the witch. One Tarongan woman had a powerful *somang* with her one day at market where she met a famous witch in the crowd. He glared at her, but her *somang* turned his evil glance back, and he fainted there in the market. His guilt was in this way clearly demonstrated, as was the efficacy of the *somang*.

There is probably no Tarongan who does not carry a *somang*, if not habitually, at least when leaving the *barrio*, and whose house is not protected by another *somang* and two or more *anibs*. Even animals are provided with *anibs*. Chickens are thus protected against epidemics, and when a pig disease is believed approaching, wooden crosses are sometimes placed beside the pig trough.

That class of talismans which is *for* rather than *against* specific events is called *talibagot* and presumed to bring good luck. These may be hung in the house or carried on one's person, as are *anibs*, and most Tarongans have one, but the variety is tremendous. There are a few generally recognized *talibagot*, such as the stone "lightning's tooth," which brings good luck. A man living near the mountains has one which he rubs over his dogs' noses before deer hunting and which has proved very useful.

Any unusual thing is as likely to be *talibagot* as *anib*. For example, a tooth of a child born with teeth brings good luck, a caul saved after birth brings luck to the family's financial dealings, and so on. If the unusual is not classifiable immediately, however, such as the birth of a child with one finger missing, the true meaning of the event may become clear with time. For example, a child in Ikan, the youngest of nine, was born with a large egglike swelling between his eyes. Shortly after his birth the family, which had been very poor, began to improve its economic status and is now doing well. The child, therefore, was considered a *talibagot* and the favorite of the family.

In addition to an acceptance of omens and talismans, Tarongans share in the widespread belief in exuvial magic. The first fingernail cuttings of a child placed in crevices of the house ladder will ensure that a child have a good grasp and not fall; a whisker pulled from a new puppy and buried under the house ladder will keep a dog from straying. Beliefs about exuviae are not associated with witchcraft, however: A person cannot be harmed through his hair cuttings or fingernail parings.

Harmful magic or witchcraft is, however, believed in by Tarongans. Typically a witch is a man or woman who has powers, presumably inherited, to do great harm to others. Although he may harm others unintentionally, he usually does so purposefully.

Witchcraft attacks produce illnesses ranging from chills or fever to death and are most often due to unprovoked malice on the part of the witch. Understandably, these people are feared and hated, but the pattern of coping with them is avoidance as far as is practicable and the use of *somangs*. To confront a witch with evidence of her treachery and demand retraction of her evil is unthinkable, for, angered, "Who knows what she might not do—she could kill us all!" * In effect witches are dealt with in much the same way as are malicious supernaturals— by avoidance, reliance on *anibs*, and, if these fail, the arcane knowledge of the *sirkano*.

The specific methods of bewitching vary; some witches are thought to use mysterious and potent objects, others apparently do not. In either case it is the innate power of the witch that propels the evil force into the victim, the object providing the specific kind of illness or acting only as a reinforcement. If one is a witch, all the necessary power with which to do harm is present—magic objects and devices serve only to elaborate and refine.

If the evil is to be transmitted through the air, this may be accomplished by a "fierce look," by a pushing gesture of the hand, or by a slight stamp of a pointing foot. Media other than air are also popular, and a bamboo slat of the floor between witch and victim may carry evil; drinking water or food can easily be contaminated; indeed, anything the witch may have handled is suspect as a transmitting device for his poisons. The only limit to a witch's power is the necessity for at least initial contact with the victim or the transmitting object, and it is this essential factor that enables avoidance to function as a protective device.

Daya, the adjacent eastern *barrio*, has previously been mentioned as a residence of many witches. And Maria, the only witch living in Tarong, is a daughter of a Dayan couple particularly notorious as "poisoners." She has caused tremors and unpleasant, painful swellings about the neck, face, and arms of two Tarongan women, in both cases by "looking strangely." The first occurrence was the result of a quarrel with a neighbor over some cloth, the second apparently for no particular reason.

I was coming along the lane, bringing faggots home, when I met Maria coming toward me. I moved as close to the other edge of the lane as possible and we passed without speaking. But she looked at me strangely, as if I were her enemy. By the time I reached home my neck was so sore I could

* The courts of law apparently allay this fear in the cities. During the field period the trial of an alleged witch provided an engrossing spectacle to residents of the provincial capitol (defendant and plaintiff both were teachers in the city high school).

barely talk or eat, and it was very swollen and painful for three days. She is evil, that one—just like her father and mother.*

Toward the end of the field period another Tarongan woman became very ill, her body painfully swollen. A number of *sirkanos* were called in turn, each giving a different diagnosis but little relief. In desperation the family, which was relatively poor, called in a famous *sirkano* from the provincial capitol who immediately diagnosed witchcraft. He proved the allegation by rubbing the side of a new water jar until a picture of the witch appeared, recognizable to the patient and three other Tarongans present as a woman in an adjacent *barrio* with whom the patient had been familiar.

No reason was ever offered for the witchcraft attack, but the time was easily determined—the last time the patient had used the then-unrecognized witch's sewing machine, about five days prior to noticeable swellings and pains. That this woman was trying to kill the Tarongan woman was clear, for the latter was very weak and obviously critically ill. The *sirkano's* series of treatments (tremendously expensive) did provide relief, however, and the patient was walking unaided within three weeks. Asked what she would do if, walking along a path, she should meet the witch who had nearly succeeded in killing her, the Tarongan woman answered, "If I meet her, I will talk naturally, but I will try to avoid her."

There is one other class of harmful persons who, although using no magical aids, are nevertheless a source of dread to Tarongans. These are the *agtoyo*, men of great strength and cunning, who, during the dry season, ride on horseback along the roads, lassoing and kidnapping the unwary. Their purpose is to provide victims for the bridgebuilders who reputedly drop the body or blood of one person into each foundation post, thus giving the bridge extra strength to withstand floods.

Some local customs give plausibility to such a practice: when a new house is built, a 10- or 20-centavo piece and a little wine are usually placed in at least one corner post hole, and often in all; and within memory of middle-aged Tarongans, when a government flood control dam was built on the Tarong-boundary creek, the blood of a pig was used in its foundation.

Although a number of Tarongans doubt the existence of *agtoyo*, the largest number of adults fear them, and if news circulates that a bridge is to be rebuilt, Tarongans are not often met walking alone on

* It should be mentioned here that, to the field team's eyes, Maria was one of the most attractive, pleasant, and intelligent women in Tarong. Nor did any other individual pointed out as a witch have any noticeable pecularities of appearance or behavior.

the paths, even during daylight hours. The feeling in the provincial capitol during one such period was also strong: high school students refused to walk to or from school alone and rumors of kidnappings circulated constantly. Fear of these kidnappers is strong enough to have made the following account of the attempt on the life of an Ikan man thoroughly credible: The elderly man, walking along the national highway at noon with his grandson, came to a part of the road which cut through a brushy hill. With no warning both felt ropes cast about them, pulling them toward the trees. The old man managed to draw his bolo and slash the ropes. He and the boy fled along the road to the nearest *sari-sari* store, where they collapsed, terror-stricken and exhausted. Neighbors hearing their story nodded gravely and said: "You were very lucky to escape the *agtoyo!*"

❧
❧
❧

Chapter 8

Health and Medicine

HEALTH AND MEDICAL CARE

The health of the average Tarongan is good, perhaps because of a widely varied diet. Teeth and bones are sturdy; severe dysentery is uncommon and malaria nonexistent. The most prevalent ailments are minor skin diseases, tropical ulcers, infections and intestinal worms— none of which are normally serious. Sprains and broken bones do, occur but with surprising infrequency. A large number of Tarongans reach old age, most functioning actively throughout this period although gradual loss of eyesight is a common complaint of the aged. Colds resulting in pneumonia are a danger during the cool wet season when long hours must be spent in knee-deep water, but current treatment of pneumonia by antibiotics has lowered the fatality rate of this disease.

Standards of cleanliness in Tarong are high: baths are taken frequently, hair is washed once or twice a week, clothing is changed at least once a day, and bedding is thoroughly aired and washed. Houses are neat and clean. Food and water are kept free of foreign matter, dishes are carefully washed, sun-dried and always wiped immediately before use. Garbage that cannot be fed to yard animals is disposed of in *sitio* dumps and the toilets, though often placed disconcertingly near wells, are some distance from the houses and relatively odorless. The only Tarongan habits which appear unsanitary to Western eyes are spitting and urination wherever convenient by children and adults, but the unsanitary aspects of this latter practice are questionable in view of the hot sun and airiness of the living areas.

Since the smallpox outbreak shortly after World War I, there has been no major epidemic, probably because of the free inoculation program in the school, which was established in Tarong at approximately this time. Sponsored by the Bureau of Public Schools, not only smallpox but also a series of cholera-dysentery-typhoid inoculations are given yearly to all schoolchildren and to as many preschool children and adults as request them. Unfortunately, a large number of young children are brought to the school for one of the series but no more; "they cry" say the parents.

During each school year the children are supposed to be inspected once by a doctor and a dentist and two or three times by a nurse. The nurse also lectures on general cleanliness, use of the school toilets and personal hygiene and checks on drinking facilities, and so on. Hygiene suggestions are geared to *barrio* equipment: for example, salt and betel nut husks are recommended to brush the teeth. Schoolteachers are pressed into first aid training and supplied with some equipment. However, the program is understaffed, and although the personnel do a remarkably good job, the number of visits and their length are insufficient for the scope of the program, and its most important effect remains the reduction of epidemic diseases.

There are two other government-sponsored health projects with whom the Tarongan comes in contact: one is the DDT team. The second is a yearly visit by a dentist, officially to take care of indigents as a part of the national aid for indigents program, but who in fact takes care of any adult who requests the service, since the term indigent is impossible to define practically. This definitional problem has led to so much difficulty in the weekly distribution of powdered milk, presumably to indigents through the schools, that the schoolteachers, fearful of starting arguments between families, simply distribute the milk equally to all schoolchildren—about a tablespoon per child, which they eat like candy.

The effect on the average Tarongan of all these people bent on improving his health is confusing. Mobile units appear, peer into throats, and disappear. One day a jeep drives up to the school and all the children are given injections; a week later another group comes and gives more injections to anyone in sight; then the first jeep reappears with another round of inoculations, and so on. To the Tarongan, often dubious of the value of injections and seeing them, at best, as a sort of internal *anib,* one should be enough; after all, one *anib* usually protects against disease in general, and he is not likely to see any sense in undergoing more. One family, by analogy with *anibs,* assumed that the inoculation of one member sufficed to protect all household members. The schoolteachers try to coax Tarongans, especially mothers of young children, to come for injections and examinations, but it is a time-consuming and usually fruitless task—only the captive school-children can be assumed thoroughly inoculated.

NONPROFESSIONAL TREATMENT

Common ailments such as colds and stomach upset are not attributed directly to the supernaturals and home remedies are used, often administered by old women.

Tremors, tics, dizziness, delirium or coma are thought to be caused by soul loss. Sudden shock or fright is thought to detach part or all of an individual's soul. Since a child's soul is weakly attached to his body, he is especially susceptible to this type of illness. To avoid such loss, an adult returning home from any trip with a child will call, "Come, Maria, do not stay." Or should a child fall, water will be splashed on the spot and some given to the child to drink, to keep his soul intact after the jolt.

If, in spite of precautions, soul loss does occur, the usual remedy is as follows: a used piece of the child's clothing is waved from the porch or house ladder as the name of the child is called; then cloth is placed over the child like a blanket. If a number of such attempts to bring back the soul do not succeed, a *sirkano* specializing in the treatment of soul loss must be summoned. A similar type of cure is used if a child becomes sick when his parent is away and the illness is interpreted as yearning for the parent. A soiled shirt or some such article of clothing will be sent to the child.

Related to illness due to soul loss are other maladies thought to occur when "something is missed." Any change of routine, even the change in seasons, may cause a state of unrest and vague physical upset. Something inside the individual looks for that which is gone and he becomes sick. The effect of such neglect varies and is usually less severe in adulthood.

Many illnesses are thought to be caused by spirits of the dead who visit their former abode. These ancestor spirits may cause acute indigestion, chills, perhaps fever. Successful therapy consists of smoking the individual with a mixture of ragbits, charcoal, and brown sugar and then whipping the body slightly with leafy twigs. If the patient is a visitor, the soiled clothing of a household member may also be placed over the patient, presumably superimposing that person's personality on the patient. This second personality, being familiar to the spirit, is of no great interest and the spirit will soon leave.

Such tricking of supernaturals is the basis of a number of standard ceremonies performed to prevent or alleviate illness caused by *not-humans*. If two consecutive children have died during their infancies, for example, it is probably due to the jealousy of *not-humans*. The next child, therefore, is baptized while still very young, and, in the Church, it is decided who will perform the "throwing away." For the child is then left at the side of the road on the way home by the chosen person, as if thrown away. One of the followers casually picks it up and brings it along, slipping the child surreptitiously into the house. This practice is said to deceive the *not-humans* into thinking that the child is unwanted so that they also will not take it. The child is thereafter called by a name derived from the "throwing away."

A child's name may also be changed to cure deformities or abnormal development such as upper teeth appearing before lower ones. The child is made to perform some adult task and is renamed after some aged relative of the child.

MEDICAL SPECIALISTS AND THEIR CURES

When the illness is sudden and severe, or when home remedies do not work, the aid of a specialist is sought. Tarongan medical practitioners are numerous and highly specialized—approximately one out of every 20 adults has some specific healing ability or knowledge. All are part-time practitioners receiving small payments, if any, and treating their fellow Tarongans primarily as a matter of social responsibility. In general, an individual's medical practice is confined to his own *sitio*, although some especially talented doctors travel to neighboring *sitios*, and in the case of the one Tarongan *sirkano*, to adjacent *barrios*.

At present Tarong offers the services of three midwives, four *ilots* (massage-curers), and one *sirkano*. Midwives may be male or female, but the three now practicing in Tarong are men and this situation is not uncommon in the area. Midwifery is considered a skill which may be learned by anyone, usually by assisting another.

Most of the *ilots*, like the midwives, enter the profession by at first practicing on members of their own family. This is particularly true of the *ilots* who specialize in caring for women after childbirth. There are two such persons now in Tarong, and they are both grandmothers who have themselves born many children and observed many births. One of them reported she first practiced when one of her grandchildren was born and no *ilot* was available. The other woman had been taught by her mother-in-law, who was a professional.

There are some *ilots*, however, who are thought to have inherent powers, which are often attributed to birth accidents. Only one such *ilot* is a resident of Tarong. His ability is attributed to his having been a breech birth, and entails the skill to massage away obstacles caught in the throat. He had successfully removed a chicken bone in this manner shortly before the field period.

For the third category of medical specialists, the *sirkano* or shaman, training or experience is thought to be of little or no importance, since he enters this profession as a consequence of a call from the *not-humans*. They choose, generally with no warning, the one they desire as a communicant. Therefore, he needs no period of training or apprenticeship.

As is not infrequently the case with shamans the world over, Idot, the only practicing Tarongan *sirkano*, is a deviant. Some say he is half-witted, others that "something is wrong inside his head." Whatever the cause, Idot's behavior is erratic, frequently unrealistic, and extremely deviant. It is said that even before his contract with the *not-humans*, he was strange. He never went to school. At 25, as a result of contact with the spirits, he became very violent, chasing his father through the house with his bolo.

Although no longer violent, Idot's very appearance is unusual, and children clearly fear him. A large and strong man, he walks with long strides, his back straight, head high—a bearing in marked contrast to the rags in which he is invariably clothed. He maintains a fixed half-smile that can be completely unnerving and may be either taciturn or loquacious but, when talking to someone, stares with unblinking eyes. His stare is not blank but rather like the unself-conscious and curious stare of a child, which may be one of the reasons for the assumption of incomplete mental development. His speech, however, shows at least adequate facility, though delivered with great rapidity, a marked lack of the usual inflections, and frequent lapses into complete irrationality.

Idot displays still further behavioral peculiarities, for example, he does not really live at home, but sleeps here and there, sometimes even in the fields. He drinks his fees and dresses in rags. Some of his patients pay him in clothes rather than money but still he wears rags. He rarely farms or participates in social life. Much of his time is spent on the mountain in Bantai, where he visits his friends the *not-humans* and hunts for medicines. His most unusual characteristic is his social isolation. He wanders about the four *barrios* in which he has patients, visiting them and picking up tidbits of information which may be useful in later diagnoses and treatments. Generally he is alone, smiling his grim smile and either greeting politely each passerby or staring through them, depending on his mood.

Although these aberrancies detract from Idot's popularity as a *sirkano*, the nearest alternative *sirkano* within six *barrios* is in the next municipality. On the other hand, Idot is related to most Tarongans; obligations and ease of access assure him a practice, and his reputation is growing with the number of cases he successfully treats.

All Idot's treatments follow roughly the same course, but more elaboration may be required for severe cases. First the precise nature of the ailment, and therefore its cause, must be determined. This is generally a matter of inspection of symptoms and often inquiry. For example, the likelihood of *not-humans* being the cause increases if the patient has recently been in an area frequented by them. Idot's reputation is enhanced when the spirits are the ones who tell him where the contact had occurred. His chance observations when wandering the area can thus be fruitful.

One elaborate diagnosis is the magical one determining the presence or absence of soul loss, which as mentioned previously, occurs most commonly in children but occasionally also in adults. It involves complicated maneuvers with rice grains in water.

The *sirkano's* treatment of ills is essentially the same kind of medication and magic as Tarongans use for their minor ills. Additionally, however, the *sirkano* can directly consult *not-humans* and in this way determine how they may be placated if their anger has caused the illness. For example, Damiana, the wife of Pasqual Navarro, was alone in the house at sunset when she saw a man at the window. "I was very angry—I was going to run and strike him, but he vanished and I became terrified." Damiana cried out and fell fainting to the floor. Her sister, who lives next door, heard her cry and ran to help. The women who quickly gathered massaged her until she regained consciousness; then she told them what had happened. Damiana was still shaky, and one side of her body, including the arm and leg, was stiff and painful to move.

Idot was called, and he diagnosed soul loss as a result of the shock of seeing a *not-human*. He tied the diagnostic rice grains into a pleat of Damiana's clothing under her arm and had her drink a little of the coconut water used during diagnosis, dropping a number of small silver coins into the rest. He then applied a mash of oil and special small roots, found in a cave in the mountain of Bantai, to her temple and waist—Idot's usual treatment for soul loss. To ease the stiffness he gathered large, fresh leaves of a certain oily plant, heated them over the stove and placed them in layers along the stiff side, leg, and arm, covering them well with cloths.

Since the cause of Damiana's fright was a spirit, Idot went into the darkest places of the *sitio*-hill, calling to and talking with *not-humans*. The now large group at Damiana's had been cautioned not to leave until Idot returned, so that no one knew precisely what happened, but his voice could be heard in conversation at some distance.

When Idot returned, he instructed that an offering be made to the *not-humans*. He selected two young women to cook a chicken and the most common spirit offering, sticky rice cooked in coconut milk. When this had been done, he picked two young men to accompany him to the offering place. Eight betel chews, four cigars, two clam shells, each containing nine grains of rice, and a bamboo tube of wine were taken; Idot saying loudly as they left the house, "I hope this cures her right away!" The offering was placed next to the main *sitio* path, on an upright bamboo stake. Afterward the cooked food was served to those neighbors still gathered in the house.

Most offerings follow this pattern; they are composed of pieces of chicken or eggs, rice, wine, often betel or tobacco, and, very occasionally, coins of small value will be included. They are placed at a spirit-designated spot, or at the one where the contact had occurred, and are left on their distinctive stakes until the wind, rain, or daring schoolboys remove them. There is no concern with their fate, since the spirits have made their meal of the essence of the food by then. These offerings, being requested by the spirits, suffice to appease their anger and to ensure their leaving the patient in peace to recover.

Applications of medicine may continue for a number of days, and, if the illness is severe, additional offerings may be made. At the successful conclusion of most treatments, a hair washing is performed as a cleansing ceremony and a restorative. For this, a special lye is made, often including wine. All members of the household then squat around the lye basin while the *sirkano* begins the washing of their hair, working from the oldest to the youngest. After all have finished washing and rinsing their hair, they change all their clothing. The soiled clothes are hung in the sun, where they remain for two days and nights.

The hair washing also has curative powers, being performed in hopes of replenishing that "something missing with you" which is the cause of deformities at birth, disfiguring boils, and postillness deformations. This hair washing is performed in the same manner except that the *sirkano* places a coin in the lye basin before beginning to wash, and the owner of the house must match it. And during the washing, neighbors prepare special rice which all then gather to eat—none must be taken away or the deformity will go with it.

Despite the *sirkano's* efforts, occasionally the spirits will not relent or the soul will not return; the patient worsens and death seems imminent. Often this is the time the Poblacion Western-style doctor is called, and, obviously, it is often too late for him to save the patient. The result of this habit is that many Tarongans associate death and the Western doctor—to call him is to admit defeat and prepare for immediate death.

When the doctor is called, he is met with various attitudes which interfere with his course of treatment. Dietary restrictions are, in general, ignored. Salves, ointments, and so on will be applied to anyone in the *barrio* experiencing a similar pain and in varying quantities to the patient; instructions for the use of internal medicines are often modified—if one pill is good, two are better, and so the whole bottleful at one time will cure the patient more effectively. Even the very use of medication is questionable, for an unpleasant-tasting medicine or stinging ointment may well be thrown out, especially if the patient is a child and complains.

The doctor's only recourse is to take the patient to his clinic (being costly, this is limited to serious cases and is emotionally disturbing for all) or to use only medication that can be injected. Idot spoke truthfully when he said, "The doctor's medicine is piercing with needles." This means that for many treatments doctors are forced to come to the patient a number of times, which highly inconvenient obligation they cheerfully assume for fees within *barrio* reach and often for fees not a great deal higher than those the *sirkano* receives for similar cases.

An account of a severe illness, directly caused by *not-humans*, will typify the methods of the major medical practitioners as well as Tarongans' current attitudes toward them. One Saturday morning during the dry season, Ariston Navarro, Rufino's father, wanted to gather hay.

Finding that someone had borrowed his sled, he grew furious and decided to plow a field in preparation for cane planting instead. Anger apparently spurring him on, he plowed all morning, returning home at noon when, exhausted, he lay down on the porch. His wife Dominga called him to come eat, but he did not reply and, going to where he lay, she found him unconscious. She called for help to neighbors pounding rice nearby, and they in turn called men from the fields to help carry Ariston into the *sala*, where he was placed on pillows.

Within moments Ariston's younger brother, the midwife, who also administers first aid, arrived and supervised the "holding"—three men pressed firmly just above Ariston's waist and at the sides of his neck, holding back the life which goes down and out of the body at death. The house filled as men in the fields and women in their kitchens heard the news and, dropping their tasks, ran to help. The holders exhorted each other to "Hold it!" and "Don't let him!" when Ariston, still unconscious, gasped for breath. Speculations and opinions as to the cause of the illness varied; perhaps an unknown ancestor spirit had called him, lonesome in that place where he now was; perhaps it was *not-humans;* perhaps something he had eaten was affecting him; or perhaps it was what the doctors call "attack."

Someone called Idot and he came, but nothing was decided until Rufino, the eldest son, could be located. On arriving, he replaced one of the holders and tried to make his father recognize and speak to him. He did not succeed, and, after much consultation, the field team was requested to bring a Poblacion doctor. The holding was steadily maintained by various men in rotation until the doctor arrived. At that time Idot rather ostentatiously left the house and went off.

The doctor examined Ariston, the holders maintaining their pressure till the doctor asked them to "please not choke him." He determined that Ariston had suffered a heart attack probably due to high blood pressure, leaving slight paralysis in the right side. He gave Ariston three injections to dissolve possible blood clots and a few pills along with specific instructions on their use and left. Amid interminable discussions, many of the group returned to their work, but a sizable gathering of close relatives remained throughout the night.

Later in the evening this number was augmented by the old women of the *sitio* and the young marriageable boys and girls, who played cards on Ariston's bed with gaiety, smiled on by their gossiping elders. Everything possible was being done to ensure Ariston's comfort of mind and to assure him that all his kin and friends were helping him by their presence. During the night, smoke of various mixtures was blown over him as a protection against ancestor-spirit contact and the doctor's pills were pulverized and forced, along with rice, into his mouth during his occasional waking moments.

The next day, Sunday, Ariston was slightly better but now and then pointed to something outside with great excitement. His sons feared that he saw *not-humans* and debated calling Idot. But in case it might, after all, be soul loss, one of the sons waved one of Ariston's soiled shirts from the porch, calling his name many times. By mid-afternoon Ariston could talk a bit, and slowly they pieced together what had probably caused his attack. Ariston had tried to lead his carabao through a narrow dike opening toward the wallow, an area known to be often inhabited by *not-humans*. The carabao balked, apparently sensing their presence, and Ariston unthinkingly whipped the animal with a switch, undoubtedly hitting a *not-human* as well. If *not-humans* were, therefore, the cause of the ailment, Idot must be called immediately, but he could not be found after a search of some hours. Annoyed at the family's lack of faith in his abilities, Idot, when the doctor arrived, had gone to the mountain in Bantai, where he remained that night, Sunday, and part of Monday.

Since it was then evening, the group decided that an offering must be made quickly, Idot or no, and the following items were assembled, partly under Ariston's direction: 2 clam shells, each holding 9 grains of rice in coconut oil, 2 rolled cigars, 2 betel chews complete with nut, lime, and leaf, and a tube of wine. One of the sons, alone, took the offering to the place described and left it there, returning quickly without looking back. A short distance from this spot, the son reported that he had seen a large snake which he could have killed if he had his bolo. When this statement was later reported to Idot, he replied: "If you had killed it, you would surely have found your father dead when you got back to the house."

Monday morning Ariston felt no better and could barely move his right arm and leg. Fearful that the offering had been insufficient or that his son might have dropped some of it, he insisted that the offering be repeated. As soon as this had been done, the sons again searched for Idot. This time he was found, and he came in midafternoon, expressing great surprise at the call: "But I thought the doctor from Poblacion had surely cured him by now?"

Ariston assured him that he did not trust the doctor and that, had he been capable of deciding, Idot would have been consulted. Idot listened to the story of the probable striking of *not-humans* and agreed it was unquestionably an illness caused by them. He pressed his hands over Ariston's body, murmuring repeatedly: "You will soon be all right. You will do the usual things again soon."

At sunset Idot began his treatment. He went into the yard, reversed the ladder, then circled the house, talking presumably to *not-humans* in a gibberish of Latin, English, and Tagalog. Now and then he raised his voice in anger and struck at the air with his bolo. Coming back into the house, where a number of people had now gathered, he ordered two white chickens killed. This being done, he selected two young women to prepare one hard-boiled egg, rice, and the chickens, the latter to be stewed with no flavorings, such as salt or pickled fish, since the salt and vinegar in the fish are *anibs* against the *not-humans* and would hardly be acceptable to them in an offering.

During these preparations Idot twice left the house to talk to and argue with the *not-humans,* refreshing himself liberally with wine. On returning to the house the last time, he turned the house ladder upside down, then went to Ariston and again pressed his hands over his body, murmuring, "You will be all right. Sure, you will be all right." When the food was ready, Idot selected two young men to bring some of it, along with a tube of wine, to the offering place—the same one at which the earlier offerings had been left.

Returning, he placed more of the food on four plates, ordering the chicken cooking-pot destroyed. The plates were then placed on four chairs set in the center of the *sala* and glasses of wine set with them. Idot, enjoining silence, went to the porch door, calling loudly to the *not-humans,* "Come now, it's all here!" Going back to the plates he muttered to himself, inspecting the food. Then at the porch door again, he repeated, "Come now, it's all here!" While the assembled visitors shifted uneasily and were nervously quiet, Idot nodded and murmured to unseen spirits coming to partake of the spirit of the food. After a few moments he turned toward the door, calling, "Please, those of you who are at the door—please come in and eat!"

Fear of such intimate contact with *not-humans* was sufficient to keep all humans except Idot rigid against the walls for at least 10 minutes. At the end of this period, during which no one spoke except Idot, who conversed with the *not-humans,* he went into the yard to make sure all the spirits had partaken of the food.

Returning, he told the group that they had finished and that the food should be reheated and eaten by the visitors. But "all must be consumed—no part of it must be left for the next meal or taken out of the house to a neighbor or any place." With this, the treatment was complete. Only one occurrence marred the ceremony—one of the female assistants, young and nervous, laughed at Idot a number of times. Arriving home shortly after eating, she experienced such violent stomach cramps that she cried loudly. Idot, passing her house on his way home, heard her and remarked to a companion that "it was her laughing that caused it." Whatever its cause, the very timely stomach cramps had a sobering effect on later assistants, who never smiled when they performed their duties.

Tuesday Idot did not visit his patient, who was noticeably better, eating well, talking with far less difficulty, and praising Idot highly. Although Ariston's arm and leg were still stiff, they could be moved with comfort. On Wednesday morning Idot came to perform the hair washing, and Ariston was sufficiently recovered to walk to the well for this ceremony. The cost of Idot's treatment, including wine and food, was 10 pesos, to which the grateful Dominga added a shirt.

DEATH AND FUNERARY PRACTICES

Eight months after the attack just described, Ariston Navarro suffered another. It was now September and during one of the chilly nights Ariston had a heart attack that left him almost completely paralyzed and only partly conscious. When he was discovered early in the morning, one neighbor, fearing imminent death, left immediately to fetch the priest. As before, his sons and neighbors converged about his bed, many of his relatives maintaining a steady wailing. Idot not being available, a *sirkano* from the adjacent municipality was called, and when the priest had left, this *sirkano* diagnosed the cause of the attack as a gust of "bad air" * which hit him on the stomach as he lay sleeping too near an open window. The condition could be cured by massaging his stomach with wine and certain leaves and holding nine prayer meetings, an unusual suggestion, and the only time during the field period that prayers were said for anyone other than the dead.

Although this was done, the first prayers being chanted that evening, a Poblacion doctor was also called the next day. His diagnosis was the same as for the preceding attack, and injections were again given. Since the illness was severe—Ariston was unconscious most of the time—relatives from farther and farther away arrived in waves, each trying to speak with him, forcing bits of rice into his mouth, and discussing the diagnoses.

Late this second day Idot came and agreed that sleeping in front of

* This air may be encounterd anywhere, usually at night. It is thought by some to be the accumulation of "all the uncured illnesses of all time."

the open window had been involved. However, he added, it was clearly caused by *not-humans:* the spirits, not bad air, had reached him through the window. Idot then spoke to the *not-humans,* applied a leaf poultice to Ariston's stomach, and performed an offering ceremony essentially like the one he had performed after the first attack.

During the next eight days, prayers continued with the usual rice candy served at the last meeting. Idot hovered, and the Poblacion doctor made two more calls; at no time were there fewer than 10 people in the house and often there were 40 to 50. Nevertheless, Ariston showed no improvement. The following week it was clear that he was failing and the house filled with visitors (and the weary but faithful neighbors) every evening during this period. A political rally at which Rufino, Ariston's eldest son, was to be an important speaker had been scheduled in Tarong for the Monday of the following week, but by noon of that day the rally was rescheduled for Ikan, since "the old people say he will probably die before sundown."

That night the house overflowed with visitors. Idot remained through the night, trying to intercede with the *not-humans,* but in the words of one of Ariston's sons, "What can he do? They are angry and will not listen." There was sporadic wailing by the immediate family; at all times Ariston was flanked by six to eight persons sitting on the bed, and smoke was blown over him every hour or so, but no further prayers were said, for the prescribed series of nine had been completed. However, the old man continued to breathe, harshly and irregularly, throughout the night, a large number of relatives remaining to take a turn at his bedside so that others might sleep.

The next morning, a little before 8 o'clock, Ariston died. The trumpeted death call of an attendant old woman—"Jesus, Maria, Apo"—carried throughout the *sitio,* and every man, woman, and child within hearing ran to the house. While Dominga collected appropriate clothing, the others tidied the house, moved the bed parallel to the ridgepole—head toward the shrine—and spread over it a mat and a clean white blanket. Ariston's sons hurriedly washed and dressed the body on the porch. Within 20 minutes of his death Ariston had been dressed in three sets of clothes, the uppermost his best, carefully saved for great occasions, and laid on the bed, a crucifix in his hands, a handkerchief around his jaw to hold it in place until he stiffened, and, to prevent rapid decay, a copper coin on his mouth and a dish of vinegar beneath the bed.

Two of Ariston's male cousins left immediately for Poblacion to buy a casket and make funeral arrangements while a few others went to nearby *sitios* and *barrios* to carry news of his death. This done and the body prepared, formal mourning could begin: all close relatives, male and female, covered their heads with black scarves, one corner clamped firmly between their teeth; Dominga led the keening, expected of all adult female relatives and close male relatives, the length of time and frequency depending primarily on the degree of relationship. The black mourning cloth is pulled over the head and face and the keener, kneeling or sitting at the side of the beds, wails the laments of the living, consolations to the one who has died, and gives him messages to those who have died previously, the chanting frequently interrupted by racking, anguished sobs.

At a wake for an old woman, for example, another old woman told the corpse, between sobs that shook her body and bent her head to her knees: "Take charge of my son, killed on the battlefield at Cervantes. You will now act as his mother. If I had the power I would come with you so I could also see my son. . . ." Mourning the death of a 7-day-old baby, one woman, considered an accomplished keener, called on the spirit of her nephew who had died when 5 to: "Take care of this little one who could not withstand the hardships of life. Holding her by the hand, teach her to walk and to play and how to laugh, for she does not yet know these things."

The already exhausted Dominga keened without interruption for 45 minutes, at which time her sons and female relatives called, "Enough, *nanang*" and pulled her away to soothe and console her. One of the sons took her place, then another and so on. The first and most closely related mourners are genuinely grief stricken, keening and sobbing with abandon and sometimes fainting. Later mourners keen with less fervor in a more formal fashion and are generally little affected emotionally although their sobs are more dramatic. From them it is a sign of respect due any relative or neighbor and tangible evidence of good will to the bereaved family.

The keening was maintained until the men returned 2½ hours later with the casket, a simple, painted wooden box. Ariston was moved to the mat and blanket-lined casket, which was then placed on the bed, a candle near his head. Dominga, seeing her husband one step closer to the grave, began again to keen and sob wildly, a few other women joining her. However, lamentations soon diminished and occurred only sporadically through the afternoon as neighbors went to their own homes to eat, take care of essential chores, and dress for the evening wake; the women in all black if possible, men partially so.

At dusk a bonfire was lit in the yard where a number of men gathered to chat and make the wooden cross for Ariston's grave. Jars of wine were bought, and the wine offered throughout the funeral period

—not to drink would give offense. During the evening well over 100 visitors arrived, about a third of whom stayed all night. All who were relatives or neighbors brought gifts of money or food—a basket of rice, a chicken, some vegetables—whatever could be spared to help defray the funeral expenses. Because of the prominence of the family, even the Poblacion mayor and a party of councilors came to visit and play cards in the yard. Inside the house, keening, of course, resumed as the distant relatives arrived, and continued till dawn. Only children were put to bed in odd corners; all adults remained awake.

The yard was never empty during the night, and at 4 A.M., a pig was butchered by the light of borrowed pressure lamps and cooked, along with a noodle dish and rice, for breakfast. At 5, a band consisting of a bass drum, a small drum, cymbals, two saxophones, two clarinets, three cornets (two alternating with trombones) and a tuba arrived in the *barrio*, loudly playing "sad music" as it walked along the paths.

For the next three hours the band played, breakfast was served, and preparations were made for removing the coffin, during which time close relatives maintained a steady, vigorous keening, which rose to a frantic peak at about 8 when the coffin was closed. It was covered with a number of blankets and taken out of the house on bamboo shoulder poles, and wine was immediately sprinkled on the floor beneath the bed where the coffin had rested to "drive away the heaviness of death." At the top of the house ladder, the bearers paused while a rooster, its throat slashed, was tossed to the ground as a sign to the spirits that a male had died (for a female, a hen is killed in the same way).

The coffin was carried across the paddies, followed by the band, which played a considerably altered version of Chopin's *Funeral March* as a funeral dirge, and approximately 70 mourning adults and children of all ages. Perhaps 20 of this number followed the coffin only as far as the schoolhouse, the others accompanying it to the cemetery. Near the highway a black-draped wagon drawn by four men waited.

While the funeral party walked slowly to the church, the neighbors and distant relatives who had remained at the house of the deceased worked feverishly to prepare the funeral feast. The porch and yard as well as the *sala* of the house were filled with benches, tables, and chairs garnered from every house in the *sitio*. Another pig was butchered along with goats and chickens, and tubsful of vegetables were sliced. Pots of rice were cooked over three open fire pits in the yard, and innumerable small pots filled with varieties of meat-vegetable stews boiled in nearby kitchens.

Meanwhile the funeral party had reached the church. The wagon was pulled part way down the center aisle where, this being an expensive *barrio* funeral, a number of candles were lit, and, over the opened coffin, the priest performed the customary brief service. The coffin was then closed and pulled outside the church. Here it was removed from the wagon, again opened and the grave-cross propped against it while the closest relatives, their heads carefully covered by the black cloths, corners still clamped between their teeth, grouped around the coffin for the important formal photograph which would later take its place on the household walls along with photographs of the older dead.

Closing the coffin and replacing it on the wagon, the procession continued through Poblacion to the walled cemetery at the edge of town. At the side of the grave the coffin was again opened, the shoes removed (the returning spirit walks noisily if buried in Western shoes) but left in the coffin. In Ariston's case, two new blankets and the usual good suit of work clothes and woven hat were packed in around his body. A final brief keening and the coffin was closed for the last time and lowered into the grave, the waiting gravediggers immediately shoveling dirt onto it as the mourners quickly left.

The funeral party then returned to the house of the deceased and the feast. As the first arrivals were seen on the path, a small rice-straw fire was lit near the foot of the house ladder, over which each arrival stepped before entering in case some evil ghost had clung to him. Then, while final food preparations were made, wine was served and the guests chatted in the *sala*, on the porch, and in the yard. By the time the elaborate feast was ready, at least 100 adults and innumerable small children were milling in and about the house, and food was served in three sittings. Dominga, who had slept little since Ariston's illness began and almost not at all the previous three nights, was staggering but managed to greet and talk with most of her guests.

During the afternoon, groups of men sat on the porch and in several nearby yards, chatting and playing cards while the women gossiped over the dishes they washed on the back porch and in the yard, a task not completed until after 4 o'clock. As dusk approached, visitors left a few at a time, and neighbors wandered off to their chores, only seven of the immediate family remaining at the deceased's house.

Soon after the evening meal, a few of the neighbors returned for the first of the nine-day prayers. But, the prayers having been quickly chanted, they left, for Dominga was barely able to sit upright, and the entire *sitio* was exhausted from the preceding days' unrest. One son with his family remained to sleep with Dominga for the remaining prayer nights, and during this period there was intense but covert competition between two of her sons to insert one of their children into the household, for Dominga's income is ample. At length a grand-

Sitio East.

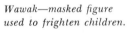

View from lane entering Tarong.

House and yard; mother and daughter pounding rice; son threshing rice.

Wawak—masked figure used to frighten children.

Leveling a new paddy.

Planting seed rice.

Harvesting rice.

Removing fish from a harvested and drying paddy; fish trap in center.

Women carrying harvest
shares of rice home.

Five- and 7-year-old boys harvesting rice.

Training fighting cocks.

Playing with beetle-powered noisemaker.

Serving at large feast;
banana stalk "plates" in foreground.

Girl with grandmother at great-grandmother's wake. Flywisk in woman's hand.

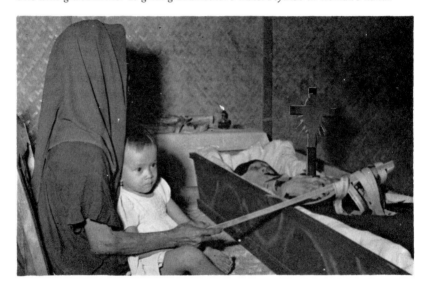

Kitchen stove, family-style meal.

Boy carrying younger brother.

daughter, the child of Dominga's least successful son, was selected and moved into the house, joining her older brother who had been resident as an "adopted" son for a few years.

The second prayer meeting was equally brief and sparsely attended, but by the third the number was up to 20 and the fourth was heavily attended, people having caught up with work and sleep. During this night and the next, the house echoed to the shouts of cardplayers, but the sixth, seventh, and eighth nights were quieter, harvesting having begun. The ninth, and last night, the house was again filled for the usual cardgame, talk, and food. It is noteworthy that although the largest group assembles for the last evening, one is expected to have attended at least one and preferably more of the previous prayer meetings if he does not want others to say "he comes only to eat."

On the third morning after burial, Ariston's closest relatives, ordered by degree of relationship, went to the well where Ariston's widowed daughter-in-law performed a hair washing, using wine in addition to lye. A similar hair washing was also performed on the morning of the ninth day but without wine. Both ceremonies serve to prevent headache and the depression associated with mourning-grief.

Two weeks after the funeral, although Dominga was heard keening occasionally, as widows are expected to, mourning was generally indicated only by wearing black or partially black clothing. Mourning black is worn for differing lengths of time, depending on the degree of relationship to the deceased: for a husband or wife, 1 year; a mother or child, 9 months because "this long are you pregnant"; a father, 7 months, since "all he has to do is author the child"; a brother or sister, 5 months; and a grandparent, 3 months. Relatives more distant than this require black only for the wake-funeral period, as do friends and neighbors.

After another series of nine prayer meetings, always arranged to terminate one month after the death, mourning was essentially completed, signalized by making a cross of wine on the forehead of the mourners. If a family can afford the expense, another nine nights of prayer on the first and sometimes also on subsequent anniversaries of the death are celebrated. Official mourning can be ended by only one prayer meeting but nine nights is preferred.

Ariston's funeral was an elaborate and expensive one, but even for poor families the pattern is the same. The only variations in these funerary practices are occasioned by deaths of children under 7. Such a child is "already an angel" and is thought to go immediately to Heaven. The usual pattern of wake, funeral, feast, and prayer meetings is followed, but all mourning clothing is white rather than black. The funeral cart is dispensed with and the band plays "happy music."

The child's funeral clothing is elaborated and its eyes propped open so that "it may find its way to heaven."

Stillbirths and miscarriages are not mourned although the approximately full-term child dead at birth is usually baptized by an old woman. But if the child is taken to the cemetery for burial, "one must sin, lying that it died on the way or it cannot be buried there." Miscarriages occurring before the fetus is human in form are discarded with no ceremony; beyond this period they are wrapped, placed in a box, often baptized and buried, along with the placenta, under the house, most commonly just behind the house ladder "where there is shade."

Most disruptive to the community is the death of young to middle-aged parents of nuclear families. The wife's death leaves children to be distributed, frequently provoking interminable squabbles and sometimes deep rifts through the kin group. But her death does not generally affect her husband's or her children's economic position, and if his mother or spinster sister can move in to care for the children, the adjustment may be effected quickly and painlessly. On the other hand, the death of the male head of a nuclear family is clearly the most disruptive; his death causes either loss to the patrilineal kin group of his children, tenancy right, and property, if the widow returns to her own family, or severe strain if she remains, and the property must be grudgingly managed on a share basis by his brothers or father until the sons mature. When there is no property, the loss of a husband consigns the widow and children to irredeemable poverty unless she can remarry or make a living by trading—a difficult task.

❈
❈
❈

Chapter 9

Formal Education

The Tarong school was established about 40 years ago. It is part of the Philippine public education system, which is under national administration, the government setting schedules, curricula, paying teachers' salaries, providing textbooks, supplying the necessary buildings and, presumably, additional materials. Maintenance and labor for further construction are supplied by the area served by the school. The Tarong school draws children from three *barrios* for its first to fourth primary grades and from six *barrios* for the fifth and sixth elementary grades.

The school is primarily Tarong's responsibility and the only formal agency of Tarongan unity in whose activities all *sitios* have an equal share. The other *barrios* using the school, especially the adjacent Bantai, do supply help, but since the official name is the Tarong Elementary School, only Tarongans feel it is really their school. The problems of collecting materials and promises of labor are tremendous but partly overcome by the support of two formal *barrio* organizations whose aims are primarily the maintenance of the school.

The most important of these organizations is the Parent-Teacher Association, similar only in name to the American counterpart. Tarong's PTA is open to all members of the school district, and in theory its purpose is the discussion and effecting of *barrio* and school programs. In fact, the PTA is a sort of men's work group consisting of a number of *barrio* leaders who have accepted the specific responsibility of maintenance and construction. The head schoolteacher, Mariano, who functions much like a principal, works with these men, explaining projects and ways of obtaining donations of materials he cannot get from the government; these leaders, in turn, prod their kin groups and friends to work and donate.

Mariano is now trying to establish a dependable work group of about a dozen men from Tarong and Bantai who will devote one day a week during lighter work periods to school maintenance. Daily cleaning of the building and grounds is done by the pupils. Despite Tarongans' great pride in the school, dependable and steady cooperation is readily offered by few, and a large part of Mariano's daily hours in the *barrio* are spent pleading for visible support of the school. He has the additional task of persuading various men to plow and harrow the school experimental garden during the heavy work seasons when time is grudgingly spent away from the fields.

The other organization, originally a part of the PTA, but now its female counterpart, is the Tarong Women's Club. It is a volunteer group, numbering about 20 active members from Bantai and Tarong, whose purpose is gathering funds for building and classroom materials and working out programs for both community and school, primarily in the field of home economics. Fund raising is the most stressed activity. The Women's Club raises money largely through its active members, a number of whom are local leaders who can press their relatives for donations. At Christmas time, the Women's Club, the teachers, and the schoolchildren canvass all the school-served *barrios,* the children singing carols and the adults recording gifts and pledges of money, chickens, and so on.

There are a few other methods of raising money and supplies for school needs: levies of cash, plants, food, and so forth on the pupils; sale of produce from the school garden; auction dances at the schoolhouse. The fifth grade also operates a tiny store, selling Coca-Cola and hard candies to schoolchildren.

That these money-making and labor-recruiting schemes do have eventual effect is illustrated by the new and attractive, well-built, bamboo home economics building, the model house associated with Philippine elementary schools. It was built to replace an older, deteriorated structure, during the first half of the field period, entirely by local labor using supplies donated by the PTA and Women's Club. This project was slow to start but aroused great enthusiasm as the building grew, so much so that when the field team suggested a goat feast for a small *tagnawa* group building a shelter at the schoolhouse for their car, the group suggested the equivalent money be spent for the few sheets of galvanized iron needed to complete the roof on the home economics building.

Although the primary role of a Tarongan in relation to the school is supportive, the school provides more than simply the education of his children. Via the teachers, the school is the agency through which national *barrio* self-improvement projects and ideological programs are presented to the *barrio.* The teacher is thus in a position to affect greatly the attitude of Tarongans toward the national government and its agencies.

The Tarong school has two primary grade teachers and two for the elementary grades, one of whom is Mariano, the head schoolteacher and only man. Two of these teachers are new, but Mariano and the other elementary teacher have been in Tarong for almost 10 years and have an intimate knowledge of all its families.

Teachers enjoy great prestige in the *barrio* both because of their status as teachers and, often more important, because of their social status in Poblacion terms, for by far the largest number of teachers are from landed families. One of the current Tarong schoolteachers is from the adjacent *barrio* Ikan and the daughter of a wealthy family; the others are all from Poblacion, to which they return by bus every evening, and all but one received their training in Manila.

With this background the teacher is perforce a community leader —"Listen to the teacher, he knows" is said to adults as well as to children. Because Tarong has neither radios nor newspapers and Poblacion contacts are limited, the schoolteacher functions as the major link to the outside world, informing about and explaining international and national events, even interpreting local ones.

And the schoolteacher, in and out of the classroom, is the most potent source of new ideas in Tarong. He suggests and demonstrates in the school garden new farming methods and crops; he introduces new ideas of livestock care and breeding; he encourages health and *barrio* improvement measures.

The new ideas brought into the *barrio* have not been uniformly successful; many admittedly are neither sensible—for example, cement toilets, nor useful—home canning—to Tarongans. The reading center once set up at the school has also been abandoned because of adult illiteracy and inability to obtain reading materials. Still, a few chicken coops have appeared; fruit trees are being planted in good number; benches have been placed along paths in the *sitios;* toilets are somewhat more carefully constructed and placed; many women bring their babies to the mobile health unit, and no house is complete without a few ornamental shrubs and hanging flowerpots.

The schoolteacher, like the *barrio* leaders and kin-neighborhood group members, is also obligated to repay the support of his followers by extending his own support and help to any Tarongans who may need them. He attends parties, advises in land transactions, explains democracy before each election, encourages the acceptance of vaccinations from the visiting health unit. Additionally, he must, by devious methods, entice enough children from surrounding *barrios* to his school to keep up the minimum enrollment, for Tarongans would be humiliated and angered if their school were closed. He owes the *barrio* his loyalty. Tarongans recently rose up in a united wrathful body against one of their teachers who was suspected of luring pupils to a rival elementary school in a nearby *barrio*. But, as is true throughout the mutual obligation system, these obligations are willingly accepted in no small part for the pleasure inherent in the friendly social relations they entail.

Almost all children attend the Tarong school for the first four years, but slightly over one third do not complete the sixth grade as there are more expenses in the last two grades and the children are now old enough to be economically productive. But if a family can manage it, they take pride in their children's graduation from sixth grade. There is a recognized value in even this level of scholarship, for it enables the child to read and write some English and Tagalog, all of which are becoming increasingly useful for a Tarongan farmer.

Further education, which means Poblacion Institute, the high school, confers prestige on its recipient and is highly desired but, because of the expenses of Poblacion living, tuition, books, and so on, is restricted to a few. About a quarter of Tarong's households either had sent or are now sending at least one son or daughter to Poblacion Institute. This number itself is evidence of the tremendous value placed on formal education. High school diplomas hang proudly on *sala* walls.

Eight households had managed to send one or more boys or girls to provincial colleges (two to a Manila university), generally to get teachers' certificates, which allow working within the public school system. To do this, loans are made, land may be mortgaged or even sold, but the child's social position is assured if he can obtain one of the scarce jobs for college-trained people. Even if his future wages are not very high, he will move in circles where a number of sidelines can considerably increase his income. A child who receives such an education may expect little as a marriage settlement if his education took all the family savings and probably some of its land, and he will be expected to repay as much as possible. Undoubtedly the additional tobacco money now coming into Tarongan households will increase the number of children sent to high school and college, especially if land prices rise above their present level, but it is unlikely that job opportunities for these people will increase in the immediate future.

Part II

Socialization

✤
✤
✤
✤
✤
✤

Chapter 10

Pregnancy and Childbirth

CONCEPTION

As previously indicated, Tarongan marriages are stable and, with rare exceptions, satisfying for both partners. This is due in part to the nature of sexual relations. A girl is expected to be chaste until marriage, but courtship patterns reinforce rather than conflict with this value. Prudery certainly is not present, but neither is titillation; sexual experience before marriage is almost nonexistent for boys as well as girls, but knowledge is widespread.

A certain degree of modesty is retained after marriage, men and women customarily undressing privately. The frequency of intercourse is not a matter of importance, being at the discretion of the man, for it is he who should initiate sexual activity. (It is not proper for women to evidence desire, but once activity is initiated, they are expected to respond.) In general, intercourse may range from once a day to once a week, about three times a week being an agreed-on modal frequency for couples with children. "No oftener than once a day, though I've been married a long time" said one woman, but added, "Occasionally twice a day would be quite all right."

Intercourse usually takes place at night for the sake of privacy, especially if there are children. "The man just goes near (the commonest euphemism) the woman and nothing is said—there is no need for conversation." This last comment brought roars of laughter from a group of five women informants, whose ribald comments indicated clearly that they used methods of encouraging and arousing their men without technically being unwomanly. The only taboos on intercourse are for a brief post-partum period and during the monthly menses —although even here it is not so much prohibited as not quite proper.

Despite the willingness to discuss sexual matters with the field team and a male interpreter, such discussion is not common at mixed-sex group affairs, and sexual joking is in terms of elaborate metaphor and innuendo. Such forthright talk is reserved for intimate groups of the same sex.

Given these attitudes toward sexual relations, and a near complete lack of knowledge regarding birth control and abortion, it is not surprising that Tarongan marriages usually result in the steady production of children spaced roughly two years apart. This is explicitly approved. As one old man said: "When a child is old enough to say Mother and Father, he is asking them for a younger sibling."

This production rate is maintained throughout the woman's child-bearing years. Occasionally one finds a mother and her married daughter sitting side by side, each nursing her latest offspring. Such age differences, of course, lead to nephews who are older than their uncles. Children in such a case call each other sibling.

Conception is the natural and desired outcome of marriage; as a favorite saying goes: "Go hand in hand, go hand in hand, later on a child." Sterility is pitiful, and a childless couple receive great sympathy and most often a young relative to raise. There is disagreement as to the cause of childlessness—some (especially the men) attributing it always to a lack in the woman, some (especially the women) saying that men also may be sterile—"perhaps they have only one testis."

If a woman is not conceiving, the only known remedy is to obtain from a *sirkano* roots, barks, and leaves, which are then boiled and drunk as cleansing agents. Such cleansing is also the specific function of the menstrual flow, according to the midwife: it "washes out impurities, for the woman must be clean to bear children."

PREGNANCY

Once conception has occurred, no deliberate control over the child's characteristics can be exercised by the parents. What the child will be—boy or girl, healthy or unhealthy, normal or malformed—these are primarily determined by luck. Specific characteristics must be obviously shared by a relative to be granted hereditary status. Twins appear "when two ova develop at the same time," but the reason for this is unknown—a matter of luck.

Conception, especially the first, is always considered a happy event, though tempered by concern in poor households. Nevertheless, there is no announcement of pregnancy except to the husband and probably the mother. Neighbors may quickly guess, but unless they ask, a woman does not volunteer such information. Nor is there much time devoted to hoping for special characteristics in the child—even the sex is not important unless the family has produced far more girls than boys or vice versa.

An even number of boys and girls is thought best, some preferring a girl first "so she could help launder clothes and do housework when the others come along," others preferring a boy first "so he could help in the fields and we would have more money to support a growing family." It is of interest that the preferences expressed in each family almost invariably coincided with the sex of their first-born. The boys seemed to have a slight edge when preferences were expressed before the birth of the first child.

Pregnancy is diagnosed when a woman misses her usual menstrual period; however, if she has not resumed the cycle after the birth of her last child, it may be diagnosed by nausea, specific cravings associated with pregnancy or perhaps only by a noticeable swelling of the abdomen. In the last case the date of delivery is determined by guesswork; normally it is expected nine months from the day when the menses should have occurred.

The period of pregnancy is potentially dangerous for the woman— she is "in death's balance." The major source of danger is the jealousy of the *not-humans,* who will cause miscarriage, even death, by striking the woman. Any pregnant woman, for example, should avoid going out of the house at night, and, if it is necessary for her to go, she should carry a number of *anibs*.

The pregnant woman must also avoid close contact with death: she must leave the house if someone is dying and stay elsewhere until after the funeral; she may attend the wake and funeral (if she is careful to leave the house before the corpse) but only as a guest —she must not touch the body; she must also avoid washing her hair on at least the subsequent Tuesday and Friday, the generally unlucky days. There is particular danger if she should even hear of the death of another pregnant woman and, should this occur, she must immediately wash her hair in lye and wine—"This will counteract the pull, so you will not be the next."

There is no clear sexual prohibition during pregnancy, the frequency of activity depending on the woman. There is some agreement that intercourse is not wise for at least two months prior to delivery. However, one woman laughingly said that, if there was no intercourse during this period, "it is due to mechanical difficulties, not prohibition."

The only foods prohibited during pregnancy are "bitter substances," such as bitter medicine, for they may abort. A few women suggest avoiding sweets, which "make the baby fat and hard to deliver." In this regard, some also say the woman should not submerge herself in water for long or there will be "too much water" and thus a difficult birth. Various effects on delivery also are predicted by some because of sitting in doorways, lying in certain positions, and so on.

Work prohibitions are few—the pregnant woman should not carry excessively heavy loads nor work in extreme heat, which is said to "cook the foetus," producing miscarriage. Nevertheless, rather than urging rest, such statements as the following are typical: "Do not siesta, for if you do, there will be more water and delivery will be hard" and "Work is good for you and makes delivery easier. Rice pounding makes the foetus fall into proper position." In fact, the pregnant woman to a large extent determines her work schedule to suit her girth, though none seem to rest unduly—one woman was observed slowly but contently harvesting rice two days before her delivery of good-sized twins. Although the necessity of field work (especially of rice harvesting) in poor families contributes significantly to the high incidence of miscarriages, these do not noticeably affect the health of the women, who invariably conceive again within a short time.

During the first three-month period nausea, especially on arising in the morning, is common, as well as marked displays of temperament, which are politely ignored or excused by neighbors and kin. This is also the time of strong, persistent cravings, which gradually taper off during the fourth and fifth months of pregnancy. Usually the desires are for specific foods but may be for people, places, pictures, or anything.

These desires "come from the child" and may vary with each pregnancy. They must be satisfied for the child's well-being, but they may create a permanent effect. Deformities at birth are always attributed to cravings and always on the principle of like effecting like. For example, one of the children in Sitio East has two fingers of one hand grown together—the result of her mother's craving for bananas (which commonly evidence this kind of growth); one boy has permanently crippled legs which are bent at the knee and upon which he can slide but neither walk nor crawl—this has been interpreted by some as the effect of a craving either for shrimp or for a picture of Christ kneeling in the garden of Gethsemene. Despite these explanations, little concern with prediction of possible effects of current cravings was shown.

All informants agree that men too may have a craving period, though less intense and of much shorter duration, beginning almost immediately after conception. It is manifested by lassitude, vague illness, and may or may not be accompanied by specific food desires. However, these same women said that, in fact, their husbands evidenced no such symptoms and no men were found who had experienced such cravings, although most had heard of it.

The craving complex, along with its associated nausea and touchiness, gradually disappears as the child "gains strength, for now it begins to move." In the fifth month of pregnancy the child is considered fully formed and "human—it has ears." In this connection it will be remembered that a miscarried child of five months or under is disposed of with no ceremony, but if born after this point it is carefully buried under the house. Despite the precautions against miscarriages, however, and the dangers associated with pregnancy, the behavior of the Tarongan expectant mother is not notably fearful. She is pleased, a bit smug, and prone to backache.

CHILDBIRTH

As her delivery date approaches, the expectant Tarongan woman prepares little for the event: an old mat and odd pieces of cloth are cleaned, and stored until needed; rags are braided to be burnt later (the *anib anglem*); a bamboo-slat bed used after birth is borrowed or brought from under the house to be stood on edge on the porch —if it is laid down before parturition it will bring bad luck. Baby clothes are made unless there are enough hand-me-downs, but the infant requires few beyond wrapping-cloths and caps.

Little fuss is made over delivery; after all, birth is a "natural thing" and trouble is not usually anticipated. Neighboring women and a few relatives will come to give help and moral support, but there is no such gathering as during an illness. This is less true of first births, which mark a change in status for the new father as well as the new mother; both will have greater independence from the family now and may move into the first house of their own.

As previously mentioned, it is such first births which put the mother-in-law in a position of highly responsible authority, testing her ability in this role. Reputedly, tension at the birth of the eldest son's first child is high.

It has also been mentioned that within Tarong itself there are three practicing midwives. Only one of these, Prudencio, is actually professional, the others limiting their services to their own children except in emergencies. Prudencio practices throughout the whole of Tarong and parts of all the surrounding *barrios*. Prudencio's fee is low, at most 5 pesos for a nonrelative, 2 or less for relatives. Normally one midwife is sufficient, but if difficulties arise, more may be summoned. In the case of one woman, four midwives were brought before she succeeded in delivering. Increasingly, in such cases, the woman is taken to a Poblacion doctor.

When questioned about their skills, midwives answer, "I watched and then tried to see if I could do it also," illustrating the non-supernatural nature of midwifery. Only Prudencio appears to have had something like an apprenticeship, as a young man assisting a renowned old woman who was a distant relative. His first delivery alone was the birth of his fourth child. Prudencio is cautious, has a good "beside manner," and is the most popular midwife.

Not until the first labor pains are final preparations made: a coconut is cracked, its meat grated and boiled to extract the oil, and a few bitter *ampilaya* leaves are crushed and tied in a clean cloth pouch, then soaked in the oil for later use. The midwife, the mother-in-law, a few neighboring women, and, if possible, a female relative, preferably a sister of the parturient woman, are notified. There is an attempt to keep young children of the household out of the room, but in the confusion of delivery they may be removed only if literally underfoot. The husband's presence about the house is essential, both for the performance of certain tasks and especially as a precaution against his angering *not-humans* at such a crucial time.

All informants agreed that two types of individuals must be rigidly excluded from a delivery room: one who has a cowlick on the forehead will make delivery difficult; one who was a breech birth will cause the child to be born this way also. It is interesting to note, however, that one of the women of Sitio East was assisted during delivery by her husband, a breech birth.

There were a number of births during the field period, one of which was attended by a member of the field team, and it is the description of this delivery we will present, supplemented by material drawn from observations and discussions of others. (Additionally, a set of twins, the first in 16 years, was born during the field period and no deviation from observed birth practices was noticed.)

Early one morning Josefa (a 38-year-old woman of Sitio East) announced her first labor pains. Telling her husband so that he would not go to the fields, she quickly went to bathe at the well before the cramps became too severe. Her three older children were sent off to school, one detouring to Bantai to notify Josefa's married sister who had agreed to housekeep for a week, since she had no young children to care for.

About 9:00 the midwife (Prudencio) was called. He came and talked with Josefa, whose cramps were about five minutes apart and who was complaining of severe back pains. Prudencio encouraged her to walk around, even sweep the floor until her cramps became too strong, since Josefa was known to have difficult births for which moderate exercise is considered helpful. He then went home, suggesting that she would probably not deliver until after lunch. Josefa walked about for a little as instructed, then sat on a chair, then alternated, obviously uncomfortable. She finally sat on the floor, legs to one side, her youngest child (not quite 2) in her lap, and her sister rubbed her back while her husband busied himself in the yard with chores.

By 11:00 Josefa's cramps were increasing in frequency. Her sister brought the birth mat, cloths, and *anglem* ropes to the kitchen. They discussed the relative merits of the methods of easing difficult births. The most common of these methods are: the husband may be called on to invert the house ladder; naturally hatched eggshells may be boiled in water, which is then drunk; a little dried horse manure may be burned, the ashes then dropped in water and drunk—"The idea of eating filth should cause the woman's body to push the filth out and the child with it"; crushed ginger may be applied to the belly when the pains are severe—"It is hot and will cause the baby to move."

The two last-mentioned techniques were decided upon, and before eating at 11:30, Josefa drank some of the burned manure. Then she ate a light meal, sitting at the low table on the kitchen porch with the family. The schoolchildren clamored to stay home, and it was agreed that they could, provided they took care of the two preschoolers and stayed out of the way.

It is said that births usually occur in the *sala* where there is more room, but deliveries in the kitchen are really more common because the kitchen floor is easier to clean and because the stove keeps the room hot. Accordingly, after eating, Josefa went into the very small kitchen and lay down on the mat, where Prudencio joined her about 12:00 to apply crushed ginger. The window shutters were closed against both *not-humans* and dangerous drafts, allowing little light in and no heat out; the stove roared, and a pot of water was put on to boil.

Josefa, now in evident pain and grimacing during her cramps, lay on the mat on her back, a small pillow under her head, her knees drawn up and covered with a blanket. Prudencio squatted next to her, applying pressure with both hands at a point just above the belly, this done during each cramp. Josefa's husband squatted across from Prudencio, holding his wife's arm; her sister, next to Prudencio, held the other. There was desultory conversation for over half an hour during which time the tableaux remained unchanged except for the occasional movements of Josefa's sister, who poured a bowlful of vinegar, arranged cloths, chased out the cat and the youngest child, who was fascinated by the proceedings.

Pressure above the belly, according to Prudencio, keeps the blood from going up. "At the center of the body are the two main paths of upward blood movement. There you must hold. If the pressure is not strong enough, the woman may see darkness because of the upward rush of blood. She may then sleep unto her death." Should such dizziness occur, vinegar is sprinkled on a winnowing tray, inverted over the stove, and when hot it is held over the woman's face. This treatment forces the blood down.

Occasionally Prudencio laid his hands on Josefa's belly, explaining that "until we feel the feet kick, we do not know if it is coming the right way. All children are face up inside the mother, but turn sideways as they come out. They are very small, and the first blast of air blows them up, like an egg. But there is no kicking there if it is a breech birth."

Josefa's cramps were growing severe, and several times she moaned, "God! God! It hurts!" Prudencio soothed her, once asking "Didn't your others hurt also?" He motioned to Josefa's mother-in-law, just entering the room, to help, and she placed some of the cloths under Josefa's buttocks, exposing no more than her lower legs and replacing the blanket immediately.

By 12:45 Josefa seemed no closer to delivery and was groaning during each cramp. After a discussion of additional ways to ease delivery, the eldest daughter was instructed to "mess the last thing put in order" by Josefa; in this case the rice she had pounded the preceding afternoon was stirred up. Had Josefa sewn any baby clothes, these would have been unseamed, but she had sewn none—perhaps the result of bitter experience during previous deliveries.

Josefa's sister-in-law, inquiring from her nearby kitchen window, was told to come, and when she had entered the now-crowded kitchen, she helped Prudencio and the husband to pull Josefa to a kneeling position. Resting on her heels she waited, Prudencio's arms tight about her waist. With the next cramp, he pushed down with great pressure but no result.

Prudencio then took a cloth, twisted it into a rope and wound it tightly about Josefa's waist. He pushed downward again with the next cramp, Josefa moaned loudly and the water sac broke. Pleased and with exclamations of "There!" "Almost finished," everyone helped Josefa lie down in the same position as before. Relieved, Josefa said, "It is hot. Fan me." While her husband complied, her sister squatted before her (had this been Josefa's first delivery, this position would have been the mother-in-law's), quickly replaced the cloths and arranged more into a pad. The bowl of vinegar was moved closer to the stove, and all the assistants squatted about Josefa, her husband and sister-in-law holding her arms, her mother-in-law and sister bracing her bent legs (still covered by the blanket).

Prudencio knelt next to her and pressed firmly on the center of her body as before, pushing downward also as the labor contractions began. After eight or so strong pushes, during which time Josefa strained but made no outcry and the blanket remained intact, the baby, a girl, was delivered onto the pad-covered hands of Josefa's sister (1:20 P.M.). The baby, crying lustily, was laid between its mother's legs while Prudencio retied the band about Josefa's waist "to keep the blood from flowing to her head" and the bowl of hot vinegar was held under her nose to counteract faintness. Although the waist band may be loosened the next day, it is not removed until normal activities are resumed.*

The painful part of childbirth now over, the group relaxed and joked with Josefa who, beaming, wanted to know the sex of her child. They teasingly refused to tell her, so giggling, she raised herself on her elbows for a moment to look at it. One of the children, brought through the door by the baby's cries, now ladled a pan of boiling water for Prudencio's scissors. Within a few moments the placenta was naturally expelled. The umbilical cord is never cut until the placenta is expelled; death is believed to result from this.

The most frequent difficulty in childbirth is said to be the child's "refusal to breathe." Forcing blood down the umbilical cord is the only known remedy, and if not immediately effective, the placenta itself is placed on the coals of the stove and rubbed; more warm blood is forced down to the child. According to Prudencio this treatment is not unusual. In one case "the placenta had already shrunk to ashes before the baby cried." Should the child never breathe despite this treatment, the subsequent procedures are not altered except for omission of the cord cutting and *anglem* burning, since the latter is for the child's protection.

Probably the second most commonly encountered difficulty is retarded expulsion of the placenta, and the four remedies known are tried in the following order. Pressure is applied along with slight, careful pulling of the umbilical cord. If this has no effect, the woman blows as hard as possible into a bottle; the strain resulting should force out the placenta. It was claimed that one Sitio East woman kept this up for more than half an hour before the next method was tried. It consists of heating the wooden handle of a ladle until very hot, then pressing it into the woman's naval area. The woman referred to developed infected burns from this treatment, indicating it was continued for some time before the last successful if unusual method was used. The husband's shorts were sprinkled with vinegar, heated over the stove and spread over the woman's abdomen.

These dangers past, Prudencio pushed the blood in the umbilical cord down to the child, tied the cord in two places and cut between the ties. The cord was traditionally cut with a knife or preferably a sharpened piece of bamboo from the house wall but is now generally cut with scissors.

As the umbilical cord of Josefa's baby was being cut, her sister

---

* Obstetrical surgery is almost unknown, only one case of perineal cutting (by fingernail) being reported.

lit one of the twisted-cloth ropes in a bowl near Josefa's head. This *anib* should burn until the cord falls off the child, for it counteracts the smell of childbirth so that the *not-humans* cannot take the child's life. Similarly, ashes were placed on the cut end of the umbilicus, then oil. Both are smeared around the navel area, the cord wrapped and covered by a belly band.

Prudencio then put the placenta into a pot (which must have a perfect rim), covering it with the "eye" half of a coconut shell, and set it next to the burning *anib*. (If the shell-half without a hole were used, the baby would be subject to colds, nasal and throat ailments.) There is no examination of the placenta. "The midwife feels the stomach and can tell if it's all out." For a first birth, however, a tiny piece of the placenta is charred, pulverized, and mixed with water for the new mother to drink. The effect is variously interpreted as insurance for future successful childbearing and as prevention of shock subsequent to delivery.

At some convenient time that day, the husband takes the placenta-pot to some out of the way place and hangs it in a tree (a recent Poblacion custom adds a paper and pencil to ensure future scholarship). There is no further interest in it unless the child, while still very young, develops respiratory difficulties. In this case the father knocks it down to cure the child.

Having disposed of the placenta, Prudencio turned again to the child. He sponged it with warm water and wrapped it well and put on a little cap. Smiling proudly at the now sleepy child, he handed it to Josefa's sister-in-law, who placed it on a vinegared winnowing tray and bounced it lightly up and down "so it will not be easily frightened."

Josefa was now given warm water to drink, a bitter root to chew to alleviate nausea, and a cigar. The shutters were opened slightly, and the baby was given the *ampilaya*—oil pouch to suck, everyone laughing as it made faces at the bitterness. This pouch is thought to cleanse the black mucous from the bowels and it is offered whenever the child cries for the first few days of its life.

For about 15 minutes the group in the kitchen, joined by two neighbors and the children of the house, chatted happily and fussed over the baby. Payment for Prudencio was not discussed, since Josefa's family is both poor and related to him. Her husband is in Prudencio's work group and can repay there. The men were then sent off and the slat bed laid down in the *sala*, its foot raised 12 to 15 inches above the floor, the head about 2 feet ("so the blood will not go to the head") and the baby moved to it. Josefa was then cleaned, trussed with cloths, and helped to the bed, where she soon slept. The remaining women gradually left as Josefa's sister began preparations for the meat soup which is thought to be good for a new mother. Shooing the perplexed youngest child out of the kitchen ahead of her, she told the girl, "You will now eat the chicken waiting (tied) under the house" which, judging from the child's delight, was adequate compensation.

⚶
⚶
⚶

Chapter 11

The Post-Partum Period

After delivery, the Tarongan woman enters two post-partum periods: the *dalagan* and the *tangad*. Although up to one month the two periods are concurrent, their identity is never confused, for both the nature of the requirements and their purposes are distinct.

Compared to the agreement found in regard to birth practices, there is considerable variation in reported *dalagan* and especially *tangad* observance. But the variations, like those relating to talismans, are matters of specifics, not principles. The purposes of the post-partum regulations and their general descriptions are uniformly accepted.

DALAGAN

The *dalagan* period takes its name from the inclined bed used after delivery and is said to be for the benefit of both mother and child. The regulations, in fact, have more to do with maintenance of the mother's health than the child's and the period is characterized by confinement and "roasting" of the mother. She and her infant must stay on their *dalagan* bed for 11 to 30 days. The mother may get up only to eliminate. Even then she must be sure to keep herself well covered with a blanket so the wind cannot strike her.

Nothing cold must touch mother or child. The shutters are kept at least partially closed; food and water are warmed; the child is carefully wrapped and capped; a fire is maintained in a stove placed somewhere in the room, most often next to the bed so that the woman can cook a bit and tend the fire when she must be left alone. The only exception to this confinement is made for baptism, which may be performed during the *dalagan* if the child does not seem strong. In this case, the mother remains at home and the baby is taken to the Church by relatives.

Because of the enforced inactivity, neighbors visit frequently, and a mother-in-law, sister, or adolescent daughter is in attendance when possible. During planting or harvesting season, however, the new mother and her husband may well have to manage by themselves. In this case, the husband is expected to take over the woman's duties —bringing firewood and water, cooking until the wife is able, even washing if necessary, although another woman will almost always volunteer for this task.

It is noteworthy that husbands rarely complain about these added duties, in fact, during one interview two fathers jokingly challenged each other's right to claim the best-kept *"dalagan* house," much to the amusement of their wives. Beyond this, the husband has no specific duties during the *dalagan* or *tangad*.

Before the morning meal on the day following delivery and thenceforth every morning of the *dalagan,* the *ilot of childbirth* comes to massage the new mother. This masseuse is very welcome, all women agreeing that they feel much better, when she has finished. The *ilot* massages the extremities with coconut oil along major veins (distal to proximate direction) and, with an upward motion, the back and chest and especially the abdomen ("This puts the uterus back in place"). The massage is vigorous and thorough, lasting half an hour or longer.

Also on this first or the following day, after the warm morning bath, most women expose themselves, a portion at a time, to the heat of the stove "to stop the blood." Heating at the stove is continued until about the ninth day when the mother washes her hair with warm water. On this day the "roasting" begins, a process which "fixes the uterus in position" and alleviates birth soreness.

After a good meal to fortify her for the ordeal, the woman sits on a cane-bottom (or bamboo-slat) chair draped in a blanket from head to floor, while a bowl of glowing hot coals is placed under her. There she "roasts" until the coals are cold. This is repeated daily until the end of the *dalagan.* Tarongan women complain little of delivery but loudly bemoan the discomfort of "roasting," many insisting it is the most arduous part of childbirth.

Beyond the minimum 11 days, the precise length of the *dalagan* depends on the condition of the mother, how many previous births have occurred and how much heat she can endure each "roasting" period. Josefa, for example, remained *dalagan* 15 days because she could not stand too much heat.

Final determination is by the *ilot* in conjunction with the mother-in-law and other women of the household. As she massages the woman every morning, she judges how recovered she is by the firmness of the abdominal muscles, a duty never taken lightly, for should the woman become ill at some later date, insufficient "roasting" during *dalagan* may well be diagnosed as the cause of her illness. *Ilots,* tend, therefore, to be very conservative in their estimate of the required time for exposure, an attitude very annoying to active young mothers who have already borne two or three children. Table 4 gives a summary of the usual *dalagan* periods with number of massages, number of "roasting" sessions, and length of *tangad* period. It will be noted that the length of *dalagan* period and the number of required treatments decrease with the number of previous children.

Table 4 Post-Partum Requirements

LENGTH OF DALAGAN PERIOD, IN DAYS		NO. OF VISITS OF MASSEUSE (*ilot*)	NO. OF "ROASTING" PERIODS	TANGAD, IN MONTHS
Premature babies				
1–5 months	1–5	1–3	1–4	0–1
6–8 months	6–7	5–7	4–6	2–3
Full term				
1st child	27–30	27–30	18–21	5
2nd child	22–25	22–25	13–16	5
3rd child	19–21	19–21	10–12	5
4th child	15–17	15–17	6–8	5
5th, etc.	11–15	11–15	2–6	5

After *dalagan* is over, the woman remains warmly dressed for three days, the cooling-off period, during which time she generally remains indoors. The period formally ends with a cold bath and hair wash. After this, most women feel sexual relations are again proper but some prefer to wait longer. The usual time for resumption of intercourse seems to be four to six weeks after delivery.

Some women say that on the day of the cold bath the mother should pound one mortarful of rice although she should not resume her regular pounding for at least another two weeks. For a month she is encouraged to limit herself to light work, and heavy lifting is prohibited. She wears a tight, protective band around her hips and sometimes another around her chest while she works.

The post-partum period is characterized by effective care for the physical well-being of the mother and by essentially no concern for supernatural dangers. The period of pregnancy is just the opposite, with almost the entire emphasis on avoidance of supernatural danger and little concern with physical care. This difference may explain the apparently low incidence of postbirth complications and high incidence of miscarriage.

TANGAD

In addition to the *dalagan,* at delivery the new mother enters the five-month period of *tangad* (literally "to take care"). It is believed that both mother and child are now especially vulnerable to ills and care must be taken. Despite the mother's presumed benefits from this care, transgressions almost always harm the child so that, in effect, the *dalagan* maintains the health of the mother, the *tangad* that of the child.

Tangad is a set of regulations, all but one referring to food and all designed to ensure an ample, nourishing milk supply. The exception referred to is the prohibition against both child and mother being in the sun too long, since the child will either be directly affected or will "suck in the heat," both of which produce fever and illness.

For at least the first two or three births, a mother's observation of *tangad* regulations is entirely in the hands of her watchful, responsible mother-in-law. Slight variations in rules between household groups is not surprising, but the following classifications are universal even if their constituents vary: The recommended foods are few, largely of the plain, nourishing type and, specifically, unripe papaya, which is eaten to induce and increase the flow of breast milk "because wherever you cut the papaya, (white) juice flows from it." A diet rich in vegetables and fish is useful also in this regard as is a brew of herbs sold by the mountain people, but these herbs are neither common nor requisite. Inimical to good milk and thus to the child are what translate as sour, tasty, and slippery foods. Slippery foods are okra, various seaweeds, mushrooms, and so forth, all of which cause the uterus to "slip." Tasty is a category not equivalent to any English term but includes oily foods whose flavor is strong, for instance, peanuts, canned fish, and fatty meat.

A few specific foods, such as octopus and squash blossom (which is thought to cause tuberculosis in the mother), are also excluded from the diet, but these vary considerably. Opinion also differs regarding sweets other than ripe fruit, which is usually acceptable; some women say no sweets should be eaten; most say a small quantity with a meal will do no harm after *dalagan;* a few feel that unless the child is unquestionably affected, sweets are entirely permissible. The refusal of cautious mothers-in-law to allow any sweets during *tangad* is a frequently mentioned source of annoyance to daughters-in-law raised in more permissive households.

Although the food regulations are not really restrictive, the heat regulation is in that it forces the Tarongan mother to stay close to home. Because she must feed the baby whenever it cries, she cannot leave it for long. One cannot expect one's neighbors to be always feeding one's child and especially at this age it is frowned on unless necessary.

All women with unweaned children are somewhat limited, but the *tangad* is especially curtailing as is evident in the women's occasional complaints that they have not been to market for months, that they missed a party in the next *barrio,* and so on. Nevertheless, the complaints remain occasional and not very serious, for *tangad* neighbors often gather during the day with their infants and the mother may attend parties, dances, and wakes within the *sitio.* Only the economically active, trading women and wives of poor tenant farmers find the *tangad* onerous. Since there is a tendency toward laxity in *tangad* observation near the end of the period, these women usually cut short the *tangad* (and *dalagan* as well) and arrange their return to normal life as quickly as possible.

The typical Tarongan woman, by the end of her first *tangad,* is accustomed to the limitations and as infant succeeds infant at her breast she grows less interested in direct participation in the outside-*sitio* world, finding her time occupied with increasing duties at home, which give her increased status among her immediate kin neighbors.

＊
＊
＊

Chapter 12

Infancy

KAYANNAK, THE NEWBORN

All informants agree that the Tarongan newborn leads a secluded life next to his mother on the *dalagan* in a dim, warm, quiet room. Nothing could be farther from the truth. His mother is remarkably active on the *dalagan*. When not directly engaged in cooking, sewing, and disciplining the older children, she loudly directs activities in all parts of the household. Neighbors and in-laws stop in to see and pat the new baby. Its older siblings clamber over the *dalagan,* in part to play with the baby, in part just to be included in all the fuss; the just-weaned elder child is very likely to become as permanent a figure on the bed as the newborn. Even the first-born child does not escape Tarongan sociability, for his young cousin-neighbors will invade, begging to hold and play with him.

But whatever the *dalagan* room may lack in quiet, it certainly makes up in affection. Tarongan babies are helpless, irresponsible, charming little creatures, hence they are quickly nurtured, carefully protected, and smothered with affection by anyone and everyone. The babies thrive on this treatment.

It is during this period of being newborn that most decisions are made as to cause and treatment of deformities or irregularities the child may exhibit. Generally these are assumed to be irremediable. For those rare cases of serious impairment, hair washing ceremonies may be held but there is not great faith in this treatment. If it is the child's luck to be born this way, there is nothing to be done about it. And perhaps it will be good luck, who can tell?

Given a reasonably healthy infant, the only perceivable anxiety is that concerning sufficiency and quality of milk. Colostrum is considered neither milk nor good food for the baby, and is squeezed out.

Before the mother's milk comes, whenever the infant is not pacified by the bitter oil pouch, some nursing mother in the neighborhood will come and feed it. A woman still *tangad* is preferred, but if all are past *tangad,* one of them can still nurse the child although she will avoid the sun for those few days so as not to make the child ill.

The ability to suck is assumed—"the child sucks in the uterus"— and only one occurence of inability to suck was remembered. In this case the child's lips were repeatedly stimulated by the bitter oil pouch and within a day it sucked. Occasionally colostrum seeps out of the breast too slowly and true milk is not produced. For this, a young puppy whose eyes are not yet open is procured to suck out the colostrum. The deaths of one woman's first two children were attributed to insufficient cleansing of the breasts. A puppy may also be used to suck out an inverted nipple. Only one Tarongan woman suffered from inverted nipples, and this treatment had succeeded for one breast but not the other, her five children having been fed from one breast only. This was considered unfortunate, not because of possible milk shortage, but because the breasts should be alternated, since the child's head will be flattened on one side if habitually fed at one breast. In practice, shifting the child's position seemed to result from stiffness of the arm rather than from concern for the child's head.

For the occasional mother whose milk is insufficient, supplementary canned or powdered milk may be bought, but the expense and trouble involved, along with rapid spoilage, make supplementary feedings by another nursing mother more practical. Again it is preferable if the woman is *tangad.* If milk is given by one mother to another, in a container (when distance is a problem or when the child is very young), the recipient must give a token payment or the donor's breasts will dry. A little polished rice, which is chewed and massaged on the breasts, is considered payment in full. Related to this belief is the statement: "If the breast milk drips and is just left and maybe cockroaches, insects get into it—then the breast dries up." These explanations were given for the otherwise inexplicable drying of two Tarongan women who later produced milk aplenty. To give milk without payment indicates you do not value it, just as leaving remnants for the cockroaches does.

Should a mother die during delivery, the infant is usually raised by a still-nursing mother. Less frequently, rice is pounded to a fine flour, which is then boiled until thick; sugar is added and this formula fed by bottle. This rice mixture is considered very nourishing and, though exceedingly tedious to prepare, even a mother having sufficient milk will occasionally prepare it to supplement a puny infant's diet.

The special term for the newborn, *kayannak,* is used only for the first two weeks or less of his life—in other words until the time the umbilical cord falls off—the symbolic separation of mother and child. Because of its earlier life-giving function, the umbilicus is accorded considerable attention during this period. It is believed that the child cries more before the cord falls off, the naval area being sore and tender. In part to relieve this soreness and in larger part as protection from *not-humans,* the use of the belly-band and ash-oil applications begun at delivery are continued. *Anglem anibs,* lit at delivery, should also be maintained.

Even after the cord has fallen off, it is still considered a part of the child. Therefore it is wrapped in cotton and hung somewhere about the house (generally in a window) where the wind will strike it to toughen the child's chest-belly region so that it will withstand cold winds when he is of an age to be clothed in no more than a shirt. But after this initial hanging no further note is taken of the cord and it is blown away by the winds of the next monsoon. An interesting variant of Poblacion origin is the wrapping of the cord in the same bundle as those of his siblings "so they will be harmonious."

Daily applications of ash and oil to the navel are maintained until it is completely healed, often a matter of a few weeks. After the umbilicus has healed, the newborn and most dangerous period is over: the child is now simply *tagibi* (baby) until the age of weaning. This division of infancy effects a change in relationship between the child and the supernatural world, not between the child and his family. All it means in terms of daily care is that the smoke *anib* and ash-oil applications are eliminated. But to the parents, the use of *tagibi* means a successful birth, for the newborn is seen as a provisional infant, not yet a separate stable entity.

TAGIBI, THE BABY

Tarongan mothers were asked: "When your child was a baby and he cried, what did you usually do?" The answers were uniformly a laugh at such an incomprehensible question and "I fed him." These answers were observably accurate. During infancy the child's desire to suck is consistently indulged: the breast is given to children whenever they cry and for as long as they evidence interest or continued distress.

This feeding pattern is not materially altered until weaning. Due to mothers' abilities to feed their babies while doing a number of tasks, the child may be fed while the mother is lying down, sitting up, standing, or squatting. One arm around a baby who straddles a hip by four months is sufficient, and a child quickly learns to hold tightly to his mother's blouse as he eats. But no matter what task is interfered with, the breast is never removed until the child is satiated or at least comforted.

The attitude toward one's child being nursed by another mother varies once the mother's milk supply is stable. A few women said: "I do not like to have my child suck from another mother if I can help it"; most felt it was perfectly all right although they seldom did it. But one group of women was notable for its communal nursing. These four sisters-in-law all had children roughly the same ages, lived in one family housing group and were relatively poor, which meant frequent field work for the women. During busy seasons one of these nursing women (usually the one with the youngest child) could be found taking care of all the children under school age—eight of them, four not yet weaned—assisted perhaps by a few of the older siblings. This pattern of child care and communal nursing is, for economic reasons, most practiced in poor family groups.

During at least the *tangad* and longer if she is not needed for field work, the infant's mother is rarely out of his sight; indeed, ideally he is seldom out of contact with her when he is awake. Infants are held unless they are asleep; even then the child sleeps with his mother while she is *dalagan* and between his parents after this until the next child is born. During the day a basketry hammock may be used to rock him to sleep, but very little commotion is required to ensure being picked up and rocked in a lap.

One specific restriction is that the child sleep only on his back or side, for if a child were to sleep on his stomach he would "turn his back" on his parents when older. The child with only young or no siblings and few grandparents or aunts receives perhaps somewhat less constant attention. But even in such households, and they are very few in number, the *tangad* heat regulations keep the mother about the house for half of the first year of the child's life.

The largest part of the infant's waking day is spent lying, sitting, or semistanding in the lap of a relatively attentive and certainly nurturant adult. No child this age is ever left to cry, and a child or adult allowing a baby to cry longer than, say, six squalls will be scolded sharply by any other adult in the vicinity. We observed not only parents and husbands but even older children mildly rebuke a busy mother for occasionally crooning to a crying child instead of picking him up.

In general, when a child cries, the mother first offers the breast. Should the child not be hungry and refuse the breast as consolation, she will bounce him in her lap or rock him astride her hip. If these fail, distracting objects and noises will be introduced: pattings, crooning, clapping, odd noises, objects about the house or yard, anything which might amuse, will be tried by one or another caretaker. A chronically colicky baby can thus thoroughly disrupt the functioning of an entire household.

Although there is no systematic effort to determine the cause of crying, generally one or another of these techniques will be effective. As the child grows older and is given more often to the care of siblings or grandparents, distracting techniques rival the breast in frequency of use.

Daily care of an infant is not laborious but is time consuming in that it requires near-constant attention. Beginning in the *dalagan* period, the infant is washed at least once daily, usually by immersing in a basin of water. During the five-month *tangad* period, the water is warmed, but after this, the water is used directly from the well or, at most, allowed to stand in the sun a short while. Infants frequently object to this sudden shift but accustom themselves to it within a few days.

When the child is old enough to sit unsupported, he is placed in a larger basin of water on the porch and allowed to splash about under the watchful eye of an adult. This daily bath, generally given during the later part of the morning, is a great pleasure to children, and no youngster at any age was ever heard to object.

Until the child's fontanel closes, oil is applied to it after each bath so the wind will not strike it, which would result in a protrusive deformation in that area. As further protection, a stocking cap may be worn during the first few months of life, particularly if it is the cold season. Cloths, blankets, or other garments are presumably wrapped around the child if the weather requires it, but such wrapping is rarely observed, cold or hot, beyond the first few months of life.

Clothing is essentially the same for boys and girls: a shirt or dress of some sort, usually reaching no lower than the navel for boys, just covering the buttocks for girls. The infant is covered loosely, if at all, below the waist. When he urinates, the puddle is wiped up or the cloth is changed; if the mother's clothing is wet, it is ignored. While interviewing or chatting with mothers of infants, we noticed that in almost all instances of the child's wetting the mother, her response was to merely shift the child to a dry part of the lap and shift the wet portion of the skirt so that it would dry. There was no verbal or facial recognition of the incident. Excretions from nose, eyes, and so on are simply wiped away, no importance being attached to them.

Precautions are taken, however, against the mother's clothes being soiled by feces. A folded cloth is kept under the buttocks of infants, and after defecation, the cloth is replaced. Babies able to sit with support are placed on the bamboo porch when they show signs of imminent defecation, and the feces are then washed through the floor with water. At 6 months or so, training is begun by moving the child to a corner of the kitchen porch over the waste-puddle for both urination and defecation.

The only pain deliberately inflicted on a child is the minor one of piercing girls' ears, generally in the first or second month. A red thread is put through the holes and fastened with a dab of beeswax. At 6 months it is considered safe to use a small gold ring, but younger babies pull at such things and may rip the ear lobes.

Tarongans are concerned not only with the infant's physical wellbeing but also with his comfort. Cooling baths, sufficient tempting food, avoidance of dangerous or dirty objects, all are thought to contribute to the comfort of the child. Fans are used to cool sleeping children and mosquito nets are placed over the hammocks by roughly half the mothers, more to keep off disturbing flies than to prevent mosquito bites. All mothers sprinkle young babies liberally with talcum powder to soothe the skin and prevent prickly heat.

Thus infancy is characterized by indulgence, constant attention, and few, if any, demands on the child. Maturation is seen as a leisurely process, a bit different for each child, and one which does not admit acceleration. There is no specific encouragement of talking, walking, or other skills although there is sometimes admiration for a child whose development is markedly rapid. In any case, neither speed nor slowness in maturation is seen as affected by parental desires (training) or parental abilities (heredity). "Babies do what they will. It is of no use to press them. They do not yet understand what is wanted. This is the time for parents to be patient. Their turn will come later when there is more understanding."

During at least the first month of the child's life he receives most of this affectionate caretaking from his mother, but even at this early age other relatives play an active role. As the child grows older, the number and frequency of other caretakers increase. The following figures, corrected in one instance by observation, are representative: 8 of the 24 sample mothers reported that another woman took more care of her child than she did herself—"I did little more than feed him."

Another 8 could not say who did most of the caretaking, "We all here (in the immediate house cluster) took care. I fed him, but when he was older that was almost all I did. There were many here to help.'

Analysis of the 16 mothers who were not principal caretakers shows that in all cases the mothers lived with parents, maiden aunts, older children, and sisters-in-law either within the same household or in immediately adjacent households. Only one of these women lived out side the three largest *sitios* and in this case her mother-in-law was a resident of the household.

Of the eight mothers who were principal caretakers, three lived in isolated houses or small *sitios* with no appropriate surrogates nearby. Three were wealthy, did little work, and needed surrogates seldom; the other two were busy women who used surrogates but did not get along too well with their neighbors and preferred to do as much of their own caretaking as possible. Age of the child, beyond the *tangad* period, does not seem to affect the use or nonuse of surrogates.

In no household did a mother have sole responsibility for her children—it would be unthinkable. Any adult or older child will immediately rescue a crying baby if his mother cannot reach him quickly. During meal preparation especially, when the women are busy in the kitchens, older siblings and fathers gather in the yard, a baby on each lap, to supervise the preschool children and chat about the day's work.

Men are no less affectionate and indulgent to their children than women, though a bit less demonstrative. One doting middle-aged grandfather was rarely seen away from the fields without his infant grandson in his arms. When the child was taken by his mother on a lengthy visit to another province, this man was inconsolable until he hit on the idea of substituting his recently weaned niece. When he was encountered at an evening dance, the sleeping girl in his arms, he answered our question with tears in his eyes: "They have taken my boy away."

In general, the amount of caretaking expected of a father depends on the number of available female surrogates. If the house is relatively isolated and the family nuclear, the father may well hold the baby whenever he is not in the fields, bathe it, change its clothes, feed it tidbits. If the house has many women or older girls, he will rarely do more than play with the child while it is still young.

One woman put it this way: "When the fathers come home from the fields, the carabao get their first attention, the children their second." All fathers play with and carry their children some of the time and would be furious if it was suggested that this was woman's work. When informants say "We all take care of our children" they mean we *all,* and grandfathers are almost as often surrogates as grand-mothers.

The only practice inconsistent with the general indulgence of young children is a variety of adult "playing" with children, done almost entirely by women and starting as soon as the child can want something. Some object (or even person) the child may value is taken by an adult, who acts as if she were going to leave with it. As she goes toward the door she smilingly asks the child: "I will go now and take this, ah?" If there is no response, variations of the question are repeated until the child perceives a potential loss and makes an outcry. At the first sign of clear distress (a howl or angry roar) the women laugh, give the object back and say: "No, no—we are only playing." The game may start again with a new object within a few minutes.

Children learn to "play" by making a loud and immediate outcry, enjoyed by all present. Whether this is an excuse for hostility on the part of the adults or perceived in some way as helping the child learn to "take a kidding" we do not know, for no amount of probing could get past the "play" interpretation. But it was noticeable that the game was limited almost exclusively to women and indulged in most frequently by those with no young children at home.

This picture of socialization does not change much until weaning, usually between 2 and 3 years. Until then modifications are made in accordance with the child's development, but the attitudes toward him remain essentially the same: he is a helpless creature with no sense. Sometime before the first birthday he is baptized and a feast given, but the event is no more than a party. Certainly the child's status relevant to the group is not affected.

The assumption at this stage is that little learning is possible. Obviously the Tarongan child does learn how to be sociable very rapidly and reacts with delight to large numbers of people who are familiars, but since this is thought a normal reaction, it goes unmarked. Similarly, a child who picks up the mannerisms of nurturance early will be highly rewarded for this good behavior. But the emphasis is on taking care of and protecting a "senseless" child. Protection and care are primarily defined as keeping the child out of danger (away from porch-edges, out of reach of stones, dirt, out of the hot sun, away from spirit places, etc.) and feeding him properly.

Protection from danger is, in effect, a series of prohibitions on the child's movements, gradually redefined as the child matures (though invariably lagging behind his potentialities) and enforced largely by simple removal of the child from an unsafe place. Removal rather than prevention (that is, the use of play pens or other restrictive devices) presupposes a constant attendant, and this duty now is increasingly shared by older siblings. They trot the babies about on their hips even while playing and are completely responsible though rather summary in their treatment.

One result of this protective outlook is that a young child is rarely able to explore his environment fully. If his caretaker has a task to finish or a game to play, he may be whisked off on a hip at any moment. If his crawlings or toddlings interfere with other activities, he is picked up and held or deposited in a more convenient place. If he howls in objection, the breast is offered or he is bounced about and played with. At this age aggression is not recognized as such—at most it calls forth: "Oh, he does not like!" The Tarongan infant soon exhibits a greater passivity toward his environment than the average American child but a far greater pleasure in sociable interaction with others of any age.

Some encouragement is given to skills like climbing house ladders and walking, but only under conditions of comparative safety and convenience for the caretaker. In this regard, sibling care is beneficial, for children tire of carrying their younger siblings and are more likely than their mothers to let them crawl and walk about the house and yard.

Siblings are also quite likely to set the child down in the midst of an older age-group game and play along. Generally the children watch with interest for quite a time before they grow restive and must, with a sigh, be replaced on their caretaker's hip or lap. Sometimes their involuntary participation can be very active: we observed more than one instance of a hip-baby being bobbed about in a frenzied game of tag until its mother noticed also!

Despite the fact that mothers say supplementary food is not introduced until about one year, from 4 months on most babies can be seen now and then gnawing drumsticks, store cookies or fruit. Tidbits of fish, fruit, and so forth are also popped into their mouths as are soft bits of mealtime rice. Parents say foods given to young children should be easy to digest, but, judging from observations, anything may be given to the child if he is able to chew it. After about a year, the soft portions of the rice from the center of the pot are presented to the child at each meal and, as he eats more, whatever else the family may be eating is also offered.

By 1½ years, mother's milk is a small part of the baby's diet, although the breast is still in frequent use as a pacifier. By 3 or earlier, the child's diet is that of the adult except that between-meal snacks are far more common. There is a pervasive concern with sufficiency of food, both for children and adults, as is noticeable in case of illness, the seriousness of which is often gauged by the patient's lack of desire for food. If a family is poor, all are expected to give up without complaint some of their portion to satisfy the younger members, those under 7 or 8. Up to this age, even complaints about monotonous food will produce coaxing to eat with tempting bits of fish, eggs, fruit if available, or promised rewards of one kind or another.

Initially the child is fed from the mother's fingers but between 1 and 2 years, the child will be given a bowl of rice and encouraged to feed himself, usually while seated on an adult's lap. Mothers complain about the length of this training process, since neatness in eating is the goal—a difficult one when eating rice with the fingertips. Most children acquire this skill by the age of 3, but parents continue for a number of years to complain of food wasted through carelessness.

Sucking the thumb or fingers is neither encouraged nor consistently discouraged in infancy. However, in an older child, if habitual, it signifies the child is "not endowed with the usual amount of sense." When the child is a year or so and able to play in the yard, the thumb or finger is lightly slapped away, "Dirty, dirty," accompanying the gesture. This casual treatment seems to be effective, for no child was ever seen sucking his thumb past very early infancy. Possibly the handiness of the breast makes such sucking superfluous. Putting of sticks, stones, and such objects in the mouth merits the same treatment more vigorously applied; the child soon learns to place nothing in his mouth not offered by a responsible caretaker.

Toilet training is intensified some time before weaning, usually at about 1½ years when the child is able to understand simple verbal instruction and express his need to urinate or defecate. As soon as the child is able to walk he is directed to the porch corner frequently and chided for mistakes. With the problems of distance and buttons or zippers being absent, bladder control is accomplished with no upset and by 3 at the latest. After this, children are encouraged to use the outhouse although most do not bother except for defecation. Bedwetting is less easily controlled, but generally by 4, lapses are only occasional and merit no more than a light scolding. A few mothers reported the following practice: "When he wet the blanket, I waited until morning and as soon as he opened his eyes, I covered him all over with the blanket. But you must not take it off—let him pull it off himself. This acts like *anib* and they do not wet it any more."

Bowel control is handled in the same fashion except that use of the outhouse instead of the porch is encouraged earlier, that is, by 2 (with an attendant for safety). Lapses also occasion sharper scolding, even a slap if the child is past the permissible age (4 at the latest). One mother was overheard scolding a 3-year-old for defecating in the yard: "It is so dirty and shameful for passers-by to see this mess scattered about." A flat stick is the usual toilet paper, and mothers say it is some time before children gain proficiency in its use. But bowel, like bladder control, is attained with no apparent resistance, only one mother reporting any difficulty with any child. In this case a boy of about 5 had developed the unusual habit of climbing a low fruit tree in the yard in order to defecate. The mother vacillated between amusement and alarm at the practice.

By the time toilet training is completed, boys are given short pants, but girls may not wear underpants for another year or two, since their dresses are long enough to satisfy modesty requirements and soap and cloth are expensive. The responsibility for meeting girls' modesty requirements is assumed by their caretakers, who twitch skirts down whenever necessary. Girls, however, are not allowed freedom of leg movement as are boys, and, beginning at birth, caretakers make sure that their legs are together when sitting, the skirt covering the genitals. This repeated shifting of position or covering the girls' genitals when exposed is sufficient to train girls fairly well by 4 or 5. An added reinforcement goes into effect as soon as the girl is old enough to play outside: it is a prerogative of young boys to lightly pinch girls' genitals if they are exposed. This privilege is exercised with hilarity and enthusiasm and is a most effective training method.

Of the 24 sample mothers, 17 reported no incidence of masturbation at any age. Three said it had occurred with their boys only during infancy: "With Mario (1½ years) and Andres (11 months)—we take the hand, slap it and say 'Do not fondle your penis—it is bad.'" Three mothers reported that their boys of 2 and 3 years sometimes did this, earning a slap: "A few times I saw him pushing the foreskin back and gave a sharp slap to the hand and a sharp look." One mother reported that her 2-year-old daughter, "sometimes rolls her sex organ back and forth in her fingers. . . . I scold and whip the hand." This activity is attributed by some to insufficient cleansing of the genitals; most assume it is inherently pleasurable but must be prohibited before it becomes a habit.

Aside from what is seen as a deliberate playing with genitals, there is little concern with any evidence of sexuality in infancy. Erection of the penis during sleep brings a smile, no more. One grandmother noticed the erect penis of her 1½-year-old charge who was sitting on her lap. Without interrupting the conversation and with a smile, she tapped the tip of his penis with her forefinger until it subsided; no further comment was made.

Beyond initial toilet, table manners, and modesty training, no demands are made on the unweaned child save that of remaining in sight of some responsible person at all times—a duty which falls more to these persons than the child. During this period, problems are met largely by distracting the child, pacifying it, and indulging its whims whenever possible.

A well-fed, happy baby is the ideal, and any expression of pleasure on the part of the infant is highly rewarding to Tarongans. Nevertheless, adults are usually content with a placid stare. Games which might provoke a laugh are most often played with the baby to distract him from some infantile misery, but mothers or caretakers who have no pressing duties or are simply feeling affectionate may begin such interaction.

A favorite with very young children is peek-a-boo with a cloth or merely the hands held before the face. By the time the baby is able to crawl, it has become more elaborate, and siblings often pop in and out from a hiding place behind a partition, shrieking peek-a-boo, at which racket Tarongan babies are invariably delighted.

Toys are very rare—an occasional piece of broken household equipment considered safe, sticks, stones, perhaps a homemade gourd or tin can rattle. A favorite is a 3-inch coconut beetle to which a string leash is attached. Fathers occasionally find these beetles in the coconut trees and bring them home to delight their young children.

While playthings of this sort are approved, there is no concern at their scarcity. The child is expected to find amusement in playing with others or in simply being with others, old or young. Babies, just able to crawl, will be sat down facing each other and told by their caretakers to "Go play now. You play now with your cousin." If one of the babies smiles at the other or crawls toward him, the caretakers beam at the child and each other. This is clearly a good baby.

A number of games are universally played between young children and their sibling caretakers. The peek-a-boo of infancy grows more elaborate, culminating in the schoolchild's hide-and-seek. Hand games are common: a typical one popular with 1- to 3-year-olds is *kondoyot*. Two or more pairs of hands are layered above each other, each lightly pinching the one beneath, the whole moved up and down to a chanted *kondoyot, kondoyot*. Suddenly one breaks away from the pile, and if he succeeds in catching the head of any other slow-reacting player, he is permitted to tousle it thoroughly. These games are enjoyed, but, at least until the age of weaning, play for the child is fortuitous and at the whim of his caretakers.

❧
❧
❧

Chapter 13

Weaning and the Preschool Child

Weaning rudely awakens the young Tarongan to the harsher realities of childhood by putting an abrupt end to his indulgence, his primary position in the household hierarchy, and the solicitous care hitherto surrounding him. He who was master of the household is now but a beggar at the gates. While a neutral eye might find this picture over-drawn, most Tarongan weanlings do not. Their world has unpleasantly changed overnight, and their attempts to restore it are often confused, generally ill-directed, and always futile.

The reason for this emotional chaos is not due solely to weaning from the breast. Because of the convergence at this time of a number of cultural directives, the Tarongan weanling is faced not only with loss of the breast but also with loss of his ownership of his mother, loss of the prerogative of irresponsibility, and loss of his immunity from punishment. He is not merely refused the breast but is pushed off the lap and all it symbolizes.

The 24 sample mothers were interviewed about the reason for and the method of weaning each of their children in order to obtain as large a range as possible. The following analyses were based on this expanded sample of 83 children.

Sixty-five children, that is, 78% of the sample, were weaned because of pregnancy; of the remaining 18 weaned for other reasons, half were last-born children. In other words, only 9 children of the 83 were weaned for such reasons as illness of the mother, necessity for a trip, and work load. By far the most common period for weaning is between the fifth month of pregnancy and birth: 48, or 74%, of the 65 children weaned due to pregnancy were weaned during this period, 13 not being weaned until delivery.

Since the precise age of weaning is dictated by pregnancy more often than by rule, there is great variability: ages run from 1 to 4 years. But to wean later than 4 is laughable and most women feel 3 should really end the nursing period. All mothers agree that 2 or 2½ is the ideal age and that weaning before 2 is unfair deprivation, but due to necessity, 9 children were reportedly weaned by 1½ and another 19 before they were 2. The mother of one of these children, weaned because of her mother's hospitalization, volunteered this comment: "When Norma (now 5) sees a child being breast fed, she seems sad; she was so young."

The modal reported age of weaning is a little over 2 years; approximately 75% of the children being weaned between just under 2 and 2½ years. This, of course, reflects the childbearing pattern, siblings being 2 to 2½ years apart. There is another clustering of children weaned at 3, a reflection largely of miscarriages before weaning and last children, who tend to be weaned later.

It should be kept in mind that these ages are of questionable accuracy. Mothers' memories of any specific event are likely to be faulty: it is not easy to report the age at weaning of two deceased and nine living children, the oldest of whom is now in his twenties. The data do represent approved norms, and we feel they are reasonably accurate for gross analysis, but the error in any specific case may be as great as a year.

Once pregnant, weaning is unavoidable, but the exact date is often determined by a specific event: the occurrence of a party, a grandmother or aunt's decision to take over the responsibility, an unusually tempting supply of goodies, mangoes, little fish, and so on. When the weaning date has been set, even the pity a mother feels for a young child does not soften the blow, and weaning is accomplished within two or three days. Only exceptional relenting occurs: of the 83 children, only 4 (all past modal age) had succeeded in forcing a postponement of their weaning. Three were finally weaned at the time of delivery of the next child when "they had to give up crying"; the other, a last child, was subdued only after three postponements and with the concerted efforts of five households.

There is no attempt to prepare the child. One day he is told that he must no longer nurse and, cry as he will, he does not after that. A few mothers try to mitigate the usual crying by weaning their children to a bottle for a time, but for most, this is too expensive, and the traditional method is used. Typically, the mother goes away for one day, during which time some female relative of whom the child is fond, an aunt or grandmother, takes the child to her house, plies him with goodies, eggs, candy, or fish, and distracts him. At this point the child is not usually upset by his mother's absence, since he is being over-indulged by an accustomed surrogate and does not require milk for nourishment any longer.

When she comes home, however, and he goes to her expecting milk, he is told: "You must no longer suck. It is not good, see?" and the mother shows him her breast to which ginger, pepper, or manure is applied, often in the child's presence. If the child is expected to be tractable, he may merely be told one of these substances has been ap-plied or that the breast is swollen, which implies diseased. One woman used mercurochrome, telling her child that she was hurt and bleeding so that he would not suck. The child patted her, asked her if it hurt much and never complained; at least one other mother was planning to try this apparently useful tactic.

The greatest trouble arises during the night, for if the child con-tinues to sleep with the mother, it begs and cries for the breast. The repetition of "It is with manure! It is odorous." or more applications of pepper or ginger result in increased howling. Older children may beg their mothers to wash it off; younger ones sometimes scream with pain after attempts to suck.

When the child cries during the night, he is again offered goodies and frightened by threats if he does not stop. There is a tendency to be more lenient with young children, but older ones are scolded and threatened if they persist in crying even after tidbits have been offered.

To avoid problems at night, the child is sent to sleep in another room or house with the aunt or grandmother (occasionally the father or older sibling), who is referred to as "the one who is weaning him." Twice as many children slept with another adult but in their own house as slept in another house, due in part to the unavailability of grandmothers and aunts living in separate households and in part to an unwillingness to upset the child still more by separation from home as well as mother. Only nine children slept with their mothers during weaning; six were children of the only mother who preferred this method and who had devised a threat effective enough in the circum-stances, a threat which will be described later.

These sleeping arrangements are continued until the child gives up looking for the breast, usually two to four days. Not infrequently, and especially when weaning coincides with delivery, the child may con-tinue to sleep in the household of the weaning agent, dividing his waking time between this house and his own. Permanent adoption may result, particularly if it is a second child being taken care of by a grandparent.

A clearer picture should be given of the frightening techniques mentioned, since weaning is generally the first time the child has been exposed to a concentrated use of them. They are threats of harm from supernatural beings, ranging from "La! Those who are *not human* will come and take your heart!" to "Christ will cut out your tongue!" The most common being invoked is the *Wawak,* a bogeyman who comes to take (kill, eat, etc.) bad children. The mother previously referred to who slept with her children during weaning used a chair covered with a dark cloth set at the far end of the room. "When they wake and cry for the breast, I point to the figure and whisper: 'Do not suck any more, because *Wawak* forbids it!' and they sleep already. All my children took only one night to wean."

A painted wood *Wawak* mask is owned by one woman and widely borrowed. Once or twice a year she puts it on, covers herself with a black cloak, and stalks the *barrio* at dusk "so that children will be good and kind and not selfish any more." This woman is a consummate actress and her slow, stalking walk is spine-chilling. Children watch the apparition paralyzed, then run screaming to their mothers who hide and protect them, extracting promises of future good behavior in return.

One exposure to the *Wawak* is sufficient to make threats and noises made by a household member at the wall or window effective for a number of months, and only during an occasional weaning does the mask have to be brought out. Another reason for the effectiveness of all such threats (and the *Wawak* works until 8 or 9) is the fact that the *Wawak* is the only supernatural being whom the adults themselves do not believe exists. All other threats have the ring of conviction and the *Wawak* fits comfortably into this belief system. When children see adult women run from a roadside field because of kidnapping *agtoyo,* it is hardly surprising to find that children run screaming from "La, there is a *Wawak!*" without waiting to verify the statement.

This abrupt, rather severe weaning method results in intense crying and unhappiness for a number of days, followed by a sullen, miserable, whining period that lasts from a few weeks to a number of months. Early in the field period we succumbed to the charms of a 2-year-old neighbor girl, far more attractive and good-natured than most children her age. To our surprise, over a period of a few days she changed alarmingly: she was never seen smiling, whined constantly, objected to everything, and had temper tantrums. We asked a neighbor what the trouble was, thinking perhaps the child was ill. "No, she is just being weaned," answered the woman. "Then they cry."

Some women say older children, 3½ to 4, "just stop when you tell them." We witnessed two weanings of children over 3; one child fussed more than most, the other was very calm. A few mothers do report such easy weaning as the following: "I had many ripening mangoes, boxes of them. I told him (a boy of about 2) 'Do not suck any more and I will give you all of these.' This worked well. Whenever he wanted to suck, I said: 'No, you have a mango instead.' Then he was satisfied and did not want the breast any more, just mangoes. So I let him go on till they were all gone and by then he did not look for it any more."

Most mothers report no special difficulties weaning their children, two to four nights of complaining and crying being considered usual. No child is ever expeced to bear unhappiness or discomfort stoically; for that matter, adults do not exhibit fortitude in frustrating situations. Only cases involving unceasing crying, violent rage, and considerable interference with sleeping and eating were singled out by their mothers as difficult.

For example, the weaning history of one of these children, a girl over 3 and the last-born child, runs as follows: weaning was attempted three times. First her aunt next door took her to her house to sleep, but the child screamed all night and had to be brought back to her mother, who applied pepper to her breasts and offered candy instead. The girl refused the candy and cried violently, demanding the pepper be washed off; her mother finally relented. A month later they tried again with the same result. Soon after this, close relatives came to visit from another province (the mother's home) and when they left, took the girl with them for two days and one night. While there, she was stuffed with favorite foods and told: "Do not suck. The breast is odorous, dirty." She did not cry much but when she returned, again demanded the breast. Her mother applied pepper, and despite it the girl attempted to suck three times. Her rage gradually subsided as she was stuffed with candy and cookies, threatened with the *Wawak* mask, and scolded for her babyish behavior. The next day she "did not look for any more."

There were 15 children reported to be difficult to wean in our sample of 83, occurring in 13 families and ranging in age from 1½ to over 3 years. This group was evenly divided as to sex of child; the children were not weaned in any systematically different fashion, nor were they less used to surrogates, which might make sudden separation from the mother more difficult. One was a last-born child, one an only child. There was, however, a high percentage of first-born children: 8 of the 15 were first-born; only 3, second-born; 2, third; and 2, fourth.

In terms of birth position of the total sample, 33% of the first-borns were difficult to wean while only 14% of the second-borns, 18% of the third-borns, and 22% of the fourth-borns were so categorized.

That a first-born child should stand a greater chance of difficulty during weaning is not surprising: he has been the only indulged child, and in a number of these cases the child is immediately replaced by another at his mother's breast; his mother is inexperienced and upset by his crying and may vacillate or be overly punitive; aunts, grand-mothers, and other interested persons invariably help more during the weaning of a first child because "the mother does not yet know."

But it should be noted that mothers may simply remember first-born children's development more clearly although this did not seem par-ticularly true in other training areas. A few mothers reported diffi-culties with two children in widely separated birth positions, conclud-ing, "Some children are difficult to wean—no reason—they cry more."

Once weaning is accomplished, mothers are relieved, for the crying and whining create sympathy and irritation at the same time. Breasts are swollen and painful, another source of annoyance. Some women wear flowers of the male papaya strung between their breasts, which prevents fever or sickness from the pain: "Wear until the flower dries so the breast will dry with it." Others say if such a flower is placed under the stove, its drying will encourage the rapid drying of the breasts. Avoidance of this pain is a factor in many womens' preference for weaning at birth. It was also noticeable that delivery settled a num-ber of difficult weanings—apparently the reality of the new infant and its obvious necessity for food force the weanling to accept his changed status. Or perhaps this is merely the result of *dalagan* mothers having more time to devote to soothing a weanling than busy pregnant mothers.

One fact must be stated emphatically: Tarongan weanlings do not vent their hostility on the newborn even when it is his birth which has pushed them from the breast. Their tantrums and rage are directed solely at their mothers; in general, they show little interest in their newborn siblings. Perhaps this results from severe punishment for ex-pressed hostility or more likely from the weanlings' view of the world as one in which babies are produced at a steady rate for no apparent reason and with no apparent control.

Whenever weaning is accomplished, arrival of the new sibling is not far off and with it final emotional weaning from the mother. In effect, this process is begun and often completed before birth, since the weaning method results in mothers avoiding close contact with the child during this period. The child, having lost his right to clamber into his mother's lap for comfort whenever he likes, usually responds by whining for attention, incessant pestering of household members, and general ill humor. Before weaning, whining would have brought soothing attention, concern for possible illness, and attempts to pacify. Now he is scolded sharply. Since the weanling is generally too young to have developed "sense," his responsibility is simple—not to cause unnecessary trouble. This means he must attach himself to another caretaker. This caretaker is generally an aunt or grandmother resident in the household or kin group, a sibling, or even a father, although the child is still too young for this to be a satisfactory substitute. In those cases where the postweaning caretaker is the same person who was the primary preweaning caretaker, the emotional transition is smoothed. Occasionally the child grasps firmly at a sympathetic sibling who takes over the mother's role. One of our sample children, a very mature girl of 10, took over the care of her young sister who was weaned at the birth of the next child. In the mother's words: "Marina takes care of her sister now. Since she was weaned, they sleep together and when Marina went away she cried for her. She calls her 'my mother Marina.' "

More often than not there is no really satisfactory mother substitute, and the child casts about, alternately whining and demanding, for attention. He eventually obtains it from the socially approved source—the neighbor-kin group, both adults and peers. The child's relationship with this group now changes from general friendliness to close identification based on his pressing needs. The larger group, however, can never be as fully nurturant as was the mother or her surrogate, and the child's demands may not always be met. Through such setbacks he learns what he can demand and when such demands are most effective. He also develops anxieties about his status with the group, since the sense of belonging is doubly important to him now. He develops a diffuse dependence on the group, a kind of large family which is never lost. When a child makes this adjustment, he is no longer a baby.

Because of his changed status, the preschool weanling derives some compensations for what he has lost. Foremost is a greater amount of space autonomy: having been kept under close surveillance and considerably restricted in his movements, he now has the freedom of all the *sitio* yards and the immediately adjacent paths although under no conditions should he wander to the fields. This increased play space facilitates interaction with *sitio* children living outside his immediate housing group, and occasionally large groups of children from all parts of the *sitio* will play noisy games together in some central yard.

Just as adults are expected to want companionship, so the assumption is made with children. A child playing alone must be lonely. The most striking thing about Tarongan children's play is that it is almost never solitary. Play groups are encouraged if they are not voluntarily formed. Older children, especially those whose freedom is somewhat curtailed by a hip-baby, often organize junior versions of school games —fantastic games labeled basketball or baseball but bearing little resemblance to the originals. As many as 20 children ranging in age from toddlers to 10 years were observed in such riotous games. One attempt to instill in such a group a newly learned military drill was the most hilarious travesty imaginable, and all the adults of the *sitio* came out to watch and laugh.

The daily play group, however, consists of cousins of the same age from adjacent households. The weaned child is with them whenever he is not sleeping, eating, or away from home with some adult. If it rains, the peer group moves on to one of the porches. He is not out of sight of adults, but neither is he watched—rather, various responsible adults and siblings keep an eye on the group as a whole.

When the schoolchildren come home, they take an active part in the daily play of their young relatives, encouraging the usual childhood games of hide and seek, tag, drop the handkerchief, and so forth. They also expend much time and patience teaching the new members of the play group the rules and skills required in a variety of stick-tossing, rock-hitting games. They even act as "carabao," dragging sledloads of shrieking youngsters behind them. Preschoolers exhibit as much impatience when classes run late as do the schoolchildren themselves. It should be noted that, in general, in all games winning is incidental and in many games the idea is dispensed with. When necessary, players often take turns "winning," distorting the games completely from our point of view.

The preschooler's caretakers are many, and, in effect, all the children of the housing group belong to all the households. A child desiring a drink of water, assistance in fixing a plaything, or a little sympathy over a skinned knee may go home for it or to a grandmother or to any of a variety of "aunties." The choice is often decided on the basis of proximity, sometimes on the known weakness of certain women in the matter of tidbits. When men act as caretakers they play with the children with evident pleasure, sometimes indulging a child's whims to the great annoyance of its mother.

In the same way, any of the group of adults will chastise any child observed misbehaving: "We all help to raise our children" is a recurrent statement from mothers and fathers who clearly find this a satisfying system. No mother need worry overmuch if her child does stray a bit far from home, for she knows that any adult seeing him headed for possible trouble will prevent it, scold him for his irresponsibility, and send him home, thus reinforcing her own warnings.

The increase in free play with other children at this age necessitates certain rules regarding expression of aggression, modesty, and sex play, nurturance, obedience, and the like. Discipline prior to this is more likely to mean removal of the child rather than punishment. The situation now requires responsibility from the child, and a variety of rewards and punishments may be employed. But it must be remembered that the child does not yet have enough "sense" to be allowed full freedom, and responsibility ultimately rests with his caretakers.

Aggression in the preweaning child is barely recognized, meriting only a mild "No, No" and removal. Now that the child is more often alone with his peers, quarrels are more likely to start, and they meet with strong disapproval: "Open quarreling and fighting, if allowed to become a habit, will result in bad children, respecting no one, troublemakers. With boys, it is more natural, but girls should behave better. By the time they go to school it should be no more." A child may express anger toward his peers verbally, but physical displays will be stopped by an adult before they become serious. The usual technique is physical removal with a thorough scolding and perhaps a slap added. This is especially true if the aggression is directed toward a younger child or toward an adult who is not an intimate of the child.

Although his cartakers are many and their attitudes somewhat varied, the Tarongan child has a generally consistent picture of what is expected of him. Probably the most important things he must learn during his preschool period, besides curbing his aggressive impulses, are responsibility and obedience.

Responsibility is an important attribute of a Tarongan adult and a prized quality in a child. Training begins fairly early; by 5, boys and girls are seen carrying water in small jars, feeding the stove fire, walking a baby in the yard, taking their own baths, even cutting rice —but always under close supervision. During this preschool period a child may begin to take care of the one or two family goats, a simple matter of periodically resetting the stake to which they are tethered and bringing them home to shelter at night and during a rain. He may also help feed the chickens and pick vegetables. Such economically useful activities bring praise, and as the child grows older, these responsibilities are gradually increased.

The preschooler, however, "has to be told—he cannot just do it yet." Incentives to accomplishment may be special foods or new clothes or, most often, praise. One mother, impressed by her daughter's ability to wash dishes, was heard saying: "Ah now, that is very good. Soon you will do them all for me, eh my *balasangko?*" The use of *balasangko* to a preschooler is gross flattery, the term properly referring to a young lady of marriageable age. Since all Tarongan children, while enjoying their childhood, are impatient to become adults, up-aging is a common form of praise, and little girls smile and preen when addressed in this manner.

At some point during this period, depending on how rapidly subsequent children are produced, the next youngest sibling is placed in the preschooler's care. Generally all that is expected is that the older child play with and keep watch over the younger (often a cranky weanling). Should the child hurt himself or need assistance, the older child is expected to convey the request to an older person, but some preschoolers take considerable responsibility for their siblings. Nor is this a matter for girls only: boys are given equal opportunity to care for their younger siblings and exhibit the same range of responses as the girls.

Responses do, of course, vary enormously. Some 5-year-olds are as nurturant as their parents and even more patient. Others find a 2- or 3-year-old tagging at their heels a very trying burden and say so at every opportunity. But there are advantages, not the least of which is the chance to be subtly aggressive toward someone a notch lower in the authority-hierarchy, this always being done in the name of discipline. And to children living in a housing group relatively devoid of preschoolers, their younger siblings are also their only playmates.

Aside from the activities mentioned, children's help at this age is generally considered play by adults. Still, by observation and play practice, the children rapidly become familiar with adult techniques and reflect these in their daily play: building twig houses, cooking, cutting cane, stringing tobacco, dancing, all are intensely re-enacted from yard to yard. The best index to current adult activity is the content of preschoolers' play, and the ingenuity they show in finding substitutes for adult implements when they cannot be borrowed is remarkable.

Sardine and other cans are fitted with strings for pulling, occasionally covered with banana-stalk tops and even fitted with wheels of some sort. Complete cooking sets are manufactured from castoff bits of pottery; mortars and pestles are readily found in rocks and sticks; sleds are lashed together from odd lengths of bamboo; thatch and bamboo houses are erected and re-erected after their inevitable collapse; one child, a first-grade boy in this case, had developed a wonderfully realistic stethoscope from pieces of inner tubing and a jar cover.

A few girls this age had received miniature cooking sets (sold in Poblacion market), including stove and pots, but they were admonished to play carefully with them, since they were expensive. Generally the children seem happier with equipment of their own manufacture, for they can do what they like with it. Also, the more generalized form of these toys makes for easy utility as a variety of things.

At some indefinable point, responsibility for carrying out tasks becomes a matter of the child's initiation. The desire of children to take on this different kind of responsibility, that of initiating tasks, is viewed by Tarongans with the same ambivalence with which it is seen in adults. It is obviously necessary that a child develop self-reliance, but too much self-initiation can lead to obstinacy, uncooperativeness and, especially at this age, impractical or disastrous acts. The result of the parents' uncertainty as to how much the child should do by himself is reflected in the diversity of responses to questions about these activities, a diversity greater than for any other questioned training area.

In general, keeping in mind the wide range of variation, the preschool child should attempt no more on his own than his caretakers tell him he can now do, such as bathing, feeding chickens, changing clothes; in other words, activities which can do little damage even when handled by a 5-year-old. If the child desires to help wash dishes, bring firewood from the pile, or hold the baby, he should request permission, which is likely to be refused unless the mother has time to supervise. Should the child run into difficulty carrying out a task or even when playing, he is encouraged to ask for help rather than solve it himself, the latter course being a scolding offense, since "it is a waste of time—they do it wrong and then we have to do it over."

In spite of this attitude children of 4 and 5 constantly try to do things they are not considered old enough to do. Parents punish them, but Tarongan children have spirit and are usually back at it when their tears have dried. Children in isolated nuclear families are allowed more freedom in these attempts, not because of parental preference but because of parental inability to supervise closely.

The training does have effect in the matter of requesting help, perhaps because the child does not want to do things the wrong way. By 5, few youngsters try more than twice to solve a problem alone; and it is not necessary, for an adult or older child is always near to help. Gradually the lesson of reliance on others for all but essentials is learned and is particularly noticeable when the child enters new and unfamiliar situations.

Obedience is, by our standards, lax. But to a Tarongan mother, obedience is more a matter of dependability than prompt compliance. If the child has been told to bring something to her, even if three requests are necessary, if it is eventually brought, the child is obedient. Disobedience is usually avoidance of a task. Children may suddenly desire to visit an aunt at such times and are likely to get away with it. But outright refusal is viewed as a severe transgression and punished accordingly.

We happened one day to record a good example of the reluctant obedience of Marino, one of the sample children. He was a school-child of 7, but the expectations in regard to this aspect of obedience do not change even through adulthood and his behavior is as typical of 4-year-olds as it is of 18-year-olds. It was approaching dusk and Marino had been asked by his grandmother, a resident of his household, to bring home the goat tethered a short distance down the road. Marino wandered slowly across the road to the schoolyard fence where he tossed a few stones before entering the yard. There he strolled idly about, then examined the flagpole minutely. Smiling broadly, he shinnied to its top where he clung for a minute or so, looking about the *sitio*. Sliding down suddenly, he bounced on the base, then began to climb again. When he was half way to the top, his grandmother came out of the house and screamed across the road: "Ay, Marino! You go get the goat now! *Okinam!* (curse word) You get down from there!"

Marino looked at his grandmother, now shaking her fist at him, and slowly slid down the flagpole. Slowly, very slowly, he strolled to the gate, swung on it a few times, then walked reluctantly down the road past his grandmother who shook her fist again and stood glaring at him, arms akimbo. The period between the initial request and final compliance was eight minutes, a not atypical time lapse.

Disciplinary techniques are not subtle: scolding, slapping, pinching are the most common punishments at this stage; threats of *Wawak*, policemen, and so on are used to prevent punishable or dangerous behavior; rewards are predominantly verbal or edible. Sharing toys or food with other children, for example, is highly approved, as is helping another child who needs assistance. Either, noticed by adults, will gain lavish praise for the child and perhaps a cooky or bit of fruit. Rewards other than praise are less consistently given than punishments. Tidbits on market day may be promised and never materialize; promised goodies or clothes may, in fact, be what the parents planned to buy in any case.

Children learn this quickly and take such promises skeptically, and when they are disappointed by such parental failures, they accept them with the same resigned, good-humored shrug adults use in similar situations. Perhaps because it is never suggested to Tarongan children that adults (or children) should be perfect, they accept human frailities with better grace than many Western adults. Also, there is no ethical framework to justify bitterness and unforgiving enmity; Tarongans can give vent to great anger, but they rarely hate.

There is some sex differentiation at this age, but it is minor except, as mentioned earlier, in the matter of modesty. Sex play barely exists, only 17 instances being reported for the 83 children. These were all interpreted as teasing; as one mother said, "It probably would not have been, except his cousins (male) wear pants late, not until they begin school." The teasing interpretation seems sensible, since the incidents were almost evenly divided between cross-sex and same-sex and the activity as reported was "grabbing" and "pinching."

The most noticeable differences in treatment of boys and girls are in areas of initial training for later mature performance. For example, girls now often go with their mothers to the well when they wash clothes. There they play, help, and get their daily bath. Boys of this age clamor to be taken by their fathers when they water the carabao and bathe at the end of a hot work day. Many a boy of 4 or 5 could be found just before dusk strutting proudly behind the carabao led by his father, switching it officiously and ineffectually with a stick to hurry it to the well. When work pressures are reduced, fathers will sometimes take young sons along with them to the well for their early morning bath, a very grown-up activity if one is to judge by the boys' behavior.

Older children encourage the helpful attempts of their younger siblings and cousins, often allowing them to assist in sweeping the yard, pounding pig feed, taking care of an infant, and so forth. Although the older children also construe these attempts as play, their laughter at mistakes and teasing instructions, combined with considerable patience, are effective teaching devices. Many Tarongans recognize this; for example, one mother, when asked how her child learned a skill, said his siblings taught him, pointing out that the child's siblings had "more time, and for them it is play."

Preschoolers are also found in the fields when their parents are working, at candy parties, even at evening wakes and parties, where they stay awake as long as possible and are finally put to sleep in corners. Despite overtiredness and a crabby disposition the next day, no parent would force a preschooler to stay home when an exciting event was occurring in his own *sitio*, although rarely would a child this age be taken to an evening affair at any distance.

But now that the child does not need mother's milk, he may be taken on many short daytime trips out of the *barrio*. Grandmothers are especially prone to scoop up one of their grandchildren (most often a girl since "they behave better than the boys") and take her along on a visit to the next *barrio* or even on a trip to Poblacion. Aunts or older sisters making social visits in and out of the *barrio* frequently take a youngster along for company. Men are less likely to do this, for their visits are often for business or political reasons and children might be too distracting. In most situations where American women would hunt for a baby sitter, the Tarongan woman hunts for a toddler to take with her. Asked about this, one old woman, grandmother to 17, patted her hip and said, "I cannot walk upright without my usual load."

Although much attention is paid to young children within the family circle, once infancy is past they are expected to "be ashamed" before visitors. This means the child must never pass in front of a guest, must never unnecessarily interrupt a conversation, should be seen but not heard, at least in the immediate vicinity of a visitor. Theoretically these rules include all nonfamily guests but are enforced only when the guest is a person of importance or a stranger to the household. Young children are very shy before strangers, whose appearance is relatively infrequent and associated with a shaming technique which will be discussed shortly.

The child begins, say parents, to get "sense" at about 4 and by 6 should have it. "Sense" is roughly the ability to profit by instruction, including both developmental ability and the desire to use it. But it is best to train when the child is young: "Like the old tree which is already bent, you cannot unbend." Tarongan parents love their children intensely, and having a fine family is a source of great pride, but it is better to have no children at all than bad ones, for the blame is almost always attributed to bad training. Discipline is firm therefore, though never harsh.

During this period, then, the child is gradually trained to accept responsibility, to curb some of his impulses, and to be obedient. But the training is coaxing rather than demanding and is taken lightly by the adults; mild scoldings or teasings are sufficient for most lapses, praise, the usual reward for accomplishment. Transgressions of clear prohibitions will result in a sharp slap with a twig, slipper, or hand, and now the child will be left to scream away his rage: "Whipping is the helpmate of your mouth." As one mother put it: "Candy in the first hand, a whip in the other."

The child quickly learns that, as in adult life, intention is not so important as action and its results. For example, if two children quarrel, both are assumed at fault, and punishment is evenly distributed unless one is much older. "He started it" is almost never heard from a Tarongan child. In the same way, an overturned pot is an overturned pot, and the fact that the guilty child was trying to help cook does not replace the food or her mother's good humor.

But there is a positive side to this lack of concern with motives. Discontent can be expressed openly as long as there is compliance. For the child the benefits are obvious: he can grumble, complain, procrastinate, yet still be rewarded for his eventual completion of a chore. He is not called upon to "want to help mother"; he is only asked to help when she catches him.

One other disciplinary technique is first used during this preschool period—ostracism and its weaker version, group teasing. Having been thrown on the mercy of the peer and neighbor group at weaning, the threatened loss of this precarious security now creates severe anxiety and, as a rule, rapid capitulation. Life without the peer group is unthinkable, especially to preschoolers, for despite their occasional trips, they are painfully shy with strangers and not at all comfortable away from their immediate housing group.

Although these tactics are most characteristic of older siblings and peers, the parents also find threatened ostracism and teasing effective disciplinary techniques. One vivid example of teasing-discipline by adults occurred at an afternoon party. A quarrel broke out in the yard between two *sitio*-mates, first cousins, over the sharing of a few marbles one of the boys had recently received. Thirty or more laughing children and adults (including the parents) soon gathered in a circle around the recalcitrant boy of 6 and teased him mercilessly until he was sobbing. Finally he threw the marbles at the other boy and ran home, after which the episode was forgotten by the adults, although probably not by the boy. Such experiences result in rapid learning to share, but also a tendency, on the few occasions possible, to cache belongings secretly for one's own use.

Another disciplinary measure of a teasing nature should be mentioned, since it also appears during this period. Visiting adults of high status, most frequently men, are used by the mothers. A mother will suggest, with a glance at her children who are watching the awesome stranger from the sidelines, that "the children are naughty." The visitor agrees, then turns to the paralyzed children and, prompted by parental asides, sternly catechizes them about their recent misdeeds. The children, of course, do not answer nor are they expected to, but they soon cry or show unmistakable signs of agonizing embarrassment and fear. When this point is reached, the visitor laughs as do the other adults present; the mother whispers warnings and soothing words to the children, and the group goes on with its discussion. This technique not only validates the authority of the parents and neighbors but also fortuitously reinforces the child's picture of them as nurturant in contrast to the outside, hostile world.

In summary, we can let one preschooler speak for herself and her just-weaned sister. This 5-year-old girl, Merlinda, was unusually verbal for her age but in other respects seemed to be a typical Tarongan child. When interviewed by one of the field team, she took advantage of the opportunity to boast and complain at length to a sympathetic adult.

Merlinda has a 2½-year-old sister, Minda, and a newborn baby brother. In addition, a school-age boy and girl who are first cousins to Merlinda live in the household. These cousins act as older siblings to Merlinda. The following remarks were spontaneous additions to her answers to the interview questions and need little interpretation.

When I go anywhere—"Where did you go?" Mother would ask if I did not come when she called me. . . . My mother would call me and ask me to rock the baby, but sometimes she lets me polish the floor. Sometimes she tells me my father would like to tell me something, but he does not tell me anything. "Your father would like to tell you something," she says and when I arrive home he is not there. I do not always believe her.

Auntie has been gone for some time now. She has not yet come back. I asked her to buy Coca Cola for me. But she will forget again.

"When we have plenty of fruit or such, we scare Minda (sister) with a ghost and then say the ghost has eaten all of it. Actually they (apparently adult household members) hid it.

There were plenty of peanuts in our house before. Minda ate and ate. She would not have stopped if we did not scare her with *Wawak*. When I made a doll for Minda, she called it baby. "It does not have hands" I said. "There are" she said. "Stupid" I said. *"Okinam"* (curse word) she said to me.

Even when she (Minda) wants to have some guavas, "There is *Wawak*" we say and sometimes she runs and hides. Sometimes she is not afraid of *Wawak*. When Tomeng (her great grandmother) died, she went downstairs (outside at dusk). The reason why I am easily afraid is they have been scaring and scaring me. My baby brother will also be afraid. When he is lying on his back on the floor, he gets scared very easily.

When Minda teased the baby, he cried. I kicked Minda. Mother scolded me. I ran to hide under the house. *"Okinam, pipit"* (curse words) she (Minda) continued to shout. I went to Melie's place (next door).

My hiding place is under our house. Mother, one time, could not locate me. I was already very near her. Sometimes I hide at Melie's place. I tell her not to tell I am there. One time Minda came to hide with me. She cried.

It is good for Minda not to be here (at interview). She will only be just a hindrance. She wants me to have her on my lap. Even when we ride in the bus.

I will first tease Minda. I will tease her that all these lemon and butterballs are mine. (Candy given during interview.)

I am always angry . . . The goat is the one. I take a stick and hit and hit it.

I can fill a big jar of water alone. All by myself. . . . Minda urinates in her sleeping place. I do not any more. I get up.

Father went to harvest rice in the south on our land there. I was going to join him. He said: "You want to come, Merlinda?" "No, because I am rocking the baby to sleep" I said to him.

Manang (the girl cousin) went to help wash clothes. She did not go to school. I help her wash at times.

I get mad because they stick it (the peg holding the goat rope) so deep sometimes. Sometimes I whip and whip the goat. I said I will break the rope —"I will cut it with a bolo" I was saying. Grandmother heard me and came over and untied it. Grandmother is very kind . . . When I had a hardship, grandmother said: "You are torturing the small child."

Minda looks for someone to sleep with at night. One night I did not like to sleep near her. She slept near one of her male cousins. I do not like to sleep near him. He is always teasing me. Sometimes I sleep between father and mother. Sometimes I sleep next to the wall.

When Grandfather Ariston (really great uncle) died (two weeks before interview), I went to the prayers. But I did not pray. It was during the day . . . when Tomeng (great grandmother) died, there were many people in our house. Like it is in the market, our house. There was a small child. When she came near Tomeng, she cried. She was afraid.

I used to go to the room of Tomeng. I was asking for the little mortar and pestle she had. She said: "Take it when I will die, grandchild." She gave it to me when she died. She asked for the little mortar and pestle to be brought over. "Will you bring over the little mortar and pestle for me to give to my grandchild" she said. She would not yet be dead if she were not again a child (senile), isn't it so?

I had a dream. Tomeng was dead then. I was cooking noodles (for the funeral feast). Her funeral was the following day. I washed the dishes. I helped make the wreath.

The other dream was about grandfather Ariston. I was playing. They were cooking (the funeral feast).

When I dream I am afraid. I pull my blanket completely over me. I crowd myself to mother. When Tomeng died I was not afraid. I had a large blanket with beautiful embroidery that time.

I slept at Auntie Lus's in Ikan only once. They have very nice food. That is why I do whatever they tell me to do. They even bought a beautiful hat for the baby.

✿
✿
✿

Chapter 14

The Schoolchild

By 6, hopefully, the child has "sense" and can profit from instruction. If he has matured sufficiently in this regard, during his sixth year he will begin school; if slow to mature, he will wait another year. Or perhaps a child will wait, with parental approval if not suggestion, for a slightly younger cousin-companion if there are no children from his *sitio* in the first grade. This lack of concern with age characterizes the school, and differences of three years in one grade go unremarked, partly because poor families send only a few of their children to school in any one year. Stay-at-homes are alternated so that all, eventually, get through at least fourth grade though they may be 12 or 13 by that time.

To the 6-year-old, starting school is an exciting event, symbolizing the attainment of a new maturational level. Understandably he shows considerable nervousness: as he walks to school in the wake of his elder siblings or cousins he smoothes his new, clean clothes, perhaps peers at his first shoes, which feel strange, self-consciously waggles his book bag, and alternately giggles and gulps. On arriving, he is turned over to his teacher and told to be good; then the older children run off, leaving him immobile and big-eyed.

But as the other children, big and small, continue to ignore him, he relaxes and examines every detail of the room from the spot where he would stay all day did not the teacher direct, shove, and prod the new children into seats, two to a desk. After they are settled, the sophisticated second graders saunter in to their side of the room to make up the full complement of 30 pupils. The third and fourth grades in Tarong, 30 pupils in all, also share a classroom but the fifth and sixth, about 20 pupils each, have separate small buildings.

Within each grade boys sit on one side of the group, girls on the other. It is interesting to note that the teachers' assumptions about the intrinsic tractability of girls is not strikingly borne out the first few weeks of school, but by the end of the year the girls' side is always quieter and better behaved. The first day's bedlam and confusion fray teachers' nerves, but order is at last created. The children sit quietly with clasped hands on their desks, rather fearfully watching the teacher, who takes his or her place at the front of the room as, painfully, education begins.

Of necessity Ilocano is the initial medium of instruction, but as soon as possible during the first semester both English and the recently adopted National Language, a Tagalog dialect, are introduced. Considerable experimentation was in progress, however, to maximize ease of teaching these languages. In 1955 all textbooks, except for those used in teaching National Language, were in English.

The effect of all this linguistic confusion is that Ilocano is used throughout the six years, gradually yielding to English as the students become more adept in its use, but the latter is rarely fluent. National Language remains a mystery to Tarongans, who for practical and ethnic reasons are far more motivated to learn English. Since they are never taught to read Ilocano, they are, as the saying goes "illiterate in three languages." (see Prator, 1950)

The curriculum, aside from language instruction, is similar to that of an American school, but the teaching technique has been somewhat modified. Young children are embarrassed if called on to perform alone whether at school or home, and parents encourage this shyness: "He (or she) is ashamed," they say with some pride, for boldness in so young a child indicates inadequate training. As a result of the socialization techniques discussed—strangers' scoldings, peer-group teasings, and so on—this acute fear and embarrassment are reinforced until the child freezes and is "ashamed" any time he is isolated from his group.

Partly for this reason and partly because competition is minimized in the schools to fit *barrio* attitudes toward accomplishment, teaching in the early grades is a matter of the teacher reciting what is to be learned or asking a question and the students chorusing in response. Punishments are for misbehavior rather than for failure to perform adequately and range from slaps to tongue-lashings. In either case they are invariably public, shaming, and effective, resulting in head-hanging, frequent tears, and at least momentary improvement in behavior.

Not until the third grade is there much individual recitation, but it increases steadily thereafter. Even sixth-grade students, however, do not carry over their new-found poise to social situations outside the schoolhouse, nor would their parents be pleased if they attempted to do so. Girls, particularly, must be shy and easily "ashamed" from now well into adulthood. The male interpreter for the field team found that, for girls from 6 to 12 or so, extracting an answer to the question "Is your mother home?" was often impossible despite the fact that the same girls proudly recited in class for the benefit of the visitors.

A desire for adequacy and no more persists through the sixth grade. It reflects, of course, adult values and effectively negates all teacher pressures for competitive excellence save in the few cases of children known to be going on to high school. For these children, school grades are seen as potentially valuable, and their peers accept this as practical for them.

The desire for adequacy rather than excellence is obvious from the behavior of the children, and the teachers complain about it. Their pleas for children to try to excell seem to be heard, for in response to the questions, "Do you want your school work to be better than that of other children?" and "Do you want your work (i.e. chores) to be better than that of others your age?" all but a few children promptly answered "Yes." They also almost unanimously agreed that they would be unhappy, ashamed, and so forth, if their work were the worst. Then they also unanimously agreed, except for some of the students planning on high school, that if their work, in school or out, were adequate, they would be quite satisfied and happy. As one of the children said: "We should all be the same. Then we will all be friends."

The adult world is further mirrored in the matter of mutual obligations: all children assume that one helps one's classmates, especially those from the same *sitio,* in tests, recitations, school chores, and homework. While this leads to fine interpersonal relations among the students, it creates severe grading problems for the teacher. Her class presents to her five clusters of identical test or homework papers, providing a far better sociogram than a test of individual knowledge. Parenthetically, grades at the end of the year are announced publicly at the graduation ceremonies, a shaming technique related to those previously described.

The school year is the same as the American school year, but modified to suit the climate, summer vacation being April and May. Classes begin at 7:45 in the morning and continue until 4:30 in the afternoon, although the schedule is flexible. There is a two and one-half hour lunch period since, except for the height of the work seasons, few children bring their lunch to school. Normally only those from the farthest *barrios* served by the school cannot walk home to eat, and many of these children have an eating arrangement with relatives closer to the school.

During the busy harvest and planting seasons, the school is emptier and busier. Many of the older children stay home to help, or to baby-tend while their mothers work in the fields, and teachers view their less than half-full classrooms unhappily. Those who do attend during these work periods almost all bring lunches, for no one is at home to prepare a noon meal. Teachers view with equal unhappiness the groups of boys flinging fruit pits or peels at each other, the overturned dishes of rice. Cleaning up the schoolyard is a standard feature of the day during the work seasons.

Given six hours of school a day, the new children rapidly recover their normal sociability and within a few weeks only traces of visible uneasiness remain, most noticeable in the presence of older fifth and sixth graders and teachers. Additionally, many hours of classes are spent reciting in chorus, outside working on the schoolgrounds, classroom cleaning, and games, all of which reduce shyness.

But in spite of the relatively smooth adjustment to the new situation, the child never really identifies with the school as a whole or even one of its classrooms. As we pointed out before, Tarongan children are not notably self-reliant and are distinctly other-reliant when difficulties of any kind are encountered. In the new school world, *sitio*-mates cling tightly together.

Gradually conversation and joking between *sitio*-groups increase, encouraged by the casualness of much Tarongan school activity. But we were unable during months of observation to find one example of a child relying for help on a non-kin child from another *sitio* until the third grade. Even past this point such reliance is the exception, not the rule. This maintenance of *sitio* identity is one of the reasons that school leaders, as we know them, simply do not exist in Tarong's classrooms.

Play groups in and out of the classroom are also largely *sitio*-defined. There is conversation, joking, even occasional sharing of work, but no intimate friendship across *sitio* lines unless the children involved are close relatives and familiars already. The situation is, of course, none too pleasant for the occasional child with no *sitio*-mates: he is the loneliest child in Tarong and generally, like his adult counterpart, attaches himself to the neighbor-kin group closest to him.

Such a selective principle creates friendship groups differing markedly from those we see in our own rigidly age-graded schools: Tarongan play groups at primary school level typically cross grades easily and involve children of both sexes and various ages, all having *sitio*-residence in common. This group walks to and from school together and plays together in school when possible as well as doing chores and playing together at home. It is no more than the lineal descendant of the adult *sitio* kin-neighbor group, stratified on the same bases and exerting the same kind of influence on its members, a miniature *sitio* as it were.

For example, the relative socio-economic positions of the parents have considerably more effect on their children's interactions now than they have had. Even preschoolers are told, with greater severity, to stop quarreling if their playmate is the child of a wealthy *sitio* landowner. Such subtlety is generally lost on the young child, but he reacts to it more appropriately by the time he is a third or fourth grader.

The child whose clothes are new and of good quality, whose lunch contains some meat or an egg, and who thinks in terms of graduation to high school, is more assured than his less fortunate classmates, enjoys more praise from his teachers, and tends to lead his playmates, more because of their deference than his desire. But he is no bully; such behavior would be intolerable in a child regardless of status.

Although children of school age are learning, as part of their social reality, to be somewhat status-conscious, this consciousness should not be overestimated. There is no class division in Tarong, only minor gradations along a predominantly economically determined scale, and the equality of *sitio* living minimizes such differences. The playmates of the wealthiest child in Tarong were not others of similar wealth but his considerably poorer *sitio*-mates.

Adults reinforce this friendship-group structure. When mothers were asked which children they would prefer to have their own play with, the answer was the same for school children and preschoolers: "These ones here—the cousins." In this way the child is encouraged to identify non*sitio* members and nonrelatives as "others" and there-fore potentially hostile. Aggression begins to be noticeably directed toward these others and away from the in-group, but for the first few years at school the new situation and general prohibitions inhibit overt display.

A typical example of *sitio*-kin solidarity in the face of a threat occurred in one of the observations made of a group of boys who had paused on the way home from school to play the Tarong version of pitching pennies. Seven boys, representing the first to fifth grades, were involved; five were from Sitio East, two from another. As one of the Sitio East kibbitzing boys, Catalino, saw an older player from the other *sitio* start to pick up a coin, he called: "That is taken." The player, Andres, turned to Catalino angrily, saying: "You have no business in this, you crazy one! You want me to slap you?"

Immediately an older player from Sitio East, second cousin to Catalino, turned to Andres and roared: "Don't talk like that to him or I will be the one to slap you!" Andres went on playing and the disagreement was forgotten, but such disputes can and often do lead to fights between older boys from different *sitios* or *barrios*. It is also worth noting that Catalino and his defender were not especially close friends, there being a four-year age gap between them, but both accepted the defence without comment as the natural and proper response to Andres' threat.

The *sitio* friendship group can close itself to outsiders in non-threatening situations as well. Friendly advances cannot properly be rebuffed but may well be coldly tolerated merely for the sake of politeness, a treatment guaranteed to ward off most Tarongan children. We observed two girls (third and fourth graders) who were *sitio*-mates playing jacks on the porch of the main school building after classes had been dismissed for the day. The girls were lackadaisically but happily playing when a fourth-grade girl from another *barrio* came over and sat down with them, saying, "I will join you?" as if conferring a favor. One of the players, Anita, said: "Hynh! You are very good," with considerable annoyance; the other reluctantly handed over the ball to let the newcomer begin a game. The girl played for about four minutes without error. During this time the original players spoke exactly two words. She was a very good player and was clearly enjoying her superior performance.

At length the ball hit a crack in the cement and rolled out of reach. The newcomer got up to retrieve it and stopped to talk to some friends, at which point Anita jumped up and got the ball. She and her friend watched as the newcomer walked away with her group, then happily returned to their game, this time enjoying the play noisily. During the next few minutes the girls joked and chatted with passing friends until the girl who had joined them returned, followed by a first grader, Nelly.

The newcomer said loudly, as she seated herself: "Ah, I'll join you also." Anita glowered, then loudly proclaimed: "Yes, la! Nelly will join us also. Let's have teams. Nelly will be my companion!" This pointed preference for a young first grader rather than for the fourth-grade newcomer was received, as it was intended, as a vicious insult, and the newcomer glared at Anita but did not leave. Most Tarongans would have left after the initial silent treatment, but this girl was of sterner stuff. Another girl joined the game, and Anita, with evident distaste, left the group and was soon followed by her friend.

Being a schoolchild has a minimum of effect on the child after he leaves the schoolyard. He and his *sitio*-mates dawdle or hurry home, depending on the weather and the ripeness of wild fruit along the way. In general, each clump of children sticks together and pays scant attention to any other group using the same or nearby paths. Occasionally some of the older children will shout back and forth, or a daring boy will tease one of the girls from the other side of a water-filled paddy while she giggles and her older brothers or cousins happily shout threats back across the paddy.

Once home, each child runs into his house to deposit books, display papers, or deliver school messages. Good school clothes are removed and everyday clothes, in some cases little more than patched rags, are put on before going out to chores or play. This step is never neglected. One of the severest whippings we saw was given to a schoolboy who had played too roughly on the way home and had badly ripped a new shirt. Since no *barrio* mother ever sends her child to school in home-woven cloth, the expense of dressing a schoolchild is a drain on small cash incomes and a frequently mentioned reason for removal of a child at the completion of fourth grade.

Only one parent in the *barrio* admitted to not caring if his children attended school or not. With the exception of this man, parents sent their children through as many grades as they could afford. They also gave verbal support to school requirements and regulations as brought home by their children and listened with interest to their reports of classroom activities. But here parental responsibility ends. It is the teacher's duty to teach and the child's duty to prepare his lessons, and few parents see any necessity for interference. The only exceptions in Tarong were two households where one of the parents understood enough English to be of real help to his children, though even here the help was sporadic.

No child, to our knowledge, could ever really study at home. Since few of the parents concern themselves with school work, and since family living patterns make individual withdrawal nearly impossible, the necessity of a modicum of light and peace for study was neither understood nor provided. Besides, activities other than play occupy the schoolchild at home, and here the parent steps firmly into the teacher's role.

The skills learned in school during the four primary years are academic save for some gardening and thus are divorced from the realities of the *barrio*. But at home the child is now old enough to be trained specifically in regard to the practical aspects of *barrio* living. Greater responsibility for goat and chicken care, food preparation, sibling care, house cleaning, water carrying, and so forth is now expected of the children, regardless of sex. Sharing of toys, food, and such is expected of even preschoolers, but intransigence in this matter will now be viewed with alarm.

In that increased responsibility is a sign of increased maturity, the children welcome such chores, at least until they become customary and no longer exciting. Although schoolchildren report little concern with "having their work better than others," they want very much to be part of the adult world. In answer to the question, "What do you like to do best?", 80% mentioned work activities, predominantly those which this age group is not capable of accomplishing without adult assistance. And in answer to a question about parental punishments, almost half the children said they had been repeatedly punished for doing things they had been told were too difficult for them. If anything, this figure is low, judging by the interviews with the mothers.

A major chore for schoolchildren is baby tending. Once the children have changed clothes after school, busy mothers and grandmothers anxious to collect firewood or vegetables before dusk or to begin the evening meal, set babies, but not young infants, before them with a sharp: "Now take care of your *ading!*" The older children put the youngster on a hip and run off to play. The younger children find this too tiring and content themselves with a chore "helper" or by playing in groups around or with the baby who is generally toddling or close to toddling age. The rule seems to be the older the child, the younger the sibling he cares for. Between 4:30 and 6:00 or so, the central yard-path space of the largest *sitio* was another schoolyard, holding throughout its length as many as 36 children, only eight being over 10 years of age.

Since baby tending is a requirement for all children and careful care is highly rewarded, Tarongan children show little objection to this duty and generally are both nurturant and ingenious in thinking of games and toys to amuse their charges. A baby's laugh rewards his older sibling almost as much as it does his mother. But, admittedly, almost as rewarding is the chance of justifiably punishing the younger children who are under supervision, and schoolchildren can be severe taskmasters.

Boys do not escape child tending even when there are girls in the family, for their taking over the job can free an older girl for field work or preparation of pig food or the family meal. In households short of girls, the boys take care of their siblings as a matter of course. But when older girls have tended to all the youngsters, the family may suddenly realize a schoolboy's lack of experience in this field and train him.

One of our most amusing observations involved such training of a 7½-year-old boy, Simeon, at an informal late-afternoon candy party. Almost all the members of three households were present, among them Simeon's tired, cranky, teething baby brother Pico. Pico was being soothed and rocked by his mother, Marina, who suddenly called to Simeon, "Here, put him to sleep," in a challenging tone. Simeon smiled and swaggered over, took the baby and went into the next room where a hammock was strung up. The eldest girl of the household ran after him, saw to it that the baby was laid down properly in the hammock, and cautioned Simeon to rock it gently. As she left the room, Simeon began to sing a rousing march in rhythm with his rocking.

In the next room all the adults were grinning. Marina, requesting conspiratorial conversational cover-up by pantomine, sat next to the door where she could hear but not be seen. Despite the singing and rocking, Pico was soon roaring again. Simeon rocked more violently and sang still louder, his voice drowning Pico's wails. At this, a younger cousin, Jose, left the group to join Simeon.

After some consultation with the equally inexperienced Jose, Simeon cradled and patted Pico in his arms as he himself sat in the hammock. Jose pushed the hammock as one would push a swing, both he and Simeon singing loudly while Pico's wails rose above the din. Marina was now peering through the door crack, convulsed with laughter, and the other women joined her, giggling at the peephole. Jose's older brother went to the door where he stood watching critically, finally bursting into laughter too. He then replaced Jose and convinced Simeon, by example, that gentle patting, cooing, and rocking were more effective.

It is of interest to note that, as in this example, in many training situations it is peers and older siblings or cousins who step in to solve problems, parents contenting themselves with occasional verbal instructions. Although the children see themselves as helping, they are in fact doing most of the training. Throughout childhood and adulthood the peer group maintains this never-stated but very important function, which creates still another layer of *sitio* connective tissue.

Now that the child is becoming useful and no longer requires the care and supervision he did as a preschooler, a grandparent or sometimes an aunt may think about adoption. This term is not really accurate, since adoption is never legal and means little more in most cases than moving the child's official residence next door. It certainly implies no separation from the parents.

Parents will not allow adoption of their first-born, but the second child, especially if the second of the same sex, is a favorite for this purpose. The process is gradual. The grandparents coax the child to eat with them more often, fuss over him a great deal more than his busy parents can, buy him expensive tidbits, nice clothes, encourage him to sleep at their house. After a period of six months to a year, during which time the child resides in both households, he either takes up permanent residence in the newer household or, if unwilling, is passed over in favor of the next child.

Ten of the 64 Tarongan children between 1 and 10 years of age were involved in such a transition; all but two were schoolchildren. These children seemed more or less willing, but a few of the parents were reluctant to let them go. Two cases involved cross-*barrio* moves. In no case did a child seem upset by impending adoption nor, as we have indicated, is there any reason for it. The child is not rejected by his parents, who continue to help him when necessary; rather, he is sought after by a friendly relative.

Equally undisturbing is the opposite situation. To facilitate weaning, a child may be taken to live with an aunt or grandmother, a step which may develop into permanent adoption. If the child stays on, a coaxing process must be instituted by the parents, generally at about 5 or 6, to entice the child back home. This is usually accomplished by gifts of clothing, special foods, money, and the like. Occasionally this leads to a none too pleasant rivalry between the two households, which the sought-after child uses to advantage. At least two *barrio* children were in the midst of this kind of dispute at the time of the field period, one a preschooler, the other a third grader; in both cases a childless aunt was involved.

As children reach 8 or 9 there is an increasing separation by sex, both in play, especially at school, and in chores. Girls and boys of this age respond very differently to questions regarding their reactions to another's teasing and both react differently if the "other" is a member of the opposite sex. When asked what they would do if another boy hit them, boys give more overtly aggressive answers, saying, "I'll fight with him" or "I'll hit him." Girls say they may "tease back" another girl but are just as likely to leave the scene and report the incident. The answers change strikingly when the teaser is of the opposite sex: boys "ignore" the aggression, girls "ignore" or "report"; neither admit to fighting or even "teasing back."

Although play groups often consist of boys and girls of all ages, especially for structured games like volley ball, at this age girls become absorbed in quieter games, like jacks and hopscotch, while boys preempt tops, marbles, pitching pennies, bolo tossing, and the rougher forms of tag, wrestling, and such. Boys are also more likely to scavenge for wild fruits and edible insects. They catch a beetle, which is much like a June bug, and fasten a string to it. It whirrs about, making a very satisfactory noise which may be improved by attaching it to an empty kerosene can.

Training also begins to be differentiated by sex. Boys now are taken to the fields more often by their fathers to learn agricultural skills and animal care while girls are taught to cook and wash clothes. But this specialization is never complete, reflecting the adult lack of concern with rigid sexual division of labor. In fact, there is deliberate training of the boys in cooking and child care although boys are usually slightly older than girls when they learn these tasks. Girls also may help with field work and animal care, especially in a household short of boys.

Responsibility for children's behavior now begins to be divided between the parents in reference to chores and minor matters, since it is far more practical. Parents try to avoid conflicting orders or censure and generally succeed, for there is rarely a difference of opinion concerning ordinary matters. Occasionally a serious decision affecting the entire family must be made, for example, the question of how much education the family can afford for which children, and then no action is taken before agreement or at least grudging acceptance is obtained from all adult and teen-age children. Even schoolchildren are expected to participate in these discussions, though little weight may be given to their opinions.

Disciplinary techniques change gradually as a child matures. Frightening by threats of *Wawak*, ghosts, and so on is reduced, and by fourth grade most children no longer believe the *Wawak* threats and are less easily frightened by the others. Realistic dangers from the kidnapping *Agtoyo, not-humans,* and roaming carabao are emphasized instead. Spankings give way to ridicule, slaps to sharp comments, lavish praise and goodies to sparser but carefully evaluated compliments.

Mothers are still inclined to be impatient with ill-done chores and to scold and slap with little restraint. Many schoolchildren apparently had this in mind when they were asked what they did when their mothers punished them, for the commonest answer was "run." But few reported anger after punishment, and a short sulking period was usually the only observable aftermath. The father's discipline is less often exercised, less situationally determined, and less emotionally expressive but is reported by most mothers to be more feared and more effective.

By about third grade—apparently now seeing their future roles more clearly—boys become rather truculent toward the only group defined as fightable, the "others" at school. Parents disapprove of such fighting, but the disapproval is openly tempered with admiration if the aggression is successful or at least does not result in torn clothes. Not surprisingly, there are fights between boys' groups walking to and from school, sometimes rather nasty ones involving rocks and sticks but never, to our knowledge, bolos, though most boys carry them. Girls do not evidence such open hostility and cross *sitio*, even *barrio*, lines more readily than boys; such friendships, though few in absolute number, increase steadily until maturity. Since a girl may well live in another *sitio* or *barrio* after marriage, this early lessening of out-group hostility on her part may represent a practical assessment of her future role.

Separation of the sexes becomes more marked in the fifth and sixth grades, which emphasize agricultural science and industrial arts for the boys and home economics for girls. Play groups at this point are definitely single-sexed, the girls acting (when they remember) like young ladies and enjoying being teased by the now very masculine boys. Peer-group power over its self-conscious members by the use of ridicule, shaming, and teasing is reaching its peak, only surpassed in adolescence.

At home, too, the now pubescent girls are scolded and cajoled into ladylike behavior by their mothers, and modesty rules are rigidly enforced. Girls this age go to bathe in pairs and take turns so that any one of them is screened by another, a pattern continuing throughout adolescence. Despite this emphasis on decorum, parents at no time expect even girls to inhibit their emotional responses beyond a minimum. A certain degree of control over one's emotions is expected to develop throughout the school years, but impassivity in the face of provocation is not a Tarongan ideal.

Having noticed parents hushing children's complaints and exuberance in the presence of visitors, we were surprised at responses to the question: Should children express themselves verbally and show their feelings or not? The 24 mothers unanimously agreed that it was proper and desirable, so that "we can know what is their emotion." Judging from observation, such expression is best evidenced within the intimate family group.

Probing further into specific emotions and the propriety of their expression in childhood, we found the answers were consistent and revealed a great deal about the adult's view of children. Anger is expressed with least approval, only four mothers feeling it was permissible. One woman's comment appeared to sum up the general attitude: "No, they should not show anger because they are not doing any responsible work. Why should they get angry?"

Crying is assumed to be "not without cause" and 10 of the 24 women felt it was better for the child to go ahead and cry rather than to attempt to suppress it, if indeed he could. As a mother of nine resignedly put it: "They may cry, because they do not seem to be given to anything other than crying, children as they are." The majority of the mothers felt crying should be stopped at once by soothing or scolding, depending on the age. "Would you derive pleasure from the crying of a child?" a mother asked.

Laughter presents just the opposite picture. By nature it is pleasing: "One smiles at a baby to make it laugh. This makes you happy, no?" Therefore it is quite proper: "It is good if they are given to laughing. Isn't it true that when they laugh, you are drawn into laughing also?" Nine mothers, however, felt constrained to point out that too much laughter, especially if raucous or inappropriate, should be stopped. The attitude toward all emotional expression is one of general permissiveness unless, as with anger or raucous laughter, such expression comes into conflict with social proscription.

There are two expectations, which are interrelated in the process of growing up to adolescence: one is the increasingly responsible behavior required of a child; the other is his increasingly fuller participation in family and *sitio* affairs. Both are rewarding to the individual as well as necessary for the maintenance of the social unit.

As we have tried to indicate, responsibility, and this includes steadiness and dependability, is a characteristic much admired by Tarongans and is always rewarded one way or another. Since Tarongan children are not encouraged to do things beyond their abilities, they can often be rewarded immediately after having mastered a task by being given considerable responsibility for that task. Responsibility is not thrust on a reluctant child who has already taken for granted the ability required, but rather becomes a reward for developing that ability.

Fuller participation in *sitio* life is also a reward for responsible, dependable behavior. At parties, for example, schoolchildren are free to help as well as play with each other as long as their behavior is within reason, and they merrily chase through the yards, snoop in the kitchens, fetch water, and dump firewood on the porches while their envious preschool siblings are held firmly at an adults's side.

Participation increases intensively as it increases extensively. The child is now old enough to understand most of the events in the adult world and his values are sufficiently adult so that he reacts to them in a more or less appropriate manner. The clearest example of this was the differential age-group responses of children at the funeral preparations for an old man who was kin to them all.

Preschoolers and many young schoolchildren watched the confusion and wailing with no emotion save curiosity and uneasiness at the sight of adult tears. Schoolchildren, on the other hand, mingled with the adults, appeared genuinely sorrowful, and rather frightened by this first-hand contact with death. One 7-year-old boy in particular was noticeably shaken by the death of this kinsman, which seemed to bring the first real understanding of death. He was solemn and, in a quiet way, very brave. Adolescents show none of this uneasiness and, like their parents, indicate sadness but acceptance of the inevitable.

Perhaps in no sphere of activity are adult values taken over so quickly as in those which are economically productive. Five-year-olds help harvest rice, 7-year-olds are given a goat or two to raise, schoolchildren are made well aware of the value of their clothes and appreciate what little spending money they may be allowed. One of the most striking examples of a child's concern with family finances occurred a few days before we left Tarong. Seated on the porch of good friends in the *sitio,* one of the field team chatted about our farewell party and arranged to buy a goat that their 7½-year-old son Simeon had raised. He was sent off to our house to get the money, 9 pesos, an honor accorded him because, as his mother put it, "He cared for the goat as if it were his little brother."

In a very few moments Simeon dashed back, ecstatically clutching a sheaf of 1 peso notes. His delight in the sale was due to his ability to raise a goat so well that it brought a good price for the family, since there is in these cases never any question of the money being given to the child. He may receive a special tidbit or fancier piece of clothing but never all the proceeds of the sale, and even extras were scarce in this large family. Simeon dumped the notes in his mother's lap with a gleeful: "It is money!"

His mother smiled indulgently, then handed two of the notes to

Bartolome, a neighbor, saying: "This is Ome's cut," a joke based on his telling us of the whereabouts of an appropriate goat for the party. We all laughed and the joke was repeated. Simeon, watching two of his hard-earned, proudly presented peso notes go into Ome's pocket, burst into miserable sobs. Tears literally streaming down his face, he turned and ran to the ladder.

His mother caught him and explained that it was merely the repayment of a loan. When he had at length stopped sobbing, she showed him the remainder of the money, at which he growled: "Ta! I will tear it to pieces!" His mother soothed him, saying: "Tearing the rest? That is how it should end? No, that is only payment of money I borrowed."

Eventually Simeon subsided but sulked and was unhappy during the rest of the visit. Later his mother said of his behavior: "I think he wants to hang the money on the wall next to the diplomas!" And though she was joking, she was quite right. To Simeon, those 9 pesos for the first goat he had sold had been the shining evidence of his ability to help maintain his family, a symbol of maturity.

Given this early acceptance of adult values, childhood as we think of it, carefree and irresponsible, ends early: graduation from sixth grade formally marks its conclusion. The graduation ceremonies are elaborate and lengthy, replete with tableaux, folk dancing, and an essay by the valedictorian. Everyone attends. Poblacion dignitaries make uplifting speeches, and the children, dressed in new white clothes, stand stiffly and proudly on the decorated stage as they are ushered with pomp into adolescence.

⚘
⚘
⚘

Chapter 15

The Adolescent

The period between pubescence and marriage witnesses no changes not foreshadowed in late childhood. Nor do Tarongans in this age range show any interest in creating their own social world, rejecting adult values. Rather, they are motivated to become adults as quickly and completely as they are allowed. Throughout adolescence, maturity is evidenced by more responsible behavior, which is rewarded by greater autonomy and a position of increasing importance in family councils until, at marriage, adulthood is formally attained.

Even before adolescence, at some point during the last school years, the companion stage begins. Girls and boys pair off with one of their own age and sex, from whom they are thereafter inseparable. They go everywhere together and share everything; since they are usually *sitio*-mates and most often cousins, they may eat and sleep together, alternating between their houses.

While children are young there may be more than one companion. But especially after graduation from school, when their days are spent in the company of their immediate neighbors, the choices are necessarily narrowed to one or perhaps two. This is not to say such pairs do not interact with others of their age, for they do at all social gatherings, at work, and at play. Rather, these pairs are the irreducible units; either member will go to great lengths to be with the other.

Objectively this custom is often interfering. For example, on arrival in Tarong we offered to pay a certain sum for the services of a young girl to baby-sit, fetch water, and so on. Instead we got two companions who had agreed to split the offered wages, for either would have been miserable working alone. The parents of the girls saw nothing strange in this, however, for they often modified their own work schedules somewhat in order to pick tobacco, plow a field, or plant seedling rice in company with others.

The friendships engendered during this period are intense, and since physical gestures are acceptable modes of expression in Tarong, pairs of boys and girls are never seen without linked arms or arms about each other's waists. Even among adults touching is an expression of friendship, and adult men or women will at times stand with an arm around each other or walk hand-in-hand. This is never seen between sexes, however. As far as we could judge, these *barrio* companions engaged in no overt homosexual acts, and much of their conversations directly or indirectly concerned the opposite sex.

At adolescence a boy takes his place as a "becoming-a-young-man," developing social assurance, tentatively participating in *sitio* decisions and working with his father, uncles and work-group members in the fields. He works as well as a man by 16, but how soon a boy is granted the status of manhood depends largely on his own abilities to function as a mature adult: one *barrio* boy was still a boy at

18; another was a man at 16. A cause of slower acceptance is high school attendance. Schoolboys cannot be men, and Tarongans even speak of the occasional college attenders as boys.

No particular attention is paid to physiological signs of maturity, since they are an expected concommitant of growth, but when sexual maturity is clear, at 14 or 15, the boy will begin to attend dances and parties as a participant, a role he has looked forward to for many envious years. His parents will now begin to evaluate potential wives and talk seriously of how much land and money they can afford to give him at marriage. He will begin to boss his younger siblings and strut a bit, watching carefully to gauge the effect.

An important modification of an adolescent boy's behavior is required by the injunctions against fighting, which are now taken seriously. Except in self-defense or after great provocation, adolescent boys should not fight. Parents agree that "by 16 or so, fights between boys are serious, maybe fatal. They are not schoolboys quarreling any more." They therefore warn their sons against thoughtless speech which might offend and against provocative acts, even when insulted. This advice is not always heeded, but open fighting among adolescent boys is fairly uncommon. Struck by the sudden shift in boys' expression of anger, we questioned further, and one man summed up general opinion with: "They know that those who are against them may wield weapons and they are not usually ready to run into serious trouble."

The requirement of caution in expressing hostility is also increasingly demanded of the boy in relation to his family. Childish anger directed toward a parent was either laughed at or punished. An angry boy who is almost a man can no longer be laughed at, and punishments at this age are neither physical nor easy to enforce. The boy himself is therefore required to express his anger in a suitably adult way out of respect for his parents and, probably more effective, fear of loss of their economic and social support. An angry son may argue, even raise his voice, but he must neither shout nor lift his hand against his parents.

Illustrative of the pressures for holding hostility to a decent minimum were the cries of horror greeting a story widely circulated in the *barrio* although its protagonists lived outside Tarong. The adolescent boy of the family one day threatened his father with a bolo and his cursing stopped only when the constabulary arrived, having been summoned by terrified neighbors. Tarongans, after much discussion, decided the boy had been taken by a fit of madness and reminded each other of similar madness induced by *not-humans* before they bestowed the ability to heal.

Less dramatic lapses from good conduct or foolish behavior are handled by the now-familiar and still effective ridicule techniques. Shaming is not usually public, but within a very short time the entire *sitio* knows "what Pedro did!" This age group is extremely sensitive to ridicule, and most boys would prefer being beaten in a fight to being laughed at. Tarongans are aware of this sensitivity; perhaps it has been forced on them by adolescent violence in reaction to taunting. Adults and other adolescents show more politeness and caution in scolding, teasing, and so forth with this age group than with any other.

One instance impressed us: at a small dance, which only a few neighboring *sitios* were attending, an impromptu program began while the band rested. Various adolescents and adults were cajoled and "forced" to sing or play the guitar. The audience was polite but comfortable and enjoying the program. Then a shy visiting boy was really forced to participate, and he faced the ring of spectators in obvious terror. He sang horribly. He seemed to know it, for he looked more miserable with each cracked note. The audience tensed and maintained the polite, respectful silence they would have accorded the mayor had he decided to sing at a similar gathering. No movement that could have been construed as derisive was made; each face was carefully blank. When the boy finished, he was applauded heartily—the decrease in tension was almost as audible.

Adolescence is a period of growing intimacy between a father and his son, for the boy works closely with his father, is often taken with him on trips to Poblacion or nearby *barrios*. He may begin to accompany his father and uncles to the town cockfights, where he learns the rules of betting. But "a chicken does not grow into a rooster by sitting in the nest," and parents are easily cajoled into permitting a son of 16 or so to go to Poblacion with his companions, and they will provide a little money to spend there.

A Tarongan does not worry about the problems of age and the relinquishing of authority to the next generation until the time is close at hand. He sees no threat in his son's approaching manhood as long as he evidences a willingness to work with his parents until his turn as a family leader will have been earned.

A girl, too, takes on increasing responsibilities during her early adolescence; the important requirement now is that she be a good worker and womanly, which implies an even greater shyness with men than she has previously shown. There is no public recognition of onset of the menses, which generally occurs at 12 or 13, but it is a long-awaited, crucial event for the girl. Now she will be called by a diminutive of the coveted term "young woman," and be teased about her near-readiness for marriage.

For the girl who is menstruating, there is no required change in everyday routine. If she does not feel well, she will be excused from some chores, and if her pains are severe, or if she has pain in her breasts, both common at initial menstruation, a decoction of crushed leaves in wine may be given. There are a few generally accepted prohibitions: most women do not wash their hair at this time, and some will not immerse themselves in water; excessive heat also is dangerous.

Two or three days before the flow begins, women say they have a desire for sour things, but once the flow has started, sour and tasty foods are forbidden, though not as many foods are excluded from the diet as during the postbirth *tangad* period. Also, as was reported for *tangad* regulations, there is disagreement about the effects of sweets.

The prohibitions for the menstruating girl are not onerous, and the privileges attendant on her new status are satisfying. At wakes she will take her place among the women, wearing a black veil; at feasts she will serve food and water to guests; and, most important of all, she now may participate at dances and parties.

Girls and boys this age are encouraged to dance in public only with their siblings and first cousins if at all. Most are far too "ashamed" and content themselves with avidly watching from the dancers' benches. But during their leisure moments, girls and even boys may be seen trying out dance steps with their same-sex companions while their young siblings tease them enviously. At intimate gatherings, impromptu practice dances may be held whenever someone present owns or has borrowed a guitar. Parents spur their children on with praises or taunts; older adolescents and young adults try to instruct; young children excitedly imitate the dancers and get underfoot.

Since Tarongan dancing is a simple version of a fox trot, such practice over a period of a year or two engenders enough confidence in adolescents for them to timidly initiate and accept requests in public. Old people say adolescents used to dance at 14 and were married at 16; now the usual age for participating in the regular dances seems to be 15 or 16, although 14-year-olds take part in intimate *sitio* dances.

The same year or two of side-line observation before full participation holds for card playing. At all gatherings aside from dances, that is, at feasts, wakes, and prayer meetings, a social cardgame is sure to begin. There is some variety, but all involve as many marriageable boys and girls as possible and are played for the amusement of the forfeits accompanying loss of a game. Gambling is never a part of these games.

The girls are little restricted in this situation, which no doubt also accounts for the popularity of cardgames. Despite the fact that the games are played in the center of a brightly lit *sala* or porch, the players are seated on the floor in a pattern of alternating sexes and the noise of the game masks low-pitched conversations.

As with dancing, young adolescents cajole older siblings into letting them practice with intimate groups that gather now and then at a house in the evening. Such groups may be merely companions or may be the excuse for a suitor to visit his choice. In that the games are simple and the players less individually noticeable, young adolescents are likely to be playing cards at the larger gatherings a year or more before they will dance at an equivalently public party.

Dancing and cardgames give adolescents a chance to become acquainted, but that is as far as their pursuit can go. Of primary importance is the maintenance of a girl's chastity, and to guard her well she is rarely sent alone on errands or to work in the fields. For the adolescent girl the companion is of great utility as a chaperone. As one mother put it: "When she is a young woman (i.e. by 14), she should always have a constant companion. Then if there is a lover or admirer, this one would be a deterrent to any untoward behavior."

Even such a young companion seems to be sufficient, for although a girl this age might turn her head in order not to witness her companion flirt, or perhaps hold hands with a boy, she would be too shocked as well as thoroughly terrified of punishment to overlook further intimacies.

As true courting approaches—from 15 on—girls and boys alike spend longer and longer at their toilets before parties. New clothes and good shoes are wheedled from secretly approving parents. Grandmothers give up their valuable earrings. Secrets are whispered incessantly.

Many giggling conversations concern sex, for sex training is surprisingly meager in view of the adults' lack of self-consciousness about sexual matters. A child's questions are simply not answered or he is told he should not be asking such "foolish things." The response to such questions is always the same, and presumably the adolescent child should know nothing of such matters. Yet parents say: "Oh, by then they know. You do not have to teach these things, they all know." One parent added: "By 12 or 13, sexual activity is already a plaything of their fancy."

Apparently the chances of the child's overseeing his parents' sexual activities and those of animals, along with the constant exposure of children's genitals and the casual discussion of such matters by adults, enables understanding despite lack of explanation. Adolescent Tarongans certainly understood and looked forward with zest to sexual relations although it is most improbable that any had experienced them.

Given the lack of first-hand experience and the sexual excitation of the courtship period, it is not surprising that the subject is of great interest to adolescent Tarongans. Equally understandable is their embarrassment with potential marriage partners. Girls chatting together sound very adult when they speak of marriage, but let the older brother of one of them appear and the others dissolve into giggles and hang their heads. By 18 or so, girls recover somewhat, at least in groups, and flirt vivaciously from behind their fans.

Boys like to brag of their boldness, but due to *barrio* chaperonage, their stories must be woefully curtailed. A stolen kiss on the way home from a dance would be as much as most could ever claim. A few boys who work out of the *barrio* frequently or who go to school in Poblacion may brag of intimacies with women, since their listeners cannot offer proof to the contrary. But all such tales are accepted with incredulity. After the visit of an attractive girl from another province, one of the *barrio* boys claimed he had once been allowed to put his hand on her thigh. This was the high point of his bragging, but no one believed the story. Incredulity is probably justified, for there is a striking difference in manner between these adolescents and mature males who, even if not married, have managed to arrange sexual contacts.

The creation of a family of one's own is a major goal to Tarongans; the courtship period is thus the turning point of their lives. This is particularly true for girls, since their futures depend on attracting solid, substantial, and dependable workers. Still, romantic love stories read aloud in porch corners are not wasted on Tarongan adolescents, and the strikingly handsome son of a poor, unsuccessful family was looked at with admiration by every girl in the *barrio* and glared at by every mother. So too was the pretty, "modern" daughter of the *barrio* lieutenant watched by the young men, whose mothers grumbled about extravagant tastes and "bold looks."

A pleasing courtship custom is serenading. On moonlight nights, groups of three or more young men with guitars stroll from girl's house to girl's house, always including those currently preferred by one or another of the group but often others as well. The girl so honored listens to their songs from the safety of the *sala,* and, if her parents approve of the boys, they may be invited onto the porch for refreshment, where the girl will join them, laughing and blushing at the circumlocutions and elaborate poesy in which Ilocano courtship is phrased.

The object of courtship being to court or be courted, Tarongan parents bent on marrying their children soon urge them to go to every wake, prayer meeting, party, or dance which they can properly attend. The surrounding *sitios* limit choices, and the young people are packed off in safely large groups to such affairs at nearby and not so near *barrios* where they can represent the family as well as shop for a spouse.

Quarrels between groups of boys from different *barrios* occasionally arise at dances, but hostility is generally held to a minimum. Not only have out-*sitio* and out-*barrio* contacts increased through participation in adult activities, but one might well wish to marry a girl from another *barrio* and quarreling with her neighbors will not help such a suit. The girls, as we mentioned earlier, are likely to have schoolgirl friendship ties with these *barrios* and are quickly made welcome.

If a boy or girl next door is a well-liked second cousin, however- parental pressures are strong in this direction, and many such marriages do occur. There is a growing tendency for adolescents of 18 or 19 to make their own choices and even reach agreements without consultation with their parents. Although such agreements are rarely refused outright by either set of parents, they are not pleased with this lack of consideration. Parents feel, and perhaps rightly, that their evaluations of prospective sons-in-law or daughters-in-law are sounder than those of their romantic, naive children.

Preferences between adolescents are recognized and discussed, but it is difficult for the outsider to see evidence of them. Although animated at parties, both boys and girls are woodenly aloof at dances and, to judge by the most prized appearance, can just manage to bring themselves to request or accept a dance. Dancing itself is hardly conducive to romance, since it consists of stolidly moving around a cleared yard-space, the partners at least a foot apart, each gazing intently and rather unhappily over the other's shoulder. Yet it is at these dances, we were told, that one could see a declaration of interest on the part of the boy and a refusal or temporary approval from the girl.

Using every possible clue, including how many times the girl fluttered her fan between dances, we were unable to guess accurately. One night we had made records of dancing partners and jokingly suggested to an old man near us that the three partnership combinations that had not occurred were the ones who were courting. He laughed and assured us that one of these pairs would be married before long and he was, as usual, right.

One young man admitted that the boys themselves were not always sure of the girls' sentiments and they sometimes resorted to a test: if a boy asks a girl not to attend some affair and she does not go, it is proof of her interest in him as a suitor. But to judge by the never-ending gossip between adolescent companions of both sexes, anxiety about the loved one's affections is high and any gesture or remark is endlessly analyzed for hidden meanings. Hopefully all doubts are resolved at the next dance where the dancers make their choices, boys approach their parents to begin negotiations, and girls lie awake wondering when a go-between will come.

BIBLIOGRAPHY

Beyer, H. O. The Philippines before Magellan. *Asia,* 1921, **21,** 861–892, 924–970.

———. Historical introduction. In E. A. Manuel, *Chinese Elements in the Tagalog Language.* Manila: Filipiniana Publications, 1948, pp. ix–xxv.

Beyer, H. O. and de Veyra, J. C. *Philippine Saga.* Manila: Capitol Publishing House, 1952.

Blair, Emma H. and Robertson, J. A. *The Philippine Islands.* Cleveland: Arthur H. Clark, 1903–1909, vols. 1–55.

Bureau of the Census and Statistics. *Statistical Handbook of the Philippines, 1903–1953.* Manila: 1954.

———. *Census of the Philippines, 1948.* Manila: 1951.

Bureau of Printing. *Civil Code of the Philippines.* Manila: 1954.

Cole, F-C. The Tinguian. *Field Museum of Natural History, Anthropological Series,* 1922, **14,** 2.

———. *The Peoples of Malaysia.* New York: van Nostrand, 1945.

Krieger, H. W. *People of the Philippines.* Smithsonian Institution War Background Series. Washington, D.C.: Smithsonian Institution, 1942.

Kroeber, A. L. *Peoples of the Philippines.* (2nd ed.) New York: American Museum of Natural History, 1943.

Manuel, E. A. *Chinese Elements in the Tagalog Language.* Manila: Filipiniana Publications, 1948.

McKaughan, H. and Forster, Jannette. *Ilocano: An Intensive Language Course.* Glendale, Calif.: Summer Institute of Linguistics, 1952.

Nydegger, W. F. Tarong: A Philippine barrio. Unpublished Ph.D. thesis, Cornell University, 1960.

Phelan, J. L. *The Hispanization of the Philippines.* Madison, Wis.: University of Wisconsin Press, 1959.

Pigafetta, A. First voyage around the world. Translated by J. A. Robertson. In E. H. Blair and J. A. Robertson, *The Philippine Islands.* Cleveland: Arthur H. Clark, 1906, vols. 33 and 34.

Prator, C. H., Jr. Language teaching in the Philippines. United States Educational Foundation in the Philippines, 1950.

Sande, F. Relation of the Filipinas Islands, 1576. Translated by Rachel King. In E. H. Blair and J. A. Robertson, *The Philippine Islands.* Cleveland: Arthur H. Clark, 1903, vol. 4.

Spencer, J. E. *Land and People in the Philippines: Geographic Problems in Rural Economy.* Berkeley: University of California Press, 1952.

Subcontractor's Monograph, *The Philippines,* Human Relations Area Files, Inc., New Haven, Conn., 1955.

Tangco, M. The Christian peoples of the Philippines. *University of the Philippines Natural and Applied Science Bulletin,* 1951, 11, 1.

Tolentino, A. M. *The Government of the Philippines.* Manila: R. P. Garcia Co., 1950.

The New Englanders

of Orchard Town, U.S.A.

❧
❧
❧
❧
❧
❧

John L. Fischer

Ann Fischer

Contents

About the Authors

In selecting the sample for study we included a group of families in a New England town so that we would have bench marks for comparison. Although it is difficult for "natives" to collect ethnographic data which is comparable to that collected by an individual of a different culture, the account of Orchard Town, presented with a format similar to that of the other ethnographies, will give the reader some idea of how a Rājpūt from Khalapur or an Okinawan from Taira would react to the description of his life.

John and Ann Fischer were assigned the difficult task of conducting the study in a New England community. John Fischer, a Ph.D. in anthropology in social relations at Harvard, and his wife had spent three years in the Caroline Islands in the Pacific where he had served as the district anthropologist on Truk and Ponape and later as a native affairs officer. Ann Fischer had gathered material for a doctoral thesis for the Harvard Anthropology Department on Trukese mothers and their infants. Their two daughters, Nikko and Mary Anne, were born on the islands and spent their early years with Trukese children. We felt, therefore, that the family would have an objectivity about New England which would help them to do a comparable study in their own society. They moved into a community and selected a group of families who were largely members of a Baptist church situated near their house. John Fischer volunteered his services as a Sunday School teacher. The yard of their house, which was large and inviting, was a gathering place for many of the children. The Fischers had by far the hardest job, from one point of view, for their informants quite understandably felt that the Fischers knew the answers to the questions they asked. The mothers were interested in child rearing but more concerned with the particular than the general. The Fischers had difficulty in convincing them that they were not "authorities" and that the project was designed to learn from them rather than to conduct a clinic. Although it was easy to evaluate individual differences, it was difficult to see the large patterns. We have often thought that, unlike the other teams, who had college graduate "native" assistants, the Fischers would have found it profitable if they had had a non-Western European assistant to gather the cultural material.

John Fischer is now a member of the Department of Sociology and Anthropology at Tulane University.

Part I

The Ethnographic Background

✵
✵
✵
✵
✵
✵

Chapter 1

The Setting

Before beginning this field study, we were residing in New England while finishing our doctoral work in anthropology. In choosing a community to study, we first defined a general area containing a couple of dozen communities which seemed to be relatively small and stable. We then reconnoitered until we found one meeting the general requirements and with suitable and strategically located living quarters for our year of study. To preserve the anonymity of the people involved, we shall refer to the community involved as North Village and to the officially organized town in which it is located as Orchard Town.

Since Orchard Town was within a reasonable traveling distance of our home at the time, we were able to visit it from time to time before actually moving there. Our initial introduction to the people of Orchard Town came through the then Superintendent of Schools. He had studied at the Harvard Graduate School of Education, with which we were affiliated during our study. Although this superintendent left to take a foreign job shortly after we met him, before leaving he introduced us (at his farewell party) to some of the officials connected with the schools and to other townspeople.

We made no special efforts to give publicity to our study, since we wished to preserve the anonymity of the town and people as far as possible. However, we explained the general purposes of our work without hesitation to anyone who asked, child or adult. In general, we told people that we were studying what it was like to be a child in North Village, that we planned to watch the children doing different things, and to ask people questions, about the children in particular and the community in general as the setting in which the children grew up. In the process of obtaining interviews from the mothers and children, all parents in the 24 families of the sample were necessarily informed that we wished to study one of their children in detail. The only formal publicity the project received in town was a speech given to the local PTA, a flourishing organization, by Beatrice Whiting, after we had been engaged in fieldwork for several months. In this speech she described the general purposes of the project and something about the fieldwork in the other five cultures.

We met more people through the local Protestant church than in any other fashion. All of the families in our sample either had some connection with the church or associated with people connected with the church. The minister, who, incidentally, was taking graduate work in religious psychology, was especially understanding of the purposes of our study and helpful in introducing us to people around town.

Since we were studying our own culture, or a not very unusual variant of it, we were in a different position from most anthropological fieldworkers. As residents, and later registered voters, of the town, we were considered by most people to be as capable of assuming the general duties of citizens as anyone else. There was little difficulty in arranging genuine participation in many aspects of the life of the community. The male ethnographer, for instance, taught Sunday School to a group of fourth-grade boys every Sunday during the school year. The difficulty was rather in trying to maintain free access to opposing groups in the community by avoiding too full participation in some of them. As members of the culture ourselves, we had constantly to check our tendency to choose sides on issues dividing the community, since we also tended to feel that it was proper for us to participate and that we were as qualified as anyone else to pass judgment. Thus not only did people in the community itself tend to think of us as not too exceptional and as equally liable to civic obligations as anyone else, but also we ourselves felt more obliged to participate than we would have in studying a foreign culture.

Unlike fieldworkers in many foreign cultures, we had little entertainment value for members of the town. If anything, our academic background seemed a little dull or stuffy to some of the townspeople.

In studying our own culture we found it difficult to get people to make generalizations about life in the town. Cultural questions would be reinterpreted as questions about individual differences within the culture or they would be airily dismissed with the statement, no doubt often correct, "Oh, you know how it is." A foreign ethnographer would probably have been more successful in getting the people to talk more generally about their community and its life, but on the other hand would probably have been slower to appreciate differences between various people.

We were fortunate in our choice of living quarters. We were able to rent the first floor of a house with a large yard which had the reputation of being a sort of playground for the neighborhood children. The yard had a broad lawn, a sandbox and sandpile, a swing attached to a high tree branch, and other attractions for children. The house faced the North Village green and was located next to the Protestant church. The business block was father down the street beyond the church. A number of the families in our sample lived within easy walking distance of our home, although others lived in newer houses on the outskirts of the village.

Orchard Town was settled and organized as a town in the colonial period, and native residents express pride at the part their ancestors and predecessors played in the Revolutionary War. Through most of its history Orchard Town has been primarily a farming town with some small local factories and craftsmen. After the initial period of settlement, the population has remained rather constant throughout most of its history, but recently, with the suburban expansion of nearby cities, the population has been increasing as city workers have moved in and bought homes. At the same time, with improvements in the nationwide transport of farm products, local farming has suffered by competition with areas favored with better soil and climate and is now much reduced in scope.

There are three major centers of population in Orchard Town, which we label here North Village (the community which we studied), Center Village, and Depot Village. The original center of the town was Center Village, and it is here that the town hall is still located. North Village and Depot Village both grew larger after the railroad was laid through them in the mid-nineteenth century. The railroad bypassed Center Village because of the protests of some of the inhabitants, and Center Village is now somewhat smaller than the other two.

The long-time residents of Orchard Town—and it is these in whom we were especially interested—like to think of the town as rural and as exemplifying the rural New England virtues of friendliness, self-respectability, moderately paced living, conservatism in respect for the law, and freedom from pretentiousness. At the same time, they recognize with mixed feelings that the nature of the community is changing because of the rapid growth produced by immigration from the cities. The increased population has made it impossible to fit all the citizens into the town hall at town meeting, has overcrowded school buildings —even though new ones have been built—and otherwise taxed public facilities. The newcomers, initially at least, tend to be more "liberal" politically and tend to have numerous ideas as to town improvements which appear unnecessary to many long-time residents. Some of the latter lament the passing of the old order and talk about moving farther out, while others welcome the growth and change, though not without nostalgia, as offering new life and opportunities for improvement.

Physically the people of Orchard Town present no apparent differences from a somewhat mixed Old American group elsewhere in the country. In emotional types, also, they greatly resemble the people in other established American groups. Any trends toward differences from Americans in other parts of the country can probably be attributed to regional rather than specifically local differences—to New England versus other parts of the country rather than to Orchard Town versus other nearby towns. Characteristics which seem to help distinguish Orchard Town people, and probably rural and small-town New Englanders generally, from the population of other parts of the country include among others a greater tolerance for personal eccentricity, a somewhat greater interest in the past, a relative lack of ostentation, and often a certain reserve or dignity of manner with strangers. All these characteristics appear to be more marked in the older people than the younger. They are in accord with the popular stereotype of New Englanders but it is our impression that while the people of Orchard Town did fulfill the stereotype to a certain degree, they are basically quite similar in character to small-town people in many parts of the country.

The population of Orchard Town is not very stable and is becoming less so; it is a mobile one. To a certain extent this has perhaps always been true. The first minister of the North Village Protestant church, for instance, resigned to go to California at the time of the 1848 Gold

Rush. The villagers have relatives in far parts of the country. The father of one informant worked on the Panama Canal and that of another visited Samoa as a sailor. Furthermore, many of the present villagers have themselves lived in various parts of the country, and, of course, during World War II, men who joined the Armed Services traveled to distant parts of the world.

A rough idea of the origin of the population can be gained from a sample of 85 parents, composed of one parent for each of 85 children entering the first grade in the year 1953. Usually the parent given is the father, although in some cases if the mother filled out the report, she did so for herself. The children and their parents come from all parts of Orchard Town, not just North Village, but it seems likely that the proportions in the sample would apply about as well to North Village as to the town as a whole. Of this sample, 8 (roughly 10%) were born in Orchard Town; 16 in nearby small towns; 12 in small towns in some part of New England—adding to a total of 36 with some kind of New England, small-town background. Thirty-three more were born in New England cities of varying size, making a total of 69 out of 85 from some part of New England. Four more were born in other eastern states, 5 more were born in far states, 4 were born in Canada, and the remaining 3 were born in Europe—note that 16 out of 85 were *not* born in New England, about one fifth of the population. However, an even smaller ratio are genuine natives of the town; moreover, some of the "natives" in this categorization, that is, people born in Orchard Town itself, were born of foreign parents.

Another thing to note about the population is that it is growing, and it is expected to continue to grow. There has been a very gradual growth in the population ever since the beginning of the town, but the greatest growth has taken place within the last few years, since World War II. Most of the recent growth appears to be accounted for by new people moving into the town. The population of the town as a whole at the time of our study was nearly 5000, of which about 1600 lived in North Village. Population throughout most of the town's history was about half this.

Orchard Town is located on the edge of the commuting area of one of the large New England cities. In addition to North Village, the town includes the two other principal centers of population: the Center, where the town hall is located, and Depot Village, the most important train stop. The description here will be limited mainly to the village studied, North Village. Certain important features and places which are not in any one of the village centers should be noted, however. Two of these are the main highway and the railroad which bisect the town. Another is the town dump, to which most residents of Orchard Town, in whichever village they reside, must pay frequent visits because there is no collecting service for trash. There is also the high school and, adjoining it, a primary school for the first two grades only. This is located roughly midway between the three centers of population. There are also a few small factories which are located between the centers of population.

Legally, Orchard Town is divided into three precincts, the three centers of population corresponding to a precinct. Besides its legal distinctness, North Village has the following attributes of a community· it has a school (for third to sixth grade, at the time of the study); it has a Protestant and Catholic church, a fire house, a small business district, a small green or square, and a railroad station at which some trains stop. Some people use the train for commuting to the city and have for many years, although train service is not as frequent as it used to be when driving was more difficult.

North Village has only about four principal streets. Two of these are state routes and are maintained mostly by the state. Many of the new houses are located on some of the small side streets. The main highway, which is used by commuters to the big city, is located about a mile from the center of North Village. Traffic is heavy and moves fast along the main highway but under rather strict police control on the lesser highways. Traffic is very light on the side streets and moves slowly, for most of the streets are narrow and poorly paved.

The center of North Village (see map 1) contains a small green on which the Protestant church is located. Adjacent to the green and church is a small, block-long business district. The green is quite small, and it is there only because a wealthy local resident gave this plot of ground to the town, within the lifetime of many now living; it is not the sort of large, planned green which is found in many New England towns. Such a green is found in Orchard Town only in Center Village. Originally there was a house on the site of the North Village green. This was torn down to make the green. A cemetery is located on the edge of the village.

The business district contains two grocery stores, one small restaurant, another lunch place with a fountain, a drugstore, a clothing store selling ready-made clothing (especially children's clothing), a materials store selling cloth for clothes and drapes, a barber shop (with one barber), a beauty shop (one beauty operator), a hardware store, and another store, very popular with the children, which sells principally stationery, magazines, newspapers, candy, and toys. There is a small railroad station, which is open for the convenience of passengers

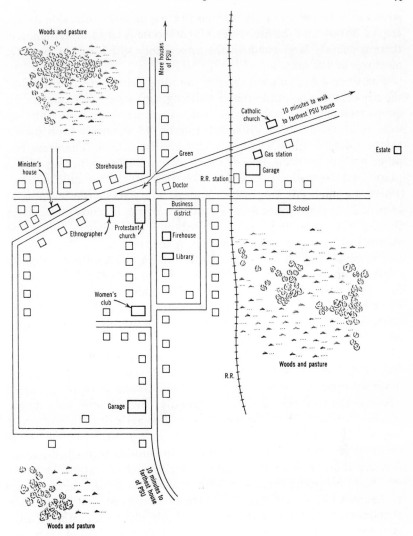

Map 1. Center of North Village.

waiting for trains but which no longer sells tickets. Across the railroad tracks from the rest of the business district there is a gas station, a garage, a trucking company, and a storage place for farm products. On the green there is also a building now used for apple storage, which was formerly the hall of a men's fraternal society. The Catholic church is on the other side of the railroad tracks, opposite the gas station.

Around the corner from the business district, on one of the side streets, are the library and the firehouse. The firehouse is two stories high, and there is a fairly large room in the upper story which can be used for meetings by the firemen.

There are a few other important buildings elsewhere in the town: the school, the community center building, and some other commercial establishments. The community center itself was organized while we were residing in North Village. Formerly the Women's Club owned the building; originally it was a Universalist church. There are two other garages in town, one of which is quite small. There is also a place with frozen-food lockers, which individuals are able to rent. There is a small gift shop, which appears to do very little business, at least with local people. There is another very small candy and grocery store, a metal pipe shop, and a paint shop. These other buildings and enterprises are all located on the principal streets.

The remaining structures in North Village are dwellings. Most of these are single-family units, although some of the older, larger houses have been divided into apartments. There is also a postwar apartment block in the center of town, covered with grey asphalt and imitation brick siding. There are at least three other buildings in town which were constructed expressly as apartments.

The natural terrain of Orchard Town is rather typical of parts of New England. It is hilly although not extremely so. It is poorly drained; there are many small ponds and swamps; there are small streams. Most of the land was originally covered over with forest. Much of this was cleared by the farmers when agriculture was of prime importance, but in recent years forests have been encroaching on the meadows and fields. The many stone walls running through the forest indicate the extent of this advance. Fields and old apple orchards, which are becoming overgrown with young trees, are further evidence of the same trend. Although it may seem paradoxical, as a result of the abandonment of farming there are probably more wild animals, such as skunks and deer, in Orchard Town now than a hundred years ago.

A number of ponds and lakes provide swimming in the summer and skating in the winter. These ponds, together with numerous small streams, offer opportunities for fishing, although, according to old inhabitants, the quality of fishing around Orchard Town has decreased in the last generation because of water pollution. Trout fishermen can easily travel to better fishing grounds in nearby areas.

The woods and fields of Orchard Town offer hunting of game birds and even some deer. The meadows and farms are also valued as places for collecting wild berries, especially bluberries. One of the most popular places for collecting blueberries is at the bog at the town dump. The town dump is located at one side of this bog, and it is being gradually filled in by the refuse which the citizens dispose of there. This is covered over periodically with sand and eventually will form a plot of dry land. Berries are said to be less common now than a generation ago, because cow pastures, which were once a very suitable site for wild berries, have been partially overgrown by shrubs.

The climate of Orchard Town is typical of New England. An inland town, it does not have the moderating effect of the ocean in the summer; summers get rather hot. In winter, temperatures go well below freezing at times, and snow, although not uncommon, seldom covers the ground for more than a few weeks.

The dwelling is one of the cultural features which most sharply distinguishes New England from the other societies described in this volume. It has brick chimneys, doors with hinges, latches, and locks, hardwood floors, woven rugs, upholstered chairs and couches, glass windows which let in the light and keep out the cold, central heating, running hot and cold water, indoor flush toilets, indoor bathtubs and showers, automatic refrigeration, gas or electric stoves, telephone, radio, television, basements, second stories, and attics. The New England house shares with that of other societies the separation of the dwelling into rooms which are used for different functions, such as cooking, sleeping, eating, and entertaining.

Although two of the families in the sample lived in apartment houses, the rest were divided about equally between old New England two-story houses and modern single-story houses. (See Figure 1 for plan of typical house and yard.) The former were larger and more costly to maintain. In addition to kitchen, bathrooms, bedrooms, and living rooms, these old houses were likely to have parlors, pantries, studies, and attics. The basements of these old houses were more likely to have been root cellars which were modified when the furnace was installed and therefore seldom used as a play area for the children or for television as is the case with the basements in the modern house. The outbuildings associated with the old houses are more likely to be barns than garages. Finally, large shade trees are likely to surround the old houses, making them cooler in summer.

The kitchen is probably the most important room in the New England house. Nearly all the families in our sample have a kitchen which contains a gas or electric stove, a refrigerator, an electric washing machine, and a sink with running hot and cold water. Around the walls are dressers, cupboards, and shelves for the storage of cooking and eating utensils. In addition, most of the kitchens contain a table and

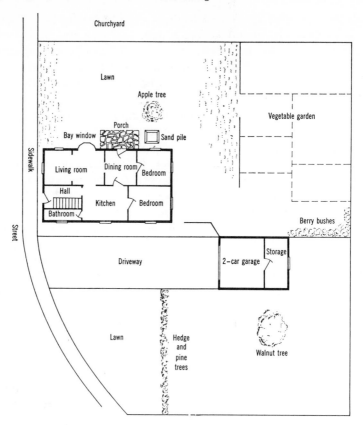

Figure 1. Plan of typical house showing ground floor and yard.

chairs at which most family meals are eaten, the dining room or dining-living space being used only for formal dinner parties. Since cooking, eating, and washing all occur in the kitchen, this is the center of family life during the daytime. In the evenings after supper this center generally moves to the living room or to the TV room.

The New Englander's inability to throw anything away, for "it might come in handy sometime," puts a strain on the house and out-buildings. The attic is generally filled with materials of little practical use. Similarly, every available bit of extra space in the basement, closets, garage, or barn is crammed with broken furniture which might some day be repaired, old clothes sometimes used by the children for "dressing up," baby carriages, "which will be perfectly good for the grandchildren," and the like. Sometimes extra buildings or additions are built just to provide more storage space.

Most of the houses are surrounded by large yards, many of which contain swings and sandpiles. Flower beds and decorative bushes are generally to be seen on the street side of the yard and fruit orchards, berry patches, and vegetable gardens in the backyard.

The above description of house and yard applies to Orchard Town people for most of the year, but most of the North Village families in our sample also spend some time in the summer at a "camp." The stay at the camp serves as an annual period of relaxation from the restrictions at the house and from the stimulation of television or other mass media. A *real* camp was defined as surrounded by forest, no electricity, no plumbing, no television or radio, and with the nearest road a half mile away. Some of the camps are within a few miles of Orchard Town and within commuting distance of home. Others are as far as a day's drive away. In any case, the camps seem to be very isolated and in a place with different neighbors. Living conditions at camp are quite different from those at home, and the children as well as the rest of the family look forward to their annual stay there.

☀
☀
☀

Chapter 2

Basic Economy

Most of the economic activities which take place inside Orchard Town are services or are concerned with the distribution of products. There are a few small factories in town, but the specialization and centralization of industry have largely taken labor out of Orchard Town and into bigger neighboring communities. This process has increased with the years and has slowly changed the basic economy from an original farming community supplying many of its own needs to one dependent on its integration with the economy of the nation.

Only two of the fathers in our sample are self-employed. One runs a chicken farm, and the other is a consultant. The remainder are all salaried employees or wage earners. Many of the occupations would fall in the category of skilled labor, but the range is from truck drivers to bankers. The sample is just about evenly split between white-collar and blue-collar jobs.

Nearly all the men commuted to their work, some of them going to the metropolitan area each day. The fathers therefore are seldom present for the noonday meal except on weekends.

The basic economy of Orchard Town, like the economy of much of the nation, is remarkably stable throughout the seasons. Man-made rest periods cause much more variation in the scheduling of the basic economy than the climate or the seasonal round. Every week the basic economy slows down for Saturday and Sunday. It also slows down for national holidays.

There is some seasonal difference in that men's work slackens during the summer. Stores are closed on Wednesday afternoons, and many men take summer vacations a few weeks during the summer or they may take longer weekends during the summer. Summer is to a certain extent the time for consumption of the winter savings.

Another variation in the summer is that some families do supplementary vegetable gardening. In former days women used to can their own vegetables, but they do not do this as much now. Some seasonal foods are preserved, especially delicacies such as strawberries and blueberries, which though available at other seasons in the stores, would be more expensive than one would wish to pay. At present, roughly the same food is available all year in the stores, since it is shipped in from far parts of the country.

The basic necessities of life as well as many of the amenities are distributed adequately throughout the population of Orchard Town. There is practically no real danger of famine or food shortage or lack of housing or clothing or other lack in the basic economy, although most of the inhabitants have a desire for more luxurious food, better-looking clothes, bigger houses, bigger TV sets, better cars, and the like. There are a number of restrictions on the consumption of food by the children, but these restrictions are not based on the danger of shortage of food. Children do not have to worry about being inadequately clothed in terms of protection from the weather, although they may be concerned about whether their clothes look as well as other children's.

Old people who lack savings are in a difficult economic position, but they receive government aid if necessary. Even they have no serious lack of the basic requirements of food, clothing, and shelter.

A few people in the town have a relatively low standard of living, since they have to live on money from relief funds. Most of these, however, are old people who do not live in households with children. Our sample, therefore, contains none of these people. Most of the families in the sample live on an income which does not allow any savings to be made beyond payments on a home mortgage and insurance payments. Perhaps 6 families in the 24 would be an exception to this rule. On the other hand, probably none of the 24 families could be said to be in debt, beyond the amount of the mortgage on their homes. Some families do a very small amount of installment buying.

Most of the wealth which is consumed is distributed throughout the population through the medium of entrepreneurs. Most goods are acquired by purchase through known entrepreneurs, and therefore shopping is an important activity. Women do most of the shopping. They must buy food regularly, and they use these trips to the store for food to do other forms of shopping as well. Practically all families in town have a car of some sort, and the women use it at certain times at least to go shopping. Usually the women themselves drive. If they do not, the husbands drive them shopping on weekends or evenings when the stores are open. There is no regular means of transportation except for the privately owned car and occasional trains which take passengers into the city. Most people rarely buy anything from a distance as far away as the city. Shopping for large quantities is usually done in nearby towns; for small quantities it is done in North Village.

The largest share of the family income is spent on goods which are immediately or almost immediately consumable—food and clothing. Although food is mainly purchased at the stores, door-to-door vendors are another source of food. Milk, eggs, bakery products, a little fish, and a few vegetables are sold this way. Home-grown vegetables and poultry supply some needs. Facilities for food storage are good. Canned and dried foods can be stored indefinitely in cupboards, and perishable food is stored in the refrigerator. Some families have locker space in the freezer plant where they can store other perishable foods for a long period. Many foods can be purchased already prepared for consumption.

There is not much food available in the fields or in the yards, but what little there is is not strongly prohibited to children. Children would be advised not to pick fruit belonging to other people, but it is not felt very serious for children to take these for their own consumption in season. It would be more serious for children to take vegetables from the vegetable gardens, but they would feel less desire to do this. Children are supposed to get most of their food at meal-times, but they are allowed some sweets and fruits in between meals and are also given small sums of money which they use mostly to purchase gum and candy. A child's between-meal food, or the money for it, may come either from his own home or from his friends.

Houses are very permanent. If preserved from fire, they last almost indefinitely. There are houses in town which are probably two centuries old. Although houses need periodic repairs, they do not fall down and are rarely torn down. The most common way to get a house is to buy one. Some families in our sample had inherited their houses. Recently many new houses have been built.

Within the nuclear family, labor is divided between adults and children and between men and women. The division of labor by generation can usually be dismissed simply by saying that the adults do most of the labor and the children do very little. Children used to do more and in some conservative families still do a significant amount of work around the home, but compared with other cultures the children of Orchard Town do not do very much.

The economic function of the men of the family is to provide the greater part of the cash and also to take care of repairs around the house and sometimes even to construct the house. Four fathers in the sample of 24 had largely built their own homes. The woman's function is to do routine housework, purchase food, and prepare it. It is considered desirable to have a variety of foods for the evening meal, and this increases the time spent in food preparation. Most women have sewing machines and make some articles of clothing for themselves and their children. Many of them also spend some time mending and knitting. These activities are not considered as important as cleaning the house and preparing the food. Women are also responsible for laundering the clothes and for cleaning and decorating the house. Many of the women have jobs or ways of earning supplemental cash. Some of the ways in which the women in our sample supplied extra cash for the family were: baby-sitting, running a nursery school, giving riding lessons, dressmaking, and serving as secretarial help for their husbands.

Occupational specialization among the men is great and has increased considerably in the last few generations as the economy of Orchard Town has been integrated with the national economy. Of a group of neighbors, each man usually has a different occupation or works in a different place away from contact with his neighbors.

In contrast to earlier days, there is a greater tendency for the men to be employed in fairly large organizations. There have been work-shops or small factories in Orchard Town for generations, but the older establishments were mostly smaller ones.

In contrast to farming and small, locally unique business enter-prises, most modern jobs demand that the individual get along with people, that he be on the good side of the customers or on the good side of the boss. One resident told a local small businessman jokingly, "You are just as ornery underneath as I am, my friend, but you don't exude it as we do; you are too afraid of losing that dollar, and you're right, you'd lose it too. There's lots of people would stop coming to you if they got angry at you."

Most people think of a job primarily as a means of getting cash. However, there is a concern, varying with individuals, for doing something or having some kind of job that is of service to others. Professional people, such as teachers, doctors, ministers, and lawyers, tend to express this concern or to obtain a certain amount of credit for it from other people.

⚹

⚹

⚹

Chapter 3

Kinship and Marriage

As has been shown in many studies of American culture, kinship is not very important in regulating human relations outside of the nuclear family. This is true because there is little interaction with other relatives. The nuclear family is formed by marriage and ideally produces children. The husband, wife, and their children generally live in a separate dwelling unit. Widowed parents of the husband or wife are possible additions to the household, although such additions are regarded with distaste by most people. In our sample only one such instance was noted out of 24 families—a widowed mother's mother. An unmarried mother's sister provided another case of an added member to the household.

Although there were no cases of the extended family household that was so common in New England during colonial days, there were several cases in which grandparents lived in an apartment attached to the house of one of their children. There were three cases of such an arrangement in our sample. In two cases the daughter was involved and in the other the son.

There seems to be some tendency for couples to reside in the wife's community if the husband's occupation permits this. Transportation is efficient enough for men to commute from some distance. Living in the locality where the wife has friends or relatives is much preferable, since the woman spends most of her day in or near the home. Five of the families of our sample exhibited this matrilocal residential pattern, whereas by contrast only one family was patrilocal, that is, the father born in Orchard Town and the mother from away. In 3 of the families, both parents were brought up in Orchard Town. In the remaining 15 families, both parents were brought up elsewhere, usually somewhere in New England so that grandparents if still living could be visited by a drive of a few hours at most. In only two families did both parents come from outside New England, and even in one of these the maternal grandparents had moved to a nearby town.

Within the nuclear family all children are legally equal. They are supposed to inherit equally and should be treated equally. One informant noted that another family in trying to achieve this equality of children had slighted the more competent child in an effort to raise a less competent child to equality.

Marriage is monogamous and for life. It is in no sense a contract between the two families but rather a contract between the two individuals involved—the well-known contract to love, honor and obey and cleave only unto this spouse so long as they both live. A divorced woman may take her children, if any, and return to live with her parents, however. One divorced woman and her two daughters were living with her parents, an arrangement which allowed the woman to work for the support of her children. Often, however, the child who has left to marry and then returns to his family finds his place in the family is not as it used to be and leaves to live alone or with friends. There were a few divorced and remarried individuals in the community. None of these were included in our sample. The general sentiment is against divorce.

All marriages are not considered equally preferable. Preferred marriages are those between persons of near equal age and status. There is some sentiment against marriage between persons of different religion or race. There is some intermarriage between Protestants and Catholics involving Catholics of both Irish and Italian background.

These latter mostly came from a nearby town. Little other inter-marriage occurs partly because there are few representatives of other races or religions in or near Orchard Town.

Adoption is a very rare phenomenon in North Village. It happened once during our year of residence, and no other cases were recorded by us. Legal adoption, however, is such a long and difficult process that it is only undertaken by those who are truly desperate to have children.

The kin terms for mother, father, grandmother, grandfather, uncle, and aunt, either in their formal or familiar (mother or mom) terms, are used in address to indicate respect. Paternal or maternal grand-parents are distinguished by coupling the appropriate surname with a kin term, for example, Grandpa Jones, whereas uncles and aunts are particularized by coupling the given name with the kin term, for example, Uncle George. First and second cousins are generally recognized as kin, but beyond this they are recognized only as being a distant relative, and personal compatibility is more important than kinship in determining their relationships. One man used the term "barnyard relation" for a remote cousin living in the vicinity. One high school girl whose family are long-time residents in the town said, "I'm related to everybody, not first cousins or anything."

Kinship terms usually applied to blood relatives are sometimes extended to affinals. This is particularly true of the uncles and aunts of one's spouse. Parents-in-law are also sometimes referred to as "mother" and "father" with surnames sometimes added. In other cases first names are used, and still others manage to avoid addressing their parents-in-law at all.

✢
✢
✢

Chapter 4

Social Organization

To a certain extent people living in adjacent houses form neighbor groups regardless of status differences. Neighbors would speak to each other on the streets and, especially in the warmer parts of the year, might talk with each other in their yards. There are also informal friendship groups among the women who visit each other during the day and talk to each other on the telephone. These are not identical with the local neighbor groups although they may include neighbors. The attitudes toward neighbors are summarized in the statement of one woman: "The old ladies are good neighbors; they are quiet."

There are a number of voluntary associations and clubs in Orchard Town and in North Village. Those connected with the church are described more fully, in connection with religion; the PTA (Parent-Teacher Association) is described in connection with education; economic organizations are described in connection with basic economy. The remainder considered here are more concerned with recreation or civic improvement. More prominent associations include the American Legion, Veterans of Foreign Wars, Masons, the Odd Fellows, Voluntary Fire Department, bowling teams, Sportsmen's Club, the Community Center, the Eastern Star (which is the Women's Auxiliary of the Masons), the Women's Club, the Garden Club, the Hospital Auxiliary. There are also local people who canvass for contributions for the Red Cross and for the United Community Service or the Red Feather Campaign in which Orchard Town participates with a number of other towns. Many of the organizations, of course, are not limited to North Village or Orchard Town members. The Fire Department is theoretically an all-town affair, but it has separate branches in each of the population centers. The firehouse used to be open and used to be a popular meeting place for men to play cards, including men not members of the Fire Department. Now it is much less used than formerly. In other parts of Orchard Town the Couple's Club, which periodically gives parties at the homes of its members, is connected with a church; however, in North Village this is not so. One informant said that this was because of some Catholic members who would not be able to attend if the club should become connected with a church. The Community Center is organized for the entire town, but it is located in North Village, and more North Village people participate in it than those from other parts of town. This has been very recently organized, and it is too early to describe its permanent functions and its membership. The Women's Club was limited ostensibly to North Village and a small nearby township during the period of our study. There is another Women's Club for the rest of Orchard Town. The Women's Club had about 70 members, 7 officers or directors, and 24 committees of one or more members each. There were also a few honorary and complimentary members.

None of the associations in Orchard Town are formally socially exclusive, although certain of them contain a somewhat larger proportion of high-status members than others. This reflects the official denial of social-class distinctions characteristic of small New England towns. Church membership, which often reflects such distinction, does so to a certain extent in Orchard Town as a whole but less so in North Village. Nearly all the Protestant families living in this section go to the local Baptist church rather than to the more prestigeful Unitarian and Episcopal churches in other parts of the town. Several high-status families go to the latter, however.

Although the formal social structure of North Village is open and democratic and there are no organized and self-conscious social classes, there is nevertheless considerable range in occupation and education, two of the more direct indices of socio-economic status. It has been previously noted that occupations range, from semiskilled to professional. Education shows a similar variation. The fathers of our sample varied in their educational background from grammar school only to college graduates. Table 1 shows the educational backgrounds of the parents of our sample.

As might be expected, most husbands and wives had similar educational backgrounds. Nine of the 24 had reached an identical level. Interestingly enough, women who had more schooling than their husbands outnumbered by 9 to 5 men who had more schooling than their wives.

Table 1. The educational background of the mothers and fathers of our sample

	MOTHERS	FATHERS
College plus graduate school	2	0
College graduate	2	5
Some college	6	5
High school plus business or vocational training	4	3
High school graduate	9	10
Some high school	1	0
Grade school or less	0	1

Using an adaptation of the formula developed by Warner, Meeker et al. (1949) to estimate socio-economic status from education and occupation, the range of the families of our sample was from upper lower to upper middle class, with the bulk falling into upper lower or lower middle—what some sociologists combine under the term "the common man."

The occupations listed by the members of the senior high school class in 1954 in the yearbook as their ambitions give a rough picture of the rank to which high school students aspire. Occupations of high rank include: hotel manager (1), accountant (1), engineer (4), interior decorator (1). Occupations of moderate rank would include military (4), mechanic or machinist (2), farmer (1) conservation officer (1). One boy also listed his ambition to become a motion picture projectionist, which seems somewhat lower than the others. Ambitions of the girls all were rather moderate: 8 office workers, 6 teachers, 2 nurses, 2 airline hostesses, 1 lab technician. One wanted to do something with horses; another had listed no ambition, which perhaps meant to get married.

Courses taken by the senior class in 1954 also give some indication of aspired rank. Eight boys were taking straight college courses, 4 were taking a college commercial course, and 4 were taking a general course, a total of sixteen boys. Of 23 girls, 8 were taking a straight college course, 12 a college commercial course, 3 a general course. The boys are about equally divided between a college course and other courses. The girls are about twice as many "other" as straight college course.

The belief that men and women are ideally equal is widespread. This does not mean that they are equally suited or expected to do the same things, but it does mean that there is very little apparent difference in privileges between the sexes. This is partially true because women's status depends in large part on the men with whom they are associated or to whom they are related. It may also be true that a woman without a man in her nuclear family suffers in prestige. We can say that the things women do, the roles they play, do not in themselves affect their status unless they do them especially poorly. Their status, instead, depends on whose child or whose wife they happen to be. It is very difficult to detect any considerable difference in status between a man and his wife in a given household. There is some feeling that since the status of the entire family depends in large measure on the status of the man, he should be helped, kept happy, or whatever may be necessary to enable him to boost the status of the family. On the other hand, most families would not endure quietly any great presumptiveness on the part of the man of the family.

In spite of relative equality of status, the roles of men and women in the community are largely separated. The important town officers as well as the important officials of state government are nearly always men. Women, however, hold certain offices which are considered appropriate for women. For instance, there are women holding positions of library trustee and there have been women candidates elected for the school board and the welfare board. However, there apparently has never been a woman selectman, a woman moderator, or a woman town clerk. In the church, also, the most important church officers—the trustees, the deacons, and the minister—have always been men. There are other positions, however, in the church organization which women may hold, such as superintendent of the Sunday School.

Economically women's primary responsibility is supposed to be the home. Many women work, bringing in extra cash, in addition to their work as housewife, but the men are supposed to be the main bread-winner. The total family status is considered to be higher if the woman does not work for cash.

There is a tendency in the home for major expenditures to be decided on jointly by husband and wife. However, this varies considerably from family to family. Women exercise the main control over the regular expenses of running the household.

Women have more to do with education than men do, up through the sixth grade at least. Schoolteachers in the lower grades are all women, as are the principals. The mothers of the schoolchildren also appear to take more interest than the fathers. There are room mothers who represent the parents at school but no room fathers. Women are also active in the Parent Teachers Association, although there is a tradition in Orchard Town of having a male for president of the PTA.

Polite manners require a man to show respect for a woman. He is supposed to stand when a woman enters the room, open doors for her, and let her precede him into a room. Training in the practice of "girls first" starts at an early age in the home and is carried on in the school.

The sex-role distinctions extend down into childhood from about the sixth year. Boys are supposed to act aggressive, cause more trouble, be rougher and more athletic than girls. Girls are expected to stay out of fights but to be verbally quite aggressive. Boys are expected to be more interested in things than in personalities and, therefore, less sensitive than girls. Girls and women are expected to grow and mature more quickly than men. One informant stated, "Girls are grown up at 16, but men not until 40." Girls are eager to attend the ballroom dancing class, while the "less mature" boys are reluctant. Although boys are troublesome creatures as youths, in maturity it is often jokingly remarked that the reverse is true, for instance, in one joke two men were talking about their wives. The first said, "Mine is an angel." The second man said, "Boy, you're lucky! Mine is still living." The fighting of boyhood is not expected to continue into manhood, while the cattiness of girlhood is said to increase with age.

One may also note that girls sometimes wear boys' clothes, either clothes actually belonging to a male member of their family or clothes made for women but in imitation of men's clothes, such as slacks. The reverse does not occur. Also, at one of the high school dances some couples were composed of two girls, but no couple was observed consisting of two boys. One of the faculty expressed disapproval of pairs of girls dancing but said that it was difficult to ban this completely as long as the girls were allowed to buy single tickets to the dances, which some do.

In sum, men and women are difficult to compare regarding status. Their roles are different, but the scales of prestige for them are so ambiguous that either sex can and does, usually in fun, claim priority.

☙
☙
☙

Chapter 5

Property

Few people in Orchard Town consider themselves rich or wealthy, but nearly all of them are fairly well off. One indication of the view which people of North Village hold of their economic status is that one of the Sunday School teachers took her class on a special trip to a city mission or social work agency to see "poor" children.

Main streets inside the village, schools, firehouses, libraries, greens, the dump, police cars, fire engines and the town hall are owned by the town. Management of these properties and their construction are fought over bitterly in the town meetings. Any mismanagement is highly criticized. Taxpayers dislike spending their dollars on mistakes. New taxes have to be levied and bonds issued to pay for new town properties. As far as the schools are concerned, the state pays a large share of the cost of their construction and operation. In return, the state has something to say about their management. Townspeople do not like this aspect of state aid.

Many of the stores are owned by local people who also manage them. There is also a business block in town which is owned by a landlord who rents these properties to store managers. The factories in Orchard Town are not owned by residents of the town. Businessmen from other communities have purchased factory buildings in Orchard Town because of reasonable rents and available labor. Storage and warehouses are owned by Orchard Town families.

The major property of most families consists of the house which they occupy with its furnishings and the land on which it is built with perhaps some extra land, a car, some business equipment if they are in business for themselves, usually some savings, and insurance policies. Of the 24 families in our sample, all but two owned or were buying their living quarters. A few families in town, including two in our sample, occupy part of their house and rent rooms or apartments to other individuals for additional income. Property is valued not only in itself but also as a sign of relative social status. The most important kinds of property for this purpose are house, house furnishings, car, and clothes.

Many landowners have a jealous regard for their property rights. This does not always mean, however, that any person walking on another's land is regarded as trespassing, for the town is "open" for hunting. That is, an owner must post his land with "no hunting" signs to prevent others from legally hunting upon it. Some owners of tracts of undeveloped land have posted their property against hunting, but these are in a minority.

There is now a zoning law restricting certain types of construction, but a sizable minority were opposed to the passing of this law on the ground that it interfered with property rights. While we were in town, some surveyors from the state highway department came and surveyed for the widening of one of the streets. One landowner was disturbed when the surveyors walked on his lawn and told them they had no right to set up their equipment there without his permission. However, he relented when the surveyors told him that he could put them off but not for long since they could get a warrant if necessary. Another man pulled up a speed limit sign which the state highway department had erected by the side of the road on his lawn. He said his property extended to the road and that the road was not state property but town property anyway. Later the sign was observed in place.

Although people are free to go on undeveloped land, adults would be careful not to go into other people's yards without some good reason. Children under the age of about 14 are much freer to go into other people's yards to play or to go through them on the way to some other place. Adults would not take a short-cut across some other person's yard unless they were very close neighbors and on good terms.

Sentiment about ownership of family land or houses is found among long-time residents or natives of the town, but such people are in the minority. Nevertheless, some of these people hold a considerable part of the area of the town, and they may feel disturbed about minor changes in the landscape. One landowner, for instance, looking out the window of her ancestral home, complained to one of us that a barn about a mile away had been moved. This, she said, spoiled the view. Stories are told admiringly of a family in a nearby town owning land which the original ancestors received from the Indians and, in another town nearby, of a family who received their land from grants from one of the English kings. These are very exceptional cases, however.

At present, inheritance of property is divided among the nuclear family if possible. If there are no children, a surviving spouse inherits all property unless otherwise specified by will. If there are children, the property is usually divided giving one-third to the widow and two-thirds to the children unless otherwise specified. Real estate inherited from parents would normally be sold and converted into cash unless one of the children is living in the parental home. In this case there would probably be an attempt to give each child an equal inheritance by giving all the money or other property to the other children and by selling some of the land if there were some extra land.

The most common pattern is to convert as much of the property as possible to cash by selling it. Practically all forms of property can be sold fairly readily. At present, real estate has a relatively high value and is easily converted into cash. This is possible because of the suburban expansion into Orchard Town. One house on which we have information, for instance, was sold to the current owners by the previous owners in 1953 for a price about 80% more than the previous owners paid for it in 1946.

Since the variety of material objects is much greater in American culture than in most cultures, perhaps a word should be injected here as to the relationship of Orchard Town people to material objects. Accumulation of objects goes on in most families at a very fast rate. Those living in old houses, which often have storage sheds, have a greater opportunity to keep objects which are no longer functional in a particular household. Occasionally, if some outsider has need of some of these objects, they are given away. Most of the time they are neglected or forgotten. Most are no longer in style. However, being old and out-dated are not always disadvantages and, in this area, often raise the value of an object. Community organizations have fairs and auctions to which such objects may be donated. This keeps a certain number of the objects in circulation. Other such objects sometimes are thrown in the town dump, where they may be rescued by those who want them. In this, rescuers are often especially proud of getting something for nothing, and the object starts over again its round from living room to attic to dump.

Expensive equipment is not acquired lightly or hastily. Long-range plans are generally made for the gradual accumulation of money enough to buy a new car or washing machine or a camera. There is some feeling that with the acquisition of the next object, life will be much more pleasant. Some of these expensive items are purely functional, but more often a more expensive item is particularly aesthetically pleasing or is important in achieving or maintaining status by expressing "good" taste.

Occasionally eccentric individuals are found who seem to have been overtrained in the accumulation of property and would be regarded as misers by the townspeople. One old woman, for instance, is said to have filled her room up with a large amount of old newspapers which she saved. Even her bed was partly covered with piles of these newspapers.

Wealthy people are possibly more often the object of gossip than are people who are not wealthy. Perhaps a very small amount of awe and respect is given them by adults. Children may be warned to avoid trespassing on their property more than that of others.

❋
❋
❋

Chapter 6

Political Organization

Orchard Town, like other towns in the United States, has a complex political structure. All political statuses, town, state, and national, are, in theory at least, either elective or appointive. There are no ascriptive statuses. Persons appointed to political positions are supposed to be appointed on the basis of their qualifications, although it is recognized that personal relationships also play an important part. Persons elected to office are also supposed to be chosen by the voters for their qualifications, although here again it is recognized that the personal appeal of the candidate and his relationship with members of his constituency play an important part in his election.

The informal power structure of the Orchard Town local government corresponds fairly well with the formal power structure. Other things being equal, the voice of the financially successful probably carries more weight in the town meetings than that of the financially unsuccessful person. There is some feeling that wealth and success are a fairly good measure of intelligence. Counterbalancing this, however, is the feeling that wealth may be a sign of stinginess or concentrated pursuit of one's own self-interest.

Until quite recently there was a feeling that town officials should be people of long-time residence. The older residents still retain this feeling, but because of the large influx of new residents, this sentiment is no longer as significant politically as it was perhaps ten years ago. The old residents have an advantage with respect to their real estate taxes. Real estate values have not been reassessed for taxes for a number of years, although real estate values have risen considerably over this period. There is no formal organization of either the new people or the old, which lessens the effect of either as a block.

More significant than a split between new and old are the splits which occur, or have occurred, on a number of important issues brought up at the town meetings in the history of the town. Some of those listed by the local historian include: the location of the railroad, bounty for Civil War soldiers, site of the high school, zoning, and the formation of a regional school district.

Although all political status is theoretically achievable, the townspeople have elected members of one family to be town clerk for several generations. We might speak of this as an informal ascribed office. Note that the service aspect of the town clerk job is more prominent than the power aspect, which may explain why the people have not demanded a change in this office. There is no doubt, moreover, that members of this family would not continue to be elected if they showed any major abuse of their office or if they were obviously incompetent. This situation calls attention to the fact that for many of the town offices, theoretically elective, there is usually only one candidate nominated.

Important town issues are decided at the town meetings. At these an elected town moderator presides. Other elected officials sit at the front of the meeting house and are frequently requested to or voluntarily give pertinent information on the issues which are to be considered. All voters in the town are eligible to attend the meeting and to speak freely on any issue which is of interest to them. Each year there is an annual town meeting and usually several special town meetings. Minor decisions and the implementation of decisions made at the town meeting are handled by the Board of Selectmen or the appropriate town official or committee. The town moderator presides but has no other duties, as such, and is not a member of the Board of Selectmen.

There is a total of about 50 elected town officers, counting a number of trustees of the town funds. And, in addition to these, there are about 90 appointed officers, the appointments being made by the selectmen.

A list of the functions of the town would include the following: the gathering of taxes and license fees, especially real estate taxes; the assessing of real estate for tax purposes; the running of the schools from first grade through high school; the maintaining of surfaced and lighted town roads and taking care of the trees along these roads; the maintaining of the fire department with several branches; the maintaining of a police force to preserve law and order and protect property. There is a board of health which is responsible for the sanitation of the town, which includes garbage collection and supervision of the town dump and also control of contagious diseases. There are also a town library, a town forest, and two town cemeteries. The town maintains various records, including records of birth, marriages, and deaths. The town supervises national, state, and town elections for its citizens. Of the various functions of the town government in 1954, roughly the following outlays of town funds were made: education took nearly half, police and fire departments and related function took 12%, charities 10% (this being especially for old age assistance), road maintenance 7%, Board of Health activities 4%, general government 3%, and the remainder miscellaneous.

Most town meetings and meetings of the various committees of the town officials operate with rather formal procedures, and full records are kept. Participants often bring up points of order. At one town meeting which we attended, one citizen maintained that the whole meeting was illegal, because it had not been properly called, in view of some obscure requirement which no one else seemed to know about.

The town is one small unit in a much larger political structure which extends to the federal or national level. The town is divided into three precincts as previously mentioned. There is a water district which includes North Village and parts of the rest of the town, but not the entire town. It also includes parts of a neighboring town. The political structure of the water district is modeled on the town government. During our residence, the town voted to form a regional school district with a neighboring town. This enabled greater financial assistance from the state for the operation of schools, especially the high school.

The town is one of a number of towns in a county, but the county is politically unimportant. Certain courts are organized on a county basis, and the agricultural extension service is organized for the county.

The state government is considerably more important than that of the county. The state maintains an extensive system of roads, including most of the principal roads in Orchard Town, except for short stretches in the center of villages. The state also collects taxes and licenses people in a number of occupations. It provides some financial support to the town, especially in running the schools and in charities. The town was given its original charter by the state, and changes in the charter or the by-laws have to be approved by the state attorney-general before going into effect. State laws are important in Orchard Town as well as in other towns of the state. But on the other hand, one hears expressions that the state is corrupt or that its officers are all politicians, people who lack talent except for knowing how to advance in the state or national government.

The national government is at the next level above the state government although there is also a feeling of a sort of regional unit consisting of the six New England States. This regional unit, however, has little formal organization. The national government is very important in the life of the people in Orchard Town. There is a post office, a branch of the federal government, in each of the three village centers. The federal government levies a large income tax.

The military activity of the national government is of concern to most males in Orchard Town. Most able-bodied men of the proper age have served in the Armed Services during World War II and younger men have prospects of Selective Service.

The people in Orchard Town have a part in electing representatives to the state and national legislatures. They are interested in both state and national affairs. A number of people are concerned about getting people out to vote in order to throw the total state vote to the Republican Party. There are no similar Democratic workers in the town. Party affiliations are not formally involved in the town elections, although there is some feeling that there is something strange about a man who is not a Republican.

There are many more Republicans than Democrats in the town, and apparently some who vote Democratic do not reveal this for political or business reasons. Also, some people moving into town from the city who were originally Democrats are reported to have shifted to the Republican Party after several years of residence in town. One old-time resident of the town said, "There are about 50 Democrats in Orchard Town I think." This would be out of a total population, children included, of nearly 5000. Actually, the number of people who voted in 1952 for Eisenhower in the whole town amounted to over 1700 and the number who voted for Stevenson was about 350. The proportion in North Village was roughly comparable to this. It can be seen that this informant's estimate of the number of Democrats was too low, but it indicates the political atmosphere of the town.

Most of the voters in Orchard Town regard themselves as at least moderately conservative politically. Although they are suspicious at times of big business, they are even more so of communism or socialism. They are concerned about the interference of the national government in state affairs and the interference of the state in town affairs. While they recognize the need for both state and national governments, they do not want state or national governments to expand in influence. The townspeople feel that they, individually and jointly, should be allowed to take care of their own affairs as much as possible.

One of the ministers in town reported that during the period of great concern with the national security and communist infiltration, he had commented unfavorably on Senator McCarthy in a sermon. He cited the sermon as one of the few that he had given on which he had personally received unfavorable comment from members of his congregation. As far as we could determine, there are no Communists in Orchard Town. Yet, before our arrival in town, it is reported that one of the local political leaders had accused a number of people of being Communists or at least Communist sympathizers. How extreme the actual informal accusations were we cannot say, since those not in sympathy with the accusations would tend to exaggerate them to make them appear to be more absurd.

There are few formal rules of respect for holders of political office except at town meetings and under certain circumstances. At town meetings, the officials and other persons who expect to make speeches or motions usually are dressed in dark suits, speak of each other as mister, and use somewhat parliamentary language. When speaking from the floor, one man may refer to another by his official title, "the Chairman of the School Committee," rather than by his name, but this is by no means a hard and fast rule. Outside of official proceedings there is not much more respect shown for holders of political office other than that to which they would be entitled as adult citizens in good standing.

✹
✹
✹

Chapter 7

Social Control

Informal social control in Orchard Town is generally indirect, in the form of gossip, avoidance, or exclusion, rather than direct. We observed no instances in which one adult publicly criticized another to his face except in a bantering or teasing manner. Spouses sometimes criticized one another in the presence of guests, but this was felt to be improper behavior and was embarrassing to the guests. Gossip, although not intended as such, is in fact very effective in ensuring value consensus and conformity. Mrs. A tells Mrs. B what she thinks of Mrs. C for leaving her children without a baby sitter. Whether or not Mrs. B agrees, she seldom will challenge Mrs. A on her statement, but the exchange will influence Mrs. B if at a later date she is tempted to leave her children without a sitter. She will know what Mrs. A will say about her.

Informal ostracism is also frequently used as a means of social control in Orchard Town. This takes the form of "cutting," "being cool to," or failing to invite to a social gathering one whose behavior is disapproved.

A final indirect method of social control which is sometimes employed in Orchard Town consists of the criticism of someone to one of his friends or relatives with the expectation that this will in some way be passed on to the deviant.

Children may occasionally function as agents of adult social control, since they sometimes repeat remarks of their parents which the parents would make only among themselves. They, also, do not have the hesitation of adults to use direct criticism. It was reported, also, that the children used to tease one man cruelly for his drinking. It was believed by some that this contributed to his final suicide.

What sort of matters are the concern of gossip, criticism, or informal social control? One of the most important is lack of industriousness. An able-bodied man who does not work and is not striving to better himself and the position of his family would be shunned and regarded with scorn unless he had enough income to maintain his family and himself comfortably. Even then, he would come in for some criticism if he did not work.

Personal cleanliness and a general cleanliness of the home are another subject of informal social control. A person who did not mow his lawn, for instance, would be severely criticized. People also ought to keep their hedges trimmed and have dead limbs on trees removed, have their houses painted, and so forth. A woman should keep her house clean and pick up things on occasions when visitors are expected.

Excessive drinking is generally disapproved, and a large number of the older people and the regular churchgoers are opposed to any form of alcoholic beverage. Many people who do drink do so privately, deferring to the feeling of those opposed to drinking.

Considerable informal pressure is exerted against parents of children who are disrespectful to adults, destructive of property, or in other ways deviate from the values of the community.

Prevention of crime is urged and carried out by most people in locking up property which might be stolen. One teen-age boy was urged by his mother not to tell anyone over the telephone that he was alone in the house when he was left to sit with younger siblings. Crowds of loafers are not allowed to gather. Crowds of teen-age boys are broken up if they become noisy and disorderly. At night children and women of all ages avoid going out alone, unless they are driving in a car.

Most of the formal law enforcement in Orchard Town is concerned with traffic offenses. In 1954 the police reported nearly 500 arrests and prosecutions for various motor vehicle offenses and less than 30 offenses of all other types. Common punishment for motor vehicle offenses is a fine. For driving under the influence of liquor, the punishment is the loss of license either temporarily or permanently. For serious motor vehicle offenses, the punishment, of course, may be imprisonment. This is rather rare. Not all of the 500 traffic offenses involved residents of Orchard Town. Many of them were no doubt people of other towns who were driving through. However, it must be remembered that people of Orchard Town themselves do a lot of driving through other towns where they are subject to arrest for traffic offenses, so the figure is not quite so misleading as it may seem.

In 1954, of the less than 30 miscellaneous offenses, 11 were for drunkenness, and no other category was larger than 2. Orchard Town people feel that crimes are, as a rule, committed by outsiders or by young boys who are potential delinquents. There is a widespread sentiment that young boys and men, especially in the big cities, but some in the town as well, are getting out of control; "You never heard of the crimes then that you do nowadays."

Three institutions are particularly used for formal social control. They are the police, the court, and the jail. A generation ago in Orchard Town there was no regular police force. Certain men were elected Constables. The job of Constable was and still is a supplementary one, and today these men do very little. They are active only on special occasions. There are also two full-time and two part-time policemen who are employed on a regular basis.

Until recently all police were elected, and their continuity in office depended on public approval—approval of both their integrity as a policeman and their reasonableness as a human being. A policeman's job does not pay unusually well. Compared with other jobs in private industry or business, it is a respectable job but not one of high prestige. Orchard Town people feel confident of the integrity of their own policemen, but it is generally recognized that police in the larger cities can often be bribed into not giving tickets for traffic violations.

The nearest court is in an adjoining town. The most common contact with the court system for the people of Orchard Town is for traffic offenses and after that for civil suits. Few residents of Orchard Town are involved in criminal cases either as defendants or witnesses. Many of them serve on juries from time to time, however. Potential civil suits involving financial damages are often settled informally out of court. People express the opinion that lawyers are expensive and that the damages awarded in court are liable to be excessive.

There is no jail in Orchard Town, although there is a state penal institution in a nearby town. Orchard Town people have practically no contact with this institution. Television and movies, of course, present images of both courts and jails which are realistic and taken as such by the children and adults. Nevertheless, there is a feeling that courts and jails are things which belong primarily to the city and not to small towns. The police rarely have occasion to take drastic action against local people—adults or children. Cases of North Village children being sent to the reform school are not frequent and have involved families who are more or less marginal socially.

Both young people and adults feel that teenagers of the town, especially the young men and boys, are tempted to become "delinquent" because "there is nothing to do." Some examples of delinquency cited were: putting a lighted cigarette in a mail box and painting the windshield of a car. One informant said that one boy was sent to reform school after an outburst of such activity and that things then quieted down.

⚘
⚘
⚘

Chapter 8

Religion

In North Village there are two churches, one Protestant, which is officially a Baptist church but in practice is largely a community church, and one Roman Catholic church. People of various denominational backgrounds attend the Baptist church. Most people regard blurring of denominational boundaries among Protestants as a good thing. At the communion service, for instance, in the North Village Protestant church, the minister regularly invites visitors, regardless of denomination, to join in the consumption of the grape juice and bread. The North Village church participates in a regional group of Protestant churches as well as in a regional group of Baptist churches. It is our impression that the activity connected with the denominational group is remaining about constant, while the activity with other nearby Protestant churches in the local group is increasing. For example, the local Protestant churches exchange ministers. If one of their ministers becomes sick, they may get a minister from a nearby church of another denomination. They also hold joint services at Christmas, Thanksgiving, and so on.

Most of the population of Orchard Town, perhaps 90%, is nominally Protestant. Lines of cleavage between the various Protestant denominations are not too sharp. It is not unusual for a family or an individual to shift from one denomination to another because of personal relationships with the minister or other people in a church. The various Protestant churches in the three centers of Orchard Town also hold joint services and cooperate in other ways.

There is little cooperation between Catholic and Protestants as religious groups. At town affairs, the high school graduation, Catholic and Protestant ministers may be together to offer prayers, one offering the invocation and the other the final blessing. In daily life, however, there are many social and business contacts between individual Catholics, especially the older residents, and Protestants.

Although we were told that with respect to our study, "The Catholics don't like to be left out of things," we chose not to study the Catholic families because of the difference of religious influence this would introduce. Accordingly, the Catholic church in North Village will not be discussed here.

At the North Village church the average attendance at the Sunday morning service has varied from 60 to 100 for the last decade. Considering the large Protestant population in the town, this is not many. There are more children in Sunday School, over 200 being enrolled there. Many residents and members are too old to attend church often. Others attend church very irregularly. The variation in attendance at Sunday Service during the last decade is the result of turnover in ministers. At first, many people attend to hear what the new man has to say. Then later they lose interest or sometimes get into feuds with the minister. Some people may stop attending church or they may transfer to another Protestant church in a nearby community. There is competition between the different churches for audiences and members. Many people start attending church when their children are old enough to start going to Sunday School. One woman said that she had transferred to another church because of the emphasis on Hell and damnation in the Baptist Sunday School. Actually, there is little mention of hell or damnation in the Baptist church in either the Sunday morning service or the Sunday School, but such are the rationalizations that lead to shifting membership.

At present, about the only obvious doctrinal difference of the local Baptist church with other churches is that it encourages baptism by immersion. However, members now may join without baptism on a simple confession of faith. This change was foreshadowed by earlier action. For instance, in 1920, members of other denominations were allowed to become affiliated members of the North Village church on presentation of a letter confirming that they had been previous members of another church of another denomination. In the 1940's persons of other denominations were allowed to become full members on presentation of a letter. The final step, taken during our study, was to allow persons who had never been a member of any church before to become full members of the North Village church on simple profession of faith. Children who desired to become members of the church, having gone through the Sunday School, would, however, be inducted with baptism.

The official church membership in the last decade has varied from 100 to 160. There has been less variation in the church membership than in attendance. In general, there have been considerably more members than there has been average attendance in the church. Not all the official members attend regularly, but some nonmembers attend on a fairly regular basis. In fact, perhaps half of those attending each Sunday are nonmembers.

The church is largely managed by the board of trustees, who look after the church property, and the board of deacons, who supervise the religious activities. The minister is important as a leader but is formally subject to the congregation and its officers. There are many special committees and offices. Most members of the church have been a member of one or more of these committees. These officers are all elected, but normally there is only one ticket. The Sunday School now is under the Religious Education Committee.

North Village Protestants give most of their attention to two supernatural beings, God and Jesus. While there is an occasional mention of the Trinity, the third member, the Holy Ghost, is rarely mentioned specifically. Both God and Jesus are seen as having infinite mercy. They are forgiving, but on the other hand they give little, if any, practical help. The principle difference between them is that one is the Father and the other the Son, and that Jesus the Son was at one time human. The Devil and Hell are seldom mentioned, although one minister said that he felt the idea of Hell was needed. If the question were raised, there might be some argument as to whether the Devil existed or not, but at any rate, it was agreed that he is not important and that children should hear little of him. On one occasion when the Devil happened to be mentioned in a Sunday School lesson, some of the children expressed surprise on the grounds that there really was no Devil. Angels are occasionally mentioned to children in Sunday School but little elsewhere. Saints are hardly mentioned, and there appears to be no way of adding to the number of saints.

If asked specifically, most people would probably admit that God does not help people to succeed or make them rich and probably does not cure sickness, although there is less consistency about this last. As a minister once put it, "The symbol of Christianity is a cross and not a rabbit's foot; it is no guarantee of any worldly success or even happiness."

The divinity of Jesus seems to be acknowledged or at least not contradicted openly by most churchgoers. However, considerable attention is given to the human nature of Jesus. One Sunday School teacher, talking about Jesus as a child said, "I don't mean to say that He was perfect. He was a normal person and I am sure He got into little tiffs, but still He was somewhat different from us for He was a supernatural being . . . so let's try to be like Him."

Most people do not seem to regard the Bible as infallible, although statements are made about the New Testament being the Church's guide. A sermon by the minister in which he said that he, personally, did not regard the New Testament as infallible, not to mention the whole Bible, did not seem to arouse any undue comment from the congregation. A high value is placed on the independence of both the congregation and individuals to decide what they want to believe and practice. A belief in immortality is general in the sense that if they were questioned, most people would probably subscribe to it, but it does not appear to be very important in that it is not often mentioned in the sermons or in the Sunday School material. This seems to be a belief which is activated mainly at funerals, but it does not seem to motivate individual daily behavior, since there is little belief that one will be punished for his sins after death or permanently confined to Hell or to some form of suffering for his sins.

In religious and Sunday School literature and in the sermons, little distinction is made between male and female ideals. However, the religious teachings are more consistent with female than male ideals as they are found in the culture at large. An emphasis on not retaliating or not resisting evil is found in the religious teaching which conflicts with the male ideal of self-respect. Self-respect is maintained by not letting anyone push you around, by retaliating with injury. When we asked for opinions on this conflict at a church parents' meeting, one father said, "We must read between the lines of the Bible." Usually more women than men attend church, and, also, more women are Sunday School teachers. Men who are Sunday School teachers are usually the husbands of women who are also Sunday School teachers.

In the past, New England Protestant churches have been opposed to drinking and smoking, although in the far distant past ministers were expected to receive part of their salary in rum. The temperance movement, which was strong during the late nineteenth and early twentieth century, is now mild. Many members of the church do not drink, and there are no ashtrays in the church building, but there is no active, organized temperance movement within the church. Moreover, some members of the church do drink in private or in appropriate company. Many smoke.

Legally there are so-called "blue laws" restricting work and disturbances on Sundays. Only a few adults take these very seriously. One town official told of a complaint which one citizen had made about another man: "He was hammering so that I could not even light my pipe or read my paper; don't we have any blue laws in this town?" The official commented that this man had just wanted to complain, so he let him and that was enough. However, the official himself felt that if anyone had noisy work of this sort to do, he would be advised to do it in his backyard on Sundays. Many of the parents observed had had restrictions on their own behavior on Sundays which they would not now attempt to enforce on themselves or their children. This is a noticeable change within the last couple of generations. One woman said that although her parents were not churchgoers, she still felt guilty about playing cards on Sunday. "You are supposed to grow Devil's horns and hooves for playing cards on Sundays, my mother always said."

The church also emphasizes the value of service and charity. Missionary activity is felt by many to be important and valuable, although the interest in missionary activity is expressed primarily through contributions of cash and does not as a rule involve actual proselytizing.

During the life of an individual, five points may be marked by religious services. The first occasion occurs shortly after birth when an infant's parents bring him to church for a service of parental dedication. The next point, perhaps roughly at puberty, is baptism. After this comes marriage, and after giving birth to children, the individual participates again in parental dedication as a parent. Finally, when he dies, he is given a funeral. It is not necessary for a person to participate in any of these services to be regarded as nominally Protestant.

In the early days of the North Village church, baptism was a more impressive ceremony than it is now. It was then carried out in a brook near the town. Now it is carried out in a tank or "baptistry" with water of controlled temperature. The tank is located at the front of the church, but in such a position that the audience cannot see the actual immersion. Except when in use, the tank is covered over by the floor. Most of the children in the Sunday School seem to be amused by the idea of baptism. This is an attitude which they probably obtained from their parents, who in many cases are not Baptists, and also from their playmates. When a child is baptized, he becomes a member of the church. He is not supposed to be baptized before he reaches an age when he may make a decision. This is usually after the age of 12. Theoretically children may attend communion before this, but they are discouraged if they do not "understand."

No church marriage took place while we were making our study, and none had occurred for sometime before that. It is possible that the minister had married some individuals privately that we did not hear about. Church marriages are felt to be exciting occasions, however, when they do occur.

Church funerals also are fairly rare. It seems more common to hold funerals at an undertaker's establishment or at the deceased's home. However, a few church funerals did occur while we were in North Village.

The principal religious activity of the North Village church is the regular Sunday morning service. One Sunday a month, communion is held. When we came to North Village, a Wednesday-evening prayer meeting was also held, but few people attended it, and finally it was abolished. Sunday morning services resemble other Protestant church services in the area, but the Wednesday-evening prayer meeting was a little more specialized in that it consisted largely of prayers given by the members of the congregation present. People of other denominational background did not seem to participate in this meeting much.

There are two ladies' auxiliary groups, one primarily for the older women which meets during the day for sewing and the other for young women with children which generally meets in the evening. Both groups sponsor luncheons or suppers, and programs with invited speakers who talk on subjects of general interest, especially travel, gardens, and "the home." A men's auxiliary group in the church carries on similar activities, although not as frequently. It is the official sponsor of one of the Boy Scout troops in the town. The men try to meet one evening a month except during the summer. Neither of the men's or women's groups do very much directly in the way of religious activity. They sometimes make some kind of contribution to the church facilities. For instance, on one occasion it is recorded that the ladies' group provided carpets and cushions for the pews. Religious elements in their meetings are usually restricted to an initial prayer, a final benediction, and grace before meals.

While we were living in North Village for our study, one of the Congregational churches in another part of Orchard Town and a Universalist church each put on church shows in the North Village

Women's Club building. The purpose of these was to raise funds for improvements to the church buildings. It was said that the Baptist church did not put on a church show itself because of the feeling of some of the older people that this was an inappropriate way for a church to raise money. But some members of the Baptist church participated in the other church shows, and many also attended both shows, so the sentiment against church shows cannot be said to be very strong or general. The Catholic church and some of the other Protestant churches in and around Orchard Town also have whist parties as a fund-raising activity. The Baptist church does not have these.

The Baptist church raises money by an annual bazaar or fair put on by the ladies' auxiliary at which home-prepared food, handiwork, and other small articles are sold. Direct appeals for money are also favored. While we were in the village, the North Village church put on a building-fund campaign. This was organized by a national organization which specializes in showing churches how to get money from their members most effectively. The essence of the plan was to obtain pledges from people or regularly weekly contributions for a period of roughly three years. Also certain individuals, including the canvassers, were supposed to announce their pledges publicly. Some people expressed some embarrassment about this, although most of the active church members seemed to feel that the plan was necessary and did not openly oppose it.

−

Chapter 9

Health and Medicine

The residents of Orchard Town subscribe to the scientific theories of Western medicine to explain disease. Although only the doctors are expected to control medical knowledge, every adult in Orchard Town has a rich store of convictions about the cause and cure of all but the most unusual diseases.

Germs are thought to cause most diseases. Germs are sensed as tiny invisible animals that swarm around sick people, particularly when they sneeze, cough, or exhale. For this reason, sick people are generally isolated and avoided. A person who sneezes is expected to cover his mouth and nose and to turn the head while coughing. Germs are also believed to infest dirt of any kind and feces in particular. For this reason, children at an early age are taught to wash their hands before eating.

Despite all these precautions, a person may get sick because his resistance is weak, and the attacking germs can overcome his defenses. This condition is generally described as being "run down" and may be caused by a faulty diet, worry, or by "overdoing things," for example, working or playing too hard. In addition, susceptibility to certain specific diseases may be influenced by prior action of the patient. Thus colds and pneumonia are thought to be brought on by getting one's feet wet or sitting in drafts or not dressing warmly enough. Some people believe that eating too many sweets or too much sugar will bring on diabetes, swallowing gum will cause appendicitis, and improper diet during adolescence leads to acne.

Good health is thought to be engendered by a good diet, proper exercise, and the avoidance of excess. Many people also take vitamin pills or other elixirs presumed to prevent "tired blood" or "that rundown feeling." Talks on diet are popular with women's groups. At one of these, the speaker asserted that children's I.Q. scores were greatly influenced by nutrition. "If you feed your child properly, he will do better in school and later life as well," she stated. She also quoted with approval the following motto on overeating, "Always be hungry, never relax, or you'll be sorry."

Regular bowel movements are thought to be necessary for good health. Constipation is believed by many to be dangerous, and medicines are taken to counteract it.

No matter how one feels, a person is not defined as being really sick unless he has a fever. For this reason a thermometer is standard equipment in any household. So strong is the New England value placed on work and achievement that anyone who stays home from school or work is considered to be a malingerer unless he can show a temperature of over 100 degrees. When one has a fever, however, he is defined as being sick, goes to bed, and has someone call the doctor. If the patient is defined as having a minor illness, he is treated at home, but if he is seriously ill, he will be taken to a hospital.

The common cold is epidemic in Orchard Town during the winter and is considered to be a minor ailment, one often treated by home remedies. People have different cold cures which they favor. There is a constant succession of remedies. Someone tries a new remedy and recommends it to friends, and it becomes popular but later may be abandoned for a still newer remedy. The statement is also heard at times, "Nothing can cure the common cold."

Smoking is believed to be a potential cause of bad health. Children are not allowed to smoke and not allowed to purchase cigarettes by law. Children are told that smoking will stunt their growth, although one boy in our sample, age 9, calmly denied this. Orchard Town people shared the recent national concern about smoking as a cause of lung cancer, and some people cut down on their cigarette smoking during our study.

The people of Orchard Town regard their town as a relatively healthy place compared to the cities and also compared to some other towns in the general vicinity. According to the town report for 1954, there were 44 deaths that year, the youngest person being 43, the oldest person 93, and the median being 72. Deaths of younger people have occurred in other years, but once a person is born, he has an excellent chance of surviving to adulthood.

The town and state governments officially subscribe to the importance of the early detection of physical disorders and disease. Schoolchildren are given periodical physical examinations, special eye and hearing examinations, and, recently, dental examinations. The parents are notified of the results of these examinations. Until recently there was no dentist in Orchard Town, and this meant that the teeth of many children were not well cared for. Children showed some resistance to wearing glasses when the glasses were shown to be necessary by the eye examination. Boys "don't want to be bothered," while the girls tend to be concerned about glamour, at least at high school age. The school nurse reported that the recent decorative varieties of glasses had made eyeglasses more popular with the girls and that it was also possible to motivate the boys to wear glasses by saying, "Don't you want to drive a car?"

Small pox vaccinations are required for schoolchildren by state law and generally are accepted by the parents. Nearly 90% of the parents with children in the first two grades gave their consent for their children to receive the Salk polio vaccine in 1955 in spite of the concern that it might accidently produce polio.

Dread diseases of past generations, such as tuberculosis and typhoid fever, have been largely eliminated or controlled when they occur. Certain childhood diseases are regarded as almost inevitable: chicken pox, measles, mumps, and whooping cough. Serious complications from these now seem to be better controlled than they were formerly, and there appears to be much less concern over a long quarantine period for children with these diseases than there was formerly. A considerable number of children in our sample had their tonsils removed or were expected to have their tonsils removed to control sore throat. The children seem to accept this operation fairly well. For very young children, virus pneumonia and respiratory infections are a source of worry. One reason here is that three young babies, less than one year old, were said to have died of virus pneumonia in the town in a recent year, two of them quite unexpectedly.

Chapter 10

Recreation

A number of activities which might be considered adult recreation have already been considered in the discussion of voluntary associations, under Social Organization. These will not be discussed again here.

Some forms of adult recreation involve both the husband and the wife and may also involve the other members of the family. Some families invite friends or relatives over occasionally for dinner or for some sort of after-dinner refreshment in the evening or occasionally in the daytime on Sundays or holidays. During the warmer part of the year guests may be invited to a "cook-out." "Cook-out" is especially used to refer to meals in one's backyard, where families have a small stone fireplace or barbecue pit.

In the summer the whole family may drive to certain places in nearby towns which sell both bulk ice cream and fountain specialties. Often each member of the family will get something at the fountain, and the family will take home a couple of quarts of ice cream to put in the refrigerator.

Many adults go to movies fairly frequently either by themselves or with the whole family. There is now a drive-in theater in Orchard Town out in the country, near North Village, to which the whole

family may go on a warm evening. There are also conventional thea-
ters in nearby towns.

Occasionally adults, especially men, buy tickets to watch spectator
sports in the city, such as baseball, basketball, or football. Children.
especially older boys, may be taken along if the event is in the daytime.

Both men and women occasionally attend theatrical productions in
the city. Perhaps more common is attending the local church amateur
shows, of which there have been two or three a year recently. Some
people pride themselves on "never" going into the city.

Many residents of Orchard Town enjoy listening to music on television, radio, or records, but few play musical instruments. Those who
attend church sing the hymns in church, but there is also music provided by the choir. On some social occasions there is group singing of
traditional popular songs. Group leaders consider singing a good way
to get a crowd interested in interacting. At one public gathering the
following words were sung to the song, "It's a Long Road to Tipperary":

> It's a good time to get acquainted.
> It's a good time to know.
> Who is sitting close beside you.
> So just smile and say hello.
> Goodbye, chilly shoulder,
> Goodbye, glassy stare.
> When we all join in (shake hand of person next to you),
> And pull together,
> We are sure to get there.

Singing such songs seems to fulfill a general need to appear happy in
public and to have flashing smiles. Although people are often embarrassed and appear to hesitate, they usually "thaw out" and "get
into the swing of things."

Some families, especially those with children, have pets, usually
dogs. Adults treat their pets affectionately, but they often give utili-
tarian reasons for having them, for example, a dog is a good watch
dog or a cat keeps the place free of mice. Some adults enjoy bird-
watching and have bird-feeding stations outside their windows. This
seems to be more popular among long-time residents.

The telephone has become important in the recreational life of the
women in Orchard Town. Women often break their round of chores
by exchanging daily experiences, gossip, and recipes. The men tend
to feel that the telephone should be used for necessary communication
only, and, partly for this reason, the women usually call one another
while their husbands are at work.

It is said that the depot, the firehouse, and the barber shop were places where men foregathered to exchange gossip and to discuss the affairs of the town, the state, and the nation. The traditional gathering of rural America, the crackerbarrel group, no longer exists in Orchard Town. The old timers talk about the olden days with nostalgia and wonder "what the world is coming to." Many blame the radio, television, and even the automobile for this turn of events.

The depot and firehouse provided a place for men to play cards after hours. A generation ago, when the North Village barbershop had a pool table in the back room, it was a recreational gathering place for both men and boys. Now it is illegal to have pool tables and loitering in barber shops is discouraged. One of the functions of the state inspector is to make surprise visits from time to time to prevent such loitering.

The all male poker game for money is also pretty much a thing of the past. Card playing has been taken over by women as a club recreation or as a family pastime. Bridge and whist are the favorite games, and they are not played for money but for prizes provided by the hostess or the club.

Dancing is a form of recreation enjoyed by many of the younger adults and most of the teenagers. Square dancing seems to be about as popular with the adults as ballroom dancing. During our stay, few ballroom dances were held in North Village for adults. We attended what was supposed to be the first square dance ever held in the North Village Protestant church vestry. We heard no overt criticism of this, although some of the people dancing made remarks about how daring they were being.

Auctions may be regarded as a form of recreation. Although only economically important to the owner whose property is being auctioned off, the auction may be of minor economic importance to the spectators. Individuals attend not because of something they need and hope to find there but to see what interesting or curious articles may be offered for sale. Much time at auctions is devoted to the sale of miscellaneous household ornaments.

Generally there are more women than men at auctions because they are usually held during the day when men are at work. However, when men are able to attend, they also seem to enjoy themselves. Antique-shop dealers and antique collectors, which latter category includes a large part of the population, especially the women, eagerly attend auctions and often bid high prices for "genuine antiques." Some men who are handy with tools and have time available attend auctions to buy broken furniture which they repair and use or dispose of as they see fit.

The auctioneers are generally professionals who are engaged for the occasion. People go as much to watch the auctioneers as to buy things. The auctioneers deliberately spice up the proceedings with humor, of which the following are examples: "This came off the hill; nice section up there." An auctioneer offering some perfume for bidding thrust the bottle to the audience and said, "I want every lady to put a little bit on her coat, but don't any of the men put it on!"

Children also attend auctions if they are not at school. There seem to be more auctions held in the summer than in the winter. Children may enter the bidding for small articles. While the auctioneers are allowed to indulge in various sorts of humor, one sort of humor which is not allowed to either adults or children is fake or joke bidding. No violation of this rule was observed at any of the auctions. Vendors of soft drinks and coffee often attend auctions and do a thriving business.

Gardening and fixing up the yard and house are treated as recreation rather than work by many. Such matters as how to lay flagstones or the best fertilizer for roses are frequent topics of conversation between neighbors and friends.

Several athletic sports, such as skiing and swimming, are enjoyed by the whole family. Others, such as hunting and fishing, are primarily male sports. Hunting takes place in the area of scrub forest owned by the Sportsmen's Club in a relatively unsettled part of town. Deer and pheasant are the most sought-after game. During the hunting season parents living outside the area of concentrated settlement worry about their children getting shot. Two families in our sample of 24 complained of hunters discharging their weapons uncomfortably near their houses. Although this is illegal, the law is difficult to enforce. Because of increasing numbers of hunters and the irresponsibility of a few in ignoring the restrictions, there seems to be increasing sentiment for closing the town to them except when the individual property owner gives permission.

Children may not use firearms, and all adults must have licenses to fish and hunt. There are limits set by law on the size and quantity of fish and animals which may be taken.

The Sportsmen's Club organizes an annual Field Day with trap shooting contests and raffles. They sell soft drinks and food and have small-scale gambling similar to that found in carnival side shows.

There is no golf course in Orchard Town, but there are golf courses in adjoining towns; some men play golf in the summer. One mother said that golf took her husband away from their son as well as from his business. She said that the father had taken their son along as caddy, but he had more or less given this up, for he did not want the son to hear the kind of language some of his golfing friends used.

Bowling is another popular male sport. There is a bowling league connected with the church. Bowlers must also go to nearby towns, but this is not difficult by automobile.

Watching fires is a popular activity, especially for men. Large crowds of spectators are reported at fires. The voluntary fire department is said to have a waiting list of applicants to join. Fires, of course, are not a planned form of recreation, although it is often suspected that they are caused by firebugs or arsonists. When they do occur, however, they are considered as very exciting occasions which are somehow important to watch even if one is in no position to help. Children are also very interested in fires and fire engines. One 7-year-old boy told an elaborate fantasy of his experience of having attended a fire with his father. His parents, however, said that he had not attended any fire and that, although his father was willing to have him go with him, the boy was afraid to go.

It should be noted, also, that fires are always reported in detail over the local radio and in both the big city and local papers along with other disasters such as drownings, auto accidents, and plane crashes. Although most New Englanders would not admit that listening to and reading such accounts were a form of recreation, they do in fact subject themselves to this sort of information every day, and it is very often a major topic of gossip and conversation. Of all the disasters which occur in the news, fires seem to be of special interest to the citizens of Orchard Town and perhaps the most feared. One couple with two small children lived for a number of years in an old house which they considered a fire trap. During this time they slept apart with the children, the wife sleeping with the daughter and the husband with the son, so that in the event of fire they would be able to help their children to escape.

Much adult recreation, when it does occur, takes parents away from their children. It is felt that adult recreation occurring in the evening is too late for children. A few children, however, from the age of about 6 on were observed attending vaudeville types of entertainment given in the town, such as the church shows or PTA shows. These were decidedly in the minority, and most families would insist that children under high school age should go to bed.

Even when the parents have some kind of recreation in the home, such as inviting guests for dinner or for a visit in the evening, the children do not participate a great deal. If the children are present at dinner, they are expected to keep reasonably quiet. After the meal they are expected to play elsewhere—go outside if the weather is good or to their bedroom or play area.

Since much adult recreation takes place at night, the parents must get a baby sitter if they have young children up to the age of 9 or 10.

Older siblings, if there are any, may serve as baby sitters or at least eliminate the need for baby sitters. Baby sitters as a rule are paid, although there is some exchange of baby sitting among parents who are friendly with each other. Some parents seem to regard the problem of finding baby sitters—that is, not simply paying for them but finding one who will be willing to come in the evening—as difficult. Because of the baby sitting problem, having young children hinders the parents from engaging in recreation.

Within the home, watching television is considered one of the main forms of recreation. One girl noted that when television was introduced, the prediction was made that it would help bring families together again, since they would watch television in the home rather than go out for amusement and recreation. This girl felt that actually television reduces the time that the family is together, since different members of the family are interested in different programs. And when the children were concentrating on a program, they were effectively removed from interacting with the adults; evening meals were rushed in order to finish in time to watch certain television programs.

The long list of recreational activities presented above may seem tedious, but it is an indication of the amount of time that the people of Orchard Town are free from either making a living or performing rituals and attending ceremonies which are thought to be necessary for their well-being or that of the community. Providing activities for leisure time may be a problem, especially for the teenagers. The remark was made by several parents that Orchard Town was a fine place for young children, but it was not very good for teenagers or young adults. One teenager said, "There is nothing to do in this town; it's dead."

Part II

Child Training

Chapter 11

The Nature of the Child in Orchard Town

The community's conception of the nature of the child has important implications for the whole system of child training. This conception of the child's nature is based on the ideas about how the child learns and how he develops. While the basic philosophy behind the socialization process in this community is constant for all families, the philosophy itself allows for a wide variety of training techniques and of goals for individual children and families.

In Orchard Town, the newborn infant is thought of as a "potential." The central concept of the child as a potential involves beliefs about the inheritance of characteristics, beliefs about the influence of parental training on the child, beliefs about the influence of the social environment and education, and beliefs about stages and norms. The interrelation of these beliefs, and the influence of the conceptual system as a whole on the socialization process is the subject of this chapter.

DEFINITION OF THE CONCEPTUAL SYSTEM

The infant as a potential is thought to be a bundle of largely inherited latent traits of emotional expression and abilities for achieving goals, which can only be realized gradually as the child develops and which may be influenced by training and growth. Most of the goals available to the children and adults of this community are thought to call for particular skills and a particular personality type, both of which must develop naturally or be influenced to develop out of the latent traits in the infant's potential. Children may have a high or low potential for the development of certain skills or personality traits. The combination of both a high potential and the best environmental influences is thought to be essential to the greatest success in achieving the goals offered to the adult.

The community members are not completely aware of their own view of the child. Evidence for this philosophy, however, is abundant in the conversation and public speeches of the people. For example,

A woman: It is in the nature of children to dawdle.
Observer: What do you mean by "the nature of children"?
Woman: It is mostly inherited, although some comes from training.
A minister in a sermon: Of course we all have different potentialities within us. We can all do a lot better than we are doing if we will follow God's way [i.e., let God show us how to develop our potentialities].
A mother: Spanking doesn't work with some children. One of my brothers was like that and my mother could never understand that. . . .
A laborer: Some people are fit to be white collar and some are not.

The beliefs about the general nature of the latent features of the potential and the method of acquisition of these latent features throw considerable light on the socialization process. The latent traits in the potential are thought to have a number of general characteristics. They are thought of as (1) fluid, (2) partially concealed, (3) being both good and bad, and (4) being more or less subject to influence from without.

Keeping the potential as fluid as possible is important for allowing the child to reach an ideal maturity. Fluidity is retained by noninterference. It is felt that adult pressure may arrest development and set the child in a mold which is not the ideal expression of his potential. Some of the fluidity of the potential is seen to be retained until the death of the individual as shown by such statements as "You keep learning until

you die," and "I learn something new everyday." The potential, however, becomes gradually actualized or "set" as the child grows. In this
way people become "types." When this happens there is thought to be
little further hope of personality change or development. Depending
on the context, people in the community are able to classify adults into
various types. For example, they may be thought of as dominated by a
particular trait—"He is a hard worker." Even children become types as
shown by statements about various children: "(He) is an underhanded
stirrer-upper," "He won't harbor a grudge, he's very open," "He's the
sneaky type, quiet about everything and a trouble-maker."

The belief that the potential is in part concealed leads to great
emphasis on techniques for the discovery and disclosure of the child's
potential. The infant is thought of as possessing innate capacities
peculiar to himself which will be revealed in the natural course of his
development, subject to the influences around him. It is thought that
the potential can be developed better if it is known or divined in
advance. Divining for the potential is highly developed in the community. There are, of course, the formal tests for intelligence, personality and achievement, but there are also more subtle techniques, such
as informal questioning of the child or observing his behavior for clues.
Clues include such things as the child showing a special interest in
something (e.g., sports or animals), or doing something particularly
well (e.g., dancing, drawing, various school subjects). After the potential has been divined parents and teachers feel more secure in taking
a particular course of action in the training of the child.

Since both good and bad features are existent in the child's potential,
it follows that a child may momentarily exhibit either his good or his
bad qualities. The child is thought to be more likely to exhibit his bad
features if he is physically tired or has had "too much" excitement. It
is also felt that good and bad aspects may be exhibited for no apparent
reason. "I was just telling you what a little devil he is and today he is
an angel." This concept of the potential as containing both good and
bad aspects is related to the two schools of child training in the town.
One school is concerned, chiefly, with curbing the bad aspects of the
child's nature; the other is concerned with developing the good aspects.

Distinctions are made between the traits in the potential on the basis
of the amount of possible influence from the environment. In addition,
it is felt that strong influences must be exerted against traits which do
not go well together. The physical features of the child are thought to
be among his more rigid traits. Even these, however, are felt to be influenced somewhat by health habits. Sex, being a rigid trait, other
traits have to be influenced from the outside to develop in accordance
with the child's sex. People may say, "What a pity! She should have

been a boy." They mean that all the potentialities this child has for being an ideal type of male are useless and that she has few potentialities for being an ideal type of female. It is considered legitimate to channel the child's development toward a masculine or feminine personality type, whereas, with less rigid traits of the potential, the child should be allowed to develop more freely. Two bad traits which are felt by adults to be present in the child at birth or shortly thereafter are the subject of vigilance on the part of the parents. These are cruelty and indifference to time. "Children tease unmercifully" is an example of a remark easily accepted by adults in the community, and these adults also make statements in reference to a child's disregard of time. It is the parent's responsibility to see that these two bad traits are under control by the time the child becomes an adult.

ACQUISITION OF THE POTENTIAL

The various features of the potential are felt to be largely inherited. Certain characteristics which are particularly thought to be acquired in this manner are: physical appearance and defects, some diseases, temperament and certain abilities. Sometimes traits are assigned to a specific progenitor, at other times they are felt to be reinforced through inheritance from a number of ancestors. Often traits are simply assigned to the father's or mother's side of the family.

A mother: "I don't know who Dick looks like. Dan is a Smith [husband's family] and Betty is a Smith. Clara looks just like me when I was a girl. I think Mary's a Smith too, she looks more like the Smiths."
Observer: "How about things other than looks?"
Mother: "The girls are all musical and that's nothing to do with me. The boys like music too, and I'm not that way at all. Grandma Smith is; she plays the organ over to the church in Westport. That is where the Smiths live."

Some other examples of inherited traits specifically mentioned by various parents included: physical defects—birthmarks, diabetic tendency, eyes out of line; disposition—temper, lowness, neatness, sensitiveness; skill—music, mathematics.

INFLUENCES ON THE DEVELOPMENT
OF THE POTENTIAL

In Orchard Town it is felt that the development of the potential can be influenced to some extent by a number of factors. First of all, the parents are considered to be important influences on the development of the child. However, other adults, the child's associates, and environmental factors are also thought to be important. In addition, development is thought to occur through a progression of stages. These stages influence the particular expression a child may give to his potential at any time. The stages are thought to be more or less inevitable and relatively inaccessible to influence.

A newborn infant, as an undeveloped potential, is very frequently viewed as a victim of his parents and elders who are in a better position than he to foresee the end product of his development. It is the duty of these elders to help the infant to realize the good aspects of his potential and to curb his bad aspects. There is relatively good agreement in the community on how to do this.

First, the parent is responsible for not doing anything which would prevent the child's natural unfolding in the future for the sake of personal convenience in the present. The parent should not impose his own standards upon the child any more than is necessary to curb his bad aspects until the child is old enough to evaluate parental standards in terms of his own nature. The statement is made in the church guide, "Enjoy your child; do not push him into development." The parent, ideally, acts as a kind of pleased observer who watches the child unfold.

Secondly, a parent is supposed to understand the child's potential insofar as this is possible. Irreparable damage is thought to occur if the child does not unfold his potentialities at the right time, so parents need to have some knowledge of norms. Norms are quite obvious after a child enters school, but even before this the parent is aware of how much the child is supposed to have accomplished at a certain age, either through the use of books as guides or through observing other children. If the child is not "normal" then it is the parent's duty to assist the child to reach the highest standard possible.

Spoiledness, laziness, nervousness, rebelliousness, discipline problems and lack of appetite are traits which in various degrees are thought to be emphasized by parental treatment of the child. Parents may try to explain these in other ways, but teachers and other members of the community feel the parent is at fault. Lack of discipline is thought to cause both spoiling and laziness, and forcing the child is thought to develop nervousness, rebelliousness, discipline problems and lack of appetite. The physical growth and health of the child are specifically parental responsibilities to the extent that it is a parental duty to see that the child has proper nourishment, avoids illnesses by dressing properly and keeps away from children with contagious diseases. It is also the parents' duty to divine and aid the development of the child's potential.

A mother: "I wish he would express a strong interest which is based on reality because I think that if you know what a child's main interest is you can feed into it right away. But I haven't located it and I don't want to impose one on him. He is quite verbal. I think children are born with the ability to spell or not to spell."

There is much evidence that the members of the community believe that traits may be acquired by members of the community through a shared physical and social environment. Numerous statements were recorded to the effect that the children or the adults of the town were of such and such a character. Here is an example of a statement by a teacher, who feels that this town in some way influences its children differently from other places:

The children in this town are not very demonstrative. The Polish children in the city are very respectful of their teacher. They will run from a distance to see their teacher. When I first came to this town I was teaching at the central school and as I was waiting for the bus I said "Good morning, boys and girls" to some children who were waiting for the bus and they just ignored me.

This belief in the ability to acquire traits from or be influenced by one's associates leads the parents to try to be good "models" for the child and to try to keep the child away from or teach him to evaluate bad models.

Education is felt as a very important influence on the development of the potential. Although a child may have a very desirable potential, no one believes it can be realized if the child does not acquire the requisite skills through education. As a means of education, the school is evaluated differently by different status groups in the community. The lower status parents feel that the town school is good, and a means of rising in the status hierarchy. Higher status parents often feel that the school in the town is actually inferior to home influence in educating their children.

The concept of stages has important influences on the child training system. There is a strong belief that a child goes through a series of stages which are common to all children or almost all children. The stages are considered to be almost, but not completely unalterable. Certain children, because of their nature, are thought not to go through certain stages, or, a clever parent is able to alter the effects of the stages. A mother says:

They all go through a whiny stage. When they are able to they go through a holding-on-to-mother's-skirts stage. Sam is at the stage where he doesn't want me to leave at night. He cries when his father leaves at night. Bill's in the cry-baby stage now. Don't they go through the same stages over and over?

At six they go through a stage of thinking nobody loves them. When Bill was six he didn't want any affection. He didn't want you to kiss him or anything, and now he likes to be loved.

Although the child may, at any stage, appear to be a particular type of person, this may be deceiving, since stages, by their nature, inevitably pass. The parent is asked to remember this. Making an issue of some bad trait may damage the potential with useless forcing, since the trait will disappear with the disappearance of the stage. Serious or criminal behavior, however, must never be ignored as "just a stage." It is to be noted that all stages are not bad. Good stages are sometimes taken as indicators of good potentials to which a child may eventually return after passing through a bad stage. Words used with reference to describing a stage through which a child was passing included: nervous, irritable, pleasant, happy, giving-away, imitative, can't concentrate, can't join in games, can learn about Jesus, can't mix sexes in learning, fascinated with babies, noisier, harder to handle, rebellious, and messy. At times, grade in school was used as the basis of definition of a stage.

CONSEQUENCES OF THE THEORY
ON PARENTS AND ELDERS

The fact that the child is viewed as a potential which the parents have the duty to assist in its development, and the related ideas about the potential, result in certain consequences for the emotional aspects of the parent-child relationship. If the child is viewed as a potential which the parents are supposed to develop, parents often react to having children as they would to having any responsibility. The emphasis on parental responsibility for the child in this community appears to be stronger than in other groups of our acquaintance. Here the responsibility for the child is focused on the two parents rather than spread over an extended family. Parents probably find it easier to take responsibility for a child whose potential is seen as similar to their own. For one thing, in terms of the view of the concealed nature of the child, this similarity of child-parent nature makes it easier for the parent to divine the concealed potential.

Sometimes, perhaps because of the concealed nature of the child's potential, parents in the community come to feel that they are victimizing their children. The parent is never quite certain whether or not he is doing his best for the child. Anxieties are alleviated by finding out what the child's potential is—insofar as this is possible.

The feeling of responsibility, if accompanied by a certain amount of lack of success in training a child, may lead parents to anxiety about their own adequacies which in turn leads them to force the child into certain channels of development. Since forcing is contrary to the belief system, this often leads to further anxiety. The ideas of stages, norms and the inheritance of characteristics act as convenient guide-posts to the parents and as comfortable explanations for the behavior of the child.

IDEAL CHILD FOR EACH AGE AND SEX GROUP

Although children with different potentials might be expected to behave differently, there are a certain number of characteristics which might be considered as ideal in a child of a particular age and sex. Some of the traits which were felt to be ideal are presented in summary form below. The data is not extensive on this subject. Unfortunately, no questions were asked which were directly related to it.

Ideal infant (both sexes): The ideal infant cries very little, and then only to indicate the pain of sticking pins. He has no physical defects, eats well, needs no entertainment. He goes happily to all adults. He has a nice odor about him (no odor of vomiting, feces, etc.) and is not ugly.

Ideal preschooler (male): This child is ideally aggressive in defending himself, but is not aggressive otherwise. He trains easily (bedtime, toilet, eating, etc.) and gets along with other children. He is not spoiled, or shy, or a show-off.

Ideal preschooler (female): She is not aggressive. She stands up for her rights only verbally. She, also, is not spoiled, shy, or a show-off. She trains easily and shows feminine tendencies like an interest in dolls, babies, etc. She likes to appear very helpful to her mother. However the female role is not quite as sharply defined as the male role at this age and during grade school. The female "tomboy" is censured less than the male "sissy."

Ideal school-age boy: A poem from the second-grade blackboard at school gives an idealistic prescription for the school-age child, both male and female:

> *Whole Duty of Children*
> A child should always say what's true,
> And speak when he is spoken to,
> And behave mannerly at table;
> At least as far as he is able.

This poem probably represents current adult standards of "company behavior" for their children and should not be taken too seriously as reflecting the actual expectations of the adults as to their children's daily behavior, although there is certainly some increase in parental standards when the children go to school.

A child of this age to be ideal must not be "sneaky"; he must appear alert. (This no doubt gives the impression that he has a high potential.) Although quiet is needed in the schoolroom, a too-quiet child is not admired either by parents or teachers. One statement relating to this was, "He was so quiet I didn't know who he was." Other similar remarks indicate that although teachers are constantly emphasizing orderliness and quiet, this is not entirely congruent with their picture of the ideal child. (A too submissive child gives evidence of a damaged potential, perhaps.)

An ideal school-age boy should be open, liked by both adults and peers. If he gets into troubles these must be of such a nature that they can be excused by the phrase "he is a typical boy." He should be willing to fight for his rights and be able to do so. He should also be willing to defend weaker children, not be a bully, and yet not be self-righteous, a tattle tale, etc.

Ideal school-age girl: This child, ideally should never engage in physical aggression. She should be alert, popular with boys and girls, not a scapegoat, and not rebellious. She should be neat, pretty or cute, get good marks in school, but not appear to be a "brain." Ideally she is shorter than most girls her age. She runs errands and helps mother willingly. She likes feminine games (dolls, etc.) and feminine frills.

DIFFERENTIAL STATUS OF AGE AND SEX GROUPS

There is no clear preference for any one age or sex group in comparison to others. This sort of preference seems to be idiosyncratic. It is probably due to factors peculiar to the individual's own childhood situation and not to any definite trend in the group. There are, however, a few opinions about age and sex factors. These will be discussed in this section.

Age

Adults vary on their preference for one age group or another. There seems to be a tendency for men to "be afraid of" infants and to prefer children with whom they can play. A number of women also reported that they did not care for the infant as much as for the child. One man reported that children's attitudes toward their parents changed after age six. Before that age, he said, children felt that parents were wonderful, and therefore he preferred the before-six age. This is probably not a feeling which is shared by any majority. At least one woman said she preferred older children because "they can take more care of themselves."

Children's looks are considered to deteriorate as they get out of the pre-school age, but children are rarely spoken of as liked or disliked on the basis of looks. At the same time as children take on the appearance of what is called "the awkward age" they are put into a kind of affective ice-box. Parents show less loving pleasure in their children as they grow older, but this is not to say that they do not like them.

The different stages or ages (insofar as these are congruent) are felt to have different contents. Some of the aspects of each of the ages may be liked while other aspects are disliked. The age which seems to produce the most anxiety in parents is that of early puberty. At this time the child has to cope more actively with his sexuality and from various reports he is rarely able to get the approval of his parents in this respect. In most families a barrier to free speech grows up at this time between parents and children. Parents have to relinquish a good deal of control over their children and they usually do so with anxiety.

Sex

Just as adult preference for an age group is an individual matter, preference as to the sex of the child varies. Remarks of a few parents suggest a tendency for fathers to want a boy and perhaps a slight tendency for women to want a girl. Two women who have only male children said they would have preferred girls before they had any children, but when they had boys they weren't disappointed. One said,

I always thought a little girl would be so much fun to dress, but I wouldn't change Tom [her youngest boy] for a million dollars; [calling the child's attention to the conversation] Would I, Tom? I asked Tom how much he loved me and he said "bigger than the whole world."

The second woman said that although she wanted a girl she wanted a boy for her husband's sake. Other women reported that they wanted a boy first or that they preferred boys. One woman who had three boys and one girl had a very strong preference for boys. She said that her one girl was more aggressive than all of her boys and that "(the girl) could knock all of the boys' heads together." The girl is not the oldest child in the family. Another woman felt that her husband "favors the girls" (they have one boy and two girls). The ideal family, perhaps, is considered to be one that has both sexes among its children.

Girls are described variously as "feminine," "not leaders," "never think of anything" (male peer speaking); while boys are people "you just can't insult," "bossy," "active," "real or typical boys," "the ones that really make trouble" (18–20-year-old boys). Boys should not be "effeminate," but girls may "play with boys as equals" without criticism, although the preference seems to be for girls who play the feminine role in the presence of boys. A speaker said to the "Ladies' Circle," "Boys can be so unpleasant parents lose patience with them." Perhaps all but the sexual aspects of child training are considered to be easier for the parent if the child is a girl. "A son is a son till he gets him a wife but a daughter's a daughter all of her life" is an opinion which is expressed often.

Most children, themselves, do not overtly express dissatisfaction with their sex whichever it may be. One girl said in a game, "I don't like to be men. I don't want to be a king. I want to be a queen or a princess." Sometimes there are aggressive feelings between the two sexes, especially envy of boys by girls. An older high school girl is very resentful of what she feels is a preference for boys in a school official. She says of him:

Everything is for the boys—nothing is for the girls. She then listed all the uniforms and equipment boys get and girls get "nothing!" He has made a rule that the girls have to have on gym suits everyday when they play games. This is "too cold in winter." The girls have resolved to practice hard and win first place in the area in athletics and then "if he doesn't praise us we're going to praise ourselves." The girls' gym teacher got very "brave" [in defending the girls] and got up in an assembly and told everyone how loyal the girls were about coming to cheer for the boys and how nobody came when the girls played a game.

Boys at times expressed resentment against older sisters, who had authority over them, but in general their resentment seemed less than that that of girls toward boys. Thus, while there is a conscious satisfaction in whichever sex role falls to one's lot, there is still a definite aggressive element in attitudes toward the opposite sex. Evidently the difference in the roles is sufficiently great to cause some jealousy about certain aspects of the opposite role.

SPECIAL STATUSES OF CHILDREN

A number of special statuses are found among the children in the town. The special statuses may be classified as: related to accidents of birth or conception and the inheritance of physical traits; related to the peculiar position of a child in the social system, such as sibling position or lack of true parents; and related to special types of training to which the child has been subjected. The special statuses are discussed below under these three headings.

Special Statuses Related to Accidents of Birth

A list of this class of statuses, taken from casual notes made throughout the year of fieldwork follows: slow or retarded children; twins; runts or children far below average in size; blue babies; deaf children; children born with heart ailments or under perilous conditions such as caesareans. Each of these statutes receive special treatment at times in the socialization process.

A child who is very much retarded mentally finds himself unable to keep up with his peers in school. If he is not too retarded he may be either kept back in school or put in slow groups in reading and arithmetic. If he is much retarded, he may be sent to a special school for retarded children or receive tutoring by people in the community who are paid to teach such children. If retardation is associated with personality or other difficulties the slow child is often the butt of teasing and ridicule by his peers and the exasperation of his parents and teachers. If he is just slow and does not stand out from the group as a disciplinary or social problem he may go more or less unnoticed, be shy, and remain as far as possible in the background of group activities. There were no seriously retarded children in our sample. If a child is merely below average in intelligence and his parents have no high aspirations for him there is generally very little problem. Parents do want their children to keep up with their age-grade in school and all parents in the sample who had children in danger of not-passing in school made special efforts to help them with their study. In one case at least this study took the child away from her peer group during informal play times.

A deaf child in the community associates freely with her peers. She is reported by adults to "use" her deafness at times to avoid hearing things she finds unpleasant. Thus, she represents a special discipline problem. She wears a hearing-aid and she is an expert lip-reader. So adeptly has the child managed her handicap that the observer would not have known of her deafness except for the visible hearing aid. She is not shy or withdrawn.

Children who are weak at birth receive special attention in their early months. This is almost inevitably true even when parents consciously try to avoid giving special attention to such a child. Such special attention is felt to be detrimental and to be likely to "spoil" children. Here is one mother's story of how she fed a child while she was paralyzed with the fear that he might die if he did not eat.

He didn't like the bottle too well; he didn't like to eat. I might have done it [started him drinking from a cup] to try something different to get some food into him. Because they told me if I could get enough food into him I might be able to keep him alive. They told me not to force him to eat, but I did. They told me he wasn't going to live anyway. He used to hold the food in his mouth and let it come out his nose so I used to hold his mouth and his nose and in order to breathe he had to swallow it. [The sequel to this is that the child is very much alive and leading a very normal life at present—age 5.]

A male child who is smaller than most children has a special status. One child's entire personality is considered by the people in the community to have been shaped by his small size. It is felt that he is constantly under pressure to prove himself physically to be as capable as other children, because of his small size.

Twins are generally welcomed. If one child is wanted, two are considered to be especially desirable. A woman who had twins reported her pleasure and her difficulties; these twins were in another special status, the first boys after three girls:

I don't know if the doctor said I wasn't going to have twins because he knew I didn't want them or not. I just thought it was awful hard to take care of them, and it is for the first six months; pretty hard for the first year; then it's not too bad.
They knew I was going to have twins after the first one was born . . . Poor George didn't know how I was going to feel about it. He was thrilled. Grandpa was more than thrilled because he had no grandsons and my sister was thrilled because she wanted a boy too—but two boys in the family!! . . . I wanted a boy so I was thrilled that it was a boy, and, after I got over the shock of it, it was a thrill to have two—one would have been spoiled. . . . It took the whole family to take care of them.

Twins, finding companionship in each other, are apparently less inclined to wander from home. These particular twins are likely to support each other in difficulty, act as consciences for each other, and probably to a greater extent than other siblings will tell their parents on each other.

Special Statuses Related to Position in the Social System

A list of some of these found in the community follows: only child, oldest child, youngest child, illegitimate child, adopted child, state child (boarding out with people in the town), children with a parent dead or missing, children of old age, step-children, children whose parents are employed as ministers, garbage collectors, teachers in the local system and possibly children of parents in a few other occupations.

Only children are considered to be in great danger of "spoiling." Although there were a number of only children in the community, only one was held up as an example of an only child. It was said of him by many people:

> He is an only child and an only grandchild, and always had things other kids didn't have, like projectors, and he was always wanting to show them off, which frequently disrupted things much to the annoyance of the children. The children, also, don't like him very much.

A teacher said of another only child: "He is a show-off, being the only child. Usually whenever we have a visitor he starts showing off."

Parents as a general rule feel that they have been "stricter" with their first-born in all of his training than they are with following children. Youngest children, like only children are felt to be in danger of being "spoiled." Youngest children in large families often do have a financial advantage over more deprived older ones. The older ones grow up, get jobs, and buy things for young siblings which they were not able to have in their own youth.

Children born late in the life of the parent generally have a special status. Women reported enjoying their children more after they themselves had reached a more substantial age. A late child was at times embarrassing to one woman who, while enjoying him, found that in public places she often overheard people saying, "they must be his grandparents."

There were a number of cases of illegitimacy or suspected illegitimacy in the community. This was a fact which was mentioned in talking about a child, but there was no particular feeling against him. It was felt, however, that the unfortunate circumstances of his birth usually led to personality problems in the child himself. The child is not condemned, but parents of illegitimate children are not always so fortunate.

One child was adopted during the period of our stay in the town. If there were other adopted children, they were unknown to us. This child's parents were delighted to have him and were expected by the community to spoil him.

A number of "state" children board with various families in the town who receive remuneration for their care. At least one of these families keeps such children isolated from the other children of the town for fear parents would be worried that state children would be a bad influence. None of these families were interviewed. Some "state" children were reported to be nice children.

One family was observed casually who had one parent, a mother. The mother was considered to be trying to do a good job under very difficult conditions. The children were in a rather poor status position with regard to their peers, although they were well-behaved children by community standards. Adults "felt sorry" for the children. One man in the community sometimes invited the boy to go along with him and his son on outings, serving as a kind of substitute father. With special friends these children were well-received, but with the rougher element in the community they were the butt of teasing. Another family which had recently acquired a step-mother had children who were not considered to be good playmates by the more conservative and conforming members of the community. The children were also not popular with their peers.

A good many of the effects on the child of incomplete or substituted families, then, probably arises out of idiosyncratic factors in the personality of the individual child, and his lot varies accordingly. He has, however, "one strike against him" before he starts. People expect him to have problems.

Children whose parents have special occupations may have special statuses. Ministers' children are always gossiped about, condemned more for wrong-doing and praised more for good behavior than other children. As the minister's wife said, "No matter what we do we will be criticized." Ministers' families also cannot make the social distinctions in their social life that other community members make, so that their children must be indiscriminately exposed to good and bad influences. Garbage collectors' children are often taunted about their father's occupation by some children. Children of teachers are probably expected by their parents to be especially well-behaved in order to advertise the parent's worth as a teacher.

Special Statuses Related to Training

A partial list of these special statuses as given by parents is: problem child, whipping boy, stinker, hoodlum, and spoiled child.

An adult recalls that there were problem children in school with him.

. . . problem children . . . they were basically not interested . . . Baseball or fishing was the source of the turmoil . . . Some of them were not too bright . . . One did a lot of whittling around school . . . carved his initials on the banisters. Another slapped a teacher once . . .

Mothers often reported that their first child had always been a problem. Problem child in this sense meant difficult to socialize. A child who is spoken of as a problem is not generally thought of as an out and out delinquent. This idea usually does not even enter the picture, but occasionally it is felt that a problem child is in danger of becoming a delinquent. This would put him in a different status category. The cause of the problem child is generally felt to be the lack of experience of the mother in dealing with children or bad techniques in dealing with them. In these cases some kind of unpleasantness gets started between parents and child at an early age and tends to continue throughout life. It is so emotionally and unconsciously based, judging from reports, that it is seldom completely overcome. One woman reported that she had a much better relationship with her first-born son since he had been gone from home a greater part of each day to a nearby private school. Another woman said of her first-born daughter, "we have always gotten on each other's nerves." A father reported that a kind of submerged hostile battle was constantly going on between himself and his oldest son. These children were all felt to be problem children to a greater or less extent. None of them were considered to be "bad" or delinquent children.

One informant, on seeing a small boy, said, "There is a 'stinker,' a 'bugger.' " The observer asked what a bugger was, and got the following reply:

He's just mean as far as the rest of the kids go . . . He used to come by here and ring the door bell all the time . . . All the kids seem afraid of him. He rules everybody. He used to hit little Jonathan all the time.

Since this boy does not come from the type of family (which seems to be essential to and) which produces "hoodlums" he is only known as a "stinker."

Hoodlums may be considered to be such while not actually being, or they may be real hoodlums. "They (the children of a certain family) were considered hoodlums. Some didn't let their kids play with them. They weren't really hoodlums." Hoodlums are evidently members of lower-status families and of families who are reputed to neglect their children. Lower status alone is not sufficient to indicate that a particular child will be considered to be a hoodlum. If some children in such a family show signs of delinquency, the other children in the same family will generally be classed with the delinquent as a "hoodlum." Such a child is generally isolated as far as possible from the children of conforming families. He is generally found in association with other "hoodlums." Stinkers, on the other hand, are found in association with children of conforming families and are generally found in families which are not lowest in status.

For one reason or another, a child may become a special focus of the hostility of an adult. There is sometimes just such a child in a classroom. He may be particularly demanding of adults in general and used to having his way with them, or have characteristics which happen to strike a particular teacher unfavorably. Such a child may be called a "whipping boy" (or girl). The following incident is typical of the school experience of one such child.

> After recess two boys had been fighting while waiting in line for the teacher to unlock the door, which had closed. The teacher sounded very angry about their fighting. One boy said, "I was already there and he tried to push me out of my place." Stanley [the whipping boy] said, "He punched me so I punched him." The teacher apparently decided on the basis of this brief questioning and previous experience that Stanley was at fault. She told him to put his head down on his desk for five minutes. "I don't want to see you."

✻
✻
✻

Chapter 12

Pregnancy and Childbirth

Most women of Orchard Town welcome the idea of having a child. There is some preference for the first child to be a boy, although there is also a definite sentiment for having a mixture of sexes among one's children. Moreover, boys are considered more difficult to control in childhood, and a mother with more than a couple of boys is the object of sympathetic concern.

However, while children are desired, pregnancy itself is regarded by some as uncomfortable and restrictive. Cravings for large amounts of strange foods are normally expected. A woman's legs sometimes swell. The appearance of pregnant women is widely regarded as awkward and embarrassing.

Women are supposed to be careful during pregnancy for the sake of the fetus. They should try to avoid any heavy physical exertion for fear of causing an abortion or miscarriage. Some women have a tendency to miscarry, and several women expressed worries about miscarriage. The doctor may prescribe hormone treatment and bed rest for threatened miscarriage. Pregnant women should also try to avoid exposure to contagious diseases and should remain in the best possible health. One mother reported that she stopped smoking when she was pregnant for the child's sake. The belief is often jokingly mentioned that if the mother is frightened by anything in pregnancy, the baby will show some mark of it. However, all regarded this as a superstition which no modern parent would take seriously.

While some indulgence of special food cravings is thought permissible, it is believed that pregnant women must control a tendency to overeat. The women have a general fear of becoming too fat anyway, and an excessive gain in weight is considered to be especially undesirable during pregnancy. If a pregnant woman eats too much, she will not only gain weight herself but her baby may be too large, and labor will be difficult. Nevertheless, both parents are proud of having a baby that is bigger than average.

Nowadays birth almost always takes place in a hospital in a nearby town, since there is none in Orchard Town itself. During our field work, one woman in town caused some raised eyebrows by her insistence that she wanted to give birth to her next baby at home. Her doctor said that this was the first home delivery he had had. But even a generation ago, home deliveries were not uncommon.

There is little danger of maternal mortality. If birth is difficult, an operation is resorted to. One woman in town had had three children by Caesarean operation without complications.

The women do not appear to enjoy their confinement at the hospital. The isolation and enforced rest annoy them. One mother complained of the attitude of some of the assistants at the hospital: "They carry the babies around like sacks of flour." A volunteer worker at the hospital felt that not enough attention was paid to the infants' crying.

Even after the mother returns home from the hospital she is considered somewhat weak and incapable of her full regular work. If possible, a grandmother or other relative may come to visit or a high school girl or an older woman may be hired on an hourly basis for a while to help out some with the housework.

There is no special ceremony at the time to celebrate the birth of a child or the return of the mother from the hospital. Both parents are proud of the birth and receive congratulations from friends and relatives. The parents may send out cards announcing the birth.

✢
✢
✢

Chapter 13

Infancy

In the beginning of infancy the mother-child relationship is built mainly around the question of care of the infant: feeding it and keeping it clean, warm, medicated, and out of harm's way. The infant is considered to be especially susceptible to a number of dangers including contagious diseases, chilling, suffocation, and physical accidents, especially falling on its head.

Infants may be fed initially by bottle or breast. Ten out of our 24 sample children were nursed for a time by their mothers. The length of nursing ranged from a few days to five months, at which time bottle feeding was substituted. One child was said to have disliked bottle feeding as a result of forcible weaning from the breast.

Some mothers said they simply could not nurse their babies, while others expressed varying degrees of distaste or revulsion toward nursing. Even the mothers who did nurse their children usually worried about whether they had enough milk. There is some indication that mothers blame themselves for lack of milk and their inability to nurse. Such a feeling of self-depreciation is reflected in the statement of one, "I am not a good mother, and, of course, I will not be adequate to the test of mothers—feeding my child." Most mothers who nursed were not reluctant to wean their children from the breast, although one mother who lacked enough milk to continue nursing her baby said she "thought the world had come to an end" when she realized she must stop.

A few years ago most children were on a feeding schedule. However, recently "demand feeding" has become popular. In our sample all but one of the children 5 years of age or younger at the time of the study were reported to have been fed on demand, while all but two of the older children were said to have been fed on schedule.

Mothers have a wide variety of interpretations of the meaning of demand and scheduled feeding. Some mothers said they had scheduled feeding, yet reported they would vary as much as half an hour from the schedule. Other mothers would have considered this to be no schedule at all. These took pride in being "on the dot" in their feeding. They reported proudly that they adjusted their own activities to their schedule for the infant. The interpretation of demand, on the other hand, often was that the child was supposed to set up a schedule in his first few weeks after which the mother would follow the child's schedule faithfully, just as she would have followed a schedule she had set up herself.

One of the difficulties of full demand feeding is that it lets the infant develop the habit of waking in the middle of the night and crying for food. Most babies sometimes wake in the night anyway, and this is considered to be very trying for the mother and for the father as well if, as occasionally happens, he helps quiet the child. Feeding in the middle of the night is not easy if it involves heating a bottle and is not considered necessary for the child's development, and some mothers even look with disfavor on giving a baby a bottle to go to sleep on the grounds that he will become too attached to the bottle this way and weaning will be difficult.

The infant sleeps in a crib for a year or more. The crib is usually at first put in the parent's bedroom to facilitate care at night and to avoid disturbing any other members of the household. However, if space were available, most parents would probably prefer to put the baby in a separate bedroom of its own near theirs. It is not uncommon for parents to take the baby into their bed to quiet it, although most would try to put it back in its crib later and not let the baby sleep regularly with them.

Cleanliness is regarded as important, both for the baby's health and for its comfort. The babies wear diapers until toilet training is fairly well completed, and the diapers are changed frequently in theory and usually so in practice, although there may be some delay since the mother is usually busy with work around the house.

Infants are bathed daily although older children usually bathe less frequently. Some babies resent the bathing initially and cry, perhaps more from the restriction on their movement than anything. The baby's hands and face are washed several times a day, after and often before eating, and after playing with anything dirty.

Babies are generally kept clothed both for modesty and to keep the baby warm. We saw only one baby naked in the course of a year, and this one was having a bath. The babies at times seem to be over-clothed, although on hot days in the summer they may wear only diapers.

Adults consider it natural and largely inevitable for babies to cry a lot, although the crying is disliked and happy babies are admired. The mother's treatment of crying depends on her interpretation of what is bothering the baby. Often it is felt the baby is simply crying for companionship, as when the mother has been playing with it and leaves to do some housework. Indulgence of crying for companionship is felt to be bad, for it leads to a spoiled child. Moreover, letting the baby "cry it out" is good not only for its character but also may help exercise its lungs.

Babies are thought to cry frequently because of stomach pains due to either hunger or colic. A baby on demand feeding is fed when it cries and the mother thinks it is hungry. Very probably it will often get food to stop it from crying when it is not in fact hungry. A baby on scheduled feeding does not usually succeed in breaking its schedule by crying for food, but it may be given a rubber pacifier to suck on. If it is not too hungry or is really crying for other reasons anyway, the pacifier may distract it enough to stop the crying. Most babies are in fact quite fat and evidently get plenty to eat. One wonders how often Orchard Town babies really cry from hunger.

A baby may be thought to be crying from colic if it is known to have had plenty of food and rejects further food. A mother may treat this by "burping" the baby—putting it on her shoulder and patting its back. Colic is regarded as a problem for which there is no sure, rapid solution.

Constipation is also believed to be a common cause of crying by many mothers. The remedies for this are suppositories, enemas, and laxatives, although laxatives are perhaps passing out of favor.

Teething is thought to make babies cross and to lead to crying. Some parents feel that not too much can be done about this; others believe teething rings are effective.

Some babies cry at the appearance of strangers. Adults laugh at this, and the stranger will usually try to reassure the baby, often successfully.

Chapter 14

Early Socialization

Although concern for meeting the physical needs of her baby dominates the mother's early interaction with her child, a positive concern
with training and controlling the infant in certain respects emerges
at an early age.

As soon as the baby is "ready," the mother tries to replace the bottle
by the cup (if the mother has nursed her baby initially, the breast has
been replaced by the bottle before this). Mothers recognize various
signs of "readiness": when a child can hold a cup, when it can sit up
in a high chair, or when the child refuses the bottle or throws it away.
In any case most people feel uncomfortable to see a child feeding from
a bottle much after the time it begins to walk.

Supplementary food may be introduced a few weeks after birth.
This is generally orange juice, canned baby food, and cereal. At first
the mother feeds the baby with a spoon, but as soon as it is ready she,
at least in theory, encourages it to feed itself. Some mothers begin by
giving the child a spoon to hold and play with while the mother continues feeding him. When the child begins to pick up food with his
spoon, his hands are guided by the mother. Gradually the mother releases her hold on the cup and the spoon, and the child is feeding
himself. An alternative method is to allow the child to begin to eat
with his fingers, leaving a spoon nearby so that the child may experiment with using it. This last method enables independent feeding to
begin very early.

These methods may be considered as ideals. Quite a number of
mothers seem to be successful in carrying them out, although some find
them too much trouble. Among the mothers who do not tolerate the
"messy" eating stage, finger feeding is discouraged by staying with the
child, restraining his hands and pushing the spoon into his mouth
Even these mothers, however, recognize the other methods as ideal.

They say, "I know you are supposed to do it that way, but I just never could stand the mess." After the age of 2 the "messy" feeding period is passed, and most of the children are then allowed to feed themselves.

According to the mothers, most children were weaned gradually from the bottle as they learned to drink from a cup and to eat solid food. Eventually a point was reached where the baby tired of the bottle and threw it away repeatedly when offered. Few mothers reported any difficulties in this process. Those who did felt they were not serious and said something like "I guess he howled some."

Although mothers feel that feeding should be enjoyable and weaning an easy and enjoyable experience—they have read this and heard it at many times—it is nevertheless true that anxiety is noticeable in both of these activities. They may say, "It won't matter when he's 50, when he was weaned, who will know?" This suggests that it is a matter to be hidden if the child is slow in weaning. Even if the mother is able to resist the temptation to wean an older child forcibly, relatives may take over. The mother of one child in the sample went off for a brief vacation. Her sister and the child's father then told the child that there were no bottles left. Only three of the 24 children were reported to have still had a bottle at 2 years of age. A summary of the reported ages of weaning is given in the following table.

It can be seen that the majority of boys are weaned between 9 months and a year (8 out of 12). Half the girls were also weaned at this age, but 3 girls were said to have been weaned at 18 months.

	BOYS	GIRLS
5–6 months	1	1
9–10 months	3	3
1 year	5	3
1½ years	1	3
2 years	1	1
Over 2 years	1	

All weaning and feeding problems are felt to be the responsibility of the parents. Since the parents tend to blame themselves, and feel that others blame them in this area of training, guilt, anxiety, and feelings of inferiority are the concomitants.

As in other areas of training there is thought to be an ideal time to begin toilet training. However, different signs that the child is "ready" for training are used by different mothers. These may be sitting up, walking, understanding what the mother says, and so on.

The process of toilet training includes giving the child the "idea" by sitting him on a potty or toilet, grunting and running water, waiting for his "regular" time to put him on the toilet, or putting him on just after urination or defecation has occurred. In other words, the attempt is made to associate the process of urination and defecation with the toilet. The ideal is often expressed that in doing this, the mother should not force the child in any way. Forcing in toilet training is considered to be responsible for making a child rebellious; in addition, it makes toilet training difficult if not impossible.

In practice, mothers generally follow the ideal rules of toilet training when they have a child who is "easy to train." With a child who is difficult to train, the ideal is very distant from the real practice, and more severe measures are used.

We list below our impressions as to the frequency of certain toilet training techniques mentioned by mothers as occurring in the community:

Holding pot on lap and small baby on pot while feeding—rare
Putting on pot at regular times after child is able to sit up—frequent
Use of suppositories, soapsticks, or enemas at regular times—one fourth to one third of all mothers used these for bowel training
Spanking—occasional
Shaming—very frequent
Rubbing nose in feces—occasional
Praising for proper performance—very frequent
Taking up at night—frequent
Restriction of water after 4 or 5 P.M.—frequent
Promise of rewards for not wetting bed—frequent with bed wetting problems

As in feeding problems, parents also feel responsible about lack of success in toilet training. If the child was slow in learning, they felt that they had started toilet training either too late or too early. At other times they worried that they had been too strict. Mothers generally said that they were more "relaxed" with their later children, and in some cases the later children were more easily trained. Mothers do not, however, accept total responsibility for slow toilet training, since they believe that some children are just "naturally" (constitutionally) hard to train. They cite different children in the family who had similar treatment but varied greatly in ease of training.

The following table gives the mothers' rough memories on the time of completion of toilet training during the day. Most mothers noted the approximate nature of these answers.

It will be seen that the spread of ages for boys is much greater than for girls. Girls were trained more consistently at 2–2½.

	BOYS	GIRLS
11 months to 1 year	2	
1½ years	2	4
2–2½ years	3	8
3 years	1	
4 years	1	
5 years	1	
Over 5 years	2	

Mothers reported, however, that the age at which children were able to stay dry all night was much later. Four of the boys in the sample still wet occasionally. Two are 5, one is 7, and one is 10. Five of the girls still wet: three 4-year-olds, one 7-year-old, and one 8-year-old.

There is a suggestion in the data that if early toilet training is severe enough and consistent, it may be completed early in childhood regardless of constitutional factors. Mothers who took an early and strong stand on toilet training according to their reports succeeded in training the child at an early age. It was the mothers who wavered between leniency and strictness who tended to be least successful in toilet training.

Somewhere between two or three months to a year when the baby is thought to need less attention at night its crib is moved into another room. If it has an older sibling, the baby usually shares the sibling's room. The baby may still cry during the night and on such occasions be taken back into the parents' bed if it is not easily quieted.

Both parents, but especially the mother, are delighted by signs of physical and social maturity in the baby. Parents will compare their children as to the age when they learned to walk, talk, feed themselves, and so on and some even kept elaborate records in the form of "baby books." The mother talks to the baby from birth whenever she is doing things with it and encourages its laughing, gurgling, and foreshadowings of speech with smiles and words of praise. When the baby begins to talk, among its first words are "Mama," "Daddy," (or "Papa"), and "bye." At first the mother waves the baby's hand while saying "bye," but soon the baby learns to do both by himself.

A mother also may hold the baby while it practices walking. Much of the day the baby may be in a crib or playpen with sides of a convenient height for the baby to grasp and practice standing or walking.

At times the mother may stimulate motor activity by jiggling the baby on her knee or by other physical play. Some adults, especially men, may lift the baby over their heads or swing it around. The baby comes to like this eventually, and this sort of roughhousing continues in later childhood between men and boys, though not so long for girls.

The baby is given a number of toys which encourage motor activity, such as rattles, and later bouncing horses and wheeled toys which jingle or make other pleasant noises when pulled or pushed. Some of these are advertised as aiding the baby's physical development by encouraging exercise.

Although parents are annoyed by the baby's clumsiness and "racket," they believe that healthy, psychologically adjusted babies are noisy and active. Accordingly, the baby gets a certain amount of unintentional reward for being noisy and active, since the parents often show pleasure at these signs of good health (in turn presumably derived from good parental care).

As the baby grows and becomes more physically active, it comes into more contact with other people. There is less worry about exposing it to colds and other infectious diseases, although care would be taken to avoid visitors with an obvious severe cold. Women start taking the babies with them around town to friends' houses or on short shopping trips, and the mother also begins to leave the baby for short periods with friends, relatives, or occasionally paid baby-sitters. Nevertheless, the baby is with the mother more than anyone else and will generally cry for a while at the mother's departure.

The older baby's first contacts with new people are more with adults than with other children. If brought together with another baby of the same age the two would fight, it is thought. Older children may enjoy trying to amuse the baby if they happen to be confined with it, but in free situations they usually desert it for their own pastimes. We frequently observed a couple of fifth-grade girls wheeling some neighbors' babies, but they seemed to interact little with the babies and to be interested primarily in earning pocket money. If the baby has an older sibling, however, it will see this child around a fair amount of the time and probably sleep in the same room with it, even though the sibling may do little either for or to the baby. This lack of interaction with older siblings is reinforced by the parents since they generally discourage older siblings (unless quite markedly older) from assuming responsibility for infants on the grounds that the older child will be irresponsible and that it would also be imposing unduly on him or her. It is thought to be too trying for an older child to face the baby's antisocial behavior and maintain reasonable control over it.

A major problem is the baby's tendency to pick up any small loose object to play with, whether another child's toy or some possession of the parents'. Depending on the baby's age, the value and fragility of the object, and the importance of its owner, the mother may retrieve it forcibly, upon which the baby generally cries angrily, or wait until the baby abandons it in the hope of avoiding a "scene." If the latter, she will apologize to the owner that the baby "doesn't know any better." Older siblings do not always accept this apology calmly.

When frustrated in this or other ways, a baby may attack an adult physically by hitting, kicking, or biting. Biting is the most severely disapproved, and although expected, it is punished. Some mothers bite the child back; others say "No! No!," cry out in pain, or spank the child. If biting continues into childhood, as it had in the case of one 3-year-old, it is punished by neighbors not allowing their children to play with the offender.

Because of the ease with which the baby lapses into antisocial behavior, prolonged social life is not considered desirable for babies and is felt to tire them. Most of them spend a good part of each day alone in a crib or playpen or in a fenced-in yard. Children learn early in Orchard Town that interaction with others is spaced, separated by periods of withdrawal.

In addition to tiring the baby, it is believed that too much social attention can "spoil" him. Certain types of unpleasant behavior, interpreted by adults to mean that the infant wants social attention, are deliberately ignored. Crying is often one of these. The value here is inculcated that people are ready to share time with a pleasant person and are unwilling to spend time with an unpleasant one. Unpleasantness must be hidden from others by means of a social mask or, alternatively, one can withdraw from others.

Such contacts as the baby has with other human beings are not marked by close bodily contacts as in many societies. There are two opposing needs considered here—one the early need for warmth supplied by close bodily contact, and the other the pleasure in the free movement of limbs. In this society the second is highly satisfied at the expense of the first. Ample clothing also intervenes between mother and child. There are freedom and a certain privacy in this. These things continue to be valued in adult social life. At the same time there are often feelings that something desirable is missing from social relations. Perhaps what is missing is the satisfaction of the need for close contact with another human being.

Chapter 15

Early Childhood

The period of early childhood begins when the child has learned to walk and talk effectively and lasts until he enters school in first grade. (There is no public kindergarten in town.) This time is felt to be the most important stage of character formation. Traits that are begun here are believed to carry through life. If the child does not receive certain basic training during the preschool period, training is thought to become much more difficult later.

Accordingly, the emphasis in the mother's behavior toward the child now shifts from care to training and control. The child no longer needs to be fed each spoonful of food, has learned to go to the toilet when appropriate (at least most of the time), and can walk around and get for himself toys or other things he wants. Even where he needs his mother's help, he can ask her promptly in words instead of simply crying and waiting for her to divine his wish.

RELATIONSHIP WITH FAMILY

The child's social relationships become less exclusive at this time. Within the family he has more to do with his father and older siblings when they are around the house, for he is now able to seek them out at will and talk with them. The father and siblings find the child more interesting at this age than in infancy and are more willing to spend some time with him.

Outside of the family the child is thought to be lonely if he does not have playmates of his own age. Children usually have a few such playmates living close by with whom they play regularly and freely during the day. However, the child of this age is still felt unable to meet the world in general independently, and he is therefore restricted to his immediate neighborhood.

TECHNIQUES OF DISCIPLINE

These children are highly aware that they have graduated from the rank of "baby" and are likely to exhibit considerable scorn of babies, whether a neighbor's child or a younger sibling. This feeling of superiority is the residue of the parents' praise for advanced behavior and their inciting the child by remarks like "Only *babies* do that. *You're* not a baby." The frequency of these remarks at this age, however, suggests that in adult minds, at least, there is concern lest the children lapse into babyish ways.

Proper discipline is felt to be especially important for a preschool child, and physical punishment is used more often in this period than at any other time. Initially children respond to the stronger discipline by temper tantrums. With these there is a shift in the parents' feelings toward the child from indulgence to some hostility toward his antisocial acts. Negatives become more common in the parents' speech with the child: "No! No!"

A typical mother shows some worry about others learning of the full extent of her troubles in controlling her child. In public she may tell him to stop doing something quite sweetly, addressing him as "dear," "darling," and so forth; when at home she might spank or speak more peremptorily for the same offense.

Because of the child's newly acquired mobility, it is no longer easy to confine him to safe parts of his environment, such as a playpen or crib. Moreover, narrow confinement would be considered undesirable for the child, since he is thought to need physical exercise and "space." Discipline which compels the child to observe restrictions on numerous acts well within his physical abilities becomes important not only for character molding but for the immediate control of the child.

SLEEPING ARRANGEMENTS AND
ATTITUDES TOWARD SLEEP

Children of this age have already been moved out of the parents' room for sleeping. However, it is not unusual for small children to crawl in bed with their parents during the night or in the early morning. In any case, parents are careful not to allow their young children to see them having intercourse. One woman reported that when she was a child she would—over her mother's objections—get in bed at times with her older brother for warmth and comfort. Presumably some of the current generation of children do this same thing, but we did not inquire as to frequency. Apart from questions of impropriety, parents would feel that the children would interfere with each other's sleep by sleeping in the same bed or even in the same room.

Most preschool children, however, sleep in a bedroom containing two beds, twin or bunk. Of the 10 children of preschool age in the sample, 6 sleep in the same room with siblings of the same sex, 3 with siblings of different sex, and 1 sleeps in a room alone, for he has no siblings living at home. There is some feeling that ideally children of opposite sex ought to have different rooms even at this age, but this is not considered important enough to warrant buying or building a new house if the present house is not big enough. Children change into special sleeping garments before they go to bed for the night. The most usual garment for both boys and girls is a pair of warm pajamas, although little girls may at times sleep in nightgowns.

Parents believe it is important for children of any age to get plenty of sleep in order to "grow." If left to themselves, children, it is thought, would not get enough sleep and would try to stay up as late as older people. This would be bad for their health and make them cross and hard to manage. Preschool children are accordingly put to bed at an early hour in the evening and are allowed to sleep as late as they will in the morning. One suspects also that a desire to have the children out of the way in order to free time for the parents to engage in their own activities is a stronger motive in putting children to bed early than many would like to admit.

Many children resist being put to sleep. When siblings sleep in the same room, they often whisper to each other regularly for half an hour or more and get into arguments as to who is keeping whom awake. Children also think of various excuses to get out of bed (e.g., go to the toilet) or call their mother (e.g., get a drink of water). One mother, who put her children to bed right after supper, regularly camped at the head of the stairs every night until the children had calmed down.

Many preschool children take a nap in the afternoon or are at least put in a room for a nap and expected to remain lying in bed reasonably quiet for an hour or so. Mothers often took naps at the same time. Some children object to taking naps, especially if they know one of their friends does not have to. However, the afternoon nap does not seem to be as much a focus of mother-child struggle as evening bedtime. Most children stop taking regular naps before they enter first grade.

MORNING ROUTINE

In the morning, preschool children have considerable freedom as to when they will get up. Most of them are neither required to get up by a certain time nor required to stay in bed until a certain time. Rising times were reported as varying from 6 A.M. to 9:30 A.M. If children are in the habit of getting up before their parents do, especially on weekends, they are taught early in this period to play quietly in parts of the house where they will not disturb their sleeping parents.

In some families, the father leaves early in the morning for work and often does not see his young children before leaving. In families where the father gets up early, however, children are more likely to go to bed earlier and therefore may be up in time to see father briefly before he starts off for work. It may be that rising time has grown later in North Village in the last half century and that formerly children were forced to get up early in the morning for breakfast.

Some preschool children dress before and some immediately after breakfast. If they are confined to the house because of recent illness, or even bad weather, in some families they may stay in their night clothes all or part of the day. But it is felt improper for a well child to remain in sleeping clothes much after breakfast on an average day.

CLOTHING AND DRESSING

The typical preschool dress is shirt, blue jeans or trousers, underwear, and sneakers or rubber-soled shoes. On hot summer days some children, mostly girls, wear shorts rather than long trousers. Short-sleeved shirts are also more common in the summer, and at this time boys, but almost never girls, may go around in the neighborhood without a shirt. Shoes are worn outside at all times. In the winter the children may put on a sweater over their shirt if the house is drafty and must put on extra outdoor clothing to go outside. On cold days they are expected to put on a snowsuit or a heavy jacket and snow pants and rubber overshoes if the ground is covered with snow or is muddy.

In general, children wear the same clothing throughout the day, but all of them have dress-up clothes for special occasions. On these occasions the little girls may appear in stiff petticoats and dresses, patent leather shoes, frilly hats, and even white gloves and a small purse, while the boys are more likely to have a white cotton shirt in place of the usual colored or patterned one, leather shoes in place of the usual sneakers, and a small jacket which matches their trousers. Miniature ties for boys are also worn occasionally.

There is much variation among young children as to how much they dress themselves. Even the most competent may require their mother's help with a few troublesome items, such as socks, shoestrings or buckles, and shirts with tight necks. Some mothers try to get their children to dress themselves as soon as possible in order to relieve the mother of this chore. Other mothers like to help the child, and still others are not satisfied with the way the child gets his own clothes on. Apart from the mother's attitude, mothers mentioned that children with an older sibling would often learn from the latter when much parental instruction had been seemingly fruitless. Moreover, all mothers appeared to give lip service at least that the child should learn to dress himself when he showed himself ready.

Of the children in our sample, some liked to dress themselves and resented help from the mother. Others asked for or were pleased to have the mother's help. If, as often happened, a child was dawdling with his dressing and the mother wanted to take him someplace, she would often take over and do it for him. Some remarks made by the mothers about the children dressing themselves follow:

I didn't set any time, I just waited until she wanted to do it. I was trying to teach her to tie at a time when I thought she should know but she didn't learn it even though I worked and worked, and then about a year later she started doing it. I found that true with her in almost everything.

I guess I did get him to dress himself by the time to go to school, but the other boobs I had to dress. On tying shoes his younger sister did it before he did and he finally got shamed into it, although he could have done it if he'd wanted to bother.

I dressed him longer than you should dress a child. As you can see, he's been babied. When he started I just helped and then I'd say, "Let's see you go; see if you can be a big man," and then I'd help him. He could do it by himself, but I like to help him.

She can dress herself, but I don't let her if I can help it. She gets everything on backwards.

Among the boys in the sample, the earliest reported time of starting to dress oneself was 1½ to 2 years of age. The latest age for completing taking over this responsibility was 6. Girls, in general, started dressing

Main street, Orchard Town.

*Modern dwelling
showing frontyard
with carriage and playpen.*

Five-month-old boy in playpen in front of house.

Sisters painting at kitchen table, ages 4½ and 3½.

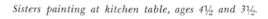

*Old style
New England dwelling.*

Family saying grace before evening meal.

After dinner in Orchard Town living room.

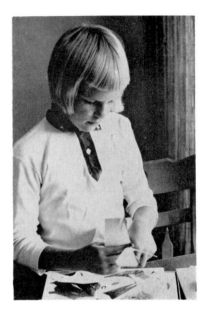

*Seven-year-old girl
cutting out models of birds.*

Children watching TV.

*Mother feeding
3-months-old infant.*

*Eight-year-old girl entertaining
neighbor's 2-year-old boy.*

Nine-year-old girl playing hospital.

Eight-year-old girl with family pet.

Father and son launching model plane.

Brothers and sisters playing in backyard,
showing swing set, wading pool, and sandbox.

themselves a little earlier and took over the responsibility completely sooner than did boys. Four girls were reported as starting to dress themselves at 2 to 2½ years. In any case, it is considered that children should be able to dress themselves by the time they start to school, and this ideal is usually achieved in plenty of time for most items of clothing.

MODESTY

Apart from the problem of getting clothes on the children, there is the further problem of keeping them on. At this age the children themselves are aware of the rules for modesty but lack enough motivation to observe them at all times. On hot summer days or in the warmth of the well-heated homes, the young children are tempted to remove all or some of their clothes. Besides the desire for physical comfort there is a fair amount of conscious exhibitionism, which the children try to conceal from adults, not always successfully. One boy aged 4 was observed showing his penis to a girl about the same age, and both were giggling. At this particular time they did not happen to be caught. One mother told proudly how her son had reported similar acts by his friends (he himself disapproving), while another mother merely commented, "Oh, all boys have to do that." Another mother reported that she had had to speak a couple of times to her two daughters, aged 4 and 7, who had turned upside down in front of their older brother, aged 12.

Most parents do not react so strongly to the child exposing himself at home among the family, but improper exposure by children outside the home is something parents appear to be very much concerned with, although they also subscribe to the belief that one "should not make an issue of modesty." We would conclude that in this area ideal and actual behavior are widely separated.

For instance, one mother who reported that she never made an issue of modesty told how she had made her daughter, when small, walk down the street naked in punishment for taking her clothes off outside repeatedly. One case was recorded of a mother keeping a 3-year-old girl in the house for a week as punishment for undressing outside. Almost all parents said that although they were not concerned with modesty, their neighbors were.

Within the home most (but not all) parents take reasonable precautions so that their children do not see them naked. Locks are always found on bathroom doors and are frequently used. However, they try not to make an issue of this also. They feel that the last generation of parents was too strict. This generation of parents feels that they have the "casual" approach.

My mother and father were the type who never let their children see them without their clothes on, and they wouldn't so much as kiss each other on the mouth in front of us—no demonstrativeness. I'm not that extreme. I believe that if your children come into the room and you are putting your clothes on that you should go on about it casually and not make an issue of it. That way they don't think anything about it. My children take it as a casual thing.

MEALS AND DIET

When the preschool child comes to breakfast in the morning, mother is generally in the kitchen, father has left for work, and, if he has older brothers or sisters, they have usually already left for school. Very few families eat their breakfasts together. Some preschoolers often get their own breakfast if it is simple enough (toast or dry cereal). Mothers want their children to have "balanced diets," but breakfast alone does not have to include all the necessary food elements. One mother said she did not worry about what her child ate for breakfast so long as she drank her orange juice and milk.

Children and other members of the family all get three meals a day and generally eat them on schedule, although schedules vary somewhat from family to family. In contrast to breakfast, lunch is almost always eaten together, except that the father is usually absent. The evening dinner is the most elaborate meal except on Sundays, when the noon meal may be larger.

Standards for table manners vary from family to family, but all families have some behavior on which they insist. These apply especially to the evening meal when the whole family is together. Proper table manners are seen as making the child more acceptable socially. This is clearly illustrated by one mother.

I don't often praise them but when children are here who don't have good table manners, I'll say, "Now, you see, you don't like that. Now you know what other people think when you go out in public and don't eat right."

Some of the activities which are socially unacceptable at the table are listed by this mother.

Now I have been beginning to give her a little salad, which is all tossed, and I let her pick out the onion. I say, "Well, just put it to one side and don't speak about it. I'll beat the brains out of the next one that makes one of those disgusting noises" [laughing]. I try to keep control over the conversation. Of course, they do forget. . . . I feel that I should give way a little bit, but I don't because I feel that if they're going to sit at the table with us I have to insist for my sake. Now my son is the one who will drop food onto the table. My daughter doesn't. She doesn't like to have to chew up meat either. . . . I have told her that things don't look nice and I suppose I make a face. . . . I think they do want to imitate too, don't you know, and they do like to go out occasionally too, and I'll say, "Well, I don't see how you expect us to take you out to a restaurant if you can't do so and so. . . ." I just ask her to do it. I don't have to get after her too much. And, of course, I do overlook. If it's something like putting her arms up in the air, and I just wanta break her of the habit I poke her and whisper at her and that's partly so that my son won't make any remarks, because he's highly scornful in his way with her. So I make believe I'm her pal in telling her so he won't. Just like if you whisper in nursery school the kids will shut up."

Most children are subject to considerable pressure from their parents to eat a "balanced diet" at meals. Children may be required to eat certain foods considered especially critical nutritionally, such as milk, meat, and vegetables. Some families have the rule that a child must at least taste everything on his plate. One family was reported to let the child eat what he pleased every day of the week, but on Sunday he was required to "clean his plate." Parents also try to get children to eat by persuasion, telling them how good the food tastes or how much it will do for them. "Carrots make your hair curly" was heard from one grandmother, although most mothers would probably try to be more "scientific" than this and say something about vitamins, minerals, and proteins.

Some mothers forbid eating between meals, but more allowed snacks now and then. One child in the sample seemed free to climb up and get food from shelves or take it from the refrigerator whenever he chose. One mother was never heard to refuse food to her children whenever they asked. However, many mothers try to limit the amount of food a child has between meals in order to get him to eat his meals.

Families differed greatly on giving sweets to children, although nearly every child was reported to have a "sweet tooth" and was subject to some restrictions as to quantity and occasion. Parents believe that eating too many sweet things tends to produce tooth decay, destroys the appetite for more wholesome foods, and may lead to an undesired obesity. There are generally restrictions on eating candy, cookies, or ice cream immediately before meals, and permission for eating them after meals may depend on eating certain required foods at mealtime. Some mothers never brought a sweet into the house so as not to tempt the child with them. In some families it was taboo for the observer to give either gum or lollypops to children, while in others it was allowed as a special treat, and in still others the mother trusted the observer's discretion.

One of the latter mothers always had a large supply of lollypops and ice cream, and her children were in general indifferent to these. This was the mother mentioned above who was never seen to refuse her children food. Although she was exceptional in her methods, we have no reason to suspect that she disagreed with the general view that children should not eat too many sweets. Perhaps she could be so permissive partly because her children had not developed a craving for sweets.

All children, even those given considerable freedom in between-meal snacks, are taught not to ask for food at neighbors' houses. One mother said with pride that she knew she could trust her daughter not to ask for something even though she might want it very much. Even the ceremonial begging which takes place at Halloween called "Trick or Treat" make some parents nervous. Some parents, especially those who try to restrict eating between meals, are angry if a neighbor offers a child food. Neighbors who do give food to others' children try to ascertain in advance how the mother feels about this and follow her wishes. The neighbor may also check apologetically with the mother later to make sure she has not done wrong.

TOILET TRAINING

Toilet training is generally well under way by late infancy, but certain refinements continue to be taught into the preschool period. Many children of this age wet their pants from time to time. Punishment for such a slip is often severe. Younger preschool children may call their mothers to wipe their bottoms after defecating, although they normally learn to do this themselves before entering school. They are also taught during this period to close the door when they go to the toilet, flush it after they are finished, and wash their hands. When a child goes to the bathroom, the mother often listens for the noise of the toilet and faucet. If she does not hear them, she reminds the child, who generally obeys without too much fuss. Constipation and irregularity in defecation (ideally once a day after breakfast) continue to be regarded as a problem with some children. Anal suppositories and enemas may continue to be used, but the mere threat of them is more frequent than actual use, and this is often sufficient to "inspire" the child to defecate.

RELATIONSHIP TO MOTHER

The preschool child continues to spend most of his time under the supervision of his mother in some sense, although some of this supervision is rather nominal, as when the mother is busy with housework and the child playing outside in his own or a close neighbor's yard.

Some children spend much of their time during the day tagging along after their mothers around the house. Mothers vary in their reaction to this. Some mothers say they cannot work if a child is anywhere near them. Others like having the child ironing nearby on a toy ironing board as the weekly ironing is being done or having a small boy on a chair beside them deciding for the mother what kind of a "fence" to put around a pie.

All children see enough of their mothers at work to learn how to do some simple tasks, and from time to time they ask to be allowed to do these. The mother is often too busy and refuses, but if the task is not dangerous, and if she is not too pressed for time, she may let the child take over. Most such work is considered to be more for the child's amusement and for the long-run value of his character than for any immediate practical value. Speed and perfection are not expected. One mother said:

> You give them something to do. If it's something new you don't know how well they're capable of doing it. If they get it done you know they tried. That goes with the child. Some child might get it done quicker and well. You can't criticize the child who tries and doesn't do it as well, if they've tried as hard.

CHORES

Children of this age are at times required to do a few chores, however. They are expected to pick up their toys at times, although not without prompting. If the mother is in a hurry with her housework, she may send the child to fetch things elsewhere around the house. Some children are asked to take their dishes off the table. A child who would regularly do these or other chores without reminders is unimaginable to Orchard Town mothers. There is, moreover, no rule that a child must do any chore regularly and unfailingly. Mothers say, "I'm afraid I feel that the important thing is to know they can do it." However, if a child refuses to do small chores like this when requested, he will be scolded, and punishment or threats are often applied, although it is thought desirable to avoid these if possible. With toys to be picked up, for instance, either parent may threaten to throw them away if the child leaves them there.

Even though children do little "work" themselves, they soon learn a sharp distinction between work and play, or being busy and free, by observing their mothers and other adults. And they can see the contrast between the tense face of a mother who has gone through a stretch of housework and child care, and the vivacious face of one who has been attending a club meeting with her friends. From such observations and from casual remarks the child learns that much work is considered unpleasant by adults. The mother's irregularity and reluctance in assigning her children chores probably communicate the same lesson in a different way.

INDOOR ACTIVITIES

Young children have a number of unsupervised indoor activities in which they may engage by themselves while their mother is "busy" at various times between breakfast and evening meal. They may play indoors for limited periods when the weather is good or all day when it is bad. When playing indoors they sometimes play by themselves and sometimes with one or two children of close neighbors. However, mothers usually do not allow groups of more than two or three children to play together indoors, for they are considered to be too noisy and hard to control.

GAMES

Some young children are fond of playing various purchased board games when the weather is bad. In these the players move counters along toward the goal on the basis of some chance mechanism. We saw some very simplified board games which children of the age of 4 and up seemed to understand sufficiently to play. Small children play these sometimes with their friends and other times with older members of their family.

Drawing is a common indoor activity. Children start scribbling on paper at a rather early age. They are left alone with crayons and pencils as soon as they have learned not to draw on the walls or furniture. Children enjoy coloring books, which their parents may buy for them. In Sunday School children regard coloring and drawing as activities which are more enjoyable than the regular educational activities. Parents generally react to the children's drawings with indiscriminate praise and amusement. Coloring books in which children fill in outline pictures with crayons are especially popular.

TOYS

Children of Orchard Town, like most American children, have a large number of toys to play with. There are certain toys or playthings which it is felt that all children should have and which, in fact, nearly all children do have. There are others which only a few children have. In the opinion of the majority of adults in the community, children with many more toys than average are "spoiled" or in danger of being spoiled.

Many of the toys are used indoors part or all of the time. Most important are blocks, artificial stuffed animals, miniature trucks and cars. For girls, dolls and accessories are important, while for boys, toy pistols and guns are very popular, and toy soldiers and accessories are also fairly common. Girls also often want toy pistols and borrow them from boys, although parents hesitate to give girls this sort of thing. Most people agree that boys should not play with true (human) dolls, although stuffed animals are regarded as suitable toys for small boys. As soon as children learn to walk they are given variously shaped toys with wheels to pull around or push. These are perhaps more toys of late infancy than early childhood. Older preschool children do not play with these "walking" toys much.

Toy musical instruments are a fairly common sort of toy but are rarely used as practice instruments for learning how to play adult musical instruments. Their main significance is as noise makers, often to the annoyance of the parents who originally presented them to their children.

Young children, particularly, often break their toys, and this is a source of chagrin to the parents. Breakage is punished only verbally, usually with such remarks as "You won't get another one."

PETS

Most of the children in our sample had pets of some sort. About half had dogs, and somewhat fewer had cats. Two families had horses, and the children of these families were popular with the other children for this as well as other reasons. The children of neighbors enjoyed watching the horses even when they did not ride on them. Some families had lesser forms of pets, such as rabbits, hamsters, parakeets, canaries, goldfish, and tropical fish.

Dogs and cats are the objects alternately of rough affection and wrath from young children. It is considered important to train children not to abuse them. Children are taught early not to anger dogs, and adults try to restrain pets to protect both the children and the animals. People express pity for animals who are subjected to the pummeling of young children. Most of these household pets have gentle natures, in contrast to the aggressive and hungry dogs found in many societies. One child in the community had maltreated his pet dog, which died as a result. This child was criticized bitterly, and the criticism was recollected and renewed when the child was given a new dog a few years later.

TELEVISION

One important indoor activity, which is new with this generation of children, is watching television. Many children in the sample spent much time each morning watching "Ding Dong School" at 10:00 A.M., and "Big Brother" at 12:15. One boy, aged 4, regularly joined Big Brother in his daily salute to the flag and toast to President Eisenhower with a glass of milk. He became very angry with his mother if his milk was not on hand for the occasion. Some children answered questions Miss Frances asked them on "Ding Dong School" as though they could really talk to her. This was a source of some learning, especially of etiquette.

Parents had not made up their minds how they felt about television. Some thought their children progressed rapidly in understanding and speaking because of it. An older woman criticized, "When I was young we made our own good time; now the children sit glued to television." Most parents of preschool children, however, allowed them considerable freedom in watching television during the daytime. In general, when they were allowed indoors, they were allowed to watch television, although they were encouraged to spend much time outdoors in acceptable weather.

OUTSIDE PLAY

Parents encourage their children to play outside in the yard as much as possible except in wet or very cold weather. There is somewhat less freedom about going outside in winter because it is necessary to put on warm clothes. The parents want the children outside for their health, as they say, for the "fresh air and sunshine" *and also* for "peace and quiet" in the house. Orchard Town parents especially urge their children to play outside, and perhaps the community attracts residents who want this for their children. Except for infants, play in the yard is not usually supervised by an adult. However, for children of preschool age there is always an adult in the house, usually the mother. Even small children may be put out in the yard to play in good weather while the mother goes about her work inside, listening for the child's cry.

The area in which the child is free to move at will increases gradually as he grows older. For a child to the age of 3 or 4, this may be only a few yards adjoining his own yard. Playing away from home is somewhat controlled by the environment. Some children live in more dangerous environments than others. Also, some children live great distances from places where they might play with other children. Most of the 4-year-olds are allowed to go across a quiet street to play. Until they go to school, however, most children stay at home or in neighbors' yards to play. One 4-year-old girl goes to the store, across a busy street, about two blocks from home. She seems to be entirely reliable and capable. Crossing streets which have been forbidden, playing with knives and matches, and going long distances from home without permission are all severely punished.

PLAYMATES

When preschool children play outside, they are most commonly playing with one or a few other young children. During school hours their playmates are necessarily of about the same age, but during vacation or after school they often tag along after the younger schoolchildren, who condescend to pay them some attention if they are not too busy.

Nearly all young children have tricycles, and many also have wagons and scooters. The tricycles, which are very popular, are invariably called "bikes" by their owners and often by older children and adults. However, true two-wheeled bicycles are not generally obtained until the child reaches school age. Preschool children spend much of their time "going places" with their tricycles or wagons, although these places are within a strictly delimited area close to the home.

Preschool children either have a sandbox or sandpile of their own or have access to one in a neighbor's yard and spend much time making roads, bridges, and tunnels, over and through which they run toy trucks and cars. At other times they also mold the sand into animal figures, houses, "cupcakes," and so on. For these purposes they use either special toy shovels, buckets, and molds or various kitchen utensils.

In their play in the sandbox, children get into arguments from time to time over the use of toys. These arguments are nearly always about taking turns, not about ownership. The children know remarkably well who owns which toy. They will remember ownership of new-found toys which have been lost in the bushes for months. The arguments sometimes degenerate into fights, but any loud screaming usually brings out the mother in whose yard the children are playing. Mothers encourage their children to share their toys and be generous, but they also encourage proper care of toys and respect for the property rights of other children. At the end of the day major toys should be returned to the owner's home.

THEFT

The children's attitudes toward each other's toys reflect the general respect for property rights which parents strive to instill in them. Taking something belonging to another, even as a teasing gesture, usually brings a reprimand from the parents if they see it, and intentional theft brings more severe punishment. A typical punishment would be for the parent to accompany the culprit in returning the stolen goods to the owner with an apology. In one instance the mother of the culprit in addition prohibited her child from visiting the owner's house again. Children who have a reputation for thievery are also watched carefully by former victims, who usually discourage or prevent them from entering their houses more than other children.

In spite of punishments and reprimands, there is a considerable amount of petty theft by some children in the community. Some children, preschool and older, are given to theft of small amounts of candy from the local stores. Some adults feel that preschool children should not be punished too severely for occasional thefts of this sort, for it is considered that they "do not understand yet." Theft between children, as distinguished from "borrowing without request," appears to be considerably rarer than theft from adults and is controlled by the children themselves as well as by parents.

Preschool children, especially the younger ones, play few if any formal organized games with each other of the sort which school-age children play. The boys, however, tag along with the older children playing "Cowboys" and shoot their toy pistols imitatively. Young boys, but not girls, do a fair amount of playful wrestling with each other, an activity which continues on into school age.

PLAY GROUPS AND FRIENDS

In general, children of this age play with whatever other young children live close to them. There is some split by sex when enough playmates are available, but there is little restriction according to status differences of parents. However, children give signs of being aware of status differences at an early age. We noticed that one boy, aged 4, identified the make of a large number of cars, which are important symbols of status. He was also concerned about which cars are better and repeatedly informed the ethnographers, "Our Oldsmobile can crash your old Nash."

Although mothers are little concerned about the social prestige of the families of the young children's playmates, they do not consider all playmates equally desirable. But the discrimination is primarily along the lines of character and manners rather than wealth or prestige of parents, although wealth and prestige do influence adult relationships. A "fresh," "sneaky," or "cynical" playmate is a "bad influence" which might affect the child's character unfavorably if he associated too much with such a friend. Mothers do not as a rule overtly forbid all contact with "bad influences," but discourage them.

Well, there have been a lot of friends. I don't believe you should say, "You can't play with this one and you can't play with that one." That sort of drives them to it. I have told them why I don't like certain children. There are a few around here, I didn't say she can't play with them. I don't like them around. Now I like to have her play with Sue. They seem to get along good together. . . . Meg's [a sneaky child] the one I really would rather she didn't play with. I don't tell her that, I just don't want Meg in my house again. If they play they can play outside. I don't care too much for the Roe kids, but they don't come here often.

Some mothers who find that their children are playing too much with "bad influences" arrange at times to have the children pay visits to "good influences" in friends' homes.

Parents want their children to be popular with their playmates and not be bullies, but they also want them to "stand up for their rights" enough so they will not be mistreated. Parents allow more antisocial behavior toward children they do not approve of. A child who was unpopular with adults was observed being excluded from a game of tag by an older boy. The parent of the older boy was present and ignored this. This was incongruent with this parent's stated values. The unpopularity of the victim was evidently the parent's reason for ignoring the act.

Young children are apt to demand their own way when playing with children their own age. Mothers said that they do not interfere under these circumstances unless someone gets hurt or angry. However, they urge children to "take turns" having their own way with each other. They also point out repeatedly that other children will not like them if they are "bossy" or do not let other children "have a turn." When someone goes home angry, one mother says, "I don't blame them, when are you gonna learn to take turns?" Mothers are proud if their children are "able to be bossy without antagonizing friends."

SPECIAL ACTIVITIES

The preschool child's daily routine of informal, unsupervised play is interrupted at times by special activities with the mother or, on weekends and in vacation, with other members of the family. When the mother goes to buy groceries or on other errands, she generally takes her young child along if there is no one at home to baby-sit.

It is customary for women with young children to visit each other. These visits and similar visits to the child's home by other women provide an occasion for training the child in certain elements of etiquette. Children are instructed to make a little polite conversation with the members of the family whom they visit and especially to thank them for the "nice time" on leaving. Punishment for bad manners is not lacking. A child who broke wind when one of us was present was instructed to apologize and leave the room immediately and to go to the toilet. The same child had a piece of gum taken away from her when she forgot to say "thank you." Preschool children taken along at these times are expected to play more or less by themselves and not interrupt adult conversation or activities. If possible, children should leave the room when adults want to talk to each other; this is partly to avoid interruptions. Some mothers excused short interruptions on the ground that children forget what they are going to say so quickly.

Besides these visits and errands where the child is an appendage to an adult there are some special recreational excursions more specifically for the child's entertainment. Parents may take young children to museums, zoos, the circus when it visits a nearby city, to the movies, or other shows in the city. During the summer many children spend much time swimming in the local ponds. Here they are usually under nominal adult supervision, that is, an adult is in sight, will tell them not to go out too far in the water, to come out if they seem to be getting cold, but otherwise will do little in the way of supervision of specific activity. Mothers are responsible for most of these recreational excursions, but the father may also be involved on weekends or during his vacation.

RELATIONSHIP TO SIBLINGS

In the middle afternoon, after a nap if any, older brothers and sisters and other older neighborhood children come home from school. Some older siblings are old enough for the mother to leave in charge of the preschool child while she goes on an errand. Children under 12 are not considered capable of having complete charge of a small child. Five or 6 years age difference is not considered to be enough to make an older sibling a good disciplinarian. However, such siblings are often left in charge of younger brothers and sisters for short periods with varying expectations. The mother will direct the older child "to correct, but not to punish"; "to watch and protect but not to punish; I'll take care of that when I get home." One mother gives stronger authority to the oldest sibling, "If she is put in charge the younger child is told she must mind her." A 12-year-old boy, who is often left in charge of three younger sisters, is said by his mother to be "an old crab and demands more than necessary when sitting . . . the kids resent it if it's unreasonable."

Older children are expected to report on dangerous undertakings or major disobediences of their younger brothers and sisters, but they must be careful not to "tell on" them too much. With less serious offenses, the parents are more liable to reprimand the tale bearer rather than the offender. Older children are not usually allowed to hit or hurt a younger one unless the younger one "asks for it." Asking for it consists of prolonged teasing or using a valued possession of an older sibling without permission. The general attitude here is stated by one mother, who says:

> Jeffrey [3 years old] sometimes slams little Raymond one. Last night they were sitting at the table and Raymond did something Jeffrey didn't like and Jeffrey hit him. I'm always saying to him, "You're not his mother; you leave him alone. I'll punish him."

Brothers and sisters who are only a couple of years apart are felt to have important relations which affect the development of each. They may amuse, teach, encourage, or "tattle" on each other. Two brothers, three years apart, amuse each other. "When they are in bed they sing and tell stories to each other and they then go to sleep." Sometimes these two help each other. A girl of 7 and her brother, aged 5, were often in a teacher-pupil relation. The mother of this boy and girl tells how this worked out.

> We have certain restrictions. We had to take the books out of the bookcase so the children wouldn't pull them out. Cynthia crawled and Charlie did not. But it was easier to train Charlie not to pull out the books because Cynthia would interest him in something else. Cynthia learned the alphabet from her blocks [and a baby sitter]. Later she sang the ABC song to Charlie. She has taught him to print and has tried to teach him to write, but I don't encourage that.

In another case the youngest of three girls does very advanced things for her age. The mother feels that the older girls are responsible for the rapid progress.

> Gail [aged 4] counts by 2's to 12 and by 10's to 100. She's been doing this for some time. It's funny to hear these things coming out of such a little thing. She picks them up from her older sisters. I didn't teach them to her.

Jealousy is thought to be the natural thing between siblings of close age if one receives some attention from the parents that the other does not. Parents try not to give one something without doing the same for the other.

A few extra years often tend to make an older sibling what parents consider to be "officious" toward his younger brothers and sisters. Such officious older siblings often act as the voice of conscience for all younger children in the family. Many older siblings are often very generous toward young brothers and sisters. Older children sometimes like to give the younger ones the benefits they feel they missed as children.

RELATIONSHIP TO FATHER

In the evening shortly before supper the father usually comes home. Three fathers in the sample traveled in their work and were home only a part of each week. Other fathers were occasionally away on business. On the other hand, seven sample fathers had jobs which allowed their children to accompany them at times during the week. These included tree work, selling eggs and produce house to house, painting, and construction.

The behavior of fathers toward their children is as varied as the time which they spend with them. Some fathers are enthusiastic about their work and spend little time at home and less still with their children. Others are felt to have a "tough row to hoe," and the mother may take as much responsibility around the home as she can to lighten their load. She may ask the children to leave the father in peace when he is at home. Still other fathers seek out their children and try to relieve the mother of duties, especially if there are a number of preschool children in the family.

Some fathers like to roughhouse with their children, and these especially enjoy preschool children. They would be afraid of treating a fragile infant in this way.

On weekends and in their brief vacations almost all fathers do odd jobs around their homes—repairs, mowing the lawn, or other heavy work in the yard. Most families own their homes, and the men seem to enjoy working around the house. The children, especially the boys, may tag along and help a little if the father is willing.

The father may also do some "baby-sitting" at times when he is home while the mother goes on errands or participates in womens' groups.

RELATIONSHIP TO ADULTS OUTSIDE THE FAMILY

Relations with adults outside the family are limited mostly to certain relatives and the mothers of playmates whom the preschool child visits. Each mother soon learns the standards which her neighbors set for their children, and most women conscientiously try to support each other in these matters. In emergencies neighbors occasionally help each other out with baby-sitting on a roughly reciprocal basis. However, it is expected that normally the mother herself will be responsible for her child and will be close enough so that she can hear him scream if he is in trouble.

GRANDMOTHERS

Many families have a grandmother or an aunt living nearby, who occasionally or frequently assumes the role of caretaker for the children. Some of these are almost complete mother substitutes, but others can be trusted with only the smallest child-care duties. Many grandparents, contrary to our expectations, are either ineffective or unwilling caretakers of their grandchildren. However, when a relative is involved in child-training, it is most usually the mother's mother. In six families in the sample, the mother's mother had occasional or frequent care of her grandchildren. Parents' sisters, brothers, and parents' aunts are sometimes reported as assisting in child care.

Grandmothers do not always love their grandchildren whole-heartedly. One grandmother was convinced that the observers represented substantiation of her own claim that the grandchild needed a psychiatrist. And some grandchildren do not like their grandparents.

My father's mother was a very funny person. I did not love her at all. She didn't let us call her Grandmother. We had to call her Nanna. She didn't want anybody to know she was a grandmother.

Pleasant relations with grandparents, however, are also frequent. One mother says, "All three of my children love my husband's mother to pieces. She is very good to them." One grandfather pleases his daughter-in-law: "But Grandpa doesn't think a child is good for much unless he works. It doesn't do children any harm to have the training like that [working with grandfather]."

If both parents and grandparents are present, discipline is generally left to the parents. Many mothers resent correction of their children by a grandparent. Others will allow it in the house of the grandparent. One grandparent, a mother's mother, who lived with the family, often "scolded" her grandchildren. The mother of the family said, "I think one person scolding a kid is enough, but sometimes we all get going and the kid gets off."

Although a grandmother often does not approve of the mother's discipline, she usually does not take disciplinary action herself. If grandparents have charge of a child, they generally try to distract the child rather than discipline him. Grandparents who want grandchildren to visit them report to the parent that the child "was wonderful."

BABY SITTERS

If a close relative is not available, all families will have a neighbor or a baby sitter who will take the mother's place on occasion. Some mothers only have a "sitter" in extreme emergencies; others will have one three or four hours each day. Baby sitters must be 12 years old to be left alone with a child, and preferably older. An unacceptable baby sitter is a girl who invites her male friends into the child's home while she is sitting. Mothers do not wish to be responsible for what may happen to a young girl under such circumstances. Some mothers will only have a baby sitter after the children are asleep, but this is not general.

In the new areas of town there are a number of groups of women who exchange baby sitting, especially daytime sitting, when a young child may be "parked" at a neighbor's house. Such a mother would be considered the most competent baby sitter.

There are a very few young male baby sitters in the town. These are all boys under 17 years of age, often relatives. Sometimes a kindly older woman will baby-sit for her younger women friends at no charge. Mothers generally would not call on such a woman except in an emergency, when no one else was available.

Baby sitters have varying authority. They are expected to see that the children behave but usually have no authority to punish. One mother, however, views this authority as necessary. "I tell the sitter she may, if she has to, spank. I know how kids can nag at you until you want just one swat." Another mother tells how her most frequent baby sitter "talks rough, but the children know how she means it."

While none of the preschool children in our sample were attending regular kindergarten during the course of our study, some did attend the Sunday School kindargarten or nursery while their parents went to church or their older brothers and sisters attended Sunday School proper. Little is demanded of preschool children in Sunday School. In the main, an effort is made to amuse them and keep them quiet so that they will not interfere with other activities. The main educational value of the Sunday School nursery and kindergarten is thought to be in accustoming the child to regular church attendance. When first left in the church nursery by their parents, many children cry loud and long. If it is warm weather and the windows are open, the crying can be heard plainly in the church, and the mother may have to return and quiet the child or remove him.

MOTHER'S ATTITUDE TOWARD
HER PARENTAL RESPONSIBILITIES

During the preschool period the mother continues to be the most important person in the child's life, although playmates, older siblings, and the father are of increasing importance. The mothers themselves accept the cultural doctrine of the importance of their child-care responsibilities, especially for younger children. Even when mother takes time off from these duties, she does so, ideally, for short periods when responsibilities are at a minimum. Thus many women report proudly that, "No one else has ever put my children to bed," or "No one else has ever had to feed my children." Mothers are supposed to supply love for their children. They are almost wholly responsible for their children's well-being—physical, mental, social.

Of course, none of the mothers studied conformed perfectly to their ideals of maternal behavior in actual practice. There are those who enjoy their responsibilities more than others and who make more elaborate and careful plans for their children. There are others who perform their duties with resignation. One woman reported that she "finally realized that I would have to give up my personal ambitions for the sake of the happiness of the whole family" and that she would have to accept this sacrifice more cheerfully. For the first few years she reported that she had found herself moody and discontented, clinging to her private ambitions.

Most mothers are able to express their own feelings toward the role they occupy. They say, "I often think I should never have been a mother" or "This is what I waited for all my life." Mothers often quite freely admit feelings of guilt in regard to responsibilities; they assign their failures to emotional or personal factors in themselves. They are constantly assessing their performances in terms of some ideal standard. The sanctions on the mother's behavior are important in this constant assessment. If mothers step beyond community standards, the force of gossip comes into play. A woman does not necessarily hear the gossip about herself, but she may imagine it from her private assessment of her own performance. It is not unusual for gossip to be repeated to her by a "friend." Whether or not a mother hears the stories told about her, she knows that no one is free from this sort of criticism, and she may hear others criticized for acts which she knows she has performed herself. From minor hints she may make conclusions which lead her to shift her behavior slightly. But the chief punisher of most deviating mothers is their own conscience.

If something happens to a mother, a substitute must be found immediately. Most people in the community cannot afford a paid mother substitute, and therefore a widower quickly remarries. There were no unmarried men with young children in the town. However, it is felt by most that no one is really able to substitute for the actual mother. Here is a statement by a woman who experienced a step-mother.

My true mother died when I was little and my stepmother was not very much of a success. I don't think stepmothers usually are, do you? I have called both my stepmothers by their first names. Definitely not "Mother"! I think you only have one mother. Not that I didn't like them. They were both all right, but they didn't take the place of my own mother.

MOTHER-CHILD INTERACTION

Analysis of behavioral observations collected during the study indicates that the mother's interaction with her preschool child is more generally involved with controlling the child by suggestions, command, or discipline than she is with helping. The behavioral observations also indicate that the more negative the mother is in dealing with the child—by negative we mean refusals of permission, criticism, etc.—the more negative the child is in response to the mother. There is also some indication that a mother is more likely to "push" a son in his activities than to push a daughter. In addition, the male children in the sample were much less verbal than the female children. Mothers are apt to try to draw out such a quiet son.

AUTHORITY OF THE FATHER

While the mother is in all families in charge of the preschool child more than the father by virtue of the fact that she is present more, in over half the families in our sample the father was said to exercise considerable authority over the child when he was present. Where this occurs it is a change from infancy, where the father, whatever his relations with his wife, has little to do with the child except occasional play and minor caretaking. In eight of the sample families the father tended to take the entire responsibility for discipline when he was around. On the other hand, in ten families the mother continued to do the disciplining even in the father's presence, while in the remainder the two parents shared authority.

When the authority is divided, the father will usually be the one to take final action. A mother who feels that she has been unsuccessful in getting her children to behave may invoke the father's name: "When Dad hears about this he's gonna be cross too," "I'll tell Dad when he gets home," "Do you want me to tell your Daddy?" "Your father will hear about this." Children are said to react differently. Some are afraid of father learning about bad behavior; others say, "Go ahead and tell him." In some families, as one woman says, "I would be wasting my breath saying 'wait until Daddy gets home,' because they know nothing's gonna happen when Daddy gets home."

Even when this technique is effective, mothers show some reluctance to invoke the father's name. It is generally felt that children should be punished on the spot as they misbehave, and it is an admission of failure for the mother to have to threaten the father's punishment. Moreover, some fathers seem to resent this disruption of their own relationship with the children, and some mothers are reluctant to call on their husbands for fear that they may punish the children too severely. One mother compared her own techniques of discipline to her husband's in describing the following incident:

Tim broke a window at the neighbors. It was on a Thursday that he threw a stone and broke the window. The neighbor said to him, "Until you tell your mother you can't come back and play here." But Tim just stayed home and didn't tell us. Finally on Sunday the neighbor told us. I talked to my husband. Spanking wouldn't have done any good then; it was too long afterwards. My husband said we should take money from his allowance until it was paid for. But I said his punishment had been the scolding and not playing with the neighbor's boys. My husband would like to spank. Tim doesn't like to be spanked. . . . My husband has a heavy voice and it makes the children fear him. I say, you don't want them to fear you. We feared our father. . . . My husband is in favor of punishment. He thinks if they do something bad you should spank 'em or shake 'em to pieces. I don't see it that way.

The father's name is most often invoked in his absence when something in his precinct has been violated by the child, such as the use of his forbidden tools. One woman says that it is no use side-stepping most issues by mentioning father and so, "I use him on his hard and fast rules—just on the things he's strict on—he's a great one to say, 'Go ask your mother.' "

The relations between the parents are affected by the amount of discipline and care each is responsible for, and these relations in turn affect the children. The observers felt that almost all women with husbands who refused or participated grudgingly in child care and training had some resentment toward their husbands. This may be largely displaced onto the child, who is felt to be too much of a burden. The mildest cases of resentment are expressed by the women as "understanding" father's refusal to participate while still not liking it. More extreme cases of resentment often result in much bitterness.

Whatever the distribution between parents of authority over children, most parents agree that it is important to conceal disagreements from the children and present a united front. However, in at least half of the families indications were noted of some overt disagreement between parents as to standards of children's behavior. This seems to be especially characteristic of the early years of marriage.

RESPECT TO ADULTS

It is during the preschool period when most parents attempt to start instilling respect for adults. Tantrums, immoderate crying, or any open aggression against a parent, verbal or physical, all meet with parent's opposition.

Tantrums occur occasionally in preschool children, although in full-blown form they are rare or nonexistent in most school-age children. The common belief that they appear more frequently with a child whose mother indulges demands made in tantrums seems to be well justified. At an early age the mother may laugh tolerantly at the child's tantrums, but as school age approaches, more severe punishments are used. A teacher in a kindergarten to which a few North Village children had gone said:

Once in a while one has a tantrum, and you would have to pick them up bodily [and remove them from the room]. There should be no raising of the voice [of the teacher] except to make oneself heard. [Laughs]. [Mothers of children of this age would be less restrained.]

More common than full temper tantrums among children of this age is a tendency toward fussy crying when frustrated in some desire by a parent. All parents find this annoying at some point and come to feel somewhat like the mother who said: "That gets my goat; I mean fussy crying, not if he's really hurt. I get cross myself." Crying can be ignored by some parents, and is, when it is "attention crying," but more mothers are impelled to take some action.

She used to scream when I tried to correct her. So I'd take her into our great big bathroom and say, "Well, if you're gonna cry, you can cry in there where I can't hear you." . . . I never could stand a kid screaming when you corrected it. . . . I'll say, "Now you're not gonna start being a cry baby now, are you?" and if she's crying to get her own way, I'll say, "If you cry, I'll spank you." I never have, I don't have to.

Other parents in the same situation feel that crying is a necessity, but nevertheless annoying to the parent, and will tell the child, "Put your hand over your mouth" or "If you must cry, will you please cry in a quieter tone of voice." However, sensitivity is more allowable in girls than boys. Parents apparently sympathize with girls who have hurt feelings but try to get boys to be "brave little fellows."

DIRECT AGGRESSION AGAINST PARENTS

Preschool children at times react to parental frustration by direct aggression against the parents. Any serious attempts at physical aggression are usually punished by spanking or isolation. However, angry remarks by the child may be punished by sarcastic retorts or, occasionally, ignored if not too prolonged and repetitive, or if the child is known to be upset about something. Some parents try at times to eliminate the causes of anger or distract from the conflict situation. About half of the mothers say they want their children to be able to admit it when they are irritated and angry but to control the feeling to the extent that they can reach a reasonable solution to the problem.

Even joking or play aggression toward the parents usually meets with some retaliation. Parents fear joking may get out of hand if not controlled. A little more aggression is allowed toward parents in public because parents are embarrassed to punish a child publicly. One 4-year-old boy sometimes called his mother an "old witch." This was considered to be a family joke, and it is unknown whether the mother punished this in private. One boy showed a lot of fantasy aggression toward his mother. He had many plans to scare her and so on. This was considered funny. One child sometimes speaks of "those lousy parents." Other people are amused by this although they might disapprove of it in their own child.

AGGRESSION TOWARD PEERS

A child's expression of anger toward his peers is much less subject to parental reprimand than anger toward the parents, especially for boys. Arguing and mild physical fighting may even be encouraged by parents as defensive measures if they feel that another child is dominating or bullying their own child. This is especially common with fathers and sons. There are definite parental limits on children's aggression toward peers, however. Children should not use profane or obscene words and must be careful in their fighting not to cause serious permanent injury to the other child. Throwing rocks or using sticks and clubs is generally taboo and severely punished if discovered. Very little attempt is made to control playful aggression of children toward peers as long as it does not degenerate into bullying or result in too much "excitement." In one observation a child busily prepared "poison" clay cookies for a small guest expected in the afternoon. This was considered to be funny. Parents themselves would not participate in such fantasies if asked by their children, and generally pretend not to see or hear them, but they do not overtly censure the child for them.

PARENTAL ATTITUDE TOWARD HAPPINESS

Parents, especially mothers, are concerned that their children should give evidence of happiness and positive emotion. If the child has been to a neighbor's house, the standard questions on return include "Did you have a good time?" If a child appears to be sad about something, or perhaps merely thoughtful, the parent is likely to ask, "What's the matter with you?" and advise the child to smile. If they have time, they may play with him a little to make him feel better.

On the other hand, excessively boisterous good spirits are also frowned on. Parents usually reprimand loud shouting by children, especially if by girls and in the house.

Children anticipating special events often get quite excited, too much so according to some parents. Some were even said to get so excited that they did not enjoy the events themselves. One or two families solve this by not telling the child about the event in advance. Almost all parents take the precaution of not telling children about a prospective event unless it is certain to take place. They feel that the pain of disappointment is too great for children to bear and recall their own disappointments in childhood. One mother said that she was "tempted to paddle" when the child gets "all worked up" but that she restrains herself. Evidently too much excitement is regarded as exhausting and threatening to discipline and scheduling.

The desire to have the child give evidence of happiness is connected with the parents' desire to prove to themselves that they have done their duty and that the child is accordingly developing properly. A related manifestation is a certain amount of encouragement to the child for "showing off" his accomplishments to the parents and interested visitors. Showing off is encouraged more in early childhood than at any other period in the child's life, and most children develop the propensity sufficiently that by the time they enter school controls must be imposed by both parents and teachers. In the preschool period, however, controls on excessively prolonged showing off are relatively mild. The parents may simply cease paying attention to the child, put on a disgusted face, or suggest to him that he is making a fool of himself.

A certain amount of showing off in early childhood is considered desirable in order to overcome the child's shyness of people outside the family, although the term itself, a "show-off" is derogatory. Parents do not want their children to be unnecessarily afraid of anyone or of anything, and showing off develops social courage in the child and may encourage specific learning.

The intentional cultivation of irrational fears of strange people or places as a device for keeping children out of places they should not be is recognized as a possible effective technique but is considered to be lazy and unscrupulous on the part of the adult and damaging to the child's confidence in the world. One mother criticized a relative, saying:

Aunt May used to say to her "Oh don't go in there, it's dark!" . . . You could tell them they might stumble over things without any light on, that they should be careful, but I don't see scaring them that way. She also picked up a fear of mice from May. Even now she has a lot of fears and is scared to go upstairs.

SUMMARY

To summarize the major developments in early childhood (preschool), the child becomes more sociable and develops significant relationships with persons outside his household, especially with the small neighborhood play group, but also with adult neighbors and relatives. Along with this the child acquires fairly good control of overt intense aggression. He can meet an increasing number of needs by himself. Differentiation between boys and girls starts to be important in this period: boys are supposed to be physically aggressive in self-defense while girls are supposed to defend themselves only verbally; boys' pastimes are supposed to be more athletic, while girls are supposed to be more interested in imitating or trying to help their mother.

$$\maltese$$
$$\maltese$$
$$\maltese$$

Chapter 16

First and Second Grades

When a child reaches the age of 6, or just before his sixth birthday, his life changes; he is now eligible for first grade and required by law to attend school. For six hours a day he is away from home with a new adult in charge, a teacher rather than his mother, and a large group of same-aged peers. Most of the time he is confined to one room and is required to sit in a chair for long periods of time, leaving the room only with the permission of the teacher. He must wait his turn to speak and do what is required of him by the teacher and schedule. He is ready to begin his formal training in certain basic skills highly valued by American culture and to receive training in differential sex-role behavior. Schedules and clocks become important pressures in his life.

MORNING ROUTINE

On school days children now have to be prompt about getting up in the morning, for they must be at school on time. One boy, aged 7, is said, during the school year, to wake up at 7:00 along with his parents and have breakfast. He usually dresses, after finishing his breakfast, in time to catch the school bus at 7:55, arriving at school at 8:25.

Another mother reports that her daughter of the same age arises at 6:30. The alarm goes off in the parents' room at 6:45. From 6:45 to 7:30 the children play in their bedroom, playing on their beds often. Breakfast is ready at 7:30; it takes about ten minutes. The girl dresses herself, gets on the school bus at 8:00, and gets to school about 8:25. It is clear that there is not much time for interaction with either parent before leaving for school.

If possible, children of school age are more likely to have bedrooms of their own than preschool children, but, again, most of the children in the sample with siblings of the same sex were sleeping in the same room with them. One mother expressed concern that her daughter, aged 7, still had to sleep in a room with her son, aged 5, because the father had not yet finished off additional sleeping space upstairs in their house.

Children do not generally wash themselves extensively in the morning because they have often had a bath the previous evening and gone to bed clean. However, they may brush their teeth before going off to school.

Most children of school age dress themselves. Mothers feel that it is inappropriate to help them and report feeling guilty if they do. The mother feels she may legitimately help comb hair, or braid it in the case of a girl, and she may button back buttons. A few children in the sample were reported to receive "more help than they should." It is felt that boys of this age are apt to "dawdle" in getting dressed or undressed, a source of irritation to the mother.

Even when children dress themselves, the mother may still lay out the child's clothes for him, although some mothers even allow the children of early school age to pick out their clothes for the day by themselves. One mother felt that her daughter would best learn how to choose suitable combinations of clothes to wear by being given freedom at this age and allowed to experience criticism for poor choices. However, in any case, at this age children are generally not allowed to choose which clothes the mother will buy for them, although she may take into account their preferences.

Some have special "school clothes" for their children, which are worn only in school or when going someplace out of the neighborhood. After school these children then change into "play clothes," with which they may be more careless. Other parents may dress their children as well, but do not have such a marked division between school and play clothes.

Before girls reach school age they sometimes wear trousers to play in, especially in cold weather. However, once they reach school age, they regularly wear skirts, differentiating them clearly in dress from the boys. This sex distinction in dress is one sign suggesting that the early grades of school are regarded as the time when children learn most about public sex roles. Children are not expected to learn about the "facts of life" at this time, but it is thought that they come to recognize the general psychological and behavioral differences between the sexes and learn the appropriate type of behavior for their own sex.

Once a child starts school, eating a good breakfast becomes more important. A typical breakfast for one child consisted of orange juice, cocoa, egg, or cereal. The "energy" from breakfast is supposed to last the child through the morning at school. With a preschooler this is less of a problem, for the mother may allow a snack or arrange an early lunch if she feels the child needs it. One mother said she believed that her children were not doing as well as they might in school because they were eating poorly.

THE SCHOOL BUS

At the time of our study nearly all first and second grade children went to school by bus, since the school was located in a sparsely settled area intermediate between the three centers of population of the town. The bus stopped at definite places on a fixed schedule. The schedule and route were changed each year, however, so that no one part of town is always the earliest.

Most North Village parents felt that the elementary school was within possible but not easy walking distance for their children, and that by this age the children could, if necessary, manage the traffic on the local roads. Most parents tried to avoid giving their children the idea that it was safe to miss the bus. One mother said, "Don't come back home if you miss the bus; just start walking." This mother was chagrined to find that her dawdling daughter had not learned her lesson from this, for a friendly neighbor had picked her up on the street and driven her to school. However, some mothers would "break down" and take a late child to school in the family car, perhaps ostensibly on the ground that walking would be too slow.

The children's behavior on the bus is a problem at times for the driver, who is supposed to keep order at the same time that he drives. One threat which he can invoke is to put unruly children off the bus and make them walk. There were no instances of children being put off the bus on the way to school, but there were a few instances of this happening on the way home. One mother was very angry when her son was disciplined by being put off the bus. She felt it was the bus driver's responsibility to bring him home or to notify her that he was walking.

SCHOOL SCHEDULE

On arrival at school the children go immediately to their rooms, take off their coats, and go to their seats to wait for the opening exercises. The teacher often uses this time before formal opening to talk informally with the class as a group. The children may also read to themselves or color in their workbooks individually at this time. Quiet talking is allowed.

Opening exercises vary somewhat according to the teacher's preferences but generally include a recital of the Lord's Prayer (Protestant version) and the pledge of allegiance to the flag by the children, all standing, the reading of a Bible passage by the teacher (especially one of the more popular psalms), and the singing of a hymn or "My Country 'Tis of Thee." The children recite the prayer and pledge rapidly in wooden fashion, although the teachers themselves read and recite expressively. These exercises are legally required, and while there appears to be little interest in them, there is also little opposition to them. The elementary school principal said that one child, whose parents were Jehovah's Witnesses, had been excused from the recitation of the pledge of allegiance with little question.

Each teacher prepares her own schedule for covering the required material in the curriculum and submits this to the principal for approval periodically. The actual order of subjects for any one day in a class depends partly on the teacher's preferences and partly on whether there are any special subjects which interrupt the regular routine. The special subjects include physical education, music, and art. Each class receives a half-hour visit every other week from a special instructor in these subjects who works with all the classes in the Orchard Town school system. However, the regular teachers are supposed to allow some additional class time apart from the special periods for art and music, and this they generally do.

The teachers tend to have the subjects demanding the most attention at the beginning of the school day but also tend to intersperse periods of concentrated attention with simpler activities. Reading or arithmetic is a common first subject, while penmanship, drawing, spelling, and so on, would tend to come later.

READING

For reading, but not other subjects, the elementary children are divided into three groups on the basis of ability. The teacher works with each group in turn at a special table in the front of the room, while the rest of the children are at their seats busy with their workbooks or, if these are finished, drawing, reading, or playing with small educational games or puzzles.

The general pattern of teaching is for the teacher to alternate between explaining things to the class and calling on the children to
answer questions or read certain passages. When she is dealing with
the whole class, she may ask the children to volunteer to answer by
raising their hands to avoid the confusion of several simultaneous answers or she may again ask a specific child to answer or recite. In the
small reading groups, the children generally read in turn, going
around the table, and answer questions freely and informally. Most
children are eager to "show off" their knowledge, especially when they
perceive another child is in difficulty, and when the teacher has asked
one child to recite, she often has some trouble restraining the other
children from volunteering an answer.

At 10 o'clock the first grade has fifteen minutes of recess, which is
immediately followed by a period of the same length for the second
grade. Before going out to recess, the teachers remind the children to
go to the "basement" if they need to. "Basement" is a euphemism for
toilet. In the new all-town elementary school everything is on one floor,
but in the old separate village schools the toilet was in the basement.

RECESS

Recess is rather disorganized. The children spend most of their time
running around chasing each other. Boys and girls generally stay on
separate sides of the building. The sexes do mix a little near the end
of the building, and the teachers do little to prevent this, but in general the children themselves seem to desire the separation and maintain it.

The principal had tried to arrange organized games for the first and
second graders during recess and said she had had no trouble doing
this in earlier times when the older classes were in the same school and
the young children could follow the model of the older grades whom
they saw playing games. However, the attempt to organize games for
the large number of elementary children without this model had in
the main failed. Perhaps the greater number of children of the same
age all together on one playground also hindered organization of
games. It may also be that organized games would work with more
adult supervision. At any one recess two of the four first or second
grade teachers are out on the playground, one for the boys and
one for the girls, while the other two are free to remain inside and
prepare materials.

The children are taught organized games in the special weekly gym period and play them with interest at this time. The teacher-pupil ratio here is more favorable, since only one room has gym at a time. Also, boys and girls are mixed in the gym period, which seems to calm down the boys somewhat.

The children always go outside at recess unless it is snowing hard or raining. On very cold, windy, winter days the recess period may be shortened a little by teachers, however, and if the playground is covered with deep snow, the children may simply march in a line around the cleared roads and paths.

There is some difference between boys' and girls' activities in recess. Jumping rope is popular mainly with girls. Both sexes play with balls. The boys form "gangs" under the leadership of a physically powerful (and often intellectually backward) boy and go charging about the playground playfully scaring nonmembers. Serious fights do not generally issue from these gang activities, perhaps partly because the teachers try to keep them somewhat under control. Many boys of this age, whether members of a gang or not, regard the gangs as very important.

Once in a while two boys will get into a fight on the playground. One fight which was observed involved an argument over a place in line as the children line up to go back in their rooms. A teacher stopped it promptly and scolded the fighters severely. Teachers are generally less sympathetic than parents to claims of self-defense.

LUNCH

Lunch for both grades takes place at 11:30 in order to clear the lunchroom for the junior high and high school children who also use the same room. The first grade goes in about five minutes ahead of the second, which follows when they can be served. Teachers see that the children all wash their hands before going to lunch.

Most children take advantage of the hot lunch served by the school at a nominal cost, although parents are free to have the children carry their lunch to school, and a few children do this. These children do not go through the full cafeteria line and eat together at a separate table. Some children also eat a candy bar or other snack at recess, and one teacher often gave her children crackers at this time.

The school authorities and some of the parents expressed the belief that the school lunch program is educational as well as simply supplying needed food. They believe that the school lunches help the children learn to eat a variety of foods and a well-balanced diet. Since the school receives federal aid for lunches, the menus must meet certain specifications as to quantity and types of food. The weekly menu at the school cafeteria is published in the local paper and duplicated to be taken home to parents so that the mother can avoid preparing the same food at home on the same day and ensure a variety of food for the child.

At school some of the teachers put a little pressure on children to eat, although probably considerably less than at home on the average. For example, the teacher may ask a girl, "Did you finish your milk?" In the cafeteria there is a rule that children may not have seconds until they have eaten everything on their tray. Parents generally seem to approve of this, although some think it amusing that a child had to finish his dessert before getting a second helping of a main course.

After lunch, for which twenty minutes are allowed, there is another recess period and free period. Possibly the point of this is to duplicate the longer lunch periods of the older grades, where some children go home for lunch. The second grade is out for twenty minutes starting at 11:50, and the first grade is out for a similar period starting at 12:10 after spending the preceding twenty minutes in leisure activities in their rooms. Activities in the noon recess are similar to the earlier morning recess.

CLASSES AFTER LUNCH

After the noon recess there is still some class time left. This is a time for activities regarded by the children as more "fun"—drawing or music, spelling or arithmetic "bees" where the class may be divided up into teams which compete in answering the teacher's questions, and so forth. In conclusion, the teacher often reads a story to the children, to which most of them listen attentively.

At the end of the school day the children reassemble in bus groups, that is, the children going to the various villages, who are scattered among the four classrooms in each grade, assemble in a single room, most often not their own. This a time of some tension, for the children are supposed to be orderly but are liable to get into arguments about places in line or whether they have on their outdoor clothes properly. Some of the teachers at this time appear to be more critical of children from other rooms than of their own children. The feeling was occasionally expressed by some that their colleagues handled these children less competently than they would. The teacher's attitude toward children from another room appears to be much like a parent's attitude toward children from another family and is indicative of the sort of personal attachment which teachers in the early grades develop toward their pupils.

RELATIONSHIP TO TEACHER

While most of the first and second grade teachers might be regarded as "motherly" individuals, there are important differences in the relationships of mothers and teachers to their children. On the one hand, the teacher has a less intense relationship to her pupils than the mother. She has close contact with them for only one year and also has nearly 30 small children at a time as opposed to one or a few which a mother might have. But, on the other hand, the teacher demands much more of the child than the mother does, at least at this age. She requires him to spend much time in "school work"—which he may not always want to do—and prevents him from doing a number of other things which would interfere with his own work or, worse yet, the work of other members of his class.

The child soon learns that he may not talk as freely as at home. He may not talk out loud when the teacher is talking and when other children are reciting. Elementary teachers do not invariably require their pupils to raise their hands whenever they want to say something to the class, but when several children wish to talk at once, the teacher invokes the hand-raising rule to preserve order. The teacher likes to encourage each child to contribute to class discussion and recitation. This means that the children must "take turns" in talking and that opportunities to "show off" are limited. Moreover, while the teachers try to avoid open criticism of a child who is doing his best, however poor that may be, their praise of a child's remarks or recitation is not so lavish or indiscriminate as many parents'. The children themselves are jealous of each other for receiving the teacher's attention or praise, and criticism which the teacher herself leaves unsaid may be uttered by the other children.

The teacher imposes restrictions on the children's physical movement as well as on their talking. During recitation periods the children involved are supposed to sit quietly in their seats, and even in periods when the child is supposed to be working by himself, the teacher may require him to obtain permission before leaving his seat to go to the toilet, sharpen a pencil, and so on.

Both parents and teachers recognize that it is hard for children to keep still in school. The first grade teachers especially seemed tolerant of minor infractions. When nothing is happening to which the children should be attending, they are allowed to talk quietly or whisper to each other. At other times whispering, if noticed at all, often brings reproof or reminder. Talking over work assignments with other pupils is discouraged officially, although one visiting mother expressed surprise at how much one teacher permitted children to help each other.

TEACHING TECHNIQUES

In addition to the various restrictions on the children's activity, the teacher makes many positive demands with regard to school work. The child is asked to finish various lessons within a specified time, and he is asked to do them with a reasonable degree of understanding. If his attention wanders and he fails to do his work through apparent lack of serious intent, the teacher may mention his failure before the class. If he does the required work well, he will very probably be praised strongly before the class, and the teacher may show his paper or other work to the class as a model.

Skillfully allotted verbal praise and, to a lesser extent, fairly mild ridicule are the main disciplinary techniques now used by Orchard Town teachers from the elementary grades on. Some corporal punishment was used in the school days of the parents of the present children, but this has now practically vanished. However, some instances which some people interpreted as corporal punishment continue to occur occasionally. One teacher, for instance, was vaguely alleged to have knocked two boys' heads together "or maybe hit them on the head with a book." One teacher described another teacher shaking a child but felt this had little effect on the child. A few young children reported corporal punishment. These reports often seem exaggerated.

In extreme cases of disorder or disobedience a child may be moved to a corner of the room or sent to the hall for a while or to see the principal. The principal may simply repeat the scolding already administered by the teacher or may notify the child's mother.

Making a child stay after school is not used as a punishment in the first two grades, probably because this would make the child miss his bus, and the teacher could not easily assume the responsibility for getting him home.

Verbal praise is sometimes supplemented, in the early grades especially, with charts listing the members of the class on which the teacher pastes stars by the children's names as tokens of recognition for their good behavior, neatness, or other nonscholastic virtues. One second grade teacher allowed the children to choose who would get a star and who should not and pointed out to them, "Your own peers are choosing." Evidently one of the purposes of this was to eliminate a feeling on the part of the children who did not receive stars that they were being treated unfairly by the teacher.

Another form of positive reward which the teachers use is in the assignment of minor tasks about the classroom, such as passing out and collecting papers, erasing the blackboard, or running small errands for the teacher. Children regard being assigned such tasks as a sign that the teacher trusts them and thinks well of them, and the teachers use the assignment of tasks quite explicitly to reward children who are well behaved or have done well scholastically. No instances were observed of a teacher asking for volunteers in assigning some job or some minor errand and not getting a response from the class. As a rule, not everyone responds, but each time there are practically always a number of children from whom the teacher may select one. Probably, however, children who volunteer too frequently or who are chosen by the teacher too frequently would be derided as "teacher's pet."

EMOTIONAL DISTURBANCES

The sudden change from home to school, with its greater demands, produces signs of emotional disturbance in some of the children. A few children, for instance, start to wet their pants in school, apparently after having learned to control themselves adequately at home. It is perhaps significant that one first grade teacher who was especially patient and fairly permissive reported that she had never had children with this problem. Teachers are on the alert for this kind of thing and urge children, on occasion, to go to the toilet. The children feel, rightly or wrongly, that they have to ask permission to leave the room to go to the toilet. This is not supposed to be so in some rooms in the first two grades, and perhaps children confuse this with the need to ask permission to get a drink of water. At lunch time, even in the third to sixth grades, teachers were heard to remind children to go to the toilet.

Some children show other signs of emotional disturbance about the demands of school. One girl was frequently absent because of illnesses which her mother admitted were at least in part feigned. But this mother said proudly, "Even with all her absences she can keep up with the others." One boy, who is thought of by his parents and teachers to be a "genius," is said to cry when he does not get the highest mark in his class. Another cried when his cat did not win a prize in a school pet show.

ATTEMPTS TO MAKE SCHOOL ENJOYABLE

Perhaps in part to compensate for these demands on the children, elementary teachers make a conscious effort to make school enjoyable for their pupils. Attempts are made with humor to entice the children to study. An elementary arithmetic workbook, for instance, was entitled "Jolly Numbers." Or, again, for writing practice a humorous poem may be given, as the following:

> Is a caterpillar ticklish?
> Well it is always my belief
> That he giggles as he wiggles
> Across a hairy leaf.

Apart from this attempt to rouse interest in what is thought of as basically "work," there is also the introduction of certain activities which the children think of primarily as "fun." These would include singing favorite songs, telling the teacher and class about interesting experiences out of school, drawing and coloring, playing with puzzles, and so on, for children who have finished other work.

Of course, Orchard Town teachers are not unique in their attempt to make school enjoyable for young children; they simply exemplify a national trend in this respect. In fact, the system does not claim to keep up with the latest educational fashions and has never reached the extremes of indulgence of pupils attained by some other schools at the height of the progressive movement.

This concern with making schools enjoyable is not limited to professional teachers but is widespread among the parents of the community. The new elementary school building and other new buildings planned at the time of our study also reflect the same general attitude on the part of the community. Most people regarded it as axiomatic that the new buildings should be more comfortable and attractive to the children than the old schools.

Teachers evidently sense the concern of the majority of parents that their children should enjoy school. There seemed to be an assumption that if a parent or other adult came to visit a class, he or she would want to see, most of all, evidence that the children were having a good time. Thus one teacher, whose classroom one of us visited for the first time, interrupted her regular class work to show how one of her brighter pupils could organize a play around a Russian folk tale, choosing some of the other children in the class as actors. Another teacher commented about her class during a sort of recreational period, which may well have been arranged or prolonged for the observer's benefit, saying "See how relaxed they are; I think it is wonderful!"

Attempts to interest the children in school by such indulgence reduce the time available for conventional study. Whether for this reason or because of the general hurried pace of American life, some of the teachers repeatedly expressed the feeling, "There is not enough time."

It is hard to know how much effect the teacher's efforts to make school attractive have, but most of the children seem to come to accept school as largely pleasant or at least not highly unpleasant. Truancy is not a serious problem now in Orchard Town. The parents want their children to attend school, and there are not too many attractions outside the school to entice the children to "play hookey."

PARENT TEACHER RELATIONSHIP

Although control of the child at this age for much of the weekday is relinquished by the parents to the teacher, the parents' continuing concern for their child is manifested in part by an interest in what the teacher is doing. Parents tend to be most active in the Parent-Teacher Association when they have a child in the early grades. Some mothers visit their children's classes in grade school to see how they are making out and to become acquainted with the teacher. The institution of a "room mother" flourished in the first two grades. This is a mother of one of the children who helps the teacher arrange special celebrations of holidays.

Parents are always concerned about reports that the teacher has disciplined their child, although their reaction varies from resentment to approval. The opposition of these two agents of discipline is not as strong as it might be, though, since the children do not report most of their punishments to their parents. We were more likely to hear about these than the parents. If parents are particularly upset by some action on the part of the teacher, the mother often "goes down to school to have it out" with her. In these instances they generally tend to feel that the teacher is just as much at fault as the child, even after they hear the teacher's side of the story. Some parents try to side with the teacher, feeling that the child is the sufferer when the disciplinarians are at odds or even that the teacher is probably right. Often, however, parents feel teachers misunderstand their children and therefore are bad teachers, while teachers feel parents have "spoiled" the children in some respect.

COMPARING CHILDREN

Both parents and teachers keep track of the childrens' work, compare the work of various children with each other, and on occasion call their findings to the attention of the children—as a reward to successful children and as a standard of achievement for the less successful. One parent reported that when she went to school, her teacher used to tell her, "All your brothers and sisters got A's; why can't you?"

Currently both parents and teachers have some tendency to be careful about openly comparing children with each other on the subject of academic achievement because of the belief that children will be "hurt" if they are not able to meet the standards set by other children. However, because of numerous parental remarks in the preschool period, the children come to school with a keen sensitivity as to how they stand in comparison with other children of their age, and it is not difficult for them to infer their approximate relative scholastic standing even if the teacher refrains from open direct comparison. For one thing, papers are often graded on a numerical point system and, if not, then with letters. Children can and do compare these. While the teachers do not always single out the least successful student for ridicule, they often, perhaps, achieve a similar effect by singling out the best student for special praise.

We have previously noted the division of the class into three reading groups according to individual ability. These are most important in first and second grades, for learning to read takes up more of the school day there than in the higher grades. In fact, by fifth grade this division is dropped. Everyone, including the children, knows which reading group is the best one, the worst, and the intermediate, although the teachers go out of their way to avoid mentioning this as a rule. Some teachers refer to the reading groups by the book they may be reading at the time. One teacher numbered the groups but reversed the order of the numbering, that is, the "first" reading group was actually the lowest in ability. In the first and second grades some give the reading groups names, such as Busy Bees, Butterflies, Bluebirds, and Pigeons.

Both parents and teachers at times make invidious comparisons without fully realizing what they are doing. In the following example the teacher intended to encourage the child by publicly noting improvement in her work, but one may wonder if this was actually the main effect.

Well, Susan, you ought to be complimented. Look at the difference from the work she did yesterday. [Teacher holds up Susan's book and shows the class. She then shows the class Susan's work of yesterday.] Do any of you like the work she did yesterday?
Several children: Awful! Awful!
Don't you like to do good work, Susan?
Susan [softly, as if embarrassed]: Yes.

AFTER SCHOOL PLAY

As soon as children get off the school bus, they generally go home promptly and report to their mothers before they do anything else. On the way back from school they may have arranged to play with other schoolmates after checking in at home. The mothers generally approve of these plans, but if a child succumbs to the temptation to go directly to a friend's house without reporting first, he is severely punished. The punishment would be especially severe if the friend lived in another part of the village and the child were not in the habit of visiting there.

When the children get home, many mothers are in the habit of giving them a cookie, glass of milk, or other snack. Perhaps the mothers feel that the children have not been given as much food as they need in school. Some of these same mothers also give their children a little food to take to school in the morning for a snack at recess time.

If the weather is at all suitable, the children usually go outside to play with friends immediately after their snack or, in some families, after changing into play clothes.

PLAYMATES

Playmates are generally chosen from the other children of the same sex in the neighborhood. However, the range of houses which the elementary school child may visit freely is somewhat larger than preschool child's range, and by special arrangements he may at times visit school friends who live in other parts of town. Play groups of children of this age at home, as at school recess, are usually segregated by sex. However, the age segregation found at school is not found at home. We regularly observed children of this age playing with children as much as three or four years older or younger. The population of Orchard Town is dispersed enough so that a strict age segregation would leave many children without any nearby playmates of the same sex.

Perhaps one important reason for the segregation of sexes in play at this age is that by now physical aggression, both playful and serious, has practically ceased in girls while it continues to be important in boys. The elementary school girls at any rate say that they want to play by themselves because the boys are too "rough."

Play groups of grade school children after school are usually small, although a child may have a fairly large number of children with whom he plays during the year. For one thing, the mothers discourage large play groups by not allowing them access to the house. But apart from this there is no very clear authority structure in the play groups, and in groups of more than two or three children there is trouble in deciding what the group is to do. In a group of two or three, the children are held together by a need for companionship, and the compromise of differences is fairly simple, but larger groups can, and easily do, break into smaller groups without leaving any child without a playmate.

Although it is true that the play groups have no formal authority, first and second grade children are keenly aware of relative status, and certain children are more admired than others. This status is based much more on individual achievement and personality traits than on the socio-economic status in the community of adult members of the family. When children of this age meet for the first time, therefore, they are concerned with establishing their relative achievements. We give below an example of this kind of behavior in a conversation which took place between a 6-year-old girl visiting our house for the first time and our elder daughter (then aged 4).

Daughter: I can climb a ladder. [There is a ladder resting on a fence.]
Girl: *I* can climb a ladder—*that* ladder.
Daughter: I can climb *any* ladder.
Girl: So can I. Can you dance?
Daughter: No.
Girl: *I* can dance.
Daughter: I can dance around in a circle.
Girl: Oh, I can do *that.* I can *really* dance—ballet dance.
Daughter: I can do Farmer-in-the-Dell.
Girl: Oh anybody can do *that.* . . . I had my nursery school at home and my mother was the teacher and another lady. . . . I can go on a trapeze.
Daughter: I can sit on a trapeze.
Girl: Oh, that's easy. I'll tell you what I can do: I can *write.* Can you?
Daughter: No.

Girl: I can read, too. Can you read?
Daughter: No.
Girl: Can you keep quiet? (Laughing) *I* can.
Daughter: I *don't.*
Girl: . . . the teacher wants you to keep quiet. She says "keep quiet, shut up."
(But some children) . . . even talk louder when she says that. . . . I got
three teeth out. Have you got any out?
Daughter: I haven't even got a rotten tooth.
Girl: *I* don't have any rotten teeth. When you get two teeth out you get
twenty cents and when you get one tooth out you get ten cents. (Laughs)

There is no sudden change in play activity around home once the
children enter school. However, organized outdoor games, such as tag,
hide-and-seek, varieties of baseball (for the boys) which require only
a few players, and so on, become of some importance. The children
learn some of these games in gym periods at school but more of them
from older playmates around the neighborhood whom they have observed playing such games although they were excluded from them.

There are also a number of relatively unorganized recreational activities or games played, but even here there are often many rules and
restrictions of the activities. For instance, "Cowboys" appears to be
a rather formless game, if it can even be called a game, but still it has
certain rules: sides must be chosen, and the children at least try to
come to some agreement as to when someone is properly "shot dead."
Children of the ages which we studied all occasionally play "Cowboys,"
although children over the age of 6 played this more often, and boys
played more than girls. Two adult informants said that they believed
that children played "Cowboys" much more now than they used to
because of watching Westerns on television. One wonders if it is not a
modern version of "cops-and-robbers."

"Cowboys" is usually played outside, although a large barn or large
basement or a place large enough for hiding and making surprise "attacks" is a possible setting. An ordinary playroom or bedroom is not
satisfactory for this. An area of several adjoining yards is ideal. Children make limits or bounds within which the players are supposed to
stay.

SUPERVISION OF PLAY AND CONTROL OF AGGRESSION

There is somewhat less adult supervision of the school age children's
play than of the preschool children's play. People feel that their children need to learn how to get along with others in these groups and

that adult interference or protection may prevent the child from learning this important lesson. Adult intervention is generally regarded as undesirable "as long as nobody is getting hurt."

Parents will not only control their own impulses to intervene and settle quarrels of their children with their playmates but will also often refuse to intervene even when requested by the child. Both mothers and fathers, but especially fathers, may encourage a son to fight against another boy of equal size and age in retaliation. Girls are not encouraged to fight physically but are encouraged to stand up for their rights in verbal argument.

There are definite limits on the sort of physical fighting permitted for boys, however. Kicking, throwing rocks, and hitting with objects other than one's hands are forbidden. During our year of observation one boy hit another on the head with a milk bottle. The offending boy was punished by making him stay at home in his own yard. Siblings of the injured boy went about the neighborhood hinting that doctor bills would be sent to the parents of the offending boy. No doctor was actually called in the case, however.

Very little physical fighting, either play or serious, was observed among girls of elementary school age or older. They fought neither with boys nor with each other. Some exceptions were occasional snowball fights in the winters, the playful roughhousing of three sisters, carefully supervised by the mother, and the playful chasing of some 10-year-old girls. All of these were less violent than similar activity of boys of the same ages.

Roughhousing between boys is permitted in the yard but usually causes some anxiety. A parent may warn, "You better stop or somebody's gonna get hurt." When the weather permitted, groups of young boys would gather on our back lawn to "wrestle." Occasionally such play battles ended on a sour note and someone would go angrily home. Snowballing is also permitted within the same bounds as roughhousing. If someone gets hurt or angry, the game breaks up.

On the rare occasions when a parent intervenes, he will generally discipline a play group only by reprimanding his own children. Occasionally a parent may rebuke a neighbor's child, but this is probably an impulsive act stemming from sudden anger and apt to be resented by the child's parents if they learn of it. One woman said of such an impulsive neighbor, "We are not speaking to each other. We found that we were being told what we could do even in our yard." On the other hand, as long as the neighbors exercise restraint in dealing with a couple's children, the parents try to make their children behave in a manner acceptable to the neighbors. As one mother said:

If the neighbors don't approve of something, I try to give the kids their side of it too. That's why I think the child has it so doggone hard, because they're called to account by so many people. If I don't teach them, they're going to learn it from somebody outside anyway.

PARENTAL CRITICISM OF PLAY

Although parents try to give the play groups considerable autonomy, they do continue to exercise some influence, mostly indirect, on their elementary school child's choice of playmates. Mothers sometimes make critical remarks to their child about undesired playmates and also show differential hospitality to neighbor's children according to their suitability as playmates from the point of view of morals and manners.

Another parental consideration affecting the composition of play groups is a feeling that each set of neighborhood parents should take its share of responsibility for supervision of the neighborhood children. One's own children, it is felt, should not spend too much time visiting the neighbors and "making trouble for them," and, reciprocally, the neighbors should not let their children spend too much time away from home. Thus, while absolute rules, such as "You must never go to the Doe's," are rare, a mother may very well say, "Don't go over to the Doe's today, you've been spending too much time over there," or she may be less hospitable to the Doe children if she thinks they have been spending too much time at her own house.

SOLITARY ACTIVITIES

There are a few solitary activities in which some children spend a considerable amount of their free time. Watching television is one of these, although often two or three children watch a program together. Also, as soon as they learn to read fairly well (often by second grade), many children spend some time in the house reading children's books. There is a branch of the town library in North Village which has children's books and is open at certain hours. Parents who buy books for their children often give these to the town library when their children have outgrown or become tired of them. Such reading, of course, is unsupervised except that parents may encourage their children to take out books, probably in the hope of improving their reading ability.

Children who take piano lessons are required to spend a certain amount of time each day practicing. Piano lessons may be started at the elementary school level. Probably a minority of the children actually take piano lessons, since not all homes have pianos or the money to pay the teacher, and since there is a feeling that the child should want to take lessons before he is allowed to do so. Of the 24 families in our sample, at least 3 had children taking lessons. The piano teachers are mainly a few housewives who give lessons to earn extra income. As a rule, parents do not teach their own children.

SPECIAL ACTIVITIES

Activities on Saturdays and during school vacations are much like after-school activities except that there is more time for the mother to take the children on occasional special trips, such as to the movies, to ponds for swimming in warm weather, and so forth.

SUNDAY SCHOOL

Sundays bring a change for many elementary school children in that this is the age of greatest attendance at Sunday School. Starting with children of this age, the Sunday School proceedings are divided into two parts: a worship service, where the children sing hymns and listen to prayers and Bible readings, and the school proper, where the children are separated into classes similar to the public school classes. The teachers—adults who have volunteered for the job—consider that the main point of the class period is to tell the children a Bible story or other moral anecdote. Much of the class time is also spent on coloring religious pictures or otherwise illustrating the lessons.

During our year of observation, the various classes were crowded together in a relatively small space, and the teachers had a problem keeping order. Most of them were considerably less efficient than public school teachers in maintaining order, but this was at least partly because they were more restricted in their disciplinary measures. Since Sunday School is not compulsory or universally attended, an offended child can try to persuade his parents to take him to another Protestant Sunday School in one of the nearby communities or to let him drop it completely. The teachers have to tread a narrow line between maintaining enough semblance of order to conduct their lessons and chasing away their pupils by disciplinary measures. Each year a few children drop out or shift Sunday Schools because they have been offended by a teacher.

The elementary schoolchildren show interest in some features of Sunday School, especially in singing certain well-known rhythmic hymns, such as "The Old Rugged Cross," and in drawing and coloring. However, older children, especially boys, rapidly lose interest; most have dropped out by the age of 11.

HOLIDAYS

The regular daily routine is also altered by certain holidays which receive special attention from teachers and parents and by short vacations from school. The children are aware of most of these holidays before entering school but acquire an increasing interest in them in school.

The first major special day affecting children in the school year is Halloween. This used to be an occasion for adult toleration of childish pranks, but by the year of our study Halloween was very dull. A few store windows and house windows were soaped or waxed, but we noticed no other pranks. According to one father, "trick-or-treat" started in Orchard Town about 1950. Before then children just played tricks and did not beg for candy or other refreshments. At present they dress up in costumes and go around ringing doorbells and collecting food. Some parents organized a group of children to go around and ask for contributions to the Children's Relief Fund, feeling that it was a waste of children's time and parents' money for children to beg for candy, and that helping to buy milk for needy children in other parts of the world was a more worthy activity. One girl, aged 8, commented on this: "Ah, them poor kids, do we have to do this for them every year?" It is too early to say whether this one experience in collecting will become an established custom of Halloween, as some adults hope and expect.

The next major holiday affecting children is Thanksgiving. This is an occasion for a family gathering. If there are any grandparents or uncles and aunts living within a convenient distance, a joint family dinner is usually held. There is a large meal with a traditional menu: roast turkey, cranberries, pudding, squash, and mincemeat pie, and so on. Thanksgiving is a fairly pleasurable occasion for children, for they are often the object of attention of older visiting relatives.

At Christmas time, parties are given at church and at school. The mothers of the children supply quantities of cookies and similar items, to ensure a good Christmas party. Children imitate the custom of adults by sending greeting cards to their friends. They sometimes make a few Christmas cards in school as part of their art work. On Christmas Eve about seven children from the church went around singing Christmas Carols during our field period.

New Year's Eve is not a children's ceremony, but the practice of making New Year's resolutions is known and indulged in mostly by children, although not taken very seriously.

The major children's holiday in February is Valentine's Day. No day off from school is given for this day, but it is an occasion for special art work and the exchange of valentine greeting cards in school. Most children give a valentine to friends in their classroom and neighborhood. Comments of a teasing nature begin to be made at this time about giving valentines to a child of the opposite sex.

Of the patriotic holidays in the school year, the most important for children is Memorial Day, when there are parades by veterans' groups and family visits to the cemetery to put flowers on the graves of deceased relatives.

Easter is an important holiday although again it does not involve vacation from school. On Easter Sunday most families attend church even if they do not regularly attend the ordinary Sunday services. All of the children have new clothing for this occasion.

There is one major holiday during the summer vacation, namely, the Fourth of July or Independence Day. A generation or more ago this was, like Halloween, an occasion for tolerated pranks by children. One popular prank for older children and adolescents used to be ringing the church bell. However, long-time residents say that the Fourth is nothing like it used to be. Firecrackers are not permitted legally, and few are shot off, although there are licensed displays of fireworks in the evening in nearby towns to which some parents take their children.

RELATIONSHIP TO MOTHER

On entry into elementary school, the family relationships of the child change most with respect to the mother. Since the children can do more for themselves and are absent in school much of the time, the mother becomes less important and does less for the child. Some children seem to become more critical of their parents, especially their mothers, at this time, perhaps because they accept their teacher as a "wiser" authority.

Parents simultaneously feel that the children are less lovable once they are out of the preschool age. This is not to say, of course, that parents stop liking their children once they enter school, but they do become more reserved in their expression of affection to them. This decrease in open expression of affection is, moreover, a gradual process, not a sudden and dramatic event, and during the first two grades of school especially, there is much carry-over of the warm relationship of the mother to the preschool child.

SUMMARY

We may summarize the elementary school period briefly as involving the following developments:

1. The child becomes increasingly self-reliant.
2. He is initiated into "work" at school, although at home he continues to contribute little toward performance of household chores.
3. The prestige of both his teacher and his peers waxes while the prestige of his parents, and especially his mother, wanes somewhat.
4. Play groups split by sex, and there is an accompanying behavioral differentiation. The children express considerable aversion for the behavior of the opposite sex.
5. Children have an opportunity in school to compare themselves with a large number of peers with respect to certain standards set up by teachers, parents, and peers. They have already been motivated to make such comparisons before entering school but now have constant occasion to do so.
6. Children have their aggressive tendencies fairly well controlled and become more sociable and start to "make friends" on a larger scale than before.

⚹
⚹
⚹

Chapter 17

Later Childhood: Third through Sixth Grades

During the year of our residence in Orchard Town, children attending the third to sixth grades were marked off as a group by attending the local village schools rather than a centralized town school. This was regarded as a temporary arrangement, which would eventually be stopped when a centralized school for children from all of the component villages had been constructed. However, this grouping of the grades seems useful to us as a device for marking the later stage of childhood, a period which in any case has a certain unity and meaning for the people of Orchard Town apart from this accident of school attendance. Moreover, the break between second and third grades at the beginning of this period did not begin with the recent establishment of the centralized primary school. Previously, for many years, up into the childhood of some students in high school at the time of our study, first and second grades were combined and taught by a single teacher (as were the third and fourth, fifth, and sixth), due to the small size of the classes. However, during the year of our study, the average class size of the elementary grades was around 30, and all grades were taught separately.

The period of third to sixth grades is in many respects similar to first and second grades, and many remarks made in the previous chapter apply with little change to children in the third to sixth grades. We note below mainly the major differences between the two periods.

During our year of study, paradoxically, many older children were under a little less pressure to get up promptly in the morning than the first and second graders. This is because most of the older children lived near enough to the local village school to walk or ride their bicycles if they missed the school bus. The school bus was, nevertheless, well patronized, especially in cold or bad weather, even by children who lived within a few blocks of the school.

RIDING TO SCHOOL ON BICYCLES

Being able to ride a bicycle to school is one of the big distinguishing marks of late childhood. No first or second graders were allowed to do this during the period of study, although probably some were permitted to do so in earlier years when these grades were in the nearby village schools.

Freedom in riding a bicycle to school coincides with a general increased freedom to visit friends in others parts of town or to go out into the countryside. Children might receive their two-wheelers in first or second grade but would initially be restricted to riding them around the neighborhood.

SCHOOL SCHEDULE

The school schedule for third to sixth grade is similar to that of the first two grades. The following fourth grade schedule will serve as an example:

8:30— 8:40	Opening exercises
8:40— 9:10	Reading group A
9:10— 9:40	Reading group B
9:40—10:00	Reading group C
10:00—10:20	Recess
10:20—11:45	Arithmetic
11:45—12:30	Lunch and noon recess
12:30—12:50	Spelling
12:50— 1:25	Language (English)
1:25— 2:00	Social studies
2:00— 2:15	Music, drawing, penmanship, etc.

Lunchtime presents a different routine in the lower grades. In the small local schools there is no cafeteria. Most children bring sandwiches and eat at school in the classroom with the teacher. If they live near enough, they are free to go home for lunch, but only a few do this regularly. It is our impression that most children prefer to eat lunch at school with their classmates. Those children who stay at school eat their lunch quickly and go out to play games with their class for the rest of the noon recess.

As was mentioned in the previous chapter, the older children normally spend their recess periods in organized games. Some of these games they learn from their regular teacher or from the gym teacher, who visits them an hour every other week. Often the class chooses which game they want to play in a short discussion and vote led by the teacher. Formally organized games also become more important in children's play outside of school at this age, although since the play groups continue to be rather small, games involving sizable teams are played mostly in school or under adult supervision of some sort.

TEACHING TECHNIQUES

The formal schedule of subjects changes little from second to higher grades, but the teachers feel free to demand more of the pupils. In the first two grades, the children have presumably adjusted to the school routine, and it is now possible to demand more concentrated effort from them. Special indulgences, such as parties to celebrate holidays, decline in importance although they do not vanish. The supply of materials to occupy the time of pupils who finish their lessons rapidly now consists mostly of books to read. Standards of order and quiet in the classroom are stricter. Teachers in these grades occasionally kept unruly children after school and had them copy over appropriate moral sentences on the board. Another similar punishment was to keep the child inside at recess.

Teachers from third grade on are less indulgent toward their pupils' desire to monopolize class time by "showing off" their knowledge or abilities. The desire to "show off" remains, as evidenced by the frantic hand waving of many children when the teacher asks a question or asks for volunteers for some classroom chore, but teachers insist with greater effect that answers should not be given out of order and provide little time for children to tell about their fantasies or personal experiences not directly connected with the lesson. Teachers from fourth grade on sometimes express minor annoyance at too much hand waving, even for "legitimate" purposes, such as volunteering an answer.

Teachers give evidence of the increased importance of peer pressures by consciously manipulating the class sentiment to compel the desired behavior in unruly pupils and also sometimes by themselves taking a child-peer role in maintaining discipline. One teacher was said to make the children do "Consequences" as a punishment, for example, to get up in class and sing a song or say a poem. Another teacher was said to confiscate marbles which students showed in the classroom and make the owner win them back from her.

Training in the proper care and maintainance of property is important in the school, as in most families. A fourth grade teacher, for instance, placed considerable emphasis on the shining of shoes, and both parents and children commented favorably on this. Another way in which the school helps to encourage respect for the care of property is by having the children themselves help to buy the playground equipment, such as soccer balls, baseballs, and bats. This is done through an annual seed sale. Children volunteer to take packages of seeds and sell them from door to door throughout the town, and profits from this sale of seeds helped to pay for the playground equipment. Evidently the sum attained is not sufficient to pay a very large proportion of the actual cost for the equipment, but such behavior is felt desirable as a training device.

PARENTAL ATTITUDE TOWARD ACHIEVEMENT

Most parents expect their children to meet certain minimum standards of scholastic achievement, although they try to adjust these to what they consider the child's abilities. A good standard is one which is capable of being reached by the child with some effort. Some remarks which illustrate this include:

I think he does well enough for his age.
I know he could do better.
You can't expect a young one to do things as well as an adult would.

It is felt that a child who is not very intelligent may be made too nervous by pushing him beyond his ability. If the child becomes nervous, even otherwise possible goals cannot be reached.

One mother tells how she changed her techniques on discovering that her daughter had a low "potential."

When I first saw she wasn't doing well in reading, I was quite cross. This made her very nervous. Then I realized she didn't have much memory span and I tried to have patience with her, and I would say, "Now I know you don't know, but let's try to find out."

Although she lowered her intellectual standards, this same mother felt it was unnecessary to change another goal: "You may not be able to get A's in reading and arithmetic, but you can get an A in conduct."

But parents are often slow to admit that their child's ability is low. Other reasons are sought, reasons that may indeed be the basis of the child's lack of success. The reason for failure that produces the greatest anger and punishment from parents is the feeling that the child is not trying. It may even be that the parent feels that the child wishes to be an embarrassing representative of the parent—to get even with the parent in some way. One parent reports about such a child:

He could do better than he does (in school) if he could learn to mind his own business a little more. We get disgusted because he's capable. He's no genius, but he could do better than he does. . . . Well, we've worked at home with him on it. Mostly it's a case, if he just paid attention, his marks would come up. We took his bike away after the first marking period until the second set of marks came out. . . . I'd get so impatient working with him here at home that I'd do more harm than good because sometimes he'd do it and other times he would just fool around.

In one child, several of the factors which might cause conflict in the realm of achievement behavior were combined. The child was a member of a highly upwardly mobile family whose mother and father had risen considerably in status. One received a strong impression that the child was regarded as a representative of the parents but also that the child was hostile to the parents. Here is what the mother says about her dissatisfaction with the child's work:

Well, I'm afraid I'm not very satisfied. She doesn't get all A's in school. She doesn't perform her tasks to perfection. She's inclined to be a little lazy. The only thing she really does well is something that captures her interest. . . . Her room is always carelessly done. She leaves things setting if I don't put them over the sink [when she does dishes]. She usually shoves the dishpan under the counter wet. Sometimes she has to do things over two or three times before she does them right.

Parents feel that it is more important for boys to "do well" than it is for girls, since a girl may gain status and popularity through personal beauty. Mothers say:

I feel that my son is more important than my daughters. So we spend much more time on his education.

I don't feel my girls will ever be any great shakes anyway. They'll probably get married.

For a girl, her achievement will generally be measured in terms of that of her husband.

CHORES

In later childhood parents demand a little more from their children in tasks and errands around the house, but these demands are not great. Children are expected to keep their rooms orderly when reminded. They are also often expected to help wash dishes. Delaying actions are not uncommon according to both observations and mothers' reports. The following mother's report will serve as an example of the chores of a 10-year-old boy and his performance of them.

In the morning he is supposed to get up, shove the heat up and put the dogs out; and almost always I have to call down and almost always one or the other or both haven't been done. This morning I called down about the heat and later I called again, and he said, "You told me about that before," and I said, "Yes, but did you take care of it?" I heard him go over and turn the heat up, and then he said, "Yes."

Some parents pay their children small sums for doing work at home, but other parents do not, often on the ground that child-training experts oppose it, for payment would prevent the children from feeling their responsibilities as family members. Still others have tried payments but later abandoned them as an ineffective incentive for consistent performance, at least payments of the size the parents are willing to offer.

Perhaps one reason why parents demand so little work from the children around the house is because they hope for so much from them in their schoolwork and in other forms of competition with their peers.

AFTER SCHOOL ACTIVITIES

After-school activities are in many ways similar to those of elementary schoolchildren. Indeed, in neighborhood play groups there is no sharp boundary between the two age groups. The third to sixth graders, however, have more freedom as to the area in which they may play. If they have a little pocket money, they are free to go to a store to buy gum, candy, inexpensive toys, and so on. In good weather boys of this age may tramp through the surrounding woods and fields, collecting birds' eggs, fishing, swimming in shallow ponds (perhaps without parental knowledge), and so forth.

Boys would like BB guns and 22-caliber rifles which would really shoot, but police regulations prevent this and are enforced. Most parents also would probably be hesitant about giving their sons such weapons. Many boys, however, look forward to the time when they will be old enough to own a 22 or a more powerful weapon and hunt with these.

ORGANIZED ACTIVITIES

Also, from third grade on the children become increasingly involved in various organized activities. These include the "Scouts," the church junior choir (third grade up), baseball teams, dancing classes, and so on.

Scouts are important for most boys and girls but are perhaps thought of as more educational than recreational. Scouts and the adult leaders take themselves quite seriously at times. One adult leader said in a speech at a troop dinner, "Our requirements are not easy, but one cannot learn to survive in the forest by performing simple tasks."

Scouts are divided into two major age grades, in addition to having these groups further divided according to many achieved statuses. The younger children are "Brownies" or "Cub Scouts" while the older children are in Boy or Girl Scouts proper.

There have been Boy Scouts in Orchard Town for a generation or so, but the Girl Scouts are more recent. Scouts are active during both the school year and the vacation. The Girl Scouts have a day camp during vacation where the girls spend most of their time in organized games and activities.

Most children from the religiously active families participate in the junior choir from third through fifth grades. There are a few children in the junior choir after the fifth grade also. The junior choir has an evening rehearsal once a week and sings occasionally at the Sunday morning services and also on special occasions, such as Christmas, Easter, and at special gatherings of children's choirs of other churches.

The children's baseball teams are known as the "Minor League" (for boys from about fifth grade) and the "Little League" (for somewhat older boys). Each team is sponsored by a local business firm or fraternal association. Boys must try out to become eligible. The adult coach and supervisors provide regular attention, although the interest of many parents is rather perfunctory. At one Minor League game which one of us attended, the spectators numbered a couple of dozen, scarcely more than the number of players.

In the summer during vacation time there have been organized swimming classes sponsored by the Red Cross in a nearby town. Also there have been classes at a Y.M.C.A. in a nearby town.

The dancing classes are another instance of organized recreation and education outside of school. Children begin attending at the age of about 10. During the year of our study there were two dancing classes in town: a square dancing class sponsored by the North Village Woman's Club and a ballroom dancing class sponsored by the Center Club. This caused some confusion, for the boys preferred the square dancing class and the girls preferred the ballroom dancing class.

The dancing classes were interesting from the point of view of teaching social etiquette in groups. The teacher demonstrates the social graces as well as the dancing. He instructs the children to "go right up and make yourself known." He tries to be amusing to impress the children and to keep their attention. The following excerpt is taken from an observation of the dancing group.

You are not boys and girls, because in this class you are ladies and gentlemen. I don't think I have to refer to each individual as far as conduct is concerned. I refer to you as a group. It's not just the class, it's (conduct) important in everyday life." "Now, when you sit down, gentlemen, you don't sit down like this [demonstrates sloppy sitting]; you sit down in one piece. Girls generally do not cross the knees, but gentlemen may cross their knees this way. There's a place for your feet—it's not on the furniture, of course. I'd like to see the gentlemen stand up and sit down in one piece. What about the fellow on the end there? He's tired before he starts. Now the girls."

"Gentlemen, stand up and walk across the hall and ask a girl to be your partner. [Boys got up and rushed across to get their favorite girls.] You'd think this was a track meet! You go and ask Alberta and she says, "Thank you." Gentlemen, will you kindly take your partner back to her seats and thank her again for the dance. Let's go to your seats walking.

During the dance the teacher was careful to see that all the girls had male partners at one time or another, and he did his best to see that none of the children were wallflowers.

INTEREST IN THE OPPOSITE SEX

The existence of the dancing school for children around the age of 10 is symptomatic of an increasing interest in the opposite sex on the part of both boys and girls, after the earlier period of strong antipathy in first and second grades. This heterosexual interest develops progressively in late childhood, although individual children differed considerably in the age at which they began to manifest an interest. According to a woman who gave lectures to Sunday School teachers throughout the area, there was also considerable variation between communities in the average age at which boys and girls began to take an interest in each other. By fourth grade some of the boys would admit with embarrassment that they had a "girl friend," although, as far as we could see, these relationships consisted mainly of secret admiration and overt teasing, and the couple saw little of each other outside of school.

By fifth grade some of the couples were playing together at times after school, usually in larger groups. We heard of one fifth grader who had wanted to take his "girl" to an afternoon movie show. His mother discouraged this, however. Judging from a small amount of observation of one fifth grade couple in a play group, teasing was still prominent in the relationship, but "serious" talk and play could also take place.

MODESTY

A sense of modesty about exposure of the unclothed body grows stronger in late childhood, although simple knowledge of the rules of modesty exists before this. One mother reported a rumor of an incident at school where a group of 9- or 10-year-old boys and girls dared one girl to pull up her dress. But supposedly this was in cold weather when she was wearing trousers under the dress. One 9-year-old who had the reputation of being rather uninhibited told of an incident where he had been swimming in a pond in his underpants and had had to hide behind some brush on an island so some girls who came by would not see him. A child of this age who was openly exhibitionistic would be disapproved of as being "dirty."

It is unclear to us how much sexual knowledge these children have. They at least have the idea of some sort of attraction between a boy and a girl. They also have the idea that there are activities about which it is inappropriate to speak. On one occasion one of us listened to some jokes which some 10-year-olds considered "dirty." However, these jokes were mostly about elimination or involved words which were considered blasphemous, such as "Hell." One joke involved a misinterpretation of the function of brassieres. There were no jokes which involved sexual intercourse. It is hard to say what is meant by a 10-year-old who says to his friend, "You learned a lot from her, eh?"

Children are not supposed to use bad language, which includes both obscene language and certain forms of blasphemy. One incident was reported where a boy called something "cock-eyed penis," and his mother hit him in the mouth and "it shocked him." Another mother reported washing her daughter's mouth out with soap for "bad language." Just what this was was unspecified. It may have involved the daughter talking back to her as well as obscenity, if it involved obscenity at all.

Kissing is a subject of joking, especially with children from 9 or so on. It is also a subject of horseplay. One incident was reported where some 11-year-old girls were trying to catch a 10-year-old boy to kiss him. The boy was supposedly trying to escape them because his own girl friend was not involved. At this age girls may show some initiative in joking or horseplay, but a few years later such joking or horseplay would not be approved of and would be rare if it occurred at all. Some young girls, who were playing "Truth or Consequences," were observed joking among themselves about sexual subjects and asking each other such questions as "Would you like to kiss so-and-so?" or "Would you like to go in the tunnel of love with him?" or "Do you like such-and-such a boy?" The questioned girl would sometimes try to deny this, but then she would be made to do something as a payment of consequences for saying something unbelievable.

SEX ROLE

The resumption of interest, in late childhood, in persons of the opposite sex suggests that the first two grades of school in Orchard Town are the principal period for the establishment of what might be termed the public sex role. Once the children are confirmed in this, they can again turn their attention toward members of the opposite sex with little danger of inappropriate imitation.

However, it is true that signs of envy of the opposite sex remain, especially on the part of girls. Some girls express resentment of the greater freedom given to boys of school age, and they also may feel they have to do more work at home than boys. Perhaps in compensation for this, the rules about crossing sex-role lines are more lenient for girls than for boys. We observed some instances of a boy playing girls' games. The criticism of this by other children was more severe than criticism of girls playing boys' games or doing things which are considered primarily boys' activities. One may also note that girls sometimes wear boys' clothes, either clothes actually belonging to a male member of their family or clothes made for women, but in imitation of men's clothes, such as slacks. The reverse does not occur.

SUNDAY SCHOOL

A majority of the sample children in later childhood continued to go to Sunday School, although often with more resistance than younger children. The boys especially became increasingly disorderly with age, hitting each other on the head with hymnals and engaging in other "horseplay."

In addition to Sunday School proper, children are encouraged to attend the regular adult morning service, although only a few actually do. The minister is in the habit of giving a special children's sermon, usually a historical or biographical incident, or fable or fairytale illustrating some moral point. Children are free to leave during the hymn before the sermon begins, but older children usually remain through the entire service if they come at all.

Most children who attend Sunday School regularly do so because their parents insist on it. However, the Sunday School authorities try to arouse the children's interest in various ways with some success. Attendance pins were given to children who had perfect attendance records, with allowance made for legitimate excuses. The use of the attendance pin as an incentive for coming to Sunday School, however, has been abandoned by a number of other nearby Protestant churches and is regarded with mixed feelings by members of the North Village church.

Certain events during the year also arouse genuine interest in the children. Of these the most important is probably the Christmas party. Some children are suspected of attending Sunday School several Sundays before Christmas in order to justify their appearance at the Christmas party and then stopping for the rest of the year. The year of our study, the Christmas party consisted of a movie and ice cream for the children, followed by the appearance of Santa Claus handing out presents. Children's Sunday, which occurred at the end of the Sunday School year in June, is another occasion which interests the children. On this occasion certificates of graduation are given to the children; attendance awards are given; children finishing the third grade are given a Bible, and every child receives a small potted plant. No special significance is given for this plant.

SUMMARY

To summarize the developments of the children in later childhood, there are:

1. Growing independence from the parents, although partly by a transfer of dependence to the teacher.
2. Increased parental and school demands for personal achievement or success but less indulgence of "showing off."

3. More formal organization of activity, even of play with peers, which often consists of formal games.
4. Growing pressure from one's own agemates to conform to the current fashions and growing sensitivity to this pressure.
5. Effective control of aggressive tendencies. Serious physical fighting is rare, almost entirely between boys, and even in the heat of anger is usually controlled enough to prevent serious injury.
6. Growing attraction between the sexes.

BIBLIOGRAPHY

Warner, W. L., Meeker, M., et al. *Social Class in America.* Chicago: Science Research Associates, 1949.

Index